The First Amendment

ASPEN CASEBOOK SERIES

The First Amendment

Cases and Theory

Fourth Edition

Ronald J. Krotoszynski, Jr.
John S. Stone Chair and Professor of Law
University of Alabama School of Law

Lyrissa Barnett Lidsky
Raymond & Miriam Ehrlich Chair in U.S. Constitutional Law
University of Florida Frederic G. Levin College of Law

Caroline Mala Corbin
Professor of Law and Dean's Distinguished Scholar
University of Miami School of Law

Timothy Zick
John Marshall Professor of Government and Citizenship
William & Mary Law School

To contact Customer Service, e-mail customer.service@aspenpublishing.com, call 1-800-950-5259, or mail correspondence to:

Aspen Publishing
Attn: Order Department
PO Box 990
Frederick, MD 21705

Printed in the United States of America.

1 2 3 4 5 6 7 8 9 0

ISBN 978-1-5438-2668-5

Library of Congress Cataloging-in-Publication Data

Names: Krotoszynski, Ronald J., 1967- author. | Lidsky, Lyrissa Barnett, 1968- author. | Corbin, Caroline Mala, author. | Zick, Timothy, author.
Title: The First Amendment : cases and theory / Ronald J. Krotoszynski, Jr., John S. Stone Chair and Professor of Law, University of Alabama, School of Law; Lyrissa Barnett Lidsky, Raymond & Miriam Ehrlich Chair in U.S. Constitutional Law, University of Florida Frederic G. Levin College of Law; Caroline Mala Corbin, Professor of Law and Dean's Distinguished Scholar University of Miami School of Law; Timothy Zick, John Marshall Professor of Government and Citizenship William & Mary Law School.
Description: Fourth edition. | Frederick : Aspen Publishing, 2022. | Series: Aspen casebook series | Includes bibliographical references and index. | Summary: "Law school casebook providing comprehensive coverage of the Speech, Press, Assembly, Petition, and Religion clauses of the First Amendment"— Provided by publisher.
Identifiers: LCCN 2022020840 | ISBN 9781543826685 (hardcover) | ISBN 9781543826692 (ebook)
Subjects: LCGFT: Casebooks (Law)
Classification: LCC KF4770 .K74 2022 | DDC 342.7308/5—dc23/eng/20220630
LC record available at https://lccn.loc.gov/2022020840

About Aspen Publishing

Aspen Publishing is a leading provider of educational content and digital learning solutions to law schools in the U.S. and around the world. Aspen provides best-in-class solutions for legal education through authoritative textbooks, written by renowned authors, and breakthrough products such as Connected eBooks, Connected Quizzing, and PracticePerfect.

The Aspen Casebook Series (famously known among law faculty and students as the "red and black" casebooks) encompasses hundreds of highly regarded textbooks in more than eighty disciplines, from large enrollment courses, such as Torts and Contracts to emerging electives such as Sustainability and the Law of Policing. Study aids such as the *Examples & Explanations* and the *Emanuel Law Outlines* series, both highly popular collections, help law students master complex subject matter.

Major products, programs, and initiatives include:

- **Connected eBooks** are enhanced digital textbooks and study aids that come with a suite of online content and learning tools designed to maximize student success. Designed in collaboration with hundreds of faculty and students, the Connected eBook is a significant leap forward in the legal education learning tools available to students.
- **Connected Quizzing** is an easy-to-use formative assessment tool that tests law students' understanding and provides timely feedback to improve learning outcomes. Delivered through CasebookConnect.com, the learning platform already used by students to access their Aspen casebooks, Connected Quizzing is simple to implement and integrates seamlessly with law school course curricula.
- **PracticePerfect** is a visually engaging, interactive study aid to explain commonly encountered legal doctrines through easy-to-understand animated videos, illustrative examples, and numerous practice questions. Developed by a team of experts, PracticePerfect is the ideal study companion for today's law students.
- The **Aspen Learning Library** enables law schools to provide their students with access to the most popular study aids on the market across all of their courses. Available through an annual subscription, the online library consists of study aids in e-book, audio, and video formats with full text search, note-taking, and highlighting capabilities.
- Aspen's **Digital Bookshelf** is an institutional-level online education bookshelf, consolidating everything students and professors need to ensure success. This program ensures that every student has access to affordable course materials from day one.
- **Leading Edge** is a community centered on thinking differently about legal education and putting those thoughts into actionable strategies. At the core of the program is the Leading Edge Conference, an annual gathering of legal education thought leaders looking to pool ideas and identify promising directions of exploration.

Dedicated to the memory of Judge Frank M. Johnson, Jr. (1918-1999) and Professor William W. Van Alstyne (1934-2019)—with sincere gratitude and appreciation for their inspiring First Amendment tutelage and unwavering commitment to the freedom of speech.

—R.K.

To my husband Howard Lidsky, for his love, support, and conversation.

—L.L.

For Michael, with gratitude and love.

—C.M.C.

To my First Amendment students—past, present, and future.

—T.Z.

Summary of Contents

Contents xi
Preface xxvii
Acknowledgments xxxi

PART I FREEDOM OF EXPRESSION 1

Chapter 1. The History, Values, and Content of the First Amendment 3
Chapter 2. Categorical Exclusions: Unprotected Speech 31
Chapter 3. Content Neutrality 89
Chapter 4. "Secondary Effects" and Expressive Conduct 135
Chapter 5. Regulation of Speech on Government Property 175
Chapter 6. Compelled Speech and Expressive Association 243
Chapter 7. Commercial Speech 313
Chapter 8. Regulation of the Mass Media 367
Chapter 9. Tort Law and the First Amendment 469
Chapter 10. The Conflict Between Free Speech and Promoting Equality, Civility, Dignity, and Mutual Respect 521
Chapter 11. The Regulation of Sexually Explicit Speech 579
Chapter 12. The Government as Speaker, Employer, and Educator 631

PART II THE RELIGION CLAUSES 725

Chapter 13. Introduction to the Religion Clauses 727
Chapter 14. Free Exercise of Religion: Exemptions 739
Chapter 15. Free Exercise of Religion: Funding 803
Chapter 16. Statutory Protection of Religious Liberty 823
Chapter 17. Free Exercise of Religion: Institutions 845
Chapter 18. Defining and Enforcing the Establishment Clause 877
Chapter 19. The Establishment Clause and Voluntary Religious Accommodations 891

Chapter 20.	**The Establishment Clause and Government Financing of Religion**	909
Chapter 21.	**The Establishment Clause and Public Schools**	957
Chapter 22.	**The Establishment Clause and Government Endorsement of Religion**	995

Table of Cases **1043**
Table of Authorities **1055**
Index **1063**

Contents

Preface xxvii

Acknowledgments xxxi

PART I FREEDOM OF EXPRESSION 1

Chapter 1 The History, Values, and Content of the First Amendment 3

A. The History of Free Expression in England and the Early Years of the Republic 5
  1. England 6
    a. Licensing 6
    b. Seditious Libel 7
  2. The Early American Republic 9
    a. Generally 9
    b. The Adoption of the First Amendment 10
  3. The Sedition Act of 1798 11
  4. From the Sedition Act to World War I 13

B. First Amendment Values 14
  1. Self-Governance 15
    Notes and Questions 17
  2. Truth and the Marketplace of Ideas 17
    Notes and Questions 18
  3. Autonomy/Self-Fulfillment 19
    Notes and Questions 20
  4. Dissent 21
    Notes and Questions 21
  5. Anti-Theory 22

C. Implementing the Freedom of Speech 23
  1. Speech vs. Conduct 23
  2. Content Discrimination 24
  3. Access to Public Property 24

4. Vague and Overly Broad Laws 25
a. Overbreadth 25
b. Vagueness 26
c. Facial and As-Applied Challenges to Laws 26
5. Prior Restraint 27
6. Extra-Doctrinal Influences on the Law 28

Chapter 2 Categorical Exclusions: Unprotected Speech **31**

A. Subversive Speech: Advocacy of Unlawful Action 32
1. Opposition to War: The "Clear and Present Danger" Standard 33
Schenck v. United States *33*
Notes and Questions 35
Abrams v. United States *37*
Notes and Questions 41
2. Agitators, Anarchists, and Revolutionaries: Criminal Syndicalism 42
Gitlow v. New York *43*
Notes and Questions 45
Whitney v. California *46*
Notes and Questions 50
An Extended Note on the Cold War Smith Act Prosecutions 51
3. The Modern "Incitement" Standard 54
Brandenburg v. Ohio *54*
Notes and Questions 57
Hess v. Indiana *58*
Notes and Questions 60
Theory-Applied Problem 63
B. "Fighting Words" and Other Categorical Exclusions 65
Chaplinsky v. New Hampshire *65*
Notes and Questions 66
An Extended Note on the Post-*Chaplinsky* Fighting-Words Doctrine 68
C. "True Threats" 70
Watts v. United States *71*
Notes and Questions 73
United States v. Stevens *75*
Notes and Questions 78
Theory-Applied Problems 79

D. The Limits of the Categorical Approach: Depictions of Animal Cruelty, Video Game Violence, and Lies 81

United States v. Stevens *81*

Other Potential Categories: Violent Video Games and Lies 84

Notes and Questions 86

An Extended Note on Defining Protected Speech—Possible Lessons from Canada 86

Chapter 3 Content Neutrality 89

A. The Content-Neutrality Principle — Origins and Rationales 90

Police Department of Chicago v. Mosley *90*

Notes and Questions 92

B. The Modern Approach to Content Neutrality 93

Reed v. Town of Gilbert *94*

Notes and Questions 103

Theory-Applied Problems 105

C. Applying Strict Scrutiny to Content-Based Laws 105

Brown v. Entertainment Merchants Ass'n *106*

Notes and Questions 108

United States v. Alvarez *109*

Notes and Questions 112

Holder v. Humanitarian Law Project *112*

Notes and Questions 117

D. Speaker Identity Distinctions 117

Citizens United v. Federal Election Commission *118*

Notes and Questions 127

E. Content-Neutral Speech Regulations and Intermediate Scrutiny 128

Ward v. Rock Against Racism *129*

Notes and Questions 133

Chapter 4 "Secondary Effects" and Expressive Conduct 135

A. Regulating the "Secondary Effects" of Speech 135

Renton v. Playtime Theatres, Inc. *135*

Notes and Questions 137

B. Regulating Conduct with an Expressive Element 139

1. Draft Card Burning 139

United States v. O'Brien *140*

Notes and Questions 144

2. Flag Desecration 146
Spence v. Washington *146*
Notes and Questions 151
Texas v. Johnson *153*
Notes and Questions 158
Theory-Applied Problems 160
3. Nude Dancing 161
Barnes v. Glen Theatre *162*
Notes and Questions 169
City of Erie v. Pap's A.M. *169*
Notes and Questions 173

Chapter 5 Regulation of Speech on Government Property 175

A. The Concept of the Public Forum: Foundational Cases 176
Hague v. CIO *176*
Notes and Questions 178
Cox v. New Hampshire *179*
Notes and Questions 180
Cantwell v. Connecticut *181*
Notes and Questions 183
B. Regulating Speech in the Public Forum: Time, Place, and Manner Regulations 184
Clark v. Community for Creative Non-Violence *184*
Notes and Questions 187
Frisby v. Schultz *189*
Notes and Questions 192
McCullen v. Coakley *193*
Notes and Questions 200
Theory-Applied Problem—Funeral Protests 201
C. Policing Conflict in the Public Forum: The Problem of the Hostile Audience 202
Feiner v. New York *203*
Notes and Questions 206
Edwards v. South Carolina *207*
Notes and Questions 210
Forsyth County v. Nationalist Movement *212*
Notes and Questions 217
Theory-Applied Problem — Portland Permit 217

D. Forum Analysis: Which Public Properties and Facilities Do Speakers Have Access To? 218
Perry Education Ass'n v. Perry Local Educators' Ass'n 218
Notes and Questions 221
Cornelius v. NAACP Legal Defense and Education Fund 223
Notes and Questions 229
Hodge v. Talkin 230
Notes and Questions 238
Theory-Applied Problems 239
E. When Should Speakers Have Access to *Private* Property? 240

Chapter 6 Compelled Speech and Expressive Association 243

A. Introduction 243
B. Compelled Speech 244
1. Compelled Government Orthodoxy 244
West Virginia State Board of Education v. Barnette 244
Notes and Questions 248
An Extended Note Regarding *Wooley v. Maynard* ("Live Free or Die") 248
Notes and Questions 249
2. Compelled Disclosure of Information 250
National Institute of Family and Life Advocates v. Becerra 250
Notes and Questions 258
Theory-Applied Problem — "Branded" Driver's Licenses 259
3. The Right Not to Publish the Speech of Others 260
Miami Herald v. Tornillo 260
Notes and Questions 263
PruneYard Shopping Center et al. v. Robins 264
Notes and Questions 268
Hurley v. Irish-American Gay, Lesbian & Bisexual Group of Boston 269
Notes and Questions 272
4. The Right Not to Pay for the Speech of Others 272
Janus v. American Federation of State, County, and Municipal Employees, Council 31 272
Notes and Questions 278
An Extended Note on Speech Exactions 279
5. The Right to Communicate Anonymously 282
McIntyre v. Ohio Elections Commission 282
Notes and Questions 286
Theory-Applied Problems — Anonymity and Accountability 288

C. The Right of Association 288
1. The Right to Associate for Expressive Purposes 288
NAACP v. Alabama *288*
Notes and Questions 292
2. The Right *Not* to Associate 293
Roberts v. United States Jaycees *293*
Notes and Questions 299
Boy Scouts of America v. Dale *300*
Notes and Questions 309
Theory-Applied Problem — Falun Gong in the Park 310

Chapter 7 Commercial Speech 313

A. The Historical Approach 314
Valentine v. Chrestensen *314*
Railway Express Agency, Inc. v. New York *316*
Notes and Questions 316
B. The New Understanding 317
An Extended Note on the Origins of First Amendment Protection for Commercial Speech 318
Notes and Questions 320
Central Hudson Gas & Electric Corp. v. Public Service Commission of New York *320*
Notes and Questions 324
Theory-Applied Problem 326
An Extended Note on *Posadas* and the Use of Commercial Speech Regulations in Lieu of Direct Regulations 326
Notes and Questions 328
Sorrell v. IMS Health Inc. 331
Notes and Questions 337
C. Limitations on the Ability of Government to Regulate Commercial Speech Because of Its Commercial Nature 340
1. The Rule Prohibiting Discrimination Against Commercial Speech as Such 341
City of Cincinnati v. Discovery Network, Inc. *341*
Notes and Questions 345
2. *Discovery Network* Applied?: Offensive Trademarks and Off-Label Rx Drug Marketing 346
Theory-Applied Problem 351
D. The Problem of Defining Commercial Speech 351
Bolger v. Youngs Drug Products Corp *352*
Notes and Questions 354

First National Bank of Boston v. Bellotti 356
Notes and Questions 360
An Extended Note on Commercial Versus Noncommercial Use of a Celebrity's Persona Without Permission or Consent 360
Theory-Applied Problem 362
An Extended Note on *Citizens United v. FEC* 362
Theory-Applied Problem 365

Chapter 8 Regulation of the Mass Media 367

A. Regulation of the Press 369
Mills v. Alabama 369
Notes and Questions 371
B. Media Newsgathering and Access Rights 372
1. Reporter's Privilege Against Compelled Disclosure of Confidential Sources 373
Branzburg v. Hayes 373
Notes and Questions 382
An Extended Note on Government Secrecy, Subpoenas, and the Investigation of Leaks 385
Theory-Applied Problem: Subpoena of Telephone Records 387
2. Access to Courtrooms 387
Richmond Newspapers, Inc. v. Virginia 387
Notes and Questions 394
An Extended Note on Expansion of the Right of Access After *Richmond Newspapers* 395
Theory-Applied Problem: Closure to Protect Children 397
3. Access to Government Institutions 397
Houchins v. KQED, Inc. 398
Notes and Questions 403
C. Prior Restraints 403
1. The Presumption of Unconstitutionality 403
Near v. Minnesota 404
Notes and Questions 408
2. The National Security Exception 410
New York Times Co. v. United States 410
Notes and Questions 411
Theory-Applied Problem: A National Security Hypothetical 412
An Extended Note on "Subsequent Punishment" of Leakers 412
Theory-Applied Problem: Wikileaks 413
Theory Applied Problem: Injunctions as Remedies for Defamation? 413

3. Free Press/Fair Trial 414
Nebraska Press Ass'n v. Stuart 414
Notes and Questions 422
Theory-Applied Problem: Protecting the Fair Trial Right 422
D. Regulation of Broadcasters 423
Notes and Questions 428
FCC v. Pacifica Foundation 429
Notes and Questions 433
Federal Communications Commission v. Fox Television Stations, Inc. 434
Notes and Questions 439
E. Regulation of Cable System Operators 441
Turner Broadcasting System, Inc. v. FCC ("Turner I") 441
Notes and Questions 449
An Extended Note on Indecency on Cable Television 450
United States v. Playboy Entertainment Group, Inc. 451
Notes and Questions 456
F. Regulation of the Internet and New Media 456
Reno v. ACLU 456
Notes and Questions 459
G. The Future of Big Tech Regulation 461
Biden v. Knight First Amendment Inst. at Columbia Univ. 462

Chapter 9 Tort Law and the First Amendment 469

A. First Amendment Limitations on the Tort of Defamation 469
1. Defamation of Public Officials 471
New York Times Co. v. Sullivan 471
Notes and Questions 478
2. Defamation of Public Figures: The Extension of the *Sullivan* Rules 481
3. Defamation of Private Figures Involved in Matters of Public Concern 482
Gertz v. Robert Welch, Inc. 482
Notes and Questions 487
4. Defamation of Private Figures Involved in Matters of Private Concern 488
5. The Constitutional "Privilege" Protecting Opinion 490
Milkovich v. Lorain Journal Co. 490
Notes and Questions 494
Theory-Applied Problem: A Restaurant Review 498
Theory-Applied Problem—Hashtag Libel 498
6. Should *New York Times v. Sullivan* Be Overruled? 499

B. First Amendment Limitations on Intentional Infliction of Emotional Distress 499

Hustler Magazine, Inc. v. Falwell *500*

Notes and Questions 503

Snyder v. Phelps *504*

Notes and Questions 507

Theory-Applied Problem: Funeral Protests 507

Theory-Applied Problem: Intentional Infliction and Public Concern 507

C. First Amendment Limitations on Imposing Liability for Publishing True Information 508

The Florida Star v. B. J. F. *508*

Notes and Questions 513

An Extended Note on Defining "Unlawfully Obtained" 515

D. First Amendment Limitations on Imposing Liability Based on Newsgathering Methods 516

Cohen v. Cowles Media Co. *516*

Notes and Questions 519

Chapter 10 The Conflict Between Free Speech and Promoting Equality, Civility, Dignity, and Mutual Respect 521

A. The Ancien Régime: Group Libel Regulations and the First Amendment 523

Beauharnais v. Illinois *523*

Notes and Questions 527

Kunz v. New York *529*

Notes and Questions 532

An Extended Note on Terry Jones and Targeted Incitement: The Example of Koran Burning 534

B. A Contemporary Example of Regulations Aimed at Promoting Social Equality: Title VII As a Limit on Free Speech 535

Hishon v. King & Spalding *535*

Notes and Questions 537

Meritor Savings Bank v. Vinson *537*

Notes and Questions 539

Theory-Applied Problem 541

C. Government Efforts to Promote Civility and the First Amendment 542

Cohen v. California *542*

Notes and Questions 546

Gooding v. Wilson *548*

Rosenfeld v. New Jersey *549*

Notes and Questions 551

D. Government Efforts to Prohibit Hate Speech and Racialized Threats 553
R. v. Keegstra *554*
Notes and Questions 560
An Introductory Note to *Mitchell* and *Black* 561
R. A.V. v. City of St. Paul, Minnesota *562*
Notes and Questions 566
Wisconsin v. Mitchell *568*
Notes and Questions 570
Virginia v. Black *571*
Notes and Questions 576
Theory-Applied Problem 577

Chapter 11 The Regulation of Sexually Explicit Speech **579**

A. Limitations on the Targeted Regulation of Sexually Explicit Materials 582
Miller v. California *582*
Notes and Questions 587
American Booksellers Ass'n, Inc. v. Hudnut *589*
Notes and Questions 592
R. v. Butler *594*
Notes and Questions 600
An Extended Note on the Problem of "Revenge Porn" 601
Theory-Applied Problem 602
An Extended Note On Sexually Explicit Expressive Conduct: Nude Dancing and the First Amendment 603
Notes and Questions 606
B. Children and Pornography 607
New York v. Ferber *608*
Notes and Questions 612
Theory-Applied Problem 614
An Extended Note on *Stanley v. Georgia* and *Osborne V. Ohio:* Privacy in the Home and the First Amendment 615
Notes and Questions 617
Theory-Applied Problem 618
C. New Media and Sexually Explicit Speech 619
Ashcroft v. Free Speech Coalition *619*
Notes and Questions 627
An Extended Note on "Childproofing" the Internet 629
Theory-Applied Problem: Sexting and Cyberstalking 629

Chapter 12 The Government as Speaker, Employer, and Educator 631

A. Government-Subsidized Speech and Government Speech 632

Rust v. Sullivan 632

Notes and Questions 635

Legal Services Corp. v. Velazquez 636

Rosenberger v. Rector & Visitors of the University of Virginia 638

Notes and Questions 642

National Endowment for the Arts v. Finley 642

Notes and Questions 646

Pleasant Grove City, Utah v. Summum 646

Notes and Questions 651

Walker v. Texas Division, Sons of Confederate Veterans, Inc. 652

Notes and Questions 659

An Extended Note on Government as Speaker and Speech Subsidizer 660

Theory-Applied Problem: The Men's Club 661

Theory-Applied Problem: Public School Banners 661

B. Speech by Government Employees 662

Pickering v. Board of Education 662

Connick v. Myers 664

Garcetti v. Ceballos 668

Notes and Questions 673

Lane v. Franks 675

Notes and Questions 679

U.S. Civil Service Commission v. National Ass'n of Letter Carriers 682

Notes and Questions 684

An Extended Note on Loyalty Oaths and Political Patronage 685

Theory-Applied Problem 688

C. Public Schools and Libraries 688

Tinker v. Des Moines Independent Community School District 688

Notes and Questions 691

Bethel School District No. 403 v. Fraser 692

An Extended Note on the "Vulgarity" Exception to *Tinker* 694

Hazelwood School District v. Kuhlmeier 697

Notes and Questions 700

Morse v. Frederick 702

Notes and Questions 706

Theory-Applied Problems 708

Board of Education v. Pico 710
Notes and Questions 716
United States v. American Library Ass'n 717
Notes and Questions 723

PART II THE RELIGION CLAUSES 725

Chapter 13 Introduction to the Religion Clauses 727

A. The Religion Clauses 727
B. Saturday Sabbath and Sunday Closing Laws 728
Braunfeld v. Brown 728
Notes and Questions 731
McGowan v. Maryland 732
Notes and Questions 734
Estate of Thornton v. Caldor, Inc. 735
Notes and Questions 738

Chapter 14 Free Exercise of Religion: Exemptions 739

A. Pre-*Smith* Caselaw 740
1. The Belief/Conduct Dichotomy 740
Reynolds v. United States 741
Notes and Questions 743
2. Protection of Religious Conduct 744
Sherbert v. Verner 744
Notes and Questions 748
Wisconsin v. Yoder 749
Notes and Questions 754
An Extended Note on "Strict in Theory but Feeble in Fact" 755
Notes and Questions 757
B. The *Smith* Standard 758
Employment Division, Department of Human Resources v. Smith 758
Notes and Questions 765
Church of the Lukumi Babalu Aye, Inc. v. City of Hialeah 766
Notes and Questions 772
Theory-Applied Problem 773
C. Exemptions and Religious Discrimination 773
1. The Fall of "Neutral and Generally Applicable" 774
South Bay United Pentecostal Church v. Newsom 774
Roman Catholic Diocese of Brooklyn v. Cuomo 776

Tandom v. Newsom 780
Notes and Questions 782
2. The Rise of Religious "Discrimination" 783
Masterpiece Cakeshop, Ltd v. Colorado Civil Rights Commission 783
Notes and Questions 790
Fulton v. City of Philadelphia 790
Notes and Questions 800
An Extended Note on Sincerity 800
Notes and Questions 802

Chapter 15 Free Exercise of Religion: Funding 803

A. Play in the Joints 803
Locke v. Davey 803
Notes and Questions 806
B. Discrimination Against Religion 807
Trinity Lutheran Church of Columbia, Inc. v. Comer 807
Espinoza v. Montana Department of Revenue 815
Notes and Questions 821

Chapter 16 Statutory Protection of Religious Liberty 823

A. The Religious Freedom Restoration Act (RFRA) and the Religious Land Use and Institutionalized Persons Act (RLUIPA) 823
B. Cases 825
Gonzales v. O Centro Espírita Beneficente União do Vegetal 825
Notes and Questions 827
Burwell v. Hobby Lobby Stores, Inc. 827
Notes and Questions 839
Holt v. Hobbs 840
Notes and Questions 842
Theory-Applied Problem 843
Theory-Applied Problem 843

Chapter 17 Free Exercise of Religion: Institutions 845

A. Church Property Disputes 846
Watson v. Jones 846
Notes and Questions 850
Presbyterian Church in the United States v. Mary Elizabeth Blue Hull Memorial Presbyterian Church 850
Notes and Questions 854

Jones v. Wolf 855
Notes and Questions 861
B. Employment Disputes 861
An Extended Note on *Serbian Eastern Orthodox Diocese v. Milivojevich* 861
Notes and Questions 863
Hosanna-Tabor Evangelical Lutheran Church and School v. Equal Employment Opportunity Commission 864
Notes and Questions 867
Our Lady of Guadalupe v. Morrissey-Berru 868
Notes and Questions 874
Theory-Applied Problem 874

Chapter 18 Defining and Enforcing the Establishment Clause 877

A. Early Efforts to Define the Separation of Church and State 879
Everson v. Board of Education 881
James Madison, "Memorial and Remonstrance Against Religious Assessments" 883
Notes and Questions 885
B. Modern Tests for Impermissible Religious Establishments 886
1. The "*Lemon* Test" 886
2. The Endorsement Analysis 886
3. The Coercion Analysis 887
4. The History and Tradition Analysis 887
Theory-Applied Problems 888

Chapter 19 The Establishment Clause and Voluntary Religious Accommodations 891

Play in the Joints 891
Texas Monthly, Inc. v. Bullock 891
Notes and Questions 894
Corporation of the Presiding Bishop of the Church of Jesus Christ of Latter-Day Saints v. Amos 895
Notes and Questions 900
Cutter v. Wilkinson 901
Notes and Questions 904
An Extended Note on the Vietnam-Era Conscientious Objector Cases *Seeger* and *Welsh* 906
Theory-Applied Problem 908

Chapter 20 The Establishment Clause and Government Financing of Religion 909

A. Separation Versus Neutrality: *Everson v. Board of Education* 910
Everson v. Board of Education of Ewing TP. et al. *910*
Notes and Questions 916
B. Tax Deductions for Religious Organizations 917
Walz v. Tax Commission of the City of New York *917*
Texas Monthly, Inc. v. Bullock *921*
Notes and Questions 921
C. Direct Aid 921
Bowen, Secretary of Health & Human Services v. Kendrick *923*
Notes and Questions 929
Mitchell v. Helms *930*
Notes and Questions 937
Trinity Lutheran Church of Columbia, Inc. v. Comer *939*
Notes and Questions 939
D. Voucher Programs 940
Zelman v. Simmons-Harris *940*
Notes and Questions 950
An Extended Note on Standing to Challenge Government Financing of Religion 952
Theory-Applied Problem 955

Chapter 21 The Establishment Clause and Public Schools 957

A. Government Endorsement of Religion in the Public Schools: School Prayer 958
Engel v. Vitale *958*
School District of Abington Township v. Schempp *961*
Stone v. Graham *964*
Notes and Questions 965
An Extended Note on the Constitutional Status of "Moment of Silence" Requirements in the Public Schools 966
Lee v. Weisman 968
Santa Fe Independent School District v. Doe 974
Notes and Questions 977
B. Government Endorsement of Religion in the Public Schools: Religion in the Public School Curriculum 978
Epperson v. Arkansas *978*
An Extended Note on the *Scopes* Trial 981

Edwards v. Aguillard 982
Notes and Questions 985
C. Religious Speech in Public Schools 988
Widmar v. Vincent 988
Lamb's Chapel v. Center Moriches Union Free School District 989
Notes and Questions 991
An Extended Note on Open Access Requirements 992
Theory-Applied Problems 993

Chapter 22 The Establishment Clause and Government Endorsement of Religion 995

A. Government-Sponsored Religious Displays 995
Lynch v. Donnelly 995
An Extended Note on Government-Sponsored Seasonal Holiday Displays 1002
Notes and Questions 1003
McCreary County, Kentucky v. American Civil Liberties Union of Kentucky 1004
Van Orden v. Perry 1007
Notes and Questions 1013
American Legion v. American Humanist Association 1015
Notes and Questions 1024
B. Government-Sponsored Prayers Outside School 1024
Marsh v. Chambers 1024
Notes and Questions 1030
Town of Greece v. Galloway 1031
Notes and Questions 1037
C. Government/Religion Power Sharing 1038
Larkin v. Grendel's Den 1038
An Extended Note on *Board of Education of Kiryas Joel v. Grumet* 1039
Notes and Questions 1040

Table of Cases 1043

Table of Authorities 1055

Index 1063

PREFACE

It may come as a surprise to many students entering law school that an entire course could be devoted to a single amendment of the United States Constitution. On the other hand, it may also come as a surprise to other students that most of the jurisprudence discussed in this casebook is of relatively recent vintage—much of it dating back to the Warren and Burger Courts. The Supreme Court devoted very little attention to the First Amendment prior to World War I. Since that time, however, the First Amendment has become one of the most frequently litigated components of the Constitution. In fact, during the current Roberts Court era, the First Amendment has become a powerful tool to challenge federal, state, and local regulations that affect communication in any conceivable way, including, for example, restrictions on the sale of physicians' prescription data and offering consumers discounts for cash purchases. From the modern perspective, the First Amendment has become such a central part of our social, political, and religious interaction in the United States that it is difficult to envision an American society without it. In an increasingly diverse culture, which is witnessing an explosion of new media through which conflicting opinions can be disseminated, the First Amendment will almost certainly remain an important—indeed central—focal point of constitutional litigation.

This casebook surveys a broad range of contemporary First Amendment jurisprudence, including cases relating to each of the major concerns of the modern amendment—freedom of speech, press, assembly, association, and religion. The right of petition, although one of the five main clauses of the First Amendment, has not (at least to date) played an important doctrinal or jurisprudential role in securing expressive and religious freedoms in the United States. The two modern cases that squarely address the meaning and scope of the Petition Clause both declined to articulate and apply a specific jurisprudence of the clause. *See* Borough of Duryea v. Guarnieri, 564 U.S. 379, 387-399 (2011) (holding that the Petition Clause does not confer any special protection on complaints by government employees about their treatment by their employers because "[p]etitions, no less than speech, can interfere with the efficient and effective operation of the government" and noting that the rights of petition and free speech "share substantial common ground"); McDonald v. Smith, 472 U.S. 479, 482, 485 (1985) (holding that the Petition Clause does not create any greater right of public comment that contains false factual assertions than do the Free Speech or Free Press Clauses because the Petition Clause is "cut from the same cloth" as these parallel rights). *But cf.* Adderley v. Florida, 385 U.S. 39, 52 (1966) (Douglas, J., dissenting) (arguing that the Petition Clause should be interpreted to provide enhanced access to government property, such as a county jail, when speech and assembly have a clear petitioning component). Indeed, the nontextual implied right to freedom of association plays a more central role in contemporary First Amendment law and theory. Accordingly, the Petition Clause does not receive independent treatment in this book. However, should the Petition Clause come to play a more meaningful role in securing expressive freedoms in the United States, the authors will certainly include dedicated coverage of this clause in a future edition.

This casebook is organized around substantial excerpts of the Supreme Court's most significant First Amendment decisions. We have edited the cases relatively lightly in an effort to let the Justices' own words lead students through the doctrine. In addition to the main cases, notes after many of the cases provide short excerpts or summaries of other relevant Supreme Court decisions and important academic commentary, along with references to some lower court decisions regarding matters on which the Supreme Court has not yet spoken. The chapters all include Theory Applied Problems after major sections and subsections to help focus students' attention on the particular applications and internal conflicts of the doctrine. The Theory Applied Problems provide an easy and reliable way to assess students' mastery of the relevant governing legal rules, principles, and theory.

A few words about our approach to contextualizing First Amendment problems and jurisprudence are in order. First, we have made a conscious effort to address the interplay of historical and political events and First Amendment doctrine. In our view, consideration of the historical and political context of free speech and religious freedom cases helps to illuminate the concerns that can motivate judges to accept or reject constitutional claims. Second, in several important areas, we incorporate decisions from foreign constitutional courts because we believe that these materials provide a helpful contrast with the U.S. approach to common legal problems. Looking at a problem from a comparative perspective often yields useful insights into the (often unstated) policies and objectives of contemporary First Amendment jurisprudence. In sum, considering both history and how other nations address common legal problems can help to foster better understanding of contemporary U.S. First Amendment jurisprudence, and this book incorporates and reflects this point of view.

We have organized this casebook with the intention of first providing students with a general background of overriding First Amendment concepts before turning to more specific areas in which the Supreme Court has developed and applied specialized rules. Modern First Amendment law can be very frustrating for the uninitiated because the lines between the various specialized rules and standards are often unclear. Indeed, the Supreme Court's consistent drift from general, open-ended principles to frame and decide First Amendment cases toward a vast sea of three- and four-part tests that apply only in very specific, limited circumstances provides one of the larger themes of this casebook. As you explore these materials, you should consider whether highly context-specific, complex, multipronged balancing tests better secure fundamental liberties than would more general, open-ended tests.

In some respects, attempting to understand First Amendment law is like learning to play three-dimensional chess. In many situations raising First Amendment issues, more than one set of rules will seem to apply. Any given case may raise generalized First Amendment concerns (such as the rule that the government may almost never engage in content or viewpoint regulation), coupled with specific rules developed for particular factual scenarios (such as the rules regarding obscenity, fighting words, threats, or government-subsidized speech), which are further complicated by special procedural rules (such as the expedited litigation requirements of *Freedman v. Maryland*), special remedial rules (such as the Court's strong discouragement of injunctive prior restraints), and even special statutory-construction mandates (such as the Court's unusual willingness to consider facial overbreadth challenges to statutes impinging on free speech). The First Amendment even has special real estate rules for government property, which dictate when and how that property must be opened to speakers wishing to express themselves to other members of the public. Learning to navigate the often conflicting crosscurrents of First Amendment law is one of the student's main tasks in a First Amendment course, and this casebook is designed to make that task easier.

The basic organization of the book divides the discussion of the First Amendment between the Speech Clauses, which are covered in Part I (the first twelve chapters), and the Religion Clauses, which are covered in Part II (the next ten chapters). Within the speech chapters, the discussion moves from an overview of the general theory and structure of the First Amendment to the specific doctrines that apply to particular areas of speech.

The first three chapters provide an overview of the history and theory of the First Amendment, along with a discussion of the basic rules regarding content and viewpoint regulation by the government. These chapters also provide a basic understanding of the government's role in regulating political expression, which is the topic that the Supreme Court addressed in its earliest First Amendment cases, and which remains at the heart of free speech jurisprudence. Chapter 4 examines two complications that have arisen under content neutrality principles – regulation of the "secondary effects" of speech and application of the First Amendment to "expressive conduct." Chapter 5 discusses the general rules that apply to government when it acts as an owner or proprietor of public properties; the chapter also examines timely concerns about government's response to hostile audiences and the potential for violence in the public square. Chapter 6 covers the general rules regarding compelled and anonymous speech and also addresses First Amendment doctrines relating to "expressive association." Chapters 7 through 12 move from the general to the particular, discussing a variety of different First Amendment doctrines that relate to specific types of speech, including commercial speech, media regulation, defamation, group libel, fighting words, erotica, government employees, and government-subsidized speech. In the Fourth Edition, we have worked diligently to update and streamline our coverage of the Supreme Court's principal free speech decisions, including the addition of new material on current constitutional controversies surrounding defamation reform and the regulation of new communications technologies, questions associated with the free speech effects of privately owned dominant social media platforms and search engines, revenge porn, the shrinking public space available for expressive activities, and the consistent and persistent growth in the constitutional protection afforded to various and sundry forms of commercial speech.

Part II discusses the Religion Clauses. The first chapter is an introduction to both clauses. The next four chapters discuss religious liberty protected by the Free Exercise Clause and statutes, and the remaining five chapters examine the Establishment Clause. In Chapter 13, Part II opens with a general overview of the history and theory of the Establishment and Free Exercise Clauses. Chapter 14 then turns to the meaning of "free exercise" and considers whether the Free Exercise

Clause should protect religiously motivated conduct no less than it protects religious belief, noting how the answer has changed over time. Chapter 15 explores a new doctrine, namely the free exercise right to government funding. Chapter 16 considers statutory enactments that convey individual exemptions from neutral laws of general applicability when such laws impede religiously motivated conduct. Chapter 17 examines the ability of religious entities, such as churches, temples, and mosques, to seek and obtain exemptions from generally applicable laws through doctrines such as the ministerial exemption.

Chapter 18 provides an introduction and overview to the Establishment Clause; this chapter considers the various general tests that the Supreme Court has deployed to prevent religious establishments. Chapter 19 examines how the Establishment Clause impacts efforts by the federal and state governments to accommodate religiously motivated beliefs and conduct. Chapter 20 discusses cases involving government financing of religion, including indirect financing of religious K-12 schools through voucher programs, as well as direct financing via government grants to religious organizations that provide social services. The distinct problems and issues associated with bringing religious beliefs and practices into the K-12 public schools receive sustained coverage in Chapter 21. Finally, Chapter 22 considers the constitutional limits applicable to government efforts to promote religion in other contexts. In sum, the Fourth Edition provides a completely updated and comprehensive survey of the Supreme Court's complex and fast-evolving Religion Clauses jurisprudence.

As this brief summary indicates, the complexities of the interrelationships between the many First Amendment standards and doctrines are daunting. Fortunately, the entertainment value of cases raising First Amendment issues is quite high. The reader will find in the materials that follow a gallery of rogues and heroes, dissenters and visionaries, and more than a few simple oddballs. The cast of characters includes Communists and Ku Klux Klansmen, cross burners, funeral protestors, punk rock bands seeking edgy trademarks, draft-card burners and anti-war protestors, atheists and evangelicals, Eugene V. Debs and Richard Nixon, Larry Flynt and Catherine McKinnon, Reverend Fred Phelps and Madalyn Murray O'Hair, and devout Jehovah's Witnesses and the purveyors of violent video games. In one sense it is their First Amendment that this book discusses, but in a more important sense this colorful cast has helped the Court define the scope of expressive and religious freedom enjoyed by the entire society. The authors of this casebook believe that we have rendered the story of the First Amendment in a way that makes it both coherent and digestible. Whether we have succeeded in that task is for the reader to decide, but at the very least we feel certain that no one will find this material boring.

Ronald J. Krotoszynski, Jr.

Lyrissa Barnett Lidsky

Caroline Mala Corbin

Timothy Zick

June 2022

Acknowledgments

I have genuinely enjoyed working with my dedicated and talented co-authors, Lyrissa Lidsky, Caroline Mala Corbin, and Tim Zick; one could not ask for better collaborators on a project of this size and scope. Moreover, it has been wonderful to have a colleague as smart, thoughtful, and careful as Professor Tim Zick, our new co-author on the Fourth Edition. It is commonplace, perhaps to the point of cliché, to say that working with one's co-authors has been a pleasure, but in this instance, the sentiment happens to be both genuine and heartfelt. I also must note that, even with the passage of time, I continue to miss the wise counsel and good humor of our former co-author, Steve Gey, who passed away in 2011. In addition, all of us also want to acknowledge, with thanks and appreciation, the outstanding work of Professor Chris Wells on the three prior editions of this casebook. Over the years, I have learned much about the First Amendment from the scholarship of Professors Gey, Wells, Lidsky, Corbin, and Zick. This casebook is immeasurably stronger because of the synergy of our collective efforts. I acknowledge with gratitude the support of Dean Mark Brandon and the University of Alabama School of Law, which greatly facilitated my work on this project. I also should note the support of the University of Alabama Law School Foundation, which provided generous financial support for this project in the form of summer research grants. Finally, the four of us wish to acknowledge the thoughtful and constructive reviews and suggestions provided by our First Amendment colleagues on various iterations of the casebook; the book has benefitted significantly from the insights and observations of our colleagues in the field who took the time and energy to provide feedback on the three earlier editions of First Amendment: Cases and Theory. Although we do not know your names (the Aspen Publishers review process is anonymous), we wish to thank you for your assistance — the Fourth Edition of this casebook will be a more effective pedagogical tool because of your labors. R.K.

Thank you to my research assistant Alexandra Bass for her help with updating and editing. L.L.

I am thankful for the opportunity to work with colleagues who I really respect and really like. C.M.C.

Thanks to my terrific co-authors for inviting me to join the Fourth Edition. T.Z.

Ronald J. Krotoszynski, Jr.

Lyrissa Barnett Lidsky

Caroline Mala Corbin

Timothy Zick

June 2022

PART I

FREEDOM OF EXPRESSION

Chapter 1

The History, Values, and Content of the First Amendment

Table of Contents

- A. The History of Free Expression in England and the Early Years of the Republic
  - 1. England
    - a. Licensing
    - b. Seditious Libel
  - 2. The Early American Republic
    - a. Generally
    - b. The Adoption of the First Amendment
  - 3. The Sedition Act of 1798
  - 4. From the Sedition Act to World War I
- B. First Amendment Values
  - 1. Self-Governance
  - 2. Truth and the Marketplace of Ideas
  - 3. Autonomy/Self-Fulfillment
  - 4. Dissent
  - 5. Anti-Theory
- C. Implementing the Freedom of Speech
  - 1. Speech vs. Conduct
  - 2. Content Discrimination
  - 3. Access to Public Property
  - 4. Vague and Overly Broad Laws
    - a. Overbreadth
    - b. Vagueness
    - c. Facial and As-Applied Challenges to Laws
  - 5. Prior Restraint
  - 6. Extra-Doctrinal Influences on the Law

The First Amendment of the United States Constitution establishes that "Congress shall make no law . . . abridging the freedom of speech, or of the press; or the right of the people peaceably to assemble, and to petition the government for a redress of grievances." Although this language seems straightforward and uncompromising, little about the amendment has proven to be so easy. Despite Justice Black's famous claim that "[n]either as offered nor as adopted is the language of this Amendment anything less than absolute," see Hugo L. Black, *The Bill of Rights*, 35 N.Y.U. L. Rev. 865, 874 (1960), the Supreme Court has never treated the First Amendment as absolutely protecting expression.

Numerous laws restricting speech exist with the Court's approval. For example, the state can criminalize incitement of lawless activity, Brandenburg v. Ohio, 395 U.S. 444 (1969), and ban the distribution of obscenity, Miller v. California, 413 U.S. 15 (1973). As well, laws criminalizing bribery, fraud, perjury, and other speech crimes have never been thought to raise First Amendment concerns. Nor has the law of contracts or the law of evidence. Speech that occurs in these contexts might be characterized as "uncovered," hence the First Amendment simply does not "show up." Frederick Schauer, *The Boundaries of the First Amendment: A Preliminary Exploration of Constitutional Salience*, 117 Harv. L. Rev. 1765, 1769-74 (2004). The Court has never ventured to explain why these forms of speech are not "covered" by the First Amendment.

The state can also regulate the time, place, and manner of protest gatherings in public forums, like streets and parks, Cox v. New Hampshire, 312 U.S. 569 (1941), and impose even greater restrictions on expression taking place on other public property, such as libraries or prisons, Adderley v. Florida, 385 U.S. 39 (1966). On the other hand, the Court has held government officials may not ban advocacy of illegal action even if it ostensibly causes harm. *Brandenburg, supra.* Nor, as a general rule, can the state punish speech because it offends the listener. Cohen v. California, 403 U.S. 15 (1971). And although the state can regulate the time, place, and manner of public protests, it cannot charge protestors differential fees based upon possible expenses associated with keeping order. Forsyth County, Ga. v. Nationalist Movement, 505 U.S. 123 (1992).

How does the Court justify differential treatment of incitement and advocacy of illegal activity, or obscenity and offensive speech, or time, place, and manner regulations and fees imposed upon protests? Many factors influence the Court, including the possible harm resulting from particular speech, the state's purpose for restraining speech, the form of the state's regulation, the form of the speech, the historical context of the speech, and the cost to society of overly restrictive speech regulations. Unfortunately, the Court has never explained with clarity or consistency the relationship between these influences and its doctrinal rules, or even the relationship of one doctrinal rule to another. Over time, the Court's free speech doctrine has developed into "a vast Sargasso Sea of drifting and entangled values, theories, rules, exceptions [and] predilections . . . [requiring] determined interpretive effort to derive a useful set of constitutional principles by which to evaluate regulations of expression." Robert C. Post, *Racist Speech, Democracy, and the First Amendment*, 32 Wm. & Mary L. Rev. 267, 278 (1991).

To complicate matters, the Court has never clearly defined when activity is sufficiently expressive to warrant First Amendment protection. While the Court has acknowledged that "expressive conduct" falls within the auspices of the First Amendment, it has struggled to define the parameters of such conduct. Burning a flag to protest government action counts, Texas v. Johnson, 491 U.S. 397 (1989), as does burning one's draft card to protest the Vietnam War, United States v. O'Brien, 391 U.S. 367 (1968). But nude dancing is only "marginally" within the parameters of the First Amendment. Barnes v. Glen Theatre, Inc., 501 U.S. 560 (1991). How does the Supreme Court arrive at such conclusions? Furthermore, a great deal of what one thinks of as "expression"—for example, proxy statements under the securities laws or requests that another person help one with a crime (that is, criminal solicitation)—never even receive First Amendment scrutiny. *See, e.g.*, Schauer, *supra.* Why? The Supreme Court has been remarkably silent about how and why it draws these "boundaries." *Id.*

The Court has decided relatively few cases concerning regulation of speech in digital forums that now play a prominent role in contemporary culture and politics. It has invalidated overbroad laws regulating "indecent" and "patently offensive" online speech, Reno v. American Civil Liberties Union, 521 U.S. 844 (1997), and banning convicted sex offenders from accessing a variety of websites, Packingham v. North Carolina, 137 S. Ct. 1730 (2017). The Court has acknowledged the "vast democratic fora of the Internet, *Reno, supra,* and characterized the migration of speech to social media as "a revolution of historic proportions, *Packingham, supra.* However, it has exercised extreme caution in addressing the relationship between the First Amendment and the Internet.

All that said, principles and themes emerge from the Court's jurisprudence that aid interpretation of its doctrine and inform discussion of contemporary free speech and press issues. This book identifies and discusses those principles and themes as it applies them to various areas of free speech doctrine. It begins in this chapter with overviews of the history associated with the First Amendment, the values underlying protection of expression, and certain doctrinal themes that consistently emerge in the Court's decisions.

A. *THE HISTORY OF FREE EXPRESSION IN ENGLAND AND THE EARLY YEARS OF THE REPUBLIC*

Consider the following hypothetical:

> You are a small internet service provider that has received a national security letter, an administrative subpoena issued by the FBI, seeking to gather all information about the internet activities of one of your customers that the FBI believes is "relevant to a foreign counter-intelligence investigation," including their complete web browsing activity, the IP addresses of everyone the customer has communicated with, and records of online purchases. Under federal law, you are required to turn over the information to the FBI. Furthermore, you are prohibited from challenging the subpoena in a court of law or from ever disclosing to any other person that you have received it. *See* The USA Patriot Act § 505, Pub. L. No. 107-56, 115 Stat. 272 (2001).

As you read the history below, consider how it bears on the above hypothetical. To what extent does the First Amendment prohibit or allow national security letters? How do the struggles over English licensing and the law of seditious libel in England and the early Republic reflect on the subpoena issue?

1. *England*

Prior to and including the late eighteenth century, English officials attempted to suppress "dangerous" or "offensive" speech, ostensibly for the preservation of the country or the welfare of its citizens. For example, libels of private persons were frequently punished as breaches of the peace. *See* 4 William Blackstone, *Commentaries on the Laws of England* *150. In addition, the Crown and Parliament also attempted to punish expression criticizing government officials, government policies, and religion. *See* Leonard W. Levy, *Emergence of a Free Press* 4-8 (1985). Two forms of regulation emerged as most effective—licensing and prosecutions for seditious libel.

a. Licensing

The fifteenth century invention of the printing press saw increased distribution of written literature and a concomitant rise in the Crown's interest in regulating the distribution of potentially "dangerous" publications. Medieval laws punishing treason, heresy, libel, and spreading "false news" against the king (Scandalum Magnatum) were already available to suppress pernicious expression. However, such laws allowed only piecemeal regulation and the Crown wanted a more unified mechanism of regulation. Beginning in the sixteenth century, the Crown claimed the authority to license printed materials as a matter of royal prerogative (powers vested in the monarch alone). Those wanting to publish printed materials had to submit their work to licensing authorities who could censor portions of it prior to granting a license. Publication without licensors' approval was punishable in the prerogative courts (those associated with the Crown). The Crown justified licensing because "the stability of the government and the peace of the realm demanded strict control" of published materials. Fredrick Seaton Siebert, *Freedom of the Press in England 1476-1776* at 22 (1952). However, few standards guided censors in their decisions, placing publishers at the mercy of government officials' arbitrary determinations.

Licensing laws were controversial. Many English libertarians argued against them, claiming they were detrimental to personal liberty and good government. The English Levellers (a radical democratic movement formed during the seventeenth century English civil wars) argued that a free press was "essential unto Freedom . . . for what may not be done to that people who may not speak or write, but at the pleasure of Licensers." "The Humble Petition of Firm and Constant Friends," in *Leveller Manifestoes of the Puritan Revolution* 326, 328 (Don M. Wolfe ed., 1944). Similarly, John Milton argued that licensing laws would discourage learning, prove fruitless in preventing the spread of "evil," and placed too much faith in the infallibility of licensors. John Milton, "Areopagitica," in *Areopagitica and of Education* 5, 21 (George H. Sabine ed., 1951).

Licensing laws nonetheless remained the primary mechanism for suppressing printed expression through the seventeenth century. In 1694, Parliament did not renew the licensing laws upon their expiration, primarily because they were expensive, imposed an undue burden on printers, were often widely ignored, and were difficult to enforce systematically. In effect, licensing expired for "reasons of expediency rather than of conviction on moral or philosophical grounds" regarding the necessity of a free press. Siebert, *supra*, at 261.

b. Seditious Libel

While licensing waned as a mechanism of enforcement in the seventeenth century, other legal instruments of suppression came to the fore. Government officials initially attempted to prosecute speech under the treason laws, which prohibited (1) imagining or plotting the death of the King, (2) making war against the King, or (3) aiding the King's enemies. By the end of the seventeenth century, judges found that writings and printings critical of the Crown could provide the "overt act" necessary for successful treason prosecutions. For example, citizens were tried for publishing materials arguing that the King should be accountable to his subjects.

While government officials initially believed that "constructive treason" prosecutions were appropriate methods of suppressing publications critical of the government, prosecutions were difficult for several reasons. Much anti-government literature was not extreme enough to be considered treasonable; juries believed the death penalty to be an unduly harsh punishment; and Parliament enacted a law substantially reforming the procedures used at treason trials, thus providing greater protection for those accused of the crime. For discussion, see Siebert, *supra*, at 264-269; Philip Hamburger, *The Development of the Law of Seditious Libel and the Control of the Press*, 37 Stan. L. Rev. 661, 666, 717-23 (1985).

The English government thus increasingly turned to seditious libel prosecutions. Such prosecutions had been available to the government for at least a century as a subset of libel and defamation prosecutions, which had developed to prevent breaches of the peace. In the late sixteenth and early seventeenth centuries, the government pursued seditious libel prosecutions primarily when they involved written statements that tended to injure a specific official's reputation. Consequently, such prosecutions were similar to those involving libels of private individuals.

In 1605, Attorney General Edward Coke's prosecution of Lewis Pickering for publishing a defamatory poem about two Archbishops of Canterbury marked a significant change regarding libel concerning government officials. In his report of the case, Coke noted the consequences of libels against private persons versus government officials:

> If it be against a private man it deserveth a severe punishment, for although the Libel be made against one, yet it inciteth all those of the same family, kindred or society to revenge, and so may be the cause [by consequence of] quarrels and breach of the peace, and may be the cause of shedding of blood and of great inconvenience; if it be against a Magistrate, or other public person, it is a greater offence; for it concerneth not onely the breach of the peace, but also the scandal of the government; for

> what greater scandal of government can there be than to have corrupt or wicked Magistrates to be appointed and constituted but the King to govern his Subjects under him? And greater imputation to the State cannot be, than to suffer such corrupt men to sit in the sacred seat of Justice, or to have any medling in or concerning the administration of Justice.

Case de Libellis Famosis, 5 Coke 125a, 125a (1605). The case also established that criminal libels such as the one involved need not be false to be punished nor did the victim need to be alive for the government to punish the libel. *Id.* at 125a-125b. Although the Pickering case was prosecuted as a straightforward libel, the case's central propositions (dispensing with truth as a defense and establishing that libel against government officials caused greater mischief than private libels) were important building blocks in the transformation of seditious libel as a crime.

During the seventeenth and early eighteenth centuries, prosecutions of seditious libel began to change. Government officials urged that any writing critical of government, not just writing aimed at specific officials, qualified as seditious libel. Eventually, the courts recognized officials' claims. In *Queen v. Tutchin,* the publisher of a periodical, *The Observator,* was prosecuted for publishing general accusations that national leaders took bribes of French gold and that military officials were corrupt. In response to defendant's argument that libel required statements about a particular person, Lord Holt declared it would be "a very strange doctrine: to say it is not a libel reflecting on the government[.] [E]ndeavouring to possess the people that the government is maladministered by corrupt persons . . . is certainly a reflection on the government." Queen v. Tutchin, 90 Eng. Rep. 1133 (Q.B. 1704). Lord Holt enlarged the definition of seditious libel, permanently bringing it out from under the auspices of traditional libel and making it a separate crime. His justification echoed Coke's reasons for distinguishing between private libels and libels of specific government officials:

> If people should not be called to account for possessing the people with an ill opinion of the government, no government can subsist; for it is very necessary for all governments that the people should have a good opinion of it. And nothing can be worse to any government than to endeavour to procure animosities as to the management of it. This has been always looked upon as a crime, and no government can be safe without it be punished.

Id.

As with earlier versions of seditious libel, judges found the truth of the published matter immaterial to the charge of seditious libel. In addition, they implied the knowledge and malice required for the crime came from the statement's defamatory content. In other words, the courts assumed the defendants had the necessary bad intent simply from the fact that the statement was defamatory; no other proof of intent was required. Some publishers attempted to evade the law's requirements by publishing satires or ironical statements that did not explicitly criticize government officials. But the courts made clear that such writings could still be punished as seditious libel. *See* Queen v. Dr. Brown, 88 Eng. Rep. 911 (Q.B. 1706). However, a jury rather than a judge had to find ironic or satirical writing libelous since it was not clearly malicious.

Detractors argued that the law of seditious libel gave judges too much leeway to find simple criticism of the government dangerous. For example, John Trenchard and Thomas Gordon, writing under the pseudonym "Cato," argued that "[w]hen words used in their true and proper sense, and understood in their literal and natural meaning, import nothing that is criminal; then to strain their genuine signification to make them intend sedition (which possibly the author might intend too) is such a stretch of discretionary power, as must subvert all the principles of free government, and overturn every species of liberty." Cato, "Second Discourse Upon Libels," 3 *Cato's Letters* No. 101. Trenchard and Gordon acknowledged that "men ought to speak well of their governors . . . while their governors deserve to be well spoken of; but [for officials] to do public mischief, without hearing of it, is only the prerogative and felicity of tyranny. . . . The administration of government is nothing else, but the attendance of trustees of the people upon the interest and affairs of the people. . . . Only the wicked governors of men dread what is said of them." Cato, "Of Freedom of Speech: That the Same Is Inseparable from Publick Liberty," in 1 *Cato's Letters* No. 15.

Despite criticism of seditious libel law, it eventually became settled practice. In 1769, Blackstone summarized the state of freedom of the press in England:

> The liberty of the press is indeed essential to the nature of a free state; but this consists in laying no previous restraints upon publications, and not in freedom from censure for criminal matter when punished. . . . To subject the press to the restrictive power of a licenser, as was formerly done . . . is to subject all freedom of sentiment to the prejudices of one man, and make him the arbitrary and infallible judge of all controverted points in learning, religion, and government. But to punish (as the law does at present) any dangerous or offensive writings, which, when published, shall on a fair and impartial trial be adjudged of a pernicious tendency, is necessary for the preservation of peace and good order, of government and religion, the only solid foundations of civil liberty.

Blackstone, *supra*, at *151-152. Accordingly, although prior restraints in the form of licensing schemes were considered antithetical to free expression, laws imposing subsequent punishment, such as seditious libel laws, were not.

2. *The Early American Republic*

a. Generally

There is some debate as to whether Blackstone's view prevailed in the colonies when the First Amendment was adopted. Licensing in the colonies, as in England, was considered inconsistent with free expression. The law of seditious libel, however, was another matter. Like much of English common law, the law of seditious libel passed over to the colonies. However, there were few seditious libel prosecutions in eighteenth century America. The most famous of these—the prosecution of John Peter Zenger for publishing remarks critical of the Governor General of New York in 1735—was an important milestone in such prosecutions. Zenger's counsel argued, against all existing precedent at the time, that Zenger should not be convicted because his publications were based in fact. Although truth had never been a defense to libel and Zenger's publication was a classic example of words often punished as seditious libel, the jury returned a "not guilty" verdict. The *Zenger* verdict signaled the depth of popular opposition to seditious libel laws used to punish criticism of the government. Accordingly, elected assemblies more commonly used "breaches of parliamentary privilege" (essentially, the power to find people in contempt) to punish statements critical of the legislature and the government. But even that tool became ineffective due to popular opposition. *See generally* Levy, *supra*, at 16-61, David A. Anderson, *The Origins of the Press Clause*, 30 UCLA L. Rev. 455, 509-515 (1983).

Thus, the law allowed substantial punishment of seditious libel but its practical effect was unclear. During the eighteenth century, newspapers and publications frequently printed material critical of the government with few repercussions. Nevertheless, colonists were not always principled in their willingness to extend protection to speech they disliked, especially as the rift between England and the colonies grew. Speech criticizing the royalist government was widely tolerated while loyalist speech was not. *See* Levy, *supra*, at 173-183; Anderson, *supra*, at 495; David M. Rabban, *The Ahistorical Historian: Leonard Levy on Freedom of Expression in Early American History*, 37 Stan. L. Rev. 795, 842 (1985); Richard Buel, "Freedom of the Press in Revolutionary America: The Evolution of Libertarianism, 1760-1820," in *The Press and the American Revolution* 59, 71-72, 74-75 (Bernard Bailyn & John Hench eds., 1980).

b. The Adoption of the First Amendment

First Amendment scholars debate whether the Framers of the First Amendment intended to adopt the Blackstonian view regarding freedom of expression. Zechariah Chafee expressed the standard libertarian sentiment that the Framers "intended to wipe out the common law of sedition, and make further prosecutions for criticism of government, without any incitement to law-breaking, forever impossible in the United States of America." Zechariah Chafee, *Freedom of Speech in War Time*, 32 Harv. L. Rev. 932, 947 (1919). Chaffee argued that since licensing schemes had expired in England in 1695 and in the colonies by 1725, the Framers of the First Amendment intended to do more than simply prohibit prior restraints.

Legal historian Leonard Levy, however, substantially challenged Chafee's assumptions. He concluded from historical evidence that although the "Declaration of Independence severed the political connection with England[,] . . . the American states continued the English common-law system except as explicitly rejected by statute. If the revolution produced any radical libertarians on the meaning of freedom of speech and press, they were not at the Constitutional Convention or the First Congress, which drafted the Bill of Rights." Levy, *supra*, at xv. Thus, Levy concluded that the Framers' conception of freedom of expression meant to leave the law of seditious libel intact. There is much to support Levy's hypothesis. As noted above, seditious libel laws did exist and the Framers tolerated some seditious libel prosecutions. Furthermore, they never intended to abolish such prosecutions in the states. Although James Madison, the primary architect of the First Amendment, also proposed a free press clause explicitly applicable to the states, the First

Congress rejected Madison's attempts to protect free expression from state restrictions. Instead, the First Amendment expressly applies only to Congress. *See* Anderson, *supra*, at 476-478, 483.[1]

Although most scholars agree that seditious libel played a greater role in the colonies and the framing of the First Amendment than Professor Chafee acknowledges, not everyone agrees with Professor Levy. Several commentators argue that Levy's thesis misses important historical subtleties regarding the Constitution and the First Amendment. Professor David Rabban, for example, has noted that numerous prominent colonial theorists argued that the government is the servant of the people. They understood the necessity of reforming, if not totally eliminating, seditious libel prosecutions to conform to notions of popular sovereignty. These scholars argued that the common law of seditious libel should require a showing of malicious intent, truth should be a defense, and juries rather than judges should be allowed to decide whether publications were seditious. Without such changes, they believed seditious libel prosecutions interfered with popular sovereignty because officials were punishing mere criticism of government conduct rather than truly dangerous speech. *See generally* Rabban, *supra*; Anderson, *supra*; William T. Mayton, *Seditious Libel and the Lost Guarantee of Freedom of Expression*, 84 Colum. L. Rev. 91 (1984).

3. *The Sedition Act of 1798*

Enacted less than a decade after the First Amendment's adoption, the Sedition Act of 1798 produced the first significant controversy regarding the scope of First Amendment protection. The Act was adopted amid growing hostilities toward ideas generated by the French Revolution, which sparked a bitter political divide between the Federalist and Republican parties. The Federalists believed in a strong central government whose purpose was to preserve security and property rights. They had little faith in the "common man's" ability to govern, believing that citizens could voice their opinions through elections but that elected officials were better suited to the responsibility of governing. Republicans, on the other hand, were strong believers in popular government and valued liberty over security. They argued for decentralized authority over decision-making and a government directly responsive to its citizens. Federalists viewed the ideas generated by the French Revolution as a threat to the nation's security; Republicans viewed it as a continuation of American ideals of liberty and democracy.

Federalists, who were then in power, argued France would imminently attack the United States and that it was necessary to prepare for war. Republicans refused to cooperate. In congressional debates and partisan newspapers accusations flew between the two parties. Federalists accused Republicans of disloyalty and argued

---

1. Eventually, the Supreme Court read the First Amendment's freedom of speech as among the liberties protected by the Fourteenth Amendment's Due Process Clause applicable to the states. *See* Gitlow v. New York, 268 U.S. 652 (1925).

hostile foreign forces were sowing the seeds of subversion within the country. Republicans accused the Federalists of exaggerating the danger to further their political ends. To silence critics and ensure a united front at home, Federalist politicians pushed the Sedition Act of 1798, Act of July 14, 1798, 1 Stat. 596, through Congress. The Sedition Act prohibited

> writing, printing, publishing or uttering, any false, scandalous, and malicious . . . writings against the government of the United States, or either house of the Congress of the United States, or the President of the United States, with intent to defame [them]; or to bring them . . . into contempt or disrepute; or to excite against them . . . the hatred of the good people of the United States, or to stir up sedition within the United States, or to excite any unlawful combinations therein, for opposing or resisting any law of the United States, or any [lawful] act of the President of the United States.

Given earlier criticism of the law of seditious libel, the Act provided that truth *was* a defense to a charge of seditious libel, that malicious intent *was* a required element of the crime, and that *juries*, rather than judges, were to decide whether a writing was defamatory.

Republicans opposed the Act, arguing it violated the First Amendment. They argued that the people, as absolute sovereigns over the government, had a right to criticize their elected officials. The Sedition Act, they feared, would be used to suppress information critical to public decision-making and good government. This was true even with the improvements because it was simply too easy for government officials to find that an opinion criticizing the government was not true and therefore could be punished. Thus, the indeterminacy of such laws would lead to self-censorship or too much discretion in government officials to act in their self-interest. Federalists, in contrast, justified the law as necessary to preserving the nation. Although they acknowledged the government was based upon notions of popular sovereignty, they maintained that to govern effectively, elected officials must be protected from criticism. Some argued that there was even greater reason to protect government officials from criticism in a popular government than in a monarchy because "[t]o mislead the judgment of the people, where they have no power may produce no mischief [but to] mislead the judgment of the people where they have *all* the power . . . must produce the greatest possible mischief." Richard Buel, *Securing the Revolution* 256 (1972). They further argued that the technical improvements in the law provided sufficient protection for speech.

In fact, the Act was vigorously prosecuted only against Republican newspapers and other Republican supporters. In 1799, Federalist officials began an organized campaign to prosecute the leaders of all prominent Republican newspapers (timing that coincided with national elections). From 1798 through 1801, at least 25 Republicans were prosecuted under the Act. Prosecutions were based on criticism such as that found in a handbill distributed by Anthony Haswell in support of Matthew Lyon, a Republican already convicted under the Act. Haswell wrote that Lyon was held "by the oppressive hand of usurped power in a loathsome prison, suffering all the indignities which can be heaped upon him by a hard-hearted savage, who has, to the disgrace of Federalism, been elevated to a station where he can satiate his barbarity on the misery of his victims." *See* Geoffrey R. Stone, *Perilous Times, Free Speech in Wartime* 63 (2004). As was the case in many such prosecutions, the judge directed the jury to enter a guilty verdict, and truth, much as the Republicans feared, provided very little defense for such a nebulous statement. Thus, the technical improvements to the Sedition Act provided little protection for speech critical of the government.

The Supreme Court never directly ruled on the constitutionality of the Sedition Act. However, several Justices upheld its constitutionality while riding circuit in the lower courts. Most scholars agree that the unpopularity of the Act was at least partly responsible for the Federalist defeat in the 1800 elections. The Act expired in 1801, and President Thomas Jefferson eventually pardoned persons convicted under it (although, ironically, he tolerated common law and state law seditious libel prosecutions of his critics). For more in-depth discussion of the history of the Sedition Act, see Levy, *supra*, at 242-349; Stone, *supra*, at 15-78; Mayton, *supra*, at 112, 121-130; Rabban, *supra*, at 841-854. For a discussion of contemporary concerns over governmental efforts to suppress criticism of government, see Timothy Zick, *The First Amendment in the Trump Era* 27-48 (2019).

4. *From the Sedition Act to World War I*

The expiration of the Sedition Act did not resolve the dispute over whether the Framers meant to adopt the Blackstonian view or a more speech-protective view of the First Amendment. Although many came to understand the Sedition Act as a misguided exercise of power, government officials resuscitated the crime of seditious libel with some regularity. During the Civil War, for example, although no federal sedition statute was enacted, military officials issued orders prohibiting speech that expressed sympathy for the enemy, criticized the Army, or "tended to bring the war policy of the Administration into disrepute." Michael Kent Curtis, *Lincoln, Vallandigham, and Anti-War Speech in the Civil War*, 7 Wm. & Mary B. Rt. J. 105, 119-120 (1998). Citizens and politicians were arrested for anti-war sentiments under the orders. *Id.*; *see also* Stone, *supra*, at 94-126.

The Supreme Court resolved few free speech issues during the Civil War, but disputes over the meaning of the First Amendment were evident in Patterson v. Colorado, 205 U.S. 454, 462 (1907). *Patterson* involved contempt prosecutions of the owner and publisher of two newspapers in Colorado that featured a series of editorials criticizing recent Colorado Supreme Court rulings as politically motivated. The Attorney General of Colorado instituted criminal contempt proceedings in the state supreme court on the basis that the editorials "were designed, intended, and calculated to hold up to public opprobrium and to incite public contempt for this court and certain of the justices thereof, and for the purpose of leading the people of this state to distrust the fairness and impartiality of the decisions of this court." People v. New Times Pblg. Co, 35 Colo. 253, 276 (1906). Patterson (the owner) was found guilty of contempt and appealed to the United States Supreme Court.

A few points in the Court's majority opinion, written by Justice Holmes, are notable. First, Justice Holmes refused to decide whether the First Amendment protected freedom of speech from abridgement by the states in addition to the federal government. This issue "was finally decided in favor of speakers decades later. *See supra* footnote 1. Second, the majority noted that even if the First Amendment restrained states, it did not prevent Patterson's contempt conviction because

> the main purpose of such constitutional provisions is "to prevent all such *previous restraints* upon publications as had been practised by other governments," and they do not prevent the subsequent punishment of such as may be deemed contrary to the public welfare. The preliminary freedom extends as well to the false as to the true; the subsequent punishment may extend as well to the true as to the false. This was the law of criminal libel apart from statute in most cases, if not in all.
>
> . . . [T]he rule applied to criminal libels applies yet more clearly to contempts. A publication likely to reach the eyes of a jury, declaring a witness in a pending cause a perjurer, would be none the less a contempt that it was true. . . . The theory of our system is that the conclusions to be reached in a case will be induced only by evidence and argument in open court, and not by any outside influence, whether of private talk or public print. . . . [I]f a court regards [a] publication concerning a matter of law pending before it, as tending toward. . . . interference, it may punish it. . . .

205 U.S. at 458-463.

Justice Harlan dissented. He first noted that "when the 14th Amendment prohibited the states from impairing or abridging the privileges of citizens of the United States, it necessarily prohibited the states from impairing or abridging the constitutional rights of such citizens to free speech and a free press." *Id.* at 558. Justice Harlan further rejected the majority's argument that the main purpose of the First Amendment was to protect against prior restraints. "I cannot assent to that view," Justice Harlan wrote, "if it be meant that the legislature may impair or abridge the rights of a free press and of free speech whenever it thinks that the public welfare requires that to be done. The public welfare cannot override constitutional privileges, and if the rights of free speech and of a free press are, in their essence, attributes of national citizenship, as I think they are, then neither Congress nor any state, since the adoption of the 14th Amendment, can, by legislative enactments or by judicial action, impair or abridge them." *Id.* at 559.

The prosecution of speakers critical of the war effort during World War I forced the Court to revisit whether the First Amendment protected speech from statutes imposing criminal punishment. In Schenck v. United States, 249 U.S. 47 (1919), *infra* p. 30, Justice Holmes this time found that the First Amendment was not simply limited to preventing prior restraints. As Chapter 2 illustrates in greater detail, deriving a judicial standard with which to judge the constitutionality of criminal statutes is still far from easy.

B. *FIRST AMENDMENT VALUES*

Colonial defenders of free expression posited many theories supporting the broad protection of free speech. James Madison argued that freedom of the press was necessary in a democratic government where officials were servants of the people who were the ultimate sovereigns. James Madison, "Report Accompanying the Virginia Resolution," reprinted in 4 *The Debates in the Several State Conventions on the Adoption of the Federal Constitution* 569-570 (J. Elliott ed., 1836). Thomas Jefferson argued that free debate would lead to truth: "[T]ruth is great and will prevail if left to herself[;]. . . . she is the proper and sufficient antagonist to error, and has nothing to fear from the conflict unless by human interposition disarmed of her natural weapons, free argument and debate." Thomas Jefferson, "A Bill for Establishing Religious Freedoms," in 2 *The Papers of Thomas Jefferson* 545, 546 (Julian P. Boyd ed., 1950). The Continental Congress approved a declaration in 1774 stating that

> [t]he importance of [freedom of the press] consists, besides the advancement of truth, science, morality, and arts in general, in its diffusion of liberal sentiments on the administration of Government, in its ready communication of thoughts between subjects, and its consequential promotion of union among them, whereby oppressive officers are shamed or intimidated into more honourable and just modes of conducting affairs.

Address to the Inhabitants of Quebec (1774). Do these justifications, along with historical events argue for or against protecting expression? Do they stand alone as justifications for protecting free expression?

Modern theorists have taken up these themes as well. As you read the following excerpts on modern free speech values, consider how they relate to statements made contemporaneous with the adoption of the First Amendment. Does any theory satisfactorily explain why we believe free expression *should* be protected? This section also briefly refers to Supreme Court cases that cite theoretical justifications for protecting speech. The Court has never relied on a single unified principle to justify its free speech jurisprudence; rather it has relied on many different theoretical justifications. Should we search for a single overarching principle to justify protection of expression?

Recall the national security letter hypothetical above. Do the values discussed below shed light on whether such subpoenas are consistent with the First Amendment?

1. *Self-Governance*

Alexander Meiklejohn is the most famous modern proponent of the self-governance rationale:

> We Americans . . . believe in self-government. . . . When self-governing men demand freedom of speech they are not saying that every individual has an unalienable right to speak whenever, wherever, however, he chooses. . . . [T]he vital point . . . is that no suggestion of policy shall be denied a hearing because it is on one side of the issue rather than another. . . . [T]hough citizens may, on other grounds, be barred from speaking, they may not be barred because their views are thought to be false or dangerous. No plan of action shall be outlawed because someone in control thinks it unwise, unfair, un-American. . . . And the reason for this equality of status in the field of ideas lies deep in the very

> foundations of the self-governing process. When men govern themselves, it is they—and no one else—who must pass judgment upon unwisdom and unfairness and danger. . . . Just so far as, at any point, the citizens who are to decide an issue are denied acquaintance with information or opinion or doubt or disbelief or criticism which is relevant to that issue, just so far as the result must be ill-considered, ill-balanced planning for the general good. *It is the mutilation of the thinking process of the community against which the First Amendment to the Constitution is directed.* The principle of the freedom of speech springs from the necessities of the program of self-government.

Alexander Meiklejohn, *Free Speech and Its Relation to Self-Government* 15-16, 24-27 (1948) (emphasis in original).

The Supreme Court has emphasized the self-governance rationale in various cases. In reversing a conviction for violating a statute prohibiting the display of a red flag as a symbol of opposition to organized government, the Court in Stromberg v. California, 283 U.S. 359, 369 (1931), stated that

> [t]he maintenance of the opportunity for free political discussion to the end that government may be responsive to the will of the people and that changes may be obtained by lawful means, an opportunity essential to the security of the Republic, is a fundamental principle of our constitutional system.

In reversing a libel verdict brought against the *New York Times* by an Alabama municipal official, the Court in New York Times Co. v. Sullivan, 376 U.S. 254, 270 (1964), relied on "a profound national commitment to the principle that debate on public issues should be uninhibited, robust, and wide-open, and that it may well include vehement, caustic, and sometimes unpleasantly sharp attacks on government and public officials."

Recently, in Citizens United v. Federal Election Commission, 558 U.S. 310 (2010), the Supreme Court, by a 5–4 vote, invalidated key provisions of the Bipartisan Campaign Reform Act of 2002 because, in the majority's view, the law prohibited core political speech (albeit by corporate entities). In holding that strict limits on uncoordinated political advocacy by corporations violate the First Amendment, Justice Anthony Kennedy explained that "the First Amendment protects speech and speaker, and the ideas that flow from each." *Id.* at 341. Moreover, "political speech must prevail against laws that would suppress it, whether by design or inadvertence." *Id.* at 340-41. The *Citizens United* Court emphasized the centrality of speech to democratic self-government, explaining that "[t]he First Amendment has its fullest and most urgent application to speech uttered during a campaign for political office." *Id.* at 339.

Citizens United justifies providing robust First Amendment protection for corporate political speech on the theory that "[s]peech is an essential mechanism of democracy, for it is the means to hold officials accountable to the people." *Id.* Because "[t]he right of citizens to inquire, to hear, to speak, and to use information to reach consensus is a precondition to enlightened self-government and a necessary means to protect it," *id.*, even political speech by corporations enjoys robust constitutional protection. Thus, Congress's concerns about the possibility of corporate political speech either distorting the democratic process or creating a strong impression of corruption were not sufficient justifications to sustain a flat statutory ban on corporate electioneering speech.

NOTES AND QUESTIONS

1. *The meaning of self-governance.* Does Meiklejohn's theory imply that *only* speech pertaining to public issues or public functions is protected by the First Amendment? *See* Zechariah Chafee, *Book Review*, 62 Harv. L. Rev. 891, 896 (1949) (arguing that Meiklejohn's theory ignored the Framers' interest in religious, scientific, poetic, artistic, and dramatic expression). Meiklejohn later wrote that his concept of self-governance was broader than Chafee claimed, noting that "[s]elf-government can exist only insofar as the voters acquire the intelligence, integrity, sensitivity, and generous devotion to the general welfare that, in theory, casting a ballot is assumed to express[.]" Alexander Meiklejohn, *The First Amendment Is an Absolute*, 1961 Sup. Ct. Rev. 245, 255-257. How does Meikeljohn's second statement distinguish speech from other human activities, such as trading on the stock market or engaging in sexual activities, that "also form personality [and] teach and create attitudes?" Robert Bork, *Neutral Principles and Some First Amendment Problems*, 47 Ind. L.J. 1, 27 (1971).
2. *Self-Governance and the checking value.* Perhaps the self-governance rationale is somewhat different from Meiklejohn's conception. Professor Vince Blasi argues that "[t]he central premise of the checking value [of free speech] is that the abuse of official power is an especially serious evil [due to government's special] capacity to employ legitimized violence. . . . Under [this] view of democracy, the role of the ordinary citizen is not so much to contribute on a continuing basis to the formation of public policy as to retain a veto power to be employed when the decisions of officials pass certain bounds." Vincent Blasi, *The Checking Value in First Amendment Theory*, 1977 Am. B. Found. Research J. 521, 527-542. Does Blasi's thesis more or less satisfactorily support a self-governance rationale than Meiklejohn's?

2. *Truth and the Marketplace of Ideas*

John Stuart Mill first elaborated on the search for truth rationale in *On Liberty*:

> [T]he peculiar evil of silencing the expression of an opinion is, that it is robbing the human race; posterity as well as the existing generation; those who dissent from the opinion, still more who hold it. If the opinion is right, they are deprived of the opportunity of exchanging error for truth: if wrong, they lose, what is almost as great a benefit, the clearer perception and livelier impression of truth, produced by its collision with error. . . .
>
> First, if any opinion is compelled to silence, that opinion may, for aught we can certainly know, be true. To deny this is to assume our own infallibility.

> Second, though the silenced opinion be an error, it may and very commonly does, contain a portion of the truth; and since the general or prevailing opinion on any subject is rarely or never the whole truth, it is only by the collision of adverse opinions that the remainder of the truth has any chance of being supplied.
>
> Thirdly, even if the received opinion be not only true, but the whole truth; unless it is suffered to be, and actually is, vigorously and earnestly contested, it will, by most of those who receive it, be held in the manner of prejudice, with little comprehension or feeling of its rational grounds. And not only this but, fourthly, the meaning of the doctrine itself will be in danger of being lost, or enfeebled, and deprived of its vital effect on the character and conduct: the dogma being a mere formal profession, inefficacious for good, but cumbering the ground, and preventing the growth of any real and heartfelt conviction, from reason or personal experience.

John Stuart Mill, *On Liberty* 87, 118 (David Bromwich & George Kale eds., 2003).

Justice Holmes picked up this thread in his dissenting opinion in Abrams v. United States, 250 U.S. 616 (1919), arguing that

> [p]ersecution for the expression of opinions seems to me perfectly logical. If you have no doubt of your premises or your power and want a certain result with all your heart you naturally express your wishes in law and sweep away all opposition. To allow opposition by speech seems to indicate that you think the speech impotent, as when a man says that he has squared the circle, or that you do not care whole heartedly for the result, or that you doubt either your power or your premises. But when men have realized that time has upset many fighting faiths, they may come to believe even more than they believe the very foundations of their own conduct that the ultimate good desired is better reached by *free trade in ideas— that the best test of truth is the power of the thought to get itself accepted in the competition of the market, and that truth is the only ground upon which their wishes safely can be carried out.* That at any rate is the theory of our Constitution. It is an experiment, as all life is an experiment. Every year if not every day we have to wager our salvation upon some prophecy based upon imperfect knowledge.

Id. at 630.

NOTES AND QUESTIONS

1. *The meaning of "truth."* Do Holmes's theory and Mills's vision of the truth differ? For discussion, see Kent Greenawalt, *Free Speech Justifications*, 89 Colum. L. Rev. 119 (1989); G. Edward White, *Justice Holmes and the Modernization of Free Speech Jurisprudence: The Human Dimension*, 80 Cal. L. Rev. 391, 439 (1992).
2. *"Objective" truth?* Does such a thing as objective "truth" exist? What does the controversy over the Sedition Act of 1798 suggest about the difficulty of ascertaining objective truth and using it as a basis for protecting speech?

3. *Protecting falsity.* On the other hand, what good does it serve to protect patently false speech such as statements "The Holocaust did not occur" or "The earth is flat"?
4. *"The marketplace" metaphor.* Do the assumptions of the "free trade in ideas" and the "marketplace" reflect the realities of contemporary society? Do certain social, interest, and political groups wield disproportionate power in speech marketplaces? Do these disparities call for interventions by the state or others in speech marketplaces? Do private social media companies "censor" speech in digital marketplaces in ways that are problematic? Are there sufficient controls such that "truth" and "falsity" can be distinguished in these new marketplaces, or does the modern social media marketplace demonstrate that lies, misinformation, and disinformation can and likely will flourish in a free and unfettered marketplace of ideas? Again, what does that likelihood suggest about legislative or regulatory interventions in social media marketplaces?

3. Autonomy/Self-Fulfillment

Recall the Continental Congress's "Address to the Inhabitants of Quebec," *supra*, and its reference to the "advancement of truth, science, morality, and arts in general." Non-political justifications for protecting speech were rare in colonial times as free expression was discussed primarily in political terms. Some Justices, however, have occasionally invoked individual-centered or autonomy-centered rationales to justify protection of speech. Note how these rationales differ from *collective* justifications such as self-government and the search for truth. Most famously, Justice Brandeis opined that "[t]hose who won our independence believed that the final end of the state was to make men free to develop their faculties, and that in its government the deliberative forces should prevail over the arbitrary. . . . They believed liberty to be the secret of happiness and courage to be the secret of liberty." Whitney v. California, 274 U.S. 357, 375 (1927) (Brandeis, J., concurring).

Autonomy, however, is a notoriously malleable concept. It can take on vastly different meanings depending on one's views. David Richards argues that

> the significance of free expression rests on the central human capacity to create and express symbolic systems, such as speech, writing, pictures, and music. Freedom of expression permits and encourages the exercise of these [capacities]. In so doing, it nurtures and sustains the self-respect of the mature person. . . . The value of free expression, in this view, rests on its deep relation to self-respect arising from autonomous self-determination without which the life of the spirit is meager and slavish.

David A.J. Richards, *Free Speech and Obscenity Law: Toward a Moral Theory of the First Amendment*, 123 U. Pa. L. Rev. 45, 62 (1974). Martin Redish, on the other hand, argues that

> the constitutional guarantee of free speech ultimately serves only one true value, which I have labeled "individual self-realization[.]" . . . [Self-realization] can be interpreted to refer either to development of the individual's

> powers and abilities—an individual "realizes" his or her full potential—or to the individual's control of his or her own destiny through making life-affecting decisions—an individual "realizes" the goals in life that he or she has set. . . .
>
> That the first amendment serves only one ultimate value, however, does not mean that the majority of values thought by others to be fostered by free speech—the "political process," "checking," and "marketplace-of-ideas" values—are invalid. . . . [T]hese other values, though perfectly legitimate, are in reality subvalues of self-realization. To the extent that they are legitimate, each can be explained by—and only by—reference to the primary value: individual self-realization.

Martin H. Redish, *The Value of Free Speech*, 130 U. Pa. L. Rev. 591, 593-594 (1982). Finally, Christina Wells claims that

> [a]utonomy . . . is not about atomistic individuals but about social creatures entitled to respect for their dignity. . . . [A system of free expression based upon such autonomy] would not focus on the rights of the speaker qua speaker but on the integrity of our thought processes as individuals and members of the community. Our thought processes are integral to our capacity for deliberation and self-governance. Ensuring their integrity is thus a necessary aspect of any system of laws built upon [this conception] of autonomy. Given that we develop our thought processes by communicating with others, and thereby our capacity for self-governance, protecting public expression is especially important. . . .
>
> A system of free expression based on [this conception of autonomy], however, would not merely concern itself with protection against government suppression. Because the State's purpose is to preserve the dignity of its citizen, such a system would also ensure that citizens use speech consistently with autonomy. The State can and should regulate speech, that by attempting to override the thought processes of other individuals, disrespects their rational capacities. Such speech does not facilitate, but rather detracts from, the public exercise of reason and is therefore the proper subject of the State's coercive powers.

Christina E. Wells, *Reinvigorating Autonomy: Freedom and Responsibility in the Supreme Court's First Amendment Jurisprudence*, 32 Harv. C.R.-C.L. L. Rev. 159, 161, 169-170 (1997).

NOTES AND QUESTIONS

1. *Speaker versus audience.* Do these individual authors locate the autonomy rationale in the speaker or in the listener? Does it make a difference from a First Amendment perspective if we think of the right as a "speaker's" right or a "listener's" right?
2. *The Supreme Court's approach.* The Supreme Court has not been consistent in locating free speech as a speaker's or listener's right. Compare Bridges v. California, 314 U.S. 252, 270 (1941) (stating that "it is a

prized American privilege to speak one's mind") and First National Bank v. Bellotti, 435 U.S. 765, 791 n.31 (1981) (stating that "[t]he First Amendment rejects the highly paternalistic approach of statutes . . . which restrict what people may hear").

4. *Dissent*

In the years surrounding the American Revolution, "dissent" played a large role in furthering revolutionary ideals. Dissenting churches that broke with the Church of England circulated religious literature with revolutionary themes while preachers gave revolutionary sermons. *See* Patricia U. Bonomi, "Religious Dissent and the Case for American Exceptionalism" at 31-55 in *Religion in a Revolutionary Age* (Ronald Hoffman & Peter J. Albert eds., 1994). Thomas Paine's *Common Sense,* which argued for freedom from British rule in language infused with dissenting Protestant beliefs, was the best-selling book of its kind at the time.

Professor Steven Shiffrin is the strongest proponent of the notion that "the value of dissent should be given greater prominence in free speech and press law." Steven H. Shiffrin, *The First Amendment, Democracy, and Romance* 100-101 (1990). According to Professor Shiffrin, "dissent and the threat of dissent make hierarchy less oppressive. Dissent communicates the fears, hopes, and aspirations of the less powerful to those in power. It sometimes chills the abuse of power; it sometimes paves the way for change by those in power or of those in power." *Id.* at 96. Such speech also fosters community engagement rather than atomistic individualism because "[d]issenters seek converts and colleagues." *Id.* at 91-93. Finally, Shiffrin argues that dissent fosters the emergence of truth even though "[d]issenters are often wrong." Nevertheless, because truth does not necessarily prevail in the marketplace of ideas, dissent is necessary to create "a robust, burgeoning marketplace." *Id.* at 95-96. For discussion of how contemporary restrictions on dissent, in particular imposition of civil costs and liabilities on protesters' speech, affect dissent see Timothy Zick, *The Costs of Dissent: Protest and Civil Liabilities,* 89 Geo. Wash. L. Rev. 233 (2021).

NOTES AND QUESTIONS

1. *The meaning of dissent.* Does dissent encompass the right to engage in "speech that criticizes existing customs, habits, traditions, institutions, or authorities" or only speech that is the "popularly disdained view"? *Id.* at 77. Steven H. Shiffrin, *Dissent, Injustice, and the Meanings of America* xi, 77 (1999). Or must dissent be "part of a social practice that challenges unjust hierarchies with the prospect of promoting progressive change"? *Id.* at 42. Do these definitions matter in terms of the scope of protection to be afforded dissent?
2. *Is dissent different?* Do the values of dissent identified above separate it from other theories of the First Amendment, such as self-government and the search for truth?

3. *Distrust of government.* Are there special reasons to distrust government in the realm of speech regulation? Frederick Schauer has posited, "Freedom of speech is based in large part on a distrust of the ability of government to make the necessary distinctions, a distrust of governmental determinations of truth and falsity, an appreciation of the fallibility of political leaders, and of somewhat deeper distrust of governmental power in a more general sense." Frederick Schauer, *Free Speech: A Philosophical Enquiry* (1982). Should we be concerned that suppression of dissent will lead to entrenched power or discrimination against unorthodox political and other views?

5. Anti-Theory

Does a neutral, theoretical principle support the First Amendment, or are the values identified above really politics in disguise? Consider the following excerpt:

> [I]f you have *any* answer to the question ["What is the First Amendment for?"], *any* answer at all, you are necessarily implicated in a regime of censorship. . . . [W]hen you say the First Amendment is for something—perhaps for giving truth the chance to emerge, or for providing the minds of citizens with the materials necessary for growth or self-realization, or for keeping the marketplace of ideas open in a democratic society—it becomes not only possible but inevitable that at some point you will ask of some instance of speech whether it in fact serves its high purpose or whether it does the opposite, retarding the search for truth, stunting the growth of mature judgment, fouling the marketplace.
>
> Although free-speech values supposedly stand alone and are said to be independent of circumstance and political pressure, they only become thick enough to provide a direction for decisionmaking when definitions and distinctions borrowed from particular circumstances (and borrowed selectively in relation to some substantive agenda) are presupposed as to their content. You must determine what you mean by "expression" or what is and is not a "free flow" or what does and does not constitute "self-realization" in relation to what notion of the self before any of these so-called principles will have any bite. And since these are not determinations those principles can make for themselves, when they do have bite, when invoking them actually gets you somewhere, it will be because inside them is the outside—substantive values, preferred outcomes, politics—from which they are rhetorically distinguished.

Stanley Fish, "The Dance of Theory," in *Eternally Vigilant: Free Speech in the Modern Era* 199, 223 (Lee C. Bollinger & Geoffrey R. Stone eds., 2002) (emphasis in original). Is Professor Fish saying that theoretical justifications for protecting speech are unhelpful, or is he simply saying that they are not—in and of themselves—"neutral"? How would recognition of their "non-neutrality" potentially advance discussion regarding the goals of the First Amendment?

C. *IMPLEMENTING THE FREEDOM OF SPEECH*

The previous readings involved the text, historical groundings, and philosophical discussion of the values supporting the First Amendment. How do those inform doctrines *implementing* the First Amendment? This book will discuss in some detail the Supreme Court's complex and evolving standards involving free expression. This chapter, however, provides a brief overview of the overarching legal themes that have dominated the Court's attention—speech vs. conduct, content discrimination, access to public property, prior restraints, vague and overly broad laws, and problems associated with facial and as-applied challenges.

When reading through the next several subsections, recall the national security letter hypothetical above and consider how it might implicate the legal doctrines set forth below.

1. *Speech vs. Conduct*

The First Amendment bars the government from "abridg[ing]" the "freedom of speech." Does this mean First Amendment applies only to speech in the literal sense or does it extend to expressive conduct? At what point does speech become so like conduct that the First Amendment no longer protects it?

Professor Thomas Emerson noted the importance of answering these questions in constructing a definition of "freedom of expression":

> The first task is to formulate in detail the distinction between "expression" and "action." . . . [T]he whole theory and practice of freedom of expression—the realization of any of the values it attempts to secure—rests upon this distinction. Hence the starting point for any legal doctrine must be to fix this line of demarcation.

Thomas I. Emerson, *Toward a General Theory of the First Amendment* 60 (1966). Unfortunately, the Court's jurisprudence regarding when conduct is sufficiently expressive to trigger First Amendment scrutiny is thin at best. It is often not clear as a practical matter where the line is between speech and action. As Professor Emerson noted, that line "at many points . . . becomes obscure. Expression often takes place in a context of action, or is closely linked with it, or is equivalent in its impact." *Id.* Is a political protest or demonstration speech, conduct, or both? What about "flipping someone the bird" or "liking" a comment or post on Facebook? Is the design of a home, including its architectural features, expressive? Is baking a cake conduct or expression?

Despite this lack of clarity, the speech/conduct distinction permeates much of the discussion surrounding the First Amendment. The thorny question of when conduct amounts to expression within the Court's jurisprudence is considered in Chapter 4, along with the scope of government power to regulate expressive conduct. But the speech/conduct distinction also permeates the discussion of whether speech has passed the bounds of expression and into the realm of unprotected conduct. *See, e.g.*, Roth v. United States, 354 U.S. 476, 514 (1957) (Douglas, J., dissenting) (discussing speech that is "so closely brigaded with illegal action as to be an inseparable part of it"). The cases in Chapter 2 involve advocacy of illegal activity, threats, and "fighting words." In these contexts, as with cases involving expressive conduct, the Court and scholars refer to unprotected speech as "conduct," but it is more often a shorthand way of saying "unprotected" or "low value" than it is an attempt to distinguish conduct from literal speech.

As you read the following chapters, keep in mind the question of whether the distinction between speech and conduct is helpful in determining whether the First Amendment should extend to the expression at issue.

2. *Content Discrimination*

According to the Supreme Court, the "government has no power to restrict expression because of its message, its ideas, its subject matter, or its content." Police Dept. of the City of Chicago v. Mosley, 408 U.S. 92, 95 (1972). Why is the Court so concerned about government regulation of the content of expression?

Chapter 3 discusses the Court's doctrine pertaining to content regulation. The Court has settled on a test that distinguishes statutes based on whether they explicitly regulate speech because of its content ("content-based" laws) or whether they affect speech but do not regulate based on what the speech says ("content-neutral" laws). The former are subject to stringent review called "strict scrutiny" while the latter statutes are subject to less rigorous review called "intermediate scrutiny." Turner Broadcasting v. FCC, 512 U.S. 622 (1994).

As noted above, the Court allows content discrimination if the speech is "unprotected" or "low value." However, the Court has found only a few categories of speech to be "low value," which it loosely describes as speech that is "no essential part of any exposition of ideas." Chaplinsky v. New Hampshire, 315 U.S. 568, 572 (1942). Thus far, the Court explicitly recognizes as "low value" only incitement to violence, threats, fighting words, defamation, obscenity, and child pornography. *See* United States v. Stevens, 559 U.S. 460, 468 (2010); *Brown v. Entertainment Merchants Ass'n,* 564 U.S. 786, 791 (2011). Nevertheless, arguments over whether regulated speech falls into an existing category or whether one can draw analogies to existing low value speech categories are still quite common because, if successful, they allow states to engage in permissible content discrimination.

3. *Access to Public Property*

The right to speak has little meaning if individuals or groups do not have access to public property, especially large public spaces such as parks. *See* Timothy Zick, *Speech Out of Doors: Preserving First Amendment Liberties in Public Places* (2008). Originally, the Court was unsympathetic to speakers' desire for access to public property, effectively giving the government the same rights as private property owners to exclude speakers. Ultimately, however, it found that streets, parks, and sidewalks have "immemorially been held in trust for the use of the public and, time out of mind, have been used for purposes of assembly, communicating thoughts between citizens, and discussing public questions." Hague v. CIO, 307 U.S. 496 (1939). Nevertheless, government officials may still have interests in regulating access based on neutral considerations of "time, place, and manner."

To what extent must government officials make available for expressive purposes other government property such as government offices, public libraries, or mailboxes? The Court has grappled, not altogether successfully, with the extent to which property other than streets, parks, and sidewalks must be available for expressive purposes. Chapter 5 discusses access to public properties and related issues in greater depth.

4. *Vague and Overly Broad Laws*

Laws can violate the Constitution not simply because they suppress speech based on content but because they proscribe too much speech or do not give fair notice as to what they attempt to regulate. The Court's doctrines of overbreadth and vagueness are designed to assess whether such laws are consistent with the First Amendment.

a. Overbreadth

Overbreadth doctrine starts from the assumption that government officials may legitimately proscribe some speech—e.g., government officials may regulate "low value" speech. Nevertheless, the overbreadth doctrine allows courts to strike down laws that are "draft[ed] . . . so broadly that they prohibit, or could prohibit, substantial amounts of constitutionally protected expression." Alan K. Chen, *Statutory Speech Bubbles, First Amendment Overbreadth, and Improper Legislative Purpose,* 38 Harv. C.R.-C.L. L. Rev. 31, 40 (2003). Overbreadth doctrine allows a person whose speech could permissibly be regulated to challenge a law as overly broad because the law might chill the speech of third-party non-litigant speakers. *See* Members of City Council of City of Los Angeles v. Taxpayers for Vincent, 466 U.S. 789 (1984); Gooding v. Wilson, 405 U.S. 518 (1972). As the Court has explained:

> Many persons, rather than undertake the considerable burden (and sometimes risk) of vindicating their rights through case-by-case litigation, will choose simply to abstain from protected speech—harming not only themselves but society as a whole, which is deprived of an uninhibited marketplace of ideas. Overbreadth adjudication, by suspending all enforcement of an over inclusive law, reduces these social costs caused by the withholding of protected speech.

Virginia v. Hicks, 539 U.S. 113, 119 (2003).

As the Court has observed, "Application of the overbreadth doctrine . . . is, manifestly, strong medicine. It has been employed by the Court sparingly and only as a last resort." Broadrick v. Oklahoma, 413 U.S. 601, 613 (1973). The Court has required challengers to show that a law is "substantially" overbroad. *Hicks,* 539 U.S. at 123-124. Thus, the overbreadth "must not only be real, but substantial as well, judged in relation to the statute's plainly legitimate sweep." *Broadrick*, 413 U.S. at 615. In all overbreadth challenges, the Court has been willing to uphold a law if the state's highest court has construed it narrowly enough so that it does not apply to protected speech. *See* Brockett v. Spokane Arcades, Inc., 472 U.S. 491 (1985).

b. Vagueness

An overly broad law can often also be challenged as vague. Such challenges are actually due process challenges with special consideration of free speech issues. Vague laws are problematic for several reasons:

> First, because we assume that man is free to steer between lawful and unlawful conduct, we insist that laws give the person of ordinary intelligence a reasonable opportunity to know what is prohibited, so that he may act accordingly. Vague laws may trap the innocent by not providing fair warning. Second, if arbitrary and discriminatory enforcement is to be prevented, laws must provide explicit standards for those who apply them. A vague law impermissibly delegates basic policy matters to policemen, judges, and juries for resolution on an ad hoc and subjective basis, with the attendant dangers of arbitrary and discriminatory application. Third, but related, where a vague statute "abut(s) upon sensitive areas of basic First Amendment freedoms," it "operates to inhibit the exercise of (those) freedoms." Uncertain meanings inevitably lead citizens to "steer far wider of the unlawful zone" . . . than if the boundaries of the forbidden areas were clearly marked.

Grayned v. City of Rockford, 408 U.S. 104, 108-109 (1972). The prevention of arbitrary and discriminatory enforcement of laws affecting speech is a consistent theme in the Court's discussion of the vagueness doctrine. *See* United States v. Williams, 535 U.S. 285 (2010); Holder v. Humanitarian Law Project, 561 U.S. 1 (2010); Smith v. Goguen, 415 U.S. 566 (1974).

As with overbreadth challenges, a state court can narrowly interpret a law to remove the vagueness problem. *See Williams*, 535 U.S. 285. Clear statutory definitions and settled legal meanings also may save an otherwise vague law. *Id.* at 306. Furthermore, a statute is not vague merely because one can envision a close case regarding speech that may fall within its scope. *Id.* at 305-306. "What renders a statute vague is not the possibility that it will sometimes be difficult to determine whether the incriminating fact it establishes has been proved; but rather the indeterminacy of precisely what that fact is." *Id.* at 306.

Unlike overbreadth challenges, an individual engaging in conduct a statute clearly proscribes cannot "complain of the vagueness of the law as applied to the conduct of others." *Humanitarian Law Project*, 130 S. Ct. at 2719. "[A] vagueness challenge does not turn on whether a law applies to a substantial amount of protected expression." *Id.*

c. Facial and As-Applied Challenges to Laws

As a procedural matter, individuals or entities wanting to challenge laws as violating the First Amendment have two possible approaches available to them. They can challenge the law as "facially" invalid or they can challenge the law "as applied" to their particular speech. In general, a facial challenge considers the restriction's application to *all* conceivable parties, while an as-applied challenge tests the application of that restriction to the facts of *a plaintiff's* concrete case.

Thus, in a facial challenge, a plaintiff argues that the statute could *never* be applied in a valid manner. In the First Amendment context, this argument translates into a claim that the statute creates an unacceptable risk of the suppression of ideas. Thus, "[w]hen asserting a facial challenge, a party seeks to vindicate not only his own rights, but those of others who may also be adversely impacted by the statute in question." City of Chicago v. Morales, 527 U.S. 41, 55 n.22 (1999); *Taxpayers for Vincent,* 466 U.S. at 789. Parties raising an as-applied challenge to the statute, on the other hand, argue that it is unconstitutional as applied to the party's own conduct.

Both the vagueness and overbreadth doctrines give rise to facial attacks. Specifically, "the overbreadth doctrine permits the facial invalidation of laws that inhibit the exercise of First Amendment rights if the impermissible applications of the law are substantial." *Morales,* 527 U.S. at 53. Further, a statute is subject to facial invalidation if "it fails to establish standards for the police and public that are sufficient to guard against the arbitrary deprivation of liberty interests." *Id.* at 53. Thus, "[w]hen vagueness permeates that text of . . . a law, it is subject to facial attack." *Id.* at 55.

If there are some conceivable instances of constitutional application, courts are more likely to entertain an as-applied challenge, but it is not always easy to tell when each challenge should be used. "[T]he distinction between facial and as-applied challenges is not so well defined that it has some automatic effect or that it must always control the pleadings and disposition in every case involving a constitutional challenge." Citizens United v. FEC, 130 S. Ct. 876, 893 (2009).

5. *Prior Restraint*

Although the Court eventually found that the First Amendment applied to subsequent punishment of speech as well as prior restraints, see Schenck v. United States, 249 U.S. 47 (1919), it nevertheless maintains a special antipathy to regulations amounting to prior restraints. Such regulations are the "most serious and least tolerable infringement of First Amendment rights." Nebraska Press Ass'n v. Stuart, 427 U.S. 539, 559 (1976). We know that the unfettered licensing schemes of sixteenth and seventeenth century England amounted to prior restraints, see *supra* Part I.A.1, but the Court has extended the concept to other forms of regulation. "[A]dministrative and judicial orders forbidding certain communications when issued in advance of the time that such communications are to occur" generally amount to prior restraints. Alexander v. United States, 509 U.S. 544, 550 (1993). Arbitrary decision-making and chilling of protected speech are primary concerns of the prior restraint doctrine. *See* Citizens United v. FEC, 130 S. Ct. 876, 895-96 (2009). Chapter 5, *infra,* discusses these issues in greater depth.

Nevertheless, the Court does not find all administrative and judicial orders to be prior restraints. It has upheld licensing schemes requiring protestors to apply for permits prior to their activities if those schemes provide objective criteria for officials to apply; regulate only time, place, and manner of the protests; and are unrelated to content. *See* Cox v. New Hampshire, 312 U.S. 569 (1941); Thomas v. Chicago Park Dist., 534 U.S. 316 (2002). Similarly, the Court has upheld content-neutral injunctions that regulate only the time, place, and manner of speech rather than suppressing it altogether. *See* Madsen v. Women's Health Ctr., Inc., 512 U.S. 753 (1994).

As you read, consider why courts disfavor some licensing schemes and injunctions and not others. For commentary on the Court's doctrine, see Vincent Blasi, *Toward a Theory of Prior Restraint: The Central Linkage,* 66 Minn. L. Rev. 11, 35-43 (1981); William T. Mayton, *Toward a Theory of First Amendment Process: Injunctions Against Speech, Subsequent Punishment, and the Costs of the Prior Restraint Doctrine,* 67 Cornell L. Rev. 245, 275 (1982); Frederick Schauer, *Fear, Risk and the First Amendment: Unraveling the Chilling Effect,* 58 B.U. L. Rev. 685, 725-730 (1978).

6. *Extra-Doctrinal Influences on the Law*

Given the brevity of the First Amendment, much decision-making regarding its scope and content is left to the courts, and ultimately the Supreme Court, as to whether speech is protected or unprotected. What influences the Court's decisions?

On the one hand, we know that the Court's jurisprudence protects core political speech and also extends some protection to commercial speech, sexually explicit speech, libel, offensive speech, and advocacy of illegal conduct. Even speech that can be punished, such as threats, incitement, fighting words, and obscenity, must meet carefully laid out judicial standards prior to suppression or punishment. On the other hand, as Professor Frederick Schauer notes, the Court apparently ignores whole areas of expression or states, with little or no discussion, that they are outside the purview of the First Amendment:

> The history of the First Amendment is the history of its boundaries. . . . Once the First Amendment shows up, much of the game is over. But the question whether the First Amendment shows up at all is rarely addressed, and the answer is too often simply assumed. . . .
>
> Though many cases involve the First Amendment, many more do not. The acts, behaviors, and restrictions not encompassed by the First Amendment at all—the events that remain wholly untouched by the First Amendment—are the ones that are simply not covered by the First Amendment. It is not that the speech is not protected. Rather, the entire event—an event that often involves "speech" in the ordinary language sense of the word—does not present a First Amendment issue at all, and the government's action is consequently measured against no First Amendment standard whatsoever. The First Amendment just does not show up.
>
> When the First Amendment does show up, the full arsenal of First Amendment rules, principles, standards, distinctions, presumptions, tools, factors, and three-part tests becomes available to determine whether the particular speech will actually wind up being protected. . . . But the fact that the[se] tests . . . are the ones to be applied reflects the coverage of the First Amendment. . . .

By contrast, no First Amendment-generated level of scrutiny is used to determine whether the content-based advertising restrictions of the Securities Act of 1933 are constitutional, whether corporate executives may be imprisoned under the Sherman Act for exchanging accurate information about proposed prices with their competitors, whether an organized crime leader may be prosecuted for urging that his subordinates murder a mob rival, or whether a chainsaw manufacturer may be held liable in a products liability action for injuries caused by mistakes in the written instructions accompanying the tool. Each of these examples involves some punishment for speech, and each involves liability based both on the content and on the communicative impact of the speech. And yet no First Amendment degree of scrutiny appears. In these and countless other instances, the permissibility of regulation—unlike the control of incitement, libel, and commercial advertising—is not measured against First Amendment-generated standards. . . . [Indeed], an argument from the First Amendment would be seen as an argument from the wrong area of law; and in which, consequently, no First Amendment principle guards, even to a limited extent, against infringement. Questions about the boundaries of the First Amendment are not questions of strength—the degree of protection that the First Amendment offers—but rather are questions of scope—whether the First Amendment applies at all. . . .

Schauer, *supra*, at 1766-71.

Chapter 2

Categorical Exclusions: Unprotected Speech

Table of Contents

A. Subversive Speech: Advocacy of Unlawful Action
   1. Opposition to War: The "Clear and Present Danger" Standard
   2. Agitators, Anarchists, and Revolutionaries: Criminal Syndicalism
   3. The Modern "Incitement" Standard
B. "Fighting Words" and Other Categorical Exclusions
C. "True Threats"
D. The Limits of the Categorical Approach: Depictions of Animal Cruelty, Violent Video Games, and Lies

Over time, the Supreme Court has defined the boundaries of the First Amendment's free speech and free press guarantees in part by recognizing certain categories or classes of expression that are categorically excluded from protection on a wholesale basis. That is, the Court has identified certain content as categorically outside the protection of the First Amendment. The Court has not always been explicit about its reasoning in defining these excluded categories. It has explained that "some utterances are no essential part of any exposition of ideas, and are of such slight social value as a step to truth" that they are unprotected. Chaplinsky v. New Hampshire, 315 U.S. 568, 572 (1942). The Court has also implicitly reasoned that the state's interests in regulating some kinds of expression are so powerful that it can be wholly excluded from "the freedom of speech." For example, it is well accepted that governments can punish offenses such as fraud or perjury.

This chapter examines three content categories the Court has recognized as unprotected under the First Amendment—incitement to unlawful action, fighting words, and true threats. These three do not exhaust the categorical exclusion approach. However, they provide a basis for critically analyzing the Court's approach to categorical exclusion and provide a general framework for thinking about the scope of the Free Speech Clause. Although they differ in various respects, all three categories address the problem of speech that portends violence and thus implicates government interests in public order and safety. Other categories, such as defamation, obscenity, and child pornography, implicate different government interests and are discussed in subsequent chapters.

As we will discover, the categorical approach has limits. The Court has not recognized an excluded content category since 1982, when child pornography was added to the list. New York v. Ferber, 458 U.S. 747 (1982). In recent cases, it has consistently rejected government arguments that additional categories, including depictions of animal cruelty, violent video games, and lies, should be categorically excluded from the First Amendment's protection. The cases and questions in this chapter reflect the Court's willingness (or lack thereof) to identify certain speech as "low value" and thus deserving of little or no First Amendment protection. They also reflect the difficulty in maintaining a strict definition of low-value categories and judges' continuing problems in identifying whether speech falls into a particular category.

A. *SUBVERSIVE SPEECH: ADVOCACY OF UNLAWFUL ACTION*

The Supreme Court faced its first significant test involving "dangerous" speech during World War I. The War was unpopular with many Americans, which posed a significant problem for the Wilson administration. Several organizations, including pacifist groups, labor unions, progressive groups, and the Socialist Party of America, openly spoke against the War, calling for public opposition through protests, demonstrations, and petitions. Nathan Fine, *Labor and Farmer Parties in the United States, 1828-1928*, at 13-14 (1928). *See also* Robert Justin Goldstein, *Political Repression in Modern America: From 1870 to 1976*, at 105-108 (2001). Such organizations, though often radical in nature and not popular with Americans generally, saw substantial increases in membership during the War. Goldstein, *supra*, at 105. Opposition to the War, however, was not limited to radical organizations, as citizens in the Midwest and South were also hostile or apathetic to the War and the draft. *Id.* at 105, 107.

Concerned that vocal opposition to the draft would paralyze the War effort, the Wilson administration tried to quell anti-war sentiment. Through the Committee on Public Information, the administration produced propaganda designed to create support for the war, including portrayals of German spies and saboteurs as lurking within the United States and of Russian Bolsheviks as German agents. Such propaganda also attempted to persuade Americans that "conscription, bond sales, and 'liberty cabbage' were the greatest national blessings since the Bill of Rights." Harry N. Scheiber, *The Wilson Administration and Civil Liberties* 16 (1960); *see also* Geoffrey R. Stone, *Perilous Times, Free Speech in Wartime* 153-155 (2004). President Wilson linked groups opposing the war (many of whose members were immigrants) to German spies, although no evidence of such a connection existed. The Wilson administration also asked private citizens to report suspicious or disloyal activity directly to the Department of Justice; the program triggered thousands of accusations of disloyalty. Goldstein, *supra*, at 110-113; Stone, *supra*, at 156-157.

In June 1917, shortly after the United States entered World War I, the administration successfully lobbied Congress to pass the Espionage Act of 1917. Among other things, the Act made it a crime, "when the United States is at war," for any person to (1) "make or convey false reports or false statements with intent to interfere with" the military success of the United States or to "promote the success of its enemies," or (2) "wilfully cause or attempt to cause insubordination, disloyalty, mutiny, [or] refusal of duty," in the United States military, or (3) "wilfully obstruct the recruiting or enlistment service of the United States." Violation of the Act was punishable by a fine of up to $10,000 and a prison sentence of up to 20 years. Act of June 15, 1917, ch. 30, tit. I., § 3, 40 Stat. 217, 219. The Espionage Act also gave the postmaster the power to exclude from the mails any matter that violated the Act. 40 Stat. at 230-231.

Less than a year later, the Wilson administration again lobbied Congress for more restrictive laws, claiming that the Espionage Act's requirements posed too onerous a burden on the government and that a law directed specifically at seditious utterances was necessary. Scheiber, *supra*, at 23-24. Congress passed the Sedition Act of 1918, which amended the Espionage Act of 1917 to make it a crime to (1) willfully utter, print, write, or publish any disloyal, profane, scurrilous, or abusive language about the form of government of the United States, the Constitution, the United States military, the United States flag, or the uniforms of the United States military; (2) to urge curtailment of production of materials necessary to the war effort; and (3) to support the cause of any country at war with the United States or oppose the cause of the United States. Act of May 16, 1918, ch. 75, § 1, 40 Stat. 553.

In the next several years, over 2,000 people were prosecuted under the Espionage and Sedition Acts, with more than half such prosecutions resulting in conviction. Lower courts generally dealt with such cases under the then-prevailing common law "bad tendency" test. Under that standard, speech could be criminalized if it had any *tendency*, however remote, to lead to violent or other unlawful activity. See, e.g., Shaffer v. United States, 255 F. 886 (9th Cir. 1919).

The Supreme Court eventually resolved whether these prosecutions were consistent with the First Amendment. In doing so, it faced many of the same questions regarding regulation of speech that government officials in England and the early American Republic faced (*see supra* Chapter 1.A). The Court wrestled with questions involving whether government officials can suppress "dangerous" speech to protect the security and safety of its citizens and the extent to which such a security rationale can be abused. Although incitement of illegal activity is only a small part of free speech doctrine, the principles involved are central to the Court's modern approach to freedom of speech. Among other concerns, in these initial cases the Supreme Court addressed the categorical treatment of speech that "incites" others to violate the law, whether the government's national security concerns can categorically outweigh free speech rights, and the justifications and values that support freedoms of speech and press.

1. *Opposition to War: The "Clear and Present Danger" Standard*

Schenck v. United States

249 U.S. 47 (1919)

Mr. Justice Holmes delivered the opinion of the Court.

[Schenck, who was secretary general of the Socialist party, was convicted of conspiracy to violate Section 3 of the Espionage Act of 1917 "by causing and attempting to cause insubordination" in the military and by attempting "to obstruct the recruiting and enlistment service of the United States, when the United States was at war with the German Empire." Specifically, Schenck was convicted for conspiring "to have printed and circulated to men who had been called and accepted for military service . . . a document set forth and alleged to be calculated to cause such insubordination and obstruction."] . . .

The document in question upon its first printed side recited the first section of the Thirteenth Amendment, said that the idea embodied in it was violated by the conscription act and that a conscript is little better than a convict. In impassioned language it intimated that conscription was despotism in its worst form and a monstrous wrong against humanity in the interest of Wall Street's chosen few. It said, "Do not submit to intimidation," but in form at least confined itself to peaceful measures such as a petition for the repeal of the act. The other and later printed side of the sheet was headed "Assert Your Rights." It stated reasons for alleging that any one violated the Constitution when he refused to recognize "your right to assert your opposition to the draft," and went on, "If you do not assert and support your rights, you are helping to deny or disparage rights which it is the solemn duty of all citizens and residents of the United States to retain." It described the arguments on the other side as coming from cunning politicians and a mercenary capitalist press, and even silent consent to the conscription law as helping to support an infamous conspiracy. It denied the power to send our citizens away to foreign shores to shoot up the people of other lands, and added that words could not express the condemnation such cold-blooded ruthlessness deserves, etc., winding up, "You must do your share to maintain, support and uphold the rights of the people of this country." Of course the document would not have been sent unless it had been intended to have some effect, and we do not see what effect it could be expected to have upon persons subject to the draft except to influence them to obstruct the carrying of it out. The defendants do not deny that the jury might find against them on this point.

But it is said, suppose that that was the tendency of this circular, it is protected by the First Amendment to the Constitution. Two of the strongest expressions are said to be quoted respectively from well-known public men. It well may be that the prohibition of laws abridging the freedom of speech is not confined to previous restraints, although to prevent them may have been the main purpose, as intimated in Patterson v. Colorado, 205 U.S. 454, 462. We admit that in many places and in ordinary times the defendants in saying all that was said in the circular would have been within their constitutional rights. But the character of every act depends upon the circumstances in which it is done. The most stringent protection of free speech would not protect a man in falsely shouting fire in a theatre and causing a panic. . . .

The question in every case is whether the words used are used in such circumstances and are of such a nature as to create a clear and present danger that they will bring about the substantive evils that Congress has a right to prevent. It is a question of proximity and degree. When a nation is at war many things that might be said in time of peace are such a hindrance to its effort that their utterance will not be endured so long as men fight and that no Court could regard them as protected by any constitutional right. It seems to be admitted that if an actual obstruction of the recruiting service were proved, liability for words that produced that effect might be enforced. The statute of 1917 in section 4 punishes conspiracies to obstruct as well as actual obstruction. If the act, (speaking, or circulating a paper,) its tendency and the intent with which it is done are the same, we perceive no ground for saying that success alone warrants making the act a crime. Goldman v. United States, 245 U.S. 474, 477. . . .

Judgments affirmed.

NOTES AND QUESTIONS

1. *Prior restraint v. subsequent punishment.* In *Schenck,* Justice Holmes acknowledges that "[i]t well may be that the prohibition of laws abridging the freedom of speech is not confined to previous restraints, although to prevent them may have been the main purpose. . . ." As discussed in Chapter 1, before and after ratification it was not clear whether the First Amendment's protection was limited solely to prohibiting prior restraints on expression. Holmes's statement is an early indication that the First Amendment also limits laws that punish speech after the fact.
2. Schenck *and "clear and present danger."* Justice Holmes announced the "clear and present danger" test for the first time in *Schenck.* What do these terms mean? Was the danger "clear" in *Schenck*? Was it "present"? Is "clear and present danger," as applied, any different from the "bad tendency" test? Would the following expression be protected under the "clear and present danger" standard as articulated by Justice Holmes in *Schenck*?
   a. distributing a pamphlet teaching that "Christians should not kill in wars";
   b. stating that "men conscripted to Europe are virtually condemned to death and everyone knows it";
   c. circulating a pamphlet urging the re-election of a Congressman who had voted against conscription.
3. *Intent and "clear and present danger."* What role does intent to bring about harm play in Justice Holmes's formulation of the test? What evidence of such intent is necessary?
4. *The "fire in a crowded theater" analogy.* What principle is Justice Holmes trying to establish with his statement in *Schenck* that "the most stringent protection of free speech would not protect a man in falsely shouting fire in a theatre and causing a panic?" Note Holmes's reference is to *falsely* shouting "Fire!" Would the First Amendment protect a speaker who shouted "Fire"! if the theater was in fact ablaze? Is this analogy helpful in determining the scope of freedom of speech? How closely does it resemble the facts in *Schenck*?
5. *Applications of "clear and present danger."* One week after the Court handed down *Schenck,* the following decisions were handed down. Are these cases simply applications of *Schenck*'s clear and present danger test, or do they go further in authorizing government to criminalize subversive speech and dissent? What, if any, light do they shed on what Holmes meant by "clear and present danger"?

a. Frohwerk v. United States, 249 U.S. 204 (1919): Jacob Frohwerk, a copy-editor/publisher of the *Missouri Staats-Zeitung* (a German-language newspaper), was convicted of violating the Espionage Act and sentenced to ten years in prison for attempting to cause "disloyalty" and "refusal of duty" by articles produced in his newspaper. Frohwerk's articles called the war "a monumental and inexcusable mistake," and stated that the deaths of American soldiers were "outright murder." Intending to "warn the American people," he wrote of Germany's "undiminished strength" and "unconquerable spirit." Frohwerk blamed involvement in the war on Wall Street, claiming that our soldiers have "sold our honor, our very souls," so "a few men and corporations might amass unprecedented fortunes." Frohwerk wrote against the draft riots in Oklahoma and elsewhere, but allegedly used "language that might be taken to convey an innuendo of a different sort." He called the legal remedies for opposing the draft "all very well for those . . . past the draft age and [without] boys to be drafted," and he questioned criminal convictions of those who followed "the first impulse of nature: self-preservation." He also made "a remark to the effect that when rulers scheme to use it for their own purposes, loyalty serves to perpetuate wrong." 249 U.S. at 207-208.

   Justice Holmes, writing for a unanimous Court, admitted that there appeared to be no "special effort [by the defendant] to reach men who were subject to the draft." He also acknowledged that "it may be that all this might be said or written even in time of war in circumstances that would not make it a crime." *Id.* at 208. Nevertheless, Holmes upheld the conviction. After noting *Schenck*'s applicability, he stated that "it is impossible to say that it might not have been found that the circulation of the paper was in quarters where a little breath would be enough to kindle a flame and that the fact was known and relied upon by those who sent the paper out." *Id.* at 209.

b. Debs v. United States, 249 U.S. 211 (1919): Eugene Debs, leader of the Socialist party and presidential candidate, was convicted and sentenced to ten years in prison under the Espionage Act for obstructing or attempting to obstruct military recruitment as a result of a speech made in July 1918. In his speech, which focused primarily on "Socialism, its growth, and a prophecy of its ultimate success," Debs opposed the war, praised persons convicted of hindering the draft, and espoused his belief that capitalism caused the war. 249 U.S. at 212-215. He also stated that "he had to be prudent and not say all that he thought, thus intimating to his hearers that they might infer that he meant more." *Id.* at 214. He told his listeners that "you need to know you are fit for something better than slavery and cannon fodder." *Id.* Authorities focused their attention on Debs because he was a prominent public figure and ran with some success as a third-party candidate for president. Immediately prior to giving his speech, Debs had visited with inmates convicted of attempt to inhibit the draft.

Delivering the opinion of the court, Justice Holmes declared that *Schenck* had "disposed of" Debs' First Amendment claim. Holmes dismissed the idea that the defendant was punished for his views on Socialism. Rather, Holmes argued, "if a part of the manifest intent of the more general utterances was to encourage those present to obstruct the recruiting service and if in passages such encouragement was directly given, the immunity of the general theme may not be enough to protect the speech." *Id.* at 212-213. According to Justice Holmes, if the "probable effect" of "one purpose of the speech, whether incidental or not does not matter, was to oppose [the] war," the speech "would not be protected." *Id.* at 214-215. Holmes thus upheld the lower court's jury instruction, which allowed conviction if "the words used had, as their natural tendency and reasonably probable effect, to obstruct the recruiting service" and the defendant so intended. *Id.* at 216.

6. *Free speech in wartime.* Should we give less protection to criticism of the government's actions during periods of war? Or should we be more vigilant during wartime, when government may be most likely to suppress speech based on pretext? *See* Vincent Blasi, *The Pathological Perspective and the First Amendment*, 85 Colum. L. Rev. 449 (1985).

Abrams v. United States

250 U.S. 616 (1919)

Mr. Justice CLARKE delivered the opinion of the Court.

[Defendants were Russian immigrants to the United States who distributed both publicly and secretively leaflets criticizing the United States government's decision to send troops to Russia as part of the effort against Germany during World War I. Defendants perceived the United States government's actions to be an effort to put down the Russian Revolution. Defendants circulated two leaflets criticizing the government's actions and calling for a general strike. They threw some of the 5,000 leaflets from a window of a building where one of the defendants was employed. The Court noted the leaflets "were circulated in the greatest port of our land, from which great numbers of soldiers were at the time taking ship daily, and in which great quantities of war supplies of every kind were at the time being manufactured for transportation overseas." As a result of circulating the leaflets, defendants were prosecuted for violating the Sedition Act of 1918, for publishing "disloyal, scurrilous and abusive language about the form of government of the United States," using language "intended to incite, provoke and encourage resistance to the United States" during the war, and conspiring "to urge, incite and advocate curtailment of production of things and products, to wit, ordnance and ammunition, necessary and essential to the prosecution of the war." The Supreme Court dismissed the argument that the defendants' speech was protected by the First Amendment, citing *Schenck* and *Frohwerk.* The Court then considered the sufficiency of the evidence supporting the convictions.] . . .

The first of the two articles attached to the indictment is conspicuously headed, "The Hypocrisy of the United States and her Allies." After denouncing President Wilson as a hypocrite and a coward because troops were sent into Russia, it proceeds to assail our government in general, saying:

> His [the President's] shameful, cowardly silence about the intervention in Russia reveals the hypocrisy of the plutocratic gang in Washington and vicinity.

It continues:

> He [the President] is too much of a coward to come out openly and say: "We capitalistic nations [including the U.S.] cannot afford to have a proletarian republic in Russia."

. . . [T]he circular culminates in:

> The Russian Revolution cries: Workers of the World! Awake! Rise! Put down your enemy and mine! Yes friends, there is only one enemy of the workers of the world and that is CAPITALISM. . . .

The second of the articles was printed in the Yiddish language and in the translation is headed, "Workers—Wake Up." After referring to "his Majesty, Mr. Wilson, and the rest of the gang, dogs of all colors!" it continues:

> Workers, Russian emigrants, you who had the least belief in the honesty of [the U.S] government . . . , must now throw away all confidence, must spit in the face the false, hypocritic, military propaganda which has fooled you so relentlessly, calling forth your sympathy, your help, to the prosecution of the war. . . .

[T]the spirit [of the leaflet] becomes more bitter as it proceeds to declare that—

> America and her Allies have betrayed [the Workers]. Their robberish aims are clear to all men. The destruction of the Russian Revolution, that is the politics of the march to Russia. *Workers, our reply to the barbaric intervention has to be a general strike! An open challenge* only will let the government know that not only the Russian Worker fights for freedom, but also *here in America lives the spirit of Revolution.*

This is not an attempt to bring about a change of administration by candid discussion, for no matter what may have incited the outbreak on the part of the defendant anarchists, the manifest purpose of such a publication was to create an attempt to defeat the war plans of the government of the United States, by bringing upon the country the paralysis of a general strike, thereby arresting the production of all munitions and other things essential to the conduct of the war. . . .

These excerpts sufficiently show, that while the immediate occasion for this particular outbreak of lawlessness, on the part of the defendant alien anarchists, may have been resentment caused by our government sending troops into Russia as a strategic operation against the Germans on the eastern battle front, yet the plain purpose of their propaganda was to excite, at the supreme crisis of the war, disaffection, sedition, riots, and, as they hoped, revolution, in this country for the purpose of embarrassing and if possible defeating the military plans of the government in Europe. Thus it is clear not only that some evidence but that much persuasive evidence was before the jury tending to prove that the defendants were guilty as charged in both the third and fourth counts of the indictment and under the long established rule of law hereinbefore stated the judgment of the District Court must be affirmed.

Mr. Justice HOLMES, dissenting.

. . . With regard to [the allegation that the defendants intend to hinder the war effort] it seems too plain to be denied that the suggestion to workers in the ammunition factories that they are producing bullets to murder their dearest, and the further advocacy of a general strike, both in the second leaflet, do urge curtailment of production of things necessary to the prosecution of the war within the meaning of the [Espionage and Sedition Acts]. But to make the conduct criminal that statute requires that it should be "with intent by such curtailment to cripple or hinder the United States in the prosecution of the war." It seems to me that no such intent is proved.

I am aware of course that the word "intent" as vaguely used in ordinary legal discussion means no more than knowledge at the time of the act that the consequences said to be intended will ensue. . . . But, when words are used exactly, a deed is not done with intent to produce a consequence unless that consequence is the aim of the deed. It may be obvious, and obvious to the actor, that the consequence will follow, and he may be liable for it even if he regrets it, but he does not do the act with intent to produce it unless the aim to produce it is the proximate motive of the specific act, although there may be some deeper motive behind.

It seems to me that this statute must be taken to use its words in a strict and accurate sense. They would be absurd in any other. A patriot might think that we were wasting money on aeroplanes, or making more cannon of a certain kind than we needed, and might advocate curtailment with success, yet even if it turned out that the curtailment hindered and was thought by other minds to have been obviously likely to hinder the United States in the prosecution of the war, no one would hold such conduct a crime. . . .

I never have seen any reason to doubt that the questions of law that alone were before this Court in *Schenck, Frohwerk,* and *Debs* were rightly decided. . . . [T]he United States constitutionally may punish speech that produces or is intended to produce a clear and imminent danger that it will bring about forthwith certain substantive evils that the United States constitutionally may seek to prevent. The power undoubtedly is greater in time of war than in time of peace because war opens dangers that do not exist at other times.

But as against dangers peculiar to war, as against others, the principle of the right to free speech is always the same. It is only the present danger of immediate evil or an intent to bring it about that warrants Congress in setting a limit to the expression of opinion where private rights are not concerned. Congress certainly cannot forbid all effort to change the mind of the country. Now nobody can suppose that the surreptitious publishing of a silly leaflet by an unknown man, without more, would present any immediate danger that its opinions would hinder the success of the government arms or have any appreciable tendency to do so. Publishing those opinions for the very purpose of obstructing, however, might indicate a greater danger and at any rate would have the quality of an attempt. So I assume that the second leaflet if published for the purposes [of hindering the war effort] might be punishable. But it seems pretty clear to me that nothing less than that would bring these papers within the scope of this law.

I do not see how anyone can find the intent required by the statute in any of the defendant's words. The second leaflet is the only one that affords even a foundation for the charge, and there, without invoking the hatred of German militarism expressed in the former one, it is evident from the beginning to the end that the only object of the paper is to help Russia and stop American intervention there against the popular government—not to impede the United States in the war that it was carrying on. To say that two phrases taken literally might import a suggestion of conduct that would have interference with the war as an indirect and probably undesired effect seems to me by no means enough to show an attempt to produce that effect. . . .

In this case sentences of twenty years imprisonment have been imposed for the publishing of two leaflets that I believe the defendants had as much right to publish as the Government has to publish the Constitution of the United States now vainly invoked by them. Even if I am technically wrong and enough can be squeezed from these poor and puny anonymities to turn the color of legal litmus paper; I will add, even if what I think the necessary intent were shown; the most nominal punishment seems to me all that possibly could be inflicted, unless the defendants are to be made to suffer not for what the indictment alleges but for the creed that they avow[.] . . .

Persecution for the expression of opinions seems to me perfectly logical. If you have no doubt of your premises or your power and want a certain result with all your heart you naturally express your wishes in law and sweep away all opposition. To allow opposition by speech seems to indicate that you think the speech impotent, as when a man says that he has squared the circle, or that you do not care whole heartedly for the result, or that you doubt either your power or your premises. But when men have realized that time has upset many fighting faiths, they may come to believe even more than they believe the very foundations of their own conduct that the ultimate good desired is better reached by free trade in ideas—that the best test of truth is the power of the thought to get itself accepted in the competition of the market, and that truth is the only ground upon which their wishes safely can be carried out. That at any rate is the theory of our Constitution. It is an experiment, as all life is an experiment. Every year if not every day we have to wager our salvation upon some prophecy based upon imperfect knowledge. While that experiment is part of our system I think that we should be eternally vigilant against attempts to check the expression of opinions that we loathe and believe to be fraught with death, unless they so imminently threaten immediate interference with the lawful and pressing purposes of the law that an immediate check is required to save the country.

I wholly disagree with the argument of the Government that the First Amendment left the common law as to seditious libel in force. History seems to me against the notion. I had conceived that the United States through many years had shown its repentance for the Sedition Act of 1798 (Act July 14, 1798, c. 73, 1 Stat. 596), by repaying fines that it imposed. Only the emergency that makes it immediately dangerous to leave the correction of evil counsels to time warrants making any exception to the sweeping command, 'Congress shall make no law abridging the freedom of speech.' Of course I am speaking only of expressions of opinion and exhortations, which were all that were uttered here, but I regret that I cannot put into more impressive words my belief that in their conviction upon this indictment the defendants were deprived of their rights under the Constitution of the United States.

[Justice BRANDEIS's concurring opinion is omitted.]

NOTES AND QUESTIONS

1. *Justice Holmes and the evolution of "clear and present danger."* Is Holmes's version of the "clear and present danger" test in *Abrams* different from that in *Schenck* decided earlier in 1919? Several prominent scholars and judges publicly and privately criticized his reasoning in *Schenck* and related cases. Most scholars believe Holmes's attitude changed owing to this criticism and as he watched what he believed to be government and judicial excess with respect to suppression of expression. *See, e.g.*, David Rabban, *The Emergence of Modern First Amendment Doctrine*, 50 U. Chi. L. Rev. 1205 (1983); G. Edward White, *Justice Holmes and the Modernization of Free Speech Jurisprudence: The Human Dimension*, 80 Cal. L. Rev. 391 (1992). *But see* Zechariah Chafee, Jr., *Free Speech in the United States* 86 (1941). For a careful examination of Holmes's evolution concerning "clear and present danger," *see* Thomas Healy, *The Great Dissent: How Oliver Wendell Holmes Changed His Mind—and Changed the History of Free Speech in America* (2013).
2. *The* Masses *decision.* Judge Learned Hand was one of the prominent critics of the "clear and present danger" standard. Hand believed it allowed judges to be swayed by passion. *See* Gerald Gunther, *Learned Hand and the Origins of Modern First Amendment Doctrine: Some Fragments of History*, 27 Stan. L. Rev. 719, 749 (1975). Two years before *Abrams*, Judge Hand, then a federal district court judge, overturned an Espionage Act conviction in Masses Publishing Co. v. Patten, 244 F. 535 (S.D.N.Y. 1917). Hand concluded use of the mails to distribute a revolutionary journal, "The Masses," did not violate the terms of the Espionage Act. He placed special emphasis on the words used by the defendants, which criticized participation in the war in terms much like those used in *Schenck* and other early Supreme Court cases. Hand wrote: "If one stops short of urging upon others that it is their duty or their interest to resist the law, it seems to me one should not be held to have attempted to cause its violation. If that be not the test, I can see no escape from the conclusion that under this section every political agitation which can be shown to be apt to create a seditious temper is illegal."
   a. Is it better to focus on the express *words* of incitement (as does Hand) or the possible *effects* of incitement (as does the "clear and present danger" test) when determining whether to punish speech?
   b. How would the speakers in Question 1 after *Schenck* have fared under Hand's approach in *Masses?*
   c. Hand's decision in *Masses* was overturned on appeal in an opinion stating that "this court does not agree that [Judge Hand's] test is the law." Masses Publg. Co. v. Patten, 246 F. 24 (2d Cir. 1917).

3. *"Immediacy."* Justice Holmes's *Abrams* dissent adds an immediacy requirement to the "clear and present danger" test. What are the advantages for speakers of adding an "immediacy" requirement to the "clear and present danger" test? What does "immediacy" mean in this context?
4. *The marketplace of ideas.* Holmes's dissent is famous for its exposition of the idea the best test for truth is competition in the "marketplace of ideas." Does the marketplace or search for truth justification support the "clear and present danger" standard or require something more speech-protective?
5. *Sedition.* Justice Holmes rejects the Government's argument that "the First Amendment left the common law as to seditious libel in force." Holmes refers to the Sedition Act of 1798, discussed in Chapter 1, which made it a crime to criticize the government of the United States with intent to defame it or bring it into contempt or disrepute. More than four decades after *Abrams*, the Supreme Court would agree with Holmes. *See* New York Times Co. v. Sullivan, 376 U.S. 254, 273-76 (1964). Is punishing Abrams under the Espionage Act equivalent to punishing him for "seditious libel" or did his speech go further?

2. *Agitators, Anarchists, and Revolutionaries: Criminal Syndicalism*

Following World War I, the United States entered a period of intense anti-radicalism. The Russian Revolution sparked fears of a possible Communist revolution within the United States. At the same time, the Russian Revolution catalyzed growth in American radical movements, such as the Socialist Party, and in various labor organizations (some of which were associated with radical movements), thus increasing tensions between such movements and those fearing the spread of radicalism. In 1919–1920, a series of protests, strikes, and bombings or attempted bombings attributed to radical forces further increased fear and hysteria around the country. Americans began to call for greater security measures.

During 1919, at least 27 states passed "red flag" laws (laws barring the display of flags as a sign of opposition to organized government), 16 states passed criminal syndicalism laws (laws prohibiting advocacy of overthrow of the government), and 12 states passed anarchy and sedition laws. Approximately 1,400 people were arrested under such laws, resulting in about 300 convictions. The "Red Scare" also led to massive efforts to round up and deport aliens believed to pose a radical threat. State and federal officials staged raids of radical organizations around the country. In January 1920, the infamous Palmer Raids, named after Attorney General A. Mitchell Palmer, involved the arrests of between 5,000 and 10,000 people who were allegedly members of radical organizations. Those arrested included almost every local and national leader of these organizations and included many American citizens, although the raids were ostensibly targeted at aliens. Many citizens were turned over to officials for prosecution under criminal syndicalism laws, although most were eventually freed due to lack of evidence. For more discussion of the Red Scare, see Robert Justin Goldstein, *Political Repression in Modern America: From 1870 to 1976*, at 139-163 (2001); Geoffrey R. Stone, *Perilous Times: Free Speech in Wartime* 220-230 (2004); Zechariah Chafee, Jr., *Free Speech in the United States* 141-240 (1941); Robert Murray, *Red Scare: A Study in National Hysteria, 1919-1920* (1964).

Gitlow v. New York

268 U.S. 652 (1925)

[The Court upheld the conviction of Benjamin Gitlow for violating New York's Criminal Anarchy Act. Enacted in the wake of the assassination of President McKinley in 1901, the law made it a felony to advocate, advise, or teach the "duty, necessity, or propriety of overthrowing or overturning organized government by force or violence, or by assassination of the executive head or of any of the executive officials of government, or by any unlawful means." The trial established Gitlow was a member of the Left Wing Section of the Socialist Party ("LWS"), a dissenting branch formed to oppose its policy of "moderate Socialism." Gitlow was convicted of violating the Act based on publication and circulation of materials labeled the "Left Wing Manifesto" and the paper "The Revolutionary Age."]

Mr. Justice SANFORD delivered the opinion of the Court.

The statute does not penalize the utterance or publication of abstract "doctrine" or academic discussion having no quality of incitement to any concrete action. It is not aimed against mere historical or philosophical essays. It does not restrain the advocacy of changes in the form of government by constitutional and lawful means. What it prohibits is language advocating, advising or teaching the overthrow of organized government by unlawful means. These words imply urging to action. . . .

The Manifesto, plainly, is neither the statement of abstract doctrine nor, as suggested by counsel, mere prediction that industrial disturbances and revolutionary mass strikes will result spontaneously in an inevitable process of evolution in the economic system. It advocates and urges in fervent language mass action which shall progressively foment industrial disturbances and through political mass strikes and revolutionary mass action overthrow and destroy organized parliamentary government. It concludes with a call to action in these words: "The proletariat revolution and the Communist reconstruction of society—*the struggle for these*—is now indispensable. . . . The Communist International calls the proletariat of the world to the final struggle!" . . . [T]he jury were warranted in finding that the Manifesto advocated not merely the abstract doctrine of overthrowing organized government by force, violence and unlawful means, but action to that end[.]

For present purposes we may and do assume that freedom of speech and of the press—which are protected by the First Amendment from abridgment by Congress—are among the fundamental personal rights and "liberties" protected by the due process clause of the Fourteenth Amendment from impairment by the States. . . .

It is a fundamental principle, long established, that the freedom of speech and of the press which is secured by the Constitution, does not confer an absolute right to speak or publish, without responsibility, whatever one may choose, or an unrestricted and unbridled license that gives immunity for every possible use of language and prevents the punishment of those who abuse this freedom. *Schenck*; *Frohwerk*; *Debs*. . . .

[A] State may punish utterances endangering the foundations of organized government and threatening its overthrow by unlawful means. These imperil its own existence as a constitutional State. . . . By enacting the present statute the State has determined, through its legislative body, that utterances advocating the overthrow of organized government by force, violence and unlawful means, are so inimical to the general welfare and involve such danger of substantive evil that they may be penalized in the exercise of its police power. That determination must be given great weight. . . . [T]he case is to be considered "in the light of the principle that the State is primarily the judge of regulations required in the interest of public safety and welfare"; and that its police "statutes may only be declared unconstitutional where they are arbitrary or unreasonable attempts to exercise authority vested in the State in the public interest." [U]tterances inciting to the overthrow of organized government by unlawful means, . . . by their very nature, involve danger to the public peace and to the security of the State. They threaten breaches of the peace and ultimate revolution. And the immediate danger is none the less real and substantial, because the effect of a given utterance cannot be accurately foreseen. . . . It cannot be said that the State is acting arbitrarily or unreasonably when in the exercise of its judgment as to the measures necessary to protect the public peace and safety, it seeks to extinguish [a] spark without waiting until it has enkindled the flame or blazed into the conflagration . . .

We cannot hold that the present statute is an arbitrary or unreasonable exercise of the police power of the State unwarrantably infringing the freedom of speech or press; and we must and do sustain its constitutionality.

This being so it may be applied to every utterance—not too trivial to be beneath the notice of the law—which is of such a character and used with such intent and purpose as to bring it within the prohibition of the statute. In other words, when the legislative body has determined generally, in the constitutional exercise of its discretion, that utterances of a certain kind involve such danger of substantive evil that they may be punished, the question whether any specific utterance coming within the prohibited class is likely, in and of itself, to bring about the substantive evil, is not open to consideration. It is sufficient that the statute itself be constitutional and that the use of the language comes within its prohibition.

It is clear that the question in such cases is entirely different from that involved in those cases where the statute merely prohibits certain acts involving the danger of substantive evil, without any reference to language itself, and it is sought to apply its provisions to language used by the defendant for the purpose of bringing about the prohibited results. . . . In such case it has been held that the general provisions of the statute may be constitutionally applied to the specific utterance of the defendant if its natural tendency and probable effect was to bring about the substantive evil which the legislative body might prevent. *Schenck*; *Debs*. And the general statement in *Schenck* that the "question in every case is whether the words used are used in such circumstances and are of such a nature as to create a clear and present danger that they will bring about the substantive evils,"—upon which great reliance is placed in the defendant's argument—was manifestly intended, as shown by the context, to apply only in cases of this class, and has no application to those like the present, where the legislative body itself has previously determined the danger of substantive evil arising from utterances of a specified character. . . .

Affirmed.

Mr. Justice HOLMES, dissenting.

. . . I think that the criterion sanctioned by the full Court in *Schenck* applies: "The question in every case is whether the words used are used in such circumstances and are of such a nature as to create a clear and present danger that they will bring about the substantive evils that [the State] has a right to prevent." . . . If what I think the correct test is applied it is manifest that there was no present danger of an attempt to overthrow the government by force on the part of the admittedly small minority who shared the defendant's views. It is said that this manifesto was more than a theory, that it was an incitement. Every idea is an incitement. It offers itself for belief and if believed it is acted on unless some other belief outweighs it or some failure of energy stifles the movement at its birth. The only difference between the expression of an opinion and an incitement in the narrower sense is the speaker's enthusiasm for the result. Eloquence may set fire to reason. But whatever may be thought of the redundant discourse before us it had no chance of starting a present conflagration. If in the long run the beliefs expressed in proletarian dictatorship are destined to be accepted by the dominant forces of the community, the only meaning of free speech is that they should be given their chance and have their way.

If the publication of this document had been laid as an attempt to induce an uprising against government at once and not at some indefinite time in the future it would have presented a different question. The object would have been one with which the law might deal, subject to the doubt whether there was any danger that the publication could produce any result, or in other words, whether it was not futile and too remote from possible consequences. But the indictment alleges the publication and nothing more.

NOTES AND QUESTIONS

1. *Incorporation.* Although the text of the First Amendment applies only to Congress, *Gitlow* assumed that the freedoms of speech and press "are among the fundamental personal rights and 'liberties' protected by the Due Process Clause of the Fourteenth Amendment." Since that brief statement in 1925 the Court has repeatedly cited *Gitlow* as the foundational case finding that the First Amendment freedoms are "fundamental components of the liberty safeguarded by the Due Process Clause" and thus applicable against the states. *See, e.g.*, First Nat'l Bank v. Bellotti, 425 U.S. 765, 780 (1978); NAACP v. Alabama ex rel. Patterson, 357 U.S. 449, 460 (1958); Stromberg v. California, 283 U.S. 359, 368 (1931).
2. *Deference to legislative pronouncements of danger.* Do you agree with Justice Sanford's claims that the "clear and present danger" standard is inapplicable because the statute at issue is specifically directed at speech, unlike the statutes in *Schenck* and *Abrams*, which were aimed at conduct? Doesn't a law aimed directly at certain types of communications pose a greater danger to freedom of speech than a law that targets conduct but incidentally affects speech? Does the majority's approach in *Gitlow* grant legislatures too much power to criminalize speech critical of government? Or are legislatures better able to assess the dangers associated with certain kinds of communications than courts? If judges are no better than anyone else

at estimating the possible harms of speech during times of crisis, should they simply defer to government officials because they are better placed to make decisions regarding security? *See, e.g.*, William H. Rehnquist, *All the Laws But One: Civil Liberties in Wartime* 205 (1998). Or, to the contrary, should judges craft rigid legal rules that can withstand those periods of pathology? *See* Vincent Blasi, *The Pathological Perspective and the First Amendment*, 85 Colum. L. Rev. 449, 474 (1985).

3. *More on Holmes's "marketplace of ideas."* Justice Holmes writes that "if in the long run the beliefs expressed in proletarian dictatorship are destined to be accepted by the dominant forces of the community, the only meaning of free speech is that they should be given their chance and have their way." Does that approach downplay the *gravity* of the danger some ideas present? Does white supremacist ideology deserve a chance to persuade in the "marketplace"? What about Holocaust denialism? Can Justice Holmes's marketplace rationale in *Abrams* be squared with the current widespread problem of misinformation and disinformation on social media platforms and elsewhere?
4. *The marketplace and totalitarian ideologies.* Should the First Amendment protect totalitarian ideologies that are themselves intolerant of free speech and democratic principles? For arguments, see Robert Bork, *Neutral Principles and Some First Amendment Problems*, 47 Ind. L.J. 1 (1971); Steven D. Smith, *Radically Subversive Speech and the Authority of Law*, 94 Mich. L. Rev. 348 (1995).

Whitney v. California

274 U.S. 357 (1927)

Mr. Justice Sanford delivered the opinion of the Court.

[Anita Whitney was convicted of violating the California Criminal Syndicalism Act, which stated:

> Section 1. The term "criminal syndicalism" as used in this act is hereby defined as any doctrine or precept advocating, teaching or aiding and abetting the commission of crime, sabotage (which word is hereby defined as meaning willful and malicious physical damage or injury to physical property), or unlawful acts of force and violence or unlawful methods of terrorism as a means of accomplishing a change in industrial ownership or control or effecting any political change.
>
> Sec. 2. Any person who: . . . Organizes or assists in organizing, or is or knowingly becomes a member of, any organization, society, group or assemblage of persons organized or assembled to advocate, teach or aid and abet criminal syndicalism; . . . is guilty of a felony and punishable by imprisonment.

Specifically, Whitney was charged with and convicted of organizing and assisting in organizing, and knowingly becoming a member of an organization that assembled to advocate or teach criminal syndicalism. At trial the evidence showed that

Whitney was a member of the Oakland branch of the Socialist Party. At the national convention in 1919, the Socialist Party split and the Oakland delegation adhered to the "radical group," which separately formed the Communist Labor Party of America ("CLP"). The CLP adopted a platform that, among other things, called for organizing workers in a "revolutionary class struggle to conquer the capitalist state and for the overthrow of capitalist rule, ultimately to establish a Dictatorship of the Proletariat." Whitney became a member of the CLP and attended its national convention as a delegate later that year. She was a member of various committees and signed a resolution that recognized the need to develop political power by voting for CLP candidates in elections and urging workers to vote for such candidates. Although this resolution was rejected by the CLP, Whitney remained at the convention. However, she testified that she never intended for the CLP to be an instrument of terrorism or violence nor was it her purpose to violate any known law.]

[The] Syndicalism Act as applied in this case [is not] repugnant to the due process clause as a restraint of the rights of free speech, assembly, and association. . . . [*See Gitlow.*] . . . The essence of the offense denounced by the Act is the combining with others in an association for the accomplishment of the desired ends through the advocacy and use of criminal and unlawful methods. It partakes of the nature of a criminal conspiracy. . . . That such united and joint action involves even greater danger to the public peace and security than the isolated utterances and acts of individuals is clear. We cannot hold that, as here applied, the Act is an unreasonable or arbitrary exercise of the police power of the State, unwarrantably infringing any right of free speech, assembly or association, or that those persons are protected from punishment by the due process clause who abuse such rights by joining and furthering an organization thus menacing the peace and welfare of the State.

Affirmed.

Mr. Justice BRANDEIS, concurring.

. . . [T]he statute [under which Ms. Whitney is punished] create[s] . . . a crime very unlike the old felony of conspiracy or the old misdemeanor of unlawful assembly. The mere act of assisting in forming a society for teaching syndicalism, of becoming a member of it, or assembling with others for that purpose is given the dynamic quality of crime. . . . Thus the accused is to be punished, not for attempt, incitement or conspiracy, but for a step in preparation, which, if it threatens the public order at all, does so only remotely. The novelty in the prohibition introduced is that the statute aims, not at the practice of criminal syndicalism, nor even directly at the preaching of it, but at association with those who propose to preach it. . . .

[A]lthough the rights of free speech and assembly are fundamental, they are not in their nature absolute. Their exercise is subject to restriction, if the particular restriction proposed is required in order to protect the state from destruction or from serious injury, political, economic or moral. That the necessity which is essential to a valid restriction does not exist unless speech would produce, or is intended to produce, a clear and imminent danger of some substantive evil which the state constitutionally may seek to prevent has been settled. *See Schenck.*

It is said to be the function of the Legislature to determine whether at a particular time and under the particular circumstances the formation of, or assembly with, a society organized to advocate criminal syndicalism constitutes a clear and present danger of substantive evil; and that by enacting the law here in question the Legislature of California determined that question in the affirmative. *Compare Gitlow.* The Legislature must obviously decide, in the first instance, whether a danger exists which calls for a particular protective measure. But where a statute is valid only in case certain conditions exist, the enactment of the statute cannot alone establish the facts which are essential to its validity. . . .

This court has not yet fixed the standard by which to determine when a danger shall be deemed clear; how remote the danger may be and yet be deemed present; and what degree of evil shall be deemed sufficiently substantial to justify resort to abridgment of free speech and assembly as the means of protection. To reach sound conclusions on these matters, we must bear in mind why a state is, ordinarily, denied the power to prohibit dissemination of social, economic and political doctrine which a vast majority of its citizens believes to be false and fraught with evil consequence.

Those who won our independence believed that the final end of the state was to make men free to develop their faculties, and that in its government the deliberative forces should prevail over the arbitrary. They valued liberty both as an end and as a means. They believed liberty to be the secret of happiness and courage to be the secret of liberty. They believed that freedom to think as you will and to speak as you think are means indispensable to the discovery and spread of political truth; that without free speech and assembly discussion would be futile; that with them, discussion affords ordinarily adequate protection against the dissemination of noxious doctrine; that the greatest menace to freedom is an inert people; that public discussion is a political duty; and that this should be a fundamental principle of the American government.[1] They recognized the risks to which all human institutions are subject. But they knew that order cannot be secured merely through fear of punishment for its infraction; that it is hazardous to discourage thought, hope and imagination; that fear breeds repression; that repression breeds hate; that hate menaces stable government; that the path of safety lies in the opportunity to discuss freely supposed grievances and proposed remedies; and that the fitting remedy for evil counsels is good ones. Believing in the power of reason as applied through public discussion, they eschewed silence coerced by law—the argument of force in its worst form. Recognizing the occasional tyrannies of governing majorities, they amended the Constitution so that free speech and assembly should be guaranteed.

Fear of serious injury cannot alone justify suppression of free speech and assembly. Men feared witches and burnt women. It is the function of speech to free men from the bondage of irrational fears. To justify suppression of free speech there must be reasonable ground to fear that serious evil will result if free speech is practiced. There must be reasonable ground to believe that the danger

---

1. Compare Thomas Jefferson: "We have nothing to fear from the demoralizing reasonings of some, if others are left free to demonstrate their errors and especially when the law stands ready to punish the first criminal act produced by the false reasonings; these are safer corrections than the conscience of the judge." Quoted by Charles A. Beard, *The Nation*, July 7, 1926, Vol. 123, P. 8. Also in first Inaugural Address: "If there be any among us who would wish to dissolve this union or change its republican form, let them stand undisturbed as monuments of the safety with which error of opinion may be tolerated where reason is left free to combat it."

apprehended is imminent. There must be reasonable ground to believe that the evil to be prevented is a serious one. Every denunciation of existing law tends in some measure to increase the probability that there will be violation of it.[5] Condonation of a breach enhances the probability. Expressions of approval add to the probability. Propagation of the criminal state of mind by teaching syndicalism increases it. Advocacy of lawbreaking heightens it still further. But even advocacy of violation, however reprehensible morally, is not a justification for denying free speech where the advocacy falls short of incitement and there is nothing to indicate that the advocacy would be immediately acted on. The wide difference between advocacy and incitement, between preparation and attempt, between assembling and conspiracy, must be borne in mind. In order to support a finding of clear and present danger it must be shown either that immediate serious violence was to be expected or was advocated, or that the past conduct furnished reason to believe that such advocacy was then contemplated.

Those who won our independence by revolution were not cowards. They did not fear political change. They did not exalt order at the cost of liberty. To courageous, self-reliant men, with confidence in the power of free and fearless reasoning applied through the processes of popular government, no danger flowing from speech can be deemed clear and present, unless the incidence of the evil apprehended is so imminent that it may befall before there is opportunity for full discussion. If there be time to expose through discussion the falsehood and fallacies, to avert the evil by the processes of education, the remedy to be applied is more speech, not enforced silence. Only an emergency can justify repression. Such must be the rule if authority is to be reconciled with freedom. Such, in my opinion, is the command of the Constitution. It is therefore always open to Americans to challenge a law abridging free speech and assembly by showing that there was no emergency justifying it.

Moreover, even imminent danger cannot justify resort to prohibition of these functions essential to effective democracy, unless the evil apprehended is relatively serious. Prohibition of free speech and assembly is a measure so stringent that it would be inappropriate as the means for averting a relatively trivial harm to society. A police measure may be unconstitutional merely because the remedy, although effective as means of protection, is unduly harsh or oppressive. Thus, a state might, in the exercise of its police power, make any trespass upon the land of another a crime, regardless of the results or of the intent or purpose of the trespasser. It might, also, punish an attempt, a conspiracy, or an incitement to commit the trespass. But it is hardly conceivable that this court would hold constitutional a statute which punished as a felony the mere voluntary assembly with a society formed to teach that pedestrians had the moral right to cross uninclosed, unposted, waste lands and to advocate their doing so, even if there was imminent danger that advocacy would lead to a trespass. The fact that speech is likely to result in some violence or in destruction of property is not enough to justify its suppression. There must be the probability of serious injury to the State. Among free men, the deterrents ordinarily to be applied to prevent crime are education and punishment for violations of the law, not abridgment of the rights of free speech and assembly. . . .

---

5. Compare Judge Learned Hand in *Masses Publishing Co. v. Patten*, 244 F. 535, 540.

Whenever the fundamental rights of free speech and assembly are alleged to have been invaded, it must remain open to a defendant to present the issue whether there actually did exist at the time a clear danger, whether the danger, if any, was imminent, and whether the evil apprehended was one so substantial as to justify the stringent restriction interposed by the Legislature. . . . The legislative [declaration] creates merely a rebuttable presumption that these conditions have been satisfied.

Whether in 1919, when Miss Whitney did the things complained of, there was in California such clear and present danger of serious evil, might have been made the important issue in the case. She might have required that the issue be determined either by the court or the jury. She claimed below that the statute as applied to her violated the federal Constitution; but she did not claim that it was void because there was no clear and present danger of serious evil, nor did she request that the existence of these conditions of a valid measure thus restricting the rights of free speech and assembly be passed upon by the court or a jury. On the other hand, there was evidence on which the court or jury might have found that such danger existed. I am unable to assent to the suggestion in the opinion of the court that assembling with a political party, formed to advocate the desirability of a proletarian revolution by mass action at some date necessarily far in the future, is not a right within the protection of the Fourteenth Amendment. In the present case, however, there was other testimony which tended to establish the existence of a conspiracy, on the part of members of the International Workers of the World, to commit present serious crimes, and likewise to show that such a conspiracy would be furthered by the activity of the society of which Miss Whitney was a member. Under these circumstances the judgment of the State court cannot be disturbed. . . .

Mr. Justice HOLMES joins in this opinion.

NOTES AND QUESTIONS

1. *Critique of the "clear and present danger" standard.* Does the Court's treatment of the "clear and present danger" standard suggest much of what is wrong with it? Consider the following:

> The amorphous balancing required in the clear and present danger test made it particularly susceptible to [skewing]. . . . Even in its most protective form, the test does little more than restate a generalized definition of risk analysis requiring courts to assess the likelihood that speech will cause a particular event. Such a test is no guard against overestimation of an event's probability, especially one that supposedly involved violent overthrow of the government, an evil that was "as great as could be imagined."

Christina E. Wells, *Fear and Loathing in Constitutional Decision-Making*, 2005 Wis. L. Rev. 115, 201-202. Can we alter the standard to avoid these problems?

2. *Justice Brandeis and "clear and present danger."* What does Justice Brandeis's version of the test add to Holmes's discussion in *Abrams*? Do you agree with Brandeis that the "gravity" of potential harm should factor into the analysis? Should incitement to trespass or other minor offenses be protected speech? Should advocacy of acts of civil disobedience, such as blocking a highway, be protected under the First Amendment?
3. *Brandeis's* Whitney *concurrence and free speech values.* Justice Brandeis's justifications for protecting free speech are as well-known as are those in Justice Holmes's *Abrams* dissent.
   a. What point does Brandeis seem to be making about the essential link between political "truth" and self-governance? *See* Vincent Blasi, *The First Amendment and the Idea of Civic Courage*, 29 Wm. & Mary L. Rev. 653, 673-675 (1988).
   b. What vision of autonomy does Brandeis hold with his statement that "[t]hose who won our independence believed that the final end of the state was to make men free to develop their faculties"? For discussion, see Vincent Blasi, *Free Speech and Good Character*, 46 UCLA L. Rev. 1567 (1999).
4. *Brandeis's decision to concur.* Given the tenor of his opinion, Justice Brandeis's concurrence with the decision to uphold Anita Whitney's conviction is curious. Did Justice Brandeis concur for technical reasons, simply because Anita Whitney failed to raise arguments on appeal, or because there were substantive arguments supporting her conviction? *See Brandeis on Democracy* 238 (Philippa Strum ed., 1995); Ronald K.L. Collins & David M. Skover, *Curious Concurrence: Justice Brandeis's Vote in* Whitney v. California, 2005 Sup. Ct. Rev. 333 (2006).
5. Whitney *and association. Whitney* raises issues regarding First Amendment associational rights, which are discussed in Chapter 6. Although the association right is not specifically mentioned in the First Amendment, the Court has recognized its importance to free speech rights, noting that "[t]he right of peaceable assembly is a right cognate to those of free speech and free press and is equally fundamental." *DeJonge*, 299 U.S. at 364; *see also* NAACP v. Alabama, 357 U.S. 449, 460 (1958) (recognizing a First Amendment right to associate with others for expressive purposes) [*infra*, Ch. 6]. The California statute made it illegal for any person knowingly to be a member of an organization that advocated certain unlawful activity. The *Whitney* majority held that the Constitution did not protect knowing membership. Is "knowledge" the appropriate mental state, or should the court require that the defendant intend to further the organization's illegal aims? What kind of activity is sufficient to meet the "knowing membership" requirement? Was Whitney's conduct sufficient?

AN EXTENDED NOTE ON THE COLD WAR SMITH ACT PROSECUTIONS

Soon after *Gitlow* and *Whitney*, the "clear and present danger" test evolved into the speech-protective test Justices Holmes and Brandeis envisioned. The Court applied the test in a variety of cases, often to the benefit of speakers. *See, e.g.*,

Cantwell v. Connecticut, 310 U.S. 296 (1940); Thornhill v. Alabama, 310 U.S. 88 (1940); Bridges v. California, 314 U.S. 252 (1941); Schneiderman v. United States, 320 U.S. 118 (1943); Taylor v. Mississippi, 319 U.S. 583 (1943).

During the Cold War, however, the emergence of the Soviet Union as a world power under Communist government that promoted Communist revolutions in other countries led many Americans to perceive new threats to domestic peace, security, and liberty. As it did during World War I, the Supreme Court again upheld repressive legislation aimed at domestic Communists. The most famous of these cases was Dennis v. United States, 341 U.S. 494 (1951), which involved prosecution of several leaders of the Communist Party USA (CPUSA) for conspiring to advocate overthrow of the government in violation of the Smith Act, a federal law that criminalized knowingly and willfully advocating, advising, or teaching the necessity or desirability of overthrowing the government of the United States by force or violence.

In *Dennis*, the Court applied an extremely deferential version of the "clear and present danger" test to uphold the convictions of domestic Communists for allegedly conspiring to advocate the overthrow of the United States government. Although it acknowledged cases subsequent to *Gitlow* and *Whitney* "have inclined toward the Holmes-Brandeis rationale," the plurality concluded the State's interest in those cases was less substantial than in the present case. It observed the government was not required to wait "until the putsch is about to be executed, the plans have been laid and the signal is awaited" and rejected "the contention that success or probability of success is the criterion." Rather, the question was *whether the "gravity of the 'evil,' discounted by its improbability, justifies such invasion of speech as is necessary to avoid the danger."* Under that standard, the plurality concluded there was a clear and present danger of a substantive evil Congress had a right to prevent.

In the years following *Dennis*, the federal government charged at least 126 Communists with violating the Smith Act. Most of these lesser CPUSA leaders were convicted, with their convictions affirmed by appellate courts. The Supreme Court was largely uninvolved in these cases. During this period, however, many of the events that led to anti-Communist sentiment in the 1940s and early 1950s began to reverse themselves. The Korean War ended. Tensions with the Soviet Union eased after Joseph Stalin's death. And Joseph McCarthy, the charismatic crusader against domestic Communism, had been disgraced. In this atmosphere of somewhat lessening tension, the Supreme Court decided two important cases involving CPUSA leaders.

In Yates v. United States, 354 U.S. 298 (1957), the Court overturned the Smith Act convictions of 14 lesser leaders of the CPUSA for conspiracy to advocate overthrow of the government. The government's case in *Yates* proceeded along the same lines as *Dennis.* In fact, the charges and evidence in both cases were so similar that Justice Clark characterized the *Yates* defendants as "engaged in this conspiracy with the defendants in *Dennis*" and as having "served in the same army." 354 U.S. at 344-345 (Clark, J., dissenting). The *Yates* Court, however, *reversed* the defendants' convictions. Justice Harlan, writing for the majority, interpreted the Smith Act as prohibiting only incitement of violence and not "advocacy and teaching of forcible overthrow as an abstract principle divorced from any effort to instigate action to that end." 354 U.S. at 318. He concluded that the lower court's jury instructions did not adequately make that distinction. He also characterized *Dennis*'s essential holding as being "that indoctrination of a group in preparation for future violent action" and exhortation to immediate forcible overthrow is not protected when a "group is of sufficient size and cohesiveness, is sufficiently oriented towards action, and other circumstances are such" that they reasonably justify apprehension that the action will occur. *Id.* at 321. Justice Harlan found the evidence of defendant's "advocacy of action" insufficient to sustain the convictions on that rationale, describing it as "almost completely overshadowed by the hundreds of instances in the record in which overthrow, if mentioned at all, occurs in the course of doctrinal disputation so remote from action as to be almost wholly lacking in probative value." *Id.* at 327-331.

In Scales v. United States, 367 U.S. 203 (1961), the defendant was prosecuted for violating the membership clause of the Smith Act, which criminalized knowingly being a member in an organization that advocated the violent overthrow of the United States. The defendant argued that the clause violated his right of association under the First Amendment. The Court rejected the defendant's challenge, but narrowed the nature of the offense:

> It is, of course, true that quasi-political parties or other groups that may embrace both legal and illegal aims differ from a technical conspiracy, which is defined by its criminal purpose, so that all knowing association with the conspiracy is a proper subject for criminal proscription as far as First Amendment liberties are concerned. If there were a similar blanket prohibition of association with a group having both legal and illegal aims, there would indeed be a real danger that legitimate political expression or association would be impaired, but the membership clause, as here construed . . . does not make criminal all association with an organization which has been shown to engage in illegal advocacy. There must be clear proof that a defendant "specifically intend(s) to accomplish (the aims of the organization) by resort to violence." Thus the member for whom the organization is a vehicle for the advancement of legitimate aims and policies does not fall within the ban of the statute: he lacks the requisite specific intent "to bring about the overthrow of the government as speedily as circumstances would permit." Such a person may be foolish, deluded, or perhaps merely optimistic, but he is not by this statute made a criminal.

367 U.S. at 229-230. The Court upheld defendant's conviction based upon evidence that he was an active leader in the CPUSA and engaged in such activities as indoctrinating new members in the inevitability and desirability of the eventual violent overthrow of the government and in training them in specific techniques to use in possibly violent situations, such as a picket line. Justices Black, Douglas, and Brennan dissented. Justice Douglas argued that

> There is here no charge of conspiracy, no charge of any overt act to overthrow the Government by force and violence, no charge of any other criminal act. The charge is being a "member" of the Communist Party, "well-knowing" that it advocated the overthrow of the Government by force and violence, "said defendant intending to bring about such overthrow by force and violence as speedily as circumstances would permit."

> That falls far short of a charge of conspiracy. Conspiracy rests not in intention alone but in an agreement with one or more others to promote an unlawful project. No charge of any kind or sort of agreement hitherto embraced in the concept of a conspiracy is made here. . . . We legalize today guilt by association, sending a man to prison when he committed no unlawful act. . . . The case is not saved by showing that petitioner was an active member. None of the activity constitutes a crime.

Id. at 263-264 (Douglas, J., dissenting).

The Court later relied on *Scales* to hold that "[c]ivil liability may not be imposed merely because an individual belonged to a group, some members of which committed acts of violence." NAACP v. Claiborne Hardware Co., 458 U.S. 886, 920 (1982). Accordingly, the Court reversed the imposition of a large damage award on the NAACP and individuals for boycotting white businesses in Claiborne County, Mississippi, although there was evidence of violence and possibly threatening behavior as part of the boycott. As in *Scales*, the Court noted that "[f]or liability to be imposed by reason of association alone, it is necessary to establish that the group itself possessed unlawful goals and that the individual held a specific intent to further those illegal aims." *Id.* The Court also noted that this intent must be judged "'according to the strictest law,'" for "'otherwise there is a danger that one in sympathy with the legitimate aims of such an organization, but not specifically intending to accomplish them by resort to violence, might be punished for his adherence to lawful and constitutionally protected purposes, because of other and unprotected purposes which he does not necessarily share.'" *Id.* (quoting Noto v. United States, 367 U.S. 290 (1961)).

3. *The Modern "Incitement" Standard*

As noted, even prior to *Dennis*, the Supreme Court had been gradually moving toward a more protective "incitement" standard. As decisions like *Yates* and *Scales* indicated, by the 1960s the Court had become more protective of speech and associational rights. In a case arising from a prosecution under a state syndicalism law much like the one upheld in *Whitney*, the Court overruled that decision, announcing a far more speech-protective version of the "clear and present danger" standard.

Brandenburg v. Ohio

395 U.S. 444 (1969)

PER CURIAM.

The appellant, a leader of a Ku Klux Klan group, was convicted under the Ohio Criminal Syndicalism statute for "advocat(ing) . . . the duty, necessity, or propriety of crime, sabotage, violence, or unlawful methods of terrorism as a means of accomplishing industrial or political reform" and for "voluntarily assembl(ing) with any society, group, or assemblage of persons formed to teach or advocate the doctrines of criminal syndicalism." . . . He was fined $1,000 and sentenced to one to 10 years' imprisonment. . . .

The record shows that a man, identified at trial as the appellant, telephoned an announcer-reporter on the staff of a Cincinnati television station and invited him to come to a Ku Klux Klan "rally" to be held at a farm in Hamilton County. With the cooperation of the organizers, the reporter and a cameraman attended the meeting and filmed the events. Portions of the films were later broadcast on the local station and on a national network. . . .

One film showed 12 hooded figures, some of whom carried firearms. They were gathered around a large wooden cross, which they burned. No one was present other than the participants and the newsmen who made the film. Most of the words uttered during the scene were incomprehensible when the film was projected, but scattered phrases could be understood that were derogatory of Negroes and, in one instance, of Jews. Another scene on the same film showed the appellant, in Klan regalia, making a speech. The speech, in full, was as follows:

> This is an organizers' meeting. We have had quite a few members here today which are — we have hundreds, hundreds of members throughout the State of Ohio. I can quote from a newspaper clipping from the Columbus, Ohio Dispatch, five weeks ago Sunday morning. The Klan has more members in the State of Ohio than does any other organization. We're not a revengent organization, but if our President, our Congress, our Supreme Court, continues to suppress the white, Caucasian race, it's possible that there might have to be some revengeance taken.
>
> We are marching on Congress July the Fourth, four hundred thousand strong. From there we are dividing into two groups, one group to march on St. Augustine, Florida, the other group to march into Mississippi. Thank you.

The second film showed six hooded figures one of whom, later identified as the appellant, repeated a speech very similar to that recorded on the first film. The reference to the possibility of "revengeance" was omitted, and one sentence was added: "Personally, I believe the [n-word] should be returned to Africa, the Jew returned to Israel." Though some of the figures in the films carried weapons, the speaker did not.

The Ohio Criminal Syndicalism Statute was enacted in 1919. From 1917 to 1920, identical or quite similar laws were adopted by 20 States and two territories. . . . In 1927, this Court sustained the constitutionality of California's Criminal Syndicalism Act, . . . the text of which is quite similar to that of the laws of Ohio. *Whitney*. The Court upheld the statute on the ground that, without more, "advocating" violent means to effect political and economic change involves such danger to the security of the State that the State may outlaw it. . . . But *Whitney* has been thoroughly discredited by later decisions. *See Dennis*. These later decisions have fashioned the principle that the constitutional guarantees of free speech and free press do not permit a State to forbid or proscribe advocacy of the use of force or of law violation except where such advocacy is directed to inciting or producing imminent lawless action and is likely to incite or produce such action.[2]

As we said in Noto v. United States, 367 U.S. 290, 297 (1961), "the mere abstract teaching . . . of the moral propriety or even moral necessity for a resort to force and violence, is not the same as preparing a group for violent action and steeling it to such action." . . . A statute which fails to draw this distinction impermissibly intrudes upon the freedoms guaranteed by the First and Fourteenth Amendments. It sweeps within its condemnation speech which our Constitution has immunized from governmental control. Cf. *Yates.*

Measured by this test, Ohio's Criminal Syndicalism Act cannot be sustained. The Act punishes persons who "advocate or teach the duty, necessity, or propriety" of violence "as a means of accomplishing industrial or political reform"; or who publish or circulate or display any book or paper containing such advocacy; or who "justify" the commission of violent acts "with intent to exemplify, spread or advocate the propriety of the doctrines of criminal syndicalism"; or who "voluntarily assemble" with a group formed "to teach or advocate the doctrines of criminal syndicalism." Neither the indictment nor the trial judge's instructions to the jury in any way refined the statute's bald definition of the crime in terms of mere advocacy not distinguished from incitement to imminent lawless action.

Accordingly, we are here confronted with a statute which, by its own words and as applied, purports to punish mere advocacy and to forbid, on pain of criminal punishment, assembly with others merely to advocate the described type of action. Such a statute falls within the condemnation of the First and Fourteenth Amendments. The contrary teaching of *Whitney v. California* cannot be supported, and that decision is therefore overruled.

Mr. Justice BLACK, concurring.

I agree with the views expressed by Mr. Justice Douglas in his concurring opinion in this case that the "clear and present danger" doctrine should have no place in the interpretation of the First Amendment. I join the Court's opinion, which, as I understand it, simply cites [*Dennis*] but does not indicate any agreement on the Court's part with the "clear and present danger" doctrine on which *Dennis* purported to rely.

Mr. Justice DOUGLAS, concurring.

. . . I see no place in the regime of the First Amendment for any "clear and present danger" test, whether strict and tight as some would make it, or free-wheeling as the Court in *Dennis* rephrased it.

When one reads [past] opinions closely and sees when and how the "clear and present danger" test has been applied, great misgivings are aroused. First, the

---

2. It was on the theory that the Smith Act embodied such a principle and that it had been applied only in conformity with it that this Court sustained the Act's constitutionality. *Dennis.* That this was the basis for *Dennis* was emphasized in *Yates,* in which the Court overturned convictions for advocacy of the forcible overthrow of the Government under the Smith Act, because the trial judge's instructions had allowed conviction for mere advocacy, unrelated to its tendency to produce forcible action.

threats were often loud but always puny and made serious only by judges so wedded to the status quo that critical analysis made them nervous. Second, the test was so twisted and perverted in *Dennis* as to make the trial of those teachers of Marxism an all-out political trial which was part and parcel of the cold war that has eroded substantial parts of the First Amendment. . . .

The line between what is permissible and not subject to control and what may be made impermissible and subject to regulation is the line between ideas and overt acts. The example usually given by those who would punish speech is the case of one who falsely shouts fire in a crowded theatre.

This is, however, a classic case where speech is brigaded with action. They are indeed inseparable and a prosecution can be launched for the overt acts actually caused. Apart from rare instances of that kind, speech is, I think, immune from prosecution. Certainly there is no constitutional line between advocacy of abstract ideas as in *Yates* and advocacy of political action as in *Scales*. The quality of advocacy turns on the depth of the conviction; and government has no power to invade that sanctuary of belief and conscience.

NOTES AND QUESTIONS

1. *A major step*. Although brief, the *Brandenburg* opinion is a major step in the development of First Amendment law. As noted, the Court had been moving toward a more speech-protective "incitement" test prior to *Dennis* and the Smith Act cases. In *Brandenburg*, the Court explicitly overrules *Whitney* and implicitly overrules other early "incitement" precedents. As we will discover, the Court's approach to speech that incites others to commit unlawful acts has significant implications for the protection of speech and association in other contexts.
2. *The standard*. Under the modern incitement standard, advocacy of unlawful action is categorically unprotected when it is (a) *directed to* inciting or producing (b) *imminent* lawless action and (c) is *likely* to incite or produce such action. The standard requires that the government prove intent, imminence, *and* likelihood.
3. Brandenburg*'s protectiveness*. The *Brandenburg* standard seems to combine both the "clear and present danger" test's focus on the imminence and likelihood of harm and Judge Hand's approach in *Masses* requiring express or implied words of incitement, ultimately resulting in a far more speech-protective version of the "clear and present danger" standard. What is it about this version of the test that results in greater protection for speech? *See, e.g.*, Vincent Blasi, *Reading Holmes Through the Lens of Schauer: The Abrams Dissent*, 72 Notre Dame L. Rev. 1343, 1358-1359 (1997); Christina E. Wells, *Fear and Loathing in Constitutional Decision-Making*, 2005 Wis. L. Rev. 115, 206.
4. Brandenburg *and line-drawing*. How difficult will it be for law enforcement, regulators, and courts to draw appropriate lines under *Brandenburg?*
   a. It is a felony under federal law to intentionally "solicit, command, induce, or otherwise endeavor to persuade" another person to engage in a crime of violence against a person or property. 18 U.S.C. § 373. Many states have similar laws. What must prosecutors prove to convict a speaker of violating such laws?

b. Is *Brandenburg* overprotective of the clever speaker who, like Marc Antony's eulogy to Julius Caesar, masks his or her words of incitement in seemingly innocent words? *See* David Crump, *Camouflaged Incitement: Freedom of Speech, Communicative Torts, and the Borderland of the* Brandenburg *Test*, 29 Ga. L. Rev. 1 (1994).

c. Suppose a political candidate at a crowded rally, when confronted by protesters who attempt to interrupt the rally by shouting, repeatedly exhorts the crowd to "Get 'em out of here!" If the protesters are assaulted by rally attendees, can the candidate be held liable for inciting the assaults? Suppose the candidate also says, "But don't hurt 'em!" at the same time that he exhorts the crowd to remove the protesters. Do these words "neutralize" any potential incitement? *See* Nwanguma v. Trump, 903 F.3d 604, 612-613 (6th Cir. 2018) (concluding the words used by the candidate did not constitute unlawful incitement).

d. How are elements such as "imminence" and "likelihood" to be measured? Is "imminence" a matter of seconds, minutes, hours, or even days? Is "likelihood" a matter of high probability or does a more remote possibility suffice? Does *Brandenburg* unduly hamper law enforcement when faced with what may be serious threats to security and public safety? Does it require that authorities wait until the moment a criminal or other unlawful act is about to happen? Isn't that too late?

e. Is *Brandenburg* under-protective of speech, as Justice Douglas's concurrence suggests? Is that because "what is permissible and not subject to control and what may be made impermissible and subject to regulation is the line between ideas and overt acts . . ."? How difficult is it to draw that line?

Hess v. Indiana

414 U.S. 105 (1973)

PER CURIAM.

Gregory Hess appeals from his conviction in the Indiana courts for violating the State's disorderly conduct statute. [The Supreme Court of Indiana considered and rejected each of Hess' constitutional contentions, and accordingly affirmed his conviction.]

The events leading to Hess' conviction began with an antiwar demonstration on the campus of Indiana University. In the course of the demonstration, approximately 100 to 150 of the demonstrators moved onto a public street and blocked the passage of vehicles. When the demonstrators did not respond to verbal directions from the sheriff to clear the street, the sheriff and his deputies began walking up the street, and the demonstrators in their path moved to the curbs on either side, joining a large number of spectators who had gathered. Hess was standing off the street as the sheriff passed him. The sheriff heard Hess utter the word "fuck" in what he later described as a loud voice and immediately arrested him on the disorderly conduct charge. It was later stipulated that what appellant had said was "We'll take the fucking street later," or "We'll take the fucking street again." Two witnesses who were in the immediate vicinity testified, apparently without contradiction, that they heard Hess' words and witnessed his arrest. They indicated that Hess did not appear to be exhorting the crowd to go back into the street, that he was facing the crowd and not the street when he uttered the statement, that his statement did not appear to be addressed to any particular person or group, and that his tone, although loud, was no louder than that of the other people in the area.

Indiana's disorderly conduct statute was applied in this case to punish only spoken words. It hardly needs repeating that "[t]he constitutional guarantees of freedom of speech forbid the States to punish the use of words or language not within 'narrowly limited classes of speech.'" . . .

The Indiana Supreme Court placed primary reliance on the trial court's finding that Hess' statement "was intended to incite further lawless action on the part of the crowd in the vicinity of appellant and was likely to produce such action." At best, however, the statement could be taken as counsel for present moderation; at worst, it amounted to nothing more than advocacy of illegal action at some indefinite future time. This is not sufficient to permit the State to punish Hess' speech. Under our decisions, "the constitutional guarantees of free speech and free press do not permit a State to forbid or proscribe advocacy of the use of force or of law violation except where such advocacy is directed to inciting or producing *imminent* lawless action and is likely to incite or produce such action." *Brandenburg v. Ohio* (1969). (Emphasis added.) Since the uncontroverted evidence showed that Hess' statement was not directed to any person or group of persons, it cannot be said that he was advocating, in the normal sense, any action. And since there was no evidence, or rational inference from the import of the language, that his words were intended to produce, and likely to produce, *imminent* disorder, those words could not be punished by the State on the ground that they had "a 'tendency to lead to violence.'"

Accordingly, the . . . judgment of the Supreme Court of Indiana is reversed.

Mr. Justice REHNQUIST, with whom THE CHIEF JUSTICE and Mr. Justice BLACKMUN join, dissenting.

The Court's *per curiam* opinion rendered today aptly demonstrates the difficulties inherent in substituting a different complex of factual inferences for the inferences reached by the courts below. Since it is not clear to me that the Court has a sufficient basis for its action, I dissent.

It should be noted at the outset that the case was tried *de novo* in the Superior Court of Indiana upon a stipulated set of facts, and, therefore, the record is perhaps unusually colorless and devoid of life. . . .

The demonstration was of sufficient size and vigor to require the summoning of police, and both the Sheriff's Department and the Bloomington Police Department were asked to help university officials and police remove demonstrators blocking doorways to a campus building. At the time the sheriff arrived, "approximately 200-300 persons" were assembled at that particular building.

The doorways eventually were cleared of demonstrators, but, in the process, two students were placed under arrest. This action did not go unnoticed by the demonstrators. As the stipulation notes, "[i]n apparent response to these arrests, about 100-150 of the persons who had gathered as spectators went into Indiana Avenue in front of Bryan Hall and in front of the patrol car in which the two arrestees had been placed." Thus, by contrast to the majority's somewhat antiseptic description of this massing as being "[i]n the course of the demonstration," the demonstrators' presence in the street was not part of the normal "course of the demonstration" but could reasonably be construed as an attempt to intimidate and impede the arresting officers. Furthermore, as the stipulation also notes, the demonstrators "did not respond to verbal directions" from the sheriff to clear the street. Thus, the sheriff and his deputies found it necessary to disperse demonstrators by walking up the street directly into their path. Only at that point did the demonstrators move to the curbs.

The summaries of testimony establish that "Hess was standing off the street on the eastern curb of Indiana Avenue" and that he said, in the words of the trial court, "We'll take the fucking street later (or again)." The two female witnesses testified, as the majority correctly observes, that they were not offended by Hess' statement, that it was said no louder than statements by other demonstrators, "that Hess *did not appear* to be exhorting the crowd to go back into the street," that he was facing the crowd, and "that his statement *did not appear* to be addressed to any particular person or group." (Emphasis added.)

The majority makes much of this "uncontroverted evidence," but I am unable to find anywhere in the opinion an explanation of why it must be believed. Surely the sentence "We'll take the fucking street later (or again)" is susceptible of characterization as an exhortation, particularly when uttered in a loud voice while facing a crowd. The opinions of two defense witnesses cannot be considered *proof* to the contrary, since the trial court was perfectly free to reject this testimony if it so desired. Perhaps, as these witnesses and the majority opinion seem to suggest, appellant was simply expressing his views to the world at large, but that is surely not the only rational explanation.

The majority also places great emphasis on appellant's use of the word "later," even suggesting at one point that the statement "could be taken as counsel for present moderation." The opinion continues: "[A]t worst, it amounted to nothing more than advocacy of illegal action at some indefinite future time." From that observation, the majority somehow concludes that the advocacy was not directed towards inciting imminent action. But whatever other theoretical interpretations may be placed upon the remark, there are surely possible constructions of the statement which would encompass more or less immediate and continuing action against the harassed police. They should not be rejected out of hand because of an unexplained preference for other acceptable alternatives. . . .

NOTES AND QUESTIONS

1. Brandenburg *and context.* Do you agree with the majority in *Hess* that "no rational inference" could be drawn from Hess's words that he intended to incite or produce imminent disorder? Does the *per curiam* opinion properly consider the circumstances of the protest, including the size of the crowd, the actions of demonstrators, the arrests of participants, and the protesters' refusals to disperse?

2. *Rhetoric v. incitement.* Where is the line to be drawn between heated rhetoric and incitement to unlawful action? In NAACP v. Claiborne Hardware, 458 U.S. 886 (1982), the Court set aside, on First Amendment grounds, a large damages award against alleged participants in an economic boycott of white merchants by civil rights activists in a Mississippi county. The boycott sought to secure compliance with a list of demands for racial justice. One of the defendants was Charles Evers, the Field Secretary of the NAACP, who took a leading role in the boycott. One of the arguments for imposing civil liability on Evers was that "a finding that his public speeches were likely to incite lawless action could justify holding him liable for unlawful conduct that in fact followed within a reasonable period." In one speech, Evers stated boycott violators would be "disciplined" by their own people and suggested the possibility that "necks would be broken." The Court concluded Evers's "emotionally charged rhetoric" did not amount to unprotected incitement under *Brandenburg.* It observed that Evers's lengthy address "generally contained an impassioned plea for black citizens to unify, to support and respect each other, and to realize the political and economic power available to them". . . . "[T]his Court has made clear . . . that mere *advocacy* of use of force or violence does not remove speech from the protection of the First Amendment." The Court continued, "If that language had been followed by acts of violence, a substantial question would be presented whether Evers could be held liable for the consequences of that unlawful conduct. In this case, however, [almost all] acts of violence identified in 1966 occurred weeks or months after the April 1, 1966 speech; the chancellor made no finding of any violence after the challenged 1969 speech. [When an advocate's] appeals do not incite lawless action, they must be regarded as protected speech." Do you agree Evers's speech did not cross the line from "impassioned plea" to unprotected incitement?
3. *Beyond face-to-face encounters. Brandenburg, Hess,* and *Claiborne Hardware* involved a Klan rally, an antiwar protest, and a civil rights boycott, respectively. In each case, speakers and crowds occupied the same physical spaces. Does the incitement standard apply *only* to such face-to-face encounters? Can lawless action be directed over television, radio, cable, or the Internet? Does use of communications media preclude a finding of "imminence" and/or "likelihood"? If so, does this indicate *Brandenburg* should be updated or revised to take account of digital modes of communication? *See* Alexander Tsesis, *Inflammatory Speech: Offense Versus Incitement,* 97 Minn. L. Rev. 1145, 1166 (2013) ("The imminent threat of harm test is too narrow in scope to regulate the dissemination of public threats streaming on the internet."). *See also* Timothy Zick, *Falsely Shouting Fire in a Global Theater: Emerging Complexities of Transborder Expression,* 65 Vand. L. Rev. 125, 146-54 (2012) (discussing incitement that crosses national borders, including via online media).
4. *Online radicalization and terrorism.* Should *Brandenburg* be relaxed to permit regulation of online speech that inspires conversion to domestic or foreign terrorist causes? *See* Nadine Strossen, *The Regulation of Extremist*

Speech in the Era of Mass Digital Communications: Is Brandenburg *Tolerance Obsolete in the Terrorist Era?*, 36 Pepp. L. Rev. 361 (2009); Richard A. Posner, *Not a Suicide Pact: The Constitution in a Time of National Emergency* 120-25 (2006). Some nations, including the United Kingdom, prohibit publication of statements that directly or indirectly encourage, induce, or glorify acts of terrorism. British Terrorism Act of 2006, Chapter 11. Under U.S. law, speakers can be prosecuted for providing "material support" to designated foreign terrorist groups. 18 U.S.C. § 2339B. In Holder v. Humanitarian Project, 561 U.S. 1 (2010) [*infra*, p. 112], the Court upheld the "material support" law as applied to U.S. citizens and organizations who sought to facilitate the humanitarian and political activities of two groups by providing them with various forms of educational and legal assistance. Is criminalizing these speech and associational activities consistent with *Brandenburg*? (Note the majority in *Humanitarian Law Project* did not mention *Brandenburg*.)

5. *Beyond political advocacy. Brandenburg* is the Supreme Court's attempt to separate protected political advocacy from speech that crosses the line into the area of "unprotected" incitement of illegal activity. To what extent should courts extend *Brandenburg*'s standard to expression that is not political advocacy but that might cause harm, such as entertainment or speech that provides information such as bombmaking instructions? Scholars disagree profoundly on this issue. For discussion, see Kent Greenawalt, *Speech, Crime, and the Uses of Language* (1989); Rodney A. Smolla, *Should the* Brandenburg v. Ohio *Incitement Test Apply in Media Violence Tort Cases?*, 27 N. Ky. L. Rev. 1 (2000); S. Elizabeth Wilborn Malloy & Ronald J. Krotoszynski, Jr., *Recalibrating the Cost of Harm Advocacy: Getting Beyond Brandenburg*, 41 Wm. & Mary L. Rev. 1159 (2000); David A. Anderson, *Incitement and Tort Law*, 37 Wake Forest L. Rev. 957 (2002); Eugene Volokh, *Crime-Facilitating Speech*, 57 Stan. L. Rev. 1095 (2005). Consider the following applications.

   a. *Entertainment and "incited" suicide.* As part of a series about the pleasures and dangers of unusual and taboo sexual practices, *Hustler Magazine* printed "Orgasm of Death," an article discussing the practice of autoerotic asphyxia. This practice entails masturbation while "hanging" oneself in order to temporarily cut off the blood supply to the brain at the moment of orgasm. The article included details about how the act is performed and the kind of physical pleasure those who engage in it seek to achieve. The heading identified "Orgasm of Death" as part of a series on "Sexplay," discussions of "sexual pleasures [that] have remained hidden for too long behind the doors of fear, ignorance, inexperience and hypocrisy" and are presented "to increase [readers'] sexual knowledge, to lessen [their] inhibitions and—ultimately—to make [them] much better lover[s]."

      An editor's note, positioned on the page so that it was likely to be the first text the reader will see, stated: "Hustler emphasizes the often-fatal dangers of the practice of 'auto-erotic asphyxia,' and recommends that readers seeking unique forms of sexual release DO NOT ATTEMPT this method. The facts are presented here solely for an educational purpose." The magazine further had a lengthy discussion of the dangers of autoerotic asphyxiation and statistics regarding the number of people who die each year as a result of the practice.

A 14-year-old boy was found hanging in his closet with a copy of the *Hustler Magazine* article at his feet. The boy's mother sued *Hustler Magazine* for inciting the suicide and sought civil damages. Does imposition of liability satisfy the requirements of *Brandenburg*? Should *Brandenburg* be applied at all? *See* Herceg v. Hustler Magazine, 814 F.2d 1017 (5th Cir. 1987) (rejecting imposition of liability under a state law "incitement" action).

b. "*How-to" manuals.* Paladin Enterprises published a book, *Hitman: A Technical Manual for Independent Contractors*, which gave explicit and detailed instructions on how to solicit, prepare for, and commit murders (at least 130 pages of this information) without being caught. Several months after the book's publication, James Perry brutally murdered a woman and her two children. Perry was solicited to do so by the victims' husband/father. In carrying out the killings, Perry meticulously followed the directions in the book *Hitman*, which was found in his apartment at the time of his arrest. The estate of the victims sued Paladin Enterprises, the publisher of the book, for wrongful death, alleging that the publisher aided and abetted Perry in the murders. In Rice v. Paladin Enterprises, 128 F.3d 233 (4th Cir. 1997), the court held the publisher could be held liable under an "aiding and abetting" theory. Should the First Amendment be a defense in this lawsuit? Should *Brandenburg* apply in this context?

Compare the *"Hitman"* scenario to the following situation:

> A website published an article on how to deceive fingerprint identification security systems. Ellen Gates, a member of an animal rights organization, used this information to bypass a security system at an animal testing lab and free the monkeys used for testing. This action caused substantial physical damage and monetary loss to the lab, which sued the website for damages (under an aiding and abetting theory similar to the *Hitman* lawsuit).

Same questions as above. Does your answer differ from that in *"Hitman"*? If so, why? Do differences in outcome suggest that we should apply *Brandenburg* differently or that one of these scenarios simply falls outside the boundaries of the First Amendment?

THEORY-APPLIED PROBLEM

The Animal Enterprise Terrorism Act, 18 U.S.C. § 43, is a federal law that creates the following federal crime:

> **(a)** Offense.—Whoever travels in interstate or foreign commerce, or uses or causes to be used the mail or any facility of interstate or foreign commerce—
>
> **(1)** for the purpose of damaging or interfering with the operations of an animal enterprise; and
>
> **(2)** in connection with such purpose—
>
> **(A)** intentionally damages or causes the loss of any real or personal property (including animals or records) used by an animal enterprise [roughly defined as a commercial or academic enterprise that uses or sells animal products, or any zoo, aquarium, pet store or other lawful competitive animal event], or any real or personal property of a person or entity having a connection to, relationship with, or transactions with an animal enterprise; . . . or
>
> **(C)** conspires or attempts to do so;
>
> shall be punished [with the imposition of fines and/or a possible jail sentence].

Consider the statute as applied in the following situation: "Stop Animal Cruelty" ("SAC") is an organization devoted to halting animal cruelty. SAC recently targeted the activities of Animal Research Labs ("ARL"), which performs testing for companies that want to bring their products to market and specifically does so on animals (including rats, mice, and guinea pigs). SAC engages in a variety of actions, both legal and illegal, as part of their campaign to stop ARL's testing. These have included legal actions, such as political protests and leafleting, and illegal actions, such as physically assaulting researchers and burglarizing ARL's research labs.

SAC maintains a central website where it posts information and discussion of its protest activities. Thus, it posts informational items describing past protests, breakins, and harassment of ARL workers. It also hosts discussion at this website about past, present, and future actions. Comments are posted by anyone who wants to log into the discussion group. Through its website, SAC also invites its supporters to engage in "electronic civil disobedience" against ARL and other companies associated with it. Electronic civil disobedience is a coordinated campaign by many people to inundate websites, e-mail servers, and the telephone service of a company. SAC sponsors electronic civil disobedience campaigns on the first Monday of every month. SAC reminds its supporters that electronic civil disobedience is illegal, so supporters should participate only if they "are prepared to suffer potentially severe consequences."

Recently, Anna posted a "bulletin" on SAC's website calling for "direct action" against the CEO of LifeCorp, Inc., a business that contracted with ARL to test its product. The call for action further noted that "First Monday approaches. Don't let these schmucks get away with this stuff." That same day, Bart commented in the website's discussion group stating, "I am excited to see someone finally paying attention to the plight of these poor animals. Keep up the good work!" On the first Monday of the next month, LifeCorp's computers were jammed for several hours with resulting damage approximating about $10,000.

Assume that none of the following actors participated in the acts of electronic civil disobedience but that they are members of SAC. Anna is arrested for violating the federal law based on her post on the website. Does she have a First Amendment defense? Bart is arrested for his comments in the discussion group on the website. Does he have a First Amendment defense?

B. *"FIGHTING WORDS" AND OTHER CATEGORICAL EXCLUSIONS*

Thus far, the materials reflect the Supreme Court's difficulty in establishing an acceptable test for punishing speech that incites illegal action. This line-drawing problem extends beyond incitement to other kinds of speech. One manner of dealing with these difficult line-drawing problems is to create bright-line or categorical rules. As we have seen, a court might carve out a specific category of speech, such as incitement, and treat it as "unprotected." When speech falls into one of these categories or classes, no balancing or further inquiry is required; the speech is outside the protection of the First Amendment. The categorical approach arguably avoids ad hoc decision making by judges and juries who otherwise must make decisions pertaining to controversial speech without adequate guidelines. Chaplinsky v. New Hampshire, 315 U.S. 568 (1942), below, was the first Supreme Court decision to explicitly rely on a "two-level" theory of the First Amendment. According to the Court, "[t]here are certain well-defined and narrowly limited classes of speech, the prevention and punishment of which has never been thought to raise any Constitutional problem." The materials in this and the next section examine the Court's attempts to construct categories of unprotected speech beyond incitement, specifically "fighting words" and "true threats." Other categories or classes of unprotected or "low-value" speech, including defamation, commercial speech, obscenity, and child pornography, are considered in subsequent chapters.

Chaplinsky v. New Hampshire

315 U.S. 568 (1942)

Mr. Justice MURPHY delivered the opinion of the Court.

. . . Chaplinsky [a member of the religious sect known as Jehovah's Witnesses] was distributing the literature of his sect on the streets of Rochester on a busy Saturday afternoon. Members of the local citizenry complained to the City Marshal, Bowering, that Chaplinsky was denouncing all religion as a "racket." Bowering told them that Chaplinsky was lawfully engaged, and then warned Chaplinsky that the crowd was getting restless. Some time later a disturbance occurred and the traffic officer on duty at the busy intersection started with Chaplinsky for the police station, but did not inform him that he was under arrest or that he was going to be arrested. On the way, they encountered Marshal Bowering who had been advised that a riot was under way and was therefore hurrying to the scene. Bowering repeated his earlier warning to Chaplinsky who then [said to him "You are a God damned racketeer" and "a damned Fascist and the whole government of Rochester are Fascists or agents of Fascists"].

Chaplinsky's version of the affair was slightly different. He testified that when he met Bowering, he asked him to arrest the ones responsible for the disturbance. In reply Bowering cursed him and told him to come along. Appellant admitted that he said the words charged in the complaint with the exception of the name of the Deity. . . .

[Chaplinsky was charged with and convicted for violation of Chapter 378, Section 2, of the Public Laws of New Hampshire: "No person shall address any offensive, derisive or annoying word to any other person who is lawfully in any street or other public place, nor call him by any offensive or derisive name, nor make any noise or exclamation in his presence and hearing with intent to deride, offend or annoy him, or to prevent him from pursuing his lawful business or occupation."]

[I]t is well understood that the right of free speech is not absolute at all times and under all circumstances. There are certain well-defined and narrowly limited classes of speech, the prevention and punishment of which has never been thought to raise any Constitutional problem. These include the lewd and obscene, the profane, the libelous, and the insulting or "fighting" words—those which by their very utterance inflict injury or tend to incite an immediate breach of the peace. It has been well observed that such utterances are no essential part of any exposition of ideas, and are of such slight social value as a step to truth that any benefit that may be derived from them is clearly outweighed by the social interest in order and morality. "Resort to epithets or personal abuse is not in any proper sense communication of information or opinion safeguarded by the Constitution, and its punishment as a criminal act would raise no question under that instrument." Cantwell v. Connecticut, 310 U.S. 296 (1940).

On the authority of its earlier decisions, the state court declared that the statute's purpose was to preserve the public peace, no words being "forbidden except such as have a direct tendency to cause acts of violence by the person to whom, individually, the remark is addressed." It was further said: "The word 'offensive' is not to be defined in terms of what a particular addressee thinks. . . . The test is what men of common intelligence would understand would be words likely to cause an average addressee to fight. . . . The English language has a number of words and expressions which by general consent are 'fighting words' when said without a disarming smile. . . . Such words, as ordinary men know, are likely to cause a fight. So are threatening, profane or obscene revilings. Derisive and annoying words can be taken as coming within the purview of the statute as heretofore interpreted only when they have this characteristic of plainly tending to excite the addressee to a breach of the peace. . . . The statute, as construed, does no more than prohibit the face-to-face words plainly likely to cause a breach of the peace by the addressee, words whose speaking constitute a breach of the peace by the speaker—including 'classical fighting words', words in current use less 'classical' but equally likely to cause violence, and other disorderly words, including profanity, obscenity and threats." . . .

A statute punishing verbal acts, carefully drawn so as not unduly to impair liberty of expression, is not too vague for a criminal law. . . .

Nor can we say that the application of the statute to the facts disclosed by the record substantially or unreasonably impinges upon the privilege of free speech. Argument is unnecessary to demonstrate that the appellations "damn racketeer" and "damn Fascist" are epithets likely to provoke the average person to retaliation, and thereby cause a breach of the peace. . . .

Affirmed.

NOTES AND QUESTIONS

1. *Definition. Chaplinsky* uses various formulations to describe "fighting words." The Court seems to require the use of certain words that, when

directed to an individual, would cause a reasonable person to respond with violence. Professor John Hart Ely characterized the category as consisting of words constituting "a quite unambiguous invitation to a brawl." John Hart Ely, *Democracy and Distrust* 114 (1980).

2. *"Abusive remarks" and provocation.* In Cantwell v. Connecticut, 310 U.S. 296 (1940) [*infra*, Ch. 5], the speaker was convicted of the common law offense of inciting a breach of the peace. The facts, as described by the Court, were as follows: "Jesse Cantwell . . . stopped two men in the street, asked, and received, permission to play a phonograph record, and played the record 'Enemies,' which attacked the religion and church of the two men, who were Catholic. Both were incensed by the contents of the record and were tempted to strike Cantwell unless he went away. On being told to be on his way he left their presence. There was no evidence he was personally offensive or entered into any argument with those he interviewed." The Court held Cantwell's speech "raised no such clear and present menace to public peace and order as to render him liable to conviction of the common law offense in question." In reaching its conclusion, the Court observed Cantwell did not use any "profane, indecent, or abusive remarks directed to the person of the hearer" and exhibited "no assault or threatening of bodily harm, no truculent bearing, no intentional discourtesy, no personal abuse." Are *Cantwell* and *Chaplinsky* distinguishable? If so, on what basis?
3. *Fighting words and "emotional injury."* Is the prevention of "inflict[ion of] injury" (presumably emotional injury) sufficient to justify punishment of speech? As we will see, the Court has indicated in several post-*Chaplinsky* decisions that mere "infliction of injury" does not remove speech from First Amendment protection. Nor, as discussed below, is the mere use of profanity sufficient, as upsetting as some may find it; as subsequent cases made clear, profanity is generally protected speech. Thus, the "fighting words" category is limited to words delivered in a manner likely to cause an imminent breach of peace. Is this concept too narrow? Should "fighting words" encompass words that are intended to inflict psychological injury?
4. *Fighting words as non-communication? Chaplinsky* states that "fighting words" are "no essential part of any exposition of ideas." Why? Are they more akin to a physical assault? What is it about such words that place them wholly outside the First Amendment? For commentary, see Alexander Bickel, *The Morality of Consent* 72 (1975); Stephen W. Gard, *Fighting Words as Free Speech*, 58 Wash. U. L.Q. 531, 542 (1980); Martin Redish, *The Value of Free Speech*, 130 U. Pa. L. Rev. 591, 626 (1982); Mark C. Rutzick, *Offensive Language and the Evolution of First Amendment Protection*, 9 Harv. C.R.-C.L. L. Rev. 1, 10 (1974).
5. *Police officers as "reasonable addressees."* Should police officers, such as Marshal Bowering, be expected not to respond violently to abusive remarks? *See* City of Houston v. Hill, 482 U.S. 451 (1987) (observing "the First Amendment protects a significant amount of verbal criticism and challenge directed at police officers," but the "freedom verbally to challenge police action is not without limits").

6. *The "low-value" list. Chaplinsky* designated "the lewd and obscene, the profane, the libelous, and the insulting or "fighting" words" as low-value categories of speech. Note the Court does not cite any authority for its list. Some have questioned whether the classes of speech the Court identified were in fact historically excluded from protection. *See* Genevieve Lakier, *The Invention of Low-Value Speech*, 128 Harv. L. Rev. 2166 (2015). In any event, over time *Chaplinsky*'s list of unprotected classes or categories of speech has undergone significant changes. For example, under modern First Amendment doctrine "lewd" and "profane" speech is generally protected by the First Amendment. *See,e.g.*, Cohen v. California, 403 U.S. 15 (1971) [*infra* Chapter 10]. Further, in N.Y. Times Co. v. Sullivan, 376 U.S. 254, 269 (1964), the Supreme Court announced that "libel can claim no talismanic immunity from constitutional limitations." (*See* discussion *infra*, Chapter 9.)
7. *"Low-value" methodology. Chaplinsky* justified treating "fighting words" and other specified classes or categories of speech as unprotected on the ground that they "are no essential part of any exposition of ideas, and are of such slight social value as a step to truth that any benefit that may be derived from them is clearly outweighed by the social interest in order and morality." As discussed in Section D below, in 2010 the Supreme Court described this rationale as merely "descriptive." It did not, the Court asserted, "set forth a test that may be applied as a general matter to permit the Government to imprison any speaker so long as his speech is deemed valueless or unnecessary, or so long as an ad hoc calculus of costs and benefits tilts in a statute's favor." United States v. Stevens, 559 U.S. 460, 471 (2010). As we will see, the modern Court has been deeply skeptical of the notion that other categories of speech can be treated as "low value" and hence unprotected.

AN EXTENDED NOTE ON THE POST-*CHAPLINSKY* FIGHTING-WORDS DOCTRINE

Chaplinsky is the only Supreme Court case to ever uphold a fighting-words conviction. However, the decision has not been overruled. In fact, recent cases have reaffirmed the viability of the fighting words category. *See R.A.V. v. City of St. Paul* (1992), *infra* Chapter 10. But subsequent cases appear to have substantially narrowed *Chaplinsky*'s reach. These cases reflect the Court's attempt to craft a narrow definition of fighting words that still leaves ample room for a speaker who attempts to persuade others to her point of view, even when she "resorts to exaggeration, vilification . . . and even to false statement."

For example, in Cohen v. California, 403 U.S. 15 (1971), the Court reversed the conviction of Paul Robert Cohen for wearing a jacket with the words "Fuck the Draft" across its back. Cohen had been tried and found guilty under a California statute prohibiting any person from "maliciously and willfully disturbing the peace or quiet of any neighborhood or person . . . by . . . offensive conduct." Citing *Chaplinsky*, the Court stated, "the States are free to ban the simple use, without a demonstration of additional justifying circumstances, of so-called 'fighting words,' those personally abusive epithets which, when addressed to the ordinary citizen, are, as a matter of common knowledge, inherently likely to provoke violent reaction." It further noted, however, that

> [w]hile the four-letter word displayed by Cohen in relation to the draft is not uncommonly employed in a personally provocative fashion, in this instance it was clearly not 'directed to the person of the hearer.' *Cantwell.* No individual actually or likely to be present could reasonably have regarded the words on appellant's jacket as a direct personal insult.

403 U.S. at 20. With these considerations in mind, the Court thus identified the free speech issue in stark terms: "Against this background, the issue flushed by this case stands out in bold relief. It is whether California can excise, as 'offensive conduct,' one particular scurrilous epithet from the public discourse, either upon the theory of the court below that its use is inherently likely to cause violent reaction or upon a more general assertion that the States, acting as guardians of public morality, may properly remove this offensive word from the public vocabulary. The rationale of the California court is plainly untenable. At most it reflects an 'undifferentiated fear or apprehension of disturbance (which) is not enough to overcome the right to freedom of expression.'" *Id.* at 22-23.

In Texas v. Johnson, 491 U.S. 397 (1989), *infra* p. 153, the defendant was arrested for burning a flag under a Texas law punishing anyone who desecrated a flag in a manner that would offend another person. The Court rejected the argument that the law was justified by the state's interest in preventing breaches of the peace. "[N]o disturbance of the peace actually occurred or threatened to occur because of Johnson's burning of the flag," the Court noted. The State's position, therefore, "amounts to a claim that an audience that takes serious offense at particular expression is necessarily likely to disturb the peace and that the expression may be prohibited on this basis. Our precedents do not countenance such a presumption. On the contrary, they recognize that a principal function of free speech under our system of government is to invite dispute." The Court concluded that Johnson's expressive conduct did not "fall within that small class of 'fighting words' that are 'likely to provoke the average person to retaliation, and thereby cause a breach of the peace.' No reasonable onlooker would have regarded Johnson's generalized expression of dissatisfaction with the policies of the Federal Government as a direct personal insult or an invitation to exchange fisticuffs." 489 U.S. at 408-409.

The Court has also invalidated laws that sweep within their terms offensive speech that does not constitute "fighting words." In Gooding v. Wilson, 405 U.S. 518 (1972), the defendant, who was protesting the Vietnam War at an induction center, swore at police officers trying to remove him, saying, "White son of a bitch, I'll kill you," "You son of a bitch, I'll choke you to death," and "You son of a bitch, if you ever put your hands on me again, I'll cut you all to pieces." He was convicted under a Georgia statute providing: "Any person who shall, without provocation, use to [or in the presence of another] . . . opprobrious words or abusive language, tending to cause a breach of the peace . . . shall be guilty of a misdemeanor." The Supreme Court reversed his conviction, finding that the statute's term "tending to cause a breach of the peace" did not "define the standard of responsibility with requisite narrow specificity." The Court found that past applications of the statute resulted in convictions where there was no likelihood that the person addressed would make an immediate violent response, in violation of the fighting-words doctrine defined by *Chaplinsky*. Accordingly, the Court believed that the statute left "wide open the standard of responsibility, so that it [was] easily susceptible to improper application."

What is left of *Chaplinsky*'s version of the fighting-words doctrine after these cases? Does the fact that words produce psychological injury suffice or has that aspect of *Chaplinsky*'s definition been entirely abandoned? Professor Stephen Gard has suggested that cases since *Chaplinsky* establish four required elements before fighting words can be punished: (1) provocative personal insult, (2) direct tendency to cause immediate violence, (3) face-to-face utterance, (4) directed at an individual. Gard, *supra*, at 536. *See also* Rutzick, *supra*, at 27. Is this a fair assessment of the modern cases? In what circumstances are fighting-words prosecutions most likely to be successful?

Despite the Supreme Court's general lack of attention to "fighting words," lower courts have continued to apply the doctrine. Convictions for "breach of peace," "disorderly conduct," and other public order offenses have been affirmed, in many cases based on abusive language directed at police officers. According to one study, the fighting words doctrine has been used as a justification for punishing provocative speech, especially in cases involving "racial minorities for talking back to the police." *See* Burton Caine, *The Trouble With Fighting Words:* Chaplinsky v. New Hampshire *Is a Threat to First Amendment Values and Should Be Overruled*, 88 Marq. L. Rev. 441 (2004). *See also* Mark P. Strasser, *Those Are Fighting Words, Aren't They? On Adding Injury to Insult*, 71 Case W. Res. L. Rev. 249, 250 (2020).

Does the Court's focus on violence ignore the possible other injuries that personal abuse and epithets might inflict? Wendy B. Reilly, Note, *Fighting the Fighting Words Standard: A Call for Its Destruction*, 52 Rutgers L. Rev. 947, 956 (2000) (arguing that focus on breach of peace renders verbal assaults "*not* regulable . . . when directed at someone of a more pacific bent," even though such words inflict significant psychic injury). Is the "fighting words" doctrine a hopeless anachronism that mimics the macho code of barroom brawls?

Should the Court overrule *Chaplinsky* as a moral aberration and a general threat to freedom of expression? Compare Caine, *supra*, at 445 (arguing "the fighting-words doctrine was ill-conceived, is in disarray, and poses a potent danger to speech that should command premier protection") with Kent Greenawalt, *Insults and Epithets: Are They Protected Free Speech?* 42 Rutgers L. Rev. 287, 296 (1990) ("when a speaker tries to provoke a fight, his expressive interest is slight; his remarks represent a course of action and may be punished").

C. *"TRUE THREATS"*

A third category of expression the Court has treated as "low value" is known as a "true threat." The true threat category has still not been fully developed by the Court, which has addressed it in only a few decisions. Important questions remain about the categorical definition, the distinction between "political hyperbole" and "true threats," the mental state required to convict a speaker of communicating unprotected threats, and the application of the "true threats" doctrine to online communications. The following cases provide a general framework for considering the categorial exclusion of "true threats" from First Amendment protection.

Watts v. United States

394 U.S. 705 (1969)

PER CURIAM.

After a jury trial in the United States District Court for the District of Columbia, petitioner was convicted of violating a 1917 statute [18 U.S.C. § 871(a)] which prohibits any person from "knowingly and willfully . . . (making) any threat to take the life of or to inflict bodily harm upon the President of the United States. . . ." The incident which led to petitioner's arrest occurred on August 27, 1966, during a public rally on the Washington Monument grounds. The crowd present broke up into small discussion groups and petitioner joined a gathering scheduled to discuss police brutality. Most of those in the group were quite young, either in their teens or early twenties. Petitioner, who himself was 18 years old, entered into the discussion after one member of the group suggested that the young people present should get more education before expressing their views. According to an investigator for the Army Counter Intelligence Corps who was present, petitioner responded: "They always holler at us to get an education. And now I have already received my draft classification as 1-A and I have got to report for my physical this Monday coming. I am not going. If they ever make me carry a rifle the first man I want to get in my sights is L.B.J." "They are not going to make me kill my black brothers." . . . On the basis of this statement, the jury found that petitioner had committed a felony by knowingly and willfully threatening the President. The United States Court of Appeals for the District of Columbia Circuit affirmed by a two-to-one vote. We reverse.

At the close of the Government's case, petitioner's trial counsel moved for a judgment of acquittal. He contended that there was "absolutely no evidence on the basis of which the jury would be entitled to find that (petitioner) made a threat against the life of the President." He stressed the fact that petitioner's statement was made during a political debate, that it was expressly made conditional upon an event—induction into the Armed Forces—which petitioner vowed would never occur, and that both petitioner and the crowd laughed after the statement was made. He concluded, "Now actually what happened here in all this was a kind of very crude offensive method of stating a political opposition to the President. What he was saying, he says, I don't want to shoot black people because I don't consider them my enemy, and if they put a rifle in my hand it is the people that put the rifle in my hand, as symbolized by the President, who are my real enemy." We hold that the trial judge erred in denying this motion.

Certainly the statute under which petitioner was convicted is constitutional on its face. The Nation undoubtedly has a valid, even an overwhelming, interest in protecting the safety of its Chief Executive and in allowing him to perform his duties without interference from threats of physical violence. Nevertheless, a statute such as this one, which makes criminal a form of pure speech, must be interpreted with the commands of the First Amendment clearly in mind. What is a threat must be distinguished from what is constitutionally protected speech.

. . . We do not believe that the kind of political hyperbole indulged in by petitioner fits within [the statutory definition of "true threat"]. For we must interpret the language Congress chose "against the background of a profound national commitment to the principle that debate on public issues should be uninhibited, robust, and wide open, and that it may well include vehement, caustic, and sometimes unpleasantly sharp attacks on government and public officials." New York Times Co. v. Sullivan, 376 U.S. 254, 270 (1964). The language of the political arena . . . is often vituperative, abusive, and inexact. We agree with petitioner that his only offense here was "a kind of very crude offensive method of stating a political opposition to the President." Taken in context, and regarding the expressly conditional nature of the statement and the reaction of the listeners, we do not see how it could be interpreted otherwise. . . . Court of Appeals reversed and case remanded with instructions.

Justice DOUGLAS, concurring.

The charge in this case is of an ancient vintage. The federal statute under which petitioner was convicted traces its ancestry to the Statute of Treasons (25 Edw. 3) which made it a crime to "compass or imagine the Death of . . . the King." Note, *Threats to Take the Life of the President*, 32 Harv. L. Rev. 724, 725 (1919).

. . . "Like the Statute of Treasons, section 871 was passed in a 'relatively calm peacetime spring,' but has been construed under circumstances when intolerance for free speech was much greater than it normally might be." Note, *Threatening the President: Protected Dissenter or Political Assassin*, 57 Geo. L.J. 553, 570 (1969). Convictions under 18 U.S.C. § 871 have been sustained for displaying posters urging passersby to "hang (President) Roosevelt" for declaring that "President Wilson ought to be killed. It is a wonder some one has not done it already. If I had an opportunity, I would do it myself"; [and] for declaring that "Wilson is a wooden-headed son of a bitch. I wish Wilson was in hell, and if I had the power I would put him there." In sustaining an indictment under the statute against a man who indicated that he would enjoy shooting President Wilson if he had the chance, the trial court [in United States v. Jasick, 252 F. 939, 933 (E.D. Mich. 1918)] explained the thrust of § 871:

> The purpose of the statute was undoubtedly not only the protection of the President, but also the prohibition of just such statements as those alleged in this indictment. The expression of such direful intentions and desires, not only indicates a spirit of disloyalty to the nation bordering upon treason, but is, in a very real sense, a menace to the peace and safety of the country. . . . It arouses resentment and concern on the part of patriotic citizens.

Suppression of speech as an effective police measure is an old, old device, outlawed by our Constitution.

Justice STEWART would deny the petition for certiorari.

[Justice WHITE's dissenting opinion is omitted.]

NOTES AND QUESTIONS

1. *What is a "true threat"? Watts* intimates threats fall into a category of unprotected speech, a fact later Supreme Court cases have reaffirmed. *See* R.A.V. v. City of St. Paul, 505 U.S. 377, 388 (1992) (*see infra* Chapter 10); Virginia v. Black, 538 U.S. 343 (2003) (*see infra* Chapter 10). However, does the Court ever clearly tell us what a "true threat" is?
2. *The* Watts *factors.* Although Watts did not define the category of "true threats," the Court seemed to rely on several factors in concluding Watts's speech did not constitute an unprotected true threat. The Court noted (1) the statements were made at a public political rally; (2) many in the crowd reacted to Watts's speech with laughter; and (3) Watts's threat was highly conditional ("If they ever make me carry a rifle . . ."). Based on the context, the crowd's reaction, and the conditional nature of the threat, the Court concluded Watts's speech was protected by the First Amendment.
3. *Political hyperbole and threats.* As noted earlier, *supra* p. 61, n. 2, in NAACP v. Claiborne Hardware, 458 U.S. 886 (1982), the Court concluded that Charles Evers's speeches to civil rights activists was protected political hyperbole and not unprotected incitement. *Claiborne Hardware* also addressed a claim that Evers's speeches contained unprotected threats. Recall Evers told a crowd of civil rights activists that if they did not participate in the boycott of the town's white businesses, they might be "disciplined" and raised the possibility that "necks might be broken." The Court concluded Evers's statements did not constitute an unprotected "true threat." Although it recognized that Evers's statements "might have been understood as inviting an unlawful form of discipline or, at least, as intending to create a fear of violence whether or not improper discipline was specifically intended," the Court nevertheless concluded that the statements were protected speech. The Court did not cite or discuss *Watts.* If some activists in the crowd might understand Evers's statements as "intending to create a fear of violence," shouldn't they be considered unprotected threats? Applying the *Watts* factors, is Evers's speech a true threat?
4. *Cross burning and intimidation.* In Virginia v. Black, 538 U.S. 343 (2003), the Court reviewed several convictions under a Virginia statute that criminalized the burning of a cross "with the intent of intimidating any person or group of persons." One of the defendants was charged with participating in a cross burning in connection with a Ku Klux Klan rally in an open field. Three other individuals were convicted under the Virginia law after they attempted to burn a cross on the lawn of an African American neighbor, in retaliation for a complaint the neighbor had made about the discharge of firearms on the defendants' properties. Although it ultimately reversed the convictions, the Court held the government could punish cross burning as a "true threat." After reviewing the history of cross burning, which the Court explained was used by the Klan both as a means of intimidation and as part of its ceremonies, the Court offered this definition:

> "True threats" encompass those statements where the speaker means to communicate a serious expression of an intent to commit an act of unlawful violence to a particular individual or group of individuals. See *Watts* ("political hyperbole" is not a true threat). The speaker need not actually intend to carry out the threat. . . . Intimidation in the constitutionally proscribable sense of the word is a type of true threat, where a speaker directs a threat to a person or group of persons with the intent of placing the victim in fear of bodily harm or death.

Thus, under *Watts* and *Claiborne Hardware*, political hyperbole, "vehement, caustic, and sometimes unpleasantly sharp attacks," and "vituperative, abusive, and inexact" statements are all protected speech. By contrast, according to *Black*, speech is a categorically unprotected "true threat" when the speaker intends to communicate to a particular person or group a *serious* expression of an intent to commit unlawful violence. How clear are these distinctions? Are some forms of intimidation and coercion protected speech? What makes an expression of intent to commit unlawful violence "serious"?

5. *The government's interests in punishing threats.* What interests are served by punishing threatening speech? In *Black*, the Court explained that a prohibition on true threats "protect[s] individuals from the fear of violence" and "from the disruption that fear engenders," in addition to protecting people "from the possibility that the threatened violence will occur." Are these interests sufficient to support restrictions of speech? Or do they amount to protecting audiences from merely unpleasant feelings? For commentary, see Steven G. Gey, *The Nuremberg Files and the First Amendment Value of Threats*, 78 Tex. L. Rev. 541 (2000); Steven J. Heyman, *Righting the Balance: An Inquiry into the Foundations and Limits of Freedom of Expression*, 78 B.U. L. Rev. 1275, 1323 (1998); Kenneth L. Karst, *Threats and Meanings: How the Facts Govern First Amendment Doctrine*, 58 Stan. L. Rev. 1337 (2006); Frederick Schauer, *Intentions, Conventions, and the First Amendment: The Case of Cross-Burning*, 2003 Sup. Ct. Rev. 197, 210.
6. *Speaker intent. Black* states a speaker must "mean" to send the allegedly threatening communication. However, the decision also states the speaker "need not actually intend to carry out the threat." What, if anything, do these statements suggest about the relevance of the speaker's subjective intent? Does the speaker have to intend to place the recipient in fear of bodily injury or death, or is it sufficient that a reasonable speaker would understand this would be the effect of the speech? Statutes penalizing threats often require that the speaker communicate with the "intent" to threaten another person. But when they do not, the question arises as to whether there is a constitutional requirement that government prove such intent before the speaker can be punished.

   In Elonis v. United States, 135 S. Ct. 2001(2015), the Supreme Court granted certiorari to consider the question whether, under *Black* and the First Amendment, conviction for threatening another person requires proof of a defendant's subjective intent to threaten. The Court did not decide that question; instead, it reversed the conviction on *statutory* grounds, holding that the jury was improperly instructed that the Government need prove only that a reasonable person would regard the defendant's communications as threats. Under the federal threat statute, the Court held, the speaker must have intended to issue a threat or knew the communication would be considered a threat. Should it be enough to show the defendant acted recklessly—i.e., that he or she consciously disregarded the risk that the communication transmitted would be interpreted as a true threat?

7. *Threats and context.* In *Elonis*, the speaker claimed his threatening statements, some of which were communicated on social media in the form of "rap lyrics," were protected compositions. In a concurrence, Justice Alito responded: "Elonis also claims his threats were constitutionally protected works of art. . . . To make this point, his brief includes a lengthy excerpt from the lyrics of a rap song in which a very well-compensated rapper imagines killing his ex-wife and dumping her body in a lake. . . . But context matters. Taken in context, lyrics in songs that are performed for an audience or sold in recorded form are unlikely to be interpreted as a real threat to a real person. Statements on social media that are pointedly directed at their victims, by contrast, are much more likely to be taken seriously. . . ." Do you agree with Justice Alito? Suppose a father, upset about a judge's rulings denying him visitation rights to see his daughter, records and posts a YouTube video of himself performing a song ("Daughter's Love"), in which he sings the lyrics: "Take my child and I'll take your life"; "I killed a man downrange in war. I have nothing against you, but I'm tellin' you this better be the last court date"; "So I promise you, judge, I will kill a man"; "And I guarantee you, if you don't stop, I'll kill you." True threat? *See* United States v. Jeffries, 692 F.3d 473 (6th Cir. 2012).

United States v. Stevens

881 F.3d 1249 (10th Cir. 2018)

Before TYMKOVICH, Chief Judge, HOLMES, and MATHESON, Circuit Judges.

MATHESON, Circuit Judge.

Jeffrey A. Stevens was indicted on 10 counts of interstate communication with intent to injure under 18 U.S.C. § 875(c) for posting 10 messages on the Tulsa Police Department's ("TPD") online "Citizen Complaint" form. The messages discussed committing violence against specific members of the TPD or TPD officers generally. Mr. Stevens moved to dismiss the indictment on First Amendment grounds, arguing his messages were not true threats. The district court denied the motion because a reasonable jury could construe the messages to be true threats. Mr. Stevens pled guilty to five counts conditioned on his right to appeal the denial of his motion, which he has done here.

The district court properly denied Mr. Stevens's motion. A reasonable jury could understand his messages to be true threats. . . . [W]e affirm.

I

On September 16, 2016, TPD Officer Betty Shelby shot and killed Terence Crutcher, an African-American. The shooting made national headlines and reignited a heated debate over law enforcement's use of force against minorities.

Three days after the shooting, Mr. Stevens, a Connecticut resident, sent the first of multiple anonymous messages to the TPD via an online form the public could use to complain about the TPD. This first message read:

> . . . The psychotic pile of s- - - who MURDERED the unarmed civilian who broke down is going to be executed, as are ALL psychotic s- - -bags you and other PDs hire across this Nation who murder unarmed civilians. They are all going to be killed.

Over the next three days, Mr. Stevens submitted nine more messages [similar in substance to the first]. Agents with the Federal Bureau of Investigation traced the messages to Mr. Stevens's residence. They interviewed Mr. Stevens, who confessed to sending the messages.

. . . A grand jury indicted Mr. Stevens on 10 counts of interstate communication with intent to injure in violation of 18 U.S.C. § 875(c). He moved to dismiss the indictment, alleging the First Amendment protected his statements because they were not true threats. The district court denied Mr. Stevens's motion, finding that a reasonable jury could understand his messages to be true threats. . . . He now appeals the district court's denial of his motion to dismiss the indictment.

II

Mr. Stevens was charged under 18 U.S.C. § 875(c), which provides:

> Whoever [1] transmits in interstate or foreign commerce [2] any communication containing [3] any threat to kidnap any person or any threat to injure the person of another, shall be fined under this title or imprisoned not more than five years, or both.

In addition to the elements specified in the statute, the Supreme Court recognized a fourth element concerning mens rea in Elonis v. United States, —— U.S. ——, 135 S.Ct. 2001 (2015). The Court said the government must prove the defendant transmitted the communication for the purpose of issuing a threat or with knowledge the communication would be viewed as a threat. *Id.* at 2012. The mens rea element calls for proof the speaker "intended the recipient of the threat to feel threatened." United States v. Heineman, 767 F.3d 970, 978 (10th Cir. 2014).

. . . In § 875(c) prosecutions, we have followed the Supreme Court's definition of a threat as "a serious expression of an intent to commit an act of unlawful violence to a particular individual or group of individuals." United States v. Wheeler, 776 F.3d 736, 743 (10th Cir. 2015) (quoting Virginia v. Black, 538 U.S. 343, 359 (2003)). In *Wheeler*, we said that § 875(c) "app[lies] only to 'true threats,' " which are "outside the protective scope of the First Amendment." *Id.* at 742-43; *see also* Watts v. United States, 394 U.S. 705, 707 (1969) ("What is a threat must be distinguished from what is constitutionally protected speech.") "Section 875(c), like all threat statutes, must be interpreted with the commands of the First Amendment clearly in mind." *Wheeler*, 776 F.3d at 742.

In line with the First Amendment, § 875(c)'s threat element requires proof that a reasonable person would understand the communication to be a threat. *Id.* at 743. Under the reasonable person standard, "[t]he question is whether those who hear or read the threat reasonably consider that an actual threat has been made." United States v. Dillard, 795 F.3d 1191, 1199 (10th Cir. 2015).

To answer this question, "the language [of the statements and] the context in which the statements are made . . . are [ ] relevant." *Wheeler*, 776 F.3d at 743; *see also Dillard*, 795 F.3d at 1201 (a statement is a true threat "so long as a reasonable recipient could conclude, based on the language of the communication and the context in which it is delivered, that this was in fact a veiled threat of violence by the defendant").

As to a message's language, we have warned against "rigid adherence to the literal meaning of a communication without regard to its reasonable connotations. . . ." *Dillard*, 795 F.3d at 1201. For example, "[a] defendant cannot escape potential liability simply by using the passive voice or couching a threat in terms of 'someone' committing an act of violence. . . ." *Id.*

As for context, it may include where a statement was made and how an audience reacted. *See Watts*, 394 U.S. at 708 (holding that statements made at political protest and at which the audience laughed were "political hyperbole" and not true threats); *Wheeler*, 776 F.3d at 743 (recognizing a recipient's reaction to a message is relevant).

. . . The district court examined the language and the context of the statements. It determined that, because Mr. Stevens's messages were "targeted at specific people, groups of people, and their family members," and because they "repeatedly assert[ed] that the targets of the messages are going to die unless they comply with [his] wishes," a "jury could determine that 'a reasonable person would interpret the statements to be threats.'"

Mr. Stevens sent messages describing specific acts of violence directed toward particular individuals or groups of individuals. He targeted particular individuals in five of his 10 messages—several to Officer Shelby, the TPD Officer who shot Mr. Crutcher.

. . . Here, Mr. Stevens sent multiple communications that Officer Shelby would be "executed" for shooting Mr. Crutcher. In the tenth message, for example, he wrote: "Betty is not going to get 3 yeas [sic] probation and a pension, she is getting a bullet through her brain." From the repeated statements and explicit motives that were sent to Officer Shelby's place of work, a reasonable jury . . . could conclude that Mr. Stevens's postings were true threats against Officer Shelby. It further could conclude Mr. Stevens's other messages directed at identified TPD employees were true threats.

Mr. Stevens also directed messages at groups, including TPD officers. The language and context of these messages were similar to a message aimed at Colorado police officers in *Wheeler*, 776 F.3d at 736. In that case, the defendant held strong anti-government views and was angry at police officers in Grand Junction, Colorado, because of a DUI arrest. *Id.* at 738. While in Italy, he posted messages on his Facebook account, one of which urged his "religious followers" to "kill cops, drown [sic] them in the blood of thier [sic] children, hunt them down and kill their entire bloodlines." *Id.* We held that a "rational juror considering the language and context of these posts could consider them to be true threats" because they directed "specific, deadly action against a number of individuals." *Id.* at 745.

Similar to the message in *Wheeler*, Mr. Stevens targeted messages of deadly action at TPD officers generally. Mr. Stevens's fifth message, for example, mentioned the "right to Life, Liberty & the Pursuit of Happiness" and stated: "If killing every last one of you [TPD officers] and your families . . . your wives . . . your children is what it takes to drive [that point] home, so be it." Because this message and the others were sent to the TPD and were "specific, deadly" in nature, *Wheeler*, 776 F.3d at 745, a reasonable jury could find from their language and context that they were true threats.

. . . On appeal, Mr. Stevens has preserved two arguments that his messages were not true threats: (1) his messages were political speech, and (2) he did not have the intent or ability to carry out the threat. Neither argument has merit.

First, Mr. Stevens argues his messages "protested improper police conduct in vehement terms," and the "threats were a means of expressing the opinion that a police officer killed a person without justification." The district court found, however, that even if Mr. Stevens's messages concerned "an event that garnered national attention and [was] a part of a larger political debate," this did "not preclude the communications from being true threats." We agree. . . . Even if a specific threat accompanies pure political speech, this does not shield a defendant from culpability.

Second, Mr. Stevens argues that his "location in Connecticut while sending threats to Tulsa reflects the absence of intent or ability to carry out any threat." Although we may consider the speaker's apparent intention or ability to carry out the threat in determining whether the communication was a true threat, Mr. Stevens's argument suffers from at least two problems. First, nowhere on the face of the messages is there any indication of Mr. Stevens's being located in Connecticut, and nowhere does the record show that any of the recipients knew that Mr. Stevens was located there. Second, even if a reasonable person in Tulsa who received these messages knew they came from Connecticut, he or she could reasonably conclude that Mr. Stevens had the wherewithal to travel to Tulsa and execute the threats. We therefore affirm the district court's rejection of this argument.

. . . In determining whether Mr. Stevens's statements were true threats, the district court examined the language of the communication and the context in which it is delivered. It properly concluded that a reasonable jury could find Mr. Stevens's messages to be true threats. . . . For the foregoing reasons, we affirm the district court's denial of Mr. Stevens's motion to dismiss the indictment.

NOTES AND QUESTIONS

1. *Speakers and audiences.* Note that under *Elonis*, conviction under the federal threats law requires proof the speaker intended to communicate a threat or acted with knowledge the communication would be received as a threat. Like several other courts of appeals, the Tenth Circuit interprets the First Amendment to require that a reasonable recipient *understand* the communication as a threat. As discussed earlier, *Elonis* only settled an issue of statutory interpretation regarding speaker intent under federal law. As in *Stevens*, many lower courts continue to apply a "reasonable recipient" standard.

2. *Intent and ability to carry out the threat.* Did the court in *Stevens* err in stating Stevens's ability to carry out his threats was a relevant consideration? Isn't that contrary to *Black*? Can or should courts consider ability or means to carry out threats as part of the "reasonable recipient" inquiry?
3. *Online threats.* Commentators and journalists have documented a sharp rise in threatening speech on social media. *See generally* Danielle Keats Citron, *Hate Crimes in Cyberspace* (2016). On the one hand, as *Watts* demonstrates, the First Amendment protects irresponsible and caustic expression. Presumably we can't simply lock up any speaker who engages in this kind of expression online. On the other hand, Professor Citron argues online attacks have for too long been trivialized by the media and law enforcement. These attacks, she observes, disparately affect women, women of color, and members of the LGBTQ community and undermine their civil rights. Professor Citron argues the Internet exacerbates the physical, psychological, and economic harms associated with online threats and attacks:

   > The Internet extends the life of destructive posts. Harassing letters are eventually thrown away, and memories fade in time. The web, however, can make it impossible to forget about malicious posts. Search engines index content on the web and produce it instantaneously. Indexed posts have no built-in expiration date; neither does the suffering they cause.

   One potential solution to this problem lies with social media companies, which can remove such content from platforms. Alternatively, given the "true threats" doctrine, how effective do you think criminal and/or civil law might be in responding to the problem of online threats? Suppose victims are not able to discover the identity of the person communicating the threat. Even assuming they can, law enforcement seemingly can't investigate every instance of threatening online speech. Would providing victims with civil causes of action for threatening or harassing speech provide a better alternative than criminal prosecution?

THEORY-APPLIED PROBLEMS

1. Bruce is a member of a militia who has blogged about national and local politics, especially gun control, for several years. On August 15, 2017, Bruce was arrested and charged with threatening to assault and murder all of the state Supreme Court judges in a blog post. Angered by the state Supreme Court's split decision upholding a state ban on high-capacity ammunition magazines, Bruce wrote on August 1, "Let me be the first to say this plainly: These judges deserve to be killed. Their blood will replenish the tree of liberty. A small price to pay for America's freedom." The next day, Bruce updated the post to include the names, work addresses, phone numbers, and photographs of the judges who decided the case. He also added an Internet hyperlink to a publicly available, detailed satellite map and street map of the outside of the state Supreme Court building.

Bruce previously called for assaults on judges in general, although no action appears to have resulted from that speech. Does Bruce's speech constitute a "true threat" under *Watts* and *Black*?

2. After arriving home from her job at a local bank, Billie received a telephone message on her answering machine. In the message, a man calmly informed her that his name was Larry, that he wanted to talk to her, and that he had already sent her an e-mail. Earlier that day, Larry left her a message on her voice mail at work insisting that he speak with her about a credit card dispute between Larry and the bank. After receiving the second message at home, Billie was sufficiently alarmed and notified a night supervisor at the bank. Upon arriving at work the next morning, Billie read Larry's e-mail, which contained her current and prior addresses, including the location of her parents' home. Larry also compared Billie to Chicago Judge Joan Lefkow and provided a Web link to information about the 2005 murder of Lefkow's mother and husband in their home after a member of a neo-Nazi organization posted Lefkow's home address on the Web. Larry further wrote, "I have run out of patience with you and your smug attitude." True threat?
3. During a 1995 meeting marking the anniversary of *Roe v. Wade*, the American Coalition of Life Activists (ACLA) revealed a poster listing the names and home addresses of the "Deadly Dozen," a group of doctors who performed abortions. The poster declared them guilty of "crimes against humanity" and offered $5,000 for information leading to the "arrest, conviction and revocation of license to practice medicine." The poster further stated that abortion had been a choice for East European and Jewish women during the Nazi regime and was prosecuted during the Nuremberg Trials as a war crime. The poster was also published in an affiliated magazine, *Life Advocate*, and distributed at ACLA events.

   Later in 1995, in front of the St. Louis federal courthouse, ACLA unveiled a second poster, targeting Dr. Robert Crist. The poster accused Crist of crimes against humanity and various acts of medical malpractice, including a botched abortion. The poster included Crist's home and work addresses and his photograph and offered $500 to "any ACLA organization that successfully persuades Crist to turn from his child killing through activities within ACLA guidelines."

   In January 1996, at another *Roe* anniversary event honoring prisoners convicted of anti-abortion violence, ACLA unveiled the "Nuremburg Files," a series of dossiers it had compiled on doctors, clinic employees, politicians, judges, and other abortion rights supporters. They hoped to conduct Nuremberg-like war crimes trials using "perfectly legal courts once the tide of this nation's opinion turns against the wanton slaughter of God's children." Neal Horsley, an anti-abortion activist, posted the information on a Web site. The Web site marked the names of those already victimized by anti-abortion terrorists, striking through the names of those who had been murdered and graying out the names of the wounded. ACLA's name originally appeared on the Web site, but Horsley removed it after the initiation of the lawsuit described below. The posters and Web site did not contain explicit threats against the doctors. However, similar posters prepared by others had preceded clinic violence in the past, a fact of which the doctors were aware. As a result of the posters, the doctors began wearing bulletproof vests, drawing the curtains on the windows of their homes, and accepting the protection of U.S. marshals.

Along with two Portland-based health centers, the doctors sued ACLA, 12 activists, and an affiliated organization, alleging that their threatening statements violated state and federal law, including the Freedom of Access to Clinic Entrances Act of 1994 (FACE), 18 U.S.C. § 2489, which gives aggrieved persons a right of action against whoever by "threat of force . . . intentionally . . . intimidates . . . any person because that person is or has been . . . providing reproductive health services." Are the subject communications "true threats"? *See* Planned Parenthood v. American Coalition of Life Activists, 290 F.3d 1059 (9th Cir. 2002).

D. THE LIMITS OF THE CATEGORICAL APPROACH: DEPICTIONS OF ANIMAL CRUELTY, VIDEO GAME VIOLENCE, AND LIES

The Court's incitement, fighting words, and true threats cases reflect its struggle to distinguish low-value speech from "high-value" political and other speech. Yet, despite the importance of distinguishing between low-value speech and otherwise protected speech, the Court has never developed a clear method for determining when speech is "low value" and hence unprotected. There are, the Court indicated in *Chaplinsky v. New Hampshire,* "certain well-defined and narrowly limited classes of speech, the prevention and punishment of which has never been thought to raise any Constitutional problem." Four decades later, in *Ferber v. New York,* 458 U.S. 747 (1982) (*infra* Chapter 11), the Court appeared to generally follow *Chaplinsky*'s approach when it recognized a new "category of material outside the protection of the First Amendment"—child pornography. More recently, however, the Court has emphatically rejected the argument that "new categories of unprotected speech may . . . be added to the list by a legislature that concludes certain speech is too harmful to be tolerated." Brown v. Entertainment Merchants Ass'n, 564 U.S. 786 (2011). Consider the following classes or categories of speech. Should any or all of them be treated as categorically unprotected speech? Under what circumstances does the Court suggest it might recognize a "new" category or class of unprotected expression?

United States v. Stevens

559 U.S. 460 (2010)

Chief Justice Roberts delivered the opinion of the Court.

Congress enacted 18 U.S.C. § 48 to criminalize the commercial creation, sale, or possession of certain depictions of animal cruelty. The statute does not address underlying acts harmful to animals, but only portrayals of such conduct. The question presented is whether the prohibition in the statute is consistent with the freedom of speech guaranteed by the First Amendment. . . .

I

Section 48 establishes a criminal penalty of up to five years in prison for anyone who knowingly "creates, sells, or possesses a depiction of animal cruelty," if done "for commercial gain" in interstate or foreign commerce. A depiction of "animal cruelty" is defined as one "in which a living animal is intentionally maimed, mutilated, tortured, wounded, or killed," if that conduct violates federal or state law where "the creation, sale, or possession takes place." § 48(c)(1). In what is referred to as the "exceptions clause," the law exempts from prohibition any depiction "that has serious religious, political, scientific, educational, journalistic, historical, or artistic value." § 48(b).

The legislative background of § 48 focused primarily on the interstate market for "crush videos." According to the House Committee Report on the bill, such videos feature the intentional torture and killing of helpless animals, including cats, dogs, monkeys, mice, and hamsters. H.R. Rep. No. 106-397 (1999). Crush videos often depict women slowly crushing animals to death "with their bare feet or while wearing high heeled shoes," sometimes while "talking to the animals in a kind of dominatrix patter" over "[t]he cries and squeals of the animals, obviously in great pain." *Ibid.* Apparently these depictions "appeal to persons with a very specific sexual fetish who find them sexually arousing or otherwise exciting." *Id.*, at 2-3. The acts depicted in crush videos are typically prohibited by the animal cruelty laws enacted by all 50 States and the District of Columbia. But crush videos rarely disclose the participants' identities, inhibiting prosecution of the underlying conduct.

This case, however, involves an application of § 48 to depictions of animal fighting. Dogfighting, for example, is unlawful in all 50 States and the District of Columbia, and has been restricted by federal law since 1976. Respondent Robert J. Stevens ran a business, "Dogs of Velvet and Steel," and an associated Web site, through which he sold videos of pit bulls engaging in dogfights and attacking other animals. Among these videos were Japan Pit Fights and Pick-A-Winna: A Pit Bull Documentary, which include contemporary footage of dogfights in Japan (where such conduct is allegedly legal) as well as footage of American dogfights from the 1960's and 1970's. A third video, Catch Dogs and Country Living, depicts the use of pit bulls to hunt wild boar, as well as a "gruesome" scene of a pit bull attacking a domestic farm pig. On the basis of these videos, Stevens was indicted on three counts of violating § 48. . . .

II

The Government's primary submission is that § 48 necessarily complies with the Constitution because the banned depictions of animal cruelty, as a class, are categorically unprotected by the First Amendment. We disagree.

From 1791 to the present, the First Amendment has permitted restrictions upon the content of speech in a few limited areas. These historic and traditional categories long familiar to the bar—including obscenity, defamation, fraud, incitement, and speech integral to criminal conduct—are well-defined and narrowly limited classes of speech, the prevention and punishment of which have never been thought to raise any Constitutional problem, *Chaplinsky v. New Hampshire* (1942).

The Government argues that "depictions of animal cruelty" should be added to the list. It contends that depictions of "illegal acts of animal cruelty" that are "made, sold, or possessed for commercial gain" necessarily "lack expressive value," and may accordingly "be regulated as *unprotected* speech." The claim is not just that Congress may regulate depictions of animal cruelty subject to the First Amendment, but that these depictions are outside the reach of that Amendment altogether—that they fall into a "First Amendment Free Zone."

As the Government notes, the prohibition of animal cruelty itself has a long history in American law, starting with the early settlement of the Colonies. But we are unaware of any similar tradition excluding *depictions* of animal cruelty from "the freedom of speech" codified in the First Amendment, and the Government points us to none.

The Government contends that "historical evidence" about the reach of the First Amendment is not "a necessary prerequisite for regulation today," and that categories of speech may be exempted from the First Amendment's protection without any long-settled tradition of subjecting that speech to regulation. Instead, the Government points to Congress's legislative judgment that . . . depictions of animals being intentionally tortured and killed [are] of such minimal redeeming value as to render [them] unworthy of First Amendment protection and asks the Court to uphold the ban on the same basis. The Government thus proposes that a claim of categorical exclusion should be considered under a simple balancing test: Whether a given category of speech enjoys First Amendment protection depends upon a categorical balancing of the value of the speech against its societal costs.

As a free-floating test for First Amendment coverage, that sentence is startling and dangerous. The First Amendment's guarantee of free speech does not extend only to categories of speech that survive an ad hoc balancing of relative social costs and benefits. The First Amendment itself reflects a judgment by the American people that the benefits of its restrictions on the Government outweigh the costs. Our Constitution forecloses any attempt to revise that judgment simply on the basis that some speech is not worth it.

To be fair to the Government, its view did not emerge from a vacuum. As the Government correctly notes, this Court has often *described* historically unprotected categories of speech as being "of such slight social value as a step to truth that any benefit that may be derived from them is clearly outweighed by the social interest in order and morality." *Chaplinsky*. But such descriptions are just that—descriptive. They do not set forth a test that may be applied as a general matter to permit the Government to imprison any speaker so long as his speech is deemed valueless or unnecessary, or so long as an ad hoc calculus of costs and benefits tilts in a statute's favor.

When we have identified categories of speech as fully outside the protection of the First Amendment, it has not been on the basis of a simple cost-benefit analysis. Our decisions . . . cannot be taken as establishing a freewheeling authority to declare new categories of speech outside the scope of the First Amendment. Maybe there are some categories of speech that have been historically unprotected, but have not yet been specifically identified or discussed as such in our case law. But if so, there is no evidence that "depictions of animal cruelty" is among them. We need not foreclose the future recognition of such additional categories to reject the Government's highly manipulable balancing test as a means of identifying them.

III

Because we decline to carve out from the First Amendment any novel exception for § 48, we review Stevens's First Amendment challenge under our existing doctrine. [The Court invalidated the law on the ground that it was "substantially overbroad," in part because its terms covered materials such as hunting videos, depictions of the lawful slaughter of animals, and magazines.]

OTHER POTENTIAL CATEGORIES: VIOLENT VIDEO GAMES AND LIES

United States v. Stevens is not the only recent Supreme Court decision to reject an ad hoc "cost-benefit" analysis for determining categorical exclusion. In Brown v. Entertainment Merchants Ass'n, 564 U.S. 786 (2011), the Court invalidated a California statute that prohibited the sale or rental to minors of violent video games, defined in part as games "in which the range of options available to a player includes killing, maiming, dismembering, or sexually assaulting an image of a human being." The Court first addressed whether video games were covered by the First Amendment:

> California correctly acknowledges that video games qualify for First Amendment protection. The Free Speech Clause exists principally to protect discourse on public matters, but we have long recognized that it is difficult to distinguish politics from entertainment, and dangerous to try. Like the protected books, plays, and movies that preceded them, video games communicate ideas—and even social messages—through many familiar literary devices (such as characters, dialogue, plot, and music) and through features distinctive to the medium (such as the player's interaction with the virtual world). That suffices to confer First Amendment protection.

Id. at 790.

The Government argued that violent depictions in video games constituted an unprotected category of speech under *Chaplinsky*'s two-level approach. As it had in *Stevens*, the Court rejected that argument:

> [Last Term,] in *Stevens*, we held that new categories of unprotected speech may not be added to the list by a legislature that concludes certain speech is too harmful to be tolerated. [That] holding controls this case. . . . California's argument would fare better if there were a longstanding tradition of specifically restricting children's access to depictions of violence, but there is none. Certainly the books we give children to read—or read to them when they are younger—contain no shortage of gore. Grimm's Fairy Tales, for example, are grim indeed. As her just deserts for trying to poison Snow White, the wicked queen is made to dance in red hot slippers "till she fell dead on the floor, a sad example of envy

> and jealousy." Cinderella's evil stepsisters have their eyes pecked out by doves. And Hansel and Gretel (children!) kill their captor by baking her in an oven.

Id. at 791-92; 795-96. The Court went on to hold that the California law was an invalid content-based regulation of speech. *Id.* at 799-804. [For a discussion of that holding, see *infra* Ch. 3.] In a concurrence, Justice Alito criticized the Court for "prematurely" dismissing the argument that owing to the explicit violence in some video games and their "technological characteristics" (chiefly, their interactive nature) the State may have a compelling interest in regulating depictions of violence in video games. *Id.* at 820-21 (Alito, J., concurring).

Finally, in United States v. Alvarez, 567 U.S. 709 (2012), the Court once again confronted a claim that certain speech was categorically unprotected. In *Alvarez* the Court struck down a federal statute imposing criminal punishment when an individual lies about receiving military honors, including the Congressional Medal of Honor. The plurality opinion acknowledged that defamation and fraud were existing categories of low-value speech involving false statements. However, it rejected the argument that lies *as a class* are unprotected. *Id.* at 719. The plurality noted that defamation and fraud, along with existing laws punishing perjury, making false statements to officials, and falsely representing oneself as a government official, involve "targeted prohibitions" supported by compelling interests in regulating speech that goes beyond the mere falsity of a statement—for example, maintaining the integrity of the court system (perjury) or preventing financial loss (fraud). *Id.* at 719-20. It thus rejected the government's argument that the law at issue was justified because false statements *generally* have no value. *Id.* at 720-21. Referring to *Stevens,* the plurality opinion noted:

> [P]erhaps there exist "some categories of speech that have been historically unprotected . . . but have not yet been specifically identified or discussed . . . in our case law." Before exempting a category of speech from the normal prohibition on content-based restrictions, however, the Court must be presented with "persuasive evidence that a novel restriction on content is part of a long (if heretofore unrecognized) tradition of proscription," The Government has not demonstrated that false statements generally should constitute a new category of unprotected speech on this basis.

Id. at 722. In a concurring opinion, Justice Breyer agreed the Stolen Valor Act violated the First Amendment. However, he reached that conclusion on a ground different from the one relied on by the plurality. *See id.* at 730 ("I do not rest my conclusion upon a strict categorical analysis. Rather, I base [my] conclusion upon the fact that the statute works First Amendment harm, while the Government can achieve its legitimate objectives in less restrictive ways.").

What are the implication of *Alvarez* for laws that punish fraudulent communications or various types of disinformation? Are these kinds of falsehoods part of a class of unprotected lies? *See id.* at 2554 (Breyer, J. concurring in the judgment); Lyrissa Barnett Lidsky, *Where's the Harm?: Free Speech and the Regulation of Lies,* 65 Wash. & Lee L. Rev. 1091 (2008). "After *Alvarez,* governments can punish people for making false statements of fact only when. . . ." How would you finish that sentence?

NOTES AND QUESTIONS

1. *The two-level approach.* What does the Court mean when it says *Chaplinsky*'s rationale for excluding certain classes or categories of expression from First Amendment protection is merely "descriptive"? Why does the Court consider the government's proposed test "startling and dangerous"?
2. *The end of categorical exclusions?* In addition to incitement, fighting words, and true threats, only a few other categories of speech (obscenity and child pornography) are subject to categorical exclusion, while a few others (commercial speech and defamation) are entitled to limited protection. Do the decisions in *Stevens, Brown,* and *Alvarez* mark the end of recognizing certain classes or categories of speech as unprotected under the First Amendment? Or does the Court leave the door open to recognition of additional categories? What standard must the government meet to prevail under the Court's approach? Can you think of any categories of speech that might satisfy the Court's standard?
3. *History and tradition.* Are history and tradition the proper bases upon which to determine categorical speech exclusions? Does the Court identify the boundaries of the historical inquiry? Does a tradition of regulation have to stretch back to the Founding? Is a century enough? Several decades of regulation? Does reliance on history and tradition preclude government from responding adequately to new forms of harmful expression, including speech communicated online? For discussion see Gregory P. Magarian, *The Marrow of Tradition: The Roberts Court and Categorical Speech Exclusions,* 56 Wm. & Mary L. Rev. 1339 (2015).
4. *Beyond categorical exclusions.* In terms of understanding the scope of the First Amendment, focusing on the few and narrow categorical exclusions the Court has expressly recognized can be somewhat misleading. There are entire areas of speech regulation in which the First Amendment simply does not "show up." For example, no one seriously questions the government's authority to prohibit fraud, perjury, or speech that constitutes or facilitates a criminal offense. Further, laws relating to the formation of contracts, wills and trusts, products liability, professional malpractice, corporate disclosures, and a host of other speech-related activities remain wholly untouched by the First Amendment. As Professor Schauer has explained, this situation is not owing to the application by courts of any categorical balancing approach but rather is likely a function of a variety of "political, social, cultural, historical, psychological, rhetorical, and economic forces." *See* Frederick Schauer, *The Boundaries of the First Amendment: A Preliminary Exploration of Constitutional Salience,* 117 Harv. L. Rev. 1765, 1766-71 (2004).

AN EXTENDED NOTE ON DEFINING PROTECTED SPEECH—POSSIBLE LESSONS FROM CANADA

The Canadian courts have defined the outer limits of protected expression quite broadly to include both threats of violence and child pornography. For example, in R. v. Sharpe, [2001] 1 S.C.R. 45 (Can.), the Supreme Court of Canada found that possession of child pornography was an expressive act protected by the Canadian Charter of Rights and Freedoms. Chief Justice McLachlin stated that

> [a]mong the most fundamental rights possessed by Canadians is freedom of expression. It makes possible our liberty, our creativity, and our democracy. . . . The values underlying the right to free expression include individual self-fulfillment, finding the truth through an open exchange of ideas, and the political discourse fundamental to democracy. While some types of expression, like political expression, lie closer to the core of the guarantee than others, all are vital to a free and democratic society. . . . [T]he guarantee "ensure[s] that everyone can manifest their thoughts, opinions, beliefs, indeed all expressions of the heart and mind, however unpopular, distasteful or contrary to the mainstream. Such protection . . . is 'fundamental' because in a free, pluralistic and democratic society we prize a diversity of ideas and opinions for their inherent value both to the community and to the individual." . . .
>
> The law challenged in this appeal engages mainly the justification of self-fulfillment. Child pornography does not generally contribute to the search for truth or to Canadian social and political discourse. Some question whether it engages even the value of self-fulfillment, beyond the base aspect of sexual exploitation. The concern in this appeal, however, is that the law may incidentally catch forms of expression that more seriously implicate self-fulfillment and that do not pose a risk of harm to children.
>
> As to the contention that prohibiting possession of expressive material does not raise free expression concerns, I cannot agree. The right conferred by s. 2(b) of the Charter embraces a continuum of intellectual and expressive freedom—"freedom of thought, belief, opinion, and expression." The right to possess expressive material is integrally related to the development of thought, belief, opinion, and expression. The possession of such material allows us to understand the thought of others or consolidate our own thought. Without the right to possess expressive material, freedom of thought, belief, opinion, and expression would be compromised. Thus the possession of expressive materials falls within the continuum of rights protected by s. 2(b) of the Charter.

Id. at 70-73. Writing in dissent, however, Justice L'Heureux-Dubé, joined by Justices Gonthier and Bastarache, rejected the argument that possession of child pornography constituted expressive conduct worthy of constitutional protection:

> It is clear that s. 163.1(4) restricts expression if child pornography can be considered expression. While the Crown has conceded this latter question, it is important to recognize that the right to free expression in s. 2(b) has always been considered to protect only those activities which are communicative. . . .
>
> From our jurisprudence, it is unclear whether the requirement that an activity convey or attempt to convey meaning excludes all activities which are not prima facie communicative from the scope of the right to free expression in s. 2(b). For example, this Court speculated that the parking of a car is not protected expression since it is not prima facie

> communicative activity. While it may be true that s. 2(b) guarantees the right to possess "material [that] allows us to understand the thought of others," the scope of the right . . . to create and possess self-authored works, especially those not intended for others, in order to "consolidate our own thought" is far from clear. Thus, in our view, it is unfortunate that the Crown conceded the right to free expression was violated in this appeal in all respects, thereby depriving the Court of the opportunity to fully explore the content and scope of s. 2(b) as it applies in this case.

Id. at 127-129 (L'Heureux-Dubé, J., dissenting).

Note that the Canadian approach links the scope of protected expression to a discussion of whether the expression serves the values underlying why we protect free expression. Is this a better way to approach the question of whether speech is protected or unprotected or does it just beg the question?

In Canada, finding that speech falls within the protection of section 2(b) of the Charter of Rights and Freedoms is only the first step in a two-step analysis. Section 1 of the Charter states, "[t]he *Canadian Charter of Rights and Freedoms* guarantees the rights and freedoms set out in it subject only to such reasonable limits prescribed by law as can be demonstrably justified in a free and democratic society." Canadian Charter of Rights and Freedoms, § 1. Consistent with section 1 of the Charter, courts should uphold laws that violate constitutionally protected speech if they are saved by application of section 1. *See* R. v. Oakes, [1986] S.C.R. 103 (applying a multi-factored balancing test to determine whether a statute that violates a Charter right is nevertheless valid and operative). Many laws found to violate section 2(b) are saved from invalidation by operation of section 1. Does this make the very broad interpretation of protected expression easier to understand? How does this approach differ from the United States Supreme Court's approach in cases like *Stevens*?

Chapter 3

Content Neutrality

Table of Contents

A. The Content-Neutrality Principle—Origins and Rationales

B. The Modern Approach to Content Neutrality

C. Applying Strict Scrutiny to Content-Based Laws

D. Speaker Identity Distinctions

E. Content-Neutral Speech Regulations and Intermediate Scrutiny

Chapter 2 examined the Supreme Court's difficulty in establishing an approach to defining categories or classes of "low-value" and unprotected speech. The Court clearly has found some speech to be "low value," and thus entitled to lesser or no First Amendment protection. Regarding "high-value" speech not within an excluded category, the Court has developed a set of First Amendment standards that considers *content-based* regulations presumptively invalid but allows more latitude for regulations that are *content-neutral.* As with low-value speech, the Court's content discrimination rules attempt to broadly categorize. In this instance, however, the categories relate to the types of laws enacted and applied rather than the nature of the speech at issue. Content-based regulations are subject to "strict" scrutiny, a standard that is difficult, although not impossible, for government to meet. Content-neutral laws, which address not the content of speech but non-content interests such as public safety, the attractiveness of public areas, or peace and tranquility, are judged by a more lenient, "intermediate" scrutiny standard. The chapter begins with a discussion of the origins and rationales of the content-neutrality principle. It then examines the Court's modern approach to reviewing content-based laws and application of strict scrutiny to such laws. The chapter also considers speech regulations drawn on the basis of speaker identity, in the context of regulation of corporate expenditures in political campaigns. Finally, it concludes with an examination of the general standard applicable to content-neutral speech regulations.

A. *THE CONTENT NEUTRALITY PRINCIPLE—ORIGINS AND RATIONALES*

Police Department of Chicago v. Mosley

408 U.S. 92 (1972)

Mr. Justice MARSHALL delivered the opinion of the Court.

At issue in this case is the constitutionality of the following Chicago ordinance:

> A person commits disorderly conduct when he knowingly: . . . (i) Pickets or demonstrates on a public way within 150 feet of any primary or secondary school building while the school is in session and one-half hour before the school is in session and one-half hour after the school session has been concluded, provided, that this subsection does not prohibit the peaceful picketing of any school involved in a labor dispute. . . .

The suit was brought by Earl Mosley, a federal postal employee, who for seven months prior to the enactment of the ordinance had frequently picketed Jones Commercial High School in Chicago. During school hours and usually by himself, Mosley would walk the public sidewalk adjoining the school, carrying a sign that read: "Jones High School practices black discrimination. Jones High School has a black quota." His lonely crusade was always peaceful, orderly, and quiet, and was conceded to be so by the city of Chicago.

. . . We hold that the ordinance is unconstitutional because it makes an impermissible distinction between labor picketing and other peaceful picketing. . . .

I

The city of Chicago exempts peaceful labor picketing from its general prohibition on picketing next to a school. The question we consider here is whether this selective exclusion from a public place is permitted. Our answer is "No."

Because Chicago treats some picketing differently from others, we analyze this ordinance in terms of the Equal Protection Clause of the Fourteenth Amendment. Of course, the equal protection claim in this case is closely intertwined with First Amendment interests; the Chicago ordinance affects picketing, which is expressive conduct; moreover, it does so by classifications formulated in terms of the subject of the picketing. As in all equal protection cases, however, the crucial question is whether there is an appropriate governmental interest suitably furthered by the differential treatment.

The central problem with Chicago's ordinance is that it describes permissible picketing in terms of its subject matter. Peaceful picketing on the subject of a school's labor-management dispute is permitted, but all other peaceful picketing is prohibited. The operative distinction is the message on a picket sign. But, above all else, the First Amendment means that government has no power to restrict expression because of its message, its ideas, its subject matter, or its content. Any restriction on expressive activity because of its content would completely undercut the "profound national commitment to the principle that debate on public issues should be uninhibited, robust, and wide-open." New York Times Co. v. Sullivan, 376 U.S. 254, 270 (1964).

Necessarily, then, under the Equal Protection Clause, not to mention the First Amendment itself, government may not grant the use of a forum to people whose views it finds acceptable, but deny use to those wishing to express less favored or more controversial views. And it may not select which issues are worth discussing or debating in public facilities. There is an "equality of status in the field of ideas," and government must afford all points of view an equal opportunity to be heard. Once a forum is opened up to assembly or speaking by some groups, government may not prohibit others from assembling or speaking on the basis of what they intend to say. Selective exclusions from a public forum may not be based on content alone, and may not be justified by reference to content alone.

Guided by these principles, we have frequently condemned such discrimination among different users of the same medium for expression. In Niemotko v. Maryland, 340 U.S. 268 (1951), a group of Jehovah's Witnesses were denied a permit to use a city park for Bible talks, although other political and religious groups had been allowed to put the park to analogous uses. Concluding that the permit was denied because of the city's "dislike for or disagreement with the Witnesses or their views," this Court held that the permit refusal violated "[t]he right to equal protection of the laws, in the exercise of those freedoms of speech and religion protected by the First and Fourteenth Amendments." . . .

II

This is not to say that all picketing must always be allowed. We have continually recognized that reasonable "time, place and manner" regulations of picketing may be necessary to further significant governmental interests. Similarly, under an equal protection analysis, there may be sufficient regulatory interests justifying selective exclusions or distinctions among pickets. Conflicting demands on the same place may compel the State to make choices among potential users and uses. And the State may have a legitimate interest in prohibiting some picketing to protect public order. But these justifications for selective exclusions from a public forum must be carefully scrutinized. Because picketing plainly involves expressive conduct within the protection of the First Amendment, discriminations among pickets must be tailored to serve a substantial government interest.

III

In this case, the ordinance itself describes impermissible picketing not in terms of time, place, and manner, but in terms of subject matter. The regulation "thus slip[s] from the neutrality of time, place, and circumstance into a concern about content." Kalven, *The Concept of the Public Forum:* Cox v. Louisiana, 1965 Sup. Ct. Rev. 29. This is never permitted. In spite of this, Chicago urges that the ordinance is not improper content censorship, but rather a device for preventing disruption of the school. Cities certainly have a substantial interest in stopping picketing which disrupts a school. The crucial question, however, is whether [Chicago's ordinance] advances that objective in a manner consistent with the commands of the Equal Protection Clause. It does not.

Although preventing school disruption is a city's legitimate concern, Chicago itself has determined that peaceful labor picketing during school hours is not an undue interference with school. Therefore, under the Equal Protection Clause,

Chicago may not maintain that other picketing disrupts the school unless that picketing is clearly more disruptive than the picketing Chicago already permits. If peaceful labor picketing is permitted, there is no justification for prohibiting all nonlabor picketing, both peaceful and nonpeaceful. "Peaceful" nonlabor picketing, however the term "peaceful" is defined, is obviously no more disruptive than "peaceful" labor picketing. But Chicago's ordinance permits the latter and prohibits the former. [Our precedents have condemned] such unequal treatment.

Similarly, we reject the city's argument that, although it permits peaceful labor picketing, it may prohibit all nonlabor picketing because, as a class, nonlabor picketing is more prone to produce violence than labor picketing. Predictions about imminent disruption from picketing involve judgments appropriately made on an individualized basis, not by means of broad classifications, especially those based on subject matter. Freedom of expression, and its intersection with the guarantee of equal protection, would rest on a soft foundation indeed if government could distinguish among picketers on such a wholesale and categorical basis. . . .

The Equal Protection Clause requires that statutes affecting First Amendment interests be narrowly tailored to their legitimate objectives. . . . Given what Chicago tolerates from labor picketing, the excesses of some nonlabor picketing may not be controlled by a broad ordinance prohibiting both peaceful and violent picketing. Such excesses can be controlled by narrowly drawn statutes, . . . focusing on the abuses and dealing evenhandedly with picketing regardless of subject matter. Chicago's ordinance imposes a selective restriction on expressive conduct far "greater than is essential to the furtherance of (a substantial governmental) interest." United States v. O'Brien, 391 U.S. 367, 377 (1968). Far from being tailored to a substantial governmental interest, the discrimination among pickets is based on the content of their expression. Therefore, under the Equal Protection Clause, it may not stand.

Mr. Justice BLACKMUN and Mr. Justice REHNQUIST concur in the result.

Mr. Chief Justice BURGER, concurring.

I join the Court's opinion but with the reservation that some of the language used in the discussion of the First Amendment could, if read out of context, be misleading. Numerous holdings of this Court attest to the fact that the First Amendment does not literally mean that we "are guaranteed the right to express any thought, free from government censorship." This statement is subject to some qualifications, as for example those of Roth v. United States, 354 U.S. 476 (1957) [obscenity, *infra* Chapter 11]; Chaplinsky v. New Hampshire, 315 U.S. 568 (1942) [fighting words, *supra* Chapter 2]. *See also* New York Times Co. v. Sullivan, 376 U.S. 254 (1964) [defamation, *infra* Chapter 9].

NOTES AND QUESTIONS

1. *Equal protection and free speech.* The decision in *Mosley* is based on the Equal Protection Clause, although the Court notes the equal protection claim is "closely intertwined with First Amendment interests." What is the relationship between the two constitutional provisions in this context?

What, if anything, does understanding the content-neutrality principle as rooted in equal protection principles tell us about the problem of content discrimination? Do the equal protection and free speech guarantees protect against similar types of discriminatory government action? Do equality concerns suggest there should be special First Amendment concerns for dissident and minority speakers, or should all speakers, from religious minorities to multinational corporations, enjoy the benefits of the content-neutrality rule? For a discussion of the "dynamic" relationship between freedom of speech and equal protection, see Timothy Zick, *The Dynamic Free Speech Clause: Free Speech and Its Relation to Other Constitutional Rights* (2018), Ch. 5.

2. *"Above all else." Mosley* states that "above all else, the First Amendment means that government has no power to restrict expression because of its message, its ideas, its subject matter, or its content." Chief Justice Burger takes issue with that statement, suggesting it cannot be taken literally. Is he right? In addition to the examples of content discrimination cited by the Chief Justice, what about criminal punishment of perjury, bribery, and solicitation of crime? If Justice Marshall's statement cannot be taken literally, what does it mean?
3. *Content neutrality—rationales.* Why does the Court say content-based regulations presumptively violate the Equal Protection Clause and First Amendment? What makes them "suspect" for free speech purposes? Do they undermine self-government? Interfere with the search for truth in the "marketplace of ideas"? Inhibit speaker autonomy? Reflect governmental paternalism or possible biases? All the above? For discussion of the content-neutrality principle, see Geoffrey R. Stone, *Content Regulation and the First Amendment*, 25 Wm. & Mary L. Rev. 189, (1983); Martin H. Redish, *The Content Distinction in First Amendment Analysis*, 34 Stan. L. Rev. 113 (1981).
4. *"Message," "idea," "subject matter," and "content."* Do these terms refer to different regulatory targets or considerations? What is the relationship between "subject matter" and "idea" or "message"? Are these the same thing? What specific type of restriction was at issue in *Mosley*? Would a restriction on speech "concerning abortion" offend *Mosley*'s content-neutrality principle? Would a regulation that prohibits only statements "advancing a pro-choice perspective"?

B. THE MODERN APPROACH TO CONTENT NEUTRALITY

The content-neutrality principle relied on in *Mosley* is simple enough to articulate: content-based speech regulations are subject to heightened scrutiny, whereas content-neutral regulations (such as those relating to the time, place, or manner of expression) are subject to less exacting judicial scrutiny. But what renders a regulation or law "content-based"? Is it that the government's *purpose* is censorial? If so, how does one discern the government's purpose? Is it only viewpoint-based discrimination that is prohibited, or does the content neutrality principle extend also to subject matter distinctions? Are regulations that target certain classes or types of speakers content-based? The Court's decisions have explored these and other questions about content neutrality, as have countless lower court decisions. This examination led to some confusion and inconsistency in application of the content-neutrality principle. In *Reed v. Town of Gilbert* (2015), which follows, the Court attempted to clarify the matter. Did it succeed?

Reed v. Town of Gilbert

576 U.S. 155 (2015)

Justice THOMAS delivered the opinion of the Court.

The town of Gilbert, Arizona (or Town), has adopted a comprehensive code governing the manner in which people may display outdoor signs. Gilbert, Ariz., Land Development Code (Sign Code or Code), ch. 1, § 4.402 (2005). . . .

I

A

The Sign Code prohibits the display of outdoor signs anywhere within the Town without a permit, but it then exempts 23 categories of signs from that requirement. These exemptions include everything from bazaar signs to flying banners. Three categories of exempt signs are particularly relevant here.

The first is "Ideological Sign[s]." This category includes any "sign communicating a message or ideas for noncommercial purposes that is not a Construction Sign, Directional Sign, Temporary Directional Sign Relating to a Qualifying Event, Political Sign, Garage Sale Sign, or a sign owned or required by a governmental agency." Of the three categories discussed here, the Code treats ideological signs most favorably, allowing them to be up to 20 square feet in area and to be placed in all "zoning districts" without time limits.

The second category is "Political Sign[s]." This includes any "temporary sign designed to influence the outcome of an election called by a public body." The Code treats these signs less favorably than ideological signs. The Code allows the placement of political signs up to 16 square feet on residential property and up to 32 square feet on nonresidential property, undeveloped municipal property, and "rights-of-way." These signs may be displayed up to 60 days before a primary election and up to 15 days following a general election.

The third category is "Temporary Directional Signs Relating to a Qualifying Event." This includes any "Temporary Sign intended to direct pedestrians, motorists, and other passersby to a 'qualifying event.'" A "qualifying event" is defined as any "assembly, gathering, activity, or meeting sponsored, arranged, or promoted by a religious, charitable, community service, educational, or other similar non-profit organization." The Code treats temporary directional signs even less favorably than political signs. Temporary directional signs may be no larger than six square feet. They may be placed on private property or on a public right-of-way, but no more than four signs may be placed on a single property at any time. And, they may be displayed no more than 12 hours before the "qualifying event" and no more than 1 hour afterward.

B

Petitioners Good News Community Church (Church) and its pastor, Clyde Reed, wish to advertise the time and location of their Sunday church services. The Church is a small, cash-strapped entity that owns no building, so it holds its services at elementary schools or other locations in or near the Town. In order to inform the public about its services, which are held in a variety of different locations, the Church began placing 15 to 20 temporary signs around the Town, frequently in the public right-of-way abutting the street. The signs typically displayed the Church's name, along with the time and location of the upcoming service. Church members would post the signs early in the day on Saturday and then remove them around midday on Sunday. The display of these signs requires little money and manpower, and thus has proved to be an economical and effective way for the Church to let the community know where its services are being held each week.

This practice caught the attention of the Town's Sign Code compliance manager, who twice cited the Church for violating the Code. The first citation noted that the Church exceeded the time limits for displaying its temporary directional signs. The second citation referred to the same problem, along with the Church's failure to include the date of the event on the signs. . . .

[After unsuccessfully trying to informally resolve the issue], petitioners filed a complaint in the United States District Court for the District of Arizona, arguing that the Sign Code abridged their freedom of speech in violation of the First and Fourteenth Amendments. The District Court denied the petitioners' motion for a preliminary injunction. The Court of Appeals for the Ninth Circuit affirmed[.] . . .

We granted certiorari and now reverse.

II

A

. . . Under [the First Amendment], a government, including a municipal government vested with state authority, "has no power to restrict expression because of its message, its ideas, its subject matter, or its content." Police Dept. of Chicago v. Mosley, 408 U.S. 92, 95 (1972). Content-based laws — those that target speech based on its communicative content — are presumptively unconstitutional and may be justified only if the government proves that they are narrowly tailored to serve compelling state interests.

Government regulation of speech is content based if a law applies to particular speech because of the topic discussed or the idea or message expressed. This commonsense meaning of the phrase "content based" requires a court to consider whether a regulation of speech "on its face" draws distinctions based on the message a speaker conveys. Some facial distinctions based on a message are obvious, defining regulated speech by particular subject matter, and others are more subtle, defining regulated speech by its function or purpose. Both are distinctions drawn based on the message a speaker conveys, and, therefore, are subject to strict scrutiny.

Our precedents have also recognized a separate and additional category of laws that, though facially content neutral, will be considered content-based regulations of speech: laws that cannot be "'justified without reference to the content of the regulated speech,'" or that were adopted by the government "because of disagreement with the message [the speech] conveys," Ward v. Rock Against Racism, 491 U.S. 781, 791 (1989). Those laws, like those that are content based on their face, must also satisfy strict scrutiny.

B

The Town's Sign Code is content based on its face. It defines "Temporary Directional Signs" on the basis of whether a sign conveys the message of directing the public to church or some other "qualifying event." It defines "Political Signs" on the basis of whether a sign's message is "designed to influence the outcome of an election." And it defines "Ideological Signs" on the basis of whether a sign "communicat[es] a message or ideas" that do not fit within the Code's other categories. It then subjects each of these categories to different restrictions.

The restrictions in the Sign Code that apply to any given sign thus depend entirely on the communicative content of the sign. If a sign informs its reader of the time and place a book club will discuss John Locke's Two Treatises of Government, that sign will be treated differently from a sign expressing the view that one should vote for one of Locke's followers in an upcoming election, and both signs will be treated differently from a sign expressing an ideological view rooted in Locke's theory of government. More to the point, the Church's signs inviting people to attend its worship services are treated differently from signs conveying other types of ideas. . . . On its face, the Sign Code is a content-based regulation of speech. We thus have no need to consider the government's justifications or purposes for enacting the Code to determine whether it is subject to strict scrutiny.

In reaching the contrary conclusion, the Court of Appeals offered several theories to explain why the Town's Sign Code should be deemed content neutral. None is persuasive.

[1] The Court of Appeals first determined that the Sign Code was content neutral because the Town "did not adopt its regulation of speech [based on] disagree[ment] with the message conveyed," and its justifications for regulating temporary directional signs were "unrelated to the content of the sign." In its brief to this Court, the United States similarly contends that a sign regulation is content neutral—even if it expressly draws distinctions based on the sign's communicative content—if those distinctions can be "'justified without reference to the content of the regulated speech.'" Brief for United States as *Amicus Curiae* 20, 24.

But this analysis skips the crucial first step in the content-neutrality analysis: determining whether the law is content neutral on its face. A law that is content based on its face is subject to strict scrutiny regardless of the government's benign motive, content-neutral justification, or lack of "animus toward the ideas contained" in the regulated speech. Cincinnati v. Discovery Network, Inc., 507 U.S. 410, 429 (1993). We have thus made clear that "'[i]llicit legislative intent is not the *sine qua non* of a violation of the First Amendment,'" and a party opposing the government "need adduce 'no evidence of an improper censorial motive.'" Although "a content-based purpose may be sufficient in certain circumstances to show that a regulation is content based, it is not necessary." Turner Broadcasting System, Inc. v. FCC, 512 U.S. 622, 642 (1994). In other words, an innocuous justification cannot transform a facially content-based law into one that is content neutral.

That is why we have repeatedly considered whether a law is content neutral on its face *before* turning to the law's justification or purpose. . . . Because strict scrutiny applies either when a law is content based on its face or when the purpose and justification for the law are content based, a court must evaluate each question before it concludes that the law is content neutral and thus subject to a lower level of scrutiny.

. . . Innocent motives do not eliminate the danger of censorship presented by a facially content-based statute, as future government officials may one day wield such statutes to suppress disfavored speech. That is why the First Amendment expressly targets the operation of the laws—*i.e.*, the "abridg[ement] of speech"—rather than merely the motives of those who enacted them. The vice of content-based legislation . . . is not that it is always used for invidious, thought-control purposes, but that it lends itself to use for those purposes.

[2] The Court of Appeals next reasoned that the Sign Code was content neutral because it "does not mention any idea or viewpoint, let alone single one out for differential treatment." . . .

This analysis conflates two distinct but related limitations that the First Amendment places on government regulation of speech. Government discrimination among viewpoints—or the regulation of speech based on "the specific motivating ideology or the opinion or perspective of the speaker"—is a "more blatant" and "egregious form of content discrimination." Rosenberger v. Rector and Visitors of Univ. of Va., 515 U.S. 819, 829 (1995). But it is well established that the First Amendment's hostility to content-based regulation extends not only to restrictions on particular viewpoints, but also to prohibition of public discussion of an entire topic.

Thus, a speech regulation targeted at specific subject matter is content based even if it does not discriminate among viewpoints within that subject matter. For example, a law banning the use of sound trucks for political speech—and only political speech—would be a content-based regulation, even if it imposed no limits on the political viewpoints that could be expressed. The Town's Sign Code likewise singles out specific subject matter for differential treatment, even if it does not target viewpoints within that subject matter. Ideological messages are given more favorable treatment than messages concerning a political candidate, which are themselves given more favorable treatment than messages announcing an assembly of like-minded individuals. That is a paradigmatic example of content-based discrimination.

[3] Finally, the Court of Appeals characterized the Sign Code's distinctions as turning on "'the content-neutral elements of who is speaking through the sign and whether and when an event is occurring.'" That analysis is mistaken on both factual and legal grounds.

To start, the Sign Code's distinctions are not speaker based. The restrictions for political, ideological, and temporary event signs apply equally no matter who sponsors them. If a local business, for example, sought to put up signs advertising the Church's meetings, those signs would be subject to the same limitations as such signs placed by the Church. And if Reed had decided to display signs in support of a particular candidate, he could have made those signs far larger—and kept them up for far longer—than signs inviting people to attend his church services. If the Code's distinctions were truly speaker based, both types of signs would receive the same treatment.

In any case, the fact that a distinction is speaker based does not, as the Court of Appeals seemed to believe, automatically render the distinction content neutral. Because "[s]peech restrictions based on the identity of the speaker are all too often simply a means to control content," Citizens United v. Federal Election Comm'n, 558 U.S. 310, 340 (2010), we have insisted that "laws favoring some speakers over others demand strict scrutiny when the legislature's speaker preference reflects a content preference." Thus, a law limiting the content of newspapers, but only newspapers, could not evade strict scrutiny simply because it could be characterized as speaker based. . . . Characterizing a distinction as speaker based is only the beginning—not the end—of the inquiry.

Nor do the Sign Code's distinctions hinge on "whether and when an event is occurring." The Code does not permit citizens to post signs on any topic whatsoever within a set period leading up to an election, for example. Instead, come election time, it requires Town officials to determine whether a sign is "designed to influence the outcome of an election" (and thus "political") or merely "communicating a message or ideas for noncommercial purposes" (and thus "ideological"). That obvious content-based inquiry does not evade strict scrutiny review simply because an event (*i.e.*, an election) is involved.

And, just as with speaker-based laws, the fact that a distinction is event based does not render it content neutral. . . . A regulation that targets a sign because it conveys an idea about a specific event is no less content based than a regulation that targets a sign because it conveys some other idea. Here, the Code singles out signs bearing a particular message: the time and location of a specific event. . . .

III

Because the Town's Sign Code imposes content-based restrictions on speech, those provisions can stand only if they survive strict scrutiny, "'which requires the Government to prove that the restriction furthers a compelling interest and is narrowly tailored to achieve that interest,'" Arizona Free Enterprise Club's Freedom Club PAC v. Bennett, 564 U.S. 721, 734 (2011). Thus, it is the Town's burden to demonstrate that the Code's differentiation between temporary directional signs and other types of signs, such as political signs and ideological signs, furthers a compelling governmental interest and is narrowly tailored to that end.

The Town cannot do so. It has offered only two governmental interests in support of the distinctions the Sign Code draws: preserving the Town's aesthetic appeal and traffic safety. Assuming for the sake of argument that those are compelling governmental interests, the Code's distinctions fail as hopelessly underinclusive.

Starting with the preservation of aesthetics, temporary directional signs are "no greater an eyesore" than ideological or political ones. Yet the Code allows unlimited proliferation of larger ideological signs while strictly limiting the number, size, and duration of smaller directional ones. The Town cannot claim that placing strict limits on temporary directional signs is necessary to beautify the Town while at the same time allowing unlimited numbers of other types of signs that create the same problem.

The Town similarly has not shown that limiting temporary directional signs is necessary to eliminate threats to traffic safety, but that limiting other types of signs is not. The Town has offered no reason to believe that directional signs pose a greater threat to safety than do ideological or political signs. If anything, a sharply worded ideological sign seems more likely to distract a driver than a sign directing the public to a nearby church meeting.

In light of this underinclusiveness, the Town has not met its burden to prove that its Sign Code is narrowly tailored to further a compelling government interest. . . .

IV

Our decision today will not prevent governments from enacting effective sign laws. The Town asserts that an "'absolutist'" content-neutrality rule would render "virtually all distinctions in sign laws . . . subject to strict scrutiny," but that is not the case. Not "all distinctions" are subject to strict scrutiny, only *content-based* ones are. Laws that are *content neutral* are instead subject to lesser scrutiny.

The Town has ample content-neutral options available to resolve problems with safety and aesthetics. For example, its current Code regulates many aspects of signs that have nothing to do with a sign's message: size, building materials, lighting, moving parts, and portability. And on public property, the Town may go a long way toward entirely forbidding the posting of signs, so long as it does so in an evenhanded, content-neutral manner. . . .

We reverse the judgment of the Court of Appeals and remand the case for proceedings consistent with this opinion.

It is so ordered.

Justice BREYER, concurring in the judgment.

I join Justice Kagan's separate opinion. Like Justice Kagan I believe that categories alone cannot satisfactorily resolve the legal problem before us. The First Amendment requires greater judicial sensitivity both to the Amendment's expressive objectives and to the public's legitimate need for regulation than a simple recitation of categories, such as "content discrimination" and "strict scrutiny," would permit. In my view, the category "content discrimination" is better considered in many contexts, including here, as a rule of thumb, rather than as an automatic "strict scrutiny" trigger, leading to almost certain legal condemnation.

To use content discrimination to trigger strict scrutiny sometimes makes perfect sense. There are cases in which the Court has found content discrimination an unconstitutional method for suppressing a viewpoint. And there are cases where the Court has found content discrimination to reveal that rules governing a traditional public forum are, in fact, not a neutral way of fairly managing the forum in the interest of all speakers.

But content discrimination, while helping courts to identify unconstitutional suppression of expression, cannot and should not *always* trigger strict scrutiny. To say that it is not an automatic "strict scrutiny" trigger is not to argue against that concept's use. I readily concede, for example, that content discrimination, as a conceptual tool, can sometimes reveal weaknesses in the government's rationale for a rule that limits speech. If, for example, a city looks to litter prevention as the rationale for a prohibition against placing newsracks dispensing free advertisements on public property, why does it exempt other newsracks causing similar litter? I also concede that, whenever government disfavors one kind of speech, it places that speech at a disadvantage, potentially interfering with the free marketplace of ideas and with an individual's ability to express thoughts and ideas that can help that individual determine the kind of society in which he wishes to live, help shape that society, and help define his place within it.

Nonetheless, in these latter instances to use the presence of content discrimination automatically to trigger strict scrutiny and thereby call into play a strong presumption against constitutionality goes too far. That is because virtually all government activities involve speech, many of which involve the regulation of speech. Regulatory programs almost always require content discrimination. And to hold that such content discrimination triggers strict scrutiny is to write a recipe for judicial management of ordinary government regulatory activity. . . .

I recognize that the Court could escape the problem by watering down the force of the presumption against constitutionality that "strict scrutiny" normally carries with it. But, in my view, doing so will weaken the First Amendment's protection in instances where "strict scrutiny" should apply in full force.

The better approach is to generally treat content discrimination as a strong reason weighing against the constitutionality of a rule where a traditional public forum, or where viewpoint discrimination, is threatened, but elsewhere treat it as a rule of thumb, finding it a helpful, but not determinative legal tool, in an appropriate case, to determine the strength of a justification. I would use content discrimination as a supplement to a more basic analysis, which, tracking most of our First Amendment cases, asks whether the regulation at issue works harm to First Amendment interests that is disproportionate in light of the relevant regulatory objectives. . . . Admittedly, this approach does not have the simplicity of a mechanical use of categories. But it does permit the government to regulate speech in numerous instances where the voters have authorized the government to regulate and where courts should hesitate to substitute judicial judgment for that of administrators.

Here, regulation of signage along the roadside, for purposes of safety and beautification is at issue. There is no traditional public forum [such as a public street or park] nor do I find any general effort to censor a particular viewpoint. Consequently, the specific regulation at issue does not warrant "strict scrutiny." Nonetheless, for the reasons that Justice Kagan sets forth, I believe that the Town of Gilbert's regulatory rules violate the First Amendment. I consequently concur in the Court's judgment only.

Justice ALITO, with whom Justice KENNEDY and Justice SOTOMAYOR join, concurring.

[As] the Court shows, the regulations at issue in this case are replete with content-based distinctions, and as a result they must satisfy strict scrutiny. This does not mean, however, that municipalities are powerless to enact and enforce reasonable sign regulations. I will not attempt to provide anything like a comprehensive list, but here are some rules that would not be content based:

> Rules regulating the size of signs. These rules may distinguish among signs based on any content-neutral criteria, including any relevant criteria listed below.

Rules regulating the locations in which signs may be placed. These rules may distinguish between free-standing signs and those attached to buildings.

Rules distinguishing between lighted and unlighted signs.

Rules distinguishing between signs with fixed messages and electronic signs with messages that change.

Rules that distinguish between the placement of signs on private and public property.

Rules distinguishing between the placement of signs on commercial and residential property.

Rules distinguishing between on-premises and off-premises signs.

Rules restricting the total number of signs allowed per mile of roadway.

Rules imposing time restrictions on signs advertising a one-time event. Rules of this nature do not discriminate based on topic or subject and are akin to rules restricting the times within which oral speech or music is allowed.

Properly understood, today's decision will not prevent cities from regulating signs in a way that fully protects public safety and serves legitimate esthetic objectives.

Justice KAGAN, with whom Justice GINSBURG and Justice BREYER join, concurring in the judgment.

Countless cities and towns across America have adopted ordinances regulating the posting of signs, while exempting certain categories of signs based on their subject matter. . . .

Given the Court's analysis, many sign ordinances of that kind are now in jeopardy. . . . [A]lthough the majority holds out hope that some sign laws with subject-matter exemptions "might survive" [strict scrutiny], the likelihood is that most will be struck down. . . . To clear that high bar, the government must show that a content-based distinction "is necessary to serve a compelling state interest and is narrowly drawn to achieve that end." So on the majority's view, courts would have to determine that a town has a compelling interest in informing passersby where George Washington slept. And likewise, courts would have to find that a town has no other way to prevent hidden-driveway mishaps than by specially treating hidden-driveway signs. (Well-placed speed bumps? Lower speed limits? Or how about just a ban on hidden driveways?) The consequence—unless courts water down strict scrutiny to something unrecognizable—is that our communities will find themselves in an unenviable bind: They will have to either repeal the exemptions that allow for helpful signs on streets and sidewalks, or else lift their sign restrictions altogether and resign themselves to the resulting clutter.

Although the majority insists that applying strict scrutiny to all such ordinances is "essential" to protecting First Amendment freedoms, I find it challenging to understand why that is so. This Court's decisions articulate two important and related reasons for subjecting content-based speech regulations to the most exacting standard of review. The first is "to preserve an uninhibited marketplace of ideas in which truth will ultimately prevail." McCullen v. Coakley, 573 U.S. 464, 476 (2014). The second is to ensure that the government has not regulated speech "based on hostility—or favoritism—towards the underlying message expressed." R.A.V. v. City of St. Paul 505 U.S. 377, 386 (1992). Yet the subject-matter exemptions included in many sign ordinances do not implicate those concerns. Allowing residents, say, to install a light bulb over "name and address" signs but no others does not distort the marketplace of ideas. Nor does that different treatment give rise to an inference of impermissible government motive.

We apply strict scrutiny to facially content-based regulations of speech, in keeping with the rationales just described, when there is any "realistic possibility that official suppression of ideas is afoot." Davenport v. Washington Ed. Assn., 551 U.S. 177, 189 (2007). That is always the case when the regulation facially differentiates on the basis of viewpoint. It is also the case (except in non-public or limited public forums) when a law restricts "discussion of an entire topic" in public debate. . . . Subject-matter regulation, in other words, may have the intent or effect of favoring some ideas over others. When that is realistically possible—when the restriction "raises the specter that the Government may effectively drive certain ideas or viewpoints from the marketplace"—we insist that the law pass the most demanding constitutional test.

But when that is not realistically possible, we may do well to relax our guard so that "entirely reasonable" laws imperiled by strict scrutiny can survive. . . .

And indeed we have done just that: Our cases have been far less rigid than the majority admits in applying strict scrutiny to facially content-based laws—including in cases just like this one. In Members of City Council of Los Angeles v. Taxpayers for Vincent, 466 U.S. 789 (1984), the Court declined to apply strict scrutiny to a municipal ordinance that exempted address numbers and markers commemorating "historical, cultural, or artistic event[s]" from a generally applicable limit on sidewalk signs. After all, we explained, the law's enactment and enforcement revealed "not even a hint of bias or censorship." *See also* Renton v. Playtime Theatres, Inc., 475 U.S. 41, 48 (1986) [*infra* p. 135] (applying intermediate scrutiny to a zoning law that facially distinguished among movie theaters based on content because it was "designed to prevent crime, protect the city's retail trade, [and] maintain property values . . . , not to suppress the expression of unpopular views"). And another decision involving a similar law provides an alternative model. In City of Ladue v. Gilleo, 512 U.S. 43 (1994), the Court assumed *arguendo* that a sign ordinance's exceptions for address signs, safety signs, and for-sale signs in residential areas did not trigger strict scrutiny. We did not need to, and so did not, decide the level-of-scrutiny question because the law's breadth made it unconstitutional under any standard.

. . . The Town of Gilbert's defense of its sign ordinance—most notably, the law's distinctions between directional signs and others—does not pass strict scrutiny, or intermediate scrutiny, or even the laugh test. The Town, for example, provides no reason at all for prohibiting more than four directional signs on a property while placing no limits on the number of other types of signs. Similarly, the Town offers no coherent justification for restricting the size of directional signs to 6 square feet while allowing other signs to reach 20 square feet. The best the Town could come up with at oral argument was that directional signs "need to be smaller because they need to guide travelers along a route." Why exactly a smaller sign better helps travelers get to where they are going is left a mystery. The absence of any sensible basis for these and other distinctions dooms the Town's ordinance under even the intermediate scrutiny that the Court typically applies to "time, place, or manner" speech regulations. Accordingly, there is no need to decide in this case whether strict scrutiny applies to every sign ordinance in every town across this country containing a subject-matter exemption.

I suspect this Court and others will regret the majority's insistence today on answering that question in the affirmative. As the years go by, courts will discover that thousands of towns have such ordinances, many of them "entirely reasonable." And as the challenges to them mount, courts will have to invalidate one after the other. (This Court may soon find itself a veritable Supreme Board of Sign Review.) And courts will strike down those democratically enacted local laws even though no one—certainly not the majority—has ever explained why the vindication of First Amendment values requires that result. Because I see no reason why such an easy case calls for us to cast a constitutional pall on reasonable regulations quite unlike the law before us, I concur only in the judgment.

NOTES AND QUESTIONS

1. *Content neutrality—methodology. Reed* articulates a framework for analyzing content neutrality. First examine the face or text of the law or regulation. If it expressly discriminates based on either subject matter or viewpoint, the law is content-based—regardless of any benign government purpose or motive. Even if the law or regulation is facially content-neutral, consider whether the government has justified or applied the regulation based on content. For example, breach of peace and other public order laws do not facially regulate speech based on its content, but if the government's purpose in applying these laws turns on the government's hostility to the speaker's expression the laws will be treated as content-based. Laws that regulate certain classes of speakers or types of events may also be treated as content-based if the classifications reflect a content preference or serve as a proxy for speech content. If a law is content-based for any of the foregoing reasons, it is subject to strict scrutiny—i.e., the government must demonstrate a "compelling interest" for the law and establish that is it "narrowly tailored" to further that interest. The tailoring requirement is exacting: the law must be necessary to further the government's interest and the least speech-restrictive alternative available. If a law is content-neutral, a less rigorous "intermediate" scrutiny standard applies.
2. *Justifications for strict scrutiny.* In their concurring opinions in *Reed*, Justices Breyer and Kagan discuss reasons why the Court has subjected content-based speech regulations to strict scrutiny. Justice Breyer characterizes such laws as "potentially interfering with the free marketplace of ideas and with an individual's ability to express thoughts and ideas that can help that individual determine the kind of society in which he wishes to live, help shape that society, and help define his place within it." Justice Kagan likewise relies on "marketplace" justifications. She also adds that content-based laws raise concerns about governmental hostility to certain viewpoints or messages. Does the sign code in *Reed* raise such concerns? Can you think of other reasons to be skeptical of subject matter-based and viewpoint-based speech regulations?

3. *Content-neutral alternatives.* In *Reed*, some of the Justices were concerned that the majority's approach unduly tied the hands of local officials. Do you agree? Does *Reed* require that localities justify, under strict scrutiny, *all* signage regulations? The majority and Justice Alito both suggested governments retain ample authority to regulate in furtherance of aesthetics, traffic safety, and other interests. Do you agree?
4. *Other existing content-based regulations.* In his concurring opinion, Justice Breyer mentions "examples of speech regulated by government that inevitably involve content discrimination, but where a strong presumption against constitutionality has no place." Consider requirements for content that must be included on labels of certain consumer electronics, a regulation requiring pilots to ensure that each passenger has been briefed on flight procedures, and a state law requiring petting zoos to post a sign at every exit "strongly recommending that persons wash their hands upon exiting the petting zoo area." Are all these laws subject to strict scrutiny after *Reed*? If so, does that suggest a more flexible approach is needed? Is the answer to apply the "strict scrutiny" standard more flexibly to allow some of these regulations? Or is it to adopt a different standard, as Justice Breyer suggests?
5. *Viewpoint-based versus subject-matter-based restrictions. Reed* affirms that laws are "content-based" when they discriminate based on *either* the viewpoint or subject matter of speech. Although *Reed* holds either type of regulation merits strict scrutiny, the Court has been particularly skeptical of viewpoint-based speech regulations. *See, e.g.*, Kingsley International Pictures Corp. v. Regents, 360 U.S. 684 (1959) (holding state may not deny a license to a film, *Lady Chatterly's Lover*, "because that picture advocates an idea—that adultery under certain circumstances may be proper behavior"); R.A.V. v. City of St. Paul, 505 U.S. 377 (1992) (invalidating city ordinance that prohibited symbols that tend to arouse anger or alarm because it prohibited fighting words by bigots but not against them). Some of the Justices in *Reed* argued that not all subject matter-based regulations merit strict scrutiny. Does that make sense? Subject matter restrictions aim at entire subjects rather than specific viewpoints—for example, a law regulating only signs with commercial content. Given their broad scope, are these kinds of regulations arguably *more* dangerous than those that single out only specific viewpoints? For a discussion of this issue, *see* Geoffrey R. Stone, *Restrictions of Speech Because of Its Content: The Peculiar Case of Subject-Matter Restrictions*, 46 U. Chi. L. Rev. 81 (1978); Daniel A. Farber, *Content Regulation and the First Amendment: A Revisionist View*, 68 Geo. L.J. 727 (1980). As subsequent chapters will discuss, although both subject matter and viewpoint discriminatory speech regulations are generally treated the same under First Amendment doctrine, there are certain contexts in which subject matter distinctions are permitted but viewpoint distinctions are not. For that reason, you should be able to distinguish between subject matter and viewpoint-based speech restrictions.

THEORY-APPLIED PROBLEMS

Determine whether each of the laws described below constitutes a content-based (subject matter or viewpoint) or content-neutral regulation of speech.

1. A town ordinance requires a permit to post a permanent sign but does not require a permit for "safety signs" such as "Blind Pedestrian Crossing" and "Hidden Driveway."
2. A State law requires payment to a State Crime Victims Board of "any proceeds due to a person accused of, convicted of, or admitting to a crime, for the production of a book or other work describing the crime." *See* Simon & Schuster, Inc. v. Members of New York State Crime Victims Board, 502 U.S. 105 (1991).
3. The District of Columbia code prohibits the display within 500 feet of a foreign embassy of any sign "tending to bring that foreign government into public odium or public disrepute." *See* Boos v. Barry, 485 U.S. 312 (1988).
4. A state statute makes it unlawful within the vicinity of a health care facility for anyone to "knowingly approach" within eight feet of another person, without that person's consent, "for the purpose of passing a leaflet or handbill to, displaying a sign to or engaging in oral protest, education, or counseling with such other person." *See* Hill v. Colorado, 530 U.S. 703 (2000).
5. Concerned that aggressive panhandling is deterring shoppers and tourists from visiting its downtown area, a city adopts an ordinance that prohibits "panhandling" in the city's downtown historic district. The ordinance prohibits "oral requests for immediate payment of money" but allows "signs requesting money" and "oral requests to send money later." *See* Norton v. City of Springfield, 803 F.3d 411 (7th Cir. 2015).

C. APPLYING STRICT SCRUTINY TO CONTENT-BASED LAWS

As *Reed* states, content-based laws are subject to a "strict scrutiny" standard that requires government demonstrate speech regulations are "narrowly tailored to serve compelling governmental interests." In *Reed*, the Court concluded the sign code provisions could not be justified under this standard. How demanding is strict scrutiny? Consider that only *once* has a Supreme Court majority upheld a content-based regulation of "high-value" speech. *See* Holder v. Humanitarian Law Project, 561 U.S. 1 (2010) (below). On just a couple other occasions, a plurality of the Court has upheld content-based speech regulations. *See* Burson v. Freeman, 504 U.S. 191 (1992) (plurality) (upholding state law prohibiting the solicitation of votes, the display of political posters or signs, and the distribution of political campaign materials within 100 feet to the entrance of a polling place); Williams-Yulee v. Florida Bar, 575 U.S. 433 (2013) (plurality) (upholding state judicial conduct rule prohibiting judicial candidates from personally soliciting campaign funds).

In short, it is very rare, although not unheard of, for a content-based law to survive strict scrutiny. Consider the application of strict scrutiny in the following decisions.

Brown v. Entertainment Merchants Ass'n

564 U.S. 786 (2011)

[Recall from Chapter 2 that the Court rejected the government's argument that depictions of violence in video games are categorically unprotected speech. The Court then determined that as a content-based speech regulation, California's law restricting the sale of violent video games to minors had to satisfy strict scrutiny.]

Justice SCALIA delivered the opinion of the Court. . . .

III

Because the Act imposes a restriction on the content of protected speech, it is invalid unless California can demonstrate that it passes strict scrutiny—that is, unless it is justified by a compelling government interest and is narrowly drawn to serve that interest. The State must specifically identify an "actual problem" in need of solving, and the curtailment of free speech must be actually necessary to the solution. That is a demanding standard. It is rare that a regulation restricting speech because of its content will ever be permissible.

California cannot meet that standard. At the outset, it acknowledges that it cannot show a direct causal link between violent video games and harm to minors. Rather, relying upon our decision in Turner Broadcasting System, Inc. v. FCC, 512 U.S. 622 (1994), the State claims that it need not produce such proof because the legislature can make a predictive judgment that such a link exists, based on competing psychological studies. But reliance on *Turner Broadcasting* is misplaced. That decision applied *intermediate scrutiny* to a content-neutral regulation. California's burden is much higher, and because it bears the risk of uncertainty, ambiguous proof will not suffice.

The State's evidence is not compelling. California relies primarily on the research of Dr. Craig Anderson and a few other research psychologists whose studies purport to show a connection between exposure to violent video games and harmful effects on children. These studies have been rejected by every court to consider them, and with good reason: They do not prove that violent video games cause minors to act aggressively (which would at least be a beginning). Instead, "[n]early all of the research is based on correlation, not evidence of causation, and most of the studies suffer from significant, admitted flaws in methodology." They show at best some correlation between exposure to violent entertainment and minuscule real-world effects, such as children's feeling more aggressive or making louder noises in the few minutes after playing a violent game than after playing a nonviolent game.

Even taking for granted Dr. Anderson's conclusions that violent video games produce some effect on children's feelings of aggression, those effects are both small and indistinguishable from effects produced by other media. In his testimony in a similar lawsuit, Dr. Anderson admitted that the "effect sizes" of children's exposure to violent video games are "about the same" as that produced by their exposure to violence on television. And he admits that the *same* effects have been found when children watch cartoons starring Bugs Bunny or the Road Runner, or when they play video games like Sonic the Hedgehog that are rated "E" (appropriate for all ages), or even when they "vie[w] a picture of a gun."

Of course, California has (wisely) declined to restrict Saturday morning cartoons, the sale of games rated for young children, or the distribution of pictures of guns. The consequence is that its regulation is wildly underinclusive when judged against its asserted justification, which in our view is alone enough to defeat it. Underinclusiveness raises serious doubts about whether the government is in fact pursuing the interest it invokes, rather than disfavoring a particular speaker or viewpoint. Here, California has singled out the purveyors of video games for disfavored treatment—at least when compared to booksellers, cartoonists, and movie producers—and has given no persuasive reason why.

The Act is also seriously underinclusive in another respect—and a respect that renders irrelevant the contentions of the concurrence and the dissents that video games are qualitatively different from other portrayals of violence. The California Legislature is perfectly willing to leave this dangerous, mind-altering material in the hands of children so long as one parent (or even an aunt or uncle) says it's OK. And there are not even any requirements as to how this parental or avuncular relationship is to be verified; apparently the child's or putative parent's, aunt's, or uncle's say-so suffices. That is not how one addresses a serious social problem.

California claims that the Act is justified in aid of parental authority: By requiring that the purchase of violent video games can be made only by adults, the Act ensures that parents can decide what games are appropriate. At the outset, we note our doubts that punishing third parties for conveying protected speech to children *just in case* their parents disapprove of that speech is a proper governmental means of aiding parental authority. Accepting that position would largely vitiate the rule that only in relatively narrow and well-defined circumstances may government bar public dissemination of protected materials to minors.

But leaving that aside, California cannot show that the Act's restrictions meet a substantial need of parents who wish to restrict their children's access to violent video games but cannot do so. The video-game industry has in place a voluntary rating system designed to inform consumers about the content of games. The system, implemented by the Entertainment Software Rating Board (ESRB), assigns age-specific ratings to each video game submitted: EC (Early Childhood); E (Everyone); E10+ (Everyone 10 and older); T (Teens); M (17 and older); and AO (Adults Only—18 and older). The Video Software Dealers Association encourages retailers to prominently display information about the ESRB system in their stores; to refrain from renting or selling adults-only games to minors; and to rent or sell "M" rated games to minors only with parental consent. In 2009, the Federal Trade Commission (FTC) found that, as a result of this system, "the video game industry outpaces the movie and music industries" in "(1) restricting target-marketing of mature-rated products to children; (2) clearly and prominently disclosing rating information; and (3) restricting children's access to mature-rated products at retail." FTC, Report to Congress, Marketing Violent Entertainment to Children 30 (Dec. 2009). This system does much to ensure that minors cannot purchase seriously violent games on their own, and that parents who care about the matter can readily evaluate the games their children bring home. Filling the remaining modest gap in concerned parents' control can hardly be a compelling state interest.

And finally, the Act's purported aid to parental authority is vastly overinclusive. Not all of the children who are forbidden to purchase violent video games on their own have parents who *care* whether they purchase violent video games. While some of the legislation's effect may indeed be in support of what some parents of the restricted children actually want, its entire effect is only in support of what the State thinks parents *ought* to want. This is not the narrow tailoring to "assisting parents" that restriction of First Amendment rights requires. . . .

NOTES AND QUESTIONS

1. *"Low-value" v. "high-value" speech regulation.* Note the Court in *Entertainment Merchants Assn.* first determined whether violent video game depictions fell into a class or category of excluded "low-value" expression. *See* Chapter 2. Answering that question in the negative, the Court then determined whether California regulated "high-value" speech based on its content. Since the law was facially content-based, the Court applied strict scrutiny.
2. *Strict scrutiny of ends.* When government regulates speech based on content, it must demonstrate a "compelling interest" for doing so. In *Entertainment Merchants Assn.*, the Court states the government "must specifically identify an 'actual problem' in need of solving." What compelling interests does the state identify? Does the Court conclude these interests are "compelling"? Does the Court explain how it decides whether an interest is "compelling"? Does *Entertainment Merchants Assn.* indicate government must establish a causal connection between every content-based law and the harms it seeks to regulate for the government's interest to be considered "compelling"? Should a correlation between certain types of speech and certain kinds of harms suffice?
3. *Strict scrutiny of means.* Content-based speech regulations must be "narrowly tailored" to further a compelling governmental interest. In *Entertainment Merchants Assn.*, the Court states "the curtailment of free speech must be actually necessary to the solution." Further, in determining whether California's law is "narrowly tailored" the Court examines whether it is "underinclusive" or "overinclusive" in scope, and whether there are less speech-restrictive alternatives. What makes the California law "underinclusive" or "overinclusive"? What "less restrictive" alternatives does the Court say were available to California?
4. *Too strict?* Is the strict scrutiny standard, as applied in *Entertainment Merchants Assn.*, too strict? Should California be required to produce the kind of empirical evidence the Court demands to defend its ban on the sale of violent video games to minors? Even if the restriction applies only to a certain potentially harmful subject matter and does not suppress any viewpoint conveyed by the video games?

United States v. Alvarez

567 U.S. 709 (2012)

[Recall from Chapter 2 that *Alvarez* involved the constitutionality of a federal law that criminalized lying about the receipt of military honors. The plurality rejected the government's argument that such falsehoods fall into a category of "low value" or unprotected speech. It then applied strict scrutiny. In a concurring opinion, Justice Breyer, joined by Justice Kagan, applied a "proportionality" standard that is similar to "intermediate" scrutiny.]

Justice KENNEDY announced the judgment of the Court and delivered an opinion, in which The CHIEF JUSTICE, Justice GINSBURG, and Justice SOTOMAYOR join.

Lying was his habit. Xavier Alvarez, the respondent here, lied when he said that he played hockey for the Detroit Red Wings and that he once married a starlet from Mexico. But when he lied in announcing he held the Congressional Medal of Honor (or Medal), respondent ventured onto new ground; for that lie violates a federal criminal statute, the Stolen Valor Act of 2005. 18 U.S.C. § 704.

I

. . . Respondent challenges the statute as a content-based suppression of pure speech, speech not falling within any of the few categories of expression where content-based regulation is permissible. The Government defends the statute as necessary to preserve the integrity and purpose of the Medal, an integrity and purpose it contends are compromised and frustrated by the false statements the statute prohibits. The Government's arguments cannot suffice to save the statute. . . .

IV

[As a content-based prohibition on speech, the Act is subject to the] "most exacting scrutiny." Although the objectives the Government seeks to further by the statute are not without significance, the Court must, and now does, find the Act does not satisfy exacting scrutiny.

The Government is correct when it states military medals "serve the important public function of recognizing and expressing gratitude for acts of heroism and sacrifice in military service," and also "'foste[r] morale, mission accomplishment and esprit de corps' among service members." . . .

These interests are related to the integrity of the military honors system in general, and the Congressional Medal of Honor in particular. Although millions have served with brave resolve, the Medal, which is the highest military award for valor against an enemy force, has been given just 3,476 times. Established in 1861, the Medal is reserved for those who have distinguished themselves "conspicuously by gallantry and intrepidity at the risk of his life above and beyond the call of duty." The stories of those who earned the Medal inspire and fascinate. . . . The Government's interest in protecting the integrity of the Medal of Honor is beyond question.

But to recite the Government's compelling interests is not to end the matter. The First Amendment requires that the Government's chosen restriction on the speech at issue be "actually necessary" to achieve its interest. There must be a direct causal link between the restriction imposed and the injury to be prevented. The link between the Government's interest in protecting the integrity of the military honors system and the Act's restriction on the false claims of liars like respondent has not been shown. . . . It must be acknowledged that when a pretender claims the Medal to be his own, the lie might harm the Government by demeaning the high purpose of the award, diminishing the honor it confirms, and creating the appearance that the Medal is awarded more often than is true. Furthermore, the lie may offend the true holders of the Medal. From one perspective it insults their bravery and high principles when falsehood puts them in the unworthy company of a pretender.

Yet these interests do not satisfy the Government's heavy burden when it seeks to regulate protected speech. The Government points to no evidence to support its claim that the public's general perception of military awards is diluted by false claims such as those made by Alvarez. Cf. *Entertainment Merchants Assn.* (analyzing and rejecting the findings of research psychologists demonstrating the causal link between violent video games and harmful effects on children). As one of the Government's amici notes "there is nothing that charlatans such as Xavier Alvarez can do to stain [the Medal winners'] honor." Brief for Veterans of Foreign Wars of the United States et al. as Amici Curiae 1. This general proposition is sound, even if true holders of the Medal might experience anger and frustration. . . .

The Government has not shown, and cannot show, why counterspeech would not suffice to achieve its interest. The facts of this case indicate that the dynamics of free speech, of counterspeech, of refutation, can overcome the lie. Respondent lied at a public meeting. Even before the FBI began investigating him for his false statements Alvarez was perceived as a phony. Once the lie was made public, he was ridiculed online, and a fellow board member called for his resignation. There is good reason to believe that a similar fate would befall other false claimants. Indeed, the outrage and contempt expressed for respondent's lies can serve to reawaken and reinforce the public's respect for the Medal, its recipients, and its high purpose. The acclaim that recipients of the Congressional Medal of Honor receive also casts doubt on the proposition that the public will be misled by the claims of charlatans or become cynical of those whose heroic deeds earned them the Medal by right.

The remedy for speech that is false is speech that is true. This is the ordinary course in a free society. The response to the unreasoned is the rational; to the uninformed, the enlightened; to the straight-out lie, the simple truth. See *Whitney* (1927) (Brandeis, J., concurring) ("If there be time to expose through discussion the falsehood and fallacies, to avert the evil by the processes of education, the remedy to be applied is more speech, not enforced silence"). The theory of our Constitution is "that the best test of truth is the power of the thought to get itself accepted in the competition of the market," Abrams v. United States, 250 U.S. 616, 630 (1919) (Holmes, J., dissenting). The First Amendment itself ensures the right to respond to speech we do not like, and for good reason. Freedom of speech and thought flows not from the beneficence of the state but from the inalienable rights of the person. And suppression of speech by the government can make exposure of falsity more difficult, not less so. Society has the right and civic duty to engage in open, dynamic, rational discourse. These ends are not well served when the government seeks to orchestrate public discussion through content-based mandates.

. . . The American people do not need the assistance of a government prosecution to express their high regard for the special place that military heroes hold in our tradition. Only a weak society needs government protection or intervention before it pursues its resolve to preserve the truth. Truth needs neither handcuffs nor a badge for its vindication.

In addition, when the Government seeks to regulate protected speech, the restriction must be the "least restrictive means among available, effective alternatives." There is, however, at least one less speech-restrictive means by which the Government could likely protect the integrity of the military awards system. A Government-created database could list Congressional Medal of Honor winners. Were a database accessible through the Internet, it would be easy to verify and expose false claims. It appears some private individuals have already created databases similar to this, and at least one database of past winners is online and fully searchable. The Solicitor General responds that although Congress and the Department of Defense investigated the feasibility of establishing a database in 2008, the Government "concluded that such a database would be impracticable and insufficiently comprehensive." Without more explanation, it is difficult to assess the Government's claim, especially when at least one database of Congressional Medal of Honor winners already exists.

The Government may have responses to some of these criticisms, but there has been no clear showing of the necessity of the statute, the necessity required by exacting scrutiny.

[In a concurring opinion, Justice BREYER, joined by Justice KAGAN, concluded the Stolen Valor Act's provisions were not adequately tailored to the government's "substantial" interest in protecting the integrity of the military honors system. In terms of tailoring the Act to this interest, Justice Breyer observed that Congress could enact a less speech-restrictive law targeting a narrower list of military honors, target lies that cause specific monetary or other harms, or rely on a database of medal recipients.]

Justice ALITO, with whom Justice SCALIA and Justice THOMAS join, dissenting.

I

. . . Both the plurality and Justice Breyer argue that Congress could have preserved the integrity of military honors by means other than a criminal prohibition, but Congress had ample reason to believe that alternative approaches would not be adequate. The chief alternative recommended is the compilation and release of a comprehensive list or database of actual medal recipients. If the public could readily access such a resource, it is argued, imposters would be quickly and easily exposed, and the proliferation of lies about military honors would come to an end.

This remedy, unfortunately, will not work. The Department of Defense has explained that the most that it can do is to create a database of recipients of certain top military honors awarded since 2001. Because a sufficiently comprehensive database is not practicable, lies about military awards cannot be remedied by what the plurality calls "counterspeech." Without the requisite database, many efforts to refute false claims may be thwarted, and some legitimate award recipients may be erroneously attacked. In addition, a steady stream of stories in the media about the exposure of imposters would tend to increase skepticism among members of the public about the entire awards system. This would only exacerbate the harm that the Stolen Valor Act is meant to prevent. . . .

NOTES AND QUESTIONS

1. *Compelling interests.* According to the Court, is the Stolen Valor Act supported by "compelling" interests? What are they? Is it clear how the Court determines whether these interests are "compelling"?
2. *Narrow tailoring.* As *Alvarez* states, strict scrutiny requires that government adopt the "least restrictive means among available, effective alternatives." Suppose the alternatives are not very or at all effective. Is "counterspeech" generally an effective alternative to criminalizing lies about military honors? Is a comprehensive database of military honors an effective alternative, considering one does not currently exist?
3. *Regulating falsehoods and disinformation.* What does the analysis in *Alvarez* suggest with regard to government efforts to regulate lies, disinformation, and other forms of falsehood in online and other contexts? Is the government likely to have a "compelling" interest in regulating falsehoods in general, or in specific contexts? Given the alternative of counterspeech, are such laws likely to be deemed narrowly tailored to further such interests?

Holder v. Humanitarian Law Project

561 U.S. 1 (2010)

Chief Justice ROBERTS delivered the opinion of the Court.

Congress has prohibited the provision of "material support or resources" to certain foreign organizations that engage in terrorist activity. 18 U.S.C. § 2339B(a)(1). That prohibition is based on a finding that the specified organizations "are so tainted by their criminal conduct that any contribution to such an organization facilitates that conduct." [*See* 18 U.S.C. § 2339B (Findings and Purpose)]. The plaintiffs in this litigation seek to provide support to two such organizations. Plaintiffs claim that they seek to facilitate only the lawful, nonviolent purposes of those groups, and that applying the material-support law to prevent them from doing so violates the Constitution. . . .

I

This litigation concerns 18 U.S.C. § 2339B, which makes it a federal crime to "knowingly provid[e] material support or resources to a foreign terrorist organization." Congress has amended the definition of "material support or resources" periodically, but at present it is defined as follows:

> "[T]he term 'material support or resources' means any property, tangible or intangible, or service, including currency or monetary instruments or financial securities, financial services, lodging, training, expert

advice or assistance, safehouses, false documentation or identification, communications equipment, facilities, weapons, lethal substances, explosives, personnel (1 or more individuals who may be or include oneself), and transportation, except medicine or religious materials." 18 U.S.C. § 2339A(b)(1).

The authority to designate an entity a "foreign terrorist organization" rests with the Secretary of State. 8 U.S.C. §§ 1189(a)(1), (d)(4). She may, in consultation with the Secretary of the Treasury and the Attorney General, so designate an organization upon finding that it is foreign, engages in "terrorist activity" or "terrorism," and thereby "threatens the security of United States nationals or the national security of the United States." §§ 1189(a)(1), (d)(4). "'[N]ational security' means the national defense, foreign relations, or economic interests of the United States." § 1189(d)(2). An entity designated a foreign terrorist organization may seek review of that designation before the D.C. Circuit within 30 days of that designation. § 1189(c)(1). . . .

[In 1977, the Secretary of State designated 30 groups as foreign terrorist organizations, including Turkey's Kurdistan Workers' Party (PKK) and the Liberation Tigers of Tamil Eelam (LTTE) of Sri Lanka. Evidence was presented regarding both parties' political aims of creating independent states in their respective countries and of numerous, violent attacks by both parties, including attacks that harmed Americans. Individual U.S. citizens and domestic organizations, [including] the Humanitarian Law Project (HLP) (a human rights organization with consultative status to the United Nations), filed a lawsuit in federal court claiming that they wanted to provide support for the humanitarian and political activities of the PKK and LTTE in the form of monetary contributions, other tangible aid, legal training, and political advocacy, but that they could not do so for fear of prosecution under § 2339B.]

V

. . . Plaintiffs claim that Congress has banned their "pure political speech." It has not. Under the material-support statute, plaintiffs may say anything they wish on any topic. . . . As the Government states: "The statute does not prohibit independent advocacy or expression of any kind." Section 2339B also "does not prevent [plaintiffs] from becoming members of the PKK and LTTE or impose any sanction on them for doing so." Congress has not, therefore, sought to suppress ideas or opinions in the form of "pure political speech." Rather, Congress has prohibited "material support," which most often does not take the form of speech at all. And when it does, the statute is carefully drawn to cover only a narrow category of speech to, under the direction of, or in coordination with foreign groups that the speaker knows to be terrorist organizations. . . .

The Government, [however], is wrong that the only thing actually at issue in this litigation is conduct. . . . [Section] 2339B regulates speech on the basis of its content. Plaintiffs want to speak to the PKK and the LTTE, and whether they may do so under § 2339B depends on what they say. If plaintiffs' speech to those groups imparts a "specific skill" or communicates advice derived from "specialized knowledge"—for example, training on the use of international law or advice on petitioning the United Nations—then it is barred. . . . We accordingly apply more rigorous scrutiny.

Everyone agrees that the Government's interest in combating terrorism is an urgent objective of the highest order. Plaintiffs' complaint is that the ban on material support, applied to what they wish to do, is not "necessary to further that interest." The objective of combating terrorism does not justify prohibiting their speech, plaintiffs argue, because their support will advance only the legitimate activities of the designated terrorist organizations, not their terrorism.

Whether foreign terrorist organizations meaningfully segregate support of their legitimate activities from support of terrorism is an empirical question. When it enacted § 2339B in 1996, Congress made specific findings regarding the serious threat posed by international terrorism. One of those findings explicitly rejects plaintiffs' contention that their support would not further the terrorist activities of the PKK and LTTE: "[F]oreign organizations that engage in terrorist activity are so tainted by their criminal conduct that *any contribution to such an organization* facilitates that conduct." § 301(a)(7) (emphasis added). . . .

Material support meant to "promot[e] peaceable, lawful conduct" can further terrorism by foreign groups in multiple ways. . . . Such support frees up other resources within the organization that may be put to violent ends. It also importantly helps lend legitimacy to foreign terrorist groups—legitimacy that makes it easier for those groups to persist, to recruit members, and to raise funds all of which facilitate more terrorist attacks. . . . Providing foreign terrorist groups with material support in any form also furthers terrorism by straining the United States' relationships with its allies and undermining cooperative efforts between nations to prevent terrorist attacks. . . .

Our precedents, old and new, make clear that concerns of national security and foreign relations do not warrant abdication of the judicial role. We do not defer to the Government's reading of the First Amendment, even when such interests are at stake. . . . But when it comes to collecting evidence and drawing factual inferences in this area, "the lack of competence on the part of the courts is marked" and respect for the Government's conclusions is appropriate. . . . The Government, when seeking to prevent imminent harms in the context of international affairs and national security, is not required to conclusively link all the pieces in the puzzle before we grant weight to its empirical conclusions. . . .

We turn to the particular speech plaintiffs propose to undertake. First, plaintiffs propose to "train members of [the] PKK on how to use humanitarian and international law to peacefully resolve disputes." Congress can, consistent with the First Amendment, prohibit this direct training. It is wholly foreseeable that the PKK could use the "specific skill[s]" that plaintiffs propose to impart as part of a broader strategy to promote terrorism. The PKK could, for example, pursue peaceful negotiation as a means of buying time to recover from short-term setbacks, lulling opponents into complacency, and ultimately preparing for renewed attacks. A foreign terrorist organization introduced to the structures of the international legal system might use the information to threaten, manipulate, and disrupt. This possibility is real, not remote.

Second, plaintiffs propose to "teach PKK members how to petition various representative bodies such as the United Nations for relief." The Government acts within First Amendment strictures in banning this proposed speech because it teaches the organization how to acquire "relief," which plaintiffs never define with any specificity, and which could readily include monetary aid. . . . Money is fungible and Congress logically concluded that money a terrorist group such as the PKK obtains using the techniques plaintiffs propose to teach could be redirected to funding the group's violent activities. . . .

All this is not to say that any future applications of the material-support statute to speech or advocacy will survive First Amendment scrutiny. It is also not to say that any other statute relating to speech and terrorism would satisfy the First Amendment. In particular, we in no way suggest that a regulation of independent speech would pass constitutional muster, even if the Government were to show that such speech benefits foreign terrorist organizations. We also do not suggest that Congress could extend the same prohibition on material support at issue here to domestic organizations. We simply hold that, in prohibiting the particular forms of support that plaintiffs seek to provide to foreign terrorist groups, § 2339B does not violate the freedom of speech. . . .

The judgment of the United States Court of Appeals for the Ninth Circuit is affirmed in part and reversed in part, and the cases are remanded for further proceedings consistent with this opinion.

It is so ordered.

Justice BREYER, with whom Justices GINSBURG and SOTOMAYOR join, dissenting.

. . . Not even the "serious and deadly problem" of international terrorism can require *automatic* forfeiture of First Amendment rights. . . . If the statute is constitutional in this context, it would have to come with a strong justification attached. . . .

The Government does identify a compelling countervailing interest, namely, the interest in protecting the security of the United States and its nationals from the threats that foreign terrorist organizations pose by denying those organizations financial and other fungible resources. I do not dispute the importance of this interest. But I do dispute whether the interest can justify the statute's criminal prohibition. To put the matter more specifically, precisely how does application of the statute to the protected activities before us *help achieve* that important security-related end?

The Government makes two efforts to answer this question. *First,* the Government says that the plaintiffs' support for these organizations is "fungible" in the same sense as other forms of banned support. Being fungible, the plaintiffs' support could, for example, free up other resources, which the organization might put to terrorist ends.

The proposition that the two very different kinds of "support" are "fungible," however, is not *obviously* true. There is no *obvious* way in which undertaking advocacy for political change through peaceful means or teaching the PKK and LTTE, say, how to petition the United Nations for political change is fungible with other resources that might be put to more sinister ends in the way that donations of money, food, or computer training are fungible. . . .

The Government has provided us with no empirical information that might convincingly support this claim. Instead, the Government cites only to evidence that Congress was concerned about the "fungible" nature in general of resources, predominately money and material goods. . . . The most one can say in the Government's favor about these statements is that they *might* be read as offering highly general support for its argument. The statements do not, however, explain in any detail how the *plaintiffs'* political-advocacy-related activities might actually be "fungible" and therefore capable of being diverted to terrorist use. . . .

Second, the Government says that the plaintiffs' proposed activities will "bolste[r] a terrorist organization's efficacy and strength in a community" and "undermin[e] this nation's efforts to *delegitimize and weaken* those groups." . . . [W]ere the law to accept a "legitimating" effect, in and of itself and without qualification, as providing sufficient grounds for imposing such a ban, the First Amendment battle would be lost in untold instances where it should be won. . . . The argument applies as strongly to "independent" as to "coordinated" advocacy. . . .

Nor can the Government overcome these considerations simply by narrowing the covered activities to those that involve *coordinated,* rather than *independent,* advocacy. . . . I am not aware of any form of words that might be used to describe "coordination" that would not, at a minimum, seriously chill not only the kind of activities the plaintiffs raise before us, but also the "independent advocacy" the Government purports to permit. And, as for the Government's willingness to distinguish *independent* advocacy from *coordinated* advocacy, the former is *more* likely, not *less* likely, to confer legitimacy than the latter. [The] distinction "coordination" makes is arbitrary in respect to furthering the statute's purposes. . . .

In my own view, the majority's arguments stretch the concept of "fungibility" beyond constitutional limits. Neither Congress nor the Government advanced these particular hypothetical claims. I am not aware of any case in this Court—not [*Gitlow*], not [*Schenck*], not [*Abrams*], not the later Communist Party cases decided during the heat of the Cold War—in which the Court accepted anything like a claim that speech or teaching might be criminalized lest it, *e.g.*, buy negotiating time for an opponent who would put that time to bad use. . . .

I believe that a construction [of the statute] that would avoid the constitutional problem is "fairly possible." In particular, I would read the statute as criminalizing First-Amendment-protected pure speech and association only when the defendant knows or intends that those activities will assist the organization's unlawful terrorist actions. Under this reading, the Government would have to show, at a minimum, that such defendants provided support that they knew was significantly likely to help the organization pursue its unlawful terrorist aims. . . .

This reading of the statute protects those who engage in pure speech and association ordinarily protected by the First Amendment. But it does not protect that activity where a defendant purposefully intends it to help terrorism or where a defendant knows (or willfully blinds himself to the fact) that the activity is significantly likely to assist terrorism. . . . *Cf. Brandenburg.* At the same time, this reading does not require the Government to undertake the difficult task of proving which, as between peaceful and nonpeaceful purposes, a defendant specifically preferred; knowledge is enough. . . .

Having interpreted the statute to impose the *mens rea* requirement just described, I would remand the cases so that the lower courts could consider more specifically the precise activities in which the plaintiffs still wish to engage and determine whether and to what extent a grant of declaratory and injunctive relief were warranted. . . .

That is why, with respect, I dissent.

NOTES AND QUESTIONS

1. *Not strict enough?* The Court has acknowledged that upholding a content-based law is an extremely rare occurrence. *Humanitarian Law Project* is the *only* case in which a Supreme Court majority upholds a content-based law under strict scrutiny. Is the Court appropriately skeptical of the content-based "material support" law? Did the government present strong empirical evidence that expressive forms of support like education and more tangible forms such as donating money or providing weapons are "fungible"? Did the majority require the same kind of empirical showing that it insisted on in *Entertainment Merchants Assn.*? Is "respect" for the government's national security interests warranted? Does the Court's distinction between "independent" and "coordinated" speech provide the requisite "narrow tailoring" under strict scrutiny?
2. *Strict scrutiny breakdown?* A few other content-based laws have survived application of strict scrutiny. Consider Williams-Yulee v. Florida Bar, 575 U.S. 433 (2015). In *Williams-Yulee,* the Court upheld a content-based Florida ethics canon barring judicial candidates from personally soliciting campaign donations. The plurality concluded the government's interest in maintaining the public's confidence in an impartial judiciary was "compelling." It applied the "narrow tailoring" requirement flexibly, such that government was not required to address other judicial expression that also implicated its compelling interests. The Court observed that "a law need not address all aspects of a problem in one fell swoop." In dissent, Justice Kennedy observed: "The Court's evisceration of [strict scrutiny] now risks long-term harm to what was once the Court's own preferred First Amendment test." Justice Scalia's dissent described the Court's approach in *Williams-Yulee* as "the appearance of strict scrutiny." Finally, Justice Alito's dissent derided the Court's judgment as "seriously impair[ing] strict scrutiny." What "long-term harms" might follow a "watering-down" of the strict scrutiny standard? Is there a connection between the dissenters' concerns in *Williams-Yulee* and those expressed by Justice Kagan in *Reed* regarding application of strict scrutiny to *all* content-based laws?

D. SPEAKER IDENTITY DISTINCTIONS

Reed v. Town of Gilbert suggested that certain speaker-based speech regulations may be content-based and hence subject to strict scrutiny. Suppose governments favor or disfavor corporate speakers to "level the playing field" or "equalize" opportunities to engage in political discourse. Should such regulations be viewed as invalid content-based suppressions of speech or justified interventions in the political marketplace? First Amendment theorist Alexander Meiklejohn posited that government interventions in the marketplace of political ideas could enhance and improve the process of democratic self-government. *See* Alexander Meiklejohn, *Free Speech and Its Relation to Self-Government* 22-23 (1948) (arguing that the marketplace of political ideas might require government regulation, with the government serving as a "chairman or moderator" who will "call[ ] the meeting to order" and then structure it by ensuring that "certain rules of order will be observed."). From this vantage point, government regulations that equalize the ability of would-be speakers to communicate enhance rather than distort the marketplace of political ideas. This approach also ensures that the electorate enjoys broad exposure to diverse and conflicting points of view. To date, however, the Supreme Court has emphatically rejected this approach and generally invalidated government efforts to equalize speakers through regulation. In the campaign finance context, the Court has concluded that money facilitates political expression, Buckley v. Valeo, 424 U.S. 1 (1976), and has invalidated efforts to restrict independent campaign expenditures by corporations and wealthy candidates. (Rules governing contributions and coordinated expenditures are more complex and typically receive coverage in classes on election law.) Citizens United v. Federal Election Comm'n, 558 U.S. 310 (2010), excerpted below, illustrates the Court's approach to speaker-based restrictions on political speech.

Citizens United v. Federal Election Commission

558 U.S. 310 (2010)

KENNEDY, J., delivered the opinion of the Court.

[*Citizens United* involved a highly critical and partisan documentary about the Democratic presidential candidate Hillary Clinton. The documentary was sponsored by Citizens United, a nonprofit corporation devoted to advancing conservative causes. Citizens United planned to offer the movie on a pay-per-view or "video-on-demand" basis in the weeks preceding the 2008 presidential primary. However, the Federal Election Commission found that the movie was an "electioneering communication" under a federal law (the BCRA), which prohibited corporations and unions from making independent expenditures from general treasury funds for "electioneering communications," defined as publicly distributed "broadcast, cable or satellite communication[s]" referring to a "clearly identified candidate" for federal elective office, within 30 days of a primary or 60 days of a general election. The BCRA allowed corporations and unions to make electioneering communications or engage in express advocacy for or against candidates, but only if they established "separate segregated funds" limited to donations from the corporation's employees or stockholders or the union's members. Relatively few took advantage of this provision, however, because of the difficulty of establishing such funds.

The district court granted summary judgment for the FEC, denying Citizens United's request for declaratory and injunctive relief. The Supreme Court granted certiorari and held, by a 5-4 margin, that the BCRA's ban on electioneering communications by corporations and unions was unconstitutional and that the government may not prevent them from tapping into their general treasury funds to support or oppose candidates for federal elective office, so long as the expenditures of funds are not coordinated with candidates. The decision not only allowed corporations to engage in electioneering communications; it also allowed them to engage in political speech during elections on an equal footing with individual citizens by allowing for payments for political advertisements from general treasury funds. In reaching its broad holding, the Court overturned two prior cases: McConnell v. Federal Election Comm'n, 540 U.S. 93 (2003), which had upheld the principal features of the BCRA, and Austin v. Michigan Chamber of Commerce, 494 U.S. 652 (1990), which had supported banning independent expenditures by corporations and unions to support or oppose candidates.]

III

The First Amendment provides that "Congress shall make no law . . . abridging the freedom of speech." Laws enacted to control or suppress speech may operate at different points in the speech process. The following are just a few examples of restrictions that have been attempted at different stages of the speech process-all laws found to be invalid: restrictions requiring a permit at the outset, Watchtower Bible & Tract Soc. of N.Y., Inc. v. Village of Stratton, 536 U.S. 150, 153 (2002); imposing a burden by impounding proceeds on receipts or royalties, Simon & Schuster, Inc. v. Members of N.Y. State Crime Victims Bd., 502 U.S. 105, 108, 123 (1991); seeking to exact a cost after the speech occurs, New York Times Co. v. Sullivan, 376 U. S., at 267; and subjecting the speaker to criminal penalties, Brandenburg v. Ohio, 395 U.S. 444, 445 (1969) *(per curiam).*

The law before us is an outright ban, backed by criminal sanctions. Section 441b makes it a felony for all corporations—including nonprofit advocacy corporations—either to expressly advocate the election or defeat of candidates or to broadcast electioneering communications within 30 days of a primary election and 60 days of a general election. Thus, the following acts would all be felonies under § 441b: The Sierra Club runs an ad, within the crucial phase of 60 days before the general election, that exhorts the public to disapprove of a Congressman who favors logging in national forests; the National Rifle Association publishes a book urging the public to vote for the challenger because the incumbent U.S. Senator supports a handgun ban; and the American Civil Liberties Union creates a Web site telling the public to vote for a Presidential candidate in light of that candidate's defense of free speech. These prohibitions are classic examples of censorship.

Section 441b is a ban on corporate speech notwithstanding the fact that a PAC created by a corporation can still speak. A PAC is a separate association from the corporation. So the PAC exemption from § 441b's expenditure ban, § 441b(b)(2), does not allow corporations to speak. Even if a PAC could somehow allow a corporation to speak—and it does not—the option to form PACs does not alleviate the First Amendment problems with § 441b. PACs are burdensome alternatives; they are expensive to administer and subject to extensive regulations. . . .

. . . This might explain why fewer than 2,000 of the millions of corporations in this country have PACs. PACs, furthermore, must exist before they can speak. Given the onerous restrictions, a corporation may not be able to establish a PAC in time to make its views known regarding candidates and issues in a current campaign.

Section 441b's prohibition on corporate independent expenditures is thus a ban on speech. As a "restriction on the amount of money a person or group can spend on political communication during a campaign," that statute "necessarily reduces the quantity of expression by restricting the number of issues discussed, the depth of their exploration, and the size of the audience reached." *Buckley v. Valeo*[]. Were the Court to uphold these restrictions, the Government could repress speech by silencing certain voices at any of the various points in the speech process. If § 441b applied to individuals, no one would believe that it is merely a time, place, or manner restriction on speech. Its purpose and effect are to silence entities whose voices the Government deems to be suspect.

Speech is an essential mechanism of democracy, for it is the means to hold officials accountable to the people. The right of citizens to inquire, to hear, to speak, and to use information to reach consensus is a precondition to enlightened self-government and a necessary means to protect it. The First Amendment "'has its fullest and most urgent application' to speech uttered during a campaign for political office."

For these reasons, political speech must prevail against laws that would suppress it, whether by design or inadvertence. Laws that burden political speech are "subject to strict scrutiny," which requires the Government to prove that the restriction "furthers a compelling interest and is narrowly tailored to achieve that interest." While it might be maintained that political speech simply cannot be banned or restricted as a categorical matter, the quoted language [from a prior case] provides a sufficient framework for protecting the relevant First Amendment interests in this case. We shall employ it here.

Premised on mistrust of governmental power, the First Amendment stands against attempts to disfavor certain subjects or viewpoints. Prohibited, too, are restrictions distinguishing among different speakers, allowing speech by some but not others. As instruments to censor, these categories are interrelated: Speech restrictions based on the identity of the speaker are all too often simply a means to control content.

Quite apart from the purpose or effect of regulating content, moreover, the Government may commit a constitutional wrong when by law it identifies certain preferred speakers. By taking the right to speak from some and giving it to others, the Government deprives the disadvantaged person or class of the right to use speech to strive to establish worth, standing, and respect for the speaker's voice. The Government may not by these means deprive the public of the right and privilege to determine for itself what speech and speakers are worthy of consideration. The First Amendment protects speech and speaker, and the ideas that flow from each.

. . . [I]t is inherent in the nature of the political process that voters must be free to obtain information from diverse sources in order to determine how to cast their votes. . . .

We find no basis for the proposition that, in the context of political speech, the Government may impose restrictions on certain disfavored speakers. Both history and logic lead us to this conclusion.

[A.1.] The Court has recognized that First Amendment protection extends to corporations.

This protection has been extended by explicit holdings to the context of political speech. Under the rationale of these precedents, political speech does not lose First Amendment protection "simply because its source is a corporation." *Bellotti*; *see Pacific Gas & Elec. Co. v. Public Util. Comm'n of Cal.*, (plurality opinion). The Court has thus rejected the argument that political speech of corporations or other associations should be treated differently under the First Amendment simply because such associations are not "natural persons."

In *Buckley*, the Court addressed various challenges to the Federal Election Campaign Act of 1971 (FECA) as amended in 1974. [*Buckley* upheld limits on direct contributions to candidates based on prevention of corruption and the appearance of corruption, since large contributions could be used to "secure a political quid pro quo"; however, *Buckley* struck down limits on independent expenditures because they did not serve the government's anti-corruption interests. *Buckley* failed to address the FECA's ban on independent expenditures by corporations and unions, which was recodified] at 2 U.S.C. § 441b four months after *Buckley* was decided. Section 441b is the independent expenditure restriction challenged here.

Less than two years after *Buckley, Bellotti* reaffirmed the First Amendment principle that the Government cannot restrict political speech based on the speaker's corporate identity. *Bellotti* could not have been clearer when it struck down a state-law prohibition on corporate independent expenditures related to referenda issues[.] . . . [*Bellotti*] rested on the principle that the Government lacks the power to ban corporations from speaking.

Bellotti did not address the constitutionality of the State's ban on corporate independent expenditures to support candidates. In our view, however, that restriction would have been unconstitutional under *Bellotti*'s central principle: that the First Amendment does not allow political speech restrictions based on a speaker's corporate identity.

Thus the law stood until *Austin. Austin* "uph[eld] a direct restriction on the independent expenditure of funds for political speech for the first time in [this Court's] history." 494 U.S., at 695 (Kennedy, J., dissenting). There, the Michigan Chamber of Commerce sought to use general treasury funds to run a newspaper ad supporting a specific candidate. Michigan law, however, prohibited corporate independent expenditures that supported or opposed any candidate for state office. A violation of the law was punishable as a felony. The Court sustained the speech prohibition.

To bypass *Buckley* and *Bellotti*, the *Austin* Court identified a new governmental interest in limiting political speech: an antidistortion interest. *Austin* found a compelling governmental interest in preventing "the corrosive and distorting effects of immense aggregations of wealth that are accumulated with the help of the corporate form and that have little or no correlation to the public's support for the corporation's political ideas."

[B.] The Court is thus confronted with conflicting lines of precedent: a pre-*Austin* line that forbids restrictions on political speech based on the speaker's corporate identity and a post-*Austin* line that permits them. No case before *Austin* had held that Congress could prohibit independent expenditures for political speech based on the speaker's corporate identity. . . .

If the First Amendment has any force, it prohibits Congress from fining or jailing citizens, or associations of citizens, for simply engaging in political speech. If the antidistortion rationale were to be accepted, however, it would permit Government to ban political speech simply because the speaker is an association that has taken on the corporate form. The Government contends that *Austin* permits it to ban corporate expenditures for almost all forms of communication stemming from a corporation. If *Austin* were correct, the Government could prohibit a corporation from expressing political views in media beyond those presented here, such as by printing books. The Government responds "that the FEC has never applied this statute to a book," and if it did, "there would be quite [a] good as-applied challenge." Tr. of Oral Arg. 65 (Sept. 9, 2009). This troubling assertion of brooding governmental power cannot be reconciled with the confidence and stability in civic discourse that the First Amendment must secure.

Political speech is "indispensable to decisionmaking in a democracy, and this is no less true because the speech comes from a corporation rather than an individual." *Bellotti*. . . . *Buckley* rejected the premise that the Government has an interest "in equalizing the relative ability of individuals and groups to influence the outcome of elections." *Buckley* was specific in stating that "the skyrocketing cost of political campaigns" could not sustain the governmental prohibition. The First Amendment's protections do not depend on the speaker's "financial ability to engage in public discussion."

. . . The rule that political speech cannot be limited based on a speaker's wealth is a necessary consequence of the premise that the First Amendment generally prohibits the suppression of political speech based on the speaker's identity.

. . . It is irrelevant for purposes of the First Amendment that corporate funds may "have little or no correlation to the public's support for the corporation's political ideas." All speakers, including individuals and the media, use money amassed from the economic marketplace to fund their speech. The First Amendment protects the resulting speech, even if it was enabled by economic transactions with persons or entities who disagree with the speaker's ideas.

Austin's antidistortion rationale would produce the dangerous, and unacceptable, consequence that Congress could ban political speech of media corporations. Media corporations are now exempt from § 441b's ban on corporate expenditures. Yet media corporations accumulate wealth with the help of the corporate form, the largest media corporations have "immense aggregations of wealth," and the views expressed by media corporations often "have little or no correlation to the public's support" for those views. Thus, under the Government's reasoning, wealthy media corporations could have their voices diminished to put them on par with other media entities. . . .

. . . *Austin* interferes with the "open marketplace" of ideas protected by the First Amendment. It permits the Government to ban the political speech of millions of associations of citizens. *See* Statistics of Income 2 (5.8 million for-profit corporations filed 2006 tax returns). Most of these are small corporations without large amounts of wealth. *See* Supp. Brief for Chamber of Commerce of the United States of America as *Amicus Curiae* 1, 3 (96% of the 3 million businesses that belong to the U.S. Chamber of Commerce have fewer than 100 employees); M. Keightley, Congressional Research Service Report for Congress, Business Organizational Choices: Taxation and Responses to Legislative Changes 10 (2009) (more than 75% of corporations whose income is taxed under federal law, see 26 U.S.C. § 301, have less than $1 million in receipts per year). This fact belies the Government's argument that the statute is justified on the ground that it prevents the "distorting effects of immense aggregations of wealth." It is not even aimed at amassed wealth.

The censorship we now confront is vast in its reach. The Government has "muffle[d] the voices that best represent the most significant segments of the economy." And "the electorate [has been] deprived of information, knowledge and opinion vital to its function." By suppressing the speech of manifold corporations, both for-profit and nonprofit, the Government prevents their voices and viewpoints from reaching the public and advising voters on which persons or entities are hostile to their interests. Factions will necessarily form in our Republic, but the remedy of "destroying the liberty" of some factions is "worse than the disease." The Federalist No. 10, p. 130 (B. Wright ed. 1961) (J. Madison). Factions should be checked by permitting them all to speak, and by entrusting the people to judge what is true and what is false.

The purpose and effect of this law is to prevent corporations, including small and nonprofit corporations, from presenting both facts and opinions to the public. . . . References to massive corporate treasuries should not mask the real operation of this law. Rhetoric ought not obscure reality.

. . . When Government seeks to use its full power, including the criminal law, to command where a person may get his or her information or what distrusted source he or she may not hear, it uses censorship to control thought. This is unlawful. The First Amendment confirms the freedom to think for ourselves.

What we have said also shows the invalidity of other arguments made by the Government. For the most part relinquishing the antidistortion rationale, the Government falls back on the argument that corporate political speech can be banned in order to prevent corruption or its appearance. . . . [But l]imits on independent expenditures, such as § 441b, have a chilling effect extending well beyond the Government's interest in preventing *quid pro quo* corruption. . . .

. . . When *Buckley* identified a sufficiently important governmental interest in preventing corruption or the appearance of corruption, that interest was limited to *quid pro quo* corruption. The fact that speakers may have influence over or access to elected officials does not mean that these officials are corrupt[.] Reliance on a "generic favoritism or influence theory . . . is at odds with standard First Amendment analyses because it is unbounded and susceptible to no limiting principle."

The appearance of influence or access, furthermore, will not cause the electorate to lose faith in our democracy. By definition, an independent expenditure is political speech presented to the electorate that is not coordinated with a candidate. The fact that a corporation, or any other speaker, is willing to spend money to try to persuade voters presupposes that the people have the ultimate influence over elected officials. . . .

. . . If elected officials succumb to improper influences from independent expenditures; if they surrender their best judgment; and if they put expediency before principle, then surely there is cause for concern. We must give weight to attempts by Congress to seek to dispel either the appearance or the reality of these influences. The remedies enacted by law, however, must comply with the First Amendment; and, it is our law and our tradition that more speech, not less, is the governing rule. An outright ban on corporate political speech during the critical preelection period is not a permissible remedy. Here Congress has created categorical bans on speech that are asymmetrical to preventing *quid pro quo* corruption.

. . . For the reasons above, it must be concluded that *Austin* was not well reasoned. . . . *Austin* is undermined by experience since its announcement. Political speech is so ingrained in our culture that speakers find ways to circumvent campaign finance laws. . . . Our Nation's speech dynamic is changing, and informative voices should not have to circumvent onerous restrictions to exercise their First Amendment rights. Speakers have become adept at presenting citizens with sound bites, talking points, and scripted messages that dominate the 24-hour news cycle. Corporations, like individuals, do not have monolithic views. On certain topics corporations may possess valuable expertise, leaving them the best equipped to point out errors or fallacies in speech of all sorts, including the speech of candidates and elected officials.

Rapid changes in technology—and the creative dynamic inherent in the concept of free expression—counsel against upholding a law that restricts political speech in certain media or by certain speakers. Today, 30-second television ads may be the most effective way to convey a political message. Soon, however, it may be that Internet sources, such as blogs and social networking Web sites, will provide citizens with significant information about political candidates and issues. Yet, § 441b would seem to ban a blog post expressly advocating the election or defeat of a candidate if that blog were created with corporate funds. The First Amendment does not permit Congress to make these categorical distinctions based on the corporate identity of the speaker and the content of the political speech.

. . . *Austin* should be and now is overruled. We return to the principle established in *Buckley* and *Bellotti* that the Government may not suppress political speech on the basis of the speaker's corporate identity. No sufficient governmental interest justifies limits on the political speech of nonprofit or for-profit corporations. . . .

Chief Justice ROBERTS filed a concurring opinion, in which Justice ALITO joined.

Justice SCALIA filed a concurring opinion, in which Justice ALITO joined and Justice THOMAS joined in part.

Justice STEVENS, with whom Justice GINSBURG, Justice BREYER, and Justice SOTOMAYOR join, concurring in part and dissenting in part.

The real issue in this case concerns how, not if, the appellant may finance its electioneering. Citizens United is a wealthy nonprofit corporation that runs a political action committee (PAC) with millions of dollars in assets. Under the Bipartisan Campaign Reform Act of 2002 (BCRA), it could have used those assets to televise and promote *Hillary: The Movie* wherever and whenever it wanted to. It also could have spent unrestricted sums to broadcast *Hillary* at any time other than the 30 days before the last primary election. Neither Citizens United's nor any other corporation's speech has been "banned." All that the parties dispute is whether Citizens United had a right to use the funds in its general treasury to pay for broadcasts during the 30–day period. The notion that the First Amendment dictates an affirmative answer to that question is, in my judgment, profoundly misguided. Even more misguided is the notion that the Court must rewrite the law relating to campaign expenditures by *for-profit* corporations and unions to decide this case.

The basic premise underlying the Court's ruling is its iteration, and constant reiteration, of the proposition that the First Amendment bars regulatory distinctions based on a speaker's identity, including its "identity" as a corporation. While that glittering generality has rhetorical appeal, it is not a correct statement of the law. Nor does it tell us when a corporation may engage in electioneering that some of its shareholders oppose. It does not even resolve the specific question whether Citizens United may be required to finance some of its messages with the money in its PAC. The conceit that corporations must be treated identically to natural persons in the political sphere is not only inaccurate but also inadequate to justify the Court's disposition of this case.

In the context of election to public office, the distinction between corporate and human speakers is significant. Although they make enormous contributions to our society, corporations are not actually members of it. They cannot vote or run for office. Because they may be managed and controlled by nonresidents, their interests may conflict in fundamental respects with the interests of eligible voters. The financial resources, legal structure, and instrumental orientation of corporations raise legitimate concerns about their role in the electoral process. Our lawmakers have a compelling constitutional basis, if not also a democratic duty, to take measures designed to guard against the potentially deleterious effects of corporate spending in local and national races.

. . . Like its paeans to unfettered discourse, the Court's denunciation of identity-based distinctions may have rhetorical appeal but it obscures reality.

. . . Apart perhaps from measures designed to protect the press, [the text of the First Amendment] might seem to permit no distinctions of any kind. Yet in a variety of contexts, we have held that speech can be regulated differentially on account of the speaker's identity, when identity is understood in categorical or institutional terms. The Government routinely places special restrictions on the speech rights of students, prisoners, members of the Armed Forces, foreigners, and its own employees. When such restrictions are justified by a legitimate governmental interest, they do not necessarily raise constitutional problems. In contrast to the blanket rule that the majority espouses, our cases recognize that the Government's interests may be more or less compelling with respect to different classes of speakers, cf. Minneapolis Star & Tribune Co. v. Minnesota Comm'r of Revenue, 460 U.S. 575, 585) (1983) ("[D]ifferential treatment" is constitutionally suspect "*unless* justified by some special characteristic" of the regulated class of speakers (emphasis added)), and that the constitutional rights of certain categories of speakers, in certain contexts, "'are not automatically coextensive with the rights'" that are normally accorded to members of our society.

The free speech guarantee thus does not render every other public interest an illegitimate basis for qualifying a speaker's autonomy; society could scarcely function if it did. It is fair to say that our First Amendment doctrine has "frowned on" certain identity-based distinctions, particularly those that may reflect invidious discrimination or preferential treatment of a politically powerful group. But it is simply incorrect to suggest that we have prohibited all legislative distinctions based on identity or content. Not even close.

. . . As we have unanimously observed, legislatures are entitled to decide "that the special characteristics of the corporate structure require particularly careful regulation" in an electoral context. Not only has the distinctive potential of corporations to corrupt the electoral process long been recognized, but within the area of campaign finance, corporate spending is also "furthest from the core of political expression, since corporations' First Amendment speech and association interests are derived largely from those of their members and of the public in receiving information." Campaign finance distinctions based on corporate identity tend to be less worrisome, in other words, because the "speakers" are not natural persons, much less members of our political community, and the governmental interests are of the highest order. Furthermore, when corporations, as a class, are distinguished from noncorporations, as a class, there is a lesser risk that regulatory distinctions will reflect invidious discrimination or political favoritism.

If taken seriously, our colleagues' assumption that the identity of a speaker has *no* relevance to the Government's ability to regulate political speech would lead to some remarkable conclusions. Such an assumption would have accorded the propaganda broadcasts to our troops by "Tokyo Rose" during World War II the same protection as speech by Allied commanders. More pertinently, it would appear to afford the same protection to multinational corporations controlled by foreigners as to individual Americans: To do otherwise, after all, could "'enhance the relative voice'" of some (*i.e.,* humans) over others (*i.e.,* nonhumans). Under the majority's majority's view, I suppose it may be a First Amendment problem that corporations are not permitted to vote, given that voting is, among other things, a form of speech.

In short, the Court dramatically overstates its critique of identity-based distinctions, without ever explaining why corporate identity demands the same treatment as individual identity. Only the most wooden approach to the First Amendment could justify the unprecedented line it seeks to draw.

. . . On numerous occasions we have recognized Congress' legitimate interest in preventing the money that is spent on elections from exerting an "'undue influence on an officeholder's judgment'" and from creating "'the appearance of such influence,'" beyond the sphere of *quid pro quo* relationships. Corruption can take many forms. Bribery may be the paradigm case. But the difference between selling a vote and selling access is a matter of degree, not kind. And selling access is not qualitatively different from giving special preference to those who spent money on one's behalf. Corruption operates along a spectrum, and the majority's apparent belief that *quid pro quo* arrangements can be neatly demarcated from other improper influences does not accord with the theory or reality of politics. It certainly does not accord with the record Congress developed in passing BCRA, a record that stands as a remarkable testament to the energy and ingenuity with which corporations, unions, lobbyists, and politicians may go about scratching each other's backs—and which amply supported Congress' determination to target a limited set of especially destructive practices.

. . . *Austin* recognized that there are substantial reasons why a legislature might conclude that unregulated general treasury expenditures will give corporations "unfai[r] influence" in the electoral process, and distort public debate in ways that undermine rather than advance the interests of listeners. The legal structure of corporations allows them to amass and deploy financial resources on a scale few natural persons can match.

. . . Corporate "domination" of electioneering can generate the impression that corporations dominate our democracy. When citizens turn on their televisions and radios before an election and hear only corporate electioneering, they may lose faith in their capacity, as citizens, to influence public policy. A Government captured by corporate interests, they may come to believe, will be neither responsive to their needs nor willing to give their views a fair hearing. The predictable result is cynicism and disenchantment: an increased perception that large spenders "'call the tune'" and a reduced "'willingness of voters to take part in democratic governance.'" To the extent that corporations are allowed to exert undue influence in electoral races, the speech of the eventual winners of those races may also be chilled. Politicians who fear that a certain corporation can make or break their reelection chances may be cowed into silence about that corporation. On a variety of levels, unregulated corporate electioneering might diminish the ability of citizens to "hold officials accountable to the people," and disserve the goal of a public debate that is "uninhibited, robust, and wide-open," New York Times Co. v. Sullivan, 376 U.S. 254, 270 (1964).

. . . None of this is to suggest that corporations can or should be denied an opportunity to participate in election campaigns or in any other public forum (much less that a work of art such as *Mr. Smith Goes to Washington* may be banned), or to deny that some corporate speech may contribute significantly to public debate. What it shows, however, is that *Austin*'s "concern about corporate domination of the political process," reflects more than a concern to protect governmental interests outside of the First Amendment. It also reflects a concern to *facilitate* First Amendment values by preserving some breathing room around the electoral "marketplace" of ideas, the marketplace in which the actual people of this Nation determine how they will govern themselves. The majority seems oblivious to the simple truth that laws such as § 203 do not merely pit the anticorruption interest against the First Amendment, but also pit competing First Amendment values against each other. There are, to be sure, serious concerns with any effort to balance the First Amendment rights of speakers against the First Amendment rights of listeners. But when the speakers in question are not real people and when the appeal to "First Amendment principles" depends almost entirely on the listeners' perspective, it becomes necessary to consider how listeners will actually be affected.

. . . In a democratic society, the longstanding consensus on the need to limit corporate campaign spending should outweigh the wooden application of judge-made rules. The majority's rejection of this principle "elevate[s] corporations to a level of deference which has not been seen at least since the days when substantive due process was regularly used to invalidate regulatory legislation thought to unfairly impinge upon established economic interests." *Bellotti*, 435 U.S., at 817, n. 13 (White, J., dissenting). At bottom, the Court's opinion is thus a rejection of the common sense of the American people, who have recognized a need to prevent corporations from undermining self-government since the founding, and who have fought against the distinctive corrupting potential of corporate electioneering since the days of Theodore Roosevelt. It is a strange time to repudiate that common sense. While American democracy is imperfect, few outside the majority of this Court would have thought its flaws included a dearth of corporate money in politics.

NOTES AND QUESTIONS

1. *Speaker-based restrictions.* Is the law in *Citizens United* based on the content of speech or is it a content-neutral time, place, or manner regulation? Recall the Court's statement in *Reed* that "[c]haracterizing a distinction

as speaker based is only the beginning—not the end—of the inquiry." As the Court observed: "Thus, a law limiting the content of newspapers, but only newspapers, could not evade strict scrutiny simply because it could be characterized as speaker based." Is the distinction drawn by the law in *Citizens United* of this character? Or is it more similar to the speaker-based distinctions Justice Stevens identifies, which the Court has allowed?

2. *Strict scrutiny.* Do you agree the government lacks a compelling interest in limiting corporate expenditures in political campaigns? Why does the Court reject anti-distortion as a compelling interest? Should the *appearance* of corruption be sufficient to justify the law's corporate expenditure limits?
3. *Money as/and speech.* The Court has not said the money *is* speech. However, it did say in *Buckley* that "virtually every means of communicating ideas in today's mass society requires the expenditure of money." Does regulation of the conditions necessary to effective communication constitute regulation of speech? Or is regulation of corporate campaign expenditures more akin to regulation of property?
4. *Corporate speech.* As the Court notes in *Citizens United*, although they are not natural persons, corporations are protected by the First Amendment. This protection extends to unions, media organizations, and other entities. In his partial dissent, Justice Stevens argues that "corporate domination of politics" poses a "distinctive threat to democratic integrity," thus justifying restrictions on independent corporate expenditures in campaigns. Do you agree? Or should corporate speech be protected, as the majority argued, owing to the contributions it makes to political discourse?
5. *Mistrust of government as the basis for* Citizens United. Is the Court correct in stating that the First Amendment is "premised on mistrust of government"? What is the basis of this mistrust: government fallibility, government tyranny, or something else? Does this mistrust adequately justify the result in the case?
6. *Meiklejohn vs. the Court.* Who has the better argument—Alexander Meiklejohn or the Supreme Court? Does government regulation that seeks to ensure a diverse and open marketplace of political ideas succeed only in distorting or tilting the political playing field? Or, in the era of fake news and dominant social media platforms like Facebook ("Meta") and Twitter, is government regulation essential to ensuring a fair and open process of democratic deliberation?

E. CONTENT-NEUTRAL SPEECH REGULATIONS AND INTERMEDIATE SCRUTINY

As we have seen, First Amendment doctrine draws a distinction between content-based laws, which are presumptively invalid, and content-neutral speech regulations. Time, place, and manner regulations are one type of content-neutral speech regulation. This type of regulation, which is discussed in greater detail in

Chapter 5, is introduced here as a point of contrast to content-based regulations. Time, place, and manner regulations are subject to an "intermediate" standard of judicial scrutiny. Note the significant differences between the "strict" and "intermediate" levels of scrutiny in the following decision.

Ward v. Rock Against Racism

491 U.S. 781 (1989)

Justice KENNEDY delivered the opinion of the Court.

In the southeast portion of New York City's Central Park, about 10 blocks upward from the park's beginning point at 59th Street, there is an amphitheater and stage structure known as the Naumberg Acoustic Bandshell. The bandshell faces west across the remaining width of the park. In close proximity to the bandshell, and lying within the directional path of its sound, is a grassy open area called the Sheep Meadow. The city has designated the Sheep Meadow as a quiet area for passive recreations like reclining, walking, and reading. Just beyond the park, and also within the potential sound range of the bandshell, are the apartments and residences of Central Park West.

This case arises from the city's attempt to regulate the volume of amplified music at the bandshell so the performances are satisfactory to the audience without intruding upon those who use the Sheep Meadow or live on Central Park West and in its vicinity. The city's regulation requires bandshell performers to use sound-amplification equipment and a sound technician provided by the city. The challenge to this volume control technique comes from the sponsor of a rock concert. The trial court sustained the noise control measures, but the Court of Appeals for the Second Circuit reversed. We granted certiorari to resolve the important First Amendment issues presented by the case.

. . . [W]e decide the case as one in which the bandshell is a public forum for performances in which the government's right to regulate expression is subject to the protections of the First Amendment. Our cases make clear, however, that even in a public forum the government may impose reasonable restrictions on the time, place, or manner of protected speech, provided the restrictions "are justified without reference to the content of the regulated speech, that they are narrowly tailored to serve a significant governmental interest, and that they leave open ample alternative channels for communication of the information." Clark v. Community for Creative Non-Violence, 468 U. S. 288, 293 (1984). We consider these requirements in turn.

A

The principal inquiry in determining content neutrality, in speech cases generally and in time, place, or manner cases in particular, is whether the government has adopted a regulation of speech because of disagreement with the message it conveys. The government's purpose is the controlling consideration. A regulation that serves purposes unrelated to the content of expression is deemed neutral, even if it has an incidental effect on some speakers or messages but not others.

Government regulation of expressive activity is content neutral so long as it is "*justified* without reference to the content of the regulated speech." *Community for Creative Non-Violence* (emphasis added).

The principal justification for the sound-amplification guideline is the city's desire to control noise levels at bandshell events, in order to retain the character of the Sheep Meadow and its more sedate activities, and to avoid undue intrusion into residential areas and other areas of the park. This justification has nothing to do with content and it satisfies the requirement that time, place, or manner regulations be content neutral.

The only other justification offered below was the city's interest in "ensur[ing] the quality of sound at Bandshell events." Respondent urges that this justification is not content neutral because it is based upon the quality, and thus the content, of the speech being regulated. In respondent's view, the city is seeking to assert artistic control over performers at the bandshell by enforcing a bureaucratically determined, value-laden conception of good sound. . . .

While respondent's arguments that the government may not interfere with artistic judgment may have much force in other contexts, they are inapplicable to the facts of this case. The city has disclaimed in express terms any interest in imposing its own view of appropriate sound mix on performers. To the contrary, as the District Court found, the city requires its sound technician to defer to the wishes of event sponsors concerning sound mix.

. . . The city's regulation is narrowly tailored to serve a significant governmental interest. Despite respondent's protestations to the contrary, it can no longer be doubted that government "ha[s] a substantial interest in protecting its citizens from unwelcome noise." City Council of Los Angeles v. Taxpayers for Vincent, 466 U. S. 789, 806 (1984). This interest is perhaps at its greatest when government seeks to protect the well-being, tranquility, and privacy of the home, but it is by no means limited to that context, for the government may act to protect even such traditional public forums as city streets and parks from excessive noise. We think it also apparent that the city's interest in ensuring the sufficiency of sound amplification at bandshell events is a substantial one. The record indicates that inadequate sound amplification has had an adverse affect on the ability of some audiences to hear and enjoy performances at the bandshell. The city enjoys a substantial interest in ensuring the ability of its citizens to enjoy whatever benefits the city parks have to offer, from amplified music to silent meditation.

The Court of Appeals recognized the city's substantial interest in limiting the sound emanating from the bandshell. The court concluded, however, that the city's sound-amplification guideline was not narrowly tailored to further this interest, because "it has not [been] shown . . . that the requirement of the use of the city's sound system and technician was the *least intrusive means* of regulating the volume." (Emphasis added.) In the court's judgment, there were several alternative methods of achieving the desired end that would have been less restrictive of respondent's First Amendment rights.

The Court of Appeals erred in sifting through all the available or imagined alternative means of regulating sound volume in order to determine whether the city's solution was "the least intrusive means" of achieving the desired end. This less-restrictive-alternative analysis . . . has never been a part of the inquiry into the validity of a time, place, and manner regulation. Instead, our cases quite clearly hold that restrictions on the time, place, or manner of protected speech are not invalid "simply because there is some imaginable alternative that might be less burdensome on speech." United States v. Albertini, 472 U. S. 675, 689 (1985).

The Court of Appeals apparently drew its least-intrusive-means requirement from United States v. O'Brien, 391 U.S. 367 (1968) [*infra* Chapter 4], the case in which we established the standard for judging the validity of restrictions on expressive conduct. The court's reliance was misplaced, however, for we have held that the *O'Brien* test "in the last analysis is little, if any, different from the standard applied to time, place, or manner restrictions." *Community for Creative Non-Violence*. . . .

Lest any confusion on the point remain, we reaffirm today that a regulation of the time, place, or manner of protected speech must be narrowly tailored to serve the government's legitimate, content-neutral interests but that it need not be the least restrictive or least intrusive means of doing so. Rather, the requirement of narrow tailoring is satisfied "so long as the . . . regulation promotes a substantial government interest that would be achieved less effectively absent the regulation." To be sure, this standard does not mean that a time, place, or manner regulation may burden substantially more speech than is necessary to further the government's legitimate interests. Government may not regulate expression in such a manner that a substantial portion of the burden on speech does not serve to advance its goals. . . . So long as the means chosen are not substantially broader than necessary to achieve the government's interest, however, the regulation will not be invalid simply because a court concludes that the government's interest could be adequately served by some less-speech-restrictive alternative. The validity of [time, place, or manner] regulations does not turn on a judge's agreement with the responsible decisionmaker concerning the most appropriate method for promoting significant government interests or the degree to which those interests should be promoted.

It is undeniable that the city's substantial interest in limiting sound volume is served in a direct and effective way by the requirement that the city's sound technician control the mixing board during performances. Absent this requirement, the city's interest would have been served less well, as is evidenced by the complaints about excessive volume generated by respondent's past concerts. The alternative regulatory methods hypothesized by the Court of Appeals reflect nothing more than a disagreement with the city over how much control of volume is appropriate or how that level of control is to be achieved. The Court of Appeals erred in failing to defer to the city's reasonable determination that its interest in controlling volume would be best served by requiring bandshell performers to utilize the city's sound technician.

The city's second content-neutral justification for the guideline, that of ensuring "that the sound amplification [is] sufficient to reach all listeners within the defined concert-ground," also supports the city's choice of regulatory methods. By providing competent sound technicians and adequate amplification equipment, the city eliminated the problems of inexperienced technicians and insufficient sound volume that had plagued some bandshell performers in the past. No doubt this concern is not applicable to respondent's concerts, which apparently were characterized by more-than-adequate sound amplification. [However,] the regulation's effectiveness must be judged by considering all the varied groups that use the bandshell, and it is valid so long as the city could reasonably have determined that its interests overall would be served less effectively without the sound-amplification guideline than with it. Considering these proffered justifications together, therefore, it is apparent that the guideline directly furthers the city's legitimate governmental interests and that those interests would have been less well served in the absence of the sound-amplification guideline. . . .

C

The final requirement, that the guideline leave open ample alternative channels of communication, is easily met. Indeed, in this respect the guideline is far less restrictive than regulations we have upheld in other cases, for it does not attempt to ban any particular manner or type of expression at a given place or time. Cf. *Frisby v. Schultz,* 487 U.S. 474 (1988); *Community for Creative Non-Violence.* Rather, the guideline continues to permit expressive activity in the bandshell, and has no effect on the quantity or content of that expression beyond regulating the extent of amplification. That the city's limitations on volume may reduce to some degree the potential audience for respondent's speech is of no consequence, for there has been no showing that the remaining avenues of communication are inadequate.

The city's sound-amplification guideline is narrowly tailored to serve the substantial and content-neutral governmental interests of avoiding excessive sound volume and providing sufficient amplification within the bandshell concert ground, and the guideline leaves open ample channels of communication. Accordingly, it is valid under the First Amendment as a reasonable regulation of the place and manner of expression. The judgment of the Court of Appeals is reversed.

Justice BLACKMUN concurs in the result.

Justice MARSHALL, with whom Justice BRENNAN and Justice STEVENS join, dissenting.

No one can doubt that government has a substantial interest in regulating the barrage of excessive sound that can plague urban life. Unfortunately, the majority plays to our shared impatience with loud noise to obscure the damage that it does to our First Amendment rights. Until today, a key safeguard of free speech has been government's obligation to adopt the least intrusive restriction necessary to achieve its goals. By abandoning the requirement that time, place, and manner regulations must be narrowly tailored, the majority replaces constitutional scrutiny with mandatory deference. The majority's willingness to give government officials a free hand in achieving their policy ends extends so far as to permit, in this case, government control of speech in advance of its dissemination.

My complaint is with the majority's serious distortion of the narrow tailoring requirement. Our cases have not, as the majority asserts, "clearly" rejected a less-restrictive-alternative test. On the contrary, just last Term, we held that a statute is narrowly tailored only "if it targets and eliminates no more than the exact source of the 'evil' it seeks to remedy." *Frisby.* While there is language in a few opinions which, taken out of context, supports the majority's position, in practice, the Court has interpreted the narrow tailoring requirement to mandate an examination of alternative methods of serving the asserted governmental interest and a determination whether the greater efficacy of the challenged regulation outweighs the increased burden it places on protected speech. . . .

The Court's past concern for the extent to which a regulation burdens speech more than would a satisfactory alternative is noticeably absent from today's decision. The majority requires only that government show that its interest cannot be served as effectively without the challenged restriction. It will be enough, therefore, that the challenged regulation advances the government's interest only in the slightest, for any differential burden on speech that results does not enter the calculus. Despite its protestations to the contrary, the majority thus has abandoned the requirement that restrictions on speech be narrowly tailored in any ordinary use of the phrase. . . .

True, the majority states that "[g]overnment may not regulate expression in such a manner that a substantial portion of the burden on speech does not serve to advance its goals." But this means that only those regulations that "engage in the gratuitous inhibition of expression" will be invalidated. Moreover, the majority has robbed courts of the necessary analytic tools to make even this limited inquiry. The Court of Appeals examined "how much control of volume is appropriate [and] how that level of control is to be achieved," but the majority admonishes that court for doing so, stating that it should have "defer[red] to the city's reasonable determination." The majority thus instructs courts to refrain from examining how much speech may be restricted to serve an asserted interest and how that level of restriction is to be achieved. If a court cannot engage in such inquiries, I am at a loss to understand how a court can ascertain whether the government has adopted a regulation that burdens substantially more speech than is necessary.

Had the majority not abandoned the narrow tailoring requirement, the Guidelines could not possibly survive constitutional scrutiny. Government's interest in avoiding loud sounds cannot justify giving government total control over sound equipment, any more than its interest in avoiding litter could justify a ban on handbill distribution. In both cases, government's legitimate goals can be effectively and less intrusively served by directly punishing the evil—the persons responsible for excessive sounds and the persons who litter. Indeed, the city concedes that it has an ordinance generally limiting noise but has chosen not to enforce it.

By holding that the Guidelines are valid time, place, and manner restrictions, notwithstanding the availability of less intrusive but effective means of controlling volume, the majority deprives the narrow tailoring requirement of all meaning. Today, the majority enshrines efficacy but sacrifices free speech.

NOTES AND QUESTIONS

1. *Strict v. intermediate scrutiny.* What are the principal differences between "strict" scrutiny and the "intermediate" scrutiny standard applied in *Rock Against Racism*? Does "intermediate" scrutiny give too much deference to government speech regulators? In *Rock Against Racism* the dissenters sharply criticized the majority's application of the "narrow tailoring" requirement. Do you agree the standard, as interpreted, prevents courts from effectively reviewing time, place, or manner regulations? If government is aiming at noise reduction but incidentally affects expression is there less reason to be skeptical of its judgments and policies?

2. *Levels of scrutiny.* As the decisions in this chapter demonstrate, the Court has adopted a "tiered" approach to judicial scrutiny of speech regulations. Not all Justices are comfortable with this approach. In his concurrence in *Alvarez,* Justice Breyer suggests the "tiers" are merely benchmarks and advocates for what he refers to as a "proportionality" approach. That approach would focus on "the seriousness of the speech-related harm the provision will likely cause, the nature and importance of the provision's countervailing objectives, the extent to which the provision will tend to achieve those objectives, and whether there are other, less restrictive ways of doing so." *Alvarez,* 567 U.S. at 730 (Breyer, J., concurring). Is that a better or clearer standard than either strict or intermediate scrutiny?
3. *The effect of content-neutral speech regulations. Rock Against Racism* applies less rigorous scrutiny to content-neutral speech regulations. But are content-neutral restrictions less worrisome in terms of First Amendment values than content-based ones? Consider the following observations:

> The most puzzling aspect of the distinction between content-based and content-neutral restrictions is that either restriction reduces the sum total of information or opinions disseminated. . . . Whatever rationale one adopts for the constitutional protection of speech, the goals behind the rationale are undermined by any limitation on expression, content-based or not. For example, if one adopts the principle that the purpose of the first amendment is to facilitate the democratic process by making individuals better informed voters, regulations that limit expression on content-neutral grounds should be as suspect as content-based regulations, since they may also undermine this value. . . .
>
> The content distinction is conceptually and pragmatically untenable and should therefore be abandoned. . . . Instead, the courts should subject all restrictions on expression to the same critical scrutiny traditionally reserved for regulations drawn in terms of content.

Martin H. Redish, *The Content Distinction in First Amendment Analysis,* 34 Stan. L. Rev. 113, 128-129, 142 (1981).

Chapter 4

"Secondary Effects" and Expressive Conduct

Table of Contents

A. Regulating the "Secondary Effects" of Speech

B. Regulating Conduct with an Expressive Element

1. Draft Card Burning
2. Flag Desecration
3. Nude Dancing

Chapter 3 examined the First Amendment's content neutrality doctrine. This chapter focuses on some complications the Court has encountered in applying the content neutrality principle. The Court has struggled to explain why zoning laws targeting sexually explicit content should nevertheless receive a less exacting level of judicial scrutiny. Localities have justified these laws based on the "secondary effects" associated with adult theaters, which purportedly include sexual assault and other crimes. The Court has also encountered difficulties applying the content neutrality standard to regulations of conduct that have an expressive element. The latter cases raise two questions: (1) whether the conduct should be considered "speech," such that its regulation triggers the First Amendment, and (2) if so, what standard of scrutiny should apply to regulations of expressive conduct.

A. *REGULATING THE "SECONDARY EFFECTS" OF SPEECH*

Renton v. Playtime Theatres, Inc.

475 U.S. 41 (1986)

Justice Rehnquist delivered the opinion of the Court.

[The city of Renton, Washington, enacted a zoning ordinance that prohibited adult motion picture theaters—defined as those showing films with "specified sexual activities"—from locating within 1,000 feet of any residential zone, family dwelling, church, park, or school. Playtime Theatres, Inc. sought a declaratory judgment that the Renton ordinance violated the First and Fourteenth Amendments and an injunction against the ordinance's enforcement.]

. . . The Renton ordinance . . . does not ban adult theaters altogether, but merely provides that such theaters may not be located within 1,000 feet of any residential zone, single- or multiple-family dwelling, church, park, or school. The ordinance is therefore properly analyzed as a form of time, place, and manner regulation.

Describing the ordinance as a time, place, and manner regulation is, of course, only the first step in our inquiry. This Court has long held that regulations enacted for the purpose of restraining speech on the basis of its content presumptively violate the First Amendment. *See* Police Dep't v. Mosley, 408 U.S. 92 (1972). On the other hand, so-called "content-neutral" time, place, and manner regulations are acceptable so long as they are designed to serve a substantial governmental interest and do not unreasonably limit alternative avenues of communication.

At first glance, the Renton ordinance . . . does not appear to fit neatly into either the "content-based" or the "content-neutral" category. To be sure, the ordinance treats theaters that specialize in adult films differently from other kinds of theaters. Nevertheless, as the District Court concluded, the Renton ordinance is aimed not at the *content* of the films shown at "adult motion picture theatres," but rather at the *secondary effects* of such theaters on the surrounding community. The . . . City Council's "*predominate* concerns" were with the secondary effects of adult theaters, and not with the content of adult films themselves.

[This] finding as to "predominate" intent . . . is more than adequate to establish that the city's pursuit of its zoning interests here was unrelated to the suppression of free expression. The ordinance by its terms is designed to prevent crime, protect the city's retail trade, maintain property values, and generally "protec[t] and preserv[e] the quality of [the city's] neighborhoods, commercial districts, and the quality of urban life," not to suppress the expression of unpopular views. . . .

In short, the Renton ordinance is completely consistent with our definition of "content-neutral" speech regulations as those that "are *justified* without reference to the content of the regulated speech." The ordinance does not contravene the fundamental principle that underlies our concern about "content-based" speech regulations: that "government may not grant the use of a forum to people whose views it finds acceptable, but deny use to those wishing to express less favored or more controversial views." *Mosley*. . . .

The appropriate inquiry in this case, then, is whether the Renton ordinance is designed to serve a substantial governmental interest and allows for reasonable alternative avenues of communication. It is clear that the ordinance meets such a standard. . . . [A] city's "interest in attempting to preserve the quality of urban life is one that must be accorded high respect."

. . . Finally, turning to the question whether the Renton ordinance allows for reasonable alternative avenues of communication, we note that the ordinance leaves some 520 acres, or more than five percent of the entire land area of Renton, open to use as adult theater sites. . . . Respondents argue, however, that some of the land in question is already occupied by existing businesses, that "practically none" of the undeveloped land is currently for sale or lease, and that in general there are no "commercially viable" adult theater sites within the 520 acres left open by the Renton ordinance. . . .

. . . That respondents must fend for themselves in the real estate market, on an equal footing with other prospective purchasers and lessees, does not give rise to a First Amendment violation. And although we have cautioned against the enactment of zoning regulations that have "the effect of suppressing, or greatly restricting access to, lawful speech," we have never suggested that the First Amendment compels the Government to ensure that adult theaters, or any other kinds of speech-related businesses for that matter, will be able to obtain sites at bargain prices. . . .

Reversed.

Justice BLACKMUN concurs in the result.

Justice BRENNAN, with whom Justice MARSHALL joins, dissenting.

. . . The Court asserts that the ordinance is "aimed not at the *content* of the films shown at 'adult motion picture theatres,' but rather at the *secondary effects* of such theaters on the surrounding community," and thus is simply a time, place, and manner regulation. This analysis is misguided. . . . The fact that adult movie theaters may cause harmful "secondary" land-use effects may arguably give Renton a compelling reason to regulate such establishments; it does not mean, however, that such regulations are content neutral.

The ordinance discriminates on its face against certain forms of speech based on content. Movie theaters specializing in "adult motion pictures" may not be located within 1,000 feet of any residential zone, single- or multiple-family dwelling, church, park, or school. Other motion picture theaters, and other forms of "adult entertainment," such as bars, massage parlors, and adult bookstores, are not subject to the same restrictions. This selective treatment strongly suggests that Renton was interested not in controlling the "secondary effects" associated with adult businesses, but in discriminating against adult theaters based on the content of the films they exhibit. The Court ignores this discriminatory treatment, declaring that Renton is free "to address the potential problems created by one particular kind of adult business," and to amend the ordinance in the future to include other adult enterprises. However, because of the First Amendment interests at stake here, this one-step-at-a-time analysis is wholly inappropriate. . . .

Even assuming that the ordinance should be treated like a content-neutral time, place, and manner restriction, I would still find it unconstitutional. . . . [R]espondents are not on equal footing with other prospective purchasers and lessees, but must conduct business under severe restrictions not imposed upon other establishments. . . . [R]espondents do not ask Renton to guarantee low-price sites for their businesses, but seek only a reasonable opportunity to operate adult theaters in the city. By denying them this opportunity, Renton can effectively ban a form of protected speech from its borders. The ordinance "greatly restrict[s] access to . . . lawful speech" and is plainly unconstitutional.

NOTES AND QUESTIONS

1. Renton *and* Reed. The *Renton* majority's treatment of the zoning ordinance appears to be at odds with *Reed v. Town of Gilbert* (*supra* Chapter 3). *Reed* states that a facially discriminatory law is content-based regardless of any content-neutral justification for its enactment. The *Reed* majority ignored *Renton* and certainly did not explicitly overrule it. Justice Kagan's

concurring opinion in *Reed* treated *Renton* as reflecting the Court's "flexibility" in approaching content-based regulations. Does *Renton* survive *Reed*?

2. *"Erogenous zoning."* In *Renton*, the Court sustained a zoning ordinance that limited adult businesses to within "1,000 feet of another regulated use." A decade earlier, the Court upheld an ordinance restricting adult businesses from locating within "500 feet of a residential use." Young v. American Mini Theatres, Inc., 427 U.S. 50, 72-73 (1976). More recently, the Court upheld an ordinance that prohibited more than one adult entertainment business in the same building. City of Los Angeles v. Alameda Books, Inc., 535 U.S. 425 (2002). The net effect of these regulations, which disperse or concentrate regulated establishments, can make large portions of a city essentially "off limits" to adult businesses. How does the Court respond to this concern in *Renton*? What message do these decisions send to local zoning officials?
3. *Speech and downstream "effects."* Under the logic of "secondary effects," speech may be regulated even if it is not intrinsically harmful because it produces harmful "effects." That logic could apply to a lot of expression. For example, leafleting produces litter on public streets and sidewalks. Governments have, from time to time, attempted to regulate or ban leafleting because of its secondary effect of causing increased litter. However, in contexts other than "adult entertainment," the Court has rejected such arguments out of hand. Instead, the Court has counseled local and state governments to punish those who litter, rather than silence those seeking to distribute pamphlets and engage in other expression. *See, e.g.*, Schneider v. New Jersey, 308 U.S. 147 (1939) (invalidating ban on public distribution of leaflets). Why doesn't the Court apply that principle in *Renton*?
4. *Speech regulation and "secondary effects."* What dangers are associated with more broadly applying the "secondary effects" rationale referred to in *Renton*? Consider the following:

   > Restrictions on free expression are rarely defended on the ground that the state simply didn't like what the defendant was saying; reference will generally be made to some danger beyond the message, such as a danger of riot, unlawful action or violent overthrow of the government. Thus in *Brandenburg* the state's defense was not that the speech in question was distasteful, though it surely was, but rather that speeches of that sort were likely to induce people to take the law into their own hands.

   John Hart Ely, *Flag Desecration: A Case Study in the Roles of Categorization and Balancing in First Amendment Analysis*, 88 Harv. L. Rev. 1482, 1496 (1975); *see also* David Hudson, Jr., *The Secondary Effects Doctrine: "The Evisceration of First Amendment Freedoms,"* 37 Washburn L.J. 55, 93 (1997).
5. *The limits of secondary effects.* The Court has not extended the "secondary effects" rationale beyond zoning ordinances targeting adult establishments and public indecency laws as applied to nude dancing (*see* discussion *infra*). Even concerning the zoning of adult establishments, in the Court's most recent decision on the subject, *Alameda Books*, only a plurality relied on "secondary effects." In other contexts, the Court has explicitly rejected

secondary effects reasoning. *See* City of Cincinnati v. Discovery Network, Inc., 507 U.S. 410 (1993) (rejecting secondary effects analysis as inapplicable to law banning distribution of commercial news racks on public sidewalks); Boos v. Barry, 485 U.S. 312 (1988) (law banning offensive displays near foreign embassies was not aimed at secondary effects, but rather at the primary effect of the audience's reaction to speech); R.A.V. v. City of St. Paul, 505 U.S. 377 (1992) (law prohibiting certain kinds of symbolic fighting words was not aimed at the secondary effects of speech).

B. *REGULATING CONDUCT WITH AN EXPRESSIVE ELEMENT*

The Supreme Court has recognized that the First Amendment extends to "more than simply the right to talk and to write." Dallas v. Stanglin, 490 U.S. 19, 25 (1989). What counts as communication for purposes of the Free Speech Clause? Some cases are easy—so easy, in fact, that we never stop to consider whether the activity in question counts as speech: distributing leaflets, giving an address at a political rally, marching in a parade, and showing a motion picture on environmental issues all count as obvious attempts at communication or "speech." Other acts lack any serious communicative element—chewing gum, taking out the garbage, or driving down an Interstate highway. Some physical acts can be communicative or non-communicative depending upon the context in which they occur. Burning a flag, for example, may be a simple act of vandalism or it may be an act of protest against government policies. *See* Texas v. Johnson, 491 U.S. 397 (1989); Spence v. Washington, 418 U.S. 405 (1974). Camping overnight in a park may be a recreational activity or a symbolic act of protest against homelessness, *see* Clark v. Community for Creative Non-Violence, 468 U.S. 288 (1984), or economic conditions, *see www.occupywallstreet.org.* The act of dancing may also be a recreational activity, *see Stanglin,* or it may be expressive of some thought or idea, *see, e.g.,* Barnes v. Glen Theatre, Inc., 501 U.S. 560 (1991) (finding nude dancing to be expressive conduct "marginally" within the "outer perimeters of the First Amendment"). What are the boundaries of the concept of "expressive conduct"? Does it extend even to some criminal actions, such that perpetrators can claim they are exercising First Amendment rights?

Assuming an act is sufficiently "expressive," how should laws that burden expressive conduct be analyzed under the First Amendment? How does the content discrimination framework discussed in Chapter 3 apply to such laws? This section explores how the Court determines when conduct is sufficiently expressive to trigger First Amendment scrutiny and examines the First Amendment standards that apply to regulations of expressive conduct.

1. *Draft Card Burning*

Prior to and during the Vietnam war, young men at age eighteen were required by law to register with their local draft boards. Each was classified according to his fitness for service and issued a draft card noting his name, age, and draft status. During the mid-1960s, young men burned their draft cards as an iconic way of protesting the Vietnam war. In 1965, Congress amended federal law to make it a crime to knowingly destroy or mutilate a draft card. The law was challenged in the following case.

United States v. O'Brien

391 U.S. 367 (1968)

Mr. Chief Justice WARREN delivered the opinion of the Court.

On the morning of March 31, 1966, David Paul O'Brien and three companions burned their Selective Service registration certificates on the steps of the South Boston Courthouse. A sizable crowd, including several agents of the Federal Bureau of Investigation, witnessed the event. . . .

For this act, O'Brien was indicted, tried, convicted, and sentenced in the United States District Court for the District of Massachusetts. He did not contest the fact that he had burned the certificate. He stated in argument to the jury that he burned the certificate publicly to influence others to adopt his antiwar beliefs, as he put it, "so that other people would reevaluate their positions with Selective Service, with the armed forces, and reevaluate their place in the culture of today, to hopefully consider my position."

The indictment upon which he was tried charged that he "willfully and knowingly did mutilate, destroy, and change by burning (his) Registration; in violation of [50 U.S.C. § 462(b)]." Section 462(b) is part of the Universal Military Training and Service Act of 1948. Section 462(b)(3) . . . was amended by Congress in 1965 . . . so that at the time O'Brien burned his certificate an offense was committed by any person, "who forges, alters, *knowingly destroys, knowingly mutilates*, or in any manner changes any such certificate. . . ." [The Court alternatively refers to the law as § 12(b)(3), which refers to the Act rather than the United States Code. –EDS.]

[T]he Court of Appeals for the First Circuit held the 1965 Amendment unconstitutional as a law abridging freedom of speech. At the time the Amendment was enacted, a regulation of the Selective Service System required registrants to keep their registration certificates in their "personal possession at all times." Wilful violations of regulations promulgated pursuant to the Universal Military Training and Service Act were made criminal by statute. The Court of Appeals, therefore, was of the opinion that conduct punishable under the 1965 Amendment was already punishable under the nonpossession regulation, and consequently that the Amendment served no valid purpose; further, that in light of the prior regulation, the Amendment must have been "directed at public as distinguished from private destruction." On this basis, the court concluded that the 1965 Amendment ran afoul of the First Amendment by singling out persons engaged in protests for special treatment. . . .

We hold that the 1965 Amendment is constitutional both as enacted and as applied. We therefore vacate the judgment of the Court of Appeals and reinstate the judgment and sentence of the District Court. . . .

I

. . . We note at the outset that the 1965 Amendment plainly does not abridge free speech on its face, and we do not understand O'Brien to argue otherwise. Amended § 12(b)(3) on its face deals with conduct having no connection with speech. It prohibits the knowing destruction of certificates issued by the Selective Service System, and there is nothing necessarily expressive about such conduct. The Amendment does not distinguish between public and private destruction, and it does not punish only destruction engaged in for the purpose of expressing views. *Compare* Stromberg v. California, 283 U.S. 359 (1931). A law prohibiting destruction of Selective Service certificates no more abridges free speech on its face than a motor vehicle law prohibiting the destruction of drivers' licenses, or a tax law prohibiting the destruction of books and records.

O'Brien nonetheless argues that the 1965 Amendment is unconstitutional in its application to him, and is unconstitutional as enacted because what he calls the "purpose" of Congress was "to suppress freedom of speech." We consider these arguments separately.

II

O'Brien first argues that the 1965 Amendment is unconstitutional as applied to him because his act of burning his registration certificate was protected "symbolic speech" within the First Amendment. His argument is that the freedom of expression which the First Amendment guarantees includes all modes of "communication of ideas by conduct," and that his conduct is within this definition because he did it in "demonstration against the war and against the draft."

We cannot accept the view that an apparently limitless variety of conduct can be labeled "speech" whenever the person engaging in the conduct intends thereby to express an idea. However, even on the assumption that the alleged communicative element in O'Brien's conduct is sufficient to bring into play the First Amendment, it does not necessarily follow that the destruction of a registration certificate is constitutionally protected activity. This Court has held that when "speech" and "nonspeech" elements are combined in the same course of conduct, a sufficiently important governmental interest in regulating the nonspeech element can justify incidental limitations on First Amendment freedoms. To characterize the quality of the governmental interest which must appear, the Court has employed a variety of descriptive terms: compelling; substantial; subordinating; paramount; cogent; strong. Whatever imprecision inheres in these terms, we think it clear that a government regulation is sufficiently justified if it is within the constitutional power of the Government; if it furthers an important or substantial governmental interest; if the governmental interest is unrelated to the suppression of free expression; and if the incidental restriction on alleged First Amendment freedoms is no greater than is essential to the furtherance of that interest. We find that the 1965 Amendment to § 12(b)(3) of the Universal Military Training and Service Act meets all of these requirements, and consequently that O'Brien can be constitutionally convicted for violating it.

The constitutional power of Congress to raise and support armies and to make all laws necessary and proper to that end is broad and sweeping. . . . Pursuant to this power, Congress may establish a system of registration for individuals liable for training and service, and may require such individuals within reason to cooperate in the registration system. The issuance of certificates indicating the registration and eligibility classification of individuals is a legitimate and substantial administrative aid in the functioning of this system. And legislation to insure the continuing availability of issued certificates serves a legitimate and substantial purpose in the system's administration. . . .

Many . . . purposes [in addition to notification] would be defeated by the certificates' destruction or mutilation. Among these are:

1. The registration certificate serves as proof that the individual described thereon has registered for the draft. The classification certificate shows the eligibility classification of a named but undescribed individual. . . . Correspondingly, the availability of the certificates for such display relieves the Selective Service System of the administrative burden it would otherwise have in verifying the registration and classification of all suspected delinquents. . . .

2. The information supplied on the certificates facilitates communication between registrants and local boards, simplifying the system and benefiting all concerned. To begin with, each certificate bears the address of the registrant's local board, an item unlikely to be committed to memory. Further, each card bears the registrant's Selective Service number, and a registrant who has his number readily available so that he can communicate it to his local board when he supplies or requests information can make simpler the board's task in locating his file. . . .

3. Both certificates carry continual reminders that the registrant must notify his local board of any change of address, and other specified changes in his status. The smooth functioning of the system requires that local boards be continually aware of the status and whereabouts of registrants, and the destruction of certificates deprives the system of a potentially useful notice device.

4. The regulatory scheme involving Selective Service certificates includes clearly valid prohibitions against the alteration, forgery, or similar deceptive misuse of certificates. The destruction or mutilation of certificates obviously increases the difficulty of detecting and tracing abuses such as these. Further, a mutilated certificate might itself be used for deceptive purposes. . . .

We think it apparent that the continuing availability to each registrant of his Selective Service certificates substantially furthers the smooth and proper functioning of the system that Congress has established to raise armies. We think it also apparent that the Nation has a vital interest in having a system for raising armies that functions with maximum efficiency and is capable of easily and quickly responding to continually changing circumstances. For these reasons, the Government has a substantial interest in assuring the continuing availability of issued Selective Service certificates.

It is equally clear that the 1965 Amendment specifically protects this substantial governmental interest. We perceive no alternative means that would more precisely and narrowly assure the continuing availability of issued Selective Service certificates than a law which prohibits their wilful mutilation or destruction. . . . The 1965 Amendment prohibits such conduct and does nothing more. In other words, both the governmental interest and the operation of the 1965 Amendment are limited to the noncommunicative aspect of O'Brien's conduct. The governmental interest and the scope of the 1965 Amendment are limited to preventing harm to the smooth and efficient functioning of the Selective Service System. When O'Brien deliberately rendered unavailable his registration certificate, he wilfully frustrated this governmental interest. For this noncommunicative impact of his conduct, and for nothing else, he was convicted.

The case at bar is therefore unlike one where the alleged governmental interest in regulating conduct arises in some measure because the communication allegedly integral to the conduct is itself thought to be harmful. In *Stromberg*, for example, this Court struck down a statutory phrase which punished people who expressed their "opposition to organized government" by displaying "any flag, badge, banner, or device." Since the statute there was aimed at suppressing communication it could not be sustained as a regulation of noncommunicative conduct. . . .

III

O'Brien finally argues that the 1965 Amendment is unconstitutional as enacted because what he calls the "purpose" of Congress was "to suppress freedom of speech." We reject this argument because under settled principles the purpose of Congress, as O'Brien uses that term, is not a basis for declaring this legislation unconstitutional.

It is a familiar principle of constitutional law that this Court will not strike down an otherwise constitutional statute on the basis of an alleged illicit legislative motive. . . .

Inquiries into congressional motives or purposes are a hazardous matter. When the issue is simply the interpretation of legislation, the Court will look to statements by legislators for guidance as to the purpose of the legislature, because the benefit to sound decision-making in this circumstance is thought sufficient to risk the possibility of misreading Congress' purpose. It is entirely a different matter when we are asked to void a statute that is, under well-settled criteria, constitutional on its face, on the basis of what fewer than a handful of Congressmen said about it. What motivates one legislator to make a speech about a statute is not necessarily what motivates scores of others to enact it, and the stakes are sufficiently high for us to eschew guesswork. We decline to void essentially on the ground that it is unwise legislation which Congress had the undoubted power to enact and which could be reenacted in its exact form if the same or another legislator made a "wiser" speech about it. . . .

There was little floor debate on this legislation in either House. Only Senator Thurmond commented on its substantive features in the Senate. After his brief statement, and without any additional substantive comments, the bill, H.R. 10306, passed the Senate. In the House debate only two Congressmen addressed themselves to the Amendment—Congressmen Rivers and Bray. The bill was passed after their statements without any further debate by a vote of 393 to 1. It is principally on the basis of the statements by these three Congressmen that O'Brien makes his congressional "purpose" argument. We note that if we were to examine legislative purpose in the instant case, we would be obliged to consider not only these statements but also the more authoritative reports of the Senate and House Armed Services

Committees. The portions of those reports explaining the purpose of the Amendment are reproduced in the Appendix in their entirety. While both reports make clear a concern with the "defiant" destruction of so-called "draft cards" and with "open" encouragement to others to destroy their cards, both reports also indicate that this concern stemmed from an apprehension that unrestrained destruction of cards would disrupt the smooth functioning of the Selective Service System. . . .

[T]he Court of Appeals . . . should have affirmed the judgment of conviction entered by the District Court.

Mr. Justice MARSHALL took no part in the consideration or decision of these cases.

[Justice HARLAN's concurring opinion is omitted.]

[Justice DOUGLAS's dissenting opinion is omitted.]

It is so ordered.

NOTES AND QUESTIONS

1. *Questioning the speech/conduct distinction.* Is burning a draft card as part of a political protest "speech"? Is it possible to distinguish speech from conduct for First Amendment purposes? Consider the following positions by two eminent legal scholars. Who has the better argument?

   > The guiding principle must be to determine which element is predominant in the conduct under consideration. Is expression the major element and the action only secondary? Or is the action the essence and the expression incidental? The answer, to a great extent, must be based on a common-sense reaction, made in light of the functions and operations of a system of freedom of expression.

   Thomas I. Emerson, *The System of Freedom of Expression* 80 (1970).

   > [B]urning a draft card to express opposition to the draft is an undifferentiated whole, 100% action and 100% expression. It involves no conduct that is not at the same time communication, and no communication that does not result from conduct. Attempts to determine which element 'predominates' will therefore inevitably degenerate into question-begging judgments about whether the activity should be protected.

   John Hart Ely, *Flag Desecration: A Case Study in the Roles of Categorization and Balancing in First Amendment Analysis*, 88 Harv. L. Rev. 1482, 1495 (1975).
2. *When is conduct sufficiently expressive?* In *O'Brien* the Court assumes the burning of the draft card is sufficiently expressive to merit First Amendment consideration. However, it also cautions that "[w]e cannot accept the view that an apparently limitless variety of conduct can be labeled 'speech' whenever the person engaging in the conduct intends thereby to express

an idea." Clearly, not every form of conduct is expressive. But note the Court does not offer any test or standard by which to determine whether conduct is sufficiently expressive to constitute "speech" under the First Amendment. In *Spence v. Washington* (1974), *infra* p. 146, the Court offers one possible standard for making this determination.

3. *The* O'Brien *standard.* As discussed in Chapter 3, the Supreme Court has developed a "tiered scrutiny" approach to speech regulations. Under that approach, if a law is content-based strict scrutiny applies. However, as *Ward v. Rock Against Racism* (p. 129, *supra*) shows, content-neutral "time, place, or manner" speech regulations are subject to a less demanding "intermediate" scrutiny standard. *O'Brien* sets forth an early version of an "intermediate scrutiny" standard, applicable to conduct regulations that incidentally burden expression. Under *O'Brien,* laws that incidentally burden expression but are content-neutral—meaning the governmental interest is "unrelated to the suppression of free expression"—must further an important or substantial governmental interest and any incidental restriction on speech must be "no greater than essential" to the furtherance of that interest. As we will see, the Court has stated there is little, if any, difference between the *O'Brien* and "time, place, and manner" standards. Clark v. Community for Creative Non-Violence, 468 U.S. 288 (1984).
4. *Applying intermediate scrutiny in* O'Brien. Did the government meet its burden under the four-factor test in *O'Brien*? Congress clearly has the power to enact laws raising and supporting armies. *See* U.S. Const., art. I. Are the government's interests "substantial" or "important," or were they "plausible but little more"? *See* Ely, *supra,* at 1486 n.17. Was the federal law "no greater than is essential" to further the government's interests? What other alternatives did the government have? What other avenues or channels of communication were open to O'Brien?
5. *Motive versus purpose.* Was the legislature's reason for enacting the law in *O'Brien* "unrelated to free expression"? Suppose there was evidence that many members of Congress wanted to prevent draft card burning, which was a common form of protesting the Vietnam War, owing to its perceived negative effect on wartime morale and public support for the war. Should the central question be what the legislature aimed at, or what it hit? Note the Court concludes the federal law is content-neutral and declines to inquire into what it calls the "motive" of the legislature. The Court obviously must inquire into governmental *purpose* when determining whether a law is content-based or content-neutral. What does the Court examine to determine purpose, and how is this different from legislative motivation? For discussion, see Robert Post, *Recuperating First Amendment Doctrine,* 47 Stan. L. Rev. 1249, 1268 (1995). Why is the Court so reluctant to inquire into the subjective motivation of legislators when in other constitutional areas it considers the motivation of administrative and executive decisions? *See, e.g.*, Yick Wo v. Hopkins, 118 U.S. 356 (1886).

2. *Flag Desecration*

Concerns about mistreatment of, or disrespect for, the U.S. flag date to before World War I. In 1907, before the Supreme Court applied the First Amendment to the states, the Supreme Court upheld the conviction of a company that had printed the American flag on the label of a beer bottle in violation of a state law criminalizing use of the flag in advertisements. Halter v. Nebraska, 205 U.S. 34 (1907). Later during the Vietnam War era, the Court reversed the conviction of Sidney Street for uttering contemptuous words about the flag as he burned it. Street v. New York, 394 U.S. 576 (1969). The Court did not decide whether Street could be convicted solely for burning the flag, as opposed to speaking contemptuously about it. In *Spence v. Washington* (1974), which follows, the Court directly addressed the use of the U.S. flag to express opposition to war.

Spence v. Washington

418 U.S. 405 (1974)

PER CURIAM.

Appellant displayed a United States flag, which he owned, out of the window of his apartment. Affixed to both surfaces of the flag was a large peace symbol fashioned of removable tape. Appellant was convicted under a Washington statute forbidding the exhibition of a United States flag to which is attached or superimposed figures, symbols, or other extraneous material. The Supreme Court of Washington affirmed appellant's conviction. It rejected appellant's contentions that the statute under which he was charged, on its face and as applied, contravened the First Amendment, as incorporated by the Fourteenth Amendment, and was void for vagueness. . . . We reverse on the ground that as applied to appellant's activity the Washington statute impermissibly infringed protected expression.

I

On May 10, 1970, appellant, a college student, hung his United States flag from the window of his apartment on private property in Seattle, Washington. The flag was upside down, and attached to the front and back was a peace symbol (i.e., a circle enclosing a trident) made of removable black tape. The window was above the ground floor. The flag measured approximately three by five feet and was plainly visible to passersby. The peace symbol occupied roughly half of the surface of the flag.

Three Seattle police officers observed the flag and entered the apartment house. They were met at the main door by appellant, who said: "I suppose you are here about the flag. I didn't know there was anything wrong with it. I will take it down." Appellant permitted the officers to enter his apartment, where they seized the flag and arrested him. Appellant cooperated with the officers. There was no disruption or altercation.

[Spence was charged under a Washington law that provided: "No person shall, in any manner, for exhibition or display: (1) Place or cause to be placed any word, figure, mark, picture, design, drawing or advertisement of any nature upon any flag, standard, color, ensign or shield of the United States or of this state . . . or (2) Expose to public view any such flag, standard, color, ensign or shield upon which shall have been printed, painted or otherwise produced, or to which shall have been attached, appended, affixed or annexed any such word, figure, mark, picture, design, drawing or advertisement."]

The State based its case on the flag itself and the testimony of the three arresting officers, who testified that they had observed the flag displayed from appellant's window and that on the flag was superimposed what they identified as a peace symbol. Appellant took the stand in his own defense. He testified that he put a peace symbol on the flag and displayed it to public view as a protest against the invasion of Cambodia and the killings at Kent State University, events which occurred a few days prior to his arrest. He said that his purpose was to associate the American flag with peace instead of war and violence: "I felt there had been so much killing and that this was not what America stood for. I felt that the flag stood for America and I wanted people to know that I thought America stood for peace."

Appellant further testified that he chose to fashion the peace symbol from tape so that it could be removed without damaging the flag. The State made no effort to controvert any of appellant's testimony.

The trial court instructed the jury in essence that the mere act of displaying the flag with the peace symbol attached, if proved beyond a reasonable doubt, was sufficient to convict. There was no requirement of specific intent to do anything more than display the flag in that manner. The jury returned a verdict of guilty. The court sentenced appellant to 10 days in jail, suspended, and to a $75 fine. . . .

II

A number of factors are important in the instant case. First, this was a privately owned flag. In a technical property sense it was not the property of any government. We have no doubt that the State or National Governments constitutionally may forbid anyone from mishandling in any manner a flag that is public property. But this is a different case. Second, appellant displayed his flag on private property. He engaged in no trespass or disorderly conduct. Nor is this a case that might be analyzed in terms of reasonable time, place, or manner restraints on access to a public area. Third, the record is devoid of proof of any risk of breach of the peace. It was not appellant's purpose to incite violence or even stimulate a public demonstration. There is no evidence that any crowd gathered or that appellant made any effort to attract attention beyond hanging the flag out of his own window. Indeed, on the facts stipulated by the parties there is no evidence that anyone other than the three police officers observed the flag.

Fourth, the State concedes, as did the Washington Supreme Court, that appellant engaged in a form of communication. Although the stipulated facts fail to show that any member of the general public viewed the flag, the State's concession is inevitable on this record. The undisputed facts are that appellant "wanted people to know that I thought America stood for peace." To be sure, appellant did not choose to articulate his views through printed or spoken words. It is therefore necessary to determine whether his activity was sufficiently imbued with elements of communication to fall within the scope of the First and Fourteenth Amendments, for as the Court noted in [*United States v. O'Brien*], "(w)e cannot accept the view that an apparently limitless variety of conduct can be labeled 'speech' whenever the person engaging in the conduct intends thereby to express an idea." But the nature of appellant's activity, combined with the factual context and environment in which it was undertaken, lead to the conclusion that he engaged in a form of protected expression.

The Court for decades has recognized the communicative connotations of the use of flags. . . . In many of their uses flags are a form of symbolism comprising a "primitive but effective way of communicating ideas . . . ," and "a short cut from mind to mind." West Virginia State Board of Education v. Barnette, 319 U.S. 624, 632 (1943). On this record there can be little doubt that appellant communicated through the use of symbols. The symbolism included not only the flag but also the superimposed peace symbol.

Moreover, the context in which a symbol is used for purposes of expression is important, for the context may give meaning to the symbol. *See* Tinker v. Des Moines Independent Community School District, 393 U.S. 503 (1969). In *Tinker*, the wearing of black armbands in a school environment conveyed an unmistakable message about a contemporaneous issue of intense public concern—the Vietnam hostilities. In this case, appellant's activity was roughly simultaneous with and concededly triggered by the Cambodian incursion and the Kent State tragedy, also issues of great public moment. A flag bearing a peace symbol and displayed upside down by a student today might be interpreted as nothing more than bizarre behavior, but it would have been difficult for the great majority of citizens to miss the drift of appellant's point at the time that he made it.

It may be noted, further, that this was not an act of mindless nihilism. Rather, it was a pointed expression of anguish by appellant about the then-current domestic and foreign affairs of his government. An intent to convey a particularized message was present, and in the surrounding circumstances the likelihood was great that the message would be understood by those who viewed it.

We are confronted then with a case of prosecution for the expression of an idea through activity. Moreover, the activity occurred on private property, rather than in an environment over which the State by necessity must have certain supervisory powers unrelated to expression. Accordingly, we must examine with particular care the interests advanced by appellee to support its prosecution.

. . . [W]e think it appropriate to review briefly the range of various state interests that might be thought to support the challenged conviction[.] The first interest at issue is prevention of breach of the peace. In our view, the Washington Supreme Court correctly rejected this notion. It is totally without support in the record.

We are also unable to affirm the judgment below on the ground that the State may have desired to protect the sensibilities of passersby. It is firmly settled that under our Constitution the public expression of ideas may not be prohibited merely because the ideas are themselves offensive to some of their hearers. Moreover, appellant did not impose his ideas upon a captive audience. Anyone who might have been offended could easily have avoided the display. Nor may appellant be punished for failing to show proper respect for our national emblem. *West Virginia State Board of Education v. Barnette, supra.*

We are brought, then, to the state court's thesis that Washington has an interest in preserving the national flag as an unalloyed symbol of our country. The court did not define this interest; it simply asserted it. Mr. Justice REHNQUIST's dissenting opinion today . . . adopts essentially the same approach. Presumably, this interest might be seen as an effort to prevent the appropriation of a revered national symbol by an individual, interest group, or enterprise where there was a risk that association of the symbol with a particular product or viewpoint might be taken erroneously as evidence of governmental endorsement. Alternatively, it might be argued that the interest asserted by the state court is based on the uniquely universal character of the national flag as a symbol. For the great majority of us, the flag is a symbol of patriotism, of pride in the history of our country, and of the service, sacrifice, and valor of the millions of Americans who in peace and war have joined together to build and to defend a Nation in which self-government and personal liberty endure. It evidences both the unity and diversity which are America. For others the flag carries in varying degrees a different message. "A person gets from a symbol the meaning he puts into it, and what is one man's comfort and inspiration is another's jest and scorn." *Barnette, supra,* at 632-33. It might be said that we all draw something from our national symbol, for it is capable of conveying simultaneously a spectrum of meanings. If it may be destroyed or permanently disfigured, it could be argued that it will lose its capability of mirroring the sentiments of all who view it.

But we need not decide in this case whether the interest advanced by the court below is valid. We assume, arguendo, that it is. The statute is nonetheless unconstitutional as applied to appellant's activity. There was no risk that appellant's acts would mislead viewers into assuming that the Government endorsed his viewpoint. To the contrary, he was plainly and peacefully protesting the fact that it did not. Appellant was not charged under [Washington's flag desecration statute], nor did he permanently disfigure the flag or destroy it. He displayed it as a flag of his country in a way closely analogous to the manner in which flags have always been used to convey ideas. Moreover, his message was direct, likely to be understood, and within the contours of the First Amendment. Given the protected character of his expression and in light of the fact that no interest the State may have in preserving the physical integrity of a privately owned flag was significantly impaired on these facts, the conviction must be invalidated.

The judgment is reversed.

It is so ordered.

Judgment reversed.

[Mr. Justice BLACKMUN concurs in the result.]

[The concurring opinion of Mr. Justice DOUGLAS is omitted.]

Mr. Chief Justice BURGER, dissenting.

If the constitutional role of this Court were to strike down unwise laws or restrict unwise application of some laws, I could agree with the result reached by the Court. That is not our function, however, and it should be left to each State and ultimately the common sense of its people to decide how the flag, as a symbol of national unity, should be protected.

Mr. Justice REHNQUIST, with whom THE CHIEF JUSTICE and Mr. Justice WHITE join, dissenting.

The Court holds that a Washington statute prohibiting persons from attaching material to the American flag was unconstitutionally applied to appellant. Although I agree with the Court that appellant's activity was a form of communication, I do not agree that the First Amendment prohibits the State from restricting this activity in furtherance of other important interests. . . .

"(T)he right of free speech is not absolute at all times and under all circumstances." Chaplinsky v. New Hampshire, 315 U.S. 568, 571 (1942). This Court has long recognized, for example, that some forms of expression are not entitled to any protection at all under the First Amendment, despite the fact that they could reasonably be thought protected under its literal language. The Court has further recognized that even protected speech may be subject to reasonable limitation when important countervailing interests are involved. Citizens are not completely free to commit perjury, to libel other citizens, to infringe copyrights, to incite riots, or to interfere unduly with passage through a public thoroughfare. The right of free speech, though precious, remains subject to reasonable accommodation to other valued interests.

Since a State concededly may impose some limitations on speech directly, it would seem to follow a fortiori that a State may legislate to protect important state interests even though an incidental limitation on free speech results. Virtually any law enacted by a State, when viewed with sufficient ingenuity, could be thought to interfere with some citizen's preferred means of expression. But no one would argue, I presume, that a State could not prevent the painting of public buildings simply because a particular class of protesters believed their message would best be conveyed through that medium. Had appellant here chosen to tape his peace symbol to a federal courthouse, I have little doubt that he could be prosecuted under a statute properly drawn to protect public property.

. . . The State of Washington is hardly seeking to protect the flag's resale value, and yet the Court's emphasis on the lack of actual damage to the flag suggests that this is a significant aspect of the State's interest. Surely the Court does not mean to imply that appellant could be prosecuted if he subsequently tore the flag in the process of trying to take the tape off. Unlike flag-desecration statutes, which the Court correctly notes are not at issue in this case, the Washington statute challenged here seeks to prevent personal use of the flag, not simply particular forms of abuse. The State of Washington has chosen to set the flag apart for a special purpose, and has directed that it not be turned into a common background for an endless variety of superimposed messages. The physical condition of the flag itself is irrelevant to that purpose.

The true nature of the State's interest in this case is not only one of preserving "the physical integrity of the flag," but also one of preserving the flag as "an important symbol of nationhood and unity." . . . It is the character, not the cloth, of the flag which the State seeks to protect.

The value of this interest has been emphasized in recent as well as distant times. . . . What appellant here seeks is simply license to use the flag however he pleases, so long as the activity can be tied to a concept of speech, regardless of any state interest in having the flag used only for more limited purposes. I find no reasoning in the Court's opinion which convinces me that the Constitution requires such license to be given.

The fact that the State has a valid interest in preserving the character of the flag does not mean, of course, that it can employ all conceivable means to enforce it. It certainly could not require all citizens to own the flag or compel citizens to salute one. *Barnette*, 319 U.S. at 624. It presumably cannot punish criticism of the flag, or the principles for which it stands, any more than it could punish criticism of this country's policies or ideas. But the statute in this case demands no such allegiance. Its operation does not depend upon whether the flag is used for communicative or noncommunicative purposes; upon whether a particular message is deemed commercial or political; upon whether the use of the flag is respectful or contemptuous; or upon whether any particular segment of the State's citizenry might applaud or oppose the intended message. It simply withdraws a unique national symbol from the roster of materials that may be used as a background for communications. Since I do not believe the Constitution prohibits Washington from making that decision, I dissent.

NOTES AND QUESTIONS

1. *When is conduct sufficiently expressive?* In *Spence*, the Court states conduct is expressive when (1) an "intent to convey a particularized message was present," and (2) "in the surrounding circumstances the likelihood was great that the message would be understood by those who viewed it." Would O'Brien's burning of his draft card qualify as "speech" under this standard? Would displaying a rainbow flag? What about carrying a firearm openly in public places? The Court has stated that where some explanatory speech is necessary to enable the audience to understand the intended message, this "is strong evidence that the conduct at issue . . . is not so inherently expressive that it warrants protection." Rumsfeld v. Forum for Acad. & Institutional Rights, 547 U.S. 47, 66 (2006).
2. *The scope of* Spence. The Supreme Court does not apply the *Spence* standard in every expressive conduct case. In some cases, the government concedes conduct is expressive, while in others (including *O'Brien* itself) the Court simply assumes so. In these instances, there is no need to apply the *Spence* standard. However, when the matter is contested, *Spence* is commonly relied upon to determine whether conduct is "expressive." The Court has applied *Spence* in modern decisions and the standard is frequently applied by lower courts. *See, e.g.*, Burns v. Town of Palm Beach, 999 F.3d 1317, 1336-38 (11th Cir. 2021) (applying *Spence* to determine whether architectural design for a planned mansion was expressive).
3. *The requirement of a "particularized message."* The Court has not always required a "*particularized*" message be conveyed by the speaker or understood by the audience. In Hurley v. Irish-American Gay, Lesbian and Bisexual Group of Boston, 515 U.S. 557 (1995) [*infra* p. 269], for example, the Court concluded a St. Patrick's Day parade was expressive even though it communicated a wide variety of messages. As the Court reasoned: "[A] narrow, succinctly articulable message is not a condition of constitutional protection, which if confined to expressions conveying a particularized message, would never reach the unquestionably shielded painting

of Jackson Pollock, music of Arnold Schonberg, or Jabberwocky verse of Lewis Carroll." Are some acts, like parading and demonstrating, *inherently* expressive? Is artistic expression exempted from the *Spence* standard?

4. Spence *and free speech boundaries.* The *Spence* standard has its critics. As scholars have observed, the standard does a poor job of explaining the "boundaries" of the Free Speech Clause as it pertains to expressive conduct. For example, graffiti that defaces property would appear to satisfy the *Spence* standard but is surely not within the ambit of the First Amendment. The same is true of crimes motivated by political views, including riots and political assassinations. Those who rioted at the U.S. Capitol on January 6, 2021 could assert they had an intent to convey a political message and that it was likely to be understood by audiences. However, the rioters' claim of First Amendment protection would get nowhere in the federal courts. Why not? *See* Robert Post, *Recuperating First Amendment Doctrine*, 47 Stan. L. Rev. 1249, 1265 (1995). In these respects, *Spence* is part of a broader problem, namely the lack of an overarching theory or approach to defining the "coverage" of the First Amendment. *See* Amanda Shanor, *First Amendment Coverage*, 93 N.Y.U. L. Rev. 318 (2018); Frederick Schauer, *The Boundaries of the First Amendment: A Preliminary Exploration of Constitutional Salience*, 117 Harv. L. Rev. 1765 (2004).
5. *Criminal acts as expression.* The Supreme Court of Canada appears to recognize that criminal acts can be expressive insofar as its own Charter is concerned. Writing for the majority in R. v. Keegstra, [1990] 3 S.C.R. 697 (Can.), Chief Justice Dickson explained that

> all activities conveying or attempting to convey meaning are considered expression for the purposes of s. 2(b); the content of expression is irrelevant in determining the scope of this Charter provision. Stated at its highest, an exception has been suggested where meaning is communicated directly via physical violence, the extreme repugnance of this form to free expression values justifying such an extraordinary step. Section 319(2) of the Criminal Code prohibits the communication of meaning that is repugnant, but the repugnance stems from the content of the message as opposed to its form. For this reason, I am of the view that hate propaganda is to be categorized as expression so as to bring it within the coverage of s. 2(b).

Id. at 732. Does this mean that in Canada threats of violence or perhaps acts of violence, if intended to convey a meaning, are constitutionally protected expression? Chief Justice Dickson suggests that threats of violence, and perhaps acts of violence, do enjoy protection as expressive conduct although other portions of the Canadian Charter may allow restrictions:

> While the line between form and content is not always easily drawn, in my opinion threats of violence can only be so classified by reference to the content of their meaning. As such, they do not fall within [any] exception . . . , and their suppression must

> be justified under s. 1. As I do not find threats of violence to be excluded from the definition of expression envisioned by s. 2(b), it is unnecessary to determine whether the threatening aspects of hate propaganda can be seen as threats of violence, or analogous to such threats, so as to deny it protection under s. 2(b).

Id. at 733. Is this a more intellectually honest way of approaching the problem of expressive conduct? Or are there reasons to set more concrete boundaries that exclude violent acts from free speech coverage? For more discussion, see Ronald J. Krotoszynski, Jr., *The First Amendment in Cross-Cultural Perspective: A Comparative Legal Analysis* 29-36 (2006).

6. *Flag desecration and free speech. Spence* was one of several cases in which the Court avoided answering whether the First Amendment prohibits government from banning conduct that conveys a negative or derogatory message about the flag or disagrees with its messages of "nationhood" and "national unity." That question was squarely presented in *Texas v. Johnson* (1989), which follows.

Texas v. Johnson

491 U.S. 397 (1989)

Justice Brennan delivered the opinion of the Court. . . .

While the Republican National Convention was taking place in Dallas in 1984, respondent Johnson participated in a political demonstration dubbed the "Republican War Chest Tour." . . . The demonstration ended in front of Dallas City Hall, where Johnson unfurled the American flag, doused it with kerosene, and set it on fire. While the flag burned, the protestors chanted: "America, the red, white, and blue, we spit on you." After the demonstrators dispersed, a witness to the flag burning collected the flag's remains and buried them in his backyard. No one was physically injured or threatened with injury, though several witnesses testified that they had been seriously offended by the flag burning.

Of the approximately 100 demonstrators, Johnson alone was charged with a crime. The only criminal offense with which he was charged was the desecration of a venerated object in violation of Tex. Penal Code Ann. § 42.09(a)(3) (1989).[1]

---

1. Texas Penal Code Ann. § 42.09 (1989) provides in full:

§ 42.09. Desecration of Venerated Object

(a) A person commits an offense if he intentionally or knowingly desecrates:

(1) a public monument;

(2) a place of worship or burial; or

(3) a state or national flag.

(b) For purposes of this section, "desecrate" means deface, damage, or otherwise physically mistreat in a way that the actor knows will seriously offend one or more persons likely to observe or discover his action.

(c) An offense under this section is a Class A misdemeanor.

After a trial, he was convicted, sentenced to one year in prison, and fined $2,000. . . .

Johnson was convicted of flag desecration for burning the flag rather than for uttering insulting words. This fact somewhat complicates our consideration of his conviction under the First Amendment. We must first determine whether Johnson's burning of the flag constituted expressive conduct, permitting him to invoke the First Amendment in challenging his conviction. *See, e.g.*, Spence v. Washington, 418 U.S. 405 (1974). If his conduct was expressive, we next decide whether the State's regulation is related to the suppression of free expression. *See, e.g., O'Brien.* If the State's regulation is not related to expression, then the less stringent standard we announced in *United States v. O'Brien* for regulations of noncommunicative conduct controls. If it is, then we are outside of *O'Brien*'s test, and we must ask whether this interest justifies Johnson's conviction under a more demanding standard. . . .

Especially pertinent to this case are our decisions recognizing the communicative nature of conduct relating to flags. Attaching a peace sign to the flag, *Spence*; refusing to salute the flag, West Virginia State Board of Education v. Barnette, 319 U.S. 624, 632 (1943); and displaying a red flag, Stromberg v. California, 283 U.S. 359 (1931), we have held, all may find shelter under the First Amendment. . . . That we have had little difficulty identifying an expressive element in conduct relating to flags should not be surprising. The very purpose of a national flag is to serve as a symbol of our country; it is, one might say, "the one visible manifestation of two hundred years of nationhood." Smith v. Goguen, 415 U.S. 566, 603 (1974).

We have not automatically concluded, however, that any action taken with respect to our flag is expressive. Instead, in characterizing such action for First Amendment purposes, we have considered the context in which it occurred. In *Spence*, for example, we emphasized that Spence's taping of a peace sign to his flag was "roughly simultaneous with and concededly triggered by the Cambodian incursion and the Kent State tragedy." . . .

The State of Texas conceded for purposes of its oral argument in this case that Johnson's conduct was expressive conduct, and this concession seems to us . . . prudent. . . . Johnson burned an American flag as part—indeed, as the culmination—of a political demonstration that coincided with the convening of the Republican Party and its renomination of Ronald Reagan for President. The expressive, overtly political nature of this conduct was both intentional and overwhelmingly apparent. . . .

In order to decide whether *O'Brien's* test applies here . . . we must decide whether Texas has asserted an interest in support of Johnson's conviction that is unrelated to the suppression of expression. If we find that an interest asserted by the State is simply not implicated on the facts before us, we need not ask whether *O'Brien*'s test applies. The State offers two separate interests to justify this conviction: preventing breaches of the peace and preserving the flag as a symbol of nationhood and national unity. We hold that the first interest is not implicated on this record and that the second is related to the suppression of expression. . . .

Texas claims that its interest in preventing breaches of the peace justifies Johnson's conviction for flag desecration. However, no disturbance of the peace actually occurred or threatened to occur because of Johnson's burning of the flag. [The] only evidence offered [at trial] to show the reaction to Johnson's actions was the testimony of several persons who had been seriously offended by the flag-burning.

The State's position, therefore, amounts to a claim that an audience that takes serious offense at particular expression is necessarily likely to disturb the peace and that the expression may be prohibited on this basis. Our precedents do not countenance such a presumption. We have not permitted the Government to assume that every expression of a provocative idea will incite a riot, but have instead required careful consideration of the actual circumstances surrounding such expression. [*Brandenburg.*] To accept Texas's arguments that it need only demonstrate "the potential for a breach of the peace," and that every flag-burning necessarily possesses that potential, would be to eviscerate our holding in *Brandenburg*. This we decline to do.

[Nor] does Johnson's expressive conduct fall within that small class of "fighting words" that are "likely to provoke the average person to retaliation, and thereby cause a breach of the peace." [*Chaplinsky.*] No reasonable onlooker would have regarded Johnson's generalized expression of dissatisfaction with the policies of the Federal Government as a direct personal insult or an invitation to exchange fisticuffs. We thus conclude that the State's interest in maintaining order is not implicated on these [facts].

The State also asserts an interest in preserving the flag as a symbol of nationhood and national unity. . . . We are equally persuaded that this interest is related to expression in the case of Johnson's burning of the flag. The State, apparently, is concerned that such conduct will lead people to believe either that the flag does not stand for nationhood and national unity, but instead reflects other, less positive concepts, or that the concepts reflected in the flag do not in fact exist, that is, that we do not enjoy unity as a Nation. These concerns blossom only when a person's treatment of the flag communicates some message, and thus are related "to the suppression of free expression" within the meaning of *O'Brien*. We are thus outside of *O'Brien*'s test altogether.

It remains to consider whether the State's interest in preserving the flag as a symbol of nationhood and national unity justifies Johnson's conviction.

. . . Johnson was not . . . prosecuted for the expression of just any idea; he was prosecuted for his expression of dissatisfaction with the policies of this country, expression situated at the core of our First Amendment values.

Moreover, Johnson was prosecuted because he knew that his politically charged expression would cause "serious offense." If he had burned the flag as a means of disposing of it because it was dirty or torn, he would not have been convicted of flag desecration under this Texas law: federal law designates burning as the preferred means of disposing of a flag "when it is in such condition that it is no longer a fitting emblem for display," 36 U.S.C. § 176(k), and Texas has no quarrel with this means of disposal. The Texas law is thus not aimed at protecting the physical integrity of the flag in all circumstances, but is designed instead to protect it only against impairments that would cause serious offense to others. . . . Johnson's political expression was restricted because of the content of the message he conveyed. We must therefore subject the State's asserted interest in preserving the special symbolic character of the flag to "the most exacting scrutiny."

Texas argues that its interest in preserving the flag as a symbol of nationhood and national unity survives this close analysis. . . . [T]he State emphasizes the "'special place'" reserved for the flag in our Nation. The State's argument is not that it has an interest simply in maintaining the flag as a symbol of *something*, no matter what it symbolizes; indeed, if that were the State's position, it would be difficult to see how that interest is endangered by highly symbolic conduct such as Johnson's. Rather, the State's claim is that it has an interest in preserving the flag as a symbol of *nationhood* and *national unity*, a symbol with a determinate range of meanings. According to Texas, if one physically treats the flag in a way that would tend to cast doubt on either the idea that nationhood and national unity are the flag's referents or that national unity actually exists, the message conveyed thereby is a harmful one and therefore may be prohibited.[9]

If there is a bedrock principle underlying the First Amendment, it is that the government may not prohibit the expression of an idea simply because society finds the idea itself offensive or disagreeable. . . . [N]othing in our precedents suggests that a State may foster its own view of the flag by prohibiting expressive conduct relating to it. . . .

. . . To conclude that the government may permit designated symbols to be used to communicate only a limited set of messages would be to enter territory having no discernible or defensible boundaries. Could the government, on this theory, prohibit the burning of state flags? Of copies of the Presidential seal? Of the Constitution? In evaluating these choices under the First Amendment, how would we decide which symbols were sufficiently special to warrant this unique status? To do so, we would be forced to consult our own political preferences, and impose them on the citizenry, in the very way that the First Amendment forbids us to do.

There is, moreover, no indication—either in the text of the Constitution or in our cases interpreting it—that a separate juridical category exists for the American flag alone. . . . The First Amendment does not guarantee that other concepts virtually sacred to our Nation as a whole—such as the principle that discrimination on the basis of race is odious and destructive—will go unquestioned in the marketplace of ideas. We decline, therefore, to create for the flag an exception to the joust of principles protected by the First Amendment.

It is not the State's ends, but its means, to which we object. It cannot be gainsaid that there is a special place reserved for the flag in this Nation, and thus we do not doubt that the government has a legitimate interest in making efforts to "preserv[e] the national flag as an unalloyed symbol of our country." *Spence*. . . . To say that the government has an interest in encouraging proper treatment of the flag, however, is not to say that it may criminally punish a person for burning a flag as a means of political protest. . . .

The way to preserve the flag's special role is not to punish those who feel differently about these matters. It is to persuade them that they are wrong. . . . We can imagine no more appropriate response to burning the flag than waving one's

---

9. Texas claims that "Texas is not endorsing, protecting, avowing or prohibiting any particular philosophy." If Texas means to suggest that its asserted interest does not prefer Democrats over Socialists, or Republicans over Democrats, for example, then it is beside the point, for Johnson does not rely on such an argument. He argues instead that the State's desire to maintain the flag as a symbol of nationhood and national unity assumes that there is only one proper view of the flag. Thus, if Texas means to argue that its interest does not prefer *any* viewpoint over another, it is mistaken; surely one's attitude toward the flag and its referents is a viewpoint.

own, no better way to counter a flag burner's message than by saluting the flag that burns, no surer means of preserving the dignity even of the flag that burned than by—as one witness did here—according its remains a respectful burial. We do not consecrate the flag by punishing its desecration, for in doing so we dilute the freedom that this cherished emblem represents. . . . [*Affirmed.*]

Chief Justice REHNQUIST, with whom Justice WHITE and Justice O'CONNOR join, dissenting. . . .

The American flag . . . is not simply another "idea" or "point of view" competing for recognition in the marketplace of ideas. Millions and millions of Americans regard it with an almost mystical reverence regardless of what sort of social, political, or philosophical beliefs they may have. I cannot agree that the First Amendment invalidates the Act of Congress, and the laws of 48 of the 50 States, which make criminal the public burning of the flag. . . .

. . . [T]he public burning of the American flag by Johnson was no essential part of any exposition of ideas, and at the same time it had a tendency to incite a breach of the peace. Johnson was free to make any verbal denunciation of the flag that he wished; indeed, he was free to burn the flag in private. He could publicly burn other symbols of the Government or effigies of political leaders. He did lead a march through the streets of Dallas, and conducted a rally in front of the Dallas City Hall. He engaged in a "die-in" to protest nuclear weapons. He shouted out various slogans during the march, including: "Reagan, Mondale which will it be? Either one means World War III"; "Ronald Reagan, killer of the hour, Perfect example of U.S. power"; and "red, white and blue, we spit on you, you stand for plunder, you will go under." For none of these acts was he arrested or prosecuted; it was only when he proceeded to burn publicly an American flag stolen from its rightful owner that he violated the Texas statute. . . .

The result of the Texas statute is obviously to deny one in Johnson's frame of mind one of many means of "symbolic speech." Far from being a case of "one picture being worth a thousand words," flag burning is the equivalent of an inarticulate grunt or roar that, it seems fair to say, is most likely to be indulged in not to express any particular idea, but to antagonize others. . . . The Texas statute deprived Johnson of only one rather inarticulate symbolic form of protest—a form of protest that was profoundly offensive to many—and left him with a full panoply of other symbols and every conceivable form of verbal expression to express his deep disapproval of national policy. Thus, in no way can it be said that Texas is punishing him because his hearers—or any other group of people—were profoundly opposed to the message that he sought to convey. . . .

Justice STEVENS, dissenting.

. . . The statutory prohibition of flag desecration does not "prescribe what shall be orthodox in politics, nationalism, religion, or other matters of opinion or force citizens to confess by word or act their faith therein." West Virginia Board of Education v. Barnette, 319 U.S. 624, 642 (1943). . . . Nor does the statute violate "the government's paramount obligation of neutrality in its regulation of protected communication." Young v. American Mini Theatres, Inc., 427 U.S. 50, 70 (1976) (plurality opinion). The content of respondent's message has no relevance whatsoever to the case. The concept of "desecration" does not turn on the substance of the message the actor intends to convey, but rather on whether those who view the *act* will take serious offense. Accordingly, one intending to convey a message of respect for the flag by burning it in a public square might nonetheless be guilty of desecration if he knows that others—perhaps simply because they misperceive the intended message—will be seriously offended. Indeed, even if the actor knows that all possible witnesses will understand that he intends to send a message of respect, he might still be guilty of desecration if he also knows that this understanding does not lessen the offense taken by some of those witnesses. . . . The case has nothing to do with "disagreeable ideas." It involves disagreeable conduct that, in my opinion, diminishes the value of an important national asset.

The Court is therefore quite wrong in blandly asserting that respondent "was prosecuted for his expression of dissatisfaction with the policies of this country, expression situated at the core of our First Amendment values." Respondent was prosecuted because of the method he chose to express his dissatisfaction with those policies. Had he chosen to spray-paint—or perhaps convey with a motion picture projector—his message of dissatisfaction on the facade of the Lincoln Memorial, there would be no question about the power of the Government to prohibit his means of expression. The prohibition would be supported by the legitimate interest in preserving the quality of an important national asset. Though the asset at stake in this case is intangible, given its unique value, the same interest supports a prohibition on the desecration of the American flag.*

[Justice KENNEDY's concurring opinion is omitted.]

NOTES AND QUESTIONS

1. *Analyzing expressive conduct regulations.* The Court's opinion in *Johnson* provides a general framework for analyzing the regulation of conduct claimed to be expressive. The Court's analysis proceeds in four steps: (1) Did Johnson engage in "speech" (expressive conduct) when he burned the flag"? (2) If so, did Johnson's "speech" fall into an unprotected "low-value" category

* The Court suggests that a prohibition against flag desecration is not content neutral because this form of symbolic speech is only used by persons who are critical of the flag or the ideas it represents. In making this suggestion the Court does not pause to consider the far-reaching consequences of its introduction of disparate-impact analysis into our First Amendment jurisprudence. It seems obvious that a prohibition against the desecration of a gravesite is content neutral even if it denies some protesters the right to make a symbolic statement by extinguishing the flame in Arlington Cemetery where John F. Kennedy is buried while permitting others to salute the flame by bowing their heads. Few would doubt that a protester who extinguishes the flame has desecrated the gravesite, regardless of whether he prefaces that act with a speech explaining that his purpose is to express deep admiration or unmitigated scorn for the late President. Likewise, few would claim that the protester who bows his head has desecrated the gravesite, even if he makes clear that his purpose is to show disrespect. In such a case, as in a flag burning case, the prohibition against desecration has absolutely nothing to do with the content of the message that the symbolic speech is intended to convey.

such as incitement or fighting words? (3) Assuming Johnson engaged in "speech" that is not categorically excluded from protection, is the Texas law content-based or content-neutral? and (4) Depending on the answer to (3), apply the appropriate standard of scrutiny. The Court determines Johnson engaged in speech not within any excluded content category. Since its answer to (3) is that the Texas law is content-based the Court applies strict scrutiny rather than *O'Brien.*

2. "*Related to the suppression of free expression*"—Johnson *and communicative impact.* The *O'Brien* standard applies when a law regulating conduct is "unrelated to the suppression of free expression." If the government's interests are indeed "related to the suppression of expression," the regulation is subject to strict scrutiny. *Johnson* relies on this distinction to subject the Texas law to strict scrutiny. What does it mean for a law to "relate to the suppression of free expression"? Given the wording of the statute, is the Texas law content-based or is the term "offend" neutral as to the content of expression? Alternatively, is the Texas statute content-based because of the way it was *applied*? Does the concept of "communicative impact"—that is, attempts to regulate expressive conduct or speech based upon the message's impact on the audience—explain *Johnson*'s willingness to discard *O'Brien*'s framework?
3. *Flag burning redux.* Soon after the Supreme Court handed down its 5–4 decision in *Texas v. Johnson,* Congress passed the Flag Protection Act of 1989, 18 U.S.C. § 700(a), which punished by fine and/or imprisonment anyone who "knowingly mutilates, defaces, physically defiles, burns, maintains on the floor or ground, or tramples upon any flag of the United States." 18 U.S.C. § 700(a)(1). The law exempted from punishment, however, "any conduct consisting of the disposal of a flag when it has become worn or soiled." 18 U.S.C. § 700(a)(2). In United States v. Eichman, 496 U.S. 310 (1990), the Court, by a vote of 5–4, invalidated the Act. Appellants in *Eichman* burned flags to protest the government's domestic and foreign policy, in one instance, and passage of the Flag Protection Act, in another. They were arrested for violating the Act in both instances, but the lower courts found that the Act facially and as applied to them violated the First Amendment. The Supreme Court affirmed. It reasoned that "[a]lthough the Flag Protection Act contains no explicit content-based limitation on the scope of prohibited conduct, it is nevertheless clear that the Government's asserted *interest* is "related 'to the suppression of free expression,' *Johnson,* and concerned with the content of such expression. The Government's interest in protecting the 'physical integrity' of a privately owned flag rests upon a perceived need to preserve the flag's status as a symbol of our Nation and certain national ideals." Are the statutes in *Johnson* and *Eichman* equally problematic from a First Amendment perspective? Arguably, the *Johnson* statute was facially content-based or at least applied in a content-based manner. But isn't the statute in *Eichman* facially neutral—instead focusing on "mutilation" or "defacement"? Or does the Act's application still turn on the reaction of viewers to the act of flag burning?

4. *Related to the suppression of free expression—symbolism.* Can one protect the flag's symbolic effect without interfering with the speaker's message? Consider the following argument:

> [While attempts to protect symbolism] do not single out certain messages for proscription, they do single out one set of messages, namely the set of messages conveyed by the American flag, for protection. . . . Orthodoxy of thought can be fostered not simply by placing unusual restrictions on "deviant" expression but also by granting unusual protection to expression that is officially acceptable. An "improper use" statute, neutral respecting the messages it would inhibit though it may be, is not analogous to a law prohibiting the interruption of speeches. It is, at best, analogous to a law prohibiting the interruption of patriotic speeches, and that is a law that is hardly "unrelated to the suppression of free expression."

Ely, *supra*, at 1506-1507.

5. *Protecting symbolism—government property.* In *Johnson,* Justice Stevens argues that the government can protect the flag from desecration just as it can protect memorials. Is the analogy between the flag and the Lincoln Memorial persuasive? Would prosecution under a general law protecting public property from physical defacement rest on the "offense" of the audience? Would the analogy have been stronger or weaker if Justice Stevens had compared flag desecration to destroying the bald eagle (our national bird) for expressive purposes? *See* Geoffrey R. Stone, *Flagburning and the Constitution,* 75 Iowa L. Rev. 111 (1990).
6. *Speech or conduct.* Is Justice Rehnquist's reference in *Johnson* to flag burning as an "inarticulate grunt or roar" an argument that flag desecration is more like conduct than communication? Again, can one ban the *conduct* of flag desecration without having an impact on the speaker's *message?*
7. *A constitutional amendment?* Since *Eichman,* Congress has repeatedly attempted to pass a constitutional amendment prohibiting flag desecration. In 2006, an amendment reading, "The Congress shall have the power to prohibit the physical desecration of the flag of the United States," fell a single vote short of the necessary support needed in the Senate to send it to the states for ratification. The amendment passed the House of Representatives earlier in the year. Is the flag *sui generis* so that an exception should be made? Would such an amendment avoid litigation, or does the text of the above proposal still raise thorny interpretive issues?

THEORY-APPLIED PROBLEMS

1. Thomas Hogue and Jason Wick are planning their wedding ceremony. They went to a locally owned bakery—Sweets-for-the-Sweet—to order a cake. This bakery is widely known as the best baker of wedding cakes in town. However, Linda Mossman, the owner of Sweets (as it is locally known) refused to provide a cake for Hogue and Wick's wedding. She cited her sincerely held religious beliefs, which prevented her from being

complicit in the sin of homosexuality. Hogue and Wick argue that Mossman's refusal amounts to discrimination under state laws that prevent discrimination in the provision of services based on race, gender, religion, sexual orientation and disability. Mossman argues that forcing her to provide a wedding cake amounts to a requirement that she endorse Hogue and Wick's lifestyle—i.e., that she express approval of their lifestyle through her provision of services. Is Mossman's baking of a wedding cake expressive conduct that triggers First Amendment scrutiny?

2. The City of Richmond, facing a financial shortfall because tax receipts failed to equal estimated revenue used to prepare the annual budget, decided to increase the number of paid parking zones in the city. The Shockoe Bottom area of Richmond, a funky warehouse district featuring vintage clothing boutiques, nouveau cuisine eateries, and other upscale diversions, has traditionally featured free street parking in most zones and free street parking after 5 P.M. on weekdays and Saturdays in all legal street parking spots. As part of Richmond's effort to increase revenue, the city turned all legal street spaces in Shockoe Bottom into metered parking only, and applied the meters until midnight six nights a week (only Sunday was excepted).

   The Shockoe Bottom Merchants Association (SBMA) opposed the city's decision to expand the times and locations of metered parking in the neighborhood. The SBMA organized a mass protest, encouraging all visitors to the neighborhood to "Stiff the Meter!" As part of the campaign, visitors to the area were encouraged to violate the new paid parking rules after 5 P.M. and in spaces that were formerly free parking. The SBMA also produced "Stiff the Meter!" magnetic stickers, which it encouraged visitors to place on the meters in lieu of paying for parking.

   On May 16, 2017, the City of Richmond organized a massive parking enforcement dragnet operation, writing more than $3,452 in parking violation tickets. SBMA, on behalf of those who park in the neighborhood, appeared in municipal court to contest the charges, seeking class action status for all persons parked in Shockoe Bottom after 5 P.M. on May 16, 2017.

   The SBMA argued that the violators were engaged in a mass protest of the city's outrageous and unfair new parking regulations in the neighborhood. The organization further argued that the enforcement effort was a viewpoint- and content-based effort to retaliate against persons who opposed the new parking rules. The city attorney, in formal filings, argued that the City of Richmond was simply attempting to enforce its entirely lawful parking regulations and that the citations should stand.

   You sit as the municipal judge assigned to hear the contested parking tickets. How should you rule on the First Amendment defense to the citations?

3. *Nude Dancing*

As *O'Brien* states, laws that regulate conduct with an expressive dimension are considered content-neutral so long as they are "unrelated to the suppression of free expression." As we have seen, in some contexts application of that standard has proven difficult and controversial. The cases that follow, which involve prohibitions on public nudity, combine the Court's decisions concerning regulation of the "secondary effects" of speech and its decisions concerning regulation of symbolic conduct.

Barnes v. Glen Theatre

501 U.S. 560 (1991)

REHNQUIST, C.J., announced the judgment of the Court and delivered an opinion, in which O'CONNOR, J., and KENNEDY, J., join.

Respondents are two establishments in South Bend, Indiana, that wish to provide totally nude dancing as entertainment, and individual dancers who are employed at these establishments. They claim that the First Amendment's guarantee of freedom of expression prevents the State of Indiana from enforcing its public indecency law to prevent this form of dancing. We reject their claim.

. . . The Kitty Kat Lounge, Inc. (Kitty Kat), is located in the city of South Bend. It sells alcoholic beverages and presents "go-go dancing." Its proprietor desires to present "totally nude dancing," but an applicable Indiana statute regulating public nudity requires that the dancers wear "pasties" and "G-strings" when they dance. The dancers are not paid an hourly wage, but work on commission. They receive a 100 percent commission on the first $60 in drink sales during their performances. Darlene Miller, one of the respondents in the action, had worked at the Kitty Kat for about two years at the time this action was brought. Miller wishes to dance nude because she believes she would make more money doing so.

Respondent Glen Theatre, Inc., is an Indiana corporation with a place of business in South Bend. Its primary business is supplying so-called adult entertainment through written and printed materials, movie showings, and live entertainment at an enclosed "bookstore." The live entertainment at the "bookstore" consists of nude and seminude performances and showings of the female body through glass panels. Customers sit in a booth and insert coins into a timing mechanism that permits them to observe the live nude and seminude dancers for a period of time. One of Glen Theatre's dancers, Gayle Ann Marie Sutro, has danced, modeled, and acted professionally for more than 15 years, and in addition to her performances at the Glen Theatre, can be seen in a pornographic movie at a nearby theater.

Respondents sued in the United States District Court for the Northern District of Indiana to enjoin the enforcement of the Indiana public indecency statute, Ind. Code § 35-45-4-1 (1988), asserting that its prohibition against complete nudity in public places violated the First Amendment. . . .

[T]he District Court concluded that "the type of dancing these plaintiffs wish to perform is not expressive activity protected by the Constitution of the United States," and rendered judgment in favor of the defendants. . . . [A] panel of [the Seventh Circuit] reversed the District Court, holding that the nude dancing involved here was expressive conduct protected by the First Amendment. The Court of Appeals then heard the case en banc and rendered a series of comprehensive and thoughtful opinions. . . . The majority concluded that nonobscene nude dancing performed for entertainment is expression protected by the First Amendment, and that the public indecency statute was an improper infringement of that expressive activity because its purpose was to prevent the message of eroticism and sexuality conveyed by the dancers. We granted certiorari . . . and now hold that the Indiana statutory requirement that the dancers in the establishments involved in this case must wear pasties and G-strings does not violate the First Amendment.

Several of our cases contain language suggesting that nude dancing of the kind involved here is expressive conduct protected by the First Amendment. . . . These statements support the conclusion of the Court of Appeals that nude dancing of the kind sought to be performed here is expressive conduct within the outer perimeters of the First Amendment, though we view it as only marginally so. This, of course, does not end our inquiry. We must determine the level of protection to be afforded to the expressive conduct at issue, and must determine whether the Indiana statute is an impermissible infringement of that protected activity.

Indiana, of course, has not banned nude dancing as such, but has proscribed public nudity across the board. The Supreme Court of Indiana has construed the Indiana statute to preclude nudity in what are essentially places of public accommodation such as the Glen Theatre and the Kitty Kat Lounge. In such places, respondents point out, minors are excluded and there are no nonconsenting viewers. Respondents contend that while the State may license establishments such as the ones involved here, and limit the geographical area in which they do business, it may not in any way limit the performance of the dances within them without violating the First Amendment. The petitioners contend, on the other hand, that Indiana's restriction on nude dancing is a valid "time, place, or manner" restriction under cases such as Clark v. Community for Creative Non-Violence, 468 U.S. 288 (1984).

The "time, place, or manner" test was developed for evaluating restrictions on expression taking place on public property which had been dedicated as a "public forum," Ward v. Rock Against Racism, 491 U.S. 781, 791 (1989), although we have on at least one occasion applied it to conduct occurring on private property. *See* Renton v. Playtime Theatres, Inc., 475 U.S. 41 (1986). In *Clark* we observed that this test has been interpreted to embody much the same standards as those set forth in United States v. O'Brien, 391 U.S. 367 (1968), and we turn, therefore, to the rule enunciated in *O'Brien*. . . .

Applying the four-part *O'Brien* test . . . we find that Indiana's public indecency statute is justified despite its incidental limitations on some expressive activity. The public indecency statute is clearly within the constitutional power of the State and furthers substantial governmental interests. It is impossible to discern, other than from the text of the statute, exactly what governmental interest the Indiana legislators had in mind when they enacted this statute, for Indiana does not record legislative history, and the State's highest court has not shed additional light on the statute's purpose. Nonetheless, the statute's purpose of protecting societal order and morality is clear from its text and history. Public indecency statutes of this sort are of ancient origin and presently exist in at least 47 States. Public indecency, including nudity, was a criminal offense at common law, and this Court recognized the common-law roots of the offense of "gross and open indecency" in Winters v. New York, 333 U.S. 507, 515 (1948). . . . Public indecency statutes such as the one before us reflect moral disapproval of people appearing in the nude among strangers in public places. . . .

This and other public indecency statutes were designed to protect morals and public order. The traditional police power of the States is defined as the authority to provide for the public health, safety, and morals, and we have upheld such a basis for legislation. . . .

Thus, the public indecency statute furthers a substantial government interest in protecting order and morality.

This interest is unrelated to the suppression of free expression. Some may view restricting nudity on moral grounds as necessarily related to expression. We disagree. . . .

Respondents contend that even though prohibiting nudity in public generally may not be related to suppressing expression, prohibiting the performance of nude dancing is related to expression because the State seeks to prevent its erotic message. Therefore, they reason that the application of the Indiana statute to the nude dancing in this case violates the First Amendment, because it fails the third part of the *O'Brien* test, viz: the governmental interest must be unrelated to the suppression of free expression.

But we do not think that when Indiana applies its statute to the nude dancing in these nightclubs it is proscribing nudity because of the erotic message conveyed by the dancers. Presumably numerous other erotic performances are presented at these establishments and similar clubs without any interference from the State, so long as the performers wear a scant amount of clothing. Likewise, the requirement that the dancers don pasties and G-strings does not deprive the dance of whatever erotic message it conveys; it simply makes the message slightly less graphic. The perceived evil that Indiana seeks to address is not erotic dancing, but public nudity. The appearance of people of all shapes, sizes and ages in the nude at a beach, for example, would convey little if any erotic message, yet the State still seeks to prevent it. Public nudity is the evil the State seeks to prevent, whether or not it is combined with expressive activity.

The fourth part of the *O'Brien* test requires that the incidental restriction on First Amendment freedom be no greater than is essential to the furtherance of the governmental interest. As indicated in the discussion above, the governmental interest served by the text of the prohibition is societal disapproval of nudity in public places and among strangers. The statutory prohibition is not a means to some greater end, but an end in itself. It is without cavil that the public indecency statute is "narrowly tailored"; Indiana's requirement that the dancers wear at least pasties and G-strings is modest, and the bare minimum necessary to achieve the State's purpose.

The judgment of the Court of Appeals accordingly is

Reversed.

SCALIA, J., concurring in the judgment.

I agree that the judgment of the Court of Appeals must be reversed. In my view, however, the challenged regulation must be upheld, not because it survives some lower level of First Amendment scrutiny, but because, as a general law regulating conduct and not specifically directed at expression, it is not subject to First Amendment scrutiny at all. . . .

Indiana's statute is in the line of a long tradition of laws against public nudity, which have never been thought to run afoul of traditional understanding of "the freedom of speech." Public indecency—including public nudity—has long been an offense at common law. Indiana's first public nudity statute, Rev. Laws of Ind., ch. 26, § 60 (1831), predated by many years the appearance of nude barroom dancing. It was general in scope, directed at all public nudity, and not just at public nude expression; and all succeeding statutes, down to the present one, have been the same. Were it the case that Indiana *in practice* targeted only expressive nudity, while turning a blind eye to nude beaches and unclothed purveyors of hot dogs and machine tools, . . . it might be said that what posed as a regulation of conduct in general was in reality a regulation of only communicative conduct. Respondents have adduced no evidence of that. Indiana officials have brought many public indecency prosecutions for activities having no communicative element. . . .

The purpose of Indiana's nudity law would be violated, I think, if 60,000 fully consenting adults crowded into the Hoosier Dome to display their genitals to one another, even if there were not an offended innocent in the crowd. Our society prohibits, and all human societies have prohibited, certain activities not because they harm others but because they are considered, in the traditional phrase, "*contra bonos mores*," *i.e.*, immoral. In American society, such prohibitions have included, for example, sadomasochism, cockfighting, bestiality, suicide, drug use, prostitution, and sodomy. While there may be great diversity of view on whether various of these prohibitions should exist (though I have found few ready to abandon, in principle, all of them), there is no doubt that, absent specific constitutional protection for the conduct involved, the Constitution does not prohibit them simply because they regulate "morality." *See* Bowers v. Hardwick, 478 U.S. 186, 196 (1986) (upholding prohibition of private homosexual sodomy enacted solely on "the presumed belief of a majority of the electorate in [the jurisdiction] that homosexual sodomy is immoral and unacceptable"). The purpose of the Indiana statute, as both its text and the manner of its enforcement demonstrate, is to enforce the traditional moral belief that people should not expose their private parts indiscriminately, regardless of whether those who see them are disedified. Since that is so, the dissent has no basis for positing that, where only thoroughly edified adults are present, the purpose must be repression of communication.

Since the Indiana regulation is a general law not specifically targeted at expressive conduct, its application to such conduct does not in my view implicate the First Amendment. . . .

All our holdings (though admittedly not some of our discussion) support the conclusion that "the only First Amendment analysis applicable to laws that do not directly or indirectly impede speech is the threshold inquiry of whether the purpose of the law is to suppress communication. If not, that is the end of the matter so far as First Amendment guarantees are concerned; if so, the court then proceeds to determine whether there is substantial justification for the proscription." Such a regime ensures that the government does not act to suppress communication, without requiring that all conduct-restricting regulation (which means in effect all regulation) survive an enhanced level of scrutiny. . . .

Indiana may constitutionally enforce its prohibition of public nudity even against those who choose to use public nudity as a means of communication. The State is regulating conduct, not expression, and those who choose to employ conduct as a means of expression must make sure that the conduct they select is not generally forbidden. For these reasons, I agree that the judgment should be reversed.

SOUTER, J., concurring in the judgment.

Not all dancing is entitled to First Amendment protection as expressive activity. This Court has previously categorized ballroom dancing as beyond the Amendment's protection, Dallas v. Stanglin, 490 U.S. 19, 24–25 (1989), and dancing as aerobic exercise would likewise be outside the First Amendment's concern. But dancing as a performance directed to an actual or hypothetical audience gives expression at least to generalized emotion or feeling, and where the dancer is nude or nearly so the feeling expressed, in the absence of some contrary clue, is eroticism, carrying an endorsement of erotic experience. Such is the expressive content of the dances described in the record.

Although such performance dancing is inherently expressive, nudity *per se* is not. It is a condition, not an activity, and the voluntary assumption of that condition, without more, apparently expresses nothing beyond the view that the condition is somehow appropriate to the circumstances. But every voluntary act implies some such idea, and the implication is thus so common and minimal that calling all voluntary activity expressive would reduce the concept of expression to the point of the meaningless. A search for some expression beyond the minimal in the choice to go nude will often yield nothing: a person may choose nudity, for example, for maximum sunbathing. But when nudity is combined with expressive activity, its stimulative and attractive value certainly can enhance the force of expression, and a dancer's acts in going from clothed to nude, as in a striptease, are integrated into the dance and its expressive function. Thus I agree with the plurality and the dissent that an interest in freely engaging in the nude dancing at issue here is subject to a degree of First Amendment protection.

I also agree with the plurality that the appropriate analysis to determine the actual protection required by the First Amendment is the four-part enquiry described in United States v. O'Brien,391 U.S. 367 (1968), for judging the limits of appropriate state action burdening expressive acts as distinct from pure speech or representation. I nonetheless write separately to rest my concurrence in the judgment, not on the possible sufficiency of society's moral views to justify the limitations at issue, but on the State's substantial interest in combating the secondary effects of adult entertainment establishments of the sort typified by respondents' establishments.

. . . In my view, the interest asserted by petitioners in preventing prostitution, sexual assault, and other criminal activity, although presumably not a justification for all applications of the statute, is sufficient under *O'Brien* to justify the State's enforcement of the statute against the type of adult entertainment at issue here.

At the outset, it is clear that the prevention of such evils falls within the constitutional power of the State, which satisfies the first *O'Brien* criterion. The second *O'Brien* prong asks whether the regulation "furthers an important or substantial governmental interest." The asserted state interest is plainly a substantial one; the only question is whether prohibiting nude dancing of the sort at issue here "furthers" that interest. I believe that our cases have addressed this question sufficiently to establish that it does.

In Renton v. Playtime Theatres, Inc., 475 U.S. 41 (1986), we upheld a city's zoning ordinance designed to prevent the occurrence of harmful secondary effects, including the crime associated with adult entertainment, by protecting approximately 95% of the city's area from the placement of motion picture theaters emphasizing "'matter depicting, describing or relating to "specified sexual activities" or "specified anatomical areas" . . . for observation by patrons therein.'"

The type of entertainment respondents seek to provide is plainly of the same character as that at issue in *Renton* . . . It therefore is no leap to say that live nude dancing of the sort at issue here is likely to produce the same pernicious secondary effects as the adult films displaying "specified anatomical areas" at issue in *Renton.* . . . [T]he State of Indiana could reasonably conclude that forbidding nude entertainment of the type offered at the Kitty Kat Lounge and the Glen Theatre's "bookstore" furthers its interest in preventing prostitution, sexual assault, and associated crimes. . . . The statute as applied to nudity of the sort at issue here therefore satisfies the second prong of *O'Brien.*

The third *O'Brien* condition is that the governmental interest be "unrelated to the suppression of free expression," and, on its face, the governmental interest in combating prostitution and other criminal activity is not at all inherently related to expression. . . . Because the State's interest in banning nude dancing results from a simple correlation of such dancing with other evils, rather than from a relationship between the other evils and the expressive component of the dancing, the interest is unrelated to the suppression of free expression. . . .

The fourth *O'Brien* condition, that the restriction be no greater than essential to further the governmental interest, requires little discussion. Pasties and a G-string moderate the expression to some degree, to be sure, but only to a degree. Dropping the final stitch is prohibited, but the limitation is minor when measured against the dancer's remaining capacity and opportunity to express the erotic message. Nor, so far as we are told, is the dancer or her employer limited by anything short of obscenity laws from expressing an erotic message by articulate speech or representational means; a pornographic movie featuring one of respondents, for example, was playing nearby without any interference from the authorities at the time these cases arose.

Accordingly, I find *O'Brien* satisfied and concur in the judgment.

Justice White, with whom Justice Marshall, Justice Blackmun, and Justice Stevens join, dissenting.

The first question presented to us in this case is whether nonobscene nude dancing performed as entertainment is expressive conduct protected by the First Amendment. The Court of Appeals held that it is, observing that our prior decisions permit no other conclusion. Not surprisingly, then, the plurality now concedes that "nude dancing of the kind sought to be performed here is expressive conduct within the outer perimeters of the First Amendment. . . ." This is no more than recognizing, as the Seventh Circuit observed, that dancing is an ancient art form and "inherently embodies the expression and communication of ideas and emotions." Miller v. Civil City of South Bend, 904 F.2d 1081, 1087 (1990) (en banc). . . .

. . . The purpose of forbidding people to appear nude in parks, beaches, hot dog stands, and like public places is to protect others from offense. But that could not possibly be the purpose of preventing nude dancing in theaters and barrooms since the viewers are exclusively consenting adults who pay money to see these dances. The purpose of the proscription in these contexts is to protect the viewers from what the State believes is the harmful message that nude dancing communicates.

The plurality nevertheless holds that the third requirement of the *O'Brien* test, that the governmental interest be unrelated to the suppression of free expression, is satisfied because in applying the statute to nude dancing, the State is not "proscribing nudity because of the erotic message conveyed by the dancers." The plurality suggests that this is so because the State does not ban dancing that sends an erotic message; it is only nude erotic dancing that is forbidden. The perceived evil is not erotic dancing but public nudity, which may be prohibited despite any incidental impact on expressive activity. This analysis is transparently erroneous.

In arriving at its conclusion, the plurality concedes that nude dancing conveys an erotic message and concedes that the message would be muted if the dancers wore pasties and G-strings. Indeed, the emotional or erotic impact of the dance is intensified by the nudity of the performers. . . . [T]he nudity of the dancer is an integral part of the emotions and thoughts that a nude dancing performance evokes. The sight of a fully clothed, or even a partially clothed, dancer generally will have a far different impact on a spectator than that of a nude dancer, even if the same dance is performed. The nudity is itself an expressive component of the dance, not merely incidental "conduct." . . .

This being the case, it cannot be that the statutory prohibition is unrelated to expressive conduct. Since the State permits the dancers to perform if they wear pasties and G-strings but forbids nude dancing, it is precisely because of the distinctive, expressive content of the nude dancing performances at issue in this case that the State seeks to apply the statutory prohibition. It is only because nude dancing performances may generate emotions and feelings of eroticism and sensuality among the spectators that the State seeks to regulate such expressive activity, apparently on the assumption that creating or emphasizing such thoughts and ideas in the minds of the spectators may lead to increased prostitution and the degradation of women. But generating thoughts, ideas, and emotions is the essence of communication. The nudity element of nude dancing performances cannot be neatly pigeonholed as mere "conduct" independent of any expressive component of the dance.

That fact dictates the level of First Amendment protection to be accorded the performances at issue here. In Texas v. Johnson, 491 U.S. 397, 411–412 (1989), the Court observed: "Whether Johnson's treatment of the flag violated Texas law thus depended on the likely communicative impact of his expressive conduct. . . . We must therefore subject the State's asserted interest in preserving the special symbolic character of the flag to 'the most exacting scrutiny.'" Content based restrictions "will be upheld only if narrowly drawn to accomplish a compelling governmental interest." Nothing could be clearer from our cases.

. . . As I see it, our cases require us to affirm absent a compelling state interest supporting the statute. Neither the plurality nor the State suggest that the statute could withstand scrutiny under that standard.

NOTES AND QUESTIONS

1. *A divided Court.* The *Barnes* Court was unable to muster a majority for any particular rationale. Clearly, however, a majority was not prepared to protect nude dancing in absolute terms. Instead, a state interest in public decency would justify denying a liquor license to an all-nude club or prohibiting completely such an establishment in South Bend (or elsewhere in Indiana).
2. *Speech/conduct and nude dancing.* The plurality states that it views nude dancing as "expressive conduct within the outer perimeters of the First Amendment, though we view it as only marginally so." Do you agree? What precisely is the intended message of such a dance? Is the audience very likely to understand it? *See* Timothy Zick, *Cross Burning, Cockfighting, and Symbolic Meaning: Toward a First Amendment Ethnography*, 45 Wm. & Mary L. Rev. 2261 (2004). What are the implications of locating a form of expressive conduct at the "outer perimeters of the First Amendment"?
3. *"Secondary effects."* Justice Souter's concurring opinion in *Barnes* relies on the "secondary effects" rationale articulated in *Renton.* What evidence is there that the "secondary effects" purportedly associated with adult movie theaters are also present in the context of nude dancing establishments? Does or should the "secondary effects" rationale apply to a *ban* on a certain type of speech, rather than a mere displacement of it? Consider the Court's decision in *Pap's A.M.*, below.
4. *Generally applicable regulations of conduct.* Justice Scalia reasons that "as a general law regulating conduct and not specifically directed at expression, [the public indecency law] is not subject to First Amendment scrutiny at all." Do you agree? How would Justice Scalia's approach apply to the draft card law in *O'Brien* and the flag desecration law in *Johnson*? Does his approach effectively preclude review of laws regulating conduct that have only incidental effects on expression?

The Supreme Court was unable to produce a single majority opinion in *Barnes,* leaving the area more unsettled than some Justices thought wise. Almost ten years later, the Supreme Court agreed to review another ban on public nudity as applied to nude dancing.

City of Erie v. Pap's A.M.

529 U.S. 277 (2000)

O'CONNOR, J., announced the judgment of the Court and delivered the opinion of the Court with respect to Parts I and II, and an opinion with respect to Parts III and IV, in which THE CHIEF JUSTICE, KENNEDY, J., and BREYER, J., join.

The city of Erie, Pennsylvania, enacted an ordinance banning public nudity. Respondent Pap's A.M. (hereinafter Pap's), which operated a nude dancing establishment in Erie, challenged the constitutionality of the ordinance and sought a permanent injunction against its enforcement. The Pennsylvania Supreme Court, although noting that this Court in Barnes v. Glen Theatre, Inc., 501 U.S. 560 (1991), had upheld an Indiana ordinance that was "strikingly similar" to Erie's, found that the public nudity sections of the ordinance violated respondent's right to freedom of expression under the United States Constitution. This case raises the question whether the Pennsylvania Supreme Court properly evaluated the ordinance's constitutionality under the First Amendment. We hold that Erie's ordinance is a content-neutral regulation that satisfies the four-part test of United States v. O'Brien, 391 U.S. 367 (1968). Accordingly, we reverse the decision of the Pennsylvania Supreme Court and remand for the consideration of any remaining issues.

On September 28, 1994, the city council for the city of Erie, Pennsylvania, enacted Ordinance 75-1994, a public indecency ordinance that makes it a summary offense to knowingly or intentionally appear in public in a "state of nudity." Respondent Pap's, a Pennsylvania corporation, operated an establishment in Erie known as "Kandyland" that featured totally nude erotic dancing performed by women. To comply with the ordinance, these dancers must wear, at a minimum, "pasties" and a "G-string." On October 14, 1994, two days after the ordinance went into effect, Pap's filed a complaint against the city of Erie, the mayor of the city, and members of the city council, seeking declaratory relief and a permanent injunction against the enforcement of the ordinance.

The Court of Common Pleas of Erie County granted the permanent injunction and struck down the ordinance as unconstitutional. On cross appeals, the Commonwealth Court reversed the trial court's order.

The Pennsylvania Supreme Court granted review and reversed, concluding that the public nudity provisions of the ordinance violated respondent's rights to freedom of expression as protected by the First and Fourteenth Amendments. . . .

The city of Erie petitioned for a writ of certiorari, which we granted. . . .

Being "in a state of nudity" is not an inherently expressive condition. As we explained in *Barnes*, however, nude dancing of the type at issue here is expressive conduct, although we think that it falls only within the outer ambit of the First Amendment's protection. *See* Barnes v. Glen Theatre, Inc., 501 U.S. at 565-566 (plurality opinion); Schad v. Mount Ephraim, 452 U.S. 61, 66 (1981).

To determine what level of scrutiny applies to the ordinance at issue here, we must decide "whether the State's regulation is related to the suppression of expression." Texas v. Johnson, 491 U.S. 397, 403 (1989); see also United States v. O'Brien, 391 U.S., at 377. If the governmental purpose in enacting the regulation is unrelated to the suppression of expression, then the regulation need only satisfy the "less stringent" standard from *O'Brien* for evaluating restrictions on symbolic speech. *Texas v. Johnson, supra,* at 403; *United States v. O'Brien, supra,* at 377. If the government interest is related to the content of the expression, however, then the regulation falls outside the scope of the *O'Brien* test and must be justified under a more demanding standard. *Texas v. Johnson, supra,* at 403. . . .

Even if we had not already rejected the view that a ban on public nudity is necessarily related to the suppression of the erotic message of nude dancing, we would do so now because the premise of such a view is flawed. The State's interest in preventing harmful secondary effects is not related to the suppression of expression. In trying to control the secondary effects of nude dancing, the ordinance seeks to deter crime and the other deleterious effects caused by the presence of such an establishment in the neighborhood. . . .

Similarly, even if Erie's public nudity ban has some minimal effect on the erotic message by muting that portion of the expression that occurs when the last stitch is dropped, the dancers at Kandyland and other such establishments are free to perform wearing pasties and G-strings. Any effect on the overall expression is *de minimis.* And as Justice Stevens eloquently stated for the plurality in Young v. American Mimi Theatres, Inc., 427 U.S. 50, 70 (1976), "even though we recognize that the First Amendment will not tolerate the total suppression of erotic materials that have some arguably artistic value, it is manifest that society's interest in protecting this type of expression is of a wholly different, and lesser, magnitude than the interest in untrammeled political debate," and "few of us would march our sons and daughters off to war to preserve the citizen's right to see" specified anatomical areas exhibited at establishments like Kandyland. If States are to be able to regulate secondary effects, the *de minimis* intrusions on expression such as those at issue here cannot be sufficient to render the ordinance content based.

We conclude that Erie's asserted interest in combating the negative secondary effects associated with adult entertainment establishments like Kandyland is unrelated to the suppression of the erotic message conveyed by nude dancing. The ordinance prohibiting public nudity is therefore valid if it satisfies the four-factor test from *O'Brien* for evaluating restrictions on symbolic speech.

Applying that standard here, we conclude that Erie's ordinance is justified under *O'Brien*. . . .

We hold, therefore, that Erie's ordinance is a content-neutral regulation that is valid under *O'Brien.* Accordingly, the judgment of the Pennsylvania Supreme Court is reversed, and the case is remanded for further proceedings.

It is so ordered.

[Justice SCALIA's concurring opinion joined by Justice THOMAS is omitted.]

SOUTER, J., concurring in part and dissenting in part.

I . . . agree with the analytical approach that the plurality employs in deciding this case. Erie's stated interest in combating the secondary effects associated with nude dancing establishments is an interest unrelated to the suppression of expression under United States v. O'Brien, 391 U.S. 367 (1968), and the city's regulation is thus properly considered under the *O'Brien* standards. I do not believe, however, that the current record allows us to say that the city has made a sufficient evidentiary showing to sustain its regulation, and I would therefore vacate the decision of the Pennsylvania Supreme Court and remand the case for further proceedings. . . .

The record before us now does not permit the conclusion that Erie's ordinance is reasonably designed to mitigate real harms. This does not mean that the required showing cannot be made, only that, on this record, Erie has not made it. I would remand to give it the opportunity to do so. Accordingly, although I join with the plurality in adopting the *O'Brien* test, I respectfully dissent from the Court's disposition of the case.

STEVENS, J., with whom GINSBURG, J., joins, dissenting.

Far more important than the question whether nude dancing is entitled to protection of the First Amendment are the dramatic changes in legal doctrine that the Court endorses today. Until now, the "secondary effects" of commercial enterprises featuring indecent entertainment have justified only the regulation of their location. For the first time, the Court has now held that such effects may justify the total suppression of protected speech. Indeed, the plurality opinion concludes that admittedly trivial advancements of a State's interests may provide the basis for censorship. The Court's commendable attempt to replace the fractured decision in Barnes v. Glen Theatre, Inc., 501 U.S. 560 (1991), with a single coherent rationale is strikingly unsuccessful; it is supported neither by precedent nor by persuasive reasoning. . . .

The plurality relies on the so-called "secondary effects" test to defend the ordinance. The present use of that rationale, however, finds no support whatsoever in our precedents. Never before have we approved the use of that doctrine to justify a total ban on protected First Amendment expression. On the contrary, we have been quite clear that the doctrine would not support that end. . . .

The reason we have limited our secondary effects cases to zoning and declined to extend their reasoning to total bans is clear and straightforward: A dispersal that simply limits the places where speech may occur is a minimal imposition, whereas a total ban is the most exacting of restrictions. The State's interest in fighting presumed secondary effects is sufficiently strong to justify the former, but far too weak to support the latter, more severe burden. . . .

The Court's use of the secondary effects rationale to permit a total ban has grave implications for basic free speech principles. Ordinarily, laws regulating the primary effects of speech, *i.e.*, the intended persuasive effects caused by the speech, are presumptively invalid. Under today's opinion, a State may totally ban speech based on its secondary effects—which are defined as those effects that "happen to be associated" with speech . . . Because the category of effects that "happen to be associated" with speech includes the narrower subset of effects caused by speech, today's holding has the effect of swallowing whole a most fundamental principle of First Amendment jurisprudence.

The plurality's mishandling of our secondary effects cases is not limited to its approval of a total ban. It compounds that error by dramatically reducing the degree to which the State's interest must be furthered by the restriction imposed on speech, and by ignoring the critical difference between secondary effects caused by speech and the incidental effects on speech that may be caused by a regulation of conduct.

In what can most delicately be characterized as an enormous understatement, the plurality concedes that "requiring dancers to wear pasties and G-strings may not greatly reduce these secondary effects." To believe that the mandatory addition of pasties and a G-string will have *any* kind of noticeable impact on secondary effects requires nothing short of a titanic surrender to the implausible. It would be more accurate to acknowledge, as Justice Scalia does, that there is no reason to believe that such a requirement "will at all reduce the tendency of establishments such as Kandyland to attract crime and prostitution, and hence to foster sexually transmitted disease." Nevertheless, the plurality concludes that the "less stringent" test announced in United States v. O'Brien, 391 U.S. 367 (1968), "requires only that the regulation further the interest in combating such effects." It is one thing to say, however, that *O'Brien* is more lenient that the "more demanding standard" we have imposed in cases such as Texas v. Johnson, 491 U.S. 397 (1989). It is quite another to say that the test can be satisfied by nothing more than the mere possibility of *de minimis* effects on the neighborhood. . . .

It is clear beyond a shadow of a doubt that the Erie ordinance was a response to a more specific concern than nudity in general, namely, nude dancing of the sort found in Kandyland. Given that the Court has not even tried to defend the ordinance's total ban on the ground that its censorship of protected speech might be justified by an overriding state interest, it should conclude that the ordinance is patently invalid. For these reasons, as well as the reasons set forth in Justice White's dissent in *Barnes*, I respectfully dissent.

NOTES AND QUESTIONS

1. *Secondary effects revisited.* Even after a second bite at the apple, the Supreme Court could not muster a clean majority in favor of a single rationale for permitting the regulation of nude dancing. However, a plurality of the Supreme Court invokes the "secondary effects" of nude dancing as a basis for prohibiting the speech. Justice Souter joins that approach but calls for a more robust evidentiary showing of "secondary effects."
2. *Seminude versus fully nude — the "last stitch."* Is the message of an almost nude dancer the same as that of a totally nude dancer? If not, is the difference really a function of the "secondary effects" of dancers with G-strings and pasties versus dancers without these accouterments? Did Erie (or the Supreme Court) make a persuasive case that the risk of fights, prostitution, and drug dealing correlates positively with the absence of pasties and G-strings and that the use of pasties and G-strings by erotic dancers directly lowers these undesirable secondary effects?
3. *Content discrimination and nude dancing.* Is nudity disfavored because of its message of unbridled eroticism and sexuality? Public nudity exists in a variety of public accommodations in Erie — presumably including country clubs, high school and college locker rooms, and health spas. If nudity, per se, were the issue, why doesn't Erie regulate nudity in other places of public accommodation? Doesn't this selective regulation strongly suggest that the government's concern isn't really related to the hypothetical secondary effects caused by nude dancing? Note, too, on the question of content or viewpoint discrimination, that nudity incident to a major Broadway play or musical, such as *Equus* or *Hair*, does not seem to trigger the same censorial impulse either on the part of local officials or the courts.
4. *Low value?* The Court's decisions in *Barnes* and *Pap's A.M.* seem to reflect a judgment that the speech in question is "low value" and hence not worthy of full First Amendment protection. The Court locates nude dancing at the "outer ambit" of the First Amendment's protection. Does that judgment help explain the Court's willingness to rely on "secondary effects" and *O'Brien* in cases like *Renton* and *Pap's A.M.*?

Chapter 5
Regulation of Speech on Government Property

Table of Contents

A. The Concept of the Public Forum: Foundational Cases
B. Regulating Speech in the Public Forum: Time, Place, and Manner Regulations
C. Policing Conflict in the Public Forum: The Problem of the Hostile Audience
D. Forum Analysis: Which Public Properties and Facilities Do Speakers Have Access To?
E. When Should Speakers Have Access to *Private* Property?

Although expression has migrated to private digital forums like social media, access to public places remains critically important to preserving First Amendment rights and maintaining a robust culture of free expression. This chapter examines First Amendment doctrines concerning government regulation of expression in properties owned and managed by government. To what extent does the First Amendment limit the government's authority to regulate speech when it acts as an owner or proprietor of property?

The Supreme Court originally found that the First Amendment was no obstacle to government regulation in this area. In Commonwealth v. Davis, 162 Mass. 510 (1895), *aff'd sub nom.* Davis v. Massachusetts, 167 U.S. 43 (1897), Oliver Wendell Holmes, Jr., then writing as a Judge for the Massachusetts Supreme Judicial Court, wrote that "[f]or the legislature absolutely or conditionally to forbid public speaking in a highway or public park is no more an infringement of the rights of a member of the public than for the owner of a private house to forbid it in his house. . . . [If] the legislature may end the right of the public to enter upon the public place by putting an end to the dedication to public uses[,] [s]o it may take the lesser step of limiting the public use to certain purposes." 162 Mass. at 511. The Supreme Court affirmed, finding that the Constitution "does not destroy the power of the states to enact police regulations as to the subjects within their control and does not have the effect of creating a particular and personal right in the citizen to use public property in defiance of the constitution and laws of the state. . . . The [government's] right to absolutely exclude all right to use necessarily includes the authority to determine under what circumstances such use may be availed of, as the greater power contains the lesser." 167 U.S. at 47-48.

As the Supreme Court's modern First Amendment doctrine began to mature, however, the Court reconsidered whether speakers had a right to access public properties for the purpose of exercising expressive rights. The Court ultimately rejected the notion that government officials have absolute authority over public property when it comes to the exercise of speech and assembly rights. This chapter begins with some of the foundational cases relating to regulation of expression in public places. It then considers several doctrines rooted in these early cases that continue to limit the government's authority to restrict speech in public places—the "prior restraint" doctrine as applied to permitting and licensing requirements; the "time, place, and manner" standard applicable to content-neutral speech regulations; and the "public forum" doctrine, which determines which public properties are open to expressive activities and on what terms.

A. *THE CONCEPT OF THE PUBLIC FORUM: FOUNDATIONAL CASES*

Hague v. CIO

307 U.S. 496 (1939)

Mr. Justice ROBERTS delivered an opinion in which Mr. Justice BLACK concurred.* . . .

[Individual citizens and labor organizations sued officials of Jersey City, New Jersey, alleging that a city ordinance giving the Director of Public Safety the ability to grant or deny permits for gatherings on public land or in public buildings violated the First and Fourteenth Amendments. They argued that the ordinance was void and was enforced against them in a discriminatory manner because of their beliefs. The citizens and labor organizations sought an injunction barring enforcement of the ordinance. After trial on the merits the District Court ruled in favor of the citizens and labor organizations. City officials petitioned the Supreme Court for a writ of certiorari.]

. . . The question now presented is whether freedom to disseminate information concerning the provisions of the National Labor Relations Act, to assemble peaceably for discussion of the Act, and of the opportunities and advantages offered by it, is a privilege or immunity of a citizen of the United States secured against State abridgment by Section 1 of the Fourteenth Amendment; and whether the Judicial Code affords redress in a federal court for such abridgment. . . .

---

* Justice Roberts delivered a plurality opinion joined by Justice Black. Justice Stone delivered a separate opinion in which Justice Reed concurred. Chief Justice Hughes also concurred. Justices McReynolds and Butler filed dissenting opinions. Justices Frankfurter and Douglas did not participate in the decision.—EDS.

Although it has been held that the Fourteenth Amendment created no rights in citizens of the United States, but merely secured existing rights against state abridgment, it is clear that the right peaceably to assemble and to discuss these topics, and to communicate respecting them, whether orally or in writing, is a privilege inherent in citizenship of the United States which the Amendment protects. . . .

. . . [In] the light of the facts found, privileges and immunities of the individual respondents as citizens of the United States, were infringed by the petitioners, by virtue of their official positions, under color of ordinances of Jersey City, unless, as petitioners contend, the city's ownership of streets and parks is as absolute as one's ownership of his home, with consequent power altogether to exclude citizens from the use thereof, or unless, though the city holds the streets in trust for public use, the absolute denial of their use to the respondents is a valid exercise of the police power.

The findings of fact negative the latter assumption. In support of the former the petitioners rely upon Davis v. Massachusetts, 167 U.S. 43. . . . [*Davis*] seems to be grounded on the holding of the State court that the Common "was absolutely under the control of the legislature," and that it was thus "conclusively determined there was no right in the plaintiff in error to use the common except in such mode and subject to such regulations as the legislature, in its wisdom, may have deemed proper to prescribe." . . .

The ordinance there in question apparently had a different purpose from that of the one here challenged, for it was not directed solely at the exercise of the right of speech and assembly, but was addressed as well to other activities, not in the nature of civil rights, which doubtless might be regulated or prohibited as respects their enjoyment in parks. In the instant case the ordinance deals only with the exercise of the right of assembly for the purpose of communicating views entertained by speakers, and is not a general measure to promote the public convenience in the use of the streets or parks.

We have no occasion to determine whether, on the facts disclosed, the *Davis* case was rightly decided, but we cannot agree that it rules the instant case. Wherever the title of streets and parks may rest, they have immemorially been held in trust for the use of the public and, time out of mind, have been used for purposes of assembly, communicating thoughts between citizens, and discussing public questions. Such use of the streets and public places has, from ancient times, been a part of the privileges, immunities, rights, and liberties of citizens. The privilege of a citizen of the United States to use the streets and parks for communication of views on national questions may be regulated in the interest of all; it is not absolute, but relative, and must be exercised in subordination to the general comfort and convenience, and in consonance with peace and good order; but it must not, in the guise of regulation, be abridged or denied.

We think the court below was right in holding the ordinance . . . void upon its face. It does not make comfort or convenience in the use of streets or parks the standard of official action. It enables the Director of Safety to refuse a permit on his mere opinion that such refusal will prevent "riots, disturbances or disorderly assemblage." It can thus, as the record discloses, be made the instrument of arbitrary suppression of free expression of views on national affairs for the prohibition of all speaking will undoubtedly "prevent" such eventualities. But uncontrolled official suppression of the privilege cannot be made a substitute for the duty to maintain order in connection with the exercise of the right. . . .

As the ordinance is void, the respondents are entitled to a decree so declaring and an injunction against its enforcement by the petitioners. They are free to hold meetings without a permit and without regard to the terms of the void ordinance. . . .

[The concurring opinions of Justice STONE and Chief Justice HUGHES are omitted.]

[The dissenting opinions of Justices MCREYNOLDS and BUTLER are omitted.]

NOTES AND QUESTIONS

1. *The "public forum."* "Wherever the title of streets and parks may rest they have immemorially been held in trust for the use of the public and, time out of mind, have been used for purposes of assembly, communicating thoughts between citizens, and discussing public questions." This language from Justice Roberts' plurality opinion in *Hague* birthed the concept of the "public forum." In contrast to Holmes's earlier suggestion that a city, like any private property owner, possesses a right to exclude others from its property, Roberts suggested the public "has a kind of First Amendment easement" to access public streets and public parks for expressive purposes. *See* Harry Kalven, Jr., *The Concept of the Public Forum:* Cox v. Louisiana, 1965 Sup. Ct. Rev. 1. Over time, the Court has added public sidewalks to the category of places used "time out of mind" for speech and assembly. *See* United States v. Grace, 461 U.S. 171, 180 (1983) (invalidating speech restrictions on public sidewalks bordering U.S. Supreme Court building). As discussed in Section D, under the Court's modern "public forum" doctrine places that fall into this category are referred to as "traditional" public forums.
2. *Minimal access rights.* The Hughes Court's decisions not only recognized the concept of the "public forum," but also preserved a degree of minimal access for speakers. For example, in early public forum decisions the Court invalidated local ordinances that flatly banned distribution of leaflets on public streets and door-to-door solicitation. *See* Lovell v. City of Griffin, 303 U.S. 444 (1938); Schneider v. New Jersey, 308 U.S. 147 (1939). As the Court explained, these means of communication were "essential to the poorly financed causes" of minority and dissident speakers. Martin v. Struthers, 319 U.S. 141, 146 (1943). Indeed, many early ordinances targeted religious proselytizing by Jehovah's Witnesses. See Shawn Francis Peters, *Judging Jehovah's Witnesses: Religious Persecution and the Dawn of the Rights Revolution* (2000).
3. *"Instruments of arbitrary suppression"—prior restraints.* Note Justice Roberts's concern in *Hughes* that the Jersey City ordinance vested unbridled discretion in the Director of Safety to suppress speech and assembly activities. Roberts writes, "uncontrolled official suppression of the privilege cannot be made a substitute for the duty to maintain order in connection with the exercise of the right." In other early decisions, the Court invalidated licensing schemes that vested unbridled discretion in local officials to regulate speech. See, e.g., Lovell v. Griffin, 303

U.S. 444 (1938). Standardless licensing schemes have long been considered a form of presumptively invalid prior restraint on expression. One concern is that the lack of standards for granting or denying a license will cause speakers to self-censor. *See, e.g.*, City of Lakewood v. Plain Dealer Publg. Co., 486 U.S. 750, 757 (1988). The Court has also observed that a lack of standards allows officials to use post hoc and content-based justifications for suppressing speech and assembly. *Id.* at 758; Cox v. Louisiana, 379 U.S. 536, 557 (1965). Numerous cases after *Hague* have reiterated the principle that standardless licensing systems are presumptively unconstitutional prior restraints. *See, e.g.*, Kunz v. New York, 340 U.S. 290 (1951); Shuttlesworth v. City of Birmingham, 394 U.S. 147 (1969); Thomas v. Chicago Park Dist., 534 U.S. 316 (2002).*See also* Elena Kagan, *Private Speech, Public Purpose: The Role of Governmental Motive in First Amendment Doctrine*, 63 U. Chi. L. Rev. 415, 459 (1996); Thomas I. Emerson, *The Doctrine of Prior Restraint*, 20 Law & Contemp. Probs. 648 (1955).

Cox v. New Hampshire

312 U.S. 569 (1941)

[The Court unanimously affirmed the convictions of five Jehovah's Witnesses for violating a state law prohibiting any "parade or procession" upon a public street without first obtaining a permit from local authorities and paying a license fee of not more than three hundred dollars a day. The defendants had marched on busy city sidewalks carrying signs bearing such slogans as "Religion is a Snare and a Racket" and "Serve God and Christ the King." They did not apply for a permit and none was issued.]

Chief Justice HUGHES delivered the opinion of the Court.

The authority of a municipality to impose regulations in order to assure the safety and convenience of the people in the use of public highways has never been regarded as inconsistent with civil liberties. [The] control of travel on the streets of cities is the most familiar illustration of this recognition of social need. Where a restriction of the use of highways in that relation is designed to promote the public convenience in the interest of all, it cannot be disregarded by the attempted exercise of some civil rights which in other circumstances would be entitled to protection. One would not be justified in ignoring the familiar red traffic light because he thought it his religious duty to disobey the municipal [command]. As a regulation of the use of the streets for parades and processions is a traditional exercise of control by local government, the question in a particular case is whether that control is exerted so as not to deny or unwarrantedly abridge the right of assembly and the opportunities for the communication of thought and the discussion of public questions immemorially associated with resort to public places.

In the instant case, we are aided by the opinion of the Supreme Court of the State, [which] defined the limitations of authority conferred for the granting of licenses. [T]he state court considered and defined the duty of the licensing authority and the rights of appellants to a license for their parade, with regard only to considerations of time, place and manner so as to conserve the public convenience. The obvious advantage of requiring application for a permit [was] giving the public authorities notice in advance so as to afford the opportunity for proper policing. [Moreover,] the license served to prevent confusion by overlapping parades, [to] secure convenient use of the streets by other travelers, and to minimize the risk of disorder. [If] a municipality has authority to control the use of its public streets for parades or processions, as it undoubtedly has, it cannot be denied authority to give consideration, without unfair discrimination, to time, place and manner in relation to the other proper uses of the streets. We find it impossible to say that the limited authority conferred by the licensing provisions of the statute in question as thus construed by the state court contravened any constitutional right. [There] is no evidence that the statute has been administered otherwise than in the fair and non-discriminatory manner which the state court has construed it to [require].

Affirmed.

NOTES AND QUESTIONS

1. *Limits on expression in the public forum.* In *Cox,* the Court made clear that speech rights in the public forum are not absolute. It recognized the State's interest in regulating public order and upheld the permit requirement as a valid "time, place, and manner" regulation (*see infra* Section B). In other early public forum cases, the Court identified several additional interests governments can validly invoke to regulate expressive activities in the public forum. Consider Kovacs v. Cooper, 336 U.S. 77 (1949), which upheld an ordinance that prohibited the use of sound trucks or any other "loudspeaker or sound amplifier" or any tool that emitted "loud or raucous noises" upon city streets or public places. The plurality held that the ordinance did not violate the First Amendment because "[t]here is no restriction upon the communication of ideas or discussion of issues" and "the need for reasonable protection in the homes or business houses from the distracting noises of vehicles equipped with such sound amplifying devices justifies the ordinance."
2. *Permit schemes.* As *Cox* shows, the Court has long recognized that officials can regulate speech to maintain public safety and order. To gauge possible conflicts with other activities, impact on traffic, and need for law enforcement involvement, governments often require persons or groups to obtain permits in advance of a demonstration, rally, or other event. Do permit requirements force speakers to "bow to the very authorities" they may be challenging? Do they create opportunities for subtle official harassment of speakers? What, if any, effect do permit requirements have on spontaneous forms of expression in the public forum? For consideration of these issues, see C. Edwin Baker, *Unreasoned Reasonableness: Mandatory Parade Permits and Time, Place and Manner Regulations,* 78 Nw. U. L. Rev. 937, 969 (1983).
3. *Limiting official discretion and content neutrality.* *Cox* holds that permitting schemes are valid so long as official discretion to grant or deny the permit is sufficiently constrained by neutral criteria. What qualifies as a neutral

"time, place, and manner" standard of decision in this context? The Court has held it is appropriate for an official to consider that the permit was not fully completed, that the permit contains material falsehoods, and that the activity for which the permit is requested conflicts with another activity already planned for a particular location. *See Thomas*, 534 U.S. at 318 n.1 (upholding ordinance with similar criteria). What about a standard allowing officials to deny a permit because the proposed activity "would present an unreasonable danger to the health or safety" of others, including government employees or the public? *See id.* (upholding ordinance with similar standard). Is this standard consistent with *Hague*? Is it content-neutral?

4. *Permit fees. Cox* held that municipalities could charge flat permit fees to "take into account the greater public expense of policing" events that draw significant crowds. Are there any First Amendment limits on either the amount or nature of such fees? For discussion see Section C, *infra*.

Cantwell v. Connecticut

310 U.S. 296 (1940)

Mr. Justice ROBERTS delivered the opinion of the Court.

[Jesse Cantwell, a Jehovah's Witness, was arrested and convicted of the common law offense of inciting a breach of the peace].

The facts which were held to support the conviction of Jesse Cantwell on the [inciting breach of peace] count were that he stopped two men in the street, asked, and received, permission to play a phonograph record, and played the record "Enemies," which attacked the religion and church of the two men, who were Catholics. Both were incensed by the contents of the record and were tempted to strike Cantwell unless he went away. On being told to be on his way he left their presence. There was no evidence that he was personally offensive or entered into any argument with those he interviewed.

The court held that the charge was not assault or breach of the peace or threats on Cantwell's part, but invoking or inciting others to breach of the peace, and that the facts supported the conviction of that offense. . . .

Conviction on the fifth count was not pursuant to a statute evincing a legislative judgment that street discussion of religious affairs, because of its tendency to provoke disorder, should be regulated, or a judgment that the playing of a phonograph on the streets should in the interest of comfort or privacy be limited or prevented. Violation of an Act exhibiting such a legislative judgment and narrowly drawn to prevent the supposed evil, would pose a question differing from that we must here answer.[9] . . . Here, however, the judgment is based on a common law concept of the most general and undefined nature. . . .

The offense known as breach of the peace embraces a great variety of conduct destroying or menacing public order and tranquility. It includes not only violent acts but acts and words likely to produce violence in others. . . . When clear and

9. Compare Gitlow v. New York, 268 U.S. 652, 670, 671; Thornhill v. Alabama, 310 U.S. 88.

present danger of riot, disorder, interference with traffic upon the public streets, or other immediate threat to public safety, peace, or order, appears, the power of the state to prevent or punish is obvious. Equally obvious is it that a state may not unduly suppress free communication of views, religious or other, under the guise of conserving desirable conditions. Here we have a situation analogous to a conviction under a statute sweeping in a great variety of conduct under a general and indefinite characterization, and leaving to the executive and judicial branches too wide a discretion in its application.

Having these considerations in mind, we note that [Cantwell] was upon a public street, where he had a right to be, and where he had a right peacefully to impart his views to others. There is no showing that his deportment was noisy, truculent, overbearing or offensive. He requested of two pedestrians permission to play to them a phonograph record. The permission was granted. It is not claimed that he intended to insult or affront the hearers by playing the record. It is plain that he wished only to interest them in his propaganda. The sound of the phonograph is not shown to have disturbed residents of the street, to have drawn a crowd, or to have impeded traffic. Thus far he had invaded no right or interest of the public or of the men accosted.

The record played by Cantwell embodies a general attack on all organized religious systems as instruments of Satan and injurious to man; it then singles out the Roman Catholic Church for strictures couched in terms which naturally would offend not only persons of that persuasion, but all others who respect the honestly held religious faith of their fellows. The hearers were in fact highly offended. One of them said he felt like hitting Cantwell and the other that he was tempted to throw Cantwell off the street. The one who testified he felt like hitting Cantwell said, in answer to the question "Did you do anything else or have any other reaction?" "No, sir, because he said he would take the victrola and he went." The other witness testified that he told Cantwell he had better get off the street before something happened to him and that was the end of the matter as Cantwell picked up his books and walked up the street.

Cantwell's conduct, in the view of the court below, considered apart from the effect of his communication upon his hearers, did not amount to a breach of the peace. One may, however, be guilty of the offense if he commit acts or make statements likely to provoke violence and disturbance of good order, even though no such eventuality be intended. Decisions to this effect are many, but examination discloses that, in practically all, the provocative language which was held to amount to a breach of the peace consisted of profane, indecent, or abusive remarks directed to the person of the hearer. Resort to epithets or personal abuse is not in any proper sense communication of information or opinion safeguarded by the Constitution[.] . . .

We find in the instant case no assault or threatening of bodily harm, no truculent bearing, no intentional discourtesy, no personal abuse. On the contrary, we find only an effort to persuade a willing listener to buy a book or to contribute money in the interest of what Cantwell, however misguided others may think him, conceived to be true religion. In the realm of religious faith, and in that of political belief, sharp differences arise. In both fields the tenets of one man may seem the rankest error to his neighbor. To persuade others to his own point of view, the pleader, as we know, at times, resorts to exaggeration, to vilification of men who have been, or are, prominent in church or state, and even to false statement. But the people of this nation have ordained in the light of history, that, in spite of the probability of excesses and abuses, these liberties are, in the long view, essential to enlightened opinion and right conduct on the part of the citizens of a democracy. . . .

Although the contents of the record not unnaturally aroused animosity, we think that, in the absence of a statute narrowly drawn to define and punish specific conduct as constituting a clear and present danger to a substantial interest of the State, the petitioner's communication, considered in the light of the constitutional guarantees, raised no such clear and present menace to public peace and order as to render him liable to conviction of the common law offense in question.

The judgment affirming the convictions on the third and fifth counts is reversed and the cause is remanded for further proceedings not inconsistent with this opinion. So ordered.

Reversed and remanded.

NOTES AND QUESTIONS

1. *Offensive and provocative speech in the public forum.* In *Cantwell* and other early decisions, the Court affirmed that speakers could not be denied access to public streets and parks merely because some considered their speech offensive or unwelcome. The Court observed Jesse Cantwell "was upon a public street, . . . where he had a right peacefully to impart his views to others." However, according to the Court, "When clear and present danger of riot, disorder, interference with traffic upon the public streets, or other immediate threat to public safety, peace, or order, appears, *the power of the state to prevent or punish is obvious.*" Could Cantwell have been arrested if he had interfered with pedestrian movement on public sidewalks or played his record in the middle of the street? If he had played the record so loudly that it interfered with the conduct of regular business in shops lining the streets? How clear must physical danger or harm be for the state to punish a provocative speaker? Suppose Cantwell had played his record even after the audience denied permission for him to do so—is that a sufficient "menace" to public order? For a discussion of the limits of provocative speech in the public forum, see Timothy Zick, *Managing Dissent*, 95 Wash. U. L. Rev. 1423 (2018).
2. *Beyond offense.* Suppose Cantwell had less "peacefully" imparted his views. The Court notes there was no "threatening of bodily harm, no truculent bearing, no intentional discourtesy, no personal abuse." As discussed in Chapter 2, threats of bodily harm and profane language directed to specific onlookers may constitute unprotected "true threats" or "fighting words." If Cantwell had a "truculent bearing" or showed a degree of "intentional discourtesy" to his audience would his speech still be protected? If Cantwell's audience had reacted violently to his speech, could police order him to stop playing his record? Consider the "hostile audience" precedents discussed *infra* Section C.

B. *REGULATING SPEECH IN THE PUBLIC FORUM: TIME, PLACE, AND MANNER REGULATIONS*

Chapter 3 explained that when government regulates speech based on its content, courts apply "strict scrutiny" and the law is usually (although not always) invalidated. By contrast, when governments regulate speech on content-neutral grounds, the restrictions are subject to a form of "intermediate scrutiny." The *O'Brien* standard, which is applicable to regulations of expressive conduct (Chapter 4), is one example of this kind of scrutiny. "Time, place, and manner" regulations are another common type of content-neutral speech restriction. As the name suggests, such regulations limit when, where, and how speech can occur. In *Cox*, the Court upheld the permit scheme as a valid content-neutral regulation of the time, place, and manner of expression. Governments typically defend such regulations by pointing to a variety of content-neutral interests including public safety, public order, tranquility, aesthetics, and residential privacy. Consider the ends and means invoked by governments to restrict public speech in the following cases.

Clark v. Community for Creative Non-Violence

468 U.S. 288 (1984)

Justice WHITE delivered the opinion of the Court.

The issue in this case is whether a National Park Service regulation prohibiting camping in certain parks violates the First Amendment when applied to prohibit demonstrators from sleeping in Lafayette Park and the Mall in connection with a demonstration intended to call attention to the plight of the homeless. We hold that it does not and reverse the contrary judgment of the Court of Appeals.

I

The Interior Department, through the National Park Service, is charged with responsibility for the management and maintenance of the National Parks and is authorized to promulgate rules and regulations for the use of the parks in accordance with the purposes for which they were established. . . . Lafayette Park is a roughly 7-acre square located across Pennsylvania Avenue from the White House. Although originally part of the White House grounds, President Jefferson set it aside as a park for the use of residents and visitors. It is a "garden park with a . . . formal landscaping of flowers and trees, with fountains, walks and benches." . . . The Mall is a stretch of land running westward from the Capitol to the Lincoln Memorial some two miles away. It includes the Washington Monument, a series of reflecting pools, trees, lawns, and other greenery. It is bordered by, inter alia, the Smithsonian Institution and the National Gallery of Art. Both the Park and the Mall were included in Major Pierre L'Enfant's original plan for the Capital. Both are visited by vast numbers of visitors from around the country, as well as by large numbers of residents of the Washington metropolitan area.

Under the regulations involved in this case, camping in National Parks is permitted only in campgrounds designated for that purpose. 36 CFR § 50.27(a) (1983).

No such campgrounds have ever been designated in Lafayette Park or the Mall. . . . Demonstrations for the airing of views or grievances are permitted in the Memorial-core parks, but for the most part only by Park Service permits. . . . Temporary structures may be erected for demonstration purposes but may not be used for camping. . . .

In 1982, the Park Service issued a renewable permit to respondent Community for Creative Non-Violence (CCNV) to conduct a wintertime demonstration in Lafayette Park and the Mall for the purpose of demonstrating the plight of the homeless. The permit authorized the erection of two symbolic tent cities: 20 tents in Lafayette Park that would accommodate 50 people and 40 tents in the Mall with a capacity of up to 100. The Park Service, however, relying on the above regulations, specifically denied CCNV's request that demonstrators be permitted to sleep in the symbolic tents.

CCNV and several individuals then filed an action to prevent the application of the no-camping regulations to the proposed demonstration, which, it was claimed, was not covered by the regulation. . . . The District Court granted summary judgment in favor of the Park Service. The Court of Appeals, sitting en banc, reversed. . . .

II

We need not differ with the view of the Court of Appeals that overnight sleeping in connection with the demonstration is expressive conduct protected to some extent by the First Amendment. We assume for present purposes, but do not decide, that such is the case, *cf.* United States v. O'Brien, 391 U.S. 367 (1968), but this assumption only begins the inquiry. Expression, whether oral or written or symbolized by conduct, is subject to reasonable time, place, or manner restrictions. We have often noted that restrictions of this kind are valid provided that they are justified without reference to the content of the regulated speech, that they are narrowly tailored to serve a significant governmental interest, and that they leave open ample alternative channels for communication of the information.

It is also true that a message may be delivered by conduct that is intended to be communicative and that, in context, would reasonably be understood by the viewer to be communicative. . . . Symbolic expression of this kind may be forbidden or regulated if the conduct itself may constitutionally be regulated, if the regulation is narrowly drawn to further a substantial governmental interest, and if the interest is unrelated to the suppression of free speech. *O'Brien.*

Petitioners submit . . . the regulation forbidding sleeping is defensible either as a time, place, or manner restriction or as a regulation of symbolic conduct. We agree [that the regulations,] . . . including the ban on sleeping, are clearly limitations on the manner in which the demonstration could be carried out. . . .

[I]t is not disputed here that the prohibition on camping, and on sleeping specifically, is content-neutral and is not being applied because of disagreement with the message presented. Neither was the regulation faulted, nor could it be, on the ground that without overnight sleeping the plight of the homeless could not be communicated in other ways. The regulation otherwise left the demonstration intact, with its symbolic city, signs, and the presence of those who were willing to take their turns in a day-and-night vigil. Respondents do not suggest that there was, or is, any barrier to delivering to the media, or to the public by other means, the intended message concerning the plight of the homeless. . . .

It is also apparent to us that the regulation narrowly focuses on the Government's substantial interest in maintaining the parks in the heart of our Capital in an attractive and intact condition, readily available to the millions of people who wish to see and enjoy them by their presence. To permit camping . . . would be totally inimical to these purposes[.] . . .

. . . Absent the prohibition on sleeping, there would be other groups who would demand permission to deliver an asserted message by camping in Lafayette Park. Some of them would surely have as credible a claim in this regard as does CCNV, and the denial of permits to still others would present difficult problems for the Park Service. With the prohibition, however, as is evident in the case before us, at least some around-the-clock demonstrations lasting for days on end will not materialize, others will be limited in size and duration, and the purposes of the regulation will thus be materially served. Perhaps these purposes would be more effectively and not so clumsily achieved by preventing tents and 24-hour vigils entirely in the core areas. But the Park Service's decision to permit nonsleeping demonstrations does not, in our view, impugn the camping prohibition as a valuable, but perhaps imperfect, protection to the parks. . . .

[T]he foregoing analysis demonstrates that the Park Service regulation is sustainable under the four-factor standard of [*O'Brien*], for validating a regulation of expressive conduct, which, in the last analysis is little, if any, different from the standard applied to time, place, or manner restrictions.[8] . . .

We are unmoved by the Court of Appeals' view that the challenged regulation is unnecessary, and hence invalid, because there are less speech-restrictive alternatives that could have satisfied the Government interest in preserving park lands. There is no gainsaying that preventing overnight sleeping will avoid a measure of actual or threatened damage to Lafayette Park and the Mall. The Court of Appeals' suggestions that the Park Service minimize the possible injury by reducing the size, duration, or frequency of demonstrations would still curtail the total allowable expression in which demonstrators could engage, whether by sleeping or otherwise, and these suggestions represent no more than a disagreement with the Park Service over how much protection the core parks require or how an acceptable level of preservation is to be attained. We do not believe, however, that either [*O'Brien*] or the time, place, or manner decisions assign to the judiciary the authority to replace the Park Service as the manager of the Nation's parks or endow the judiciary with the competence to judge how much protection of park lands is wise and how that level of conservation is to be attained.

Accordingly, the judgment of the Court of Appeals is *reversed.*

---

8. Reasonable time, place, or manner restrictions are valid even though they directly limit oral or written expression. It would be odd to insist on a higher standard for limitations aimed at regulable conduct and having only an incidental impact on speech. Thus, if the time, place, or manner restriction on expressive sleeping, if that is what is involved in this case, sufficiently and narrowly serves a substantial enough governmental interest to escape First Amendment condemnation, it is untenable to invalidate it under *O'Brien* on the ground that the governmental interest is insufficient to warrant the intrusion on First Amendment concerns or that there is an inadequate nexus between the regulation and the interest sought to be served. . . .

Justice MARSHALL, with whom Justice BRENNAN joins, dissenting.

. . . Although sleep in the context of this case is symbolic speech protected by the First Amendment, it is nonetheless subject to reasonable time, place, and manner restrictions. I agree with the standard enunciated by the majority[.] . . . I conclude, however, that the regulations at issue in this case, as applied to respondents, fail to satisfy this standard. . . .

According to the majority, the significant Government interest advanced by denying respondents' request to engage in sleep-speech is the interest in "maintaining the parks in the heart of our capital in an attractive and intact condition, readily available to the millions of people who wish to see and enjoy them by their presence." . . . That interest is indeed significant. However, neither the Government nor the majority adequately explains how prohibiting respondents' planned activity will substantially further that interest. . . .

. . . The majority cites no evidence indicating that sleeping engaged in as symbolic speech will cause *substantial* wear and tear on park property. Furthermore, the Government's application of the sleeping ban in the circumstances of this case is strikingly underinclusive. The majority acknowledges that a proper time, place, and manner restriction must be "narrowly tailored." Here, however, the tailoring requirement is virtually forsaken inasmuch as the Government offers no justification for applying its absolute ban on sleeping yet is willing to allow respondents to engage in activities—such as feigned sleeping—that [are] no less burdensome. . . .

The disposition of this case impels me to make two additional observations. First, in this case, as in some others involving time, place, and manner restrictions, the Court has dramatically lowered its scrutiny of governmental regulations once it has determined that such regulations are content-neutral. The result has been the creation of a two-tiered approach to First Amendment cases: while regulations that turn on the content of the expression are subjected to a strict form of judicial review, regulations that are aimed at matters other than expression receive only a minimal level of scrutiny. . . .

Second, the disposition of this case reveals a mistaken assumption regarding the motives and behavior of government officials who create and administer content-neutral regulations. . . . The Court evidently assumes that the balance struck by officials is deserving of deference so long as it does not appear to be tainted by content discrimination. What the Court fails to recognize is that public officials have strong incentives to overregulate even in the absence of an intent to censor particular views. This incentive stems from the fact that of the two groups whose interests officials must accommodate—on the one hand, the interests of the general public and, on the other, the interests of those who seek to use a particular forum for First Amendment activity—the political power of the former is likely to be far greater than that of the latter. . . .

For the foregoing reasons, I respectfully dissent.

[Chief Justice BURGER's concurring opinion is omitted.]

NOTES AND QUESTIONS

1. O'Brien *vs. time, place, and manner.* In *CCNV*, the Court refers to the four-part test from United States v. O'Brien, 391 U.S. 367 (1968), *supra* p. 140.

As discussed in Chapter 4, the *O'Brien* standard is an intermediate scrutiny standard applicable to regulations of expressive conduct. The time, place, and manner standard, which is also a form of intermediate scrutiny, is described somewhat differently from the *O'Brien* standard (for example, the Court says time, place, and manner regulations must leave open "alternative channels of communication," a requirement not expressly stated in *O'Brien*). Nevertheless, in *CCNV* the Justices agreed that the *O'Brien* test "is little, if any, different from the standard applied to time, place, or manner restrictions." Both standards require that content-neutral speech regulations burden no more speech than necessary to further important or significant governmental interests.

2. *Aesthetics and preservation.* Do you think "maintaining the parks in the heart of our Capital in an attractive and intact condition" constitutes a "substantial" governmental interest for purposes of reviewing the speech regulation in *CCNV*? Does the Court explain why it views such an interest as "substantial"? The Court has recognized "aesthetic" interests as substantial in other cases. In Metromedia, Inc. v. San Diego, 453 U.S. 490 (1981), seven Justices concluded that the city's interest in preserving and improving the appearance of the city would be sufficient to justify a flat ban on all billboards. *See also* City Council of Los Angeles v. Taxpayers for Vincent, 466 U.S. 789 (1984) (upholding Los Angeles ordinance that banned signs on public property owing to the "visual assault on the citizens of Los Angeles").
3. *"Narrow tailoring." Rock Against Racism* [*supra* p. 129, Chapter 3] stated "that a regulation of the time, place, or manner of protected speech must be narrowly tailored to serve the government's legitimate, content-neutral interests but that it need not be the least restrictive or least intrusive means of doing so. Rather, the requirement of narrow tailoring is satisfied 'so long as the . . . regulation promotes a substantial government interest that would be achieved less effectively absent the regulation.'" *Id.* How does this form of "narrow tailoring" differ from the standard under "strict" scrutiny?
4. *"Intermediate" scrutiny.* Does *CCNV* allow for appropriate and meaningful judicial review of time, place, and manner regulations? Or do you agree with the dissenters that the majority "dramatically lowered its scrutiny of governmental regulations once it . . . determined that such regulations are content-neutral"? Under the standard as applied, does content neutrality seem more like a "ceiling" rather than a "floor" in terms of judicial review of speech regulations? In other words, once a regulation is determined to be content-neutral does *CCNV* suggest courts will not engage in meaningful review?
5. *Deference to forum proprietors. CCNV* strongly suggests that courts should defer to public forum administrators concerning how best to accommodate speech on public properties. Is deference to the forum administrator appropriate so long as officials regulate in a content-neutral manner? Or do officials "have strong incentives to overregulate even in the absence of an intent to censor particular views"? David Goldberger, *Judicial Scrutiny in Public Forum Cases: Misplaced Trust in the Judgment of Public Officials*, 32 Buff. L. Rev. 175, 207-208 (1983).

Frisby v. Schultz

487 U.S. 474 (1988)

Justice O'Connor delivered the opinion of the Court.

Brookfield, Wisconsin, has adopted an ordinance that completely bans picketing "before or about" any residence. This case presents a facial First Amendment challenge to that ordinance.

[Appellees] are individuals strongly opposed to abortion and wish to express their views on the subject by picketing on a public street outside the Brookfield residence of a doctor who apparently performs abortions at two clinics in neighboring towns. Appellees and others engaged in precisely that activity, assembling outside the doctor's home on at least six occasions between April 20, 1985, and May 20, 1985, for periods ranging from one to one and a half hours. The size of the group varied from 11 to more than 40. The picketing was generally orderly and peaceful; the town never had occasion to invoke any of its various ordinances prohibiting obstruction of the streets, loud and unnecessary noises, or disorderly conduct. Nonetheless, the picketing generated substantial controversy and numerous complaints. . . .

[O]n May 15, 1985, [the town enacted] the following flat ban on all residential picketing:

> It is unlawful for any person to engage in picketing before or about the residence or dwelling of any individual in the Town of Brookfield.

The ordinance itself recites the primary purpose of this ban: "the protection and preservation of the home" through assurance "that members of the community enjoy in their homes and dwellings a feeling of well-being, tranquility, and privacy." The Town Board believed that a ban was necessary because it determined that "the practice of picketing before or about residences and dwellings causes emotional disturbance and distress to the occupants . . . [and] has as its object the harassing of such occupants." . . . The ordinance also evinces a concern for public safety, noting that picketing obstructs and interferes with "the free use of public sidewalks and public ways of travel." . . .

Our prior holdings make clear that a public street does not lose its status as a traditional public forum simply because it runs through a residential neighborhood. . . .

[The] residential character of those streets may well inform the application of the relevant test, but it does not lead to a different test; the antipicketing ordinance must be judged against the stringent standards we have established for restrictions on speech in traditional public fora[.] . . .

[W]e accept the lower courts' conclusion that the Brookfield ordinance is content neutral. Accordingly, we turn to consider whether the ordinance is "narrowly tailored to serve a significant government interest" and whether it "leave[s] open ample alternative channels of communication." . . .

Because the last question is so easily answered, we address it first. Of course, before we are able to assess the available alternatives, we must consider more carefully the reach of the ordinance. The precise scope of the ban is not further described within the text of the ordinance, but in our view the ordinance is readily subject to a narrowing construction that avoids constitutional difficulties. Specifically, the use of the singular form of the words "residence" and "dwelling" suggests that the ordinance is intended to prohibit only picketing focused on, and taking place in front of, a particular residence. . . .

So narrowed, the ordinance permits the more general dissemination of a message. As appellants explain, the limited nature of the prohibition makes it virtually self-evident that ample alternatives remain: "Protestors have not been barred from the residential neighborhoods. They may enter such neighborhoods, alone or in groups, even marching. . . . They may go door-to-door to proselytize their views. They may distribute literature in this manner . . . or through the mails. They may contact residents by telephone, short of harassment."

We readily agree that the ordinance preserves ample alternative channels of communication and thus move on to inquire whether the ordinance serves a significant government interest. We find that such an interest is identified within the text of the ordinance itself: the protection of residential privacy. "The State's interest in protecting the well-being, tranquility, and privacy of the home is certainly of the highest order in a free and civilized society." Carey v. Brown, 447 U.S. 455, 471 (1980). . . . Although in many locations, we expect individuals simply to avoid speech they do not want to hear, *cf.* Erznoznik v. City of Jacksonville, 422 U.S. 205 (1975); Cohen v. California, 403 U.S. 15 (1971), the home is different. . . . [A] special benefit of the privacy all citizens enjoy within their own walls . . . is an ability to avoid intrusions. Thus, we have repeatedly held that individuals are not required to welcome unwanted speech into their own homes and that the government may protect this freedom. . . . There simply is no right to force speech into the home of an unwilling listener.

It remains to be considered, however, whether the Brookfield ordinance is narrowly tailored to protect only unwilling recipients of the communications. A statute is narrowly tailored if it targets and eliminates no more than the exact source of the "evil" it seeks to remedy. . . . A complete ban can be narrowly tailored, but only if each activity within the proscription's scope is an appropriately targeted evil. For example, in [*City Council of Los Angeles v.*] *Taxpayers for Vincent* [466 U.S. 789, (1984)] we upheld an ordinance that banned all signs on public property because the interest supporting the regulation, an esthetic interest in avoiding visual clutter and blight, rendered each sign an evil. Complete prohibition was necessary because "the substantive evil—visual blight—[was] not merely a possible byproduct of the activity, but [was] created by the medium of expression itself."

The same is true here. The type of focused picketing prohibited by the Brookfield ordinance is fundamentally different from more generally directed means of communication that may not be completely banned in residential areas. . . . Here, in contrast, the picketing is narrowly directed at the household, not the public. The type of picketers banned by the Brookfield ordinance generally do not seek to disseminate a message to the general public, but to intrude upon the targeted resident, and to do so in an especially offensive way. Moreover, even if some such picketers have a broader communicative purpose, their activity nonetheless inherently and offensively intrudes on residential privacy. The devastating effect of targeted picketing on the quiet enjoyment of the home is beyond doubt. . . .

In this case, for example, appellees subjected the doctor and his family to the presence of a relatively large group of protesters on their doorstep in an attempt to force the doctor to cease performing abortions. But the actual size of the group is irrelevant; even a solitary picket can invade residential privacy. . . . The offensive and disturbing nature of the form of the communication banned by the Brookfield ordinance thus can scarcely be questioned. . . .

The First Amendment permits the government to prohibit offensive speech as intrusive when the "captive" audience cannot avoid the objectionable speech. . . . The target of the focused picketing banned by the Brookfield ordinance is just such a "captive." The resident is figuratively, and perhaps literally, trapped within the home, and because of the unique and subtle impact of such picketing is left with no ready means of avoiding the unwanted speech. . . . Thus, the "evil" of targeted residential picketing . . . is "created by the medium of expression itself." . . . Accordingly, the Brookfield ordinance's complete ban of that particular medium of expression is narrowly tailored.

Reversed.

Justice BRENNAN, with whom Justice MARSHALL joins, dissenting.

. . . The mere fact that speech takes place in a residential neighborhood does not automatically implicate a residential privacy interest. . . .

Without question there are many aspects of residential picketing that, if unregulated, might easily become intrusive or unduly coercive. Indeed, some of these aspects are illustrated by this very case. . . . [S]logan-shouting protesters regularly converged on Dr. Victoria's home and, in addition to protesting, warned young children not to go near the house because Dr. Victoria was a "baby killer." Further, the throng repeatedly trespassed onto the Victorias' property and at least once blocked the exits to their home. . . .

Surely it is within the government's power to enact regulations as necessary to prevent such intrusive and coercive abuses. Thus, for example, the government could constitutionally regulate the number of residential picketers, the hours during which a residential picket may take place, or the noise level of such a picket. [S]ubstantial regulation is permitted to neutralize the intrusive or unduly coercive aspects of picketing around the home. But to say that picketing may be substantially regulated is not to say that it may be prohibited in its entirety. Once size, time, volume, and the like have been controlled to ensure that the picket is no longer intrusive or coercive, only the speech itself remains, conveyed perhaps by a lone, silent individual, walking back and forth with a sign. . . . Such speech, which no longer implicates the heightened governmental interest in residential privacy, is nevertheless banned by the Brookfield law. Therefore, the ordinance is not narrowly tailored. . . .

Justice STEVENS, dissenting.

"GET WELL CHARLIE—OUR TEAM NEEDS YOU."

In Brookfield, Wisconsin, it is unlawful for a fifth grader to carry such a sign in front of a residence for the period of time necessary to convey its friendly message to its intended audience. . . .

The picketing that gave rise to the ordinance enacted in this case was obviously intended to do more than convey a message of opposition to the character of the doctor's practice; it was intended to cause him and his family substantial psychological distress. . . . I do not believe that picketing for the sole purpose of imposing psychological harm on a family in the shelter of their home is constitutionally protected. I do believe, however, that the picketers have a right to communicate their strong opposition to abortion to the doctor, but after they have had a fair opportunity to communicate that message, I see little justification for allowing them to remain in front of his home and repeat it over and over again simply to harm the doctor and his family. Thus, I agree that the ordinance may be constitutionally applied to the kind of picketing that gave rise to its enactment.

On the other hand, the ordinance is unquestionably "overbroad" in that it prohibits some communication that is protected by the First Amendment. . . .

My hunch is that the town will probably not enforce its ban against friendly, innocuous, or even brief unfriendly picketing, and that the Court may be right in concluding that its legitimate sweep makes its overbreadth insubstantial. But there are two countervailing considerations that are persuasive to me. The scope of the ordinance gives the town officials far too much discretion in making enforcement decisions; while we sit by and await further developments, potential picketers must act at their peril. . . .

[Justice WHITE's opinion concurring in the judgment is omitted.]

NOTES AND QUESTIONS

1. *The "well-being, tranquility, and privacy of the home." Frisby* recognizes the government's significant interest in protecting residential privacy and tranquility. The Court has asserted that when they are in public places, audiences must typically avert their eyes and close their ears to speech that offends. *See* Cohen v. California, 403 U.S. 15 (1971) (*infra* Chapter 10). However, as *Frisby* shows, the home is treated differently. The Court has recognized that government has an important interest in preventing residents from being held "captive" to speech that "invades a significant privacy interest in an essentially intolerable manner." *Cohen.*
2. *Alternative means of communication.* In *Frisby*, the Court assumes demonstrating on public streets and sidewalks provides an adequate alternative to the prohibited "targeted picketing." Does it? Isn't focusing on the doctor's residence central to the message of the picketers? How elastic is the concept of "alternative channels"? So long as a speaker has *some* opportunity, in some place, to communicate a message is this requirement satisfied? Don't speakers always have *some* alternative, including use of the mails or posting their messages to social media?
3. *Medium bans.* Is it problematic, from a First Amendment standpoint, for government to effectively *ban* a particular form of expression such as picketing residences or camping in parks? In early public forum cases, the Court was quite skeptical of outright bans on leafletting and other means of expression relied on by "poorly financed" speakers. *See* Schneider v New Jersey, 308 U.S. 147 (1939) (invalidating an ordinance banning the distribution of leaflets). However, in more recent decisions, including *Frisby*, the Court has reasoned that banning an entire medium of expression is a "narrowly tailored" regulation if the medium itself creates a substantive evil the government has the power to address. Does that allow or encourage government to define the evil in a way that authorizes a medium ban?

McCullen v. Coakley

134 S. Ct. 2518 (2014)

Chief Justice ROBERTS delivered the opinion of the Court. . . .

I

[T]he Massachusetts Legislature amended [a] statute in 2007. The statute now provides:

> "No person shall knowingly enter or remain on a public way or sidewalk adjacent to a reproductive health care facility within a radius of 35 feet of any portion of an entrance, exit or driveway of a reproductive health care facility or within the area within a rectangle created by extending the outside boundaries of any entrance, exit or driveway of a reproductive health care facility in straight lines to the point where such lines intersect the sideline of the street in front of such entrance, exit or driveway."

A "reproductive health care facility," in turn, is defined as "a place, other than within or upon the grounds of a hospital, where abortions are offered or performed."

The 35-foot buffer zone applies only "during a facility's business hours," and the area must be "clearly marked and posted." In practice, facilities typically mark the zones with painted arcs and posted signs on adjacent sidewalks and streets. . . .

The Act exempts four classes of individuals: (1) "persons entering or leaving such facility"; (2) "employees or agents of such facility acting within the scope of their employment"; (3) "law enforcement, ambulance, firefighting, construction, utilities, public works and other municipal agents acting within the scope of their employment"; and (4) "persons using the public sidewalk or street right-of-way adjacent to such facility solely for the purpose of reaching a destination other than such facility." . . .

Some of the individuals who stand outside Massachusetts abortion clinics are fairly described as protestors, who express their moral or religious opposition to abortion through signs and chants or, in some cases, more aggressive methods such as face-to-face confrontation. Petitioners take a different tack. They attempt to engage women approaching the clinics in what they call "sidewalk counseling," which involves offering information about alternatives to abortion and help pursuing those options. . . . McCullen and the other petitioners consider it essential to maintain a caring demeanor, a calm tone of voice, and direct eye contact during these exchanges. Such interactions, petitioners believe, are a much more effective means of dissuading women from having abortions than confrontational methods such as shouting or brandishing signs, which in petitioners' view tend only to antagonize their intended audience. . . .

Petitioners at all three clinics claim that the buffer zones have considerably hampered their counseling efforts. Although they have managed to conduct some counseling and to distribute some literature outside the buffer zones—particularly at the Boston clinic—they say they have had many fewer conversations and distributed many fewer leaflets since the zones went into effect.

The second statutory exemption allows clinic employees and agents acting within the scope of their employment to enter the buffer zones. Relying on this exemption, the Boston clinic uses "escorts" to greet women as they approach the clinic, accompanying them through the zones to the clinic entrance. Petitioners claim that the escorts sometimes thwart petitioners' attempts to communicate with patients by blocking petitioners from handing literature to patients, telling patients not to "pay any attention" or "listen to" petitioners, and disparaging petitioners as "crazy."

In January 2008, petitioners sued Attorney General Coakley and other Commonwealth officials. They sought to enjoin enforcement of the Act, alleging that it violates the First and Fourteenth Amendments, both on its face and as applied to them. The District Court denied petitioners' facial challenge after a bench trial based on a stipulated record. The Court of Appeals for the First Circuit affirmed.

We granted certiorari.

II

By its very terms, the Massachusetts Act regulates access to "public way[s]" and "sidewalk[s]." Such areas occupy a "special position in terms of First Amendment protection" because of their historic role as sites for discussion and debate. United States v. Grace, 461 U.S. 171, 180 (1983).

It is no accident that public streets and sidewalks have developed as venues for the exchange of ideas. Even today, they remain one of the few places where a speaker can be confident that he is not simply preaching to the choir. With respect to other means of communication, an individual confronted with an uncomfortable message can always turn the page, change the channel, or leave the Web site. Not so on public streets and sidewalks. There, a listener often encounters speech he might otherwise tune out. . . . [T]his aspect of traditional public fora is a virtue, not a vice. . . .

Consistent with the traditionally open character of public streets and sidewalks, we have held that the government's ability to restrict speech in [traditional public forums] is "very limited." In particular, the guiding First Amendment principle that the "government has no power to restrict expression because of its message, its ideas, its subject matter, or its content" applies with full force in a traditional public forum. Police Dept. of Chicago v. Mosley, 408 U.S. 92, 95 (1972). As a general rule, in such a forum the government may not "selectively . . . shield the public from some kinds of speech on the ground that they are more offensive than others." Erznoznik v. Jacksonville, 422 U.S. 205, 209 (1975).

We have, however, afforded the government somewhat wider leeway to regulate features of speech unrelated to its content. "[E]ven in a public forum the government may impose reasonable restrictions on the time, place, or manner of protected speech, provided the restrictions 'are justified without reference to the content of the regulated speech, that they are narrowly tailored to serve a significant governmental interest, and that they leave open ample alternative channels for communication of the information.'" Ward v. Rock Against Racism, 491 U.S. 781, 791 (1989). . . .

III . . .

The Act applies only at a "reproductive health care facility," defined as "a place, other than within or upon the grounds of a hospital, where abortions are offered or performed." Given this definition, petitioners argue, "virtually all speech affected by the Act is speech concerning abortion," thus rendering the Act content based.

We disagree. To begin, the Act does not draw content-based distinctions on its face. The Act would be content based if it required "enforcement authorities" to "examine the content of the message that is conveyed to determine whether" a violation has occurred. But it does not. Whether petitioners violate the Act "depends" not "on what they say" but simply on where they say it. Indeed, petitioners can violate the Act merely by standing in a buffer zone, without displaying a sign or uttering a word.

It is true, of course, that by limiting the buffer zones to abortion clinics, the Act has the "inevitable effect" of restricting abortion-related speech more than speech on other subjects. But a facially neutral law does not become content based simply because it may disproportionately affect speech on certain topics. On the contrary, "[a] regulation that serves purposes unrelated to the content of expression is deemed neutral, even if it has an incidental effect on some speakers or messages but not others." *Ward*. The question in such a case is whether the law is "'justified without reference to the content of the regulated speech.'" Renton v. Playtime Theatres, Inc., 475 U.S. 41, 48 (1986).

The Massachusetts Act is. Its stated purpose is to "increase forthwith public safety at reproductive health care facilities." Respondents have articulated similar purposes before this Court—namely, "public safety, patient access to healthcare, and the unobstructed use of public sidewalks and roadways." It is not the case that "[e]very objective indication shows that the provision's primary purpose is to restrict speech that opposes abortion."

We have previously deemed the foregoing concerns to be content neutral. Obstructed access and congested sidewalks are problems no matter what caused them. A group of individuals can obstruct clinic access and clog sidewalks just as much when they loiter as when they protest abortion or counsel patients.

To be clear, the Act would not be content neutral if it were concerned with undesirable effects that arise from "the direct impact of speech on its audience" or "[l]isteners' reactions to speech." *See* Boos v. Barry, 485 U.S. 312 (1988). If, for example, the speech outside Massachusetts abortion clinics caused offense or made listeners uncomfortable, such offense or discomfort would not give the Commonwealth a content-neutral justification to restrict the speech. All of the problems identified by the Commonwealth here, however, arise irrespective of any listener's reactions. . . .

. . . [P]etitioners note that these interests "apply outside every building in the State that hosts any activity that might occasion protest or comment," not just abortion clinics. By choosing to pursue these interests only at abortion clinics, petitioners argue, the Massachusetts Legislature evinced a purpose to "single[ ] out for regulation speech about one particular topic: abortion."

We cannot infer such a purpose from the Act's limited scope. The broad reach of a statute can help confirm that it was not enacted to burden a narrower category of disfavored speech. At the same time, however, "States adopt laws to address the problems that confront them. The First Amendment does not require States to regulate for problems that do not exist." The Massachusetts Legislature amended the Act in 2007 in response to a problem that was, in its experience, limited to abortion clinics. . . . In light of the limited nature of the problem, it was reasonable for the Massachusetts Legislature to enact a limited solution. When selecting among various options for combating a particular problem, legislatures should be encouraged to choose the one that restricts less speech, not more. . . .

Petitioners also argue that the Act is content based because it exempts four classes of individuals, one of which comprises "employees or agents of [a reproductive healthcare] facility acting within the scope of their employment." This exemption, petitioners say, favors one side in the abortion debate and thus constitutes viewpoint discrimination—an "egregious form of content discrimination," . . .

There is nothing inherently suspect about providing some kind of exemption to allow individuals who work at the clinics to enter or remain within the buffer zones. In particular, the exemption cannot be regarded as simply a carve-out for the clinic escorts; it also covers employees such as the maintenance worker shoveling a snowy sidewalk or the security guard patrolling a clinic entrance.

Given the need for an exemption for clinic employees, the "scope of their employment" qualification simply ensures that the exemption is limited to its purpose of allowing the employees to do their jobs. . . . The limitation . . . makes clear . . . that exempted individuals are allowed inside the zones only to perform those acts authorized by their employers. There is no suggestion in the record that any of the clinics authorize their employees to speak about abortion in the buffer zones. . . .

It would be a very different question if it turned out that a clinic authorized escorts to speak about abortion inside the buffer zones. In that case, the escorts would not seem to be violating the Act because the speech would be within the scope of their employment. The Act's exemption for clinic employees would then facilitate speech on only one side of the abortion debate—a clear form of viewpoint discrimination that would support an as-applied challenge to the buffer zone at that clinic. But the record before us contains insufficient evidence to show that the exemption operates in this way at any of the clinics, perhaps because the clinics do not want to doom the Act by allowing their employees to speak about abortion within the buffer zones.

We thus conclude that the Act is neither content nor viewpoint based and therefore need not be analyzed under strict scrutiny.

IV

Even though the Act is content neutral, it still must be "narrowly tailored to serve a significant governmental interest." The tailoring requirement does not simply guard against an impermissible desire to censor. The government may attempt to suppress speech not only because it disagrees with the message being expressed, but also for mere convenience. Where certain speech is associated with particular problems, silencing the speech is sometimes the path of least resistance. But by demanding a close fit between ends and means, the tailoring requirement prevents the government from too readily "sacrific[ing] speech for efficiency."

For a content-neutral time, place, or manner regulation to be narrowly tailored, it must not "burden substantially more speech than is necessary to further the government's legitimate interests." *Ward*. Such a regulation, unlike a content-based restriction of speech, "need not be the least restrictive or least intrusive means of" serving the government's interests. But the government still "may not regulate expression in such a manner that a substantial portion of the burden on speech does not serve to advance its goals."

A

As noted, respondents claim that the Act promotes "public safety, patient access to healthcare, and the unobstructed use of public sidewalks and roadways." Petitioners do not dispute the significance of these interests. We have, moreover, previously recognized the legitimacy of the government's interests in "ensuring public safety and order, promoting the free flow of traffic on streets and sidewalks, protecting property rights, and protecting a woman's freedom to seek pregnancy-related services." Schenck v. Pro–Choice Network of Western N.Y., 519 U.S. 357, 376 (1997). The buffer zones clearly serve these interests.

At the same time, the buffer zones impose serious burdens on petitioners' speech. At each of the three Planned Parenthood clinics where petitioners attempt to counsel patients, the zones carve out a significant portion of the adjacent public sidewalks, pushing petitioners well back from the clinics' entrances and driveways. The zones thereby compromise petitioners' ability to initiate the close, personal conversations that they view as essential to "sidewalk counseling."

For example, in uncontradicted testimony, McCullen explained that she often cannot distinguish patients from passersby outside the Boston clinic in time to initiate a conversation before they enter the buffer zone. And even when she does manage to begin a discussion outside the zone, she must stop abruptly at its painted border, which she believes causes her to appear "untrustworthy" or "suspicious." Given these limitations, McCullen is often reduced to raising her voice at patients from outside the zone—a mode of communication sharply at odds with the compassionate message she wishes to convey. . . .

The buffer zones have also made it substantially more difficult for petitioners to distribute literature to arriving patients. . . . In short, the Act operates to deprive petitioners of their two primary methods of communicating with patients.

The Court of Appeals and respondents are wrong to downplay these burdens on petitioners' speech. . . . [W]hile the First Amendment does not guarantee a speaker the right to any particular form of expression, some forms—such as normal conversation and leafletting on a public sidewalk—have historically been more closely associated with the transmission of ideas than others. . . . When the government makes it more difficult to engage in these modes of communication, it imposes an especially significant First Amendment burden.

Respondents also emphasize that the Act does not prevent petitioners from engaging in various forms of "protest"—such as chanting slogans and displaying signs—outside the buffer zones. That misses the point. Petitioners are not protestors. They seek not merely to express their opposition to abortion, but to inform women of various alternatives and to provide help in pursuing them. . . . It is thus no answer to say that petitioners can still be "seen and heard" by women within the buffer zones. If all that the women can see and hear are vociferous opponents of abortion, then the buffer zones have effectively stifled petitioners' message. . . .

B

The buffer zones burden substantially more speech than necessary to achieve the Commonwealth's asserted interests. . . .

. . . The Commonwealth's interests include ensuring public safety outside abortion clinics, preventing harassment and intimidation of patients and clinic staff, and combating deliberate obstruction of clinic entrances. The Act itself contains a separate provision . . . that prohibits much of this conduct. That provision subjects to criminal punishment "[a]ny person who knowingly obstructs, detains, hinders, impedes or blocks another person's entry to or exit from a reproductive health care facility." If Massachusetts determines that broader prohibitions along the same lines are necessary, it could enact legislation similar to the federal Freedom of Access to Clinic Entrances Act of 1994 (FACE Act), which subjects to both criminal and civil penalties anyone who "by force or threat of force or by physical obstruction, intentionally injures, intimidates or interferes with or attempts to injure, intimidate or interfere with any person because that person is or has been, or in order to intimidate such person or any other person or any class of persons from, obtaining or providing reproductive health services." Some dozen other States have done so. If the Commonwealth is particularly concerned about harassment, it could also consider an ordinance such as the one adopted in New York City that not only prohibits obstructing access to a clinic, but also makes it a crime "to follow and harass another person within 15 feet of the premises of a reproductive health care facility."

The Commonwealth points to a substantial public safety risk created when protestors obstruct driveways leading to the clinics. That is, however, an example of its failure to look to less intrusive means of addressing its concerns. Any such obstruction can readily be addressed through existing local ordinances. *See, e.g.*, Worcester, Mass., Revised Ordinances of 2008, ch. 12, § 25(b) ("No person shall stand, or place any obstruction of any kind, upon any street, sidewalk or crosswalk in such a manner as to obstruct a free passage for travelers thereon").

All of the foregoing measures are, of course, in addition to available generic criminal statutes forbidding assault, breach of the peace, trespass, vandalism, and the like. . . .

Respondents contend that the alternatives we have discussed suffer from two defects: First, given the "widespread" nature of the problem, it is simply not "practicable" to rely on individual prosecutions and injunctions. But far from being "widespread," the problem appears from the record to be limited principally to the Boston clinic on Saturday mornings. Moreover, by their own account, the police appear perfectly capable of singling out lawbreakers. . . .

The second supposed defect in the alternatives we have identified is that laws [we have identified] require a showing of intentional or deliberate obstruction, intimidation, or harassment, which is often difficult to prove. As Captain Evans predicted in his legislative testimony, fixed buffer zones would "make our job so much easier."

Of course they would. But that is not enough to satisfy the First Amendment. . . . A painted line on the sidewalk is easy to enforce, but the prime objective of the First Amendment is not efficiency. In any case, we do not think that showing intentional obstruction is nearly so difficult in this context as respondents suggest.

To determine whether a protestor intends to block access to a clinic, a police officer need only order him to move. If he refuses, then there is no question that his continued conduct is knowing or intentional. . . .

The judgment of the Court of Appeals for the First Circuit is reversed, and the case is remanded for further proceedings consistent with this opinion.

It is so ordered.

Justice SCALIA, with whom Justice KENNEDY and Justice THOMAS join, concurring in the judgment. . . .

[P]etitioners maintain that the Act targets abortion-related—for practical purposes, abortion-opposing—speech because it applies outside abortion clinics only (rather than outside other buildings as well).

. . . It blinks reality to say, as the majority does, that a blanket prohibition on the use of streets and sidewalks where speech on only one politically controversial topic is likely to occur—and where that speech can most effectively be communicated—is not content based. Would the Court exempt from strict scrutiny a law banning access to the streets and sidewalks surrounding the site of the Republican National Convention? Or those used annually to commemorate the 1965 Selma–to–Montgomery civil rights marches? Or those outside the Internal Revenue Service? Surely not. . . .

Does a statute become "justified without reference to the content of the regulated speech" simply because the statute itself and those defending it in court *say* that it is? Every objective indication shows that the provision's primary purpose is to restrict speech that opposes abortion.

I begin, as suggested above, with the fact that the Act burdens only the public spaces outside abortion clinics. One might have expected the majority to defend the statute's peculiar targeting by arguing that those locations regularly face the safety and access problems that it says the Act was designed to solve. But the majority does not make that argument because it would be untrue. As the Court belatedly discovers in Part IV of its opinion, although the statute applies to all abortion clinics in Massachusetts, only one is known to have been beset by the problems that the statute supposedly addresses. The Court uses this striking fact (a smoking gun, so to speak) as a basis for concluding that the law is insufficiently "tailored" to safety and access concerns (Part IV) rather than as a basis for concluding that it is not *directed* to those concerns at all, but to the suppression of antiabortion speech. That is rather like invoking the eight missed human targets of a shooter who has killed one victim to prove, not that he is guilty of attempted mass murder, but that *he has bad aim.*

Whether the statute "restrict[s] more speech than necessary" in light of the problems that it allegedly addresses is, to be sure, relevant to the tailoring component of the First Amendment analysis (the shooter doubtless did have bad aim), but it is also relevant—powerfully relevant—to whether the law is really directed to safety and access concerns or rather to the suppression of a particular type of speech. Showing that a law that suppresses speech on a specific subject is so far-reaching that it applies even when the asserted non-speech-related problems are not present is persuasive evidence that the law is content based. In its zeal to treat abortion-related speech as a special category, the majority distorts not only the First Amendment but also the ordinary logic of probative inferences.

The structure of the Act also indicates that it rests on content-based concerns. The goals of "public safety, patient access to healthcare, and the unobstructed use of public sidewalks and roadways," are already achieved by an earlier-enacted subsection of the statute, which provides criminal penalties for "[a]ny person who knowingly obstructs, detains, hinders, impedes or blocks another person's entry to or exit from a reproductive health care facility." As the majority recognizes, that provision is easy to enforce. Thus, the speech-free zones carved out by subsection (b) add nothing to safety and access; what they achieve, and what they were obviously designed to achieve, is the suppression of speech opposing abortion. . . .

The provision at issue here was indisputably meant to serve the same interest [as in Hill v. Colorado, 530 U.S. 703 (2000)] in protecting citizens' supposed right to avoid speech that they would rather not hear. . . . In concluding that the statute is content based and therefore subject to strict scrutiny, I necessarily conclude that *Hill* should be overruled. Reasons for doing so are set forth in the dissents in that case[.] . . . Protecting people from speech they do not want to hear is not a function that the First Amendment allows the government to undertake in the public streets and sidewalks. . . .

Petitioners [also] contend that the Act targets speech opposing abortion (and thus constitutes a presumptively invalid viewpoint-discriminatory restriction) for another reason as well: It exempts "employees or agents" of an abortion clinic "acting within the scope of their employment."

It goes without saying that "[g]ranting waivers to favored speakers (or . . . denying them to disfavored speakers) would of course be unconstitutional." Thomas v. Chicago Park Dist., 534 U.S. 316 (2002). The majority opinion sets forth a two-part inquiry for assessing whether a regulation is content based, but when it comes to assessing the exemption for abortion-clinic employees or agents, the Court forgets its own teaching. Its opinion jumps right over the prong that asks whether the provision "draw[s] . . . distinctions on its face" and instead proceeds directly to the purpose-related prong, asking whether the exemption "represent[s] a governmental attempt to give one side of a debatable public question an advantage in expressing its views to the people." . . .

Is there any serious doubt that *abortion-clinic employees or agents* "acting within the scope of their employment" near clinic entrances may—indeed, often will—speak in favor of abortion ("You are doing the right thing")? Or speak in opposition to the message of abortion opponents—saying, for example, that "this is a safe facility" to rebut the statement that it is not? The Court's contrary assumption is simply incredible. . . .

I concur only in the judgment that the statute is unconstitutional under the First Amendment.

[Justice Alito's opinion concurring in the judgment is omitted.]

NOTES AND QUESTIONS

1. *Content-based or content-neutral?* Is the Massachusetts statute in *McCullen* content-based or content-neutral? Which opinion has the better argument on that point, the majority's or Justice Scalia's concurrence?

2. *"Protesters" v. "sidewalk counselors."* Why do you think the Court draws an explicit distinction between "protesters" and "sidewalk counselors" like McCullen? Are "protesters" entitled to fewer First Amendment protections in the public forum? Does it matter that, from the perspective of the patients, the sidewalk counselors' speech may be as or even more unwelcome than the speech of "protesters"? Is the main problem with the law that it severely burdens or even bans some forms of pamphleteering?
3. *Intermediate scrutiny.* How does *McCullen*'s application of intermediate scrutiny compare to the standard's application in earlier cases, such as *CCNV* and *Frisby*? Does the decision suggest the intermediate scrutiny standard may have real bite? How deferential is the Court to Massachusetts' asserted interests and its chosen means of furthering them? Justice Scalia frequently complained that the Court altered First Amendment standards in ways that disfavored anti-abortion speakers. Is the Court arguably doing just the opposite in *McCullen*? *See* Timothy Zick, *Justice Scalia and Abortion Speech*, 15 First Amend. L. Rev. 288 (2017).
4. *A right to be let alone?* In Hill v. Colorado, 530 U.S. 703 (2000), the Court upheld a Colorado law that prohibited anyone within 100 feet of a health care facility from knowingly approaching within eight feet of another person, without that person's consent, "for the purpose of passing a leaflet or handbill to, displaying a sign to, or engaging in oral protest, education, or counseling with such other person." The Court concluded that the Colorado law was content-neutral. In the course of its decision, the majority noted that the state's interest in protecting the health and welfare of its citizens might "justify a special focus on unimpeded access to health care facilities and the avoidance of potential trauma to patients associated with confrontational protests." 530 U.S. at 715. The Court relied in part on "[t]he unwilling listener's interest in avoiding unwanted communication." In *McCullen*, Massachusetts did not rely on protecting a "right to be let alone" in public places. Does *McCullen* implicitly undermine or reject this "privacy" interest? Is protecting audiences from unwanted speech after an offer to communicate has been declined a content-neutral government interest?

THEORY-APPLIED PROBLEM—FUNERAL PROTESTS

Okla. Stat. Ann., tit. 21, Oklahoma Funeral Picketing § 1380. Act—Findings—Purposes—Definitions—Penalties—Damages

A. This section shall be known and may be cited as the "Oklahoma Funeral Picketing Act."

1. The Legislature finds that:

a. it is generally recognized that families have a substantial interest in organizing and attending funerals for deceased relatives,

b. the interests of families in privately and peacefully mourning the loss of deceased relatives are violated when funerals are targeted for picketing and other public demonstrations,

c. picketing of funerals causes emotional disturbance and distress to grieving families who participate in funerals, and

d. full opportunity exists under the terms and provisions of this section for the exercise of freedom of speech and other constitutional rights at times other than the period from two hours before the scheduled commencement of funeral services until two hours after the actual completion of the funeral services.

B. The purposes of this section are to:

1. Protect the privacy of grieving families during the period from two hours before the scheduled commencement of the funeral services until two hours after the actual completion of the funeral services; and

2. Preserve the peaceful character of cemeteries, mortuaries and churches from two hours before the scheduled commencement of funeral services until two hours after the actual completion of the funeral services.

C. As used in this section:

1. "Funeral" means the ceremonies, processions and memorial services held in connection with the burial or cremation of the dead; and

2. "Picketing" means protest activities engaged in by a person or persons within one thousand (1,000) feet of a cemetery, mortuary, church or other place where any portion of a funeral service is held during the period from two hours before the scheduled commencement of funeral services until two hours after the actual completion of the funeral services.

D. It is unlawful for any person to engage in picketing within one thousand (1,000) feet of any cemetery, church, mortuary or other place where any portion of a funeral service is held during the period from two hours before the scheduled commencement of funeral services until two hours after the actual completion of the funeral services.

E. Any person violating the provisions of this section shall be guilty of a misdemeanor and upon conviction thereof shall be punished by a fine of not more than Five Hundred Dollars ($500.00), or by imprisonment in the county jail not more than thirty (30) days, or by both such fine and imprisonment.

F. Notwithstanding the penalties provided in subsection E, any district court may enjoin conduct proscribed by this section and may in any such proceeding award damages, including punitive damages attorney fees or other appropriate relief against the persons found guilty of actions made unlawful by this section.

Is this law content-based or content-neutral? Does it satisfy the applicable standard of scrutiny? What arguments would you make on behalf of the state, and on behalf of any challengers arrested or convicted for protesting on a public sidewalk within the prohibited areas and during the prohibited times?

C. *POLICING CONFLICT IN THE PUBLIC FORUM: THE PROBLEM OF THE HOSTILE AUDIENCE*

In *Cantwell v. Connecticut* (1940), the Supreme Court stated that when speech creates a "clear and present danger of riot, disorder, interference with traffic upon the public streets, or other immediate threat to public safety, peace, or order" . . . "the power of the State to prevent or punish is obvious." The State's power to "prevent or punish" is presumably not limited to the context in which the speaker's *supporters* pose some threat to order and safety, as when a speaker incites imminent violence. Audiences who *oppose* the speaker's views may also pose a threat to public safety and order. Suppose counter-protesters threaten to physically attack a speaker because they are offended or upset by the content of the speech. Can law enforcement order the speaker to stop communicating? If so, does that permit a "hostile audience" to effectively silence an unpopular or provocative speaker and impose a kind of "heckler's veto"? These issues have proven difficult to resolve, in part because solutions are highly context-specific, but also owing to the Court's lack of clear guidance. *See* Frederick Schauer, *Costs and Challenges of the Hostile Audience*, 94 Notre Dame L. Rev. 1671 (2019). Two issues have proven particularly nettlesome: (1) What is the proper role of law enforcement when faced with a hostile audience? (2) Can the negative effects of audience hostility be dealt with in advance, for example through permitting or shifting the costs of protest onto speakers and groups? Consider whether or to what extent the following cases provide answers to these questions.

Feiner v. New York

340 U.S. 315 (1951)

Mr. Chief Justice Vinson delivered the opinion of the Court.

On the evening of March 8, 1949, petitioner Irving Feiner was addressing an open-air meeting at the corner of South McBride and Harrison Streets in the City of Syracuse. At approximately 6:30 p.m., the police received a telephone complaint concerning the meeting, and two officers were detailed to investigate. One of these officers went to the scene immediately, the other arriving some twelve minutes later. They found a crowd of about seventy-five or eighty people, both [Black] and white, filling the sidewalk and spreading out into the street. Petitioner, standing on a large wooden box on the sidewalk, was addressing the crowd through a loud-speaker system attached to an automobile. Although the purpose of his speech was to urge his listeners to attend a meeting to be held that night in the Syracuse Hotel, in its course he was making derogatory remarks concerning President Truman, the American Legion, the Mayor of Syracuse, and other local political officials.

The police officers made no effort to interfere with petitioner's speech, but were first concerned with the effect of the crowd on both pedestrian and vehicular traffic. They observed the situation from the opposite side of the street, noting that some pedestrians were forced to walk in the street to avoid the crowd. Since traffic was passing at the time, the officers attempted to get the people listening to petitioner back on the sidewalk. The crowd was restless and there was some pushing, shoving and milling around. One of the officers telephoned the police station from a nearby store, and then both policemen crossed the street and mingled with the crowd without any intention of arresting the speaker.

At this time, petitioner was speaking in a "loud, high-pitched voice." He gave the impression that he was endeavoring to arouse the [Black] people against the whites, urging that they rise up in arms and fight for equal rights. The statements before such a mixed audience "stirred up a little excitement." Some of the onlookers made remarks to the police about their inability to handle the crowd and at least one threatened violence if the police did not act. There were others who appeared to be favoring petitioner's arguments. Because of the feeling that existed in the crowd both for and against the speaker, the officers finally "stepped in to prevent it from resulting in a fight." One of the officers approached the petitioner, not for the purpose of arresting him, but to get him to break up the crowd. He asked petitioner to get down off the box, but the latter refused to accede to his request and continued talking. The officer waited for a minute and then demanded that he cease talking. Although the officer had thus twice requested petitioner to stop over the course of several minutes, petitioner not only ignored him but continued talking. During all this time, the crowd was pressing closer around petitioner and the officer. Finally, the officer told petitioner he was under arrest and ordered him to get down from the box, reaching up to grab him. Petitioner stepped down, announcing over the microphone that "the law has arrived, and I suppose they will take over now." In all, the officer had asked petitioner to get down off the box three times over a space of four or five minutes. Petitioner had been speaking for over a half hour. On these facts, petitioner was specifically charged with [disorderly conduct, a misdemeanor].

. . . We are not faced here with blind condonation by a state court of arbitrary police action. The courts below recognized petitioner's right to hold a street meeting at this locality, to make use of loud-speaking equipment in giving his speech, and to make derogatory remarks concerning public officials and the American Legion. They found that the officers in making the arrest were motivated solely by a proper concern for the preservation of order and protection of the general welfare, and that there was no evidence which could lend color to a claim that the acts of the police were a cover for suppression of petitioner's views and opinions. Petitioner was thus neither arrested nor convicted for the making or the content of his speech. Rather, it was the reaction which it actually engendered.

The language of Cantwell v. Connecticut, 310 U. S. 296 (1940), is appropriate here. "The offense known as breach of the peace embraces a great variety of conduct destroying or menacing public order and tranquility. It includes not only violent acts but acts and words likely to produce violence in others. No one would have the hardihood to suggest that the principle of freedom of speech sanctions incitement to riot or that religious liberty connotes the privilege to exhort others to physical attack upon those belonging to another sect. When clear and present danger of riot, disorder, interference with traffic upon the public streets, or other immediate threat to public safety, peace, or order, appears, the power of the State to prevent or punish is obvious." 310 U. S. at 308. The findings of the New York courts as to the condition of the crowd and the refusal of petitioner to obey the police requests, supported as they are by the record of this case, are persuasive that the conviction of petitioner for violation of public peace, order and authority does not exceed the bounds of proper state police action. This Court respects, as it must, the interest of the community in maintaining peace and order on its streets. We cannot say that the preservation of that interest here encroaches on the constitutional rights of this petitioner.

. . . We are well aware that the ordinary murmurings and objections of a hostile audience cannot be allowed to silence a speaker, and are also mindful of the possible danger of giving overzealous police officials complete discretion to break up otherwise lawful public meetings. "A State may not unduly suppress free communication of views, religious or other, under the guise of conserving desirable conditions." *Cantwell.* But we are not faced here with such a situation. It is one thing to say that the police cannot be used as an instrument for the suppression of unpopular views, and another to say that, when as here the speaker passes the bounds of argument or persuasion and undertakes incitement to riot, they are powerless to prevent a breach of the peace. Nor in this case can we condemn the considered judgment of three New York courts approving the means which the police, faced with a crisis, used in the exercise of their power and duty to preserve peace and order. . . . [T]he imminence of greater disorder coupled with petitioner's deliberate defiance of the police officers convince us that we should not reverse this conviction in the name of free speech.

Affirmed.

Mr. Justice BLACK, dissenting.

The record before us convinces me that petitioner, a young college student, has been sentenced to the penitentiary for the unpopular views he expressed on matters of public interest while lawfully making a street-corner speech in Syracuse, New York. The end result of the affirmance here is to approve a simple and readily available technique by which cities and states can with impunity subject all speeches, political or otherwise, on streets or elsewhere, to the supervision and censorship of the local police. I will have no part or parcel in this holding which I view as a long step toward totalitarian authority.

The Court's opinion apparently rests on this reasoning: The policeman, under the circumstances detailed, could reasonably conclude that serious fighting or even riot was imminent; therefore he could stop petitioner's speech to prevent a breach of peace; accordingly, it was "disorderly conduct" for petitioner to continue speaking in disobedience of the officer's request. As to the existence of a dangerous situation on the street corner, it seems far-fetched to suggest that the "facts" show any imminent threat of riot or uncontrollable disorder. It is neither unusual nor unexpected that some people at public street meetings mutter, mill about, push, shove, or disagree, even violently, with the speaker. Indeed, it is rare where controversial topics are discussed that an outdoor crowd does not do some or all of these things. Nor does one isolated threat to assault the speaker forebode disorder. Especially should the danger be discounted where, as here, the person threatening was a man whose wife and two small children accompanied him and who, so far as the record shows, was never close enough to petitioner to carry out the threat.

Moreover, assuming that the "facts" did indicate a critical situation, I reject the implication of the Court's opinion that the police had no obligation to protect petitioner's constitutional right to talk. The police of course have power to prevent breaches of the peace. But if, in the name of preserving order, they ever can interfere with a lawful public speaker, they first must make all reasonable efforts to protect him. Here the policemen did not even pretend to try to protect petitioner. According to the officers' testimony, the crowd was restless but there is no showing of any attempt to quiet it; pedestrians were forced to walk into the street, but there was no effort to clear a path on the sidewalk; one person threatened to assault petitioner but the officers did nothing to discourage this when even a word might have sufficed. Their duty was to protect petitioner's right to talk, even to the extent of arresting the man who threatened to interfere. Instead, they shirked that duty and acted only to suppress the right to speak.

Finally, I cannot agree with the Court's statement that petitioner's disregard of the policeman's unexplained request amounted to such "deliberate defiance" as would justify an arrest or conviction for disorderly conduct. On the contrary, I think that the policeman's action was a "deliberate defiance" of ordinary official duty as well as of the constitutional right of free speech. For at least where time allows, courtesy and explanation of commands are basic elements of good official conduct in a democratic society. Here petitioner was "asked" then "told" then "commanded" to stop speaking, but a man making a lawful address is certainly not required to be silent merely because an officer directs it. Petitioner was entitled to know why he should cease doing a lawful act. Not once was he told. I understand that people in authoritarian countries must obey arbitrary orders. I had hoped that there was no such duty in the United States.

In my judgment, today's holding means that as a practical matter, minority speakers can be silenced in any city. Hereafter, despite the First and Fourteenth Amendments, the policeman's club can take heavy toll of a current administration's public critics. Criticism of public officials will be too dangerous for all but the most courageous.

Mr. Justice DOUGLAS, with whom Mr. Justice MINTON concurs, dissenting.

Public assemblies and public speech occupy an important role in American life. One high function of the police is to protect these lawful gatherings so that the speakers may exercise their constitutional rights. When unpopular causes are sponsored from the public platform, there will commonly be mutterings and unrest and heckling from the crowd. When a speaker mounts a platform it is not unusual to find him resorting to exaggeration, to vilification of ideas and men, to the making of false charges. But those extravagances, as we emphasized in *Cantwell*, do not justify penalizing the speaker by depriving him of the platform or by punishing him for his conduct.

A speaker may not, of course, incite a riot any more than he may incite a breach of the peace by the use of "fighting words." *See* Chaplinsky v. New Hampshire, 315 U. S. 568. But this record shows no such extremes. It shows an unsympathetic audience and the threat of one man to haul the speaker from the stage. It is against that kind of threat that speakers need police protection. If they do not receive it and instead the police throw their weight on the side of those who would break up the meetings, the police become the new censors of speech. Police censorship has all the vices of the censorship from city halls which we have repeatedly struck down.

NOTES AND QUESTIONS

1. *The "heckler's veto."* Did law enforcement's ordering Feiner to cease speaking allow a hostile audience to effectively censor a speaker? Does the answer depend on whether Feiner crossed some boundary between protected and unprotected expression? Did he engage in incitement to unlawful action? Fighting words? Is the mere prospect of "disorder"

sufficient to allow law enforcement to order a speaker from communicating further? If so, won't counter-protesters possess an effective "veto" over any public speaker?

2. *A duty to protect the speaker?* In his dissent in *Feiner*, Justice Black wrote: "But if, in the name of preserving order, [police] ever can interfere with a lawful public speaker, they first must make all reasonable efforts to protect him." According to Justice Black, what should the officers have done when confronted with the prospect of a violent reaction from onlookers? Is the principal duty of law enforcement in these circumstances to protect speech or public order?

Edwards v. South Carolina

372 U.S. 229 (1963)

Mr. Justice STEWART delivered the opinion of the Court.

The petitioners, 187 in number, were convicted in a magistrate's court in Columbia, South Carolina, of the common-law crime of breach of the peace. Their convictions were ultimately affirmed by the South Carolina Supreme Court. We granted certiorari to consider the claim that these convictions cannot be squared with the Fourteenth Amendment of the United States Constitution.

There was no substantial conflict in the trial evidence. Late in the morning of March 2, 1961, the petitioners, [Black] high school and college students, met at the Zion Baptist Church in Columbia. From there, at about noon, they walked in separate groups of about 15 to the South Carolina State House grounds, an area of two city blocks open to the general public. Their purpose was "to submit a protest to the citizens of South Carolina, along with the Legislative Bodies of South Carolina, our feelings and our dissatisfaction with the present condition of discriminatory actions against Negroes, in general, and to let them know that we were dissatisfied and that we would like for the laws which prohibited Negro privileges in this State to be removed."

Already on the State House grounds when the petitioners arrived were 30 or more law enforcement officers, who had advance knowledge that the petitioners were coming. Each group of petitioners entered the grounds through a driveway and parking area known in the record as the "horseshoe." As they entered, they were told by the law enforcement officials that "they had a right, as a citizen, to go through the State House grounds, as any other citizen has, as long as they were peaceful." During the next half hour or 45 minutes, the petitioners, in the same small groups, walked single file or two abreast in an orderly way through the grounds, each group carrying placards bearing such messages as "I am proud to be a Negro" and "Down with segregation."

During this time a crowd of some 200 to 300 onlookers had collected in the horseshoe area and on the adjacent sidewalks. There was no evidence to suggest that these onlookers were anything but curious, and no evidence at all of any threatening remarks, hostile gestures, or offensive language on the part of any member of the crowd. The City Manager testified that he recognized some of the onlookers, whom he did not identify, as "possible trouble makers," but his subsequent testimony made clear that nobody among the crowd actually caused or threatened any trouble. There was no obstruction of pedestrian or vehicular traffic within the State House grounds. No vehicle was prevented from entering or leaving the horseshoe area. Although vehicular traffic at a nearby street intersection was slowed down somewhat, an officer was dispatched to keep traffic moving. There were a number of bystanders on the public sidewalks adjacent to the State House grounds, but they all moved on when asked to do so, and there was no impediment of pedestrian traffic. Police protection at the scene was at all times sufficient to meet any foreseeable possibility of disorder.

In the situation and under the circumstances thus described, the police authorities advised the petitioners that they would be arrested if they did not disperse within 15 minutes. Instead of dispersing, the petitioners engaged in what the City Manager described as "boisterous," "loud," and "flamboyant" conduct, which, as his later testimony made clear, consisted of listening to a "religious harangue" by one of their leaders, and loudly singing "The Star Spangled Banner" and other patriotic and religious songs, while stamping their feet and clapping their hands. After 15 minutes had passed, the police arrested the petitioners and marched them off to jail. . . .

. . . [I]t is clear to us that in arresting, convicting, and punishing the petitioners under the circumstances disclosed by this record, South Carolina infringed the petitioners' constitutionally protected rights of free speech, free assembly, and freedom to petition for redress of their grievances. The circumstances in this case reflect an exercise of these basic constitutional rights in their most pristine and classic form. The petitioners felt aggrieved by laws of South Carolina which allegedly "prohibited Negro privileges in this State." They peaceably assembled at the site of the State Government and there peaceably expressed their grievances "to the citizens of South Carolina, along with the Legislative Bodies of South Carolina." Not until they were told by police officials that they must disperse on pain of arrest did they do more. Even then, they but sang patriotic and religious songs after one of their leaders had delivered a "religious harangue." There was no violence or threat of violence on their part, or on the part of any member of the crowd watching them. Police protection was "ample."

This, therefore, was a far cry from the situation in Feiner v. New York, 340 U. S. 315, where two policemen were faced with a crowd which was "pushing, shoving and milling around," *id.*, at 317, where at least one member of the crowd "threatened violence if the police did not act," *id.*, at 317, where "the crowd was pressing closer around petitioner and the officer," *id.*, at 318, and where "the speaker passes the bounds of argument or persuasion and undertakes incitement to riot." *Id.*, at 321. And the record is barren of any evidence of "fighting words." *See Chaplinsky.*

. . . .The Fourteenth Amendment does not permit a State to make criminal the peaceful expression of unpopular views. [As we said in Terminiello v. Chicago, 337 U.S. 1, 4-5 (1949),] "a function of free speech under our system of government is to invite dispute. It may indeed best serve its high purpose when it induces a condition of unrest, creates dissatisfaction with conditions as they are, or even stirs people to anger. Speech is often provocative and challenging. It may strike at prejudices and preconceptions and have profound unsettling effects as it presses for acceptance of an idea. That is why freedom of speech . . . is . . . protected against censorship or punishment, unless shown likely to produce a clear and present danger of a serious substantive evil that rises far above public inconvenience, annoyance, or unrest. . . . There is no room under our Constitution for a more restrictive view. For the alternative would lead to standardization of ideas either by legislatures, courts, or dominant political or community groups." As in the *Terminiello* case, the courts of South Carolina have defined a criminal offense so as to permit conviction of the petitioners if their speech "stirred people to anger, invited public dispute, or brought about a condition of unrest. A conviction resting on any of those grounds may not stand." *Id.*, at 5.

For these reasons we conclude that these criminal convictions cannot stand.

Reversed.

Mr. Justice CLARK, dissenting.

Petitioners, of course, had a right to peaceable assembly, to espouse their cause and to petition, but in my view the manner in which they exercised those rights was by no means the passive demonstration which this Court relates; rather, as the City Manager of Columbia testified, "a dangerous situation was really building up" which South Carolina's courts expressly found had created "an actual interference with traffic and an imminently threatened disturbance of the peace of the community." . . .

. . . Certainly the city officials would be constitutionally prohibited from refusing petitioners access to the State House grounds merely because they disagreed with their views. But here South Carolina's courts have found: "There is no indication whatever in this case that the acts of the police officers were taken as a subterfuge or excuse for the suppression of the appellants' views and opinions." It is undisputed that the city officials specifically granted petitioners permission to assemble, imposing only the requirement that they be "peaceful." Petitioners then gathered on the State House grounds, during a General Assembly session, in a large number of almost 200, marching and carrying placards with slogans such as "Down with segregation" and "You may jail our bodies but not our souls." Some of them were singing.

The activity continued for approximately 45 minutes, during the busy noon-hour period, while a crowd of some 300 persons congregated in front of the State House and around the area directly in front of its entrance, known as the "horseshoe," which was used for vehicular as well as pedestrian ingress and egress. During this time there were no efforts made by the city officials to hinder the petitioners in their rights of free speech and assembly; rather, the police directed their efforts to the traffic problems resulting from petitioners' activities. It was only after the large crowd had gathered, among which the City Manager and Chief of Police recognized potential trouble-makers, and which together with the students had become massed on and around the "horseshoe" so closely that vehicular and pedestrian traffic was materially impeded, that any action against the petitioners was taken. Then the City Manager, in what both the state intermediate and Supreme Court found to be the utmost good faith, decided that danger to peace and safety was imminent. Even at this juncture no orders were issued by the City Manager for the police to break up the crowd, now about 500 persons, and no arrests were made. Instead, he approached the recognized leader of the petitioners and requested him to tell the various groups of petitioners to disperse within 15 minutes, failing which they would be arrested. Even though the City Manager might have been honestly mistaken as to the imminence of danger, this was certainly a reasonable request by the city's top executive officer in an effort to avoid a public brawl. But the response of petitioners and their leader was defiance rather than cooperation. . . .

For the next 15 minutes the petitioners sang "I Shall Not Be Moved" and various religious songs, stamped their feet, clapped their hands, and conducted what the South Carolina Supreme Court found to be a "noisy demonstration in defiance of [the dispersal] orders." Ultimately, the petitioners were arrested, as they apparently planned from the beginning, and convicted on evidence the sufficiency of which the Court does not challenge. The question thus seems to me whether a State is constitutionally prohibited from enforcing laws to prevent breach of the peace in a situation where city officials in good faith believe, and the record shows, that disorder and violence are imminent, merely because the activities constituting that breach contain claimed elements of constitutionally protected speech and assembly. To me the answer under our cases is clearly in the negative.

. . . In *Cantwell*, this Court recognized that "[w]hen clear and present danger of riot, disorder, interference with traffic upon the public streets, or other immediate threat to public safety, peace, or order, appears, the power of the State to prevent or punish is obvious." And in *Feiner*, we upheld a conviction for breach of the peace in a situation no more dangerous than that found here. There the demonstration was conducted by only one person and the crowd was limited to approximately 80, as compared with the present lineup of some 200 demonstrators and 300 onlookers. . . . Only one person—in a city having an entirely different historical background—was exhorting adults. Here 200 youthful [Black] demonstrators were being aroused to a "fever pitch" before a crowd of some 300 people who undoubtedly were hostile. Perhaps their speech was not so animated but in this setting their actions, their placards reading "You may jail our bodies but not our souls" and their chanting of "I Shall Not Be Moved," accompanied by stamping feet and clapping hands, created a much greater danger of riot and disorder. It is my belief that anyone conversant with the almost spontaneous combustion in some Southern communities in such a situation will agree that the City Manager's action may well have averted a major catastrophe.

. . . [T]o say that the police may not intervene until the riot has occurred is like keeping out the doctor until the patient dies. I cannot subscribe to such a doctrine. I would affirm the convictions.

NOTES AND QUESTIONS

1. *Stirring to anger and inviting dispute*. Two years before *Feiner*, the Court decided Terminiello v. Chicago, 337 U.S. 1 (1949). The decision, which the *Edwards* Court quoted from extensively, reversed a breach of peace conviction based on an improper charge to the jury and did not expressly address the "hostile audience" problem. However, its reasoning relates closely to the "hostile audience" scenario. The speaker, Father Arthur Terminiello, was well known for speeches and writings warning that the United States must be saved from communists and Jews. Prior to a

scheduled speech at an auditorium in the predominantly Jewish Chicago neighborhood of Albany Park, an angry audience gathered outside the auditorium. Terminiello denounced the crowd as "snakes," "slimy scum," and used other epithets. The Court noted a "cordon of police officers was assigned to the meeting to maintain order; but they were not able to prevent several disturbances. The crowd outside was angry and turbulent." Some outside broke the windows of the meeting hall and physically attacked those who sought to go inside. The trial judge construed the breach of peace statute, under which Terminiello was charged after a disturbance relating to his speech, to allow conviction for speech that "stirs the public to anger, invites dispute, brings about a condition of unrest, or creates a disturbance." The Supreme Court reversed the conviction on the ground that such speech is fully protected. Does allowing provocative speech that stirs others to anger and "invites dispute" invite a dangerous "battle for the streets"? In his dissent in *Terminiello,* Justice Jackson invoked "[r]ecent European history" to condemn the tactics of both the speaker and counter-demonstrators. Justice Jackson wrote: "Terminiello's victory today certainly fulfills the most extravagant hopes of both right and left totalitarian groups, who want nothing so much as to paralyze and discredit the only democratic authority that can curb them in their battle for the streets." Should public officials have the power to cancel or restrict speeches or demonstrations that are likely to or have become violent or disruptive?

2. "*A far cry from* Feiner?" In *Edwards,* the Court distinguished *Feiner* on the ground that the circumstances present in that case were "a far cry from *Feiner.*" Note the descriptions of events differ markedly in the majority and dissenting opinions. What facts does the majority rely on to determine whether an improper "heckler's veto" has occurred in *Edwards*? What facts lead the dissent to conclude authorities acted properly in arresting the protestors? In Cox v. Louisiana, 379 U.S. 536 (1965), the Court relied heavily on *Edwards* to invalidate a breach of peace conviction of a civil rights demonstrator who attracted the attention of a hostile crowd. Cox, an ordained minister, led a group of 2,000 students in a peaceful march to a courthouse in Baton Rouge, Louisiana to protest the jailing of 23 students arrested for picketing stores that maintained segregated lunch counters. The Court observed that about 100 to 300 whites gathered on the sidewalk opposite the student protesters. Approximately 75 police officers were stationed on the street between the two groups. There was some "muttering" and "grumbling" by some of the white onlookers, but none threatened violence. The Court concluded "[t]his situation, like that in *Edwards,* is a far cry from the situation in [*Feiner*]." Do you agree?
3. *Protecting the speaker.* Do the *Edwards* and *Cox* decisions implicitly accept Justice Black's view that law enforcement has a duty to protect the speaker? If so, what is the *scope* of that duty? Are state and local officials obligated to devote adequate personnel and resources necessary to ensure the speech or demonstration can take place? Does any such duty extend to calling in reinforcements from other jurisdictions, if necessary to maintain order?

Are there any financial limitations on the duty to protect the speaker, or must public officials spend whatever is reasonably necessary to allow the event to proceed? Can a public speech be cancelled if authorities determine they lack the personnel and financial resources to ensure the safety of the speaker and audience? Consider whether *Forsyth County v. Nationalist Movement* (1992), below, answers these questions.

4. *Planning for provocative speech.* If a municipality has reason to believe a demonstration will lead to violence or property damage, what if anything can it do to reduce the prospect such effects will materialize? Presumably it can rely on content-neutral time, place, and manner regulations, including objective permit schemes, to ensure public order and safety. It can also enforce content-neutral breach of peace, riot, and other laws. Can authorities physically separate different speakers and groups from one another, either through the permit process or otherwise? Can a municipality confine speakers or groups to certain designated "free speech zones" to restrict their movement and keep a watchful eye on them? *See* Timothy Zick, *Speech and Spatial Tactics*, 84 Tex. L. Rev. 581 (2006); Ronald Krotoszynski, Jr., *Reclaiming the Petition Clause: Seditious Libel, "Offensive" Protest, and the Right to Petition the Government for Redress of Grievances* (2012).
5. *Distributing costs – fees.* For government officials, the cleanup, security, and other costs associated with hosting provocative speakers and groups can be considerable, sometimes running to hundreds of thousands of dollars or in some cases considerably more. In *Cox v. New Hampshire* (1941), *supra* p. 179, the Court stated that municipalities could charge flat permit fees that "take into account the greater public expense of policing" demonstrations, parades, and other events that draw significant crowds. Does the First Amendment limit imposition of such fees? Consider the following decision.

Forsyth County v. Nationalist Movement

505 U.S. 123 (1992)

Justice BLACKMUN delivered the opinion of the Court.

In this case, with its emotional overtones, we must decide whether the free speech guarantees of the First and Fourteenth Amendments are violated by an assembly and parade ordinance that permits a government administrator to vary the fee for assembling or parading to reflect the estimated cost of maintaining public order. . . .

I

Petitioner Forsyth County is a primarily rural Georgia county approximately 30 miles northeast of Atlanta. It has had a troubled racial history. In 1912, in one month, its entire African-American population, over 1,000 citizens, was driven systematically from the county in the wake of the rape and murder of a white woman and the lynching of her accused assailant. Seventy-five years later, in 1987, the county population remained 99% white.

Spurred by this history, Hosea Williams, an Atlanta city councilman and civil rights personality, proposed a Forsyth County "March Against Fear and Intimidation" for January 17, 1987. Approximately 90 civil rights demonstrators attempted to parade in Cumming, the county seat. The marchers were met by members of the Forsyth County Defense League (an independent affiliate of respondent, The Nationalist Movement), the Ku Klux Klan, and other Cumming residents. In all, some 400 counterdemonstrators lined the parade route, shouting racial slurs. Eventually, the counterdemonstrators, dramatically outnumbering police officers, forced the parade to a premature halt by throwing rocks and beer bottles.

Williams planned a return march the following weekend. It developed into the largest civil rights demonstration in the South since the 1960's. On January 24, approximately 20,000 marchers joined civil rights leaders, United States Senators, Presidential candidates, and an Assistant United States Attorney General in a parade and rally. The 1,000 counterdemonstrators on the parade route were contained by more than 3,000 state and local police and National Guardsmen. Although there was sporadic rock throwing and 60 counterdemonstrators were arrested, the parade was not interrupted. The demonstration cost over $670,000 in police protection, of which Forsyth County apparently paid a small portion.

"As a direct result" of these two demonstrations, the Forsyth County Board of Commissioners enacted Ordinance 34 on January 27, 1987. The ordinance recites that it is "to provide for the issuance of permits for parades, assemblies, demonstrations, road closings, and other uses of public property and roads by private organizations and groups of private persons for private purposes." The board of commissioners justified the ordinance by explaining that "the cost of necessary and reasonable protection of persons participating in or observing said parades, assemblies, demonstrations, road closings and other related activities exceeds the usual and normal cost of law enforcement for which those participating should be held accountable and responsible." The ordinance required the permit applicant to defray these costs by paying a fee, the amount of which was to be fixed "from time to time" by the Board. [As amended, Ordinance 34 provides] that every permit applicant "shall pay in advance for such permit, for the use of the County, a sum not more than $1,000.00 for each day such parade, procession, or open air public meeting shall take place." In addition, the county administrator was empowered to "adjust the amount to be paid in order to meet the expense incident to the administration of the Ordinance and to the maintenance of public order in the matter licensed."

In January 1989, respondent The Nationalist Movement proposed to demonstrate in opposition to the federal holiday commemorating the birthday of Martin Luther King, Jr. In Forsyth County, the Movement sought to "conduct a rally and speeches for one and a half to two hours" on the courthouse steps on a Saturday afternoon. The county imposed a $100 fee. The fee did not include any calculation for expenses incurred by law enforcement authorities, but was based on 10 hours of the county administrator's time in issuing the permit. The county administrator testified that the cost of his time was deliberately undervalued and that he did not charge for the clerical support involved in processing the application.

The Movement did not pay the fee and did not hold the rally. Instead, it instituted this action [requesting an injunction prohibiting Forsyth County from interfering with the Movement's plans. The District Court denied relief, but the Court of Appeals for the Eleventh Circuit reversed. The Court of Appeals held: "An ordinance which charges more than a nominal fee for using public forums for public issue speech, violates the First Amendment."] We granted certiorari to resolve a conflict among the Courts of Appeals concerning the constitutionality of charging a fee for a speaker in a public forum.

II

Respondent mounts a facial challenge to the Forsyth County ordinance. It is well established that in the area of freedom of expression an overbroad regulation may be subject to facial review and invalidation, even though its application in the case under consideration may be constitutionally unobjectionable. . . .

A

Respondent contends that the county ordinance is facially invalid because it does not prescribe adequate standards for the administrator to apply when he sets a permit fee. A government regulation that allows arbitrary application "is inherently inconsistent with a valid time, place, and manner regulation because such discretion has the potential for becoming a means of suppressing a particular point of view." Heffron v. International Society for Krishna Consciousness, Inc., 452 U. S. 640, 649 (1981). . . . In the present litigation, the county has made clear how it interprets and implements the ordinance. The ordinance can apply to any activity on public property—from parades, to street corner speeches, to bike races—and the fee assessed may reflect the county's police and administrative costs. Whether or not, in any given instance, the fee would include any or all of the county's administrative and security expenses is decided by the county administrator.

In this case, according to testimony at the District Court hearing, the administrator based the fee on his own judgment of what would be reasonable. . . . The administrator also explained that the county had imposed a fee pursuant to a permit on two prior occasions. The year before, the administrator had assessed a fee of $100 for a permit for the Movement. . . . The administrator also once charged bike-race organizers $25 to hold a race on county roads. . . .

Based on the county's implementation and construction of the ordinance, it simply cannot be said that there are any "narrowly drawn, reasonable and definite standards" guiding the hand of the Forsyth County administrator. The decision how much to charge for police protection or administrative time—or even whether to charge at all—is left to the whim of the administrator. There are no articulated standards either in the ordinance or in the county's established practice. The administrator is not required to rely on any objective factors. He need not provide any explanation for his decision, and that decision is unreviewable. Nothing in the law or its application prevents the official from encouraging some views and discouraging others through the arbitrary application of fees. The First Amendment prohibits the vesting of such unbridled discretion in a government official.

B

The Forsyth County ordinance contains more than the possibility of censorship through uncontrolled discretion. As construed by the county, the ordinance often requires that the fee be based on the content of the speech.

. . . The county envisions that the administrator, in appropriate instances, will assess a fee to cover "the cost of necessary and reasonable protection of persons participating in or observing said . . . activit[y]." In order to assess accurately the cost of security for parade participants, the administrator "must necessarily examine the content of the message that is conveyed," estimate the response of others to that content, and judge the number of police necessary to meet that response. The fee assessed will depend on the administrator's measure of the amount of hostility likely to be created by the speech based on its content. Those wishing to express views unpopular with bottle throwers, for example, may have to pay more for their permit.

Although petitioner agrees that the cost of policing relates to content, it contends that the ordinance is content neutral because it is aimed only at a secondary effect—the cost of maintaining public order. It is clear, however, that, in this case, it cannot be said that the fee's justification " 'ha[s] nothing to do with content.' "

The costs to which petitioner refers are those associated with the public's reaction to the speech. Listeners' reaction to speech is not a content-neutral basis for regulation. Speech cannot be financially burdened, any more than it can be punished or banned, simply because it might offend a hostile mob. *See* Terminiello v. Chicago, 337 U.S. 1 (1949).

This Court has held time and again: "Regulations which permit the Government to discriminate on the basis of the content of the message cannot be tolerated under the First Amendment." The county offers only one justification for this ordinance: raising revenue for police services. While this undoubtedly is an important government responsibility, it does not justify a content-based permit fee.

Petitioner insists that its ordinance cannot be unconstitutionally content based because it contains much of the same language as did the state statute upheld in Cox v. New Hampshire, 312 U. S. 569 (1941). Although the Supreme Court of New Hampshire had interpreted the statute at issue in *Cox* to authorize the municipality to charge a permit fee for the "maintenance of public order," no fee was actually assessed. Nothing in this Court's opinion suggests that the statute, as interpreted by the New Hampshire Supreme Court, called for charging a premium in the case of a controversial political message delivered before a hostile audience. In light of the Court's subsequent First Amendment jurisprudence, we do not read *Cox* to permit such a premium.

C

Petitioner, as well as the Court of Appeals and the District Court, all rely on the maximum allowable fee as the touchstone of constitutionality. Petitioner contends that the $1,000 cap on the fee ensures that the ordinance will not result in content-based discrimination. The ordinance was found unconstitutional by the Court of Appeals because the $1,000 cap was not sufficiently low to be "nominal."

Neither the $1,000 cap on the fee charged, nor even some lower nominal cap, could save the ordinance because in this context, the level of the fee is irrelevant. A tax based on the content of speech does not become more constitutional because it is a small tax. . . . [T]he provision of the Forsyth County ordinance relating to fees is invalid because it unconstitutionally ties the amount of the fee to the content of the speech and lacks adequate procedural safeguards; no limit on such a fee can remedy these constitutional violations.

The judgment of the Court of Appeals is affirmed.

Chief Justice REHNQUIST, with whom Justice WHITE, Justice SCALIA, and Justice THOMAS join, dissenting.

We granted certiorari in this case to consider [whether the First Amendment limits the amount of a license fee assessed pursuant to the provisions of a county parade ordinance to a nominal sum, or whether the amount of the license fee may take into account the actual expense incident to the administration of the ordinance and the maintenance of public order in the matter licensed, up to the sum of $1,000.00 per day of the activity.]

The answer seems to me quite simple, because it was authoritatively decided by this Court more than half a century ago in Cox v. New Hampshire, 312 U. S. 569 (1941). There we . . . [held] "[t]here is nothing contrary to the Constitution in the charge of a fee limited to the [expense-defraying] purpose stated. The suggestion that a flat fee should have been charged fails to take account of the difficulty of framing a fair schedule to meet all circumstances, and we perceive no constitutional ground for denying to local governments that flexibility of adjustment of fees which in the light of varying conditions would tend to conserve rather than impair the liberty sought." I believe that the decision in *Cox* squarely controls the disposition of the question presented in this case, and I therefore would explicitly hold that the Constitution does not limit a parade license fee to a nominal amount. . . .

[T]he Court concludes that the county ordinance is facially unconstitutional because it places too much discretion in the hands of the county administrator and forces parade participants to pay for the cost of controlling those who might oppose their speech. . . . The Court apparently envisions a situation where the administrator would impose a $1,000 parade fee on a group whose message he opposed, but would waive the fee entirely for a similarly situated group with whom he agreed. But the county has never rendered any "authoritative construction" indicating that officials have "unbridled discretion," in setting parade fees, nor has any lower court so found. It is true that the Constitution does not permit a system in which the county administrator may vary fees at his pleasure, but there has been no lower court finding that that is what this fledgling ordinance creates.

The Court's second reason for invalidating the ordinance is its belief that any fee imposed will be based in part on the cost of security necessary to control those who *oppose* the message endorsed by those marching in a parade. Assuming 100 people march in a parade and 10,000 line the route in protest, for example, the Court worries that, under this ordinance, the county will charge a premium to control the hostile crowd of 10,000, resulting in the kind of "heckler's veto" we have previously condemned. But there have been no lower court findings on the question whether or not the county plans to base parade fees on anticipated hostile crowds. It has not done so in any of the instances where it has so far imposed fees. And it most certainly did not do so in this case. The Court's analysis on this issue rests on an assumption that the county will interpret the phrase "maintenance of public order" to support the imposition of fees based on opposition crowds. There is nothing in the record to support this assumption, however, and I would remand for a hearing on this question.

For the foregoing reasons, I dissent.

NOTES AND QUESTIONS

1. *Permit fees and other costs. Cox v. New Hampshire* upheld an ordinance that contained a provision allowing officials to charge permit fees up to $300. Are such fees constitutional after *Forsyth County*? Can government charge a fee regardless of the speaker's ability to pay, or must it exempt those who cannot afford the fee? Is there any limit on the *amount* of the fee? *See* David Goldberger, *A Reconsideration of* Cox v. New Hampshire: *Can Demonstrators Be Required to Pay the Costs of Using America's Public Forums?*, 62 Tex. L. Rev. 403, 410-412 (1983). After *Forsyth County*, would it be permissible for government officials to require speakers who want to use a public forum to obtain an insurance policy to cover any damages? Is it permissible to require that permit applicants pay a security deposit to cover the costs of cleanup and security? *See Timothy Zick, The Costs of Dissent: Protest and Civil Liabilities*, 89 Geo. Wash. L. Rev. 233 (2021). Note the costs for providing security for a prior march in *Forsyth County* amounted to more than $600,000. Who should bear these costs, and why? Should there be some cap on the amount governments must pay to police and manage these events? If so, how would you determine the amount?
2. *Unbridled discretion and content discrimination. Forsyth County* invalidated the permit regulations on two independent grounds. First, the Court concluded the ordinance granted local officials unfettered discretion in setting the fees. As we have seen, this kind of scheme has been treated as an unlawful prior restraint on expression in public forums. Second, the Court invalidated the permit regulations because they allowed administrators to *vary* fees based on the perceived reaction of the audience to the speech. The Court referred to the concern, reflected in decisions including *Feiner* and *Edwards*, that government reliance on hostile audience reaction to limit speech imposes a content-based "heckler's veto." Insofar as the fee is based on official's perception of the provocative nature of the speech it is content-based. The Court concluded offsetting security and cleanup expenses are not compelling reasons justifying a variable fee.

THEORY-APPLIED PROBLEM — PORTLAND PERMIT

The city of Portland enacted the following ordinance: "It is unlawful for any person to conduct or participate in any organized entertainment, demonstration, or public gathering, or to make any address in a park without a written permit issued by the Parks Commissioner." The ordinance also requires that permit applicants pay a security deposit "equal to the estimated cost of policing, cleaning up, and restoring the park upon conclusion of the applicant's use or activity." Five individuals chose to protest a city decision to close a local elementary school. They decided to gather in a park in downtown Portland one weekend. The city had already issued an exclusive-use permit to an Art Show that weekend for the entire park. When a police officer discovered the protestors and that they did not have a permit, she asked them to leave. When they refused, she told them she would arrest them for violating the permit ordinance. They chose to stay, so she arrested them. Is the Portland ordinance constitutional, facially and as applied to the protestors?

D. *FORUM ANALYSIS: WHICH PUBLIC PROPERTIES AND FACILITIES DO SPEAKERS HAVE ACCESS TO?*

Hague v. CIO (1939) suggested speakers have a First Amendment right, rooted in tradition, to access (at least) public streets and public parks for expressive purposes. Subsequent decisions have confirmed access rights to these places while also addressing various others. This section covers the Court's jurisprudence regarding whether and under what circumstances government must make public property available for expressive purposes and, if so, on what terms. These rules and standards constitute the "public forum" doctrine. Prior to *Perry Education Ass'n v. Perry Local Educators' Ass'n* (1983), below, the Court reviewed speech and assembly claims involving a multitude of public places including public library reading rooms, the grounds of a public jailhouse, military bases, postal mailboxes, and the advertising space on municipal buses. However, its decisions did not chart a clear or consistent path. In *Perry*, the Court provided a synthesis of modern public forum doctrine.

Perry Education Ass'n v. Perry Local Educators' Ass'n

460 U.S. 37 (1983)

Justice WHITE delivered the opinion of the Court.

. . . The Metropolitan School District of Perry Township, Ind., operates a public school system of 13 separate schools. Each school building contains a set of mailboxes for the teachers. Interschool delivery by school employees permits messages to be delivered rapidly to teachers in the district. The primary function of this internal mail system is to transmit official messages among the teachers and between the teachers and the school administration. In addition, teachers use the system to send personal messages and individual school building principals have allowed delivery of messages from various private organizations.[2]

---

2. Local parochial schools, church groups, YMCAs, and Cub Scout units have used the system. The record does not indicate whether any requests for use have been denied, nor does it reveal whether permission must separately be sought for every message that a group wishes delivered to the teachers.

Prior to 1977, both the Perry Education Association (PEA) and the Perry Local Educators' Association (PLEA) represented teachers in the school district and apparently had equal access to the interschool mail system. In 1977, PLEA challenged PEA's status as *de facto* bargaining representative for the Perry Township teachers by filing an election petition with the Indiana Education Employment Relations Board (Board). PEA won the election and was certified as the exclusive representative, as provided by Indiana law.

. . . Following the election, PEA and the school district negotiated a labor contract in which the school board gave PEA "access to teachers' mailboxes in which to insert material" and the right to use the interschool mail delivery system to the extent that the school district incurred no extra expense by such use. The labor agreement noted that these access rights were being accorded to PEA "acting as the representative of the teachers" and went on to stipulate that [PEA would have exclusive access rights over other unions]. . . .

The exclusive access policy applies only to use of the mailboxes and school mail system. PLEA is not prevented from using other school facilities to communicate with teachers. PLEA may post notices on school bulletin boards; may hold meetings on school property after school hours; and may, with approval of the building principals, make announcements on the public address system. Of course, PLEA also may communicate with teachers by word of mouth, telephone, or the United States mail. . . .

. . . There is no question that constitutional interests are implicated by denying PLEA use of the interschool mail system. . . . The First Amendment's guarantee of free speech applies to teacher's [sic] mailboxes as surely as it does elsewhere within the school, Tinker v. Des Moines School District, 393 U.S. 503 (1969), and on sidewalks outside, Police Department of Chicago v. Mosely, 408 U.S. 92 (1972). But this is not to say that the First Amendment requires equivalent access to all parts of a school building in which some form of communicative activity occurs. . . . The existence of a right of access to public property and the standard by which limitations upon such a right must be evaluated differ depending on the character of the property at issue.

In places which by long tradition or by government fiat have been devoted to assembly and debate, the rights of the state to limit expressive activity are sharply circumscribed. At one end of the spectrum are streets and parks which "have immemorially been held in trust for the use of the public, and, time out of mind, have been used for purposes of assembly, communicating thoughts between citizens, and discussing public questions." *Hague v. CIO.* In these quintessential public forums, the government may not prohibit all communicative activity. For the state to enforce a content-based exclusion it must show that its regulation is necessary to serve a compelling state interest and that it is narrowly drawn to achieve that end. . . . The state may also enforce regulations of the time, place, and manner of expression which are content-neutral, are narrowly tailored to serve a significant government interest, and leave open ample alternative channels of communication. . . .

A second category consists of public property which the state has opened for use by the public as a place for expressive activity. The Constitution forbids a state to enforce certain exclusions from a forum generally open to the public even if it was not required to create the forum in the first place. Widmar v. Vincent, 454

U.S. 263 (1981) (university meeting facilities); City of Madison Joint School District v. Wisconsin Public Employment Relations Comm'n, 429 U.S. 167 (1976) (school board meeting); Southeastern Promotions, Ltd. v. Conrad, 420 U.S. 546 (1975) (municipal theater).[7] Although a state is not required to indefinitely retain the open character of the facility, as long as it does so it is bound by the same standards as apply in a traditional public forum. Reasonable time, place and manner regulations are permissible, and a content-based prohibition must be narrowly drawn to effectuate a compelling state interest.

Public property which is not by tradition or designation a forum for public communication is governed by different standards. We have recognized that the "First Amendment does not guarantee access to property simply because it is owned or controlled by the government." United States Postal Service v. Greenburgh Civic Ass'n, 453 U.S. 114, (1981). In addition to time, place, and manner regulations, the state may reserve the forum for its intended purposes, communicative or otherwise, as long as the regulation on speech is reasonable and not an effort to suppress expression merely because public officials oppose the speaker's view. . . .

The school mail facilities at issue here fall within this third category. . . . The internal mail system, at least by policy, is not held open to the general public. It is instead PLEA's position that the school mail facilities have become a "limited public forum" from which it may not be excluded because of the periodic use of the system by private non-school connected groups, and PLEA's own unrestricted access to the system prior to PEA's certification as exclusive representative.

Neither of these arguments is persuasive. The use of the internal school mail by groups not affiliated with the schools is no doubt a relevant consideration. If by policy or by practice the Perry School District has opened its mail system for indiscriminate use by the general public, then PLEA could justifiably argue a public forum has been created. This, however, is not the case. As the case comes before us, there is no indication in the record that the school mailboxes and interschool delivery system are open for use by the general public. Permission to use the system to communicate with teachers must be secured from the individual building principal. There is no court finding or evidence in the record which demonstrates that this permission has been granted as a matter of course to all who seek to distribute material. We can only conclude that the schools do allow some outside organizations such as the YMCA, Cub Scouts, and other civic and church organizations to use the facilities. . . .

Moreover, even if we assume that by granting access to the Cub Scouts, YMCAs, and parochial schools, the school district has created a "limited" public forum, the constitutional right of access would in any event extend only to other entities of similar character. While the school mail facilities thus might be a forum generally open for use by the Girl Scouts, the local boys' club and other organizations that engage in activities of interest and educational relevance to students, they would not as a consequence be open to an organization such as PLEA, which is concerned with the terms and conditions of teacher employment. . . .

---

7. A public forum may be created for a limited purpose such as use by certain groups, e.g., *Widmar* (student groups), or for the discussion of certain subjects, e.g., *City of Madison Joint School District* (school board business).

. . . In the Court of Appeals' view . . . , the access policy adopted by the Perry schools favors a particular viewpoint, that of the PEA, on labor relations, and consequently must be strictly scrutinized regardless of whether a public forum is involved. There is, however, no indication that the school board intended to discourage one viewpoint and advance another. We believe it is more accurate to characterize the access policy as based on the *status* of the respective unions rather than their views. Implicit in the concept of the nonpublic forum is the right to make distinctions in access on the basis of subject matter and speaker identity. . . . The touchstone for evaluating these distinctions is whether they are reasonable in light of the purpose which the forum at issue serves. . . .

The differential access provided PEA and PLEA is reasonable because it is wholly consistent with the district's legitimate interest in "preserv[ing] the property . . . for the use to which it is lawfully dedicated." *Postal Service*, 453 U.S. at 129-130. Use of school mail facilities enables PEA to perform effectively its obligations as exclusive representative of *all* Perry Township teachers. Conversely, PLEA does not have any official responsibility in connection with the school district and need not be entitled to the same rights of access to school mailboxes. [Moreover], exclusion of the rival union may reasonably be considered a means of insuring labor peace within the schools. Finally, the reasonableness of the limitations on PLEA's access to the school mail system is also supported by the substantial alternative channels that remain open for union-teacher communication to take place. . . . There is no showing here that PLEA's ability to communicate with teachers is seriously impinged by the restricted access to the internal mail system. . . .

The judgment of the Court of Appeals is

Reversed.

Justice BRENNAN, with whom Justice MARSHALL, Justice POWELL, and Justice STEVENS join, dissenting. . . .

. . . This case does not involve an "absolute access" claim. It involves an "equal access" claim. As such it does not turn on whether the internal school mail system is a "public forum." In focusing on the public forum issue, the Court disregards the First Amendment's central proscription against censorship, in the form of viewpoint discrimination, in any forum, public or nonpublic. . . .

. . . [I]t is clear that the exclusive access policy discriminates on the basis of viewpoint. The Court of Appeals found that "the access policy adopted by the Perry schools, in form a speaker restriction, favors a particular viewpoint on labor relations in the Perry [schools]: the teachers inevitably will receive from [the petitioner] self-laudatory descriptions of its activities on their behalf and will be denied the critical perspective offered by [the respondents]." This assessment of the effect of the policy is eminently reasonable. . . .

NOTES AND QUESTIONS

1. *Development of public forum doctrine. Perry* provides a synthesis of a "public forum" doctrine that developed over the course of several decades. In prior cases, protesters and other speakers had been granted access to certain public properties. *See Edwards* (1963) (p. 207, *supra*) (grounds of

the South Carolina State House); Brown v. Louisiana, 383 U.S. 131 (1966) (public library reading room). But in other cases, the Court rejected speakers' access claims. *See* Adderley v. Florida, 385 U.S. 39 (1966) (upholding breach of peace convictions of protesters who assembled on the curtilage of a jailhouse); Lehman v. Shaker Heights, 418 U.S. 298 (1974) (plurality) (upholding exclusion of campaign ads from advertising space on city buses); Greer v. Spock, 424 U.S. 828 (1976) (upholding regulations that barred political activities, including speeches and demonstrations, on the grounds of a military base); U.S. Postal Service v. Council of Greenburgh Civic Ass'ns, 453 U.S. 114 (1981) (finding that a letter box is not a "public forum"). The Court's precedents failed to articulate a consistent approach. Some cases turned on whether the speech in question was "basically compatible" with the functions of the property in question, while others relied on an assessment of the property's character and function.

2. *Public forum methodology. Perry* represents the Court's modern "categorical" approach. To determine whether speech in a public place is protected by the First Amendment, the public forum doctrine requires that one (1) identify the specific place or property a speaker seeks access to, (2) determine which category of "forum" the place or property belongs to, and (3) apply the First Amendment standards for that category of forum. In traditional and designated public forums, general First Amendment content neutrality doctrines apply. In properties neither traditionally nor by designation generally open to expressive activities, speech regulations must be "reasonable" and viewpoint neutral.
3. *Categories of public forums. Perry* identifies three general categories or types of public forum—"*traditional*," "*designated*," and "*non-public*." As *Perry* suggests, however, government can create public forums in which only certain speakers or subject matters are permitted (*see Perry*, n. 7). Is the status or subject matter forum a subset of the designated public forum or a "non-public" forum? Is it a separate type or category of forum, perhaps a "limited" public forum? The Court has not been consistent in terms of the labels it uses to describe this category. In cases following *Perry*, the Court has sometimes referred to "non-public" and "limited" public forums interchangeably, while at other times it has simply left "non-public" forums out of the categorical description. *See, e.g.*, Christian Legal Society v. Martinez, 561 U.S. 661, 679 n.11 (2010) (mentioning "traditional," "designated," and "limited" public forums). Regardless of label, as noted, in forums that are neither traditionally nor by designation generally open to expressive activity speech regulations must be "reasonable" and viewpoint neutral.
4. *"Traditional" public forums—sidewalks. Hague* identified public streets and public parks as forums open "immemorially" for expressive purposes. What about public sidewalks? It has long been accepted that under the *Perry* framework, public sidewalks are also "traditional" or "quintessential" public forums. United States v. Grace, 461 U.S. 171 (1983). *See also* Frisby v. Shultz, *supra* p. 189; McCullen v. Coakley, *supra* p. 193. But be careful—not *all* sidewalks are traditional public forums. In United States v. Kokinda, 497 U.S. 720 (1990) (plurality), the Court held that in contrast to the municipal sidewalk running parallel to a postal building, the sidewalk used to access

the building itself was a "non-public" forum. The plurality reasoned that the postal sidewalk was not "like" other sidewalks in terms of its functions and physical characteristics. Unlike public sidewalks, the postal sidewalk functioned to facilitate access to the post office and postal business. The dissenting Justices in *Kokinda* argued the Court had relied on "wooden distinctions that obscured important free speech and assembly concerns.

5. *"Designated" public forums. Perry* indicates that if a public property is "generally open to the public" for purposes of expressive activity, the First Amendment significantly limits governmental control over speech in such a place. Although they do exist, the Court's precedents do not provide many examples of "designated" public forums. *See* Southeastern Promotions, Ltd. v. Conrad, 420 U.S. 546 (1975) (noting that local public theaters had been made generally available for theatrical productions, and thus officials could not exclude the production "Hair"). As we will see, a "designated" public forum is created only when there is clear evidence government intends to invite the public at large to use a place for expressive purposes. Can you imagine why such designations might be relatively rare?
6. *Critiques of public forum doctrine.* Many scholars have criticized, on various grounds, the Court's public forum doctrine. Some scholars have argued forum categorization diverts judges' attention from central First Amendment concerns. See, e.g., Farber & Nowak, *The Misleading Nature of Public Forum Analysis: Content and Context in First Amendment Adjudication*, 70 Va. L. Rev. 1219 (1984). Other commentators have argued the Court's approach allows too little access to government properties not traditionally used for expressive purposes, such as libraries, courthouses, and prisons but still important to the exercise of First Amendment rights. Geoffrey R. Stone, *Fora Americana*, 1974 Sup. Ct. Rev. 233, 238. Still others have argued public forum doctrine ignores the dynamic and complex relationship speakers have with "place" and the critical role location plays in communicating thoughts and ideas. Timothy Zick, *Space, Place and Speech: The Expressive Topography*, 74 Geo. Wash. L. Rev. 439 (2006); Timothy Zick, *Speech Out of Doors: Preserving First Amendment Liberties in Public Places* (2008). Public forum doctrine also has its defenders. Some have justified the doctrine as a means of generalizing about the kinds of places where government distortion of expression is most concerning. Lillian BeVier, *Rehabilitating Public Forum Doctrine: In Defense of Categories*, 1993 Sup. Ct. Rev. 79. Think about these criticisms and defenses as you read the cases that follow.

Cornelius v. NAACP Legal Defense and Education Fund

473 U.S. 488 (1985)

Justice O'Connor delivered the opinion of the Court.

This case requires us to decide whether the Federal Government violates the First Amendment when it excludes legal defense and political advocacy organizations from participation in the Combined Federal Campaign (CFC or Campaign), a charity drive aimed at federal employees.

I

The CFC is an annual charitable fundraising drive conducted in the federal workplace during working hours largely through the voluntary efforts of federal employees. At all times relevant to this litigation, participating organizations confined their fundraising activities to a 30-word statement submitted by them for inclusion in the Campaign literature. Volunteer federal employees distribute to their co-workers literature describing the Campaign and the participants along with pledge cards. Contributions may take the form of either a payroll deduction or a lump-sum payment made to a designated agency or to the general Campaign fund. . . . Through the CFC, the Government employees contribute in excess of $100 million to charitable organizations each year.

. . . [In response to several lawsuits,] President Reagan took several steps to restore the CFC to what he determined to be its original purpose. [An Executive Order provided that the] CFC was designed to lessen the Government's burden in meeting human health and welfare needs by providing a convenient, nondisruptive channel for federal employees to contribute to nonpartisan agencies that directly serve those needs. The Order limited participation to "voluntary, charitable, health and welfare agencies that provide or support direct health and welfare services to individuals or their families," and specifically excluded those "[a]gencies that seek to influence the outcomes of elections or the determination of public policy through political activity or advocacy, lobbying, or litigation on behalf of parties other than themselves."

Respondents brought this action challenging their threatened exclusion under the new Executive Order. They argued that the denial of the right to seek designated funds violates their First Amendment right to solicit charitable contributions. . . .

II

The issue presented is whether respondents have a First Amendment right to solicit contributions that was violated by their exclusion from the CFC. Assuming that such solicitation is protected speech, we must identify the nature of the forum, because the extent to which the Government may limit access depends on whether the forum is public or nonpublic. Finally, we must assess whether the justifications for exclusion from the relevant forum satisfy the requisite standard. . . .

A

[The Court concludes that charitable solicitation of funds is a form of protected speech.]

B

The conclusion that the solicitation which occurs in the CFC is protected speech merely begins our inquiry. Even protected speech is not equally permissible in all places and at all times. Nothing in the Constitution requires the Government freely to grant access to all who wish to exercise their right to free speech on every type of Government property without regard to the nature of the property or to the disruption that might be caused by the speaker's activities. . . . [T]he Court has adopted a forum analysis as a means of determining when the Government's interest in limiting the use of its property to its intended purpose outweighs the interest of those wishing to use the property for other purposes. Accordingly, the extent to which the Government can control access depends on the nature of the relevant forum. . . .

To determine whether the First Amendment permits the Government to exclude respondents from the CFC, we must first decide whether the forum consists of the federal workplace, as petitioner contends, or the CFC, as respondents maintain. Having defined the relevant forum, we must then determine whether it is public or nonpublic in nature.

Petitioner contends that a First Amendment forum necessarily consists of tangible government property. [However, we] agree with respondents that the relevant forum for our purposes is the CFC. Although petitioner is correct that as an initial matter a speaker must seek access to public property or to private property dedicated to public use to evoke First Amendment concerns, forum analysis is not completed merely by identifying the government property at issue. Rather, in defining the forum we have focused on the access sought by the speaker. When speakers seek general access to public property, the forum encompasses that property. In cases in which limited access is sought, our cases have taken a more tailored approach to ascertaining the perimeters of a forum within the confines of the government property. For example, *Perry Education Ass'n* examined the access sought by the speaker and defined the forum as a school's internal mail system and the teachers' mailboxes, notwithstanding that an "internal mail system" lacks a physical situs. Similarly, in Lehman v. City of Shaker Heights, 418 U. S. 298, 300 (1974), where petitioners sought to compel the city to permit political advertising on city-owned buses, the Court treated the advertising spaces on the buses as the forum.

Here, as in *Perry*, respondents seek access to a particular means of communication. Consistent with the approach taken in prior cases, we find that the CFC, rather than the federal workplace, is the forum. This conclusion does not mean, however, that the Court will ignore the special nature and function of the federal workplace in evaluating the limits that may be imposed on an organization's right to participate in the CFC. *See Perry*.

Having identified the forum as the CFC, we must decide whether it is nonpublic or public in nature. [The Court recites *Perry*'s description of the public forum categories.]

The government does not create a public forum by inaction or by permitting limited discourse, but only by intentionally opening a nontraditional forum for public discourse. Accordingly, the Court has looked to the policy and practice of the government to ascertain whether it intended to designate a place not traditionally open to assembly and debate as a public forum. The Court has also examined the nature of the property and its compatibility with expressive activity to discern the government's intent. . . .

Not every instrumentality used for communication, however, is a traditional public forum or a public forum by designation. The First Amendment does not guarantee access to property simply because it is owned or controlled by the government. We will not find that a public forum has been created in the face of clear evidence of a contrary intent, nor will we infer that the government intended to create a public forum when the nature of the property is inconsistent with expressive activity. . . . In cases where the principal function of the property would be disrupted by expressive activity, the Court is particularly reluctant to hold that the government intended to designate a public forum. Accordingly, we have held that military reservations, Greer v. Spock, 424 U.S. 828 (1976), and jailhouse grounds, Adderley v. Florida, 385 U.S. 39 (1966), do not constitute public fora.

Here the parties agree that neither the CFC nor the federal workplace is a traditional public forum. Respondents argue, however, that the Government created a limited public forum for use by all charitable organizations to solicit funds from federal employees. Petitioner contends, and we agree, that neither its practice nor its policy is consistent with an intent to designate the CFC as a public forum open to all tax-exempt organizations. The Government's consistent policy has been to limit participation in the CFC to "appropriate" voluntary agencies and to require agencies seeking admission to obtain permission from federal and local Campaign officials. Although the record does not show how many organizations have been denied permission throughout the 24-year history of the CFC, there is no evidence suggesting that the granting of the requisite permission is merely ministerial. The Civil Service Commission and, after 1978, the Office of Personnel Management developed extensive admission criteria to limit access to the Campaign to those organizations considered appropriate. Such selective access, unsupported by evidence of a purposeful designation for public use, does not create a public forum.

Nor does the history of the CFC support a finding that the Government was motivated by an affirmative desire to provide an open forum for charitable solicitation in the federal workplace when it began the Campaign. The historical background indicates that the Campaign was designed to minimize the disruption to the workplace that had resulted from unlimited ad hoc solicitation activities by *lessening* the amount of expressive activity occurring on federal property. Indeed, the [Government] stringently limited expression to the 30-word statement included in the Campaign literature. The decision of the Government to limit access to the CFC is not dispositive in itself; instead, it is relevant for what it suggests about the Government's intent in creating the forum. The Government did not create the CFC for purposes of providing a forum for expressive activity. That such activity occurs in the context of the forum created does not imply that the forum thereby becomes a public forum for First Amendment purposes.

An examination of the nature of the Government property involved strengthens the conclusion that the CFC is a nonpublic forum. The federal workplace, like any place of employment, exists to accomplish the business of the employer. It follows that the Government has the right to exercise control over access to the federal workplace in order to avoid interruptions to the performance of the duties of its employees. In light of the Government policy in creating the CFC and its practice in limiting access, we conclude that the CFC is a nonpublic forum.

C

Control over access to a nonpublic forum can be based on subject matter and speaker identity so long as the distinctions drawn are reasonable in light of the purpose served by the forum and are viewpoint neutral. *Perry*. Although a speaker may be excluded from a nonpublic forum if he wishes to address a topic not encompassed within the purpose of the forum, or if he is not a member of the class of speakers for whose especial benefit the forum was created, the government violates the First Amendment when it denies access to a speaker solely to suppress the point of view he espouses on an otherwise includible subject. The Court of Appeals found it unnecessary to resolve whether the government's denial of access to respondents was viewpoint based, because it determined that respondents' exclusion was unreasonable in light of the purpose served by the CFC.

[The Court of Appeals agreed with respondents that] the reasonableness standard is satisfied only when there is some basic incompatibility between the communication at issue and the principal activity occurring on the Government property. Respondents contend that the purpose of the CFC is to permit solicitation by groups that provide health and welfare services. By permitting such solicitation to take place in the federal workplace, respondents maintain, the Government has concluded that such activity is consistent with the activities usually conducted there. Because respondents are seeking to solicit such contributions and their activities result in direct, tangible benefits to the groups they represent, the Government's attempt to exclude them is unreasonable.

[W]e conclude that respondents may be excluded from the CFC. The Government's decision to restrict access to a nonpublic forum need only be *reasonable;* it need not be the most reasonable or the only reasonable limitation. In contrast to a public forum, a finding of strict incompatibility between the nature of the speech or the identity of the speaker and the functioning of the nonpublic forum is not mandated. Even if some incompatibility with general expressive activity were required, the CFC would meet the requirement because it would be administratively unmanageable if access could not be curtailed in a reasonable manner. Nor is there a requirement that the restriction be narrowly tailored or that the Government's interest be compelling. The First Amendment does not demand unrestricted access to a nonpublic forum merely because use of that forum may be the most efficient means of delivering the speaker's message. Rarely will a nonpublic forum provide the only means of contact with a particular audience. Here, as in *Perry*, the speakers have access to alternative channels, including direct mail and in-person solicitation outside the workplace, to solicit contributions from federal employees.

The reasonableness of the Government's restriction of access to a nonpublic forum must be assessed in the light of the purpose of the forum and all the surrounding circumstances. Here the President could reasonably conclude that a dollar directly spent on providing food or shelter to the needy is more beneficial than a dollar spent on litigation that might or might not result in aid to the needy. Moreover, avoiding the appearance of political favoritism is a valid justification for limiting speech in a nonpublic forum. [The Court notes the Government submitted several letters from federal employees and managers expressing concern about the inclusion of groups termed "political" or "nontraditional" in the CFC.] . . . Although the avoidance of controversy is not a valid ground for restricting speech in a public forum, a nonpublic forum by definition is not dedicated to general debate or the free exchange of ideas. The First Amendment does not forbid a viewpoint-neutral exclusion of speakers who would disrupt a nonpublic forum and hinder its effectiveness for its intended purpose.

D

On this record, the Government's posited justifications for denying respondents access to the CFC appear to be reasonable in light of the purpose of the CFC. The existence of reasonable grounds for limiting access to a nonpublic forum, however, will not save a regulation that is in reality a facade for viewpoint-based discrimination. . . .

Petitioner argues that a decision to exclude all advocacy groups, regardless of political or philosophical orientation, is by definition viewpoint neutral. Exclusion of groups advocating the use of litigation is not viewpoint-based, petitioner asserts, because litigation is a means of promoting a viewpoint, not a viewpoint in itself. . . .

Petitioner contends that controversial groups must be eliminated from the CFC to avoid disruption and ensure the success of the Campaign. As noted *supra*, we agree that these are facially neutral and valid justifications for exclusion from the nonpublic forum created by the CFC. Nonetheless, the purported concern to avoid controversy excited by particular groups may conceal a bias against the viewpoint advanced by the excluded speakers. . . . [Since the issue] whether the Government excluded respondents because it disagreed with their viewpoints was neither decided below nor fully briefed before this Court, [w]e decline to decide in the first instance whether the exclusion of respondents was impermissibly motivated by a desire to suppress a particular point of view. Respondents are free to pursue this contention on remand.

III

We conclude that the Government does not violate the First Amendment when it limits participation in the CFC in order to minimize disruption to the federal workplace, to ensure the success of the fundraising effort, or to avoid the appearance of political favoritism without regard to the viewpoint of the excluded groups. Accordingly, we reverse the judgment of the Court of Appeals that the exclusion of respondents was unreasonable, and we remand this case for further proceedings consistent with this opinion.

Justice MARSHALL took no part in the consideration or decision of this case.

Justice POWELL took no part in the decision of this case.

Justice BLACKMUN, with whom Justice BRENNAN joins, dissenting.

I agree with the Court that the CFC is not a traditional public forum. I cannot accept, however, the Court's circular reasoning that the CFC is not a limited public forum because the Government intended to limit the forum to a particular class of speakers. Nor can I agree with the Court's conclusion that distinctions the Government makes between speakers in defining the limits of a forum need not be narrowly tailored and necessary to achieve a compelling governmental interest. Finally, I would hold that the exclusion of the several respondents from the CFC was, on its face, viewpoint-based discrimination. Accordingly, I dissent. . . .

[A dissenting opinion by Justice STEVENS is omitted.]

NOTES AND QUESTIONS

1. *Identifying the relevant forum.* In *Cornelius,* is the relevant place for purposes of public forum analysis the CFC campaign or the federal workplace? What difference might the answer to that question make in terms of forum analysis?
2. *The role of government intent.* As the Court explains in *Cornelius,* whether government has created a "designated" public forum depends on a demonstration of its clear intent to do so. What evidence is relevant to establishing the government's intent? Is the fact that some speech has occurred in the forum sufficient to create a designated public forum? Does allowing government to control access in this manner create an incentive for it to open at least *some* places to expressive activity? Or does focusing on governmental intent provide a basis for broadly excluding speakers from public places?
3. *Access to the "limited"/non-public forum.* In his dissent, Justice Blackmun complained that the Court had effectively nullified the concept of a "limited" public forum. He asserted the Court's analysis "makes it *virtually* impossible to prove that a forum restricted to a particular class of speakers is a limited public forum. If the Government does not create a limited public forum unless it intends to provide an 'open forum' for expressive activity, and if the exclusion of some speakers is evidence that the Government did not intend to create such a forum, no speaker challenging denial of access will ever be able to prove that the forum is a limited public forum." Do you agree with Justice Blackmun that the concept of a "limited" public forum is circular?
4. *"Reasonable" and viewpoint neutral.* In a "limited" public forum, speech regulations must only be "reasonable" and viewpoint-neutral. What factors or considerations are relevant to the "reasonableness" inquiry? In *Cornelius,* the majority remanded the case for a determination whether the CFC exclusion was viewpoint-based. In his dissent, Justice Blackmun concluded the CFC's limitation was viewpoint-based because it singled out certain advocacy groups based on how they chose to provide services to the public. Do you agree? Consider Rosenberger v. Rector & Visitors of University of Virginia, 515 U.S. 819 (1995), in which the Court concluded a public university engaged in viewpoint discrimination in a limited public forum. The case involved a program of mandatory student fees used to fund student extracurricular activities. The Court concluded the activities fee program was a "limited" public forum. It invalidated as viewpoint-based a guideline that prohibited the use of funds for any "religious activities," defined as any activity "that primarily promotes or manifests a particular belief in or about a deity or an ultimate reality." Is that exclusion viewpoint-neutral, in the sense that it declines to fund all positions regarding religion? Or is the exclusion of "religious" perspectives itself a form of viewpoint discrimination?
5. *"Metaphysical" fora.* As *Cornelius* shows, the forum doctrine applies not just to physical properties but to charitable funding campaigns and other resources government makes available. In Christian Legal Society v.

Martinez, 561 U.S. 661 (2010), the Court upheld Hastings Law School's nondiscrimination policy for registered student organizations, which required that recognized student organizations accept "all comers" into their groups. Christian Legal Society, which excluded certain students based on their sexual orientation, argued the "all comers" policy violated its First Amendment rights. The Court treated the Registered Student Organization (RSO) program as the relevant forum and concluded it was a "limited" public forum. The Court held that the nondiscrimination policy was "textbook neutral" and that it was reasonable because it "ensures that the leadership, educational, and social opportunities afforded by [RSOs] are available to all students," "helps Hastings police the written terms of its Nondiscrimination Policy without inquiring into an RSO's motivation for membership restrictions," "encourages tolerance, cooperation, and learning among students," and "conveys the Law School's decision 'to decline to subsidize with public monies and benefits conduct of which the people of California disapprove.'" The Court also noted the all-comers policy left open ample alternative opportunities for CLS to communicate, including access to school facilities to conduct meetings and the use of chalkboards.

6. *When is forum doctrine "out of place"?* As expansive as public forum doctrine is, there are certain contexts in which the Court has doubted its application or held it does not apply. For example, in Pleasant Grove City v. Summum, 555 U.S. 460 (2009), *infra* Chapter 12, the Supreme Court found public forum principles "out of place" in the context of a city's decision to exclude a privately donated religious monument from a municipal park. The Court, in an opinion by Justice Alito, concluded that the monuments donated to the city were a form of "government speech" as to which public forum and other free speech doctrines do not apply. (The government speech doctrine is discussed in Chapter 12.) The Court has also hesitated to apply public forum principles where government actors exercise broad discretion in terms of excluding speakers from certain kinds of places. In United States v. American Library Ass'n, 539 U.S. 194 (2003), library patrons, librarians, and others challenged a federal law requiring that public libraries filter publicly accessible Internet terminals for obscenity, child pornography, and material harmful to minors as a condition of receiving federal funds. The Court rejected public forum principles as "incompatible" with the discretion public libraries have in choosing material suitable for patrons. *See also* AETC v. Forbes, 523 U.S. 666 (1998) (cautioning that public forum principles ordinarily do not apply to public television stations' editorial judgments concerning private speech presented to viewers).

Hodge v. Talkin

799 F.3d 1145 (D.C. Cir. 2015)

Before: HENDERSON and SRINIVASAN, Circuit Judges, and WILLIAMS, Senior Circuit Judge.

Opinion of the Court filed by SRINIVASAN, Circuit Judge.

For more than sixty-five years, a federal statute has restricted the public's conduct of expressive activity within the building and grounds of the Supreme Court. The law contains two prohibitions within the same sentence. The first makes it unlawful "to parade, stand, or move in processions or assemblages in the Supreme Court Building or grounds" (the Assemblages Clause). The second makes it unlawful "to display in the Building and grounds a flag, banner, or device designed or adapted to bring into public notice a party, organization, or movement" (the Display Clause). 40 U.S.C. § 6135. The statute defines the Supreme Court "grounds" to extend to the public sidewalks forming the perimeter of the city block that houses the Court.

In United States v. Grace, 461 U.S. 171 (1983), the Supreme Court held the statute's Display Clause unconstitutional as applied to the sidewalks at the edge of the grounds. The Court found "nothing to indicate to the public that these sidewalks are part of the Supreme Court grounds" or that they "are in any way different from other public sidewalks in the city." Like other public sidewalks, consequently, the sidewalks surrounding the Court qualify as a "public forum" for First Amendment purposes, an area in which "the government's ability to permissibly restrict expressive conduct is very limited." But the Court left for another day the constitutionality of the statute's application to the rest of the grounds, including the Court's plaza: the elevated marble terrace running from the front sidewalk to the staircase that ascends to the Court's main doors.

We confront that issue today. The plaintiff in this case, Harold Hodge, Jr., seeks to picket, leaflet, and make speeches in the Supreme Court plaza, with the aim of conveying to the Court and the public what he describes as "political messages" about the Court's decisions. Hodge claims that the statute's Assemblages and Display Clauses, by restricting his intended activities, violate his rights under the First Amendment. The district court, persuaded by his arguments, declared the statute unconstitutional in all its applications to the Court's plaza. We disagree and conclude that the Assemblages and Display Clauses may be constitutionally enforced in the plaza. . . .

I

The federal statute in issue, 40 U.S.C. § 6135, makes it unlawful "to parade, stand, or move in processions or assemblages in the Supreme Court Building or grounds, or to display in the Building and grounds a flag, banner, or device designed or adapted to bring into public notice a party, organization, or movement." Another provision defines "the Supreme Court grounds" to extend to the curbs of the four streets fixing the boundary of the city block in which the Court is situated. 40 U.S.C. § 6101(b). The statute thus encompasses "not only the building," but also "the plaza and surrounding promenade, lawn area, and steps," together with "[t]he sidewalks comprising the outer boundaries of the Court grounds." *Grace.*

. . . The Court's main entrance faces west towards First Street Northeast, across which sits the United States Capitol. Eight marble steps, flanked on either side by marble candelabra, ascend from the concrete sidewalk along First Street Northeast to the Court's elevated marble plaza: an oval terrace that is 252 feet long (at the largest part of the oval) and 98 feet wide (inclusive of the front eight steps). The terrace is paved in gray and white marble in a pattern of alternating circles and squares similar to that of the floor of the Roman Pantheon. The plaza contains two fountains, two flagpoles, and six marble benches. Another thirty-six steps lead from the plaza to the building's portico and the magnificent bronze doors that are the main entrance into the building. A low marble wall surrounds the plaza and also encircles the rest of the building. And the plaza's white marble matches the marble that makes up the low wall, the two staircases, the fountains, and the building's façade and columns.

On January 28, 2011, Harold Hodge, Jr., stood in the plaza approximately 100 feet from the building's front doors. He hung from his neck a two-by-three-foot sign displaying the words "The U.S. Gov. Allows Police To Illegally Murder And Brutalize African Americans And Hispanic People." After a few minutes, a Supreme Court Police officer approached Hodge and told him he was violating the law. Hodge declined to leave. After three more warnings, the officer arrested him. On February 4, 2011, Hodge was charged with violating 40 U.S.C. § 6135.

In January 2012, Hodge filed the present action in federal district court. His complaint alleges that he "desires to return to the plaza area . . . and engage in peaceful, non-disruptive political speech and expression in a similar manner to his activity on January 28, 2011." In addition to again wearing a sign, Hodge wishes to "picket, hand out leaflets, sing, chant, and make speeches, either by himself or with a group of like-minded individuals." Hodge says that the "political message that [he] would like to convey would be directed both at the Supreme Court and the general public, and would explain how decisions of the Supreme Court have allowed police misconduct and discrimination against racial minorities to continue." Hodge's complaint . . . claims that the Assemblages and Display Clauses amount to unconstitutional restrictions of speech. . . .

III

A

Hodge's desired activities in the Supreme Court plaza—picketing, leafleting, and speechmaking—lie at the core of the First Amendment's protections. Still, he does not have an automatic entitlement to engage in that conduct wherever (and whenever) he would like. Rather, the "Government, 'no less than a private owner of property, has the power to preserve the property under its control for the use to which it is lawfully dedicated.'" That principle finds voice in the Supreme Court's "forum analysis," which determines when a governmental entity, in regulating property in its charge, may place limitations on speech.

. . . We find the Supreme Court plaza to be a nonpublic forum. The Court's analysis in *Grace* directly points the way to that conclusion. In finding that the sidewalks marking the perimeter of the Court's grounds are a public forum, the Court emphasized that there is "no separation, no fence, and no indication whatever to persons stepping from the street to the curb and sidewalks" that "they have entered some special type of enclave." Although certain sidewalks might constitute nonpublic forums if they serve specific purposes for particular public sites (such as providing solely for internal passage within those sites, see United States v. Kokinda, 497 U.S. 720 (1990) (plurality opinion)), the *Grace* Court viewed the Supreme Court's perimeter sidewalks to be "indistinguishable from any other sidewalks in

Washington, D.C." The Court therefore saw "nothing to indicate to the public that these sidewalks are part of the Supreme Court grounds" in particular. As a result, there is "no reason why they should be treated any differently" from the mine-run of public sidewalks, which are "considered, generally without further inquiry, to be public forum property."

Grace's analysis makes evident that the Supreme Court plaza, in contrast to the perimeter sidewalks, is a nonpublic forum. [In *Grace*,] the Court considered it of pivotal significance that there was "nothing to indicate to the public that these sidewalks are part of the Supreme Court grounds," or that "they have entered some special type of enclave." The opposite is very much true of the Court's plaza.

The plaza's appearance and design vividly manifest its architectural integration with the Supreme Court building, as well as its separation from the perimeter sidewalks and surrounding area. The plaza is elevated from the sidewalk by a set of marble steps. A low, patterned marble wall—the same type of wall that encircles the rest of the building—surrounds the plaza platform and defines its boundaries. And the plaza and the steps rising to it are composed of white marble that contrasts sharply with the concrete sidewalk in front of it, but that matches the staircase ascending to the Court's front doors and the façade of the building itself.

. . . From the perspective of a Court visitor (and also the public), the "physical and symbolic pathway to [the Supreme Court] chamber begins on the plaza." Cass Gilbert, the Supreme Court's architect, conceived of the plaza, staircase, and portico leading to the massive bronze entry doors as an integrated "processional route" culminating in the courtroom. Commenting on that design, a sitting Justice has written that, "[s]tarting at the Court's western plaza, Gilbert's plan leads visitors along a carefully choreographed, climbing path that ultimately ends at the courtroom itself." *Statement Concerning the Supreme Court's Front Entrance*, 2009 J. Sup.Ct. U.S. at 831 (Breyer, J.).

In short, . . . there is everything to indicate to the public that the plaza is an integral part of [the Supreme Court] grounds. The plaza's features convey in many distinctive ways that a person has entered some special type of enclave. And in serving as what amounts to the elevated front porch of the Supreme Court building (complete with a surrounding railing), the plaza—like the building from which it extends, and to which it leads—is a nonpublic forum.

[This] conclusion is consistent with the treatment of courthouses more generally. The area surrounding a courthouse traditionally has not been considered a forum for demonstrations and protests. In Cox v. Louisiana, 379 U.S. 559 (1965), the Supreme Court rejected a First Amendment challenge to a Louisiana law prohibiting picketing or parades "in or near" courthouses if aimed to impede the administration of justice or influence a court officer. The Court found there to be "no question that a State has a legitimate interest in protecting its judicial system from the pressures which picketing near a courthouse might create."

Importantly, the Supreme Court plaza's status as a nonpublic forum is unaffected by the public's unrestricted access to the plaza at virtually any time. Indeed, in *Grace* itself, the Court emphasized that "property is not transformed into 'public forum' property merely because the public is permitted to freely enter and leave the grounds at practically all times." The same is true of open-air monuments held by this court to be nonpublic forums. As our court observed in reference to the interior of the Jefferson Memorial, "[t]hat the Memorial is open to the public does not alter its status as a nonpublic forum. Visitors are not invited for expressive purposes, but are free to enter only if they abide by the rules that preserve the Memorial's solemn atmosphere." Although those visitors may "regularly talk loudly, make noise, and take and pose for photographs, . . . none of this conduct rises to the level of a conspicuous demonstration." Much the same could be said of the Supreme Court plaza.

. . . With regard to any suggestion that the Court's plaza could be considered some kind of park, [we have held in prior cases that] our country's many national parks are too vast and variegated to be painted with a single brush for purposes of forum analysis. . . . [W]e [have] recognized . . . many areas within national parks never have been dedicated to free expression and public assembly. Here, Hodge makes no argument that the Supreme Court plaza is defined as a "park" for any reason under the law. And regardless, the plaza, like courthouse grounds in general, has never been dedicated to the public's conduct of assemblages, expressive activity, and recreation in the manner of a traditional park.

None of this is to say that Congress could not *choose* to dedicate the Supreme Court plaza as a forum for the robust exercise of First Amendment activity by the general public. The plaza could be transformed into a setting for demonstrations and the like. And if Congress were to open up the plaza as a public forum, the space would become subject to the same First Amendment rules that govern across the street on the grounds of the Capitol. But whereas the Capitol grounds are a public forum by requirement of the First Amendment, the Supreme Court plaza would become a public forum by choice of Congress. The difference exists because judges are not politicians. And although politicians are expected to be appropriately responsive to the preferences of the public—and therefore are expected to accommodate public expression on the grounds of the legislative chamber—the same is not true of judges. So while Congress *could* elect to dedicate the Court's plaza as a public forum, Congress has not done so. To the contrary, Congress has restricted expressive activity in the plaza through statutes like § 6135.

Nor have the Supreme Court's own enforcement practices transformed the plaza into a nonpublic forum. The Court's allowance of two forms of highly circumscribed expressive activity in the plaza—attorneys and litigants addressing the media immediately after a Supreme Court argument, and the occasional granting of approval to conduct filming on the plaza for commercial or professional films relating to the Court—is immaterial. The "government does not create a public forum by inaction or by permitting limited discourse, but only by intentionally opening a nontraditional forum for public discourse." *Cornelius.*

For the same reason, it is of no moment that the Supreme Court Police in certain situations might opt to allow demonstrators onto the plaza for a brief period, presumably in an effort to exercise enforcement authority with responsible (and viewpoint-neutral) discretion in unique circumstances. For instance, notwithstanding the Court Police's usual practice of strict enforcement, the Police apparently did not attempt to prevent a crowd of about 200 demonstrators from briefly surging up the off-limits steps of the U.S. Supreme Court late one night last fall as part of nationwide protests against a Missouri grand jury's decision not to indict the police officer who fatally shot a Ferguson teenager. The protesters evidently moved on after about fifteen minutes, and the Police made no arrests. The fact that the protesters made their way onto the plaza for a quarter of an hour did not somehow transform the plaza into a public forum for all time. Rather, the plaza was then, and remains now, a nonpublic forum.

B

Having concluded that the Supreme Court plaza is a nonpublic forum, we now examine whether the Assemblages and Display Clauses survive . . . [the] much more limited review governing speech restrictions in such areas. Under that review, the restrictions need only be reasonable, as long as [they are] not an effort to suppress the speaker's activity due to disagreement with the speaker's view.

There is no suggestion that either clause discriminates on the basis of viewpoint. The Assemblages Clause makes it unlawful "to parade, stand, or move in processions or assemblages," and the Display Clause makes it unlawful to "display" a "flag, banner, or device designed or adapted to bring into public notice a party, organization, or movement." 40 U.S.C. § 6135. Whatever the scope of expressive activities within the reach of those prohibitions (a matter we explore in greater depth below), they operate without regard to the communication's viewpoint. Demonstrations supporting the Court's decisions and demonstrations opposing them are equally forbidden in the plaza.

The question, then, is whether the restrictions are reasonable in light of the government's interest in preserving the property for its intended purposes. *See Perry*. We find that they are.

[1] The government puts forward two primary interests in support of § 6135's application in the Supreme Court plaza. First, the government argues that the statute helps maintain the decorum and order befitting courthouses generally and the nation's highest court in particular. Second, the government contends that the statute promotes the appearance and actuality of a Court whose deliberations are immune to public opinion and invulnerable to public pressure. Precedent lies with the government as to both interests.

With respect to the first, in *Grace*, the government relied on the statute's purpose "to provide for the . . . maintenance of proper order and decorum" in the Supreme Court grounds. The Supreme Court concluded that the Display Clause bore an insufficient nexus to that interest under the strict standards applicable in a traditional public forum. But for present purposes, what matters is that the Court did not denigrate the necessity . . . to maintain proper order and decorum within the Supreme Court grounds. The Court's opinion therefore has been cited for the proposition that it is proper to weigh the need to maintain the dignity and purpose of a public building.

That need fully applies to the Supreme Court plaza. As the actual and figurative entryway to the Supreme Court building and ultimately the courtroom, the plaza is one of the integrated architectural elements [that] does its part to encourage contemplation of the Court's central purpose, the administration of justice to all who seek it. And as the public's staging ground to enter the Supreme Court building and engage with the business conducted within it, the plaza, together with the building to which it is integrally connected, is an area in which the government may legitimately attempt to maintain suitable decorum for a courthouse.

The second interest the government invokes here was also recognized in *Grace*. There, the Court described the interest in preserving the appearance of a judiciary immune to public pressure as follows:

> Court decisions are made on the record before them and in accordance with the applicable law. The views of the parties and of others are to be

> presented by briefs and oral argument. Courts are not subject to lobbying, judges do not entertain visitors in their chambers for the purpose of urging that cases be resolved one way or another, and they do not and should not respond to parades, picketing or pressure groups.

. . . [It] may have become fashionable in certain quarters to assume that any reference to an apolitical judiciary free from outside control and influence, should be met with a roll of one's eyes, or perhaps to view any suggestion to that effect as antiquated or quaintly idealistic. If so, the government's interest in preserving (or restoring) the public's impression of a judiciary immune to outside pressure would have only gained in salience. . . . Unlike the executive or the legislature, the judiciary "has no influence over either the sword or the purse; . . . neither force nor will but merely judgment." The Federalist No. 78, p. 465 (C. Rossiter ed. 1961) (A. Hamilton) (capitalization altered). The judiciary's authority therefore depends in large measure on the public's willingness to respect and follow its decisions.

[2] Unlike in a public forum, there is no requirement in a nonpublic forum "that the restriction be narrowly tailored" to advance the government's interests. *Cornelius.* Rather, the government's "decision to restrict access to a nonpublic forum need only be *reasonable*," and even then, "it need not be the most reasonable or the only reasonable limitation." *Id.* Judged by those standards, § 6135, as applied to the Supreme Court plaza, reasonably serves the government's interests in maintaining order and decorum at the Supreme Court and in avoiding the impression that popular opinion and public pressure affect the Court's deliberations.

To begin with, restricting expressive assemblages and displays promotes a setting of decorum and order at the Supreme Court. Congress could reasonably conclude that demonstrations and parades in the plaza, or the display of signs and banners, would compromise the sense of dignity and decorum befitting the entryway to the nation's highest court. . . .

The statute also promotes the understanding that the Court resolves the matters before it without regard to political pressure or public opinion. Allowing demonstrations directed at the Court, on the Court's own front terrace, would tend to yield the opposite impression: that of a Court engaged with — and potentially vulnerable to — outside entreaties by the public. At the least, the *appearance* of a Court subject to political pressure might gain increasing hold.

This case illustrates the point. Hodge tells us he wants to use the plaza to send a "political message . . . directed . . . at the Supreme Court" explaining how its decisions "have allowed police misconduct and discrimination against racial minorities to continue." Congress may act to prevent just those sorts of conspicuous efforts on the courthouse grounds to pressure the Court to change its decision-making — efforts that could well foster an impression of a Court subject to outside influence. Reserving the plaza as a demonstration-free zone counters the sense that it is appropriate to appeal to the Court through means other than "briefs and oral argument." It thereby protects the judicial process, and the Supreme Court's unique role within that process, from being misjudged in the minds of the public.

Insofar as the prohibitions of the Assemblages and Display Clauses may reach beyond what is strictly necessary to vindicate those interests, Congress is allowed a degree of latitude in a nonpublic forum. The Supreme Court's admonition that a restriction "need not be the most reasonable or the only reasonable limitation" captures that understanding.

Hodge . . . [also] argues . . . the Assemblages and Display Clauses are unreasonably *broad* in prohibiting various conduct in the Supreme Court plaza that should remain permissible. The prohibitions' terms, the argument runs, carry the capacity to sweep in a range of expressive activity bearing an inadequate connection to the government's interests. For instance, a solitary, peaceful protester unassumingly holding an inconspicuous sign in the corner of the plaza, perhaps on a day when the Court conducts no business, might seem an unlikely candidate to raise substantial concerns about breaching appropriate decorum in the Supreme Court grounds or engendering a misperception regarding the Court's receptiveness to outside influences.

It is often possible, however, to formulate hypothetical applications of a challenged statute that may call into question the law's efficacy in those discrete instances. But "the validity of [a] regulation depends on the relation it bears to the overall problem the government seeks to correct, not on the extent to which it furthers the government's interests in an individual case." Ward v. Rock Against Racism, 491 U.S. 781 (1989). It bears reemphasis in this regard that restrictions of expressive activity in a nonpublic forum need not satisfy any least-restrictive-means threshold, and "a finding of strict incompatibility between the nature of the speech . . . and the functioning of the nonpublic forum is not mandated." *Cornelius.* Rather, Congress may prophylactically frame prohibitions at a level of generality as long as the lines it draws are reasonable, even if particular applications within those lines would implicate the government's interests to a greater extent than others. . . . Congress therefore was under no obligation to fashion § 6135's reach so as to encompass only those forms of expressive activity in the Supreme Court plaza that most acutely implicate the government's concerns. Congress could paint with a broader brush.

With respect to expressive activity that *does* fall within the statute's prohibitions, it is a mark in favor of the statute's reasonableness that the barred activity can be undertaken in an adjacent forum—the sidewalk running along First Street Northeast. The Supreme Court's decisions have counted it significant that other available avenues for the . . . exercise [of] First Amendment rights lessen the burden of a restriction in a nonpublic forum. The sidewalk area fronting the Supreme Court along First Street is over fifty feet deep. And demonstrations, protests, and other First Amendment activities regularly occur there, as is often seen in pictures. The public generally must pass through the sidewalk to enter the plaza, moreover, arming someone engaged in expressive activity on the perimeter with exposure to the vast majority of people who go onto the platform.

Hodge makes no argument that the sidewalk in front of the Court is a physically inadequate or less effective forum for communicating his message. Instead, Hodge contends that the sidewalk's availability should count as a strike *against* the statue's reasonableness. He reasons that the adverse effects of First Amendment activity in the plaza would also be felt from the same activity on the adjacent sidewalk, rendering the distinction between the two an unreasonable one. We are unpersuaded. . . . [The] government could . . . conclude that protests in the Supreme Court plaza and protests on the public sidewalk present markedly different appearances to the public. . . . Congress could conclude that the public might form a different impression about the Court's susceptibility to public opinion if it saw a Court seemingly inviting demonstrators onto its own front porch (as opposed to a Court tolerating demonstrators on a public sidewalk "indistinguishable from any other sidewalks in Washington, D.C."

* * *

In the end, unless demonstrations are to be freely allowed inside the Supreme Court building itself, a line must be drawn somewhere along the route from the street to the Court's front entrance. But where? At the front doors themselves? At the edge of the portico? At the bottom of the stairs ascending from the plaza to the portico? Or perhaps somewhere in the middle of the plaza? Among the options, it is fully reasonable for that line to be fixed at the point one leaves the concrete public sidewalk and enters the marble steps to the Court's plaza, where the "physical and symbolic pathway to [the] chamber begins."

Of course, this case would be decidedly different if the line—wherever exactly it lay—were geared to shield the Supreme Court from having to face criticism just outside its own front door. A law that discriminated on the basis of viewpoint in that way would plainly infringe the First Amendment even in a nonpublic forum. Section 6135, however, bans demonstrations and displays in the plaza regardless of whether they support or oppose (or even concern) the Court.

The statute requires that result because *all* demonstrations on the Court's front porch—even those seeking to give the Court a pat on the back, not a slap in the face—could fuel the impression of a Court responsive to public opinion or outside influence, and could compromise the decorum and order suitable in the entryway to a courthouse, the nation's highest. . . . For all those reasons, § 6135 is a reasonable, viewpoint-neutral—and thus permissible—means of vindicating the government's important interests in the Supreme Court plaza.

For the foregoing reasons, we reverse the judgment of the district court.

NOTES AND QUESTIONS

1. *Public expression and public places.* Is the D.C. Circuit's decision consistent with the fundamental concept of the "public forum"? Is a plaza generally open to the public, including for some expressive activity, truly "nonpublic"? Is the government's interest in preserving the appearance of judicial impartiality and "decorum" sufficient to exclude protests, demonstrations, and other expression from such a place? Are sidewalks adjacent to the plaza adequate alternatives of communication given Hodge's message? Does the appeals court undervalue the extent to which speakers rely on location to communicate? More broadly, does *Hodge* highlight a shrinking of the "expressive topography," or the public space deemed available for expressive activities? *See* Timothy Zick, *Speech Out of Doors: Preserving First Amendment Liberties in Public Places* (2009).
2. *The seat of government: legislatures and courthouses.* In *Edwards v. South Carolina, supra* p. 207, the Supreme Court treated the South Carolina State House grounds as a traditional public forum. *Hodge* likewise describes the grounds around the U.S Capitol as a traditional public forum. However, courthouse plazas have been categorized as nonpublic forums in *Cox v. Louisiana,* relied on in *Hodge,* and of course in *Hodge* itself. Do you agree there are reasons to treat legislative and judicial plazas differently under public forum doctrine? If so, what are those reasons?
3. *City centers, national parks, and monuments.* In Berger v. City of Seattle, 569 F.3d 1029 (9th Cir. 2009) (en banc), the court held the Seattle Center was

a traditional public forum akin to a public park. The Seattle Center is a centrally located 80-acre public space that is home to the Space Needle, museums, sports arenas, theaters, a performance hall, and 23 acres of outdoor public park space. Does it make sense to treat Seattle Center, an entertainment space, like a public park but the Supreme Court plaza as a "non-public" forum? As *Hodge* indicates, some courts have declined to treat national parks, or areas within national parks, as traditional or designated public forums. In Boardley v. U.S. Dep't of Interior, 615 F.3d 508 (D.C. Cir. 2010), the D.C. Circuit observed:

> The protections of the First Amendment do not rise or fall depending on the characterization ascribed to a forum by the government. ". . . Mount Rushmore does not become a public forum merely by being called a 'national park' any more than it would be transformed into a nonpublic forum if it were labeled a 'museum.' The dispositive question is not what the forum is *called*, but what *purpose* it serves, either by tradition or specific designation. What makes a park a traditional public forum is not its grass and trees, but the fact that it has 'immemorially been held in trust for the use of the public and, time out of mind, ha[s] been used for purposes of assembly, communicating thoughts between citizens, and discussing public questions.' Thus, to establish that a national park (in whole or part) is a traditional public forum, Boardley must show that, like a typical municipal park, it has been held open by the government for the purpose of public discourse." *Id.* at 515.

As *Hodge* notes, the D.C. Circuit has also held that the inside of the Jefferson Memorial in Washington, D.C. is a "nonpublic" forum. Oberwetter v. Hilliard, 639 F.3d 545 (D.C. Cir. 2011). The court observed that "[n]ational memorials are places of public commemoration, not freewheeling forums for open expression, and thus the government may reserve them for purposes that preclude expressive activity. . . ." Can the federal government close all memorials in the D.C. area to speech activity, provided it does so on a viewpoint-neutral basis?

THEORY-APPLIED PROBLEMS

1. The Roosevelt Center performing arts complex is in a busy section of Old York City, a large metropolis. The Arts Plaza (Plaza), located in front of the arts complex, is a large outdoor square that serves as the centerpiece of the Roosevelt Center complex. The Plaza is bounded by various arts and other public buildings, including an opera house, a theater, and a public library. The Plaza opens onto a major downtown thoroughfare and can be reached by climbing a short flight of stairs. Public entranceways also connect to the Plaza from the sidewalks surrounding Roosevelt Center. These entranceways facilitate access to the Plaza and its surrounding buildings, and permit pedestrians to cross the Plaza on their way to other destinations in the downtown neighborhood.

Public access to the Plaza is unrestricted. There are several benches in the Plaza, which are typically used by the public for sitting, reading, and eating lunch. There is also a scenic walkway surrounded by grass and trees, which people stroll and run along. During early morning and some evening hours, small groups of people use the Plaza to engage in meditation and exercise. The original design of the Plaza specified that there should be a "large plaza space serving as a forecourt for the Center and an impressive entryway for public access to the Center." The Parks Department, which has jurisdiction over the Plaza, has adopted regulations that restrict events on the Plaza to those "having a performance, entertainment, or artistic component." Members of a labor union want to hold a rally on the Plaza but have been informed the event does not comply with the Parks Department regulation. What kind of forum is the Plaza? Is the Parks Department regulation valid as applied to the union's members?

2. The General Services Administration (GSA) is a federal government agency that operates a Facebook page describing the mission of the GSA and issuing "status updates" about its actions and operations. Citizens can make comments on the Facebook page as long as they are linked to the topic of the status updates. What kind of forum is the GSA's Facebook page? To what extent can the GSA delete comments on its Facebook page?
3. Bland City has bi-weekly City Council meetings where issues on the agenda related to city governance are raised. Bland City recently adopted "rules of decorum" for city council meetings that forbade persons addressing the council from making "personal, impertinent, slanderous or profane remarks that disrupt, disturb or otherwise impede the orderly conduct of City Council meetings." Are such rules consistent with the forum created? Can Bland City remove a speaker from a meeting for giving the Nazi salute to a city official who has taken an action with which they are unhappy?

E. *WHEN SHOULD SPEAKERS HAVE ACCESS TO* PRIVATE *PROPERTY?*

The foregoing cases all examined access to *public* properties and resources. Do speakers have any First Amendment claim of access to *private* properties?

In Marsh v. Alabama, 326 U.S. 501 (1946), the Court considered whether a state could "impose criminal punishment on a person who undertakes to distribute religious literature on the premises of a company-owned town contrary to the wishes of the town's management." The town, a suburb of Mobile, Alabama, known as Chickasaw, had the characteristics of other American towns, except that it was owned by the Gulf Shipbuilding Corporation. The Court held that a Jehovah's Witness could distribute religious literature on the town's sidewalks because the town served a "public function" creating state action.

Two decades later, in Amalgamated Food Employees v. Logan Valley Plaza, Inc., 391 U.S. 308 (1968), the Court found unconstitutional a state court injunction prohibiting a union from picketing at a private shopping mall. According to the Court, "[t]he similarities between the business block in *Marsh* and the shopping center in the present case are striking. . . . The general public has unrestricted access to the mall property. The shopping center here is clearly the functional equivalent of the business district of Chickasaw involved in *Marsh*. . . . We see no reason why access to a business district in a company town for the purpose of exercising First Amendment rights should be constitutionally required, while access for the same purpose to property functioning as a business district should be limited simply because the property surrounding the 'business district' is not under the same ownership." *Id.* at 318-319. The Court held that an injunction banning all trespass at the mall had the effect of prohibiting speech on the mall premises and was not consistent with the First Amendment. *Id.* at 323-334.

Just a few years later, however, the Court in Lloyd Corp. v. Tanner, 407 U.S. 551 (1972), "distinguished" *Logan Valley*, holding that exclusion of persons distributing leaflets from a largely enclosed shopping mall did not violate the First Amendment. *Lloyd* involved a challenge to the mall's complete ban on handbilling as applied to anti-war leafleters. The mall had strictly enforced its anti-handbilling policy against all groups. Five people distributing anti-war leaflets were told to leave or they would be arrested for trespass. The individuals left the premises to avoid arrest but later brought a suit seeking to have the mall's policy declared invalid under the First Amendment. The lower courts, relying on *Marsh* and *Logan Valley* agreed with the leafleters. The Supreme Court reversed.

The majority opinion noted that "the facts of this case are significantly different" from *Logan Valley*. That case, the opinion noted, "extended *Marsh* to a shopping center situation in a different context from the company town setting, but it did so only in a context where the First Amendment activity was related to the shopping center's operations. . . . The opinion was carefully phrased to limit its holding to the picketing involved, where the picketing was 'directly related in its purpose to the use to which the shopping center property was being put' and where the store was located in the center of a large private enclave with the consequence that no other reasonable opportunities for the pickets to convey their message to their intended audience were available." *Id.* at 563-564.

The majority further rejected respondents' argument that the shopping mall's open nature created a First Amendment right of access: "The handbilling by respondents in the malls of Lloyd Center had no relation to any purpose for which the center was built and being used. It is nevertheless argued by respondents that, since the Center is open to the public, the private owner cannot enforce a restriction against handbilling on the premises. The thrust of this argument is considerably broader than the rationale of *Logan Valley*. It requires no relationship, direct or indirect, between the purpose of the expressive activity and the business of the shopping center. The message sought to be conveyed by respondents was directed to all members of the public, not solely to patrons of Lloyd Center or of any of its operations. Respondents could have distributed these handbills on any public street, on any public sidewalk, in any public park, or in any public building in the city of Portland." *Id.* at 564. Accordingly, the Court ruled against the respondents, concluding that "this Court has never held that a trespasser or an uninvited guest may exercise general rights of free speech on property privately owned." *Id.* at 568.

The dissent argued that *Logan Valley* and *Lloyd* were indistinguishable:

> For many persons who do not have easy access to television, radio, the major newspapers, and the other forms of mass media, the only way they can express themselves to a broad range of citizens on issues of general public concern is to picket, or to handbill, or to utilize other free or relatively inexpensive means of communication. The only hope that these people have to be able to communicate effectively is to be permitted to speak in those areas in which most of their fellow citizens can be found. One such area is the business district of a city or town or its functional equivalent. And this is why respondents have a tremendous need to express themselves within Lloyd Center.

Id. at 580-581.

In Hudgens v. NLRB, 424 U.S. 507 (1976), the Court went beyond *Lloyd*'s attempt to merely distinguish *Logan Valley* on its facts and flatly stated that "the rationale of *Logan Valley* did not survive the Court's decision in the *Lloyd* case." *Id.* at 518. In rejecting the union picketers' claims of a right of access to shopping center property, the Court concluded that "under the present state of the law the constitutional guarantee of free expression has no part to play in a case such as this." *Id.* at 520. After *Hudgens,* can a mall owner exclude a patron because she does not like the message on the patron's T-shirt?

Should owners of private property with characteristics of public forums (that is, quasi-public forums) have complete control over who has a right to access the properly for expressive purposes? Should it matter that private property with such characteristics takes up valuable open space and is often financed, in part, with public funds? *See* Zick, *Speech Out of Doors,* at 165-66 (describing the Mall of America in Minneapolis, Minnesota, which draws 37 million annual visitors and was financed with more than $100 million in public funds). Should quasi-public forums be made available to speakers on matters of national interest and public concern? *See,e.g.,* Gregory P. Magarian, *The First Amendment, The Public-Private Distinction and Nongovernmental Suppression of Wartime Political Debate,* 73 Geo. Wash. L. Rev. 101, 103-104 (2004).

The advent of the Internet raises issues pertaining to speakers' rights of access to private property. Must YouTube, Twitter, or other social media platforms refrain from discriminating against speakers much as the government does, or do they have the same rights as private property owners? For discussion, see Prager University v. Google LLC, 951 F.3d 991 (9th Cir. 2020) (holding that YouTube does not serve a "public function" and, like other private property owners, is not bound by First Amendment content neutrality rules). Should social media platforms be subject to First Amendment restrictions? Are they more akin to public accommodations like malls or to daily newspapers and other media? Does their outsize power to moderate user content argue in favor of treating social media platforms as "public forums"?

Chapter 6

Compelled Speech and Expressive Association

Table of Contents

A. Introduction

B. Compelled Speech

  1. Compelled Government Orthodoxy
  2. Compelled Disclosure of Information
  3. The Right Not to Publish the Speech of Others
  4. The Right Not to Pay for the Speech of Others
  5. The Right to Communicate Anonymously

C. The Right of Association

  1. The Right to Associate for Expressive Purposes
  2. The Right *Not* to Associate

A. *INTRODUCTION*

The First Amendment protects expressive rights beyond the right to speak. It also provides robust (though not absolute) protection against being compelled by government to speak, to publish the speech of others, to pay for the speech of others, and to disclose one's identity. This chapter examines these First Amendment rights, which have increasingly been the subject of litigation and inform important policy discussions from abortion to the regulation of social media platforms. The chapter examines another right not explicitly mentioned in the First Amendment's text but, like the right not to speak, long considered "ancillary" to the freedom of speech—the right of "expressive association." Recognition of this right reflects the fact that individual expressive rights can be more effectual when exercised collectively. Finally, the Supreme Court has recognized a First Amendment right *not* to associate with others, comparable to the right not to speak. Precedents concerning the right not to associate have focused primarily on tensions between antidiscrimination laws, which require equal access to "public accommodations," and a group's right to choose its own members.

B. *COMPELLED SPEECH*

A corollary of the First Amendment's right to speak is the right *not* to speak. The right not to speak encompasses a right to keep one's ideas to oneself and a right not to be compelled to voice the ideas of others. Consider the justifications and implications of this right in the cases that follow.

1. *Compelled Government Orthodoxy*

World War II forms the historical backdrop to the opinion below, which was decided in 1943 and addressed the constitutionality of a West Virginia law requiring schoolchildren to "salute the flag" and recite the Pledge of Allegiance on a regular basis. The case overturned a 1940 Supreme Court decision on the same subject, Minersville School District v. Gobitis, 310 U.S. 586 (1940).

West Virginia State Board of Education v. Barnette

319 U.S. 624 (1943)

Mr. Justice JACKSON delivered the opinion of the Court. . . .

[On January 9, 1942, the West Virginia State Board of Education adopted a resolution requiring all students and teachers to participate on a regular basis in saluting the flag and reciting the Pledge of Allegiance. Appellees sought an injunction in district court to restrain enforcement against Jehovah's Witnesses.] The Witnesses are an unincorporated body teaching that the obligation imposed by law of God is superior to that of laws enacted by temporal government. Their religious beliefs include a literal version of Exodus, Chapter 20, verses 4 and 5, which says: "Thou shalt not make unto thee any graven image, or any likeness of anything that is in heaven above, or that is in the earth beneath, or that is in the water under the earth; thou shalt not bow down thyself to them nor serve them." They consider that the flag is an "image" within this command. For this reason they refuse to salute it.

Children of this faith have been expelled from school and are threatened with exclusion for no other cause. Officials threaten to send them to reformatories maintained for criminally inclined juveniles. Parents of such children have been prosecuted and are threatened with prosecutions for causing delinquency.

[The School Board moved to dismiss, and three judges of the District Court decided the case on the pleadings, restraining enforcement as to Jehovah's Witnesses. The Board appealed directly to the Supreme Court.]

The freedom asserted by these appellees does not bring them into collision with rights asserted by any other individual. It is such conflicts which most frequently require intervention of the State to determine where the rights of one end and those of another begin. But the refusal of these persons to participate in the ceremony does not interfere with or deny rights of others to do so. Nor is there any question in this case that their behavior is peaceable and orderly. The sole conflict is between authority and rights of the individual. The State asserts power to condition access to public education on making a prescribed sign and profession and at the same time to coerce attendance by punishing both parent and child. The latter stand on a right of self-determination in matters that touch individual opinion and personal attitude.

As the present Chief Justice said in dissent in the [*Minersville School District v.*] *Gobitis* case, the State may "require teaching by instruction and study of all in our history and in the structure and organization of our government, including the guaranties of civil liberty which tend to inspire patriotism and love of country." 310 U.S. at 604. Here, however, we are dealing with a compulsion of students to declare a belief. They are not merely made acquainted with the flag salute so that they may be informed as to what it is or even what it means. The issue here is whether this slow and easily neglected route to aroused loyalties constitutionally may be short-cut by substituting a compulsory salute and slogan. . . .

There is no doubt that, in connection with the pledges, the flag salute is a form of utterance. Symbolism is a primitive but effective way of communicating ideas. The use of an emblem or flag to symbolize some system, idea, institution, or personality, is a short cut from mind to mind. Causes and nations, political parties, lodges and ecclesiastical groups seek to knit the loyalty of their followings to a flag or banner, a color or design. . . . Associated with many of these symbols are appropriate gestures of acceptance or respect: a salute, a bowed or bared head, a bended knee. A person gets from a symbol the meaning he puts into it, and what is one man's comfort and inspiration is another's jest and scorn.

. . . Here it is the State that employs a flag as a symbol of adherence to government as presently organized. It requires the individual to communicate by word and sign his acceptance of the political ideas it thus bespeaks. Objection to this form of communication when coerced is an old one, well known to the framers of the Bill of Rights.

It is also to be noted that the compulsory flag salute and pledge requires affirmation of a belief and an attitude of mind. It is not clear whether the regulation contemplates that pupils forego any contrary convictions of their own and become unwilling converts to the prescribed ceremony or whether it will be acceptable if they simulate assent by words without belief and by a gesture barren of meaning. It is now a commonplace that censorship or suppression of expression of opinion is tolerated by our Constitution only when the expression presents a clear and present danger of action of a kind the State is empowered to prevent and punish. It would seem that involuntary affirmation could be commanded only on even more immediate and urgent grounds than silence. But here the power of compulsion is invoked without any allegation that remaining passive during a flag salute ritual creates a clear and present danger that would justify an effort even to muffle expression. To sustain the compulsory flag salute we are required to say that a Bill of Rights which guards the individual's right to speak his own mind, left it open to public authorities to compel him to utter what is not in his mind.

Whether the First Amendment to the Constitution will permit officials to order observance of ritual of this nature does not depend upon whether as a voluntary exercise we would think it to be good, bad or merely innocuous. Any credo of nationalism is likely to include what some disapprove or to omit what others think essential, and to give off different overtones as it takes on different accents or interpretations. If official power exists to coerce acceptance of any patriotic creed, what it shall contain cannot be decided by courts, but must be largely discretionary with the ordaining authority, whose power to prescribe would no doubt include power to amend.

. . . Free public education, if faithful to the ideal of secular instruction and political neutrality, will not be partisan or enemy of any class, creed, party, or faction. . . .

The Fourteenth Amendment, as now applied to the States, protects the citizen against the State itself and all of its creatures—Boards of Education not excepted. These have, of course, important, delicate, and highly discretionary functions, but none that they may not perform within the limits of the Bill of Rights. That they are educating the young for citizenship is reason for scrupulous protection of Constitutional freedoms of the individual, if we are not to strangle the free mind at its source and teach youth to discount important principles of our government as mere platitudes.

. . . The very purpose of a Bill of Rights was to withdraw certain subjects from the vicissitudes of political controversy, to place them beyond the reach of majorities and officials and to establish them as legal principles to be applied by the courts. One's right to life, liberty, and property, to free speech, a free press, freedom of worship and assembly, and other fundamental rights may not be submitted to vote; they depend on the outcome of no elections.

. . . National unity as an end which officials may foster by persuasion and example is not in question. The problem is whether under our Constitution compulsion as here employed is a permissible means for its achievement.

Struggles to coerce uniformity of sentiment in support of some end thought essential to their time and country have been waged by many good as well as by evil men. Nationalism is a relatively recent phenomenon but at other times and places the ends have been racial or territorial security, support of a dynasty or regime, and particular plans for saving souls. As first and moderate methods to attain unity have failed, those bent on its accomplishment must resort to an ever-increasing severity. As governmental pressure toward unity becomes greater, so strife becomes more bitter as to whose unity it shall be. Probably no deeper division of our people could proceed from any provocation than from finding it necessary to choose what doctrine and whose program public educational officials shall compel youth to unite in embracing. Ultimate futility of such attempts to compel coherence is the lesson of every such effort from the Roman drive to stamp out Christianity as a disturber of its pagan unity, the Inquisition, as a means to religious and dynastic unity, the Siberian exiles as a means to Russian unity, down to the fast failing efforts of our present totalitarian enemies. Those who begin coercive elimination of dissent soon find themselves exterminating dissenters. Compulsory unification of opinion achieves only the unanimity of the graveyard.

It seems trite but necessary to say that the First Amendment to our Constitution was designed to avoid these ends by avoiding these beginnings. There is no mysticism in the American concept of the State or of the nature or origin of its authority. We set up government by consent of the governed, and the Bill of Rights denies those in power any legal opportunity to coerce that consent. Authority here is to be controlled by public opinion, not public opinion by authority.

The case is made difficult not because the principles of its decision are obscure but because the flag involved is our own. Nevertheless, we apply the limitations of the Constitution with no fear that freedom to be intellectually and spiritually diverse or even contrary will disintegrate the social organization. To believe that patriotism will not flourish if patriotic ceremonies are voluntary and spontaneous instead of a compulsory routine is to make an unflattering estimate of the appeal of our institutions to free minds. We can have intellectual individualism and the rich cultural diversities that we owe to exceptional minds only at the price of occasional eccentricity and abnormal attitudes. When they are so harmless to others or to the State as those we deal with here, the price is not too great. But freedom to differ is not limited to things that do not matter much. That would be a mere shadow of freedom. The test of its substance is the right to differ as to things that touch the heart of the existing order.

If there is any fixed star in our constitutional constellation, it is that no official, high or petty, can prescribe what shall be orthodox in politics, nationalism, religion, or other matters of opinion or force citizens to confess by word or act their faith therein. If there are any circumstances which permit an exception, they do not now occur to us.

We think the action of the local authorities in compelling the flag salute and pledge transcends constitutional limitations on their power and invades the sphere of intellect and spirit which it is the purpose of the First Amendment to our Constitution to reserve from all official control. [Affirming injunction against enforcement of the West Virginia Regulation.]

[Justice Roberts's and Justice Reed's dissenting opinion is omitted.]

Justice Black and Justice Douglas, concurring.

. . . Words uttered under coercion are proof of loyalty to nothing but self-interest. Love of country must spring from willing hearts and free minds, inspired by a fair administration of wise laws enacted by the people's elected representatives within the bounds of express constitutional prohibitions. These laws must, to be consistent with the First Amendment, permit the widest toleration of conflicting viewpoints consistent with a society of free men.

Neither our domestic tranquility in peace nor our martial effort in war depend on compelling little children to participate in a ceremony which ends in nothing for them but a fear of spiritual condemnation. If, as we think, their fears are groundless, time and reason are the proper antidotes for their errors. The ceremonial, when enforced against conscientious objectors, more likely to defeat than to serve its high purpose, is a handy implement for disguised religious persecution. As such, it is inconsistent with our Constitution's plan and purpose.

[Justice Murphy's concurring opinion is omitted.]

Justice Frankfurter, dissenting.

One who belongs to the most vilified and persecuted minority in history is not likely to be insensible to the freedoms guaranteed by our Constitution. Were my purely personal attitude relevant I should whole-heartedly associate myself with the general libertarian views in the Court's opinion, representing as they do the thought and action of a lifetime. But as judges we are neither Jew nor Gentile, neither Catholic nor agnostic. We owe equal attachment to the Constitution and are equally bound by our judicial obligations whether we derive our citizenship from the earliest or the latest immigrants to these shores. As a member of this Court I am not justified in writing my private notions of policy into the Constitution, no matter how deeply I may cherish them or how mischievous I may deem their disregard. . . .

. . . Saluting the flag suppresses no belief nor curbs it. Children and their parents may believe what they please, avow their belief and practice it. It is not even remotely suggested that the requirement for saluting the flag involves the slightest restriction against the fullest opportunity on the part both of the children and of their parents to disavow as publicly as they choose to do so the meaning that others attach to the gesture of salute. All channels of affirmative free expression are open to both children and parents. Had we before us any act of the state putting the slightest curbs upon such free expression, I should not lag behind any member of this Court in striking down such an invasion of the right to freedom of thought and freedom of speech protected by the Constitution.

NOTES AND QUESTIONS

1. *Identifying the harm.* In what manner are children and their parents harmed by being forced to salute and pledge allegiance to the flag? Is forcing children to salute the flag different from forcing them to take exams in which they must accept and explain the theory of evolution? If so, how?
2. *First Amendment values.* What free speech values or justifications are furthered by recognizing a right not to speak? Does the First Amendment protect rights to think or believe? If so, how do the compulsory pledge and salute burden those rights?
3. *Attribution and disassociation.* If everyone is aware that the schoolchildren are required to salute the flag and recite the Pledge, will the message likely be attributed to the student or the state? Is it not also possible for the speakers to disclaim support for the compelled message, by retracting or attacking the message or refusing to participate? Do these considerations lessen any First Amendment harm or weaken the free speech claims? Does forcing the subjects of compulsion to object to the state's message compound the problem by compelling them to dissent?

AN EXTENDED NOTE REGARDING *WOOLEY v. MAYNARD* ("LIVE FREE OR DIE")

Wooley v. Maynard, 430 U.S. 705 (1977), involved a challenge by a Jehovah's Witness to a New Hampshire law prohibiting defacement of its "Live Free or Die" license plate. *Wooley* was ultimately framed and decided by the Supreme Court as a compelled-speech case governed by the principle enunciated in *Barnette.* Maynard objected to being compelled to display the state's "Live Free or Die" motto because it conflicted with his sincerely held religious beliefs. New Hampshire fined

Maynard when he covered the state motto on his license plate with tape. Chief Justice Burger, writing for the majority, explained:

> We begin with the proposition that the right of freedom of thought protected by the First Amendment against state action includes both the right to speak freely and the right to refrain from speaking at all. See Barnette. A system which secures the right to proselytize religious, political, and ideological causes must also guarantee the concomitant right to decline to foster such concepts. The right to speak and the right to refrain from speaking are complementary components of the broader concept of "individual freedom of mind." . . .
>
> . . . Here, as in Barnette, we are faced with a state measure which forces an individual, as part of his daily life—indeed constantly while his automobile is in public view—to be an instrument for fostering public adherence to an ideological point of view he finds unacceptable. In doing so, the State "invades the sphere of intellect and spirit which it is the purpose of the First Amendment to our Constitution to reserve from all official control."
>
> New Hampshire's statute in effect requires that appellees use their private property as a "mobile billboard" for the State's ideological message or suffer a penalty, as Maynard already has. As a condition to driving an automobile, a virtual necessity for most Americans, the Maynards must display "Live Free or Die" to hundreds of people each day. The fact that most individuals agree with the thrust of New Hampshire's motto is not the test; most Americans also find the flag salute acceptable. The First Amendment protects the right of individuals to hold a point of view different from the majority and to refuse to foster, in the way New Hampshire commands, an idea they find morally objectionable.

430 U.S. at 714-715.

The *Wooley* Court, however, did not consider this the end of the inquiry but instead went on to consider whether "the State's countervailing interest [was] sufficiently compelling to justify requiring appellees to display the state motto on their license plates" [citing United States v. O'Brien, 391 U.S. 367, 376-377 (1968)]. The Court held that the State interest underlying the defacement statute failed to outweigh the First Amendment interests of the Jehovah's Witness who did not wish to display the motto. It determined that the state's interest in vehicle identification could be achieved by "less drastic means" and that its interest in inculcating state pride was "not ideologically neutral." The Court explained that "where the State's interest is to disseminate an ideology, no matter how acceptable to some, such interest cannot outweigh an individual's First Amendment right to avoid becoming the courier for such message."

NOTES AND QUESTIONS

1. *Is* Barnette *distinguishable from* Wooley? Is the nature of the compulsion of the same kind or degree in *Wooley* as in *Barnette*? What is the orthodox

view the state is compelling Maynard to communicate? Were other citizens likely to assume Mr. Maynard endorsed the state motto simply because it was on his license plate? Couldn't Mr. Maynard simply attach a bumper sticker to his car with a message contrary to the state's?

2. *Variations on the compulsion problem.* What if the state in *Wooley* had allowed a choice of several different license plates, including one that bore the words "Choose Life"? Would providing that option violate the First Amendment rights of citizens who hold "pro-choice" views? Could the state have taxed its citizens and used the tax dollars to erect "Live Free or Die" billboards all over the state? Does use of U.S. currency, which contains the words "In God We Trust," compel speech by those who use cash to make purchases?
3. *The scope of* Barnette *and* Wooley. In both *Barnette* and *Wooley*, the Court held that governments had mandated a message or motto and compelled speakers to communicate or endorse it. The First Amendment forbids government from compelling communication or endorsement of state-sponsored political or other "orthodoxy." Is the ban on compelled speech limited to this scenario, or does it apply to other laws that directly or indirectly compel communication? Consider the scope and boundaries of the compelled speech concept as you read the cases that follow.

2. *Compelled Disclosure of Information*

Governmental regulations compel the disclosure of information in a variety of contexts—for example, in commercial, medical, business, and other areas. When, if ever, do these mandated disclosures violate the First Amendment? Consider the following decision, which involves mandatory disclosures applicable to clinics providing services to pregnant women.

National Institute of Family and Life Advocates v. Becerra

138 S. Ct. 2361 (2018)

Justice THOMAS delivered the opinion of the Court.

The California Reproductive Freedom, Accountability, Comprehensive Care, and Transparency Act (FACT Act) requires clinics that primarily serve pregnant women to provide certain notices. Licensed clinics must notify women that California provides free or low-cost services, including abortions, and give them a phone number to call. Unlicensed clinics must notify women that California has not licensed the clinics to provide medical services. The question in this case is whether these notice requirements violate the First Amendment.

I

A

. . . The California State Legislature enacted the FACT Act to regulate crisis pregnancy centers. Crisis pregnancy centers—according to a report commissioned by the California State Assembly—are pro-life (largely Christian belief-based) organizations that offer a limited range of free pregnancy options, counseling, and other services to individuals that visit a center. "[U]nfortunately," the author of the FACT Act stated, "there are nearly 200 licensed and unlicensed" crisis pregnancy centers in California. These centers "aim to discourage and prevent women from seeking abortions." The author of the FACT Act observed that crisis pregnancy centers "are commonly affiliated with, or run by organizations whose stated goal" is to oppose abortion—including "the National Institute of Family and Life Advocates," one of the petitioners here. To address this perceived problem, the FACT Act imposes two notice requirements on facilities that provide pregnancy-related services—one for licensed facilities and one for unlicensed facilities.

. . . The first notice requirement applies to "licensed covered facilities." To fall under the definition of "licensed covered facility," a clinic must be a licensed primary care or specialty clinic or qualify as an intermittent clinic under California law. A licensed covered facility also must have the primary purpose of providing family planning or pregnancy-related services. [The facility must also engage in at least two of six specified activities relating to family planning and pregnancy.]

If a clinic is a licensed covered facility, the FACT Act requires it to disseminate a government-drafted notice on site. The notice states that "California has public programs that provide immediate free or low-cost access to comprehensive family planning services (including all FDA-approved methods of contraception), prenatal care, and abortion for eligible women. To determine whether you qualify, contact the county social services office at [insert the telephone number]." This notice must be posted in the waiting room, printed and distributed to all clients, or provided digitally at check-in. The notice must be in English and any additional languages identified by state law. In some counties, that means the notice must be spelled out in 13 different languages.

The stated purpose of the FACT Act, including its licensed notice requirement, is to ensure that California residents make their personal reproductive health care decisions knowing their rights and the health care services available to them. The Legislature posited that thousands of women remain unaware of the public programs available to provide them with contraception, health education and counseling, family planning, prenatal care, abortion, or delivery. Citing the "time sensitive" nature of pregnancy-related decisions, the Legislature concluded that requiring licensed facilities to inform patients themselves would be the most effective way to convey this information. . . .

The second notice requirement in the FACT Act applies to "unlicensed covered facilities." To fall under the definition of "unlicensed covered facility," a facility must not be licensed by the State, not have a licensed medical provider on staff or under contract, and have the primary purpose of providing pregnancy-related services. [An unlicensed covered facility also must satisfy other requirements relating to pregnancy-related services.]

Unlicensed covered facilities must provide a government-drafted notice stating that "this facility is not licensed as a medical facility by the State of California and has no licensed medical provider who provides or directly supervises the provision of services." This notice must be provided on site and in all advertising materials. Onsite, the notice must be posted conspicuously at the entrance of the facility and in at least one waiting area. It must be at least 8.5 inches by 11 inches and written in no less than 48-point type. In advertisements, the notice must be in the same size or larger font than the surrounding text, or otherwise set off in a way that draws attention to it. Like the licensed notice, the unlicensed notice must be in English and any additional languages specified by state law. Its stated purpose is to ensure that pregnant women in California know when they are getting medical care from licensed professionals.

B

. . . After the Governor of California signed the FACT Act, petitioners—a licensed pregnancy center, an unlicensed pregnancy center, and an organization composed of crisis pregnancy centers—filed this suit. Petitioners alleged that the licensed and unlicensed notices abridge the freedom of speech protected by the First Amendment.

II

We first address the licensed notice. . . .

The First Amendment, applicable to the States through the Fourteenth Amendment, prohibits laws that abridge the freedom of speech. When enforcing this prohibition, our precedents distinguish between content-based and content-neutral regulations of speech. Content-based regulations "target speech based on its communicative content." *Reed v. Town of Gilbert* (2015). As a general matter, such laws are presumptively unconstitutional and may be justified only if the government proves that they are narrowly tailored to serve compelling state interests. This stringent standard reflects the fundamental principle that governments have no power to restrict expression because of its message, its ideas, its subject matter, or its content. *Id*; Police Dept. of Chicago v. Mosley, 408 U.S. 92, 95 (1972).

The licensed notice is a content-based regulation of speech. By compelling individuals to speak a particular message, such notices alter the content of their speech. Here, for example, licensed clinics must provide a government-drafted script about the availability of state-sponsored services, as well as contact information for how to obtain them. One of those services is abortion—the very practice that petitioners are devoted to opposing. By requiring petitioners to inform women how they can obtain state-subsidized abortions—at the same time petitioners try to dissuade women from choosing that option—the licensed notice plainly alters the content of petitioners' speech. . . .

. . . [O]ur precedents have applied more deferential review to some laws that require professionals to disclose factual, noncontroversial information in their commercial speech. . . . [Further,] under our precedents, States may regulate professional conduct, even though that conduct incidentally involves speech. *See, e.g.*, Planned Parenthood of Southeastern Pa. v. Casey, 505 U.S. 833, 884 (1992) (opinion of O'Connor, Kennedy, and Souter, JJ.). [In *Casey*, the Court upheld a Pennsylvania law that required physicians to inform their patients of "the nature of the procedure, the health risks of the abortion and childbirth, and the 'probable gestational age of the unborn child.'" *Id.*, at 881.] But neither line of precedents is implicated here.

. . . The licensed notice is not limited to purely factual and uncontroversial information about the terms under which services will be available. The notice in no way relates to the services that licensed clinics provide. Instead, it requires these clinics to disclose information about *state*-sponsored services—including abortion, anything but an uncontroversial topic.

... [Requiring that covered facilities provide information about abortion services] ... poses the inherent risk that the Government seeks not to advance a legitimate regulatory goal, but to suppress unpopular ideas or information. ... Professionals might have a host of good-faith disagreements, both with each other and with the government, on many topics in their respective fields. Doctors and nurses might disagree about the ethics of assisted suicide or the benefits of medical marijuana; lawyers and marriage counselors might disagree about the prudence of prenuptial agreements or the wisdom of divorce; bankers and accountants might disagree about the amount of money that should be devoted to savings or the benefits of tax reform. "[T]he best test of truth is the power of the thought to get itself accepted in the competition of the market," Abrams v. United States, 250 U.S. 616, 630 (1919) (Holmes, J., dissenting), and the people lose when the government is the one deciding which ideas should prevail.

... The licensed notice cannot survive even intermediate scrutiny. California asserts a single interest to justify the licensed notice: providing low-income women with information about state-sponsored services. Assuming that this is a substantial state interest, the licensed notice is not sufficiently drawn to achieve it.

If California's goal is to educate low-income women about the services it provides, then the licensed notice is wildly underinclusive. The notice applies only to clinics that have a "primary purpose" of "providing family planning or pregnancy-related services" and that provide two of six categories of specific services. Other clinics that have another primary purpose, or that provide only one category of those services, also serve low-income women and could educate them about the State's services. Such underinclusiveness raises serious doubts about whether the government is in fact pursuing the interest it invokes, rather than disfavoring a particular speaker or viewpoint.

Further, California could inform low-income women about its services without burdening a speaker with unwanted speech. Most obviously, it could inform the women itself with a public information campaign. California could even post the information on public property near crisis pregnancy centers. California argues that it has already tried an advertising campaign, and that many women who are eligible for publicly-funded healthcare have not enrolled. But California has identified no evidence to that effect. And regardless, a tepid response does not prove that an advertising campaign is not a sufficient alternative. Here, for example, individuals might not have enrolled in California's services because they do not want them, or because California spent insufficient resources on the advertising campaign. Either way, California cannot co-opt the licensed facilities to deliver its message for it. The First Amendment does not permit the State to sacrifice speech for efficiency.

... Contrary to the suggestion in the dissent, we do not question the legality of health and safety warnings long considered permissible, or purely factual and uncontroversial disclosures about commercial products. ...

III

We next address the unlicensed notice. California has the burden to prove that the unlicensed notice is neither unjustified nor unduly burdensome. It has not met its burden. We need not decide what type of state interest is sufficient to sustain a disclosure requirement like the unlicensed notice. California has not demonstrated any justification for the unlicensed notice that is more than purely hypothetical. The only justification that the California Legislature put forward was ensuring that pregnant women in California know when they are getting medical care from licensed professionals. At oral argument, however, California denied that the justification for the FACT Act was that women go into crisis pregnancy centers and they don't realize what they are. Indeed, California points to nothing suggesting that pregnant women do not already know that the covered facilities are staffed by unlicensed medical professionals.

Even if California had presented a nonhypothetical justification for the unlicensed notice, the FACT Act unduly burdens protected speech. The unlicensed notice imposes a government-scripted, speaker-based disclosure requirement that is wholly disconnected from California's informational interest. It requires covered facilities to post California's precise notice, no matter what the facilities say on site or in their advertisements. And it covers a curiously narrow subset of speakers. The unlicensed notice applies only to facilities that primarily provide "pregnancy-related" services. Thus, a facility that advertises and provides pregnancy tests is covered by the unlicensed notice, but a facility across the street that advertises and provides nonprescription contraceptives is excluded—even though the latter is no less likely to make women think it is licensed. This Court's precedents are deeply skeptical of laws that distinguish among different speakers, allowing speech by some but not others. Speaker-based laws run the risk that the State has left unburdened those speakers whose messages are in accord with its own views.

. . . The application of the unlicensed notice to advertisements demonstrates just how burdensome it is. The notice applies to all print and digital advertising materials by an unlicensed covered facility. These materials must include a government-drafted statement that "this facility is not licensed as a medical facility by the State of California and has no licensed medical provider who provides or directly supervises the provision of services." An unlicensed facility must call attention to the notice, instead of its own message, by some method such as larger text or contrasting type or color. This scripted language must be posted in English and as many other languages as California chooses to require. As California conceded at oral argument, a billboard for an unlicensed facility that says "Choose Life" would have to surround that two-word statement with a 29-word statement from the government, in as many as 13 different languages. In this way, the unlicensed notice drowns out the facility's own message. More likely, the detail required by the unlicensed notice effectively rules out the possibility of having such a billboard in the first place. . . .

California has offered no justification that the notice plausibly furthers. It targets speakers, not speech, and imposes an unduly burdensome disclosure requirement that will chill their protected speech. Taking all these circumstances together, we conclude that the unlicensed notice is unjustified and unduly burdensome.

Justice KENNEDY, with whom THE CHIEF JUSTICE, Justice ALITO, and Justice GORSUCH join, concurring.

I join the Court's opinion in all respects. This separate writing seeks to underscore that the apparent viewpoint discrimination here is a matter of serious constitutional concern. Viewpoint discrimination is inherent in the design and structure of this Act. This law is a paradigmatic example of the serious threat presented when government seeks to impose its own message in the place of individual speech, thought, and expression. For here the State requires primarily pro-life pregnancy centers to promote the State's own preferred message advertising abortions. This compels individuals to contradict their most deeply held beliefs, beliefs grounded in basic philosophical, ethical, or religious precepts, or all of these. And the history of the Act's passage and its underinclusive application suggest a real possibility that these individuals were targeted because of their beliefs.

. . . The California Legislature included in its official history the congratulatory statement that the Act was part of California's legacy of "forward thinking." But it is not forward thinking to force individuals to be an instrument for fostering public adherence to an ideological point of view they find unacceptable. *Wooley*. It is forward thinking to begin by reading the First Amendment as ratified in 1791; to understand the history of authoritarian government as the Founders then knew it; to confirm that history since then shows how relentless authoritarian regimes are in their attempts to stifle free speech; and to carry those lessons onward as we seek to preserve and teach the necessity of freedom of speech for the generations to come. Governments must not be allowed to force persons to express a message contrary to their deepest convictions. Freedom of speech secures freedom of thought and belief. This law imperils those liberties.

Justice BREYER, with whom Justice GINSBURG, Justice SOTOMAYOR, and Justice KAGAN join, dissenting.

The petitioners ask us to consider whether two sections of a California statute violate the First Amendment. . . . In my view both statutory sections are likely constitutional, and I dissent from the Court's contrary conclusions.

I

A

Before turning to the specific law before us, I focus upon the general interpretation of the First Amendment that the majority says it applies. It applies heightened scrutiny to the Act because the Act, in its view, is content based. By compelling individuals to speak a particular message, it claims, such notices alter the content of their speech. "As a general matter," the majority concludes, such laws are "presumptively unconstitutional" and are subject to "stringent" review.

. . . This constitutional approach threatens to create serious problems. Because much, perhaps most, human behavior takes place through speech and because much, perhaps most, law regulates that speech in terms of its content, the majority's approach at the least threatens considerable litigation over the constitutional validity of much, perhaps most, government regulation. Virtually every disclosure law could be considered content based, for virtually every disclosure law requires individuals to speak a particular message. *See Reed v. Town of Gilbert* (2015) (Breyer, J., concurring in judgment) (listing regulations that inevitably involve content discrimination, ranging from securities disclosures to signs at petting zoos). Thus, the majority's view, if taken literally, could radically change prior law, perhaps placing much securities law or consumer protection law at constitutional risk, depending on how broadly its exceptions are interpreted.

[The affected class of disclosure laws includes] numerous commonly found disclosure requirements relating to the medical profession. See, *e.g.*, Cal. Veh. Code Ann. § 27363.5 (West 2014) (requiring hospitals to tell parents about child seat belts); Cal. Health & Safety Code Ann. § 123222.2 (requiring hospitals to ask incoming patients if they would like the facility to give their family information about patients' rights and responsibilities); N.C. Gen. Stat. Ann. § 131E-79.2 (2017) (requiring hospitals to tell parents of newborns about pertussis disease and the available vaccine). The [category also includes] numerous disclosure requirements found in other areas. See, *e.g.*, N.Y.C. Rules & Regs., tit. 1, § 27-01 (2018) (requiring signs by elevators showing stair locations); San Francisco Dept. of Health, Director's Rules & Regs., Garbage and Refuse (July 8, 2010) (requiring property owners to inform tenants about garbage disposal procedures).

.... [T]the majority's general broad "content-based" test . . . invites courts around the Nation to apply an unpredictable First Amendment to ordinary social and economic regulation, striking down disclosure laws that judges may disfavor, while upholding others, all without grounding their decisions in reasoned principle.

... The Court, in justification, refers to widely accepted First Amendment goals, such as the need to protect the Nation from laws that suppress unpopular ideas or information or inhibit the marketplace of ideas in which truth will ultimately prevail. I, too, value this role that the First Amendment plays—in an appropriate case. But here, the majority enunciates a general test that reaches far beyond the area where this Court has examined laws closely in the service of those goals. And, in suggesting that heightened scrutiny applies to much economic and social legislation, the majority pays those First Amendment goals a serious disservice through dilution. Using the First Amendment to strike down economic and social laws that legislatures long would have thought themselves free to enact will, for the American public, obscure, not clarify, the true value of protecting freedom of speech.

... [B] The disclosure at issue here concerns speech related to abortion. It involves health, differing moral values, and differing points of view. Thus, rather than set forth broad, new, First Amendment principles, I believe that we should focus more directly upon precedent more closely related to the case at hand. This Court has more than once considered disclosure laws relating to reproductive health. Though those rules or holdings have changed over time, they should govern our disposition of this case.

... In *Planned Parenthood of Southeastern Pa. v. Casey* (1992), the Court considered a state law that required doctors to provide information to a woman deciding whether to proceed with an abortion. . . . In a joint opinion, the Court stated that the statutory requirements amounted to reasonable measures to ensure an informed choice, one which might cause the woman to choose childbirth over abortion. The joint opinion concluded that the statute did not violate the First Amendment. It wrote [in full]:

> All that is left of petitioners' argument is an asserted First Amendment right of a physician not to provide information about the risks of abortion, and childbirth, in a manner mandated by the State. To be sure, the physician's First Amendment rights not to speak are implicated, see *Wooley*

> *v. Maynard* (1977), but only as part of the practice of medicine, subject to reasonable licensing and regulation by the State. We see no constitutional infirmity in the requirement that the physician provide the information mandated by the State here.

Thus, the Court considered the State's statutory requirements, including the requirement that the doctor must inform his patient about where she could learn how to have the newborn child adopted (if carried to term) and how she could find related financial assistance. . . .

If a State can lawfully require a doctor to tell a woman seeking an abortion about adoption services, why should it not be able, as here, to require a medical counselor to tell a woman seeking prenatal care or other reproductive healthcare about childbirth and abortion services? . . . I find it impossible to drive any meaningful legal wedge between the law, as interpreted in *Casey*, and the law as it should be applied in this case. If the law in *Casey* regulated speech only as part of the *practice* of medicine, so too here.

Of course, one might take the majority's decision to mean that speech about abortion is special, that it involves in this case not only professional medical matters, but also views based on deeply held religious and moral beliefs about the nature of the practice. But assuming that is so, the law's insistence upon treating like cases alike should lead us to reject the petitioners' arguments. This insistence, the need for evenhandedness, should prove particularly weighty in a case involving abortion rights. That is because Americans hold strong, and differing, views about the matter. . . . For this reason too a Constitution that allows States to insist that medical providers tell women about the possibility of adoption should also allow States similarly to insist that medical providers tell women about the possibility of abortion.

II

[Regarding the mandatory disclosure applicable to unlicensed facilities], [t]he majority does not question the State's interest: ensuring that pregnant women in California know when they are getting medical care from licensed professionals. Nor could it. Such informational interests have long justified regulations in the medical context. There is no basis for finding the State's interest "hypothetical." The legislature heard that information-related delays in qualified healthcare negatively affect women seeking to terminate their pregnancies as well as women carrying their pregnancies to term, with delays in qualified prenatal care causing life-long health problems for infants. Even without such testimony, it is self-evident that patients might think they are receiving qualified medical care when they enter facilities that collect health information, perform obstetric ultrasounds or sonograms, diagnose pregnancy, and provide counseling about pregnancy options or other prenatal care. The State's conclusion to that effect is certainly reasonable.

. . . [T]he majority suggests that the Act is suspect because it covers some speakers but not others. I agree that a law's exemptions can reveal viewpoint discrimination (although the majority does not reach this point). Speaker-based laws warrant heightened scrutiny when they reflect the Government's preference for the substance of what the favored speakers have to say (or aversion to what the disfavored speakers have to say). Accordingly, where a law's exemptions facilitate speech on only one side of the abortion debate, there is a clear form of viewpoint discrimination.

There is no cause for such concern here. The Act does not, on its face, distinguish between facilities that favor pro-life and those that favor pro-choice points of view. Nor is there any convincing evidence before us or in the courts below that discrimination was the purpose or the effect of the statute. . . .

NOTES AND QUESTIONS

1. *Compelled disclosures and compelled speech.* To what extent does the majority's analysis rely on *Barnette* and *Wooley*? Is compelling licensed facilities to disclose the availability of abortion services the same, from a First Amendment standpoint, as compelling students to salute the U.S. flag? Is the state attempting to force pregnancy centers to endorse abortion, or merely to inform women that abortion is an option? Does the mere fact that the government provides a "script" violate the speaker's right not to be compelled to communicate? Or is the problem the content of the mandated disclosure, which the pregnancy centers oppose on moral and religious grounds?
2. *Content-based compulsions. NIFLA* applies a form of heightened scrutiny after determining the California law is content-based. The Court discusses a variety of compelled commercial, professional, and medical disclosures. After *NIFLA*, which of these mandatory disclosures are likely to be invalidated? Aren't *all* compelled disclosures content-based, as Justice Breyer suggests? What of the dissenters' concern that the Court's approach jeopardizes a wide variety of mandatory disclosures that implicate public health and safety concerns?
3. *Medical disclosures.* Is there a separate category of disclosures governments can mandate pursuant to the *practice of medicine* that do not offend the First Amendment? Presumably that category includes statements relating to patient informed consent, which is how the majority views the *Casey* disclosures, but how far can government go in that respect? Can it compel physicians to openly discourage certain procedures? Does or should it matter whether the mandated disclosures affect discourse between physicians and patients concerning constitutional rights such as abortion, equal protection, and the right to keep and bear arms? *See* Timothy Zick, *Rights Speech*, 48 U.C. Davis L. Rev. 1 (2014); Timothy Zick, *Professional Rights Speech*, 47 Ariz. St. L. J. 1289 (2015).
4. *Compulsion and public health.* After *NIFLA*, to what extent can governments compel product manufacturers and distributors to disclose safety and health concerns regarding their products? Do such mandated disclosures raise the concerns identified in cases such as *Barnette* and *Wooley*? Or are they the type of *factual* disclosures the *NIFLA* Court purports to accept? In R.J. Reynolds Tobacco Co. v. FDA, 696 F.3d 1205 (D.C. Cir. 2012), the court of appeals applied intermediate scrutiny and invalidated an FDA regulation requiring tobacco companies to display large, graphic warnings on cigarette packaging. Does the FDA disclosure requirement

go beyond warning consumers of potential dangers from using tobacco? Even assuming so, doesn't the government have a compelling interest in mandating such warnings?

5. *Compulsion and complicity.* Some religious adherents opposed to same-sex marriage have argued that compelling them to comply with state anti-discrimination laws violates the First Amendment right not to be compelled to speak. See, e.g., State v. Arlene's Flowers, 441 P.3d 1203, 1225-26 (Wash. 2019) (holding floral arrangement is not expressive); Masterpiece Cakeshop. Ltd. v. Colorado Civil Rights Commission, 138 S. Ct. 1719, 1743 (2018) (Thomas, J., concurring) (agreeing with plaintiff that being compelled under state law to bake a wedding cake for a gay couple communicates that "a wedding has occurred, a marriage has begun, and the couple should be celebrated"). Does compelling a pregnancy center to communicate about abortion services implicate similar concerns? Does compliance with the disclosure mandate itself suggest the pregnancy centers' support for abortion?
6. *Abortion-Related Disclosures.* As discussed in *NIFLA*, the *Casey* joint opinion dismissed First Amendment concerns relating to state requirements that physicians inform women seeking abortions of the probable gestational age of the fetus and the risks of abortion and childbirth. The opinion acknowledged the mandatory disclosures "implicate" the right not to be compelled to speak but applied only rational basis. Is the dissent correct that the California law is simply the mirror image of the Pennsylvania mandatory disclosure upheld in *Casey*? If the state can mandate that physicians speak about gestation, childbirth, and adoption, why can't they also mandate that clinics providing pregnancy-related services disclose that they don't offer certain services women may want and that they are not licensed by the state? What about other abortion-related disclosures? *See* Stuart v. Camnitz, 774 F.3d 238 (4th Cir. 2014) (invalidating provisions of the North Carolina Woman's Right to Know Act, which required abortion doctors to perform an ultrasound and display the resulting sonogram while describing the image in real time to women seeking abortions). For discussion of free speech issues relating to mandatory abortion disclosures, see Caroline Mala Corbin, *Compelled Disclosures*, 65 Ala. L. Rev. 1277 (2014).

THEORY-APPLIED PROBLEM — "BRANDED" DRIVER'S LICENSES

Concerned about protecting its citizenry from recidivist sex offenders, the State of Utopia imposes one of the strictest registration schemes in the nation on state residents who have been convicted of certain sex crimes. To ensure easy identification of registrants, the Sex Offender Registration Act (SORA) requires all sex offenders to carry "branded" identification cards. Specifically, the statute provides that convicted sex offenders must "obtain and always have in their possession a valid driver's license or identification card issued by the Utopia State Law Enforcement Agency (Agency)." The licenses and cards must "bear a designation that enables state law enforcement officers to identify the person as a sex offender." Utopia's legislature delegated to the Agency the exclusive power to promulgate any rules necessary to implement and enforce SORA. The Agency has required the face of the licenses and identification cards to bear the inscription "CRIMINAL SEX OFFENDER" in bold, red letters. Registrants must also relinquish any other identification previously issued to them by the state that does not bear the sex offender inscription. However, registrants may carry other government-issued identification that does not bear the mandated state inscription, including social security cards and U.S. passports. Does the law as interpreted by the Agency violate the First Amendment?

3. *The Right Not to Publish the Speech of Others*

The cases in this section present a different, but related, issue concerning compelled speech. Suppose government attempts to give one speaker a right of access to a publication, property, or event owned or controlled by another speaker, asserting that access will foster desirable diversity in the marketplace of ideas or serve other interests. Does this form of regulation compel speech in violation of the First Amendment?

Miami Herald v. Tornillo

418 U.S. 241 (1974)

Mr. Chief Justice BURGER delivered the opinion of the Court.

The issue in this case is whether a state statute granting a political candidate a right to equal space to reply to criticism and attacks on his record by a newspaper, violates the guarantees of a free press.

I

In the fall of 1972, appellee, Executive Director of the Classroom Teachers Association, apparently a teachers' collective-bargaining agent, was a candidate for the Florida House of Representatives. On September 20, 1972, and again on September 29, 1972, appellant printed editorials critical of appellee's candidacy. In response to these editorials appellee demanded that appellant print verbatim his replies, defending the role of the Classroom Teachers Association and the organization's accomplishments for the citizens of Dade County. Appellant declined to print the appellee's replies, and appellee brought suit in Circuit Court, Dade County, seeking declaratory and injunctive relief and actual and punitive damages in excess of $5,000. The action was premised on Florida Statute § 104.38 (1973), a "right of reply" statute. . . .[2]

---

2. "104.38 *Newspaper Assailing Candidate in an Election; Space for Reply.* If any newspaper in its columns assails the personal character of any candidate for nomination or for election in any election, or charges said candidate with malfeasance or misfeasance in office, or otherwise attacks his official record, or gives to another free space for such purpose, such newspaper shall upon request of such candidate immediately publish free of cost any reply he may make thereto in as conspicuous a place and in the same kind of type as the matter that calls for such reply, provided such reply does not take up more space than the matter replied to. Any person or firm failing to comply with the provisions of this section shall be guilty of a misdemeanor of the first degree, punishable as provided in § 775.082 or § 775.083."

[Appellant sought a declaratory judgment, and the Circuit Court held the right-of-reply section unconstitutional. The Florida Supreme Court reversed, holding that the statute furthered the "broad societal interest in the free flow of information to the public," and that it was not impermissibly vague. The court narrowed the statute by construing it to require "any reply" to be "wholly responsive to the charge made" and "neither libelous nor slanderous of the publication nor anyone else, nor vulgar nor profane." The case was remanded for further proceedings.]

III

[A.] The challenged statute creates a right to reply to press criticism of a candidate for nomination or election. The statute was enacted in 1913, and this is only the second recorded case decided under its provisions.

Appellant contends the statute is void on its face because it purports to regulate the content of a newspaper in violation of the First Amendment. Alternatively it is urged that the statute is void for vagueness since no editor could know exactly what words would call the statute into operation. It is also contended that the statute fails to distinguish between critical comment which is and which is not defamatory.

[B.] [The Court summarized virtually every argument made by proponents of access to the media. The Court noted that access advocates argued that in 1791 "[a] true marketplace of ideas existed in which there was relatively easy access to the channels of communication." By 1973, however, concentration of ownership in the media industry, the "elimination of competing newspapers in most of our large cities," and other technological and economic developments had "place[d] in a few hands the power to inform the American people and shape public opinion." The increasing power and influence of the media had also deprived the public of meaningful participation in public debate. The Court further noted that access advocates had "urged that the claim of newspapers to be 'surrogates for the public' carries with it a concomitant fiduciary obligation to account for that stewardship." The only way to enforce such an obligation, however, would be "for government to take affirmative action."]

IV

However much validity may be found in these arguments, at each point the implementation of a remedy such as an enforceable right of access necessarily calls for some mechanism, either governmental or consensual. If it is governmental coercion, this at once brings about a confrontation with the express provisions of the First Amendment and the judicial gloss on that Amendment developed over the years.

The Court foresaw the problems relating to government-enforced access as early as its decision in *Associated Press v. United States.* There it carefully contrasted the private "compulsion to print" called for by the Association's bylaws with the provisions of the District Court decree against appellants which "does not compel AP or its members to permit publication of anything which their 'reason' tells them should not be published." 326 U.S. [1, 20 n.18 (1945)]. In Branzburg v. Hayes, 408 U.S. 665, 681 (1972), we emphasized that the cases then before us "involve no intrusions upon speech or assembly, no prior restraint or restriction on what the press may publish, and no express or implied command that the press publish what it prefers to withhold." In Columbia Broadcasting System, Inc. v. Democratic National Committee, 412 U.S. 94, 117 (1973), the plurality opinion as to Part III noted:

> The power of a privately owned newspaper to advance its own political, social, and economic views is bounded by only two factors: first, the acceptance of a sufficient number of readers—and hence advertisers—to assure financial success; and, second, the journalistic integrity of its editors and publishers.

An attitude strongly adverse to any attempt to extend a right of access to newspapers was echoed by several Members of this Court in their separate opinions in that case. . . . [In a recent dissent,] Mr. Justice Stewart, joined by Mr. Justice Douglas, expressed the view that no "government agency—local, state, or federal—can tell a newspaper in advance what it can print and what it cannot."

We see that beginning with *Associated Press* the Court has expressed sensitivity as to whether a restriction or requirement constituted the compulsion exerted by government on a newspaper to print that which it would not otherwise print. The clear implication has been that any such a compulsion to publish that which "'reason' tells them should not be published" is unconstitutional. A responsible press is an undoubtedly desirable goal, but press responsibility is not mandated by the Constitution and like many other virtues it cannot be legislated.

Appellee's argument that the Florida statute does not amount to a restriction of appellant's right to speak because "the statute in question here has not prevented the Miami Herald from saying anything it wished" begs the core question. Compelling editors or publishers to publish that which "'reason' tells them should not be published" is what is at issue in this case. The Florida statute operates as a command in the same sense as a statute or regulation forbidding appellant to publish specified matter. Governmental restraint on publishing need not fall into familiar or traditional patterns to be subject to constitutional limitations on governmental powers. Grosjean v. American Press Co., 297 U.S. 233, 244-45 (1936). The Florida statute exacts a penalty on the basis of the content of a newspaper. The first phase of the penalty resulting from the compelled printing of a reply is exacted in terms of the cost in printing and composing time and materials and in taking up space that could be devoted to other material the newspaper may have preferred to print. It is correct, as appellee contends, that a newspaper is not subject to the finite technological limitations of time that confront a broadcaster but it is not correct to say that, as an economic reality, a newspaper can proceed to infinite expansion of its column space to accommodate the replies that a government agency determines or a statute commands the readers should have available.

Faced with the penalties that would accrue to any newspaper that published news or commentary arguably within the reach of the right-of-access statute, editors might well conclude that the safe course is to avoid controversy. Therefore, under the operation of the Florida statute, political and electoral coverage would be blunted or reduced. Government-enforced right of access inescapably "dampens the vigor and limits the variety of public debate," New York Times Co. v. Sullivan, *supra*, 376 U.S. at 279. The Court, in Mills v. Alabama, 384 U.S. 214, 218 (1966) stated that

> There is practically universal agreement that a major purpose of [the First] Amendment was to protect the free discussion of governmental affairs. This of course includes discussions of candidates. . . .

Even if a newspaper would face no additional costs to comply with a compulsory access law and would not be forced to forgo publication of news or opinion by the inclusion of a reply, the Florida statute fails to clear the barriers of the First Amendment because of its intrusion into the function of editors. A newspaper is more than a passive receptacle or conduit for news, comment, and advertising. The choice of material to go into a newspaper, and the decisions made as to limitations on the size and content of the paper, and treatment of public issues and public officials—whether fair or unfair—constitute the exercise of editorial control and judgment. It has yet to be demonstrated how governmental regulation of this crucial process can be exercised consistent with First Amendment guarantees of a free press as they have evolved to this time. Accordingly, the judgment of the Supreme Court of Florida is *Reversed.*

[Justices BRENNAN'S and REHNQUIST'S concurrence is omitted.]

Mr. Justice WHITE, concurring.

. . . A newspaper or magazine is not a public utility subject to "reasonable" governmental regulation in matters affecting the exercise of journalistic judgment as to what shall be printed. . . . We have learned, and continue to learn, from what we view as the unhappy experiences of other nations where government has been allowed to meddle in the internal editorial affairs of newspapers. Regardless of how beneficent-sounding the purposes of controlling the press might be, we prefer "the power of reason as applied through public discussion"—and remain intensely skeptical about those measures that would allow government to insinuate itself into the editorial rooms of this Nation's press.

. . . [T]his law runs afoul of the elementary First Amendment proposition that government may not force a newspaper to print copy which, in its journalistic discretion, it chooses to leave on the newsroom floor. . . .

NOTES AND QUESTIONS

1. *Basis of decision.* In what way does the right-of-reply statute "penalize" newspapers? Is the right-of-reply statute's interference with "the exercise of editorial control and judgment" an independent ground of decision? Could a newspaper be compelled to allow a candidate to purchase advertising at the prevailing rate to respond to an editorial "attack"?
2. *New media and right-of-reply statutes.* The Internet gives millions of citizens, most of whom have no journalism training, access to a mass medium to publish their opinions, complaints, and harsh and sometimes defamatory criticisms of their fellow citizens. Would a right-of-reply statute directed at Web sites, blogs, or social media sites such as Facebook be unconstitutional?
3. *Right of access in other media.* The Supreme Court in *Tornillo* stressed that a newspaper is private property. Broadcasters, on the other hand, may

not use the airwaves without receiving a license from the government. Does the fact that the public in essence "owns the airwaves" mean that government regulators can compel the broadcast media—radio and television—to grant a right of reply to candidates or others criticized on the airwaves? Perhaps surprisingly, the answer is yes, for reasons you will see in Chapter 8, *infra. See* Red Lion Broad. Co. v. FCC, 395 U.S. 367 (1969).

4. *Is the election context special?* Is the argument for a right of reply stronger or weaker when it is limited to a pending election? Professor Cass Sunstein, who questions the outcome or at least the rationale in *Tornillo*, suggests that the Court may have suspected that the "special problem with [the statute] was that it was limited to candidates for office," which gave the Court reason "to suspect that the law was an effort by political candidates to insulate themselves from attack." Cass R. Sunstein, *Democracy and the Problem of Free Speech* 271 n.20 (1993). Might incumbents reasonably think that they would benefit more from this type of statute than would challengers?
5. *Free press versus free speech?* Why isn't *Tornillo* clearly governed by *Barnette*? Is this a case that pits the First Amendment rights of the press against the rights of an individual speaker? Why do the First Amendment rights of the *Miami Herald* trump those of Pat Tornillo?

PruneYard Shopping Center et al. v. Robins

447 U.S. 74 (1980)

Mr. Justice REHNQUIST delivered the opinion of the Court.

We decide whether state constitutional provisions, which permit individuals to exercise free speech and petition rights on the property of a privately owned shopping center to which the public is invited, violate the shopping center owner's free speech rights under the First and Fourteenth Amendments.

I

Appellant PruneYard is a privately owned shopping center in the city of Campbell, Cal. It covers approximately 21 acres—5 devoted to parking and 16 occupied by walkways, plazas, sidewalks, and buildings that contain more than 65 specialty shops, 10 restaurants, and a movie theater. The PruneYard is open to the public for the purpose of encouraging the patronizing of its commercial establishments. It has a policy not to permit any visitor or tenant to engage in any publicly expressive activity, including the circulation of petitions, that is not directly related to its commercial purposes. This policy has been strictly enforced in a nondiscriminatory fashion.

Appellees are high school students who sought to solicit support for their opposition to a United Nations resolution against "Zionism." On a Saturday afternoon they set up a card table in a corner of PruneYard's central courtyard. They distributed pamphlets and asked passersby to sign petitions, which were to be sent to the President and Members of Congress. Their activity was peaceful and orderly and so far as the record indicates was not objected to by PruneYard's patrons.

Soon after appellees had begun soliciting signatures, a security guard informed them that they would have to leave because their activity violated PruneYard regulations. The guard suggested that they move to the public sidewalk at the PruneYard's perimeter. Appellees immediately left the premises and later filed this lawsuit in the California Superior Court of Santa Clara County. They sought to enjoin appellants from denying them access to the PruneYard for the purpose of circulating their petitions.

. . . V

Appellants contend that a private property owner has a First Amendment right not to be forced by the State to use his property as a forum for the speech of others. They state that in *Wooley v. Maynard* (1977), this Court concluded that a State may not constitutionally require an individual to participate in the dissemination of an ideological message by displaying it on his private property in a manner and for the express purpose that it be observed and read by the public. This rationale applies here, they argue, because the message of *Wooley* is that the State may not force an individual to display any message at all. . . .

Wooley, however, was a case in which the government itself prescribed the message, required it to be displayed openly on appellee's personal property that was used "as part of his daily life," and refused to permit him to take any measures to cover up the motto even though the Court found that the display of the motto served no important state interest. Here, by contrast, there are a number of distinguishing factors. Most important, the shopping center by choice of its owner is not limited to the personal use of appellants. It is instead a business establishment that is open to the public to come and go as they please. The views expressed by members of the public in passing out pamphlets or seeking signatures for a petition thus will not likely be identified with those of the owner. Second, no specific message is dictated by the State to be displayed on appellants' property. There consequently is no danger of governmental discrimination for or against a particular message. Finally, as far as appears here appellants can expressly disavow any connection with the message by simply posting signs in the area where the speakers or handbillers stand. Such signs, for example, could disclaim any sponsorship of the message and could explain that the persons are communicating their own messages by virtue of state law.

Appellants also argue that their First Amendment rights have been infringed in light of *West Virginia State Board of Education v. Barnette* (1943), and *Miami Herald Publishing Co. v. Tornillo* (1974). *Barnette* is inapposite because it involved the compelled recitation of a message containing an affirmation of belief. This Court held such compulsion unconstitutional because it "require[d] the individual to communicate by word and sign his acceptance" of government-dictated political ideas, whether or not he subscribed to them. Appellants are not similarly being compelled to affirm their belief in any governmentally prescribed position or view, and they are free to publicly dissociate themselves from the views of the speakers or handbillers.

Tornillo struck down a Florida statute requiring a newspaper to publish a political candidate's reply to criticism previously published in that newspaper. It rests on the principle that the State cannot tell a newspaper what it must print. The Florida statute contravened this principle in that it exacted a penalty on the basis of the content of a newspaper. There also was a danger in *Tornillo* that the statute would dampen the vigor and limit the variety of public debate by deterring editors from publishing controversial political statements that might trigger the application of the statute. Thus, the statute was found to be an intrusion into the function of editors. These concerns obviously are not present here.

. . . We conclude that appellants' First Amendment rights have not been infringed by the California Supreme Court's decision recognizing a right of appellees to exercise state-protected rights of expression and petition on appellants' property. The judgment of the Supreme Court of California is therefore

Affirmed.

[Concurring opinions by Justice BLACKMUN and Justice MARSHALL are omitted.]

Mr. Justice POWELL, with whom Mr. Justice WHITE joins, concurring in part and in the judgment.

I

Restrictions on property use, like other state laws, are invalid if they infringe the freedom of expression and belief protected by the First and Fourteenth Amendments. In Part V of today's opinion, the Court rejects appellants' contention that "a private property owner has a First Amendment right not to be forced by the State to use his property as a forum for the speech of others." I agree that the owner of this shopping center has failed to establish a cognizable First Amendment claim in this case. But some of the language in the Court's opinion is unnecessarily and perhaps confusingly broad. In my view, state action that transforms privately owned property into a forum for the expression of the public's views could raise serious First Amendment questions.

The State may not compel a person to affirm a belief he does not hold. *See Wooley; Barnette.* Whatever the full sweep of this principle, I do not believe that the result in *Wooley* would have changed had the State of New Hampshire directed its citizens to place the slogan "Live Free or Die" in their shop windows rather than on their automobiles. In that case, we said that "a system which secures the right to proselytize religious, political, and ideological causes must also guarantee the concomitant right to decline to foster such concepts." This principle on its face protects a person who refuses to allow use of his property as a marketplace for the ideas of others. And I can find no reason to exclude the owner whose property is "not limited to [his] personal use. . . ." A person who has merely invited the public onto his property for commercial purposes cannot fairly be said to have relinquished his right to decline to be an instrument for fostering public adherence to an ideological point of view he finds unacceptable. *Wooley.*

As the Court observes, this case involves only a state-created right of limited access to a specialized type of property. But even when no particular message is mandated by the State, First Amendment interests are affected by state action that forces a property owner to admit third-party speakers. In many situations, a right of access is no less intrusive than speech compelled by the State itself. For example, a law requiring that a newspaper permit others to use its columns imposes an unacceptable burden upon the newspaper's First Amendment right to select material for publication. *Tornillo.* Such a right of access burdens the newspaper's fundamental right to decide what to print or omit. As such, it is tantamount to compelled affirmation and, thus, presumptively unconstitutional.

The selection of material for publication is not generally a concern of shopping centers. But similar speech interests are affected when listeners are likely to identify opinions expressed by members of the public on commercial property as the views of the owner. If a state law mandated public access to the bulletin board of a freestanding store, hotel, office, or small shopping center, customers might well conclude that the messages reflect the view of the proprietor. The same would be true if the public were allowed to solicit or distribute pamphlets in the entrance area of a store or in the lobby of a private building. The property owner or proprietor would be faced with a choice: he either could permit his customers to receive a mistaken impression or he could disavow the messages. Should he take the first course, he effectively has been compelled to affirm someone else's belief. Should he choose the second, he has been forced to speak when he would prefer to remain silent. In short, he has lost control over his freedom to speak or not to speak on certain issues. The mere fact that he is free to dissociate himself from the views expressed on his property cannot restore his right to refrain from speaking at all. *Wooley.*

A property owner also may be faced with speakers who wish to use his premises as a platform for views that he finds morally repugnant. Numerous examples come to mind. A minority-owned business confronted with leaflet distributers from the American Nazi Party or the Ku Klux Klan, a church-operated enterprise asked to host demonstrations in favor of abortion, or a union compelled to supply a forum to right-to-work advocates could be placed in an intolerable position if state law requires it to make its private property available to anyone who wishes to speak. The strong emotions evoked by speech in such situations may virtually compel the proprietor to respond.

The pressure to respond is particularly apparent when the owner has taken a position opposed to the view being expressed on his property. But an owner who strongly objects to some of the causes to which the state-imposed right of access would extend may oppose ideological activities of *any* sort that are not related to the purposes for which he has invited the public onto his property. To require the owner to specify the particular ideas he finds objectionable enough to compel a response would force him to relinquish his freedom to maintain his own beliefs without public disclosure. Thus, the right to control one's own speech may be burdened impermissibly even when listeners will not assume that the messages expressed on private property are those of the owner.

II

One easily can identify other circumstances in which a right of access to commercial property would burden the owner's First and Fourteenth Amendment right to refrain from speaking. But appellants have identified no such circumstance. Nor did appellants introduce evidence that would support a holding in their favor under either of the legal theories outlined above.

On the record before us, I cannot say that customers of this vast center would be likely to assume that appellees' limited speech activity expressed the views of the

PruneYard or of its owner. The shopping center occupies several city blocks. It contains more than 65 shops, 10 restaurants, and a theater. Interspersed among these establishments are common walkways and plazas designed to attract the public. Appellees are high school students who set up their card table in one corner of a central courtyard known as the "Grand Plaza." They showed passersby several petitions and solicited signatures. Persons solicited could not reasonably have believed that the petitions embodied the views of the shopping center merely because it owned the ground on which they stood.

. . . Appellants have not alleged that they object to the ideas contained in the appellees' petitions. Nor do they assert that some groups who reasonably might be expected to speak at the PruneYard will express views that are so objectionable as to require a response even when listeners will not mistake their source. The record contains no evidence concerning the numbers or types of interest groups that may seek access to this shopping center, and no testimony showing that the appellants strongly disagree with any of them.

Because appellants have not shown that the limited right of access held to be afforded by the California Constitution burdened their First and Fourteenth Amendment rights in the circumstances presented, I join the judgment of the Court. I do not interpret our decision today as a blanket approval for state efforts to transform privately owned commercial property into public forums. Any such state action would raise substantial federal constitutional questions not present in this case.

NOTES AND QUESTIONS

1. *Distinguishing* Barnette *and* Wooley. What factors does the *PruneYard* Court rely on to distinguish the invalid compulsions in *Barnette* and *Wooley* from the access mandate in *PruneYard*? Did the size of the shopping center matter? The fact that the property was open to the public? The lack of any specific state-approved message? Would it have made a difference if the shopping center owner had expressly objected to the students' message? What opportunities did the shopping center owner have to disassociate from the students' speech?
2. *"Trivializing"* Barnette *and* Wooley. As *PruneYard* shows, the concept of compulsory speech has limits. Consider also Rumsfeld v. FAIR, 547 U.S. 47 (2006), which upheld the Solomon Amendment, a federal law that requires educational institutions receiving federal funds to give military recruiters access to universities' career services facilities "that is at least equal in quality and scope to the access . . . that is provided to any other employer." A group of law schools objected that providing access to military recruiters violated their policies against providing access to such facilities to employers that discriminate on the basis of sexual orientation (the military's "Don't Ask, Don't Tell" policy was then in force). The Court unanimously rejected the law schools' claim that requiring them to send emails, post notices on bulletin boards on an employer's behalf, or otherwise grant equal access to military recruiters constituted compelled speech. It observed: "This sort of recruiting assistance . . . is a far cry from

the compelled speech at issue in *Barnette* and *Wooley*. . . . There is nothing in this case approaching a Government-mandated pledge or motto that the school must endorse." Indeed, the Court stated, "it trivializes the freedom protected in *Barnette* and *Wooley* to claim the Solomon Amendment compels speech." Are the law schools being compelled to communicate acceptance of the military's discriminatory policy, by hosting its recruiters? Will students likely associate the military's policy or message with the law school? Can law schools communicate their rejection of that message while still complying with the Solomon Amendment?

3. *Compelled access and social media.* Some have raised concerns about content bias by social media platforms, which exercise enormous political and economic power. Could Congress mandate that social media companies carry or publish content without regard to viewpoint? Do cases like *PruneYard* support the constitutionality of such laws? What about the First Amendment rights of the platforms not to be compelled to speak or publish under cases like *Tornillo*? Are social media platforms more like newspapers or shopping malls? For arguments that treating social media platforms like "common carriers," which are compelled by law to publish information without regard to viewpoint, may survive First Amendment scrutiny see Eugene Volokh, *Treating Social Media Platforms Like Common Carriers?*, 1 Journal of Free Speech Law 377 (2021).

Hurley v. Irish-American Gay, Lesbian & Bisexual Group of Boston

515 U.S. 557 (1995)

Justice SOUTER delivered the opinion of the Court.

The issue in this case is whether Massachusetts may require private citizens who organize a parade to include among the marchers a group imparting a message the organizers do not wish to convey. We hold that such a mandate violates the First Amendment. . . .

[In 1947, the City of Boston] granted authority to organize and conduct the St. Patrick's Day-Evacuation Day Parade to the petitioner South Boston Allied War Veterans Council, an unincorporated association of individuals elected from various South Boston veterans groups. Every year since that time, the Council has applied for and received a permit for the parade, which at times has included as many as 20,000 marchers and drawn up to 1 million watchers. No other applicant has ever applied for that permit. Through 1992, the city allowed the Council to use the city's official seal, and provided printing services as well as direct funding.

In 1992, a number of gay, lesbian, and bisexual descendants of the Irish immigrants joined together with other supporters to form the respondent organization, GLIB, to march in the parade as a way to express pride in their Irish heritage as openly gay, lesbian, and bisexual individuals[.] . . . Although the Council denied GLIB's application to take part in the 1992 parade, GLIB obtained a state-court order to include its contingent, which marched "uneventfully" among that year's 10,000 participants and 750,000 spectators.

In 1993, after the Council had again refused to admit GLIB to the upcoming parade, the organization and some of its members filed this suit against the Council, the individual petitioner John J. "Wacko" Hurley, and the city of Boston, alleging violations of . . . the state public accommodations law, which prohibits "any distinction, discrimination or restriction on account of . . . sexual orientation . . . relative to the admission of any person to, or treatment in any place of public accommodation, resort or amusement." . . .

If there were no reason for a group of people to march from here to there except to reach a destination, they could make the trip without expressing any message beyond the fact of the march itself. . . . Hence, we use the word "parade" to indicate marchers who are making some sort of collective point, not just to each other but to bystanders along the way. . . . Parades are thus a form of expression, not just motion, and the inherent expressiveness of marching to make a point explains our cases involving protest marches. . . .

The protected expression that inheres in a parade is not limited to its banners and songs, however, for the Constitution looks beyond written or spoken words as mediums of expression. Noting that "[s]ymbolism is a primitive but effective way of communicating ideas," West Virginia Bd. of Ed. v. Barnette, 319 U.S. 624, 632 (1943), our cases have recognized that the First Amendment shields such acts as saluting a flag (and refusing to do so), wearing an armband to protest a war, displaying a red flag, and even "[m]arching, walking or parading" in uniforms displaying the swastika, National Socialist Party of America v. Skokie, 432 U.S. 43 (1977). As some of these examples show, a narrow, succinctly articulable message is not a condition of constitutional protection, which if confined to expressions conveying a "particularized message," *cf. Spence*, would never reach the unquestionably shielded painting of Jackson Pollock, music of Arnold Schoenberg, or Jabberwocky verse of Lewis Carroll.

Not many marches, then, are beyond the realm of expressive parades, and the South Boston celebration is not one of them. . . . To be sure, we agree with the state courts that in spite of excluding some applicants, the Council is rather lenient in admitting participants. But a private speaker does not forfeit constitutional protection simply by combining multifarious voices, or by failing to edit their themes to isolate an exact message as the exclusive subject matter of the speech. Nor, under our precedent, does First Amendment protection require a speaker to generate, as an original matter, each item featured in the communication. Cable operators, for example, are engaged in protected speech activities even when they only select programming originally produced by others. Turner Broadcasting System, Inc. v. FCC, 512 U.S. 622, 636 (1994). For that matter, the presentation of an edited compilation of speech generated by other persons is a staple of most newspapers' opinion pages, which, of course, fall squarely within the core of First Amendment security, Miami Herald Publishing Co. v. Tornillo, 418 U.S. 241, 258 (1974), as does even the simple selection of a paid noncommercial advertisement for inclusion in a daily paper, see New York Times v. Sullivan, 376 U.S. 254 (1964). The selection of contingents to make a parade is entitled to similar protection.

Respondents' participation as a unit in the parade was equally expressive. GLIB was formed for the very purpose of marching in it, as the trial court found, in order to celebrate its members' identity as openly gay, lesbian, and bisexual descendants of the Irish immigrants, to show that there are such individuals in the community, and to support the like men and women who sought to march in the New York parade. . . . GLIB understandably seeks to communicate its ideas as part of the existing parade, rather than staging one of its own.

The Massachusetts public accommodations law . . . today prohibits discrimination on the basis of "race, color, religious creed, national origin, sex, sexual orientation . . . , deafness, blindness or any physical or mental disability or ancestry" in "the admission of any person to, or treatment in any place of public accommodation, resort or amusement." Mass. Gen. Laws § 272:98 (1992). Provisions like these are well within the State's usual power to enact when a legislature has reason to believe that a given group is the target of discrimination, and they do not, as a general matter, violate the First or Fourteenth Amendments.

In the case before us, however, the Massachusetts law has been applied in a peculiar way. Its enforcement does not address any dispute about the participation of openly gay, lesbian, or bisexual individuals in various units admitted to the parade. Petitioners disclaim any intent to exclude homosexuals as such, and no individual member of GLIB claims to have been excluded from parading as a member of any group that the Council has approved to march. Instead, the disagreement goes to the admission of GLIB as its own parade unit carrying its own banner. . . . Although the state courts spoke of the parade as a place of public accommodation, once the expressive character of both the parade and the marching GLIB contingent is understood, it becomes apparent that the state courts' application of the statute had the effect of declaring the sponsors' speech itself to be the public accommodation. Under this approach any contingent of protected individuals with a message would have the right to participate in petitioners' speech, so that the communication produced by the private organizers would be shaped by all those protected by the law who wished to join in with some expressive demonstration of their own. But this use of the State's power violates the fundamental rule of protection under the First Amendment, that a speaker has the autonomy to choose the content of his own message. . . .

Petitioners' claim to the benefit of this principle of autonomy to control one's own speech is as sound as the South Boston parade is expressive. Rather like a composer, the Council selects the expressive units of the parade from potential participants, and though the score may not produce a particularized message, each contingent's expression in the Council's eyes comports with what merits celebration on that day. Even if this view gives the Council credit for a more considered judgment than it actively made, the Council clearly decided to exclude a message it did not like from the communication it chose to make, and that is enough to invoke its right as a private speaker to shape its expression by speaking on one subject while remaining silent on another. . . .

Our holding today rests not on any particular view about the Council's message but on the Nation's commitment to protect freedom of speech. Disapproval of a private speaker's statement does not legitimize use of the Commonwealth's power to compel the speaker to alter the message by including one more acceptable to others. Accordingly, the judgment of the Supreme Judicial Court is reversed, and the case is remanded for proceedings not inconsistent with this opinion.

It is so ordered.

NOTES AND QUESTIONS

1. *Parades as expressive conduct.* Note the Court's determination that the parade is an expressive event. In making that determination, the Court does not apply the *Spence* standard discussed in Chapter 4. Are parades an inherently expressive activity? Even if they do not express a cohesive or even coherent message?
2. *Speaker autonomy. Hurley* relies on a principle of speaker autonomy central to the right not to be compelled to speak. But how exactly would the inclusion of GLIB affect the parade group's own expression? If the parade does not send a single message, would GLIB's simply be one among many messages communicated by the parade?
3. Hurley *and* PruneYard. If mandating access to the private mall in *PruneYard* did not compel expression, why does mandating access to the parade in *Hurley*? Does the distinction rest on the fact that the public accommodation in *Hurley*, the parade, is itself expressive while the mall is not? Does it rest on the fact that in *Hurley*, the parade organizer expressly objected to GLIB's message while the mall owner in *PruneYard* did not object to the students' speech? In *Hurley*, who is the speech likely to be attributed to? If to the organizers, is there any way for them to disassociate from the objected-to expression in the parade context?

4. *The Right Not to Pay for the Speech of Others*

The section addresses whether governments violate the First Amendment when they compel individuals to *subsidize* speech they do not agree with. In recent years, many compelled subsidy cases have involved mandatory public sector union dues. Once a union is chosen by a majority of employees, the union collectively bargains with the employer on behalf of all employees over wages, benefits, and working conditions. Unions also typically engage in lobbying and electioneering activities. Under Supreme Court precedents preceding *Janus*, which follows, the Court had distinguished between charges for collective bargaining activities (for which contributions could be compelled from dissenting nonmembers) and "ideological" activities (for which contributions from such persons could not be compelled). Abood v. Detroit Board of Education, 431 U.S. 209 (1977). After expressing skepticism concerning *Abood* and union shop fees more generally, see Knox v. Service Employees International, 567 U.S. 298 (2012), in *Janus* the Court abandoned the distinction and overruled *Abood*.

Janus v. American Federation of State, County, and Municipal Employees, Council 31

138 S. Ct. 2448 (2018)

Justice Alito delivered the opinion of the Court.

Under Illinois law, public employees are forced to subsidize a union, even if they choose not to join and strongly object to the positions the union takes in collective bargaining and related activities. We conclude that this arrangement violates the free speech rights of nonmembers by compelling them to subsidize private speech on matters of substantial public concern. . . .

I

[A] Under the Illinois Public Labor Relations Act (IPLRA), employees of the State and its political subdivisions are permitted to unionize. If a majority of the employees in a bargaining unit vote to be represented by a union, that union is designated as the exclusive representative of all the employees. Employees in the unit are not obligated to join the union selected by their co-workers, but whether they join or not, that union is deemed to be their sole permitted representative.

Once a union is so designated, it is vested with broad authority. Only the union may negotiate with the employer on matters relating to pay, wages, hours, and other conditions of employment. And this authority extends to the negotiation of what the IPLRA calls "policy matters," such as merit pay, the size of the work force, layoffs, privatization, promotion methods, and non-discrimination policies.

Designating a union as the employees' exclusive representative substantially restricts the rights of individual employees. Among other things, this designation means that individual employees may not be represented by any agent other than the designated union; nor may individual employees negotiate directly with their employer. Protection of the employees' interests is placed in the hands of the union, and therefore the union is required by law to provide fair representation for all employees in the unit, members and nonmembers alike.

Employees who decline to join the union are not assessed full union dues but must instead pay what is generally called an "agency fee," which amounts to a percentage of the union dues. Under *Abood*, non-members may be charged for the portion of union dues attributable to activities that are "germane to [the union's] duties as collective-bargaining representative," but nonmembers may not be required to fund the union's political and ideological projects. *Id.* In labor-law parlance, the outlays in the first category are known as "chargeable" expenditures, while those in the latter are labeled "non-chargeable."

Illinois law does not specify in detail which expenditures are chargeable and which are not. The IPLRA provides that an agency fee may compensate a union for the costs incurred in the collective bargaining process, contract administration, and pursuing matters affecting wages, hours, and conditions of employment. Excluded from the agency-fee calculation are union expenditures related to the election or support of any candidate for political office.

Applying this standard, a union categorizes its expenditures as chargeable or non-chargeable and thus determines a nonmember's proportionate share[.] This determination is then audited; the amount of the "proportionate share" is certified to the employer; and the employer automatically deducts that amount from the nonmembers' wages. Nonmembers need not be asked, and they are not required to consent before the fees are deducted.

. . . As illustrated by the record in this case, unions charge nonmembers, not just for the cost of collective bargaining *per se*, but also for many other supposedly connected activities. Here, the nonmembers were told that they had to pay for lobbying, social and recreational activities, advertising, membership meetings and conventions, and litigation, as well as other unspecified services that may ultimately inure to the benefit of the members of the local bargaining unit. The total chargeable amount for non-members was 78.06% of full union dues.

[B] Petitioner Mark Janus is employed by the Illinois Department of Healthcare and Family Services as a child support specialist. The employees in his unit are among the 35,000 public employees in Illinois who are represented by respondent American Federation of State, County, and Municipal Employees, Council 31 (Union). Janus refused to join the Union because he opposes many of the public policy positions that it advocates, including the positions it takes in collective bargaining. Janus believes that the Union's behavior in bargaining does not appreciate the current fiscal crises in Illinois and does not reflect his best interests or the interests of Illinois citizens. Therefore, if he had the choice, he would not pay any fees or otherwise subsidize the Union. Under his unit's collective-bargaining agreement, however, he was required to pay an agency fee of $44.58 per month,—which would amount to about $535 per year. . . .

III

. . . [A] We have held time and again that freedom of speech "includes both the right to speak freely and the right to refrain from speaking at all." [*Wooley*; *Tornillo*]. The right to eschew association for expressive purposes is likewise protected. Roberts v. United States Jaycees, 468 U.S. 609, 623 (1984) ("Freedom of association . . . plainly presupposes a freedom not to associate") [Freedom of association is examined in Section C, *infra* – Eds]. As Justice Jackson memorably put it: "If there is any fixed star in our constitutional constellation, it is that no official, high or petty, can prescribe what shall be orthodox in politics, nationalism, religion, or other matters of opinion or *force citizens to confess by word or act their faith therein*." *Barnette* (1943) (emphasis added).

Compelling individuals to mouth support for views they find objectionable violates that cardinal constitutional command, and in most contexts, any such effort would be universally condemned. Suppose, for example, that the State of Illinois required all residents to sign a document expressing support for a particular set of positions on controversial public issues—say, the platform of one of the major political parties. No one, we trust, would seriously argue that the First Amendment permits this.

Perhaps because such compulsion so plainly violates the Constitution, most of our free speech cases have involved restrictions on what can be said, rather than laws compelling speech. But measures compelling speech are at least as threatening.

. . . Free speech serves many ends. It is essential to our democratic form of government, and it furthers the search for truth. Whenever the Federal Government or a State prevents individuals from saying what they think on important matters or compels them to voice ideas with which they disagree, it undermines these ends.

When speech is compelled, however, additional damage is done. In that situation, individuals are coerced into betraying their convictions. Forcing free and independent individuals to endorse ideas they find objectionable is always demeaning, and for this reason, one of our landmark free speech cases said that a law commanding "involuntary affirmation" of objected-to beliefs would require "even more immediate and urgent grounds" than a law demanding silence. *Barnette.*

Compelling a person to *subsidize* the speech of other private speakers raises similar First Amendment concerns. As Jefferson famously put it, "to compel a man to furnish contributions of money for the propagation of opinions which he disbelieves and abhor[s] is sinful and tyrannical." A Bill for Establishing Religious Freedom, in 2 Papers of Thomas Jefferson 545 (J. Boyd ed. 1950) (emphasis deleted and footnote omitted). We have therefore recognized that a significant impingement on First Amendment rights occurs when public employees are required to provide financial support for a union that takes many positions during collective bargaining that have powerful political and civic consequences.

. . . [B] In *Abood*, the main defense of the agency-fee arrangement was that it served the State's interest in "labor peace." By "labor peace," the *Abood* Court meant avoidance of the conflict and disruption that it envisioned would occur if the employees in a unit were represented by more than one union. In such a situation, the Court predicted, inter-union rivalries would foster dissension within the work force, and the employer could face conflicting demands from different unions. Confusion would ensue if the employer entered into and attempted to enforce two or more agreements specifying different terms and conditions of employment. And a settlement with one union would be subject to attack from [a] rival labor organization.

We assume that "labor peace," in this sense of the term, is a compelling state interest, but *Abood* cited no evidence that the pandemonium it imagined would result if agency fees were not allowed, and it is now clear that *Abood*'s fears were unfounded. [The Court here described the experience under federal law, which does not permit agency fees.] Likewise, millions of public employees in the 28 States that have laws generally prohibiting agency fees are represented by unions that serve as the exclusive representatives of all the employees. Whatever may have been the case 41 years ago when *Abood* was handed down, it is now undeniable that "labor peace" can readily be achieved through means significantly less restrictive of associational freedoms than the assessment of agency fees.

[C] In addition to the promotion of "labor peace," *Abood* cited the risk of free riders as justification for agency fees. . . . Petitioner strenuously objects to this free-rider label. He argues that he is not a free rider on a bus headed for a destination that he wishes to reach but is more like a person shanghaied for an unwanted voyage.

. . . Whichever description fits the majority of public employees who would not subsidize a union if given the option, avoiding free riders is not a compelling interest. To hold otherwise across the board would have startling consequences. Many private groups speak out with the objective of obtaining government action that will have the effect of benefiting nonmembers. May all those who are thought to benefit from such efforts be compelled to subsidize this speech? Suppose that a particular group lobbies or speaks out on behalf of what it thinks are the needs of senior citizens or veterans or physicians, to take just a few examples. Could the government require that all seniors, veterans, or doctors pay for that service even if they object? It has never been thought that this is permissible. In simple terms, the First Amendment does not permit the government to compel a person to pay for another party's speech just because the government thinks that the speech furthers the interests of the person who does not want to pay. . . . We therefore hold that agency fees cannot be upheld on free-rider grounds. . . .

VI

For the reasons given above, we conclude that public-sector agency-shop arrangements violate the First Amendment, and *Abood* erred in concluding otherwise. There remains the question whether *stare decisis* nonetheless counsels against overruling *Abood*. It does not. [The Court explained its decision to overrule *Abood* under *stare decisis* principles.]

VII

For these reasons, States and public-sector unions may no longer extract agency fees from nonconsenting employees. . . . This procedure violates the First Amendment and cannot continue. Neither an agency fee nor any other payment to the union may be deducted from a nonmember's wages, nor may any other attempt be made to collect such a payment, unless the employee affirmatively consents to pay. By agreeing to pay, non-members are waiving their First Amendment rights, and such a waiver cannot be presumed. Rather, to be effective, the waiver must be freely given and shown by clear and compelling evidence. Unless employees clearly and affirmatively consent before any money is taken from them, this standard cannot be met.

Justice KAGAN, with whom Justice GINSBURG, Justice BREYER, and Justice SOTOMAYOR join, dissenting.

For over 40 years, *Abood* struck a stable balance between public employees' First Amendment rights and government entities' interests in running their workforces as they thought proper. . . . Today, the Court succeeds in its 6-year campaign to reverse *Abood*. Its decision will have large-scale consequences. Public employee unions will lose a secure source of financial support. State and local governments that thought fair-share provisions furthered their interests will need to find new ways of managing their workforces. Across the country, the relationships of public employees and employers will alter in both predictable and wholly unexpected ways.

. . . I respectfully dissent.

II

. . . [A] *Abood*'s reasoning about governmental interests has three connected parts. First, exclusive representation arrangements benefit some government entities because they can facilitate stable labor relations. In particular, such arrangements eliminate the potential for inter-union conflict and streamline the process of negotiating terms of employment. Second, the government may be unable to avail itself of those benefits unless the single union has a secure source of funding. The various tasks involved in representing employees cost money; if the union doesn't have enough, it can't be an effective employee representative and bargaining partner. And third, agency fees are often needed to ensure such stable funding. That is because without those fees, employees have every incentive to free ride on the union dues paid by others.

. . . [O]nce a union achieves exclusive-representation status, the law compels it to fairly represent all workers in the bargaining unit, whether or not they join or contribute to the union. Because of that legal duty, the union cannot give special advantages to its own members. And that in turn creates a collective action problem of nightmarish proportions. Everyone—not just those who oppose the union, but also those who back it—has an economic incentive to withhold dues; only altruism or loyalty—as *against* financial self-interest—can explain why an employee would pay the union for its services. And so emerged *Abood*'s rule allowing fair-share agreements: That rule ensured that a union would receive sufficient funds, despite its legally imposed disability, to effectively carry out its duties as exclusive representative of the government's employees.

The majority's initial response to this reasoning is simply to dismiss it. . . . But that disregards the defining characteristic of *this* free-rider argument—that unions, unlike many other private groups, must serve members and non-members alike. Groups advocating for "senior citizens or veterans" (to use the majority's examples) have no legal duty to provide benefits to all those individuals: They can spur people to pay dues by conferring all kinds of special advantages on their dues-paying members. Unions are—by law—in a different position, as this Court has long recognized. In a way that is true of no other private group, the law *requires* the union to carry non-members. That special feature was what justified *Abood*: Where the state imposes upon the union a duty to deliver services, it may permit the union to demand reimbursement for them.

. . . [B][1] Time and again our cases have recognized that the Government has a much freer hand in dealing with its employees than with citizens at large. The government, we have stated, needs to run as effectively and efficiently as possible. That means it must be able, much as a private employer is, to manage its workforce as it thinks fit. A public employee thus must submit to "certain limitations on his or her freedom." Garcetti v. Ceballos, 547 U.S. 410, 418 (2006) [Chapter 12, *infra.*] Government workers, of course, do not wholly lose their constitutional rights when they accept their positions. But under our precedent, their rights often yield when weighed against the realities of the employment context. If it were otherwise—if every employment decision were to become a constitutional matter—the Government could not function.

Those principles apply with full force when public employees' expressive rights are at issue. . . . Again, significant control does not mean absolute authority. In particular, the Court has guarded against government efforts to "leverage the employment relationship" to shut down its employees' speech as private citizens. *Garcetti.* But when the government imposes speech restrictions relating to workplace operations, of the kind a private employer also would, the Court reliably upholds them.

Abood . . . dovetailed with the Court's usual attitude in First Amendment cases toward the regulation of public employees' speech. That attitude is one of respect—even solicitude—for the government's prerogatives as an employer. So long as the government is acting as an employer—rather than exploiting the employment relationship for other ends—it has a wide berth, comparable to that of a private employer. And when the regulated expression concerns the terms and conditions of employment—the very stuff of the employment relationship—the government really cannot lose. There, managerial interests are obvious and strong. And so government employees are . . . just employees, even though they work for the government. Except that today the government does lose, in a first for the law. Now, the government can constitutionally adopt all policies regulating core workplace speech in pursuit of managerial goals—save this single one.

[2] . . . [T]he majority's distinction between compelling and restricting speech also lacks force. The majority posits that compelling speech always works a greater injury, and so always requires a greater justification. But the only case the majority cites for that reading of our precedent is possibly (thankfully) the most exceptional in our First Amendment annals: It involved the state forcing children to swear an oath contrary to their religious beliefs. [West Virginia Bd. of Ed. v. Barnette, 319 U.S. 624 (1943).] Regulations challenged as compelling expression do not usually look anything like that—and for that reason, the standard First Amendment rule is that the difference between compelled speech and compelled silence is without constitutional significance. *See Wooley v. Maynard* (1977) (referring to "[t]he right to speak and the right to refrain from speaking" as "complementary components" of the First Amendment). And if anything, the First Amendment scales tip the opposite way when (as here) the government is not compelling actual speech, but instead compelling a subsidy that others will use for expression. . . .

IV

There is no sugarcoating today's opinion. The majority overthrows a decision entrenched in this Nation's law—and in its economic life—for over 40 years. As a result, it prevents the American people, acting through their state and local officials, from making important choices about workplace governance. And it does so by weaponizing the First Amendment, in a way that unleashes judges, now and in the future, to intervene in economic and regulatory policy. . . . [M]aybe most alarming, the majority has . . . turn[ed] the First Amendment into a sword, . . . using it against workaday economic and regulatory policy. Today is not the first time the Court has wielded the First Amendment in such an aggressive way. See, *e.g.*, National Institute of Family and Life Advocates v. Becerra, 138 S. Ct. 2361 (2018) (2018) (invalidating a law requiring medical and counseling facilities to provide relevant information to users) [*supra* p. 250]. And it threatens not to be the last. Speech is everywhere—a part of every human activity (employment, health care, securities trading, you name it). For that reason, almost all economic and regulatory policy affects or touches speech. So the majority's road runs long. And at every stop are black-robed rulers overriding citizens' choices. The First Amendment was meant for better things. It was meant not to undermine but to protect democratic governance—including over the role of public-sector unions.

NOTES AND QUESTIONS

1. *Compelled speech and compelled subsidies.* We are all taxed in ways that similarly compel us to support messages, policies, and ideas we do not agree with. Are all those taxes unconstitutional compelled subsidies under *Janus*? If not, what makes the agency fee in *Janus* different?
2. *The right not to associate.* The *Janus* majority indicates that the agency fee violates not only the right not to speak but also the dissenting employees' right not to associate with the union. The rights to associate and not to

associate are examined later in this chapter. As you consider that material, ask whether the First Amendment ought to distinguish between compelled association in the literal sense—i.e., forcing groups to accept as members those they wish to exclude—and forcing people to jointly provide financial support for speech with which they disagree. Do you think there is, or ought to be, a difference between the two situations?

3. *"Weaponizing" the First Amendment.* What does Justice Kagan mean when she says the majority in *Janus* has "weaponized" the First Amendment? Does *Janus,* like *NIFLA,* potentially invalidate a wide range of "economic" and labor regulations? Should such regulations be immune from First Amendment scrutiny? If so, why?
4. *Compulsory Bar dues.* How far does the right not to be compelled to pay mandatory dues or fees extend? After *Janus,* can states charge mandatory state Bar dues or other professional licensure fees? In Keller v. State Bar of California, 496 U.S. 1, 13–14 (1990), the Supreme Court concluded that a state Bar may use mandatory dues to subsidize activities "germane to" the goals of "regulating the legal profession and improving the quality of legal services" without running afoul of its members' First Amendment rights of free speech. That approach is consistent with *Abood,* but does it run afoul of the holding in *Janus*? *See* Crowe v. Oregon State Bar, 989 F.3d 784 (9th Cir. 2021) (upholding dismissal of compelled speech claim under *Janus* on the ground that *Keller* has not been expressly overruled, but reversing dismissal of claim that mandatory dues violate plaintiffs' right not to associate—a claim the Supreme Court did not consider in *Keller*).

AN EXTENDED NOTE ON SPEECH EXACTIONS

The Supreme Court has considered First Amendment speech and association challenges to compelled fees and subsidies in several contexts. In general, it has encountered a significant degree of difficulty defining the scope of the government's authority to compel individuals or entities to pay fees and subsidies for speech they may not agree with.

In several cases decided prior to *Janus,* the Court considered the validity of compelled fees charged for advertising agricultural products. In Glickman v. Wileman Bros., 521 U.S. 457 (1997), the Court upheld against First Amendment challenge U.S. Department of Agriculture marketing orders assessing California fruit growers for the costs of generic advertising of California nectarines, plums, and peaches. Justice Stevens, writing for the Court, found the assessments did not raise a First Amendment issue at all, but rather "simply a question of economic policy for Congress and the Executive to resolve." He continued:

> Three characteristics of the regulatory scheme at issue distinguish it from laws that we have found to abridge the freedom of speech protected by the First Amendment. First, the marketing orders impose no restraint on the freedom of any producer to communicate any message to any audience. Second, they do not compel any person to engage in any actual or symbolic speech. Third, they do not compel the producers to endorse or to finance any political or ideological views. Indeed, since all of the

> respondents are engaged in the business of marketing California nectarines, plums, and peaches, it is fair to presume that they agree with the central message of the speech that is generated by the [program.].

Justice Stevens concluded the "use of assessments to pay for advertising does not require respondents to repeat an objectionable message out of their own mouths, *Barnette*, require them to use their own property to convey an antagonistic ideological message, *Wooley*[,] force them to respond to a hostile message when they would prefer to remain silent, or require them to be publicly identified or associated with another's message. *PruneYard*. Respondents are not required themselves to speak, but are merely required to make contributions for advertising."

Justice Stevens reasoned that under appropriately deferential scrutiny, the assessments were clearly constitutional: "Generic advertising is intended to stimulate consumer demand for an agricultural product in a regulated market. That purpose is legitimate and consistent with the regulatory goals of the overall statutory scheme. [Whether] the benefits from the advertising justify its cost is a question that [involves] the exercise of policy judgments that are better made by producers and administrators than by judges."

Justice Souter, writing for himself, Chief Justice Rehnquist, and Justice Scalia, dissented. He summarized the dissenters' position:

> The legitimacy of governmental regulation does not validate coerced subsidies for speech that the government cannot show to be reasonably necessary to implement the regulation, and the very reasons for recognizing that commercial speech falls within the scope of First Amendment protection likewise justifies the protection of those who object to subsidizing it against their will. I therefore conclude that forced payment for commercial speech should be subject to the same level of judicial scrutiny as any restriction on communications in that category. Because I believe that the advertising scheme here fails that test, I respectfully dissent.

Three years later, in United States v. United Foods, 533 U.S. 405 (2001), the Court invalidated a federal law mandating that fresh mushroom handlers pay assessments used primarily to fund advertisements promoting mushroom sales. A large mushroom grower objected to being compelled to support generic mushroom advertisements, preferring to be free to convey the message that its brand of mushrooms was superior to those grown by other producers. The Court, in an opinion by Justice Kennedy speaking for six justices, distinguished *Glickman*:

> In the Government's view the assessment in this case is permitted by *Glickman* because it is similar in important respects. It imposes no restraint on the freedom of an objecting party to communicate its own message; the program does not compel an objecting party . . . itself to express views it disfavors; and the mandated scheme does not compel the expression of political or ideological views. These points were noted in *Glickman* in the context of a different kind of regulatory scheme and are not controlling of the outcome. The program sustained in *Glickman* differs from the one under review in a most fundamental respect. In *Glickman* the mandated assessments for speech were ancillary to a more comprehensive program

> restricting marketing autonomy. Here, for all practical purposes, the advertising itself, far from being ancillary, is the principal object of the regulatory scheme. [Here] the statute does not require group action, save to generate the very speech to which some handlers object. [We] have not upheld compelled subsidies for speech in the context of a program where the principal object is the speech itself. [The] cooperative marketing structure relied upon by a majority of the Court in *Glickman* to sustain an ancillary assessment finds no corollary here; the expression respondent is required to support is not germane to a purpose related to an association independent from the speech itself. [For] these and other reasons we have set forth, the assessments are not permitted under the First Amendment.

Justice Stevens, the author of *Glickman*, joined the majority and penned a separate concurrence in which he read *Glickman* as permitting a compelled subsidy "when it is ancillary, or germane, to a valid cooperative endeavor." When nothing more than commercial advertising is at stake, Justice Stevens reasoned, the assessment was "like a naked restraint on speech."

Justice Breyer dissented, joined by Justice Ginsburg and in part by Justice O'Connor, finding "[t]his case, although it involves mushrooms rather than fruit, [identical] in [all] critical respects" to *Glickman*. Justice Breyer wrote that "the advertising here relates directly, not in an incidental or subsidiary manner, to the regulatory program's underlying goal of maintaining and expanding the existing markets and uses for mushrooms." He continued: "It is difficult to see why a Constitution that seeks to protect individual freedom would consider the absence of 'heavy regulation" to amount to a special determinative reason for refusing to permit this less intrusive program." Justice Breyer found the compelled expression here, like that in *Glickman* and unlike that in *Barnette* and *Wooley*, "incapable of 'engendering any crisis of conscience.'"

In a third case involving agricultural marketing assessments, Johanns v. Livestock Mktg Ass'n, 544 U.S. 550 (2005), the Court concluded that the compelled speech, which generically promoted beef ("Beef—It's What's For Dinner"), was that of the federal government itself. The Court concluded that compelled funding of government speech did not raise First Amendment concerns. The question of when challenged speech is in fact speech by the government itself, rather than private speech coerced by government, is considered in Chapter 12.

Finally, consider the Court's resolution of the compelled subsidy issue in Board of Regents of the University of Wisconsin v. Southworth, 529 U.S. 217 (2000), which involved a university compulsory student activities fee. Students argued they were entitled to a rebate of the amount of their fee used to finance student organizations engaging in political or ideological speech to which they objected. The Court rejected their claim. Distinguishing *Abood* and *Keller* (the mandatory Bar dues case), Justice Kennedy wrote for a unanimous Court: "The standard of germane speech as applied to student speech at a university is unworkable. To insist upon asking what speech is germane would be contrary to the very goal the University seeks to pursue. It is not for the Court to say what is or what is not germane to the ideas to be pursued in an institution of higher learning." Justice Kennedy cautioned, however, that "the University must provide some protection to its students'

First Amendment interests. [The] proper measure, and the principal standard of protection for objecting students, we conclude, is the requirement of viewpoint neutrality in the allocation of funding support."

Note all the decisions in this Note preceded the Court's decision in *Janus* and many relied on *Abood*'s distinction between subsidies for "germane" versus "ideological" speech. Although *Janus* was decided in the context of union agency fees and concerns special interests such as "labor peace" and "free riding," do its general principles and conclusions undermine decisions like *Glickman, Keller,* and *Southworth*? Can the government *ever* compel individuals to subsidize speech they disagree with?

5. *The Right to Communicate Anonymously*

As should be clear by now, compulsory expression takes many forms. One potential form of compulsion relates to the disclosure of a speaker's identity. Speakers may wish to communicate without disclosing anything at all about their identities or may want to communicate using a pseudonym. However, knowledge of an author's identity arguably might assist the audience in interpreting the author's message or serve other interests. The Supreme Court has recognized a right to speak anonymously, at least in some contexts.

McIntyre v. Ohio Elections Commission

514 U.S. 334 (1995)

Justice STEVENS delivered the opinion of the Court.

. . . On April 27, 1988, Margaret McIntyre distributed leaflets to persons attending a public meeting at the Blendon Middle School in Westerville, Ohio. At this meeting, the superintendent of schools planned to discuss an imminent referendum on a proposed school tax levy. The leaflets expressed Mrs. McIntyre's opposition to the levy. There is no suggestion that the text of her message was false, misleading, or libelous. She had composed and printed it on her home computer and had paid a professional printer to make additional copies. Some of the handbills identified her as the author; others merely purported to express the views of "CONCERNED PARENTS AND TAX PAYERS." . . .

While Mrs. McIntyre distributed her handbills, an official of the school district, who supported the tax proposal, advised her that the unsigned leaflets did not conform to the Ohio election laws. . . .

. . . Five months later, the same school official filed a complaint with the Ohio Elections Commission charging that Mrs. McIntyre's distribution of unsigned leaflets violated § 599.09(A) of the Ohio Code, [which provided that any publication promoting a ballot issue was required to include the "name and residence" of the person "who issues, makes, or is responsible therefor." The Commission fined McIntyre $100. She appealed, and when the case reached the Ohio Supreme Court, the court affirmed, holding that the minor burden the election law posed on speakers was more than offset by the state interest in helping voters assess the "validity" of campaign literature and identifying disseminators of fraud, libel or false advertising.]

II

Ohio maintains that the statute under review is a reasonable regulation of the electoral process. The State does not suggest that all anonymous publications are pernicious or that a statute totally excluding them from the marketplace of ideas would be valid. This is a wise (albeit implicit) concession, for the anonymity of an author is not ordinarily a sufficient reason to exclude her work product from the protections of the First Amendment.

"Anonymous pamphlets, leaflets, brochures and even books have played an important role in the progress of mankind." Talley v. California, 362 U.S., at 64. Great works of literature have frequently been produced by authors writing under assumed names. Despite readers' curiosity and the public's interest in identifying the creator of a work of art, an author generally is free to decide whether or not to disclose his or her true identity. The decision in favor of anonymity may be motivated by fear of economic or official retaliation, by concern about social ostracism, or merely by a desire to preserve as much of one's privacy as possible. Whatever the motivation may be, at least in the field of literary endeavor, the interest in having anonymous works enter the marketplace of ideas unquestionably outweighs any public interest in requiring disclosure as a condition of entry. Accordingly, an author's decision to remain anonymous, like other decisions concerning omissions or additions to the content of a publication, is an aspect of the freedom of speech protected by the First Amendment.

The freedom to publish anonymously extends beyond the literary realm. In *Talley*, the Court held that the First Amendment protects the distribution of unsigned handbills urging readers to boycott certain Los Angeles merchants who were allegedly engaging in discriminatory employment practices. 362 U.S. at 60. Writing for the Court, Justice Black noted that "[p]ersecuted groups and sects from time to time throughout history have been able to criticize oppressive practices and laws either anonymously or not at all." Justice Black recalled England's abusive press licensing laws and seditious libel prosecutions, and he reminded us that even the arguments favoring the ratification of the Constitution advanced in the Federalist Papers were published under fictitious names. On occasion, quite apart from any threat of persecution, an advocate may believe her ideas will be more persuasive if her readers are unaware of her identity. Anonymity thereby provides a way for a writer who may be personally unpopular to ensure that readers will not prejudge her message simply because they do not like its proponent. . . . The specific holding in *Talley* related to advocacy of an economic boycott, but the Court's reasoning embraced a respected tradition of anonymity in the advocacy of political causes. This tradition is perhaps best exemplified by the secret ballot, the hard-won right to vote one's conscience without fear of retaliation.

III

. . . *Talley* does not necessarily control the disposition of this case. We must, therefore, decide whether and to what extent the First Amendment's protection of anonymity encompasses documents intended to influence the electoral process.

. . . [T]he Ohio Code does not control the mechanics of the electoral process. It is a regulation of pure speech. Moreover, even though this provision applies evenhandedly to advocates of differing viewpoints, it is a direct regulation of the content of speech. Every written document covered by the statute must contain "the name and residence or business address of the chairman, treasurer, or secretary of the organization issuing the same, or the person who issues, makes, or is responsible therefor." Ohio Rev. Code Ann. § 3599.09(A) (1988). Furthermore, the category of covered documents is defined by their content—only those publications containing speech designed to influence the voters in an election need bear the required markings. Consequently, we are not faced with an ordinary election restriction; this case "involves a limitation on political expression subject to exacting scrutiny." . . .

Indeed, as we have explained on many prior occasions, the category of speech regulated by the Ohio statute occupies the core of the protection afforded by the First Amendment: "Discussion of public issues and debate on the qualifications of candidates are integral to the operation of the system of government established by our Constitution. The First Amendment affords the broadest protection to such political expression in order 'to assure [the] unfettered interchange of ideas for the bringing about of political and social changes desired by the people.' Roth v. United States, 354 U.S. 476, 484 (1957). Although First Amendment protections are not confined to 'the exposition of ideas,' . . . , 'there is practically universal agreement that a major purpose of that Amendment was to protect the free discussion of governmental affairs, . . . of course includ[ing] discussions of candidates. . . .' Mills v. Alabama, 384 U.S. 214, 218 (1966). . . . In a republic where the people are sovereign, the ability of the citizenry to make informed choices among candidates for office is essential, for the identities of those who are elected will inevitably shape the course that we follow as a nation. . . ."

Of course, core political speech need not center on a candidate for office. . . . Indeed, the speech in which Mrs. McIntyre engaged—handing out leaflets in the advocacy of a politically controversial viewpoint—is the essence of First Amendment expression. That this advocacy occurred in the heat of a controversial referendum vote only strengthens the protection afforded to Mrs. McIntyre's expression: Urgent, important, and effective speech can be no less protected than impotent speech, lest the right to speak be relegated to those instances when it is least needed. No form of speech is entitled to greater constitutional protection than Mrs. McIntyre's.

When a law burdens core political speech, we apply "exacting scrutiny," and we uphold the restriction only if it is narrowly tailored to serve an overriding state interest. Our precedents thus make abundantly clear that the Ohio Supreme Court applied a significantly more lenient standard than is appropriate in a case of this kind.

IV

Nevertheless, the State argues that, even under the strictest standard of review, the disclosure requirement in § 3599.09(A) is justified by two important and legitimate state interests. Ohio judges its interest in preventing fraudulent and libelous statements and its interest in providing the electorate with relevant information to be sufficiently compelling to justify the anonymous speech ban. These two interests necessarily overlap to some extent, but it is useful to discuss them separately.

Insofar as the interest in informing the electorate means nothing more than the provision of additional information that may either buttress or undermine the argument in a document, we think the identity of the speaker is no different from other components of the document's content that the author is free to include or exclude. We have already held that the State may not compel a newspaper that prints editorials critical of a particular candidate to provide space for a reply by the candidate. *Tornillo*. . . . The simple interest in providing voters with additional relevant information does not justify a state requirement that a writer make statements or disclosures she would otherwise omit. Moreover, in the case of a handbill written by a private citizen who is not known to the recipient, the name and address of the author add little, if anything, to the reader's ability to evaluate the document's message. Thus, Ohio's informational interest is plainly insufficient to support the constitutionality of its disclosure requirement.

The state interest in preventing fraud and libel stands on a different footing. We agree with Ohio's submission that this interest carries special weight during election campaigns when false statements, if credited, may have serious adverse consequences for the public at large. Ohio does not, however, rely solely on § 3599.09(A) to protect that interest. Its Election Code includes detailed and specific prohibitions against making or disseminating false statements during political campaigns. These regulations apply both to candidate elections and to issue-driven ballot measures. Thus, Ohio's prohibition of anonymous leaflets plainly is not its principal weapon against fraud. Rather, it serves as an aid to enforcement of the specific prohibitions and as a deterrent to the making of false statements by unscrupulous prevaricators. Although these ancillary benefits are assuredly legitimate, we are not persuaded that they justify § 3599.09(A)'s extremely broad prohibition.

As this case demonstrates, the prohibition encompasses documents that are not even arguably false or misleading. It applies not only to the activities of candidates and their organized supporters, but also to individuals acting independently and using only their own modest resources. It applies not only to elections of public officers, but also to ballot issues that present neither a substantial risk of libel nor any potential appearance of corrupt advantage. It applies not only to leaflets distributed on the eve of an election, when the opportunity for reply is limited, but also to those distributed months in advance. It applies no matter what the character or strength of the author's interest in anonymity. Moreover, as this case also demonstrates, the absence of the author's name on a document does not necessarily protect either that person or a distributor of a forbidden document from being held responsible for compliance with the Election Code. Nor has the State explained why it can more easily enforce the direct bans on disseminating false documents against anonymous authors and distributors than against wrongdoers who might use false names and addresses in an attempt to avoid detection. We recognize that a State's enforcement interest might justify a more limited identification requirement, but Ohio has shown scant cause for inhibiting the leafletting at issue here. . . .

VI

Under our Constitution, anonymous pamphleteering is not a pernicious, fraudulent practice, but an honorable tradition of advocacy and of dissent. Anonymity is a shield from the tyranny of the majority. *See generally* J. Mill, On Liberty and Considerations on Representative Government 1, 3-4 (R. McCallum ed. 1947). It thus exemplifies the purpose behind the Bill of Rights, and of the First

Amendment in particular: to protect unpopular individuals from retaliation—and their ideas from suppression—at the hand of an intolerant society. The right to remain anonymous may be abused when it shields fraudulent conduct. But political speech by its nature will sometimes have unpalatable consequences, and, in general, our society accords greater weight to the value of free speech than to the dangers of its misuse. Ohio has not shown that its interest in preventing the misuse of anonymous election-related speech justifies a prohibition of all uses of that speech. The State may, and does, punish fraud directly. But it cannot seek to punish fraud indirectly by indiscriminately outlawing a category of speech, based on its content, with no necessary relationship to the danger sought to be prevented. . . .

Justice Scalia, with whom The Chief Justice joins, dissenting.

. . . Preferring the views of the English utilitarian philosopher John Stuart Mill to the considered judgment of the American people's elected representatives from coast to coast, the Court discovers a hitherto unknown right-to-be-unknown while engaging in electoral politics. I dissent from this imposition of free-speech imperatives that are demonstrably not those of the American people today, and that there is inadequate reason to believe were those of the society that begat the First Amendment or the Fourteenth.

. . . The law at issue here . . . forbids the expression of no idea, but merely requires identification of the speaker when the idea is uttered in the electoral context. It is at the periphery of the First Amendment. . . .

. . . [T]he usefulness of a signing requirement lies not only in promoting observance of the law against campaign falsehoods (though that alone is enough to sustain it). It lies also in promoting a civil and dignified level of campaign debate—which the State has no power to command, but ample power to encourage by such undemanding measures as a signature requirement. . . .

. . . We have approved much more onerous disclosure requirements in the name of fair elections. In Buckley v. Valeo, 424 U.S. 1 (1976), we upheld provisions of the Federal Election Campaign Act that required private individuals to report to the Federal Election Commission independent expenditures made for communications advocating the election or defeat of a candidate for federal office. Our primary rationale for upholding this provision was that it served an "informational interest" by "increas[ing] the fund of information concerning those who support the candidates." The provision before us here serves the same informational interest, as well as more important interests, which I have discussed above. . . . If *Buckley* remains the law, this is an easy case. . . .

NOTES AND QUESTIONS

1. *Anonymity and equality.* In *McIntyre*, the Court refers to the long American tradition of anonymous handbilling. That tradition has served many causes, including advocacy on behalf of civil rights. *See* Talley v. California, 362 U.S. 60 (1960). As the Court observes, throughout history anonymity has been particularly important to speakers who are members of persecuted groups.
2. *Other anonymous speech precedents. McIntyre* is not the Supreme Court's last word on the right to speak anonymously. In Watchtower Bible & Tract

Society of New York, Inc. v. Stratton, 536 U.S. 150 (2002), the Court struck down an ordinance prohibiting door-to-door canvassing without a permit from the mayor's office, holding that the ordinance was overbroad and insufficiently tailored to protect privacy or prevent fraud and crime. In Buckley v. American Constitutional Law Foundation, Inc., 525 U.S. 182, 199-200 (1999), the Court struck down a state law requiring people circulating petitions regarding issue referenda to wear identification badges.

3. *Campaign-related disclosure requirements.* The majority in *McIntyre* stressed that Ohio was attempting to regulate "pure speech" rather than "the mechanics of the electoral process." As Justice Scalia's dissent notes, the Court has "approved much more onerous disclosure requirements [than the one at issue in *McIntyre*] in the name of fair elections." *See* Buckley v. Valeo, 424 U.S. 1 (1976) (upholding Federal Election Campaign Act (FECA) disclosure requirements requiring reporting of contributions and expenditures – and the identities of those behind them – to the Federal Election Commission (FEC)); McConnell v. Federal Election Comm'n, 540 U.S. 93 (2003) (upholding expanded reporting and disclosure requirements under federal law, including requirements that the identities of those involved with "issue ads" be disclosed); Citizens United v. Federal Election Comm'n, 558 U.S. 310 (2010) (upholding campaign disclosure and disclaimer provisions, including a requirement that anyone making electioneering communications state the name of the party responsible for the communication and that it was not authorized by the candidate).

4. *Petition signatures.* Doe v. Reed, 561 U.S. 186 (2010) rejected a challenge to a state requirement that mandated disclosure of the names and addresses of citizens who had signed petitions seeking to put up for a referendum a law expanding the rights of same-sex couples. State law generally mandated referenda petition signatures be treated as "public records." Plaintiffs argued that public disclosure of petition signatures violated the First Amendment. After determining that petition-signing was a form of political expression, the Court applied "exacting scrutiny" to the public records law under *Citizens United* and *Buckley*. It concluded that the State's disclosure law was "substantially related" to its "important" interest in preserving the integrity of the electoral process, which included rooting out instances of fraud and mistakes in signature collection. The Court's decision addressed the disclosure law as applied to all petition signatures; it left open the possibility that in a narrower challenge plaintiffs could prove their First Amendment rights were burdened by disclosure. For example, it affirmed that those resisting disclosure under the First Amendment could show "a reasonable probability that the compelled disclosure [of personal information] will subject them to threats, harassment, or reprisals from either Government officials or private parties." *Buckley*. Based on the record before the Court, plaintiffs had failed to make such a showing.

THEORY-APPLIED PROBLEMS—ANONYMITY AND ACCOUNTABILITY

1. *Mask ordinances.* Assume a state passes a law forbidding the wearing of a mask in public. Would such a statute be constitutional as a public safety measure? Would a statute that forbids the wearing of a mask in any building owned or leased by the state be constitutional? *Compare* Church of the Am. Knights of the Ku Klux Klan v. Kerid, 356 F.3d 197, 206-207 (2d Cir. 2004) (ordinance upheld), *with* American Knights of the Ku Klux Klan v. City of Goshen, 50 F. Supp. 2d 835, 840-842 (N.D. Ind. 1999) (ordinance struck down).
2. *Internet anonymity.* The Internet has made it easier for citizens to speak anonymously or pseudonymously. Would a federal statute making it a crime to knowingly initiate an anonymous Internet communication with the "intent to annoy, abuse, threaten, or harass any person who receives the communication" be likely to withstand a First Amendment challenge? For more on the topic of Internet anonymity, see Jeff Kosseff, *The United States of Anonymous: How the First Amendment Shaped Online Speech* (2022); Lyrissa Barnett Lidsky & Thomas F. Cotter, *Authorship, Audiences, and Anonymous Speech,* 82 Notre Dame L. Rev. 1537 (2007). For more discussion regarding online harassment, see Danielle Keats Citron, *Hate Crimes in Cyberspace* (2014).

C. THE RIGHT OF ASSOCIATION

As noted, the First Amendment protects more than speech rights. It has also been interpreted to protect a right to associate for expressive purposes and a right not to associate. This Section examines the recognition and interpretation of these "associational" rights.

1. The Right to Associate for Expressive Purposes

The Supreme Court has recognized that assembling and acting in concert with others can facilitate the effective exercise of First Amendment rights. In NAACP v. Alabama, 357 U.S. 449 (1958), below, the Court recognized a First Amendment right to associate with others for expressive purposes. Note the right of "expressive association" is dependent on the exercise of collective rights of expression. In other words, the Court has not recognized a right of association for any reason at all or in the *abstract* but rather only in connection with participation in expressive activity.

NAACP v. Alabama

357 U.S. 449 (1958)

Mr. Justice Harlan delivered the opinion of the Court.

We review from the standpoint of its validity under the Federal Constitution a judgment of civil contempt entered against petitioner, the National Association for the Advancement of Colored People, in the courts of Alabama. The question presented is whether Alabama . . . can compel petitioner to reveal to the State's Attorney General the names and addresses of all its Alabama members and agents, without regard to their positions or functions in the Association. The judgment of contempt was based upon petitioner's refusal to comply fully with a court order requiring in part the production of membership lists. Petitioner's claim is that the order, in the circumstances shown by this record, violated rights assured to petitioner and its members under the Constitution.

Alabama has a statute similar to those of many other States which requires a foreign corporation, except as exempted, to qualify before doing business by filing its corporate charter with the Secretary of State and designating a place of business and an agent to receive service of process. The statute imposes a fine on a corporation transacting intrastate business before qualifying and provides for criminal prosecution of officers of such a corporation. The National Association for the Advancement of Colored People is a nonprofit membership corporation organized under the laws of New York. Its purposes, fostered on a nationwide basis, are those indicated by its name, and it operates through chartered affiliates which are independent unincorporated associations, with membership therein equivalent to membership in petitioner. The first Alabama affiliates were chartered in 1918. Since that time the aims of the Association have been advanced through activities of its affiliates, and in 1951 the Association itself opened a regional office in Alabama, at which it employed two supervisory persons and one clerical worker. The Association has never complied with the qualification statute, from which it considered itself exempt.

In 1956 the Attorney General of Alabama brought an equity suit in the State Circuit Court, Montgomery County, to enjoin the Association from conducting further activities within, and to oust it from, the State. Among other things the bill in equity alleged that the Association had opened a regional office and had organized various affiliates in Alabama; had recruited members and solicited contributions within the State; had given financial support and furnished legal assistance to [Black] students seeking admission to the state university; and had supported a [Black] boycott of the bus lines in Montgomery to compel the seating of passengers without regard to race. The bill recited that the Association, by continuing to do business in Alabama without complying with the qualification statute, was ". . . causing irreparable injury to the property and civil rights of the residents and citizens of the State of Alabama for which criminal prosecution and civil actions at law afford no adequate relief. . . ." On the day the complaint was filed, the Circuit Court issued *ex parte* an order restraining the Association . . . from engaging in further activities within the State and forbidding it to take any steps to qualify itself to do business therein.

. . . [T]he State moved for the production of a large number of the Association's records and papers, including bank statements, leases, deeds, and records containing the names and addresses of all Alabama "members" and "agents" of the Association. It alleged that all such documents were necessary [to determine whether petitioner was conducting business in Alabama] within the meaning of the qualification statute. . . . [T]he court ordered the production of a substantial part of the requested records, including the membership lists[.] . . . [P]etitioner did not comply with the production order, and for this failure was adjudged in civil contempt and fined $10,000. The contempt judgment provided that the fine would be subject to reduction or remission if compliance were forthcoming within five days but otherwise would be increased to $100,000. At the end of the five-day period petitioner produced substantially all the data called for by the production order except its membership lists, as to which it contended that Alabama could not constitutionally compel disclosure. . . . [The NAACP was adjudged to be in contempt and ordered to pay a fine of $100,000.] . . .

III

. . . Petitioner argues that in view of the facts and circumstances shown in the record, the effect of compelled disclosure of the membership lists will be to abridge the rights of its rank-and-file members to engage in lawful association in support of their common beliefs. It contends that governmental action which, although not directly suppressing association, nevertheless carries this consequence, can be justified only upon some overriding valid interest of the State.

Effective advocacy of both public and private points of view, particularly controversial ones, is undeniably enhanced by group association, as this Court has more than once recognized by remarking upon the close nexus between the freedoms of speech and assembly. It is beyond debate that freedom to engage in association for the advancement of beliefs and ideas is an inseparable aspect of the "liberty" assured by the Due Process Clause of the Fourteenth Amendment, which embraces freedom of speech. Of course, it is immaterial whether the beliefs sought to be advanced by association pertain to political, economic, religious or cultural matters, and state action which may have the effect of curtailing the freedom to associate is subject to the closest scrutiny.

The fact that Alabama, so far as is relevant to the validity of the contempt judgment presently under review, has taken no direct action . . . to restrict the right of petitioner's members to associate freely, does not end inquiry into the effect of the production order. In the domain of these indispensable liberties, whether of speech, press, or association, the decisions of this Court recognize that abridgment of such rights, even though unintended, may inevitably follow from varied forms of governmental action. . . .

It is hardly a novel perception that compelled disclosure of affiliation with groups engaged in advocacy may constitute as effective a restraint on freedom of association as [more direct forms governmental action]. . . . This Court has recognized the vital relationship between freedom to associate and privacy in one's associations. . . . Inviolability of privacy in group association may in many circumstances be indispensable to preservation of freedom of association, particularly where a group espouses dissident beliefs.

We think that the production order, in the respects here drawn in question, must be regarded as entailing the likelihood of a substantial restraint upon the exercise by petitioner's members of their right to freedom of association. Petitioner has made an uncontroverted showing that on past occasions revelation of the identity of its rank-and-file members has exposed these members to economic reprisal, loss of employment, threat of physical coercion, and other manifestations of public hostility. Under these circumstances, we think it apparent that compelled disclosure of petitioner's Alabama membership is likely to affect adversely the ability of petitioner and its members to pursue their collective effort to foster beliefs which they admittedly have the right to advocate, in that it may induce members to withdraw from the Association and dissuade others from joining it because of fear of exposure of their beliefs shown through their associations and of the consequences of this exposure.

It is not sufficient to answer, as the State does here, that whatever repressive effect compulsory disclosure of names of petitioner's members may have upon participation by Alabama citizens in petitioner's activities follows not from *state* action but from *private* community pressures. The crucial factor is the interplay of governmental and private action, for it is only after the initial exertion of state power represented by the production order that private action takes hold.

We turn to the final question whether Alabama has demonstrated an interest in obtaining the disclosures it seeks from petitioner which is sufficient to justify the deterrent effect which we have concluded these disclosures may well have on the free exercise by petitioner's members of their constitutionally protected right of association. Such a ". . . subordinating interest of the State must be compelling," Sweezy v. New Hampshire, 354 U. S. 234, 265 (concurring opinion). It is not of moment that the State has here acted solely through its judicial branch, for whether legislative or judicial, it is still the application of state power which we are asked to scrutinize.

It is important to bear in mind that petitioner asserts no right to absolute immunity from state investigation, and no right to disregard Alabama's laws. As shown by its substantial compliance with the production order, petitioner does not deny Alabama's right to obtain from it such information as the State desires concerning the purposes of the Association and its activities within the State. Petitioner has not objected to divulging the identity of its members who are employed by or hold official positions with it. It has urged the rights solely of its ordinary rank-and-file members. . . .

Whether there was "justification" in this instance turns solely on the substantiality of Alabama's interest in obtaining the membership lists. . . . The exclusive purpose [of the State] was to determine whether petitioner was conducting intrastate business in violation of the Alabama foreign corporation registration statute, and the membership lists were expected to help resolve this question. . . . [W]e are unable to perceive that the disclosure of the names of petitioner's rank-and-file members has a substantial bearing on [the State's interest]. As matters stand in the state court, petitioner (1) has admitted its presence and conduct of activities in Alabama since 1918; (2) has offered to comply in all respects with the state qualification statute, although preserving its contention that the statute does not apply to it; and (3) has apparently complied satisfactorily with the production order, except for the membership lists, by furnishing the Attorney General with varied business records, its charter and statement of purposes, the names of all of its directors and officers, and with the total number of its Alabama members and the amount of their dues. . . . [W]hatever interest the State may have in obtaining names of ordinary members has not been shown to be sufficient to overcome petitioner's constitutional objections to the production order.

. . . We hold that the immunity from state scrutiny of membership lists which the Association claims on behalf of its members is here so related to the right of the members to pursue their lawful private interests privately and to associate freely with others in so doing as to come within the protection of the Fourteenth Amendment. And we conclude that Alabama has fallen short of showing a controlling justification for the deterrent effect on the free enjoyment of the right to associate which disclosure of membership lists is likely to have. Accordingly, the judgment of civil contempt and the $100,000 fine which resulted from petitioner's refusal to comply with the production order in this respect must fall.

. . . For the reasons stated, the judgment of the Supreme Court of Alabama must be reversed and the case remanded for proceedings not inconsistent with this opinion.

Reversed.

NOTES AND QUESTIONS

1. *Collective expression.* In *NAACP*, the Court observes that "[e]ffective advocacy of both public and private points of view, particularly controversial ones, is undeniably enhanced by group association, as this Court has more than once recognized by remarking upon the close nexus between the freedoms of speech and assembly." How does collective action "enhance" the exercise of free speech and assembly rights?
2. *"Expressive association."* The First Amendment protects free speech and assembly rights. However, a right of "expressive association" is not mentioned in the text. For an analysis of the Court's substitution of "expressive association" for the right of peaceable assembly, see John D. Inazu, *Liberty's Refuge: The Forgotten Freedom of Assembly* (2012). Professor Inazu criticizes the Court's reliance on the message of groups or their participation in expressive activities in developing associational doctrine, arguing that this focus undervalues interests in group formation, composition, and existence. *Id.* at 2. Gay social clubs, prayer groups, and college sororities are all associations, he notes, but suppose none are likely "expressive enough" to merit First Amendment protection. *Id.* at 3. Should the First Amendment protect the practices and activities of groups without regard to whether they are engaged in expressive activities?
3. *Other disclosure mandates.* During the Civil Rights Era, the Court invalidated other efforts to compel disclosure of membership in civil rights organizations. *See* Shelton v. Tucker, 364 U.S. 479 (1960) (invalidating Arkansas law that required every teacher, as a condition of employment in a state-supported school or college, to file an annual statement "listing without limitation every organization to which he has belonged or regularly contributed within the preceding five years"); Gibson v. Florida Legislative Investigation Comm., 372 U.S. 539 (1963) (reversing the conviction of an NAACP official who refused to comply with a legislative committee's request to disclose the membership list of a local NAACP branch).
4. *Direct restrictions on expressive association.* Although they have become less commonplace, the Court has also invalidated more direct restraints on

associational activity. *See* Healy v. James, 408 U.S. 169 (1972) (invalidating efforts by state university to exclude from campus a chapter of Students for a Democratic Society); NAACP v. Button, 371 U.S. 415 (1963) (invalidating Virginia law restricting political litigation by civil rights group).

2. *The Right* Not *to Associate*

In the decades after *NAACP*, litigants and Supreme Court cases focused on the right not to associate. Attention shifted to government efforts to enforce nondiscrimination laws on organizations that asserted a right to decide with whom to associate. Do the anti-discrimination laws involved in the following cases regulate expressive association or discriminatory conduct? Does the First Amendment protect a group's right to determine its own membership? Are there any interests that would outweigh that right?

Roberts v. United States Jaycees

468 U.S. 609 (1984)

Justice BRENNAN delivered the opinion of the Court. . . .

The United States Jaycees (Jaycees), founded in 1920 as the Junior Chamber of Commerce, is a nonprofit membership corporation, incorporated in Missouri with national headquarters in Tulsa, Okla. The objective of the Jaycees, as set out in its bylaws, is to pursue

> such educational and charitable purposes as will promote and foster the growth and development of young men's civic organizations in the United States, designed to inculcate in the individual membership of such organization a spirit of genuine Americanism and civic interest, and as a supplementary education institution to provide them with opportunity for personal development and achievement and an avenue for intelligent participation by young men in the affairs of their community, state and nation, and to develop true friendship and understanding among young men of all nations. . . .

Regular membership is limited to young men between the ages of 18 and 35, while associate membership is available to individuals or groups ineligible for regular membership, principally women and older men. An associate member, whose dues are somewhat lower than those charged regular members, may not vote, hold local or national office, or participate in certain leadership training and awards programs. . . .

In 1974 and 1975, respectively, the Minneapolis and St. Paul chapters of the Jaycees began admitting women as regular members. Currently, the memberships and boards of directors of both chapters include a substantial proportion of women. As a result, the two chapters have been in violation of the national organization's bylaws for about 10 years. . . .

In December 1978, the president of the national organization advised both chapters that a motion to revoke their charters would be considered. . . . Shortly after receiving this notification, members of both chapters filed charges of discrimination with the Minnesota Department of Human Rights. The complaints alleged that the exclusion of women from full membership required by the national organization's bylaws violated the Minnesota Human Rights Act (Act), which provides in part:

> It is an unfair discriminatory practice: To deny any person the full and equal enjoyment of the goods, services, facilities, privileges, advantages, and accommodations of a place of public accommodation because of race, color, creed, religion, disability, national origin or sex.

Minn. Stat. § 363.03.

The term "place of public accommodation" is defined in the Act as "a business, accommodation, refreshment, entertainment, recreation, or transportation facility of any kind, whether licensed or not, whose goods, services, facilities, privileges, advantages or accommodations are extended, offered, sold, or otherwise made available to the public." § 363.01.

. . . [T]he national organization brought suit against various state officials, appellants here, in the United States District Court . . . [alleging that], by requiring the organization to accept women as regular members, application of the Act would violate the male members' constitutional rights of free speech and association. . . .

[T]he District Court entered judgment in favor of the state officials. On appeal, a divided Court of Appeals for the Eighth Circuit reversed. The Court of Appeals determined that, because "the advocacy of political and public causes, selected by the membership, is a not insubstantial part of what [the Jaycees organization] does," the organization's right to select its members is protected by the freedom of association guaranteed by the First Amendment. . . .

Our decisions have referred to constitutionally protected "freedom of association" in two distinct senses. In one line of decisions, the Court has concluded that choices to enter into and maintain certain intimate human relationships must be secured against undue intrusion by the State because of the role of such relationships in safeguarding the individual freedom that is central to our constitutional scheme. In this respect, freedom of association receives protection as a fundamental element of personal liberty. In another set of decisions, the Court has recognized a right to associate for the purpose of engaging in those activities protected by the First Amendment—speech, assembly, petition for the redress of grievances, and the exercise of religion. The Constitution guarantees freedom of association of this kind as an indispensable means of preserving other individual liberties.

The intrinsic and instrumental features of constitutionally protected association may, of course, coincide. . . . Still, the nature and degree of constitutional protection afforded freedom of association may vary depending on the extent to which one or the other aspect of the constitutionally protected liberty is at stake in a given case. We therefore find it useful to consider separately the effect of applying the Minnesota statute to the Jaycees on what could be called its members' freedom of intimate association and their freedom of expressive association.

The Court has long recognized that, because the Bill of Rights is designed to secure individual liberty, it must afford the formation and preservation of certain kinds of highly personal relationships a substantial measure of sanctuary from unjustified interference by the State. . . . Protecting these relationships from unwarranted state interference therefore safeguards the ability independently to define one's identity that is central to any concept of liberty.

The personal affiliations that exemplify these considerations, and that therefore suggest some relevant limitations on the relationships that might be entitled to this sort of constitutional protection, are those that attend the creation and sustenance of a family. . . . Family relationships, by their nature, involve deep attachments and commitments to the necessarily few other individuals with whom one shares not only a special community of thoughts, experiences, and beliefs but also distinctively personal aspects of one's life. . . . As a general matter, only relationships with these sorts of qualities are likely to reflect the considerations that have led to an understanding of freedom of association as an intrinsic element of personal liberty. Conversely, an association lacking these qualities—such as a large business enterprise—seems remote from the concerns giving rise to this constitutional protection. . . .

Between these poles, of course, lies a broad range of human relationships that may make greater or lesser claims to constitutional protection from particular incursions by the State. . . . We need not mark the potentially significant points on this terrain with any precision. We note only that factors that may be relevant include size, purpose, policies, selectivity, congeniality, and other characteristics that in a particular case may be pertinent. In this case, however, several features of the Jaycees clearly place the organization outside of the category of relationships worthy of this kind of constitutional protection.

The undisputed facts reveal that the local chapters of the Jaycees are large and basically unselective groups. . . . Apart from age and sex, neither the national organization nor the local chapters employ any criteria for judging applicants for membership, and new members are routinely recruited and admitted with no inquiry into their backgrounds. . . .

. . . Moreover, much of the activity central to the formation and maintenance of the association involves the participation of strangers to that relationship. Accordingly, we conclude that the Jaycees chapters lack the distinctive characteristics that might afford constitutional protection to the decision of its members to exclude women. We turn therefore to consider the extent to which application of the Minnesota statute to compel the Jaycees to accept women infringes the group's freedom of expressive association.

An individual's freedom to speak, to worship, and to petition the government for the redress of grievances could not be vigorously protected from interference by the State unless a correlative freedom to engage in group effort toward those ends were not also guaranteed. According protection to collective effort on behalf of shared goals is especially important in preserving political and cultural diversity and in shielding dissident expression from suppression by the majority. Consequently, we have long understood as implicit in the right to engage in activities protected by the First Amendment a corresponding right to associate with others in pursuit of a wide variety of political, social, economic, educational, religious, and cultural ends. In view of the various protected activities in which the Jaycees engages, that right is plainly implicated in this case.

Government actions that may unconstitutionally infringe upon this freedom can take a number of forms. Among other things, government may seek to impose penalties or withhold benefits from individuals because of their membership in a disfavored group; Healy v. James, 408 U.S. 169 (1972), it may attempt to require disclosure of the fact of membership in a group seeking anonymity; Brown v. Socialist Workers '74 Campaign Committee, 459 U.S. 87 (1982) and it may try to interfere with the internal organization or affairs of the group. By requiring the Jaycees to admit women as full voting members, the Minnesota Act works an infringement of the last type. There can be no clearer example of an intrusion into the internal structure or affairs of an association than a regulation that forces the group to accept members it does not desire. Such a regulation may impair the ability of the original members to express only those views that brought them together. Freedom of association therefore plainly presupposes a freedom not to associate.

The right to associate for expressive purposes is not, however, absolute. Infringements on that right may be justified by regulations adopted to serve compelling state interests, unrelated to the suppression of ideas, that cannot be achieved through means significantly less restrictive of associational freedoms. We are persuaded that Minnesota's compelling interest in eradicating discrimination against its female citizens justifies the impact that application of the statute to the Jaycees may have on the male members' associational freedoms.

On its face, the Minnesota Act does not aim at the suppression of speech, does not distinguish between prohibited and permitted activity on the basis of viewpoint, and does not license enforcement authorities to administer the statute on the basis of such constitutionally impermissible criteria. Nor does the Jaycees contend that the Act has been applied in this case for the purpose of hampering the organization's ability to express its views. Instead, as the Minnesota Supreme Court explained, the Act reflects the State's strong historical commitment to eliminating discrimination and assuring its citizens equal access to publicly available goods and services. That goal, which is unrelated to the suppression of expression, plainly serves compelling state interests of the highest order.

The Minnesota Human Rights Act at issue here is an example of public accommodations laws that were adopted by some States beginning a decade before enactment of their federal counterpart, the Civil Rights Act of 1875. . . .

A State enjoys broad authority to create rights of public access on behalf of its citizens. Minnesota has adopted a functional definition of public accommodations that reaches various forms of public, quasi-commercial conduct. . . . [I]n explaining its conclusion that the Jaycees local chapters are "place[s] of public accommodations" within the meaning of the Act, the Minnesota court noted the various commercial programs and benefits offered to members and stated that "[l]eadership skills are 'goods,' [and] business contacts and employment promotions are 'privileges' and 'advantages'. . . ." Assuring women equal access to such goods, privileges, and advantages clearly furthers compelling state interests.

In applying the Act to the Jaycees, the State has advanced those interests through the least restrictive means of achieving its ends. Indeed, the Jaycees has failed to demonstrate that the Act imposes any serious burdens on the male members' freedom of expressive association. . . . To be sure, as the Court of Appeals noted, a "not insubstantial part" of the Jaycees' activities constitutes protected expression on political, economic, cultural, and social affairs. . . . There is, however, no basis in the record for concluding that admission of women as full voting members will impede the organization's ability to engage in [its] protected [expressive] activities or to disseminate its preferred views. The Act requires no change in the Jaycees' creed of promoting the interests of young men, and it imposes no restrictions on the organization's ability to exclude individuals with ideologies or philosophies different from those of its existing members. Moreover, the Jaycees already invites women to share the group's views and philosophy and to participate in much of its training and community activities. Accordingly, any claim that admission of women as full voting members will impair a symbolic message conveyed by the very fact that women are not permitted to vote is attenuated at best.

[Furthermore, in] claiming that women might have a different attitude about such issues as the federal budget, school prayer, voting rights, and foreign relations, or that the organization's public positions would have a different effect if the group were not "a purely young men's association," the Jaycees relies solely on unsupported generalizations about the relative interests and perspectives of men and women. Although such generalizations may or may not have a statistical basis in fact with respect to particular positions adopted by the Jaycees, we have repeatedly condemned legal decisionmaking that relies uncritically on such assumptions. *See, e.g.*, Palmore v. Sidoti, 466 U.S. 429, 433-434 (1984). . . .

In any event, even if enforcement of the Act causes some incidental abridgment of the Jaycees' protected speech, that effect is no greater than is necessary to accomplish the State's legitimate purposes. As we have explained, acts of invidious discrimination in the distribution of publicly available goods, services, and other advantages cause unique evils that government has a compelling interest to prevent—wholly apart from the point of view such conduct may transmit. Accordingly, like violence or other types of potentially expressive activities that produce special harms distinct from their communicative impact, such practices are entitled to no constitutional protection. In prohibiting such practices, the Minnesota Act therefore "responds precisely to the substantive problem which legitimately concerns" the State and abridges no more speech or associational freedom than is necessary to accomplish that purpose.

The judgment of the Court of Appeals is

Reversed.

THE CHIEF JUSTICE and Justice BLACKMUN took no part in the decision of this case.

Justice REHNQUIST concurs in the judgment.

Justice O'CONNOR, concurring in part and concurring in the judgment.

. . . The Court declares that the Jaycees' right of association depends on the organization's making a "substantial" showing that the admission of unwelcome members "will change the message communicated by the group's speech." I am not sure what showing the Court thinks would satisfy its requirement of proof of a membership-message connection, but whatever it means, the focus on such a connection is objectionable.

Imposing such a requirement, especially in the context of the balancing-of-interests test articulated by the Court, raises the possibility that certain commercial associations, by engaging occasionally in certain kinds of expressive activities, might improperly gain protection for discrimination. . . .

The Court's readiness to inquire into the connection between membership and message reveals a more fundamental flaw in its analysis. The Court pursues this inquiry as part of its mechanical application of a "compelling interest" test [but the] . . . Court entirely neglects to establish at the threshold that the Jaycees is an association whose activities or purposes should engage the strong protections that the First Amendment extends to expressive associations.

On the one hand, an association engaged exclusively in protected expression enjoys First Amendment protection of both the content of its message and the choice of its members. Protection of the message itself is judged by the same standards as protection of speech by an individual. Protection of the association's right to define its membership derives from the recognition that the formation of an expressive association is the creation of a voice, and the selection of members is the definition of that voice. . . .

On the other hand, there is only minimal constitutional protection of the freedom of commercial association. There are, of course, some constitutional protections of commercial speech—speech intended and used to promote a commercial transaction with the speaker. But the State is free to impose any rational regulation on the commercial transaction itself. . . .

Many associations cannot readily be described as purely expressive or purely commercial. No association is likely ever to be exclusively engaged in expressive activities[.] . . . And innumerable commercial associations also engage in some incidental protected speech or advocacy. . . .

In my view, an association should be characterized as commercial, and therefore subject to rationally related state regulation of its membership and other associational activities, when, and only when, the association's activities are not predominantly of the type protected by the First Amendment. It is only when the association is predominantly engaged in protected expression that state regulation of its membership will necessarily affect, change, dilute, or silence one collective voice that would otherwise be heard. . . .

Determining whether an association's activity is predominantly protected expression will often be difficult, if only because a broad range of activities can be expressive. It is easy enough to identify expressive words or conduct that [is] strident, contentious, or divisive, but protected expression may also take the form of quiet persuasion, inculcation of traditional values, instruction of the young, and community service. The purposes of an association, and the purposes of its members in adhering to it, are doubtless relevant in determining whether the association is primarily engaged in protected expression. Lawyering to advance social goals may be speech but ordinary commercial law practice is not. A group boycott or refusal to deal for political purposes may be speech, though a similar boycott for purposes of maintaining a cartel is not. Even the training of outdoor survival skills or participation in community service might become expressive when the activity is intended to develop good morals, reverence, patriotism, and a desire for self-improvement.

The considerations that may enter into the determination of when a particular association of persons is predominantly engaged in expression are therefore fluid and somewhat uncertain. But the Court has recognized the need to draw similar lines in the past. . . .

The State of Minnesota has a legitimate interest in ensuring nondiscriminatory access to the commercial opportunity presented by membership in the Jaycees. The members of the Jaycees may not claim constitutional immunity from Minnesota's antidiscrimination law by seeking to exercise their First Amendment rights through this commercial organization.

For these reasons, I agree with the Court that the Jaycees' First Amendment challenge to the application of Minnesota's public accommodations law is meritless. I therefore concur[.]

NOTES AND QUESTIONS

1. Roberts *and expressive association.* Is the *Roberts* Court wise to link a right to expressive association with an inquiry into whether the group has a message? Who has the better approach—the majority or Justice O'Connor? Should the question be the degree to which the government-compelled association affects the group's speech, or whether the group was formed for expressive purposes? For commentary on both approaches, see Douglas O. Linder, *Freedom of Association After* Roberts v. United States Jaycees, 82 Mich. L. Rev. 1878 (1984); Seanna Valentine Shiffrin, *What Is Really Wrong with Compelled Association?*, 99 Nw. U. L. Rev. 839 (2005).
2. *The scope of* Roberts. Under the reasoning in *Roberts*, could an organization dedicated to eradicating women from the workplace exclude women, or must it accept women who adhere to that principle? What if the organization was more generally a "male supremacy" organization? Can the National Socialist Movement (a neo-Nazi group) be required to accept minorities and Jews? To what extent, if at all, does the focus in *Roberts* on the group's message allow status to be used as a proxy for message?
3. Roberts *and "private" clubs.* After Roberts, the Supreme Court upheld other laws prohibiting discrimination in clubs and organizations. In New York State Club Ass'n, Inc. v. City of New York, 487 U.S. 1 (1988), the Court upheld a New York City human rights ordinance that had the effect of banning discrimination based on race, creed, and sex in any private club that had more than "four hundred members, provide[d] regular meal service and regularly receive[d] payment . . . directly or indirectly from or on behalf of nonmembers for the furtherance of trade or business". According to the Court, such an ordinance does not affect "'in any significant way' the ability of individuals to form associations that will advocate public or private viewpoints. It does not require the clubs 'to abandon or alter' any activities that are protected by the First Amendment. If a club seeks to exclude individuals who do not share the views that the club's members wish to promote, the Law erects no obstacle to this end. Instead, the Law merely prevents an association from using race, sex, and the other specified characteristics as shorthand measures in place of what the city considers to be more legitimate criteria for determining membership." *Id.* at 13.

Boy Scouts of America v. Dale

530 U.S. 640 (2000)

Chief Justice REHNQUIST delivered the opinion of the Court.

Petitioners are the Boy Scouts of America and the Monmouth Council, a division of the Boy Scouts of America (collectively, Boy Scouts). The Boy Scouts is a private, not-for-profit organization engaged in instilling its system of values in young people. The Boy Scouts asserts that homosexual conduct is inconsistent with the values it seeks to instill. Respondent is James Dale, a former Eagle Scout whose adult membership in the Boy Scouts was revoked when the Boy Scouts learned that he is an avowed homosexual and gay rights activist. The New Jersey Supreme Court held that New Jersey's public accommodations law requires that the Boy Scouts readmit Dale. This case presents the question whether applying New Jersey's public accommodations law in this way violates the Boy Scouts' First Amendment right of expressive association. We hold that it does.

I

. . . Dale became a Boy Scout in 1981 and remained a Scout until he turned 18. By all accounts, Dale was an exemplary Scout. In 1988, he achieved the rank of Eagle Scout, one of Scouting's highest honors.

Dale applied for adult membership in the Boy Scouts in 1989. The Boy Scouts approved his application for the position of assistant scoutmaster of Troop 73. Around the same time, Dale left home to attend Rutgers University. After arriving at Rutgers, Dale first acknowledged to himself and others that he is gay. He quickly became involved with, and eventually became the copresident of, the Rutgers University Lesbian/Gay Alliance. In 1990, Dale attended a seminar addressing the psychological and health needs of lesbian and gay teenagers. A newspaper covering the event interviewed Dale about his advocacy of homosexual teenagers' need for gay role models. In early July 1990, the newspaper published the interview and Dale's photograph over a caption identifying him as the copresident of the Lesbian/Gay Alliance.

Later that month, Dale received a letter from Monmouth Council Executive James Kay revoking his adult membership. Dale wrote to Kay requesting the reason for Monmouth Council's decision. Kay responded by letter that the Boy Scouts "specifically forbid membership to homosexuals."

In 1992, Dale filed a complaint against the Boy Scouts in the New Jersey Superior Court. The complaint alleged that the Boy Scouts had violated New Jersey's public accommodations statute and its common law by revoking Dale's membership based solely on his sexual orientation. New Jersey's public accommodations statute prohibits, among other things, discrimination on the basis of sexual orientation in places of public accommodation.

The New Jersey Superior Court's Chancery Division granted summary judgment in favor of the Boy Scouts. . . . The New Jersey Superior Court's Appellate Division . . . reversed and . . . rejected the Boy Scouts' federal constitutional claims. The New Jersey Supreme Court affirmed the judgment of the Appellate Division. . . .

II

The forced inclusion of an unwanted person in a group infringes the group's freedom of expressive association if the presence of that person affects in a significant way the group's ability to advocate public or private viewpoints. New York State Club Assn., Inc. v. City of New York, 487 U.S. 1, 13 (1988). But the freedom of expressive association, like many freedoms, is not absolute. We have held that the freedom could be overridden "by regulations adopted to serve compelling state interests, unrelated to the suppression of ideas, that cannot be achieved through means significantly less restrictive of associational freedoms." Roberts v. United States Jaycees, 468 U.S. 609 (1984).

To determine whether a group is protected by the First Amendment's expressive associational right, we must determine whether the group engages in "expressive association." The First Amendment's protection of expressive association is not reserved for advocacy groups. But to come within its ambit, a group must engage in some form of expression, whether it be public or private. . . .

The Boy Scouts is a private, nonprofit organization. According to its mission statement:

> It is the mission of the Boy Scouts of America to serve others by helping to instill values in young people and, in other ways, to prepare them to make ethical choices over their lifetime in achieving their full potential.
>
> The values we strive to instill are based on those found in the Scout Oath and Law:
>
> **Scout Oath**
>
> On my honor I will do my best
> To do my duty to God and my country
> and to obey the Scout Law;
> To help other people at all times;
> To keep myself physically strong,
> mentally awake, and morally straight.
>
> **Scout Law**
>
> A Scout is: Trustworthy, Obedient, Loyal, Cheerful, Helpful, Thrifty, Friendly, Brave, Courteous, Clean, Kind, Reverent.

Thus, the general mission of the Boy Scouts is clear: "[T]o instill values in young people." The Boy Scouts seeks to instill these values by having its adult leaders spend time with the youth members, instructing and engaging them in activities like camping, archery, and fishing. During the time spent with the youth members, the scoutmasters and assistant scoutmasters inculcate them with the Boy Scouts' values—both expressly and by example. It seems indisputable that an association that seeks to transmit such a system of values engages in expressive activity. . . .

Given that the Boy Scouts engages in expressive activity, we must determine whether the forced inclusion of Dale as an assistant scoutmaster would significantly affect the Boy Scouts' ability to advocate public or private viewpoints. This inquiry necessarily requires us first to explore, to a limited extent, the nature of the Boy Scouts' view of homosexuality. . . .

The Boy Scouts explains that the Scout Oath and Law provide "a positive moral code for living; they are a list of 'do's' rather than 'don'ts.'" The Boy Scouts asserts that homosexual conduct is inconsistent with the values embodied in the Scout Oath and Law, particularly with the values represented by the terms "morally straight" and "clean."

Obviously, the Scout Oath and Law do not expressly mention sexuality or sexual orientation. And the terms "morally straight" and "clean" are by no means self-defining. Different people would attribute to those terms very different meanings. . . .

The New Jersey Supreme Court analyzed the Boy Scouts' beliefs and found that the "exclusion of members solely on the basis of their sexual orientation is inconsistent with Boy Scouts' commitment to a diverse and 'representative' membership . . . [and] contradicts Boy Scouts' overarching objective to reach 'all eligible youth.'" The court concluded that the exclusion of members like Dale "appears antithetical to the organization's goals and philosophy." But our cases reject this sort of inquiry; it is not the role of the courts to reject a group's expressed values because they disagree with those values or find them internally inconsistent.

The Boy Scouts asserts that it "teach[es] that homosexual conduct is not morally straight," and that it does "not want to promote homosexual conduct as a legitimate form of behavior." We accept the Boy Scouts' assertion. We need not inquire further to determine the nature of the Boy Scouts' expression with respect to homosexuality. But because the record before us contains written evidence of the Boy Scouts' viewpoint, we look to it as instructive, if only on the question of the sincerity of the professed beliefs.

A 1978 position statement to the Boy Scouts' Executive Committee, signed by Downing B. Jenks, the President of the Boy Scouts, and Harvey L. Price, the Chief Scout Executive, expresses the Boy Scouts' "official position" with regard to "homosexuality and Scouting:"

> **Q:** May an individual who openly declares himself to be a homosexual be a volunteer Scout leader?
>
> **A:** No. The Boy Scouts of America is a private, membership organization and leadership therein is a privilege and not a right. We do not believe that homosexuality and leadership in Scouting are appropriate. We will continue to select only those who in our judgment meet our standards and qualifications for leadership.

Thus, at least as of 1978—the year James Dale entered Scouting—the official position of the Boy Scouts was that avowed homosexuals were not to be Scout leaders.

A position statement promulgated by the Boy Scouts in 1991 (after Dale's membership was revoked but before this litigation was filed) also supports its current view:

> We believe that homosexual conduct is inconsistent with the requirement in the Scout Oath that a Scout be morally straight and in the Scout Law that a Scout be clean in word and deed, and that homosexuals do not provide a desirable role model for Scouts.

This position statement was redrafted numerous times but its core message remained consistent, [including in a 1993 position statement.] . . .

The Boy Scouts publicly expressed its views with respect to homosexual conduct by its assertions in prior litigation. For example, throughout a California case with similar facts filed in the early 1980's, the Boy Scouts consistently asserted the same position with respect to homosexuality that it asserts today. We cannot doubt that the Boy Scouts sincerely holds this view.

We must then determine whether Dale's presence as an assistant scoutmaster would significantly burden the Boy Scouts' desire to not "promote homosexual conduct as a legitimate form of behavior." As we give deference to an association's assertions regarding the nature of its expression, we must also give deference to an association's view of what would impair its expression. That is not to say that an expressive association can erect a shield against antidiscrimination laws simply by asserting that mere acceptance of a member from a particular group would impair its message. But here Dale, by his own admission, is one of a group of gay Scouts who have "become leaders in their community and are open and honest about their sexual orientation." Dale was the copresident of a gay and lesbian organization at college and remains a gay rights activist. Dale's presence in the Boy Scouts would, at the very least, force the organization to send a message, both to the youth members and the world, that the Boy Scouts accepts homosexual conduct as a legitimate form of behavior.

Hurley is illustrative on this point. [In *Hurley*, we] . . . noted that the parade organizers did not wish to exclude the GLIB members because of their sexual orientations, but because they wanted to march behind a GLIB banner. . . .

As the presence of GLIB in Boston's St. Patrick's Day parade would have interfered with the parade organizers' choice not to propound a particular point of view, the presence of Dale as an assistant scoutmaster would just as surely interfere with the Boy Scouts' choice not to propound a point of view contrary to its beliefs.

The New Jersey Supreme Court determined that the Boy Scouts' ability to disseminate its message was not significantly affected by the forced inclusion of Dale as an assistant scoutmaster because of the following findings:

> Boy Scout members do not associate for the purpose of disseminating the belief that homosexuality is immoral; Boy Scouts discourages its leaders from disseminating any views on sexual issues; and Boy Scouts includes sponsors and members who subscribe to different views in respect of homosexuality.

We disagree with the New Jersey Supreme Court's conclusion drawn from these findings.

First, associations do not have to associate for the "purpose" of disseminating a certain message in order to be entitled to the protections of the First Amendment. An association must merely engage in expressive activity that could be impaired in order to be entitled to protection. . . .

Second, even if the Boy Scouts discourages Scout leaders from disseminating views on sexual issues—a fact that the Boy Scouts disputes with contrary evidence—the First Amendment protects the Boy Scouts' method of expression. If the Boy Scouts wishes Scout leaders to avoid questions of sexuality and teach only by example, this fact does not negate the sincerity of its belief discussed above.

Third, the First Amendment simply does not require that every member of a group agree on every issue in order for the group's policy to be "expressive association." The Boy Scouts takes an official position with respect to homosexual conduct, and that is sufficient for First Amendment purposes. . . .

Having determined that the Boy Scouts is an expressive association and that the forced inclusion of Dale would significantly affect its expression, we inquire whether the application of New Jersey's public accommodations law to require that the Boy Scouts accept Dale as an assistant scoutmaster runs afoul of the Scouts' freedom of expressive association. We conclude that it does.

State public accommodations laws were originally enacted to prevent discrimination in traditional places of public accommodation—like inns and trains. Over time, the public accommodations laws have expanded to cover more places. New Jersey's statutory definition of "'[a] place of public accommodation'" is extremely broad. . . . In this case, the New Jersey Supreme Court . . . applied its public accommodations law to a private entity without even attempting to tie the term "place" to a physical location. As the definition of "public accommodation" has expanded from clearly commercial entities, such as restaurants, bars, and hotels, to membership organizations such as the Boy Scouts, the potential for conflict between state public accommodations laws and the First Amendment rights of organizations has increased.

We recognized in [*Roberts*] that States have a compelling interest in eliminating discrimination against women in public accommodations. But . . . we went on to conclude that the enforcement of these statutes would not materially interfere with the ideas that the organization sought to express. In *Roberts*, we said "[i]ndeed, the Jaycees has failed to demonstrate . . . any serious burden on the male members' freedom of expressive association." . . .

Dale contends that we should apply the intermediate standard of review enunciated in United States v. O'Brien, 391 U.S. 367 (1968), to evaluate the competing interests. There the Court enunciated a four-part test for review of a governmental regulation that has only an incidental effect on protected speech—in that case the symbolic burning of a draft card. A law prohibiting the destruction of draft cards only incidentally affects the free speech rights of those who happen to use a violation of that law as a symbol of protest. But New Jersey's public accommodations law directly and immediately affects associational rights, in this case associational rights that enjoy First Amendment protection. Thus, *O'Brien* is inapplicable.

In *Hurley*, we applied traditional First Amendment analysis to hold that the application of the Massachusetts public accommodations law to a parade violated the First Amendment rights of the parade organizers. Although we did not explicitly deem the parade in *Hurley* an expressive association, the analysis we applied there is similar to the analysis we apply here. We have already concluded that a state requirement that the Boy Scouts retain Dale as an assistant scoutmaster would significantly burden the organization's right to oppose or disfavor homosexual conduct. The state interests embodied in New Jersey's public accommodations law do not justify such a severe intrusion on the Boy Scouts' rights to freedom of expressive association. That being the case, we hold that the First Amendment prohibits the State from imposing such a requirement through the application of its public accommodations law.[4] . . .

---

4. We anticipated this result in *Hurley* when we illustrated the reasons for our holding in that case by likening the parade to a private membership organization. We stated: "Assuming the parade to be large enough and a source of benefits (apart from its expression) that would generally justify a mandated access provision, GLIB could nonetheless be refused admission as an expressive contingent with its own message just as readily as a private club could exclude an applicant whose manifest views were at odds with a position taken by the club's existing members." 515 U.S. at 580-81.

We are not, as we must not be, guided by our views of whether the Boy Scouts' teachings with respect to homosexual conduct are right or wrong; public or judicial disapproval of a tenet of an organization's expression does not justify the State's effort to compel the organization to accept members where such acceptance would derogate from the organization's expressive message. "While the law is free to promote all sorts of conduct in place of harmful behavior, it is not free to interfere with speech for no better reason than promoting an approved message or discouraging a disfavored one, however enlightened either purpose may strike the government." *Hurley.*

The judgment of the New Jersey Supreme Court is reversed, and the case is remanded for further proceedings not inconsistent with this opinion.

It is so ordered.

Justice STEVENS, with whom Justice SOUTER, Justice GINSBURG, and Justice BREYER join, dissenting. . . .

I

BSA's mission statement reads as follows: "It is the mission of the Boy Scouts of America to serve others by helping to instill values in young people and, in other ways, to prepare them to make ethical choices over their lifetime in achieving their full potential." Its federal charter declares its purpose is "to promote, through organization, and cooperation with other agencies, the ability of boys to do things for themselves and others, to train them in scoutcraft, and to teach them patriotism, courage, self-reliance, and kindred values, using the methods which were in common use by Boy Scouts on June 15, 1916." . . . In particular, the group emphasizes that "[n]either the charter nor the bylaws of the Boy Scouts of America permits the exclusion of any boy. . . .To meet these responsibilities we have made a commitment that our membership shall be representative of *all* the population in every community, district, and council." . . .

To bolster its claim that its shared goals include teaching that homosexuality is wrong, BSA directs our attention to two terms appearing in the Scout Oath and Law. The first is the phrase "morally straight," which appears in the Oath[.] [T]he second term is the word "clean," which appears in a list of 12 characteristics together constituting the Scout Law.

The Boy Scout Handbook defines "morally straight," as such:

> To be a person of strong character, guide your life with honesty, purity, and justice. Respect and defend the rights of all people. Your relationships with others should be honest and open. Be clean in your speech and actions, and faithful in your religious beliefs. The values you follow as a Scout will help you become virtuous and self-reliant.

. . . As for the term "clean," the Boy Scout Handbook offers the following:

> A Scout is CLEAN. *A Scout keeps his body and mind fit and clean. He chooses the company of those who live by these same ideals. He helps keep his home and community clean.*
>
> You never need to be ashamed of dirt that will wash off. . . .
>
> There's another kind of dirt that won't come off by washing. It is the kind that shows up in foul language and harmful thoughts.

> Swear words, profanity, and dirty stories are weapons that ridicule other people and hurt their feelings. The same is true of racial slurs and jokes making fun of ethnic groups or people with physical or mental limitations. A Scout knows there is no kindness or honor in such mean-spirited behavior. He avoids it in his own words and deeds. He defends those who are targets of insults. . . .

It is plain as the light of day that neither one of these principles—"morally straight" and "clean"—says the slightest thing about homosexuality. Indeed, neither term in the Boy Scouts' Law and Oath expresses any position whatsoever on sexual matters. . . .

More specifically, BSA has set forth a number of rules for Scoutmasters when these types of issues come up:

> You may have boys asking you for information or advice about sexual matters. . . .
>
> How should you handle such matters?
>
> Rule number 1: *You do not undertake to instruct Scouts, in any formalized manner, in the subject of sex and family life. The reasons are that it is not construed to be Scouting's proper area,* and that you are probably not well qualified to do this. . . .

In light of BSA's self-proclaimed ecumenism, furthermore, it is even more difficult to discern any shared goals or common moral stance on homosexuality. . . . "The BSA does not define what constitutes duty to God or the practice of religion. This is the responsibility of parents and religious leaders." In fact, many diverse religious organizations sponsor local Boy Scout troops. Because a number of religious groups do not view homosexuality as immoral or wrong and reject discrimination against homosexuals, it is exceedingly difficult to believe that BSA nonetheless adopts a single particular religious or moral philosophy when it comes to sexual orientation. . . .

II

The Court seeks to fill the void by pointing to a statement of "policies and procedures relating to homosexuality and Scouting," signed by BSA's President and Chief Scout Executive in 1978 and addressed to the members of the Executive Committee of the national organization. . . . [A]t most this letter simply adopts an exclusionary membership policy. But simply adopting such a policy has never been considered sufficient, by itself, to prevail on a right to associate claim.

Second, the 1978 policy was never publicly expressed—unlike, for example, the Scout's duty to be "obedient." It was an internal memorandum, never circulated beyond the few members of BSA's Executive Committee. . . . BSA's *public* posture—to the world and to the Scouts themselves—remained what it had always been: one of tolerance, welcoming all classes of boys and young men. . . .

The majority also relies on four other policy statements that were issued between 1991 and 1993. All of them were written and issued *after* BSA revoked Dale's membership. Accordingly, they have little, if any, relevance to the legal question before this Court. . . .

[A]t most the 1991 and 1992 statements declare only that BSA believed "homosexual *conduct* is inconsistent with the requirement in the Scout Oath that a Scout be morally straight and in the Scout Law that a Scout be clean in word and deed." But New Jersey's law prohibits discrimination on the basis of sexual *orientation.* And when Dale was expelled from the Boy Scouts, BSA said it did so because of his sexual orientation, not because of his sexual conduct.[8] . . .

III

[I]n *Jaycees,* we asked whether Minnesota's Human Rights Law requiring the admission of women "impose[d] any *serious burdens*" on the group's "collective effort on behalf of [its] *shared goals.*" Notwithstanding the group's obvious publicly stated exclusionary policy, we did not view the inclusion of women as a "serious burden" on the Jaycees' ability to engage in the protected speech of its choice. . . . The relevant question is whether the mere inclusion of the person at issue would "impose any serious burden," "affect in any significant way," or be "a substantial restraint upon" the organization's "shared goals," "basic goals," or "collective effort to foster beliefs." Accordingly, it is necessary to examine what, exactly, are BSA's shared goals and the degree to which its expressive activities would be burdened, affected, or restrained by including homosexuals.

The evidence before this Court makes it exceptionally clear that BSA has, at most, simply adopted an exclusionary membership policy and has no shared goal of disapproving of homosexuality. . . . In short, Boy Scouts of America is simply silent on homosexuality. There is no shared goal or collective effort to foster a belief about homosexuality at all—let alone one that is significantly burdened by admitting homosexuals. . . .

IV

The majority pretermits this entire analysis. It finds that BSA in fact "'teach[es] that homosexual conduct is not morally straight.'" This conclusion, remarkably, rests entirely on statements in BSA's briefs. Moreover, the majority insists that we must "give deference to an association's assertions regarding the nature of its expression" and "we must also give deference to an association's view of what would impair its expression." So long as the record "contains written evidence" to support a group's bare assertion, "[w]e need not inquire further." . . .

This is an astounding view of the law. . . . [N]othing in our cases calls for this Court to do any such thing. An organization can adopt the message of its choice, and it is not this Court's place to disagree with it. But we must inquire whether the group is, in fact, expressing a message (whatever it may be) and whether that message (if one is expressed) is significantly affected by a State's antidiscrimination law. . . .

---

8. At oral argument, BSA's counsel was asked: "[W]hat if someone is homosexual in the sense of having a sexual orientation in that direction but does not engage in any homosexual conduct?" Counsel answered: "[I]f that person also were to take the view that the reason they didn't engage in that conduct [was because] it would be morally wrong . . . that person would not be excluded."

There is, of course, a valid concern that a court's independent review may run the risk of paying too little heed to an organization's sincerely held views. But unless one is prepared to turn the right to associate into a free pass out of antidiscrimination laws, an independent inquiry is a necessity. . . .

In this case, no such concern is warranted. It is entirely clear that BSA in fact expresses no clear, unequivocal message burdened by New Jersey's law.

V

The majority's argument relies exclusively on *Hurley*. . . . Dale's inclusion in the Boy Scouts is nothing like the case in *Hurley*. His participation sends no cognizable message to the Scouts or to the world. Unlike GLIB, Dale did not carry a banner or a sign; he did not distribute any factsheet; and he expressed no intent to send any message. If there is any kind of message being sent, then, it is by the mere act of joining the Boy Scouts. Such an act does not constitute an instance of symbolic speech under the First Amendment.

It is true, of course, that some acts are so imbued with symbolic meaning that they qualify as "speech" under the First Amendment. *See* United States v. O'Brien, 391 U.S. 367 (1968). At the same time, however, "[w]e cannot accept the view that an apparently limitless variety of conduct can be labeled 'speech' whenever the person engaging in the conduct intends thereby to express an idea." Though participating in the Scouts could itself conceivably send a message on some level, it is not the kind of act that we have recognized as speech. Indeed, if merely joining a group did constitute symbolic speech; and such speech were attributable to the group being joined; and that group has the right to exclude that speech (and hence, the right to exclude that person from joining), then the right of free speech effectively becomes a limitless right to exclude for every organization, whether or not it engages in *any* expressive activities. That cannot be, and never has been, the law.

Furthermore, it is not likely that BSA would be understood to send any message, either to Scouts or to the world, simply by admitting someone as a member. . . . In 1992 over one million adults were active BSA members. The notion that an organization of that size and enormous prestige implicitly endorses the views that each of those adults may express in a non-Scouting context is simply mind boggling. . . .

VI

Unfavorable opinions about homosexuals "have ancient roots." Bowers v. Hardwick, 478 U.S. 186 (1986). Like equally atavistic opinions about certain racial groups, those roots have been nourished by sectarian doctrine. . . .

That such prejudices are still prevalent and that they have caused serious and tangible harm to countless members of the class New Jersey seeks to protect are established matters of fact that neither the Boy Scouts nor the Court disputes. That harm can only be aggravated by the creation of a constitutional shield for a policy that is itself the product of a habitual way of thinking about strangers. . . .

If we would guide by the light of reason, we must let our minds be bold. I respectfully dissent.

[Justice SOUTER's dissenting opinion is omitted.]

NOTES AND QUESTIONS

1. Roberts *and* Dale. Can *Dale* be squared with *Roberts*, or does it essentially change the standard applied in compelled association cases? For discussion, see Dale Carpenter, *Expressive Association and Anti-Discrimination Law After Dale: A Tripartite Approach*, 85 Minn. L. Rev. 1515 (2001).
2. Hurley *and* Dale — *the analogy*. The *Dale* majority relied on *Hurley* to explain why including Dale interfered with the Boy Scouts' message. Is *Hurley* the appropriate comparison case? When does an individual's mere presence or status communicate a message? Does admission of a Black nationalist who favors racial segregation to a group of whites that espouses racial segregation dilute or interfere with the white group's message? Does the communicative impact of a person's status depend in part on whether that status is obvious to the general public or to the recipients of the group's speech? Would *Dale* have come out differently if Dale had promised to keep his sexual orientation private, or does his mere presence as a gay man alter the Scouts' message? In that respect, is *Dale* governed by *Hurley* as the majority asserts? For discussion, see James P. Madigan, *Questioning the Coercive Effect of Self-Identifying Speech*, 87 Iowa L. Rev. 75 (2001).
3. Dale's *implications*. Does *Dale*, if "applied correctly," mean that "Title VII is flatly unconstitutional" because it forces some people to send a message of equality that they oppose? Richard Epstein, *The Constitutional Perils of Moderation: The Case of the Boy Scouts*, 74 S. Cal. L. Rev. 119, 139-140 (2000).
4. *Was there a group message?* After *Hurley* and *Dale*, how discernible must a group's expressive message be to qualify for protection under the Court's approach to freedom of association?
5. *Deference to the association*. How carefully should a court review an organization's claims that it engaged in expression and that compelled admission of a certain person or type of person would alter that expression? Does deferential review give organizations a free pass to ignore antidiscrimination laws? For discussion, see Timothy Zick, *Cross Burning, Cockfighting, and Symbolic Meaning: Toward a First Amendment Ethnography*, 45 Wm. & Mary L. Rev. 2261, 2297-99 (2004).
6. *Compelling interests*. Ultimately, does *Dale* turn on the fact that the majority believes the state has a less compelling interest in eradicating sexual orientation discrimination than discrimination based, for example, on gender? If so, what is the basis for that determination?
7. *Policy change*. In 2015, the Boy Scouts officially ended its ban on gay leaders. *See* Erick Eckholm, *Mormons Assail Boy Scouts' Shift on Gay Leaders*, N.Y. Times, July 28, 2015, at A1. The Scouts have also lifted gender-based restrictions, including exclusion based on transgender status.
8. *The limits of the compelled association right*. A federal law known as the "Solomon Amendment" requires equal access for military recruiting on campus as a condition of universities' receiving federal funds. In Rumsfeld v. Forum for Academic and Institutional Rights (FAIR), 547 U.S. 47 (2006), a group of law faculties objected that unwilling association with military employers, who then discriminated under a "Don't Ask, Don't Tell" policy, violated their right not to associate under *Dale*. The Supreme Court

unanimously rejected the law schools' argument. It distinguished *Dale* on the ground that the Solomon Amendment, unlike the public accommodation law, did not "force law schools to accept members it does not desire." "Recruiters are, by definition, outsiders who come onto campus for the limited purpose of trying to hire students—not to become members of the school's expressive association." Should the Court have accorded greater deference to the law schools' self-identified mission and message in *FAIR*? Didn't the presence of military recruiters on campus significantly dilute the law schools' anti-discrimination message?

THEORY-APPLIED PROBLEM — FALUN GONG IN THE PARK

Falun Gong ("The Practice of the Wheel of Law" in Chinese) is a "traditional Chinese spiritual discipline that includes exercise and meditation." Founded by Mr. Li Hongzhi in 1992, the organization enjoys thousands of members dispersed around the globe. Falun Gong features three main principles ("truth, compassion, and tolerance") and offers its adherents "better health, reduced stress, inner peace, and deepened morals." The organization promotes these benefits in part through the regular conduct of five meditation exercises, usually performed in a public place as part of a group.

Falun Gong has generated a significant following in Jackson, Mississippi. Its members regularly use the local municipal parks to practice the organization's meditation exercises, which, to the uninitiated, look very much like Pilates (a form of exercise focusing on flexibility and muscle strengthening). Pilates are also very popular in Jackson, Mississippi. In fact, the City of Jackson Department of Parks and Recreation ("Department"), which sponsors Pilates classes in the evening at the main city recreational center, has found that demand for its classes far exceeds supply. The Department currently has a yearlong waiting list.

Francine Jenkins, an associate at a large Jackson, Mississippi, law firm attempted to sign up for one of the Department's classes but was told that there was a one-year waiting list for the city-sponsored Pilates program. Driving home from work, Jenkins noticed a group that exercises regularly in her neighborhood park in an area known as "The Meadow." The Department permits the reservation of "The Meadow" for group activities, including rallies, picnics, and concerts. Falun Gong reserves the Meadow on Wednesday evenings, from 7 P.M. to 8 P.M. for its meditation exercises. Jenkins, unable to join the city recreation center's Pilates program, decided to join the Falun Gong group on Wednesdays. She was told, politely, but firmly, that she could not participate in the meditation exercises unless she became a member of Falun Gong. (These exercises are an integral aspect of Falun Gong's belief system as they promote its three main principles—"truth, compassion, and tolerance.") Jenkins refused because she did not subscribe to the group's beliefs. Wanting to participate in the exercises, which she thought looked interesting, Jenkins asked again if she could participate in the group's exercise period. The local chapter's leader again declined her request.

The City of Jackson enacted a comprehensive human rights ordinance in 2015 that prohibits discrimination based on "race, sex, national origin, ethnicity, religion, veteran's status, and sexual orientation" in "any place of public accommodation."

The Mississippi Supreme Court has authoritatively construed the phrase "place of public accommodation" to include both physical places and organizations that generally solicit members from the public. Jenkins, irked at being excluded from yet another exercise class, filed a complaint with the City of Jackson Civil Rights Commission, alleging a violation of the nondiscrimination ordinance. The local chapter of Falun Gong asked the Commission to dismiss the complaint. The chapter claims that all adherents of Falun Gong are welcome to participate in the group exercises but that nonmembers who reject Falun Gong's teachings are not welcome. The chapter further asserts that Jenkins expressed interest only in the exercises and not in the organization's overall spiritual message. According to the chapter, such an attitude makes it quite impossible for the organization to welcome Jenkins to their devotions.

May the Civil Rights Commission rule in favor of Jenkins without violating the First Amendment?

Chapter 7

Commercial Speech

Table of Contents

A. The Historical Approach

B. The New Understanding

C. Limitations on the Ability of Government to Regulate Commercial Speech Because of Its Commercial Nature

1. The Rule Prohibiting Discrimination Against Commercial Speech as Such
2. *Discovery Network* Applied?: Offensive Trademarks and Off-Label Rx Drug Marketing

D. The Problem of Defining Commercial Speech

To what extent should advertising enjoy serious First Amendment protection as "speech"? Before answering this question, consider the fact that prior to the 1970s, the Supreme Court routinely rejected efforts to extend free speech protection to commercial solicitations or advertisements, instead amalgamating such materials with commerce itself. For an example of this, see Railway Express Agency, Inc. v. New York City, 336 U.S. 106 (1949) (excerpted below in Section A). Indeed, Railway Express did not even attempt to litigate a First Amendment claim, resting its challenge to a ban on certain commercial advertising on the doctrine of substantive due process, on the Equal Protection Clause, and on the Interstate Commerce Clause. Thus, as late as 1949, the idea that advertising enjoys any protection as "speech" was utterly implausible—indeed, it was more plausible to raise a dormant Commerce Clause preemption argument against New York City's panel truck advertising ban!

The Supreme Court began to move away from its position that advertising does not have any free speech value (and hence protection) in the 1970s. The first major case involved advertising of a service that itself enjoyed serious constitutional protection: abortion. *See* Bigelow v. Virginia, 421 U.S. 809 (1975) (discussed below in Section B). Because a targeted advertising ban against promotion of abortion services could be seen as a burden on the underlying substantive liberty (the due process liberty interest in terminating a pregnancy), it was not clear if the speech would have enjoyed protection if the subject matter were more mundane (for example, the sale of groceries). By the early 1980s, however, it was clear that the Supreme Court had experienced a change of heart; commercial advertising no longer existed outside the protection of the Free Speech Clause.

One of the most protective lines of the Supreme Court's commercial speech jurisprudence prohibits the regulation of commercial speech when direct regulations would be equally effective at advancing the government's purpose. Thus, even if the government could ban the sale of alcohol, it cannot regulate the advertising of alcohol as a means of discouraging consumption. Similarly, regulation of commercial speech cannot be more burdensome than the regulation of noncommercial speech, unless commercial speech as a class causes the particular social problem to be remedied. In fact, the Supreme Court's protection of commercial speech seemed even more aggressive—at least in the 1980s and 1990s—than its willingness to protect noncommercial speech in public forums. This expansionary trend has been accelerating over time, with the Supreme Court deploying the First Amendment, and the commercial speech doctrine, to invalidate an ever-broader array of business regulations (for example, a state law ban on merchants advertising surcharges for credit card use).

This chapter begins by considering the historical exclusion of commercial speech from free speech protections and the Supreme Court's subsequent change of heart. It considers the special rules that limit government burdens on commercial speech. Finally, the chapter examines the problem of defining "commercial" speech. For a concept of such sweeping importance to First Amendment law, the Supreme Court has not been particularly helpful in defining precisely what makes speech "commercial" rather than "noncommercial."

A. *THE HISTORICAL APPROACH*

Valentine represents the classic pre-1970s statement on the exclusion of commercial speech from serious First Amendment protection. *Railway Express* is illustrative of how the legal community generally accepted the complete exclusion of advertising from the free speech project.

Valentine v. Chrestensen

316 U.S. 52 (1942)

Mr. Justice Roberts delivered the opinion of the Court.

The respondent, a citizen of Florida, owns a former United States Navy submarine which he exhibits for profit. In 1940 he brought it to New York City and moored it at a State pier in the East River. He prepared and printed a handbill advertising the boat and soliciting visitors for a stated admission fee. On his attempting to distribute the bill in the city streets, he was advised by the petitioner, as Police Commissioner, that this activity would violate § 318 of the Sanitary Code, which forbids distribution in the streets of commercial and business advertising matter, but was told that he might freely distribute handbills solely devoted to "information or a public protest."

Respondent thereupon prepared and showed to the petitioner, in proof form, a double-faced handbill. On one side was a revision of the original, altered by the removal of the statement as to admission fee but consisting only of commercial advertising. On the other side was a protest against the action of the City Dock Department in refusing the respondent wharfage facilities at a city pier for the exhibition of his submarine, but no commercial advertising. The Police Department advised that distribution of a bill containing only the protest would not violate § 318, and would not be restrained, but that distribution of the double-faced bill was prohibited. The respondent, nevertheless, proceeded with the printing of his proposed bill and started to distribute it. He was restrained by the police.

Respondent then brought this suit to enjoin the petitioner from interfering with the distribution. [The district court ruled in favor of Chrestensen, and the Second Circuit affirmed.]

The question is whether the application of the ordinance to the respondent's activity was, in the circumstances, an unconstitutional abridgement of the freedom of the press and of speech.

1. This court has unequivocally held that the streets are proper places for the exercise of the freedom of communicating information and disseminating opinion and that, though the states and municipalities may appropriately regulate the privilege in the public interest, they may not unduly burden or proscribe its employment in these public thoroughfares. We are equally clear that the Constitution imposes no such restraint on government as respects purely commercial advertising. Whether, and to what extent, one may promote or pursue a gainful occupation in the streets, to what extent such activity shall be adjudged a derogation of the public right of user [*sic*], are matters for legislative judgment. The question is not whether the legislative body may interfere with the harmless pursuit of a lawful business, but whether it must permit such pursuit by what it deems an undesirable invasion of, or interference with, the full and free use of the highways by the people in fulfillment of the public use to which streets are dedicated. If the respondent was attempting to use the streets of New York by distributing commercial advertising, the prohibition of the code provision was lawfully invoked against his conduct.

2. The respondent contends that, in truth, he was engaged in the dissemination of matter proper for public information, none the less so because there was inextricably attached to the medium of such dissemination commercial advertising matter. The court below appears to have taken this view, since it adverts to the difficulty of apportioning, in a given case, the contents of the communication as between what is of public interest and what is for private profit. We need not indulge nice appraisal based upon subtle distinctions in the present instance nor assume possible cases not now presented. It is enough for the present purpose that the stipulated facts justify the conclusion that the affixing of the protest against official conduct to the advertising circular was with the intent, and for the purpose, of evading the prohibition of the ordinance. If that evasion was successful, every merchant who desires to broadcast advertising leaflets in the streets need only append a civic appeal, or a moral platitude, to achieve immunity from the law's command.

The decree is

Reversed.

Railway Express Agency, Inc. v. New York

336 U.S. 106 (1949)

Mr. Justice DOUGLAS delivered the opinion of the Court.

Section 124 of the Traffic Regulations of the City of New York promulgated by the Police Commissioner provides:

> "No person shall operate, or cause to be operated, in or upon any street an advertising vehicle; provided that nothing herein contained shall prevent the putting of business notices upon business delivery vehicles, so long as such vehicles are engaged in the usual business or regular work of the owner and not used merely or mainly for advertising."

Appellant is engaged in a nation-wide express business. It operates about 1,900 trucks in New York City and sells the space on the exterior sides of these trucks for advertising. That advertising is for the most part unconnected with its own business. It was convicted in the magistrate's court and fined. The judgment of conviction was sustained in the Court of Special Sessions. The Court of Appeals affirmed without opinion by a divided vote. The case is here on appeal. . . .

The Court of Special Sessions concluded that advertising on vehicles using the streets of New York City constitutes a distraction to vehicle drivers and to pedestrians alike and therefore affects the safety of the public in the use of the streets. We do not sit to weigh evidence on the due process issue in order to determine whether the regulation is sound or appropriate; nor is it our function to pass judgment on its wisdom. See Olsen v. Nebraska, 313 U.S. 236. We would be trespassing on one of the most intensely local and specialized of all municipal problems if we held that this regulation had no relation to the traffic problem of New York City. It is the judgment of the local authorities that it does have such a relation. And nothing has been advanced which shows that to be palpably false.

The question of equal protection of the laws is pressed more strenuously on us. . . . [The court rejected the Equal Protection Clause argument.]

It is finally contended that the regulation is a burden on interstate commerce in violation of Art. I, § 8 of the Constitution. Many of these trucks are engaged in delivering goods in interstate commerce from New Jersey to New York. Where traffic control and the use of highways are involved and where there is no conflicting federal regulation, great leeway is allowed local authorities, even though the local regulation materially interferes with interstate commerce.

Affirmed.

NOTES AND QUESTIONS

1. *Commercial or noncommercial speech?* Was Chrestensen engaged in commercial or noncommercial speech? His revised leaflets included a complaint and remonstrance against the City Dock Department for refusing to rent him wharfage facilities for his submarine. If a commercial message is joined to a noncommercial message, should the speech be deemed "commercial"? Is Justice Roberts correct to assume that any other approach would effectively end regulation of commercial speech?

2. *The absence of a First Amendment claim.* Why did Railway Express not challenge a flat ban on speech? The New York City ordinance had the effect of prohibiting all speech on panel trucks, unless the speech related to the owner's business. The law was little different than a ban on political buttons or yard signs, in that it foreclosed the use of private property for speech. Does this suggest that the exclusion of commercial speech was deeply ingrained in the 1940s?
3. *Entertainment as commerce rather than speech.* In the early twentieth century, the Supreme Court emphatically rejected the contention that motion pictures, as well as "the theatre, the circus, and all other shows and spectacles, and their performances" enjoy *any* First Amendment protection. Mutual Film Corp. v. Industrial Comm'n, 236 U.S. 230, 243 (1915). Writing for a unanimous Supreme Court, Justice McKenna explained that "[w]e immediately feel that the argument is wrong or strained which extends the guaranties of free opinion and speech to the multitudinous shows which are advertised on the bill-boards of our cities and towns . . . and which seeks to bring motion pictures and other spectacles into practical and legal similitude to a free press and liberty of opinion." *Id.* at 243-244. "The judicial sense supporting the common sense of the country is against the contention." *Id.* at 244. Thus, not only commercial speech, but also motion pictures, theater performances, and other public "spectacles" fell outside "the freedom of speech" safeguarded by the First Amendment. The profit-seeking motive of theater operators plainly informed the Supreme Court's decision to deny First Amendment protection to motion picture exhibitors: "It cannot be put out of view that the exhibition of moving pictures is a business pure and simple, originated and conducted for profit, like other spectacles, not to be regarded, nor intended to be regarded by the Ohio constitution, we think, as part of the press of the country or as organs of public opinion." *Id. Mutual Film Corp.* thus incorporates and reflects the *Valentine* view that speech associated with commercial activity has no claim on the First Amendment.
4. *Commercial speech as ordinary commerce.* Until the 1970s, the Supreme Court's view was that advertising was not "speech" but rather an aspect of "commerce." After its repudiation of the *Lochner* doctrine, see Lochner v. New York, 198 U.S. 45 (1908), the Supreme Court generally sustained any regulation of commerce that, at least in theory, possessed a rational relationship to a legitimate state interest. Accordingly, during this period any regulation of commercial speech was constitutional if it had any possible rational basis (whether real or merely theoretical). In light of this, raising a free speech objection to the New York City ordinance regulating ads on panel trucks would have been utterly futile.

B. THE NEW UNDERSTANDING

In 1975, the Supreme Court took a major step away from its traditional view that advertising had no call on free speech protections. By 1980, the turn was complete and the Supreme Court had declared advertising and other forms of commercial speech to be protected speech activity. The Court never really fashioned a compelling rationale for this change of policy, other than the law and economics rationale that some listeners valued advertising as much or more than other forms of speech (whether political, artistic, literary, or scientific). The Court seemed to be taking the view that it had no business establishing consumer preferences in the marketplace of ideas, and that categorically excluding commercial speech from protection could not be justified by the "low value" of such speech activity.

The Supreme Court did suggest that the transfer of information, regardless of its content, from a willing speaker to a willing listener fell within the scope of the Free Speech Clause. In other words, if speakers and listeners acted as if commercial speech has social value, then such speech must have social value. The Justices never attempted to ground their commercial speech doctrine in the original understanding of the Free Speech Clause (that is, did Madison think commercial speech enjoyed First Amendment protection?), perhaps because such an argument was untenable in light of consistent holdings over time that amalgamated commercial speech with commerce itself. Nor did they embrace a marketplace conception of the value of speech in other areas, such as sexually explicit speech, where consumers of speech might prefer modes of speech deemed offensive or harmful to the general community.

AN EXTENDED NOTE ON THE ORIGINS OF FIRST AMENDMENT PROTECTION FOR COMMERCIAL SPEECH

The first Supreme Court case to afford significant constitutional protection was Bigelow v. Virginia, 421 U.S. 809 (1975). *Bigelow* involved a criminal conviction "for a violation of a Virginia statute that made it a misdemeanor, by the sale or circulation of any publication, to encourage or prompt the procuring of an abortion." *Id.* at 811. Bigelow's newspaper, the *Virginia Weekly*, in its February 8, 1971 issue, published an advertisement for the Women's Pavilion, a New York City reproductive health services clinic that provided abortion services (keep in mind that this was two years before *Roe*). Bigelow was subsequently charged and convicted of violating Va. Code Ann. § 18.1-63 (1960), a state law that prohibited publication of any materials that could "encourage or prompt the procuring of abortion." By a 4–2 vote, the Virginia Supreme Court affirmed Bigelow's conviction notwithstanding his argument that the First Amendment protected the newspaper's decision to publish the Woman's Pavilion's advertisement.

The Supreme Court, in an opinion by Justice Blackmun, reversed Bigelow's conviction. Blackmun explained that:

> The central assumption made by the Supreme Court of Virginia was that the First Amendment guarantees of speech and press are inapplicable to paid commercial advertisements. Our cases, however, clearly establish that speech is not stripped of First Amendment protection merely because it appears in that form.
>
> The fact that the particular advertisement in appellant's newspaper had commercial aspects or reflected the advertiser's commercial interests did not negate all First Amendment guarantees. The State was not free of constitutional restraint merely because the advertisement involved sales or "solicitations," or because appellant was paid for printing it, or because appellant's motive or the motive of the advertiser may have involved

> financial gain. The existence of "commercial activity, in itself, is no justification for narrowing the protection of expression secured by the First Amendment." *Ginzburg v. United States,* 383 U.S. 463, 474 (1966).

Id. at .818.

Unfortunately, however, *Bigelow* held the advertisement to be protected speech without actually providing a governing standard of review for regulations of commercial speech. Justice Blackmun explained that "the Virginia courts erred in their assumptions that advertising, as such, was entitled to no First Amendment protection and that appellant Bigelow had no legitimate First Amendment interest," *id.* at 825, but the Court did "not decide in this case the precise extent to which the First Amendment permits regulation of advertising that is related to activities the State may legitimately regulate or even prohibit." *Id.* Because the underlying activity being advertised, reproductive health care, relates to a fundamental right, it was unclear whether *all* commercial advertising enjoys significant First Amendment protection or only advertising related to fundamental rights enjoys such protection.

The Supreme Court's next commercial speech case, Virginia State Board of Pharmacy v. Virginia Citizens Consumer Council, Inc., 425 U.S. 728 (1976), did little to clarify matters. A Virginia state statute, Va. Code Ann. § 54-524.35 (1974), prohibited a pharmacist from "publish[ing], advertis[ing] or promot[ing], directly or indirectly, in any manner whatsoever, any amount, price, fee, premium, discount, rebate or credit terms . . . for any drugs which may be dispensed only by prescription." A three judge district court, based on "[t]he strength of the interest in the free flow of drug price information," held "the quoted portion of the statute 'void and of no effect' and enjoined the defendant-appellants, the Virginia State Board of Pharmacy and the individual members of that Board, from enforcing it." *Id.* at 750.

Once again writing for the majority, Justice Blackmun affirmed the lower court's decision invalidating the Virginia law on First Amendment grounds. He explained that "[f]reedom of speech presupposes a willing speaker" but the First Amendment's protection runs to "its source and to its recipients both." *Id.* at 756. Thus, "[i]f there is a right to advertise, there is a reciprocal right to receive the advertising, and it may be asserted by these appellees." *Id.* at 757. This clearly established that the Free Speech Clause conveys significant protection on commercial advertising.

Virginia State Board of Pharmacy embraces an audience autonomy theory of the First Amendment. Reasoning from the premise that would-be readers, not the government, get to decide how to value speech, Justice Blackmun observes that "[a]s to the particular consumer's interest in the free flow of commercial information, that interest may be as keen, if not keener by far, than his interest in the day's most urgent political debate." *Id.* at 763. In other words, readers, listeners, and viewers can determine for themselves whether or not speech merits their attention. Blackmun adds that "society also may have a strong interest in the free flow of commercial information" because advertising commonly contains information "of general public interest." *Id.* at 764.

Unfortunately, however, the majority once again failed to provide a general constitutional standard of review for government restrictions on commercial speech. Justice Blackmun merely notes that the Court "do[es] not hold that it [commercial speech] can never be regulated in any way" and "[s]ome forms of commercial speech regulation are surely permissible." *Id.* at 770. Among his examples of permissible forms of commercial speech regulation are prohibitions on false and misleading advertisements and bans on advertisements for unlawful goods or services. *See id.* at 771-73. Even if some restrictions on commercial speech can be reconciled with the First Amendment's Free Speech Clause, a state government may not seek to "completely suppress the dissemination of concededly truthful information about entirely lawful activity, fearful of that information's effect upon its disseminators and its recipients." *Id.* at 773.

It was not until the next principal case, Central Hudson Gas & Electric Corp. v. Public Service Corporation, 447 U.S. 557 (1980), handed down four years later, that a clear majority adopted a general test to determine whether a particular regulation of commercial speech violates the First Amendment.

NOTES AND QUESTIONS

1. *A clear rule: commercial speech enjoys constitutional protection.* In *Bigelow,* it was far from clear whether commercial speech enjoyed significant First Amendment protection or whether commercial speech related to a fundamental right (the liberty interest in terminating a pregnancy) enjoyed significant constitutional protection. *Virginia State Board of Pharmacy* clarifies the meaning and scope of *Bigelow* by establishing that commercial speech has categorical protection under the Free Speech Clause, regardless of the particular good or service being hawked. Thus, unlike *Bigelow, Virginia State Board of Pharmacy* is not ambiguous about the scope of the ruling: *all* commercial speech has some claim on the Free Speech Clause. Even so, many important questions remain to be addressed.
2. *Regulating commercial speech.* First, to what extent, if any, may government regulate commercial speech? Should such regulations be subject to the exact same restrictions applicable to noncommercial speech (such as content-neutral, reasonable time, place, and manner restrictions if the speech takes place on public property)? If not, precisely what rules govern regulations that fall short of a total ban on commercial speech? Moreover, is the subject matter of the speech entirely irrelevant? For example, could advertising about alcohol or tobacco be regulated more aggressively than advertising about laundry detergents? If a product arguably causes significant social harms, should government enjoy a freer hand to attempt to reduce demand for that product by limiting or even proscribing its promotion through mass media advertising?

Central Hudson Gas & Electric Corp. v. Public Service Commission of New York

447 U.S. 557 (1980)

Mr. Justice Powell delivered the opinion of the Court.

This case presents the question whether a regulation of the Public Service Commission of the State of New York violates the First and Fourteenth Amendments because it completely bans promotional advertising by an electrical utility.

In December 1973, the Commission, appellee here, ordered electric utilities in New York State to cease all advertising that "promot[es] the use of electricity." The order was based on the Commission's finding that "the interconnected utility system in New York State does not have sufficient fuel stocks or sources of supply to continue furnishing all customer demands for the 1973-1974 winter."

[After reviewing its policies on advertising in a rulemaking proceeding], the Commission declared all promotional advertising contrary to the national policy of conserving energy. It acknowledged that the ban is not a perfect vehicle for conserving energy. . . . Still, the Commission adopted the restriction because it was deemed likely to "result in some dampening of unnecessary growth" in energy consumption.

Appellant challenged the order in state court, arguing that the Commission had restrained commercial speech in violation of the First and Fourteenth Amendments. The Commission's order was upheld by the trial court and at the intermediate appellate level. The New York Court of Appeals affirmed. . . .

The Commission's order restricts only commercial speech, that is, expression related solely to the economic interests of the speaker and its audience. The First Amendment, as applied to the States through the Fourteenth Amendment, protects commercial speech from unwarranted governmental regulation. Commercial expression not only serves the economic interest of the speaker, but also assists consumers and furthers the societal interest in the fullest possible dissemination of information. In applying the First Amendment to this area, we have rejected the "highly paternalistic" view that government has complete power to suppress or regulate commercial speech. . . .

Nevertheless, our decisions have recognized "the 'common-sense' distinction between speech proposing a commercial transaction, which occurs in an area traditionally subject to government regulation, and other varieties of speech." . . . The Constitution therefore accords a lesser protection to commercial speech than to other constitutionally guaranteed expression. The protection available for particular commercial expression turns on the nature both of the expression and of the governmental interests served by its regulation.

The First Amendment's concern for commercial speech is based on the informational function of advertising. Consequently, there can be no constitutional objection to the suppression of commercial messages that do not accurately inform the public about lawful activity. The government may ban forms of communication more likely to deceive the public than to inform it, or commercial speech related to illegal activity.[6]

---

6. In most other contexts, the First Amendment prohibits regulation based on the content of the message. Two features of commercial speech permit regulation of its content. First, commercial speakers have extensive knowledge of both the market and their products. Thus, they are well situated to evaluate the accuracy of their messages and the lawfulness of the underlying activity. In addition, commercial speech, the offspring of economic self-interest, is a hardy breed of expression that is not "particularly susceptible to being crushed by overbroad regulation."

If the communication is neither misleading nor related to unlawful activity, the government's power is more circumscribed. The State must assert a substantial interest to be achieved by restrictions on commercial speech. Moreover, the regulatory technique must be in proportion to that interest. The limitation on expression must be designed carefully to achieve the State's goal. Compliance with this requirement may be measured by two criteria. First, the restriction must directly advance the state interest involved; the regulation may not be sustained if it provides only ineffective or remote support for the government's purpose. Second, if the governmental interest could be served as well by a more limited restriction on commercial speech, the excessive restrictions cannot survive.

Under the first criterion, the Court has declined to uphold regulations that only indirectly advance the state interest involved. . . .

The second criterion recognizes that the First Amendment mandates that speech restrictions be "narrowly drawn." The regulatory technique may extend only as far as the interest it serves. The State cannot regulate speech that poses no danger to the asserted state interest, nor can it completely suppress information when narrower restrictions on expression would serve its interest as well. . . .

In commercial speech cases, then, a four-part analysis has developed. At the outset, we must determine whether the expression is protected by the First Amendment. For commercial speech to come within that provision, it at least must concern lawful activity and not be misleading. Next, we ask whether the asserted governmental interest is substantial. If both inquiries yield positive answers, we must determine whether the regulation directly advances the governmental interest asserted, and whether it is not more extensive than is necessary to serve that interest.

We now apply this four-step analysis for commercial speech to the Commission's arguments in support of its ban on promotional advertising.

The Commission offers two state interests as justifications for the ban on promotional advertising. The first concerns energy conservation. Any increase in demand for electricity—during peak or off-peak periods—means greater consumption of energy. The Commission argues, and the New York court agreed, that the State's interest in conserving energy is sufficient to support suppression of advertising designed to increase consumption of electricity. In view of our country's dependence on energy resources beyond our control, no one can doubt the importance of energy conservation. Plainly, therefore, the state interest asserted is substantial. . . .

Next, we focus on the relationship between the State's interests and the advertising ban. Under this criterion, the Commission's laudable concern over the equity and efficiency of appellant's rates does not provide a constitutionally adequate reason for restricting protected speech. The link between the advertising prohibition and appellant's rate structure is, at most, tenuous. The impact of promotional advertising on the equity of appellant's rates is highly speculative. Advertising to increase off-peak usage would have to increase peak usage, while other factors that directly affect the fairness and efficiency of appellant's rates remained constant. Such conditional and remote eventualities simply cannot justify silencing appellant's promotional advertising.

In contrast, the State's interest in energy conservation is directly advanced by the Commission order at issue here. There is an immediate connection between advertising and demand for electricity. Central Hudson would not contest the advertising ban unless it believed that promotion would increase its sales. Thus, we find a direct link between the state interest in conservation and the Commission's order.

We come finally to the critical inquiry in this case: whether the Commission's complete suppression of speech ordinarily protected by the First Amendment is no more extensive than necessary to further the State's interest in energy conservation. The Commission's order reaches all promotional advertising, regardless of the impact of the touted service on overall energy use. But the energy conservation rationale, as important as it is, cannot justify suppressing information about electric devices or services that would cause no net increase in total energy use. In addition, no showing has been made that a more limited restriction on the content of promotional advertising would not serve adequately the State's interests. . . .

The Commission's order prevents appellant from promoting electric services that would reduce energy use by diverting demand from less efficient sources, or that would consume roughly the same amount of energy as do alternative sources. In neither situation would the utility's advertising endanger conservation or mislead the public. To the extent that the Commission's order suppresses speech that in no way impairs the State's interest in energy conservation, the Commission's order violates the First and Fourteenth Amendments and must be invalidated.

Accordingly, the judgment of the New York Court of Appeals is

Reversed.

Mr. Justice Blackmun, with whom Mr. Justice Brennan joins, concurring in the judgment.

I agree with the Court that the Public Service Commission's ban on promotional advertising of electricity by public utilities is inconsistent with the First and Fourteenth Amendments. I concur only in the Court's judgment, however, because I believe the test now evolved and applied by the Court is not consistent with our prior cases and does not provide adequate protection for truthful, nonmisleading, noncoercive commercial speech. . . .

I seriously doubt whether suppression of information concerning the availability and price of a legally offered product is ever a permissible way for the State to "dampen" demand for or use of the product. Even though "commercial" speech is involved, such a regulatory measure strikes at the heart of the First Amendment. This is because it is a covert attempt by the State to manipulate the choices of its citizens, not by persuasion or direct regulation, but by depriving the public of the information needed to make a free choice. As the Court recognizes, the State's policy choices are insulated from the visibility and scrutiny that direct regulation would entail and the conduct of citizens is molded by the information that government chooses to give them. . . .

It appears that the Court would permit the State to ban all direct advertising of air conditioning, assuming that a more limited restriction on such advertising would not effectively deter the public from cooling its homes. In my view, our cases do not support this type of suppression. If a governmental unit believes that use or overuse of air conditioning is a serious problem, it must attack that problem directly, by prohibiting air conditioning or regulating thermostat levels. Just as the Commonwealth of Virginia may promote professionalism of pharmacists directly, so too New York may *not* promote energy conservation "by keeping the public in ignorance."

Mr. Justice STEVENS, with whom Mr. Justice BRENNAN joins, concurring in the judgment.

Because "commercial speech" is afforded less constitutional protection than other forms of speech, it is important that the commercial speech concept not be defined too broadly lest speech deserving of greater constitutional protection be inadvertently suppressed. The issue in this case is whether New York's prohibition on the promotion of the use of electricity through advertising is a ban on nothing but commercial speech.

In my judgment one of the two definitions the Court uses in addressing that issue is too broad and the other may be somewhat too narrow. . . .

In sum, I concur in the result because I do not consider this to be a "commercial speech" case.

Mr. Justice REHNQUIST, dissenting.

. . . Given what seems to me full recognition of the holding of *Virginia Pharmacy Board* that commercial speech is entitled to some degree of First Amendment protection, I think the Court is nonetheless incorrect in invalidating the carefully considered state ban on promotional advertising in light of pressing national and state energy needs.

NOTES AND QUESTIONS

1. *The* Central Hudson *test. Central Hudson* adopts a four-part test for determining the constitutionality of a government regulation burdening commercial speech: The speech must relate to a lawful product and must not be false or misleading; if the speech meets this prerequisite, the government must proffer a "substantial" reason for the regulation, the regulation must directly advance the substantial government interest, and the regulation cannot be more extensive than necessary to achieve that interest.
2. *Is commercial speech distinguishable from other kinds of speech?* Why should commercial speech be a dispreferred stepsister of noncommercial speech? Justice Powell suggests, in footnote 6 of *Central Hudson*, that commercial speech can be more highly regulated because "commercial speakers have extensive knowledge of both the market and their products" and accordingly can "evaluate the accuracy of their messages and the lawfulness of the underlying activity." Moreover, he posits that "commercial speech, the offspring of economic self-interest, is a hardy breed of expression" that is not easily squelched. Even if both of these observations are perfectly true, that does not justify second-class status for commercial speech in theoretical terms. If people care more about the Macy's Labor Day Sale than the candidates for city council, should the government be able to suppress one category of speech simply because the government believes political speech is more important? For an argument that commercial speech should receive equal treatment, see Alex Kozinski & Stuart Banner, *Who's Afraid of Commercial Speech?*, 76 VA. L. REV. 627 (1990).

3. *Does the* Central Hudson *test work?* Does Justice Powell's four-part test do a good job of formalizing the test for determining whether regulations of commercial speech are constitutionally permissible? The first prong seems entirely sensible and flows directly from *Virginia State Board of Pharmacy*: To be protected, commercial speech must be truthful and must relate to a lawful good or service. These inquiries are fairly objective as well, making this part of the test relatively easy to apply. What about the last three factors—whether the regulation "directly advances" the government's "substantial" interest in way that "is not more extensive than necessary"? Are these aspects of the test easily applied? Objective?
4. *The substantial government interest prong.* Is it very likely that government would adopt and enforce regulations for a problem that it deems insubstantial? Or that, objectively viewed, is "insubstantial"? As you might predict, this prong does not fence out many commercial speech claims.
5. *The direct advancement prong.* The question of direct advancement is capable of easy manipulation. How perfect does the means/end fit have to be in order to satisfy this prong? A reviewing court does not have to strain very much to find this criterion met—or not. The third prong of the test, accordingly, is a major front in commercial speech battles. Similarly, whether a restriction is "more extensive than necessary" is hardly an objective inquiry. To some extent, the social value of the product being advertised, as perceived by a judge, will prefigure the degree to which a regulation goes too far. Limits on advertising cars, on the one hand, might, on a de facto basis, be harder to sustain than regulations on the sale of alcohol or medical marijuana. If one views the underlying product as lacking social merit, it is unlikely that one will find that a regulation of commercial speech regarding that product "goes too far" in light of the social benefits obtained.
6. *Lawyer advertising restrictions and "false or misleading" commercial speech.* The Supreme Court has rejected challenges to at least some state bar regulations aimed at advancing "professionalism" values and safeguarding the public from abusive or deceptive lawyer marketing practices—for example, state bar rules that flatly prohibit in-person solicitation of clients and certain kinds of deceptive lawyer advertising. *See* Ohralik v. Ohio State Bar Ass'n., 436 U.S. 447, 461-66 (1978) (upholding a ban against in-person lawyer solicitation of potential clients as a constitutionally permissible "prophylactic measure" because of "[t]he substantive evils of solicitation," which include, among other things, "stirring up litigation, assertion of fraudulent claims, debasing the legal profession, and potential harm to the solicited client in the form of overreaching, overcharging, underrepresentation, and misrepresentation"); Bates v. State Bar of Ariz., 433 U.S. 350, 383-84 (1977) (opining in dicta that "advertising claims as to the quality of services . . . are not susceptible of measurement or verification" and "accordingly, such claims may be so likely to be misleading as to warrant restriction"). On the other hand, state bar efforts to promote "professionalism" are not sufficiently weighty to justify flat bans against any and all forms of lawyer advertising. *See* Zauderer v. Office of Disciplinary Counsel, 471 U.S. 626, 647 (1985) ("An attorney may not be

disciplined for soliciting legal business through printed advertising containing truthful and nondeceptive information and advice regarding the legal rights of potential clients."). Advertising restrictions applicable to other licensed professions, such as medicine and accounting, follow the same First Amendment rules. *See, e.g.*, Edenfield v. Fane, 507 U.S. 761, 770-71 (1993) (invalidating on First Amendment grounds a Florida ban against in-person client solicitation by licensed CPAs, holding that "a governmental body seeking to sustain a restriction on commercial speech must demonstrate that the harms it recites are real and that its restriction will in fact alleviate them to a material degree," and cautioning that "mere speculation or conjecture" is not constitutionally sufficient to support a ban on otherwise truthful and non-misleading professional speech). For thoughtful overviews, discussions, and analyses of how the federal courts seek to reconcile First Amendment values with government regulation of the professions (with decidedly mixed results), see Claudia Haupt, *Professional Speech*, 125 YALE L.J. 1238 (2016) and Timothy Zick, *Professional Rights Speech*, 47 ARIZ. ST. L.J. 1289 (2015).

THEORY-APPLIED PROBLEM

The state of Indiana, concerned about the prevalence of teenagers and children using tobacco products unlawfully, enacts a statute that bans "the use or depiction of cartoon or cartoon-like characters in tobacco advertisements, whether in print, over broadcast outlets, on billboards, signs, or on packaging for tobacco products." Violations are punishable with a fine of up to $10,000, with each item bearing a prohibited cartoon or cartoon-like figure constituting an independent violation of the law. The law seeks to prohibit the use of characters, like Joe Camel, who empirical studies show make smoking more appealing to children. Indeed, a study published in the *Journal of the American Medical Association* finds that five- and six-year olds are better able to identify Joe Camel than either Mickey Mouse or Fred Flintstone.

Before the new law's effective date, R.J. Reynolds Corporation, the maker of Camel brand cigarettes, brings suit in federal district court in Indianapolis, Indiana, seeking a declaratory judgment that the new ban on cartoon or cartoon-like characters to promote tobacco products violates the First Amendment and seeking an injunction against its enforcement. At the time, tobacco products are lawful in Indiana but may only be sold to and possessed by persons at least 18 years of age. How should the district court rule?

AN EXTENDED NOTE ON *POSADAS* AND THE USE OF COMMERCIAL SPEECH REGULATIONS IN LIEU OF DIRECT REGULATIONS

In Posadas de Puerto Rico Associates v. Tourism Co., 478 U.S. 328 (1986), the Supreme Court sustained a ban on casino advertising aimed at encouraging local citizens to gamble. Because gambling could be prohibited entirely, Justice Rehnquist reasoned, the Commonwealth of Puerto Rico could take the less burdensome approach of discouraging patronage of casinos by regulating promotional advertising. He explained that

> [a]ppellant also makes the related argument that, having chosen to legalize casino gambling for residents of Puerto Rico, the legislature is prohibited by the First Amendment from using restrictions on advertising to accomplish its goal of reducing demand for such gambling. We disagree. In our view, appellant has the argument backwards. As we noted in the preceding paragraph, it is precisely because the government could have enacted a wholesale prohibition of the underlying conduct that it is permissible for the government to take the less intrusive step of allowing the conduct, but reducing the demand through restrictions on advertising. It would surely be a Pyrrhic victory for casino owners such as appellant to gain recognition of a First Amendment right to advertise their casinos to the residents of Puerto Rico, only to thereby force the legislature into banning casino gambling by residents altogether. It would just as surely be a strange constitutional doctrine which would concede to the legislature the authority to totally ban a product or activity, but deny to the legislature the authority to forbid the stimulation of demand for the product or activity through advertising on behalf of those who would profit from such increased demand. Legislative regulation of products or activities deemed harmful, such as cigarettes, alcoholic beverages, and prostitution, has varied from outright prohibition on the one hand, see, e.g., Cal. Penal Code Ann. § 647(b) (West Supp. 1986) (prohibiting soliciting or engaging in act of prostitution), to legalization of the product or activity with restrictions on stimulation of its demand on the other hand, see, e.g., Nev. Rev. Stat. §§ 244.345(1), (8) (1986) (authorizing licensing of houses of prostitution except in counties with more than 250,000 population), §§ 201.430, 201.440 (prohibiting advertising of houses of prostitution "[in] any public theater, on the public streets of any city or town, or on any public highway," or "in [a] place of business"). To rule out the latter, intermediate kind of response would require more than we find in the First Amendment.

Id. at 346-347.

In dissent, Justice Brennan rejected the "greater includes the lesser" argument, suggesting that a regulation of commercial speech presented First Amendment issues that a ban on casino gambling would not:

> The Court reasons that because Puerto Rico could legitimately decide to prohibit casino gambling entirely, it may also take the "less intrusive step" of legalizing casino gambling but restricting speech. According to the Court, it would "surely be a strange constitutional doctrine which would concede to the legislature the authority to totally ban [casino gambling] but deny to the legislature the authority to forbid the stimulation of demand for [casino gambling]" by banning advertising. I do not agree that a ban on casino advertising is "less intrusive" than an outright prohibition of such activity. A majority of States have chosen not to legalize casino gambling, and we have never suggested that this might be unconstitutional. However, having decided to legalize casino gambling, Puerto Rico's decision to ban truthful speech concerning entirely lawful activity raises serious First Amendment problems. Thus, the "constitutional

> doctrine" which bans Puerto Rico from banning advertisements concerning lawful casino gambling is not so strange a restraint—it is called the First Amendment.

Id. at 354 n.4 (Brennan, J., dissenting).

A decade later, in 44 Liquormart v. Rhode Island, 517 U.S. 484 (1996), a plurality of the Supreme Court squarely rejected the "greater includes the lesser" view that regulations (up to and including targeted bans) of commercial speech could serve as fungible substitutes for direct regulations of conduct. Writing for the plurality, Justice Stevens observed that "[f]urther consideration persuades us that the 'greater-includes-the-lesser' argument should be rejected" because "it is inconsistent with both logic and well-settled doctrine." *Id.* at 511. Justice Stevens explained the Court's reasoning as follows:

> Although we do not dispute the proposition that greater powers include lesser ones, we fail to see how that syllogism requires the conclusion that the State's power to regulate commercial activity is "greater" than its power to ban truthful, nonmisleading commercial speech. Contrary to the assumption made in *Posadas*, we think it quite clear that banning speech may sometimes prove far more intrusive than banning conduct. As a venerable proverb teaches, it may prove more injurious to prevent people from teaching others how to fish than to prevent fish from being sold. Similarly, a local ordinance banning bicycle lessons may curtail freedom far more than one that prohibits bicycle riding within city limits. In short, we reject the assumption that words are necessarily less vital to freedom than actions, or that logic somehow proves that the power to prohibit an activity is necessarily "greater" than the power to suppress speech about it.

Id. Thus, "[t]he text of the First Amendment makes clear that the Constitution presumes that attempts to regulate speech are more dangerous than attempts to regulate conduct." *Id.* at 512. Justice Stevens emphasized that this "presumption accords with the essential role that the free flow of information plays in a democratic society." *Id.* And, "[a]s a result, the First Amendment directs that government may not suppress speech as easily as it may suppress conduct, and that speech restrictions cannot be treated as simply another means that the government may use to achieve its ends." *Id.*

Because Justice Stevens only garnered four votes for his complete rejection of the *Posadas* "greater includes the lesser" reasoning, however, the question remained open as to whether government could regulate commercial speech as a proxy for regulation of the underlying substantive activity. Three years later, in *Greater New Orleans Broadcasting Association* (*infra* p. 329), a majority of the Supreme Court essentially endorsed Justice Stevens's position and rejected the "greater includes the lesser" syllogism.

NOTES AND QUESTIONS

1. *The "lesser" power to regulate commercial speech and* Posadas. If commercial speech is really "low-value" speech and is more robust than other forms of speech, should government be permitted to regulate it in lieu of adopting

direct regulations? Did the *Posadas* approach have a certain logic? As between banning gambling and banning advertising of gambling, isn't the net freedom of citizens enhanced, rather than reduced, by permitting the speech regulations?

2. *Is regulating commercial speech really the same as regulating conduct?* On the other hand, perhaps speech regulations really *are* totally different in kind than direct regulations of behavior. The First Amendment does not require a state government to permit or prohibit commercial gambling, but it does limit the ability of a state government to regulate, much less ban, speech. Thus, perhaps Justice Stevens has the better of the argument that a ban on speech is *not* simply a lesser included power. Isn't there something troubling about government attempting to trick citizens into virtuous behavior? And, if government thinks a particular behavior is socially harmful (but not harmful enough to justify a ban), government remains free to share its views in the marketplace of ideas.
3. *Growing skepticism toward commercial speech regulations.* Over time, the Supreme Court has become increasingly demanding of commercial speech restrictions and has required government to establish that targeted speech restrictions are part of a consistent larger program of regulation in order to find the third and fourth prongs of *Central Hudson* have been met.
4. *Burdening commercial speech.* Should government be required to adopt commercial speech restrictions as part of a comprehensive and internally consistent regulatory program to satisfy the third and fourth prongs of *Central Hudson*? Normally, government is permitted to address a social problem in a piecemeal fashion—not so here. If a government regulatory scheme contains numerous exceptions or provisos, it appears that restrictions on commercial speech are less likely to survive judicial review. Just as government cannot use a ban on commercial speech (in lieu of direct regulations) to discourage the sale of a good or service, so too government cannot place relatively greater weight on commercial speech restrictions (rather than direct regulations) as part of a comprehensive regulatory effort.
5. *Commercial speech regulations must be coherent.* In Greater New Orleans Broadcasting Association v. U.S., 527 U.S. 173 (1999) (GNOB), the Supreme Court struck down a ban on casino advertising over radio and television stations because the policy with riddled with exemptions that undercut its efficacy. Writing for the majority, Justice Stevens acknowledged that "[n]o one seriously doubts that the Federal Government may assert a legitimate and substantial interest in alleviating the societal ills [associated with gambling], or in assisting like-minded States to do the same." *Id.* at 186. Nevertheless, because the federal government's ban on casino advertising was riddled with exceptions that seemed to swallow the rule, the Supreme Court invalidated it under *Central Hudson. See id.* at 191 ("From what we can gather, the Government is committed to prohibiting accurate product information, not commercial enticements of all kinds, and then only when conveyed over certain forms of media and for certain types of gambling—indeed, for only certain brands of *casino* gambling—and

despite the fact that messages about the availability of such gambling are being conveyed over the airwaves by other speakers."). On these facts, the federal government could not "overcome the presumption that the speaker and the audience, not the Government, should be left to assess the value of accurate and nonmisleading information about lawful conduct." *Id.* at 195.

6. *Even more robust protection for commercial speech?* In *GNOB*, Justice Thomas concurred and noted that he "continue[d] to adhere to my view that in cases such as this, in which the government's asserted interest is to keep legal users of a product or service ignorant in order to manipulate their choices in the marketplace, the *Central Hudson* test should not be applied because such an 'interest' is *per se* illegitimate and can no more justify regulation of 'commercial speech' than it can justify regulation of 'noncommercial' speech." *Id.* at 197 (Thomas, J., concurring) (cleaned up). Does Justice Thomas have the better view? Should a presumption exist that a flat ban on truthful, non-misleading information about a lawful good or service violates the Free Speech Clause? If government is not regulating commercial speech, but banning it, would the adoption of a per se rule help to clarify the proper free speech analysis? Or is Justice Stevens correct to insist that *Central Hudson* always provides the proper method of analysis? If the results in concrete cases work more or less just like a per se rule, wouldn't it make sense for the Supreme Court to acknowledge this fact?
7. *A dead letter?* Is anything left of the *Posadas* "lesser includes the greater" approach? Consider the case of government-mandated gruesome tobacco warning labels. The FDA ordered cigarette manufacturers to place graphic warning labels on cigarette packaging. See Ellen P. Goodman, *Visual Gut Punch: Persuasion, Emotion and the Constitutional Meaning of Graphic Disclosure*, 99 Cornell L. Rev. 513 (2014). The FDA claimed that the labels were necessary to help consumers make well-informed choices about the health risks associated with the use of tobacco products; the tobacco companies argued that the FDA was trying to scare consumers into quitting smoking by using emotionally manipulative graphic images. Two U.S. Courts of Appeals considered challenges to the graphic visual labels and reached conflicting results. *Compare* Discount Tobacco City & Lottery Inc. v. U.S., 674 F.3d 509, 529-30 (6th Cir. 2012) (rejecting a facial challenge to the FDA's graphic labeling requirements and explaining that "the color graphics requirement materially advances the government's stated interest in counteracting the informational deficit regarding health hazards") *with* R.J. Reynolds Tobacco Co. v. FDA, 696 F.3d 1205, 1214 (D.C. Cir. 2012) (invalidating the FDA's graphic labeling regulations, on an as-applied basis, as unconstitutional compelled speech and holding that "a disclosure requirement is only appropriate if the government shows that, absent a warning, there is a self-evident—or at least 'potentially real'—danger that an advertisement will mislead consumers"). Did the government's power to ban tobacco altogether perhaps influence the Sixth Circuit—leading that court to uphold the graphic warning

> requirement? Or is *Discount Tobacco City* simply an example of a lower court applying the first prong of *Central Hudson* (commercial speech must be truthful and non-misleading)? Moreover, if tobacco companies intentionally misled consumers about the adverse health effects of tobacco consumption, may government require them to correct consumer information deficits that they helped to create? For a thoughtful analysis and a doctrinal proposal that government efforts to "inform" consumers cannot constitutionally extend to lobbying consumers to refrain from engaging in a lawful activity, see Jennifer M. Keighley, *Can You Handle the Truth? Compelled Commercial Speech and the First Amendment*, 15 U. Pa. J. Const. L. 539 (2012).

As the next principal case makes clear, the Supreme Court has, consistently over time, expanded the scope of protection afforded commercial speech. In fact, some legal scholars believe that the commercial speech doctrine has come to represent a modern day form of so-called *Lochner*izing. *See* Gregory P. Magarian, Managed Speech: The Roberts Court's First Amendment 53 (2017) ("The *Lochner* era and the commercial speech doctrine converge because First Amendment limits on commercial speech regulations might seem to resurrect *Lochner*."); Kathleen Sullivan, Comment, *Two Concepts of Freedom of Speech*, 124 Harv. L. Rev. 143, 143–46, 155–63 (2010) (objecting to the Supreme Court's "Lochnerian" vision for the First Amendment and the steady expansion of speech rights for corporations and commercial speakers). Should a state government be able to adopt targeted privacy protections that only burden *commercial use* of privately-held personal data? Or are restrictions on the commercial use of data, but not other uses of such personal data, an impermissible form of content discrimination?

Sorrell v. IMS Health Inc.

564 U.S. 552 (2011)

Justice Kennedy delivered the opinion of the Court.

Vermont law restricts the sale, disclosure, and use of pharmacy records that reveal the prescribing practices of individual doctors. Vt. Stat. Ann., Tit. 18, § 4631 (Supp. 2010). Subject to certain exceptions, the information may not be sold, disclosed by pharmacies for marketing purposes, or used for marketing by pharmaceutical manufacturers. Vermont argues that its prohibitions safeguard medical privacy and diminish the likelihood that marketing will lead to prescription decisions not in the best interests of patients or the State. It can be assumed that these interests are significant. Speech in aid of pharmaceutical marketing, however, is a form of expression protected by the Free Speech Clause of the First Amendment. As a consequence, Vermont's statute must be subjected to heightened judicial scrutiny. The law cannot satisfy that standard. . . .

Pharmacies, as a matter of business routine and federal law, receive prescriber-identifying information when processing prescriptions. See 21 U.S.C. § 353(b); see also Vt. Bd. of Pharmacy Admin. Rule 9.1 (2009); Rule 9.2. Many pharmacies sell this information to "data miners," firms that analyze prescriber identifying information and produce reports on prescriber behavior. Data miners lease these reports to pharmaceutical manufacturers subject to nondisclosure agreements. Detailers, who represent the manufacturers, then use the reports to refine their marketing tactics and increase sales.

In 2007, Vermont enacted the Prescription Confidentiality Law. The measure is also referred to as Act 80. It has several components. The central provision of the present case is § 4631(d).

> "A health insurer, a self-insured employer, an electronic transmission intermediary, a pharmacy, or other similar entity shall not sell, license, or exchange for value regulated records containing prescriber-identifiable information, nor permit the use of regulated records containing prescriber-identifiable information for marketing or promoting a prescription drug, unless the prescriber consents. . . . Pharmaceutical manufacturers and pharmaceutical marketers shall not use prescriber-identifiable information for marketing or promoting a prescription drug unless the prescriber consents. . . ."

[Vermont's law sought to restrict access to prescription data as part of an effort to thwart "detailing," the use of high-pressure in-office marketing visits by pharmaceutical company representatives aimed at increasing the "detailed" physician's prescribing rate for the company's proprietary drugs. The state argued that detailing has adverse affects on the cost of health care in the state, by encouraging physicians to prescribe more-expensive proprietary drugs rather than less-expensive generic equivalents. By generally prohibiting the sale of prescription data by third parties, like pharmacies, Vermont hoped to curtail the health care costs associated with successful "detailing."]

[A group of data miners, sellers of aggregated prescription data from pharmacies, and an association of pharmaceutical manufacturers, initiated a challenge to the new law, arguing that it violated the First Amendment's Free Speech Clause. Following a bench trial, the district court rejected the plaintiffs' claims and held the law to be constitutional. On appeal, the U.S. Court of Appeals for the Second Circuit reversed on First Amendment grounds, holding that Vermont's ban on the sale of prescription data for the purpose of detailing unduly restricted lawful commercial speech. The Supreme Court granted review to resolve a circuit split on this question.]

[T]he opening clause of § 4631(d) prohibits pharmacies, health insurers, and similar entities from selling prescriber-identifying information, subject to the statutory exceptions set out at § 4631(e). Under that reading, pharmacies may sell the information to private or academic researchers, see § 4631(e)(1), but not, for example, to pharmaceutical marketers. There is no dispute as to the remainder of § 4631(d). It prohibits pharmacies, health insurers, and similar entities from disclosing or otherwise allowing prescriber-identifying information to be used for marketing. And it bars pharmaceutical manufacturers and detailers from using the information for marketing. The questions now are whether § 4631(d) must be tested by heightened judicial scrutiny and, if so, whether the State can justify the law.

On its face, Vermont's law enacts content-and speaker-based restrictions on the sale, disclosure, and use of prescriber-identifying information. The provision first forbids sale subject to exceptions based in large part on the content of a purchaser's speech. For example, those who wish to engage in certain "educational communications," § 4631(e)(4), may purchase the information. The measure then bars any disclosure when recipient speakers will use the information for marketing. Finally, the provision's second sentence prohibits pharmaceutical manufacturers from using the information for marketing. The statute thus disfavors marketing, that is, speech with a particular content. More than that, the statute disfavors specific speakers, namely pharmaceutical manufacturers. As a result of these content- and speaker-based rules, detailers cannot obtain prescriber-identifying information, even though the information may be purchased or acquired by other speakers with diverse purposes and viewpoints. Detailers are likewise barred from using the information for marketing, even though the information may be used by a wide range of other speakers. For example, it appears that Vermont could supply academic organizations with prescriber-identifying information to use in countering the messages of brand-name pharmaceutical manufacturers and in promoting the prescription of generic drugs. But § 4631(d) leaves detailers no means of purchasing, acquiring, or using prescriber-identifying information. The law on its face burdens disfavored speech by disfavored speakers.

Any doubt that § 4631(d) imposes an aimed, content-based burden on detailers is dispelled by the record and by formal legislative findings. . . .

Act 80 is designed to impose a specific, content-based burden on protected expression. It follows that heightened judicial scrutiny is warranted. See Cincinnati v. Discovery Network, Inc., 507 U.S. 410, 418 (1993) (applying heightened scrutiny to "a categorical prohibition on the use of newsracks to disseminate commercial messages"). . . .

The First Amendment requires heightened scrutiny whenever the government creates "a regulation of speech because of disagreement with the message it conveys." . . . A government bent on frustrating an impending demonstration might pass a law demanding two years' notice before the issuance of parade permits. Even if the hypothetical measure on its face appeared neutral as to content and speaker, its purpose to suppress speech and its unjustified burdens on expression would render it unconstitutional. Commercial speech is no exception. A "consumer's concern for the free flow of commercial speech often may be far keener than his concern for urgent political dialogue." Bates v. State Bar of Ariz., 433 U.S. 350, 364 (1977). That reality has great relevance in the fields of medicine and public health, where information can save lives. . . .

The State asks for an exception to the rule that information is speech, but there is no need to consider that request in this case. The State has imposed content- and speaker-based restrictions on the availability and use of prescriber-identifying information. So long as they do not engage in marketing, many speakers can obtain and use the information. But detailers cannot. Vermont's statute could be compared with a law prohibiting trade magazines from purchasing or using ink. Cf. *Minneapolis Star*, 460 U.S. 575. Like that hypothetical law, § 4631(d) imposes a speaker- and content-based burden on protected expression, and that circumstance is sufficient to justify application of heightened scrutiny. As a consequence, this case can be resolved even assuming, as the State argues, that prescriber-identifying information is a mere commodity.

In the ordinary case it is all but dispositive to conclude that a law is content-based and, in practice, viewpoint-discriminatory. The State argues that a different analysis applies here because, assuming § 4631(d) burdens speech at all, it at most burdens only commercial speech. As in previous cases, however, the outcome is the same whether a special commercial speech inquiry or a stricter form of judicial scrutiny is applied. For the same reason there is no need to determine whether all speech hampered by § 4631(d) is commercial, as our cases have used that term.

Under a commercial speech inquiry, it is the State's burden to justify its content-based law as consistent with the First Amendment. To sustain the targeted, content-based burden § 4631(d) imposes on protected expression, the State must show at least that the statute directly advances a substantial governmental interest and that the measure is drawn to achieve that interest. There must be a "fit between the legislature's ends and the means chosen to accomplish those ends." As in other contexts, these standards ensure not only that the State's interests are proportional to the resulting burdens placed on speech but also that the law does not seek to suppress a disfavored message.

The State's asserted justifications for § 4631(d) come under two general headings. First, the State contends that its law is necessary to protect medical privacy, including physician confidentiality, avoidance of harassment, and the integrity of the doctor-patient relationship. Second, the State argues that § 4631(d) is integral to the achievement of policy objectives—namely, improved public health and reduced healthcare costs. Neither justification withstands scrutiny. . . .

The State contends that § 4631(d) advances important public policy goals by lowering the costs of medical services and promoting public health. If prescriber-identifying information were available for use by detailers, the State contends, then detailing would be effective in promoting brand-name drugs that are more expensive and less safe than generic alternatives. This logic is set out at length in the legislative findings accompanying § 4631(d). Yet at oral argument here, the State declined to acknowledge that § 4631(d)'s objective purpose and practical effect were to inhibit detailing and alter doctors' prescription decisions. The State's reluctance to embrace its own legislature's rationale reflects the vulnerability of its position.

While Vermont's stated policy goals may be proper, § 4631(d) does not advance them in a permissible way. As the Court of Appeals noted, the "state's own explanation of how" § 4631(d) "advances its interests cannot be said to be direct." 630 F.3d, at 277. The State seeks to achieve its policy objectives through the indirect means of restraining certain speech by certain speakers—that is, by diminishing detailers' ability to influence prescription decisions. Those who seek to censor or burden free expression often assert that disfavored speech has adverse effects. But the "fear that people would make bad decisions if given truthful information" cannot justify content-based burdens on speech. "The First Amendment directs us to be especially skeptical of regulations that seek to keep people in the dark for what the government perceives to be their own good." *44 Liquormart, supra*, at 503 (opinion of Stevens, J.); see also Linmark Associates, Inc. v. Willingboro, 431 U.S. 85, 97 (1977). These precepts apply with full force when the audience, in this case prescribing physicians, consists of "sophisticated and experienced" consumers. . . .

Vermont may be displeased that detailers who use prescriber-identifying information are effective in promoting brand-name drugs. The State can express that view through its own speech. See *Linmark*, 431 U.S., at 97; cf. § 4622(a)(1) (establishing a prescription drug educational program). But a State's failure to persuade does not allow it to hamstring the opposition. The State may not burden the speech of others in order to tilt public debate in a preferred direction. "The commercial marketplace, like other spheres of our social and cultural life, provides a forum where ideas and information flourish. Some of the ideas and information are vital, some of slight worth. But the general rule is that the speaker and the audience, not the government, assess the value of the information presented." . . .

The capacity of technology to find and publish personal information, including records required by the government, presents serious and unresolved issues with respect to personal privacy and the dignity it seeks to secure. In considering how to protect those interests, however, the State cannot engage in content-based discrimination to advance its own side of a debate.

If Vermont's statute provided that prescriber-identifying information could not be sold or disclosed except in narrow circumstances then the State might have a stronger position. Here, however, the State gives possessors of the information broad discretion and wide latitude in disclosing the information, while at the same time restricting the information's use by some speakers and for some purposes, even while the State itself can use the information to counter the speech it seeks to suppress. Privacy is a concept too integral to the person and a right too essential to freedom to allow its manipulation to support just those ideas the government prefers.

When it enacted § 4631(d), the Vermont Legislature found that the "marketplace for ideas on medicine safety and effectiveness is frequently one-sided in that brand-name companies invest in expensive pharmaceutical marketing campaigns to doctors." 2007 Vt. Laws No. 80, § 1(4). "The goals of marketing programs," the legislature said, "are often in conflict with the goals of the state." § 1(3). The text of § 4631(d), associated legislative findings, and the record developed in the District Court establish that Vermont enacted its law for this end. The State has burdened a form of protected expression that it found too persuasive. At the same time, the State has left unburdened those speakers whose messages are in accord with its own views. This the State cannot do.

The judgment of the Court of Appeals is affirmed.

It is so ordered.

Justice BREYER, with whom Justice GINSBURG and Justice KAGAN join, dissenting.

The Vermont statute before us adversely affects expression in one, and only one, way. It deprives pharmaceutical and data-mining companies of data, collected pursuant to the government's regulatory mandate, that could help pharmaceutical companies create better sales messages. In my view, this effect on expression is inextricably related to a lawful governmental effort to regulate a commercial enterprise. The First Amendment does not require courts to apply a special "heightened" standard of review when reviewing such an effort. And, in any event, the statute meets the First Amendment standard this Court has previously applied when the government seeks to regulate commercial speech. For any or all of these reasons, the Court should uphold the statute as constitutional. . . .

There are several reasons why the Court should review Vermont's law "under the standard appropriate for the review of economic regulation," not "under a heightened standard appropriate for the review of First Amendment issues." *Glickman*, 521 U.S., at 469. For one thing, Vermont's statute neither forbids nor requires anyone to say anything, to engage in any form of symbolic speech, or to endorse any particular point of view, whether ideological or related to the sale of a product.

For another thing, the same First Amendment standards that apply to Vermont here would apply to similar regulatory actions taken by other States or by the Federal Government acting, for example, through Food and Drug Administration (FDA) regulation. (And the Federal Government's ability to preempt state laws that interfere with existing or contemplated federal forms of regulation is here irrelevant.)

Further, the statute's requirements form part of a traditional, comprehensive regulatory regime. Cf. *United Foods, supra*, at 411 [U.S. v. United Foods, 533 U.S. 405, 411 (2001)]. The pharmaceutical drug industry has been heavily regulated at least since 1906. See Pure Food and Drugs Act, 34 Stat. 768. Longstanding statutes and regulations require pharmaceutical companies to engage in complex drug testing to ensure that their drugs are both "safe" and "effective." 21 U.S.C. §§ 355(b)(1), 355(d). Only then can the drugs be marketed, at which point drug companies are subject to the FDA's exhaustive regulation of the content of drug labels and the manner in which drugs can be advertised and sold. § 352(f)(2); 21 CFR pts. 201-203 (2010).

Finally, Vermont's statute is directed toward information that exists only by virtue of government regulation. Under federal law, certain drugs can be dispensed only by a pharmacist operating under the orders of a medical practitioner. 21 U.S.C. § 353(b). Vermont regulates the qualifications, the fitness, and the practices of pharmacists themselves, and requires pharmacies to maintain a "patient record system" that, among other things, tracks who prescribed which drugs. Vt. Stat. Ann., Tit. 26, §§ 2041(a), 2022(14) (Supp. 2010); Vt. Bd. of Pharmacy Admin. Rules (Pharmacy Rules) 9.1, 9.24(e) (2009). But for these regulations, pharmacies would have no way to know who had told customers to buy which drugs (as is the case when a doctor tells a patient to take a daily dose of aspirin). . . .

If the Court means to create constitutional barriers to regulatory rules that might affect the *content* of a commercial message, it has embarked upon an unprecedented task—a task that threatens significant judicial interference with widely accepted regulatory activity. Nor would it ease the task to limit its "heightened" scrutiny to regulations that only affect certain speakers. As the examples that I have set forth illustrate, many regulations affect only messages sent by a small class of regulated speakers, for example, electricity generators or natural gas pipelines.

The Court also uses the words "aimed" and "targeted" when describing the relation of the statute to drug manufacturers. But, for the reasons just set forth, to require "heightened" scrutiny on this basis is to require its application early and often when the State seeks to regulate industry. Any statutory initiative stems from a legislative agenda. Any administrative initiative stems from a regulatory agenda. The related statutes, regulations, programs, and initiatives almost always reflect a point of view, for example, of the Congress and the administration that enacted them and ultimately the voters. And they often aim at, and target, particular firms that engage in practices about the merits of which the Government and the firms may disagree. Section 2 of the Sherman Act, 15 U.S.C. § 2, for example, which limits the truthful, nonmisleading speech of firms that, due to their market power, can affect the competitive landscape, is directly aimed at, and targeted at, monopolists.

In short, the case law in this area reflects the need to ensure that the First Amendment protects the "marketplace of ideas," thereby facilitating the democratic creation of sound government policies without improperly hampering the ability of government to introduce an agenda, to implement its policies, and to favor them to the exclusion of contrary policies. To apply "heightened" scrutiny when the regulation of commercial activities (which often involve speech) is at issue is unnecessarily to undercut the latter constitutional goal. The majority's view of this case presents that risk. . . .

[I] believe that the statute before us satisfies the "intermediate" standards this Court has applied to restrictions on commercial speech. *A fortiori* it satisfies less demanding standards that are more appropriately applied in this kind of commercial regulatory case—a case where the government seeks typical regulatory ends (lower drug prices, more balanced sales messages) through the use of ordinary regulatory means (limiting the commercial use of data gathered pursuant to a regulatory mandate). The speech-related consequences here are indirect, incidental, and entirely commercial.

The Court reaches its conclusion through the use of important First Amendment categories—"content-based," "speaker-based," and "neutral"—but without taking full account of the regulatory context, the nature of the speech effects, the values these First Amendment categories seek to promote, and prior precedent. At best the Court opens a Pandora's Box of First Amendment challenges to many ordinary regulatory practices that may only incidentally affect a commercial message. At worst, it reawakens *Lochner*'s pre-New Deal threat of substituting judicial for democratic decisionmaking where ordinary economic regulation is at issue. See *Central Hudson,* 447 U.S., at 589 (Rehnquist, J., dissenting).

Regardless, whether we apply an ordinary commercial speech standard or a less demanding standard, I believe Vermont's law is consistent with the First Amendment. And with respect, I dissent.

NOTES AND QUESTIONS

1. *Ordinary commercial transactions as speech.* After *Sorrell,* are any and all commercial transactions potentially constitutionally protected commercial speech? For example, would government efforts to regulate chewing gum sales in convenience stores be subject to intermediate scrutiny, to the extent that the regulations affect the ability of a store to market chewing gum to potential customers? What about regulations of deceptive or unfair marketing practices? Or would such regulations be sustained on the first prong of *Central Hudson,* that is, the speech must be truthful and non-misleading to enjoy constitutional protection? But, if aggressive marketing techniques, like detailing, pressure physicians into prescribing more expensive yet no more effective drugs, why is such a practice not akin to a form of fraud? Is the ability of a physician to simply close

his office to detailers a sufficient response? But wouldn't this also be true of consumers with respect to deceptive marketing techniques? For a thoughtful discussion of paternalism as a basis for regulating commercial speech, see Tamara R. Piety, Brandishing the First Amendment: Commercial Expression in America (2012).

2. *Content- and viewpoint-discrimination revisited.* Justice Kennedy, writing for the majority, clearly frames the primary issue in *Sorrell* as involving both content- and viewpoint-based discrimination: "On its face, Vermont's law enacts content- and speaker-based restrictions on the sale, disclosure, and use of prescriber-identifying information." This is certainly true; yet any regulation regarding the marketing or sale of a good or service raises the same issues. For example, the Securities and Exchange Commission regulates the speech associated with initial public offerings of securities, such as shares of common stock; it disallows some speech and mandates other speech, including mandatory information that a seller must disclose to would-be buyers. Should such regulations be subject to heightened scrutiny under the First Amendment? Or does Justice Breyer have the stronger view here – namely that the government as an administrative regulator generally does not have to answer for the First Amendment effects of otherwise permissible regulatory programs? Does either approach adequately address the problems and shortcomings that would arise from adopting it? Or is a proverbial "third way" needed to address such cases? If so, how should courts articulate the governing test when deciding when to treat a regulatory regime that regulates commercial speech as triggering heightened First Amendment scrutiny?
3. *The difficulty in setting boundaries.* These boundary issues arise frequently and in myriad circumstances, yet the Supreme Court largely has failed to address them; instead, it seems to know when the First Amendment provides the relevant framework (and when it doesn't). For a very useful discussion of the problem, see Frederick Schauer, *The Boundaries of the First Amendment: A Preliminary Exploration of Constitutional Salience,* 117 Harv. L. Rev. 1765 (2004).
4. *Secondary effects and the First Amendment.* Should the First Amendment mean that the federal and state governments are simply powerless to regulate markets in information when those markets cause externalities, such as higher health care costs? In the context of nude dancing, for example, the Supreme Court has embraced the invocation of "secondary effects" as a basis for regulating—and even banning—speech (erotic dance, for example). See *supra* Chapter 4 and *infra* Chapter 11, Part C. Why should the secondary effects of nude dancing justify content-based speech restrictions when the secondary effects of pharmaceutical representatives' aggressive marketing techniques do not justify a content-based ban on the sale of prescription data?
5. *Is data collection speech?* If Vermont's regulation of a physician's prescription data is a content-based speech restriction, does this mean that any and all government regulations of the use of data are content-based speech restrictions too? And, accordingly, must survive strict judicial scrutiny under the First Amendment? For an argument that the answer

to this question is "yes," see Jane Bambauer, *Is Data Speech?*, 66 Stan. L. Rev. 57 (2014). Professor Bambauer posits that "[t]he First Amendment is, in many ways, an experiment that hinders the government from deciding what speech, and what thoughts, are good, even if most level-headed people could agree on the matter. After all, a benevolent dictator is still a dictator." *Id.* at 118, *see id.* at 60 (arguing that "the freedom of speech carries an implicit right to create knowledge" and that government regulation that substantially interferes with knowledge creation, including data collection, is "presumptively illegitimate and must withstand judicial scrutiny"). Consistent with these views, she argues that "[t]he sanctity of a freely made mind requires protection not only for speech, but also for the digestion of raw facts," *id.* at 120, meaning that data collection and data mining constitute forms of protected First Amendment activity. Do you find these arguments persuasive? Or should data collection and data mining be characterized as antecedent activities to speech?

6. *Privacy and the commercial speech doctrine.* Does the protection of personal privacy not constitute a sufficiently important government objective to sustain restrictions on the sale of a person's medical history or a doctor's prescribing habits? Moreover, after *Sorrell* is there any room left for the federal or state governments to enact statutory privacy protections? *See* Ashutosh Bhagwat, Sorrell v. IMS Health*: Details, Detailing, and the Death of Privacy*, 36 Vt. L. Rev. 855, 856 (2012) (arguing that *Sorrell* might have "dramatic, and extremely troubling, implications for a broad range of existing and proposed rules that seek to control disclosure of personal information in order to protect privacy"). Or did Vermont simply enact a poorly drafted statute, given the highly targeted nature of the ban on selling prescription data to third parties? As an alternative to regulating information markets in physician prescription data, could Vermont instead create a statutory *property interest* in prescription data and require affirmative, direct consent from the patient receiving the medications and/or the physician prescribing the medications before a pharmacy or insurance company could sell the information to a third party? In other words, would a statute that more directly and more completely advances an interest in data privacy stand a better chance of surviving judicial review against a First Amendment challenge?
7. Lochner*izing via the First Amendment?* Justice Breyer, in dissent, warned that the *Sorrell* majority was "open[ing] a Pandora's Box of First Amendment challenges to many ordinary regulatory practices that may only incidentally affect a commercial message." *Sorrell*, 564 U.S. at 602. In his view, using the First Amendment to strike down ordinary business regulations "reawakens *Lochner*'s pre-New Deal threat of substituting judicial for democratic decisionmaking where ordinary economic regulation is at issue." *Id.* Justice Breyer made the same point in a concurring opinion a six years later. *See* Expressions Hair Design v. Schneiderman, 137 S. Ct. 1144, 1152-53 (2017) (Breyer, J., concurring). He observed that "all government regulation affects speech" because "[h]uman relations take place through speech. And human relations include community activities of all kinds—commercial and otherwise." *Id.* In light of this reality,

a reviewing court should inquire into "whether, or how, a challenged statute, rule, or regulation affects an interest that the First Amendment protects" rather than automatically deploying a First Amendment rule that presumes unconstitutional any and all content-based speech regulations." *Id.* at 1152-53. By way of contrast, the majority in *Expressions Hair Design* held that a state law, N.Y. Gen. Bus. Law § 518, that prohibited merchants from advertising surcharges for the use of a credit card, triggered strict scrutiny under the First Amendment. *See Expressions Hair Design*, 137 S. Ct. at 1150-51. Chief Justice Roberts, writing for the majority, found that the law constituted a content-based regulation of speech. *Id.* at 1151 (opining that § 518 "tells merchants nothing about the amount they are allowed to collect from a cash or credit card payer" but instead "[i]n regulating the communication of prices rather than prices themselves [the statute] regulates speech"). Is prohibiting the communication of credit charge surcharges, while permitting speech that announces price discounts for cash, the sort of government speech regulation that merits strict judicial scrutiny under the First Amendment? *See* Leslie Kendrick, *First Amendment Expansionism*, 56 Wm. & Mary L. Rev. 1199, 1208-09 (2015) (noting the increasing use of the First Amendment to challenge routine business regulations, observing that "[t]hese claims mirror *Lochner*-era claims in their structure," and explaining that "[t]he difference today is that the First Amendment is so often the designated vehicle for these antiregulatory impulses"); Ronald J. Krotoszynski, Jr., *The First Amendment as a Procrustean Bed?: On How and Why Bright Line First Amendment Tests Can Stifle the Scope and Vibrancy of Democratic Deliberation*, 2020 U. Chi. Legal F. 145, 149 ("The prospect of applying strict judicial scrutiny to virtually all government social and economic regulations does bear more than a passing resemblance to *Lochner.* To the extent that government regulations affect communications related to the sale of goods or services, the potential risk of *Lochner*izing is obvious.")

C. *LIMITATIONS ON THE ABILITY OF GOVERNMENT TO REGULATE COMMERCIAL SPEECH BECAUSE OF ITS COMMERCIAL NATURE*

The Supreme Court, even as it extended protection to commercial speech in cases like *Virginia State Board of Pharmacy* and *Central Hudson*, maintained that such speech stands on the lower rung of the hierarchy of First Amendment free speech values. It has sufficient value to merit protection as "free speech" but is ostensibly not as central to the free speech project as political speech, or even artistic, literary, or scientific speech. If this is so, may government then single out commercial speech for special regulatory burdens? The answer appears to be a qualified no. Even so, cases involving the Federal Trade Commission's do-not-call registry suggest that targeted bans of commercial speech might in fact be consistent with the Free Speech Clause.

1. *The Rule Prohibiting Discrimination Against Commercial Speech as Such*

City of Cincinnati v. Discovery Network, Inc.

507 U.S. 410 (1993)

Justice STEVENS delivered the opinion of the Court.

Motivated by its interest in the safety and attractive appearance of its streets and sidewalks, the city of Cincinnati has refused to allow respondents to distribute their commercial publications through freestanding newsracks located on public property. The question presented is whether this refusal is consistent with the First Amendment. In agreement with the District Court and the Court of Appeals, we hold that it is not.

Respondent Discovery Network, Inc. is engaged in the business of providing adult educational, recreational, and social programs to individuals in the Cincinnati area. It advertises those programs in a free magazine that it publishes nine times a year. Although these magazines consist primarily of promotional material pertaining to Discovery's courses, they also include some information about current events of general interest. Approximately one-third of these magazines are distributed through the 38 newsracks that the city authorized Discovery to place on public property in 1989.

Respondent Harmon Publishing Company, Inc., publishes and distributes a free magazine that advertises real estate for sale at various locations throughout the United States. The magazine contains listings and photographs of available residential properties in the greater Cincinnati area, and also includes some information about interest rates, market trends, and other real estate matters. In 1989, Harmon received the city's permission to install 24 newsracks at approved locations. About 15% of its distribution in the Cincinnati area is through those devices.

In March 1990, the city's Director of Public Works notified each of the respondents that its permit to use dispensing devices on public property was revoked, and ordered the newsracks removed within 30 days. Each notice explained that respondent's publication was a "commercial handbill" within the meaning of § 714-1-C of the Municipal Code and therefore § 714-23 of the code prohibited its distribution on public property. [The city and publishers agreed to seek a judicial determination of the constitutionality of the city's newsrack policy.] Respondents then commenced this litigation in the United States District Court for the Southern District of Ohio.

After an evidentiary hearing the District Court concluded that "the regulatory scheme advanced by the City of Cincinnati completely prohibiting the distribution of commercial handbills on the public right of way violates the First Amendment." [T]he Court of Appeals agreed with the District Court that the burden placed on speech "cannot be justified by the paltry gains in safety and beauty achieved by the ordinance." . . .

There is no claim in this case that there is anything unlawful or misleading about the contents of respondents' publications. Moreover, respondents do not challenge their characterization as "commercial speech." Nor do respondents question the substantiality of the city's interest in safety and esthetics. It was, therefore, proper for the District Court and the Court of Appeals to judge the validity of the city's prohibition under the standards we set forth in *Central Hudson* and *Fox.* It was the city's burden to establish a "reasonable fit" between its legitimate interests in safety and esthetics and its choice of a limited and selective prohibition of newsracks as the means chosen to serve those interests.

There is ample support in the record for the conclusion that the city did not "establish the reasonable fit we require." The ordinance on which it relied was an outdated prohibition against the distribution of any commercial handbills on public property. It was enacted long before any concern about newsracks developed. Its apparent purpose was to prevent the kind of visual blight caused by littering, rather than any harm associated with permanent, freestanding dispensing devices. The fact that the city failed to address its recently developed concern about newsracks by regulating their size, shape, appearance, or number indicates that it has not "carefully calculated" the costs and benefits associated with the burden on speech imposed by its prohibition. The benefit to be derived from the removal of 62 newsracks while about 1,500-2,000 remain in place was considered "minute" by the District Court and "paltry" by the Court of Appeals. We share their evaluation of the "fit" between the city's goal and its method of achieving it.

In seeking reversal, the city argues that it is wrong to focus attention on the relatively small number of newsracks affected by its prohibition, because the city's central concern is with the overall number of newsracks on its sidewalks, rather than with the unattractive appearance of a handful of dispensing devices. It contends, first, that a categorical prohibition on the use of newsracks to disseminate commercial messages burdens no more speech than is necessary to further its interest in limiting the number of newsracks; and, second, that the prohibition is a valid "time, place, and manner" regulation because it is content neutral and leaves open ample alternative channels of communication. We consider these arguments in turn.

The city argues that there is a close fit between its ban on newsracks dispensing "commercial handbills" and its interests in safety and esthetics because every decrease in the number of such dispensing devices necessarily effects an increase in safety and an improvement in the attractiveness of the cityscape. In the city's view, the prohibition is thus *entirely* related to its legitimate interests in safety and esthetics.

We accept the validity of the city's proposition, but consider it an insufficient justification for the discrimination against respondents' use of newsracks that are no more harmful than the permitted newsracks, and have only a minimal impact on the overall number of newsracks on the city's sidewalks. The major premise supporting the city's argument is the proposition that commercial speech has only a low value. Based on that premise, the city contends that the fact that assertedly more valuable publications are allowed to use newsracks does not undermine its judgment that its esthetic and safety interests are stronger than the interest in allowing commercial speakers to have similar access to the reading public.

We cannot agree. In our view, the city's argument attaches more importance to the distinction between commercial and noncommercial speech than our cases warrant and seriously underestimates the value of commercial speech.

This very case illustrates the difficulty of drawing bright lines that will clearly cabin commercial speech in a distinct category. For respondents' publications share important characteristics with the publications that the city classifies as "newspapers." Particularly, they are "commercial handbills" within the meaning of § 714-1-C of the city's code because they contain advertising, a feature that apparently also places ordinary newspapers within the same category. Separate provisions in the code specifically authorize the distribution of "newspapers" on the public right of way, but that term is not defined. Presumably, respondents' publications do not qualify as newspapers because an examination of their content discloses a higher ratio of advertising to other text, such as news and feature stories, than is found in the exempted publications. Indeed, Cincinnati's City Manager has determined that publications that qualify as newspapers and therefore *can* be distributed by newsrack are those that are published daily and/or weekly and "*primarily* presen[t] coverage of, and commentary on, current events."

The absence of a categorical definition of the difference between "newspapers" and "commercial handbills" in the city's code is also a characteristic of our opinions considering the constitutionality of regulations of commercial speech. Fifty years ago, we concluded that the distribution of a commercial handbill was unprotected by the First Amendment, even though half of its content consisted of political protest. Valentine v. Chrestensen, 316 U.S. 52 (1942). A few years later, over Justice Black's dissent, we held that the "commercial feature" of door-to-door solicitation of magazine subscriptions was a sufficient reason for denying First Amendment protection to that activity. Breard v. Alexandria, 341 U.S. 622 (1951). Subsequent opinions, however, recognized that important commercial attributes of various forms of communication do not qualify their entitlement to constitutional protection. . . . We then held that even speech that does no more than propose a commercial transaction is protected by the First Amendment. . . .

[F]or the purpose of deciding this case, we assume that all of the speech barred from Cincinnati's sidewalks is what we have labeled "core" commercial speech and that no such speech is found in publications that are allowed to use newsracks. We nonetheless agree with the Court of Appeals that Cincinnati's actions in this case run afoul of the First Amendment. Not only does Cincinnati's categorical ban on commercial newsracks place too much importance on the distinction between commercial and noncommercial speech, but in this case, the distinction bears no relationship *whatsoever* to the particular interests that the city has asserted. It is therefore an impermissible means of responding to the city's admittedly legitimate interests.

The city has asserted an interest in esthetics, but respondent publishers' newsracks are no greater an eyesore than the newsracks permitted to remain on Cincinnati's sidewalks. Each newsrack, whether containing "newspapers" or "commercial handbills" is equally unattractive. . . .

In the absence of some basis for distinguishing between "newspapers" and "commercial handbills" that is relevant to an interest asserted by the city, we are unwilling to recognize Cincinnati's bare assertion that the "low value" of commercial speech is a sufficient justification for its selective and categorical ban on newsracks dispensing "commercial handbills." Our holding, however, is narrow. As should be clear from the above discussion, we do not reach the question whether, given certain facts and under certain circumstances, a community might be able to justify differential treatment of commercial and noncommercial newsracks. We simply hold that on this record Cincinnati has failed to make such a showing. Because the distinction Cincinnati has drawn has absolutely no bearing on the interests it has asserted, we have no difficulty concluding, as did the two courts below, that the city has not established the "fit" between its goals and its chosen means that is required by our opinion in *Fox*. It remains to consider the city's argument that its prohibition is a permissible time, place, and manner regulation. . . .

[T]he city's newsrack policy is neither content neutral nor, as demonstrated in Part III, *supra*, "narrowly tailored." Thus, regardless of whether or not it leaves open ample alternative channels of communication, it cannot be justified as a legitimate time, place, or manner restriction on protected speech.

The judgment of the Court of Appeals is

Affirmed.

Justice BLACKMUN, concurring.

I agree that Cincinnati's ban on commercial newsracks cannot withstand scrutiny under Central Hudson Gas & Electric Corp. v. Public Serv. Comm'n of N.Y., 447 U.S. 557 (1980), and Board of Trustees of State University of N.Y. v. Fox, 492 U.S. 469 (1989), and I therefore join the Court's opinion. I write separately because I continue to believe that the analysis set forth in *Central Hudson* and refined in *Fox* afford insufficient protection for truthful, noncoercive commercial speech concerning lawful activities. . . .

I am heartened by the Court's decision today to reject the extreme extension of *Central Hudson*'s logic, and I hope the Court ultimately will come to abandon *Central Hudson*'s analysis entirely in favor of one that affords full protection for truthful, noncoercive commercial speech about lawful activities.

Chief Justice REHNQUIST, with whom Justice WHITE and Justice THOMAS join, dissenting.

Concerned about the safety and esthetics of its streets and sidewalks, the city of Cincinnati decided to do something about the proliferation of newsracks on its street corners. Pursuant to an existing ordinance prohibiting the distribution of "commercial handbills" on public property, the city ordered respondents Discovery Newswork, Inc., and Harmon Publishing Company, Inc., to remove their newsracks from its sidewalks within 30 days. Respondents publish and distribute free of charge magazines that consist principally of commercial speech. Together their publications account for 62 of the 1,500-2,000 newsracks that clutter Cincinnati's street corners. Because the city chose to address its newsrack problem by banning only those newsracks that disseminate commercial handbills, rather than regulating all newsracks (including those that disseminate traditional newspapers) alike, the Court holds that its actions violate the First Amendment to the Constitution. I believe this result is inconsistent with prior precedent. . . .

[D]espite the fact that we have consistently distinguished between commercial and noncommercial speech for the purpose of determining whether the regulation of speech is permissible, the Court holds that in attempting to alleviate its newsrack problem Cincinnati may not choose to proceed incrementally by burdening only commercial speech first. Based on the different levels of protection we have accorded commercial and noncommercial speech, we have previously said that localities may not favor commercial over noncommercial speech in addressing similar urban problems, see *Metromedia, Inc. v. San Diego, supra*, at 513 (plurality opinion), but before today we have never even suggested that the converse holds true. It is not surprising, then, that the Court offers little in the way of precedent supporting its new rule. . . .

If (as I am certain) Cincinnati may regulate newsracks that disseminate commercial speech based on the interests it has asserted, I am at a loss as to why its scheme is unconstitutional because it does not also regulate newsracks that disseminate noncommercial speech. One would have thought that the city, perhaps even following the teachings of our commercial speech jurisprudence, could have decided to place the burden of its regulatory scheme on less protected speech (*i.e.*, commercial handbills) without running afoul of the First Amendment. Today's decision, though, places the city in the position of having to decide between restricting more speech—fully protected speech—and allowing the proliferation of newsracks on its street corners to continue unabated. It scarcely seems logical that the First Amendment compels such a result. . . .

NOTES AND QUESTIONS

1. *Prohibiting discrimination against commercial speech. Discovery Network* is an important, indeed landmark, commercial speech decision. Justice Stevens appears to say that regulations targeting commercial speech for adverse treatment vis-à-vis noncommercial speech are valid *only* if commercial speech contributes in a non-general way to the problem being addressed. If too many newsracks litter fair Cincinnati's streets, the problem is clutter, not the clutter created by newspapers and magazines featuring predominantly commercial speech (viz., *Harmon Homes, Thrifty Nickel*).
2. *The potential virtues of differential treatment.* Why shouldn't government be able to disprefer commercial speech when attempting to mitigate a genuine aesthetic concern? Recall that in *Railway Express Agency*, the Supreme Court permitted New York City to ban third-party advertisements on panel trucks, even though the city permitted advertisements associated with the owner's business on panel trucks. Justice Douglas suggested that the Constitution permitted New York City to address the problem of visual blight in a piecemeal fashion. If, as Justice Powell observed in *Central Hudson*, commercial speech is more robust and less socially valuable than other kinds of speech, why shouldn't government have a freer hand in regulating it?
3. *The baby and the bath water objection.* Paradoxically, does *Discovery Network* mean—as it seems to say—that free speech values would be advanced more effectively if Cincinnati banned all newsracks on city property? That would lead to an even greater burden on the marketplace of ideas, wouldn't it? Does Chief Justice Rehnquist's dissent have a point? For an argument that *Discovery Network* has the potential to do more harm than good precisely because it invites the adoption of broader speech restrictions targeting both commercial and noncommercial speech, see William W. Van Alstyne, *Remembering Melville Nimmer: Some Cautionary Notes on Commercial Speech*, 43 UCLA L. Rev. 1635 (1996).

4. *Favoring the government's own commercial speech?* In Barr v. American Ass'n of Political Consultants, 140 S. Ct. 2335 (2020) (AAPC), the Supreme Court invalidated a federal law that permitted debt collectors seeking to collect government-owned debt, but no one else, to robocall cell phone numbers without an owner's consent. The Telephone Consumer Protection Act of 1991 prohibits virtually all robocalls to cell phones. *See* 47 U.S.C. § 227(b)(1)(A)(iii) (2018). However, in 2015, "Congress carved out a new government-debt exception to the general robocall restriction" that permitted the government or its agents to make such calls. *AAPC,* 140 S. Ct. at 2345. The AAPC, comprised of campaign managers and advisers, along with two other groups, brought suit in federal court seeking the same ability for their members to make robocalls to cell phones for campaign-related communications. *Id.* Writing for a plurality, Justice Kavanaugh held that the exception for government debt-related robocalls to cell phones constituted a content-based regulation of commercial speech. *See id.* at 2346 ("Because the law favors speech made for collecting government debt over political and other speech, the law is a content-based restriction on speech."). Applying strict scrutiny to this content-based speech regulation, the plurality invalidated it (rather than expanding it to encompass the AAPC's noncommercial speech). Kavanaugh explained that "[a]lthough collecting government debt is no doubt a worthy goal, the Government concedes that it has not sufficiently justified the differentiation between government-debt collection speech and other important categories of robocall speech, such as political speech, charitable fundraising, issue advocacy, commercial advertising, and the like" to save the provision from invalidation under strict scrutiny. *Id.* at 2347. Justice Gorsuch, joined by Justice Thomas, agreed with this aspect of Kavanaugh's opinion, thereby creating a 5–4 majority for applying strict scrutiny to the government's self-serving exemption to the robocall ban, but argued that the remedy should permit the plaintiffs to speak. *See id.* at 2364-66 (Gorsuch, J. concurring in part and dissenting in part). *AACP* seems to stand for the proposition that just as the government cannot categorically favor noncommercial speech over commercial speech, neither may it constitutionally favor some commercial speech over other commercial speech. The rule prohibiting discrimination against commercial speech, announced and applied in *Discovery Network,* applies in this context too.
5. *Is commercial speech less protected than noncommercial speech?* After *Discovery Network,* as explicated and expanded by cases like *AAPC,* what, if anything, remains of the idea that commercial speech stands on a lesser free speech footing than noncommercial speech?

2. **Discovery Network** *Applied?: Offensive Trademarks and Off-Label Rx Drug Marketing*

Discovery Network holds that government may not treat commercial speech less favorably than noncommercial speech, unless the commercial speech presents social harms that the unregulated noncommercial speech of the same kind or character does not. But when does commercial speech present a sufficiently particularized threat to justify regulating or proscribing it—but not noncommercial speech of a similar stripe? The examples of offensive trademarks and off-label prescription drug marketing help to shed some light on this important question.

The Lantham Act is a federal law that permits individuals and businesses to register trademarks and, after registration, grants the holder of the trademark the exclusive right to use the trademark when associated with a particular good, service, or activity. However, the Lantham Act prohibits the Patent and Trademark Office (PTO) from registering "scandalous, disparaging, or immoral" trademarks. *See* 15 U.S.C. § 1052(a). For many years, the federal courts, notably including the U.S. Court of Appeals for the Federal Circuit, upheld this statutory limitation on trademarks and the PTO's associated policy of refusing to register trademarks that feature offensive language, sexually-explicit content, or offensive racial stereotypes. *See* In re Tam, 808 F.3d 1321, 1330 (Fed. Cir. 2015) (en banc), *aff'd*, 137 S. Ct. 1744 (2017) (providing illustrative disallowed trademarks, including "Redskins," "Amish-Homo," "Christian Prostitute," "Wet Bac," and "2 Dyke Minimum").

Prior to *Tam*, the lower federal courts uniformly had rejected First Amendment challenges to trademark denials because refusals to register a trademark did not prohibit use of the trademark; instead, such decisions simply denied the user the right to prevent others from also using the trademark. *See* In re Fox, 702 F. 3d 633, 635 (Fed. Cir. 2012); In re Boulevard Entm't, Inc., 334 F.3d 1336, 1343 (Fed. Cir. 2003). In 2015, however, the Federal Circuit changed course, holding that the PTO's refusal to grant a trademark to Simon Shiao Tam for a rock band he fronted called "The Slants," violated the First Amendment. In Re Tam, 808 F.3d at 1327-28.

In choosing the name "The Slants" for his band, Tam sought "to make a statement about racial and cultural issues." *Id.* at 1327-28. More specifically, the band's name reflected an effort "to 'reclaim' and 'take ownership' of Asian stereotypes." *Id.* at 1331. The PTO declined to register "The Slants" for a trademark because the proposed trademark was "likely disparaging to 'persons of Asian descent' under § 2(a)." *Id.* A three-judge panel, applying binding circuit precedent, affirmed the PTO's refusal to register the proposed trademark. *See id.* at 1331-33. However, after rehearing the case en banc, the full Federal Circuit reversed the panel decision, holding that section 2(a) constituted an impermissible form of viewpoint discrimination. More specifically, the PTO's enforcement of section 2(a)t "stifle[d] the use of certain disfavored messages." *Id.* at 1339. Judge Kimberly Moore added that "[s]trict scrutiny therefore governs [the court's] First Amendment assessment—and no argument has been made that the measure survives such scrutiny." *Id.* The government argued that because trademarks are commercial in nature, strict scrutiny should not apply, even if section 2(a) constitutes a viewpoint-based speech regulation. However, the Federal Circuit squarely rejected this argument, holding instead that section 2(a) "regulates expressive speech, not commercial speech, and therefore strict scrutiny is appropriate." *Id.* at 1355.

The Supreme Court granted review and affirmed the Federal Circuit's en banc decision. Matal v. Tam, 137 S. Ct. 1744 (2017). As will be explained in Chapter 12, *see infra* p. 651, Justice Alito found that trademarks do not constitute "government speech" simply because of the PTO approval process. *Id.* at 1758-60. He also rejected the government's argument that the PTO could engage in content and viewpoint discrimination because the trademark registration process is a "government program" that created a kid of limited purpose public forum. *Id.* at 1761-63. This left only the question of whether trademarks constitute "commercial speech" and therefore receive reduced First Amendment protection under *Central Hudson. See id.* at 1763-65.

Justice Alito found it unnecessary to determine definitively whether a trademark constitutes commercial speech because, even assuming that all trademarks (including the trademark that Tam sought to register) are commercial speech, the Lantham Act's proscription against offensive and disparaging trademarks was not sufficiently "narrowly drawn" to pass constitutional muster under *Central Hudson.* He argued that "a deeper problem [exists] with the argument that commercial speech may be cleansed of any expression likely to cause offense," namely, that "[t]he commercial market is well stocked with merchandise that disparages prominent figures and groups, and the line between commercial and non-commercial speech is not always clear, as this case illustrates." *Id.* at 1765. Accordingly, "[i]f affixing the commercial label permits the suppression of any speech that may lead to political or social 'volatility,' free speech would be endangered." *Id.*

Justice Kennedy, for himself and Justices Ginsburg, Sotomayor, and Kagan, concurred and reached the same result by a more direct path: "To permit viewpoint discrimination in this context is to permit Government censorship." *Id.* at 1768 (Kennedy, J., concurring). He added that "[a] law that can be directed against speech found offensive to some portion of the public can be turned against minority and dissenting views to the detriment of all." *Id.* at 1769. In Kennedy's view, "[t]he First Amendment does not entrust that power to the government's benevolence. Instead, our reliance must be on the substantial safeguards of free and open discussion in a democratic society." *Id.* Thus, for Justices Kennedy, Ginsburg, Sotomayor, and Kagan, strict scrutiny, applicable to viewpoint-based government speech regulations, provided the correct legal standard regardless of whether a trademark constitutes "commercial" or "noncommercial" speech. *See id.* at 1767-68 (noting that "[t]he parties dispute whether trademarks are commercial speech and whether trademark registration should be considered a federal subsidy" but concluding that "[h]owever that issue is resolved, the viewpoint based discrimination at issue here necessarily invokes heightened scrutiny").

In considering whether Justice Alito or Justice Kennedy has the better analytical approach, one might want to bear in mind that the PTO previously had allowed trademarks for "Aunt Jemima," "Uncle Ben," and the "Frito Bandito." See Brian D. Behnken & Gregory D. Smithers, Racism in American Popular Media: From Aunt Jemima to the Frito Bandito (2015). Given that the PTO had registered racially problematic trademarks in the past, isn't Justice Kennedy correct to posit that the PTO's long-term pattern of inconsistent and selective enforcement, i.e., viewpoint discrimination, constituted the most serious First Amendment problem with the PTO's application of section 2(a) to deny Tam a trademark for his band's name? By way of contrast, Justice Alito posits that the PTO's inconsistent enforcement standards mean that the section 2(a) is not narrowly tailored—even if one assumes that a trademark is commercial speech. Justice Kennedy's approach would presumptively disallow commercial speech regulations that turn on the viewpoint expressed by the speaker—whereas Justice Alito's approach would only seem to require more carefully drawn rules and greater consistency in enforcing those rules. Justice Kennedy's approach has the effect of rendering even more narrow the daylight between First Amendment protection for commercial and noncommercial speech and constitutes an extension of the *Discovery Network* general rule that commercial speech may not be regulated more aggressively than noncommercial speech simply because of its commercial nature.

The Food and Drug Administration's (FDA) ban against off-label prescription drug marketing efforts by drug manufacturers provides another context in which to test *Discovery Network*'s rule that government may regulate commercial speech, but not noncommercial speech, only when commercial speech presents an identifiable social harm that identical noncommercial speech does not. For many years, the federal courts routinely sustained the FDA's ban against such marketing efforts. However, the enhanced scope of protection afforded to commercial speech over time placed increasing pressure on the FDA's ban against off-label marketing by drug makers. If one views commercial speech by a drug maker as presenting a more serious risk of being false and misleading, then a targeted ban on commercial speech of this sort, by this subset of speakers, might be consistent with *Discovery Network* because it constitutes a particularized threat that noncommercial speech about off-label drug applications would not. United States v. Caronia, 703 F.3d 149 (2012), casts serious doubt on this analysis and suggests that drug makers have a First Amendment right to actively promote off-label uses of FDA-approved drugs.

In order to sell a prescription medicine, a drug manufacturer must prove its efficacy to the FDA through a series of highly demanding clinical trials. *See* Food, Drug, and Cosmetic Act (FDCA), 21 U.S.C. §§ 331, 352, 355 (prohibiting the sale or promotion of "misbranded" drugs and requiring a pharmaceutical company to prove the efficacy of a drug for a particular condition and to label a drug consistently with the drug's established efficacy). Once approved based on demonstrated clinical efficacy, the drug's manufacturer may lawfully market that drug for its demonstrated purpose. However, the FDA has taken the position that a drug manufacturer may not *itself* market a prescription drug for "off-label" purposes, even though *physicians* are entirely free to prescribe prescription drugs for off-label uses. Thus, drug makers may not affirmatively advertise or promote an FDA-approved drug for such off-label uses—even if such uses are widely-accepted within the medical community.

For many years, federal courts sustained the FDA's ban against pharmaceutical companies marketing prescription drugs for off-label use—even though this constituted a speech restriction in a circumstance where the underlying speech was accurate and truthful and where it was also perfectly lawful for a physician to prescribe the drug for the off-label use to a patient. Moreover, anyone other than the drug's maker would have been quite free to promote an off-label use of an FDA-approved drug; only the drug's maker could run afoul the FDA's "misbranding" regulations. Misbranding of drugs, including promotion of off-label uses, exposed pharmaceutical companies and their marketing staff to both civil and criminal sanctions.

In 2012, however, following the Supreme Court's decision in *Sorrell*, the U.S. Court of Appeals for the Second Circuit invalidated the FDA's efforts to prohibit pharmaceutical companies from promoting the off-label use of FDA-approved prescription drugs. *See Caronia*, 703 F.3d at 166-69. Writing for the panel majority, Judge Denny Chin explained that "[t]he government's construction of the FDCA's misbranding provisions to prohibit and criminalize the promotion of off-label drug use by pharmaceutical manufacturers is content- and speaker-based, and, therefore, subject to heightened scrutiny." *Id.* at 164-65. Turning to the *Central Hudson* four-part test, Judge Chin easily found the first and second prongs were satisfied: Caronia's speech was truthful and non-misleading and related to a lawful product and the government possessed a substantial interest in preventing misleading or inaccurate drug marketing efforts by drug makers. *Id.* at 165-66. However, the government could not meet the third and fourth prongs of *Central Hudson* because the ban against promoting off-label uses did not directly advance the government's interest in avoiding misbranded prescription drugs nor was it narrowly tailored. *See id.* at 166-69.

The key to both holdings is the fact that it is perfectly legal to prescribe FDA-approved drugs for off-label uses. As Judge Chin explained, "off-label drug usage is not unlawful, and the FDA's drug approval process generally contemplates that approved drugs will be used in off-label ways." *Id.* at 166. Thus, "even if pharmaceutical manufacturers are barred from off-label promotion, physicians can prescribe, and patients can use, drugs for off-label purposes." *Id.* Thus, because off-label drug use is legal, "it does not follow that prohibiting the truthful promotion of off-label drug usage by a particular class of speakers would directly further the government's goals of preserving the efficacy and integrity of the FDA's drug approval process and reducing patient exposure to unsafe and ineffective drugs." *Id.* at 166.

Only if one views speech about off-label uses of prescription drugs as inherently "false and misleading" could the FDA's speech ban have survived constitutional scrutiny. And, in terms of *Discovery Network*, false and misleading commercial speech about prescription drugs would at least arguably constitute a particular evil that would justify targeted regulation. Because drug makers have a strong financial incentive to promote the widest possible use of their products, drug makers have a powerful financial incentive to push toward the outer limits of plausibility in making new claims about their products that other potential speakers do not. In this sense, then, a pharmaceutical company's speech promoting off-label uses of its FDA-approved drugs presents social risks that identical speech by others does not.

However, this logic only holds true if one accepts the view that *any* effort to promote off-label uses of prescription drugs presents an unacceptable risk of self-dealing by drug makers. As Dean Rodney Smolla has argued, "[t]he arguments advanced by the FDA to defend its ban on off-label drug promotion . . . are all deeply flawed when measured against modern First Amendment principles" because "[t]hose principles no longer permit the FDA to exert its near-absolute ban on truthful, non-misleading promotional and marketing information by pharmaceutical companies and their agents regarding the off-label uses of drugs." Rodney A. Smolla, *Off Label Drug Advertising and the First Amendment*, 50 Wake Forest L. Rev. 81, 91 (2015). Accordingly, "to the extent that drug companies seek to share information about the prescribing habits of other doctors and extant medical literature regarding off-label uses, the companies, even if sharing this information for a commercial purpose, appear to be trafficking in scientific data regarding prescription habits analytically indistinguishable from the information held protected by the First Amendment in *Sorrell.*" *Id.* at 103. *But cf.* David Orentlicher, *Off-Label Drug Marketing, The First Amendment, and Federalism*, 50 Wash. U. J.L. & Pol'y 89, 103 (2016) ("First Amendment concerns should not block regulation of off-label marketing. A company's off-label promotional speech provides probative evidence of illicit conduct—the distribution of misbranded drugs—and therefore restrictions of off-label promotion should not trigger First Amendment protection.").

The FDA declined to seek Supreme Court review of the Second Circuit's *Caronia* decision but has indicated that it will continue to initiate prosecutions for "false and misleading" promotion of off-brand use of prescription drugs. *See* Marc J. Scheineson & Guillermo Cuevas, United States v. Caronia, *The Increasing Strength of Commercial Free Speech and Potential New Emphasis on Classifying Off-Label Promotion as "False and Misleading"*, 68 Food & Drug L.J. 201, 211-12 (2013). Even if other federal and state courts find *Caronia* persuasive, serious questions remain to be addressed regarding what constitutes "truthful" off-label drug advertising. *See* Kathryn Bi, Comment, *What Is "False or Misleading" Off-Label Promotion?*, 82 U. Chi. L. Rev. 975 (2015) (noting that "[t]hough off-label promotion is at the center of numerous active lawsuits and a national policy debate, courts have not yet addressed what constitutes 'false or misleading' off-label speech" and proposing a theoretical and doctrinal framework for addressing this lacuna in existing law). For a thoughtful debate on the merits of *Caronia*, see Stephanie M. Greene & Lars Noah, *Debate: Off Label Drug Promotion and the First Amendment*, 162 U. Pa. L. Rev. Online 239 (2014).

THEORY-APPLIED PROBLEM

In 2023, the Federal Trade Commission considers adopting a "do-not-track" registry, largely modeled on its do-not-call registry; the new program would require all commercial Web site operators to offer a do-not-track option to persons who visit their Web sites. The incumbent chair of the FTC explains that "despite some good actors, self-regulation of privacy has not worked adequately and is not working adequately for American consumers." The chair adds that "[w]e would like to see companies work a lot faster to make consumer choice easier." Under the new regulations, all commercial Web sites (defined as "websites that seek to sell goods or services to the general public") must have an easy-to-find and easy-to-use do-not-track function that completely disables any and all tracking software or protocols from saving the visitor's data "for marketing or other commercial purposes." You work as an assistant general counsel for Boogle, a large and highly diversified Web services company that in part generates revenue by bundling, processing, and selling data obtained from third-party commercial Web sites. The proposed FTC regulation would interrupt the supply of Web site visitors' data, and thereby the data being analyzed, bundled, and sold to advertisers. Boogle's general counsel asks you to advise her on whether any valid First Amendment objections would potentially exist to the FTC's proposed mandatory do-not-track regulations. How do you advise her? Would such a challenge likely succeed in federal court? Moreover, does the commercial speech doctrine provide the only potential First Amendment objection to such a regulation? What other First Amendment issues might be raised in litigation?

D. THE PROBLEM OF DEFINING COMMERCIAL SPEECH

One distinct problem with the Supreme Court's commercial speech doctrine is the failure of the Justices to define with any precision exactly what constitutes "commercial" as opposed to "noncommercial" speech. Does any communication from a business or corporation count as commercial speech? What if the speaker has a financial motive for speaking but the speech itself does not solicit the sale of a good or service? Should the constitutional status of speech be measured by the identity of the speaker? The following three cases take up the problem of defining precisely when speech or speakers are "commercial" in nature.

Bolger v. Youngs Drug Products Corp.

463 U.S. 60 (1983)

Justice MARSHALL delivered the opinion of the Court.

Title 39 U.S.C. § 3001(e)(2) prohibits the mailing of unsolicited advertisements for contraceptives. The District Court held that, as applied to appellee's mailings, the statute violates the First Amendment. We affirm.

Section 3001(e)(2) states that "[a]ny unsolicited advertisement of matter which is designed, adapted, or intended for preventing conception is nonmailable matter, shall not be carried or delivered by mail, and shall be disposed of as the Postal Service directs. . . ." As interpreted by Postal Services regulations, the statutory provision does not apply to unsolicited advertisements in which the mailer has no commercial interest. In addition to the civil consequences of a violation of § 3001(e)(2), 18 U.S.C. § 1461 makes it a crime knowingly to use the mails for anything declared by § 3001(e) to be nonmailable.

Appellee Youngs Drug Products Corp. (Youngs) is engaged in the manufacture, sale, and distribution of contraceptives. Youngs markets its products primarily through sales to chain warehouses and wholesale distributors, who in turn sell contraceptives to retail pharmacists, who then sell those products to individual customers. Appellee publicizes the availability and desirability of its products by various methods. This litigation resulted from Youngs' decision to undertake a campaign of unsolicited mass mailings to members of the public. In conjunction with its wholesalers and retailers, Youngs seeks to mail to the public on an unsolicited basis three types of materials:

- multi-page, multi-item flyers promoting a large variety of products available at a drugstore, including prophylactics;
- flyers exclusively or substantially devoted to promoting prophylactics;
- informational pamphlets discussing the desirability and availability of prophylactics in general or Youngs' products in particular.

In 1979 the Postal Service traced to a wholesaler of Youngs' products an allegation of an unsolicited mailing of contraceptive advertisements. The Service warned the wholesaler that the mailing violated 39 U.S.C. § 3001(e)(2). Subsequently, Youngs contacted the Service and furnished it with copies of Youngs' three types of proposed mailings, stating its view that the statute could not constitutionally restrict the mailings. The Service rejected Youngs' legal argument and notified the company that the proposed mailings would violate § 3001(e)(2). Youngs then brought this action for declaratory and injunctive relief in the United States District Court for the District of Columbia. It claimed that the statute, as applied to its proposed mailings, violated the First Amendment and that Youngs and its wholesaler were refraining from distributing the advertisements because of the Service's warning.

[The federal district court agreed with Youngs Drug that § 3001(e)(2) violated the company's free speech rights. A direct appeal to the Supreme Court followed.]

Beginning with Bigelow v. Virginia, 421 U.S. 809 (1975), this Court extended the protection of the First Amendment to commercial speech. Nonetheless, our decisions have recognized "the 'common-sense' distinction between speech proposing a commercial transaction, which occurs in an area traditionally subject to government regulation, and other varieties of speech." Thus, we have held that the Constitution accords less protection to commercial speech than to other constitutionally safeguarded forms of expression. . . .

Because the degree of protection afforded by the First Amendment depends on whether the activity sought to be regulated constitutes commercial or noncommercial speech, we must first determine the proper classification of the mailings at issue here. Appellee contends that its proposed mailings constitute "fully protected" speech, so that § 3001(e)(2) amounts to an impermissible content-based restriction on such expression. Appellants argue, and the District Court held, that the proposed mailings are all commercial speech. The application of § 3001(e)(2) to appellee's proposed mailings must be examined carefully to ensure that speech deserving of greater constitutional protection is not inadvertently suppressed.

Most of appellee's mailings fall within the core notion of commercial speech—"speech which does 'no more than propose a commercial transaction.'" Youngs' informational pamphlets, however, cannot be characterized merely as proposals to engage in commercial transactions. Their proper classification as commercial or noncommercial speech thus presents a closer question. The mere fact that these pamphlets are conceded to be advertisements clearly does not compel the conclusion that they are commercial speech. Similarly, the reference to a specific product does not by itself render the pamphlets commercial speech. Finally, the fact that Youngs has an economic motivation for mailing the pamphlets would clearly be insufficient by itself to turn the materials into commercial speech.

The combination of all these characteristics, however, provides strong support for the District Court's conclusion that the informational pamphlets are properly characterized as commercial speech. The mailings constitute commercial speech notwithstanding the fact that they contain discussions of important public issues such as venereal disease and family planning. We have made clear that advertising which "links a product to a current public debate" is not thereby entitled to the constitutional protection afforded noncommercial speech. A company has the full panoply of protections available to its direct comments on public issues, so there is no reason for providing similar constitutional protection when such statements are made in the context of commercial transactions. Advertisers should not be permitted to immunize false or misleading product information from government regulation simply by including references to public issues.

We conclude, therefore, that all of the mailings in this case are entitled to the qualified but nonetheless substantial protection accorded to commercial speech.

[The Court applied the four-part *Central Hudson* test and found § 3001(e)(2) to be overbroad because the means selected (a complete ban) were not proportionate to the advancement of the government's substantial interest in protecting minors from information about birth control.]

We thus conclude that the justifications offered by appellants are insufficient to warrant the sweeping prohibition on the mailing of unsolicited contraceptive advertisements. As applied to appellee's mailings, § 3001(e)(2) is unconstitutional. The judgment of the District Court is therefore

Affirmed.

Justice REHNQUIST, with whom Justice O' CONNOR joins, concurring in the judgment.

I agree that the judgment should be affirmed, but my reasoning differs from that of the Court. The right to use the mails is undoubtedly protected by the First Amendment, Blount v. Rizzi, 400 U.S. 410 (1971). But because the home mailbox has features which distinguish it from a public hall or public park, where it may be assumed that all who are present wish to hear the views of the particular speaker then on the rostrum, it cannot be totally assimilated for purposes of analysis with these traditional public forums. . . .

The questions whether § 3001(e)(2) directly advances these interests, and whether it is more extensive than necessary, are more problematic [than whether the government possessed a substantial reason for the ban].

Thus, under this Court's cases the intrusion generated by Youngs' proposed advertising is relatively small, and the restriction imposed by § 3001(e)(2) is relatively large. Although this restriction directly advances weighty governmental interests, it is somewhat more extensive than is necessary to serve those interests. On balance I conclude that this restriction on Youngs' commercial speech has not been adequately justified. Section 3001(e)(2) therefore violates the First Amendment as applied to Youngs and to material of the type Youngs has indicated that it plans to send, and I agree that the judgment of the District Court should be affirmed.

Justice STEVENS, concurring in the judgment.

Two aspects of the Court's opinion merit further comment: (1) its conclusion that all of the communications at issue are properly classified as "commercial speech" (*ante*, at 68); and (2) its virtually complete rejection of offensiveness as a possibly legitimate justification for the suppression of speech. My views are somewhat different from the Court's on both of these matters.

Even if it may not intend to do so, the Court's opinion creates the impression that "commercial speech" is a fairly definite category of communication that is protected by a fairly definite set of rules that differ from those protecting other categories of speech. That impression may not be wholly warranted. . . .

NOTES AND QUESTIONS

1. *The problem of defining "commercial speech." Youngs Drug* is a hard case: At least some of the flyers in question made no effort to sell goods or services. "Condoms and Human Sexuality" and "Plain Talk About Venereal Disease" would undoubtedly be fully protected speech if distributed by a chapter of Planned Parenthood rather than Youngs Drug Products Corporation. Does the commercial motive of Youngs Drug render the speech commercial in nature? If not, what precise factor leads Justice Marshall to declare all the materials to constitute commercial speech?

2. *A distinction without a difference?* If a subjective commercial motivation (as objectively determined by a reviewing court) defines "commercial speech," is the *New York Times* or *ABC World News Tonight* commercial speech? Certainly the parent corporations of both the *New York Times* and *ABC World News Tonight* hope to make money by distributing newspapers and news programs. Moreover, the content exists in part to support the sale of advertising—printed ads in the case of a newspaper and commercial air time in the case of a broadcast network. Yet, if the New York Times and ABC World News Tonight both constitute commercial speech, what is left of the residual category of "noncommercial" speech? Suppose a politician running for Congress supports increased defense spending, in part because local industrial facilities within her congressional district contract with the Pentagon for the design and construction of weapons systems. Is the candidate's speech "commercial speech" because she hopes that, if elected, she will increase the net amount of economic activity in the community?
3. *The relevant factors and the governing test. Youngs Drug* relies on three factors to make the commercial speech determination: (1) the speaker's concession in court that the pamphlets were advertisements, (2) reference to Youngs Drug products (even if generically) in the pamphlets, and (3) an economic motivation for mailing the pamphlets. Should these factors be dispositive? *See* Ronald J. Krotoszynski, Jr., *Into the Woods: Broadcasters, Bureaucrats, and Children's Television Programming*, 45 Duke L.J. 1193 (1996) (arguing that the Supreme Court's attempts to define commercial speech have failed and would lead to incoherent results if followed consistently).
4. *False and misleading commercial speech.* Justice Marshall says that "[a]dvertisers should not be able to immunize false or misleading product information from government regulation simply by including references to public issues." Is this a kind of return to *Chrestensen*'s holding that mixing commercial and noncommercial speech does not have the effect of bringing the full weight of the Free Speech Clause to bear? Consider this question in light of the First National Bank of Boston v. Bellotti, 435 U.S. 765 (1978), *infra* p. 356.
5. *Corporate "political" speech?* The Supreme Court has held that a corporation cannot be prohibited from engaging in political speech—even when it is a regulated monopoly public service service provider and charges its customers (aka the rate payers) the costs associated with disseminating its speech. *See* Consolidated Edison Co. v. Pub. Serv. Comm'n, 447 U.S. 530 (1980). New York's PSC ordered the Consolidated Edison Company, a local electricity provider, to stop including billing inserts containing speech on public policy matters. *Id.* at 532-33 ("The Consolidated Edison Company of New York . . . placed written material entitled 'Independence Is Still a Goal, and Nuclear Power Is Needed to Win the Battle' in its January 1976 billing envelope."). Consolidated Edison sued in federal court, claiming that the PSC's order violated that company's First Amendment rights. The Supreme Court squarely sided with the utility company, holding that "the restriction on bill inserts cannot be upheld on the ground that Consolidated Edison is not entitled to freedom of speech."

Id. at 533. Justice Powell explained that "[t]he Commission has limited the means by which Consolidated Edison may participate in the public debate on this question [nuclear power] and other controversial issues of national interest and importance," thereby prohibiting "discussion of controversial issues" and "strik[ing] at the heart of the freedom to speak." *Id.* At no point in his analysis does Justice Powell pause to consider whether speech advocating a corporate speaker's product (in this case electricity) should be deemed "commercial" or "noncommercial" in nature. Instead, Justice Powell takes it as self-evident that an electric company's efforts to promote nuclear power constitute "noncommercial" speech. Is this correct?

6. *Should a profit motive matter?* In fairness to Justice Powell, even the concurring and dissenting Justices in *Consolidated Edison* did not quibble with affording Consolidated Edison's speech full First Amendment protection. Thus, it seems to be the case that if a corporation speaks about a controversial issue of the day without directly seeking to sell its own products (although even this proposition is debatable in *Consolidated Edison*), the fact that a for-profit corporation is speaking does not automatically render the speech "commercial" in nature.
7. *Corporations and noncommercial speech.* Should all corporate speech be deemed "commercial" in nature? Why would a corporation seek to communicate a message with the general public unless it advances the entity's economic interests? If a corporation engages in political speech, but has a financial motive for speaking directly related to its business interests, should the speech be deemed "commercial" or "noncommercial"? The raison d'être of a corporation is ostensibly to maximize shareholder wealth. Accordingly, should the government have the power to regulate corporate speech more aggressively than noncorporate speech? Reconsider these questions in light of the next principal case—which accepts uncritically the proposition that a corporation may engage in core political speech (despite possessing a clear economic motive for speaking).

First National Bank of Boston v. Bellotti

435 U.S. 765 (1978)

Mr. Justice Powell delivered the opinion of the Court.

In sustaining a state criminal statute that forbids certain expenditures by banks and business corporations for the purpose of influencing the vote on referendum proposals, the Massachusetts Supreme Court held that the First Amendment rights of a corporation are limited to issues that materially affect its business, property, or assets. The court rejected appellants' claim that the statute abridges freedom of speech in violation of the First and Fourteenth Amendments. The issue presented in this context is one of first impression in this Court. We now reverse.

The statute at issue [§ 8] prohibits appellants, two national banking associations and three business corporations, from making contributions or expenditures "for the purpose of . . . influencing or affecting the vote on any question submitted to the voter, other than one materially affecting any of the property, business or assets of the corporation." The statute further specifies that "[n]o question submitted to the voters solely concerning the taxation of the income, property or transactions of individuals shall be deemed materially to affect the property, business or assets of the corporation." A corporation that violates § 8 may receive a maximum fine of $50,000; a corporate officer, director, or agent who violates the section may receive a maximum fine of $10,000 or imprisonment for up to one year, or both.

Appellants wanted to spend money to publicize their views on a proposed constitutional amendment that was to be submitted to the voters as a ballot question at a general election on November 2, 1976. The amendment would have permitted the legislature to impose a graduated tax on the income of individuals. After appellee, the Attorney General of Massachusetts, informed appellants that he intended to enforce § 8 against them, they brought this action seeking to have the statute declared unconstitutional. . . .

Appellants argued that § 8 violates the First Amendment, the Due Process and Equal Protection Clauses of the Fourteenth Amendment, and similar provisions of the Massachusetts Constitution. They prayed that the statute be declared unconstitutional on its face and as it would be applied to their proposed expenditures. [The Supreme Judicial Court of Massachusetts rejected these objections and sustained § 8 as applied to the plaintiffs.]

The court below framed the principal question in this case as whether and to what extent corporations have First Amendment rights. We believe that the court posed the wrong question. The Constitution often protects interests broader than those of the party seeking their vindication. The First Amendment, in particular, serves significant societal interests. The proper question therefore is not whether corporations "have" First Amendment rights and, if so, whether they are coextensive with those of natural persons. Instead, the question must be whether § 8 abridges expression that the First Amendment was meant to protect. We hold that it does.

The speech proposed by appellants is at the heart of the First Amendment's protection. . . . The referendum issue that appellants wish to address falls squarely within [the protection of the Free Speech Clause]. In appellants' view, the enactment of a graduated personal income tax, as proposed to be authorized by constitutional amendment, would have a seriously adverse effect on the economy of the State. The importance of the referendum issue to the people and government of Massachusetts is not disputed. Its merits, however, are the subject of sharp disagreement. . . .

The court below nevertheless held that corporate speech is protected by the First Amendment only when it pertains directly to the corporation's business interests. In deciding whether this novel and restrictive gloss on the First Amendment comports with the Constitution and the precedents of this court, we need not survey the outer boundaries of the Amendment's protection of corporate speech, or address the abstract question whether corporations have the full measure of rights that individuals enjoy under the First Amendment. The question in this case, simply put, is whether the corporate identity of the speaker deprives this proposed speech of what otherwise would be its clear entitlement to protection. We turn now to that question.

The court below found confirmation of the legislature's definition of the scope of a corporation's First Amendment rights in the language of the Fourteenth

Amendment. Noting that the First Amendment is applicable to the States through the Fourteenth, and seizing upon the observation that corporations "cannot claim for themselves the liberty which the Fourteenth Amendment guarantees," Pierce v. Society of Sisters, 268 U.S. 510, 535 (1925), the court concluded that a corporation's First Amendment rights must derive from its property rights under the Fourteenth.

This is an artificial mode of analysis, untenable under decisions of this Court. . . . [The Court went on to find that corporate speech makes a valuable contribution to the marketplace of ideas.]

Nor do our recent commercial speech cases lend support to appellee's business interest theory. They illustrate that the First Amendment goes beyond protection of the press and the self-expression of individuals to prohibit government from limiting the stock of information from which members of the public may draw. A commercial advertisement is constitutionally protected not so much because it pertains to the seller's business as because it furthers the societal interest in the "free flow of commercial information."

We thus find no support in the First or Fourteenth Amendment, or in the decisions of this Court, for the proposition that speech that otherwise would be within the protection of the First Amendment loses that protection simply because its source is a corporation that cannot prove, to the satisfaction of a court, a material effect on its business or property. The "materially affecting" requirement is not an identification of the boundaries of corporate speech etched by the Constitution itself. Rather, it amounts to an impermissible legislative prohibition of speech based on the identity of the interests that spokesmen may represent in public debate over controversial issues and a requirement that the speaker have a sufficiently great interest in the subject to justify communication.

Section 8 permits a corporation to communicate to the public its views on certain referendum subjects—those materially affecting its business—but not others. It also singles out one kind of ballot question—individual taxation—as a subject about which corporations may never make their ideas public. The legislature has drawn the line between permissible and impermissible speech according to whether there is a sufficient nexus, as defined by the legislature, between the issue presented to the voters and the business interests of the speaker.

In the realm of protected speech, the legislature is constitutionally disqualified from dictating the subjects about which persons may speak and the speakers who may address a public issue. . . .

The constitutionality of § 8's prohibition of the "exposition of ideas" by corporations turns on whether it can survive the exacting scrutiny necessitated by a state-imposed restriction of freedom of speech. Especially where, as here, a prohibition is directed at speech itself and the speech is intimately related to the process of governing, "the State may prevail only upon showing a subordinating interest which is compelling," "and the burden is on the government to show the existence of such an interest." Even then, the State must employ means "closely drawn to avoid unnecessary abridgement." . . .

The Supreme Judicial Court did not subject § 8 to "the critical scrutiny demanded under accepted First Amendment and equal protection principles" because of its view that the First Amendment does not apply to appellants' proposed speech. For this reason the court did not even discuss the State's interests in considering appellants' First Amendment argument. [Justice Powell rejected the justifications that the state offered in support of the law.]

Because that portion of § 8 challenged by appellants prohibits protected speech in a manner unjustified by a compelling state interest, it must be invalidated. The judgment of the Supreme Judicial Court is

Reversed.

Mr. Chief Justice BURGER, concurring.

I join the opinion and judgment of the Court but write separately to raise some questions likely to arise in this area in the future. . . .

Because the First Amendment was meant to guarantee freedom to express and communicate ideas, I can see no difference between the right of those who seek to disseminate ideas by way of a newspaper and those who give lectures or speeches and seek to enlarge the audience by publication and wide dissemination. "[T]he purpose of the Constitution was not to erect the press into a privileged institution but to protect all persons in their right to print what they will as well as to utter it. '. . . the liberty of the press is no greater and no less . . .' than the liberty of every citizen of the Republic." Pennekamp v. Florida, 328 U.S. 331, 364 (1946) (Frankfurter, J., concurring).

In short, the First Amendment does not "belong" to any definable category of persons or entities: It belongs to all who exercise its freedoms.

Mr. Justice WHITE, with whom Mr. Justice BRENNAN and Mr. Justice MARSHALL join, dissenting.

The Massachusetts statute challenged here forbids the use of corporate funds to publish views about referenda issues having no material effect on the business, property, or assets of the corporation. The legislative judgment that the personal income tax issue, which is the subject of the referendum out of which this case arose, has no such effect was sustained by the Supreme Judicial Court of Massachusetts and is not disapproved by this Court today. Hence, as this case comes to us, the issue is whether a State may prevent corporate management from using the corporate treasury to propagate views having no connection with the corporate business. The Court commendably enough squarely faces the issue but unfortunately errs in deciding it. The Court invalidates the Massachusetts statute and holds that the First Amendment guarantees corporate managers the right to use not only their personal funds, but also those of the corporation, to circulate fact and opinion irrelevant to the business placed into their charge and necessarily representing their own personal or collective views about political and social questions. I do not suggest for a moment that the First Amendment requires a State to forbid such use of corporate funds, but I do strongly disagree that the First Amendment forbids state interference with managerial decisions of this kind. . . .

I would affirm the judgment of the Supreme Judicial Court for the Commonwealth of Massachusetts.

Mr. Justice REHNQUIST, dissenting.

[Justice Rehnquist's dissenting opinion is omitted.]

NOTES AND QUESTIONS

1. *The identity of the speaker and commercial speech.* Should the identity of the speaker be dispositive? In this respect, both *Consolidated Edison* and *Bellotti* are surprising cases. In neither case does the commercial motive for the speech affect—at all—the fully protected status of the speech. Writing for the majority in both cases, Justice Powell seems simply to assume that the speech at issue was noncommercial in nature, presumably because the speech did not attempt to sell directly a good or service. Yet, ConEd's speech directly related to business objectives—the building and operation of nuclear power plants in New York State. Similarly, the First National Bank of Boston was engaged in advocacy regarding a referendum issue to advance its commercial interests. Indeed, both *Consolidated Edison* and *Bellotti* apply strict scrutiny to the laws at issue—the strictest test known to contemporary constitutional law.
2. *The relevance of* Youngs Drug. How can the outcome—and standard of review—applied in *Youngs Drug* be reconciled with the more demanding standard of review applied in *Consolidated Edison* and *Bellotti*? One might infer that the Supreme Court is simply more concerned with the value of speech to a potential audience than it is with the economic motive of a corporate speaker. This would explain the Justices considering solely the content—but not the context—of corporate speech in cases like *Bellotti* and *Consolidated Edison*. If, however, audience autonomy should serve as the controlling consideration in First Amendment theory and doctrine, what basis (if any) does the Supreme Court have for affording commercial speech less protection than noncommercial speech in the first place? Should the federal courts assume a function that they would deny to the political branches—namely deciding the social worth of particular speech activity?
3. *Should the* Central Hudson *test apply?* At a minimum, if corporate speech is, by definition, "commercial speech," should state and federal limits on corporate speech be tested under the more generous standards of *Central Hudson*? Would *Bellotti* be decided differently if the Court had applied *Central Hudson*?
4. *A relevant distinction?* Given the robust protection that the Supreme Court has afforded commercial speech, and the sometimes parsimonious protection afforded political speech in traditional public forums (under the rubric of the time, place, and manner doctrine; *see, e.g.*, Ward v. Rock Against Racism, *supra*, page 129), does the definitional question ultimately matter?

AN EXTENDED NOTE ON COMMERCIAL VERSUS NONCOMMERCIAL USE OF A CELEBRITY'S PERSONA WITHOUT PERMISSION OR CONSENT

In Jordan v. Jewel Food Stores, Inc., 743 F. 3d 509 (2014), Jewel Food Stores, Inc. (Jewel), a company that operates the Jewel-Osco grocery store chain in Chicago, Illinois, agreed to buy advertising space in *Sports Illustrated*; in exchange for the advertising buy, Jewel Food Stores received a full page in a special commemorative edition of *Sports Illustrated* celebrating Michael Jordan's induction into the Basketball Hall of Fame. Jewel's copy in this special edition featured a pair of sneakers emblazoned with Jordan's jersey number (23) and text reading "A Shoe In! After six NBA championships, scores of rewritten record books and numerous buzzer beaters, Michael Jordan's elevation in the Basketball Hall of Fame was never in doubt! Jewel-Osco salutes #23 on his many accomplishments as we honor a fellow Chicagoan who was 'just around the corner' for so many years." *Id.* at 512. The full page display, which appeared on the inside back cover of the special issue, also prominently featured Jewel-Osco's logo and slogan. Michael Jordan sued Jewel after publication of the special issue, seeking $5 million in compensatory damages, as well as additional exemplary damages, alleging a violation of federal trademark law as well as an Illinois right of publicity statute. Jewel moved for summary judgment, arguing that both Jordan's federal and state claims were precluded by the First Amendment. *Id.* at 512-13. The district court accepted Jewel's characterization of its copy as constitutionally protected noncommercial speech and entered summary judgment in the company's favor; Jordan appealed this decision.

The Seventh Circuit reversed, finding that the copy constituted commercial, rather than noncommercial, speech. Writing for the panel majority, Judge Diane Sykes observed that "[i]t's clear that the textual focus of Jewel's ad is a congratulatory salute to Jordan on his induction into the Hall of Fame" and, accordingly, "[i]f the literal import of the words were all that mattered, this celebratory tribute would be noncommercial." *Id.* at 517. However, "evaluating the text requires consideration of its context, and this truism has special force when applying the commercial-speech doctrine." *Id.* This is so because "[m]odern commercial advertising is enormously varied in form and style." *Id.* at 517-18.

On the facts presented, the copy had two functions: congratulating Jordan and promoting Jewel-Osco grocery stores. Thus, "considered in context, and without the rose-colored glasses, Jewel's ad has an unmistakable commercial function: enhancing the Jewel-Osco brand in the minds of consumers." Moreover, "[t]his commercial message is implicit but easily inferred, and is the dominant one." In consequence, the copy in the special edition constituted commercial speech. *See id.* at 519 (noting that "the ad's commercial nature is readily apparent" even though "[i]t may be generic and implicit"). Thus, the Seventh Circuit used an objective analysis to ascertain the probable subjective intent of the speaker; on the facts presented, Jewel's copy constituted "a form of image advertising aimed at promoting goodwill for the Jewel-Osco brand by exploiting public affection for Jordan at an auspicious moment in his career." *Id.*

Are you persuaded by this analysis? By way of contrast, could the University of North Carolina use Michael Jordan's image without his consent in promotional materials touting the success of its student athletes? Or would this use constitute "commercial" speech, potentially engendering trademark and right of personality liability for the university, if the university were trying to exploit Jordan's image as part of it general marketing and recruiting efforts? The *Jewel Food Stores* court observed that "[n]othing we say here is meant to suggest that a company cannot use its graphic logo or slogan in an otherwise noncommercial way without thereby transforming the communication into commercial speech." *Id.* at 520. But when a for-profit company includes the image of a public figure in corporate promotional materials, won't it be very hard pressed to prove that its motives did not encompass "image advertising"? Clearly, simply avoiding the inclusion of "an outright sales pitch," *id.*, is not enough to alter the essentially commercial nature of corporate promotional material. But what would be?

Under this broad reasoning, what, if anything, could Jewel have done to avoid having its effort to publicly congratulate Michael Jordan on his election to the Hall of Fame engender a multi-million dollar trademark and right of personality liability? Would an express disclaimer in the copy—"This Is Not an Advertisement"—have worked for Jewel? Or should we be concerned about the ability of a publicly traded corporation to appropriate a celebrity's image without incurring liability of this sort? After all, what precisely is the social value of Jewel's speech? And should this affect the balancing of the relevant interests? Could the Chicago public school district have run the same ad, in precisely the same way, without it being considered commercial speech? Why or why not? Should we generally assume that corporate speakers engage in commercial speech—at least in close cases—on the theory that most of the time, corporations act to maximize shareholder wealth?

THEORY-APPLIED PROBLEM

Perhaps, like Justice Stewart and obscenity, the Justices "know [commercial speech] when they see it." Is the definition of commercial speech simply a matter of intuition? If so, consider the following hypotheticals and analyze whether the speech is "commercial" or "noncommercial."

1. Philip Morris sponsors a traveling exhibit on the Constitution and Bill of Rights. To promote this exhibit, the company takes out large full-page ads in local papers, stating "Philip Morris Supports Freedom, You Should, Too!"
2. Absolut Vodka places print ads in a variety of magazines, featuring an Absolut vodka bottle wrapped in bright red tape, with the phrase "Absolut DC" underneath the bottle.
3. Andy Warhol creates a series of silk-screen images of Campbell's soup cans and seeks to exhibit them in a local Pittsburgh, Pennsylvania, public gallery space. The city government rejects the submission for the exhibit "because of the commercial nature of the art." Campbell's Soup, enamored of the Warhol prints, reproduces them in a variety of newspaper and magazine spreads, with "Campbell's M'm! M'm! Good!" beneath the prints.

AN EXTENDED NOTE ON *CITIZENS UNITED v. FEC*

In Citizens United v. FEC, 558 U.S. 310 (2010) (excerpted *supra* p. 118), the Supreme Court reaffirmed and extended its prior holdings that corporations are entitled to the full protection of the First Amendment when engaging in political speech. Writing for the majority, Justice Kennedy explained that

> [p]remised on mistrust of governmental power, the First Amendment stands against attempts to disfavor certain subjects or viewpoints. See, e.g., United States v. Playboy Entertainment Group, Inc., 529 U.S. 803, 813 (2000) (striking down content-based restriction). Prohibited, too, are restrictions distinguishing among different speakers, allowing speech by some but not others. See First Nat. Bank of Boston v. Bellotti, 435 U.S. 765, 784 (1978). As instruments to censor, these categories are interrelated: Speech restrictions based on the identity of the speaker are all too often simply a means to control content.
>
> Quite apart from the purpose or effect of regulating content, moreover, the Government may commit a constitutional wrong when by law it identifies certain preferred speakers. By taking the right to speak from some and giving it to others, the Government deprives the disadvantaged person or class of the right to use speech to strive to establish worth, standing, and respect for the speaker's voice. The Government may not by these means deprive the public of the right and privilege to determine for itself what speech and speakers are worthy of consideration. The First Amendment protects speech and speaker, and the ideas that flow from each.

558 U.S. at 340-41. Justice Kennedy concluded that "[w]e find no basis for the proposition that, in the context of political speech, the Government may impose restrictions on certain disfavored speakers." *Id.* at 341.

The importance of protecting core political speech from government censorship plainly serves as the linchpin of the *Citizens United* majority's logic:

> When Government seeks to use its full power, including the criminal law, to command where a person may get his or her information or what distrusted source he or she may not hear, it uses censorship to control thought. This is unlawful. The First Amendment confirms the freedom to think for ourselves.

Id. at 356.

Yet, with respect to for-profit, publicly traded corporations, the entity exists for one and only one purpose, namely, to maximize shareholder wealth. We can place to one side nonprofit entities, such as the NRA or Planned Parenthood, that use a corporate form to harness the energy of a large, broad-based membership base to influence public policy regarding matters such as gun control or family planning. Companies such as General Motors or Walmart, however, do not exist for the purpose of doing anything more than returning a profit to their investors. In what respect, then, can the "political" speech of a for-profit enterprise be deemed anything but "commercial speech"? Can speech by a for-profit corporation ever be truly noncommercial? Isn't the concept of "corporate political speech," at least with respect to for-profit enterprises, an oxymoron?

If the animating purpose of the speech is to facilitate the sale of goods or services, then the fact that the content might otherwise constitute noncommercial speech should be of no moment whatsoever. *See Youngs Drug, supra* p. 352. *Citizens United*, like *Bellotti* before it, completely elides this point and appears simply to assume that speech by for-profit corporations related to candidates and elections can and does constitute noncommercial speech, entitled to the fullest protection of the First Amendment. *See Citizens United*, 558 U.S. at 319 ("The government may regulate *corporate political speech* through disclaimer and disclosure requirements, but it may not suppress that speech altogether." (emphasis added)).

Does—or should—the profit motive affect the potential value of political speech sponsored by for-profit corporations? Alternatively, should the protected status of corporate political communications depend on the precise context and content of the speech? The identity of the speaker? Both? Neither? Or does *Citizens United* suggest that the commercial or noncommercial character of speech is not to be gleaned from the intent or purpose of the *speaker* in communicating the message but rather on the potential value and purpose of the information to the *intended audience*? Under this approach, the listener, rather than the speaker, would determine the nature of the speech as either commercial or noncommercial. But, if this is so, where does this leave *Youngs Drug*'s approach of considering the motive of the speaker in assessing how to characterize the nature of the speech being regulated?

On the other hand, in the context of *Citizens United*, would characterization of speech by for-profit corporations as "commercial speech" rather than "political speech" affect the probable outcome of a First Amendment challenge to the federal government's flat ban on such communications? In other words, would a flat ban on corporate political speech pass muster under *Central Hudson*'s four-part test? If not, then the question of whether a for-profit corporation may ever engage in noncommercial speech might be less important than it seemed upon first consideration.

Suppose, however, that the federal government sought to regulate political advertising by for-profit corporations rather than simply ban it outright, perhaps by requiring that shareholders specifically approve any such expenditures from the corporation's treasury. With respect to something short of a complete ban, the characterization of the speech being regulated as "commercial" or "noncommercial" might well prefigure the validity of the regulation.

If corporate political speech were characterized as commercial speech, however, interesting questions would immediately arise regarding how to apply the *Central Hudson* test—and particularly the first prong of the test, namely that the speech must be "truthful and non-misleading." When a 30-second television or radio spot says, "Jane Doe would be a great U.S. Senator and far better than the present incumbent," how does one assess whether the speech is "truthful and non-misleading"? Would the government itself get to make this determination? Or would this task be left to the federal courts? Or does the difficulty of ascertaining the truth or falsity of political speech mean that it is best to simply leave the question up to the marketplace to resolve? *See, e.g.*, United States v. Alvarez, 567 U.S. 709 (2012).

To date, the Supreme Court has simply assumed that speech that appears to be political in nature, even if disseminated by a for-profit corporation, is fully and completely "political speech" rather than "commercial speech." The question of how to properly characterize such speech, however, seems significantly more complicated than the Justices have acknowledged. In sum, important issues remain and seem to require a fuller exposition than they have received to date.

THEORY-APPLIED PROBLEM

Acme Cigarettes has developed "Fred the Fox" as its corporate logo. Fred the Fox appears in a wide variety of mail, print, and billboard advertisements for Acme's cigarettes. Children's advocates claim that Fred the Fox is a thinly veiled effort to market cigarettes to children, who cannot lawfully purchase, possess, or consume them. Many of the advertisements appear in California. Acme issues a press release stating that "Fred the Fox does not encourage underage smoking—empirical evidence proves this to be true." It also purchases newspaper advertising space and broadcast radio and television ads defending Fred the Fox. The Smoke-Free Children's Alliance brings a suit under the California Unfair Competition Law, alleging that Acme has intentionally misled consumers in an effort to increase sales.

Is the speech at issue "commercial" or "noncommercial"? Should it be subject to suppression in the same fashion as speech that misstates the gas mileage of a truck or claims that sugar pills cure cancer? Does *Central Hudson*'s first prong provide the answer: Such speech can be regulated because it is "false and misleading"? If so, then the characterization of the speech as "commercial" rather than "noncommercial" could well prove to be outcome determinative.

Chapter 8

Regulation of the Mass Media

Table of Contents

A. Regulation of the Press

B. Media Newsgathering and Access Rights

   1. Reporter's Privilege Against Compelled Disclosure of Confidential Sources
   2. Access to Courtrooms
   3. Access to Government Institutions

C. Prior Restraints

   1. The Presumption of Unconstitutionality
   2. The National Security Exception
   3. Free Press/Fair Trial

D. Regulation of Broadcasters

E. Regulation of Cable System Operators

F. Regulation of the Internet and New Media

G. The Future of Big Tech Regulation

The First Amendment to the U.S. Constitution protects both freedom of speech and freedom of the press, but the Supreme Court typically treats them as merely different facets of a more general right to freedom of expression. In interpreting the First Amendment's Press Clause, the Court has often stated that the press is entitled to no greater First Amendment protection than the general public, and most First Amendment decisions involving the media are grounded at least as much in the Free Speech Clause of the First Amendment as in the Press Clause.

That said, members of the mass communications media have litigated a number of seminal First Amendment cases before the Supreme Court, and the resulting jurisprudence often reflects their interests. The focus of this chapter, therefore, is on the body of case law most directly affecting the media. As you read these cases, you should pay special attention to the following questions. First, does "the press" receive special First Amendment protections under the Press Clause not accorded to other speakers under the Free Speech Clause? A second question is intertwined with the first: If "the press" receives special First Amendment protections, what is "the press"? This question has become more difficult to answer since the advent of the internet, which provides most American citizens with the ability to distribute their views through a medium of mass communication. A third question is whether newsgathering activities receive the same level of First Amendment protection as publication of the news. Finally, to what extent is the First Amendment's protection "medium-specific"? As you will see, most First Amendment principles apply equally to all media—broadcasting, print, Internet publishers, satellite, and cable programmers and operators—but a few apply differently, particularly when it comes to broadcasting, due to the special characteristics of the medium.

The Framers of the First Amendment left very little indication of whether "freedom of the press" was meant to protect the press as an institution that plays a "structural" role in enabling democratic self-governance, or whether it merely was meant to protect speech when widely disseminated by means of the printing press. If the latter is the case, anyone who "functions" as the press by distributing his or her speech to a mass audience should be able to claim protection under the Press Clause of the First Amendment as well as the Free Speech Clause. Scholars have debated whether the structural or functional definition of the press is consistent with the Framer's intent.

Leading media law scholar David Anderson contends, based on his historical research, that the Framers were influenced by contemporary state constitutions protecting freedom of the press; the Framers viewed the Press Clause as a necessary protection for the press's role in checking governmental abuses of power. In contrast, the protection of freedom of speech seems to have reflected concern for individual autonomy. *See generally* David A. Anderson, *The Origin of the Press Clause*, 30 UCLA L. Rev. 455, 534 (1983). Professor Eugene Volokh, on the other hand, contends that the Speech Clause of the First Amendment protects spoken words and the Press Clause protects printed words, that is, words that can be broadly disseminated. He looks to how the word "press" was defined both around 1791, when the First Amendment was drafted, and in 1868, when the Fourteenth Amendment was ratified, and contends that the text was understood to protect a "technology," not an industry or institution. *See generally* Eugene Volokh, *Freedom for the Press as an Industry, or the Press as a Technology? From the Framing to Today*, 160 U. Pa. L. Rev. 1 (2011).

The conception of the Press Clause as a structural protection for the press as an institution was famously advocated by Justice Potter Stewart. Justice Stewart's structural account of the Press Clause led him to argue for special First Amendment privileges for the institutional press. For example, Justice Stewart contended that the press (but not individuals) has a First Amendment privilege not to disclose confidential news sources to a grand jury. He also contended that the press (but not individuals) deserves special protections against being held liable for defamation of public officials. *See generally* Potter Stewart, *Or of the Press*, 26 Hastings L.J. 631 (1975). Justice Stewart's view has never been adopted by the Court, and, indeed, in Citizens United v. Federal Elections Comm'n, 558 U.S. 50 (2010), the Court expressly stated that the "institutional press" has no "constitutional privilege beyond that of other speakers." *But see* id. at 431 n.57 (Stevens, J., concurring in part and dissenting in part) (suggesting that the press "might be able to claim special First Amendment status" under the Press Clause).

There are powerful pragmatic reasons that the Court has tended to embrace a functional account of the Press Clause, typically extending protection to anyone who publishes to a mass audience. This functional account avoids the difficult problem of defining which members of the press qualify for special privileges, a problem that has been compounded as first the Internet and now mobile-based technologies have turned millions of ordinary citizens into publishers. That said, many of the Supreme Court's most important First Amendment decisions are shaped by the needs and interests of the institutional press, one of the few repeat players in First Amendment litigation.

Before reading the cases in this chapter, it is important to acknowledge how much the institutional press has changed since the Supreme Court decided many of them. The growth of the Internet and social media companies such as Meta (formerly Facebook), YouTube, Google, Apple, and Twitter over the last two decades produced a seismic shift in news consumption habits and the advertising revenue model undergirding the newspaper industry. A Pew Research report in 2020 revealed that newspapers made more money from circulation than from advertising for the first time, and a 2021 report revealed that more U.S. adults get news from a smartphone, computer, or tablet than from television. Consumption of news through print and radio is much less frequent than consumption online and through television. As a result of the upheaval caused by this economic and technological revolution, newsroom employment fell by 26% between 2008 and 2021. Perhaps related to the exodus of newsroom talent, a 2022 Axios report revealed that "[a] majority of people globally believe journalists (67%), government leaders (66%) and business executives (63%) are 'purposely trying to mislead people by saying things they know are false or gross exaggerations.'"

Social media function like traditional media actors in some respects: they sometimes decide what content to publish and what to withhold and they sometimes make their own contributions to public discourse. Yet their main function is to serve as a conduit for the speech of others, and they do this at a scale that no newspaper can match. This creates some unique First Amendment challenges, as you will see in this chapter.

A. *REGULATION OF THE PRESS*

As noted above, the press has been a frequent litigant in First Amendment cases in the Supreme Court. Much of this litigation has addressed the press's ability to gather and disseminate news and information. The case below, however, involves a state law imposing a limit on the press's ability to advocate for or against a government policy by publishing an election-day editorial. As you read it, consider whether the case would have come out differently if the law had been applied against an individual speaker rather than a member of the institutional press.

Mills v. Alabama

384 U.S. 214 (1966)

Mr. Justice Black delivered the opinion of the Court.

[The Alabama Corrupt Practices Act made it a crime to solicit votes for or against any ballot proposition on election day. The Birmingham Post-Herald carried an election-day editorial urging voters to support a ballot proposition replacing their existing city commission with a mayor-council system. Editor James E. Mills was arrested for violating the statute. The trial court granted a demurrer on the criminal complaint, but the Alabama Supreme Court reversed, holding that the law was a reasonable restriction imposing only a minor limitation on the press.]

I.

[The Court rejected the argument that there was no final judgment because Mills had not yet been convicted.]

II.

We come now to the merits. The First Amendment, which applies to the States through the Fourteenth, prohibits laws "abridging the freedom of speech, or of the press." The question here is whether it abridges freedom of the press for a State to punish a newspaper editor for doing no more than publishing an editorial on election day urging people to vote a particular way in the election. We should point out at once that this question in no way involves the extent of a State's power to regulate conduct in and around the polls in order to maintain peace, order and decorum there. The sole reason for the charge that Mills violated the law is that he wrote and published an editorial on election day urging Birmingham voters to cast their votes in favor of changing their form of government.

Whatever differences may exist about interpretations of the First Amendment, there is practically universal agreement that a major purpose of that Amendment was to protect the free discussion of governmental affairs. This of course includes discussions of candidates, structures and forms of government, the manner in which government is operated or should be operated, and all such matters relating to political processes. The Constitution specifically selected the press, which includes not only newspapers, books, and magazines, but also humble leaflets and circulars, see Lovell v. City of Griffin, 303 U.S. 444, to play an important role in the discussion of public affairs. Thus the press serves and was designed to serve as a powerful antidote to any abuses of power by governmental officials and as a constitutionally chosen means for keeping officials elected by the people responsible to all the people whom they were selected to serve. Suppression of the right of the press to praise or criticize governmental agents and to clamor and contend for or against change, which is all that this editorial did, muzzles one of the very agencies the Framers of our Constitution thoughtfully and deliberately selected to improve our society and keep it free. The Alabama Corrupt Practices Act by providing criminal penalties for publishing editorials such as the one here silences the press at a time it can be most effective. . . . [T]he Alabama Supreme Court nevertheless sustained the constitutionality of the law on the ground that the restrictions on the press were only 'reasonable restrictions' or at least 'within the field of reasonableness.' The court reached this conclusion because it thought the law imposed only a minor limitation on the press-restricting it only on election days-and because the court thought the law served a good purpose. It said:

> 'It is a salutary legislative enactment that protects the public from confusive last-minute charges and countercharges and the distribution of

propaganda in an effort to influence voters on an election day; when as a practical matter, because of lack of time, such matters cannot be answered or their truth determined until after the election is over.' [ ]

This argument, even if it were relevant to the constitutionality of the law, has a fatal flaw. The state statute leaves people free to hurl their campaign charges up to the last minute of the day before election. The law held valid by the Alabama Supreme Court then goes on to make it a crime to answer those 'last-minute' charges on election day, the only time they can be effectively answered. Because the law prevents any adequate reply to these charges, it is wholly ineffective in protecting the electorate 'from confusive last-minute charges and countercharges.' We hold that no test of reasonableness can save a state law from invalidation as a violation of the First Amendment when that law makes it a crime for a newspaper editor to do no more than urge people to vote one way or another in a publicly held election.

The judgment of the Supreme Court of Alabama is reversed and the case is remanded for further proceedings not inconsistent with this opinion. . . .

Mr. Justice DOUGLAS, with whom Mr. Justice BRENNAN joins, concurring [omitted].

[Justice Harlan would have dismissed the appeal for want of a final judgment.]

NOTES AND QUESTIONS

1. *Non-press speakers.* Justice Black describes the statute as a "flagrant abridgment of the constitutionally guaranteed freedom of the press," and his opinion emphasizes the press's constitutional role in the discussion of public affairs. Does that indicate that this is a press clause decision that would not necessarily apply to a non-press speaker? For example, would *Mills* preclude enforcement of a statute that forbade candidates from making last-minute accusations about their opponents?
2. *Strict scrutiny?* What test does the Supreme Court apply to resolve this case? Does the Court hold the statute unconstitutional because it is a content-based regulation of speech?
3. *Generally applicable laws.* Like other businesses, the media are subject to generally applicable laws. For example, they must obey employment laws, municipal ordinances, and pay taxes. The government does not violate the First Amendment by subjecting the media to these laws, though even generally applicable laws may be subject to enhanced scrutiny when they appear to disproportionately target or affect the press. For example, given that the power to tax is the power to destroy and that the government may attempt to use its taxing power to silence or punish those with whom it disagrees, the Supreme Court has applied heightened First Amendment scrutiny where taxes singled out the media for a burden place on no other speakers, where they disproportionately affect a small number of media, or where the tax burden is based on the content of the publication. *See* Leathers v. Medlock, 499 U.S. 439 (1990).

4. In *Citizens United v. Fed. Election Com'n*, the Supreme Court held that corporations have a right to engage in political speech just as media corporations do. The Court struck down a law prohibiting corporations from using their general treasury funds to make "electioneering communications" within 30 days of a primary election or 60 days of a general election for federal office. The statute the Court struck down had an exemption for media corporations, but the Court stated that "[d]ifferential treatment of media corporations and other corporations cannot be squared with the First Amendment." In contrast, the dissenting justices wrote: "The press plays a unique role not only in the text, history, and structure of the First Amendment but also in facilitating public discourse . . . ". Id. at 473-74 (Stevens, J., with whom Justice Ginsburg, Breyer, and Sotomayor join, concurring in part and dissenting in part). By implication, this special role might justify differential treatment of media corporations. Does the majority's holding make *Mills* less significant as a "press" case?
5. *A right to videotape police?* Courts in every federal circuit have addressed whether citizens have a constitutional right to film police performing their duties in public places. Almost all have held that such a right exists, subject to reasonable time, place, and manner restrictions. *See, e.g.*, ACLU v. Alvarez, 679 F.3d 583 (7th Cir. 2012); Fields v. City of Philadelphia, 862 F.3d 353, 360 (3d Cir. 2017). *See also* Doori Song, *Qualified Immunity and the Clear, but Unclear First Amendment Right to Film Police*, 33 Notre Dame J. of Law, Ethics & Pub'l Pol'y, 337 (2019) (collecting cases and discussing the debate over whether the constitutional right is clearly established enough to defeat officers' claims to qualified immunity for taking actions against those filming them in public).

B. *MEDIA NEWSGATHERING AND ACCESS RIGHTS*

In order to report on important events, the media must be able to gather information. The media's need to gather information gives rise to two distinct First Amendment claims. First, the media sometimes claim that the First Amendment gives them a right to be free from government interference with their information-gathering efforts. Thus, in *Branzburg v. Hayes*, below, the media claimed that a qualified privilege protected reporters from being forced to testify about the identity of their confidential sources when subpoenaed to testify before grand juries. The claim to a constitutional "reporter's privilege," in essence, is a claim that the First Amendment gives the media a right to be free from government interference with confidential source relationships.

Yet this is not the only First Amendment claim that the media make on behalf of their need to gather information. At times, the media also claim a right to receive access to information possessed or controlled by the government. The media, for example, have claimed a First Amendment right of access to criminal trials, government institutions, and civil discovery documents. The materials in this chapter deal only with First Amendment claims of access, but bear in mind that both federal and state statutes give the media access to a wide variety of government information. For example, the federal Freedom of Information Act gives citizens a right of access to a wide array of information in the hands of executive agencies. Similar legislation at the state level gives citizens access to various types of government meetings and government documents. These statutory claims should not be confused with the constitutional claims discussed below.

1. *Reporter's Privilege Against Compelled Disclosure of Confidential Sources*

Branzburg v. Hayes

408 U.S. 665 (1972)

(Together with *In re Pappas* and *United States v. Caldwell.*)

WHITE, J., wrote the opinion of the Court, in which BURGER, C.J., and BLACKMUN, POWELL, and REHNQUIST, JJ., joined.

[This case involved four consolidated cases in which reporters were subpoenaed to testify before criminal grand juries. Branzburg, a reporter for the Courier-Journal, a Louisville, Kentucky newspaper, was involved in two of the cases. One of the cases involved a story Branzburg wrote regarding the production of hashish; the story was based on his personal observations of two local residents of Jefferson County, Kentucky, synthesizing hashish from marijuana. Shortly after this story ran in the Courier-Journal, Branzburg was subpoenaed by a Jefferson County grand jury. He appeared but refused to identify anyone involved in making hashish. The state trial court ordered him to identify them and rejected his claim that the state reporters' privilege statute, the First Amendment to the U.S. Constitution, or the Kentucky Constitution protected him from having to reveal the information. He sought writs of prohibition and mandamus, which were denied by the Kentucky Court of Appeals, which also denied his writs of prohibition and mandamus in a second, similar case.]

In re Pappas [involved a reporter who gained entrance to the police-barricaded headquarters of the Black Panthers in New Bedford, Massachusetts]. As a condition of entry, Pappas agreed not to disclose anything he saw or heard inside the store except an anticipated police raid. . . . [The raid never took place, but the reporter was subpoenaed to testify before a grand jury. He] refused to answer any questions about what had taken place inside headquarters while he was there, claiming that the First Amendment afforded him a privilege to protect confidential informants and their information. A second summons was then served upon him, [but the trial judged denied his motion to quash because Massachusetts had no statutory reporter's privilege. The Supreme Judicial Court of Massachusetts affirmed.]

United States v. Caldwell . . . arose from subpoenas issued by a federal grand jury in the Northern District of California to respondent Earl Caldwell, a reporter for the New York Times assigned to cover the Black Panther Party and other black militant groups. [Caldwell was served with a subpoena that ordered him to testify before a grand jury investigating the Black Panther Party.] Respondent and his employer, the New York Times, moved to quash on the ground that the unlimited breadth of the subpoenas and the fact that Caldwell would have to appear in secret before the grand jury would destroy his working relationship with the Black Panther Party and "suppress vital First Amendment freedoms . . . by driving a wedge of distrust and silence between the news media and the militants." . . .

[The District Court denied Respondent's motion to quash, and upon Caldwell's refusal to testify, ordered him jailed for contempt. The Court of Appeals reversed the contempt order based on a qualified First Amendment privilege. The Supreme Court then granted certiorari.]

II

. . . Although the newsmen in these cases do not claim an absolute privilege against official interrogation in all circumstances, they assert that the reporter should not be forced either to appear or to testify before a grand jury or at trial until and unless sufficient grounds are shown for believing that the reporter possesses information relevant to a crime the grand jury is investigating, that the information the reporter has is unavailable from other sources, and that the need for the information is sufficiently compelling to override the claimed invasion of First Amendment interests occasioned by the disclosure. . . . The heart of the claim is that the burden on news gathering resulting from compelling reporters to disclose confidential information outweighs any public interest in obtaining the information.

We do not question the significance of free speech, press, or assembly to the country's welfare. Nor is it suggested that news gathering does not qualify for First Amendment protection; without some protection for seeking out the news, freedom of the press could be eviscerated. But these cases involve no intrusions upon speech or assembly, no prior restraint or restriction on what the press may publish, and no express or implied command that the press publish what it prefers to withhold. No exaction or tax for the privilege of publishing, and no penalty, civil or criminal, related to the content of published material is at issue here. The use of confidential sources by the press is not forbidden or restricted; reporters remain free to seek news from any source by means within the law. No attempt is made to require the press to publish its sources of information or indiscriminately to disclose them on request.

The sole issue before us is the obligation of reporters to respond to grand jury subpoenas as other citizens do and to answer questions relevant to an investigation into the commission of crime. Citizens generally are not constitutionally immune from grand jury subpoenas; and neither the First Amendment nor any other constitutional provision protects the average citizen from disclosing to a grand jury information that he has received in confidence. The claim is, however, that reporters are exempt from these obligations because if forced to respond to subpoenas and identify their sources or disclose other confidences, their informants will refuse or be reluctant to furnish newsworthy information in the future. This asserted burden on news gathering is said to make compelled testimony from newsmen constitutionally suspect and to require a privileged position for them.

It is clear that the First Amendment does not invalidate every incidental burdening of the press that may result from the enforcement of civil or criminal statutes of general applicability. Under prior cases, otherwise valid laws serving substantial public interests may be enforced against the press as against others, despite the possible burden that may be imposed. The Court has emphasized that "the publisher of a newspaper has no special immunity from the application of general laws. He has no special privilege to invade the rights and liberties of others." Associated Press v. NLRB, 301 U.S. 103, 132-133 (1937). It was there held that the Associated Press, a news-gathering and disseminating organization, was not exempt from the requirements of the National Labor Relations Act. . . .

It has generally been held that the First Amendment does not guarantee the press a constitutional right of special access to information not available to the public generally. In *Zemel v. Rusk*, for example, [a ban on travel to Cuba] was held constitutional, for "the right to speak and publish does not carry with it the unrestrained right to gather information."

Despite the fact that news gathering may be hampered, the press is regularly excluded from grand jury proceedings, our own conferences, the meetings of other official bodies gathered in executive session, and the meetings of private organizations. Newsmen have no constitutional right of access to the scenes of crime or disaster when the general public is excluded, and they may be prohibited from attending or publishing information about trials if such restrictions are necessary to assure a defendant a fair trial before an impartial tribunal. . . .

It is thus not surprising that the great weight of authority is that newsmen are not exempt from the normal duty of appearing before a grand jury and answering questions relevant to a criminal investigation. . . .

The prevailing constitutional view of the newsman's privilege is very much rooted in the ancient role of the grand jury that has the dual function of determining if there is probable cause to believe that a crime has been committed and of protecting citizens against unfounded criminal prosecutions. Grand jury proceedings are constitutionally mandated for the institution of federal criminal prosecutions for capital or other serious crimes, and "its constitutional prerogatives are rooted in long centuries of Anglo-American history." The Fifth Amendment provides that "no person shall be held to answer for a capital, or otherwise infamous crime, unless on a presentment or indictment of a Grand Jury." The adoption of the grand jury "in our Constitution as the sole method for preferring charges in serious criminal cases shows the high place it held as an instrument of justice." . . . Because its task is to inquire into the existence of possible criminal conduct and to return only well-founded indictments, its investigative powers are necessarily broad. . . . Hence, the grand jury's authority to subpoena witnesses is not only historic, but essential to its task. . . .

A number of States have provided newsmen a statutory privilege of varying breadth, but the majority have not done so, and none has been provided by federal statute. Until now the only testimonial privilege for unofficial witnesses that is rooted in the Federal Constitution is the Fifth Amendment privilege against compelled self-incrimination. We are asked to create another by interpreting the First Amendment to grant newsmen a testimonial privilege that other citizens do not enjoy. This we decline to do. Fair and effective law enforcement aimed at providing security for the person and property of the individual is a fundamental function of government, and the grand jury plays an important, constitutionally mandated role in this process. On the records now before us, we perceive no basis for holding that the public interest in law enforcement and in ensuring effective grand jury proceedings is insufficient to override the consequential, but uncertain, burden on news gathering that is said to result from insisting that reporters, like other citizens, respond to relevant questions put to them in the course of a valid grand jury investigation or criminal trial.

This conclusion itself involves no restraint on what newspapers may publish or on the type or quality of information reporters may seek to acquire, nor does it threaten the vast bulk of confidential relationships between reporters and their sources. Grand juries address themselves to the issues of whether crimes have been committed and who committed them. Only where news sources themselves are implicated in crime or possess information relevant to the grand jury's task need they or the reporter be concerned about grand jury subpoenas. Nothing before us indicates that a large number or percentage of *all* confidential news sources falls into either category and would in any way be deterred by our holding that the Constitution does not, as it never has, exempt the newsman from performing the citizen's normal duty of appearing and furnishing information relevant to the grand jury's task.

The preference for anonymity of those confidential informants involved in actual criminal conduct is presumably a product of their desire to escape criminal prosecution, and this preference, while understandable, is hardly deserving of constitutional protection. It would be frivolous to assert—and no one does in these cases—that the First Amendment, in the interest of securing news or otherwise, confers a license on either the reporter or his news sources to violate valid criminal laws. Although stealing documents or private wiretapping could provide newsworthy information, neither reporter nor source is immune from conviction for such conduct, whatever the impact on the flow of news. Neither is immune, on First Amendment grounds, from testifying against the other, before the grand jury or at a criminal trial. . . .

Thus, we cannot seriously entertain the notion that the First Amendment protects a newsman's agreement to conceal the criminal conduct of his source, or evidence thereof, on the theory that it is better to write about crime than to do something about it. . . .

The argument that the flow of news will be diminished by compelling reporters to aid the grand jury in a criminal investigation is not irrational, nor are the records before us silent on the matter. But we remain unclear how often and to what extent informers are actually deterred from furnishing information when newsmen are forced to testify before a grand jury. The available data indicate that some newsmen rely a great deal on confidential sources and that some informants are particularly sensitive to the threat of exposure and may be silenced if it is held by this Court that, ordinarily, newsmen must testify pursuant to subpoenas, but the evidence fails to demonstrate that there would be a significant constriction of the flow of news to the public if this Court reaffirms the prior common-law and constitutional rule regarding the testimonial obligations of newsmen. Estimates of the inhibiting effect of such subpoenas . . . are widely divergent and to a great extent speculative. . . . Reliance by the press on confidential informants does not mean that all such sources will in fact dry up because of the later possible appearance of the newsman before a grand jury. The reporter may never be called and if he objects to testifying, the prosecution may not insist. Also, the relationship of many informants to the press is a symbiotic one which is unlikely to be greatly inhibited by the threat of subpoena: quite often, such informants are members of a minority political or cultural group that relies heavily on the media to propagate its views, publicize its aims, and magnify its exposure to the public. Moreover, grand juries characteristically conduct secret proceedings, and law enforcement officers are themselves experienced in dealing with informers, and have their own methods for protecting them without interference with the effective administration of justice. There is little before us indicating that informants whose interest in avoiding exposure is that it may threaten job security, personal safety, or peace of mind, would in fact be in a worse position, or would think they would be, if they risked placing their trust in public officials as well as reporters. We doubt if the informer who prefers anonymity but is sincerely interested in furnishing evidence of crime will always or very often be deterred by the prospect of dealing with those public authorities characteristically charged with the duty to protect the public interest as well as his.

. . . [W]e cannot accept the argument that the public interest in possible future news about crime from undisclosed, unverified sources must take precedence over the public interest in pursuing and prosecuting those crimes reported to the press by informants and in thus deterring the commission of such crimes in the future.

We note first that the privilege claimed is that of the reporter, not the informant, and that if the authorities independently identify the informant, neither his own reluctance to testify nor the objection of the newsman would shield him from grand jury inquiry, whatever the impact on the flow of news or on his future usefulness as a secret source of information. More important, it is obvious that agreements to conceal information relevant to commission of crime have very little to recommend them from the standpoint of public policy. . . . Such conduct deserves no encomium, and we decline now to afford it First Amendment protection by denigrating the duty of a citizen, whether reporter or informer, to respond to grand jury subpoena and answer relevant questions put to him. . . .

Neither are we now convinced that a virtually impenetrable constitutional shield, beyond legislative or judicial control, should be forged to protect a private system of informers operated by the press to report on criminal conduct, a system that would be unaccountable to the public, would pose a threat to the citizen's justifiable expectations of privacy, and would equally protect well-intentioned informants and those who for pay or otherwise betray their trust to their employer or associates. . . .

We are admonished that refusal to provide a First Amendment reporter's privilege will undermine the freedom of the press to collect and disseminate news. But this is not the lesson history teaches us. . . . From the beginning of our country the press has operated without constitutional protection for press informants, and the press has flourished. . . . The obligation to testify in response to grand jury subpoenas will not threaten [] sources not involved with criminal conduct and without information relevant to grand jury investigations, and we cannot hold that the Constitution places the sources in these two categories either above the law or beyond its reach.

The argument for such a constitutional privilege rests heavily on those cases holding that the infringement of protected First Amendment rights must be no broader than necessary to achieve a permissible governmental purpose. We do not deal, however, with a governmental institution that has abused its proper function. . . . [Moreover, t]he requirements of those cases [holding] that a State's interest must be "compelling" or "paramount" to justify even an indirect burden on First Amendment rights . . . are also met here. . . .

The privilege claimed here is conditional, not absolute; given the suggested preliminary showings and compelling need, the reporter would be required to testify. Presumably, such a rule would reduce the instances in which reporters could be required to appear, but predicting in advance when and in what circumstances they could be compelled to do so would be difficult. Such a rule would also have implications for the issuance of compulsory process to reporters at civil and criminal trials and at legislative hearings. If newsmen's confidential sources are as sensitive as they are claimed to be, the prospect of being unmasked whenever a judge determines the situation justifies it is hardly a satisfactory solution to the problem. For them, it would appear that only an absolute privilege would suffice.

We are unwilling to embark the judiciary on a long and difficult journey to such an uncertain destination. The administration of a constitutional newsman's privilege would present practical and conceptual difficulties of a high order. Sooner or later, it would be necessary to define those categories of newsmen who qualified for the privilege, a questionable procedure in light of the traditional doctrine that liberty of the press is the right of the lonely pamphleteer who uses carbon paper or a mimeograph just as much as of the large metropolitan publisher who utilizes the latest photocomposition methods. Freedom of the press is a "fundamental personal right" which "is not confined to newspapers and periodicals. It necessarily embraces pamphlets and leaflets. . . . The press in its historic connotation comprehends every sort of publication which affords a vehicle of information and opinion." . . . The informative function asserted by representatives of the organized press in the present cases is also performed by lecturers, political pollsters, novelists, academic researchers, and dramatists. Almost any author may quite accurately assert that he is contributing to the flow of information to the public, that he relies on confidential sources of information, and that these sources will be silenced if he is forced to make disclosures before a grand jury. . . .

[I]n the end, by considering whether enforcement of a particular law served a "compelling" governmental interest, the courts would be inextricably involved in distinguishing between the value of enforcing different criminal laws. By requiring testimony from a reporter in investigations involving some crimes but not in others, they would be making a value judgment that a legislature had declined to make, since in each case the criminal law involved would represent a considered legislative judgment, not constitutionally suspect, of what conduct is liable to criminal prosecution. The task of judges, like other officials outside the legislative branch, is not to make the law but to uphold it in accordance with their oaths.

At the federal level, Congress has freedom to determine whether a statutory newsman's privilege is necessary and desirable and to fashion standards and rules as narrow or broad as deemed necessary to deal with the evil discerned and, equally important, to refashion those rules as experience from time to time may dictate. There is also merit in leaving state legislatures free, within First Amendment limits, to fashion their own standards in light of the conditions and problems with respect to the relations between law enforcement officials and press in their own areas. . . .

In addition, there is much force in the pragmatic view that the press has at its disposal powerful mechanisms of communication and is far from helpless to protect itself from harassment or substantial harm. . . .

Finally, as we have earlier indicated, news gathering is not without its First Amendment protections, and grand jury investigations if instituted or conducted other than in good faith, would pose wholly different issues for resolution under the First Amendment. Official harassment of the press undertaken not for purposes of law enforcement but to disrupt a reporter's relationship with his news sources would have no justification. Grand juries are subject to judicial control and subpoenas to motions to quash. We do not expect courts will forget that grand juries must operate within the limits of the First Amendment as well as the Fifth. [The Court then reversed *Caldwell*, affirmed *Branzburg v. Hayes* and *Branzburg v. Meigs*, and held that as to *In re Pappas*, petitioner was required to testify subject] to the supervision of the presiding judge as to "the propriety, purposes, and scope of the grand jury inquiry and the pertinence of the probable testimony."

Mr. Justice POWELL, concurring.

I add this brief statement to emphasize what seems to me to be the limited nature of the Court's holding. The Court does not hold that newsmen, subpoenaed to testify before a grand jury, are without constitutional rights with respect to the gathering of news or in safeguarding their sources. Certainly, we do not hold, as suggested in Mr. Justice Stewart's dissenting opinion, that state and federal authorities are free to "annex" the news media as "an investigative arm of government." The solicitude repeatedly shown by this Court for First Amendment freedoms should be sufficient assurance against any such effort, even if one seriously believed that the media—properly free and untrammeled in the fullest sense of these terms—were not able to protect themselves.

As indicated in the concluding portion of the opinion, the Court states that no harassment of newsmen will be tolerated. If a newsman believes that the grand jury investigation is not being conducted in good faith he is not without remedy. Indeed, if the newsman is called upon to give information bearing only a remote and tenuous relationship to the subject of the investigation, or if he has some other reason to believe that his testimony implicates confidential source relationships without a legitimate need of law enforcement, he will have access to the court on a motion to quash and an appropriate protective order may be entered. The asserted claim to privilege should be judged on its facts by the striking of a proper balance between freedom of the press and the obligation of all citizens to give relevant testimony with respect to criminal conduct. The balance of these vital constitutional and societal interests on a case-by-case basis accords with the tried and traditional way of adjudicating such questions.*

---

* It is to be remembered that Caldwell asserts a constitutional privilege not even to appear before the grand jury unless a court decides that the Government has made a showing that meets the three preconditions specified in the dissenting opinion of Mr. Justice Stewart. To be sure, this would require a "balancing" of interests by the court, but under circumstances and constraints significantly different from the balancing that will be appropriate under the court's decision. The newsman witness, like all other witnesses, will have to appear; he will not be in a position to litigate at the threshold the State's very authority to subpoena him. Moreover, . . . , the court—when called upon to protect a newsman from improper or prejudicial questioning—would be free to balance the competing interests on their merits in the particular case. The new constitutional rule endorsed by th[e] dissenting opinion would, as a practical matter, defeat such a fair balancing and the essential societal interest in the detection and prosecution of crime would be heavily subordinated.

In short, the courts will be available to newsmen under circumstances where legitimate First Amendment interests require protection.

Mr. Justice DOUGLAS, dissenting in *United States v. Caldwell.*

. . . A reporter is no better than his source of information. Unless he has a privilege to withhold the identity of his source, he will be the victim of governmental intrigue or aggression. If he can be summoned to testify in secret before a grand jury, his sources will dry up and the attempted exposure, the effort to enlighten the public, will be ended. If what the Court sanctions today becomes settled law, then the reporter's main function in American society will be to pass on to the public the press releases which the various departments of government issue. . . .

Mr. Justice STEWART, with whom Mr. Justice BRENNAN and Mr. Justice MARSHALL join, dissenting.

The Court's crabbed view of the First Amendment reflects a disturbing insensitivity to the critical role of an independent press in our society. The question whether a reporter has a constitutional right to a confidential relationship with his source is of first impression here, but the principles that should guide our decision are as basic as any to be found in the Constitution. While Mr. Justice Powell's enigmatic concurring opinion gives some hope of a more flexible view in the future, the Court in these cases holds that a newsman has no First Amendment right to protect his sources when called before a grand jury. The Court thus invites state and federal authorities to undermine the historic independence of the press by attempting to annex the journalistic profession as an investigative arm of government. Not only will this decision impair performance of the press' constitutionally protected functions, but it will, I am convinced, in the long run harm rather than help the administration of justice.

I

The reporter's constitutional right to a confidential relationship with his source stems from the broad societal interest in a full and free flow of information to the public. . . .

. . . A corollary of the right to publish must be the right to gather news. . . . News must not be unnecessarily cut off at its source, for without freedom to acquire information the right to publish would be impermissibly compromised. Accordingly, a right to gather news, of some dimensions, must exist. . . .

The right to gather news implies, in turn, a right to a confidential relationship between a reporter and his source. This proposition follows as a matter of simple logic once three factual predicates are recognized: (1) newsmen require informants to gather news; (2) confidentiality—the promise or understanding that names or certain aspects of communications will be kept off the record—is essential to the creation and maintenance of a news-gathering relationship with informants; and (3) an unbridled subpoena power—the absence of a constitutional right protecting, in *any* way, a confidential relationship from compulsory process—will either deter sources from divulging information or deter reporters from gathering and publishing information. . . .

[II.] Posed against the First Amendment's protection of the newsman's confidential relationships in these cases is society's interest in the use of the grand jury to administer justice fairly and effectively. The grand jury serves two important functions: "to examine into the commission of crimes" and "to stand between the prosecutor and the accused, and to determine whether the charge was founded upon credible testimony or was dictated by malice or personal ill will." . . . And to perform these functions the grand jury must have available to it every man's relevant evidence.

Yet the longstanding rule making every person's evidence available to the grand jury is not absolute. The rule has been limited by the Fifth Amendment, the Fourth Amendment, and the evidentiary privileges of the common law. . . .

Such an interest must surely be the First Amendment protection of a confidential relationship. [T]his protection does not exist for the purely private interests of the newsman or his informant, nor even, at bottom, for the First Amendment interests of either partner in the news-gathering relationship. Rather, it functions to insure nothing less than democratic decisionmaking through the free flow of information to the public, and it serves, thereby, to honor the "profound national commitment to the principle that debate on public issues should be uninhibited, robust, and wide-open." New York Times Co. v. Sullivan, 376 U.S. at 270.

In striking the proper balance between the public interest in the efficient administration of justice and the First Amendment guarantee of the fullest flow of information, we must begin with the basic proposition that because of their "delicate and vulnerable" nature, NAACP v. Button, 371 U.S., at 433, and their transcendent importance for the just functioning of our society, First Amendment rights require special safeguards.

[A.] This Court has erected such safeguards when government, by legislative investigation or other investigative means, has attempted to pierce the shield of privacy inherent in freedom of association. In no previous case have we considered the extent to which the First Amendment limits the grand jury subpoena power. . . .

The established method of "carefully" circumscribing investigative powers is to place a heavy burden of justification on government officials when First Amendment rights are impaired. . . .

Thus, when an investigation impinges on First Amendment rights, the government must not only show that the inquiry is of "compelling and overriding importance" but it must also "convincingly" demonstrate that the investigation is "substantially related" to the information sought.

Governmental officials must, therefore, demonstrate that the information sought is *clearly* relevant to a *precisely* defined subject of governmental inquiry. They must demonstrate that it is reasonable to think the witness in question has that information. And they must show that there is not any means of obtaining the information less destructive of First Amendment liberties. . . .

Accordingly, when a reporter is asked to appear before a grand jury and reveal confidences, I would hold that the government must (1) show that there is probable cause to believe that the newsman has information that is clearly relevant to a specific probable violation of law; (2) demonstrate that the information sought cannot be obtained by alternative means less destructive of First Amendment rights; and (3) demonstrate a compelling and overriding interest in the information.

This is not to say that a grand jury could not issue a subpoena until such a showing were made, and it is not to say that a newsman would be in any way privileged to ignore any subpoena that was issued. Obviously, before the government's burden to make such a showing were triggered, the reporter would have to move to quash the subpoena, asserting the basis on which he considered the particular relationship a confidential one.

[B.] The crux of the Court's rejection of any newsman's privilege is its observation that only "where news sources themselves are implicated in crime or possess information *relevant* to the grand jury's task need they or the reporter be concerned about grand jury subpoenas." But this is a most misleading construct. For it is obviously not true that the only persons about whom reporters will be forced to testify will be those "confidential informants involved in actual criminal conduct" and those having "information suggesting illegal conduct by others." As noted above, given the grand jury's extraordinarily broad investigative powers and the weak standards of relevance and materiality that apply during such inquiries, reporters, if they have no testimonial privilege, will be called to give information about informants who have neither committed crimes nor have information about crime. It is to avoid deterrence of such sources and thus to prevent needless injury to First Amendment values that I think the government must be required to show probable cause that the newsman has information that is clearly relevant to a specific probable violation of criminal law.

NOTES AND QUESTIONS

1. *Sources and privilege.* Will confidential sources "dry up" without a privilege? How much do sources rely on the existence, or absence, of a reporter's privilege in deciding whether to provide information to the media? Should this matter to the outcome of the decision? Is it subject to empirical proof?
2. *Is* Branzburg *a plurality opinion?* An important part of understanding Supreme Court decisions is "counting heads." Four members of the Court would recognize a constitutional reporter's privilege. Would Justice Powell also recognize a constitutional privilege in some circumstances? Why did Justice Powell decide to write a separate concurrence after joining the majority (five votes) decision?
3. *A surprising twist.* Many state and federal courts read *Branzburg* to create a constitutional reporter's privilege. How? By reading Justice Powell's concurrence together with the dissent, the court found five votes for creating some form of qualified constitutional privilege. Is this an honest reading of *Branzburg*? Several federal appellate courts have said no, noting that Powell joined in Justice White's opinion, and arguing that his concurrence only addresses abuse of the subpoena power rather than routine use. *See, e.g.*, United States v. Smith, 135 F.3d 963 (5th Cir. 1998); In re Grand Jury Proceedings, 5 F.3d 397 (9th Cir. 1993); In re Grand Jury Proceedings, 810 F.2d 580 (6th Cir. 1987); *see also* In re WTHR-TV, 693 N.E.2d 1 (Ind. 1998).
4. *Privilege variables.* Reporters possess valuable information that is sought in a variety of contexts other than grand jury proceedings. Reporters may be

subpoenaed to testify at criminal trials and at civil trials, and their testimony may be sought by legislative committees or administrative tribunals. The government or private litigants may seek information that is confidential or nonconfidential, published or unpublished, eyewitness observations or hearsay. Moreover, disclosure may be sought when reporters themselves are parties to litigation (as in defamation actions). Which of these variables should weigh in favor of disclosure? Jurisdictions vary in answering this question.

5. *Shield statutes.* Before *Branzburg,* 17 states had in place shield statutes (that is, statutorily enacted reporters' privileges). In 2020, forty-nine states and the District of Columbia had shield laws. Jane E. Kirtley, Shield Laws, https://www.mtsu.edu/first-amendment/article/1241/shield-laws. Although more than 100 bills to enact a shield law have been filed at the federal level, none has passed both houses of Congress. Many bills failed because the media could not agree as to the terms of such legislation. Statutes are not the only source of privilege law.
6. *Other sources of privilege.* Statutes are not the only source of privilege law. Some courts have interpreted their state constitutions or their common law to create a reporter's privilege to protect confidential sources. In addition, federal courts sometimes suggest that federal common law may be a source of privilege. Rule 501 of the Federal Rules of Evidence provides that privilege issues in federal courts "shall be governed by the principles of the common law as they may be interpreted by the courts of the United States in the light of reason and experience." However, state privilege law controls "with respect to an element of a claim or defense as to which State law supplies the rule of decision." The courts that turn to federal common law as the source for privilege rely on the same policies as those that turn to the First Amendment as the source. It should be obvious from this account of the sources of privilege that different jurisdictions enact and apply their reporter's privilege with varying degrees of fervor. These variations make the law of reporter's privilege quite complex.
7. *Reconsidering a substantive press clause.* Might the press lose something from a substantive press clause—that is, one that gives the press special rights not available to individuals under the Free Speech Clause? Several commentators have worried that if the media gain special rights because of their status as the public's eyes and ears, special responsibilities might follow. For example, special rights, such as a reporter's privilege, might come with an enforceable responsibility to provide the public with full and fair coverage of important issues. *See* Anthony Lewis, *A Preferred Position for Journalism?*, 7 Hofstra L. Rev. 595, 605 (1979); William W. Van Alstyne, *The Hazards to the Press of Claiming a "Preferred Position,"* 28 Hastings L.J. 761 (1977). Professor David Anderson has worried that the extension of special *constitutional* rights to the press might lead to the elimination of the many special *nonconstitutional* rights the press receives under existing law. Anderson concludes: "The paradox of the Press Clause is this: giving the press special constitutional protection inevitably diminishes the ability

to give the press special protection by nonconstitutional means." If the Supreme Court recognizes special constitutional press rights that must be accorded to anyone who meets the definition of press, other government entities may forgo creating statutory or administrative protections because fighting over who gets them is too difficult or too costly: "The prospect of litigating these issues, or just the burden of devising policies to avoid litigation, might dissuade agencies from attempting to accommodate the press when doing so entails the exclusion of someone else." *See* David A. Anderson, *Freedom of the Press*, 80 Tex. L. Rev. 429, 511-512 (2002); *but see* Sonja R. West, *Awakening the Press Clause*, 58 UCLA L. Rev. 1025, 1027-1029 (2011) (contending that the Press Clause should provide protection for the press as an institution).

8. *Subpoenas to website operators*: What standard applies when a platform or website receives a grand jury subpoena in a criminal case requiring it to disclose information about those who have used its website to post speech about a matter of public concern? In the only published appellate case on this issue decided as of early 2022, a website moved to quash a grand jury subpoena on grounds that compliance with the subpoena would violate its users' First Amendment rights to associational privacy and anonymous speech. In re Grand Jury Subpoena, No. 16-03-217, United States v. Glassdoor, 875 F. 3d 1179 (9th Cir. 2017). Although the website tried to distinguish its argument from the one made by the reporters in *Branzburg* on the ground that the website was vindicating its users' rights rather than its own, the Court of Appeals for the Ninth Circuit found the distinction unpersuasive. "Although [the website Glassdoor] is not a news business, as part of its business model it does gather and publish information from sources it has agreed not to identify." Thus, forcing it to comply with the subpoena would have a chilling effect similar to that of forcing reporters to comply and reveal confidential sources. The court wrote: *Branzburg* "made clear that the First Amendment does not provide reporters—or anyone else—with a privilege against responding to a grand jury's inquiries. Therefore, it doesn't matter whether the underlying claim is related to newsgathering, speech, or association. These are all First Amendment-protected activities, but none of them will prevent an individual from being required to cooperate with a good-faith grand jury investigation." The court held that the proper standard to apply to the motion to quash was *Branzburg*'s good faith standard. Since there was "no evidence that the government is on an improper fishing expedition," the website operator had to comply with the subpoena. Does this holding imply that website operators or internet platforms should receive the same treatment as traditional media when they play similar roles, or does it imply that neither new media nor traditional media deserve special First Amendment protection? Would the result be the same in a civil case? For extended discussion, see Leeza Arbatman and John Villasenor, *Anonymous Expression and "Unmasking" in Civil and Criminal Proceedings*, 23 Minn. J.L. Sci. & Tech. 77 (2022).

AN EXTENDED NOTE ON GOVERNMENT SECRECY, SUBPOENAS, AND THE INVESTIGATION OF LEAKS

When government employees leak classified information to reporters, difficult legal issues arise because the leak itself is often a crime, which means that the reporter who receives the leaked information possesses direct evidence of the commission of a crime. Yet leaks from every echelon of government are common, and many important stories would be lost without them.

One high-profile leaks case illustrates some of the legal difficulties. The case involved a prosecution brought against Jeffrey Sterling, a former member of the CIA's Iran Task Force. The government suspected that Sterling was a source for an account in journalist James Risen's book "State of War" about a botched CIA attempt to sabotage Iranian nuclear research.

The government subpoenaed Risen, on the basis that his testimony was essential to prove the case against Sterling. A district judge quashed the government's subpoena insofar as it required Risen to identify his source, U.S. v. Sterling, 818 F. Supp. 2d 945 (E.D. Va. 2011), but the Fourth Circuit reversed. U.S. v. Sterling, 724 F.3d 482 (4th Cir. 2013).

Citing *Branzburg*, the court held: "There is no First Amendment testimonial privilege, absolute or qualified, that protects a reporter from being compelled to testify by the prosecution or the defense in criminal proceedings about criminal conduct that the reporter personally witnessed or participated in, absent a showing of bad faith, harassment, or other such non-legitimate motive, even though the reporter promised confidentiality to his source." The court rejected the argument that Justice Powell's *Branzburg* concurrence had "tacit[ly] endorsed" the dissenting opinion of Justice Stewart. The court further noted that the Supreme Court "has never varied from" *Branzburg*'s holding since it was decided, and thus it was the only court authorized to recognize a reporter's privilege based in the First Amendment.

The court concluded that Risen "has 'direct information . . . concerning the commission of serious crimes.' [ ] Indeed, he can provide the *only* first-hand account of the commission of a most serious crime indicted by the grand jury—the illegal disclosure of classified, national security information by one who was entrusted by our government to protect national security, but who is charged with endangering it instead." The court also concluded that the there was no evidence that the government subpoenaed Risen's testimony in bad faith or for purposes of harassment. Instead, the government was "seek[ing] to compel evidence that Risen alone possesses—evidence that goes to the heart of the prosecution."

The court refused to recognize a reporter's privilege rooted in federal common law, again citing *Branzburg* as clear authority on the issue. The court concluded: "If Risen is to be protected from being compelled to testify and give what evidence of crime he possesses, in contravention of every citizen's duty to do so, we believe that decision should rest with the Supreme Court, which can revisit *Branzburg* and the policy arguments it rejected, or with Congress, which can more effectively and comprehensively weigh the policy arguments for and against adopting a privilege and define its scope."

Judge Roger Gregory, dissenting, argued that Risen's testimony should have been shielded by both a qualified First Amendment privilege and a federal common law privilege tailored specifically to the context of national security leaks. In order to overcome the qualified privilege, the government would have to show that the subpoenaed information was "highly material and relevant, necessary or critical to the maintenance of the claim, and not obtainable from other sources." To this inquiry, the judge would add in national security cases "consideration of two additional factors: the harm caused by the public dissemination of the information, and the newsworthiness of the information conveyed." Consideration of these additional factors would allow the privilege to be overridden in "matters of national security" in the face of "pressing governmental interests."

Applying this test in *Sterling*, the judge would have quashed the government's subpoena seeking Risen's testimony. After summarizing the evidence against Sterling in detail, the judge concluded that the government had failed to show a compelling interest in obtaining Risen's testimony regarding his confidential sources, because this testimony would be superfluous in light of the other strong evidence available to the government. Moreover, the information was available from other means.

Turning to the newsworthiness and harm inquiries, the judge concluded that the information published by Risen concerning "the United States intelligence community's efforts concerning the development of the Iranian nuclear program" to be highly newsworthy. Indeed, Risen's book suggested that the efforts were so misguided that they "may have helped Iran advance its nuclear program." Globally, the information "portends to inform the reader of a blundered American intelligence mission in Iran," an especially important topic in the wake of the U.S. invasion of Iraq based on flawed intelligence information.

The judge, however, did not assess the harm caused by the leak of the classified information but instead would have remanded to the district court, because "the Government has not clearly articulated the nature, extent, and severity of the harm resulting from the leak. Without such evidence, it is impossible for a reviewing court to determine whether the First Amendment interest in presenting newsworthy information to the public—if indeed the district court finds the information newsworthy—is outweighed by the consequences of the leak." The judge conceded that this balancing might be difficult, but "[t]he First Amendment interest in informed popular debate does not simply vanish at the invocation of the words 'national security.'" (citing United States v. Morison, 844 F.2d 1057, 1081 (4th Cir. 1988) (Wilkinson, J., concurring)).

Risen's seven-year battle not to testify ended after Attorney General Eric Holder announced prosecutors would end attempts to compel his testimony. Matt Apuzzo, *Times Reporter Will Not Be Called to Testify in Leak Case*, N.Y. Times, Jan. 12, 2015. Jeffrey Sterling was sentenced to three and half years in prison.

Does the modified balancing test tip the scales toward the Government's interest in protecting classified information or against it? To what extent would application of the modified balancing test lead to enhanced protection of confidential sources in leaks cases? To what extent would it allow federal judges to usurp the role of the legislative and executive branches?

THEORY-APPLIED PROBLEM: SUBPOENA OF TELEPHONE RECORDS

Can the federal government avoid First Amendment issues involved in subpoenaing reporters to testify about leaks simply by obtaining their telephone or email records from third-party companies? What arguments can you make on both sides of this issue? The question is not a hypothetical one. In a 2013 leaks investigation, the Justice Department secretly subpoenaed two months' worth of records from twenty of the Associated Press's phone lines. Mark Sherman, Gov't Obtains Wide AP Phone Records in Probe, Assoc. Press, May 13, 2013. Also in 2013, the Federal Bureau of Investigation obtained a search warrant for the contents of the personal email of Fox News correspondent James Rosen in 2010. (James Risen, mentioned above, and James Rosen are two different journalists.) The search warrant issued based on an assertion that the government had probable cause to believe the reporter had violated the Espionage Act by soliciting a State Department official to leak classified information. Ann E. Marimow, A Rare Peek Into a Justice Department Leak Probe, Wash. Post, May 19, 2013. The Trump administration also subpoenaed months' worth of reporters' telephone and email records in pursuing a leaks investigation in 2020. It also imposed gag orders so that the reporters would not be notified that their information was sought. The Biden administration announced that the Justice Department would no longer use this tactic in leaks investigations. *See* Ted Johnson, *Justice Department Will No Longer Subpoena Reporters' Phone and Email Records In Leak Investigations*, Deadline, June 5, 2021. See also New York Times Co. v. Gonzales, 382 F. Supp. 2d 457 (S.D.N.Y. 2005) (holding that reporters enjoyed a qualified privilege both under the First Amendment and under federal common law that prevented the government from obtaining their telephone records, particularly when it could check its own telephone records to try to uncover the leak), vacated and remanded in New York Times Co. v. Gonzales, 459 F.3d 160, 163 (2d Cir. 2006) (holding that whatever privilege might exist had been overcome as a matter of law under the facts of the case).

2. *Access to Courtrooms*

Richmond Newspapers, Inc. v. Virginia

448 U.S. 555 (1980)

Mr. Chief Justice Burger announced the judgment of the Court and delivered an opinion, in which Mr. Justice White and Mr. Justice Stevens joined.

[In 1977, the Virginia Supreme Court reversed Stevenson's conviction of second-degree murder because the trial court had improperly admitted a bloodstained shirt purportedly belonging to Stevenson into evidence. Stevenson's case was retried, but his second trial ended in a mistrial. So did his third.] It appears that the mistrial may have been declared because a prospective juror had read about Stevenson's previous trials in a newspaper and had told other prospective jurors about the case before the retrial began. Stevenson was tried in the same court for a fourth time beginning on September 11, 1978. Present in the courtroom when the case was called were appellants Wheeler and McCarthy, reporters for appellant Richmond Newspapers, Inc. Before the trial began, counsel for the defendant moved that it be closed to the public. . . .

[The prosecutor did not object, and the trial judge entered an order excluding the public and the press from the courtroom. Appellants moved to vacate and asked for a hearing.] At the closed hearing, counsel for appellants observed that no evidentiary findings had been made by the court prior to the entry of its closure order and pointed out that the court had failed to consider any other, less drastic measures within its power to ensure a fair trial. . . . [The court denied the motion to vacate, the closed trial continued, and the defendant was acquitted. The Virginia Supreme Court denied the newspaper's appeal.]

II

We begin consideration of this case by noting that the precise issue presented here has not previously been before this Court for decision. In *Gannett Co. v. DePasquale* the Court was not required to decide whether a right of access to *trials*, as distinguished from hearings on pretrial motions, was constitutionally guaranteed. The Court held that the Sixth Amendment's guarantee to the accused of a public trial gave neither the public nor the press an enforceable right of access to a pretrial suppression hearing. . . .

[H]ere for the first time the Court is asked to decide whether a criminal trial itself may be closed to the public upon the unopposed request of a defendant, without any demonstration that closure is required to protect the defendant's superior right to a fair trial, or that some other overriding consideration requires closure.

[A.] The origins of the proceeding which has become the modern criminal trial in Anglo-American justice can be traced back beyond reliable historical records. We need not here review all details of its development, but a summary of that history is instructive. What is significant for present purposes is that throughout its evolution, the trial has been open to all who cared to observe.

[The opinion traced a tradition of open public trials in England from "the days before the Norman Conquest" to the present day and then turned to the tradition of open public trials in America.]

We have found nothing to suggest that the presumptive openness of the trial, which English courts were later to call "one of the essential qualities of a court of justice" was not also an attribute of the judicial systems of colonial America. . . .

[B.] [T]he historical evidence demonstrates conclusively that at the time when our organic laws were adopted, criminal trials both here and in England had long been presumptively open. This is no quirk of history; rather, it has long been recognized as an indispensable attribute of an Anglo-American trial. Both Hale in the 17th century and Blackstone in the 18th saw the importance of openness to the proper functioning of a trial; it gave assurance that the proceedings were conducted fairly to all concerned, and it discouraged perjury, the misconduct of participants, and decisions based on secret bias or partiality.

. . . The early history of open trials in part reflects the widespread acknowledgment, long before there were behavioral scientists, that public trials had significant community therapeutic value. Even without such experts to frame the concept in words, people sensed from experience and observation that, especially in the administration of criminal justice, the means used to achieve justice must have the support derived from public acceptance of both the process and its results.

When a shocking crime occurs, a community reaction of outrage and public protest often follows. Thereafter the open processes of justice serve an important prophylactic purpose, providing an outlet for community concern, hostility, and emotion. Without an awareness that society's responses to criminal conduct are underway, natural human reactions of outrage and protest are frustrated and may manifest themselves in some form of vengeful "self-help," as indeed they did regularly in the activities of vigilante "committees" on our frontiers.

. . . To work effectively, it is important that society's criminal process "satisfy the appearance of justice," . . . , and the appearance of justice can best be provided by allowing people to observe it. . . .

People in an open society do not demand infallibility from their institutions, but it is difficult for them to accept what they are prohibited from observing. When a criminal trial is conducted in the open, there is at least an opportunity both for understanding the system in general and its workings in a particular case. . . .

In earlier times, both in England and America, attendance at court was a common mode of "passing the time." . . . Yet "[it] is not unrealistic even in this day to believe that public inclusion affords citizens a form of legal education and hopefully promotes confidence in the fair administration of justice." . . . Instead of acquiring information about trials by firsthand observation or by word of mouth from those who attended, people now acquire it chiefly through the print and electronic media. In a sense, this validates the media claim of functioning as surrogates for the public. While media representatives enjoy the same right of access as the public, they often are provided special seating and priority of entry so that they may report what people in attendance have seen and heard. This "[contributes] to public understanding of the rule of law and to comprehension of the functioning of the entire criminal justice system. . . ." Nebraska Press Assn. v. Stuart, 427 U.S., at 587 (Brennan, J., concurring in judgment).

[C.] From this unbroken, uncontradicted history, supported by reasons as valid today as in centuries past, we are bound to conclude that a presumption of openness inheres in the very nature of a criminal trial under our system of justice.

III

[A.] . . . The Bill of Rights was enacted against the backdrop of the long history of trials being presumptively open. Public access to trials was then regarded as an important aspect of the process itself; the conduct of trials "before as many of the people as chuse to attend" was regarded as one of "the inestimable advantages of a free English constitution of government." . . . In guaranteeing freedoms such as those of speech and press, the First Amendment can be read as protecting the right of everyone to attend trials so as to give meaning to those explicit guarantees. . . . Free speech carries with it some freedom to listen. "In a variety of contexts this Court has referred to a First Amendment right to 'receive information and ideas.'" Kleindienst v. Mandel, 408 U.S. 753, 762 (1972). What this means in the context of trials is that the First Amendment guarantees of speech and press, standing alone, prohibit government from summarily closing courtroom doors which had long been open to the public at the time that Amendment was adopted. . . .

It is not crucial whether we describe this right to attend criminal trials to hear, see, and communicate observations concerning them as a "right of access," . . .[11] or a "right to gather information," for we have recognized that "without some protection for seeking out the news, freedom of the press could be eviscerated." Branzburg v. Hayes, 408 U.S. 665, 681 (1972). The explicit, guaranteed rights to speak and to publish concerning what takes place at a trial would lose much meaning if access to observe the trial could, as it was here, be foreclosed arbitrarily.

[B.] The right of access to places traditionally open to the public, as criminal trials have long been, may be seen as assured by the amalgam of the First Amendment guarantees of speech and press; and their affinity to the right of assembly is not without relevance. . . . Subject to the traditional time, place, and manner restrictions, see, *e.g.*, Cox v. New Hampshire, 312 U.S. 569 (1941), streets, sidewalks, and parks are places traditionally open, where First Amendment rights may be exercised, . . . ; a trial courtroom also is a public place where the people generally—and representatives of the media—have a right to be present, and where their presence historically has been thought to enhance the integrity and quality of what takes place.

[C.] We hold that the right to attend criminal trials[17] is implicit in the guarantees of the First Amendment; without the freedom to attend such trials, which people have exercised for centuries, important aspects of freedom of speech and "of the press could be eviscerated." *Branzburg*, 408 U.S., at 681.

[D.] Having concluded there was a guaranteed right of the public under the First and Fourteenth Amendments to attend the trial of Stevenson's case, we return to the closure order challenged by appellants. The Court in *Gannett [v. DePasquale]* made clear that although the Sixth Amendment guarantees the accused a right to a public trial, it does not give a right to a private trial. Despite the fact that this was the fourth trial of the accused, the trial judge made no findings to support closure; no inquiry was made as to whether alternative solutions would have met the need to ensure fairness; there was no recognition of any right under the Constitution for the public or press to attend the trial. In contrast to the pretrial proceeding dealt with in *Gannett*, there exist in the context of the trial itself various tested alternatives to satisfy the constitutional demands of fairness. *See, e.g.*, Nebraska Press Assn.

---

11. *Procunier* and *Saxbe* are distinguishable in the sense that they were concerned with penal institutions which, by definition, are not "open" or public places. Penal institutions do not share the long tradition of openness, although traditionally there have been visiting committees of citizens, and there is no doubt that legislative committees could exercise plenary oversight and "visitation rights." *Saxbe*, 417 U.S., at 849, noted that "limitation on visitations is justified by what the Court of Appeals acknowledged as 'the truism that prisons are institutions where public access is generally limited.' 161 U. S. App. D. C., at 80, 494 F.2d, at 999. *See* Adderley v. Florida, 385 U.S. 39, 41 (1966) [jails]." *See also* Greer v. Spock, 424 U.S. 828 (1976) (military bases).

17. Whether the public has a right to attend trials of civil cases is a question not raised by this case, but we note that historically both civil and criminal trials have been presumptively open.

v. Stuart, 427 U.S., at 563-565; Sheppard v. Maxwell, 384 U.S., at 357-362. There was no suggestion that any problems with witnesses could not have been dealt with by their exclusion from the courtroom or their sequestration during the trial. Nor is there anything to indicate that sequestration of the jurors would not have guarded against their being subjected to any improper information. All of the alternatives admittedly present difficulties for trial courts, but none of the factors relied on here was beyond the realm of the manageable. Absent an overriding interest articulated in findings, the trial of a criminal case must be open to the public.

Mr. Justice POWELL took no part in the consideration or decision of this case.

Mr. Justice BRENNAN, with whom Mr. Justice MARSHALL joins, concurring in the judgment.

. . . Because I believe that the First Amendment—of itself and as applied to the States through the Fourteenth Amendment—secures . . . a public right of access [to criminal trial], I agree with those of my Brethren who hold that, without more, agreement of the trial judge and the parties cannot constitutionally close a trial to the public.

While freedom of expression is made inviolate by the First Amendment, and, with only rare and stringent exceptions, may not be suppressed, . . . the First Amendment has not been viewed by the Court in all settings as providing an equally categorical assurance of the correlative freedom of access to information.[2] Yet the Court has not ruled out a public access component to the First Amendment in every circumstance. Read with care and in context, our decisions must therefore be understood as holding only that any privilege of access to governmental information is subject to a degree of restraint dictated by the nature of the information and countervailing interests in security or confidentiality. . . .

The Court's approach in right-of-access cases simply reflects the special nature of a claim of First Amendment right to gather information. Customarily, First Amendment guarantees are interposed to protect communication between speaker and listener. When so employed against prior restraints, free speech protections are almost insurmountable. . . . But the First Amendment embodies more than a commitment to free expression and communicative interchange for their own sakes; it has a *structural* role to play in securing and fostering our republican system of self-government. Implicit in this structural role is not only "the principle that debate on public issues should be uninhibited, robust, and wide-open," New York Times Co. v. Sullivan, 376 U.S. 254, 270 (1964), but also the antecedent

---

2. A conceptually separate, yet related, question is whether the media should enjoy greater access rights than the general public. *See, e.g.*, Saxbe v. Washington Post Co., 417 U.S., at 850; Pell v. Procunier, 417 U.S., at 834-835. But no such contention is at stake here. Since the media's right of access is at least equal to that of the general public, see *ibid.*, this case is resolved by a decision that the state statute unconstitutionally restricts public access to trials. As a practical matter, however, the institutional press is the likely, and fitting, chief beneficiary of a right of access because it serves as the "agent" of interested citizens, and funnels information about trials to a large number of individuals.

assumption that valuable public debate—as well as other civic behavior—must be informed. The structural model links the First Amendment to that process of communication necessary for a democracy to survive, and thus entails solicitude not only for communication itself, but also for the indispensable conditions of meaningful communication.

However, . . . "[there] are few restrictions on action which could not be clothed by ingenious argument in the garb of decreased data flow." *Zemel v. Rusk.* An assertion of the prerogative to gather information must accordingly be assayed by considering the information sought and the opposing interests invaded.

This judicial task is as much a matter of sensitivity to practical necessities as it is of abstract reasoning. But at least two helpful principles may be sketched. First, the case for a right of access has special force when drawn from an enduring and vital tradition of public entree to particular proceedings or information. Such a tradition commands respect in part because the Constitution carries the gloss of history. More importantly, a tradition of accessibility implies the favorable judgment of experience. Second, the value of access must be measured in specifics. Analysis is not advanced by rhetorical statements that all information bears upon public issues; what is crucial in individual cases is whether access to a particular government process is important in terms of that very process.

To resolve the case before us, therefore, we must consult historical and current practice with respect to open trials, and weigh the importance of public access to the trial process itself.

[The opinion cited numerous historical sources indicating that both English common law and American colonial law had recognized a right of public trial. It then noted that the "overwhelming majority of States secure the right to public trials."]

III

Publicity serves to advance several of the particular purposes of the trial (and, indeed, the judicial) process. Open trials play a fundamental role in furthering the efforts of our judicial system to assure the criminal defendant a fair and accurate adjudication of guilt or innocence. But, as a feature of our governing system of justice, the trial process serves other, broadly political, interests, and public access advances these objectives as well. To that extent, trial access possesses specific structural significance.

The trial is a means of meeting "the notion, deeply rooted in the common law, that 'justice must satisfy the appearance of justice.'" . . . One major function of the trial, hedged with procedural protections and conducted with conspicuous respect for the rule of law, is to make that demonstration.

Secrecy is profoundly inimical to this demonstrative purpose of the trial process. Open trials assure the public that procedural rights are respected, and that justice is afforded equally. Closed trials breed suspicion of prejudice and arbitrariness, which in turn spawns disrespect for law. Public access is essential, therefore, if trial adjudication is to achieve the objective of maintaining public confidence in the administration of justice.

But the trial is more than a demonstrably just method of adjudicating disputes and protecting rights. It plays a pivotal role in the entire judicial process, and, by extension, in our form of government. Under our system, judges are not mere umpires, but, in their own sphere, lawmakers—a coordinate branch of *government.* While individual cases turn upon the controversies between parties, or involve particular prosecutions, court rulings impose official and practical consequences upon members of society at large. Moreover, judges bear responsibility for the vitally important task of construing and securing constitutional rights. Thus, so far as the trial is the mechanism for judicial factfinding, as well as the initial forum for legal decision making, it is a genuine governmental proceeding.

It follows that the conduct of the trial is pre-eminently a matter of public interest. *See* Cox Broadcasting Corp. v. Cohn, 420 U.S., at 491-492. More importantly, public access to trials acts as an important check, akin in purpose to the other checks and balances that infuse our system of government. . . .

Finally, with some limitations, a trial aims at true and accurate factfinding. Of course, proper factfinding is to the benefit of criminal defendants and of the parties in civil proceedings. But other, comparably urgent, interests are also often at stake. A miscarriage of justice that imprisons an innocent accused also leaves a guilty party at large, a continuing threat to society. Also, mistakes of fact in civil litigation may inflict costs upon others than the plaintiff and defendant. Facilitation of the trial factfinding process, therefore, is of concern to the public as well as to the parties. . . .

Popular attendance at trials, in sum, substantially furthers the particular public purposes of that critical judicial proceeding. In that sense, public access is an indispensable element of the trial process itself. Trial access, therefore, assumes structural importance in our "government of laws," Marbury v. Madison, 1 Cranch 137, 163 (1803).

IV

. . . With regard to the case at hand, our ingrained tradition of public trials and the importance of public access to the broader purposes of the trial process, tip the balance strongly toward the rule that trials be open. What countervailing interests might be sufficiently compelling to reverse this presumption of openness need not concern us now, for the statute at stake here authorizes trial closures at the unfettered discretion of the judge and parties. [Reversed.]

Mr. Justice STEWART, concurring in the judgment.

. . . In conspicuous contrast to a military base, . . . or a prison, . . . a trial courtroom is a public place. Even more than city streets, sidewalks, and parks as areas of traditional First Amendment activity, a trial courtroom is a place where representatives of the press and of the public are not only free to be, but where their presence serves to assure the integrity of what goes on.

But this does not mean that the First Amendment right of members of the public and representatives of the press to attend civil and criminal trials is absolute. Just as a legislature may impose reasonable time, place, and manner restrictions upon the exercise of First Amendment freedoms, so may a trial judge impose reasonable limitations upon the unrestricted occupation of a courtroom by representatives of the press and members of the public. Much more than a city street, a trial courtroom must be a quiet and orderly place. Moreover, every courtroom has a finite physical capacity, and there may be occasions when not all who wish to attend a trial may do so.[3] And while there exist many alternative ways to satisfy the constitutional demands of a fair trial, those demands may also sometimes justify limitations upon the unrestricted presence of spectators in the courtroom.

Since in the present case the trial judge appears to have given no recognition to the right of representatives of the press and members of the public to be present at the Virginia murder trial over which he was presiding, the judgment under review must be reversed.

[Justice Stevens's concurrence and Justice Rehnquist's dissent are omitted.]

NOTES AND QUESTIONS

1. *Value of openness as a limit on the access right.* Can it be argued that openness plays a positive role in almost every type of governmental meeting or proceeding? Should the right of access extend broadly to other types of governmental proceedings? Federal courts have recognized a right of access to civil trials. *See, e.g.*, Publicker Indus., Inc. v. Cohen, 733 F.2d 1059 (3d Cir. 1984). Does this extend to a right of access to documents? Cases such as Courthouse News Serv. v. Schaefer, 2 F.4th 318 (2021), hold that "the press and public enjoy a First Amendment right of access to newly filed civil complaints." If attorneys are given electronic access to newly filed civil complaints, must the public and journalists be given this access also?
2. *History of openness as a limit on the access right.* How valuable is a constitutional right of access that depends on historical recognition for its existence?
3. *Distinguishing* Gannett. Is *Richmond Newspapers* truly distinguishable from *Gannett v. DePasquale*, which is discussed several times in the case?
4. *Free press versus fair trial.* The conflict between a criminal defendant's Sixth Amendment right to a fair trial and the press's and public's First Amendment right to information about that trial comes up in a variety of contexts. The Supreme Court has recognized that trial publicity can, in certain circumstances, violate a criminal defendant's due process rights. Sheppard v. Maxwell, 384 U.S. 333 (1966) (involving a high-profile trial in which the trial judge allowed "newsmen" to take over the courtroom, resulting in "bedlam" and depriving the defendant "of that 'judicial serenity and calm to which [he] was entitled'" by the Due Process Clause). To safeguard the rights of the criminal defendant, the Court has encouraged trial judges to employ procedures to reduce the effect of prejudicial pretrial publicity on a defendant's fair trial right, including change of venue, postponement, extensive and searching voir dire of prospective jurors, clear instructions regarding publicity, sequestration of the jury,

3. In such situations, representatives of the press must be assured access. *Houchins v. KQED, Inc.*, 438 U.S. 1, 16 (opinion concurring in judgment).

and restraining the comments of trial participants. One option that the trial judge does not have (except perhaps in the rarest of cases) is to put a prior restraint on what the press may publish in order to protect the Sixth Amendment rights of a criminal defendant. Later in this chapter, we examine Nebraska Press Ass'n v. Stuart, 427 U.S. 539 (1976), which establishes stringent constitutional standards that a trial judge must satisfy in order to enjoin publication of prejudicial pretrial publicity.

5. *Equal rights or special rights?* The logic of *Richmond Newspapers* is premised on the notion that the public has a constitutional right to attend criminal trials, and therefore so does the press. In other words, the press receives no greater right to attend criminal trials than does the general public. Does Justice Stewart's concurrence, which suggests that the press should receive preferential seating when space is limited, turn an "equal" right of the press and the public to attend criminal trials into a "special" right of the press?

AN EXTENDED NOTE ON EXPANSION OF THE RIGHT OF ACCESS AFTER RICHMOND NEWSPAPERS

The Supreme Court expanded the right of access in a series of opinions after *Richmond Newspapers* and in the process diluted the requirement that a "history of openness" must underpin any constitutional right of access.

In Globe Newspaper Co. v. Superior Court, 457 U.S. 596 (1982), the Court struck down a state statute requiring automatic closure of the courtroom during the trial testimony of minor victims of sexual offenses. The Court held that the key inquiry was not the history of openness of a particular type of trial—such as a sex offense trial. Rather the key inquiry was whether the state could show that closure was "necessitated by a compelling governmental interest" and that its statute was "narrowly tailored to serve that interest." The Court held that mandatory closure was not justified despite the fact that protecting minors is a compelling state interest. Instead, the Court held that a trial judge must make a case-by-case determination that closure is necessary to protect this interest.

In Press-Enterprise Co. v. Superior Court, 464 U.S. 501 (1984) (*Press-Enterprise I*), the Court held that there is a constitutional right of access to attend the voir dire portion of a criminal trial. In that case, the trial judge closed all but three days of a six-week voir dire in a case involving a black defendant charged with raping and murdering a white teenager. The trial judge believed closure was necessary to protect prospective jurors' privacy. The judge not only closed the voir dire but also refused to release transcripts of voir dire after the criminal trial was over. The Supreme Court unanimously reversed. The Court acknowledged that a juror may sometimes have a compelling interest in privacy, but the Court stated that the interest could be protected by questioning the juror with regard to private matters in chambers. The Court refined the constitutional test applied in *Richmond Newspapers* and *Globe Newspaper*, stating: "The presumption of openness may be overcome only by an overriding interest based on findings that closure is essential to preserve higher values and is narrowly tailored to serve that interest. The interest is to be articulated along with findings specific enough that a reviewing court can determine whether the closure order was properly entered." How difficult will this standard be for a trial judge to satisfy? Is ensuring juror candor a more compelling interest than protecting juror privacy?

Finally, in Press-Enterprise Co. v. Superior Court, 478 U.S. 1 (1986) (*Press-Enterprise II*), the Supreme Court held that the press and public have a constitutional right of access to pretrial hearings in criminal cases. *Press-Enterprise II* involved a claim of access to a preliminary probable cause hearing in a California criminal trial; the particular type of preliminary hearing at issue appears to have been unique to California procedure as it existed in 1986. (The procedure was modified by voter initiative in 1990, making it less attractive to defendants in some cases and unavailable to them in others.) Obviously, then, the Court did not put much emphasis on the "historical tradition of openness" of this type of proceeding, instead noting only that most states provide for open preliminary hearings in criminal trials. Instead, the Court focused on "whether public access to preliminary hearings as they are conducted in California plays a significant positive role in the actual functioning of the process." The Court emphasized that the preliminary hearing is the final step in many criminal cases, and it therefore found openness of the preliminary hearing would foster most of the same positive goals as in the trial itself. The Court concluded that a qualified right of access attached to the preliminary hearing, and that the trial judge had not made the requisite findings—that "closure is essential to preserve higher values and is narrowly tailored to serve that interest"—to justify closure. It is worth noting that in both *Press-Enterprise I* and *Press-Enterprise II* the media sought access to transcripts of the proceedings. The Court decided that there was a right to attend the proceedings themselves, and, by extension, that there is a right of access to the records of open proceedings.

An additional access case is worth noting, though it deals with access to documents rather than access to a proceeding and deals with a civil rather than a criminal trial. In Seattle Times Co. v. Rhinehart, 467 U.S. 20 (1984), plaintiff, Rhinehart, and a religious group he headed sued two newspapers for libel. During discovery in the libel case, the newspapers sought information about the religious group's membership and fundraising. The trial court ordered the plaintiffs to produce the information but issued a protective order to prevent the newspapers from publishing it or otherwise disclosing it. The newspapers claimed that the protective order violated their First Amendment right to disseminate the information. The Supreme Court held, however, that "where, as in this case, a protective order is entered upon a showing of good cause as required by Rule 26(c) [of the Federal Rules of Civil Procedure], is limited to the context of pretrial civil discovery, and does not restrict the dissemination of the information if gained from other sources, it does not offend the First Amendment." Would a contrary result have given media litigants an unfair advantage in civil litigation? Why did the Court believe that the protective order here was "not the kind of classic prior restraint that requires exacting First Amendment scrutiny"?

Lower courts have not always faithfully applied the stringent constitutional standards that govern courtroom closure. In Presley v. Georgia, 558 U.S. 209 (2010), a defendant fought all the way to the Supreme Court to have his right to a public trial upheld in a per curiam decision, even though the Supreme Court had clearly recognized the right for a quarter of a century. In *Presley*, a trial court ordered courtroom closure during voir dire of prospective jurors, explaining that "it's up to the individual judge to decide what's comfortable." The judge did not articulate any "overriding interest" in closure beyond a generic risk that the defendant's uncle, who wished to be present, might sit near prospective jurors; nor did the judge consider alternatives to closure. Nonetheless, the Georgia Court of Appeals and the Georgia Supreme Court upheld closure. The Georgia Supreme Court found that "the trial court certainly had an overriding interest in ensuring that potential jurors heard no inherently prejudicial remarks from observers during voir dire," and held that the trial court was not required *sua sponte* to consider alternatives to closure, such as holding the voir dire in a bigger courtroom so that the public and prospective jurors need not be seated together. The U.S. Supreme Court reversed, holding that a criminal defendant's "Sixth Amendment right to a public trial extends to the voir dire of prospective jurors." The Court reminded lower courts that the high burden of justifying closure lies with the trial court and not with the criminal defendant: "Trial courts are obligated to take every reasonable measure to accommodate public attendance at criminal trials." Given that few litigants have the persistence or resources to appeal their cases all the way to the U.S. Supreme Court, what signal does *Presley* send to a trial judge who wishes to order closure of a criminal proceeding? *See* Daniel Levitas, *Scaling Waller: How Courts Have Eroded the Sixth Amendment Public Trial Right*, 59 Emory L.J. 493 (2009) (observing that appellate courts have upheld courtroom closures even when trial courts have not applied the appropriate constitutional standards to justify closure nor made the requisite findings prior to closure).

THEORY-APPLIED PROBLEM: CLOSURE TO PROTECT CHILDREN

Assume that a tabloid newspaper publishes a story alleging that the minor child of a celebrity suffers from severe depression and is addicted to drugs. Suit is brought on the child's behalf for the tort of defamation, and the case proceeds to trial. At trial, the child's attorney requests the trial judge to close the courtroom to outside observers, contending that the trial is likely to involve testimony about the minor child's psychological and physical health and that closure is essential to protect the child's privacy. The attorney for the tabloid does not object, and the trial judge states on the record: "Closure of the courtroom is essential to protect the minor child's privacy and to prevent him from being traumatized by subsequent publication of matters of a private nature to the public at large." Is the closure order likely to be constitutional? Why or why not?

3. Access to Government Institutions

In *Richmond Newspapers* and its progeny, the Supreme Court struggled to reach an accommodation between a First Amendment right of access to criminal trials and the Sixth Amendment rights of criminal defendants. A different accommodation must be struck in cases in which the press has asserted a right of access to governmental institutions such as prisons. Namely, the First Amendment interests must be balanced against the government's need to administer prisons to protect the safety and privacy of inmates, maintain order and discipline, and protect the security of the public.

The first cases dealing with prison access were Pell v. Procunier, 417 U.S. 817 (1974), and Saxbe v. Washington Post Co., 417 U.S. 843 (1974). *Pell* and *Saxbe* involved a ban on media interviews with specific inmates in the California prisons and in federal prisons respectively. Justice Stewart wrote for the Court in both cases, upholding the ban. Justice Stewart viewed the case as governed by the principle that the First Amendment does not "impose[] upon government the affirmative duty to make available to journalists sources of information not available to members of the public generally." The prison regulation at issue treated the press no worse than members of the general public, and it did not foreclose other avenues of gaining information about the prison system. Reporters could tour the prisons and "speak about any subject to any inmates whom they might encounter." They could also interview randomly selected inmates. Significantly, Justice Stewart noted that the ban was "not part of an attempt by the State to conceal the conditions of its prisons or to frustrate the press investigation and reporting of those conditions." Thus, the ban on individual interviews was upheld.

Four Justices dissented in *Pell* and *Saxbe*. Justice Powell, joined by Justices Brennan and Marshall, wrote in *Saxbe* that he could not "follow the Court in concluding that *any* government restriction on press access to information, so long as it is nondiscriminatory, falls outside the purview of First Amendment concern. . . . At some point official restraints on access to news sources, even though not directed solely at the press, may so undermine the function of the First Amendment that it is both appropriate and necessary to require the Government to justify such regulations in terms more compelling than discretionary authority and administrative convenience." Justice Douglas also dissented. *Pell* and *Saxbe* were 5–4 decisions. Would they have come out differently if the government had placed extensive, rather than limited, restrictions on press and public access to prisons? The case below addresses that question. Note that only seven Justices took part in the decision.

Houchins v. KQED, Inc.

438 U.S. 1 (1978)

Mr. Chief Justice BURGER announced the judgment of the Court and delivered an opinion, in which Mr. Justice WHITE and Mr. Justice REHNQUIST joined.

The question presented is whether the news media have a constitutional right of access to a county jail, over and above that of other persons, to interview inmates and make sound recordings, films, and photographs for publication and broadcasting by newspapers, radio, and television.

Petitioner Houchins, as Sheriff of Alameda County, Cal., controls all access to the Alameda County Jail at Santa Rita. Respondent KQED operates licensed television and radio broadcasting stations which have frequently reported newsworthy events relating to penal institutions in the San Francisco Bay Area. On March 31, 1975, KQED reported the suicide of a prisoner in the Greystone portion of the Santa Rita jail. The report included a statement by a psychiatrist that the conditions at the Greystone facility were responsible for the illnesses of his patient-prisoners there, and a statement from petitioner denying that prison conditions were responsible for the prisoners' illnesses.

KQED requested permission to inspect and take pictures within the Greystone facility. After permission was refused, KQED and the Alameda and Oakland branches of the National Association for the Advancement of Colored People (NAACP) filed suit under 42 U.S.C. § 1983. [They sought an injunction to prevent the sheriff from violating their First Amendment rights by excluding them. Shortly thereafter, the sheriff instituted a new prison tour program open to the public and the press.]

Each tour was limited to 25 persons and permitted only limited access to the jail. The tours did not include the disciplinary cells or the portions of the jail known as "Little Greystone," the scene of alleged rapes, beatings, and adverse physical conditions. Photographs of some parts of the jail were made available, but no cameras or tape recorders were allowed on the tours. Those on the tours were not permitted to interview inmates, and inmates were generally removed from view.

. . . [Respondents continued to seek wider access. In response to their request for a preliminary injunction, the sheriff contended] that unregulated access by the media would infringe inmate privacy, and tend to create "jail celebrities," who in turn tend to generate internal problems and undermine jail security. He also contended that unscheduled media tours would disrupt jail operations.

. . . After considering the testimony, affidavits, and documentary evidence presented by the parties, the District Court preliminarily enjoined petitioner from denying KQED news personnel and "responsible representatives" of the news media access to the Santa Rita facilities, including Greystone, "at reasonable times and hours" and "from preventing KQED news personnel and responsible representatives of the news media from utilizing photographic and sound equipment or from utilizing inmate interviews in providing full and accurate coverage of the Santa Rita facilities."

The District Court rejected petitioner's contention that the media policy then in effect was necessary to protect inmate privacy or minimize security and administrative problems. It found that the testimony of officials involved with other jails indicated that a "more flexible press policy at Santa Rita [was] both desirable and attainable." [The Court of Appeals affirmed.]

II

Notwithstanding our holding in *Pell v. Procunier*, respondents assert that the right recognized by the Court of Appeals flows logically from our decisions construing the First Amendment. They argue that there is a constitutionally guaranteed right to gather news under *Pell v. Procunier* and Branzburg v. Hayes, 408 U.S. 665, 681, 707 (1972). From the right to gather news and the right to receive information, they argue for an implied special right of access to government-controlled sources of information. This right, they contend, compels access as a *constitutional* matter. . . . Respondents contend that public access to penal institutions is necessary to prevent officials from concealing prison conditions from the voters and impairing the public's right to discuss and criticize the prison system and its administration.

III

We can agree with many of the respondents' generalized assertions; conditions in jails and prisons are clearly matters "of great public importance." *Pell v. Procunier.* Penal facilities are public institutions which require large amounts of public funds, and their mission is crucial in our criminal justice system. Each person placed in prison becomes, in effect, a ward of the state for whom society assumes broad responsibility. It is equally true that with greater information, the public can more intelligently form opinions about prison conditions. Beyond question, the role of the media is important; acting as the "eyes and ears" of the public, they can be a powerful and constructive force, contributing to remedial action in the conduct of public business. They have served that function since the beginning of the Republic, but like all other components of our society media representatives are subject to limits.

The media are not a substitute for or an adjunct of government and, like the courts, they are "ill equipped" to deal with problems of prison administration. We must not confuse the role of the media with that of government; each has special, crucial functions, each complementing—and sometimes conflicting with—the other.

The public importance of conditions in penal facilities and the media's role of providing information afford no basis for reading into the Constitution a right of the public or the media to enter these institutions, with camera equipment, and take moving and still pictures of inmates for broadcast purposes. This Court has never intimated a First Amendment guarantee of a right of access to all sources of information within government control. Nor does the rationale of the decisions upon which respondents rely lead to the implication of such a right.

Grosjean v. American Press Co., supra, and *Mills v. Alabama, supra,* emphasized the importance of informed public opinion and the traditional role of a free press as a source of public information. But an analysis of those cases reveals that the Court was concerned with the freedom of the media to *communicate* information once it is obtained; neither case intimated that the Constitution *compels* the government to provide the media with information or access to it on demand. . . .

Branzburg v. Hayes offers even less support for the respondents' position. Its observation, in dictum, that "news gathering is not without its First Amendment protections," in no sense implied a constitutional right of access to news sources. That observation must be read in context; it was in response to the contention that forcing a reporter to disclose to a grand jury information received in confidence would violate the First Amendment by deterring news sources from communicating information. There is an undoubted right to gather news "from any source by means within the law," but that affords no basis for the claim that the First Amendment compels others—private persons or governments—to supply information.

. . . The right to *receive* ideas and information is not the issue in this case. The issue is a claimed special privilege of access which the Court rejected in *Pell* and *Saxbe,* a right which is not essential to guarantee the freedom to communicate or publish.

IV

The respondents' argument is flawed, not only because it lacks precedential support and is contrary to statements in this Court's opinions, but also because it invites the Court to involve itself in what is clearly a legislative task which the

Constitution has left to the political processes. Whether the government should open penal institutions in the manner sought by respondents is a question of policy which a legislative body might appropriately resolve one way or the other.

A number of alternatives are available to prevent problems in penal facilities from escaping public attention. . . . Citizen task forces and prison visitation committees continue to play an important role in keeping the public informed on deficiencies of prison systems and need for reforms. Grand juries, with the potent subpoena power—not available to the media—traditionally concern themselves with conditions in public institutions; a prosecutor or judge may initiate similar inquiries, and the legislative power embraces an arsenal of weapons for inquiry relating to tax-supported institutions. In each case, these public bodies are generally compelled to publish their findings and, if they default, the power of the media is always available to generate public pressure for disclosure. But the choice as to the most effective and appropriate method is a policy decision to be resolved by legislative decision. We must not confuse what is "good," "desirable," or "expedient" with what is constitutionally commanded by the First Amendment. To do so is to trivialize constitutional adjudication.

Unarticulated but implicit in the assertion that media access to the jail is essential for informed public debate on jail conditions is the assumption that media personnel are the best qualified persons for the task of discovering malfeasance in public institutions. But that assumption finds no support in the decisions of this Court or the First Amendment. . . .

There is no discernible basis for a constitutional duty to disclose, or for standards governing disclosure of or access to information. Because the Constitution affords no guidelines, absent statutory standards, hundreds of judges would, under the Court of Appeals' approach, be at large to fashion ad hoc standards, in individual cases, according to their own ideas of what seems "desirable" or "expedient." We, therefore, reject the Court of Appeals' conclusory assertion that the public and the media have a First Amendment right to government information regarding the conditions of jails and their inmates and presumably all other public facilities such as hospitals and mental institutions.

. . . Petitioner cannot prevent respondents from learning about jail conditions in a variety of ways, albeit not as conveniently as they might prefer. Respondents have a First Amendment right to receive letters from inmates criticizing jail officials and reporting on conditions. Respondents are free to interview those who render the legal assistance to which inmates are entitled. They are also free to seek out former inmates, visitors to the prison, public officials, and institutional personnel, as they sought out the complaining psychiatrist here.

Moreover, California statutes currently provide for a prison Board of Corrections that has the authority to inspect jails and prisons and *must* provide a public report at regular intervals. Health inspectors are required to inspect prisons and provide reports to a number of officials, including the State Attorney General and the Board of Corrections. Fire officials are also required to inspect prisons. Following the reports of the suicide at the jail involved here, the County Board of Supervisors called for a report from the County Administrator; held a public hearing on the report, which was open to the media; and called for further reports when the initial report failed to describe the conditions in the cells in the Greystone portion of the jail.

Neither the First Amendment nor the Fourteenth Amendment mandates a right of access to government information or sources of information within the government's control. Under our holdings in *Pell v. Procunier*, and *Saxbe v. Washington Post Co.*, until the political branches decree otherwise, as they are free to do, the media have no special right of access to the Alameda County Jail different from or greater than that accorded the public generally. [Reversed and remanded.]

Mr. Justice Stewart, concurring in the judgment.

. . . The First and Fourteenth Amendments do not guarantee the public a right of access to information generated or controlled by government, nor do they guarantee the press any basic right of access superior to that of the public generally. The Constitution does no more than assure the public and the press equal access once government has opened its doors. Accordingly, I agree substantially with what the opinion of The Chief Justice has to say on that score.

We part company, however, in applying these abstractions to the facts of this case. Whereas he appears to view "equal access" as meaning access that is identical in all respects, I believe that the concept of equal access must be accorded more flexibility in order to accommodate the practical distinctions between the press and the general public.

When on assignment, a journalist does not tour a jail simply for his own edification. He is there to gather information to be passed on to others, and his mission is protected by the Constitution for very specific reasons. . . . Our society depends heavily on the press for that enlightenment. . . .

That the First Amendment speaks separately of freedom of speech and freedom of the press is no constitutional accident, but an acknowledgment of the critical role played by the press in American society. The Constitution requires sensitivity to that role, and to the special needs of the press in performing it effectively. A person touring Santa Rita jail can grasp its reality with his own eyes and ears. But if a television reporter is to convey the jail's sights and sounds to those who cannot personally visit the place, he must use cameras and sound equipment. In short, terms of access that are reasonably imposed on individual members of the public may, if they impede effective reporting without sufficient justification, be unreasonable as applied to journalists who are there to convey to the general public what the visitors see.

. . . I agree that the judgment of the Court of Appeals affirming the District Court's order must be reversed [as overbroad based on the available record]. But I would not foreclose the possibility of further relief for KQED on remand. In my view, the availability and scope of future permanent injunctive relief must depend upon the extent of access then permitted the public, and the decree must be framed to accommodate equitably the constitutional role of the press and the institutional requirements of the jail.

Mr. Justice Stevens, with whom Mr. Justice Brennan and Mr. Justice Powell join, dissenting.

. . . In this case, the record demonstrates that both the public and the press had been consistently denied any access to the inner portions of the Santa Rita jail, that there had been excessive censorship of inmate correspondence, and that there was no valid justification for these broad restraints on the flow of information. . . . An official prison policy of concealing such knowledge from the public by arbitrarily cutting off the flow of information at its source abridges the freedom of speech and of the press protected by the First and Fourteenth Amendments to the Constitution.

NOTES AND QUESTIONS

1. *Reconciling* Richmond Newspapers. Is this decision consistent with *Richmond Newspapers?* Could the test applied in that case be applied here to reach the same result?
2. *Justice Stewart's Press Clause.* What is the significance of Justice Stewart's decision? Recall that only seven Justices participated in deciding this case. On what points do Justice Stewart and the plurality opinion agree? Is an independent right of access arising under the Press Clause necessary to the decision of these cases?
3. *Choosing the relevant precedent to resolve other access issues.* Do the media have a First Amendment right of access to battlefields? Which is the relevant precedent, *Richmond Newspapers* and the Court's other courtroom access precedents, or *Houchins*? See Flynt v. Rumsfeld, 355 F.3d 697 (D.C. Cir. 2004) (refusing to apply *Richmond Newspapers* to a claim asserting First Amendment right of access by the media to accompany U.S. troops into combat).

C. PRIOR RESTRAINTS

1. The Presumption of Unconstitutionality

The classic prior restraint is a licensing law—a law that forbids a person from publishing his ideas without first receiving the permission, or "license," of a government official. The first licensing laws were a response to the spread of printing presses in the late fifteenth century. As this medium of mass communication spread, so did government attempts to control it.

In England, the government initially prohibited publishers from printing works without first receiving a license from government officials, who had the power to censor or to ban works at will. However, English licensing laws eventually came to be seen as a threat to press freedom, and they were not renewed in England after 1693. By the eighteenth century, William Blackstone's famous treatise on the English common law articulated the objection to licensing as follows:

> The liberty of the press is indeed essential to the nature of a free state; but this consists in laying no previous restraints on publications, and not in freedom from censure for criminal matter when published. Every freeman has an undoubted right to lay what sentiments he pleases before the public; to forbid this is to destroy the freedom of the press; but if he publishes what is improper, mischievous or illegal, he must take the consequences of his own temerity.

4 William Blackstone, Commentaries *151, *152 (1769).

The common law prohibition on prior restraints also was in effect in the American colonies in the eighteenth century, providing a backdrop to the adoption of the First Amendment in 1791. Indeed, the first major controversy over the meaning of the First Amendment was not about whether it prohibited prior restraints; rather, it was over whether it prohibited prior restraints as well as seditious libel—that is, criminal punishment of citizens who criticize the government.

The first controversy over the meaning of the First Amendment began just seven years after its adoption, when the Federalist Party enacted the Sedition Act of 1798. The Sedition Act was the Federalists' attempt to silence Republican newspapers and prevent Republicans from taking control of Congress and the Presidency in the election of 1800. The Sedition Act made it a crime to publish false, malicious, or scandalous items about the federal government, Congress, or the President. Conspicuously, the Sedition Act did not criminalize criticism of then–Vice President Thomas Jefferson, a Republican. Moreover, the Federalists hedged their bets against a Republican sweep of the elections of 1800 by making the Sedition Act expire in 1801. Although the Sedition Act was enforced vigorously against Republican newspapers, virtually silencing them, Thomas Jefferson won the presidency and his party took control of Congress. The Sedition Act expired and was not renewed.

Passage of the Sedition Act triggered a national debate on the meaning of press freedom. As leaders of this debate, both James Madison and Thomas Jefferson wrote extended discourses on press freedom in which they argued that the First Amendment deprived the federal government of power to punish seditious libel. Whether or not their expansive conceptions of the First Amendment were shared by a majority of Framers, they were a tremendous influence on the shape of subsequent First Amendment doctrine. (Virginia adopted Madison's arguments as "The Virginia Report of 1799-80," and Kentucky adopted Jefferson's as "The Kentucky Resolutions of 1798." Both are excerpted in Leonard Levy, *Freedom of the Press from Zenger to Jefferson* (Leonard Levy ed., 1966).)

The Supreme Court has never questioned that the First Amendment forbids prior restraints. But what is a prior restraint? Blackstone had used the term to mean a group of government officials with authority to censor or ban works prior to publication. But with the expansion of equity jurisdiction, judicial restraints on publication in the form of injunctions became more common. The Supreme Court was forced to decide whether such injunctions—often called gag orders—were also "prior restraints" forbidden by the First Amendment.

Near v. Minnesota, 283 U.S. 697 (1931), is sometimes called the Supreme Court's first great press case, and it involved a judicial restraint on publication. *Near v. Minnesota* was a 5–4 decision. As you read it, try to imagine what First Amendment jurisprudence would look like today if it had gone the other way.

Near v. Minnesota

283 U.S. 697 (1931)

[An unusual Minnesota law authorized abatement, as a public nuisance, of a "malicious, scandalous and defamatory newspaper, or other periodical."

A Minnesota prosecutor sought abatement of The Saturday Press after it published several stories alleging "that a Jewish gangster was in control of gambling, bootlegging and racketeering in Minneapolis" with the complicity of law enforcement. The Minnesota state court concluded that The Saturday Press had "made serious accusations against the public officials named. . . ." Although the abatement statute provided a defense "that the truth was published with good motives and for justifiable ends," the publisher of The Saturday Press did not assert this defense. Instead, he asserted that the abatement statute was unconstitutional. The Minnesota court nonetheless "abated" The Saturday Press as a public nuisance and entered a permanent injunction forbidding the defendants from circulating "any publication whatsoever which is a malicious, scandalous or defamatory newspaper." The Minnesota Supreme Court affirmed, concluding that the injunction did not prevent defendants "from operating a newspaper in harmony with the public welfare, to which all must yield."]

Mr. Chief Justice Hughes delivered the opinion of the Court.

. . . If we cut through mere details of procedure, the operation and effect of the statute in substance is that public authorities may bring the owner or publisher of a newspaper or periodical before a judge upon a charge of conducting a business of publishing scandalous and defamatory matter—in particular that the matter consists of charges against public officers of official dereliction—and, unless the owner or publisher is able and disposed to bring competent evidence to satisfy the judge that the charges are true and are published with good motives and for justifiable ends, his newspaper or periodical is suppressed and further publication is made punishable as a contempt. This is of the essence of censorship.

The question is whether a statute authorizing such proceedings in restraint of publication is consistent with the conception of the liberty of the press as historically conceived and guaranteed. In determining the extent of the constitutional protection, it has been generally, if not universally, considered that it is the chief purpose of the guaranty to prevent previous restraints upon publication. The struggle in England, directed against the legislative power of the licenser, resulted in renunciation of the censorship of the press. The liberty deemed to be established was thus described by Blackstone: "The liberty of the press is indeed essential to the nature of a free state; but this consists in laying no previous restraints upon publications, and not in freedom from censure for criminal matter when published. . . ." 4 Bl. Com. 151, 152. . . . The distinction was early pointed out between the extent of the freedom with respect to censorship under our constitutional system and that enjoyed in England. Here, as Madison said, "the great and essential rights of the people are secured against legislative as well as against executive ambition. They are secured, not by laws paramount to prerogative, but by constitutions paramount to laws. This security of the freedom of the press requires that it should be exempt not only from previous restraint by the Executive, as in Great Britain, but from legislative restraint also." Report on the Virginia Resolutions, Madison's Works, vol. IV, p. 543. . . .

The criticism upon Blackstone's statement has not been because immunity from previous restraint upon publication has not been regarded as deserving of special emphasis, but chiefly because that immunity cannot be deemed to exhaust the conception of the liberty guaranteed by State and Federal Constitutions. . . . [I]t is recognized that punishment for the abuse of the liberty accorded to the press is essential to the protection of the public, and that the common-law rules that subject the libeler to responsibility for the public offense, as well as for the private injury, are not abolished by the protection extended in our Constitutions. The law of criminal libel rests upon that secure foundation. . . . For whatever wrong the appellant has committed or may commit, by his publications, the state appropriately affords both public and private redress by its libel laws. As has been noted, the statute in question does not deal with punishments; it provides for no punishment, except in case of contempt for violation of the court's order, but for suppression and injunction—that is, for restraint upon publication.

The objection has also been made that the principle as to immunity from previous restraint is stated too broadly, if every such restraint is deemed to be prohibited. That is undoubtedly true; the protection even as to previous restraint is not absolutely unlimited. But the limitation has been recognized only in exceptional cases. "When a nation is at war many things that might be said in time of peace are such a hindrance to its effort that their utterance will not be endured so long as men fight and that no Court could regard them as protected by any constitutional right." Schenck v. United States, 249 U. S. 47, 52. No one would question but that a government might prevent actual obstruction to its recruiting service or the publication of the sailing dates of transports or the number and location of troops. On similar grounds, the primary requirements of decency may be enforced against obscene publications. The security of the community life may be protected against incitements to acts of violence and the overthrow by force of orderly government. The constitutional guaranty of free speech does not "protect a man from an injunction against uttering words that may have all the effect of force." Gompers v. Buck's Stove & Range Co., 221 U.S. 418. . . . These limitations are not applicable here. Nor are we now concerned with questions as to the extent of authority to prevent publications in order to protect private rights according to the principles governing the exercise of the jurisdiction of courts of equity.

. . . The fact that for approximately one hundred and fifty years there has been almost an entire absence of attempts to impose previous restraints upon publications relating to the malfeasance of public officers is significant of the deep-seated conviction that such restraints would violate constitutional right. Public officers, whose character and conduct remain open to debate and free discussion in the press, find their remedies for false accusations in actions under libel laws providing for redress and punishment, and not in proceedings to restrain the publication of newspapers and periodicals. The general principle that the constitutional guaranty of the liberty of the press gives immunity from previous restraints has been approved in many decisions under the provisions of state constitutions.

The importance of this immunity has not lessened. While reckless assaults upon public men, and efforts to bring obloquy upon those who are endeavoring faithfully to discharge official duties, exert a baleful influence and deserve the severest condemnation in public opinion, it cannot be said that this abuse is greater, and it is believed to be less, than that which characterized the period in which our institutions took shape. Meanwhile, the administration of government has become more complex, the opportunities for malfeasance and corruption have multiplied, crime has grown to most serious proportions, and the danger of its protection by unfaithful officials and of the impairment of the fundamental security of life and property by criminal alliances and official neglect, emphasizes the primary need of a vigilant and courageous press, especially in great cities. The fact that the liberty of the press may be abused by miscreant purveyors of scandal does not make any the less necessary the immunity of the press from previous restraint in dealing with official misconduct. Subsequent punishment for such abuses as may exist is the appropriate remedy, consistent with constitutional privilege.

In attempted justification of the statute, it is said that it deals not with publication per se, but with the "business" of publishing defamation. If, however, the publisher has a constitutional right to publish, without previous restraint, an edition of his newspaper charging official derelictions, it cannot be denied that he may publish subsequent editions for the same purpose. He does not lose his right by exercising it. If his right exists, it may be exercised in publishing nine editions, as in this case, as well as in one edition. If previous restraint is permissible, it may be imposed at once; indeed, the wrong may be as serious in one publication as in several. Characterizing the publication as a business, and the business as a nuisance, does not permit an invasion of the constitutional immunity against restraint. . . .

. . . The statute in question cannot be justified by reason of the fact that the publisher is permitted to show, before injunction issues, that the matter published is true and is published with good motives and for justifiable ends. If such a statute, authorizing suppression and injunction on such a basis, is constitutionally valid, it would be equally permissible for the Legislature to provide that at any time the publisher of any newspaper could be brought before a court, or even an administrative officer (as the constitutional protection may not be regarded as resting on mere procedural details), and required to produce proof of the truth of his publication, or of what he intended to publish and of his motives, or stand enjoined. If this can be done, the Legislature may provide machinery for determining in the complete exercise of its discretion what are justifiable ends and restrain publication accordingly. And it would be but a step to a complete system of censorship. . . .

Justice BUTLER, dissenting[,with whom Justices VAN DEVANTER, REYNOLDS, and SUTHERLAND concur].

. . . The Minnesota statute does not operate as a previous restraint on publication within the proper meaning of that phrase. It does not authorize administrative control in advance such as was formerly exercised by the licensers and censors, but prescribes a remedy to be enforced by a suit in equity. In this case there was previous publication made in the course of the business of regularly producing malicious, scandalous, and defamatory periodicals. The business and publications unquestionably constitute an abuse of the right of free press. The statute denounces the things done as a nuisance on the ground, as stated by the state Supreme Court, that they threaten morals, peace, and good order. There is no question of the power of the state to denounce such transgressions. The restraint authorized is only in respect of continuing to do what has been duly adjudged to constitute a nuisance. . . .

NOTES AND QUESTIONS

1. *Defining prior restraint.* Why are prior restraints considered worse than subsequent punishment of speech? What is the essence of a prior restraint? The Supreme Court rejected an attempt to characterize a restriction on speech as a prior restraint in Alexander v. United States, 509 U.S. 544 (1993). Alexander was convicted of engaging in the business of selling obscene material and of transporting four obscene magazines and three obscene videos in interstate commerce. This formed the basis for a forfeiture action under the Racketeer Influenced and Corrupt Organizations Act (RICO), which allowed the government to seize Alexander's 31 businesses, confiscate $9 million in profits, and destroy millions of dollars' worth of books and videos found in Alexander's stores. Although the Supreme Court remanded the case for determination whether the forfeiture was an "excessive fine" under the Eighth Amendment, the Court rejected the argument that the forfeiture operated as a prior restraint. The Court instead found the forfeiture to be a valid subsequent punishment akin to a prison term and fine. Chief Justice Rehnquist, writing for the Court, explained:

   > Petitioner's proposed definition of the term "prior restraint" would undermine the time-honored distinction barring speech in the future and penalizing past speech. . . . Because we have interpreted the First Amendment as providing greater protection from prior restraints than from subsequent punishments, it is important for us to delineate with some precision the defining characteristics of a prior restraint. To hold that the forfeiture order in this case constituted a prior restraint would have the opposite effect: it would blur the line separating prior restraints from subsequent punishments to such a degree that it would be impossible to determine with any certainty whether a particular measure is a prior restraint or not.

   Despite Justice's Rehnquist's admonition about defining prior restraints with precision, his opinion for the Court provided no more guidance than what is given in the quoted paragraph. Justice Kennedy, joined by Justices Blackmun and Stevens, dissented in *Alexander*, contending that the forfeiture scheme, like the abatement statute in *Near*, had the "operation and effect" of a prior restraint and raised the same dangers of "state censorship and the unacceptable chilling of protected speech." For further reading regarding prior restraints, see Martin Redish, *The Proper Role of the Prior Restraint Doctrine in First Amendment Theory*, 70 Va. L. Rev. 53 (1984); Jeffrey A. Smith, *Prior Restraint: Original Intentions and Modern Interpretations*, 28 Wm. & Mary L. Rev. 439 (1987).
2. *The collateral bar.* Most jurisdictions have a "collateral bar" rule, which prohibits a person who violates an injunction from challenging its constitutionality. The purpose of the collateral bar rule is to ensure that individuals comply with judicial orders unless they are invalidated through

judicial process. Failure to comply with an injunction may result in a conviction of criminal contempt. The collateral bar rule is the reason that the media are not free to ignore injunctions against publication, even injunctions that are almost certainly unconstitutional. The collateral bar rule may have serious consequences for free speech: an injunction may delay publication long enough so that the information loses its value, or it may prevent publication by one source even though another source is free to publish.

3. *Prior restraints versus subsequent punishments.* Professor John Jeffries contends that "there is only one respect in which injunctions plausibly can be claimed to have a First Amendment impact significantly greater than the threat of subsequent punishment. That argument is based on the traditional rule that the legality of an injunction may not be challenged by disobeying its terms. In its most uncompromising form, the traditional approach would declare that the invalidity or even unconstitutionality of a court order would be no defense in a contempt proceeding based on violation of that order." *Rethinking Prior Restraints,* 92 Yale L.J. 409, 426-433 (1983). Jeffries argues, however, that "a properly limited collateral bar rule would not be destructive of our system of freedom of expression." Courts have in fact carefully confined the collateral bar rule in cases involving prior restraints on expression, as discussed below.

4. *The transparently invalid exception to the collateral bar.* First Amendment concerns have led some courts to develop an exception to the collateral bar rule for "transparently invalid" injunctions. Most notable is In re Providence Journal Co., 820 F.2d 1354 (1st Cir. 1987) (en banc). A newspaper, the Providence Journal, obtained FBI surveillance logs of alleged mobster Raymond Patriarca, who had recently died. At the request of Patriarca's son, a trial judge temporarily enjoined publication pending a hearing to determine whether the surveillance information had been wrongfully released under the Freedom of Information Act. Despite the temporary restraining order, the Providence Journal published information from the logs. The trial judge then appointed a special prosecutor to press criminal contempt against the newspaper and its editor. They were convicted. The judge suspended an 18-month jail sentence on condition that the editor perform 200 hours of community service. The newspaper was fined $100,000. On appeal, a panel of First Circuit judges reversed. The panel relied on dicta in Walker v. City of Birmingham, 388 U.S. 307 (1967), which had affirmed contempt convictions against Martin Luther King, Jr. and others for violating an injunction against parading without a permit; however, *Walker* acknowledged that defendants may ignore a "transparently invalid" injunction. The panel held that the injunction against the Providence Journal was transparently invalid because there was no indication that the heavy presumption of unconstitutionality could be overcome, it was not authorized by statute, and it was not likely to be effective since the FBI had distributed the same information to others. The case was reheard en banc by the First Circuit, which did not vacate the panel's opinion, but which did modify it, stating that "finer tuning is available to minimize the disharmony between respect for court orders

and respect for free speech." Thus, the court stated: "It is not asking much, beyond some additional expense and time, to require a publisher, even when it thinks it is the subject of a transparently unconstitutional order of a prior restraint, to make a good-faith effort to seek emergency relief from the appellate court. If timely access to the appellate court is not available or if timely decision is not forthcoming, the publisher may then proceed to publish and challenge the constitutionality of the order in contempt proceedings." What advice would you give to a publisher who had been enjoined by a Rhode Island court in light of this decision? What if the appellate court grants review, but not expedited review? *See also* United States v. Dickinson, 465 F.2d 496 (5th Cir. 1972) ("[I]n the absence of strong indications that the appellate process is being deliberately stalled—certainly not so in this record—violation with impunity does not occur simply because immediate decision is not forthcoming, even though the communication enjoined is 'news.'"); Procter & Gamble Co. v. Bankers Trust Co., 78 F.3d 219 (6th Cir. 1996) (determining that a permanent injunction on publication was "patently invalid").

2. *The National Security Exception*

The first test of whether a prior restraint could be justified in the name of national security came in the so-called "Pentagon Papers" case, excerpted below. In the midst of the Vietnam War, the *New York Times* obtained a classified government document detailing U.S. involvement in Vietnam. The document consisted of 47 volumes (the "Pentagon Papers"), many of which gave the historical backdrop to U.S. involvement. After several months of studying the volumes, the *New York Times* published the first in a planned series of articles about the Pentagon Papers. The Justice Department sought an injunction. A New York district judge temporarily enjoined publication, and the Second Circuit granted the injunction. Meanwhile, the *Washington Post* began publishing material from the Pentagon Papers. The Justice Department again asked for an injunction, but the district judge and the Court of Appeals for the District of Columbia Circuit denied the motion. The Supreme Court issued stays to prevent either newspaper from publishing, heard oral argument, and issued the following decision five days later. Although the Court's opinion is per curiam, every Justice wrote a separate opinion.

New York Times Co. v. United States

("Pentagon Papers" Case)
403 U.S. 713 (1971)

PER CURIAM.

We granted certiorari in these cases in which the United States seeks to enjoin the New York Times and the Washington Post from publishing the contents of a classified study entitled "History of U.S. Decision-Making Process on Viet Nam Policy."

"Any system of prior restraints of expression comes to this Court bearing a heavy presumption against its constitutional validity." Bantam Books, Inc. v. Sullivan, 372 U.S. 58, 70 (1963); see also Near v. Minnesota ex rel. Olson, 283 U.S. 697 (1931). The Government "thus carries a heavy burden of showing justification for the imposition of such a restraint." . . . The District Court for the Southern District of New York in the New York Times case, and the District Court for the District of Columbia and the Court of Appeals for the District of Columbia Circuit in the Washington Post case held that the Government had not met that burden. We agree.

The judgment of the Court of Appeals for the District of Columbia Circuit is therefore affirmed. The order of the Court of Appeals for the Second Circuit is reversed, and the case is remanded with directions to enter a judgment affirming the judgment of the District Court for the Southern District of New York. The stays entered June 25, 1971, by the Court are vacated. The judgments shall issue forthwith.

NOTES AND QUESTIONS

1. *The Pentagon Papers and executive power.* As noted above, every member of the Court wrote a separate opinion in the Pentagon Papers case. Three justices would have barred the newspapers from further publication. Justice John Marshall Harlan, writing for himself, Chief Justice Warren Burger, and Justice Harry Blackmun, contended that federal courts owe deference to the executive branch in foreign affairs and that review should be limited to determining whether the dispute was with the "proper compass of the President's foreign relations power." Was the Court correct in "second-guessing" the executive branch's determination that disclosure of the Pentagon Papers could "irreparably impair national security?" Does the First Amendment demand that the Court do so?
2. *The importance of statutory authorization.* Several of the Justices wrote that they might have been willing to issue an injunction if statutory authorization were present. Why does statutory authorization matter? In his 1992 book, *Free Speech in an Open Society*, Professor Rodney Smolla explains: "The exercise of a prior restraint is such an anathema in the American First Amendment tradition that only the combined authority of the legislative and executive branch, after review by the judiciary, should be enough to sustain it."
3. *Permissible prior restraints.* Injunctions are authorized by section 502 of the Copyright Act, and are commonly granted as a remedy in copyright infringement cases. Injunctions are also commonly granted to prevent publication of trade secrets. Although courts have tended to grant injunctions in copyright and trade secret cases without applying much, if any, First Amendment scrutiny, scholars have begun to argue that courts should apply the same standards before granting preliminary injunctions in intellectual property cases that they do before granting them in defamation cases. *See* Mark A. Lemley & Eugene Volokh, *Freedom of Speech and Injunctions in Intellectual Property Cases,* 48 Duke L.J. 147 (1998).

See also State ex rel. Sports Mgmt. News, Inc. v. Nachtigal, 921 P.2d 1304 (Or. 1996) (applying traditional prior restraint analysis in a trade secrets case).

4. *Injunctions as a remedy for defamation.* Some courts have upheld an injunction requiring removal of speech already adjudicated to be defamatory at trial, while still disfavoring injunctions against similar speech by the defendant. *See, e.g.*, Kinney v. Barnes, 443 S.W. 3d 87 (2014). For discussion of post-trial injunctions as a defamation remedy, see Eugene Volokh, *Anti-Libel Injunctions*, 168 Penn. L. Rev. 73 (2019).

THEORY-APPLIED PROBLEM: A NATIONAL SECURITY HYPOTHETICAL

It is easy to imagine terrorists using information about weaknesses in our critical infrastructure or about chemical or biological weapons to kill hundreds of thousands of people. Assume that a magazine plans to run an article with a "map" of the U.S. fiber-optic network, assembled from publicly available documents. Government officials learn of the article and seek an injunction on the grounds that terrorists could use the information to cripple the business and industrial sector of the U.S. economy. How should a court rule? (The government chose to "classify" the dissertation of George Mason University graduate student Sean Gorman for precisely this reason. *See* Sean Gorman, *9/11 Turned Thesis into Time Bomb*, Pittsburgh Post-Gazette, July 13, 2003, at A11.)

AN EXTENDED NOTE ON "SUBSEQUENT PUNISHMENT" OF LEAKERS

If it is almost impossible to enjoin publication of government secrets, why not preserve them by prosecuting disclosures? Can the media be prosecuted under the Espionage Act for disclosing information related to the national defense? In United States v. Rosen, 445 F. Supp. 2d 602 (E.D. Va. 2006), a district judge rejected the First Amendment arguments of two former lobbyists charged with illegally receiving classified security information and disclosing it to Israeli officials and reporters. The defendants were lobbyists for the American Israel Public Affairs Committee (AIPAC). They allegedly received information about classified matters involving U.S. Middle East strategy from a Pentagon analyst and passed it along to Israeli officials and journalists. They were charged with violations of 18 U.S.C. § 793, which makes it a crime to willfully communicate information "relating to the national defense" when "the possessor has reason to believe [the information] could be used to the injury of the United States or to the advantage of any foreign nation" to "any person not entitled to receive it." The defendants moved to dismiss the indictments, arguing that the Espionage Act was intended to apply to government employees and others for whom disclosure would be a breach of trust, and that applying it to outsiders who owed no special obligation to help keep the government's secrets would violate the First Amendment. The trial judge concluded that application of the Espionage Act to outsiders would be constitutional in "situations in which national security is genuinely at risk." He therefore construed the definition of national defense information to mean "information potentially damaging to the United States or useful to an enemy of the United States." He also rejected the defendants' overbreadth and vagueness challenges to the statute. The government dropped the charges against two of the defendants in 2009, after the Fourth Circuit ruled that the government would have to disclose certain classified information to proceed. *See* United States v. Rosen, 557 F.3d 192 (4th Cir. 2009). [Another had pled guilty in 2005.] Jerry Markon, *U.S. Drops Case Against Ex-Lobbyists: Former AIPAC Employees Faced Espionage Charges*, Washington Post, May 2, 2009, at *http://www.washingtonpost.com/wpdyn/content/article/2009/05/01/AR2009050101310.html.*

If the lobbyists in *Rosen* could be prosecuted for disclosing classified information "leaked" by a government official, what would prevent the government from prosecuting reporters for publishing similar information? Is the potential for harm to national security less in the case of media publication? For a discussion of the dearth of First Amendment precedents to prevent such prosecutions, see William E. Lee, *Probing Secrets: The Press and Inchoate Liability for Newsgathering Crimes*, 36 Am. J. of Crim L. 129 (2009).

THEORY-APPLIED PROBLEM: WIKILEAKS

In 2010 WikiLeaks.org, an online "publisher" of leaked documents, released some 400,000 secret U.S. government documents on its website. The *Guardian* newspaper in England and the *New York Times* published some of these documents, too, which they had obtained through an arrangement with WikiLeaks founder Julian Assange. The documents included diplomatic cables, intelligence assessments, and confidential military information that Assange allegedly received from U.S. intelligence analyst, Pfc. Bradley Manning, A Pentagon official called the release of classified material by WikiLeaks a boon to "terrorist organizations" and said the release "put at risk the lives of our troops." John F. Burns and Ravi Somaiya, *WikiLeaks Founder Gets Support in Rebuking U.S. on Whistleblowers*, Oct. 23, 2010, at http://www.nytimes.com/2010/10/24/world/24london.html. The U.S. government began a criminal investigation of Julian Assange, and a grand jury returned an indictment against him. Then-Secretary of State Hillary Clinton called the disclosures "an attack against the international community." Should the government have sought an injunction against WikiLeaks, the *Guardian*, and/or the *New York Times* to prevent them from disclosing the secret and allegedly damaging documents? Why or why not? Could the *New York Times* editors responsible for publishing the leaked documents be prosecuted under the Espionage Act of 1917? The U.S. government has sought extradition of Mr. Assange, who is not a U.S. citizen and who did not release any leaked documents within the United States. If extradited, Assange faces 17 counts of espionage and one of computer misuse for obtaining and publishing classified documents. Rachel Treisman, *A Court in the U.K. says Julian Assange Can Keep Fighting his Extradition to the U.S.*, NPR, Jan. 24, 2022. For more on the legal issues surrounding disclosures by WikiLeaks, see Christina E. Wells, *Contextualizing Disclosure's Effects: WikiLeaks, Balancing, and the First Amendment*, 97 Iowa L. Rev. Bulletin 51 (2012).

THEORY-APPLIED PROBLEM: INJUNCTIONS AS REMEDIES FOR DEFAMATION?

Can a court issue a post-trial injunction requiring a defendant to remove from his website statements he made that a civil jury has found to be defamatory? What are the arguments for and against the issues of such an injunction? In Kinney

v. Barnes, 443 S.W.3d 87 (Tx. 2014), the Texas Supreme Court rejected the arguments of a plaintiff who had won a defamation judgment at trial that the defendant should be permanently enjoined from making future statements *similar* to those that a jury had determined to be defamatory. The court reasoned that the speech on the defendant's website that had been adjudicated defamatory by the jury fell into the category of speech unprotected by the First Amendment, and therefore an injunction requiring removal of that speech was not an unconstitutional prior restraint. By contrast, an injunction against future, similar speech runs the risk of chilling constitutionally protected expression: "Given the inherently contextual nature of defamatory speech, even the most narrowly crafted of injunctions risks enjoining protected speech because the same statement made at a different time and in a different context may no longer be actionable. Untrue statements may later become true; unprivileged statements may later become privileged." Noting that the U.S. Supreme Court had never "definitively addressed" the issue, the Texas Supreme Court cited the Texas Constitution as the basis for its holding regarding injunctions against future speech. What are the implications of this decision? Can a court issue a post-trial injunction requiring a defendant to remove information that has been found to invade privacy? What about a criminal record that has been expunged? What about ordering a review website to take down a review that a jury has determined to be defamatory? What about ordering a review website to take down a review after a default judgment in favor of a defamation plaintiff?

3. *Free Press/Fair Trial*

Prejudicial publicity can deprive a criminal defendant of his or her Sixth Amendment right to a fair trial. In Sheppard v. Maxwell, 384 U.S. 333 (1966), the Supreme Court reversed the conviction of a criminal defendant on this ground and recommended a number of steps trial judges should take to control prejudicial publicity in high-profile cases. These steps included, for example, sequestration of the trial, change of venue, searching voir dire of jurors exposed to publicity, orders to participants not to reveal information prior to trial, and so forth. Perhaps naturally, some judges took the direct route and began imposing restraints on the publication of prejudicial information about the criminal defendant prior to trial. That practice ended because of the following case.

Nebraska Press Ass'n v. Stuart

427 U.S. 539 (1976)

Chief Justice BURGER delivered the opinion of the Court.

The respondent State District Judge entered an order restraining the petitioners from publishing or broadcasting accounts of confessions or admission made by the accused or facts "strongly implicative" of the accused in a widely reported murder of six persons. We granted certiorari to decide whether the entry of such an order on the showing made before the state court violated the constitutional guarantee of freedom of the press.

On the evening of October 18, 1975, local police found the six members of the Henry Kellie family murdered in their home in Sutherland, Neb., a town of about 850 people. Police released the description of a suspect, Erwin Charles Simants, to the reporters who had hastened to the scene of the crime. Simants was arrested and arraigned in Lincoln County Court the following morning, ending a tense night for this small rural community.

The crime immediately attracted widespread news coverage, by local, regional, and national newspapers, radio and television stations. [Four days after the crime, the County Court, at the request of the prosecutor and defense attorney, entered an order restricting the release of information about the case.]

Simants' preliminary hearing was held the same day, open to the public but subject to the order. The County Court bound over the defendant for trial to the State District Court. The charges, as amended to reflect the autopsy findings, were that Simants had committed the murders in the course of a sexual assault.

[Petitioners moved to vacate the County Court order. After a hearing, the District Court entered a narrower restrictive order, based on his finding of] "a clear and present danger that pre-trial publicity could impinge upon the defendant's right to a fair trial." The order applied only until the jury was impaneled, and specifically prohibited petitioners from reporting five [specified] subjects. . . .

[Petitioners sought expedited appeal in the Nebraska Supreme Court, which] modified the District Court's order to accommodate the defendant's right to a fair trial and the petitioners' interest in reporting pretrial events. The order as modified prohibited reporting of only three matters: (a) the existence and nature of any confessions or admissions made by the defendant to law enforcement officers, (b) any confessions or admissions made to any third parties, except members of the press, and (c) other facts "strongly implicative" of the accused. . . . After construing Nebraska law to permit closure in certain circumstances, the court remanded the case to the District Judge for reconsideration of the issue whether pretrial hearings should be closed to the press and public.

We granted certiorari to address the important issues raised by the District Court order as modified by the Nebraska Supreme Court, but we denied the motion to expedite review or to stay entirely the order of the State District Court pending Simants' trial. We are informed by the parties that since we granted certiorari, Simants has been convicted of murder and sentenced to death. His appeal is pending in the Nebraska Supreme Court.

[The Court held that the case was not moot, since it was "capable of repetition, yet evading review."]

III

The problems presented by this case are almost as old as the Republic. Neither in the Constitution nor in contemporaneous writings do we find that the conflict between these two important rights was anticipated, yet it is inconceivable that the authors of the Constitution were unaware of the potential conflicts between the right to an unbiased jury and the guarantee of freedom of the press. The unusually able lawyers who helped write the Constitution and later drafted the Bill of Rights were familiar with the historic episode in which John Adams defended British soldiers charged with homicide for firing into a crowd of Boston demonstrators; they were intimately familiar with the clash of the adversary system and the part that passions of the populace sometimes play in influencing potential jurors. They did not address themselves directly to the situation presented by this case; their chief concern was the need for freedom of expression in the political arena and the dialogue in ideas. But they recognized that there were risks to private rights from an unfettered press. . . .

The trial of Aaron Burr in 1807 presented Mr. Chief Justice Marshall, presiding as a trial judge, with acute problems in selecting an unbiased jury. Few people in the area of Virginia from which jurors were drawn had not formed some opinions concerning Mr. Burr or the case, from newspaper accounts and heightened discussion both private and public. The Chief Justice conducted a searching voir dire of the two panels eventually called, and rendered a substantial opinion on the purposes of voir dire and the standards to be applied. See 1 Causes Celebres, Trial of Aaron Burr for Treason 404-427, 473-481 (1879); United States v. Burr, 25 Fed. Cas. No. 14,692g, p. 49 (CC Va. 1807). Burr was acquitted, so there was no occasion for appellate review to examine the problem of prejudicial pretrial publicity. Mr. Chief Justice Marshall's careful voir dire inquiry into the matter of possible bias makes clear that the problem is not a new one.

The speed of communication and the pervasiveness of the modern news media have exacerbated these problems, however, as numerous appeals demonstrate. The trial of Bruno Hauptmann in a small New Jersey community for the abduction and murder of the Charles Lindberghs' infant child probably was the most widely covered trial up to that time, and the nature of the coverage produced widespread public reaction. Criticism was directed at the "carnival" atmosphere that pervaded the community and the courtroom itself. Responsible leaders of press and the legal profession including other judges pointed out that much of this sorry performance could have been controlled by a vigilant trial judge and by other public officers subject to the control of the court. . . .

The excesses of press and radio and lack of responsibility of those in authority in the Hauptmann case and others of that era led to efforts to develop voluntary guidelines for courts, lawyers, press, and broadcasters. The effort was renewed in 1965 when the American Bar Association embarked on a project to develop standards for all aspects of criminal justice, including guidelines to accommodate the right to a fair trial and the rights of a free press. The resulting standards, approved by the Association in 1968, received support from most of the legal profession. . . . In the wake of these efforts, the cooperation between bar associations and members of the press led to the adoption of voluntary guidelines like Nebraska's.

In practice, of course, even the most ideal guidelines are subjected to powerful strains when a case such as Simants' arises, with reporters from many parts of the country on the scene. Reporters from distant places are unlikely to consider themselves bound by local standards. They report to editors outside the area covered by the guidelines, and their editors are likely to be guided only by their own standards. To contemplate how a state court can control acts of a newspaper or broadcaster outside its jurisdiction, even though the newspapers and broadcasts reach the very community from which jurors are to be selected, suggests something of the practical difficulties of managing such guidelines. . . .

IV

. . . In the overwhelming majority of criminal trials, pretrial publicity presents few unmanageable threats to this important right. But when the case is a "sensational" one tensions develop between the right of the accused to trial by an impartial jury and the rights guaranteed others by the First Amendment. The relevant decisions of this Court, even if not dispositive, are instructive by way of background.

. . . In Sheppard v. Maxwell, 384 U.S. 333, 86 S. Ct. 1507, 16 L. Ed. 2d 600 (1966), the Court focused sharply on the impact of pretrial publicity and a trial court's duty to protect the defendant's constitutional right to a fair trial. With only Mr. Justice Black dissenting, and he without opinion, the Court ordered a new trial for the petitioner, even though the first trial had occurred 12 years before. Beyond doubt the press had shown no responsible concern for the constitutional guarantee of a fair trial; the community from which the jury was drawn had been inundated by publicity hostile to the defendant. But the trial judge "did not fulfill his duty to protect (the defendant) from the inherently prejudicial publicity which saturated the community and to control disruptive influences in the courtroom." The Court noted that "unfair and prejudicial news comment on pending trials has become increasingly prevalent," and issued a strong warning:

> Due process requires that the accused receive a trial by an impartial jury free from outside influences. . . . [W]here there is a reasonable likelihood that prejudicial news prior to trial will prevent a fair trial, the judge should continue the case until the threat abates, or transfer it to another county not so permeated with publicity. In addition, sequestration of the jury was something the judge should have raised sua sponte with counsel. If publicity during the proceedings threatens the fairness of the trial, a new trial should be ordered. But we must remember that reversals are but palliatives; the cure lies in those remedial measures that will prevent the prejudice at its inception. . . . Neither prosecutors, counsel for defense, the accused, witnesses, court staff nor enforcement officers coming under the jurisdiction of the court should be permitted to frustrate its function. Collaboration between counsel and the press as to information affecting the fairness of a criminal trial is not only subject to regulation, but is highly censurable and worthy of disciplinary measures. . . .

Because the trial court had failed to use even minimal efforts to insulate the trial and the jurors from the "deluge of publicity," the Court vacated the judgment of conviction and a new trial followed, in which the accused was acquitted. . . .

The state trial judge in the case before us acted responsibly, out of a legitimate concern, in an effort to protect the defendant's right to a fair trial. What we must decide is not simply whether the Nebraska courts erred in seeing the possibility of real danger to the defendant's rights, but whether in the circumstances of this case the means employed were foreclosed by another provision of the Constitution.

V

The First Amendment provides that "Congress shall make no law . . . abridging the freedom . . . of the press," and it is "no longer open to doubt that the liberty of the press and of speech, is within the liberty safeguarded by the due process clause of the Fourteenth Amendment from invasion by state action." [*Near.*] The Court has interpreted these guarantees to afford special protection against orders that prohibit the publication or broadcast of particular information or commentary orders that impose a "previous" or "prior" restraint on speech. None of our decided cases on prior restraint involved restrictive orders entered to protect a defendant's right to a fair and impartial jury, but the opinions on prior restraint have a common thread relevant to this case.

. . . The thread running through [our prior] cases is that prior restraints on speech and publication are the most serious and the least tolerable infringement on First Amendment rights. A criminal penalty or a judgment in a defamation case is subject to the whole panoply of protections afforded by deferring the impact of the judgment until all avenues of appellate review have been exhausted. Only after judgment has become final, correct or otherwise, does the law's sanction become fully operative.

A prior restraint, by contrast and by definition, has an immediate and irreversible sanction. If it can be said that a threat of criminal or civil sanctions after publication "chills" speech, prior restraint "freezes" it at least for the time.

The damage can be particularly great when the prior restraint falls upon the communication of news and commentary on current events. Truthful reports of public judicial proceedings have been afforded special protection against subsequent punishment. See Cox Broadcasting Corp. v. Cohn, 420 U.S. 469, 492-493 (1975). For the same reasons the protection against prior restraint should have particular force as applied to reporting of criminal proceedings, whether the crime in question is a single isolated act or a pattern of criminal conduct. . . .

The extraordinary protections afforded by the First Amendment carry with them something in the nature of a fiduciary duty to exercise the protected rights responsibly, a duty widely acknowledged but not always observed by editors and publishers. It is not asking too much to suggest that those who exercise First Amendment rights in newspapers or broadcasting enterprises direct some effort to protect the rights of an accused to a fair trial by unbiased jurors.

Of course, the order at issue like the order requested in New York Times does not prohibit but only postpones publication. Some news can be delayed and most commentary can even more readily be delayed without serious injury, and there often is a self-imposed delay when responsible editors call for verification of information. But such delays are normally slight and they are self-imposed. Delays imposed by governmental authority are a different matter. . . .

As a practical matter, moreover, the element of time is not unimportant if press coverage is to fulfill its traditional function of bringing news to the public promptly.

The authors of the Bill of Rights did not undertake to assign priorities as between First Amendment and Sixth Amendment rights, ranking one as superior to the other. In this case, the petitioners would have us declare the right of an accused subordinate to their right to publish in all circumstances. But if the authors of these guarantees, fully aware of the potential conflicts between them, were unwilling or unable to resolve the issue by assigning to one priority over the other, it is not for us to rewrite the Constitution by undertaking what they declined to do. It is unnecessary, after nearly two centuries, to establish a priority applicable in all circumstances. Yet it is nonetheless clear that the barriers to prior restraint remain high unless we are to abandon what the Court has said for nearly a quarter of our national existence and implied throughout all of it. . . .

VI

We turn now to the record in this case to determine whether, as Learned Hand put it, "the gravity of the 'evil,' discounted by its improbability, justifies such invasion of free speech as is necessary to avoid the danger." United States v. Dennis, 183 F.2d 201, 212 (CA2 1950), aff'd, 341 U.S. 494(1951); *see also* L. Hand, *The Bill of Rights* 58-61 (1958). To do so, we must examine the evidence before the trial judge when the order was entered to determine (a) the nature and extent of pretrial news coverage; (b) whether other measures would be likely to mitigate the effects of unrestrained pretrial publicity; and (c) how effectively a restraining order would operate to prevent the threatened danger. The precise terms of the restraining order are also important. We must then consider whether the record supports the entry of a prior restraint on publication, one of the most extraordinary remedies known to our jurisprudence.

[A.] In assessing the probable extent of publicity, the trial judge had before him newspapers demonstrating that the crime had already drawn intensive news coverage, and the testimony of the County Judge, who had entered the initial restraining order based on the local and national attention the case had attracted. The District Judge was required to assess the probable publicity that would be given these shocking crimes prior to the time a jury was selected and sequestered. He then had to examine the probable nature of the publicity and determine how it would affect prospective jurors.

Our review of the pretrial record persuades us that the trial judge was justified in concluding that there would be intense and pervasive pretrial publicity concerning this case. He could also reasonably conclude, based on common man experience, that publicity might impair the defendant's right to a fair trial. He did not purport to say more, for he found only "a clear and present danger that pretrial publicity *could* impinge upon the defendant's right to a fair trial." (Emphasis added.) His conclusion as to the impact of such publicity on prospective jurors was of necessity speculative, dealing as he was with factors unknown and unknowable.

[B.] We find little in the record that goes to another aspect of our task, determining whether measures short of an order restraining all publication would have insured the defendant a fair trial. Although the entry of the order might be read as a judicial determination that other measures would not suffice, the trial court made no express findings to that effect; the Nebraska Supreme Court referred to the issue only by implication.

Most of the alternatives to prior restraint of publication in these circumstances were discussed with obvious approval in Sheppard v. Maxwell: (a) change of trial venue to a place less exposed to the intense publicity that seemed imminent in Lincoln County; (b) postponement of the trial to allow public attention to subside; (c) searching questioning of prospective jurors . . . to screen out those with fixed opinions as to guilt or innocence; (d) the use of emphatic and clear instructions on the sworn duty of each juror to decide the issues only on evidence presented in open court. Sequestration of jurors is, of course, always available. Although that measure insulates jurors only after they are sworn, it also enhances the likelihood of dissipating the impact of pretrial publicity and emphasizes the elements of the jurors' oaths.

. . . We have noted earlier that pretrial publicity, even if pervasive and concentrated, cannot be regarded as leading automatically and in every kind of criminal case to an unfair trial. The decided cases "cannot be made to stand for the proposition that juror exposure to information about a state defendant's prior convictions or to news accounts of the crime with which he is charged alone presumptively deprives the defendant of due process." Murphy v. Florida, 421 U.S., at 799, 95 S. Ct., at 2036. . . .

We have . . . examined this record to determine the probable efficacy of the measures short of prior restraint on the press and speech. There is no finding that alternative measures would not have protected Simants' rights, and the Nebraska Supreme Court did no more than imply that such measures might not be adequate. Moreover, the record is lacking in evidence to support such a finding.

[C.] We must also assess the probable efficacy of prior restraint on publication as a workable method of protecting Simants' right to a fair trial, and we cannot ignore the reality of the problems of managing and enforcing pretrial restraining orders. The territorial jurisdiction of the issuing court is limited by concepts of sovereignty, see, . . . ; Pennoyer v. Neff, 95 U.S. 714 (1878). The need for *in personam* jurisdiction also presents an obstacle to a restraining order that applies to publication at large as distinguished from restraining publication within a given jurisdiction.

The Nebraska Supreme Court narrowed the scope of the restrictive order, and its opinion reflects awareness of the tensions between the need to protect the accused as fully as possible and the need to restrict publication as little as possible. The dilemma posed underscores how difficult it is for trial judges to predict what information will in fact undermine the impartiality of jurors, and the difficulty of drafting an order that will effectively keep prejudicial information from prospective jurors. When a restrictive order is sought, a court can anticipate only part of what will develop that may injure the accused. But information not so obviously prejudicial may emerge, and what may properly be published in these "gray zone" circumstances may not violate the restrictive order and yet be prejudicial.

Finally, we note that the events disclosed by the record took place in a community of 850 people. It is reasonable to assume that, without any news accounts being printed or broadcast, rumors would travel swiftly by word of mouth. One can only speculate on the accuracy of such reports, given the generative propensities of rumors; they could well be more damaging than reasonably accurate news accounts. But plainly a whole community cannot be restrained from discussing a subject intimately affecting life within it.

Given these practical problems, it is far from clear that prior restraint on publication would have protected Simants' rights.

[D.] Finally, another feature of this case leads us to conclude that the restrictive order entered here is not supportable. At the outset the County Court entered a very broad restrictive order, the terms of which are not before us; it then held a preliminary hearing open to the public and the press. There was testimony concerning at least two incriminating statements made by Simants to private persons; the statement—evidently a confession that he gave to law enforcement officials—was also introduced. The State District Court's later order was entered after this public hearing and, as modified by the Nebraska Supreme Court, enjoined reporting of[, among other things, any confession or confessions made by Simants.]

To the extent that this order prohibited the reporting of evidence adduced at the open preliminary hearing, it plainly violated settled principles: "(T)here is nothing that proscribes the press from reporting events that transpire in the courtroom." Sheppard v. Maxwell, 384 U.S., at 362-363. *See also* Cox Broadcasting Corp. v. Cohn, 420 U.S. 469 (1975). The County Court could not know that closure of the preliminary hearing was an alternative open to it until the Nebraska Supreme Court so construed state law; but once a public hearing had been held, what transpired there could not be subject to prior restraint.

The third prohibition of the order was defective in another respect as well. As part of a final order, entered after plenary review, this prohibition regarding "implicative" information is too vague and too broad to survive the scrutiny we have given to restraints on First Amendment rights. . . .

[E.] Our analysis ends as it began, with a confrontation between prior restraint imposed to protect one vital constitutional guarantee and the explicit command of another that the freedom to speak and publish shall not be abridged. We reaffirm that the guarantees of freedom of expression are not an absolute prohibition under all circumstances, but the barriers to prior restraint remain high and the presumption against its use continues intact. We hold that, with respect to the order entered in this case prohibiting reporting or commentary on judicial proceedings held in public, the barriers have not been overcome; to the extent that this order restrained publication of such material, it is clearly invalid. To the extent that it prohibited publication based on information gained from other sources, we conclude that the heavy burden imposed as a condition to securing a prior restraint was not met. . . .

Justice White, concurring.

Technically there is no need to go farther than the Court does to dispose of this case, and I join the Court's opinion. I should add, however, that for the reasons which the Court itself canvasses there is grave doubt in my mind whether orders with respect to the press such as were entered in this case would ever be justifiable. . . .

Justice Brennan, with whom Justice Stewart and Justice Marshall join, concurring in the judgment.

. . . The right to a fair trial by a jury of one's peers is unquestionably one of the most precious and sacred safeguards enshrined in the Bill of Rights. I would hold, however, that resort to prior restraints on the freedom of the press is a constitutionally impermissible method for enforcing that right; judges have at their disposal a broad spectrum of devices for ensuring that fundamental fairness is accorded the accused without necessitating so drastic an incursion on the equally fundamental and salutary constitutional mandate that discussion of public affairs in a free society cannot depend on the preliminary grace of judicial censors.

. . . Recognition of any judicial authority to impose prior restraints on the basis of harm to the Sixth Amendment rights of particular defendants, especially since that harm must remain speculative, will thus inevitably interject judges at all levels into censorship roles that are simply inappropriate and impermissible under the First Amendment. Indeed, the potential for arbitrary and excessive judicial utilization of any such power would be exacerbated by the fact that judges and committing magistrates might in some cases be determining the propriety of publishing information that reflects on their competence, integrity, or general performance on the bench.

[Justice STEVENS's concurring opinion is omitted.]

NOTES AND QUESTIONS

1. *Distinguishing* Near. Why doesn't the majority opinion simply apply the presumption of unconstitutionality from *Near* or the Pentagon Papers case? Although the *Nebraska Press* standard seems lower, is it really? Can a prior restraint on the press ever meet the stringent guidelines set forth in *Nebraska Press*?
2. *Restraints on trial participants.* One alternative to restraints on the media to prevent prejudicial publicity is to impose restraints on trial participants, such as attorneys, police, and witnesses. Most states have rules limiting what attorneys involved in pending proceedings may say. The Supreme Court addressed the constitutionality of those rules in Gentile v. State Bar of Nevada, 501 U.S. 1030 (1991), which held that states may regulate attorney speech to protect the fair trial rights of criminal defendants based on a showing of a "substantial likelihood of material prejudice."
3. *Media standing.* Courts have held that the media have standing to challenge gag orders on trial participants, such as lawyers. It is not clear, however, what standard should be applied to such challenges. The Second Circuit, for example, upheld a restraint on trial participants in the face of a media challenge upon a showing of a "reasonable likelihood" that pretrial publicity would prejudice the fair trial rights of the defendants. Application of Dow Jones & Co., 842 F.2d 603 (2d Cir. 1988). The Ninth Circuit also uses that test, *see* Radio & Television News Ass'n v. U.S. Dist. Court, 781 F.2d 1443 (9th Cir. 1986), but the Sixth Circuit applies a clear and present danger standard, CBS, Inc. v. Young, 522 F.2d 234 (6th Cir. 1975).

THEORY-APPLIED PROBLEM: PROTECTING THE FAIR TRIAL RIGHT

A court martial is a military court that tries cases involving crimes committed by members of the armed forces, as defined by the Uniform Code of Military Justice. Courts martial may be conducted in secret. Assume the federal Congress, disturbed by the degree of pretrial publicity given to cases involving allegations of sexual assault within the military, passes a law called the Courts Martial Fair Trial Act. The act provides that a newspaper, broadcaster, or cable television station may not publish information concerning the existence or contents of a confession allegedly made to law enforcement officers, military officials, or others by a defendant who is to be tried by a court martial; however, the act provides an exception to allow publication of the confession if the publisher first gives notice to the defendant via his attorney of the intent to publish the confession and simultaneously publishes any statement of the defendant or his attorney regarding the alleged confession. The publisher is required to publish the response in full, provided the response does not exceed the column space or air time devoted to reporting the alleged confession. Failure to comply with the act will subject the publisher to a criminal fine not to exceed $5,000. Is the act constitutional? Why or why not? What precedent applies to resolve this issue?

D. REGULATION OF BROADCASTERS

We have considered whether the press might be treated differently than other speakers for some First Amendment purposes. We now consider whether different media might warrant differential treatment under the First Amendment. Before beginning, it is worth emphasizing that the vast majority of First Amendment protections apply equally to all media. For example, a prior restraint is presumptively unconstitutional whether it is deployed against a broadcaster, a newspaper, or an internet website. The constitutional restrictions on the tort of defamation apply whether the defendant is a provider of cable programming, a provider of broadcast programming, or a magazine publisher. However, there are some situations in which a particular medium of expression (usually broadcasting) is subject to regulation that would be unconstitutional if applied to another medium.

Broadcasting is the medium most commonly singled out for differential treatment under the First Amendment, and this differential treatment is typically justified by the technical characteristics of the electromagnetic spectrum employed by broadcasters. However, the argument that the technological features of different media justify differential First Amendment treatment has arisen in the contexts of the Internet, cable, and direct broadcast satellite. We begin with the status of broadcasting.

The electromagnetic spectrum is a unique natural resource. Utilization does not use it up or wear it out. It does not require maintenance. It is subject to pollution (interference), but once the interference is removed, the pollution and its effects disappear. It is intangible, unable to be seen or touched, and it is everywhere, in the sense that it surrounds us whether we are in a building or outside. In many ways the airwaves are like a public resource, in the sense that they are omnipresent and can be used by many people. On the other hand, the airwaves are like private property in that they can be occupied to the exclusion of others.

Five properties determine the use of the spectrum: space, time, frequency, power, and antenna height. Two broadcasters can broadcast on the same frequency at the same time if they are far enough apart, operating at low enough power, or their antennae are sufficiently low or separated by mountains that are sufficiently high. Where two users of the spectrum are not sufficiently separated by space, time, frequency, power, or antenna height, they interfere with each other. A particularly powerful signal may drown out a weaker one or, as is more commonly the case, the signals will be of less quality or even unintelligible as a result of their interference with each other.

Historically, these technological characteristics led the government to regulate broadcast media differently than other media, and history goes far toward explaining the unique First Amendment status of broadcasting. During the 1920s, technology advanced to the point where hundreds of radio stations could begin broadcasting to the public. At first, there was little or no government oversight of these broadcasters. The Supreme Court described the situation thus: "the allocation of frequencies was left entirely to the private sector, and the result was chaos." Red Lion Broad. Co. v. FCC, 395 U.S. 367 (1969). Competing stations broadcast at the same frequency in the same geographic location, and signal interference made it impossible for them to reach their listeners. It soon became apparent that governmental regulation was essential for the broadcasting system to function. Both broadcasters and government regulators turned to Congress for help.

Congress responded with the Radio Act of 1927. The Act created the Federal Radio Commission (FRC), which became the Federal Communications Commission (FCC) in 1934. The FRC (later the FCC) was responsible for allocating the electromagnetic spectrum available for commercial and public broadcasting in a manner "consistent with the public interest, convenience [and] necessity." Broadcast licenses were issued for a limited term, and licenses were to be granted and renewed as dictated by "public interest, convenience, or necessity." Broadcast licensees that carried the advertisements of one political candidate were required to give or sell equal time to opposing candidates. The Act forbade censorship of broadcast programming, while it banned obscene, indecent, or profane language.

Even though the Communications Act of 1934 soon replaced the Radio Act, the new Act retained most of the provisions governing broadcasters. The 1934 Communications Act centralized federal authority over common carriers (telephone and telegraph operators) and broadcasters in the Federal Communications Commission. Even though the Communications Act was substantially amended by the Telecommunications Competition and Deregulation Act of 1996, the FCC today continues to issue licenses to broadcasters, renew licenses periodically, ensure that broadcasters comply with technical and operations rules, and develop rules to regulate broadcasting. The FCC's exercise of its regulatory authority has given rise to a host of litigation addressing the scope of First Amendment rights of broadcasters.

Red Lion. One of the most important of cases concerning the First Amendment rights of broadcasters was Red Lion Broad. Co. v. FCC, 395 U.S. 367 (1969). In *Red Lion*, the FCC proposed to make a rule—the "personal attack" rule—out of its common law practice of insisting that when "during the presentation of views on a controversial issue of public importance, an attack is made upon the honesty, character, integrity or like personal qualities of an identified person or group, the licensee shall, within a reasonable time, [no longer than a week] after the attack" send that person or group a script or tape of the attack and "an offer of a reasonable opportunity to respond over the licensee's facilities." During the mid-1960s two cases arose challenging the "personal attack" rule. The Supreme Court addressed both cases in *Red Lion* and unanimously upheld the rule.

Justice White, writing for the Court, began by noting that each medium of communication warranted individual legal treatment:

> Just as the Government may limit the use of sound-amplifying equipment potentially so noisy that it drowns out civilized private speech, so may the

> Government limit the use of broadcast equipment. The risk of free speech of a broadcaster, the user of a sound truck, or any other individual does not embrace a right to snuff out the free speech of others.
>
> When two people converse face to face, both should not speak at once if either is to be clearly understood. But the range of the human voice is so limited that there could be meaningful communications if half the people in the United States were talking and the other half listening. Just as clearly, half the people might publish and the other half read. But the reach of radio signals is incomparably greater than the range of the human voice and the problem of interference is a massive reality. The lack of know-how and equipment may keep many from the air, but only a tiny fraction of those with resources and intelligence can hope to communicate by radio at the same time if intelligible communication is to be had, even if the entire radio spectrum is utilized in the present state of commercially acceptable technology.

The Court noted that it was this chaos in the early days that led Congress to develop a licensing system. Then, the Court concluded that the First Amendment must bend to the realities of the broadcast medium:

> Where there are substantially more individuals who want to broadcast than there are frequencies to allocate, it is idle to posit an unabridgeable First Amendment right to broadcast comparable to the right of every individual to speak, write, or publish. If 100 persons want broadcast licenses but there are only 10 frequencies to allocate, all of them may have the same "right" to a license; but if there is to be any effective communication by radio, only a few can be licensed and the rest must be barred from the airwaves. It would be strange if the First Amendment, aimed at protecting and furthering communications, prevented the Government from making radio communication possible by requiring licenses to broadcast and by limiting the number of licenses so as not to overcrowd the spectrum.
>
> . . . By the same token, as far as the First Amendment is concerned those who are licensed stand no better than those to whom licenses are refused. A license permits broadcasting, but the licensee has no constitutional right to be the one who holds the license or to monopolize a radio frequency to the exclusion of his fellow citizens. There is nothing in the First Amendment which prevents the Government from requiring a licensee to share his frequency with others and to conduct himself as a proxy or fiduciary with obligations to present those views and voices which are representative of his community and which would otherwise, by necessity, be barred from the airwaves.
>
> This is not to say that the First Amendment is irrelevant to public broadcasting. On the contrary, it has a major role to play as the Congress itself recognized in [section] 326 [of the Communications Act], which forbids FCC interference with "the right of free speech by means of radio communication." Because of the scarcity of radio frequencies, the Government is permitted to put restraints on licensees in favor of others whose views should be expressed on this unique medium. But the people as a whole

retain their interest in free speech by radio and their collective right to have the medium function consistently with the ends and purposes of the First Amendment. It is the right of the viewers and listeners, not the right of the broadcasters, which is paramount. . . . It is the purpose of the First Amendment to preserve an uninhibited marketplace of ideas in which truth will ultimately prevail, rather than to countenance monopolization of that market, whether it be by the Government itself or a private licensee . . . ; [*Times v. Sullivan*]; Abrams v. United States, 250 U.S. 616, 630 (1919) (Holmes, J., dissenting). "[S]peech concerning public affairs is more than self-expression; it is the essence of self-government." [*Garrison v. Louisiana*]. . . . It is the right of the public to receive suitable access to social, political, esthetic, moral, and other ideas and experiences which is crucial here. That right may not constitutionally be abridged either by Congress or by the FCC.

The Court then turned to the specific constraint applied to broadcasters in the case. Justice White observed that the "Government could surely have decreed that each frequency should be shared among all or some of those who wish to use it, each being assigned a portion of the broadcast day or the broadcast week." Nor could the "personal attack" rule be distinguished from the requirement that broadcasters must give or sell time to political candidates if the station has given or sold time to their opponents—a provision that had never been questioned:

Nor can we say that it is inconsistent with the First Amendment goal of producing an informed public capable of conducting its own affairs to require a broadcaster to permit answers to personal attacks occurring in the course of discussing controversial issues, or to require that the political opponents of those endorsed by the station be given a chance to communicate with the public. Otherwise, station owners and a few networks would have unfettered power to make time available only to the highest bidders, to communicate only their own views on public issues, people and candidates, and to permit on the air only those with whom they agreed. There is no sanctuary in the First Amendment for unlimited private censorship operating in a medium not open to all.

The Court next rejected the claim that if this type of obligation is imposed, licensees will eliminate coverage of important political issues. The opinion noted that broadcasters had not aired bland programming in the past and observed:

. . . [E]ven now they do not assert that they intend to abandon their efforts in this regard. It would be better if the FCC's encouragement were never necessary to induce the broadcasters to meet the responsibility. And if experience with the administration of those doctrines indicates that they have the net effect of reducing rather than enhancing the volume and quality of coverage, there will be time enough to reconsider the constitutional implications. The fairness doctrine in the past has had no such overall effect.

. . . [Moreover, if licensees] should suddenly prove timorous, the Commission is not powerless to insist that they give adequate and fair attention to public issues. It does not violate the First Amendment to treat licensees

> given the privilege of using scarce radio frequencies as proxies for the entire community, obligated to give suitable time and attention to matters of great public concern. . . . Congress need not stand idly by and permit those with licenses to ignore the problems which beset the people or to exclude from the airways anything but their own views of fundamental questions. The statute, long administrative practice, and cases are to this effect.

After rejecting claims of "vagueness," the Court also rejected the claim that even if past scarcity justified this rule, current conditions no longer did so:

> Scarcity is not entirely a thing of the past. Advances in technology, such as microwave transmission, have led to more efficient utilization of the frequency spectrum, but uses for that spectrum have also grown apace. Portions of the spectrum must be reserved for vital uses unconnected with human communication, such as radio-navigational aids used by aircraft and vessels. Conflicts have even emerged between such vital functions as defense preparedness and experimentation in methods of averting midair collisions through radio warning devices. "Land mobile services" such as police, ambulance, fire department, public utility, and other communications systems have been occupying an increasingly crowded portion of the frequency spectrum and there are, apart from licensed amateur radio operators' equipment, 5,000,000 transmitters operated on the "citizens' band" which is also increasingly congested. Among the various uses for radio frequency space, including marine, aviation, amateur, military, and common carrier users, there are easily enough claimants to permit use of the whole with an even smaller allocation to broadcast radio and television uses than now exists.
>
> . . . The rapidity with which technological advances succeed one another to create more efficient use of spectrum space on the one hand, and to create new uses for that space by ever growing numbers of people on the other, makes it unwise to speculate on the future allocation of that space. It is enough to say that the resource is one of considerable and growing importance whose scarcity impelled its regulation by an agency authorized by Congress. Nothing in this record, or in our own researches, convinces us that the resource is no longer one for which there are more immediate and potential uses than can be accommodated, and for which wise planning is essential. This does not mean, of course, that every possible wavelength must be occupied at every hour by some vital use in order to sustain the congressional judgment.

Even where gaps in coverage existed, Justice White's opinion for the Court noted:

> [E]xisting broadcasters have often attained their present position because of their initial government selection in competition with others before new technological advances opened new opportunities for further uses. Long experience in broadcasting, confirmed habits of listeners and viewers, network affiliation, and other advantages in program procurement give existing broadcasters a substantial advantage over new entrants, even where new entry is technologically possible. These advantages are the

fruit of a preferred position conferred by the Government. Some present possibility for new entry by competing stations is not enough, in itself, to render unconstitutional the Government's effort to assure that a broadcaster's programming ranges widely enough to serve the public interest.

In view of the scarcity of broadcast frequencies, the Government's role in allocating those frequencies, and the legitimate claims of those unable without governmental assistance to gain access to those frequencies for expression of their views, we hold the regulations and ruling at issue here are both authorized by statute and constitutional.

NOTES AND QUESTIONS

1. *Reconciling* Tornillo. In Miami Herald Publishing Co. v. Tornillo, which is excerpted in Chapter 6, *supra*, the Supreme Court struck down a Florida statute that purported to give a political candidate a "right of reply" when "any newspaper in its column assails the personal character" of the candidate. The Court held that the right-of-reply statute violated the First Amendment because it interfered with the editorial discretion of newspaper publishers and penalized the publication of particular types of content. Although the Court decided *Tornillo* five years after *Red Lion*, the Court did not mention *Red Lion* or attempt to distinguish it. Can you reconcile the two cases? Don't both cases involve "government-enforced access" to a medium of mass communication in the name of promoting diversity in the marketplace of ideas?
2. *Demise of the personal attack rule. Red Lion* remains an important case defining the First Amendment rights of broadcasters, but the personal attack rule is no longer in effect. *See* Radio-Television News Directors Ass'n v. FCC, 229 F.3d 269 (D.C. Cir. 2000) (issuing writ of mandamus vacating the personal attack and political editorial rules). However, the paradigm of broadcast regulation outlined in *Red Lion* continues to have validity. For now, the important point is to see how differently the Court treated broadcasting in 1969 (*Red Lion*) and print media in 1974 (*Tornillo*).
3. *Criticism of the scarcity rationale.* The scarcity rationale for broadcast regulation has received intense criticism. Many commentators, including the FCC, the U.S. Court of Appeals for the District of Columbia Circuit, scholars, and several Supreme Court Justices, have argued that the scarcity doctrine no longer justifies special constitutional treatment of government restrictions on broadcast expression. *See* Columbia Broad. Sys., Inc. v. Democratic Natl. Comm'n, 412 U.S. 94, 144 (1973) (Stewart, J., concurring); *id.* at 149 (Douglas, J., concurring); Telecommunications Research & Action Ctr. v. FCC, 801 F.2d 501 (D.C. Cir. 1986); In re Complaint of Syracuse Peace Council Against Television Station WTVH Syracuse, N.Y., 2 FCC Rec. 5043, 5048 (1987) (mem. opinion and order).
4. *Is scarcity a thing of the past?* Even if physical scarcity was once a feature of the electromagnetic spectrum, technology is quickly making it a thing of the past. *See* Tom Wheeler, *Is Spectrum Shortage a Thing of the Past*, Brookings, Oct. 5, 2020 (discussing technology that enables spectrum

sharing); Christopher S. Yoo, *The Rise and Demise of the Technology-Specific Approach to the First Amendment*, 91 Geo. L.J. 245 (2003); Kevin D. Werbach, *Supercommons: Toward a Unified Theory of Wireless Communication*, 82 Tx. L. Rev. (2004). Technology has both expanded the broadcast spectrum and erased lines between broadcasters and other media. Even the FCC has conceded "the dramatic transformation in the telecommunications marketplace provides a basis for the [Supreme] Court to reconsider its application of diminished First Amendment protection to the electronic media." In re Complaint of Syracuse Peace Council, 2 FCC Rec. 5043, 5058 (1987) (citing FCC v. League of Women Voters, 468 U.S. 364 (1984)).

5. *Justifications for broadcast regulation.* In *Red Lion*, the Court focused on the scarcity of electromagnetic spectrum as a justification for treating broadcast media differently from print media. A related justification is that the public retains ownership of the airwaves, and broadcasters are merely licensed to use them in the public interest. The Telecommunications Act of 1996, Pub. L. No. 104-104, 110 Stat. 56 (1996), 47 U.S.C. § 309(1) (2000), revised the licensing criteria employed by the FCC but still required the FCC to base license renewal in part on the public interest. The Supreme Court invoked the FCC's "'broad' mandate to assure broadcasters operate in the public interest" as a justification for a requirement that broadcasters maintain records of "politically related broadcasting requests" to aid the government in policing campaign finance restrictions. McConnell v. Federal Elections Comm'n, 540 U.S. 93, 232, 124 S. Ct. 619, 712 (2003). Scarcity and public ownership are not the only justifications advanced for regulation of broadcasting, as you will see in the case below. As you read it, consider the distinctive characteristics of the broadcast medium that allow the FCC to "channel" and censure indecent content on the airwaves.

FCC v. Pacifica Foundation

438 U.S. 726 (1978)

Mr. Justice STEVENS delivered the opinion of the Court (Parts I, II, III, and IV-C) and an opinion in which THE CHIEF JUSTICE and Mr. Justice REHNQUIST joined (Parts IV-A and IV-B).

This case requires that we decide whether the Federal Communications Commission has any power to regulate a radio broadcast that is indecent but not obscene.

A satiric humorist named George Carlin recorded a 12-minute monologue entitled "Filthy Words" before a live audience in a California theater. He began by referring to his thoughts about "the words you couldn't say on the public, ah, airwaves, um, the ones you definitely wouldn't say, ever." He proceeded to list those words and repeat them over and over again in a variety of colloquialisms. The transcript of the recording, which is appended to this opinion, indicates frequent laughter from the audience.

At about 2 o'clock in the afternoon on Tuesday, October 30, 1973, a New York radio station, owned by respondent Pacifica Foundation, broadcast the "Filthy Words" monologue. A few weeks later a man, who stated that he had heard the broadcast while driving with his young son, wrote a letter complaining to the Commission. . . .

On February 21, 1975, the Commission issued a declaratory order granting the complaint and holding that Pacifica "could have been the subject of administrative sanctions." . . .

The Commission characterized the language used in the Carlin monologue as "patently offensive," though not necessarily obscene, and expressed the opinion that it should be regulated by principles analogous to those found in the law of nuisance where the "law generally speaks to *channeling* behavior more than actually prohibiting it. . . . [The] concept of 'indecent' is intimately connected with the exposure of children to language that describes, in terms patently offensive as measured by contemporary community standards for the broadcast medium, sexual or excretory activities and organs, at times of the day when there is a reasonable risk that children may be in the audience." [The D.C. Circuit Court of Appeals reversed, and the Supreme Court granted certiorari.]

. . .

[Before reaching the First Amendment question, the Court addressed several preliminary questions. One of these was whether the FCC had statutory authority to regulate indecency. The Court concluded that it did. After analyzing the text and legislative history of § 326 of the Communications Act of 1934, the Court concluded that the statutory provision did give the Commission "authority to impose sanctions on licensees who engage in obscene, indecent, or profane broadcasting." The Court then turned to a second statutory question.]

The only other statutory question presented by this case is whether the afternoon broadcast of the "Filthy Words" monologue was indecent within the meaning of § 1464. . . .

. . . Pacifica does not quarrel with the conclusion that this afternoon broadcast was patently offensive. Pacifica's claim that the broadcast was not indecent within the meaning of the statute rests entirely on the absence of prurient appeal.

The plain language of the statute does not support Pacifica's argument. The words "obscene, indecent, or profane" are written in the disjunctive, implying that each has a separate meaning. Prurient appeal is an element of the obscene, but the normal definition of "indecent" merely refers to nonconformance with accepted standards of morality.

. . . [T]here is no basis for disagreeing with the Commission's conclusion that indecent language was used in this broadcast.

IV*

[B.] When the issue is narrowed to the facts of this case, the question is whether the First Amendment denies government any power to restrict the public broadcast of indecent language in any circumstances. For if the government has any such power, this was an appropriate occasion for its exercise.

---

* [Editor's Note: Make sure you count the votes supporting IV.A. and IV.B.!]

. . . The classic exposition of the proposition that both the content and the context of speech are critical elements of First Amendment analysis is Mr. Justice Holmes' statement for the Court in Schenck v. United States, 249 U.S. 47, 52:

> "We admit that in many places and in ordinary times the defendants in saying all that was said in the circular would have been within their constitutional rights. But the character of every act depends upon the circumstances in which it is done. . . . The most stringent protection of free speech would not protect a man in falsely shouting fire in a theatre and causing a panic. It does not even protect a man from an injunction against uttering words that may have all the effect of force. . . . The question in every case is whether the words used are used in such circumstances and are of such a nature as to create a clear and present danger that they will bring about the substantive evils that Congress has a right to prevent."

Other distinctions based on content have been approved in the years since *Schenck*. The government may forbid speech calculated to provoke a fight. . . . It may pay heed to the "'commonsense differences' between commercial speech and other varieties." . . . It may treat libels against private citizens more severely than libels against public officials. . . . Obscenity may be wholly prohibited. . . .

The question in this case is whether a broadcast of patently offensive words dealing with sex and excretion may be regulated because of its content. Obscene materials have been denied the protection of the First Amendment because their content is so offensive to contemporary moral standards. But the fact that society may find speech offensive is not a sufficient reason for suppressing it. Indeed, if it is the speaker's opinion that gives offense, that consequence is a reason for according it constitutional protection. For it is a central tenet of the First Amendment that the government must remain neutral in the marketplace of ideas. If there were any reason to believe that the Commission's characterization of the Carlin monologue as offensive could be traced to its political content—or even to the fact that it satirized contemporary attitudes about four-letter words—First Amendment protection might be required. But that is simply not this case. These words offend for the same reasons that obscenity offends. Their place in the hierarchy of First Amendment values was aptly sketched by Mr. Justice Murphy when he said: "[Such] utterances are no essential part of any exposition of ideas, and are of such slight social value as a step to truth that any benefit that may be derived from them is clearly outweighed by the social interest in order and morality." Chaplinsky v. New Hampshire, 315 U.S., at 572.

. . . [C.] We have long recognized that each medium of expression presents special First Amendment problems. And of all forms of communication, it is broadcasting that has received the most limited First Amendment protection. Thus, although other speakers cannot be licensed except under laws that carefully define and narrow official discretion, a broadcaster may be deprived of his license and his forum if the Commission decides that such an action would serve "the public interest, convenience, and necessity." Similarly, although the First Amendment protects newspaper publishers from being required to print the replies of those whom they criticize [*Tornillo*], it affords no such protection to broadcasters; on the contrary, they must give free time to the victims of their criticism [*Red Lion*].

The reasons for these distinctions are complex, but two have relevance to the present case. First, the broadcast media have established a uniquely pervasive presence in the lives of all Americans. Patently offensive, indecent material presented over the airwaves confronts the citizen, not only in public, but also in the privacy of the home, where the individual's right to be left alone plainly outweighs the First Amendment rights of an intruder. Because the broadcast audience is constantly tuning in and out, prior warnings cannot completely protect the listener or viewer from unexpected program content. To say that one may avoid further offense by turning off the radio when he hears indecent language is like saying that the remedy for an assault is to run away after the first blow. One may hang up on an indecent phone call, but that option does not give the caller a constitutional immunity or avoid a harm that has already taken place.

Second, broadcasting is uniquely accessible to children, even those too young to read. Although Cohen's written message might have been incomprehensible to a first grader [referring to Cohen v. California, 403 U.S. 15 (1971), in which the Supreme Court defended the First Amendment right to wear a "Fuck the Draft" jacket], Pacifica's broadcast could have enlarged a child's vocabulary in an instant. Other forms of offensive expression may be withheld from the young without restricting the expression at its source. Bookstores and motion picture theaters, for example, may be prohibited from making indecent material available to children. We held in Ginsberg v. New York, 390 U.S. 629, that the government's interest in the "well-being of its youth" and in supporting "parents' claim to authority in their own household" justified the regulation of otherwise protected expression. The ease with which children may obtain access to broadcast material, coupled with the concerns recognized in *Ginsberg*, amply justify special treatment of indecent broadcasting.

It is appropriate, in conclusion, to emphasize the narrowness of our holding. This case does not involve a two-way radio conversation between a cab driver and a dispatcher, or a telecast of an Elizabethan comedy. We have not decided that an occasional expletive in either setting would justify any sanction or, indeed, that this broadcast would justify a criminal prosecution. The Commission's decision rested entirely on a nuisance rationale under which context is all-important. The concept requires consideration of a host of variables. The time of day was emphasized by the Commission. The content of the program in which the language is used will also affect the composition of the audience, and differences between radio, television, and perhaps closed-circuit transmissions, may also be relevant. As Mr. Justice Sutherland wrote, a "nuisance may be merely a right thing in the wrong place—like a pig in the parlor instead of the barnyard." . . . We simply hold that when the Commission finds that a pig has entered the parlor, the exercise of its regulatory power does not depend on proof that the pig is obscene.

Mr. Justice POWELL, with whom Mr. Justice BLACKMUN joins, concurring in part and concurring in the judgment.

. . . During most of the broadcast hours, both adults and unsupervised children are likely to be in the broadcast audience, and the broadcaster cannot reach willing adults without also reaching children. This, as the Court emphasizes, is one of the distinctions between the broadcast and other media to which we often have adverted as justifying a different treatment of the broadcast media for First Amendment purposes. In my view, the Commission was entitled to give substantial weight to this difference in reaching its decision in this case.

A second difference, not without relevance, is that broadcasting—unlike most other forms of communication—comes directly into the home, the one place where people ordinarily have the right not to be assaulted by uninvited and offensive sights and sounds. . . . Although the First Amendment may require unwilling adults to absorb the first blow of offensive but protected speech when they are in public before they turn away, a different order of values obtains in the home. . . .

. . . As the foregoing demonstrates, my views are generally in accord with what is said in Part IV-C of Mr. Justice Stevens' opinion. I therefore join that portion of his opinion. I do not join Part IV-B, however, because I do not subscribe to the theory that the Justices of this Court are free generally to decide on the basis of its content which speech protected by the First Amendment is most "valuable" and hence deserving of the most protection, and which is less "valuable" and hence deserving of less protection.

Mr. Justice BRENNAN, with whom Mr. Justice MARSHALL joins, dissenting.

. . . [N]either of the factors relied on by both the opinion of my Brother Powell and the opinion of my Brother Stevens—the intrusive nature of radio and the presence of children in the listening audience—can, when taken on its own terms, support the FCC's disapproval of the Carlin monologue. These two asserted justifications are further plagued by a common failing: the lack of principled limits on their use as a basis for FCC censorship. No such limits come readily to mind, and neither of the opinions constituting the Court serve to clarify the extent to which the FCC may assert the privacy and children-in-the-audience rationales as justification for expunging from the airways protected communications the Commission finds offensive. Taken to their logical extreme, these rationales would support the cleansing of public radio of any "four-letter words" whatsoever, regardless of their context. The rationales could justify the banning from radio of a myriad of literary works, novels, poems, and plays by the likes of Shakespeare, Joyce, Hemingway, Ben Jonson, Henry Fielding, Robert Burns, and Chaucer; they could support the suppression of a good deal of political speech, such as the Nixon tapes; and they could even provide the basis for imposing sanctions for the broadcast of certain portions of the Bible.

NOTES AND QUESTIONS

1. *Self-help as remedy.* Why isn't turning off the radio or TV an adequate remedy against broadcast indecency? Is an Internet user just as likely to encounter offensive material unexpectedly?
2. *Safe harbors.* After *Pacifica*, the FCC ordered broadcasters to channel indecent programming during late-night hours when children were less likely to be in the audience. Action for Children's Television v. FCC, 58 F.3d 654 (D.C. Cir. 1995), *cert. denied*, 516 U.S. 1072 (1996), upheld the FCC's designation of "safe harbors" (10 P.M. to 6 A.M.) for indecent content on the grounds that government has a compelling interest in protecting children from indecent broadcasts and that channeling indecency into late-night hours was not an undue burden on First Amendment rights of broadcasters.

In 2003 the FCC changed its prior standard regarding broadcast indecency, which had permitted isolated uses of expletives, and began imposing indecency fines (forfeitures) on broadcasters for the airing of even a single use of an expletive. The FCC's "fleeting expletive" rule was invalidated as "arbitrary and capricious" by the Second Circuit Court of Appeals in 2007. Fox Television Stations, Inc. v. FCC, 489 F. 3d 444 (2d Cir. 2007), *rev'd*, 556 U.S. 502 (2009), but the Supreme Court reversed on administrative law grounds and remanded. On remand, the Second Circuit struck down the FCC's indecency policy in its entirety on First Amendment grounds. The Supreme Court again granted certiorari and reversed the Second Circuit in the opinion below. Note that in doing so, the Court avoids the invitation to revisit the constitutionality of its "medium-specific" approach to broadcast indecency regulation and instead decides the case on due process grounds.

Federal Communications Commission v. Fox Television Stations, Inc.

567 U.S. ___, 132 S. Ct. 2307 (2012)

Justice KENNEDY delivered the opinion of the Court.

In FCC v. Fox Television Stations, Inc., 556 U.S. 502, 529 (2009) *(Fox I)*, the Court held that the Federal Communication Commission's decision to modify its indecency enforcement regime to regulate so-called fleeting expletives was neither arbitrary nor capricious. The Court then declined to address the constitutionality of the policy, however, because the United States Court of Appeals for the Second Circuit had yet to do so. On remand, the Court of Appeals found the policy was vague and, as a result, unconstitutional. 613 F.3d 317 (2010). The case now returns to this Court for decision upon the constitutional question.

I

. . . [A.] Title 18 U.S.C. § 1464 provides that "[w]hoever utters any obscene, indecent, or profane language by means of radio communication shall be fined . . . or imprisoned not more than two years, or both." The Federal Communications Commission (Commission) has been instructed by Congress to enforce § 1464 between the hours of 6 A.M. and 10 P.M. []. And the Commission has applied its regulations to radio and television broadcasters alike, []. Although the Commission has had the authority to regulate indecent broadcasts under § 1464 since 1948 (and its predecessor commission, the Federal Radio Commission, since 1927), it did not begin to enforce § 1464 until the 1970's. []

This Court first reviewed the Commission's indecency policy in FCC v. Pacifica Foundation, 438 U.S. 726 (1978). In *Pacifica*, the Commission determined that George Carlin's "Filthy Words" monologue was indecent. It contained "'language that describes, in terms patently offensive as measured by contemporary community standards for the broadcast medium, sexual or excretory activities and organs, at times of the day when there is a reasonable risk that children may be in the audience.'" *Id.*, at 732 (quoting 56 F.C.C. 2d 94, 98 (1975)). This Court upheld the Commission's ruling. The broadcaster's statutory challenge was rejected. The Court held the Commission was not engaged in impermissible censorship . . . and that § 1464's definition of indecency was not confined to speech with an appeal to the prurient interest, []. Finding no First Amendment violation, the decision explained the constitutional standard under which regulations of broadcasters are assessed. It observed that "broadcast media have established a uniquely pervasive presence in the lives of all Americans," [], and that "broadcasting is uniquely accessible to children, even those too young to read," []. In light of these considerations, "broadcasting . . . has received the most limited First Amendment protection." []. Under this standard the Commission's order passed constitutional scrutiny. The Court did note the narrowness of its holding, explaining that it was not deciding whether "an occasional expletive . . . would justify any sanction." []; see also *id.*, at 760–761 (Powell, J., concurring in part and concurring in judgment) ("[C]ertainly the Court's holding . . . does not speak to cases involving the isolated use of a potentially offensive word in the course of a radio broadcast, as distinguished from the verbal shock treatment administered by respondent here").

From 1978 to 1987, the Commission did not go beyond the narrow circumstances of *Pacifica* and brought no indecency enforcement actions. []. Recognizing that *Pacifica* provided "no general prerogative to intervene in any case where words similar or identical to those in *Pacifica* are broadcast over a licensed radio or television station," the Commission distinguished between the "repetitive occurrence of the 'indecent' words" (such as in the Carlin monologue) and an "isolated" or "occasional" expletive, that would not necessarily be actionable. [].

In 1987, the Commission determined it was applying the *Pacifica* standard in too narrow a way. It stated that in later cases its definition of indecent language would "appropriately includ[e] a broader range of material than the seven specific words at issue in [the Carlin monologue]." [] Thus, the Commission indicated it would use the "generic definition of indecency" articulated in its 1975 *Pacifica* order, [] and assess the full context of allegedly indecent broadcasts rather than limiting its regulation to a "comprehensive index . . . of indecent words or pictorial depictions" [].

. . . In 2001, the Commission issued a policy statement intended "to provide guidance to the broadcast industry regarding [its] caselaw interpreting 18 U.S.C. § 1464 and [its] enforcement policies with respect to broadcast indecency." [] In that document the Commission restated that for material to be indecent it must depict sexual or excretory organs or activities and be patently offensive as measured by contemporary community standards for the broadcast medium. []. Describing the framework of what it considered patently offensive, the Commission explained that three factors had proved significant:

> "(1) [T]he explicitness or graphic nature of the description or depiction of sexual or excretory organs or activities; (2) whether the material dwells on or repeats at length descriptions of sexual or excretory organs or activities; (3) whether the material appears to pander or is used to titillate, or whether the material appears to have been presented for its shock value." []

As regards the second of these factors, the Commission explained that "[r]epetition of and persistent focus on sexual or excretory material have been cited consistently as factors that exacerbate the potential offensiveness of broadcasts. In contrast, where sexual or excretory references have been made once or have been passing or fleeting in nature, this characteristic has tended to weigh against a finding of indecency." []. The Commission then gave examples of material that was not found indecent because it was fleeting and isolated, [citing one FCC ruling finding "a fleeting and isolated utterance" in the context of live and spontaneous programming not actionable and another finding that fleeting language referring to sexual activity with a child was patently offensive].

[B.] It was against this regulatory background that the three incidents of alleged indecency at issue here took place. First, in the 2002 Billboard Music Awards, broadcast by respondent Fox Television Stations, Inc., the singer Cher exclaimed during an unscripted acceptance speech: "I've also had my critics for the last 40 years saying that I was on my way out every year. Right. So f*** 'em." []. Second, Fox broadcast the Billboard Music Awards again in 2003. There, a person named Nicole Richie made the following unscripted remark while presenting an award: "Have you ever tried to get cow s*** out of a Prada purse? It's not so f***ing simple." []. The third incident involved an episode of NYPD Blue, a regular television show broadcast by respondent ABC Television Network. The episode broadcast on February 25, 2003, showed the nude buttocks of an adult female character for approximately seven seconds and for a moment the side of her breast. During the scene, in which the character was preparing to take a shower, a child portraying her boyfriend's son entered the bathroom. A moment of awkwardness followed. [].

After these incidents, but before the Commission issued Notices of Apparent Liability to Fox and ABC, the Commission issued a decision sanctioning NBC for a comment made by the singer Bono during the 2003 Golden Globe Awards. Upon winning the award for Best Original Song, Bono exclaimed: "'This is really, really, f***ing brilliant. Really, really great.'" []. Reversing a decision by its enforcement bureau, the Commission found the use of the F-word actionably indecent. []. The Commission held that the word was "one of the most vulgar, graphic and explicit descriptions of sexual activity in the English language," and thus found "any use of that word or a variation, in any context, inherently has a sexual connotation." []. Turning to the isolated nature of the expletive, the Commission reversed prior rulings that had found fleeting expletives not indecent. The Commission held "the mere fact that specific words or phrases are not sustained or repeated does not mandate a finding that material that is otherwise patently offensive to the broadcast medium is not indecent." [].

[C.] [The Commission did not impose penalties on Fox or NBC on the ground that they did not have sufficient notice that such broadcasts would violate FCC policy regarding fleeting expletives, but imposed forfeitures of $27,500 on each of the 45 ABC affiliates that carried the NYPD Blue episode on the ground that the policy against nudity was sufficiently clear.]

[Fox appealed the FCC decision arguing, among other things, that the government may not punish broadcast speech that in any other medium would be protected by the First Amendment. Fox and other networks argued that changes in the media landscape, especially the growth of cable and the Internet, had made the rationale of *Pacifica* untenable. The Second Circuit did not decide the constitutional question, but vacated the rulings against Fox on the ground the Commission's reversal of policy violated the Administrative Procedures Act. In *Fox I* the Supreme Court reversed that decision and did not consider the constitutional question because it had not been decided by the court of appeals. On remand from *Fox I*, the court of appeals again held the Commission's indecency policy unconstitutional, this time on the ground that the policy failed to give broadcasters sufficient notice of what would be considered indecent. The court of appeals found the vagueness inherent in the policy had forced broadcasters to "choose between not airing . . . controversial programs [or] risking massive fines or possibly even loss of their licenses." The Second Circuit then vacated the forfeiture order against ABC.]

The Government sought review of both judgments. . . .

II

A fundamental principle in our legal system is that laws which regulate persons or entities must give fair notice of conduct that is forbidden or required. []. This requirement of clarity in regulation is essential to the protections provided by the Due Process Clause of the Fifth Amendment. [] It requires the invalidation of laws that are impermissibly vague. A conviction or punishment fails to comply with due process if the statute or regulation under which it is obtained "fails to provide a person of ordinary intelligence fair notice of what is prohibited, or is so standardless that it authorizes or encourages seriously discriminatory enforcement." []. As this Court has explained, a regulation is not vague because it may at times be difficult to prove an incriminating fact but rather because it is unclear as to what fact must be proved. [].

Even when speech is not at issue, the void for vagueness doctrine addresses at least two connected but discrete due process concerns: first, that regulated parties should know what is required of them so they may act accordingly; second, precision and guidance are necessary so that those enforcing the law do not act in an arbitrary or discriminatory way. [] When speech is involved, rigorous adherence to those requirements is necessary to ensure that ambiguity does not chill protected speech.

These concerns are implicated here because, at the outset, the broadcasters claim they did not have, and do not have, sufficient notice of what is proscribed. And leaving aside any concerns about facial invalidity, they contend that the lengthy procedural history set forth above shows that the broadcasters did not have fair notice of what was forbidden. Under the 2001 Guidelines in force when the broadcasts occurred, a key consideration was "'whether the material dwell[ed] on or repeat[ed] at length'" the offending description or depiction. []. In the 2004 *Golden Globes* Order, issued after the broadcasts, the Commission changed course and held that fleeting expletives could be a statutory violation. *Fox I,* []. In the challenged orders now under review the Commission applied the new principle promulgated in the *Golden Globes* Order and determined fleeting expletives and a brief moment of indecency were actionably indecent. This regulatory history, however, makes it apparent that the Commission policy in place at the time of the broadcasts gave no notice to Fox or ABC that a fleeting expletive or a brief shot of nudity could be actionably indecent; yet Fox and ABC were found to be in violation. The Commission's lack of notice to Fox and ABC that its interpretation had changed so the fleeting moments of indecency contained in their broadcasts were a violation of § 1464 as interpreted and enforced by the agency "fail[ed] to provide a person of ordinary intelligence fair notice of what is prohibited." []. This would be true with respect to a regulatory change this abrupt on any subject, but it is surely the case when applied to the regulations in question, regulations that touch upon "sensitive areas of basic First Amendment freedoms," [].

The Government raises two arguments in response, but neither is persuasive. As for the two fleeting expletives, the Government concedes [in its brief] that "Fox did not have reasonable notice at the time of the broadcasts that the Commission would consider non-repeated expletives indecent." The Government argues, nonetheless, that Fox "cannot establish unconstitutional vagueness on that basis . . . because the Commission did not impose a sanction where Fox lacked such notice." [].This "policy of forbearance," as the Government calls it, does not suffice to make the issue moot. Though the Commission claims it will not consider the prior indecent broadcasts "in any context," it has the statutory power to take into account "any history of prior offenses" when setting the level of a forfeiture penalty. [] Just as in the First Amendment context, the due process protection against vague regulations "does not leave [regulated parties] . . . at the mercy of *noblesse oblige*." [] Given that the Commission found it was "not inequitable to hold Fox responsible for [the 2003 broadcast]," [], and that it has the statutory authority to use its finding to increase any future penalties, the Government's assurance it will elect not to do so is insufficient to remedy the constitutional violation.

In addition, when combined with the legal consequence described above, reputational injury provides further reason for granting relief to Fox. . . . [F]indings of wrongdoing can result in harm to a broadcaster's "reputation with viewers and advertisers." . . . The challenged orders could have an adverse impact on Fox's reputation that audiences and advertisers alike are entitled to take into account.

With respect to ABC, the Government with good reason does not argue no sanction was imposed. The fine against ABC and its network affiliates for the seven seconds of nudity was nearly $1.24 million. []. The Government argues instead that ABC had notice that the scene in NYPD Blue would be considered indecent in light of a 1960 decision where the Commission declared that the "televising of nudes might well raise a serious question of programming contrary to 18 U.S.C. § 1464." []. This argument does not prevail. An isolated and ambiguous statement from a 1960 Commission decision does not suffice for the fair notice required when the Government intends to impose over a $1 million fine for allegedly impermissible speech. The Commission, furthermore, had released decisions before sanctioning ABC that declined to find isolated and brief moments of nudity actionably indecent. [The court cited an FCC decision finding full frontal nudity in Schindler's List not indecent.] This is not to say, of course, that a graphic scene from Schindler's List involving nude concentration camp prisoners is the same as the shower scene from NYPD Blue. It does show, however, that the Government can point to nothing that would have given ABC affirmative notice that its broadcast would be considered actionably indecent. It is likewise not sufficient for the Commission to assert, as it did in its order, that though "the depiction [of nudity] here is not as lengthy or repeated" as in some cases, the shower scene nonetheless "does contain more shots or lengthier depictions of nudity" than in other broadcasts found not indecent. []. This broad language fails to demonstrate that ABC had fair notice that its broadcast could be found indecent. In fact, a Commission ruling prior to the airing of the NYPD Blue episode had deemed 30 seconds of nude buttocks "very brief" and not actionably indecent in the context of the broadcast. []. In light of this record of agency decisions, and the absence of any notice in the 2001 Guidance that seven seconds of nude buttocks would be found indecent, ABC lacked constitutionally sufficient notice prior to being sanctioned.

The Commission failed to give Fox or ABC fair notice prior to the broadcasts in question that fleeting expletives and momentary nudity could be found actionably indecent. Therefore, the Commission's standards as applied to these broadcasts were vague, and the Commission's orders must be set aside.

III

It is necessary to make three observations about the scope of this decision. First, because the Court resolves these cases on fair notice grounds under the Due Process Clause, it need not address the First Amendment implications of the Commission's indecency policy. It is argued that this Court's ruling in *Pacifica* (and the less rigorous standard of scrutiny it provided for the regulation of broadcasters, []) should be overruled because the rationale of that case has been overtaken by technological change and the wide availability of multiple other choices for listeners and viewers. []. The Government for its part maintains that when it licenses a conventional broadcast spectrum, the public may assume that the Government has its own interest in setting certain standards. []. These arguments need not be addressed here. In light of the Court's holding that the Commission's policy failed to provide fair notice it is unnecessary to reconsider *Pacifica* at this time.

This leads to a second observation. Here, the Court rules that Fox and ABC lacked notice at the time of their broadcasts that the material they were broadcasting could be found actionably indecent under then-existing policies. Given this disposition, it is unnecessary for the Court to address the constitutionality of the current indecency policy as expressed in the *Golden Globes* Order and subsequent adjudications. The Court adheres to its normal practice of declining to decide cases not before it. []

Third, this opinion leaves the Commission free to modify its current indecency policy in light of its determination of the public interest and applicable legal requirements. And it leaves the courts free to review the current policy or any modified policy in light of its content and application.

The judgments of the United States Court of Appeals for the Second Circuit are vacated, and the cases are remanded for further proceedings consistent with the principles set forth in this opinion.

Justice GINSBURG, concurring in the judgment

In my view, the Court's decision in FCC v. Pacifica Foundation, [], was wrong when it issued. Time, technological advances, and the Commission's untenable rulings in the cases now before the Court show why *Pacifica* bears reconsideration. Cf. FCC v. Fox Television Stations, Inc., 556 U. S. 502-535 (2009) (Thomas, J., concurring).

Justice SOTOMAYOR took no part in the consideration or decision of these cases.

NOTES AND QUESTIONS

1. *The chilling effect of uncertainty?* Whether the First Amendment permits the FCC to punish the broadcast of fleeting expletives remains unresolved almost 30 years after the Commission announced its intention to do so. As the opinion points out, the FCC is still free to enforce an indecency

policy that provides sufficient notice to broadcasters. The vagueness problem as described by the Second Circuit was that it "forced broadcasters to 'choose between not airing . . . controversial programs [or] risking massive fines or possibly even loss of their licenses.'" Is the uncertainty as to whether the Commission has any power to regulate broadcast indecency any less likely to put broadcasters to such a choice? At some point, does the Court's "normal practice of declining to decide cases not before it" become a First Amendment issue in itself? Note that the Court did not affirm the Second Circuit decisions, but vacated and remanded. Presumably the networks can renew their First Amendment challenge there.

2. *Vagueness, overbreadth, and the need for flexibility.* Can the FCC cure the vagueness problem by decreeing that any use of certain words, or any nude depiction of certain body parts, is a violation? Is there a more nuanced solution that would pass muster?
3. *The wardrobe malfunction case.* The Supreme Court declined to hear the FCC's appeal of a Third Circuit decision vacating the Commission's $550,000 fine against CBS for airing a brief glimpse of Janet Jackson's bare breast during a "wardrobe malfunction" at the 2004 Super Bowl halftime show. FCC v. CBS Corp., 567 U.S. 953 (2012).
4. Fox *as forgone opportunity to revisit* Pacifica. Why did the Supreme Court forgo the opportunity, presented in the *Fox* cases above, to revisit *Pacifica* and the broader issue whether broadcasters receive less First Amendment protection from content-based regulation than do other media? Some commentators have speculated that Justice Sotomayor's recusal may have left the Court split 4–4 on whether to overturn *Pacifica,* and the Court ruled narrowly to avoid issuing an opinion that would not bring unanimity or clarity. *See, e.g.*, Eugene Volokh, FCC v. Fox Television *Decided Narrowly on Lack-of-Fair-Notice Grounds,* Volokh Conspiracy (June 21, 2012), http://www.volokh.com/2012/06/21/fcc-v-fox-television-decided-narrowly-on-lack-of-fair-notice-grounds (speculating that Justices Ginsburg, Thomas, Kennedy, and Kagan might have favored overruling *Pacifica,* and that Justices Scalia, Alito, Breyer, and Roberts favored upholding it); Joe Flint & David Savage, *Justices Decline to Address Bid to Overturn FCC Indecency Rules,* L.A. Times (Jun. 22, 2012), *available at* http://articles.latimes.com/2012/jun/22/business/la-fi-ct-court-indecency-20120622. When a 4-4 deadlock occurs, the case is not deemed precedential; the Court simply announces that the Court is evenly divided and affirms the lower court decision under review. The affirmance is issued to afford finality for the litigants in that particular case. In the event of such a tie, the court typically issues a *per curiam* decision. *See, e.g.*, Comment, *Supreme Court No-Clear-Majority Decisions: A Study in Stare Decisis,* 24 U. Chi. L. Rev. 99 (1956) (analyzing various types of no-clear-majority decisions and considering their treatment by subsequent courts). Regardless, the Court's narrow decision leaves the FCC free to regulate indecency as long as its policy for doing so provides constitutionally sufficient notice of the prohibited conduct. After the Court issued its ruling, commissioners of the FCC announced that they would continue to regulate broadcast indecency, within First Amendment parameters announced by the Court.

E. *REGULATION OF CABLE SYSTEM OPERATORS*

The following case, Turner Broadcasting System Inc. v. FCC, 512 U.S. 622 (1994), is known as *Turner I* because the same case later went back to the Supreme Court as *Turner II*, 520 U.S. 180 (1997). *Turner I* illustrates the importance of the distinction between content-based versus content-neutral regulations on speech, but the case is used here primarily to illustrate the Court's resolution of whether the First Amendment applies in a "medium-specific" fashion to cable operators or programmers.

Both *Turner I* and *Turner II* address the constitutionality of "must-carry" provisions in the Cable Act of 1992. The must-carry provisions require cable operators to carry the signals of local over-the-air broadcasters. These provisions were a response to the perceived negative effects of deregulation of the cable industry by the Cable Communications Policy Act of 1984. After the 1984 Act took effect, cable providers began to increase subscription rates, shift broadcasters to less desirable channels, and deny access to competitors. In response to this, and to the lobbying of a coalition of broadcasters and consumer activists, Congress passed the Cable Act of 1992 (Cable Television Consumer Protection and Competition Act of 1992). President George H.W. Bush vetoed it, but his veto was overridden.

The main issue that *Turner I* addresses is what constitutional standard applies to must-carry provisions. *Turner I* concludes that the must-carry rules are content-neutral and subject to intermediate scrutiny. It then vacates and remands to the district court for additional fact-finding and application of the standard. The case returns to the Supreme Court as *Turner II*, at which point the Supreme Court *applies* intermediate scrutiny to the must-carry provisions and deems them constitutional. In the course of reaching these issues, the Court provides its most extensive analysis of whether the unique characteristics of cable as a medium justify applying to it the regulatory paradigm outlined in *Red Lion*. As you read, consider what it tells you about how far the government can go in regulating cable to enhance diversity in the marketplace of ideas.

Turner Broadcasting System, Inc. v. FCC

("*Turner I*")
512 U.S. 622 (1994)

Justice Kennedy announced the judgment of the Court and delivered the opinion of the Court, except as to Part III-B.

. . . [A.] The role of cable television in the Nation's communications system has undergone dramatic change over the past 45 years. Given the pace of technological advancement and the increasing convergence between cable and other electronic media, the cable industry today stands at the center of an ongoing telecommunications revolution with still undefined potential to affect the way we communicate and develop our intellectual resources.

The earliest cable systems were built in the late 1940's to bring clear broadcast television signals to remote or mountainous communities. The purpose was not to replace broadcast television but to enhance it. Modern cable systems do much more than enhance the reception of nearby broadcast television stations. With the capacity to carry dozens of channels and import distant programming signals via satellite or microwave relay, today's cable systems are in direct competition with over-the-air broadcasters as an independent source of television programming.

Broadcast and cable television are distinguished by the different technologies through which they reach viewers. Broadcast stations radiate electromagnetic signals from a central transmitting antenna. These signals can be captured, in turn, by any television set within the antenna's range. Cable systems, by contrast, rely upon a physical, point-to-point connection between a transmission facility and the television sets of individual subscribers. Cable systems make this connection much like telephone companies, using cable or optical fibers strung aboveground or buried in ducts to reach the homes or businesses of subscribers. The construction of this physical infrastructure entails the use of public rights-of-way and easements and often results in the disruption of traffic on streets and other public property. As a result, the cable medium may depend for its very existence upon express permission from local governing authorities.

Cable technology affords two principal benefits over broadcast. First, it eliminates the signal interference sometimes encountered in over-the-air broadcasting and thus gives viewers undistorted reception of broadcast stations. Second, it is capable of transmitting many more channels than are available through broadcasting, giving subscribers access to far greater programming variety. More than half of the cable systems in operation today have a capacity to carry between 30 and 53 channels. 1994 Television and Cable Factbook I-69. And about 40 percent of cable subscribers are served by systems with a capacity of more than 53 channels. Newer systems can carry hundreds of channels, and many older systems are being upgraded with fiber optic rebuilds and digital compression technology to increase channel capacity.

The cable television industry includes both cable operators (those who own the physical cable network and transmit the cable signal to the viewer) and cable programmers (those who produce television programs and sell or license them to cable operators). In some cases, cable operators have acquired ownership of cable programmers, and vice versa. Although cable operators may create some of their own programming, most of their programming is drawn from outside sources. These outside sources include not only local or distant broadcast stations, but also the many national and regional cable programming networks that have emerged in recent years, such as CNN, MTV, ESPN, TNT, C-Span, The Family Channel, Nickelodeon, Arts and Entertainment, Black Entertainment Television, CourtTV, The Discovery Channel, American Movie Classics, Comedy Central, The Learning Channel, and The Weather Channel. Once the cable operator has selected the programming sources, the cable system functions, in essence, as a conduit for the speech of others, transmitting it on a continuous and unedited basis to subscribers.

In contrast to commercial broadcast stations, which transmit signals at no charge to viewers and generate revenues by selling time to advertisers, cable systems charge subscribers a monthly fee for the right to receive cable programming and rely to a lesser extent on advertising. . . .

[B.] . . . At issue in this case is the constitutionality of the so-called must-carry provisions, contained in §§ 4 and 5 of the Act, which require cable operators to carry the signals of a specified number of local broadcast television stations.

Section 4 requires carriage of "local commercial television stations," defined to include all full power television broadcasters, other than those qualifying as "noncommercial educational" stations under § 5, that operate within the same television market as the cable system. Cable systems with more than 12 active channels, and more than 300 subscribers, are required to set aside up to one-third of their channels for commercial broadcast stations that request carriage. Cable systems with more than 300 subscribers, but only 12 or fewer active channels, must carry the signals of three commercial broadcast stations.

. . . The broadcast signals carried under this provision must be transmitted on a continuous, uninterrupted basis, and must be placed in the same numerical channel position as when broadcast over the air. Further, subject to a few exceptions, a cable operator may not charge a fee for carrying broadcast signals in fulfillment of its must-carry obligations.

Section 5 of the Act imposes similar requirements regarding the carriage of local public broadcast television stations, referred to in the Act as local "noncommercial educational television stations." . . .

[C.] Congress enacted the 1992 Cable Act after conducting three years of hearings on the structure and operation of the cable television industry. The conclusions Congress drew from its factfinding process are recited in the text of the Act itself. In brief, Congress found that the physical characteristics of cable transmission, compounded by the increasing concentration of economic power in the cable industry, are endangering the ability of over-the-air broadcast television stations to compete for a viewing audience and thus for necessary operating revenues. Congress determined that regulation of the market for video programming was necessary to correct this competitive imbalance.

. . . In light of these technological and economic conditions, Congress concluded that unless cable operators are required to carry local broadcast stations, "there is a substantial likelihood that . . . additional local broadcast signals will be deleted, repositioned, or not carried"; the "marked shift in market share" from broadcast to cable will continue to erode the advertising revenue base which sustains free local broadcast television; and that, as a consequence, "the economic viability of free local broadcast television and its ability to originate quality local programming will be seriously jeopardized."

II

There can be no disagreement on an initial premise: Cable programmers and cable operators engage in and transmit speech, and they are entitled to the protection of the speech and press provisions of the First Amendment. Leathers v. Medlock, 499 U.S. 439, 444 (1991). Through "original programming or by exercising editorial discretion over which stations or programs to include in its repertoire," cable programmers and operators "seek to communicate messages on a wide variety of topics and in a wide variety of formats." . . . By requiring cable systems to set aside a portion of their channels for local broadcasters, the must-carry rules regulate cable speech in two respects: The rules reduce the number of channels over which cable operators exercise unfettered control, and they render it more difficult for cable programmers to compete for carriage on the limited channels remaining. Nevertheless, because not every interference with speech triggers the same degree of scrutiny under the First Amendment, we must decide at the outset the level of scrutiny applicable to the must-carry provisions.

[A.] We address first the Government's contention that regulation of cable television should be analyzed under the same First Amendment standard that applies to regulation of broadcast television. It is true that our cases have permitted more intrusive regulation of broadcast speakers than of speakers in other media. But the rationale for applying a less rigorous standard of First Amendment scrutiny to broadcast regulation, whatever its validity in the cases elaborating it, does not apply in the context of cable regulation.

The justification for our distinct approach to broadcast regulation rests upon the unique physical limitations of the broadcast medium. As a general matter, there are more would-be broadcasters than frequencies available in the electromagnetic spectrum. And if two broadcasters were to attempt to transmit over the same frequency in the same locale, they would interfere with one another's signals, so that neither could be heard at all. The scarcity of broadcast frequencies thus required the establishment of some regulatory mechanism to divide the electromagnetic spectrum and assign specific frequencies to particular broadcasters. In addition, the inherent physical limitation on the number of speakers who may use the broadcast medium has been thought to require some adjustment in traditional First Amendment analysis to permit the Government to place limited content restraints, and impose certain affirmative obligations, on broadcast licensees. . . .

Although courts and commentators have criticized the scarcity rationale since its inception, we have declined to question its continuing validity as support for our broadcast jurisprudence, and see no reason to do so here. The broadcast cases are inapposite in the present context because cable television does not suffer from the inherent limitations that characterize the broadcast medium. Indeed, given the rapid advances in fiber optics and digital compression technology, soon there may be no practical limitation on the number of speakers who may use the cable medium. Nor is there any danger of physical interference between two cable speakers attempting to share the same channel. In light of these fundamental technological differences between broadcast and cable transmission, application of the more relaxed standard of scrutiny adopted in *Red Lion* and the other broadcast cases is inapt when determining the First Amendment validity of cable regulation. . . .

This is not to say that the unique physical characteristics of cable transmission should be ignored when determining the constitutionality of regulations affecting cable speech. They should not. But whatever relevance these physical characteristics may have in the evaluation of particular cable regulations, they do not require the alteration of settled principles of our First Amendment jurisprudence.

Although the Government acknowledges the substantial technological differences between broadcast and cable, it advances a second argument for application of the *Red Lion* framework to cable regulation. It asserts that the foundation of our broadcast jurisprudence is not the physical limitations of the electromagnetic spectrum, but rather the "market dysfunction" that characterizes the broadcast market. Because the cable market is beset by a similar dysfunction, the Government maintains, the *Red Lion* standard of review should also apply to cable. While we agree that the cable market suffers certain structural impediments, the Government's argument is flawed in two respects. First, as discussed above, the special physical characteristics of broadcast transmission, not the economic characteristics of the broadcast market, are what underlies our broadcast jurisprudence. Second, the mere assertion of dysfunction or failure in a speech market, without more, is not sufficient to shield a speech regulation from the First Amendment standards applicable to non-broadcast media.

By a related course of reasoning, the Government and some appellees maintain that the must-carry provisions are nothing more than industry-specific antitrust legislation, and thus warrant rational basis scrutiny under this Court's "precedents governing legislative efforts to correct market failure in a market whose commodity is speech." . . . This contention is unavailing. [W]hile the enforcement of a generally applicable law may or may not be subject to heightened scrutiny under the First Amendment, [ ], laws that single out the press, or certain elements thereof, for special treatment "pose a particular danger of abuse by the State," and so are always subject to at least some degree of heightened First Amendment scrutiny. Because the must-carry provisions impose special obligations upon cable operators and special burdens upon cable programmers, some measure of heightened First Amendment scrutiny is demanded.

[B.] [T]he First Amendment, subject only to narrow and well-understood exceptions, does not countenance governmental control over the content of messages expressed by private individuals. [*R.A.V.*]; Texas v. Johnson, 491 U.S. 397, 414 (1989). Our precedents thus apply the most exacting scrutiny to regulations that suppress, disadvantage, or impose differential burdens upon speech because of its content. [ ]. Laws that compel speakers to utter or distribute speech bearing a particular message are subject to the same rigorous scrutiny. [ ]. In contrast, regulations that are unrelated to the content of speech are subject to an intermediate level of scrutiny, [ ], because in most cases they pose a less substantial risk of excising certain ideas or viewpoints from the public dialogue.

Deciding whether a particular regulation is content based or content neutral is not always a simple task. We have said that the "principal inquiry in determining content neutrality . . . is whether the government has adopted a regulation of speech because of [agreement or] disagreement with the message it conveys." [ ] See *R.A.V.* [ ] ("The government may not regulate [speech] based on hostility—or favoritism—towards the underlying message expressed"). The purpose, or justification, of a regulation will often be evident on its face. [ ] But while a content-based purpose may be sufficient in certain circumstances to show that a regulation is content based, it is not necessary to such a showing in all cases. [ ] Nor will the mere assertion of a content-neutral purpose be enough to save a law which, on its face, discriminates based on content. [ ]

As a general rule, laws that by their terms distinguish favored speech from disfavored speech on the basis of the ideas or views expressed are content based. [ ] By contrast, laws that confer benefits or impose burdens on speech without reference to the ideas or views expressed are in most instances content neutral. [ ]

[C.] Insofar as they pertain to the carriage of full power broadcasters, the must-carry rules, on their face, impose burdens and confer benefits without reference to the content of speech. Although the provisions interfere with cable operators' editorial discretion by compelling them to offer carriage to a certain minimum number of broadcast stations, the extent of the interference does not depend upon the content of the cable operators' programming. The rules impose obligations upon all operators, save those with fewer than 300 subscribers, regardless of the programs or stations they now offer or have offered in the past. Nothing in the Act imposes a restriction, penalty, or burden by reason of the views, programs, or stations the cable operator has selected or will select. The number of channels a cable operator must set aside depends only on the operator's channel capacity; hence, an operator cannot avoid or mitigate its obligations under the Act by altering the programming it offers to subscribers. Cf. *Miami Herald Publishing Co. v. Tornillo*, 418 U.S. at 256-257 (newspaper may avoid access obligations by refraining from speech critical of political candidates).

The must-carry provisions also burden cable programmers by reducing the number of channels for which they can compete. But, again, this burden is unrelated to content, for it extends to all cable programmers irrespective of the programming they choose to offer viewers. And finally, the privileges conferred by the must-carry provisions are also unrelated to content. The rules benefit all full power broadcasters who request carriage—be they commercial or noncommercial, independent or network-affiliated, English or Spanish language, religious or secular. The aggregate effect of the rules is thus to make every full power commercial and noncommercial broadcaster eligible for must-carry, provided only that the broadcaster operates within the same television market as a cable system.

It is true that the must-carry provisions distinguish between speakers in the television programming market. But they do so based only upon the manner in which speakers transmit their messages to viewers, and not upon the messages they carry: Broadcasters, which transmit over the airwaves, are favored, while cable programmers, which do not, are disfavored. Cable operators, too, are burdened by the carriage obligations, but only because they control access to the cable conduit. So long as they are not a subtle means of exercising a content preference, speaker distinctions of this nature are not presumed invalid under the First Amendment.

That the must-carry provisions, on their face, do not burden or benefit speech of a particular content does not end the inquiry. Our cases have recognized that even a regulation neutral on its face may be content-based if its manifest purpose is to regulate speech because of the message it conveys.

. . . Our review of the Act and its various findings persuades us that Congress' overriding objective in enacting must-carry was not to favor programming of a particular subject matter, viewpoint, or format, but rather to preserve access to free television programming for the 40 percent of Americans without cable.

In unusually detailed statutory findings Congress explained that because cable systems and broadcast stations compete for local advertising revenue, and because cable operators have a vested financial interest in favoring their affiliated programmers over broadcast stations, cable operators have a built-in "economic incentive . . . to delete, reposition, or not carry local broadcast signals." Congress concluded that absent a requirement that cable systems carry the signals of local broadcast stations, the continued availability of free local broadcast television would be threatened. Congress sought to avoid the elimination of broadcast television because, in its words, "such programming is . . . free to those who own television sets and do not require cable transmission to receive broadcast television signals," and because "there is a substantial governmental interest in promoting the continued availability of such free television programming, especially for viewers who are unable to afford other means of receiving programming."

By preventing cable operators from refusing carriage to broadcast television stations, the must-carry rules ensure that broadcast television stations will retain a large enough potential audience to earn necessary advertising revenue—or, in the case of noncommercial broadcasters, sufficient viewer contributions, see § 2(a)(8)(B)—to maintain their continued operation. In so doing, the provisions are designed to guarantee the survival of a medium that has become a vital part of the Nation's communication system, and to ensure that every individual with a television set can obtain access to free television programming.

. . . [O]ur precedents have held that "protecting noncable households from loss of regular television broadcasting service due to competition from cable systems," is not only a permissible governmental justification, but an "important and substantial federal interest."

The design and operation of the challenged provisions confirm that the purposes underlying the enactment of the must-carry scheme are unrelated to the content of speech. The rules, as mentioned, confer must-carry rights on all full power broadcasters, irrespective of the content of their programming. They do not require or prohibit the carriage of particular ideas or points of view. They do not penalize cable operators or programmers because of the content of their programming. They do not compel cable operators to affirm points of view with which they disagree. They do not produce any net decrease in the amount of available speech. And they leave cable operators free to carry whatever programming they wish on all channels not subject to must-carry requirements.

Appellants and the dissent make much of the fact that, in the course of describing the purposes behind the Act, Congress referred to the value of broadcast programming. In particular, Congress noted that broadcast television is "an important source of local news[,] public affairs programming and other local broadcast services critical to an informed electorate," and that noncommercial television "provides educational and informational programming to the Nation's citizens." We do not think, however, that such references cast any material doubt on the content-neutral character of must-carry. That Congress acknowledged the local orientation of broadcast programming and the role that noncommercial stations have played in educating the public does not indicate that Congress regarded broadcast programming as *more* valuable than cable programming. Rather, it reflects nothing more than the recognition that the services provided by broadcast television have some intrinsic value and, thus, are worth preserving against the threats posed by cable.

The operation of the Act further undermines the suggestion that Congress' purpose in enacting must-carry was to force programming of a "local" or "educational" content on cable subscribers. The provisions, as we have stated, benefit all full power broadcasters irrespective of the nature of their programming. In fact, if a cable system were required to bump a cable programmer to make room for a broadcast station, nothing would stop a cable operator from displacing a cable station that provides all local- or education-oriented programming with a broadcaster that provides very little. Appellants do not even contend, moreover, that broadcast programming is any more "local" or "educational" than cable programming. Cf. *Leathers v. Medlock*. . . .

. . . We likewise reject the suggestion, advanced by appellants and by Judge Williams in dissent, that the must-carry rules are content-based because the preference for broadcast stations "*automatically* entails content requirements." It is true that broadcast programming, unlike cable programming, is subject to certain limited content restraints imposed by statute and FCC regulation. But it does not follow that Congress mandated cable carriage of broadcast television stations as a means of ensuring that particular programs will be shown, or not shown, on cable systems.

As an initial matter, the argument exaggerates the extent to which the FCC is permitted to intrude into matters affecting the content of broadcast programming. The FCC is forbidden by statute from engaging in "censorship" or from promulgating any regulation "which shall interfere with the [broadcasters'] right of free speech." 47 U.S.C. § 326. . . . In particular, the FCC's oversight responsibilities do not grant it the power to ordain any particular type of programming that must be offered by broadcast stations; for although "the Commission may inquire of licensees what they have done to determine the needs of the community they propose to serve, the Commission may not impose upon them its private notions of what the public ought to hear." . . .

. . . In a regime where Congress or the FCC exercised more intrusive control over the content of broadcast programming, an argument similar to appellants' might carry greater weight. But in the present regulatory system, those concerns are without foundation. . . .

III

[A.] In sum, the must-carry provisions do not pose such inherent dangers to free expression, or present such potential for censorship or manipulation, as to justify application of the most exacting level of First Amendment scrutiny. [T]he appropriate standard by which to evaluate the constitutionality of must-carry is the intermediate level of scrutiny applicable to content-neutral restrictions that impose an incidental burden on speech. See United States v. O'Brien, 391 U.S. 367 (1968).

Under *O'Brien*, a content-neutral regulation will be sustained if

> it furthers an important or substantial governmental interest; if the governmental interest is unrelated to the suppression of free expression; and if the incidental restriction on alleged First Amendment freedoms is no greater than is essential to the furtherance of that interest. Id. at 377.

To satisfy this standard, a regulation need not be the least speech-restrictive means of advancing the Government's interests. "Rather, the requirement of narrow tailoring is satisfied 'so long as the . . . regulation promotes a substantial government interest that would be achieved less effectively absent the regulation.'" Narrow tailoring in this context requires, in other words, that the means chosen do not "burden substantially more speech than is necessary to further the government's legitimate interests."

Congress declared that the must-carry provisions serve three interrelated interests: (1) preserving the benefits of free, over-the-air local broadcast television, (2) promoting the widespread dissemination of information from a multiplicity of sources, and (3) promoting fair competition in the market for television programming. None of these interests is related to the "suppression of free expression," or to the content of any speakers' messages. And viewed in the abstract, we have no difficulty concluding that each of them is an important governmental interest.

. . . [A]ssuring that the public has access to a multiplicity of information sources is a governmental purpose of the highest order, for it promotes values central to the First Amendment. Indeed, it has long been a basic tenet of national communications policy that the widest possible dissemination of information from diverse and antagonistic sources is essential to the welfare of the public. . . . Finally, the Government's interest in eliminating restraints on fair competition is always substantial, even when the individuals or entities subject to particular regulations are engaged in expressive activity protected by the First Amendment.

[B.] That the Government's asserted interests are important in the abstract does not mean, however, that the must-carry rules will in fact advance those interests.

. . . The Government's assertion that the must-carry rules are necessary to protect the viability of broadcast television rests on two essential propositions: (1) that unless cable operators are compelled to carry broadcast stations, significant numbers of broadcast stations will be refused carriage on cable systems; and (2) that the broadcast stations denied carriage will either deteriorate to a substantial degree or fail altogether.

. . . [W]e hold that the District Court erred in granting summary judgment in favor of the Government. Because of the unresolved factual questions, the importance of the issues to the broadcast and cable industries, and the conflicting conclusions that the parties contend are to be drawn from the statistics and other evidence presented, we think it necessary to permit the parties to develop a more thorough factual record, and to allow the District Court to resolve any factual disputes remaining, before passing upon the constitutional validity of the challenged provisions. [Vacated and remanded.]

Justice O'CONNOR, with whom Justice SCALIA and Justice GINSBURG join, and with whom Justice THOMAS joins as to Parts I and III, concurring in part and dissenting in part.

. . . Preferences for diversity of viewpoints, for localism, for educational programming, and for news and public affairs all make reference to content. . . . The First Amendment does more than just bar government from intentionally suppressing speech of which it disapproves. It also generally prohibits the government from excepting certain kinds of speech from regulation because it thinks the speech is especially valuable. . . . The interest in ensuring access to a multiplicity of diverse and antagonistic sources of information, no matter how praiseworthy, is directly tied to the content of what the speakers will likely say.

NOTES AND QUESTIONS

1. *Content-neutral or content-based?* Does Congress's desire to preserve the "benefits of free, over-the-air local broadcasting" reflect a preference for particular content? How can one consider the benefits without considering the content?
2. *Distinguishing* Tornillo. Why doesn't *Miami Herald v. Tornillo* govern this case? After all, the must-carry rules certainly interfere with the editorial

discretion of cable operators. The Court suggested that one distinction is that "the cable operator exercises far greater control over access to the relevant medium." Can you think of any other distinctions between this case and *Tornillo*?

3. *Counting the votes.* Justice Stevens thought the must-carry rules should be upheld without further proceedings, but he provided the fifth vote for remand in order to provide a disposition.
4. Turner II. Upon remand of *Turner I*, the U.S. District Court for the District of Columbia conducted extensive fact-finding and then voted 2–1 to uphold the must-carry rules. The Supreme Court took the case on direct review and affirmed. Turner Broad. Sys., Inc. v. FCC, 520 U.S. 180 (1997) ("*Turner II*"). The Justices were again sharply divided, even though Justice Breyer had replaced Justice Blackmun in the interim between the two decisions. The five Justices in the majority held that the must-carry provisions satisfied *O'Brien*'s intermediate scrutiny test and were therefore constitutional. Although *Turner I* rejected the broadcast paradigm of regulation, the outcome of the *Turner* cases arguably depends on the unique characteristics of cable as medium. Justice Breyer, partially concurring in *Turner II*, made this point particularly explicit:

> [I] note (and agree) that a cable system, physically dependent upon the availability of space along city streets, at present (perhaps less in the future) typically faces little competition, that it therefore constitutes a kind of bottleneck that controls the range of viewer choice (whether or not it uses any consequent economic power for economically predatory purposes), and that *some* degree—at least a limited degree—of governmental intervention and control through regulation can prove appropriate when justified under *O'Brien* (at least when not "content based"). . . . I agree further that the burden the statute imposes upon the cable system, potential cable programmers, and cable viewers is limited and will diminish as typical cable system capacity grows over time.

Id. at 228. Would a must-carry provision for newspapers, even a content-neutral one designed to preserve a multiplicity of voices in the marketplace of ideas, survive constitutional scrutiny?

AN EXTENDED NOTE ON INDECENCY ON CABLE TELEVISION

In 1992 Congress passed the Cable Television Consumer Protection and Competition Act, 47 U.S.C. § 532(h), (j), and note following § 531. The purpose of the Act was to regulate indecent material on cable television. In Denver Area Educational Telecommunications Consortium, Inc. v. FCC, 518 U.S. 727 (1996), the Court addressed the constitutionality of three provisions of the Act. The Court struck down, 6-3, section 10(b) of the Act, which required "cable system operators to segregate certain 'patently offensive' programming, to place it on a single channel, and to block that channel from viewer access unless the viewer requests access in advance and in writing." The government contended that this so-called "segregate and block" should be judged according to the principles announced in the Court's opinion in *Pacifica*, which "does not require that regulations of indecency on television be subject to the strictest" First Amendment "standard of review." The Court refused to address this argument directly because it was clear the Act violated strict or even less than strict scrutiny because it was not the "least restrictive alternative," was not "narrowly tailored," and was "more extensive than necessary."

The Court deemed the "segregate and block" provision overly restrictive in several different respects. For example, the provision "force[d] the viewer to receive (for days or weeks at a time) all 'patently offensive' or none," and it "automatically place[d] the viewer's name on a special list." The Court also held that the provision was not narrowly tailored to protect children, a concededly compelling interest, because less restrictive means such as scrambling laws and "lockboxes"—used by parents to block particular channels—were available.

The Telecommunications Act of 1996, 47 U.S.C. § 561, attempted once more to address indecent and obscene cable programming. Section 505 of the Act gave cable operators two options. One option was to "fully scramble" or "fully block" audio and video portions of any "sexually explicit adult programming or other programming that is indecent on any channel of its service primarily dedicated to sexually-oriented programming." The other option was to limit their transmission to the hours between 10 P.M. and 6 A.M. Most cable operators chose the "time channeling" option rather than the complete scrambling option. Playboy Entertainment Group brought the following suit challenging the constitutionality of the scrambling requirement. The following decision struck down the requirement by a 5–4 vote.

United States v. Playboy Entertainment Group, Inc.

529 U.S. 803 (2000)

Justice KENNEDY delivered the opinion of the Court.

This case presents a challenge to § 505 of the Telecommunications Act of 1996, Pub. L. 104-104, 110 Stat. 136, 47 U.S.C. § 561 (1994 ed., Supp. III). Section 505 requires cable television operators who provide channels "primarily dedicated to sexually-oriented programming" either to "fully scramble or otherwise fully block" those channels or to limit their transmission to hours when children are unlikely to be viewing, set by administrative regulation as the time between 10 P.M. and 6 A.M. Even before enactment of the statute, signal scrambling was already in use. Cable operators used scrambling in the regular course of business, so that only paying customers had access to certain programs. Scrambling could be imprecise, however; and either or both audio and visual portions of the scrambled programs might be heard or seen, a phenomenon known as "signal bleed." The purpose of § 505 is to shield children from hearing or seeing images resulting from signal bleed.

To comply with the statute, the majority of cable operators adopted the second, or "time channeling," approach. The effect of the widespread adoption of time channeling was to eliminate altogether the transmission of the targeted programming outside the safe harbor period in affected cable service areas. In other words, for two-thirds of the day no household in those service areas could receive the programming, whether or not the household or the viewer wanted to do so.

Appellee Playboy Entertainment Group, Inc, challenged the statute as unnecessarily restrictive content-based legislation violative of the First Amendment. After a trial, a three-judge District Court concluded that a regime in which viewers could order signal blocking on a household-by-household basis presented an effective, less restrictive alternative to § 505. Finding no error in this conclusion, we affirm.

I

Playboy Entertainment Group owns and prepares programs for adult television networks, including Playboy Television and Spice. Playboy transmits its programming to cable television operators, who retransmit it to their subscribers, either through monthly subscriptions to premium channels or on a so-called "pay-per-view" basis. Cable operators transmit Playboy's signal, like other premium channel signals, in scrambled form. The operators then provide paying subscribers with an "addressable converter," a box placed on the home television set. The converter permits the viewer to see and hear the descrambled signal. It is conceded that almost all of Playboy's programming consists of sexually explicit material as defined by the statute. . . .

II

. . . The speech in question is defined by its content; and the statute which seeks to restrict it is content based. Section 505 applies only to channels primarily dedicated to "sexually explicit adult programming or other programming that is indecent." The statute is unconcerned with signal bleed from any other channels. . . . The overriding justification for the regulation is concern for the effect of the subject matter on young viewers. . . .

Not only does § 505 single out particular programming content for regulation, it also singles out particular programmers. . . . [T]he statutory disability applies only to channels "primarily dedicated to sexually-oriented programming." One sponsor of the measure even identified appellee by name. See 141 Cong. Rec. 15587 (1995) (statement of Sen. Feinstein) (noting the statute would apply to channels "such as the Playboy and Spice channels"). Laws designed or intended to suppress or restrict the expression of specific speakers contradict basic First Amendment principles. Section 505 limited Playboy's market as a penalty for its programming choice, though other channels capable of transmitting like material are altogether exempt.

The effect of the federal statute on the protected speech is now apparent. . . . According to the District Court, "30 to 50% of all adult programming is viewed by households prior to 10 P.M.," when the safe-harbor period begins. To prohibit this much speech is a significant restriction of communication between speakers and willing adult listeners, communication which enjoys First Amendment protection. It is of no moment that the statute does not impose a complete prohibition. The distinction between laws burdening and laws banning speech is but a matter of degree. . . .

Since § 505 is a content-based speech restriction, it can stand only if it satisfies strict scrutiny. If a statute regulates speech based on its content, it must be narrowly tailored to promote a compelling Government interest. If a less restrictive alternative would serve the Government's purpose, the legislature must use that alternative. To do otherwise would be to restrict speech without an adequate justification, a course the First Amendment does not permit.

Our precedents teach these principles. Where the designed benefit of a content-based speech restriction is to shield the sensibilities of listeners, the general rule is that the right of expression prevails, even where no less restrictive alternative exists. We are expected to protect our own sensibilities "simply by averting [our] eyes." [*Cohen v. California; Erzoznik.*] Here, of course, we consider images transmitted to some homes where they are not wanted and where parents often are not present to give immediate guidance. Cable television, like broadcast media, presents unique problems, which inform our assessment of the interests at stake, and which may justify restrictions that would be unacceptable in other contexts. See [*DAETC; Pacifica*]. No one suggests the Government must be indifferent to unwanted, indecent speech that comes into the home without parental consent. The speech here, all agree, is protected speech; and the question is what standard the Government must meet in order to restrict it. As we consider a content-based regulation, the answer should be clear: The standard is strict scrutiny. This case involves speech alone; and even where speech is indecent and enters the home, the objective of shielding children does not suffice to support a blanket ban if the protection can be accomplished by a less restrictive alternative.

. . . There is, moreover, a key difference between cable television and the broadcasting media, which is the point on which this case turns: Cable systems have the capacity to block unwanted channels on a household-by-household basis. The option to block reduces the likelihood, so concerning to the Court in *Pacifica*, that traditional First Amendment scrutiny would deprive the Government of all authority to address this sort of problem. The corollary, of course, is that targeted blocking enables the Government to support parental authority without affecting the First Amendment interests of speakers and willing listeners—listeners for whom, if the speech is unpopular or indecent, the privacy of their own homes may be the optimal place of receipt. Simply put, targeted blocking is less restrictive than banning, and the Government cannot ban speech if targeted blocking is a feasible and effective means of furthering its compelling interests. This is not to say that the absence of an effective blocking mechanism will in all cases suffice to support a law restricting the speech in question; but if a less restrictive means is available for the Government to achieve its goals, the Government must use it.

III

. . . When a student first encounters our free speech jurisprudence, he or she might think it is influenced by the philosophy that one idea is as good as any other, and that in art and literature objective standards of style, taste, decorum, beauty, and esthetics are deemed by the Constitution to be inappropriate, indeed unattainable. Quite the opposite is true. The Constitution no more enforces a relativistic philosophy or moral nihilism than it does any other point of view. The Constitution exists precisely so that opinions and judgments, including esthetic and moral judgments about art and literature, can be formed, tested, and expressed. What the Constitution says is that these judgments are for the individual to make, not for the Government to decree, even with the mandate or approval of a majority. Technology expands the capacity to choose; and it denies the potential of this revolution if we assume the Government is best positioned to make these choices for us.

. . . There is little hard evidence of how widespread or how serious the problem of signal bleed is. Indeed, there is no proof as to how likely any child is to view a discernible explicit image, and no proof of the duration of the bleed or the quality of the pictures or sound. To say that millions of children are subject to a risk of viewing signal bleed is one thing; to avoid articulating the true nature and extent of the risk is quite another. Under § 505, sanctionable signal bleed can include instances as fleeting as an image appearing on a screen for just a few seconds. The First Amendment requires a more careful assessment and characterization of an evil in order to justify a regulation as sweeping as this. . . .

In addition, market-based solutions such as programmable televisions, VCR's, and mapping systems (which display a blue screen when tuned to a scrambled signal) may eliminate signal bleed at the consumer end of the cable. . . .

. . . The Government also failed to prove [that voluntary blocking at the request of the cable subscriber, available under § 504] would be an ineffective alternative to § 505. . . . There is no evidence that a well-promoted voluntary blocking provision would not be capable at least of informing parents about signal bleed (if they are not yet aware of it) and about their rights to have the bleed blocked (if they consider it a problem and have not yet controlled it themselves).

. . . It is no response that voluntary blocking requires a consumer to take action, or may be inconvenient, or may not go perfectly every time. A court should not assume a plausible, less restrictive alternative would be ineffective; and a court should not presume parents, given full information, will fail to act. If unresponsive operators are a concern, moreover, a notice statute could give cable operators ample incentive, through fines or other penalties for noncompliance, to respond to blocking requests in prompt and efficient fashion.

[The Government then contended voluntary blocking was insufficient because "[t]here would certainly be parents—perhaps a large number of parents—who out of inertia, indifference, or distraction, simply would take no action to block signal bleed, even if fully informed of the problem and even if offered a relatively easy solution."]

Even upon the assumption that the Government has an interest in substituting itself for informed and empowered parents, its interest is not sufficiently compelling to justify this widespread restriction on speech. The Government's argument stems from the idea that parents do not know their children are viewing the material on a scale or frequency to cause concern, or if so, that parents do not want to take affirmative steps to block it and their decisions are to be superseded. The assumptions have not been established; and in any event the assumptions apply only in a regime where the option of blocking has not been explained. The whole point of a publicized § 504 would be to advise parents that indecent material may be shown and to afford them an opportunity to block it at all times, even when they are not at home and even after 10 P.M. Time channeling does not offer this assistance. The regulatory alternative of a publicized § 504, which has the real possibility of promoting more open disclosure and the choice of an effective blocking system, would provide parents the information needed to engage in active supervision. The Government has not shown that this alternative, a regime of added communication and support, would be insufficient to secure its objective, or that any overriding harm justifies its intervention.

. . . Basic speech principles are at stake in this case. When the purpose and design of a statute is to regulate speech by reason of its content, special consideration or latitude is not accorded to the Government merely because the law can somehow be described as a burden rather than outright suppression. We cannot be influenced, moreover, by the perception that the regulation in question is not a major one because the speech is not very important. The history of the law of free expression is one of vindication in cases involving speech that many citizens may find shabby, offensive, or even ugly. It follows that all content-based restrictions on speech must give us more than a moment's pause. If television broadcasts can expose children to the real risk of harmful exposure to indecent materials, even in their own home and without parental consent, there is a problem the Government can address. It must do so, however, in a way consistent with First Amendment principles. Here the Government has not met the burden the First Amendment imposes. . . .

Justice BREYER, with whom THE CHIEF JUSTICE, Justice O'CONNOR, and Justice SCALIA join, dissenting.

The majority first concludes that the Government failed to prove the seriousness of the problem—receipt of adult channels by children whose parents did not request their broadcast. This claim is flat-out wrong. For one thing, the parties concede that basic RF scrambling does not scramble the audio portion of the program. For another, Playboy itself conducted a survey of cable operators who were asked: "Is your system in full compliance with Section 505 (no discernible audio or video bleed)?" To this question, 75% of cable operators answered "no." . . .

I would add to this empirical evidence the majority's own statement that "*most* cable operators had 'no practical choice but to curtail'" adult programming by switching to nighttime only transmission of adult channels. *If signal bleed is not a significant empirical problem, then why, in light of the cost of its cure, must so many cable operators switch to night time hours?* There is no realistic answer to this question. I do not think it realistic to imagine that signal bleed occurs just enough to make cable operators skittish, without also significantly exposing children to these images.

. . . The majority's second claim—that the Government failed to demonstrate the absence of a "less restrictive alternative"—presents a closer question. The specific question is whether § 504's "opt-out" amounts to a "less restrictive," but *similarly* practical and *effective*, way to accomplish § 505's child-protecting objective. . . .

. . . Unlike the majority, I believe the record makes clear that § 504's opt-out is not a similarly effective alternative. Section 504 (opt-out) and § 505 (opt-in) work differently in order to achieve very different legislative objectives. Section 504 gives parents the power to tell cable operators to keep any channel out of their home. Section 505 does more. Unless parents explicitly consent, it inhibits the transmission of adult cable channels to children whose parents may be unaware of what they are watching, whose parents cannot easily supervise television viewing habits, whose parents do not know of their § 504 "opt-out" rights, or whose parents are simply unavailable at critical times. In this respect, § 505 serves the same interests as the laws that deny children access to adult cabarets or X-rated movies. These laws, and § 505, all act in the absence of direct parental supervision.

This legislative objective is perfectly legitimate. Where over 28 million school age children have both parents or their only parent in the work force, where at least 5 million children are left alone at home without supervision each week, and where children may spend afternoons and evenings watching television outside of the home with friends, § 505 offers independent protection for a large number of families. . . . [G]overnment has a compelling interest in helping parents by preventing minors from accessing sexually explicit materials in the absence of parental supervision.

NOTES AND QUESTIONS

1. *Evidentiary support.* How much more evidence would Congress need about the problem of signal bleed in order to justify § 505?
2. *Opt out/opt in.* Will a provision allowing audience members to "opt out" of receiving offensive speech always be constitutionally preferable to a provision forcing audience members who wish to receive the speech to "opt in"?
3. *Cable as medium.* How much of this decision rests on the distinct technological features of cable as a medium?
4. *Regulating "bad" parenting.* Why isn't the government allowed to regulate to protect children in the face of parental indifference or inertia? If, as the evidence indicates, "fewer than 0.5% of cable subscribers requested full blocking" under § 504, does this mean that signal bleed was not a significant problem? That few parents cared about signal bleed? Or that few parents knew that full blocking was available upon request? Is the interpretation of the evidence relevant to the constitutional analysis?

F. *REGULATION OF THE INTERNET AND NEW MEDIA*

The Telecommunications Act of 1996 attempted to regulate indecency not merely on cable systems but on the internet as well. Title V of the Telecommunications Act is called the Communications Decency Act (CDA). The constitutionality of two provisions of the CDA was at issue in *Reno v. ACLU,* below. However, in addressing the constitutionality of the CDA provisions, the Court also addressed a more fundamental jurisprudential issue, namely, whether the broadcast paradigm of indecency regulation laid out in *Pacifica* also applied to the Internet.

Reno v. ACLU

521 U.S. 844 (1997)

Justice Stevens delivered the opinion of the Court.

At issue is the constitutionality of two statutory provisions enacted to protect minors from "indecent" and "patently offensive" communications on the Internet.

Notwithstanding the legitimacy and importance of the congressional goal of protecting children from harmful materials, we agree with the three-judge District Court that the statute abridges "the freedom of speech" protected by the First Amendment.

[The Court began its opinion by reiterating some of the district court's extensive factual findings about the nature of the Internet, comparing it to "a vast library including millions of readily available and indexed publications and a sprawling mall offering goods and services." The Court also noted that "[f]rom the publishers' point of view, it constitutes a vast platform from which to address and hear from a world-wide audience of millions of readers, viewers, researchers, and buyers. Any person or organization with a computer connected to the Internet can 'publish' information." The Court then turned to the challenged provisions of the CDA: the "indecent transmission" provision and the "patently offensive display" provision. The first, § 223(a), prohibited knowing transmission of obscene or indecent messages to any recipient under 18 years of age. The second provision, § 223(d), prohibited knowing sending or displaying of patently offensive messages in a manner available to a person under 18 years of age. That section defined such messages as "any comment, request, suggestion, proposal, image, or other communication that, in context, depicts or describes, in terms patently offensive as measured by contemporary community standards, sexual or excretory activities or organs, regardless of whether the user of such service placed the call or initiated the communication." It then provided for affirmative defenses for those who take good-faith measure to restrict access by minors and for those who restrict access through certain age or credit card verification systems.]

In *Ginsberg*, we upheld the constitutionality of a New York statute that prohibited selling to minors under 17 years of age material that was considered obscene as to them even if not obscene as to adults. . . . [W]e relied not only on the State's independent interest in the well-being of its youth, but also on our consistent recognition of the principle that "the parents' claim to authority in their own household to direct the rearing of their children is basic in the structure of our society." In four important respects, the statute upheld in *Ginsberg* was narrower than the CDA. First, we noted in *Ginsberg* that "the prohibition against sales to minors does not bar parents who so desire from purchasing the magazines for their children." Under the CDA, by contrast, neither the parents' consent—nor even their participation—in the communication would avoid the application of the statute. Second, the New York statute applied only to commercial transactions, whereas the CDA contains no such limitation. Third, the New York statute cabined its definition of material that is harmful to minors with the requirement that it be "utterly without redeeming social importance for minors." The CDA fails to provide us with any definition of the term "indecent" as used in § 223(a)(1) and, importantly, omits any requirement that the "patently offensive" material covered by § 223(d) lack serious literary, artistic, political, or scientific value. Fourth, the New York statute defined a minor as a person under the age of 17, whereas the CDA, in applying to all those under 18 years, includes an additional year of those nearest majority.

In *Pacifica*, we . . . concluded that the ease with which children may obtain access to broadcasts, "coupled with the concerns recognized in *Ginsberg*," justified special treatment of indecent broadcasting.

As with the New York statute at issue in *Ginsberg*, there are significant differences between the order upheld in *Pacifica* and the CDA. First, the order in *Pacifica*, issued by an agency that had been regulating radio stations for decades, targeted a specific broadcast that represented a rather dramatic departure from traditional program content in order to designate when—rather than whether—it would be permissible to air such a program in that particular medium. The CDA's broad categorical prohibitions are not limited to particular times and are not dependent on any evaluation by an agency familiar with the unique characteristics of the Internet. Second, unlike the CDA, the Commission's declaratory order was not punitive; we expressly refused to decide whether the indecent broadcast "would justify a criminal prosecution." Finally, the Commission's order applied to a medium which as a matter of history had "received the most limited First Amendment protection," in large part because warnings could not adequately protect the listener from unexpected program content. The Internet, however, has no comparable history. Moreover, the District Court found that the risk of encountering indecent material by accident is remote because a series of affirmative steps is required to access specific material.

. . . In Southeastern Promotions, Ltd. v. Conrad, 420 U.S. 546, 557, 43 L. Ed. 2d 448, 95 S. Ct. 1239 (1975), we observed that "each medium of expression . . . may present its own problems." Thus, some of our cases have recognized special justifications for regulation of the broadcast media that are not applicable to other speakers. In these cases, the Court relied on the history of extensive government regulation of the broadcast medium; the scarcity of available frequencies at its inception; and its "invasive" nature.

Those factors are not present in cyberspace. Neither before nor after the enactment of the CDA have the vast democratic fora of the Internet been subject to the type of government supervision and regulation that has attended the broadcast industry. Moreover, the Internet is not as "invasive" as radio or television. The District Court specifically found that "communications over the Internet do not 'invade' an individual's home or appear on one's computer screen unbidden. Users seldom encounter content 'by accident.'" It also found that "almost all sexually explicit images are preceded by warnings as to the content," and cited testimony that "'odds are slim' that a user would come across a sexually explicit sight by accident."

. . . [U]nlike the conditions that prevailed when Congress first authorized regulation of the broadcast spectrum, the Internet can hardly be considered a "scarce" expressive commodity. It provides relatively unlimited, low-cost capacity for communication of all kinds. The Government estimates that "as many as 40 million people use the Internet today, and that figure is expected to grow to 200 million by 1999." This dynamic, multifaceted category of communication includes not only traditional print and news services, but also audio, video, and still images, as well as interactive, real-time dialogue. Through the use of chat rooms, any person with a phone line can become a town crier with a voice that resonates farther than it could from any soapbox. Through the use of Web pages, mail exploders, and newsgroups, the same individual can become a pamphleteer. As the District Court found, "the content on the Internet is as diverse as human thought." We agree with its conclusion that our cases provide no basis for qualifying the level of First Amendment scrutiny that should be applied to this medium.

. . . The breadth of the CDA's coverage is wholly unprecedented. Unlike the regulations upheld in *Ginsberg* and *Pacifica*, the scope of the CDA is not limited to commercial speech or commercial entities. Its open-ended prohibitions embrace all nonprofit entities and individuals posting indecent messages or displaying them on their own computers in the presence of minors. The general, undefined terms "indecent" and "patently offensive" cover large amounts of nonpornographic material with serious educational or other value. Moreover, the "community standards" criterion as applied to the Internet means that any communication available to a nation-wide audience will be judged by the standards of the community most likely to be offended by the message. The regulated subject matter includes any of the seven "dirty words" used in the Pacifica monologue, the use of which the Government's expert acknowledged could constitute a felony. It may also extend to discussions about prison rape or safe sexual practices, artistic images that include nude subjects, and arguably the card catalogue of the Carnegie Library.

. . . Under the CDA, a parent allowing her 17-year-old to use the family computer to obtain information on the Internet that she, in her parental judgment, deems appropriate could face a lengthy prison term. See 47 U.S.C. A. § 223(a)(2) (Supp. 1997). Similarly, a parent who sent his 17-year-old college freshman information on birth control via e-mail could be incarcerated even though neither he, his child, nor anyone in their home community, found the material "indecent" or "patently offensive," if the college town's community thought otherwise.

The breadth of this content-based restriction of speech imposes an especially heavy burden on the Government to explain why a less restrictive provision would not be as effective as the CDA. It has not done so. . . . Particularly in the light of the absence of any detailed findings by the Congress, or even hearings addressing the special problems of the CDA, we are persuaded that the CDA is not narrowly tailored if that requirement has any meaning at all.

. . . We agree with the District Court's conclusion that the CDA places an unacceptably heavy burden on protected speech, and that the defenses do not constitute the sort of "narrow tailoring" that will save an otherwise patently invalid unconstitutional provision. In *Sable*, we remarked that the speech restriction at issue there amounted to "'burning the house to roast the pig.'" The CDA, casting a far darker shadow over free speech, threatens to torch a large segment of the Internet community.

Justice O'Connor, with whom The Chief Justice joins, concurring in the judgment in part and dissenting in part. [Omitted.]

NOTES AND QUESTIONS

1. *Defining minors.* Is one of the problems with the CDA provisions that they make no distinctions between 17-year-olds and 7-year-olds? If so, how should Congress remedy this problem?
2. *A medium-specific First Amendment.* Is the First Amendment "medium specific"? Or is there one set of First Amendment standards for broadcasters and a different set of standards for all other media? Is "intrusiveness" (in the sense that one can be subjected to indecent material without warning or consent) still a valid rationale for tolerating more regulation of a medium than might otherwise be allowed?

3. *Protecting minors by restricting adults.* How much may a regulation designed to protect children infringe upon nonobscene speech before it is declared invalid?
4. *Community standards and the internet.* Is the application of a "community standards" criterion to define indecency inherently unconstitutional when applied to the Internet, which crosses all geographical boundaries?
5. *Mobile access and invasiveness.* Today most children have access to smart phones, iPads, or other mobile devices that offer instant access and browsing capability. Does this make the Internet as invasive as radio or television?
6. *Video games as medium.* In Brown v. Entertainment Merchants Ass'n, 564 U.S. 786 (2011), the Supreme Court rejected the argument that the medium of video games should receive a reduced level of First Amendment protection. The case involved a constitutional challenge to a California statute prohibiting sale or rental of violent video games to minors. The state argued that the interactive graphic nature of such games justified the prohibition, but the Court struck down the California law as a content-based restriction on speech. The Court's opinion conceded that video games have little to do with protection of discourse on public matters, but the Court granted full First Amendment protection, stating: "[W]e have long recognized that it is difficult to distinguish politics from entertainment, and dangerous to try." The Court found no relevant distinction between the video games and the "books, plays, and moves that preceded them.": "video games communicate ideas—and even social messages—through many familiar literary devices (such as characters, dialogue, plot, and music) and through features distinctive to the medium (such as the player's interaction with the virtual world)." The opinion further rejected the notion that violent speech fell into a category of low-value or unprotected speech, even when aimed at children. As Justice Scalia noted in his opinion for the Court, many of the classics of children's literature "contain no shortage of gore. Grimm's Fairy Tales, for example, are grim indeed." Thus, without compelling evidence showing that violent video games cause actual harm to minors, the California law failed strict scrutiny. For further discussion of the Roberts Court's lack of receptiveness to arguments for "medium-specific" First Amendment protections, see Lyrissa Barnett Lidsky, *Not A Free Press Court?*, 2012 B.Y.Y.L. Rev. 1819 (2012).
7. *Medium-specific standards applied to video-on-demand?* In Citizens United v. Federal Elections Commission, 558 U.S. 310 (2010), excerpted in Chapter 6, the Court refused to apply different First Amendment standards to "movies shown through video-on-demand" than it applied to "television ads" simply because users must take affirmative steps to obtain video-on-demand. The Court stated:

> While some means of communication may be less effective than others at influencing the public in different contexts, any effort by the Judiciary to decide which means of communications are to be preferred for the particular type of message and speaker

> would raise questions as to the courts' own lawful authority. Substantial questions would arise if courts were to begin saying what means of speech should be preferred or disfavored. And in all events, those differentiations might soon prove to be irrelevant or outdated by technologies that are in rapid flux. []
>
> Courts, too, are bound by the First Amendment. We must decline to draw, and then redraw, constitutional lines based on the particular media or technology used to disseminate political speech from a particular speaker.

G. *THE FUTURE OF BIG TECH REGULATION*

In *Reno v. ACLU*, the Supreme Court analogized internet service providers to print publishers rather than broadcasters and struck down a portion of the Communications Decency Act designed to protect minors from indecent and patently offensive content on the Internet. *Reno* did not affect a separate portion of the Communications Decency Act that gave Internet service providers immunity from liability for defamatory and many other types of harmful content posted by their users. Subsection 230(c)(1) provides that "[n]o provider or user of an interactive computer service shall be treated as the publisher or speaker of any information provided by another information content provider." The title and legislative history of the CDA suggest that Congress meant to establish a policy that tech platforms would not be subject to liability as "publishers" of content posted by third parties just because they exercise a limited degree of editorial control over content. Indeed, Congress wanted to incentivize platforms to remove indecent content without fear of liability. But court decisions interpreted subsection 230(c)'s broadly worded text to grant the platforms almost complete immunity from liability for content posted by their users. (The immunity does not extend to publication of copyrighted material.)

Amid growing dissatisfaction with Big Tech actors, Congress has proposed bills to deter anticompetitive behavior, "strengthen privacy, protect children online, curb misinformation, restrain targeted advertising and regulate artificial intelligence and cryptocurrencies." Cecelia Kang and David McCabe, *Efforts to Rein in Big Tech May Be Running Out of Time,* N.Y. Times, Jan. 20, 2022.

Big Tech's content moderation practices have generated criticism from all quarters. Some argue that the platforms must do more to eliminate harmful speech online. In other words, they argue for more "censorship." Others argue that Big Tech must do less restricting of conservative viewpoints online. In other words, they argue for less "censorship" by Big Tech. There is a growing consensus that Big Tech distorts public discourse, and at least 72% of the American public believes that Big Tech platforms, such as Google, Facebook, Instagram, Twitter, and YouTube, "actively censor political views that those companies find objectionable." Public Attitudes Toward Technology Companies, Pew Research Center (June 28, 2018), https://www.pewinternet.org/2018/06/28/public-attitudes-toward-technology-companies/.

Legislators have proposed a variety of bills to rein in Big Tech. Florida and Texas passed bills requiring platforms not to censor or ban speakers based on viewpoint. Both were enjoined as violating the First Amendment. NetChoice, LLC v. Moody, No. 4:21CV220-RH-MAF, 2021 WL 2690876 (N.D. Fla. June 30, 2021); NetChoice, LLC v. Paxton, No. 1:21-CV-840-RP, 2021 WL 5755120 (W.D. Tex. Dec. 1, 2021).

Under existing First Amendment principles, Big Tech platforms are not state actors, despite the high degree of power they wield in the marketplace of ideas. Instead, they are private speakers, which allows them to use "editorial discretion" to block or edit disfavored speech or promote favored speech on their platforms.

Some argue that these existing First Amendment principles must be revisited. In the following case, a lower court relied on a decision by the U.S. Court of Appeals for the Second Circuit in holding that President Donald Trump violated the First Amendment rights of some of his critics by blocking them from responding to his tweets on Twitter. By the time the case reached the Supreme Court, Trump was no longer in office and had been banned by Twitter for violating its terms of service. Therefore, the Supreme Court granted certiorari only in order to vacate the judgment and remand to the Second Circuit to dismiss the case as moot. Justice Thomas used his concurrence as an opportunity to consider whether the Court may be forced to revisit its First Amendment jurisprudence to address the growing power of Big Tech over public discourse.

Biden v. Knight First Amendment Inst. at Columbia Univ.

593 U.S. __ (2021)

Justice THOMAS, concurring. . . .

Donald Trump, then President of the United States, blocked several users from interacting with his Twitter account. They sued. The Second Circuit held that the comment threads were a "public forum" and that then-President Trump violated the First Amendment by using his control of the Twitter account to block the plaintiffs from accessing the comment threads. *Knight First Amdt. Inst. at Columbia Univ. v. Trump*, 928 F.3d 226 (2019). But Mr. Trump, it turned out, had only limited control of the account; Twitter has permanently removed the account from the platform.

Because of the change in Presidential administration, the Court correctly vacates the Second Circuit's decision. I write separately to note that this petition highlights the principal legal difficulty that surrounds digital platforms—namely, that applying old doctrines to new digital platforms is rarely straightforward. Respondents have a point, for example, that some aspects of Mr. Trump's account resemble a constitutionally protected public forum. But it seems rather odd to say that something is a government forum when a private company has unrestricted authority to do away with it.

The disparity between Twitter's control and Mr. Trump's control is stark, to say the least. Mr. Trump blocked several people from interacting with his messages. Twitter barred Mr. Trump not only from interacting with a few users, but removed him from the entire platform, thus barring *all* Twitter users from interacting with his messages. Under its terms of service, Twitter can remove any person from the platform—including the President of the United States—"at any time for any or no reason."

. . . Today's digital platforms provide avenues for historically unprecedented amounts of speech, including speech by government actors. Also unprecedented, however, is the concentrated control of so much speech in the hands of a few private parties. We will soon have no choice but to address how our legal doctrines apply to highly concentrated, privately owned information infrastructure such as digital platforms.

I

On the surface, some aspects of Mr. Trump's Twitter account resembled a public forum. A designated public forum is "property that the State has opened for expressive activity by part or all of the public." International Soc. for Krishna Consciousness, Inc. v. Lee, 505 U.S. 672, 678 (1992). Mr. Trump often used the account to speak in his official capacity. And, as a governmental official, he chose to make the comment threads on his account publicly accessible, allowing any Twitter user—other than those whom he blocked—to respond to his posts.

Yet, the Second Circuit's conclusion that Mr. Trump's Twitter account was a public forum is in tension with, among other things, our frequent description of public forums as "government-controlled spaces." Minnesota Voters Alliance v. Mansky, 585 U.S. ——, —— (2018); [ ]; [ ]. Any control Mr. Trump exercised over the account greatly paled in comparison to Twitter's authority, dictated in its terms of service, to remove the account "at any time for any or no reason." Twitter exercised its authority to do exactly that.

Because unbridled control of the account resided in the hands of a private party, First Amendment doctrine may not have applied to respondents' complaint of stifled speech. See Manhattan Community Access Corp. v. Halleck, 587 U.S.——, ——, 139 S.Ct. 1921, 1930 (2019) (a "private entity is not ordinarily constrained by the First Amendment"). Whether governmental use of private space implicates the First Amendment often depends on the government's control over that space. For example, a government agency that leases a conference room in a hotel to hold a public hearing about a proposed regulation cannot kick participants out of the hotel simply because they express concerns about the new regulation. [ ]. But government officials who informally gather with constituents in a hotel bar can ask the hotel to remove a pesky patron who elbows into the gathering to loudly voice his views. The difference is that the government controls the space in the first scenario, the hotel, in the latter. Where, as here, private parties control the avenues for speech, our law has typically addressed concerns about stifled speech through other legal doctrines, which may have a secondary effect on the application of the First Amendment.

[A.] If part of the problem is private, concentrated control over online content and platforms available to the public, then part of the solution may be found in doctrines that limit the right of a private company to exclude. Historically, at least two legal doctrines limited a company's right to exclude.

First, our legal system and its British predecessor have long subjected certain businesses, known as common carriers, to special regulations, including a general requirement to serve all comers. [Adam] Candeub, *Bargaining for Free Speech: Common Carriage, Network Neutrality, and Section 230,* 22 Yale J. L. & Tech. 391, 398–403 (2020); see also Burdick, *The Origin of the Peculiar Duties of Public Service Companies,* Pt. 1, 11 Colum. L. Rev. 514 (1911). Justifications for these regulations have varied. Some scholars have argued that common-carrier regulations are justified only when a carrier possesses substantial market power. Others have said that no substantial market power is needed so long as the company holds itself out as open to the public. [ ]. And this Court long ago suggested that regulations like those placed on common carriers may be justified, even for industries not historically recognized as common carriers, when "a business, by circumstances and its nature, . . . rise[s] from private to be of public concern." See German Alliance Ins. Co. v. Lewis, 233 U.S. 389, 411 (1914) (affirming state regulation of fire insurance rates). At that point, a company's "property is but its instrument, the means of rendering the service which has become of public interest."

This latter definition of course is hardly helpful, for most things can be described as "of public interest." But whatever may be said of other industries, there is clear historical precedent for regulating transportation and communications networks in a similar manner as traditional common carriers. Telegraphs, for example, because they "resemble[d] railroad companies and other common carriers," were "bound to serve all customers alike, without discrimination." [ ].

In exchange for regulating transportation and communication industries, governments—both State and Federal—have sometimes given common carriers special government favors. For example, governments have tied restrictions on a carrier's ability to reject clients to "immunity from certain types of suits" or to regulations that make it more difficult for other companies to compete with the carrier (such as franchise licenses). By giving these companies special privileges, governments place them into a category distinct from other companies and closer to some functions, like the postal service, that the State has traditionally undertaken.

Second, governments have limited a company's right to exclude when that company is a public accommodation. This concept—related to common-carrier law—applies to companies that hold themselves out to the public but do not "carry" freight, passengers, or communications. [ ]. It also applies regardless of the company's market power.

[B.]Internet platforms of course have their own First Amendment interests, but regulations that might affect speech are valid if they would have been permissible at the time of the founding. The long history in this country and in England of restricting the exclusion right of common carriers and places of public accommodation may save similar regulations today from triggering heightened scrutiny—especially where a restriction would not prohibit the company from speaking or force the company to endorse the speech. There is a fair argument that some digital platforms are sufficiently akin to common carriers or places of accommodation to be regulated in this manner.

In many ways, digital platforms that hold themselves out to the public resemble traditional common carriers. Though digital instead of physical, they are at bottom communications networks, and they "carry" information from one user to another. A traditional telephone company laid physical wires to create a network connecting people. Digital platforms lay information infrastructure that can be controlled in much the same way. And unlike newspapers, digital platforms hold themselves out as organizations that focus on distributing the speech of the broader public. Federal law dictates that companies cannot "be treated as the publisher or speaker" of information that they merely distribute. 110 Stat. 137, 47 U.S. C. § 230(c).

The analogy to common carriers is even clearer for digital platforms that have dominant market share. Similar to utilities, today's dominant digital platforms derive much of their value from network size. The Internet, of course, is a network. But these digital platforms are networks within that network. The Facebook suite of apps is valuable largely because 3 billion people use it. Google search—at 90% of the market share—is valuable relative to other search engines because more people use it, creating data that Google's algorithm uses to refine and improve search results. These network effects entrench these companies. Ordinarily, the astronomical profit margins of these platforms—last year, Google brought in $182.5 billion total, $40.3 billion in net income—would induce new entrants into the market. That these companies have no comparable competitors highlights that the industries may have substantial barriers to entry.

To be sure, much activity on the Internet derives value from network effects. But dominant digital platforms are different. Unlike decentralized digital spheres, such as the e-mail protocol, control of these networks is highly concentrated. Although both companies are public, one person controls Facebook (Mark Zuckerberg), and just two control Google (Larry Page and Sergey Brin). No small group of people controls e-mail.

Much like with a communications utility, this concentration gives some digital platforms enormous control over speech. When a user does not already know exactly where to find something on the Internet—and users rarely do—Google is the gatekeeper between that user and the speech of others 90% of the time. It can suppress content by deindexing or downlisting a search result or by steering users away from certain content by manually altering autocomplete results. [ ]. Facebook and Twitter can greatly narrow a person's information flow through similar means. And, as the distributor of the clear majority of e-books and about half of all physical books, Amazon can impose cataclysmic consequences on authors by, among other things, blocking a listing.

It changes nothing that these platforms are not the sole means for distributing speech or information. A person always could choose to avoid the toll bridge or train and instead swim the Charles River or hike the Oregon Trail. But in assessing whether a company exercises substantial market power, what matters is whether the alternatives are comparable. For many of today's digital platforms, nothing is.

If the analogy between common carriers and digital platforms is correct, then an answer may arise for dissatisfied platform users who would appreciate not being blocked: laws that restrict the platform's right to exclude. When a platform's unilateral control is reduced, a government official's account begins to better resemble a "government-controlled spac[e]." *Mansky*, 585 U.S., at ——, ; see also *Southeastern Promotions*, 420 U.S., at 547, 555, 95 S.Ct. 1239 (recognizing that a private space can become a public forum when leased to the government). Common-carrier regulations, although they directly restrain private companies, thus may have an indirect effect of subjecting government officials to suits that would not otherwise be cognizable under our public-forum jurisprudence.

This analysis may help explain the Second Circuit's intuition that part of Mr. Trump's Twitter account was a public forum. But that intuition has problems.

First, if market power is a predicate for common carriers (as some scholars suggest), nothing in the record evaluates Twitter's market power. Second, and more problematic, neither the Second Circuit nor respondents have identified any regulation that restricts Twitter from removing an account that would otherwise be a "government-controlled space."

Even if digital platforms are not close enough to common carriers, legislatures might still be able to treat digital platforms like places of public accommodation. Although definitions between jurisdictions vary, a company ordinarily is a place of public accommodation if it provides "lodging, food, entertainment, or other services to the public . . . in general." Black's Law Dictionary 20 (11th ed. 2019) (defining "public accommodation"); accord, 42 U.S. C. § 2000a(b)(3) (covering places of "entertainment"). Twitter and other digital platforms bear resemblance to that definition. This, too, may explain the Second Circuit's intuition. Courts are split, however, about whether federal accommodations laws apply to anything other than "physical" locations. *Compare, e.g.,* Doe v. Mutual of Omaha Ins. Co., 179 F.3d 557, 559 (C.A.7 1999) (Title III of the Americans with Disabilities Act (ADA) covers websites), with Parker v. Metropolitan Life Ins. Co., 121 F.3d 1006, 1010–1011 (C.A.6 1997) (en banc) (Title III of the ADA covers only physical places); see also 42 U.S. C. §§ 2000a(b)–(c) (discussing "physica[l] locat[ions]").

Once again, a doctrine, such as public accommodation, that reduces the power of a platform to unilaterally remove a government account might strengthen the argument that an account is truly government controlled and creates a public forum. But no party has identified any public accommodation restriction that applies here.

II.

The similarities between some digital platforms and common carriers or places of public accommodation may give legislators strong arguments for similarly regulating digital platforms. . . . That is especially true because the space constraints on digital platforms are practically nonexistent (unlike on cable companies), so a regulation restricting a digital platform's right to exclude might not appreciably impede the platform from speaking. Yet Congress does not appear to have passed these kinds of regulations. To the contrary, it has given digital platforms "immunity from certain types of suits," with respect to content they distribute, but it has not imposed corresponding responsibilities, like nondiscrimination, that would matter here.

None of this analysis means, however, that the First Amendment is irrelevant until a legislature imposes common carrier or public accommodation restrictions—only that the principal means for regulating digital platforms is through those methods. Some speech doctrines might still apply in limited circumstances, as this Court has recognized in the past.

For example, although a "private entity is not ordinarily constrained by the First Amendment," *Halleck,* 587 U.S., at ——, ——, 139 S.Ct., at 1930, it is if the government coerces or induces it to take action the government itself would not be permitted to do, such as censor expression of a lawful viewpoint. Consider government threats. "People do not lightly disregard public officers' thinly veiled threats to institute criminal proceedings against them if they do not come around."

Bantam Books, Inc. v. Sullivan, 372 U.S. 58 (1963). The government cannot accomplish through threats of adverse government action what the Constitution prohibits it from doing directly. See *ibid.*; Blum v. Yaretsky, 457 U.S. 991, 1004–1005 (1982). Under this doctrine, plaintiffs might have colorable claims against a digital platform if it took adverse action against them in response to government threats.

But no threat is alleged here. What threats would cause a private choice by a digital platform to "be deemed . . . that of the State" remains unclear. *Id.*, at 1004. And no party has sued Twitter. The question facing the courts below involved only whether a government actor violated the First Amendment by blocking another Twitter user. That issue turns, at least to some degree, on ownership and the right to exclude.

* * *

The Second Circuit feared that then-President Trump cut off speech by using the features that Twitter made available to him. But if the aim is to ensure that speech is not smothered, then the more glaring concern must perforce be the dominant digital platforms themselves. As Twitter made clear, the right to cut off speech lies most powerfully in the hands of private digital platforms. The extent to which that power matters for purposes of the First Amendment and the extent to which that power could lawfully be modified raise interesting and important questions. This petition, unfortunately, affords us no opportunity to confront them.

CHAPTER 9

TORT LAW AND THE FIRST AMENDMENT

TABLE OF CONTENTS

A. First Amendment Limitations on the Tort of Defamation
   1. Defamation of Public Officials
   2. Defamation of Public Figures: The Extension of the *Sullivan* Rules
   3. Defamation of Private Figures Involved in Matters of Public Concern
   4. Defamation of Private Figures Involved in Matters of Private Concern
   5. The Constitutional "Privilege" Protecting Opinion
   6. Should *New York Times v. Sullivan* Be Overruled?
B. First Amendment Limitations on Intentional Infliction of Emotional Distress
C. First Amendment Limitations on Imposing Liability for Publishing True Information
D. First Amendment Limitations on Imposing Liability Based on Newsgathering Methods

Tort law implicates First Amendment values when it attempts to impose liability on those who make or publish statements that allegedly harm the reputation, privacy, or emotional tranquility of others. This chapter first examines the interaction between First Amendment law and torts that impose liability for harms caused by publication, including the torts of defamation, intentional infliction of emotional distress, and public disclosure of private facts. The chapter then examines the interaction between the First Amendment and the so-called "newsgathering torts."

A. *FIRST AMENDMENT LIMITATIONS ON THE TORT OF DEFAMATION*

The term *defamation* encompasses the twin torts of libel and slander. As a rule of thumb, defamation in written or any other relatively permanent form is libel; defamation in spoken or other "impermanent" form is slander. Libel and slander are civil actions, allowing private litigants who have been defamed to recover monetary damages for harm to their reputations. Defamation, therefore, is concerned with policing the boundaries of free expression and forcing speakers to pay for harm caused by their speech. For obvious reasons, the press is a common target of defamation actions, and fear of tort liability shapes many editorial decisions. But individual speakers also are subject to defamation actions, and social media, along with the unpopularity of the press, seem to have made defamation actions more common.

Until 1964, the tort of defamation was purely a matter of state law: defamatory speech, like fighting words and obscenity, was deemed to be outside the scope of First Amendment protection. As in 1964, the common law of most states today requires plaintiffs seeking recovery for defamation to prove the existence of (1) a defamatory communication by the defendant, (2) "of and concerning" the plaintiff, and (3) publication by the defendant to at least one third party. Note that the common law typically has not required a libel plaintiff to prove actual harm to his or her reputation,[1] but instead allows juries to award "presumed damages" based on the nature of the defamatory statement made by the defendant. This unusual feature of the common law tort is justified by the difficulty of proving harm to reputation.

Reputation, the interest protected by defamation, is a sociological or relational construct. In other words, one's reputation is defined by how one is perceived by others. Therefore, the tort defines a defamatory communication as one that "tends to harm" an individual's reputation in the eyes of his or her community or, increasingly, reasonable persons who receive it. In order to be defamatory, a communication must go beyond mere name-calling and actually call into question a plaintiff's moral fiber. Hence, it is ordinarily defamatory to call an individual an adulterer, a domestic abuser, or a murderer, but it is not defamatory to call him a jerk or a neat freak or even to state falsely that he has died.

Because this is a First Amendment casebook rather than a Torts casebook, we will not dwell on the intricacies of tort law, but instead will focus on the Supreme Court's "constitutionalization" of defamation law since 1964. We also will not focus on statutory alterations to the tort, such as the federal statutory immunity provided to tech platforms for defamatory communications made by their users, or the various state statutes that allow defendants to seek dismissal of frivolous defamation actions at early stages of litigation.

You should be aware, nonetheless, that defendants often are able to defeat defamation cases based on tort law or statutes alone, without reference to the First Amendment. Even before the Supreme Court began to constitutionalize defamation law, tort law had developed a variety of privileges designed to protect freedom of expression. For example, although one who repeats the defamatory statement of another will ordinarily be liable as if he had originated it (this is known as the "republication rule"), the common law recognizes a privilege that protects a person

---

1. Slander plaintiffs typically must be able to put an actual dollar figure on their losses unless they show that the slander falls into one of four categories known as slander per se. The four categories concern allegations of lack of chastity, unfitness for one's business or profession, having contracted a loathsome disease, and commission of a crime.

who repeats or "republishes" a defamatory statement made by someone else in the course of an official government proceeding. Even today, the media often rely on this tort privilege—the "fair and accurate report privilege"—to avoid liability for defamation when reporting on governmental affairs. Moreover, by 1964, tort law provided that a defendant could defend against a defamation action by establishing the truth of his publication. In fact, the defendant did not ordinarily have to prove that each and every fact in his publication was literally true. So long as the defendant could establish "substantial truth"—that the gist or sting of the slightly inaccurate statement was the same as the true facts—the defendant could evade defamation liability. In considering the Supreme Court's seminal decision in *New York Times v. Sullivan,* you should consider why the Supreme Court determined that tort law did not do enough to protect press freedom. You should also consider *Sullivan* in the context of the civil rights movement and consider what would have been the fate of that movement if the half-million-dollar defamation verdict imposed against the New York Times by the Alabama courts had been allowed to survive.

1. Defamation of Public Officials

New York Times Co. v. Sullivan

376 U.S. 254 (1964)

Justice BRENNAN delivered the opinion of the Court.

We are required in this case to determine for the first time the extent to which the constitutional protections for speech and press limit a State's power to award damages in a libel action brought by a public official against critics of his official conduct. . . .

[L.B. Sullivan, a city commissioner in Montgomery, Alabama, sued the New York Times Company and four Black clergymen for libel based on a full-page advertisement published in the New York Times in 1960. The ad asked readers to help fund the civil rights movement and decried an "unprecedented wave of terror" in the South. The ad listed the names of 64 persons, including the clergymen, who purportedly endorsed its content. Sullivan's libel claim focused on two of the ad's ten paragraphs:]

> "In Montgomery, Alabama, after students sang 'My Country, 'Tis of Thee' on the State Capitol steps, their leaders were expelled from school, and truckloads of police armed with shotguns and tear-gas ringed the Alabama State College Campus. When the entire student body protested to state authorities by refusing to re-register, their dining hall was padlocked in an attempt to starve them into submission.". . .
>
> "Again and again the Southern violators have answered Dr. King's peaceful protests with intimidation and violence. They have bombed his home almost killing his wife and child. They have assaulted his person. They have arrested him seven times—for 'speeding,' 'loitering' and similar 'offenses.' And now they have charged him with 'perjury'—a felony under which they could imprison him for ten years. . . ."

[Sullivan contended that the ad accused him of overseeing a campaign of violence in his capacity as supervisor of the police. His witnesses testified that they understood the ad to refer to him, and he showed that he had not participated in the events attributed to the police. He did not put on evidence establishing pecuniary losses resulting from the libel, but instead sought recovery of presumed damages. The Times conceded that the ad contained inaccuracies: the students sang the National Anthem rather than "My Country, 'Tis of Thee"; nine students were expelled for demanding service at a lunch counter in the county courthouse, not for leading a demonstration; the police never literally "ringed" the campus; and Dr. King had been arrested four times, not seven. The trial judge instructed the jury that the statements in the ad were libelous per se (that is, libelous on their face) and not privileged. He also instructed that the jury could impose liability if it found petitioners had published the statements "of and concerning" Sullivan. The judge also told jury members they could award presumed and punitive damages even if no actual damages were shown and punitive damages could be awarded if they found "evidence of actual malice or malice in fact." The jury returned a verdict of $500,000, and the judge did not require the jury to designate which portion, if any, of the award constituted punitive damages. The Supreme Court of Alabama affirmed.]

I

We may dispose at the outset of two grounds asserted to insulate the judgment of the Alabama courts from constitutional scrutiny. The first is the proposition relied on by the State Supreme Court—that "The Fourteenth Amendment is directed against State action and not private action." That proposition has no application to this case. Although this is a civil lawsuit between private parties, the Alabama courts have applied a state rule of law which petitioners claim to impose invalid restrictions on their constitutional freedoms of speech and press. . . . The second contention is that the constitutional guarantees of freedom of speech and of the press are inapplicable here, at least so far as the Times is concerned, because the allegedly libelous statements were published as part of a paid, "commercial" advertisement. . . . The publication here was not a "commercial" advertisement. . . . It communicated information, expressed opinion, recited grievances, protested claimed abuses, and sought financial support on behalf of a movement whose existence and objectives are matters of the highest public interest and concern. . . . Any other conclusion would discourage newspapers from carrying "editorial advertisements" of this type, and so might shut off an important outlet for the promulgation of information and ideas by persons who do not themselves have access to publishing facilities—who wish to exercise their freedom of speech even though they are not members of the press. . . .

II . . .

The question before us is whether [Alabama libel law], as applied to an action brought by a public official against critics of his official conduct, abridges the freedom of speech and of the press that is guaranteed by the First and Fourteenth Amendments.

Respondent relies heavily, as did the Alabama courts, on statements of this Court to the effect that the Constitution does not protect libelous publications. Those statements do not foreclose our inquiry here. None of the cases sustained the use of libel laws to impose sanctions upon expression critical of the official conduct of public officials. . . . Like insurrection, contempt, advocacy of unlawful acts, breach of the peace, obscenity, solicitation of legal business, and the various other formulae for the repression of expression that have been challenged in this Court, libel can claim no talismanic immunity from constitutional limitations. It must be measured by standards that satisfy the First Amendment. . . .

[W]e consider this case against the background of a profound national commitment to the principle that debate on public issues should be uninhibited, robust, and wide-open, and that it may well include vehement, caustic, and sometimes unpleasantly sharp attacks on government and public officials. *See* Terminiello v. Chicago, 337 U.S. 1, 4. . . . The present advertisement, as an expression of grievance and protest on one of the major public issues of our time, would seem clearly to qualify for the constitutional protection. The question is whether it forfeits that protection by the falsity of some of its factual statements and by its alleged defamation of respondent. Authoritative interpretations of the First Amendment guarantees have consistently refused to recognize an exception for any test of truth—whether administered by judges, juries, or administrative officials—and especially one that puts the burden of proving truth on the speaker. The constitutional protection does not turn upon "the truth, popularity, or social utility of the ideas and beliefs which are offered." N.A.A.C.P. v. Button, 371 U.S. 415, 445. As Madison said, "Some degree of abuse is inseparable from the proper use of every thing; and in no instance is this more true than in that of the press." 4 Elliot's Debates on the Federal Constitution (1876), p. 571. . . .

[E]rroneous statement is inevitable in free debate, and . . . it must be protected if the freedoms of expression are to have the "breathing space" that they "need . . . to survive. . . . [As the Circuit Court of Appeals for the District of Columbia wrote in Sweeney v. Patterson, 128 F.2d 457, 458 (D.C. Cir.), *cert. denied*, 317 U.S. 67 (1942)]:

> "Cases which impose liability for erroneous reports of the political conduct of officials reflect the obsolete doctrine that the governed must not criticize their governors. . . . The interest of the public here outweighs the interest of appellant or any other individual. The protection of the public requires not merely discussion, but information. Political conduct and views which some respectable people approve, and others condemn, are constantly imputed to Congressmen. Errors of fact, particularly in regard to a man's mental states and processes, are inevitable. . . . Whatever is added to the field of libel is taken from the field of free debate."

Injury to official reputation affords no more warrant for repressing speech that would otherwise be free than does factual error. Where judicial officers are involved, this Court has held that concern for the dignity and reputation of the courts does not justify the punishment as criminal contempt of criticism of the judge or his decision. Bridges v. California, 314 U.S. 252. This is true even though the utterance contains "half-truths" and "misinformation." Such repression can be justified, if at all, only by a clear and present danger of the obstruction of justice. If judges are to be treated as "men of fortitude, able to thrive in a hardy climate," surely the same must be true of other government officials, such as elected city commissioners. Criticism of their official conduct does not lose its constitutional protection merely because it is effective criticism and hence diminishes their official reputations.

If neither factual error nor defamatory content suffices to remove the constitutional shield from criticism of official conduct, the combination of the two elements is no less inadequate. This is the lesson to be drawn from the great controversy over the Sedition Act of 1798, which first crystallized a national awareness of the central meaning of the First Amendment. . . .

Although the Sedition Act was never tested in this Court, the attack upon its validity has carried the day in the court of history. Fines levied in its prosecution were repaid by Act of Congress on the ground that it was unconstitutional. . . . The invalidity of the Act has also been assumed by Justices of this Court. These views reflect a broad consensus that the Act, because of the restraint it imposed upon criticism of government and public officials, was inconsistent with the First Amendment.

. . . What a State may not constitutionally bring about by means of a criminal statute is likewise beyond the reach of its civil law of libel. The fear of damage awards under a rule such as that invoked by the Alabama courts here may be markedly more inhibiting than the fear of prosecution under a criminal statute. Alabama, for example, has a criminal libel law which subjects to prosecution "any person who speaks, writes, or prints of and concerning another any accusation falsely and maliciously importing the commission by such person of a felony, or any other indictable offense involving moral turpitude," and which allows as punishment upon conviction a fine not exceeding $500 and a prison sentence of six months. Presumably a person charged with violation of this statute enjoys ordinary criminal-law safeguards such as the requirements of an indictment and of proof beyond a reasonable doubt. These safeguards are not available to the defendant in a civil action. The judgment awarded in this case—without the need for any proof of actual pecuniary loss—was one thousand times greater than the maximum fine provided by the Alabama criminal statute, and one hundred times greater than that provided by the Sedition Act. And since there is no double-jeopardy limitation applicable to civil lawsuits, this is not the only judgment that may be awarded against petitioners for the same publication.[18] Whether or not a newspaper can survive a succession of such judgments, the pall of fear and timidity imposed upon those who would give voice to public criticism is an atmosphere in which the First Amendment freedoms cannot survive. . . .

The state rule of law is not saved by its allowance of the defense of truth. . . . Allowance of the defense of truth, with the burden of proving it on the defendant,

---

18. The Times states that four other libel suits based on the advertisement have been filed against it by others who have served as Montgomery City Commissioners and by the Governor of Alabama; that another $500,000 verdict has been awarded in the only one of these cases that has yet gone to trial; and that the damages sought in the other three total $2,000,000.

does not mean that only false speech will be deterred. Even courts accepting this defense as an adequate safeguard have recognized the difficulties of adducing legal proofs that the alleged libel was true in all its factual particulars. Under such a rule, would-be critics of official conduct may be deterred from voicing their criticism, even though it is believed to be true and even though it is in fact true, because of doubt whether it can be proved in court or fear of the expense of having to do so. They tend to make only statements which "steer far wider of the unlawful zone." Speiser v. Randall, 357 U.S. at 526. The rule thus dampens the vigor and limits the variety of public debate. It is inconsistent with the First and Fourteenth Amendments.

The constitutional guarantees require, we think, a federal rule that prohibits a public official from recovering damages for a defamatory falsehood relating to his official conduct unless he proves that the statement was made with "actual malice"—that is, with knowledge that it was false or with reckless disregard of whether it was false or not. An oft-cited statement of a like rule, which has been adopted by a number of state courts, is found in the Kansas case of Coleman v. MacLennan, 78 Kan. 711, 98 P. 281 (1908). . . .

Such a privilege for criticism of official conduct is appropriately analogous to the protection accorded a public official when *he* is sued for libel by a private citizen. In Barr v. Matteo, 360 U.S. 564, 575, this Court held the utterance of a federal official to be absolutely privileged if made "within the outer perimeter" of his duties. The States accord the same immunity to statements of their highest officers, although some differentiate their lesser officials and qualify the privilege they enjoy. But all hold that all officials are protected unless actual malice can be proved. The reason for the official privilege is said to be that the threat of damage suits would otherwise "inhibit the fearless, vigorous, and effective administration of policies of government" and "dampen the ardor of all but the most resolute, or the most irresponsible, in the unflinching discharge of their duties." Analogous considerations support the privilege for the citizen-critic of government. It is as much his duty to criticize as it is the official's duty to administer. As Madison said, "the censorial power is in the people over the Government, and not in the Government over the people." It would give public servants an unjustified preference over the public they serve, if critics of official conduct did not have a fair equivalent of the immunity granted to the officials themselves.

We conclude that such a privilege is required by the First and Fourteenth Amendments.

III

We hold today that the Constitution delimits a State's power to award damages for libel in actions brought by public officials against critics of their official conduct. Since this is such an action, the rule requiring proof of actual malice is applicable. While Alabama law apparently requires proof of actual malice for an award of punitive damages, where general damages are concerned malice is "presumed." Such a presumption is inconsistent with the federal rule. . . . Since the trial judge did not instruct the jury to differentiate between general and punitive damages, it may be that the verdict was wholly an award of one or the other. But it is impossible to know, in view of the general verdict returned. Because of this uncertainty, the judgment must be reversed and the case remanded.

Since respondent may seek a new trial, we deem that considerations of effective judicial administration require us to review the evidence in the present record to determine whether it could constitutionally support a judgment for respondent. This Court's duty is not limited to the elaboration of constitutional principles; we must also in proper cases review the evidence to make certain that those principles have been constitutionally applied. This is such a case, particularly since the question is one of alleged trespass across "the line between speech unconditionally guaranteed and speech which may legitimately be regulated." *Speiser.* In cases where that line must be drawn, the rule is that we "examine for ourselves the statements in issue and the circumstances under which they were made to see . . . whether they are of a character which the principles of the First Amendment, as adopted by the Due Process Clause of the Fourteenth Amendment, protect." *Pennekamp v. Florida,* 328 U.S. 331, 335. We must "make an independent examination of the whole record," so as to assure ourselves that the judgment does not constitute a forbidden intrusion on the field of free expression.

Applying these standards, we consider that the proof presented to show actual malice lacks the convincing clarity which the constitutional standard demands, and hence that it would not constitutionally sustain the judgment for respondent under the proper rule of law. The case of the individual petitioners requires little discussion. Even assuming that they could constitutionally be found to have authorized the use of their names on the advertisement, there was no evidence whatever that they were aware of any erroneous statements or were in any way reckless in that regard. The judgment against them is thus without constitutional support.

As to the Times, we similarly conclude that the facts do not support a finding of actual malice. . . . The Times' failure to retract upon respondent's demand, although it later retracted upon the demand of Governor Patterson, is . . . not adequate evidence of malice for constitutional purposes. Whether or not a failure to retract may ever constitute such evidence, there are two reasons why it does not here. *First,* the letter written by the Times reflected a reasonable doubt on its part as to whether the advertisement could reasonably be taken to refer to respondent at all. *Second,* it was not a final refusal, since it asked for an explanation on this point—a request that respondent chose to ignore. . . . It may be doubted that a failure to retract which is not itself evidence of malice can retroactively become such by virtue of a retraction subsequently made to another party. But in any event that did not happen here, since the explanation given by the Times' Secretary for the distinction drawn between respondent and the Governor was a reasonable one, the good faith of which was not impeached.

Finally, there is evidence that the Times published the advertisement without checking its accuracy against the news stories in the Times' own files. The mere presence of the stories in the files does not, of course, establish that the Times "knew" the advertisement was false, since the state of mind required for actual malice would have to be brought home to the persons in the Times' organization having responsibility for the publication of the advertisement. With respect to the failure of those persons to make the check, the record shows that they relied upon their knowledge of the good reputation of many of those whose names were listed as sponsors of the advertisement, and upon the letter from A. Philip Randolph, known to them as a responsible individual, certifying that the use of the names was authorized. . . .

We also think the evidence was constitutionally defective in another respect: it was incapable of supporting the jury's finding that the allegedly libelous statements were made "of and concerning" respondent. Respondent relies on the words of the advertisement and the testimony of six witnesses to establish a connection between it and himself. . . . There was no reference to respondent in the advertisement, either by name or official position. . . . [Moreover, the statements about the police] were false only in that the police had been "deployed near" the campus but had not actually "ringed" it and had not gone there in connection with the State Capitol demonstration, and in that Dr. King had been arrested only four times [rather than seven]. The ruling that these discrepancies between what was true and what was asserted were sufficient to injure respondent's reputation may itself raise constitutional problems, but we need not consider them here. Although the statements may be taken as referring to the police, they did not on their face make even an oblique reference to respondent as an individual. Support for the asserted reference must, therefore, be sought in the testimony of respondent's witnesses. But none of them suggested any basis for the belief that respondent himself was attacked in the advertisement beyond the bare fact that he was in overall charge of the Police Department and thus bore official responsibility for police conduct. . . . [Thus, proof that the ad pertained to Sullivan relied]"on the bare fact of respondent's official position."

This proposition has disquieting implications for criticism of governmental conduct. For good reason, "no court of last resort in this country has ever held, or even suggested, that prosecutions for libel on government have any place in the American system of jurisprudence." . . . The present proposition would sidestep this obstacle by transmuting criticism of government, however impersonal it may seem on its face, into personal criticism, and hence potential libel, of the officials of whom the government is composed. There is no legal alchemy by which a State may thus create the cause of action that would otherwise be denied for a publication which, as respondent himself said of the advertisement, "reflects not only on me but on the other Commissioners and the community." Raising as it does the possibility that a good-faith critic of government will be penalized for his criticism, the proposition relied on by the Alabama courts strikes at the very center of the constitutionally protected area of free expression. We hold that such a proposition may not constitutionally be utilized to establish that an otherwise impersonal attack on governmental operations was a libel of an official responsible for those operations. Since it was relied on exclusively here, and there was no other evidence to connect the statements with respondent, the evidence was constitutionally insufficient to support a finding that the statements referred to respondent.

The judgment of the Supreme Court of Alabama is reversed and the case is remanded to that court for further proceedings not inconsistent with this opinion.

Justice Black, with whom Justice Douglas joins, concurring.

. . . I vote to reverse exclusively on the ground that the Times and the individual defendants had an absolute, unconditional constitutional right to publish in the Times advertisement their criticisms of the Montgomery agencies and officials. . . .

The half-million-dollar verdict does give dramatic proof, however, that state libel laws threaten the very existence of an American press virile enough to publish unpopular views on public affairs and bold enough to criticize the conduct of public officials. The factual background of this case emphasizes the imminence and enormity of that threat. . . . [B]riefs before us show that in Alabama there are now pending eleven libel suits by local and state officials against the Times seeking $5,600,000, and five such suits against the Columbia Broadcasting System seeking $1,700,000. Moreover, this technique for harassing and punishing a free press—now that it has been shown to be possible—is by no means limited to cases with racial overtones; it can be used in other fields where public feelings may make local as well as out-of-state newspapers easy prey for libel verdict seekers. . . .

Justice GOLDBERG, with whom Justice DOUGLAS joins, concurring in the result.

. . . In my view, the First and Fourteenth Amendments to the Constitution afford to the citizen and to the press an absolute, unconditional privilege to criticize official conduct despite the harm which may flow from excesses and abuses. . . .

NOTES AND QUESTIONS

1. *The effect of presumed damages.* The New York Times had a very small circulation in Alabama in 1960. Fewer than 400 copies of the edition with the allegedly libelous advertisement circulated in Alabama, only 35 of which were circulated in Montgomery County. Should this have been relevant to Sullivan's damages? What damages do you think Sullivan actually suffered? Would it have been possible to provide adequate breathing room for First Amendment interests simply by capping the amount of damages recoverable in libel actions or by abolishing the doctrine of presumed damages?
2. *Does false speech have constitutional value?* In a footnote, the majority opinion cited John Stuart Mill's *On Liberty* for the proposition that "[e]ven a false statement may be deemed to make a valuable contribution to public debate, since it brings about 'the clearer perception and livelier impression of truth, produced by its collision with error.'" What other rationales justify protecting false speech? Why does the Court refuse to give absolute protection to false speech about public officials? In Garrison v. Louisiana, 379 U.S. 64 (1964), the Court held that the actual malice standard also applied when the State attempted to punish libel as a criminal offense. There, the Court stated that "the use of the known lie as a tool is at once at odds with the premises of democratic government and with the orderly manner in which economic, social, or political change is to be effected."
3. *Shifting the burden of proof of falsity to plaintifffs?* Does the Court's holding—that plaintiffs who are public officials must prove actual malice—implicitly shift the burden of proof on falsity to the plaintiff? Many lower courts believed so, and in Philadelphia Newspapers, Inc. v. Hepps, 475 U.S. 767 (1986), the Supreme Court made it clear that the plaintiff must indeed prove falsity as part of a prima facie case of defamation in all cases involving matters of public concern.
4. *Constitutionalizing the identification element?* Was the Court's determination that the advertisement was not "of and concerning" Sullivan an intrusion into the fact-finding function of the jury? Why or why not? Tort law

traditionally assigns the jury the job of determining whether the allegedly defamatory statement made by the defendant actually referred to the plaintiff. The identification element is not an obstacle when the defendant identifies the plaintiff by name, but sometimes the defendant identifies the plaintiff only by physical or other personal characteristics, and the plaintiff must show that some audience members would reasonably understand the defamatory statement to refer to the plaintiff. Plaintiffs may also face problems in proving the identification element when the defendant makes a defamatory statement about a group of which the plaintiff is a part. A defamatory statement about a small group may defame every member of that group, but a defamatory statement about a large group will not be deemed to "identify" each member of that group, because the defamatory "sting" will be too diffuse to attach to each member as an individual.

5. *Hate speech and group libel.* Although hate speech is not a constitutional category, some states have statutes that make it a crime to defame a class of people because of their race or religion. Although the Supreme Court, 5-4, upheld the constitutionality of a "group libel" statute in Beauharnais v. Illinois, 343 U.S. 250 (1952), subsequent decisions such as R.A.V. v. City of St. Paul, 505 U.S. 377 (1992) make the constitutionality of such statutes highly suspect.
6. *State action.* In an omitted portion of the opinion, the Court stated: "[T]he Alabama courts have applied a state rule of law which petitioners claim to impose invalid restrictions on their constitutional freedoms of speech and press. It matters not that that law has been applied in a civil action and that it is common law only, though supplemented by statute. The test is not the form in which state power has been applied but, whatever the form, whether such power has in fact been exercised." Where (or what) was the state action here?
7. *Procedural protection for defamation defendants (convincing clarity /independent review).* Although the substantive protections of *Sullivan*, particularly the actual malice rule, are obviously important, the procedural protections are critical as well. The requirement that the plaintiff prove actual malice with convincing clarity (rather than the usual preponderance) tilts the scales in favor of defendants. At least in cases under the Federal Rules of Civil Procedure, the convincing clarity requirement means that a judge must determine at summary judgment "whether the evidence in the record could support a reasonable jury finding either that the plaintiff has shown actual malice by clear and convincing evidence or that the plaintiff has not." Anderson v. Liberty Lobby, Inc., 477 U.S. 242 (1986). Moreover, the requirement that appellate courts "independently review the record as a whole" to ensure that actual malice has been proved with convincing clarity further tilts the scale toward defendants. This requirement stems from Bose Corp. v. Consumers Union, 466 U.S. 485 (1984). The Supreme Court explained that the requirement that appellate courts independently review the record to support the finding of actual malice "reflects a deeply held conviction that judges—and particularly members

of this Court—must exercise such review in order to preserve the precious liberties established and ordained by the Constitution. The question whether the evidence in the record in a defamation case is of the convincing clarity required to strip the utterance of First Amendment protection is not merely a question for the trier of fact. Judges, as expositors of the Constitution, must independently decide whether the evidence in the record is sufficient to cross the constitutional threshold that bars the entry of any judgment that is not supported by clear and convincing proof of 'actual malice.'"

8. *Proving actual malice.* In order for a plaintiff to establish actual malice, the Supreme Court has said that "[t]here must be sufficient evidence to permit the conclusion that the defendant in fact entertained serious doubts as to the truth of his publication." St. Amant v. Thompson, 390 U.S. 727 (1968). In other words, actual malice focuses on the mental state of the defendant at the time of publication, especially his subjective awareness of falsity. Actual malice may be found, for example, where the defendant invents a story, bases it on "an unverified anonymous telephone call," publishes information "so inherently improbable that only a reckless man would have put [it] in circulation," or where the defendant publishes despite "obvious reasons to doubt the veracity of [an] informant or the accuracy of his reports." On the other hand, the Supreme Court has held that actual malice may not be based merely on evidence that the defendant failed to investigate fully before publication; however, "the purposeful avoidance of the truth is in a different category." Harte-Hanks Communs, Inc. v. Connaughton, 491 U.S. 657 (1989). In addition, a plaintiff cannot show actual malice by showing only that the defendant acted out of bad motive, ill will, or spite (that is, common law malice), though these can be relevant to show knowledge or reckless disregard for falsity when coupled with other evidence. By the same token, the defendant's lack of objectivity, the adoption of a sarcastic tone, the reliance on a single source, or the misinterpretation of available data will not, by themselves, be enough to establish actual malice. Time, Inc. v. Pape, 401 U.S. 279 (1971). Finally, the plaintiff may not show actual malice by establishing that the defendant knew of a mere technical falsehood in the publication. Thus, even a showing that a reporter deliberately altered a direct quotation by the plaintiff is not a showing of actual malice, unless the material meaning is changed in a way that is defamatory. Masson v. New Yorker Magazine, 501 U.S. 496 (1991). As these examples make clear, mere professional negligence or neglect of good journalistic practices does not equate with actual malice. In fact, the Supreme Court has said that actual malice cannot be shown by proof of even "highly unreasonable conduct constituting an extreme departure from the standards of investigation and reporting ordinarily adhered to by responsible publishers." Curtis Publg. Co. v. Butts, 388 U.S. 130 (1967).
9. *Who is a public official?* After *Sullivan*, a plaintiff who is determined to be a public official will rarely be able to surmount the constitutional obstacles necessary to prevail in a libel suit. Therefore, the determination

of whether a plaintiff is a public official is a critical one. The Supreme Court has defined the category of public officials to apply "at the very least to those among the hierarchy of government employees who have, or appear to the public to have, substantial responsibility for or control over the conduct of governmental affairs." Rosenblatt v. Baer, 383 U.S. 75 (1966). A person will be deemed a public official "[w]here [that person's] position in government has such apparent importance that the public has an independent interest in the qualifications and performance of the person who holds it, beyond the general public interest in the qualifications and performance of all government employees." A low-level government employee does not become a public official simply because a news story about him attracts public attention; he must be a public official by virtue of his position of potential influence over governmental policy. Is a police officer a public official? (Typically yes.) What about a fireman or a school principal? (Sometimes yes and sometimes no.)

2. *Defamation of Public Figures: The Extension of the* Sullivan *Rules*

In 1967 the Supreme Court extended *Sullivan*'s protections to cases involving public figures suing for libel. Curtis Publishing Co. v. Butts and Associated Press v. Walker, decided together, 388 U.S. 130 (1967), both involved plaintiffs who had gained prominence in their selected spheres of influence. Wally Butts was the athletic director and former coach of the University of Georgia. In fact, it was this prominent position that made the ensuing defamatory newspaper story about him newsworthy, for the story stated that he had "fixed" a football game by telling a rival coach his secret plays. Walker, on the other hand, was prominent partly by virtue of his former position as an Army general, but more pertinently by virtue of his political activism. Walker resigned from the military to protest federal intervention in the South to support civil rights. Walker sued for defamation after a news wire report stated that he had instigated and participated in a riot against the federal marshals supporting the registration of Black student James Meredith at the University of Mississippi. The question before the Supreme Court was whether the *Sullivan* actual malice rule should apply to Butts and Walker. In a fractured opinion, a majority of the Court said yes.

Chief Justice Warren, joined by four other justices, justified application of the actual malice rule to public figures by pointing to the significant public interest in both of the plaintiffs. Warren further explained that "what we have commonly considered to be the private sector" has become increasingly powerful and has even taken over some governmental functions. This shift of power to the private sector means that "many who do not hold public office at the moment are nevertheless intimately involved in the resolution of important public questions or, by reason of their fame, shape events in areas of concern to society at large."

The political power and influence wielded by public figures gives the public a "legitimate and substantial interest in the[ir] conduct." This alone might justify treating them like public officials for purposes of defamation law. Yet the Court also reasoned that it was fair to subject public figures to the actual malice rule because public figures, like public officials, have "ready access" to the media "both to influence policy and to counter criticism of their views and activities." In other words, public figures have tools other than tort law to deal with defamatory falsehoods. Moreover, public scrutiny of public figures may be even more important than public scrutiny of public officials, precisely because public figures are not subject to the political process. Thus, the proper balance between protecting "uninhibited debate" about public figures and safeguarding an individual's reputation is properly struck by adoption of the actual malice rule.

The Court did more than extend the actual malice rule to public figures; it also extended the other procedural protections of press freedom developed in *Sullivan.* Public figures, like public officials, must both prove actual malice by clear and convincing evidence and prove falsity. And courts must independently review cases in which public figures are involved to ensure the plaintiff has adduced adequate evidence of actual malice to justify a judgment in his or her favor. As we shall see in the following sections, application of these procedural safeguards has dramatically reduced defamation recoveries for a broad class of plaintiffs.

3. *Defamation of Private Figures Involved in Matters of Public Concern*

Once the *Sullivan* rules extended to public-figure plaintiffs, there was increasing pressure to extend them to all cases involving matters of public concern. In other words, there was pressure to shift emphasis from the status of the plaintiff to the subject matter discussed in the allegedly defamatory publication. Although the Supreme Court in Rosenbloom v. Metromedia, Inc., 403 U.S. 29 (1971), initially appeared to endorse this approach, it firmly rejected it in *Gertz,* below. As you read *Gertz,* pay attention to the passages defining the different types of public figures and explaining why public figures and private figures deserve different legal treatment. Private figures, like the plaintiff in *Gertz,* are defined by *not* being public figures.

Gertz v. Robert Welch, Inc.

418 U.S. 323 (1974)

Justice Powell delivered the opinion of the Court.

. . . [Petitioner Elmer Gertz represented the Nelson family in civil litigation against Nuccio, a Chicago policeman convicted of murdering their son.]

Respondent publishes American Opinion, a monthly outlet for the views of the John Birch Society. . . . [T]he managing editor of American Opinion commissioned an article on the murder trial of Officer Nuccio. . . . In March 1969 respondent published the resulting article under the title "FRAME-UP: Richard Nuccio And The War On Police." The article purports to demonstrate that [Nuccio's] prosecution was part of the Communist campaign against the police.

. . . Notwithstanding petitioner's remote connection with the prosecution of Nuccio, respondent's magazine portrayed him as an architect of the "frame-up." According to the article, the police file on petitioner took "a big, Irish cop to lift."

The article stated that petitioner had been an official of the "Marxist League for Industrial Democracy, originally known as the Intercollegiate Socialist Society, which has advocated the violent seizure of our government." It labeled Gertz a "Leninist" and a "Communist-fronter." . . .

The implication that petitioner had a criminal record was false. . . . There was also no basis for the charge that petitioner was a "Leninist" or a "Communist-fronter." And he had never been a member of the "Marxist League for Industrial Democracy" or the "Intercollegiate Socialist Society."

The managing editor of American Opinion made no effort to verify or substantiate the charges against petitioner. Instead, he appended an editorial introduction stating that the author had "conducted extensive research into the Richard Nuccio Case." . . .

Petitioner filed a diversity action for libel. [Following a jury verdict for petitioner of $50,000, the district court entered a judgment notwithstanding the verdict on the ground that *Sullivan*'s actual malice rule applied to "discussion of any public issue," and the Seventh Circuit affirmed.]

The principal issue in this case is whether a newspaper or broadcaster that publishes defamatory falsehoods about an individual who is neither a public official nor a public figure may claim a constitutional privilege against liability for the injury inflicted by those statements. . . .

We begin with the common ground. Under the First Amendment there is no such thing as a false idea. However pernicious an opinion may seem, we depend for its correction not on the conscience of judges and juries but on the competition of other ideas. But there is no constitutional value in false statements of fact. Neither the intentional lie nor the careless error materially advances society's interest in "uninhibited, robust, and wide-open" debate on public issues. They belong to that category of utterances which "are no essential part of any exposition of ideas, and are of such slight social value as a step to truth that any benefit that may be derived from them is clearly outweighed by the social interest in order and morality." *Chaplinsky v. New Hampshire*, [] . . .

Although the erroneous statement of fact is not worthy of constitutional protection, it is nevertheless inevitable in free debate. . . . Our decisions recognize that a rule of strict liability that compels a publisher or broadcaster to guarantee the accuracy of his factual assertions may lead to intolerable self-censorship. . . .

The need to avoid self-censorship by the news media is, however, not the only societal value at issue. If it were, this Court would have embraced long ago the view that publishers and broadcasters enjoy an unconditional and indefeasible immunity from liability for defamation. Such a rule would, indeed, obviate the fear that the prospect of civil liability for injurious falsehood might dissuade a timorous press from the effective exercise of First Amendment freedoms. Yet absolute protection for the communications media requires a total sacrifice of the competing value served by the law of defamation.

The legitimate state interest underlying the law of libel is the compensation of individuals for the harm inflicted on them by defamatory falsehood. We would not lightly require the State to abandon this purpose, for, as Mr. Justice Stewart has reminded us, the individual's right to the protection of his own good name "reflects no more than our basic concept of the essential dignity and worth of every human being—a concept at the root of any decent system of ordered liberty. . . ."

The *New York Times* standard defines the level of constitutional protection appropriate to the context of defamation of a public person. Those who, by reason of the notoriety of their achievements or the vigor and success with which they seek the public's attention, are properly classed as public figures and those who hold governmental office may recover for injury to reputation only on clear and convincing proof that the defamatory falsehood was made with knowledge of its falsity or with reckless disregard for the truth. This standard administers an extremely powerful antidote to the inducement to media self-censorship of the common-law rule of strict liability for libel and slander. And it exacts a correspondingly high price from the victims of defamatory falsehood. . . . For the reasons stated below, we conclude that the state interest in compensating injury to the reputation of private individuals requires that a different rule should obtain with respect to them.

Theoretically, of course, the balance between the needs of the press and the individual's claim to compensation for wrongful injury might be struck on a case-by-case basis. . . . But this approach would lead to unpredictable results and uncertain expectations, and it could render our duty to supervise the lower courts unmanageable. Because an *ad hoc* resolution of the competing interests at stake in each particular case is not feasible, we must lay down broad rules of general application. . . .

With that caveat we have no difficulty in distinguishing among defamation plaintiffs. The first remedy of any victim of defamation is self-help — using available opportunities to contradict the lie or correct the error and thereby to minimize its adverse impact on reputation. Public officials and public figures usually enjoy significantly greater access to the channels of effective communication and hence have a more realistic opportunity to counteract false statements than private individuals normally enjoy.[18] Private individuals are therefore more vulnerable to injury, and the state interest in protecting them is correspondingly greater.

More important than the likelihood that private individuals will lack effective opportunities for rebuttal, there is a compelling normative consideration underlying the distinction between public and private defamation plaintiffs. An individual who decides to seek governmental office must accept certain necessary consequences of that involvement in public affairs. He runs the risk of closer public scrutiny than might otherwise be the case. And society's interest in the officers of government is not strictly limited to the formal discharge of official duties. As the Court pointed out in *Garrison v. Louisiana*, the public's interest extends to "anything which might touch on an official's fitness for office. . . . Few personal attributes are more germane to fitness for office than dishonesty, malfeasance, or improper motivation, even though these characteristics may also affect the official's private character."

Those classed as public figures stand in a similar position. Hypothetically, it may be possible for someone to become a public figure through no purposeful action of his own, but the instances of truly involuntary public figures must be

18. Of course, an opportunity for rebuttal seldom suffices to undo harm of defamatory falsehood. Indeed, the law of defamation is rooted in our experience that the truth rarely catches up with a lie. But the fact that the self-help remedy of rebuttal, standing alone, is inadequate to its task does not mean that it is irrelevant to our inquiry.

exceedingly rare. For the most part those who attain this status have assumed roles of special prominence in the affairs of society. Some occupy positions of such persuasive power and influence that they are deemed public figures for all purposes. More commonly, those classed as public figures have thrust themselves to the forefront of particular public controversies in order to influence the resolution of the issues involved. In either event, they invite attention and comment.

Even if the foregoing generalities do not obtain in every instance, the communications media are entitled to act on the assumption that public officials and public figures have voluntarily exposed themselves to increased risk of injury from defamatory falsehood concerning them. No such assumption is justified with respect to a private individual. He has not accepted public office or assumed an "influential role in ordering society." He has relinquished no part of his interest in the protection of his own good name, and consequently he has a more compelling call on the courts for redress of injury inflicted by defamatory falsehood. Thus, private individuals are not only more vulnerable to injury than public officials and public figures; they are also more deserving of recovery.

For these reasons we conclude that the States should retain substantial latitude in their efforts to enforce a legal remedy for defamatory falsehood injurious to the reputation of a private individual. . . .

We hold that, so long as they do not impose liability without fault, the States may define for themselves the appropriate standard of liability for a publisher or broadcaster of defamatory falsehood injurious to a private individual. . . . [This approach] recognizes the strength of the legitimate state interest in compensating private individuals for wrongful injury to reputation, yet shields the press and broadcast media from the rigors of strict liability for defamation. At least this conclusion obtains where, as here, the substance of the defamatory statement "makes substantial danger to reputation apparent." . . .

[W]e endorse this approach in recognition of the strong and legitimate state interest in compensating private individuals for injury to reputation. But this countervailing state interest extends no further than compensation for actual injury. For the reasons stated below, we hold that the States may not permit recovery of presumed or punitive damages, at least when liability is not based on a showing of knowledge of falsity or reckless disregard for the truth.

The common law of defamation is an oddity of tort law, for it allows recovery of purportedly compensatory damages without evidence of actual loss. Under the traditional rules pertaining to actions for libel, the existence of injury is presumed from the fact of publication. Juries may award substantial sums as compensation for supposed damage to reputation without any proof that such harm actually occurred. The largely uncontrolled discretion of juries to award damages where there is no loss unnecessarily compounds the potential of any system of liability for defamatory falsehood to inhibit the vigorous exercise of First Amendment freedoms. Additionally, the doctrine of presumed damages invites juries to punish unpopular opinion rather than to compensate individuals for injury sustained by the publication of a false fact. More to the point, the States have no substantial interest in securing for plaintiffs such as this petitioner gratuitous awards of money damages far in excess of any actual injury.

We would not, of course, invalidate state law simply because we doubt its wisdom, but here we are attempting to reconcile state law with a competing interest grounded in the constitutional command of the First Amendment. It is therefore appropriate to require that state remedies for defamatory falsehood reach no farther than is necessary to protect the legitimate interest involved. It is necessary to restrict defamation plaintiffs who do not prove knowledge of falsity or reckless disregard for the truth to compensation for actual injury. We need not define "actual injury," as trial courts have wide experience in framing appropriate jury instructions in tort actions. Suffice it to say that actual injury is not limited to out-of-pocket loss. Indeed, the more customary types of actual harm inflicted by defamatory falsehood include impairment of reputation and standing in the community, personal humiliation, and mental anguish and suffering. Of course, juries must be limited by appropriate instructions, and all awards must be supported by competent evidence concerning the injury, although there need be no evidence which assigns an actual dollar value to the injury.

We also find no justification for allowing awards of punitive damages against publishers and broadcasters held liable under state-defined standards of liability for defamation. . . . [P]unitive damages are wholly irrelevant to the state interest that justifies a negligence standard for private defamation actions. They are not compensation for injury. Instead, they are private fines levied by civil juries to punish reprehensible conduct and to deter its future occurrence. In short, the private defamation plaintiff who establishes liability under a less demanding standard than that stated by *New York Times* may recover only such damages as are sufficient to compensate him for actual injury.

[R]espondent contends that we should affirm the judgment below on the ground that petitioner is either a public official or a public figure. There is little basis for the former assertion. [Respondent] argues that petitioner's appearance at the coroner's inquest rendered him a "de facto public official." Our cases recognize no such concept. Respondent's suggestion would sweep all lawyers under the *New York Times* rule as officers of the court and distort the plain meaning of the "public official" category beyond all recognition. We decline to follow it.

Respondent's characterization of petitioner as a public figure raises a different question. . . . Petitioner has long been active in community and professional affairs. He has served as an officer of local civic groups and of various professional organizations, and he has published several books and articles on legal subjects. Although petitioner was consequently well known in some circles, he had achieved no general fame or notoriety in the community. None of the prospective jurors called at the trial had ever heard of petitioner prior to this litigation, and respondent offered no proof that this response was atypical of the local population. We would not lightly assume that a citizen's participation in community and professional affairs rendered him a public figure for all purposes. Absent clear evidence of general fame or notoriety in the community, and pervasive involvement in the affairs of society, an individual should not be deemed a public personality for all aspects of his life. It is preferable to reduce the public-figure question to a more meaningful context by looking to the nature and extent of an individual's participation in the particular controversy giving rise to the defamation.

In this context it is plain that petitioner was not a public figure. He played a minimal role at the coroner's inquest, and his participation related solely to his representation of a private client. He took no part in the criminal prosecution of Officer Nuccio. Moreover, he never discussed either the criminal or civil litigation with the press and was never quoted as having done so. He plainly did not thrust himself into the vortex of this public issue, nor did he engage the public's attention in an attempt to influence its outcome. We are persuaded that the trial court did not err in refusing to characterize petitioner as a public figure for the purpose of this litigation.

We therefore conclude that the *New York Times* standard is inapplicable to this case and that the trial court erred in entering judgment for respondent. Because the jury was allowed to impose liability without fault and was permitted to presume damages without proof of injury, a new trial is necessary. We reverse and remand for further proceedings in accord with this opinion.

NOTES AND QUESTIONS

1. *Rejecting the public concern test?* Why did the majority in *Gertz* reject a rule that would focus on the status of the speech (that is, whether the speech was of public concern) rather than the status of the plaintiff (whether the plaintiff is a public or private figure)?
2. *Who is a public figure?* Public figures come in three different types, all of which have additional defining criteria. The three types are (1) "general" public figures, who have achieved such pervasive fame or notoriety that they are public figures "for all purposes and in all contexts"; (2) limited-purpose public figures, who are public figures only for purposes of discussion of a particular controversy in which they have become involved; and (3) "involuntary" public figures, who are thrust into a controversy through no action of their own and become public figures only for purposes of discussion of that controversy.
3. *What is an "actual injury"?* The best guidance on this issue comes from Time, Inc. v. Firestone, 424 U.S. 448 (1976). There the plaintiff relied on the testimony of her minister, physician, attorney, and friends to establish that she had suffered mental anguish, but she did not provide any evidence of reputational harm. The Supreme Court held that *Gertz* did not forbid recovery, even absent evidence of pecuniary injury to reputation. Does *Firestone* suggest that the requirement that private-figure plaintiffs like Gertz must prove actual injury (if they do not prove actual malice) is not that onerous?
4. *Establishing negligence.* Must the plaintiff establish that the defendant failed to behave as a "reasonable publisher or broadcaster" or merely that the defendant failed to behave as a reasonable person? Does it matter whether the standard is professional negligence or ordinary care?
5. *Setting a constitutional "floor."* It is important to remember that *Gertz* sets a First Amendment minimum and that states are free to impose a fault standard greater than negligence if they choose. New York, for example, requires private plaintiffs to show that the publisher "acted in a grossly irresponsible manner," at least where the defamation concerns a matter of "legitimate public concern." Chapadeau v. Utica Observer-Dispatch, Inc., 341 N.E.2d 569 (N.Y. 1975); Gaeta v. New York News, Inc., 465 N.E.2d 802 (N.Y. 1984).

6. *The outcome of* Gertz. When the *Gertz* case was retried, the plaintiff proved actual malice, and a jury award of $100,000 in compensatory damages and $300,000 in punitive damages was affirmed on appeal. Gertz v. Robert Welch, Inc., 680 F.2d 527 (7th Cir. 1982).
7. *Proof of falsity.* At common law truth was a defense to libel, to be pleaded and proved by the defendant. The Supreme Court in Philadelphia Newspapers, Inc. v. Hepps, 475 U.S. 767 (1986), clarified that public officials and public figures must prove falsity in order to recover for defamation. More surprisingly, the Court held that private-figure plaintiffs suing over speech on a matter of public concern must also prove falsity. In other words, in the common situation where such speech cannot be proved true or false, the plaintiff will lose. The rationale for putting the burden of proving falsity on the plaintiff was that where the evidence is ambiguous as to whether particular speech is true or false, the balance should tip "in favor of protecting true speech." Thus, the media will not be chilled from publishing speech on matters of public concern just because they fear they will not be able to later prove its truth to a jury's satisfaction.
8. *Applying* Gertz *to bloggers.* In Obsidian Financial Group LLC v. Cox, 740 F.3d 1284 (9th Cir. 2014), the Ninth Circuit, falling in line with other circuits, held that the requirements of *Gertz* apply to lawsuits against bloggers no less than lawsuits against traditional media. The defendant blogger in the case maintained a site called obsidianfinancesucks.com, which was devoted to "one-sided" and hyperbolic criticism of the plaintiff Obsidian Finance. Nonetheless, the court concluded that "[t]he protections of the First Amendment do not turn on whether the journalist was a trained journalist, formally affiliated with traditional news entities, engaged in conflict-of-interest disclosure, went beyond just assembling others' writings, or tried to get both sides of the story." The court noted that every other circuit to address the issue had held that First Amendment protections in libel cases apply equally to the institutional press and individual speakers. It cited cases from the Second, Third, Fourth, Eighth, Tenth, and D.C. Circuits. For discussion of how social-media cases are reshaping libel doctrine, see Lyrissa Barnett Lidsky & RonNell Andersen Jones, *Of Reasonable Readers and Unreasonable Speakers: Libel Law in a Networked World*, 23 Va. J. Soc. Pol'y & L. 155 (2016).

4. *Defamation of Private Figures Involved in Matters of Private Concern*

In Dun & Bradstreet v. Greenmoss Builders, 472 U.S. 749 (1985), the Supreme Court held, in a plurality decision, that not all defamation actions are subject to First Amendment limitations. In *Dun & Bradstreet*, a construction contractor sued for defamation after five of its creditors received a false credit report stating that the contractor had filed for bankruptcy. The defamation occurred because a 17-year-old employee of the credit-reporting agency, who had been paid to review state bankruptcy petitions, mistakenly attributed the bankruptcy of one of the plaintiff's former employees to the plaintiff itself. The credit-reporting agency made no attempt to verify the information before reporting it to five subscribers of its credit report, who were contractually bound not to reveal the contents to anyone else. The plaintiff won a verdict of $50,000 in compensatory or presumed damages and $300,000 in punitive damages on its defamation claim. The defendant Dun & Bradstreet moved for a new trial on the grounds that the trial court did not properly instruct the jury that punitive damages could not be awarded without proof of actual malice. In other words, the basis for the motion was that the constitutional requirements set forth in *Gertz v. Robert Welch, Inc.*, had not been met.

In a plurality decision, the United States Supreme Court agreed that Dun & Bradstreet was not entitled to the protections of *Gertz.* The Court based its decision on the conclusion that the case involved "speech on matters of purely *private* concern," and distinguished *Gertz* as involving a matter of undoubted *public* concern. In a case involving a private-figure plaintiff and a matter of merely private concern, the plurality opinion held that "permitting recovery of presumed and punitive damages . . . absent a showing of 'actual malice' does not violate the First Amendment."

The plurality's rationale was that a different balance must be struck in cases where the type of speech involves only matters of private concern. The speech at issue in these cases is "less important" from a First Amendment standpoint than speech on matters of public concern: Private-concern speech is less essential to the "free and robust debate of public issues" or to a "meaningful dialogue of ideas concerning self-government." On the other side of the balance, the state interest in awarding presumed and punitive damages as an "effective" remedy for defamation is higher in cases involving matters of private concern, given the difficulties plaintiffs face in proving actual damages even where "'it is all but certain that serious harm has resulted in fact.'"

Although the plurality did not spell out the practical implications of this decision, its reasoning suggested that states may impose strict liability on defendants who defame private plaintiffs concerning matters of private concern. In other words, the *Dun & Bradstreet* decision may mean that in a limited class of cases, the states may simply require a plaintiff to prove the traditional common law elements of defamation—the publication of a defamatory statement of and concerning the plaintiff—without regard to fault.

However, the reach of the Court's decision is limited because its analysis indicated that cases involving purely private-concern speech will be rare, and a majority of state courts actually require some degree of fault in all cases as a matter of tort law. The Court indicated that "content, form and context" are determinative in deciding whether speech is of public concern or of private concern. Based on these factors, Dun & Bradstreet's credit report was private because it was "solely in the individual interest of the speaker and its specific business audience." Almost by definition, the credit report made no contribution to "the free flow of commercial information" because the audience for the speech consisted only of the five paid subscribers who were contractually bound not to disseminate the information more widely. The Court also emphasized that the speech deserved no special constitutional protection due to the allegedly "hardy" nature of commercial speech in general. Because credit-reporting agencies will have powerful market incentives to continue publishing and to verify the accuracy of reports, they will presumably not be unduly chilled by the imposition of defamation liability for false reports. For further clarification on what constitutes a matter of public concern, see the discussion in *Snyder v. Phelps*, excerpted later in this chapter.

5. *The Constitutional "Privilege" Protecting Opinion*

What if a plaintiff seeks to recover damages for the publication of material that is neither true nor false? In *Gertz v. Robert Welch*, the Supreme Court stated in dicta that "[u]nder the First Amendment there is no such thing as a false idea." Many lower courts interpreted this dictum as creating a privilege against defamation liability for anything that might be labeled opinion. In the following case, the Supreme Court chastises the lower courts for providing too much protection for opinion and set parameters for the so-called opinion privilege. The key inquiry, according to the Court, is whether a publication implies an assertion of objective fact. As you read, make sure to discern what two categories of statements the Court identifies as not implying an assertion of objective fact.

Milkovich v. Lorain Journal Co.

497 U.S. 1 (1990)

Chief Justice Rehnquist delivered the opinion of the Court.

. . . This lawsuit is before us for the third time in an odyssey of litigation spanning nearly 15 years. Petitioner Milkovich, now retired, was the wrestling coach at Maple Heights High School in Maple Heights, Ohio. In 1974, his team was involved in an altercation at a home wrestling match with a team from Mentor High School. Several people were injured. In response to the incident, the Ohio High School Athletic Association (OHSAA) held a hearing at which Milkovich and H. Don Scott, the Superintendent of Maple Heights Public Schools, testified. Following the hearing, OHSAA placed the Maple Heights team on probation for a year and declared the team ineligible for the 1975 state tournament. OHSAA also censured Milkovich for his actions during the altercation. Thereafter, several parents and wrestlers sued OHSAA in the Court of Common Pleas of Franklin County, Ohio, seeking a restraining order against OHSAA's ruling on the grounds that they had been denied due process in the OHSAA proceeding. Both Milkovich and Scott testified in that proceeding. The court overturned OHSAA's probation and ineligibility orders on due process grounds.

The day after the court rendered its decision, respondent [Ted] Diadiun's column appeared in the News-Herald, a newspaper which circulates in Lake County, Ohio, and is owned by respondent Lorain Journal Co. The column bore the heading "Maple beat the law with the 'big lie,'" beneath which appeared Diadiun's photograph and the words "TD Says." The carryover page headline announced ". . . Diadiun says Maple told a lie." The column contained the following passages:

> "'. . . [A] lesson was learned (or relearned) yesterday by the student body of Maple Heights High School, and by anyone who attended the Maple-Mentor wrestling meet of last Feb. 8.

"'A lesson which, sadly, in view of the events of the past year, is well they learned early.

"'It is simply this: If you get in a jam, lie your way out.

"'If you're successful enough, and powerful enough, and can sound sincere enough, you stand an excellent chance of making the lie stand up, regardless of what really happened.

"'The teachers responsible were mainly head Maple wrestling coach, Mike Milkovich, and former superintendent of schools H. Donald Scott.

. . . "'Anyone who attended the meet, whether he be from Maple Heights, Mentor, or impartial observer, knows in his heart that Milkovich and Scott lied at the hearing after each having given his solemn oath to tell the truth.

"'But they got away with it.

"'Is that the kind of lesson we want our young people learning from their high school administrators and coaches?

"'I think not.'"

Petitioner commenced a defamation action against respondents in the Court of Common Pleas of Lake County, Ohio, alleging that the headline of Diadiun's article and the nine passages quoted above "accused plaintiff of committing the crime of perjury, an indictable offense in the State of Ohio, and damaged plaintiff directly in his life-time occupation of coach and teacher, and constituted libel per se." The action proceeded to trial, and the court granted a directed verdict to respondents on the ground that the evidence failed to establish the article was published with "actual malice" as required by *New York Times Co. v. Sullivan.* [While Milkovich's appeals were ongoing, the Ohio Supreme Court upheld a grant of summary judgments against Principal Scott, on the grounds that Diadiun's column was constitutionally protected opinion. Subsequently, the Ohio Court of Appeals upheld a grant of summary judgment against Milkovich, concluding that it was bound by the Ohio Supreme Court's analysis in Scott's case. The U.S. Supreme Court granted certiorari and reversed.]

. . . Respondents would have us recognize . . . still another First-Amendment-based protection for defamatory statements which are categorized as "opinion" as opposed to "fact." For this proposition they rely principally on the following dictum from our opinion in *Gertz:*

> "Under the First Amendment there is no such thing as a false idea. However pernicious an opinion may seem, we depend for its correction not on the conscience of judges and juries but on the competition of other ideas. But there is no constitutional value in false statements of fact."

Judge Friendly appropriately observed that this passage "has become the opening salvo in all arguments for protection from defamation actions on the ground of opinion, even though the case did not remotely concern the question." Cianci v. New Times Publishing Co., 639 F.2d 54, 61 (2d Cir. 1980). Read in context, though, the fair meaning of the passage is to equate the word "opinion" in the second sentence with the word "idea" in the first sentence. Under this view, the language was merely a reiteration of Justice Holmes' classic "marketplace of ideas" concept. *See* Abrams v. United States, 250 U.S. 616, 630 (1919) (dissenting opinion)

("The ultimate good desired is better reached by free trade in ideas— . . . the best test of truth is the power of the thought to get itself accepted in the competition of the market").

Thus, we do not think this passage from *Gertz* was intended to create a wholesale defamation exemption for anything that might be labeled "opinion." . . . Not only would such an interpretation be contrary to the tenor and context of the passage, but it would also ignore the fact that expressions of "opinion" may often imply an assertion of objective fact.

If a speaker says, "In my opinion John Jones is a liar," he implies a knowledge of facts which lead to the conclusion that Jones told an untruth. Even if the speaker states the facts upon which he bases his opinion, if those facts are either incorrect or incomplete, or if his assessment of them is erroneous, the statement may still imply a false assertion of fact. Simply couching such statements in terms of opinion does not dispel these implications; and the statement, "In my opinion Jones is a liar," can cause as much damage to reputation as the statement, "Jones is a liar." As Judge Friendly aptly stated: "[It] would be destructive of the law of libel if a writer could escape liability for accusations of [defamatory conduct] simply by using, explicitly or implicitly, the words 'I think.'" It is worthy of note that at common law, even the privilege of fair comment did not extend to "a false statement of fact, whether it was expressly stated or implied from an expression of opinion." *Restatement (Second) of Torts, § 566*, Comment *a* (1977).

Apart from their reliance on the *Gertz* dictum, respondents do not really contend that a statement such as, "In my opinion John Jones is a liar," should be protected by a separate privilege for "opinion" under the First Amendment. But they do contend that in every defamation case the First Amendment mandates an inquiry into whether a statement is "opinion" or "fact," and that only the latter statements may be actionable. They propose that a number of factors developed by the lower courts (in what we hold was a mistaken reliance on the *Gertz* dictum) be considered in deciding which is which. But we think the "'breathing space'" which "'freedoms of expression require in order to survive,'" is adequately secured by existing constitutional doctrine without the creation of an artificial dichotomy between "opinion" and fact.

Foremost, we think [*Philadelphia Newspapers, Inc. v.*] *Hepps* stands for the proposition that a statement on matters of public concern must be provable as false before there can be liability under state defamation law, at least in situations, like the present, where a media defendant is involved. Thus, unlike the statement, "In my opinion Mayor Jones is a liar," the statement, "In my opinion Mayor Jones shows his abysmal ignorance by accepting the teachings of Marx and Lenin," would not be actionable. *Hepps* ensures that a statement of opinion relating to matters of public concern which does not contain a provably false factual connotation will receive full constitutional protection.

Next, the *Bresler-Letter Carriers-Falwell* line of cases provides protection for statements that cannot "reasonably [be] interpreted as stating actual facts" about an individual. *Falwell*, 485 U.S. at 50. This provides assurance that public debate will not suffer for lack of "imaginative expression" or the "rhetorical hyperbole" which has traditionally added much to the discourse of our Nation.

The *New York Times-Butts-Gertz* culpability requirements further ensure that debate on public issues remains "uninhibited, robust, and wide-open." *New York Times*, 376 U.S. at 270. Thus, where a statement of "opinion" on a matter of public concern reasonably implies false and defamatory facts regarding public figures or officials, those individuals must show that such statements were made with knowledge of their false implications or with reckless disregard of their truth. Similarly, where such a statement involves a private figure on a matter of public concern, a plaintiff must show that the false connotations were made with some level of fault as required by *Gertz*. Finally, the enhanced appellate review required by *Bose Corp.* provides assurance that the foregoing determinations will be made in a manner so as not to "constitute a forbidden intrusion of the field of free expression." *Bose Corp.*, 466 U.S. at 499 (quotation omitted).

We are not persuaded that, in addition to these protections, an additional separate constitutional privilege for "opinion" is required to ensure the freedom of expression guaranteed by the First Amendment. The dispositive question in the present case then becomes whether a reasonable factfinder could conclude that the statements in the Diadiun column imply an assertion that petitioner Milkovich perjured himself in a judicial proceeding. We think this question must be answered in the affirmative. As the Ohio Supreme Court itself observed: "The clear impact in some nine sentences and a caption is that [Milkovich] 'lied at the hearing after . . . having given his solemn oath to tell the truth.'" This is not the sort of loose, figurative, or hyperbolic language which would negate the impression that the writer was seriously maintaining that petitioner committed the crime of perjury. Nor does the general tenor of the article negate this impression.

We also think the connotation that petitioner committed perjury is sufficiently factual to be susceptible of being proved true or false. A determination whether petitioner lied in this instance can be made on a core of objective evidence by comparing, *inter alia*, petitioner's testimony before the OHSAA board with his subsequent testimony before the trial court. . . .

The numerous decisions discussed above establishing First Amendment protection for defendants in defamation actions surely demonstrate the Court's recognition of the Amendment's vital guarantee of free and uninhibited discussion of public issues. But there is also another side to the equation; we have regularly acknowledged the "important social values which underlie the law of defamation," and recognized that "society has a pervasive and strong interest in preventing and redressing attacks upon reputation." Rosenblatt v. Baer, 383 U.S. 75 (1966). [Reversed and remanded.]

Justice BRENNAN, with whom Justice MARSHALL joins, dissenting.

. . . Although I agree with the majority that statements must be scrutinized for implicit factual assertions, the majority's scrutiny in this case does not "hold the balance true," between protection of individual reputation and freedom of speech. The statements complained of neither state nor imply a false assertion of fact, and, under the rule the Court reconfirms today, they should be found not libel "as a matter of constitutional law." Readers of Diadiun's column are signaled repeatedly that the author does not actually know what Milkovich said at the court hearing and that the author is surmising, from factual premises made explicit in the column, that Milkovich must have lied in court.

NOTES AND QUESTIONS

1. *The role of context.* In *Milkovich*, the Supreme Court failed to specify what role, if any, context plays in determining whether an allegedly defamatory statement "implies an assertion of objective fact." Must lower courts consider context in deciding whether a statement "cannot reasonably be interpreted as stating actual facts"? In deciding whether it is "provably false"? More recent decisions involving hyperbole include Bauer v. Brinkman, 958 N.W.2d 194 (Iowa 2021) (the word "slumlord" used in a social media was post was hyperbole given context of "emotionally charged responses," profane language, and tone that was "pointed, exaggerated, and heavily laden with emotional rhetoric and moral outrage, thus alerting readers that the statements [were] expressions of personal judgment) (internal quotations omitted). But see Deeb v. Saati, 778 Fed. App'x 683 (11th Cir. 2019), in which the phrases "alleged money launderers" and "Barons of the bleaching of the city" who, the social media post said, would be "handcuffed and en route to the American prisons" were not necessarily hyperbole/opinion, even though the bulk of the social media post ("stream-of-consciousness sermonizing about values") would be.
2. *The media/nonmedia distinction in the age of the Internet.* The Court in *Milkovich* again "reserved judgment" on the question of whether the protection for statements that are not provably false applies to nonmedia defendants. 497 U.S. at 20 n.6. Does the logic of *Milkovich* suggest that its protections should extend only to media defendants? Why? Does the media/nonmedia distinction deserve re-examination in light of the growth of blogs and other novel forms of communication that blur the line between media and nonmedia speakers?
3. *Do false statements of fact have constitutional value?* In United States v. Alvarez, 567 U.S. 709 (2012), the Supreme Court struck down the Stolen Valor Act, a federal statute making it a crime for a person to falsely claim that she received a military decoration authorized by Congress. The decision affirmed that the government lacks the power to censor lies—even highly offensive ones—absent a showing of significant harm. Six justices concluded that the false statements prohibited by the Stolen Valor Act were not "in a general category that is presumptively unconstitutional." A plurality of four justices applied strict scrutiny to reach this result. Although "[t]he Government's interest in protecting the integrity of the Medal of Honor is beyond question," the government could not show the Act was "actually necessary" to achieve that interest. The government showed no evidence that lies about military awards would dilute their meaning, and "counterspeech" could easily be deployed against false claims. In addition, "[a] Government-created database" listing soldiers who received medals or honors was a less restrictive alternative to criminalization of speech.

The two justices who joined the plurality in invalidating the Act differed as to the appropriate level of constitutional scrutiny of restrictions on false speech such as lies about military honors: they applied "intermediate scrutiny" or "proportionality" analysis and determined that the harm to speech interests was "disproportionate" to the Act's advancement of the government's interest in upholding the integrity of its military awards.

4. *Online review sites.* In Seaton v. TripAdvisor, 728 F.3d 592 (6th Cir. 2013), plaintiff, Kenneth Seaton, the sole owner of Grand Resort Hotel and Convention, sued TripAdvisor for defamation, false light, and invasion of privacy for placing his hotel on its "2011 Dirtiest Hotels List." TripAdvisor filed a motion to dismiss, asserting that its placement of the Grand Resort on the list constituted non-actionable opinion. The district court granted TripAdvisor's motion to dismiss. The Sixth Circuit affirmed, holding that TripAdvisor's placement of Seaton's hotel on its dirtiest hotels list was "not capable of being understood as defamatory." The court based this conclusion, first, on the fact that the "superlative" adjective "dirtiest" was "loose, hyperbolic language." Second, the court looked at the "general tenor" of the list, which billed itself as a product of user reviews rather than "scientific study," with the user reviews being full of hyperbole and subjective accounts of travelers' experiences. Finally, the court placed the TripAdvisor list in the "broader context" of online rankings. TripAdvisor's compilation of user comments was part of broader online trend: "[T]op ten" lists and the like appear with growing frequency on the web." Thus, "a reasonable observer understands that placement on and ranking within the bulk of such lists constitutes opinion, not a provable fact." Although the plaintiff contended that TripAdvisor employed a flawed methodology for ranking user comments, the court found that "the subjective weighing of factors cannot be proven false and therefore cannot be the basis of a defamation claim." Indeed, the court's opinion repeatedly stressed the subjectivity of such rankings as a basis for affirming dismissal of plaintiff's claim. See also Spencer v. Glover, 397 P.3d 780 (Utah App. 2017) (online review by client calling former attorney "worst ever" held non-defamatory opinion when read in context).

5. *An injunction remedy for online defamation.* In Kinney v. Barnes, 443 S.W.3d 87 (Tex. 2014), the Texas Supreme Court held that a court may issue a post-trial injunction requiring a defendant to remove from his website statements he made that a civil jury has found to be defamatory. However, the court held that an injunction on future speech of a similar nature was an unconstitutional prior restraint that ran the risk of chilling constitutionally protected expression. The court cited the "inherently contextual nature of defamatory speech" as problematic, explaining "even the most narrowly crafted of injunctions risks enjoining protected speech because the same statement made at a different time and in a different context may no longer be actionable. Untrue statements may later become true; unprivileged statements may later become privileged." In sum, this case stands for the general recognition that "the appropriate remedy for defamation is damages, not injunctive relief." What are implications of this

decision? Can a court issue a post-trial injunction requiring a defendant to remove information that has been found to invade privacy? What about a criminal record that has been expunged?

6. *Libel and the Press Clause.* What do the libel cases discussed in this chapter suggest about whether the Press Clause of the First Amendment provides "special rights" to the press not already provided by the Speech Clause? Is this message consistent with that expressed in the line of cases developed in Chapter 8, which dealt with mass media and the First Amendment?

7. *Statutory modifications of the "republication rule" in the Internet age.* For purposes of defamation law, a defendant "publishes" a statement when he originates or repeats defamatory material to at least one third person. Publication can be accomplished by written, oral, broadcast, photographic, printed, or other means. A person is liable for the "republication"—that is, the repetition—of another's defamatory statement as if he originated it. For example, a newspaper that publishes a defamatory letter to the editor can be sued for defamation for the contents of that letter. The rationale for the republication rule is that otherwise media and others could defame at will merely by finding someone to whom they can attribute a defamatory statement. The "republication rule" is sometimes modified to protect those who repeat (or "publish") the statements of others. For example, a tort privilege protects the media when they fairly and accurate report on open public meetings, and the actual malice rule acts as a constitutional privilege protecting one who repeats information learned from others as long as he or she does not knowingly or recklessly disregard the falsity of the repeated information.

   The "republication rule" is deeply at odds with the practices of Internet communications. The Internet has developed a culture of more or less uninhibited repetition of information originated by others. Early on, Congress recognized that defamation lawsuits threatened to stifle free speech in this then-new medium, and it stepped in to insulate Internet service providers from defamation and other tort liability when they act merely as intermediaries allowing the "republication" of speech originated by others. Congress provided, in Section 230 of the Communications Decency Act (CDA), that: "No provider or user of an interactive computer service shall be treated as the publisher or speaker of any information provided by another information content provider." 47 U.S.C. § 230(c)(1). As interpreted by courts, Section 230 broadly bars lawsuits seeking to hold any Internet service provider liable for "publishing" or refusing to remove content originated by other speakers. *See, e.g.*, Zeran v. America Online, Inc., 129 F.3d 327 (4th Cir. 1997) (barring lawsuit against AOL for delay in removing defamatory messages posted by unidentified third party).

   A few courts have attempted to limit the broad scope of Section 230 immunity. In Fair Housing Council of San Fernando Valley v. Roommates.com LLC, 521 F.3d 1157, 36 Med. L. Rptr. 1545 (9th Cir. 2008) (en banc), for example, the U.S. Court of Appeals for the Ninth Circuit held, 8-3, that a Web site's active involvement in soliciting the content supplied by its users deprived the Web site's operators of CDA immunity in a housing discrimination action. The Web site offered a "roommate-matching" service and required users of the service to answer questionnaires with information about gender identity, sexual orientation, and whether children would be living in the user's household. The Ninth Circuit held that three aspects of the Roommates.com Web site deprived it of CDA immunity. First, requiring users to answer questions about their sex, family status, and sexual orientation made Roommates.com an "information content provider" rather than a conduit for information supplied by third parties. Second, the creation of user profiles based on answers to the required questionnaire made Roommates.com an information "developer" rather than a "passive transmitter of information provided by others." Third, the creation of a search engine that allowed "discriminatory filtering" by users—that is, filtering based on gender and other illegal criteria—made Roommates.com "forfeit any immunity to which it was otherwise entitled." The court distinguished the search engine function of Roommates.com from search engines functions such as Google's, which "provide neutral tools to carry out what may be unlawful or illicit searches." The court also stressed that "an editor's minor changes to the spelling, grammar and length of third-party content do not strip him of Section 230 immunity." For other cases expressing dissatisfaction with the broad scope of Section 230 immunity in cases like *Zeran*, see Doe v. GTE Corp., 347 F.3d 655 (7th Cir. 2003); Chicago Lawyers' Committee for Civil Rights Under the Law, Inc. v. Craigslist, Inc., 519 F.3d 666 (7th Cir. 2008). What are the implications of this case for defamation law? What about sites that solicit online gossip, like TheDirty.com? Other cases applying § 230 include Klayman v. Zuckerberg, 753 F.3d 1354 (D.C. Cir. 2014) (applying 230 immunity); Jones v. Dirty World Entertainment, 755 F.3d 398 (6th Cir. 2014) (granting immunity); J.S. v. Village Voice Media Holdings, 359 P.3d 714 (Wash. 2015) (rejecting blanket immunity); Doe v. Backpage.com, 817 F.3d 12 (1st Cir. 2016), cert. denied, 137 S.Ct. 622 (2017); Gonzalez v. Google, 2 F.4th 871 (9th Cir. 2021) (reluctantly applying statutory immunity while asserting that it is "likely premised on an antiquated understanding of the extent to which it is possible to screen content posted by third parties.").

8. *Libel law abroad.* Libel laws in other countries are less favorable—often far less favorable—to defendants than those of the United States. The Supreme Court of Canada recently reduced the disparity with its decision in Grant v. Torstar Corp. (Can.), [2009] 3 S.C.R. 640. The *Torstar* decision makes a new defense available to Canadian libel defendants publishing in both traditional and new media. The defense protects "responsible communication on matters of public interest." In determining whether publication was "responsible," courts examine how diligently the defendant has attempted to verify the defamatory statement prior to publishing. Factors include the "seriousness of the allegation"; the "public importance of the matter"; "urgency"; the "status and reliability of the source"; "whether the plaintiff's side of the story was sought and accurate reported"; whether "inclusion of the defamatory statement was justifiable"; whether the statement was reported for "the fact that it was made" as opposed to its truth; and "any other relevant circumstances." The Canadian Supreme Court

explicitly rejected the "American approach of protecting all statements about public figures, unless the plaintiff can show malice" and instead adopted the "middle road . . . chosen by courts in Australia, New Zealand, South Africa and the United Kingdom." The Court believed this "middle road" "represents a reasonable and proportionate response to the need to protect reputation while sustaining the public exchange of information that is vital to modern Canadian society."

9. *Libel tourism deterrence.* The term "libel tourism" is sometimes used to describe plaintiffs' attempt to forum-shop for a jurisdiction with the most favorable libel laws. Ordinarily, unless the defendant has assets in the forum jurisdiction, a plaintiff who wins a libel case abroad can collect it only by having a U.S. court enforce the foreign judgment. Congress passed the SPEECH Act in 2010 to protect U.S. citizens from the threat of foreign libel judgments. *See* Securing the Protection of our Enduring and Established Constitutional Heritage Act, 28 U.S.C. §§ 4101-4105 (2010). The Act provides, among other things, that U.S. courts may not enforce foreign judgments unless (1) the law applied in the foreign court provided at least as much protection to free expression as U.S. law, or (2) the speech would have subjected the speaker to liability for defamation under U.S. law, even if the foreign jurisdiction's law was not as protective of expression as U.S. law.

THEORY-APPLIED PROBLEM: A RESTAURANT REVIEW

Assume that a restaurant critic for the Ohio Post reviews a new steakhouse called Chops. The critic pans the restaurant, stating that "my strip steak was miserably tough and fatty." The owner of Chops sues for libel. Rate the owner's chances of success in light of *Milkovich.* What if the owner can prove that the critic ordered a steak sandwich made with flank steak, an inferior cut, rather than a strip steak? What if the owner can prove that on the date the critic claims to have eaten the strip steak the critic actually ordered only salmon?

THEORY-APPLIED PROBLEM—HASHTAG LIBEL

A company named Able Business Co. sues a competitor for libel, based on the competitor's social media posts that say: "We support the USA 100 percent. We encourage you to ask our competitor, Able Business Co., about its support. #MADEINCHINA #RedDragon." Is this statement defamatory? Is it protected by the constitutional privilege for opinion, assuming that Able Business Co. is a registered U.S. corporation with its principal place of business and the overwhelming majority of its supplier in the U.S.? *See* AvePoint, Inc. v. Power Tools, Inc., 981 F. Supp. 2d 496 (W.D. Va. 2013).

Assume a social media "influencer" begins a campaign to help reduce the stigma of being a victim of child abuse. The influencer writes about his experiences with the hashtag #AbuseSurvivor. Thousands of people post about their experiences using the hashtag, though many just post #AbuseSurvivor. An outraged parent of one of the posters denies the allegation and sues for defamation. Is the adult child's use of the hashtag defamatory? A number of lawsuits were brought by people identified as alleged sexual harassers in the #Me,Too movement, which gained traction in 2017. *See* Shaina Weisbrot, 23 CUNY L. Rev. 332 (2020) (collecting cases).

6. *Should* New York Times v. Sullivan *Be Overruled?*

In McKee v. Cosby, Jr. 139 S.Ct. 675 (2019) (Thomas, J., concurring in denial of certiorari), Justice Clarence Thomas filed an opinion calling for the Supreme Court to reconsider and overrule *New York Times v. Sullivan's* actual malice standard. Justice Thomas called the *Sullivan* case and the subsequent decisions extending it as "policy-driven decisions masquerading as constitutional law." He asserted that the Court in *Sullivan* "made no attempt to base [its actual-malice rule] on the original understanding" of the First and Fourteenth Amendments, and that "States are perfectly capable of striking an acceptable balance between encouraging robust public discourse and providing a meaningful remedy for reputational harm." Given the foundational status of the case, Justice Thomas's call to overrule it at first seemed quixotic, even though several prior Justices had questioned the standard's extension to public figures. Yet Justice Thomas's opinion reopened scholarly and judicial debate over whether *Sullivan* still makes sense in the mass media environment of the early twenty-first century. *See, e.g.*, David Logan, *Rescuing our Democracy by Rethinking* New York Times Co. v. Sullivan, 81 Ohio St. L.J. 759 (2020).

Just a few years later, Justice Neil Gorsuch joined in Thomas's call for overruling *Sullivan* and its progeny. Berisha v. Lawson, 141 S.Ct. 2424 (2021) (Gorsuch, J., dissenting from denial of certiorari). In addition to criticizing the decision on originalism grounds, Justice Gorsuch observed that "[s]ince 1964 . . . our Nation's media landscape has shifted in ways few could have foreseen." In particular, he pointed to a study showing the spread of disinformation across social networks, at the same time that the economic model undergirding newsgathering and editorial oversight in more traditional media had faltered. He also asserted that the actual-malice rule, which was supposed to be a "high bar to recovery" has become "an effective immunity from liability." He cited an article Justice Elena Kagan published before joining the Supreme Court questioning whether the actual-malice rule "cuts against the [democracy-enhancing] values underlying the decision."

B. *FIRST AMENDMENT LIMITATIONS ON INTENTIONAL INFLICTION OF EMOTIONAL DISTRESS*

Typically intentional infliction of emotional distress is actionable when a defendant, through "outrageous" conduct, intentionally or recklessly inflicts severe emotional distress on the plaintiff. *See Restatement (Second) of Torts* § 46. In the following case, a public-figure plaintiff based his claim of intentional infliction on an outrageous parody advertisement.

Hustler Magazine, Inc. v. Falwell

485 U.S. 46 (1989)

Chief Justice REHNQUIST delivered the opinion of the Court.

. . . Respondent Jerry Falwell, a nationally known minister who has been active as a commentator on politics and public affairs, sued petitioner [Hustler Magazine] and its publisher, petitioner Larry Flynt, to recover damages for invasion of privacy, libel, and intentional infliction of emotional distress. The District Court directed a verdict against respondent on the privacy claim, and submitted the other two claims to a jury. The jury found for petitioners on the defamation claim, but found for respondent on the claim for intentional infliction of emotional distress and awarded damages [or $100,000 in compensatory damages and $50,000 in punitives against each petitioner]. We now consider whether this award is consistent with the First and Fourteenth Amendments of the United States Constitution.

The inside front cover of the November 1983 issue of Hustler Magazine featured a "parody" of an advertisement for Campari Liqueur that contained the name and picture of respondent and was entitled "Jerry Falwell talks about his first time." This parody was modeled after actual Campari ads that included interviews with various celebrities about their "first times." Although it was apparent by the end of each interview that this meant the first time they sampled Campari, the ads clearly played on the sexual double entendre of the general subject of "first times." Copying the form and layout of these Campari ads, Hustler's editors chose respondent as the featured celebrity and drafted an alleged "interview" with him in which he states that his "first time" was during a drunken incestuous rendezvous with his mother in an outhouse. The Hustler parody portrays respondent and his mother as drunk and immoral, and suggests that respondent is a hypocrite who preaches only when he is drunk. In small print at the bottom of the page, the ad contains the disclaimer, "ad parody—not to be taken seriously." . . .

. . . The jury . . . found against respondent on the libel claim, specifically finding that the ad parody could not "reasonably be understood as describing actual facts about [respondent] or actual events in which [he] participated." . . . The jury ruled for respondent on the intentional infliction of emotional distress claim. . . . On appeal, the United States Court of Appeals for the Fourth Circuit affirmed the judgment against petitioners. . . .

This case presents us with a novel question involving First Amendment limitations upon a State's authority to protect its citizens from the intentional infliction of emotional distress. We must decide whether a public figure may recover damages for emotional harm caused by the publication of an ad parody offensive to him, and doubtless gross and repugnant in the eyes of most. Respondent would have us find that a State's interest in protecting public figures from emotional distress is sufficient to deny First Amendment protection to speech that is patently offensive and is intended to inflict emotional injury, even when that speech could not reasonably have been interpreted as stating actual facts about the public figure involved. This we decline to do.

At the heart of the First Amendment is the recognition of the fundamental importance of the free flow of ideas and opinions on matters of public interest and concern. "The freedom to speak one's mind is not only an aspect of individual liberty—and thus a good unto itself—but also is essential to the common quest for truth and the vitality of society as a whole." . . . We have therefore been particularly vigilant to ensure that individual expressions of ideas remain free from governmentally imposed sanctions. . . .

The sort of robust political debate encouraged by the First Amendment is bound to produce speech that is critical of those who hold public office or those public figures who are "intimately involved in the resolution of important public questions or, by reason of their fame, shape events in areas of concern to society at large." . . . Justice Frankfurter put it succinctly in *Baumgartner v. United States*, . . . , when he said that "one of the prerogatives of American citizenship is the right to criticize public men and measures." Such criticism, inevitably, will not always be reasoned or moderate; public figures as well as public officials will be subject to "vehement, caustic, and sometimes unpleasantly sharp attacks." . . .

Of course, this does not mean that any speech about a public figure is immune from sanction in the form of damages. Since *New York Times Co. v. Sullivan*, we have consistently ruled that a public figure may hold a speaker liable for the damage to reputation caused by publication of a defamatory falsehood, but only if the statement was made "with knowledge that it was false or with reckless disregard of whether it was false or not." . . . False statements of fact are particularly valueless; they interfere with the truth-seeking function of the marketplace of ideas, and they cause damage to an individual's reputation that cannot easily be repaired by counterspeech, however persuasive or effective. But even though falsehoods have little value in and of themselves, they are "nevertheless inevitable in free debate" . . . , and a rule that would impose strict liability on a publisher for false factual assertions would have an undoubted "chilling" effect on speech relating to public figures that does have constitutional value. . . . [B]reathing space is provided by a constitutional rule that allows public figures to recover for libel or defamation only when they can prove both that the statement was false and that the statement was made with the requisite level of culpability.

Respondent argues, however, that a different standard should apply in this case because here the State seeks to prevent not reputational damage, but the severe emotional distress suffered by the person who is the subject of an offensive publication. In respondent's view . . . , so long as the utterance was intended to inflict emotional distress, was outrageous, and did in fact inflict serious emotional distress, it is of no constitutional import whether the statement was a fact or an opinion, or whether it was true or false. It is the intent to cause injury that is the gravamen of the tort, and the State's interest in preventing emotional harm simply outweighs whatever interest a speaker may have in speech of this type.

Generally speaking the law does not regard the intent to inflict emotional distress as one which should receive much solicitude, and it is quite understandable that most if not all jurisdictions have chosen to make it civilly culpable where the conduct in question is sufficiently "outrageous." But in the world of debate about public affairs, many things done with motives that are less than admirable are protected by the First Amendment. In *Garrison v. Louisiana*, we held that even when a speaker or writer is motivated by hatred or ill-will his expression was protected by the First Amendment. . . . [W]hile such a bad motive may be deemed controlling for purposes of tort liability in other areas of the law, we think the First Amendment prohibits such a result in the area of public debate about public figures.

Were we to hold otherwise, there can be little doubt that political cartoonists and satirists would be subjected to damages awards without any showing that their work falsely defamed its subject. Webster's defines a caricature as "the deliberately distorted picturing or imitating of a person, literary style, etc. by exaggerating features or mannerisms for satirical effect." . . . The appeal of the political cartoon or caricature is often based on exploration of unfortunate physical traits or politically embarrassing events—an exploration often calculated to injure the feelings of the subject of the portrayal. The art of the cartoonist is often not reasoned or evenhanded, but slashing and one-sided. One cartoonist expressed the nature of the art in these words:

> "The political cartoon is a weapon of attack, of scorn and ridicule and satire; it is least effective when it tries to pat some politician on the back. It is usually as welcome as a bee sting and is always controversial in some quarters." Long, The Political Cartoon: Journalism's Strongest Weapon, The Quill, 56, 57 (Nov. 1962).

Several famous examples of this type of intentionally injurious speech were drawn by Thomas Nast, probably the greatest American cartoonist to date, who was associated for many years during the post-Civil War era with Harper's Weekly. In the pages of that publication Nast conducted a graphic vendetta against William M. "Boss" Tweed and his corrupt associates in New York City's "Tweed Ring." It has been described by one historian of the subject as "a sustained attack which in its passion and effectiveness stands alone in the history of American graphic art." . . . Another writer explains that the success of the Nast cartoon was achieved "because of the emotional impact of its presentation. It continuously goes beyond the bounds of good taste and conventional manners." . . .

Despite their sometimes caustic nature, from the early cartoon portraying George Washington as an ass down to the present day, graphic depictions and satirical cartoons have played a prominent role in public and political debate. Nast's castigation of the Tweed Ring, Walt McDougall's characterization of presidential candidate James G. Blaine's banquet with the millionaires at Delmonico's as "The Royal Feast of Belshazzar," and numerous other efforts have undoubtedly had an effect on the course and outcome of contemporaneous debate. Lincoln's tall, gangling posture, Teddy Roosevelt's glasses and teeth, and Franklin D. Roosevelt's jutting jaw and cigarette holder have been memorialized by political cartoons with an effect that could not have been obtained by the photographer or the portrait artist. From the viewpoint of history it is clear that our political discourse would have been considerably poorer without them.

Respondent contends, however, that the caricature in question here was so "outrageous" as to distinguish it from more traditional political cartoons. There is no doubt that the caricature of respondent and his mother published in Hustler is at best a distant cousin of the political cartoons described above, and a rather poor relation at that. If it were possible by laying down a principled standard to separate the one from the other, public discourse would probably suffer little or no harm. But we doubt that there is any such standard, and we are quite sure that the pejorative description "outrageous" does not supply one. "Outrageousness" in the area of political and social discourse has an inherent subjectiveness about it which would allow a jury to impose liability on the basis of the jurors' tastes or views, or perhaps on the basis of their dislike of a particular expression. An "outrageousness" standard thus runs afoul of our longstanding refusal to allow damages to be awarded because the speech in question may have an adverse emotional impact on the audience. . . .

We conclude that public figures and public officials may not recover for the tort of intentional infliction of emotional distress by reason of publications such as the one here at issue without showing in addition that the publication contains a false statement of fact which was made with "actual malice," i.e., with knowledge that the statement was false or with reckless disregard as to whether or not it was true. This is not merely a "blind application" of the *New York Times* standard; it reflects our considered judgment that such a standard is necessary to give adequate "breathing space" to the freedoms protected by the First Amendment.

Here it is clear that respondent Falwell is a "public figure" for purposes of First Amendment law. The jury found against respondent on his libel claim when it decided that the Hustler ad parody could not "reasonably be understood as describing actual facts about [respondent] or actual events in which [he] participated." . . . The Court of Appeals interpreted the jury's finding to be that the ad parody "was not reasonably believable," and in accordance with our custom we accept this finding. Respondent is thus relegated to his claim for damages awarded by the jury for the intentional infliction of emotional *distress* by "outrageous" conduct. But for reasons heretofore stated this claim cannot, consistently with the First Amendment, form a basis for the award of damages when the conduct in question is the publication of a caricature such as the ad parody involved here. The judgment of the Court of Appeals is accordingly

Reversed.

Justice KENNEDY took no part in the consideration or decision of this case.

NOTES AND QUESTIONS

1. *First Amendment protection for satire, hyperbole, parody. Falwell* held narrowly that public figures must prove actual malice to recover for intentional infliction based on the publication of allegedly outrageous material. But the Supreme Court's later opinion in Milkovich v. Lorain Journal, 497 U.S. 1 (1990), which is excerpted in Section A.5 of this chapter, interpreted *Falwell* as protecting statements that cannot "reasonably be interpreted as stating actual facts" about an individual. The Court reasoned that such statements must be protected so that "public debate will not suffer for lack of 'imaginative expression' or the 'rhetorical hyperbole' which has traditionally added much to the discourse of our nation." Does this rationale apply only to speech about public figures?
2. *Newsgathering and emotional distress.* May a public-figure plaintiff bring a claim for intentional infliction of emotional distress if a reporter uses intrusive methods to gather information about the plaintiff?

In the case below, the plaintiff sues for intentional infliction and other torts after the defendants protest outside his son's funeral holding signs with highly offensive messages. What does the plaintiff contend is "outrageous" about the defendants' conduct in this case: the content of defendants' speech, the setting, or both?

Snyder v. Phelps

562 U.S. 443 (2011)

Chief Justice Roberts delivered the opinion of the Court.

. . . Fred Phelps founded the Westboro Baptist Church in Topeka, Kansas, in 1955. The church's congregation believes that God hates and punishes the United States for its tolerance of homosexuality, particularly in America's military. . . . [T]hey have picketed nearly 600 funerals [to spread their message, including the funeral of Marine Lance Corporal Matthew Snyder, who was killed in the line of duty in Iraq.]

Phelps became aware of Matthew Snyder's funeral and decided to travel to Maryland with six other Westboro Baptist parishioners (two of his daughters and four of his grandchildren) to picket. On the day of the memorial service, the Westboro congregation members picketed on public land adjacent to public streets near the Maryland State House, the United States Naval Academy, and Matthew Snyder's funeral. The Westboro picketers carried signs [stating:] "God Hates the USA/Thank God for 9/11," "America is Doomed," "Don't Pray for the USA," "Thank God for IEDs," "Thank God for Dead Soldiers," "Pope in Hell," "Priests Rape Boys," "God Hates Fags," "You're Going to Hell," and "God Hates You."

[The picketing took place 1,000 feet from the church. Snyder's father, the plaintiff in this tort action against Westboro, could not see what was written on the picket signs on his way to the funeral, but he saw them while watching a news broadcast of the protest later that night. He sued Phelps, his daughters, and Westboro for defamation, publicity given to private life, intentional infliction of emotional distress, intrusion upon seclusion, and civil conspiracy. A federal district court granted summary judgment for Westboro on the defamation and publicity claims. A jury found for Snyder on the intentional infliction, intrusion, and civil conspiracy claims and awarded him \$2.9 million in compensatory and \$8 million in punitive damages. The punitive were remitted to \$2.1 million. The Court of Appeals reversed on First Amendment grounds, and the Supreme Court granted certiorari.]

Whether the First Amendment prohibits holding Westboro liable for its speech in this case turns largely on whether that speech is of public or private concern, as determined by all the circumstances of the case. "[S]peech on 'matters of public concern' . . . is 'at the heart of the First Amendment's protection.'" Dun & Bradstreet, Inc. v. Greenmoss Builders, Inc., 472 U.S. 749, 758-759 (1985) (opinion of Powell, J.). . . .

. . . [W]here matters of purely private significance are at issue, First Amendment protections are often less rigorous. *Hustler.* That is because restricting speech on purely private matters does not implicate the same constitutional concerns as limiting speech on matters of public interest: "[T]here is no threat to the free and robust debate of public issues; there is no potential interference with a meaningful dialogue of ideas"; and the "threat of liability" does not pose the risk of "a reaction of self-censorship" on matters of public import. *Dun & Bradstreet.*

We noted a short time ago, in considering whether public employee speech addressed a matter of public concern, that "the boundaries of the public concern test are not well defined." San Diego v. Roe, 543 U.S. 77 (2004) (per curiam).

Although that remains true today, we have articulated some guiding principles, principles that accord broad protection to speech to ensure that courts themselves do not become inadvertent censors.

Speech deals with matters of public concern when it can "be fairly considered as relating to any matter of political, social, or other concern to the community," Connick [v. Myers, 461 U.S. 138 (1983)], or when it "is a subject of legitimate news interest; that is, a subject of general interest and of value and concern to the public," *San Diego*. The arguably "inappropriate or controversial character of a statement is irrelevant to the question whether it deals with a matter of public concern." [].

[W]e concluded in *San Diego v. Roe* that, in the context of a government employer regulating the speech of its employees, videos of an employee engaging in sexually explicit acts did not address a public concern; the videos "did nothing to inform the public about any aspect of the [employing agency's] functioning or operation." 543 U.S., at 84.

Deciding whether speech is of public or private concern requires us to examine the "'content, form, and context'" of that speech, "'as revealed by the whole record.'" *Dun & Bradstreet* (quoting *Connick*). As in other First Amendment cases, the court is obligated "to 'make an independent examination of the whole record' in order to make sure that 'the judgment does not constitute a forbidden intrusion on the field of free expression.'" In considering content, form, and context, no factor is dispositive, and it is necessary to evaluate all the circumstances of the speech, including what was said, where it was said, and how it was said.

The "content" of Westboro's signs plainly relates to broad issues of interest to society at large, rather than matters of "purely private concern." . . . While the [] messages [on Westboro's signs] may fall short of refined social or political commentary, the issues they highlight—the political and moral conduct of the United States and its citizens, the fate of our Nation, homosexuality in the military, and scandals involving the Catholic clergy—are matters of public import. The signs certainly convey Westboro's position on those issues, in a manner designed . . . to reach as broad a public audience as possible. And even if a few of the signs—such as "You're Going to Hell" and "God Hates You"—were viewed as containing messages related to Matthew Snyder or the Snyders specifically, that would not change the fact that the overall thrust and dominant theme of Westboro's demonstration spoke to broader public issues.

Apart from the content of Westboro's signs, Snyder contends that the "context" of the speech—its connection with his son's funeral—makes the speech a matter of private rather than public concern. The fact that Westboro spoke in connection with a funeral, however, cannot by itself transform the nature of Westboro's speech. . . .

. . . Westboro had been actively engaged in speaking on the subjects addressed in its picketing long before it became aware of Matthew Snyder, and there can be no serious claim that Westboro's picketing did not represent its "honestly believed" views on public issues. There was no pre-existing relationship or conflict between Westboro and Snyder that might suggest Westboro's speech on public matters was intended to mask an attack on Snyder over a private matter. []

. . . Westboro's choice to convey its views in conjunction with Matthew Snyder's funeral made the expression of those views particularly hurtful to many, especially to Matthew's father. The record makes clear that the applicable legal term—"emotional distress"—fails to capture fully the anguish Westboro's choice added to Mr. Snyder's already incalculable grief. But Westboro conducted its picketing peacefully on matters of public concern at a public place adjacent to a public street. Such space occupies a "special position in terms of First Amendment protection." United States v. Grace, 461 U.S. 171, 180 (1983). "[W]e have repeatedly referred to public streets as the archetype of a traditional public forum," noting that "'[t]ime out of mind' public streets and sidewalks have been used for public assembly and debate." Frisby v. Schultz, 487 U.S. 474, 480 (1988).

. . . Maryland now has a law imposing restrictions on funeral picketing, Md. Crim. Law Code Ann. § 10-205 (Lexis Supp. 2010), as do 43 other States and the Federal Government. To the extent these laws are content neutral, they raise very different questions from the tort verdict at issue in this case. Maryland's law, however, was not in effect at the time of the events at issue here. . . .

Simply put, the church members had the right to be where they were. Westboro alerted local authorities to its funeral protest and fully complied with police guidance on where the picketing could be staged. The picketing was conducted under police supervision some 1,000 feet from the church, out of the sight of those at the church. The protest was not unruly; there was no shouting, profanity, or violence.

The record confirms that any distress occasioned by Westboro's picketing turned on the content and viewpoint of the message conveyed, rather than any interference with the funeral itself. A group of parishioners standing at the very spot where Westboro stood, holding signs that said "God Bless America" and "God Loves You," would not have been subjected to liability. It was what Westboro said that exposed it to tort damages.

. . . The jury here was instructed that it could hold Westboro liable for intentional infliction of emotional distress based on a finding that Westboro's picketing was "outrageous." "Outrageousness," however, is a highly malleable standard with "an inherent subjectiveness about it which would allow a jury to impose liability on the basis of the jurors' tastes or views, or perhaps on the basis of their dislike of a particular expression." *Hustler*. . . . What Westboro said, in the whole context of how and where it chose to say it, is entitled to "special protection" under the First Amendment, and that protection cannot be overcome by a jury finding that the picketing was outrageous.

. . . Westboro believes that America is morally flawed; many Americans might feel the same about Westboro. Westboro's funeral picketing is certainly hurtful and its contribution to public discourse may be negligible. But Westboro addressed matters of public import on public property, in a peaceful manner, in full compliance with the guidance of local officials. The speech was indeed planned to coincide with Matthew Snyder's funeral, but did not itself disrupt that funeral, and Westboro's choice to conduct its picketing at that time and place did not alter the nature of its speech.

Speech is powerful. It can stir people to action, move them to tears of both joy and sorrow, and—as it did here—inflict great pain. On the facts before us, we cannot react to that pain by punishing the speaker. As a Nation we have chosen a different course—to protect even hurtful speech on public issues to ensure that we do not stifle public debate. That choice requires that we shield Westboro from tort liability for its picketing in this case. [Affirmed.]

NOTES AND QUESTIONS

1. *A personal assault?* In dissent, Justice Samuel Alito labeled Westboro's speech a "vicious verbal assault" and a "brutal attack." Is Justice Alito correct that there is no need to protect the speech of the Westboro protestors here because they have "almost limitless opportunities" to voice their opinions on "moral, religious, and political issues" in other contexts? Is there a First Amendment right to convey your message in the format or context where it is most likely to be heard or seen? Should the majority have given more weight to the argument that the Westboro protestors were exploiting the funeral of a private citizen to attract public attention to their repugnant views? Does it matter whether the picketing was directed to "society at large" or to the family of Matthew Snyder? *See* Steven J. Heyman, *To Drink the Cup of Fury: Funeral Picketing, Public Discourse and the First Amendment*, 45 Conn. L. Rev. 101 (2012).
2. *The constitutionality of funeral protest statutes.* Is the Court majority encouraging states to pass funeral protest statutes? The Court suggests content-neutral laws imposing reasonable time, place, and manner restrictions on funeral picketing would not violate the First Amendment. At least 41 states and the federal govern have passed statutes restricting funeral protests. *See* Christina E. Wells, *Privacy and Funeral Protest*, 87 N.C. L. Rev. 151, 158 (2008) (discussing the constitutionality of these statutes).

THEORY-APPLIED PROBLEM: FUNERAL PROTESTS

A state law makes it a misdemeanor to engage in "violent, abusive, indecent, profane, boisterous, unreasonably loud or otherwise disorderly conduct" within 500 feet of a funeral service within the hour preceding such service, during such service, or within the hour immediately following the conclusion of such service. Is this law constitutional? Why or why not? Would the law be constitutional if it were limited by adding the requirement that the conduct "tends to cause or provoke a disturbance"?

THEORY-APPLIED PROBLEM: INTENTIONAL INFLICTION AND PUBLIC CONCERN

Assume a high school student creates a Web site called "My Teacher Sux." On the site, he ridicules the teaching style, appearance, and intelligence of his math teacher. The site includes a page captioned, "Why Should My Math Teacher Die? [Joke!]" and asks visitors to the site for contributions of $20 to hire a hit man. Many of the students in the teacher's class learn of and visit the site, and one of them brings it to the teacher's attention. The teacher becomes so severely distressed he must take medical leave and cannot finish the school year. He sues the student for intentional infliction of emotional distress. Is the First Amendment a bar to recovery? The facts of this problem are based loosely on J.S. v. Bethlehem Area Sch. Dist., 807 A.2d 803 (Pa. 2002).

C. *FIRST AMENDMENT LIMITATIONS ON IMPOSING LIABILITY FOR PUBLISHING TRUE INFORMATION*

The previous cases in this chapter dealt with First Amendment limits on torts that impose liability on publishers of information alleged to be false or at least not provably true. A harder issue is presented when states attempt to impose liability based on the publication of truthful but private information. Many states recognize the tort of public disclosure of private facts, which is defined by the *Restatement (Second) of Torts § 652D* as being actionable when a defendant gives publicity to private facts about a plaintiff, the disclosure is highly offensive to a reasonable person, and the disclosure is not of public concern. Because the tort developed in the twentieth century, the tort elements reflect an attempt to accommodate the publication of newsworthy information. However, the constitutionality of the tort is cast into doubt by the following case. Can you see why?

The Florida Star v. B. J. F.

491 U.S. 524 (1989)

Justice MARSHALL delivered the opinion of the Court.

Florida Stat. § 794.03 (1987) makes it unlawful to "print, publish, or broadcast . . . in any instrument of mass communication" the name of the victim of a sexual offense. Pursuant to this statute, appellant The Florida Star was found civilly liable for publishing the name of a rape victim which it had obtained from a publicly released police report. The issue presented here is whether this result comports with the First Amendment. We hold that it does not.

I

. . . On October 20, 1983, appellee B. J. F. reported to the Duval County, Florida, Sheriff's Department (Department) that she had been robbed and sexually assaulted by an unknown assailant. The Department prepared a report on the incident which identified B. J. F. by her full name. The Department then placed the report in its pressroom. The Department does not restrict access either to the pressroom or to the reports made available therein.

[The Florida Star, a Jacksonville newspaper, sent a "reporter-trainee" to the pressroom. The trainee copied the police report, including B. J. F.'s full name.] A Florida Star reporter then prepared a one-paragraph article about the crime, derived entirely from the trainee's copy of the police report. The article included B. J. F.'s full name. It appeared in the "Police Reports" section on October 29, 1983, one of 54 police blotter stories in that day's edition. . . . In printing B. J. F.'s full name, The Florida Star violated its internal policy of not publishing the names of sexual offense victims.

On September 26, 1984, B. J. F. [sued] the Department and the Florida Star, alleging that these parties negligently violated § 794.03. Before trial, the Department settled with B. J. F. for $2,500. . . .

[At trial,] B. J. F. testified that . . . she had heard about the article from fellow workers and acquaintances; that her mother had received several threatening phone calls from a man who stated that he would rape B. J. F. again; and that these events had forced B. J. F. to change her phone number and residence, to seek police protection, and to obtain mental health counseling. In defense, The Florida Star put forth evidence indicating that the newspaper had learned B. J. F.'s name from the incident report . . . , and that the newspaper's violation of its internal rule against publishing the names of sexual offense victims was inadvertent.

[The trial judge] ruled from the bench that § 794.03 was constitutional [and] directed [a] verdict on the issue of negligence, finding the newspaper *per se* negligent based upon its violation of § 794.03. This ruling left the jury to consider only the questions of causation and damages. The jury awarded B. J. F. $75,000 in compensatory damages and $25,000 in punitive damages. [The District Court of Appeal affirmed and the Florida Supreme Court denied review.]

II

. . . The parties to this case frame their contentions in light of a trilogy of cases which have presented, in different contexts, the conflict between truthful reporting and state-protected privacy interests. In Cox Broadcasting Corp. v. Cohn, 420 U.S. 469 (1975), we found unconstitutional a civil damages award entered against a television station for broadcasting the name of a rape-murder victim which the station had obtained from courthouse records. In Oklahoma Publishing Co. v. Oklahoma County District Court, 430 U.S. 308 (1977), we found unconstitutional a state court's pretrial order enjoining the media from publishing the name or photograph of an 11-year-old boy in connection with a juvenile proceeding involving that child which reporters had attended. Finally, in Smith v. Daily Mail Publishing Co., 443 U.S. 97 (1979), we found unconstitutional the indictment of two newspapers for violating a state statute forbidding newspapers to publish, without written approval of the juvenile court, the name of any youth charged as a juvenile offender. The papers had learned about a shooting by monitoring a police band radio frequency and had obtained the name of the alleged juvenile assailant from witnesses, the police, and a local prosecutor. . . .

We conclude that imposing damages on appellant for publishing B. J. F.'s name violates the First Amendment. . . . Despite the strong resemblance this case bears to *Cox Broadcasting*, that case cannot fairly be read as controlling here. The name of the rape victim in that case was obtained from courthouse records that were open to public inspection, a fact which Justice White's opinion for the Court repeatedly noted. That role is not directly compromised where, as here, the information in question comes from a police report prepared and disseminated at a time at which not only had no adversarial criminal proceedings begun, but no suspect had been identified.

Nor need we accept appellant's invitation to hold broadly that truthful publication may never be punished consistent with the First Amendment. Our cases have carefully eschewed reaching this ultimate question, mindful that the future may bring scenarios which prudence counsels our not resolving anticipatorily. Indeed, in *Cox Broadcasting*, we pointedly refused to answer even the less sweeping question "whether truthful publications may ever be subjected to civil or criminal liability" for invading "an area of privacy" defined by the State. Respecting the fact that press freedom and privacy rights are both "plainly rooted in the traditions and significant concerns of our society," we instead focused on the less sweeping issue "whether the State may impose sanctions on the accurate publication of the name of a rape victim obtained from public records—more specifically, from judicial records which are maintained in connection with a public prosecution and which themselves are open to public inspection." We continue to believe that the sensitivity and significance of the interests presented in clashes between First Amendment and privacy rights counsel relying on limited principles that sweep no more broadly than the appropriate context of the instant case.

In our view, this case is appropriately analyzed with reference to [the] limited First Amendment principle . . . articulated in *Daily Mail* . . . : "[I]f a newspaper lawfully obtains truthful information about a matter of public significance then state officials may not constitutionally punish publication of the information, absent a need to further a state interest of the highest order." According the press the ample protection provided by that principle is supported by at least three separate considerations, in addition to, of course, the overarching "'public interest, secured by the Constitution, in the dissemination of truth.'" The cases on which the *Daily Mail* synthesis relied demonstrate these considerations.

First, because the *Daily Mail* formulation only protects the publication of information which a newspaper has "lawfully obtain[ed]," the government retains ample means of safeguarding significant interests upon which publication may impinge, including protecting a rape victim's anonymity. To the extent sensitive information rests in private hands, the government may under some circumstances forbid its nonconsensual acquisition, thereby bringing outside of the *Daily Mail* principle the publication of any information so acquired. To the extent sensitive information is in the government's custody, it has even greater power to forestall or mitigate the injury caused by its release. The government may classify certain information, establish and enforce procedures ensuring its redacted release, and extend a damages remedy against the government or its officials where the government's mishandling of sensitive information leads to its dissemination. Where information is entrusted to the government, a less drastic means than punishing truthful publication almost always exists for guarding against the dissemination of private facts.

A second consideration undergirding the *Daily Mail* principle is the fact that punishing the press for its dissemination of information which is already publicly available is relatively unlikely to advance the interests in the service of which the State seeks to act. It is not, of course, always the case that information lawfully acquired by the press is known, or accessible, to others. But where the government has made certain information publicly available, it is highly anomalous to sanction persons other than the source of its release. . . .

A third and final consideration is the "timidity and self-censorship" which may result from allowing the media to be punished for publishing certain truthful information. *Cox Broadcasting* noted this concern with overdeterrence in the context of information made public through official court records, but the fear of excessive media self-suppression is applicable as well to other information released, without qualification, by the government. A contrary rule, depriving protection to those who rely on the government's implied representations of the lawfulness of dissemination, would force upon the media the onerous obligation of sifting through government press releases, reports, and pronouncements to prune out material arguably unlawful for publication. This situation could inhere even where the newspaper's sole object was to reproduce, with no substantial change, the government's rendition of the event in question.

Applied to the instant case, the *Daily Mail* principle clearly commands reversal. The first inquiry is whether the newspaper "lawfully obtain[ed] truthful information about a matter of public significance." It is undisputed that the news article describing the assault on B. J. F. was accurate. In addition, appellant lawfully obtained B. J. F.'s name. Appellee's argument to the contrary is based on the fact that under Florida law, police reports which reveal the identity of the victim of a sexual offense are not among the matters of "public record" which the public, by law, is entitled to inspect. But the fact that state officials are not required to disclose such reports does not make it unlawful for a newspaper to receive them when furnished by the government. Nor does the fact that the Department apparently failed to fulfill its obligation under § 794.03 not to "cause or allow to be . . . published" the name of a sexual offense victim make the newspaper's ensuing receipt of this information unlawful. Even assuming the Constitution permitted a State to proscribe *receipt* of information, Florida has not taken this step. It is clear, furthermore, that the news article concerned "a matter of public significance," in the sense in which the *Daily Mail* synthesis of prior cases used that term. That is, the article generally, as opposed to the specific identity contained within it, involved a matter of paramount public import: the commission, and investigation, of a violent crime which had been reported to authorities.

The second inquiry is whether imposing liability on appellant pursuant to § 794.03 serves "a need to further a state interest of the highest order." Appellee argues that a rule punishing publication furthers three closely related interests: the privacy of victims of sexual offenses; the physical safety of such victims, who may be targeted for retaliation if their names become known to their assailants; and the goal of encouraging victims of such crimes to report these offenses without fear of exposure. . . .

At a time in which we are daily reminded of the tragic reality of rape, it is undeniable that these are highly significant interests, a fact underscored by the Florida Legislature's explicit attempt to protect these interests by enacting a criminal statute prohibiting much dissemination of victim identities. We accordingly do not rule out the possibility that, in a proper case, imposing civil sanctions for publication of the name of a rape victim might be so overwhelmingly necessary to advance these interests as to satisfy the *Daily Mail* standard. For three independent reasons, however, imposing liability for publication under the circumstances of this case is too precipitous a means of advancing these interests to convince us that there is a "need" within the meaning of the *Daily Mail* formulation for Florida to take this extreme step. . . .

First is the manner in which appellant obtained the identifying information in question. As we have noted, where the government itself provides information to the media, it is most appropriate to assume that the government had, but failed to utilize, far more limited means of guarding against dissemination than the extreme step of punishing truthful speech. That assumption is richly borne out in this case. B. J. F.'s identity would never have come to light were it not for the erroneous, if inadvertent, inclusion by the Department of her full name in an incident report made available in a pressroom open to the public. . . . Where, as here, the government has failed to police itself in disseminating information, it is clear under *Cox Broadcasting, Oklahoma Publishing,* and *Landmark Communications* that the imposition of damages against the press for its subsequent publication can hardly be said to be a narrowly tailored means of safeguarding anonymity. Once the government has placed such information in the public domain, "reliance must rest upon the judgment of those who decide what to publish or broadcast," and hopes for restitution must rest upon the willingness of the government to compensate victims for their loss of privacy and to protect them from the other consequences of its mishandling of the information which these victims provided in confidence.

That appellant gained access to the information in question through a government news release makes it especially likely that, if liability were to be imposed, self-censorship would result. Reliance on a news release is a paradigmatically "routine newspaper reporting techniqu[e]." The government's issuance of such a release, without qualification, can only convey to recipients that the government considered dissemination lawful, and indeed expected the recipients to disseminate the information further. . . .

A second problem with Florida's imposition of liability for publication is the broad sweep of the negligence *per se* standard applied under the civil cause of action implied from § 794.03. Unlike claims based on the common-law tort of invasion of privacy, civil actions based on § 794.03 require no case-by-case findings that the disclosure of a fact about a person's private life was one that a reasonable person would find highly offensive. [L]iability follows automatically from publication. This is so regardless of whether the identity of the victim is already known throughout the community; whether the victim has voluntarily called public attention to the offense; or whether the identity of the victim has otherwise become a reasonable subject of public concern—because, perhaps, questions have arisen whether the victim fabricated an assault by a particular person. Nor is there a scienter requirement of any kind under § 794.03, engendering the perverse result that truthful publications challenged pursuant to this cause of action are less protected by the First Amendment than even the least protected defamatory falsehoods: those involving purely private figures, where liability is evaluated under a standard, usually applied by a jury, of ordinary negligence. . . .

Third, and finally, the facial underinclusiveness of § 794.03 raises serious doubts about whether Florida is, in fact, serving, with this statute, the significant interests which appellee invokes in support of affirmance. Section 794.03 prohibits the publication of identifying information only if this information appears in an "instrument of mass communication," a term the statute does not define. Section 794.03 does not prohibit the spread by other means of the identities of victims of sexual offenses. An individual who maliciously spreads word of the identity of a rape victim is thus not covered, despite the fact that the communication of such information to persons who live near, or work with, the victim may have consequences as devastating as the exposure of her name to large numbers of strangers. . . .

When a State attempts the extraordinary measure of punishing truthful publication in the name of privacy, it must demonstrate its commitment to advancing this interest by applying its prohibition evenhandedly, to the smalltime disseminator as well as the media giant. Where important First Amendment interests are at stake, the mass scope of disclosure is not an acceptable surrogate for injury. A ban on disclosures effected by "instrument[s] of mass communication" simply cannot be defended on the ground that partial prohibitions may effect partial relief. Without more careful and inclusive precautions against alternative forms of dissemination, we cannot conclude that Florida's selective ban on publication by the mass media satisfactorily accomplishes its stated purpose. . . .

Justice SCALIA, concurring in part and concurring in the judgment.

I think it sufficient to decide this case to rely upon the third ground set forth in the Court's opinion: that a law cannot be regarded as protecting an interest "of the highest order," and thus as justifying a restriction upon truthful speech, when it leaves appreciable damage to that supposedly vital interest unprohibited. In the present case, I would anticipate that the rape victim's discomfort at the dissemination of news of her misfortune among friends and acquaintances would be at least as great as her discomfort at its publication by the media to people to whom she is only a name. Yet the law in question does not prohibit the former in either oral or written form. Nor is it at all clear, as I think it must be to validate this statute, that Florida's general privacy law would prohibit such gossip. Nor, finally, is it credible that the interest meant to be served by the statute is the protection of the victim against a rapist still at large—an interest that arguably would extend only to mass publication. There would be little reason to limit a statute with that objective to rape alone; or to extend it to all rapes, whether or not the felon has been apprehended and confined. In any case, the instructions here did not require the jury to find that the rapist was at large.

Justice WHITE, joined by Chief Justice REHNQUIST and Justice O'CONNOR, dissenting.

At issue in this case is whether there is any information about people, which—though true—may not be published in the press. By holding that only "a state interest of the highest order" permits the State to penalize the publication of truthful information, and by holding that protecting a rape victim's right to privacy is not among those state interests of the highest order, the Court accepts appellant's invitation, . . . to obliterate one of the most noteworthy legal inventions of the 20th century: the tort of the publication of private facts. . . . Even if the Court's opinion does not say as much today, such obliteration will follow inevitably from the Court's conclusion here. If the First Amendment prohibits wholly private persons (such as B. J. F.) from recovering for the publication of the fact that she was raped, I doubt that there remain any "private facts" which persons may assume will not be published in the newspapers or broadcast on television.

NOTES AND QUESTIONS

1. *Plaintiff must defend state's interests and means.* The Supreme Court's application of the *Daily Mail* test meant that the burden was on B. J. F. to defend the state of Florida's choice of § 794.03 as a means of protecting her

privacy. Did her tort action fail because the state interests underlying the statute were not "of the highest order," or because the statute was not narrowly tailored to achieve the state interests?

2. *Implications for the public disclosure privacy tort.* What are the implications of the decision for plaintiffs who sue defendants in tort for public disclosure of private facts? When, if ever, can tort liability be imposed for the publication of truthful information about a matter of public concern?
3. *Right to be forgotten in the European Union.* Personal privacy receives markedly more protection in Europe than in the United States. In Europe, of course, First Amendment limitations provide no shield for global media companies. For example, a 2014 decision by the European Court of Justice (the EU's highest court) recognized a privacy right unknown in the U.S, which is commonly referred to as the right to be forgotten. The court held that search engines like Google must remove certain privacy-invading links from their search results. The case arose in Spain, where a man complained that a Google search of his name turned up a 12-year-old newspaper story about proceedings against him for debt. He contended that the story, although accurate, was no longer relevant because the matter had been fully resolved. He demanded that Google remove the link that pulled up the story when users entered his name in a Google search. The Court held that the 1995 Data Protection Directive of the European Parliament gives individuals a right to insist on removal of data that are "inadequate, irrelevant, or no longer relevant, or excessive in relation to the purposes for which they were processed and in the light of the time that has elapsed Case C-131/12, Google Spain SL, Google Inc. v. Agencia Española de Protectión de Datos (AEPD), Mario Costeja Gonzáles, Court of Justice (Grand Chamber), 13 May 2014. The European Union adopted its General Data Protection Regulation, which codifies a right to request erasure of one's personal data. The Regulation went fully into effect in 2018. It regulates organizations physically or virtually present in the EU, and its protections covers EU citizens even while they reside in the U.S.; it also covers U.S. citizens who reside in the EU. See Regulation (EU) 2016/679 of the European Parliament and of the Council of April 27, 2016 on the protection of natural persons with regard to the processing of personal data and on the free movement of such data, and repealing Directive 95/46/EC (General Data Protection Regulation), Official Journal of the European Union, Vol. L119 (May 2016), 1-88.
4. *A right to be forgotten in the United States?* Traditionally, there has been little jurisprudential support for a right to be forgotten in the United States. In January 2015, for example, the Second Circuit ruled that a woman who had been arrested in 2010 and whose arrest had later been nullified could not order the arrest removed from websites. She argued that the information was now false and defamatory and, therefore, should be erased under Connecticut's Erasure Statute, which mandates that government records be erased after a nullifying prosecutorial decision; but the court found that no "amount of wishing can undo [the] historical truth" of the arrest. Martin v. Hearst Corp., 777 F.3d 546 (2d Cir. 2015). However,

judicial sentiment may be shifting. See, for example, Pierre-Paul v. ESPN, 44 Media L. Rep. 2452 (S.D. Fla. 2016) (denying dismissal of privacy claim by NFL player Jason Pierre-Paul, who sued ESPN after one of its reporters tweeted that Pierre-Paul had lost a finger in a fireworks accident and attached the medical chart as proof and holding that "Plaintiff has shown the publication of his private medical records may breach [privacy tort] limits and, thus, are not a matter of public concern." The case later settled for an undisclosed amount. See also Jackson v. Mayweather, 10 Cal. App. 5th 1240 (Cal. Ct. App. 2017) (holding that the famous boxer's girlfriend had a privacy claim after he published sonogram images of twin fetuses: "Mayweather's posting of the sonogram of the twins Jackson had been carrying before her pregnancy terminated and the summary medical report regarding her pregnancy falls outside the protection accorded a newsworthy report"); Judge v. Saltz Plastic Surgery, 367 P.3d 1006 (Utah 2016) (denying summary judgment in a case involving photographs of the plaintiff's body before and after breast augmentation surgery).

AN EXTENDED NOTE ON DEFINING "UNLAWFULLY OBTAINED"

In Bartnicki v. Vopper, 532 U.S. 514 (2001), the Supreme Court considered whether information is "unlawfully obtained" by a broadcaster who receives the information from a third party who obtained it in violation of wiretap laws. In *Bartnicki*, the chief negotiator for a local teacher's union was recorded while speaking on her cell phone to the union's president about a proposed teacher's strike. In the course of their conversation, the union president stated in regard to the school board with whom they were negotiating: "If they're not gonna move for three percent, we're gonna have to go to their homes. . . . To blow off their front porches, we'll have to do some work on some of those guys. (PAUSES) Really, um, really and truthfully because this is, you know, this is bad news. (UNDECIPHERABLE.)" The person who illegally intercepted and recorded this conversation was never identified, but an opponent of the union came into possession of the tape and turned it over to a local radio talk show host who broadcasted it on his show. It was also broadcast by another station and published by local newspapers. The union negotiator and union president sued the talk show host, his radio station, and other members of the media, alleging that each one "knew or had reason to know" that recording their private telephone conversation was a violation of Pennsylvania and federal wiretap law. The federal wiretap statute made it a crime to "intentionally disclose [], or endeavor [] to disclose, to any other person the contents of any wire, oral, or electronic communication, knowing or having reason to know that the information was obtained through the interception of a wire, oral, or electronic communication. . . ." 18 U.S.C. § 2511(1)(a). Pennsylvania's statute was similar. Both statutes authorized suits for damages. The U.S. Court of Appeals for the Third Circuit held that the wiretap statutes were content-neutral. Bartnicki v. Vopper, 200 F.3d 109 (1999). Applying intermediate scrutiny, the Third Circuit held that the statutes were invalid because they deterred more speech than necessary to protect the privacy interests at stake. The Supreme Court reached the same result by a different route. Although the Court conceded that the wiretap statutes were "content-neutral law[s] of general applicability," the Court analyzed "the [statutes'] naked prohibition against disclosures" as "a regulation of pure speech." The Court therefore applied the same exacting constitutional test that it had applied in *B.J.F.*, holding, 6-3, that as to the broadcaster, the information contained on the intercepted recording was not unlawfully obtained. The government asserted that the statute served an interest in deterring illegal interceptions of private conversations and remedying the harm caused by illegal interception. The Court, however, stated that these interests could be adequately served by punishing the person who illegally intercepted the conversation in the first place rather than "punishing disclosures of lawfully obtained information of public interest by one not involved in the initial illegality." Despite the breadth of this language, the Court emphasized that *Bartnicki* involved a narrow set of facts: Specifically, it involved public-figure plaintiffs whose illegally recorded conversations involved "truthful information of public concern." Indeed, the concurring Justices Breyer and O'Connor, whose votes were essential to make the 6–3 majority, wrote separately to emphasize that the Court's "narrow" holding rested on "special circumstances" present in the case: The fact that the broadcasters acted lawfully prior to disclosure, and the fact that the "information publicized involved a matter of *unusual* public concern, namely, a threat of potential physical harm to others" (emphasis added). The Court's decision, they wrote, did not create a broad, general "'public interest' exception" to the application of wiretap laws to members of the media. For a high-profile test case regarding the scope of the *Bartnicki* decision, *see* Boehner v. McDermott, 484 F.3d 573 (D.C. Cir. 2007). See also Dahlstrom v. Sun-Times Media, LLC., 777 F.3d 937 (7th Cir. 2015).

D. *FIRST AMENDMENT LIMITATIONS ON IMPOSING LIABILITY BASED ON NEWSGATHERING METHODS*

Sometimes plaintiffs bring tort actions based on the methods by which the media (or others) obtain information rather than based on the publication of that information. For example, plaintiffs may sue when reporters engage in trespass, fraud, or intrusions in an effort to gather information for publication. While publication receives full First Amendment protection, the Supreme Court in Cohen v. Cowles Media, which appears immediately below, held that "generally applicable laws do not offend the First Amendment simply because their enforcement against the press has incidental effects on its ability to gather the news." As you read *Cohen*, which deals with the law of promissory estoppel rather than tort law, you should attempt to reconcile it with the cases you've studied previously in this chapter.

Cohen v. Cowles Media Co.

501 U.S. 663 (1991)

[Cohen was a consultant working on a Republican gubernatorial campaign. He offered to provide reporters with court documents showing that the Democratic candidate for lieutenant governor had previously been convicted of shoplifting, but only on condition that Cohen not be identified as the source. Reporters from two different newspapers took the information from Cohen on his terms, but their editors included Cohen's name in the resulting story. Cohen lost his job as a result, and he sued both newspapers. The Minnesota Supreme Court held that (1) the reporters' arrangement with Cohen did not amount to a contract, (2) he might have a cause of action for breach of the promise of confidentiality on a theory of promissory estoppel, but (3) permitting such a judgment would violate the First Amendment. Cohen appealed.]

Justice WHITE delivered the opinion of the Court.

. . . Respondents rely on the proposition that "if a newspaper lawfully obtains truthful information about a matter of public significance then state officials may not constitutionally punish publication of the information, absent a need to further a state interest of the highest order." That proposition is unexceptionable, and it has been applied in various cases that have found insufficient the asserted state interests in preventing publication of truthful, lawfully obtained information. See, e.g., *Florida Star v. B.J.F.* . . .

This case, however, is not controlled by this line of cases but, rather, by the equally well-established line of decisions holding that generally applicable laws do not offend the First Amendment simply because their enforcement against the press has incidental effects on its ability to gather and report the news. As the cases relied on by respondents recognize, the truthful information sought to be published must have been lawfully acquired. The press may not with impunity break and enter an office or dwelling to gather news. Neither does the First Amendment relieve a newspaper reporter of the obligation shared by all citizens to respond to a grand jury subpoena and answer questions relevant to a criminal investigation, even though the reporter might be required to reveal a confidential source. *Branzburg v. Hayes*. . . . The press, like others interested in publishing, may not publish copyrighted material without obeying the copyright laws. . . . Similarly, the media must obey the National Labor Relations Act . . . and the Fair Labor Standards Act . . . ; may not restrain trade in violation of the antitrust laws . . . ; and must pay non-discriminatory taxes. . . . It is, therefore, beyond dispute that "[t]he publisher of a newspaper has no special immunity from the application of general laws. He has no special privilege to invade the rights and liberties of others." . . . Accordingly, enforcement of such general laws against the press is not subject to stricter scrutiny than would be applied to enforcement against other persons or organizations.

There can be little doubt that the Minnesota doctrine of promissory estoppel is a law of general applicability. It does not target or single out the press. Rather, insofar as we are advised, the doctrine is generally applicable to the daily transactions of all the citizens of Minnesota. The First Amendment does not forbid its application to the press.

Justice Blackmun suggests that applying Minnesota promissory estoppel doctrine in this case will "punish" respondents for publishing truthful information that was lawfully obtained. . . . This is not strictly accurate because compensatory damages are not a form of punishment. . . . If the contract between the parties in this case had contained a liquidated damages provision, it would be perfectly clear that the payment to petitioner would represent a cost of acquiring newsworthy material to be published at a profit, rather than a punishment imposed by the State. The payment of compensatory damages in this case is constitutionally indistinguishable from a generous bonus paid to a confidential news source. In any event, as indicated above, the characterization of the payment makes no difference for First Amendment purposes when the law being applied is a general law and does not single out the press. Moreover, Justice Blackmun's reliance on cases like *Florida Star v. B.J.F.* and *Smith v. Daily Mail* is misplaced. In those cases, the State itself defined the content of publications that would trigger liability. Here, by contrast, Minnesota law simply requires those making promises to keep them. The parties themselves, as in this case, determine the scope of their legal obligations, and any restrictions that may be placed on the publication of truthful information are self-imposed.

Also, it is not at all clear that respondents obtained Cohen's name "lawfully" in this case, at least for purposes of publishing it. Unlike the situation in *Florida Star*, where the rape victim's name was obtained through lawful access to a police report, respondents obtained Cohen's name only by making a promise that they did not honor. The dissenting opinions suggest that the press should not be subject to any law, including copyright law for example, which in any fashion or to any degree limits or restricts the press' right to report truthful information. The First Amendment does not grant the press such limitless protection.

Nor is Cohen attempting to use a promissory estoppel cause of action to avoid the strict requirements for establishing a libel or defamation claim. . . . Cohen is not seeking damages for injury to his reputation or his state of mind. He sought damages in excess of $50,000 for breach of a promise that caused him to lose his job and lowered his earning capacity. Thus, this is not a case like *Hustler Magazine, Inc. v. Falwell*, where we held that the constitutional libel standards apply to a claim alleging that the publication of a parody was a state-law tort of intentional infliction of emotional distress.

Respondents and amici argue that permitting Cohen to maintain a cause of action for promissory estoppel will inhibit truthful reporting because news organizations will have legal incentives not to disclose a confidential source's identity even when that person's identity is itself newsworthy. Justice Souter makes a similar argument. But if this is the case, it is no more than the incidental, and constitutionally insignificant, consequence of applying to the press a generally applicable law that requires those who make certain kinds of promises to keep them. . . . [The Court remanded to the Minnesota Supreme Court, which affirmed an award to Cohen of $200,000 on his promissory estoppel claim.]

Justice BLACKMUN, with whom Justice MARSHALL and Justice SOUTER join, dissenting.

. . . I regard our decision in *Hustler Magazine, Inc. v. Falwell* . . . to be precisely on point. . . . There was no doubt that Virginia's tort of intentional infliction of emotional distress was "a law of general applicability" unrelated to the suppression of speech. . . . As in *Hustler*, the operation of Minnesota's doctrine of promissory estoppel in this case cannot be said to have a merely "incidental" burden on speech; the publication of important political speech is the claimed violation. Thus, as in *Hustler*, the law may not be enforced to punish the expression of truthful information or opinion. In the instant case, it is undisputed that the publication at issue was true.

To the extent that truthful speech may ever be sanctioned consistent with the First Amendment, it must be in furtherance of a state interest "of the highest order." Because the Minnesota Supreme Court's opinion makes clear that the State's interest in enforcing its promissory estoppel doctrine in this case was far from compelling . . . I would affirm that court's decision.

[Justice Souter also dissented, in an opinion in which Justice Marshall, Justice Blackmun, and Justice O'Connor joined. He argued that "the State's interest in enforcing a newspaper's promise of confidentiality [is] insufficient to outweigh the interest in unfettered publication of the information revealed in this case. . . ."]

NOTES AND QUESTIONS

1. *Reconciling* Bartnicki. Did the reporters "unlawfully obtain" Cohen's name? Cohen offered to "leak" the negative documents concerning the Democratic candidate only if the reporters promised him confidentiality. The reporters promised confidentiality, but their editors reneged on the promise because they believed Cohen's name was part of what made the story newsworthy. What makes the reporters' method of obtaining the information unlawful? Is it clearly unlawful in a way that accepting information known to have been obtained by a third party in violation of federal law is not?
2. *Laws of general application.* Why isn't defamation a law of general application that does not offend the First Amendment when applied to the press? Is it because it is a law that directly affects publication, as opposed to newsgathering?

Chapter 10

The Conflict Between Free Speech and Promoting Equality, Civility, Dignity, and Mutual Respect

Table of Contents

A. The Ancien Régime: Group Libel Regulations and the First Amendment
B. A Contemporary Example of Regulations Aimed at Promoting Social Equality: Title VII As a Limit on Free Speech
C. Government Efforts to Promote Civility and the First Amendment
D. Government Efforts to Prohibit Hate Speech and Racialized Threats

To what extent can government restrict speech in order to advance other (constitutional) interests, such as social equality (or even mere civility) between the races, the sexes, and various religious groups? Does the First Amendment, properly read and applied, completely bar government efforts to promote social harmony in an increasingly pluralistic society by imposing limits on "hate speech"? Or, in the alternative, should free speech principles give way when necessary to protect equality and human dignity? What about baseline notions of civility in public discourse? Should government be utterly powerless to enact regulations aimed at securing these values?

Since the 1970s (and arguably since the late 1960s), the Supreme Court of the United States generally has invalidated most government efforts aimed at promoting equality, dignity, and civility, in the name of safeguarding freedom of speech. The Justices have never suggested that hate speech has any particular social value but instead have emphasized that the danger of empowering the government to censor even highly offensive speech clearly outweighs the value of creating a more civil marketplace of ideas. Justice Kennedy, for example, has noted that "[t]he

Nation well knows that one of the costs of the First Amendment is that it protects the speech we detest as well as the speech we embrace." United States v. Alvarez, 567 U.S. 709, 729 (2012). *Alvarez* involved intentional false claims about military honors, a kind of speech obviously lacking much (any?) objective social value. Even "[t]hough few might find [Alvarez's] statements anything but contemptible, his right to make those statements is protected by the Constitution's guarantee of freedom of speech and expression." *Id.* at 729-30. The Supreme Court's approach to hate speech consistently has followed this logic.

The contemporary U.S. approach advances free speech at the cost of protecting social equality, dignity, and civility. The protection of such speech undoubtedly imposes serious social costs. *See* Jeremy Waldron, *The Harm in Hate Speech* (2012) (arguing that hate speech marginalizes its victims within the political community, reduces the vibrancy and vitality of public discourse, and positing that the harms hate speech causes cannot be effectively addressed by counter speech). The United States Supreme Court's approach, however, reflects an assumption that counter speech often can serve as an effective antidote to racist, sexist, homophobic, or otherwise bigoted speech. Moreover, even if this does not hold true in all cases, hate speech should still enjoy constitutional protection "not because we doubt the speech inflicts harm, but because we fear the censorship more." Michael W. McConnell, *You Can't Say That,* N.Y. Times, June 24, 2012, BR14 (book review).

Alternative approaches to the regulation of hate speech not only exist but flourish in other industrial democracies, such as Canada and Germany. In other words, the U.S. approach of privileging hate speech in order to ensure full and robust political dialogue is not the only way to address the problem, even in a society generally committed to protecting freedom of expression. Some First Amendment scholars have questioned whether U.S. law adequately advances equality values when free speech and equality collide. *See, e.g.*, Richard Delgado, *Campus Anti-racism Rules: Constitutional Narratives in Collision,* 85 Nw. U. L. Rev. 343 (1991); Mari Matsuda, *Public Response to Racist Speech: Considering the Victim's Story,* 87 Mich. L. Rev. 2320 (1989). Other scholars, while acknowledging the importance of the equality project, question whether speech codes are an effective (let alone constitutionally permissible) response, particularly in light of the inevitably content- and viewpoint-based nature of such speech restrictions. *See, e.g.*, Steven G. Gey, *The Case Against Post-Modern Censorship Theory,* 145 U. Pa. L. Rev. 193 (1996).

The modern rule against civility codes aimed at improving social relations masks a more complicated historical picture. The U.S. Supreme Court relatively recently sustained statutes and regulations facially aimed at securing a modicum of civility in public communications. Cases like *Beauharnais,* decided in 1952, reflect a very different sensibility than cases like *Cohen* and *Gooding.* Moreover, even in the contemporary United States, the commitment to protecting free speech is not absolute. For example, Title VII prohibits the creation of "hostile work environments" based on race, gender, sexual orientation, gender identity, or religion; the creation of such an environment generally involves speech that reflects animus or hostility based on race, sex, or religion. Yet, most judges, legal academics, and practitioners do not view Title VII as impermissibly trenching on the First Amendment. *Cf.* Kinsley R. Browne, *Title VII as Censorship: Hostile-Environment Harassment and the First Amendment,* 52 Ohio St. L.J. 481 (1991); Eugene Volokh, *Freedom of Speech and Workplace Harassment,* 39 UCLA L. Rev. 1791 (1992).

This chapter considers the problem of "group libel": speech that attacks a particular group based on race, gender, sexual orientation, gender identity, religion, or other characteristics generally thought to be inappropriate bases for public or private discrimination. It then examines in some detail Title VII and cases sustaining the application of Title VII on facts that strongly implicate free speech principles. Finally, the chapter reviews major cases invalidating government efforts to promote equality, human dignity, and civility in the United States but sustaining such laws in Canada. These cases reflect the fact that the Supreme Court of Canada views legislative efforts to promote equality via speech restrictions more sympathetically than does the contemporary Supreme Court of the United States. In Canada, fear that the government will abuse the power to censor particularly noxious forms of hate speech has not prevented the creation and enforcement of bans against hate speech, notwithstanding a strong constitutional free speech guarantee.

This chapter does not seek to persuade the reader that one approach is inherently superior to another, or that a decent and just society must adopt or must not adopt particular rules or regulatory regimes. Rather, the point is to establish the fact of the conflicts between freedom of speech and the equality project, and also between free speech and efforts to secure a modicum of civility in public discourse. Any polity committed to free speech, equality, and civility will have to deal with resolving inevitable conflicts between a commitment to a full and free marketplace of ideas and a strong commitment to equal access to political, social, and economic opportunities without regard to race, sex, sexual orientation, gender identity, religion, or national origin.

A. *THE ANCIEN RÉGIME: GROUP LIBEL REGULATIONS AND THE FIRST AMENDMENT*

As late as 1952, the Supreme Court sustained a content- and viewpoint-based Illinois law that prohibited "group libel" of persons based on "race, color, creed, or religion." Invoking a history of toxic race relations in Illinois, the Supreme Court held (by a 5–4 vote) that Illinois had a legitimate interest in promoting social peace among a diverse population. Reasoning that group libel simply represented an extension of well-settled tort defamation principles applicable to individual citizens, the majority found the Illinois law sufficiently important to trump free speech principles. As later cases will make clear, the *Beauharnais* approach has not withstood the test of time. Even so, it represents a very different baseline for evaluating the consistency of hate speech regulations with the Free Speech Clause of the First Amendment.

Beauharnais v. Illinois

343 U.S. 250 (1952)

Mr. Justice FRANKFURTER delivered the opinion of the Court.

The petitioner was convicted upon information in the Municipal Court of Chicago of violating § 224a of the Illinois Criminal Code, Ill. Rev. Stat., 1949, c. 38, Div. 1, § 471. He was fined $200. The section provides:

> "It shall be unlawful for any person, firm or corporation to manufacture, sell, or offer for sale, advertise or publish, present or exhibit in any public place in this state any lithograph, moving picture, play, drama or sketch, which publication or exhibition portrays depravity, criminality, unchastity, or lack of virtue of a class of citizens, of any race, color, creed or religion which said publication or exhibition exposes the citizens of any race, color, creed or religion to contempt, derision, or obloquy or which is productive of breach of the peace or riots. . . ."

Beauharnais challenged the statute as violating the liberty of speech and of the press guaranteed as against the States by the Due Process Clause of the Fourteenth Amendment, and as too vague, under the restrictions implicit in the same Clause, to support conviction for crime. The Illinois courts rejected these contentions and sustained defendant's conviction. We granted certiorari in view of the serious questions raised concerning the limitations imposed by the Fourteenth Amendment on the power of a State to punish utterances promoting friction among racial and religious groups.

The information, cast generally in the terms of the statute, charged that Beauharnais "did unlawfully . . . exhibit in public places lithographs, which publications portray depravity, criminality, unchastity or lack of virtue of citizens of Negro race and color and which exposes [*sic*] citizens of Illinois of the Negro race and color to contempt, derision, or obloquy. . . ." The lithograph complained of was a leaflet setting forth a petition calling on the Mayor and City Council of Chicago "to halt the further encroachment, harassment and invasion of white people, their property, neighborhoods and persons, by the Negro. . . ." Below was a call for "One million self respecting white people in Chicago to unite . . . " with the statement added that "If persuasion and the need to prevent the white race from becoming mongrelized by the negro will not unite us, then the aggressions . . . rapes, robberies, knives, guns and marijuana of the negro, surely will." This, with more language, similar if not so violent, concluded with an attached application for membership in the White Circle League of America, Inc.

The testimony at the trial was substantially undisputed. From it the jury could find that Beauharnais was president of the White Circle League; that, at a meeting on January 6, 1950, he passed out bundles of the lithographs in question, together with other literature, to volunteers for distribution on downtown Chicago street corners the following day; that he carefully organized that distribution, giving detailed instructions for it; and that the leaflets were in fact distributed on January 7 in accordance with his plan and instructions. The court, together with other charges on burden of proof and the like, told the jury "if you find . . . that the defendant, Joseph Beauharnais, did . . . manufacture, sell, or offer for sale, advertise or publish, present or exhibit in any public place the lithograph . . . then you are to find the defendant guilty . . . "[.] He refused to charge the jury, as requested by the defendant, that in order to convict they must find "that the article complained of was likely to produce a clear and present danger of a serious substantive evil that rises far above public inconvenience, annoyance or unrest." Upon this evidence and these instructions, the jury brought in the conviction here for review. . . .

[T]oday, every American jurisdiction—the forty-eight States, the District of Columbia, Alaska, Hawaii and Puerto Rico—punish libels directed at individuals.

"There are certain well-defined and narrowly limited classes of speech, the prevention and punishment of which have never been thought to raise any Constitutional problem. These include the lewd and obscene, the profane, the libelous, and the insulting or "fighting" words—those which by their very utterance inflict injury or tend to incite an immediate breach of the peace. It has been well observed that such utterances are no essential part of any exposition of ideas, and are of such slight social value as a step to truth that any benefit that may be derived from them is clearly out-weighed by the social interest in order and morality." . . .

No one will gainsay that it is libelous falsely to charge another with being a rapist, robber, carrier of knives and guns, and user of marijuana. The precise question before us, then, is whether the protection of "liberty" in the Due Process Clause of the Fourteenth Amendment prevents a State from punishing such libels—as criminal libel has been defined, limited and constitutionally recognized time out of mind—directed at designated collectivities and flagrantly disseminated. There is even authority, however dubious, that such utterances were also crimes at common law. It is certainly clear that some American jurisdictions have sanctioned their punishment under ordinary criminal libel statutes. We cannot say, however, that the question is concluded by history and practice. But if an utterance directed at an individual may be the object of criminal sanctions, we cannot deny to a State power to punish the same utterance directed at a defined group, unless we can say that this is a wilful [*sic*] and purposeless restriction unrelated to the peace and well-being of the State.

Illinois did not have to look beyond her own borders or await the tragic experience of the last three decades to conclude that wilful purveyors of falsehood concerning racial and religious groups promote strife and tend powerfully to obstruct the manifold adjustments required for free, ordered life in a metropolitan, polyglot community. From the murder of the abolitionist Lovejoy in 1837 to the Cicero riots of 1951, Illinois has been the scene of exacerbated tension between races, often flaring into violence and destruction. In many of these outbreaks, utterances of the character here in question, so the Illinois legislature could conclude, played a significant part. The law was passed on June 29, 1917, at a time when the State was struggling to assimilate vast numbers of new inhabitants, as yet concentrated in discrete racial or national or religious groups—foreign-born brought to it by the crest of the great wave of immigration, and Negroes attracted by jobs in war plants and allurements of northern claims. Nine years earlier, in the very city where the legislature sat, what is said to be the first northern race riot had cost the lives of six people, left hundreds of Negroes homeless and shocked citizens into action far beyond the borders of the State. Less than a month before the bill was enacted, East St. Louis had seen a day's rioting, prelude to an outbreak, only four days after the bill became law, so bloody that it led to Congressional investigation. A series of bombings had begun which was to culminate two years later in the awful race riot which held Chicago in its grip for seven days in summer of 1919. Nor has the tension and violence between the groups defined in the statute been limited in Illinois to clashes between whites and Negroes.

In the face of this history and its frequent obligato of extreme racial and religious propaganda, we would deny experience to say that the Illinois legislature was without reason in seeking ways to curb false or malicious defamation of racial and religious groups, made in public places and by means calculated to have a powerful emotional impact on those to whom it was presented. . . .

It may be argued, and weightily, that this legislation will not help matters; that tension and on occasion violence between racial and religious groups must be traced to causes more deeply embedded in our society than the ranting of modern Know-Nothings. Only those lacking responsible humility will have a confident solution for problems as intractable as the frictions attributable to differences of race, color or religion. This being so, it would be out of bounds for the judiciary to deny the legislature a choice of policy, provided it is not unrelated to the problem and not forbidden by some explicit limitation on the State's power. That the legislative remedy might not in practice mitigate the evil, or might itself raise new problems, would only manifest once more the paradox of reform. . . .

We are warned that the choice open to the Illinois legislature here may be abused, that the law may be discriminatorily enforced; prohibiting libel of a creed or of a racial group, we are told, is but a step from prohibiting libel of a political party.[18] Every power may be abused, but the possibility of abuse is a poor reason for denying Illinois the power to adopt measures against criminal libels sanctioned by centuries of Anglo-American law. "While this Court sits" it retains and exercises authority to nullify action which encroaches on freedom of utterance under the guise of punishing libel. Of course discussion cannot be denied and the right, as well as the duty, of criticism must not be stifled. . . .

Libelous utterances not being within the area of constitutionally protected speech, it is unnecessary, either for us or for the State courts, to consider the issues behind the phrase "clear and present danger." Certainly no one would contend that obscene speech, for example, may be punished only upon a showing of such circumstances. Libel, as we have seen, is in the same class.

We find no warrant in the Constitution for denying to Illinois the power to pass the law here under attack. But it bears repeating—although it should not—that our finding that the law is not constitutionally objectionable caries no implication of approval of the wisdom of the legislation or of its efficacy. These questions may raise doubts in our minds as well as in others. It is not for us, however, to make the legislative judgment. We are not at liberty to erect those doubts into fundamental law.

Affirmed.

Mr. Justice BLACK, with whom Mr. Justice DOUGLAS concurs, dissenting.

This case is here because Illinois inflicted criminal punishment on Beauharnais for causing the distribution of leaflets in the city of Chicago. The conviction rests on the leaflet's contents, not on the time, manner or place of distribution. Beauharnais is head of an organization that opposes amalgamation and favors segregation of white and colored people. After discussion, an assembly of his group

---

18. It deserves emphasis that there is no such attempt in this statute. The rubric "race, color, creed or religion" which describes the type of group libel of which is punishable, has attained too fixed a meaning to permit political groups to be brought within it. If a statute sought to outlaw libels of political parties, quite different problems not now before us would be raised. For one thing, the whole doctrine of fair comment as indispensable to the democratic political process would come into play. *See* People v. Fuller, [238 Ill. 116, 125,] 87 N.E. 338-39 [(1909)]; Commonwealth v. Pratt, 208 Mass. 553, 559, 95 N.E. 105, 106 [(1911)]. Political parties, like public men, are, as it were, public property.

decided to petition the mayor and council of Chicago to pass laws for segregation. Volunteer members of the group agreed to stand on street corners, solicit signers to petitions addressed to city authorities, and distribute leaflets giving information about the group, its beliefs and its plans. In carrying out this program a solicitor handed out a leaflet which was the basis of this prosecution. . . .

Today's case degrades First Amendment freedoms to the "rational basis" level. It is now a certainty that the new "due process" coverall offers far less protection to liberty than would adherence to our former cases compelling states to abide by the unequivocal First Amendment command that its defined freedoms shall not be abridged. . . .

This Act sets up a system of state censorship which is at war with the kind of free government envisioned by those who forced adoption of our Bill of Rights. The motives behind the state law may have been to do good. But the same can be said about most laws making opinions punishable as crimes. History indicates that urges to do good have led to the burning of books and even to the burning of "witches." . . .

If there be minority groups who hail this holding as their victory, they might consider the possible relevancy of this ancient remark:

"Another such victory and I am undone."

Mr. Justice REED, with whom Mr. Justice DOUGLAS joins, dissenting.

[Opinion omitted.]

Mr. Justice DOUGLAS, dissenting.

Hitler and his Nazis showed how evil a conspiracy could be which was aimed at destroying a race by exposing it to contempt, derision, and obloquy. I would be willing to concede that such conduct directed at a race or group in this country could be made an indictable offense. For such a project would be more than the exercise of free speech. Like picketing, it would be free speech plus.

I would also be willing to concede that even without the element of conspiracy there might be times and occasions when the legislative or executive branch might call a halt to inflammatory talk, such as the shouting of "fire" in a school or a theater.

My view is that in any case other public interests are to override the plain command of the First Amendment, the peril of speech must be clear and present, leaving no room for argument, raising no doubts as to the necessity of curbing speech in order to prevent disaster. . . .

Mr. Justice JACKSON, dissenting.

[Justice Jackson objected to the procedures used to enforce the Illinois group libel statute.]

NOTES AND QUESTIONS

1. *The problem of discretionary enforcement of hate speech regulations.* Is the *Beauharnais* majority naïve to believe that a group libel statute will be enforced

consistently and in an even-handed fashion? And, if a "well fixed star in our constitutional constellation" mandates that government may not generally "prescribe what shall be orthodox in politics, nationalism, religion, or other matters of opinion" in the words of Justice Jackson in West Virginia State Board of Education v. Barnette, 319 U.S. 624, 642 (1942), how does one distinguish a mandatory pledge from a rule against racist speech? Don't both involve government efforts to create and enforce "orthodoxy"? Perhaps ironically, in *Beauharnais,* the same Justice Jackson, although dissenting, nevertheless seems quite sympathetic to the ends, if not the means, that the Illinois state legislature sought to advance. How can one reconcile the seemingly inconsistent results reached in *Beauharnais* and *Barnette*?

2. *No such thing as "free" speech?* Professor Stanley Fish has famously asserted that there really is no such thing as "free speech," if by "free speech" one means speech that does not impose social costs of some sort. *See* Stanley Fish, *There's No Such Thing as Free Speech, and It's a Good Thing, Too* 102-133 (1994). If this is so, is it reasonable for a state government to attempt to redistribute some of the social costs of speech activity? Suppose empirical studies show that racist stereotypes, perpetuated in part by materials of the sort that Beauharnais sought to distribute in Chicago, lead to persistent discrimination against people of color in a wide variety of contexts. If government shows clearly that such speech demonstrably causes social, economic, and political discrimination against minorities, would that justify the enactment and enforcement of a group libel law? Why should minorities bear the social cost of racist speech? Are they really the least cost avoiders?
3. *A global perspective.* On the other hand, one would do well to consider the success (or lack thereof) of hate speech codes in places that maintain and enforce them, like Canada and Germany. Germany has maintained not only comprehensive speech codes that prohibit incitement to racial hatred but also laws that protect personal honor and dignity. *See* Ronald J. Krotoszynski, Jr., *The First Amendment in Cross-Cultural Perspective: A Comparative Legal Analysis of the Freedom of Speech* 118-130 (2006) (discussing hate speech regulations in Germany). Even so, the problem of racist hate speech, after more than 70 years of aggressive enforcement of these laws, has not gone away. *Id.* at 130-131, 135-137. As a means of preventing the dissemination of hate speech and combating the social evils of racism, speech codes do not seem to be particularly effective at achieving their larger purposes.
4. *The dangers of government censorship.* Does Justice Black's dissent make an important point? Can government be trusted to prohibit only really bad speech, and not attempt to use a censorial power in favor of incumbent officeholders? For example, would an elected district attorney go after a popular local citizen who makes a racist remark in public? Suppose, however, that a Native American leader expresses admiration for Hitler and that there are relatively few Native American citizens in the district attorney's constituency. If you think one prosecution is more likely to move

forward than the other, have equality values really been well served? *See* Krotoszynski, *supra*, at 82-87 (discussing prosecution of First Nations leader David Ahenakew for incitement to racial hatred and the differential enforcement of hate speech laws in Canada).

Kunz v. New York

340 U.S. 290 (1951)

Mr. Chief Justice VINSON delivered the opinion of the Court.

New York City has adopted an ordinance which makes it unlawful to hold public worship meetings on the streets without first obtaining a permit from the city police commissioner. Appellant, Carl Jacob Kunz, was convicted and fined $10 for violating this ordinance by holding a religious meeting without a permit. The conviction was affirmed by the Appellate Part of the Court of Special Sessions, and by the New York Court of Appeals, three judges dissenting, 300 N.Y. 273, 90 N.E.2d 455 (1950). The case is here on appeal, it having been urged that the ordinance is invalid under the Fourteenth Amendment.

Appellant is an ordained Baptist minister who speaks under the auspices of the "Outdoor Gospel Work," of which he is the director. He has been preaching for about six years, and states that it is his conviction and duty to "go out on the highways and byways and preach the word of God." In 1946, he applied for and received a permit under the ordinance in question, there being no question that appellant comes within the classes of persons entitled to receive permits under the ordinance. This permit, like all others, was good only for the calendar year in which issued. In November, 1946, his permit was revoked after a hearing by the police commissioner. The revocation was based on evidence that he had ridiculed and denounced other religious beliefs in his meetings.

Although the penalties of the ordinance apply to anyone who "ridicules and denounces other religious beliefs," the ordinance does not specify this as a ground for permit revocation. Indeed, there is no mention in the ordinance of any power of revocation. However, appellant did not seek judicial or administrative review of the revocation proceedings, and any question as to the propriety of the revocation is not before us in this case. In any event, the revocation affected appellant's rights to speak in 1946 only. Appellant applied for another permit in 1947, and again in 1948, but was notified each time that his application was "disapproved," with no reason for the disapproval being given. On September 11, 1948, appellant was arrested for speaking at Columbus Circle in New York City without a permit. It is from the conviction which resulted that this appeal has been taken.

Appellant's conviction was thus based upon his failure to possess a permit for 1948. We are here concerned only with the propriety of the action of the police commissioner in refusing to issue that permit. Disapproval of the 1948 permit application by the police commissioner was justified by the New York courts on the ground that a permit had previously been revoked "for good reasons." It is noteworthy that there is no mention in the ordinance of reasons for which such a permit application can be refused. This interpretation allows the police commissioner, an administrative official, to exercise discretion in denying subsequent permit applications on the basis of his interpretation, at that time, of what is deemed to be conduct condemned by the ordinance which gives an administrative official discretionary power to control in advance the right of citizens to speak on religious matters on the streets of New York. As such, the ordinance is clearly invalid as a prior restraint on the exercise of First Amendment rights.

In considering the right of a municipality to control the use of public streets for the expression of religious views, we start with the words of Mr. Justice Roberts that "Wherever the title of streets and parks may rest, they have immemorially been held in trust for the use of the public and, time out of mind, have been used for purposes of assembly, communicating thoughts between citizens, and discussing public questions." Hague v. C.I.O., 307 U.S. 496, 515 (1939). Although this Court has recognized that a statute may be enacted which prevents serious interference with normal usage of streets and parks, Cox v. New Hampshire, 312 U.S. 569 (1941), we have consistently condemned licensing systems which vest in an administrative official discretion to grant or withhold a permit upon broad criteria unrelated to proper regulation of public places. . . .

The court below has mistakenly derived support for its conclusion from the evidence produced at the trial that appellant's religious meetings had, in the past, caused some disorder. There are appropriate public remedies to protect the peace and order of the community if appellant's speeches should result in disorder or violence. "In the present case, we have no occasion to inquire as to the permissible scope of subsequent punishment." Near v. Minnesota, 283 U.S. 697, 715 (1931). We do not express any opinion on the propriety of punitive remedies which the New York authorities may utilize. We are here concerned with suppression—not punishment. It is sufficient to say that New York cannot vest restraining control over the right to speak on religious subjects in an administrative official where there are no appropriate standards to guide his action.

Reversed.

Mr. Justice JACKSON, dissenting.

Essential freedoms are today threatened from without and within. It may become difficult to preserve here what a large part of the world has lost—the right to speak, even temperately, on matters vital to spirit and body. In such a setting, to blanket hateful and hate-stirring attacks on races and faiths under the protections for freedom of speech may be a noble innovation. On the other hand, it may be a quixotic tilt at windmills which belittles great principles of liberty. Only time can tell. But I incline to the latter view and cannot assent to the decision.

To know what we are doing, we must first locate the point at which rights asserted by Kunz conflict with powers asserted by the organized community. New York City has placed no limitation upon any speech Kunz may choose to make on private property, but it does require a permit to hold religious meetings in its streets. The ordinance, neither by its terms nor as it has been applied, prohibited Kunz, even in street meetings, from preaching his own religion or making any temperate criticism or refutation of other religions; indeed, for the year 1946, he was given a general permit to do so. His meetings, however, brought "a flood of complaints" to city authorities that he was engaging in scurrilous attacks on Catholics and Jews. On notice, he was given a hearing at which eighteen complainants appeared. The Commissioner revoked his permit and applications for 1947 and 1948 were refused. For a time he went on holding meetings without a permit in Columbus Circle, where in September, 1948, he was arrested for violation of the ordinance. He was convicted and fined ten dollars.

At these meetings, Kunz preached, among many other things of like tenor, that "The Catholic Church makes merchandise out of souls," that Catholicism is "a religion of the devil," and that the Pope is "the anti-Christ." The Jews he denounced as "Christ-killers," and he said of them "All the garbage that didn't believe in Christ should have been burnt in the incinerators. It's a shame they all weren't."

These utterances, as one might expect, stirred strife and threatened violence. Testifying in his own behalf, Kunz stated that he "became acquainted with" one of the complaining witnesses, whom he thought to be a Jew, "when he happened to sock one of my Christian boys in the puss." Kunz himself complained to the authorities, charging a woman interrupter with disorderly conduct. He also testified that when an officer is not present at his meetings "I have trouble then," but "with an officer, no trouble."

The contention which Kunz brings here and which this Court sustains is that such speeches on the streets are within his constitutional freedom and therefore New York City has no power to require a permit. He does not deny that this has been and will continue to be his line of talk. He does not claim that he should have been granted a permit; he attacks the whole system of control of street meetings and says the Constitution gives him permission to speak and he needs none from the City.

The speeches which Kunz has made and which he asserts he has a *right* to make in the future were properly held by the courts below to be out of bounds for a street meeting and not constitutionally protected. . . . Of course, if Kunz is only exercising his constitutional *rights*, then New York can neither restrain nor punish him. But I doubt that the Court's assumption will survive analysis.

This Court today initiates the doctrine that language such as this, in the environment of the street meeting, is immune from prior municipal control. We would have a very different question if New York had presumed to say that Kunz could not speak his piece in his own pulpit or hall. But it has undertaken to restrain him only if he chooses to speak at street meetings. There is a world of difference. The street preacher takes advantage of people's presence on the streets to impose his message upon what, in a sense, is a captive audience. A meeting on private property is made up of an audience that has volunteered to listen. The question, therefore, is not whether New York could, if it tried, silence Kunz, but whether it must place its streets at his service to hurl insults at the passer-by.

What Mr. Justice Holmes said for a unanimous Court in Schenck v. United States, 249 U.S. 47, 52, has become an axiom: "The most stringent protection of free speech would not protect a man in falsely shouting fire in a theatre and causing a panic." This concept was applied in one of its few unanimous decisions in recent years when, through Mr. Justice Murphy, the Court said: "There are certain well-defined and narrowly limited classes of speech, *the prevention and punishment* of which *have never been thought to raise any Constitutional problem*. These include the lewd and obscene, the profane, the libelous, and *the insulting or 'fighting' words*— those which by their very utterance inflict injury or *tend to incite* an immediate breach of the peace. . . ." (Emphasis supplied.) Chaplinsky v. New Hampshire, 315 U.S. 568, 571-572.

There held to be "insulting or 'fighting' words" were calling one a "God damned racketeer" and a "damned Fascist." Equally inciting and more clearly "fighting words," when thrown at Catholics and Jews who are rightfully on the streets of New York, are statements that "The Pope is the anti-Christ" and the Jews are "Christ-killers." These terse epithets come down to our generation weighted with hatreds accumulated through centuries of bloodshed. They are recognized words of art in the profession of defamation. They are not the kind of insult that men bandy and laugh off when the spirits are high and the flagons are low. They are not in that class of epithets whose literal sting will be drawn if the speaker smiles when he uses them. They are always, and in every context, insults which do not spring from reason and can be answered by none. Their historical associations with violence are well understood, both by those who hurl and those who are struck by these missiles. Jews, many of whose families perished in extermination furnaces of Dachau and Auschwitz, are more than tolerant if they pass off lightly the suggestion that unbelievers in Christ should all have been burned. Of course, people might pass this speaker by as a mental case, and so they might file out of a theatre in good order at the cry of "fire." But in both cases there is genuine likelihood that someone will get hurt. . . .

The question remains whether the Constitution prohibits a city from control of its streets by a permit system which takes into account dangers to public peace and order. I am persuaded that it does not do so, provided of course, that the city does not so discriminate as to deny equal protection of the law or undertake a censorship of utterances that are not so defamatory, insulting, inciting, or provocative as to be reasonably likely to cause disorder and violence. . . .

NOTES AND QUESTIONS

1. *Reconciling* Beauharnais *and* Kunz. The Supreme Court actually decided *Beauharnais* a year *after Kunz*. Even so, the *Kunz* approach better reflects the modern rule than does *Beauharnais*. Still, given that the cases are decided within a year of each other, how does one square the disparate results? Could it be that even with respect to subject matter that might fall outside the scope of the First Amendment, the rule against prior restraints makes a permissive permitting scheme more objectionable than criminal punishment after the fact? Note that Chief Justice Vinson emphasizes that "[w]e are here concerned with suppression—not punishment." Moreover, the *Kunz* majority did not "express any opinion on the propriety of punitive remedies which the New York authorities may utilize." Thus, is the result in *Kunz* really a function of prior restraint, rather than the notion that speakers have a right to bandy about racial or religious epithets on the public streets?
2. *No protection against highly offensive and insulting speech?* Is New York City (and any other government) powerless to protect random passersby from racist, sexist, or homophobic speech? Why does (or should) the First Amendment protect uncivil discourse? Does a serious commitment to freedom of expression require protection if someone calls another person a "kike," "faggot," "nigger," or "cunt" on a public street? In theory,

words of this sort might be excluded from constitutional protection under the doctrine of "fighting words," as mentioned by Justice Jackson in his dissenting opinion in *Kunz*. For better or worse, however, the modern Supreme Court, in a series of cases in the 1970s, significantly limited the potential scope of the fighting-words doctrine. *See infra* pages 548-533.

3. *The potential lessons of history.* Justice Jackson argues that the harms associated with hate speech are sufficiently serious to warrant suspending general free speech principles in order to permit government to regulate (or proscribe) such language. The standard response to this argument is that counter speech, rather than government regulation, presents a better approach. Is this realistic? If a large group of men standing on a street corner calls a lone woman walking by "a fucking dyke cunt," is it really reasonable to expect her to attempt to engage her verbal assailants in some sort of repartee? Consider too that this case, decided in 1951, comes only six years after the liberation of the Nazi death camps for Jews (and other persons deemed unworthy to live by Hitler and his minions). In other words, in all probability, Holocaust survivors, their relatives, and their friends might well have been subjected to Kunz's ravings. Should this matter in evaluating the validity of the New York City policy? Germany, to this day, maintains and enforces strict laws against anti-Semitic speech, as well as a criminal law ban on pro-Nazi speech. *See* Krotoszynski, *supra* page 528, at 118-130.

4. *A different (better) rationale for protecting low value hate speech?* Perhaps a better argument in favor of permitting Kunz to speak isn't that counter speech is an effective defense for those he victimizes but rather that the greater danger to society lies in permitting government to decide what words can, and cannot, be spoken in public. *See* Lyrissa Barnett Lidsky, *Where's the Harm: Free Speech and the Regulation of Lies*, 65 Wash. & Lee L. Rev. 1091, 1097 (2008) ("Yet even if First Amendment theory's faith in the fundamental rationality of public discourse is misplaced, distrust of government still may be a strong enough basis, standing alone, to warrant declaring any attempt to punish Holocaust denial unconstitutional."). As Justice Harlan explains in *Cohen* (*infra* page 542), the ability to control the expression of an idea ultimately implies the ability to control the idea itself. If this is so, perhaps a free society must tolerate evil boors like Kunz because a government empowered to ban words, and hence ideas, is a greater net threat to liberty and happiness than religious bigots screaming on street corners. Even if one finds this argument persuasive, however, it does not provide much consolation to those persons that people like Kunz verbally assault.

5. *The current precedential status of* Beauharnais. *Beauharnais*, although never formally reversed, has been effectively superseded by later cases, notably including New York Times Co. v. Sullivan, 376 U.S. 254 (1964), and Brandenburg v. Ohio, 395 U.S. 444 (1969). Thus, in *R.A.V.*, decided in 1992, the Supreme Court invalidated on free speech grounds a local St. Paul, Minnesota, ordinance that prohibited speech causing fear or alarm based on race, sex, or religion because the ordinance constituted a form of impermissible content and viewpoint discrimination. *See* R.A.V. v. City of St. Paul, 505 U.S. 377 (1992). [*R.A.V.* appears *infra* p. 562.] Under

the modern rule, only speech that conveys a true threat may be criminally punished. *See* Virginia v. Black, 538 U.S. 343, 359-361 (2003) [*Black* appears *infra* p. 571.] Nevertheless, vestiges of *Beauharnais* remain in contemporary free speech law. Even if direct regulations of hate speech transgress the First Amendment, the Supreme Court has sustained more nuanced efforts to punish hate speech.

AN EXTENDED NOTE ON TERRY JONES AND TARGETED INCITEMENT: THE EXAMPLE OF KORAN BURNING

Pastor Terry Jones, a fundamentalist pastor based in Gainesville, Florida, has engaged in targeted burnings of the Koran, both in Florida and elsewhere. He is the author of a self-published book, *Islam Is of the Devil* (Creation House 2010), and his church, the Dove World Outreach Center (once based in Gainesville, but now based in Tampa) sells coffee mugs and t-shirts emblazoned with this offensive slogan. Donna Koehn, *Opinions of Islam Worsen*, Tampa Trib., Sept. 10, 2010, at B1. Jones regularly conducts mass Koran burnings and also encourages others to stage similar events. Keith Morelli, *Preacher Plans to Burn Korans in Polk*, Tampa Trib., July 26, 2013, at B1.

Jones actively seeks to provoke angry reactions to his Koran burnings—presumably in order to garner media attention. For example, he attempted to burn a Koran outside the Arab International Festival in Dearborn, Michigan, but he was met with angry counterprotestors who confronted him and "hemmed him in as he tried to walk down Schaefer Road." *See* Oralandar Brand-Williams, Josh Katzenstein & Mike Wilkinson, *Dearborn Cops Pull Pastor from Crowd*, Detroit News, June 18, 2011, at A3. Jones said that "[i]t got really, really nasty" and that "[t]hey had us completely surrounded, pushing on us and blocking us." Did the police act lawfully in removing Jones and his supporters from the angry crowd?

Jones has made multiple attempts to burn a Koran in Dearborn, a community with a large percentage of residents who adhere to the Islamic faith. He was permitted to stage a rally outside Dearborn City Hall (although he did not burn a Koran at this event). Earlier, in April 2011, he attempted to stage a protest and a Koran burning outside the Islamic Center of Dearborn, but he was prevented from doing so after a jury "ruled he would likely breach the peace" and issued an injunction against the protest. Niraj Warikoo, *Florida Pastor Returning to Dearborn to Protest Islam*, Detroit Free Press, June 17, 2011, at A10. Jones refused to post a security bond after the jury's verdict and was briefly jailed until he posted the bond.

Was the Michigan state court's restraining order against Jones consistent with the First Amendment? Or did Dearborn have an obligation to permit Jones to go forward with his proposed protest and Koran burning outside the Islamic Center, despite a very high probability of violence? Moreover, should the potential effects of Jones's proposed actions worldwide be a potential basis for legal action against him? Senior U.S. government officials have argued that Jones's proposed actions create a serious security risk for U.S. military and diplomatic personnel stationed abroad. *See* Kevin Sieff, *Florida Pastor Terry Jones's Koran Burning Has Far-Reaching Effect*, Wash. Post, Apr. 2, 2011. Would speech restrictions against Jones designed to avoid harm to U.S. troops and diplomatic personnel constitute civility norms? Or something else?

In April 2012, a federal district judge issued a preliminary injunction ordering the city of Dearborn to allow Terry Jones and his followers to protest on public property adjacent to the Islamic Center of America; in August 2013 the court entered a final summary judgment order and permanent injunction in favor of Jones. Stand Up America Now v. City of Dearborn, 969 F. Supp. 2d 843 (E.D. Mich. 2013). The district court's decision does not discuss (at all) the city's claim that social unrest, including the outbreak of violence, could result from the proposed protest at the Islamic Center. Instead, Judge Denise Page Hood explains that "[i]t is well recognized that an ordinance which grants an administrative body or government official unfettered discretion to regulate the licensing of activities protected by the First Amendment is unconstitutional." *Id.* at 847. In addition, "courts have held that a clause requiring the permitee to hold the city harmless from any liability caused by the conduct of the event is unconstitutional." *Id.* Accordingly, the city's demand for an indemnification agreement was also void. Does this outcome surprise you?

On April 7, 2012, the proposed protest, under the protection of the federal district court's injunction, took place on a city-owned grassy area across the street from the Islamic Center of America—peaceably and without any arrests or other problems. *See* Niraj Warikoo, *Florida Pastor at Dearborn Protest,* Detroit Free Press, Apr. 7, 2012, available at *http://www.freep.com/article/20120407/NEWS02/120407023/Terry-Jones-Dearborn-Quran-Islam.* Does this outcome change your thinking about whether the district judge properly applied the First Amendment? On the other hand, however, in virtually all of the larger democratic world, Jones would face criminal prosecution and imprisonment for attempting to incite religious hatred. *See* Lara Marlowe, *Pastor Feels No Shame, Nor Has He Any Remorse,* Irish Times (Dublin), Apr. 6, 2011, at 11 (noting that "[i]n a different country, Pastor Terry Jones might have been arrested" and explaining that "[i]n the US, where the First Amendment guarantee of free speech is sacrosanct, Jones enjoys police protection").

B. A CONTEMPORARY EXAMPLE OF REGULATIONS AIMED AT PROMOTING SOCIAL EQUALITY: TITLE VII AS A LIMIT ON FREE SPEECH

Antidiscrimination laws, such as Title VII, obviously have effects on the exercise of free speech. For example, the question of a "hostile work environment" could turn entirely on speech in a workplace. Even so, the Supreme Court has not been sympathetic to arguments that federal and state employment nondiscrimination laws violate the First Amendment.

Hishon v. King & Spalding

467 U.S. 69 (1984)

Chief Justice Burger delivered the opinion of the Court.

We granted certiorari to determine whether the District Court properly dismissed a Title VII complaint alleging that a law partnership discriminated against petitioner, a woman lawyer employed as an associate, when it failed to invite her to become a partner.

In 1972 petitioner Elizabeth Anderson Hishon accepted a position as an associate with respondent, a large Atlanta law firm established as a general partnership. When this suit was filed in 1980, the firm had more than 50 partners and employed approximately 50 attorneys as associates. Up to that time, no woman had ever served as a partner at the firm. [In May 1978, King & Spalding denied Hishon a partnership; in December 1979, following proceedings before the EEOC, Hishon commenced a Title VII action in federal district court.]

The District Court dismissed the complaint on the ground that Title VII was inapplicable to the selection of partners by a partnership. 24 FEP Cases 1303 (1980). A divided panel of the United States Court of Appeals for the Eleventh Circuit affirmed. 678 F.2d 1022 (1982). We granted certiorari, 459 U.S. 1169 (1983), and we reverse. . . .

Several allegations in petitioner's complaint would support the conclusion that the opportunity to become a partner was part and parcel of an associate's status as an employee at respondent's firm, independent of any allegation that such an opportunity was included in associates' employment contracts. Petitioner alleges that respondent's associates could regularly expect to be considered for partnership at the end of their "apprenticeships," and it appears that lawyers outside the firm were not routinely so considered. Thus, the benefit of partnership consideration was allegedly linked directly with an associate's status as an employee, and this linkage was far more than coincidental: petitioner alleges that respondent explicitly used the prospect of ultimate partnership to induce young lawyers to join the firm. Indeed, the importance of the partnership decision to a lawyer's status as an associate is underscored by the allegation that associates' employment is terminated if they are not elected to become partners. These allegations, if proved at trial, would suffice to show that partnership consideration was a term, condition, or privilege of an associate's employment at respondent's firm, and accordingly that partnership consideration must be without regard to sex. . . .

[R]espondent argues that application of Title VII in this case would infringe constitutional rights of expression or association. Although we have recognized that the activities of lawyers may make a "distinctive contribution . . . to the ideas and beliefs of our society," NAACP v. Button, 371 U.S. 415, 431 (1963), respondent has not shown how its ability to fulfill such a function would be inhibited by a requirement that it consider petitioner for partnership on her merits. Moreover, as we have held in another context, "[i]nvidious private discrimination may be characterized as a form of exercising freedom of association protected by the First Amendment, but it has never been accorded affirmative constitutional protections." Norwood v. Harrison, 413 U.S. 455, 470 (1973). There is no constitutional right, for example, to discriminate in the selection of who may attend a private school or join a labor union. Runyon v. McCrary, 427 U.S. 160 (1976); Railway Mail Assn. v. Corsi, 326 U.S. 88, 93-94 (1945).

We conclude that petitioner's complaint states a claim cognizable under Title VII. Petitioner therefore is entitled to her day in court to prove her allegations. The judgment of the Court of Appeals is reversed, and the case is remanded for further proceedings consistent with this opinion.

It is so ordered.

[Justice POWELL's concurring opinion is omitted.]

NOTES AND QUESTIONS

1. *No serious First Amendment implications?* Is the question of First Amendment protection of "invidious private discrimination" as open and shut as Chief Justice Burger suggests? Could the Ku Klux Klan, for example, be required to admit gay men of color to its ranks? Or could a federal or state civil rights law require a religious organization that prohibits female ordination to modify its theological rules and ordain women? In the context of a large, corporate law firm, the claim of a core associational commitment to discriminate on the basis of sex does not wash. If one of King & Spalding's core organizational purposes included promoting gender discrimination, the outcome of the free association claim would probably be different. For the relevant doctrinal analysis, see *Boy Scouts v. Dale* (*supra* p. 300).
2. *Should the nature of the enterprise or organization make a difference?* Even if one can draw a clear distinction between a major corporate law firm, on the one hand, and the Ku Klux Klan or the Aryan Brotherhood, on the other, why shouldn't a major corporate law firm be able to claim the benefit of the First Amendment? If gender discrimination is something that King & Spalding wishes to promote in its hiring and promotion practices, why should the fact that it is a general partnership created to provide legal services to paying clients make any difference? Moreover, in other contexts, *e.g.*, *Bellotti, supra* page 356 and *Citizens United, supra* pages 118 and 362, the Supreme Court has rejected the idea that corporations and partnerships are not entitled to the protection of the First Amendment. Thus, if corporations and partnerships *do* enjoy First Amendment rights, why don't those rights extend to maintaining gender discriminatory or racially discriminatory workplaces?
3. *The hostile workplace theory and Title VII.* Professor Catharine MacKinnon's book, *The Sexual Harassment of Working Women* (1979), forcefully argued that the federal courts should interpret Title VII to prohibit pervasive, gender-based harassment in the workplace. In 1986, in the following case, the Supreme Court appeared to adopt MacKinnon's theory.

Meritor Savings Bank v. Vinson

477 U.S. 57 (1986)

Justice Rehnquist delivered the opinion of the Court.

This case presents important questions concerning claims of workplace "sexual harassment" brought under Title VII of the Civil Rights Act of 1964, 78 Stat. 253, as amended, 42 U.S.C. § 2000e *et seq.*

In 1974, respondent Mechelle Vinson met Sidney Taylor, a vice president of what is now petitioner Meritor Savings Bank (bank) and manager of one of its branch offices. When respondent asked whether she might obtain employment at the bank, Taylor gave her an application, which she completed and returned the next day; later that same day Taylor called her to say that she had been hired.

With Taylor as her supervisor, respondent started as a teller-trainee, and thereafter was promoted to teller, head teller, and assistant branch manager. She worked at the same branch for four years, and it is undisputed that her advancement there was based on merit alone. In September 1978, respondent notified Taylor that she was taking sick leave for an indefinite period. On November 1, 1978, the bank discharged her for excessive use of that leave.

Respondent brought this action against Taylor and the bank, claiming that during her four years at the bank she had "constantly been subjected to sexual harassment" by Taylor in violation of Title VII. She sought injunctive relief, compensatory and punitive damages against Taylor and the bank, and attorney's fees. . . .

The District Court denied relief, but did not resolve the conflicting testimony about the existence of a sexual relationship between respondent and Taylor. . . . The court ultimately found that the respondent "was not the victim of sexual harassment and was not the victim of sexual discrimination" while employed at the bank. . . .

The Court of Appeals for the District of Columbia Circuit reversed. Relying on its earlier holding in *Bundy v. Jackson* . . . [t]he court stated that a violation of Title VII may be predicated on either of two types of sexual harassment: harassment that involves the conditioning of concrete employment benefits on sexual favors, and harassment that, while not affecting economic benefits, creates a hostile or offensive working environment. . . .

In accordance with the foregoing, the Court of Appeals reversed the judgment of the District Court and remanded the case for further proceedings. A subsequent suggestion for rehearing en banc was denied, with three judges dissenting. We granted certiorari, 474 U.S. 1047 (1985), and now affirm but for different reasons.

Title VII of the Civil Rights Act of 1964 makes it "an unlawful employment practice for an employer . . . to discriminate against any individual with respect to his compensation, terms, conditions, or privileges of employment, because of such individual's race, color, religion, sex or national origin." 42 U.S.C. § 2000e-2(a)(1). The prohibition against discrimination based on sex was added to Title VII at the last minute on the floor of the House of Representatives. 110 Cong. Rec. 2577-2584 (1964). . . .

Respondent argues, and the Court of Appeals held, that unwelcome sexual advances that create an offensive or hostile working environment violate Title VII. Without question, when a supervisor sexually harasses a subordinate because of the subordinate's sex, that supervisor "discriminate[s]" on the basis of sex. Petitioner apparently does not challenge this proposition. It contends instead that in prohibiting discrimination with respect to "compensation, terms, conditions, or privileges" of employment, Congress was concerned with what petitioner describes as "tangible loss" of "an economic character," not "purely psychological aspects of the workplace environment." In support of this claim petitioner observes that in both the legislative history of Title VII and this Court's Title VII decisions, the focus has been on tangible, economic barriers erected by discrimination.

We reject petitioner's view. First, the language of Title VII is not limited to "economic" or "tangible" discrimination. The phrase "terms, conditions, or privileges of employment" evinces a congressional intent "'to strike at the entire spectrum of disparate treatment of men and women'" in employment. Los Angeles Dept. of Water and Power v. Manhart, 435 U.S. 702, 707 n.13 (1978), quoting Sprogis v. United Air Lines, Inc., 444 F.2d 1194, 1198 (CA7 1971). Petitioner has pointed to nothing in the Act to suggest that Congress contemplated the limitation urged here. . . .

Since the [EEOC's] Guidelines were issued, courts have uniformly held, and we agree, that a plaintiff may establish a violation of Title VII by proving that discrimination based on sex has created a hostile or abusive work environment. As the Court of Appeals for the Eleventh Circuit wrote in Henson v. Dundee, 682 F.2d 897, 902 (1982):

> "Sexual harassment which creates a hostile or offensive environment for members of one sex is every bit the arbitrary barrier to sexual equality at the workplace that racial harassment is to racial equality. Surely, a requirement that a man or woman run a gauntlet of sexual abuse in return for the privilege of being allowed to work and make a living can be as demeaning and disconcerting as the harshest of racial epithets." . . .

Of course, as the courts in both *Rogers* and *Henson* recognized, not all workplace conduct that may be described as "harassment" affects a "term, condition, or privilege" of employment within the meaning of Title VII. See Rogers v. EEOC, *supra*, at 238 ("mere utterance of an ethnic or racial epithet which engenders offensive feelings in an employee" would not affect the conditions of employment to sufficiently significant degree to violate Title VII); *Henson*, 682 F.2d, at 904 (quoting same). For sexual harassment to be actionable, it must be sufficiently severe or pervasive "to alter the conditions of [the victim's] employment and create an abusive working environment." *Ibid.* Respondent's allegations in this case—which include not only pervasive harassment but also criminal conduct of the most serious nature—are plainly sufficient to state a claim for "hostile environment" sexual harassment. . . .

In sum, we hold that a claim of "hostile environment" sex discrimination is actionable under Title VII, that the District Court's findings were insufficient to dispose of respondent's hostile environment claim, and that the District Court did not err in admitting testimony about respondent's sexually provocative speech and dress. . . .

Justice MARSHALL, with whom Justice BRENNAN, Justice BLACKMUN, AND Justice STEVENS join, concurring in the judgment. [Opinion omitted.]

NOTES AND QUESTIONS

1. *Private employers and harassing workplace speech.* Why do free speech concerns receive such short shrift in *Hishon* and *Meritor Savings Bank*? If the owner of a garage decorates the place of employment with images of hardcore pornography, why shouldn't the Free Speech Clause provide some measure of protection for this decision? Provided that men and women receive equal pay and benefits, should the First Amendment protect a business owner's idiosyncratic decorating concepts?
2. *Does free speech potentially limit the government's ability to promote workplace equality?* Clearly, if Congress (or a state legislature) wishes to advance equal employment at the cost of free speech, the Supreme Court will not apply the First Amendment inflexibly as an absolute bar to such legislation. Precisely why does promoting equality trump speech in this context but not

in other contexts? Are places of employment different from a home, a rally on private land, or a street march? If so, how are they different?

3. *College and university campuses.* If Congress can prohibit hostile work environments, can a state university or college prohibit hostile learning environments by enacting a campus speech code? How does a campus speech code differ (or does it?) from Title VII? Every lower federal court to consider the constitutional status of a campus speech code has invalidated the campus speech code on First Amendment grounds. Why is this so? What is the difference between preventing a hostile work environment in a place of employment and punishing racist, sexist, or homophobic speech on campus? Clearly it cannot be a difference in kind but rather must rest on a difference in the scope of the regulation. Would more narrowly tailored campus speech restrictions survive First Amendment scrutiny? Is it permissible to restrict speech only at the point that another person is forced to choose between a livelihood (or education) and another person's free speech rights? Or is pervasive harassment in a hostile environment more closely akin to a true threat? (Recall that "true threats" enjoy no First Amendment protection. See *supra* pages 70-81.)
4. *Free speech as an absolute value?* As noted in the Introduction to this chapter, a small but vocal group of First Amendment scholars have attacked *Hishon* and *Meritor Savings Bank* as being inconsistent with basic free speech principles, including both content and viewpoint neutrality. *See, e.g.*, Eugene Volokh, *How Harassment Law Restricts Free Speech*, 47 Rutgers L. Rev. 563, 574-579 (1995). These critiques have not proven persuasive to the federal courts or within the larger legal academy.
5. *Discrimination against LGBTQ and transgender persons after* Bostock. In *Bostock v. Clayton County*, 140 S. Ct. 1731 (2020), the Supreme Court held that the term "sex" as used in Title VII encompasses discrimination based on both sexual orientation and gender identity. Writing for the 6–3 majority, Justice Neil Gorsuch explained that "[a]n employer who fires an individual for being homosexual or transgender fires that person for traits or actions it would not have questioned in members of a different sex." *Id.* at 1737. When an employer discriminates on the basis of sexual orientation or gender identity, "[s]ex plays a necessary and undisguisable role in the decision, exactly what Title VII forbids." Thus, "[f]or an employer to discriminate against employees for being homosexual or transgender, the employer must intentionally discriminate against individual men and women in part because of sex." *Id.* at 1743. After *Bostock*, employers are under a general legal duty to avoid creating and maintaining a hostile work environment for LGBTQ and transgender employees. The same arguably holds true, under Title IX, with respect to hostile learning environments in public schools, colleges, and universities that receive federal funds. Title IX is an important federal civil rights law that, like Title VII, prohibits sex discrimination. *See* 20 U.S.C. § 1681 (2018); *see also* Cannon v. University of Chicago, 441 U.S. 677, 709, 717 (1979) (holding that Title IX creates an implied private right of action for victims of sex discrimination

in federally-funded educational programs). Does this mean that colleges and universities *must* adopt policies that seek to prevent the creation and maintenance of hostile learning environments on campus for LGBTQ and transgender students, faculty, and staff? How should a university general counsel try to reconcile an institution's duties under federal civil rights laws, like Title IX, with the First Amendment's Free Speech Clause?

THEORY-APPLIED PROBLEM

In July 2023, Mississippi State University (MSU) enacts a campus speech code that prohibits "speech creating a hostile learning environment based on race, sex, religion, national origin, or sexual orientation such that no reasonable person within a protected classification would reasonably be expected to remain enrolled as a full time student on campus if regularly subjected to the harassment at issue." MSU general counsel intentionally drafted language that tracks the language of the relevant hostile work environment precedents, which require an environment so toxic that no reasonable woman (in the case of gender) or no reasonable person of color (in the case of race) would tolerate the environment.

In October 2023, the MSU chapter of Kappa Beta Alpha, an undergraduate fraternity, charges its pledge class with sorting out the "bitches" from the "whores" on campus as part of the organization's mandatory pledge activities. As part of their pledge duties, the would-be KBA brothers must, on a 24-hour basis, declare any woman that they encounter to be either a "bitch" or a "whore." Cindy Who, enrolled in advanced organic chemistry, has a term paper due in 48 hours and needs to use the university library to complete the assignment. As she approaches the university library's entrance, a group of around six KBA pledges begins shouting "whore" at her. Startled, she flees the library. Who returns four hours later and is met with chants of "bitch" from a different group of equally fervent KBA pledges. She again flees and does not return. Moreover, she receives a "D" mark on her paper because she is afraid to return to the library, for fear of a third altercation with the KBA pledges. Who files a formal complaint with campus security following the second altercation. After conducting an investigation, campus security finds that more than three dozen women had been subjected to verbal abuse by the KBA pledges during the prior week at various locations on campus, including the library, the student center, the main gymnasium, and classroom buildings.

The Faculty/Student Review Board initiates formal proceedings against the KBA pledges and recommends that they be suspended from campus for at least one academic semester. MSU's provost accepts the Faculty/Student Review Board's recommendation and immediately suspends 11 freshman students from the university for one semester. The KBA pledges secure a lawyer and file a section 1983 action against the university, alleging a violation of their free speech and free association rights. The university defends the action by claiming that the students were not suspended because of their speech but because of the harassing actions. How should the district court rule? Is the MSU policy consistent with the First Amendment?

C. *GOVERNMENT EFFORTS TO PROMOTE CIVILITY AND THE FIRST AMENDMENT*

Governments at all levels (federal, state, and local), responding to the wishes of voters, have attempted to enact and enforce civility norms. The modern Supreme Court has consistently rebuffed these efforts (save in the context of Title VII). Should a commitment to freedom of expression imply an absolute rule against mandatory civility norms in public places, like a local courthouse, or at public meetings, like a school board meeting, where a captive audience, sometimes including young children, may be present?

If one believes that a meaningful commitment to freedom of expression should not imply an absolute ban on mandatory civility regulations, a serious question remains about the ability of government (and perhaps the willingness of government) to enforce such norms consistently. For example, Vice President Dick Cheney, on the floor of the United States Senate, told Senator Patrick Leahy, to "go fuck yourself." Sidney Blumenthal, *When Cheney's Mask Slips, It Reveals Bush*, The Guardian, July 1, 2004, at 25. If a federal civility law existed that prohibited use of profanity in government buildings during regular business hours, is it at all realistic to expect the Department of Justice to prosecute the Vice President? And, if it is not, would it be fair to prosecute an angry veteran who tells a local Veteran's Administration functionary in Jacksonville, Florida, to do the same thing? Even if one agrees in principle that civility norms would enhance, rather than degrade, the marketplace of ideas, how could one ensure that such rules are deployed in a content- and viewpoint-neutral fashion?

Cohen v. California

403 U.S. 15 (1971)

Mr. Justice HARLAN delivered the opinion of the Court.

This case may seem at first blush too inconsequential to find its way into our books, but the issue it presents is of no small constitutional significance.

Appellant Paul Robert Cohen was convicted in the Los Angeles Municipal Court of violating that part of California Penal Code § 415 which prohibits "maliciously and willfully disturb[ing] the peace or quiet of any neighborhood or person . . . by . . . offensive conduct. . . . He was given 30 days' imprisonment. The facts upon which his conviction rests are detailed in the opinion of the Court of Appeal of California, Second Appellate District, as follows:

> "On April 26, 1968, the defendant was observed in the Los Angeles County Courthouse in the corridor outside of division 20 of the municipal court wearing a jacket bearing the words 'Fuck the Draft' which were plainly visible. There were women and children present in the corridor. The defendant was arrested. The defendant testified that he wore the jacket knowing that the words were on the jacket as a means of informing the public of the depth of his feelings against the Vietnam War and the draft.
>
> "The defendant did not engage in, nor threaten to engage in, nor did anyone as the result of his conduct in fact commit or threaten to commit

any act of violence. The defendant did not make any loud or unusual noise, nor was there any evidence that he uttered any sound prior to his arrest." 1 Cal. App. 3d 94, 97-98, 81 Cal. Rptr. 503, 505 (1969).

In affirming the conviction the Court of Appeal held that "offensive conduct" means "behavior which has a tendency to provoke *others* to acts of violence or to in turn disturb the peace," and that the State had proved this element because, on the facts of this case, "[i]t was certainly reasonably foreseeable that such conduct might cause others to rise up to commit a violent act against the person of the defendant or attempt to forceably remove his jacket." The California Supreme Court declined review by a divided vote. We brought the case here, postponing the consideration of the question of our jurisdiction over this appeal to a hearing of the case on the merits. We now reverse. . . .

In order to lay hands on the precise issue which this case involves, it is useful first to canvass various matters which this record does *not* present.

The conviction quite clearly rests upon the asserted offensiveness of the *words* Cohen used to convey his message to the public. The only "conduct" which the State sought to punish is the fact of communication. Thus, we deal here with a conviction resting solely upon "speech," *cf.* Stromberg v. California, 283 U.S. 359 (1931), not upon any separately identifiable conduct which allegedly was intended by Cohen to be perceived by others as expressive of particular views but which, on its face, does not necessarily convey any message and hence arguably could be regulated without effectively repressing Cohen's ability to express himself. Cf. *United States v. O'Brien*, 391 U.S. 367 (1968). Further, the State certainly lacks power to punish Cohen for the underlying content of the message the inscription conveyed. At least so long as there is no showing of an intent to incite disobedience to or disruption of the draft, Cohen could not, consistently with the First and Fourteenth Amendments, be punished for asserting the evident position on the inutility or immorality of the draft his jacket reflected. Yates v. United States, 354 U.S. 298 (1957).

Appellant's conviction, then, rests squarely upon his exercise of the "freedom of speech" protected from arbitrary governmental interference by the Constitution and can be justified, if at all, only as a valid regulation of the manner in which he exercised that freedom, not as a permissible prohibition on the substantive message it conveys. . . .

In the first place, Cohen was tried under a statute applicable throughout the entire State. Any attempt to support this conviction on the ground that the statute seeks to preserve an appropriately decorous atmosphere in the courthouse where Cohen was arrested must fail in the absence of any language in the statute that would have put appellant on notice that certain kinds of otherwise permissible speech or conduct would nevertheless, under California law, not be tolerated in certain places. *See* Edwards v. South Carolina, 372 U.S. 229, 236-237, and n.11 (1963). *Cf.* Adderley v. Florida, 385 U.S. 39 (1966). No fair reading of the phrase "offensive conduct" can be said sufficiently to inform the ordinary person that distinctions between certain locations are thereby created.[3]

---

3. It is illuminating to note what transpired when Cohen entered a courtroom in the building. He removed his jacket and stood with it folded over his arm. Meanwhile, a policeman sent the presiding judge a note suggesting that Cohen be held in contempt of court. The judge declined to do so and Cohen was arrested by the officer only after he emerged from the courtroom. App. 18-19.

In the second place, as it comes to us, this case cannot be said to fall within those relatively few categories of instances where prior decisions have established the power of government to deal more comprehensively with certain forms of individual expression simply upon a showing that such a form was employed. This is not, for example, an obscenity case. . . .

There is, as noted above, no showing that anyone who saw Cohen was in fact violently aroused or that appellant intended such a result. [Accordingly, the fighting-words doctrine does not apply on these facts.]

Finally, in arguments before this Court much has been made of the claim that Cohen's distasteful mode of expression was thrust upon unwilling or unsuspecting viewers, and that the State might therefore legitimately act as it did in order to protect the sensitive from otherwise unavoidable exposure to appellant's crude form of protest. . . . The ability of government, consonant with the Constitution, to shut off discourse solely to protect others from hearing it is, in other words, dependent upon a showing that substantial privacy interests are being invaded in an essentially intolerable manner. Any broader view of this authority would effectively empower a majority to silence dissidents simply as a matter of personal predilections.

In this regard, persons confronted with Cohen's jacket were in a quite different posture than, say, those subjected to the raucous emissions of sound trucks blaring outside their residences. Those in the Los Angeles courthouse could effectively avoid further bombardment of their sensibilities simply by averting their eyes. . . .

Against this background, the issue flushed by this case stands out in bold relief. It is whether California can excise, as "offensive conduct," one particular scurrilous epithet from the public discourse, either upon the theory of the court below that its use is inherently likely to cause violent reaction or upon a more general assertion that the States, acting as guardians of public morality, may properly remove this offensive word from the public vocabulary.

The rationale of the California court is plainly untenable. At most it reflects an "undifferentiated fear or apprehension of disturbance [which] is not enough to overcome the right to freedom of expression." Tinker v. Des Moines Indep. Community School Dist., 393 U.S. 503, 508 (1969). . . .

Admittedly, it is not so obvious that the First and Fourteenth Amendments must be taken to disable the States from punishing public utterance of this unseemly expletive in order to maintain what they regard as a suitable level of discourse within the body politic. We think, however, that examination and reflection will reveal the shortcomings of a contrary viewpoint.

At the outset, we cannot overemphasize that, in our judgment, most situations where the State has a justifiable interest in regulating speech will fall within one or more of the various established exceptions, discussed above but not applicable here, to the usual rule that governmental bodies may not prescribe the form or content of individual expression. Equally important to our conclusion is the constitutional backdrop against which our decision must be made. The constitutional right of free expression is powerful medicine in a society as diverse and populous as ours. It is designed and intended to remove governmental restraints from the arena of public discussion, putting the decision as to what views shall be voiced largely into the hands of each of us, in the hope that use of such freedom will ultimately produce a more capable citizenry and more perfect polity and in the belief that no other approach would comport with the premise of individual dignity and choice upon which our political system rests. *See* Whitney v. California, 274 U.S. 357, 375-377 (1927) (Brandeis, J., concurring).

To many, the immediate consequence of this freedom may often appear to be only verbal tumult, discord, and even offensive utterance. These are, however, within established limits, in truth necessary side effects of the broader enduring values which the process of open debate permits us to achieve. That the air may at times seem filled with verbal cacophony is, in this sense not a sign of weakness but of strength. We cannot lose sight of the fact that, in what otherwise might seem a trifling and annoying instance of individual distasteful abuse of a privilege, these fundamental societal values are truly implicated. . . .

Against this perception of the constitutional policies involved, we discern certain more particularized considerations that peculiarly call for reversal of this conviction. First, the principle contended for by the State seems inherently boundless. How is one to distinguish this from any other offensive word? Surely the state has no right to cleanse public debate to the point where it is grammatically palatable to the most squeamish among us. Yet no readily ascertainable general principle exists for stopping short of that result were we to affirm the judgment below. For, while the particular four-letter word being litigated here is perhaps more distasteful than most others of its genre, it is nevertheless often true that one man's vulgarity is another's lyric. Indeed, we think it is largely because governmental officials cannot make principled distinctions in this area that the Constitution leaves matters of taste and style so largely to the individual.

Additionally, we cannot overlook the fact, because it is well illustrated by the episode involved here, that much linguistic expression serves a dual communicative function: it conveys not only ideas capable of relatively precise, detached explication, but otherwise inexpressible emotions as well. In fact, words are often chosen as much for their emotive as their cognitive force. We cannot sanction the view that the Constitution, while solicitous of the cognitive content of individual speech, has little or no regard for that emotive function which practically speaking, may often be the more important element of the overall message sought to be communicated. . . .

Finally, and in the same vein, we cannot indulge the facile assumption that one can forbid particular words without also running a substantial risk of suppressing ideas in the process. Indeed, governments might soon seize upon the censorship of particular words as a convenient guise for banning the expression of unpopular views. We have been able, as noted above, to discern little social benefit that might result from running the risk of opening the door to such grave results.

It is, in sum, our judgment that, absent a more particularized and compelling reason for its actions, the State may not, consistently with the First and Fourteenth Amendments, make the simple public display here involved of this single four-letter expletive a criminal offense. Because that is the only arguably sustainable rationale for the conviction here at issue, the judgment below must be

Reversed.

Mr. Justice Blackmun, with whom The Chief Justice and Mr. Justice Black join.

I dissent, and I do so for two reasons:

1. Cohen's absurd and immature antic, in my view was mainly conduct and little speech. And I cannot characterize it otherwise. Further, the case appears to me to be well within the sphere of *Chaplinsky v. New Hampshire*, 315 U.S. 568 (1942), where Mr. Justice Murphy, a known champion of First Amendment freedoms, wrote for a unanimous bench. As a consequence, this Court's agonizing over First Amendment values seems misplaced and unnecessary.

2. I am not at all certain that the California Court of Appeal's construction of § 415 is now the authoritative California construction. . . . Inasmuch as this Court does not dismiss this case, it ought to be remanded to the California Court of Appeal for reconsideration in the light of the subsequently rendered decision by the State's highest tribunal in *Bushman.*

Mr. Justice WHITE concurs in Paragraph 2 of Mr. Justice BLACKMUN's dissenting opinion.

NOTES AND QUESTIONS

1. *A binary choice?* Is Justice Harlan correct to suggest that the power to suppress a single curse word from public discourse necessarily leads down the road to more generalized forms of government censorship? Is this a false choice? Could government attempt to maintain civility norms without engaging in broader efforts to censor the entire culture?
2. *The emotive impact of speech.* Justice Harlan's suggestion that the emotive content of communication can be more important than its cognitive content seems persuasive, does it not? To use the facts at issue in *Cohen*, would a jacket with "Down with the Draft" or "I Oppose the Draft" or "The Draft Is Bad, M'Kay?" convey the same message as Cohen's actual jacket? And should Cohen be prevented from communicating his message in public because his preferred means of communication will likely offend at least some other citizens?
3. *A contrary approach.* Contrary to Justice Harlan's thesis, could government create and enforce civility norms in public places and at public meetings without squelching the ability of a speaker to express herself fully? Should Cohen's interest in expressing himself trump the interest of an unwilling audience in avoiding his expression? If one has unavoidable business in the local courthouse, is an admonition to "avert one's eyes" really a satisfactory response? On the other hand, the federal courts consistently have held that an adverse public reaction is *not* a permissible basis for squelching speech. Viewed from the perspective of that rule, Justice Harlan seems to have the better of the argument.
4. *The* Cohen *rule retains strong precedential force.* The Supreme Court has given absolutely no indication that it is inclined to resile from either the baseline holding or the underlying reasoning of *Cohen.* For example, in Snyder v. Phelps, 562 U.S. 443 (2011) (excerpted *supra* at p. 504) the Supreme Court held protected, on First Amendment grounds, a targeted funeral protest of a marine killed while on active duty in Iraq. Brandishing signs with slogans like "God Hates the USA/Thank God for 9/11,"

"God Hates Fags," and "Thank God for Dead Soldiers," the protest took place contemporaneously with, and proximate to, Marine Corporal Matthew Snyder's funeral services in Westminster, Maryland. Writing for the 8–1 majority, Chief Justice Roberts held that the First Amendment essentially immunizes speech in a public forum, related to a matter of public concern, from serving as the basis for tort liability—even if the speech at issue badly transgresses baseline and widely held notions of civility and personal dignity. In particular, Roberts squarely rejected the idea that the highly targeted and intentionally offensive nature of the protest removed, or even reduced, the scope of protection the protest activity enjoyed under the First Amendment:

> Given that Westboro's speech was at a public place on a matter of public concern, that speech is entitled to "special protection" under the First Amendment. Such speech cannot be restricted simply because it is upsetting or arouses contempt. "If there is a bedrock principle underlying the First Amendment, it is that government may not prohibit the expression of an idea simply because society finds the idea itself offensive or disagreeable." Texas v. Johnson, 491 U.S. 397, 414 (1989).

Id. at 1219. Moreover, the gravamen of both the intentional infliction of emotional distress and privacy tort claims relates to the *outrageousness* of the speech or the grossly offensive nature of the intrusion upon privacy. Chief Justice Roberts specifically rejected this legal standard, at least in this context, because "'[o]utrageousness,' however, is a highly malleable standard with 'an inherent subjectiveness about it which would allow a jury to impose liability on the basis of the jurors' tastes or views, or perhaps on the basis of their dislike of a particular expression.' *Hustler* [v. Falwell, 485 U.S. 46, 55 (1988)]." *Id.* That a civil jury might take such a step by imposing civil liability on an unpopular speaker or group constitutes an "unacceptable" risk and, accordingly, "the jury verdict imposing tort liability on Westboro for intentional infliction of emotional distress must be set aside." Thus, *Phelps* both applies and extends the general rule against the creation and enforcement of mandatory civility norms, whether through the criminal law (as in *Cohen*) or via civil law rules (as in *Phelps*).

5. *The dissent not written.* What does one make of the Blackmun dissent? Is it at all persuasive to characterize Cohen's wearing the jacket as "conduct" and not "speech"? Was there a better argument to be made in response to Justice Harlan's majority opinion? How about this: Does a commitment to free speech mean that a society must hold itself absolutely barred from establishing and enforcing any meaningful civility norms in public places? In other words, if a modern day Al Swearengen (the Ian McShane bar proprietor in *Deadwood*) wishes to go about the Los Angeles County courthouse cheerfully greeting passersby as "cocksuckers," may the community disallow this particular form of communication in a public building filled with a captive audience? States maintain laws against public indecency, for example—if one cannot appear nude in public, why should one be

permitted to use highly offensive language in public? Both laws aim at protecting essentially aesthetic interests that reflect long-standing cultural norms and community standards.

6. *Extending the* Cohen *rationale?* Justice Harlan wrote a thoughtful, but carefully limited, majority opinion in *Cohen.* Subsequent opinions in the *Cohen* line were far less circumscribed about the state's power to limit the use of profanity or other offensive language in public places. Consider the following cases.

Gooding v. Wilson

405 U.S. 518 (1972)

Mr. Justice BRENNAN delivered the opinion of the Court.

Appellee was convicted in Superior Court, Fulton County, Georgia, on two counts of using opprobrious words and abusive language in violation of Georgia Code Ann. § 26-6303, which provides: "Any person who shall, without provocation, use to or of another, and in his presence . . . opprobrious words or abusive language, tending to cause a breach of the peace . . . shall be guilty of a misdemeanor." Appellee appealed the conviction to the Supreme Court of Georgia on the ground, among others, that the statute violated the First and Fourteenth Amendments because vague and overbroad. The Georgia Supreme Court rejected that contention and sustained the conviction. . . .

Section 26-6303 punishes only spoken words. It can therefore withstand appellee's attack upon its facial constitutionality only if, as authoritatively construed by the Georgia courts, it is not susceptible of application to speech, although vulgar or offensive, that is protected by the First and Fourteenth Amendments, Cohen v. California, 403 U.S. 15, 18-22 (1971); Terminiello v. Chicago, 337 U.S. 1, 4-5 (1949). . . .

The constitutional guarantees of freedom of speech forbid the States to punish the use of words or language not within "narrowly limited classes of speech." Chaplinsky v. New Hampshire, 315 U.S. 568, 571 (1942). Even as to such a class, however, because "the line between speech unconditionally guaranteed and speech which may legitimately be regulated, suppressed, or punished is finely drawn," Speiser v. Randall, 357 U.S. 513, 525 (1958), "[i]n every case the power to regulate must be so exercised as not, in attaining a permissible end, unduly to infringe the protected freedom," Cantwell v. Connecticut, 310 U.S. 296, 304 (1940). In other words, the statute must be carefully drawn or be authoritatively construed to punish only unprotected speech and not be susceptible of application to protected expression. "Because First Amendment freedoms need breathing space to survive, government may regulate in the area only with narrow specificity." *NAACP v. Button, supra*, at 433. . . .

We conclude that "[t]he separation of legitimate from illegitimate speech calls for more sensitive tools than [Georgia] has supplied." Speiser v. Randall, 357 U.S. at 525. The most recent decision of the Georgia Supreme Court, *Wilson v. State, supra*, in rejecting appellee's attack on the constitutionality of § 26-6303, stated that the statute "conveys a definite meaning as to the conduct forbidden, measured by common understanding and practice." Because earlier appellate decisions applied

§ 26-6303 to utterances where there was no likelihood that the person addressed would make an immediate violent response, it is clear that the standard allowing juries to determine guilt "measured by common understanding and practice" does not limit the application of § 26-6303 to "fighting" words defined by *Chaplinsky*. Rather, that broad standard effectively "licenses the jury to create its own standard in each case." Herndon v. Lowry, 301 U.S. 242, 263 (1937). Accordingly, we agree with the conclusion of the [lower court], "[t]he fault of the statute is that it leaves wide open the standard of responsibility, so that it is easily susceptible to improper application." Unlike the construction of the New Hampshire statute by the New Hampshire Supreme Court, the Georgia appellate courts have not construed § 26-6303 "so as to avoid all constitutional difficulties." United States v. Thirty-seven Photographs, 402 U.S., at 369.

Affirmed.

Mr. Chief Justice BURGER, dissenting.

I fully join in Mr. Justice Blackmun's dissent against the bizarre result reached by the Court. It is not merely odd, it is nothing less than remarkable that a court can find a state statute void on its face, not because of its language—which is the traditional test—but because of the way courts of the state have applied the statute in a few isolated cases, decided as long ago as 1905 and generally long before this Court's decision in Chaplinsky v. New Hampshire, 315 U.S. 568 (1942). Even if all of those cases had been decided yesterday, they do nothing to demonstrate that the narrow language of the Georgia statute has any significant potential for sweeping application to suppress or deter important protected speech. . . .

Mr. Justice BLACKMUN, with whom THE CHIEF JUSTICE joins, dissenting.

It seems strange, indeed, that in this day a man may say to a police officer, who is attempting to restore access to a public building, "White son of a bitch, I'll kill you" and "You son of a bitch, I'll choke you to death," and say to an accompanying officer, "You son of a bitch, if you ever put your hands on me again, I'll cut you all to pieces," and yet constitutionally cannot be prosecuted and convicted under a state statute that makes it a misdemeanor to "use to or of another and in his presence . . . opprobrious words or abusive language, tending to cause a breach of the peace. . . ." This, however, is precisely what the Court pronounces as the law today. . . .

Rosenfeld v. New Jersey

408 U.S. 901 (1972)

PER CURIAM.

Judgment vacated and case remanded for reconsideration in light of Cohen v. California, 403 U.S. 15 (1971), and Gooding v. Wilson, 405 U.S. 518 (1972).

Mr. Chief Justice BURGER, with whom Mr. Justice BLACKMUN and Mr. Justice REHNQUIST join, dissenting.

I am constrained to express my profound disagreement with what the Court does in these three cases on the basis of Gooding v. Wilson, 405 U.S. 518 (1972).

The important underlying aspect of these cases goes really to the function of law in preserving ordered liberty. Civilized people refrain from "taking the law into their own hands" because of a belief that the government, as their agent, will take care of the problem in an organized orderly way with as nearly a uniform response as human skills can manage. History is replete with evidence of what happens when the law cannot or does not provide a collective response for conduct so widely regarded as impermissible and intolerable.

It is barely a century since men in parts of this country carried guns constantly because the law did not afford protection. In that setting, the words used in these cases, if directed toward such an armed civilian, could well have led to death or serious bodily injury. When we undermine the general belief that the law will give protection against fighting words and profane and abusive language such as the utterances involved in these cases, we take steps to return to the law of the jungle. These three cases, like *Gooding*, are small but symptomatic steps. If continued, this permissiveness will tend further to erode public confidence in the law—that subtle but indispensable ingredient of ordered liberty.

In Rosenfeld's case, for example, civilized people attending such a meeting with wives and children would not likely have an instantaneous, violent response, but it does not unduly tax the imagination to think that some justifiably outraged parent whose family were exposed to the foul mouthings of the speaker would "meet him outside" and, either alone or with others, resort to the 19th century's vigorous modes of dealing with such people. I cannot see these holdings as an "advance" in human liberty but rather a retrogression to what men have struggled to escape for a long time.

Mr. Justice POWELL, with whom THE CHIEF JUSTICE and Mr. Justice BLACKMUN join, dissenting.

It has long been established that the First and Fourteenth Amendments prohibit the States from punishing all but the most "narrowly limited classes of speech." Chaplinsky v. New Hampshire, 315 U.S. 568, 571 (1942). The right of free speech, however, has never been held to be absolute at all times and under all circumstances. To so hold would sanction invasion of cherished personal rights and would deny the states the power to deal with threats to public order. . . .

This case presents an example of gross abuse of the respected privilege in this country of allowing every citizen to speak his mind. Appellant addressed a public school board meeting attended by about 150 people, approximately 40 of whom were children and 25 of whom were women. In the course of his remarks he used the adjective "m ______ f ______" on four occasions, to describe the teachers, the school board, the town and his own country. . . .

[A] verbal assault on an unwilling audience may be so grossly offensive and emotionally disturbing as to be the proper subject of criminal proscription, whether under a statute denominating it disorderly conduct, or, more accurately, a public nuisance. . . .

The line between such rights and the type of conduct proscribed by the New Jersey statute is difficult to draw. The preservation of the right to free and robust speech is accorded high priority in our society and under the Constitution. Yet, there are other significant values. One of the hallmarks of a civilized society is the level and quality of discourse. We have witnessed in recent years a disquieting deterioration in standards of taste and civility in speech. For the increasing number of persons who derive satisfaction from vocabularies dependent upon filth and obscenities, there are abundant opportunities to gratify their debased tastes. But our free society must be flexible enough to tolerate even such a debasement provided it occurs without subjecting unwilling audiences to the type of verbal nuisance committed in this case. The shock and sense of affront, and sometimes the injury to mind and spirit, can be as great from words as from some physical attacks.

I conclude in this case that appellant's utterances fall within the proscription of the New Jersey statute, and are not protected by the First Amendment. Accordingly, I would dismiss the appeal for want of a substantial federal question.

Mr. Justice REHNQUIST, with whom THE CHIEF JUSTICE and Mr. Justice BLACKMUN join, dissenting.

In *Lewis*, the police were engaged in making an arrest of appellant's son on grounds not challenged here. While the police were engaged in the performance of their duty, appellant intervened and ultimately addressed the police officers as "g- - d - - - m - - - - - f - - - - - - police." . . .

Appellant in *Brown* spoke to a large group of men and women gathered in the University of Tulsa chapel. During a question and answer period he referred to some policemen as "m - - - - - f - - - - - fascist pig cops" and to a particular Tulsa police officer as that "black m - - - - f- - - - - pig. . . ." Brown was convicted of violating an Oklahoma statute that prohibited the utterance of "any obscene or lascivious language or word in any public place, or in the presence of females. . . ." Okla. Stat. Ann., Tit. 21, § 906 (1958). . . .

Insofar as the Court's remand is based on *Cohen, supra*, for the reasons stated in Mr. Justice Blackmun's dissenting opinion in that case, *id.*, at 27, I would not deny to these States the power to punish language of the sort used here by appropriate legislation. Appellant Lewis' words to the police officers were "fighting words," and those of appellants Rosenfeld and Brown were "lewd and obscene" and "profane" as those terms are used in Chaplinsky v. New Hampshire, 315 U.S. 568 (1942), the leading case in the field. . . .

The language used by these appellants therefore clearly falls within the class of punishable utterances described in *Chaplinsky*. . . .

I would dismiss these appeals for lack of a substantial federal question.

NOTES AND QUESTIONS

1. *No civility norms in public places?* Is it absolutely necessary to protect the use of the "f-bomb" at a school board meeting to ensure that an Orwellian thought control project does not advance? Or is the *Cohen-Gooding* doctrine best understood as a kind of prophylactic rule that overprotects marginal speech in order to ensure adequate breathing room for intemperate core political speech of a dissenting cast?
2. *Broad protection for offensive and insulting speech.* Notwithstanding *Cohen*'s insistence that the holding was limited to the specific context of a generic breach of the peace statute, *Gooding* and *Rosenfeld* make clear that *Cohen*

has a broader effect than Justice Harlan's carefully limited opinion would suggest. Along similar lines is Hess v. Indiana, 414 U.S. 105, 107-109 (1973) (holding protected, on free speech grounds, statement to local sheriff that antiwar protestors would "take the fucking street later" or "take the fucking street again").

3. *Civility norms in the public schools.* Do the public schools present a special case for the creation of mandatory civility norms? Given highly publicized incidents of bullying and mistreatment of students perceived to be "different" in some material respect, many school districts have responded by adopting codes of conduct that require students to treat each other respectfully during school hours and at school events. These codes of conduct commonly prohibit the use of offensive or degrading language (for example, typically a student may not call another student "fag" or "too gay," or otherwise use racist, sexist, homophobic, or religiously offensive language). Although students do not check their First Amendment rights at the schoolhouse door, *Tinker v. Des Moines Indep. Cmty. Sch. Dist.* (excerpted *infra* p. 608), the Supreme Court has sustained restrictions against vulgar speech at curricular events, *Bethel School Dist. No. 403 v. Fraser* (excerpted *infra* p. 692), and also restrictions against speech arguably advocating the use of illegal drugs, *Morse v. Frederick* (excerpted *infra* p. 702). These precedents would seem to support the creation and enforcement of civility codes designed to avoid disruption of the educational mission of the public schools. Although such rules are decidedly content-based (if not *viewpoint*-based), they arguably advance a compelling interest, and the speech itself is the evil to be avoided (given that the speech creates a high probability of disruption).

4. *Off-campus student speech and the First Amendment.* What about mandatory civility norms applicable to student speech that takes place off campus but which is plainly directed at an audience of students, teachers, and administrators, which also has discernable adverse effects within the public schools? The Supreme Court provided a partial answer in Mahanoy Area School Dist. v. B.L., 141 S. Ct. 2038 (2021). B.L., a freshman high school student, sent critical and profane social media messages after being denied a spot on the varsity cheerleading team. *Id.* at 2043. More specifically, she sent a Snapchat message to friends that said "Fuck school fuck softball fuck cheer fuck everything." *Id.* The school then removed B.L. from the junior varsity cheerleading team (on which she had been offered a spot). The Supreme Court, in an opinion by Justice Stephen Breyer, held that the First Amendment protected the student's scatological off-campus speech:

> Putting aside the vulgar language, the listener would hear criticism, of the team, the team's coaches, and the school—in a word or two, criticism of the rules of a community of which B. L. forms a part. This criticism did not involve features that would place it outside the First Amendment's ordinary protection. B. L.'s posts, while crude, did not amount to fighting words.

Id. at 2046. Perhaps most crucially, B.L.'s social media rant did not seriously disrupt or impede the high school's regular operations. *See id.* at 2047-48. After carefully considering several factors, including the lack of any on-campus disruption, Justice Breyer concluded, for an 8-1 majority, that the school district had violated B.L.'s First Amendment rights. *Id.* at 2046-48. He explained that "It might be tempting to dismiss B.L.'s words as unworthy of the robust First Amendment protections discussed herein. But sometimes it is necessary to protect the superfluous in order to preserve the necessary." *Id.* at 2048. Accordingly, a public school district's power to punish profane or scatological language off-campus is more circumscribed than its power to punish such language when used on campus. For a thoughtful discussion of these issues, *see* Barry P. McDonald, *Regulating Student Cyberspeech*, 77 Mo. L. Rev. 727 (2012); Mary-Rose Papandrea, *Student Speech Rights in the Digital Age*, 60 Fla. L. Rev. 1027 (2008); Nancy Willard, *School Response to Cyberbullying and Sexting: The Legal Challenges*, 2011 BYU Edu. & L.J. 75.

5. *A different (better?) approach?* Should a more targeted ban against particularly socially harmful kinds of uncivil communications that also constitute hate speech be sustained as a justifiable limit on freedom of expression? Consider Canada's answer to this question, provided in the next principal case.

D. *GOVERNMENT EFFORTS TO PROHIBIT HATE SPEECH AND RACIALIZED THREATS*

Should government efforts to prevent or punish overtly racist, sexist, homophobic, transphobic, or religiously bigoted speech be treated as presumptively unconstitutional under the *Cohen/Gooding* line of cases that invalidate mandatory civility norms as impermissible content-based speech regulations? Or is racist and other bigoted speech more self-evidently socially harmful than scatology and, therefore, a subset of low-value speech, like obscenity (*see infra* Chapter 11), that the government has a sufficiently pressing and important rationale for regulating (or even banning)? Could one plausibly characterize racist or other bigoted statements that degrade, stigmatize, and genuinely frighten those to whom they are directed as "true threats" (*see Watts, supra* p. 71)? Our neighbor to the north, Canada, has squarely embraced the idea that direct hate speech regulations can be reconciled with a robust commitment to the freedom of speech. To date, however, this approach has not gained much ground in the pages of *U.S. Reports.*

The next principal case, *Keegstra*, endorses the view that hate speech seriously impedes the ability of minorities to participate in the process of democratic self-government on a free and equal basis. The Supreme Court of Canada held that laws proscribing hate speech *enhance* and *improve* the marketplace of political ideas—and are therefore constitutional. By way of contrast, however, Justice Scalia's approach in *R.A.V.* (*see infra* p. 562), epitomizes the traditional U.S. approach, namely that direct, targeted regulations of hate speech constitute unconstitutional government content and viewpoint discrimination. Even so, however, the U.S. approach is considerably more complicated than *R.A.V.* might suggest. Although the federal courts consistently have invalidated *direct bans* on hate speech, they have *upheld* enhanced sentences for identity-based crimes (*see* Wisconsin v. Mitchell, *infra* p. 568), as well as targeted regulations against hate speech that conveys true threats (*see* Virginia v. Black, *infra* p. 571). Thus, it greatly oversimplifies current First Amendment law to posit that the government may never take hate speech into account when imposing civil or criminal sanctions. Simply put, First Amendment law in this area is more complicated.

R. v. Keegstra

[1990] 3 S.C.R. 697 (Can.)

DICKSON, C.J.

This appeal . . . raises a delicate and highly controversial issue as to the constitutional validity of s. 319(2) of the Criminal Code, R.S.C. 1985, c. C-46, a legislative provision which prohibits the wilful promotion of hatred, other than in private conversation, towards any section of the public distinguished by colour, race, religion or ethnic origin. In particular, the court must decide whether this section infringes the guarantee of freedom of expression found in s. 2(*b*) of the Canadian Charter of Rights and Freedoms in a manner that cannot be justified under s. 1 of the Charter. A secondary issue arises as to whether the presumption of innocence protected in the Charter's s. 11(*d*) is unjustifiably breached by reason of s. 319(3)(a) of the Code, which affords a defense of "truth" to the wilful promotion of hatred, but only where the accused proves the truth of the communicated statements on the balance of probabilities.

Mr. James Keegstra was a high school teacher in Eckville, Alberta, from the early 1970s until his dismissal in 1982. In 1984 Mr. Keegstra was charged under s. 319(2) (then s. 281.2(2)) of the Criminal Code with unlawfully promoting hatred against an identifiable group by communicating anti-semitic statements to his students. He was convicted by a jury in a trial before McKenzie J. of the Alberta Court of the Queen's Bench.

Mr. Keegstra's teachings attributed various evil qualities to Jews. He thus described Jews to his pupils as "treacherous," "subversive," "sadistic," "money-loving," "power hungry" and "child killers." He taught his classes that Jewish people seek to destroy Christianity and are responsible for depressions, anarchy, chaos, wars and revolution. According to Mr. Keegstra, Jews "created the Holocaust to gain sympathy" and, in contrast to the open and honest Christians, were said to be deceptive, secretive and inherently evil. Mr. Keegstra expected his students to reproduce his teachings in class and on exams. If they failed to do so, their marks suffered. . . .

[After a trial, Keegstra was convicted of violating § 319(2). On appeal, however, the Alberta Court of Appeal unanimously voted to reverse Keesgra's conviction and invalidated § 319(2) on free speech grounds.]

[In relevant part, § 319(2) provides that:]

> Every one who, by communicating statements, other than in private conversation, wilfully promotes hatred against any identifiable group is guilty of an indictable offence and is liable to imprisonment for a term not exceeding two years; or an offence punishable on summary conviction.
>
> No person shall be convicted of an offence under subsection (2) if he establishes that the statements communicated were true; if, in good faith, he expressed or attempted to establish by argument an opinion on a religious subject; if the statements were relevant to any subject of public interest, the discussion of which was for the public benefit, and if on reasonable grounds he believed them to be true; or if, in good faith, he intended to point out, for the purpose of removal, matters producing or tending to produce feelings of hatred toward an identifiable group in Canada. No proceedings for an offence under subsection (2) shall be instituted without the consent of the Attorney General. . . .

In my view, through s. 319(2) Parliament seeks to prohibit communications which convey meaning, namely, those communications which are intended to promote hatred against identifiable groups. I thus find s. 319(2) to constitute an infringement of the freedom of expression guaranteed by s. 2(*b*) of the Charter. . . .

Though the language of s. 1 appears earlier in these reasons, it is appropriate to repeat its words:

> The Canadian Charter of Rights and Freedoms guarantees the rights and freedoms set out in it subject only to such reasonable limits prescribed by law as can be demonstrably justified in a free and democratic society. . . .

Having discussed the unique and unifying role of s. 1, I think it appropriate to address a tangential matter, yet one nonetheless crucial to the disposition of this appeal: the relationship between Canadian and American approaches to the constitutional protection of free expression, most notably in the realm of hate propaganda. Those who attack the constitutionality of s. 319(2) draw heavily on the tenor of First Amendment jurisprudence in weighing the competing freedoms and interests in this appeal, a reliance which is understandable given the prevalent opinion that the criminalization of hate propaganda violates the Bill of Rights (see, e.g., L. Tribe, American Constitutional Law, 2nd ed. (1988), at p. 861, n. 2; K. Greenawalt, "Insults and Epithets: Are They Protected Speech?" (1990), 42 Rutgers L. Rev. 287, at p. 304). In response to the emphasis placed upon this jurisprudence, I find it helpful to summarize the American position and to determine the extent to which it should influence the s. 1 analysis in the circumstances of this appeal.

A myriad of sources—both judicial and academic—offer reviews of First Amendment jurisprudence as it pertains to hate propaganda. Central to most discussions is the 1952 case of Beauharnais v. Illinois, 343 U.S. 250, where the Supreme Court of the United States upheld as constitutional a criminal statute forbidding certain types of group defamation. Though never overruled, *Beauharnais* appears to have been weakened by later pronouncements of the Supreme Court (see, e.g., Garrison v. Louisiana, 379 U.S. 64 (1964); Ashton v. Kentucky, 384 U.S. 195 (1966); New York Times Co. v. Sullivan, 376 U.S. 254 (1964); Brandenburg v. Ohio, 395 U.S. 444 (1969); and Cohen v. California, 403 U.S. 15 (1971)). The trend reflected in many of these pronouncements is to protect offensive, public invective as long as the speaker has not knowingly lied and there exists no clear and present danger of violence or insurrection. . . .

Canada and the United States are not alike in every way, nor have the documents entrenching human rights in our two countries arisen in the same context. It is only common sense to recognize that, just as similarities will justify borrowing from the American experience, differences may require that Canada's constitutional vision depart from that endorsed in the United States.

Having examined the American cases relevant to First Amendment jurisprudence and legislation criminalizing hate propaganda, I would be adverse to following too closely the line of argument that would overrule *Beauharnais* on the ground that incursions placed upon free expression are only justified where there is a clear and present danger of imminent breach of peace. Equally, I am unwilling to embrace various categorizations and guiding rules generated by American law without careful consideration of their appropriateness to Canadian constitutional theory. Though I have found the American experience tremendously helpful in coming to my own conclusions regarding this appeal, and by no means reject the whole of the First Amendment doctrine, in a number of respects I am thus dubious as to the applicability of this doctrine in the context of a challenge to hate propaganda legislation.

First, it is not entirely clear that *Beauharnais* must conflict with existing First Amendment doctrine. Credible arguments have been made that later Supreme Court cases do not necessarily erode its legitimacy (*see, e.g.*, Kenneth Lasson, "Racial Defamation as Free Speech: Abusing the First Amendment" (1985), 17 Colum. Human Rights L. Rev. 11). Indeed, there exists a growing body of academic writing in the United States which evinces a stronger focus upon the way in which hate propaganda can undermine the very values which free speech is said to protect. . . .

Second, the aspect of First Amendment doctrine most incompatible with s. 319(2), at least as that doctrine is described by those who would strike down the legislation, is its strong aversion to content-based regulation of expression. I am somewhat skeptical, however, as to whether this view of free speech in the United States is entirely accurate. Rather, in rejecting the extreme position that would provide an absolute guarantee of free speech in the Bill of Rights, the Supreme Court has developed a number of tests and theories by which protected speech can be identified and the legitimacy of government regulation assessed. Often required is a content-based categorization of the expression under examination. . . .

Third, applying the Charter to the legislation challenged in this appeal reveals important differences between Canadian and American constitutional perspectives. I have already discussed in some detail the special role of s. 1 in determining the protective scope of Charter rights and freedoms. Section 1 has no equivalent in the United States, a fact previously alluded to by this court in selectively utilizing American constitutional jurisprudence. Of course, American experience should never be rejected simply because the Charter contains a balancing provision, for it is well known that American courts have fashioned compromises between conflicting interests despite what appears to be the absolute guarantee of constitutional rights. Where s. 1 operates to accentuate a uniquely Canadian vision of a free and democratic society, however, we must not hesitate to depart from the path taken in the United States. Far from requiring a less solicitous protection of Charter rights and freedoms, such independence of vision protects these rights and freedoms in a different way. As will be seen below, in my view the international commitment to eradicate hate propaganda and, most importantly, the special role given equality and multiculturalism in the Canadian Constitution necessitate a departure from the view, reasonably prevalent in America at present, that the suppression of hate propaganda is incompatible with the guarantee of free expression (in support of this view, see the comments of Professors Kathleen Mahoney and Jamie Cameron in "The James McCormick Mitchell Lecture—Language as Violence v. Freedom of Expression: Canadian and American Perspectives on Group Defamation" (1988-89), 37 Buffalo L. Rev. 337, beginning at pp. 344 and 353 respectively).

In sum, there is much to be learned from First Amendment jurisprudence with regard to freedom of expression and hate propaganda. It would be rash, however, to see First Amendment doctrine as demanding the striking down of s. 319(2). Not only are the precedents somewhat mixed, but the relaxation of the prohibition against content-based regulation of expression in certain areas indicates that American courts are not loath to permit the suppression of ideas in some circumstances. Most importantly, the nature of the s. 1 test as applied in the context of a challenge to s. 319(2) may well demand a perspective particular to Canadian constitutional jurisprudence when weighing competing interests. If values fundamental to the Canadian conception of a free and democratic society suggest an approach that denies hate propaganda the highest degree of constitutional protection, it is this approach which must be employed. . . .

In my opinion, it would be impossible to deny that Parliament's objective in enacting s. 319(2) is of the utmost importance. Parliament has recognized the substantial harm that can flow from hate propaganda, and in trying to prevent the pain suffered by target group members and to reduce racial, ethnic and religious tension in Canada has decided to suppress the wilful promotion of hatred against identifiable groups. The nature of Parliament's objective is supported not only by the work of numerous study groups but also by our collective historical knowledge of the potentially catastrophic effects of the promotion of hatred (*Jones*, [R. v. Jones, [1986] 2 S.C.R. 284], per La Forest J., at pp. 299-300). Additionally, the international commitment to eradicate hate propaganda and the stress placed upon equality and multiculturalism in the Charter strongly buttress the importance of this objective. I consequently find that the first part of the test under s. 1 of the Charter is easily satisfied and that a powerfully convincing legislative objective exists such as to justify some limit on freedom of expression. . . .

The suppression of hate propaganda undeniably muzzles the participation of a few individuals in the democratic process, and hence detracts somewhat from free expression values, but the degree of this limitation is not substantial. I am aware that the use of strong language in political and social debate—indeed, perhaps even language intended to promote hatred—is an unavoidable part of the democratic process. Moreover, I recognize that hate propaganda is expression of a type which would generally be categorized as "political," thus putatively placing it at the very heart of the principle extolling freedom of expression as vital to the democratic process. Nonetheless, expression can work to undermine our commitment to democracy where employed to propagate ideas anathemic to democratic values. Hate propaganda works in just such a way, arguing as it does for a society in which the democratic process is subverted and individuals are denied respect and dignity simply because of racial or religious characteristics. This brand of expressive activity is thus wholly inimical to the democratic aspirations of the free expression guarantee.

Indeed, one may quite plausibly contend that it is through rejecting hate propaganda that the state can best encourage the protection of values central to freedom of expression, while simultaneously demonstrating dislike for the vision forwarded by hate-mongers. In this regard, the reaction to various types of expression by a democratic government may be perceived as meaningful expression on behalf of the vast majority of citizens. I do not wish to be construed as saying that an infringement of s. 2(*b*) can be justified under s. 1 merely because it is the product of a democratic process; the Charter will not permit even the democratically elected legislature to restrict the rights and freedoms crucial to a free and democratic society. What I do wish to emphasize, however, is that one must be careful not to accept blindly that the suppression of expression must always and unremittingly detract from values central to freedom of expression (Lee C. Bollinger, The Tolerant Society: Freedom of Speech and Extremist Speech in America (1986), at pp. 87-93).

I am very reluctant to attach anything but the highest importance to expression relevant to political matters. But given the unparalleled vigour with which hate propaganda repudiates and undermines democratic values, and in particular its condemnation of the view that all citizens need be treated with equal respect and dignity so as to make participation in the political process meaningful, I am unable to see the protection of such expression as integral to the democratic ideal so central to the s. 2(*b*) rationale. Together with my comments as to the tenuous link between communications covered by s. 319(2) and other values at the core of the free expression guarantee, this conclusion leads me to disagree with the opinion of McLachlin J. that the expression at stake in this appeal mandates the most solicitous degree of constitutional protection. In my view, hate propaganda should not be accorded the greatest of weight in the s. 1 analysis.

[Chief Justice Dickson concludes that all of Section 1's requirements have been met and that Section 1 therefore saves § 319(2) from judicial invalidation on Charter grounds.]

I find that the infringement of the respondent's freedom of expression as guaranteed by s. 2(*b*) should be upheld as a reasonable limit prescribed by law in a free and democratic society. Furthering an immensely important objective and directed at expression distant from the core of free expression values, s. 319(2) satisfies each of the components of the proportionality inquiry. I thus disagree with the Alberta Court of Appeal's conclusion that this criminal prohibition of hate propaganda violates the Charter, and would allow the appeal in this respect. . . .

Insofar as its purpose is to prohibit the expression of certain meanings, s. 319(2) of the Criminal Code infringes the guarantee of freedom of expression found in s. 2(*b*) of the Charter. Given the importance of Parliament's purpose in preventing the dissemination of hate propaganda and the tenuous connection such expression has with s. 2(*b*) values, however, I have found the narrowly drawn parameters of s. 319(2) to be justifiable under s. 1. . . .

McLachlin, J. (dissenting):

The issue on this appeal is whether s. 319(2) and (3) of the Criminal Code, R.S.C. 1985, c. C-46, creating the offence of unlawfully promoting hatred, should be struck down on the ground that they infringe the guarantees of free expression and the presumption of innocence embodied in the Canadian Charter of Rights and Freedoms.

The framers of the Charter recognized both the fundamental nature of freedom of expression and the necessity of sometimes limiting it where the risks it poses are too great for society to tolerate. Its importance is reflected in the broad and untrammeled definition of expression embodied in s. 2(*b*). The guarantee of free expression is not internally limited as are certain other Charter rights (e.g., s. 8 of the Charter) or as are the equivalent guarantees in the European Convention for the Protection of Human Rights and Fundamental Freedoms, 213 U.N.T.S. 221 (1950), and the International Covenant on Civil and Political Rights, 999 U.N.T.S. 171 (1966). The guarantees of free expression in those documents explicitly permit a wide variety of limitations on free expression—limitations which the person asserting the right of free expression must observe. By contrast, the Canadian guarantee of free expression is more comprehensive. The provision is a very broad guarantee, and all expression is prima facie protected. Any infringement must be justified by the state under s. 1. Moreover, as will be observed *infra*, freedom of expression had achieved a near-constitutional status in Canada long before its specific entrenchment by the Charter. All this suggests that the framers of the Charter envisaged freedom of expression as a comprehensive, fundamental right of great importance.

At the same time, the Charter permits freedom of speech to be restricted by law where this is justified by the need to protect more important countervailing values. Thus the broad guarantee of freedom of expression in s. 2(*b*) of the Charter is made subject to s. 1 which permits such reasonable limitations on the right as may be justified in a free and democratic society. . . .

The objective of s. 319(2) of the Criminal Code is to prevent the promotion of hatred toward identifiable groups within our society. As the Attorney General of Canada puts it, the objective of the legislation is, "among other things, to protect racial, religious and other groups from the wilful promotion of hatred against them, to prevent the spread of hatred and the breakdown of racial and social harmony," and "to prevent the destruction of our multicultural society." These aims are subsumed in the twin values of social harmony and individual dignity. . . .

Given the problem of racial and religious prejudice in this country, I am satisfied that the objective of the legislation is of sufficient gravity to be capable of justifying limitations on constitutionally protected rights and freedoms. . . .

[Even so, Justice McLachlin found that Section 1 did not save § 319(2) because the provision] catches a broad range of speech and prohibits it in a broad manner, allowing only private conversations to escape scrutiny. Moreover, the process by which the prohibition is effected—the criminal law—is the severest our society can impose and is arguably unnecessary given the availability of alternative remedies. I conclude that the criminalization of hate statements does not impair free speech to the minimum extent permitted by its objectives.

. . . Viewed from the perspective of our society as a whole, the infringement of the guarantee of freedom of expression before this court is a serious one. Section 319(2) of the Criminal Code does not merely regulate the form or tone of expression—it strikes directly at its content and at the viewpoints of individuals. It strikes, moreover, at viewpoints in widely diverse domains, whether artistic, social or political. It is capable of catching not only statements like those at issue in this case, but works of art and the intemperate statement made in the heat of social controversy. While few may actually be prosecuted to conviction under s. 319(2), many fall within the shadow of its broad prohibition. These dangers are exacerbated by the fact that s. 319(2) applies to all public expression. In short, the limitation on freedom of expression created by s. 319(2) of the Criminal Code invokes all of the values upon which s. 2(*b*) of the Charter rests—the value of fostering a vibrant and creative society through the marketplace of ideas; the value of the vigorous and open debate essential to democratic government and preservation of our rights and freedoms; and the value of a society which fosters the self-actualization and freedom of its members. . . .

I turn then to the other side of the scale and the benefit to be gained by maintenance of the limitation on freedom of expression effected by s. 319(2) of the Criminal Code. As indicated earlier, there is no question but that the objectives which underlie this legislation are of a most worthy nature. Unfortunately, the claims of gains to be achieved at the cost of the infringement of free speech represented by s. 319(2) are tenuous. It is far from clear that the legislation does not promote the cause of hate-mongering extremists and hinder the possibility of voluntary amendment of conduct more than it discourages the spread of hate propaganda. Accepting the importance to our society of the goals of social harmony and individual dignity, of multiculturalism and equality, it remains difficult to see how s. 319(2) fosters them.

In my opinion, the result is clear. Any questionable benefit of the legislation is outweighed by the significant infringement on the constitutional guarantee of free expression effected by s. 319(2) of the Criminal Code. . . .

NOTES AND QUESTIONS

1. *Judicial deference to legislative judgments about the need to regulate hate speech.* The Supreme Court of Canada does not exclude hate speech from protection under section 2(b) of the Charter but appears more willing than the Supreme Court of the United States to credit legislative judgments that some speech imposes unreasonable social costs and, accordingly, may be suppressed. Of course, *Keegstra* could be seen as nothing more than a more permissive iteration of the approach reflected in *Hishon.* If advocacy or incitement to racial hatred is itself a social harm, like telemarketing fraud, gender discrimination in the workplace, or a true threat, why shouldn't government be permitted to regulate that harm?
2. *Rejecting the First Amendment's protection of hate speech.* Does the Supreme Court of Canada properly understand U.S. free speech law? If so, why does it reject the U.S. approach? In what respect is the U.S. approach found to be wanting?
3. *The U.S. approach to Keegstra's bad behavior.* Would Keegstra's behavior be lawful in the United States? Would he have kept his job as a public school

teacher? Is the real question whether, in addition to losing his job, he should also go to jail? And, if Keegstra goes to jail, is he guilty of a thought crime, or rather some sort of misappropriation of a government trust?

4. *Speech versus conduct.* In the United States, although Keegstra could not be punished directly for his anti-Semitic speech activity, if he committed an independent criminal act, his sentence could be enhanced because of his ideological motivation for the criminal act. Consider the following cases and then reconsider whether the U.S. and Canadian approaches are fundamentally inconsistent.

AN INTRODUCTORY NOTE TO *MITCHELL* AND *BLACK*

In R.A.V. v. City of St. Paul, 505 U.S. 377 (1992), the Supreme Court invalidated a local St. Paul, Minnesota, ordinance that prohibited verbal assaults based on, among other things, racial animus. Writing for a 5–4 majority, Justice Scalia explained that although fighting words were outside the scope of the Free Speech Clause's protection, and the Minnesota Supreme Court had limited the scope of the ordinance to fighting words, St. Paul nevertheless could not punish fighting words selectively based on the content or viewpoint of the message being conveyed. Justice Scalia found that limiting a prohibition on fighting words to those fighting words that cause alarm or resentment based on race constituted an impermissible form of both content and viewpoint discrimination. A broad reading of *R.A.V.* would seem to preclude similar policies that make adverse legal consequences turn on the expression of racist, sexist, homophobic, or religiously bigoted viewpoints. However, the Supreme Court has declined to extend *R.A.V.*'s reasoning to disallow enhanced penalties for otherwise unlawful behavior based on the identity of the victim and the defendant's intentional selection of the victim because of a characteristic such as race, gender, religion, or sexual orientation. *R.A.V.*, if read broadly, could have prohibited sentencing enhancements based on the victim's identity, if one viewed the victim's identity as a de facto proxy for particular ideological or political commitments. Under this view, the underlying crime constitutes a kind of expressive conduct, and the enhancement, by targeting the ideological or political motivation, punishes speech based on content and viewpoint. The argument, simply enough, would be that although government can punish an assault, it cannot punish a racist assault more severely because the enhanced penalty constitutes a kind of thought crime. On the other hand, the use of motive to enhance punishment is commonplace in the criminal law, and the punishment itself flows from the underlying crime, not from the ideology that gave rise to it. Moreover, the social effects of a hate crime might well be more severe on both the community and the victim than those of a random mugging. *Mitchell* addresses the scope of *R.A.V.*'s holding and, in an opinion authored by Chief Justice Rehnquist (who was part of the *R.A.V.* majority), distinguishes sentencing enhancements from crimes based directly on uttering racial threats. So, too, the Supreme Court has permitted punishment for expressive conduct that conveys a true threat—despite the potential chilling effect that permitting such prosecutions might create.

R.A.V. v. City of St. Paul, Minnesota

505 U.S. 377 (1992)

Justice Scalia delivered the opinion of the Court.

In the predawn hours of June 21, 1990, petitioner and several other teenagers allegedly assembled a crudely made cross by taping together broken chair legs. They then allegedly burned the cross inside the fenced yard of a black family that lived across the street from the house where petitioner was staying. Although this conduct could have been punished under any of a number of laws, one of the two provisions under which respondent city of St. Paul chose to charge petitioner (then a juvenile) was the St. Paul Bias-Motivated Crime Ordinance, St. Paul, Minn., Legis. Code § 292.02 (1990), which provides:

> Whoever places on public or private property a symbol, object, appellation, characterization or graffiti, including, but not limited to, a burning cross or Nazi swastika, which one knows or has reasonable grounds to know arouses anger, alarm or resentment in others on the basis of race, color, creed, religion or gender commits disorderly conduct and shall be guilty of a misdemeanor.

Petitioner moved to dismiss this count on the ground that the St. Paul ordinance was substantially overbroad and impermissibly content based and therefore facially invalid under the First Amendment. The trial court granted this motion, but the Minnesota Supreme Court reversed. That court rejected petitioner's overbreadth claim because, as construed in prior Minnesota cases, the modifying phrase "arouses anger, alarm or resentment in others" limited the reach of the ordinance to conduct that amounts to "fighting words," *i.e.*, "conduct that itself inflicts injury or tends to incite immediate violence . . . ," . . . and therefore the ordinance reached only expression "that the first amendment does not protect." The court also concluded that the ordinance was not impermissibly content based because, in its view, "the ordinance is a narrowly tailored means toward accomplishing the compelling governmental interest in protecting the community against bias-motivated threats to public safety and order." . . .

I

. . . [W]e accept the Minnesota Supreme Court's authoritative statement that the ordinance reaches only those expressions that constitute "fighting words" within the meaning of *Chaplinsky*. Petitioner and his *amici* urge us to modify the scope of the *Chaplinsky* formulation, thereby invalidating the ordinance as "substantially overbroad[.]" We find it unnecessary to consider this issue. Assuming, *arguendo*, that all of the expression reached by the ordinance is proscribable under the "fighting words" doctrine, we nonetheless conclude that the ordinance is facially unconstitutional in that it prohibits otherwise permitted speech solely on the basis of the subjects the speech addresses.

The First Amendment generally prevents government from proscribing speech . . . because of disapproval of the ideas expressed. Content-based regulations are presumptively invalid. . . . From 1791 to the present, however, our society, like other free but civilized societies, has permitted restrictions upon the content of speech in a few limited areas, which are "of such slight social value as a step to truth that any benefit that may be derived from them is clearly outweighed by the social interest in order and morality." *Chaplinsky*. . . .

We have sometimes said that these categories of expression are "not within the area of constitutionally protected speech[.]" . . . Such statements must be taken in context, however[.] . . . What they mean is that these areas of speech can, consistently with the First Amendment, be regulated *because of their constitutionally proscribable content* (obscenity, defamation, etc.) — not that they are categories of speech entirely invisible to the Constitution, so that they may be made the vehicles for content discrimination unrelated to their distinctively proscribable content. Thus, the government may proscribe libel; but it may not make the further content discrimination of proscribing *only* libel critical of the government. . . .

Our cases surely do not establish the proposition that the First Amendment imposes no obstacle whatsoever to regulation of particular instances of such proscribable expression, so that the government "may regulate [them] freely." . . . That would mean that a city council could enact an ordinance prohibiting only those legally obscene works that contain criticism of the city government or, indeed, that do not include endorsement of the city government. Such a simplistic, all-or-nothing-at-all approach to First Amendment protection is at odds with common sense and with our jurisprudence as well. It is not true that "fighting words" have at most a "*de minimis* " expressive content, or that their content is *in all respects* "worthless and undeserving of constitutional protection"; sometimes they are quite expressive indeed. We have not said that they constitute "*no* part of the expression of ideas," but only that they constitute "no *essential* part of any exposition of ideas." *Chaplinsky*. . . .

[T]he exclusion of "fighting words" from the scope of the First Amendment simply means that, for purposes of that Amendment, the unprotected features of the words are, despite their verbal character, essentially a "nonspeech" element of communication. Fighting words are thus analogous to a noisy sound truck. . . . [B]oth can be used to convey an idea; but neither has, in and of itself, a claim upon the First Amendment. As with the sound truck, however, so also with fighting words: The government may not regulate use based on hostility — or favoritism — towards the underlying message expressed.

Even the prohibition against content discrimination . . . is not absolute. It applies differently in the context of proscribable speech than in the area of fully protected speech. The rationale of the general prohibition, after all, is that content discrimination "raises the specter that the Government may effectively drive certain ideas or viewpoints from the marketplace." . . . But content discrimination among various instances of a class of proscribable speech often does not pose this threat.

When the basis for the content discrimination consists entirely of the very reason the entire class of speech at issue is proscribable, no significant danger of idea or viewpoint discrimination exists. Such a reason, having been adjudged neutral enough to support exclusion of the entire class of speech from First Amendment protection, is also neutral enough to form the basis of distinction within the class. . . . [T]he Federal Government can criminalize only those threats of violence that are directed against the President . . . since the reasons why threats of violence are outside the First Amendment (protecting individuals from the fear of violence, from the disruption that fear engenders, and from the possibility that the threatened violence will occur) have special force when applied to the person of the President. . . . But the Federal Government may not criminalize only those threats against the President that mention his policy on aid to inner cities. . . .

II

Applying these principles to the St. Paul ordinance, we conclude that, even as narrowly construed by the Minnesota Supreme Court, the ordinance is facially unconstitutional. Although the phrase in the ordinance, "arouses anger, alarm or resentment in others," has been limited by the Minnesota Supreme Court's construction to reach only those symbols or displays that amount to "fighting words," the remaining, unmodified terms make clear that the ordinance applies only to "fighting words" that insult, or provoke violence, "on the basis of race, color, creed, religion or gender." Displays containing abusive invective, no matter how vicious or severe, are permissible unless they are addressed to one of the specified disfavored topics. Those who wish to use "fighting words" in connection with other ideas—to express hostility, for example, on the basis of political affiliation, union membership, or homosexuality—are not covered. The First Amendment does not permit St. Paul to impose special prohibitions on those speakers who express views on disfavored subjects. . . .

In its practical operation, moreover, the ordinance goes even beyond mere content discrimination, to actual viewpoint discrimination. Displays containing some words—odious racial epithets, for example—would be prohibited to proponents of all views. But "fighting words" that do not themselves invoke race, color, creed, religion, or gender—aspersions upon a person's mother, for example—would seemingly be usable *ad libitum* in the placards of those arguing *in favor* of racial, color, etc., tolerance and equality, but could not be used by those speakers' opponents. One could hold up a sign saying, for example, that all "anti-Catholic bigots" are misbegotten; but not that all "papists" are, for that would insult and provoke violence "on the basis of religion." St. Paul has no such authority to license one side of a debate to fight freestyle, while requiring the other to follow Marquis of Queensberry rules. . . .

The content-based discrimination reflected in the St. Paul ordinance . . . does not fall within the exception for content discrimination based on the very reasons why the particular class of speech at issue (here, fighting words) is proscribable. . . . [T]he reason why fighting words are categorically excluded from the protection of the First Amendment is not that their content communicates any particular idea, but that their content embodies a particularly intolerable (and socially unnecessary) *mode* of expressing *whatever* idea the speaker wishes to convey. St. Paul has not singled out an especially offensive mode of expression—it has not, for example, selected for prohibition only those fighting words that communicate ideas in a threatening (as opposed to a merely obnoxious) manner. Rather, it has proscribed fighting words of whatever manner that communicate messages of racial, gender, or religious intolerance. Selectivity of this sort creates the possibility that the city is seeking to handicap the expression of particular ideas. That possibility would alone be enough to render the ordinance presumptively invalid, but St. Paul's comments and concessions in this case elevate the possibility to a certainty. . . .

Finally, . . . even if the ordinance regulates expression based on hostility towards its protected ideological content, [St. Paul asserts that] this discrimination is nonetheless justified because it is narrowly tailored to serve compelling state interests. Specifically, [it asserts] that the ordinance helps to ensure the basic human rights of members of groups that have historically been subjected to discrimination, including the right of such group members to live in peace where they wish. We do not doubt that these interests are compelling, and that the ordinance can be said to promote them. But the "danger of censorship" presented by a facially content-based statute . . . requires that that weapon be employed only where it is "*necessary* to serve the asserted [compelling] interest." . . .

The existence of adequate content-neutral alternatives thus "undercut[s] significantly" any defense of such a statute, . . . casting considerable doubt on the government's protestations that "the asserted justification is in fact an accurate description of the purpose and effect of the law." . . . The dispositive question in this case, therefore, is whether content discrimination is reasonably necessary to achieve St. Paul's compelling interests; it plainly is not. An ordinance not limited to the favored topics, for example, would have precisely the same beneficial effect. In fact the only interest distinctively served by the content limitation is that of displaying the city council's special hostility towards the particular biases thus singled out. That is precisely what the First Amendment forbids. . . .

Let there be no mistake about our belief that burning a cross in someone's front yard is reprehensible. But St. Paul has sufficient means at its disposal to prevent such behavior without adding the First Amendment to the fire.

The judgment of the Minnesota Supreme Court is reversed, and the case is remanded for proceedings not inconsistent with this opinion.

It is so ordered.

Justice WHITE, with whom Justice BLACKMUN and Justice O'CONNOR join, and with whom Justice STEVENS joins . . . concurring in the judgment.

I agree with the majority that the judgment of the Minnesota Supreme Court should be reversed. However, our agreement ends there. . . .

Although I disagree with the Court's analysis, I do agree with its conclusion: The St. Paul ordinance is unconstitutional. However, I would decide the case on overbreadth grounds. . . . Although the ordinance reaches conduct that is unprotected, it also makes criminal expressive conduct that causes only hurt feelings, offense, or resentment, and is protected by the First Amendment. . . . The ordinance is therefore fatally overbroad and invalid on its face . . .

[Justice BLACKMUN's opinion concurring in the judgment is omitted.]

Justice STEVENS, with whom Justice WHITE and Justice BLACKMUN join . . . concurring in the judgment.

. . . I am . . . troubled by . . . [the Court's] conclusion that the St. Paul ordinance is an unconstitutional content-based regulation of speech. Drawing on broadly worded dicta, the Court establishes a near-absolute ban on content-based regulations of expression and holds that the First Amendment prohibits the regulation of fighting words by subject matter. Thus, while the Court rejects the "all-or-nothing-at-all" nature of [its earlier categorical approach to low value speech], it promptly embraces an absolutism of its own: Within a particular "proscribable" category of expression, the Court holds, a government must either proscribe *all* speech or no speech at all. This aspect of the Court's ruling fundamentally misunderstands the role and constitutional status of content-based regulations on speech, conflicts with the very nature of First Amendment jurisprudence, and disrupts well-settled principles of First Amendment law. . . .

. . . [I] believe our decisions establish a more complex and subtle analysis, one that considers the content and context of the regulated speech, and the nature and scope of the restriction on speech. Applying this analysis and assuming, *arguendo,* (as the Court does) that the St. Paul ordinance is *not* overbroad, I conclude that such a selective, subject-matter regulation on proscribable speech is constitutional. . . .

Contrary to the suggestion of the majority, the St. Paul ordinance does *not* regulate expression based on viewpoint. . . . The St. Paul ordinance is evenhanded. In a battle between advocates of tolerance and advocates of intolerance, the ordinance does not prevent either side from hurling fighting words at the other on the basis of their conflicting ideas, but it does bar *both* sides from hurling such words on the basis of the target's "race, color, creed, religion or gender." To extend the Court's pugilistic metaphor, the St. Paul ordinance simply bans punches "below the belt"—*by either party.* It does not, therefore, favor one side of any debate. . . .

Taken together, these several considerations persuade me that the St. Paul ordinance is not an unconstitutional content-based regulation of speech. Thus, were the ordinance not overbroad, I would vote to uphold it.

NOTES AND QUESTIONS

1. *Targeted versus generic proscriptions against fighting words.* Is it ironic that the logic of Justice Scalia's position would require St. Paul to ban *more* speech rather than less speech? An ordinance that banned fighting words generically would be a permissible form of content discrimination. Justice Scalia, however, views the government's motive in banning only *some* fighting words as constitutionally problematic—a form of both content and viewpoint discrimination. Justice Stevens, on the other hand, seems to believe that banning only those fighting words that constitute a form of hate speech is not inconsistent with the First Amendment. Who has the better view? Why?
2. *Content discrimination within a category of unprotected speech.* What purpose does the Court's prohibition against content discrimination within categories of unprotected speech serve? Does it protect against distortion of public debate or possible illegitimate government purposes? Did the St. Paul ordinance pose either of these dangers? *See* Elena Kagan, *Private Speech, Public Purpose: The Role of Governmental Motive in First Amendment Doctrine,* 63 U. Chi. L. Rev. 413, 418-423 (1996).
3. *Justice Stevens's "harm" rationale.* Justice Stevens suggests that the *R.A.V.* "ordinance regulate[d] speech not on the basis of its subject matter or

the viewpoint expressed, but rather on the basis of the *harm* the speech causes." Does he present a viable alternative to the current approach to content-based regulations? Do racist, sexist, homophobic, or religiously-bigoted fighting words cause more social harm than other kinds of fighting words? If this is true, does it justify permitting government to regulate fighting words selectively? Consider carefully the Supreme Court's approach in the next principal case and whether there is a principled distinction between criminalizing speech directly or enhancing a defendant's sentence if he commits a crime motivated by a form of social bias.

4. *Viewpoint versus subject-matter?* Was the *R.A.V.* ordinance viewpoint-based as Justice Scalia claimed, or was it merely subject-matter based, as Justice Stevens claimed? Consider the following arguments:

> [The *R.A.V.* ordinance did] not draw a line between prohibited and permitted points of view. . . . [Rather,] antiwhite and antiblack statements are [treated alike]. In this respect, the law is content-based but viewpoint-neutral. [It] has regulated on the basis of subjects for discussion but not on the basis of viewpoint. . . . As a class, subject-matter restrictions [occupy] a point somewhere between viewpoint-based restrictions and content-neutral ones. [A] subject-matter restriction on unprotected speech should probably be upheld if the legislature can plausibly argue that it is counteracting harms rather than ideas. [This standard is easily satisfied in *R.A.V.* because racially hateful fighting words have] especially severe social consequences, [and there] is nothing partisan or illegitimate in recognizing that distinctive harms are produced by this unusual class of fighting words.

Cass R. Sunstein, *Democracy and the Problem of Free Speech* 188-193 (1993).

> Viewed purely on its face, the St. Paul ordinance, as construed by the Minnesota Supreme Court, appears to discriminate only on the basis of subject matter. . . . Beyond the question of facial discrimination, however, lurked another issue: Did the statute discriminate in its operation on the basis of viewpoint? . . . The St. Paul ordinance, it is true, handicaps both sides (and therefore neither side) when Jews and Catholics, whites and blacks scream slurs based on religion or race at each other. But surely race-based fighting words occur . . . in something other than this double-barreled context. In most instances, racists use race-based fighting words, and racists usually do not assail only each other. When the dispute is of this kind, the government effectively favors a side in barring only race-based fighting words.

See Elena Kagan, *The Changing Faces of First Amendment Neutrality:* R.A.V. v. St. Paul, Rust v. Sullivan, *and the Problem of Content-Based Underinclusion,* 1992 Sup. Ct. Rev. 29, 70-71.

Wisconsin v. Mitchell

508 U.S. 476 (1993)

Chief Justice Rehnquist delivered the opinion of the Court.

Respondent Todd Mitchell's sentence for aggravated battery was enhanced because he intentionally selected his victim on account of the victim's race. The question presented in this case is whether this penalty enhancement is prohibited by the First and Fourteenth Amendments. We hold that it is not.

On the evening of October 7, 1989, a group of young black men and boys, including Mitchell, gathered at an apartment complex in Kenosha, Wisconsin. Several members of the group discussed a scene from the motion picture "Mississippi Burning," in which a white man beat a young black boy who was praying. The group moved outside and Mitchell asked them: "'Do you all feel hyped up to move on some white people?'" Shortly thereafter, a young white boy approached the group on the opposite side of the street where they were standing. As the boy walked by, Mitchell said: "'You all want to fuck somebody up? There goes a white boy; go get him.'" Mitchell counted to three and pointed in the boy's direction. The group ran toward the boy, beat him severely, and stole his tennis shoes. The boy was rendered unconscious and remained in a coma for four days.

After a jury trial in the Circuit Court for Kenosha County, Mitchell was convicted of aggravated battery. That offense ordinarily carries a maximum sentence of two years' imprisonment. But because the jury found that Mitchell had intentionally selected his victim because of the boy's race, the maximum sentence for Mitchell's offense was increased to seven years under § 939.645. That provision enhances the maximum penalty for an offense whenever the defendant "[i]ntentionally selects the person against whom the crime . . . is committed . . . because of the race, religion, color, disability, sexual orientation, national origin or ancestry of that person. . . ." § 939.645(1)(b). The Circuit Court sentenced Mitchell to four years' imprisonment for the aggravated battery.

Mitchell unsuccessfully sought postconviction relief in the Circuit Court. Then he appealed his conviction and sentence, challenging the constitutionality of Wisconsin's penalty-enhancement provision on First Amendment grounds. The Wisconsin Court of Appeals rejected Mitchell's challenge, but the Wisconsin Supreme Court reversed. The Supreme Court held that the statute "violates the First Amendment directly by punishing what the legislature has deemed to be offensive thought." It rejected the State's contention "that the statute punishes only the 'conduct' of intentional selection of a victim." . . . [The Wisconsin Supreme Court reasoned that] under R.A.V. v. St. Paul, 505 U.S. 377 (1992), "the Wisconsin legislature cannot criminalize bigoted thought with which it disagrees." . . .

We granted certiorari because of the importance of the question presented and the existence of a conflict of authority among state high courts on the constitutionality of statutes similar to Wisconsin's penalty-enhancement provision, 506 U.S. 1033 (1992). We reverse. . . .

The State argues that the statute does not punish bigoted thought, as the Supreme Court of Wisconsin said, but instead punishes only conduct. While this argument is literally correct, it does not dispose of Mitchell's First Amendment challenge. To be sure, our cases reject the "view that an apparently limitless variety of conduct can be labeled 'speech' whenever the person engaging in the conduct intends thereby to express an idea." United States v. O'Brien, 391 U.S. 367, 376 (1968). Thus a physical assault is not by any stretch of the imagination expressive conduct protected by the First Amendment. *See* Roberts v. United States Jaycees, 468 U.S. 609, 628 (1984) ("[V]iolence or other types of potentially expressive activities that produce special harms distinct from their communicative impact . . . are entitled to no constitutional protection"); NAACP v. Claiborne Hardware Co., 458 U.S. 886, 916 (1982) ("The First Amendment does not protect violence").

But the fact remains that under the Wisconsin statute the same criminal conduct may be more heavily punished if the victim is selected because of his race or other protected status than if no such motive obtained. Thus, although the statute punishes criminal conduct, it enhances the maximum penalty for conduct motivated by a discriminatory point of view more severely than the same conduct engaged in for some other reason or for no reason at all. Because the only reason for the enhancement is the defendant's discriminatory motive for selecting his victim, Mitchell argues (and the Wisconsin Supreme Court held) that the statute violates the First Amendment by punishing offenders' bigoted beliefs.

Traditionally, sentencing judges have considered a wide variety of factors in addition to evidence bearing on guilt in determining what sentence to impose on a convicted defendant. The defendant's motive for committing the offense is one important factor. Thus, in many states the commission of a murder, or other capital offense, for pecuniary gain is a separate aggravating circumstance under the capital sentencing statute. But it is equally true that a defendant's abstract beliefs, however obnoxious to most people, may not be taken into consideration by a sentencing judge. Dawson v. Delaware, 503 U.S. 159 (1992). In *Dawson*, the State introduced evidence at a capital sentencing hearing that the defendant was a member of a white supremacist prison gang. Because "the evidence proved nothing more than [the defendant's] abstract beliefs," we held that its admission violated the defendant's First Amendment rights. *Id.*, at 167. In so holding, however, we emphasized that "the Constitution does not erect a *per se* barrier to the admission of evidence concerning one's beliefs and associations at sentencing simply because those beliefs and associations are protected by the First Amendment." *Id.* at 165. Thus, in Barclay v. Florida, 463 U.S. 939 (1983) (plurality opinion), we allowed the sentencing judge to take into account the defendant's racial animus towards his victim. The evidence in that case showed that the defendant's membership in the Black Liberation Army and desire to provoke a "race war" were related to the murder of a white man for which he was convicted. *See id.*, at 942-944. Because "the elements of racial hatred in [the] murder" were relevant to several aggravating factors, we held the trial judge permissibly took this evidence into account in sentencing the defendant to death. *Id.*, at 949, and n.7. . . .

Mitchell argues that the Wisconsin penalty-enhancement statute is invalid because it punishes the defendant's discriminatory motive, or reason, for acting. But motive plays the same role under the Wisconsin statute as it does under federal and state antidiscrimination laws, which we have previously upheld against constitutional challenge. . . .

Nothing in our decision last Term in *R.A.V.* compels a different result here. That case involved a First Amendment challenge to a municipal ordinance prohibiting the use of "'fighting words' that insult, or provoke violence, 'on the basis of race, color, creed, religion or gender.'" 505 U.S., at 391 (quoting St. Paul Bias-Motivated Crime Ordinance, St. Paul, Minn., Legis. Code § 292.02 (1990)). Because the ordinance only proscribed a class of "fighting words" deemed particularly offensive by the city—*i.e.*, those "that contain . . . messages of 'bias-motivated' hatred," 505 U.S. at 392—we held that it violated the rule against content-based discrimination. *See id.*, at 392-394. But whereas the ordinance struck down in *R. A. V.* was explicitly directed at expression (*i.e.*, "speech" or "messages"), *id.*, at 392, the statute in this case is aimed at conduct unprotected by the First Amendment.

Moreover, the Wisconsin statute singles out for enhancement bias-inspired conduct because this conduct is thought to inflict greater individual and societal harm. For example, according to the State and its *amici*, bias-motivated crimes are more likely to provoke retaliatory crimes, inflict distinct emotional harms on their victims, and incite community unrest. The State's desire to redress these perceived harms provides an adequate explanation for its penalty-enhancement provision over and above mere disagreement with offenders' beliefs or biases. . . .

For the foregoing reasons, we hold that Mitchell's First Amendment rights were not violated by the application of the Wisconsin penalty-enhancement provision in sentencing him. The judgment of the Supreme Court of Wisconsin is therefore reversed, and the case is remanded for further proceedings not inconsistent with this opinion.

It is so ordered.

NOTES AND QUESTIONS

1. *Reconciling* Mitchell *and* R.A.V. When one reads *Mitchell* in conjunction with *R.A.V.*, the resulting rule appears to be that although government cannot punish hate speech directly (as was the case in *Keegstra*), government may punish otherwise unlawful conduct more severely when the subjective motive for the crime involves animus based on race, gender, religion, or sexual orientation (that is, viewpoint-based considerations). This approach seems to track a widely shared cultural belief that some motives are more blameworthy than others because they impose higher social costs. For example, the *Washington Post* has opined that "crimes that target someone because of his or her race or sexual orientation are more than an offense against that individual. They are crimes that terrorize whole communities." *Protection from Hate*, Wash. Post, May 14, 2007, at A14.
2. *Sentencing and judicial discretion to consider myriad factors.* Speaking for a unanimous court, Chief Justice Rehnquist justifies this rule under the theory that sentencing, as an historical matter, has always taken into account a wide variety of factors, including the social significance of the crime. Is this a sufficient response to the objection that punishing one crime more harshly because of an ideological or political motive violates the otherwise categorical rule against viewpoint discrimination? If person A physically attacks person B because he hates minorities and person B is a minority, then an enhanced sentence could apply. If person A attacks person B because person B is a racist, no enhanced sentence would apply (because

the crime would not have been motivated by racial bias but rather on ideological antipathy). Should the intervening cause of a criminal act disable the rule against viewpoint discrimination? Representative Doc Hastings (R-Washington), an opponent of expanding federal hate crime laws, has stated that "[i]f someone commits a crime, they should be punished for that crime. Period." Perhaps, though, the intervening cause should be considered if some motivations in fact impose greater social costs on the community.

3. *A speech versus conduct dichotomy?* If one considers *Mitchell* in conjunction with *Hishon* and *Meritor Savings Bank*, the proposition that *Beauharnais* is an entirely dead letter becomes highly questionable. Rather, the Supreme Court's approach seems to be more nuanced: Although government cannot adopt direct civility regulations, it can enforce civility norms indirectly incident to other (constitutional) regulatory objectives. Government cannot criminalize or create tort liability for the expression of sexist sentiments, but it can take the expression of those sentiments into account in assessing whether an employer maintains a workplace open to both men and women. Similarly, even if government cannot create civil or criminal liability for the expression of racist, sexist, or homophobic viewpoints, it may consider animus based on race, gender, or sexual orientation when determining an appropriate punishment for a crime. It would, therefore, be an overstatement to suggest that the Free Speech Clause categorically disables government from attempting to establish and enforce civility norms; rather, it would be more accurate to say that government cannot use speech regulations as a proxy for conduct regulations aimed at creating a free and equal society.

Virginia v. Black

538 U.S. 343 (2003)

Justice O'CONNOR announced the judgment of the Court and delivered the opinion of the Court with respect to Parts I, II, and III, and an opinion with respect to Parts IV and V, in which THE CHIEF JUSTICE, Justice STEVENS, and Justice BREYER join.

I

[Barry Black, Richard Elliott, and Jonathan O'Mara were convicted of violating a Virginia statute, § 18.2-423, which provides: "It shall be unlawful for any person or persons, with the intent of intimidating any person or group of persons, to burn, or cause to be burned, a cross on the property of another, a highway or other public place. . . . Any such burning of a cross shall be prima facie evidence of an intent to intimidate a person or group of persons."

On August 22, 1998, Barry Black led a Ku Klux Klan rally on private property. During the rally, about 40 to 50 cars passed the site, and eight to ten houses were located in the vicinity of the rally. Witnesses claimed the speakers "talked real bad about the blacks and the Mexicans," and one speaker said that "he would love to take a .30/.30 and just randomly shoot the blacks." When the rally ended, the crowd circled around a 25-30 foot cross, which then was engulfed in flames. Black was charged with burning a cross with the intent of intimidating a person or group of persons, in violation of § 18.2-423. The trial court instructed the jury that "the burning of a cross by itself is sufficient evidence from which you may infer the required intent." The jury found Black guilty.

On May 2, 1998, Richard Elliott and Jonathan O'Mara attempted to burn a cross on the yard of James Jubilee, an African-American, who was Elliott's next-door neighbor. Elliott and O'Mara planted a cross on Jubilee's property and set it on fire. Their apparent motive was retaliation for Jubilee's complaints about their shooting in the backyard. Jubilee discovered the partially burned cross the next morning while pulling his car out of the driveway. After seeing the cross, Jubilee was "very nervous" because he "didn't know what would be the next phase," and because "a cross burned in your yard . . . tells you that it's just the first round." Prosecutors charged Elliott and O'Mara with attempted cross burning and conspiracy to commit cross burning. O'Mara pleaded guilty after reserving the right to challenge the constitutionality of the cross-burning statute. At Elliott's trial, . . . the court instructed the jury that the Commonwealth must prove that "the defendant intended to commit cross burning," that "the defendant did a direct act toward the commission of the cross burning," and that "the defendant had the intent of intimidating any person or group of persons." The court did not instruct the jury on the meaning of the word "intimidate," or on the prima facie evidence provision of § 18.2-423. The jury found Elliott guilty. After consolidating the cases, the Supreme Court of Virginia held the statute unconstitutional on its face because the statute was "analytically indistinguishable from the ordinance found unconstitutional in *R.A.V.*"]

II

[The Court examined at length the history of cross-burning, noting especially that "[b]urning a cross in the United States is inextricably intertwined with the history of the Ku Klux Klan" and had "been used to communicate both threats of violence and messages of shared ideology." The Klan often used such burnings as messages of intimidation or threats of impending violence. In effect, "[t]he burning cross became a symbol of the Klan itself and a central feature of Klan gatherings. . . . To this day, regardless of whether the message is a political one or whether the message is also meant to intimidate, the burning of the cross is a 'symbol of hate.'" The majority concluded this discussion noting that: "While cross burning sometimes carries no intimidating message, at other times the intimidating message is the *only* message conveyed. For example, when a cross burning is directed at a particular person not affiliated with the Klan, the burning cross often serves as a message of intimidation, designed to inspire in the victim a fear of bodily harm. . . . Indeed, as the cases of respondents Elliott and O'Mara indicate, individuals without Klan affiliation who wish to threaten or menace another person sometimes use cross burning because of this association between a burning cross and violence. In sum, while a burning cross does not inevitably convey a message of intimidation, often the cross burner intends that the recipients of the message fear for their lives. And when a cross burning is used to intimidate, few if any messages are more powerful."]

III

. . . [T]he First Amendment . . . permits a State to ban a "true threat." . . . "True threats" encompass those statements where the speaker means to communicate a serious expression of an intent to commit an act of unlawful violence to a particular individual or group of individuals. *See Watts*; *R.A.V.* The speaker need not actually intend to carry out the threat. Rather, a prohibition on true threats "protect[s] individuals from the fear of violence" and "from the disruption that fear engenders," in addition to protecting people "from the possibility that the threatened violence will occur." Intimidation in the constitutionally proscribable sense of the word is a type of true threat, where a speaker directs a threat to a person or group of persons with the intent of placing the victim in fear of bodily harm or death. . . .

. . . The First Amendment permits Virginia to outlaw cross burnings done with the intent to intimidate because burning a cross is a particularly virulent form of intimidation. Instead of prohibiting all intimidating messages, Virginia may choose to regulate this subset of intimidating messages in light of cross burning's long and pernicious history as a signal of impending violence. Thus, just as a State may regulate only that obscenity which is the most obscene due to its prurient content, so too may a State choose to prohibit only those forms of intimidation that are most likely to inspire fear of bodily harm. A ban on cross burning carried out with the intent to intimidate is fully consistent with our holding in *R.A.V.* and is proscribable under the First Amendment. . . .

IV

. . . The Supreme Court of Virginia has not ruled on the meaning of the prima facie evidence provision. It has, however, stated that "the act of burning a cross alone, with no evidence of intent to intimidate, will nonetheless suffice for arrest and prosecution and will insulate the Commonwealth from a motion to strike the evidence at the end of its case-in-chief." . . . The court in Barry Black's case instructed the jury that the provision means: "The burning of a cross, by itself, is sufficient evidence from which you may infer the required intent." . . .

The prima facie evidence provision, as interpreted by the jury instruction, renders the statute unconstitutional. . . . *Terminiello* (striking down an ambiguous statute on facial grounds based upon the instruction given to the jury). . . . As construed by the jury instruction, the prima facie provision strips away the very reason why a State may ban cross burning with the intent to intimidate. The prima facie evidence provision permits a jury to convict in every cross-burning case in which defendants exercise their constitutional right not to put on a defense. And even where a defendant like Black presents a defense, the prima facie evidence provision makes it more likely that the jury will find an intent to intimidate regardless of the particular facts of the case. The provision permits the Commonwealth to arrest, prosecute, and convict a person based solely on the fact of cross burning itself.

It is apparent that the provision as so interpreted "'would create an unacceptable risk of the suppression of ideas.'" . . . The act of burning a cross may mean that a person is engaging in constitutionally proscribable intimidation. But that same act may mean only that the person is engaged in core political speech. The prima facie evidence provision in this statute blurs the line between these two meanings of a burning cross. As interpreted by the jury instruction, the provision chills constitutionally protected political speech because of the possibility that the Commonwealth will prosecute—and potentially convict—somebody engaging only in lawful political speech at the core of what the First Amendment is designed to protect.

As the history of cross burning indicates, a burning cross is not always intended to intimidate. Rather, sometimes the cross burning is a statement of ideology, a symbol of group solidarity. It is a ritual used at Klan gatherings, and it is used to represent the Klan itself. Thus, "[b]urning a cross at a political rally would almost certainly be protected expression." . . . Cross burnings have appeared in movies such as Mississippi Burning, and in plays such as the stage adaptation of Sir Walter Scott's The Lady of the Lake.

The prima facie provision makes no effort to distinguish . . . between a cross burning done with the purpose of creating anger or resentment and a cross burning done with the purpose of threatening or intimidating a victim. . . . It may be true that a cross burning, even at a political rally, arouses a sense of anger or hatred among the vast majority of citizens who see a burning cross. But this sense of anger or hatred is not sufficient to ban all cross burnings. . . . The prima facie evidence provision in this case ignores all of the contextual factors that are necessary to decide whether a particular cross burning is intended to intimidate. The First Amendment does not permit such a shortcut. . . .

V

With respect to Barry Black, we agree with the Supreme Court of Virginia that his conviction cannot stand, and we affirm the judgment of the Supreme Court of Virginia. With respect to Elliott and O'Mara, we vacate the judgment of the Supreme Court of Virginia, and remand the case for further proceedings.

It is so ordered.

Justice SOUTER, with whom Justice KENNEDY and Justice GINSBURG join, concurring in the judgment in part and dissenting in part.

I agree with the majority that the Virginia statute makes a content-based distinction within the category of punishable intimidating or threatening expression, the very type of distinction we considered in *R.A.V.* I disagree that any exception should save Virginia's law from unconstitutionality under the holding in *R.A.V.* or any acceptable variation of it.

. . . Because of the burning cross's extraordinary force as a method of intimidation, the *R.A.V.* exception most likely to cover the statute is the first of the three mentioned there, which the *R.A.V.* opinion called an exception for content discrimination on a basis that "consists entirely of the very reason the entire class of speech at issue is proscribable." This is the exception the majority speaks of here as covering statutes prohibiting "particularly virulent" proscribable expression. . . . The Court explained that when the subcategory is confined to the most obviously proscribable instances, "no significant danger of idea or viewpoint discrimination exists" and the explanation was rounded out with some illustrative examples. None of them, however, resembles the case before us.

. . . [W]hether or not the Court should conceive of exceptions to *R.A.V.*'s general rule in a more practical way, no content-based statute should survive even under a pragmatic recasting of *R.A.V.* without a high probability that no "official suppression of ideas is afoot," 505 U.S., at 390. I believe the prima facie evidence provision stands in the way of any finding of such a high probability here. . . .

[That provision's] primary effect is to skew jury deliberations toward conviction in cases where the evidence of intent to intimidate is relatively weak and arguably consistent with a solely ideological reason for burning. . . . One can tell the intimidating instance from the wholly ideological one only by reference to some further circumstance. In the real world . . . there will always be further circumstances, and the factfinder will always learn something more than the isolated fact of cross burning. Sometimes those circumstances will show an intent to intimidate, but sometimes they will be at least equivocal, as in cases where a white supremacist group burns a cross at an initiation ceremony or political rally visible to the public. In such a case, if the factfinder is aware of the prima facie evidence provision, as the jury was in respondent Black's case, the provision will have the practical effect of tilting the jury's thinking in favor of the prosecution. . . . The provision will thus tend to draw nonthreatening ideological expression within the ambit of the prohibition of intimidating expression. . . .

It is difficult to conceive of an intimidation case that could be easier to prove than one with cross burning, assuming any circumstances suggesting intimidation are present. The provision, apparently so unnecessary to legitimate prosecution of intimidation, is therefore quite enough to raise the question whether Virginia's content-based statute seeks more than mere protection against a virulent form of intimidation. . . .

I conclude that the statute under which all three of the respondents were prosecuted violates the First Amendment, since the statute's content-based distinction was invalid at the time of the charged activities, regardless of whether the prima facie evidence provision was given any effect in any respondent's individual case. . . . I would therefore affirm the judgment of the Supreme Court of Virginia vacating the respondents' convictions and dismissing the indictments. Accordingly, I concur in the Court's judgment as to respondent Black and dissent as to respondents Elliott and O'Mara.

Justice Thomas, dissenting.

Although I agree with the majority's conclusion that it is constitutionally permissible to "ban . . . cross burning carried out with the intent to intimidate," . . . I believe that the majority errs in imputing an expressive component to the activity in question. . . . In my view, whatever expressive value cross burning has, the legislature simply wrote it out by banning only intimidating conduct undertaken by a particular means. A conclusion that the statute prohibiting cross burning with intent to intimidate sweeps beyond a prohibition on certain conduct into the zone of expression overlooks not only the words of the statute but also reality. . . .

Even assuming that the statute implicates the First Amendment, in my view, the fact that the statute permits a jury to draw an inference of intent to intimidate from the cross burning itself presents no constitutional problems. . . . The plurality fears the chill on expression because . . . the inference permits "the Commonwealth to arrest, prosecute and convict a person based solely on the fact of cross burning itself." . . . [But] Virginia law still requires the jury to find the existence of each element, including intent to intimidate, beyond a reasonable doubt. . . .

Because I would uphold the validity of this statute, I respectfully dissent.

[Justice Stevens's opinion concurring in the judgment is omitted.]

[Justice Scalia's concurring in part and dissenting in part of the judgment is omitted.]

NOTES AND QUESTIONS

1. *Is cross burning a per se threat?* Should the government, consistent with the First Amendment, be permitted to presume that *all* cross burnings convey an intent to intimidate or a "true threat? Even in the absence of any evidence—much less proof beyond a reasonable doubt—that a particular act of cross burning was directed at a particular person or group?
2. *True threats and offensive expressive conduct.* Is Justice O'Connor correct to observe (in dicta) that a state law applicable only to cross burnings intended to intimidate or threaten a specific person or group of persons would be consistent with the First Amendment? Or does Justice Souter have the better view? Namely, that a generic criminal proscription against threats of violence is all that is required to punish cross burnings that constitute true threats? And that a targeted statute simply invites juries to engage in viewpoint discrimination by punishing this behavior regardless of whether, in context, it actually conveyed a true threat? Justice Thomas, by way of contrast, argues that cross burnings are always and inherently threatening by their very nature—and are therefore specifically proscribable without violating the First Amendment. Which of these three approaches best accommodates the relevant social interests? Does the answer to this question depend on how one weighs the relative importance of the social interests at stake?
3. *Distinguishing between true threats and political beliefs.* Recall that under *Watts v. United States* (*supra* p. 71), a "true threat" is not protected speech and may be criminalized. On the other hand, ideologies that include abstract calls to violent revolution, such as Soviet-style communism, constitute protected speech—unless a specific call to violent action presents a clear and present danger of unlawful activity. *See* Brandenburg v. Ohio, *supra* p. 54.
4. *Reconciling* R.A.V., Mitchell, *and* Black. How do these three cases fit together? How far may the government go in using an ideological or political belief as a basis for imposing civil or criminal liability? Is the rule that although bigoted ideologies cannot themselves be directly proscribed, they may be *indirectly* punished when conjoined with otherwise constitutionally proscribable conduct? Notwithstanding any potential chilling effect on pure speech that might result? Is this a sensible accommodation of the relevant values? Beliefs as such are protected absolutely—but when actions are motivated by beliefs, and cause cognizable and particularized social harms because of the motivation, government may take the motive into account? Either by enhancing the punishment for a crime or creating a law targeted at a particular kind of true threat?

5. *The U.S. approach to hate speech regulation is not widely shared.* U.S. constitutional law routinely privileges the protection of freedom of speech over other important human rights values—such as dignity, equality and mutual respect. In so doing, the United States stands virtually alone among major western democracies with constitutional free speech protections in its categorical rejection of direct bans on hate speech. In other nations, including Canada, Germany, South Africa, and the United Kingdom, statutes prohibiting speech that advocates racial, gender-based, LGBTQ, transgender, or religious hatred exist, and the local domestic courts view these enactments as fully consistent with a meaningful commitment to the freedom of expression. *See* Ronald J. Krotoszynski, Jr., *Privacy Revisited: A Global Perspective on the Right to Be Left Alone* 25-30, 151-160 (2016). What risks do these nations necessarily accept as a consequence of this approach? Conversely, what risks, if any, does the Supreme Court of the United States accept as a consequence of protecting hate speech?

THEORY-APPLIED PROBLEM

Consider the following three hypotheticals, and determine whether a state appellate court should overturn the conviction if the defendant raises a First Amendment argument on appeal. In particular, what specific facts and circumstances might lead a court to sustain, or reject, free speech objections to sanctions for the offensive speech?

1. While testifying in a criminal trial for fraud and forgery in a Missouri state trial court, defendant Robert Holman repeatedly drops the "f-bomb," in statements such as "Mother fuckin' fact—I want my mother fuckin' 40 acres. This is bullshit. You know you can't have me keep this man up there and shit like that. 12 mother fuckin' jurors and stuff." The trial judge instructs Holman to cease using unnecessary profanity in court and tells the court reporter to "cease transcribing Mr. Holman's expletives." The court warns Holman to stop using profanity while testifying, on pain of being found in contempt of court, removed from the stand, and jailed (for contempt, independent of the pending criminal charges against him). Holman says he understands, then continues using the f-bomb as if it were a punctuation mark. The trial judge finds Holman in contempt of court, orders him removed from the witness stand by the bailiff, and orders him jailed for 48 hours or until such time as he will cease using gratuitous profanity in his testimony. Holman appeals the contempt citation to the Missouri Court of Appeals, alleging a violation of his free speech rights. How should the appellate court rule?
2. Timothy Boomer, after his canoe capsizes on the Rifle River, in rural Arenac County, Michigan, unleashes a fusillade of profanity, including words such as "fucking faggots," "dirty motherfuckers," and "goddamn cocksuckers." Other nearby users of the Rifle River included Tammy Smith, her husband, and her five- and two-year-old children. In addition, two sheriff's deputies also hear the tirade and issue a citation to Boomer under a Michigan law that prohibits "any person" from using "any indecent,

immoral, obscene, vulgar, or insulting language in the presence or hearing of any woman or child." Violations of section 337 of the Michigan Criminal Code constitute a simple misdemeanor, punishable by a jail term of up to 90 days and a fine up to $100. After a jury trial, Boomer is convicted of the violation, and the trial judge sentences Boomer to four days of community service and orders him to pay a fine of $75. Boomer files an appeal with the Michigan Court of Appeals. How should the appellate court rule?

3. In Rockbridge County High School, in Lexington, Virginia, Fred Jones (a white, eleventh-grade student) calls Michael Smith (a Black, tenth-grade student) "a dirty, stupid n****r" during the public high school's lunch period. Smith does not immediately react to the racist slur and simply walks away from Jones. Immediately thereafter, Smith complains about the incident to the vice principal, Gladys Miller. Later that afternoon, Miller calls Jones into her office and asks whether he used the offensive language in question. When Jones confirms that he used the language, Miller immediately suspends Jones for ten school days under the Rockbridge County School Board's policy prohibiting the use of "offensive, degrading, or harassing language" on school property or at any school-sponsored events. Jones files a section 1983 action in the local federal district court, challenging both his suspension and the Rockbridge County School Board's policy, at least as applied on these facts. How should the federal district court rule?

Chapter 11

The Regulation of Sexually Explicit Speech

Table of Contents

A. Limitations on the Targeted Regulation of Sexually Explicit Materials
B. Children and Pornography
C. New Media and Sexually Explicit Speech

It is doubtful that James Madison, author of the Bill of Rights, would have anticipated the Free Speech Clause applying to pornographic videos featuring Pamela Lee Anderson or nude photographs of Burt Reynolds. Sexually explicit speech lacks any obvious nexus with the project of democratic self-government. Indeed, even if one broadens the democratic self-government theory to encompass scientific, artistic, or literary speech, it is difficult to see how highly graphic pornographic on-line streaming services fit within the expanded universe of speech necessary to enable citizens to be self-governing.

On the other hand, the Supreme Court's move toward a marketplace paradigm for protecting free speech raises a serious issue for targeted regulations of erotica. If commercial advertising has a strong First Amendment claim to be largely free of government regulation, why shouldn't the same be true for sexually graphic forms of art or literature? If the Free Speech Clause exists to facilitate and protect a free market for speech, how can one justify government regulations aimed at suppressing or proscribing porn? Moreover, if free speech is about facilitating personal autonomy, one could easily imagine a person having a stronger interest in pornography than in President Joe Biden's proposals for corporate tax reform.

Should government have the ability to suppress speech that some within the community deem immoral or wicked? Some advocates of equal rights for women believe that pornography creates social conditions that make securing true equality with respect to gender a difficult, if not impossible, task. Even if community moral norms are not a sufficient basis for regulating erotica, are equality norms a more persuasive rationale for limiting or banning porn?

In the U.S., government regulation of sexually explicit speech rests on the idea that such speech has "low value" for First Amendment purposes. Perhaps this claim is true—although such a claim is very difficult to reconcile with theories of free expression based on speaker and audience autonomy. Nevertheless, serious definitional difficulties exist in sorting out low-value "obscenity" from high-value "art." If *Harry Potter* star Daniel Radcliffe appears nude on stage and simulates sex in the play *Equus*, the probability of government efforts to suppress the performance is quite low. On the other hand, if Bambi grinds her hips while stark naked at the Kitty Kat Club, the probability of government efforts to suppress, if not ban, the performance is quite high. "[W]hile the entertainment afforded by a nude ballet at Lincoln Center to those who can pay the price may differ vastly in content (as viewed by judges) or in quality (as viewed by critics), it may not differ in substance from the dance viewed by the person who . . . wants some 'entertainment' with his beer or shot of rye." Salem Inn, Inc. v. Frank, 501 F.2d 18, 21 n.3 (2d Cir. 1974), *aff'd in part sub nom.* Doran v. Salem Inn, Inc., 422 U.S. 922 (1975).

Traditionally, "obscene" materials, like fighting words and libels, stood completely outside the scope of the Free Speech Clause. *See* Chaplinsky v. New Hampshire, 315 U.S. 568, 571-572 (1942). Over time, however, bans enforced against serious literary and artistic works with sexual themes (for example, D.H. Lawrence's *Lady Chatterley's Lover*) raised serious definitional questions for the Supreme Court. *See, e.g.*, Kingsley Intl. Pictures Corp. v. Regents, 360 U.S. 684 (1959) (holding protected a film version of *Lady Chatterley's Lover* and noting that the First Amendment "protects advocacy of the opinion that adultery may sometimes be proper, no less than advocacy of socialism or the single tax"). Would a passage or two in a novel, or a single scene in a movie, justify the complete criminalization of a film? How could judges properly determine when a particular book, magazine, or film crossed the line from the merely indecent to the shadowlands of the obscene?

In the nineteenth century, the British case Regina v. Hicklin, [1868] L.R. 3 Q.B. 360, influenced the development of U.S. obscenity law with its highly deferential standard for measuring government efforts to suppress erotica. Under the *Hicklin* test, government could proscribe material that "depraves and corrupts those whose minds are open to such immoral influences and into whose hands a publication of this sort might fall"—children, for example. *Id.* at 371. The test asked "whether the tendency of the matter charged as obscenity is to deprave and corrupt those whose minds are open to such immoral influences." *Id.* Materials meeting this standard could be regulated—even banned—as obscenity. The *Hicklin* test "came to stand for the double proposition that obscenity was to be measured by its effect on the most susceptible, and that obscenity of the work as a whole was to be judged by the effect of isolated passages." Laurence Tribe, *American Constitutional Law* § 12-16, at 906 (2d ed. 1988).

The Supreme Court rejected the *Hicklin* standard in Roth v. United States, 354 U.S. 476 (1957). *Roth* adopted as a standard for obscenity the following test:

> [S]ex and obscenity are not synonymous. Obscene material is material which deals with sex in a manner appealing to the prurient interest. The portrayal of sex, e.g., in art, literature, and scientific works, is not itself sufficient reason to deny material the constitutional protection of freedom of speech and press.

Id. at 487-488. Although the *Roth* Court held that "obscenity is not within the protection of constitutionally protected speech or press," *id.* at 485, it also held that "[a]ll ideas having even the slightest redeeming social importance—unorthodox ideas, controversial ideas, even ideas hateful to the prevailing climate of opinion—have the full protection of the guaranties, unless excludable because they encroach upon the limited area of more important interests," *id.* at 484.

Roth thus established a tension in the governing legal doctrine: Obscene materials lie outside the scope of the First Amendment, but ideas with "the slightest redeeming social importance" enjoy protection. How then should a court evaluate a pornographic film that opens with the tasteful recitation of a sonnet by Shakespeare?

Attempting to address this conflict nine years later in Memoirs v. Massachusetts, 383 U.S. 413, 418 (1966), the Supreme Court fashioned a three-part test for defining obscenity:

> [I]t must be established that (a) the dominant theme of the material taken as a whole appeals to the prurient interest in sex; (b) the material is patently offensive because it affronts contemporary community standards relating to the description or representation of sexual matters; and (c) the material is utterly without redeeming social value.

The problem with the *Memoirs* test, obviously enough, is the ease with which a commercial pornographer could meet the third prong of the test—the material had to be "utterly without redeeming social value" to constitute obscenity—which the addition of a sonnet or bit of free verse would defeat. Writing seven years later, Chief Justice Burger described this burden as "virtually impossible to discharge under our criminal standards of proof." Miller v. California, 413 U.S. 15, 22 (1973).

Following the effort to establish a standard in *Memoirs*, a year later the Supreme Court gave up its efforts to tinker with the test and simply reverted to issuing very short opinions summarily reversing certain obscenity convictions. The first of this line, Redrup v. New York, 386 U.S. 767, 770-771 (1967), made no attempt to articulate a standard of review and instead announced that a majority of the Justices did not find particular materials to be obscene (under whatever standard that each member of the majority felt should govern). From 1967 to 1973, the Supreme Court "Redrupped" obscenity convictions without attempting to articulate a governing standard of review for obscenity. Generally, the Justices and their clerks would gather in the Supreme Court basement to view the films under review, a process that several members of the Court felt undignified. For an amusing account of this practice, see Bob Woodward & Scott Armstrong, *The Brethren: Inside the Supreme Court* 192-194 (1979). Finally, in 1973, a working majority of the Court coalesced around a "new and improved" standard for defining "obscenity." As you read through these materials, you should consider whether *Miller* sufficiently resolves the conflicting objectives of protecting ideas absolutely while not protecting prurient content at all.

Even today, serious scholars question the ability of law enforcement officers and judges to discern "obscene" materials from legitimate works of art. Thus, *Miller* did not really solve the definitional problem that has plagued obscenity doctrine for decades. Moreover, even if one could define obscenity with perfect clarity, a serious question would exist about the legitimacy of the censorial project itself. Both content and viewpoint neutrality are central components of the Supreme Court's more general free speech jurisprudence—restrictions on obscenity are both content- and viewpoint-based. Moreover, to the extent that one believes in a free, relatively unregulated marketplace of ideas, why should government have the power to exorcise one particular set of wares from the market? The evidence that sexually explicit speech imposes greater social costs than other kinds of high-risk, low-value speech (for example, public calls for race wars or the extermination of persons belonging to a particular religion) is utterly lacking. Obscenity seems to have particular cultural importance (at least for the Supreme Court), but the notion that it presents specialized risks that justify regulations up to and including complete proscription is highly contestable.

A. *LIMITATIONS ON THE TARGETED REGULATION OF SEXUALLY EXPLICIT MATERIALS*

Miller provides the standard citation for the proposition that the federal and state governments may criminalize the distribution of obscene materials. *Miller* relies on a public morals theory of justification for suppressing sexually explicit speech. This is not the only basis on which one might attempt to support regulations of erotica: In Canada, the constitutional commitment to gender equality, rather than a concern about the debasing effects of smut, supports the regulation and proscription of "degrading" and "dehumanizing" forms of erotica. *See Butler, infra* page 594.

Miller v. California

413 U.S. 15 (1973)

Burger, C.J., delivered the opinion of the Court.

This is one of a group of "obscenity-pornography" cases being reviewed by the Court in a re-examination of standards enunciated in earlier cases involving what Mr. Justice Harlan called "the intractable obscenity problem." *Interstate Circuit, Inc. v. Dallas,* 390 U.S. 676, 704 (1968) (concurring and dissenting).

Appellant conducted a mass mailing campaign to advertise the sale of illustrated books, euphemistically called "adult" material. After a jury trial, he was convicted of violating California Penal Code § 311.2(a), a misdemeanor, by knowingly distributing obscene matter, and the Appellate Department, Superior Court of California, County of Orange, summarily affirmed the judgment without opinion. Appellant's conviction was specifically based on his conduct in causing five unsolicited advertising brochures to be sent through the mail in an envelope addressed to a restaurant in Newport Beach, California. The envelope was opened by the manager of the restaurant and his mother. They had not requested the brochures; they complained to the police.

The brochures advertise four books entitled "Intercourse," "Man-Woman," "Sex Orgies Illustrated," and "An Illustrated History of Pornography," and a film entitled "Marital Intercourse." While the brochures contain some descriptive printed material, primarily they consist of pictures and drawings very explicitly depicting men and women in groups of two or more engaging in a variety of sexual activities, with genitals often prominently displayed.

This case involves the application of a State's criminal obscenity statute to a situation in which sexually explicit materials have been thrust by aggressive sales action upon unwilling recipients who had in no way indicated any desire to receive such materials. This Court has recognized that the States have a legitimate interest in prohibiting dissemination or exhibition of obscene material[2] when the mode of dissemination carries with it a significant danger of offending the sensibilities of unwilling recipients or of exposure to juveniles. It is in this context that we are called on to define the standards which must be used to identify obscene material that a State may regulate without infringing on the First Amendment as applicable to the States through the Fourteenth Amendment. . . .

Apart from the initial formulation in the *Roth* case [requiring the government to show that erotica was "utterly without redeeming social importance" in order to prohibit distribution or possession of it], no majority of the Court has at any given time been able to agree on a standard to determine what constitutes obscene, pornographic material subject to regulation under the States' police power. [] We have seen "a variety of views among the members of the Court unmatched in any other course of constitutional adjudication." *Interstate Circuit, Inc. v. Dallas,* [*supra,*] (Harlan, J., concurring and dissenting).[3] This is not remarkable, for in the area of freedom of speech and press the courts must always remain sensitive to any infringement on genuinely serious literary, artistic, political, or scientific expression. This is an area in which there are few eternal verities.

The case we now review was tried on the theory that the California Penal Code § 311 approximately incorporates the three-stage *Memoirs* test. But now the *Memoirs* test has been abandoned as unworkable by its author, and no Member of the Court today supports the *Memoirs* formulation.

---

2. This Court has defined "obscene material" as "material which deals with sex in a manner appealing to prurient interest," but the *Roth* definition does not reflect the precise meaning of "obscene" as traditionally used in the English language. Derived from the Latin *obscaenus, ob,* to, plus *caenum,* filth, "obscene" is defined in the Webster's Third New International Dictionary (Unabridged 1969) as "1a: disgusting to the senses . . . b: grossly repugnant to the generally accepted notions of what is appropriate . . . 2: offensive or revolting as countering or violating some ideal or principle." The Oxford English Dictionary (1933 ed.) gives a similar definition, "[o]ffensive to the senses, or to taste or refinement; disgusting, repulsive, filthy, foul, abominable, loathsome."

The material we are discussing in this case is more accurately defined as "pornography" or "pornographic material." "Pornography" derives from the Greek (*porné,* harlot, and *graphos,* writing). The word now means "1: a description of prostitutes or prostitution 2: a depiction (as in writing or painting) of licentiousness or lewdness: a portrayal of erotic behavior designed to cause sexual excitement." Webster's Third New International Dictionary, *supra.* Pornographic material which is obscene forms a sub-group of all "obscene" expression, but not the whole, at least as the word "obscene" is now used in our language. We note, therefore, that the words "obscene material" as used in this case, have a specific judicial meaning which derives from the *Roth* case, *i.e.,* obscene material "which deals with sex." *Roth, supra,* at 487. *See also* ALI Model Penal Code § 251.4(1) "Obscene Defined." (Official Draft 1962.)

3. In the absence of a majority view, this Court was compelled to embark on the practice of summarily reversing convictions for the dissemination of materials that at least five members of the Court, applying their separate tests, found to be protected by the First Amendment. Redrup v. New York, 386 U.S. 767 (1967). Thirty-one cases have been decided in this manner. Beyond the necessity of circumstances, however, no justification has ever been offered in support of the *Redrup* "policy." *See* Walker v. Ohio, 398 U.S. 434-435 (1970) (dissenting opinion of Burger, C.J., and Harlan, J.). The *Redrup* procedure has cast us in the role of an unreviewable board of censorship for the 50 States, subjectively judging each piece of material brought before us.

This much has been categorically settled by the court, that obscene material is unprotected by the First Amendment. . . . We acknowledge, however, the inherent dangers of undertaking to regulate any form of expression. State statutes designed to regulate obscene materials must be carefully limited. See *Interstate Circuit, Inc. v. Dallas, supra,* at 682-685. As a result, we now confine the permissible scope of such regulation to works which depict or describe sexual conduct. That conduct must be specifically defined by the applicable state law, as written or authoritatively construed. A state offense must also be limited to works which, taken as a whole, appeal to the prurient interest in sex, which portray sexual conduct in a patently offensive way, and which, taken as a whole, do not have serious literary, artistic, political, or scientific value.

The basic guidelines for the trier of fact must be: (a) whether "the average person, applying contemporary community standards" would find that the work, taken as a whole, appeals to the prurient interest, *Kois v. Wisconsin, supra,* at 230, quoting *Roth v. United States, supra,* at 489; (b) whether the work depicts or describes, in a patently offensive way, sexual conduct specifically defined by the applicable state law; and (c) whether the work, taken as a whole, lacks serious literary, artistic, political, or scientific value. We do not adopt as a constitutional standard the "*utterly* without redeeming social value" test of Memoirs v. Massachusetts, 383 U.S., at 419; that concept has never commanded the adherence of more than three Justices at one time.[7] If a state law that regulates obscene material is thus limited, as written or construed, the First Amendment values applicable to the States through the Fourteenth Amendment are adequately protected by the ultimate power of appellate courts to conduct an independent review of constitutional claims when necessary.

We emphasize that it is not our function to propose regulatory schemes for the States. That must await their concrete legislative efforts. It is possible, however, to give a few plain examples of what a state statute could define for regulation under part (b) of the standard announced in this opinion: (a) Patently offensive representations or descriptions of ultimate sexual acts, normal or perverted, actual or simulated; (b) Patently offensive representations or descriptions of masturbation, excretory functions, and lewd exhibition of the genitals.

Sex and nudity may not be exploited without limit by films or pictures exhibited or sold in places of public accommodation any more than live sex and nudity can be exhibited or sold without limit in such public places.[8] At a minimum,

---

7. "A quotation from Voltaire in the flyleaf of a book will not constitutionally redeem an otherwise obscene publication. . . ." Kois v. Wisconsin, 408 U.S. 229, 231 (1972). *See* Memoirs v. Massachusetts, 383 U.S. 413, 461 (1966) (White, J., dissenting). We also reject, as a constitutional standard, the ambiguous concept of "social importance." *See id.*, at 462 (White, J., dissenting).

8. Although we are not presented here with the problem of regulating lewd public conduct itself, the States have greater power to regulate nonverbal, physical conduct than to suppress depictions or descriptions of the same behavior. In United States v. O'Brien, 391 U.S. 367, 377 (1968), a case not dealing with obscenity, the Court held a State regulation of conduct which itself embodies both speech and nonspeech elements to be "sufficiently justified if . . . it furthers an important or substantial governmental interest; if the governmental interest is unrelated to the suppression of free expression; and if the incidental restriction on alleged First Amendment freedoms is no greater than is essential to the furtherance of that interest." *See* California v. LaRue, 409 U.S. 109, 117-118 (1972).

prurient, patently offensive depiction or description of sexual conduct must have serious literary, artistic, political, or scientific value to merit First Amendment protection. For example, medical books for the education of physicians and related personnel necessarily use graphic illustrations and descriptions of human anatomy. In resolving the inevitably sensitive questions of fact and law, we must continue to rely on the jury system, accompanied by the safeguards that judges, rules of evidence, presumption of innocence, and other protective features provide, as we do with rape, murder, and a host of other offenses against society and its individual members. . . .

Under the holdings announced today, no one will be subject to prosecution for the sale or exposure of obscene materials unless these materials depict or describe patently offensive "hard core" sexual conduct specifically defined by the regulating state law, as written or construed. We are satisfied that these specific prerequisites will provide fair notice to a dealer in such materials that his public and commercial activities may bring prosecution. . . .

Under a National Constitution, fundamental First Amendment limitations on the powers of the States do not vary from community to community, but this does not mean that there are, or should or can be, fixed, uniform national standards of precisely what appeals to the "prurient interest" or is "patently offensive." These are essentially questions of fact, and our Nation is simply too big and too diverse for this Court to reasonably expect that such standards could be articulated for all 50 States in a single formulation, even assuming the prerequisite consensus exists. When triers of fact are asked to decide whether "the average person, applying contemporary community standards" would consider certain materials "prurient," it would be unrealistic to require that the answer be based on some abstract formulation. The adversary system, with lay jurors as the usual ultimate factfinders in criminal prosecutions, has historically permitted triers of fact to draw on the standards of their community, guided always by limiting instructions on the law. To require a State to structure obscenity proceedings around evidence of a *national* "community standard" would be an exercise in futility. . . .

We conclude that neither the State's alleged failure to offer evidence of "national standards," nor the trial court's charge that the jury consider state community standards, were constitutional errors. Nothing in the First Amendment requires that a jury must consider hypothetical and unascertainable "national standards" when attempting to determine whether certain materials are obscene as a matter of fact. . . .

It is neither realistic nor constitutionally sound to read the First Amendment as requiring that the people of Maine or Mississippi accept public depiction of conduct found tolerable in Las Vegas, or New York City.

People in different States vary in their tastes and attitudes, and this diversity is not to be strangled by the absolutism of imposed uniformity. As the Court made clear in Mishkin v. New York, 383 U.S., at 508-509, the primary concern with requiring a jury to apply the standard of "the average person, applying contemporary community standards" is to be certain that, so far as material is not aimed at a deviant group, it will be judged by its impact on an average person, rather than a particularly susceptible or sensitive person—or indeed a totally insensitive one. See *Roth v. United States, supra,* at 489. Cf. the now discredited test in Regina v. Hicklin,

[1868] L.R. 3 Q.B. 360. We hold that the requirement that the jury evaluate the materials with reference to "contemporary standards of the State of California" serves this protective purpose and is constitutionally adequate. . . .

In sum, we (a) reaffirm the *Roth* holding that obscene material is not protected by the First Amendment; (b) hold that such material can be regulated by the States, subject to the specific safeguards enunciated above, without a showing that the material is "*utterly* without redeeming social value"; and (c) hold that obscenity is to be determined by applying "contemporary community standards," [] not "national standards." The judgment of the Appellate Department of the Superior Court, Orange County, California, is vacated and the case remanded to that court for further proceedings not inconsistent with the First Amendment standards established by this opinion.

Vacated and remanded.

DOUGLAS, J., dissenting.

Today we leave open the way for California to send a man to prison for distributing brochures that advertise books and a movie under freshly written standards defining obscenity which until today's decision were never the part of any law.

The Court has worked hard to define obscenity and concededly has failed. In Roth v. United States, 354 U.S. 476, it ruled that "[o]bscene material is material which deals with sex in a manner appealing to prurient interest." Obscenity, it was said, was rejected by the First Amendment because it is "utterly without redeeming social importance." The presence of a "prurient interest" was to be determined by "contemporary community standards." That test, it has been said, could not be determined by one standard here and another standard there, Jacobellis v. Ohio, 378 U.S. 184, 194, but "on the basis of a national standard." My Brother Stewart in *Jacobellis* commented that the difficulty of the Court in giving content to obscenity was that it was "faced with the task of trying to define what may be indefinable." . . .

Today the Court retreats from the earlier formulations of the constitutional test and undertakes to make new definitions. This effort, like the earlier ones, is earnest and well intentioned. The difficulty is that we do not deal with constitutional terms, since "obscenity" is not mentioned in the Constitution or Bill of Rights. And the First Amendment makes no such exception from "the press" which it undertakes to protect nor, as I have said on other occasions, is an exception necessarily implied, for there was no recognized exception to the free press at the time the Bill of Rights was adopted which treated "obscene" publications differently from other types of papers, magazines, and books. So there are no constitutional guidelines for deciding what is and what is not "obscene." The Court is at large because we deal with tastes and standards of literature. What shocks me may be sustenance for my neighbor. What causes one person to boil up in rage over one pamphlet or movie may reflect only his neurosis, not shared by others. We deal here with a regime of censorship which, if adopted, should be done by constitutional amendment after full debate by the people. . . .

BRENNAN, J., with whom STEWART, J., and MARSHALL, J., join, dissenting.

In my dissent in Paris Adult Theatre I v. Slaton, [413 U.S. 49 (1973),] I noted that I had no occasion to consider the extent of state power to regulate the distribution of sexually oriented material to juveniles or the offensive exposure of such material to unconsenting adults. In the case before us, appellant was convicted of distributing obscene matter in violation of California Penal Code § 311.2, on the basis of evidence that he had caused to be mailed unsolicited brochures advertising various books and a movie. I need not now decide whether a statute might be drawn to impose, within the requirements of the First Amendment, criminal penalties for the precise conduct at issue here. For it is clear that under my dissent in *Paris Adult Theatre I*, the statute under which the prosecution was brought is unconstitutionally overbroad, and therefore invalid on its face. "[T]he transcendent value to all society of constitutionally protected expression is deemed to justify allowing 'attacks on overly broad statutes with no requirement that the person making the attack demonstrate that his own conduct could not be regulated by a statute drawn with the requisite narrow specificity.'" Gooding v. Wilson, 405 U.S. 518, 521 (1972), quoting from Dombrowski v. Pfister, 380 U.S. 479, 486 (1965).

NOTES AND QUESTIONS

1. *Does the* Miller *test bring clarity?* Did Justice Burger succeed in articulating a bright-line test that will permit state and lower federal courts to define "obscenity" with precision? Or is the *Miller* test simply a reworking of the *Roth* test, with the addition of a "taken as a whole" requirement for "literary, artistic, political, or scientific" value? Is there a way to come up with a bright-line test for something so inherently subjective?
2. *Privacy versus public morals as rationale for regulation.* Justice Brennan, the author of the *Roth* test, dissents in *Miller*. After almost two decades of trying to articulate a viable test for obscenity, Justice Brennan concluded that this was an impossible task. Would the Supreme Court have done better to abandon the effort to define obscenity and instead focus on the problems of protecting both minors and a captive audience from sexually explicit materials? Even if government should not be permitted to ban sexually explicit materials outright, does government have a legitimate interest in protecting citizens against unwanted exposure to such materials? In other words, on the facts in *Miller*, would a privacy rationale be more persuasive than a public morals rationale?
3. *The variable obscenity standard.* The Supreme Court has endorsed a different, less protective, standard of obscenity for materials made available to minors. *See* Ginsberg v. New York, 390 U.S. 629, 637-639 (1968). Thus, materials that are not constitutionally obscene as to adults may be obscene with respect to minors. Even though the state and federal governments may enact laws to protect minors from exposure to sexually explicit materials, such regulations may not have the effect of blocking adults from accessing materials that are not legally obscene as to an adult audience. *See* Butler v. Michigan, 352 U.S. 380, 382-383 (1957).
4. *Local community standards in the internet era.* The viability of the local community standard approach for ascertaining prurience and patent offensiveness has been in serious doubt since the Supreme Court decided Ashcroft v. ACLU, 535 U.S. 564 (2002) ("Ashcroft I"), which dealt with the

constitutionality of the Child Online Protection Act (COPA), 47 U.S.C. § 231(a), federal legislation aimed at protection children from indecency online. Although no opinion in the case garnered the unqualified support of five Justices, multiple opinions, representing the views of a majority of the Supreme Court, all expressed serious concerns about the viability of a local community standard as applied to the internet. *See id.* at 576-579 (plurality opinion by Justice Thomas); *id.* at 584, 587-588 (O'Connor, J., concurring); *id.* at 591 (Breyer, J., concurring); *id.* at 593-594 (Kennedy, J., concurring). In consequence, the continuing viability of this aspect of the *Miller* test is open to serious question. In Ashcroft v. ACLU, 542 U.S. 656 (2004) ("Ashcroft II"), Justices Stevens and Ginsburg wrote a concurrence in which they emphasized that the application of community standards to define prohibited speech would "penalize speakers for making available to the general World Wide Web audience that which the least tolerant communities in America deem unfit for their children's consumption, and consider that principle a sufficient basis for deciding this case." For more on the opinions in *Ashcroft I* and *Ashcroft II* and the curious saga of the COPA, which was ultimately deemed unconstitutional, see *supra* Chapter 8.

5. *What about highly graphic depictions of violence?* Can extremely graphic depictions of violence constitute "obscenity"? The Supreme Court's answer is an emphatic "no." *See* Brown v. Entertainment Merchants Ass'n, 564 U.S. 786 (2011). One of California's principal arguments in favor of a state law banning the sale of violent video games to minors involved characterizing such games as a form of obscenity. *See id.* at 792-94. Justice Antonin Scalia, writing for the majority, squarely rejected California's "attempt to shoehorn speech about violence into obscenity." Justice Scalia explained that "[o]ur cases have been clear that the obscenity exception to the First Amendment does not cover whatever a legislature finds shocking, but only depictions of 'sexual conduct,' *Miller, supra,* at 24." *Id.* at 792-93. Thus, "[b]ecause speech about violence is not obscene, it is of no consequence that California's statute mimics the New York statute regulating obscenity for minors that we upheld in *Ginsberg v. New York,* 390 U.S. 629 (1968)." *Id.* at 793. Should violent or gruesome speech be subject to content-based regulation because of its repulsiveness? For an argument that it should not, except in very limited contexts involving government-owned property, see Eugene Volokh, *Gruesome Speech,* 100 Cornell L. Rev. 901 (2015).
6. *Licensing requirements.* A local government, incident to its comprehensive zoning rules, may adopt a mandatory licensing scheme for "adult" businesses to ensure full compliance with those regulations. *See* City of Littlejohn v. Z.J. Gifts D-4, L.L.C., 541 U.S. 774 (2004). If a local government denies or revokes a license to operate an adult business, however, the government must ensure the availability of prompt judicial review of the adverse decision and a prompt judicial determination of the merits. *Id.* at 778-781, 783-784. In addition, the licensing scheme must use "reasonably objective" and rely on

"nondiscretionary criteria unrelated to the content of the expressive materials that an adult business may sell or display." *Id.* at 783.

American Booksellers Ass'n, Inc. v. Hudnut

771 F.2d 323 (7th Cir. 1985), *aff'd mem.*, 475 U.S. 1001 (1986)

EASTERBROOK, Circuit Judge.

Indianapolis enacted an ordinance defining "pornography" as a practice that discriminates against women. "Pornography" is to be redressed through the administrative and judicial methods used for other discrimination. The City's definition of "pornography" is considerably different from "obscenity," which the Supreme Court has held is not protected by the First Amendment.

To be "obscene" under *Miller v. California*, 413 U.S. 15 (1973), "a publication must, taken as a whole, appeal to the prurient interest, must contain patently offensive depictions or descriptions of specified sexual conduct, and on the whole have no serious literary, artistic, political, or scientific value." . . .

"Pornography" under the ordinance is "the graphic sexually explicit subordination of women, whether in pictures or in words, that also includes one or more of the following:

(1) Women are presented as sexual objects who enjoy pain or humiliation; or
(2) Women are presented as sexual objects who experience sexual pleasure in being raped; or
(3) Women are presented as sexual objects tied up or cut up or mutilated or bruised or physically hurt, or as dismembered or truncated or fragmented or severed into body parts; or
(4) Women are presented as being penetrated by objects or animals; or
(5) Women are presented in scenarios of degradation, injury, abasement, torture, shown as filthy or inferior, bleeding, bruised, or hurt in a context that makes these conditions sexual; or
(6) Women are presented as sexual objects for domination, conquest, violation, exploitation, possession, or use, or through postures or positions of servility or submission or display."

Indianapolis Code § 16-3(q). The statute provides that the "use of men, children, or transsexuals in the place of women in paragraphs (1) through (6) above shall also constitute pornography under this section." The ordinance as passed in April 1984 defined "sexually explicit" to mean actual or simulated intercourse or the uncovered exhibition of the genitals, buttocks or anus. An amendment in June 1984 deleted this provision, leaving the terms undefined.

The Indianapolis ordinance does not refer to the prurient interest, to offensiveness, or to the standards of the community. It demands attention to particular depictions, not to the work judged as a whole. It is irrelevant under the ordinance whether the work has literary, artistic, political, or scientific value. The City and many amici point to these omissions as virtues. They maintain that pornography influences attitudes, and the statute is a way to alter the socialization of men and women rather than to vindicate community standards of offensiveness. And as one of the principal drafters of the ordinance has asserted, "if a woman is subjected, why should it matter that the work has other value?" Catharine A. MacKinnon, *Pornography, Civil Rights, and Speech*, 20 Harv. Civ. Rts.-Civ. Lib. L. Rev. 1, 21 (1985).

Civil rights groups and feminists have entered this case as amici on both sides. Those supporting the ordinance say that it will play an important role in reducing the tendency of men to view women as sexual objects, a tendency that leads to both unacceptable attitudes and discrimination in the workplace and violence away from it. Those opposing the ordinance point out that much radical feminist literature is explicit and depicts women in ways forbidden by the ordinance and that the ordinance would reopen old battles. It is unclear how Indianapolis would treat works from James Joyce's *Ulysses* to Homer's *Iliad*; both depict women as submissive objects for conquest and domination.

We do not try to balance the arguments for and against an ordinance such as this. The ordinance discriminates on the ground of the content of the speech. Speech treating women in the approved way—in sexual encounters "premised on equality" (MacKinnon, *supra*, at 22)—is lawful no matter how sexually explicit. Speech treating women in the disapproved way—as submissive in matters sexual or as enjoying humiliation—is unlawful no matter how significant the literary, artistic, or political qualities of the work taken as a whole. The state may not ordain preferred viewpoints in this way. The Constitution forbids the state to declare one perspective right and silence opponents. . . .

The district court held the ordinance unconstitutional. 598 F. Supp. 1316 (S.D. Ind. 1984). The court concluded that the ordinance regulates speech rather than the conduct involved in making pornography. The regulation of speech could be justified, the court thought, only by a compelling interest in reducing sex discrimination, an interest Indianapolis had not established. The ordinance is also vague and overbroad, the court believed, and establishes a prior restraint of speech. . . .

"If there is any fixed star in our constitutional constellation, it is that no official, high or petty, can prescribe what shall be orthodox in politics, nationalism, religion, or other matters of opinion or force citizens to confess by word or act their faith therein." West Virginia State Board of Education v. Barnette, 319 U.S. 624, 642 (1943). Under the First Amendment the government must leave to the people the evaluation of ideas. Bald or subtle, an idea is as powerful as the audience allows it to be. A belief may be pernicious—the beliefs of Nazis led to the death of millions, those of the Klan to the repression of millions. A pernicious belief may prevail. Totalitarian governments today rule much of the planet, practicing suppression of billions and spreading dogma that may enslave others. One of the things that separates our society from theirs is our absolute right to propagate opinions that the government finds wrong or even hateful.

. . . Under the ordinance graphic sexually explicit speech is "pornography" or not depending on the perspective the author adopts. Speech that "subordinates" women and also, for example, presents women as enjoying pain, humiliation, or rape, or even simply presents women in "positions of servility or submission or display" is forbidden, no matter how great the literary or political value of the work taken as a whole. Speech that portrays women in positions of equality is lawful, no matter how graphic the sexual content. This is thought control. It establishes an "approved" view of women, of how they may react to sexual encounters, of how the sexes may relate to each other. Those who espouse the approved view may use sexual images; those who do not, may not.

Indianapolis justifies the ordinance on the ground that pornography affects thoughts. Men who see women depicted as subordinate are more likely to treat them so. Pornography is an aspect of dominance. It does not persuade people so much as change them. It works by socializing, by establishing the expected and the permissible. In this view pornography is not an idea; pornography is the injury.

There is much to this perspective. Beliefs are also facts. People often act in accordance with the images and patterns they find around them. People raised in a religion tend to accept the tenets of that religion, often without independent examination. People taught from birth that black people are fit only for slavery rarely rebelled against that creed; beliefs coupled with the self-interest of the masters established a social structure that inflicted great harm while enduring for centuries. Words and images act at the level of the subconscious before they persuade at the level of the conscious. Even the truth has little chance unless a statement fits within the framework of beliefs that may never have been subjected to rational study.

Therefore we accept the premises of this legislation. Depictions of subordination tend to perpetuate subordination. The subordinate status of women in turn leads to affront and lower pay at work, insult and injury at home, battery and rape on the streets. . . . Pornography is a systematic practice of exploitation and subordination based on sex which differentially harms women. . . .

Yet this simply demonstrates the power of pornography as speech. All of these unhappy effects depend on mental intermediation. Pornography affects how people see the world, their fellows, and social relations. If pornography is what pornography does, so is other speech. Hitler's orations affected how some Germans saw Jews. Communism is a world view, not simply a *Manifesto* by Marx and Engels or a set of speeches. . . .

Racial bigotry, anti-semitism, violence on television, reporters' biases—these and many more influence the culture and shape our socialization. None is directly answerable by more speech, unless that speech too finds its place in the popular culture. Yet all is protected as speech, however insidious. Any other answer leaves the government in control of all of the institutions of culture, the great censor and director of which thoughts are good for us. . . .

Much of Indianapolis's argument rests on the belief that when speech is "unanswerable," and the metaphor that there is a "marketplace of ideas" does not apply, the First Amendment does not apply either. The metaphor is honored; Milton's *Areopagitica* and John Stewart Mill's *On Liberty* defend freedom of speech on the ground that the truth will prevail, and many of the most important cases under the First Amendment recite this position. The Framers undoubtedly believed it. As a general matter it is true. But the Constitution does not make the dominance of truth a necessary condition of freedom of speech. To say that it does would be to confuse an outcome of free speech with a necessary condition for the application of the amendment.

A power to limit speech on the ground that truth has not yet prevailed and is not likely to prevail implies the power to declare truth. At some point the government must be able to say (as Indianapolis has said): "We know what the truth is, yet a free exchange of speech has not driven out falsity, so that we must now prohibit falsity." If the government may declare the truth, why wait for the failure of speech? Under the First Amendment, however, there is no such thing as a false idea, Gertz v. Robert Welch, Inc., 418 U.S. 323, 339 (1974), so the government may not restrict speech on the ground that in a free exchange truth is not yet dominant.

At any time, some speech is ahead in the game; the more numerous speakers prevail. Supporters of minority candidates may be forever "excluded" from the political process because their candidates never win, because few people believe their positions. This does not mean that freedom of speech has failed.

The Supreme Court has rejected the position that speech must be "effectively answerable" to be protected by the Constitution. . . .

Any rationale we could imagine in support of this ordinance could not be limited to sex discrimination. Free speech has been on balance an ally of those seeking change. Governments that want stasis start by restricting speech. Culture is a powerful force of continuity; Indianapolis paints pornography as part of the culture of power. Change in any complex system ultimately depends on the ability of outsiders to challenge accepted views and the reigning institutions. Without a strong guarantee of freedom of speech, there is no effective right to challenge what is.

The definition of "pornography" is unconstitutional. No construction or excision of particular terms could save it. The offense of trafficking in pornography necessarily falls with the definition. We express no view on the district court's conclusions that the ordinance is vague and that it establishes a prior restraint. Neither is necessary to our judgment. We also express no view on the argument presented by several amici that the ordinance is itself a form of discrimination on account of sex. . . .

No amount of struggle with particular words and phrases in this ordinance can leave anything in effect. The district court came to the same conclusion. Its judgment is therefore

Affirmed.

NOTES AND QUESTIONS

1. *Obscenity regulation as content-based regulation.* Pornography undoubtedly imposes social costs, something that Judge Easterbrook cheerfully acknowledges in *Hudnut.* At the same time, however, graphic forms of erotica also present (often controversial) ideas about sex, human sexuality, and gender norms. The conflict first recognized in *Roth* persists to this day: Regulation of erotica reflects, to some extent, strong content and viewpoint discrimination against the ideas erotica advances. If the regulation of erotica exists because of strong hostility to its message, should the Supreme Court simply invalidate efforts to regulate it? The Supreme Court of Oregon has done so; incident to the Oregon state

constitution, Article I, § 8 ("No law shall be passed restraining the free expression of opinion, or restricting the right to speak, write, or print freely on any subject whatever; but every person shall be responsible for the abuse of this right."), it has held that sexually explicit materials are fully protected speech activity and that government may not regulate such material because it disapproves of the content or views the content as "immoral." *See* Oregon v. Henry, 732 P.2d 9, 17 (Or. 1987) ("We hold that characterizing expression as "obscenity" under any definition, be it *Roth*, *Miller*, or otherwise, does not deprive it of protection under the Oregon Constitution."). Nevertheless, the Supreme Court of Oregon also held that the state may regulate sexually explicit materials to protect the interests of "unwilling viewers, captive audiences, minors and beleaguered neighbors." *Id.* at 18. As recently as 2005, the Supreme Court of Oregon strongly reaffirmed *Henry*'s approach to the regulation of pornography. *See* State v. Ciancanelli, 121 P.3d 613, 618-620, 633-635 (Or. 2005); City of Nyssa v. Dufloth, 121 P.3d 639, 643-644 (Or. 2005). Is this a more sensible approach than *Miller*? If Judge Easterbrook is correct in positing that erotica has a strong communicative function, how can any regulations of erotica be sustained? Aren't all bans on pornography a reflection of public offense at the content? If so, how can such a regime of regulation be squared with the baseline rule that whatever else the government may do, it cannot regulate speech based on its content or viewpoint?

2. *Articulating the value (or lack thereof) of sexually explicit speech.* Before rejecting Chief Justice Burger's efforts in *Miller*, one should consider the countervailing point of view: What value does sexually explicit speech have? If free speech enjoys protection for instrumental reasons, such as advancing democratic self-government, it is difficult to see why legislatures should not be free to regulate erotica, just as they can regulate the size of shopping malls or establish deposit rules for soda cans. *See* Robert H. Bork, *Neutral Principles and Some First Amendment Problems*, 47 Ind. L.J. 1, 27-29 (1971) (arguing that "art and pornography are on a par with industry and smoke pollution" in terms of the proper scope of a legislature's regulatory powers and that "[f]reedom of non-political speech rests, as does freedom for other valuable forms of behavior, upon the enlightenment of society and its elected representatives"). *But cf.* Steven G. Gey, *The Apologetics of Suppression: The Regulation of Pornography as Act and Idea*, 86 Mich. L. Rev. 1564, 1582-1586 (1988) (offering a trenchant critique of the Bork objection to affording protection to sexually explicit speech and noting that the "disarming honesty of Bork's rendition of the morality principle has never found favor with the [Supreme] Court"). On this view, however, how could one justify protecting commercial speech but not erotica from legislative infringements?

Not all nations committed to free speech find unpersuasive the gender equality rationale for regulating at least some forms of sexually explicit speech. Consider the following landmark case from Canada.

R. v. Butler

[1992] 1 S.C.R. 452 (Can.)

SOPINKA, J.

This appeal calls into question the constitutionality of the obscenity provisions of the Criminal Code, R.S.C., 1985, c. C-46, s. 163.[1] They are attacked on the ground that they contravene s. 2(b) of the Canadian Charter of Rights and Freedoms. The case requires the Court to address one of the most difficult and controversial of contemporary issues, that of determining whether, and to what extent, Parliament may legitimately criminalize obscenity. . . .

In August 1987, the appellant, Donald Victor Butler, opened the Avenue Video Boutique located in Winnipeg, Manitoba. The shop sells and rents "hard core" videotapes and magazines as well as sexual paraphernalia. . . .

---

1. Criminal Code, R.S.C., 1985, c. C-46 § 163.

(a) Every one commits an offence who (a) makes, prints, publishes, distributes, circulates, or has in his possession for the purpose of publication, distribution or circulation any obscene written matter, picture, model, phonograph record or other thing whatever; or (b) makes, prints, publishes, distributes, sells or has in his possession for the purpose of publication, distribution or circulation a crime comic.

(b) Every one commits an offence who knowingly, without lawful justification or excuse, (a) sells, exposes to public view or has in his possession for such a purpose any obscene written matter, picture, model, phonograph record or other thing whatever, (b) publicly exhibits a disgusting object or an indecent show, (c) offers to sell, advertises or publishes an advertisement of, or has for sale or disposal, any means, instructions, medicine, drug or article intended or represented as a method of causing abortion or miscarriage, or (d) advertises or publishes an advertisement of any means, instructions, medicine, drug or article intended or represented as a method for restoring sexual virility or curing venereal diseases or diseases of the generative organs.

(c) No person shall be convicted of an offence under this section if he establishes that the public good was served by the acts that are alleged to constitute the offence and that the acts alleged did not extend beyond what served the public good.

(d) For the purposes of this section, it is a question of law whether an act served the public good and whether there is evidence that the act alleged went beyond what served the public good, but it is a question of fact whether the acts did or did not extend beyond what served the public good.

(e) For the purposes of this section, the motives of an accused are irrelevant.

(f) Where an accused is charged with an offence under the subsection (1), the fact that the accused was ignorant of the nature or presence of the matter, picture, model, phonograph record, crime comic or other thing by means of or in relation to which the offence was committed is not a defense to the charge.

(g) In this section, "crime comic" means a magazine, periodical or book that exclusively or substantially comprises matter depicting pictorially (a) the commission of crimes, real or fictitious, or (b) events connected with the commission of crimes, real or fictitious, whether occurring before or after the commission of the crime.

(h) For the purposes of this Act, any publication a dominant characteristic of which is the undue exploitation of sex, or of sex and any one or more of the following subjects, namely, crime, horror, cruelty and violence shall be deemed to be obscene.

On August 21, 1987, the City of Winnipeg Police entered the appellant's store with a search warrant and seized all the inventory. The appellant was charged with 173 counts in the first indictment: three counts of selling obscene material contrary to s. 159(2)(a) of the Criminal Code, R.S.C. 1970, c. C-34 (now s. 163(2)(a)), 41 counts of possessing obscene material for the purpose of distribution contrary to s. 159(1)(a) (now s. 163(1)(a)) of the Criminal Code, 128 counts of possessing obscene material for the purpose of sale contrary to s. 159(2)(a) of the Criminal Code and one count of exposing obscene material to public view contrary to s. 159(2)(a) of the Criminal Code.

On October 19, 1987, the appellant reopened the store at the same location. As a result of a police operation a search warrant was executed on October 29, 1987, resulting in the arrest of an employee, Norma McCord. The appellant was arrested at a later date.

A joint indictment was laid against the appellant doing business as Avenue Video boutique and Norma McCord. The joint indictment contains 77 counts under s. 159 (now s. 163) of the Criminal Code: two counts of selling obscene material contrary to s. 159(2)(a), 73 counts of possessing obscene material for the purpose of distribution contrary to s. 159(1)(a), one count of possessing obscene material for the purpose of sale contrary to s. 159(2)(a) and one count of exposing obscene material to public view contrary to s. 159(2)(a).

The trial judge convicted the appellant on eight counts relating to eight films. Convictions were entered against the co-accused McCord with respect to two counts relating to two of the films. Fines of $1,000 per offence were imposed on the appellant. Acquittals were entered on the remaining charges.

The Crown appealed the 242 acquittals with respect to the appellant and the appellant cross-appealed the convictions. The majority of the Manitoba Court of Appeal allowed the appeal of the Crown and entered convictions for the appellant with respect to all of the counts. . . .

The constitutional questions, as stated, bring under scrutiny the entirety of s. 163. However, both lower courts as well as the parties have focused almost exclusively on the definition of obscenity found in s. 163(8). Other portions of the impugned provision, such as the reverse onus provision envisaged in s. 163(3) as well as the absolute liability offence created by s. 163(6), raise substantial Charter issues which should be left to be dealt with in proceedings specifically directed to these issues. In my view, in the circumstances, this appeal should be confined to the examination of the constitutional validity of s. 163(8) only.

Before proceeding to consider the constitutional question, it will be helpful to review the legislative history of the provision as well as the extensive judicial interpretation and analysis which have infused meaning into the bare words of the statute. . . .

In order for the work or material to qualify as "obscene", the exploitation of sex must not only be its dominant characteristic, but such exploitation must be "undue". In determining when the exploitation of sex will be considered "undue", the courts have attempted to formulate workable tests. The most important of these is the "community standard of tolerance" test.

"Community Standard of Tolerance" Test

Our Court was called upon to elaborate the community standards test in Towne Cinema Theatres Ltd. v. The Queen, [1985] 1 S.C.R. 494. Dickson C.J. reviewed the case law and found (at pp. 508-9):

"The cases all emphasize that it is a standard of *tolerance* not taste, that is relevant. What matters is not what Canadians think is right for themselves to see. What matters is what Canadians would not abide other Canadians seeing because it would be beyond the contemporary Canadian standard of tolerance to allow them to see it.

Since the standard is tolerance, I think the audience to which the allegedly obscene material is targeted must be relevant. The operative standards are those of the Canadian community as a whole, but since what matters is what other people may see, it is quite conceivable that the Canadian community would tolerate varying degrees of explicitness depending upon the audience and the circumstances." [Emphasis in original.]

Therefore, the community standards test is concerned not with what Canadians would not tolerate being exposed to themselves, but what they would not tolerate other Canadians being exposed to. . . .

"Degradation or Dehumanization" Test

There has been a growing recognition in recent cases that material which may be said to exploit sex in a "degrading or dehumanizing" manner will necessarily fail the community standards test. . . .

> [F]ilms which consist substantially or partially of scenes which portray violence and cruelty in conjunction with sex, particularly where the performance of indignities degrade and dehumanize the people upon whom they are performed, exceed the level of community tolerance.

Subsequent decisions . . . held that material that "degraded" or "dehumanized" any of the participants would exceed community standards even in the absence of cruelty and violence. . . .

This type of material would, apparently, fail the community standards test not because it offends against morals but because it is perceived by public opinion to be harmful to society, particularly to women. While the accuracy of this perception is not susceptible of exact proof, there is a substantial body of opinion that holds that the portrayal of persons being subjected to degrading or dehumanizing sexual treatment results in harm, particularly to women and therefore to society as a whole. [] It would be reasonable to conclude that there is an appreciable risk of harm to society in the portrayal of such material. . . .

"Internal Necessities Test" or "Artistic Defence"

[A third test] or what has been referred to as the "artistic defence" has been interpreted to assess whether the exploitation of sex has a justifiable role in advancing the plot or the theme, and in considering the work as a whole, does not merely represent "dirt for dirt's sake" but has a legitimate role when measured by the internal necessities of the work itself. . . .

Pornography can be usefully divided into three categories: (1) explicit sex with violence, (2) explicit sex without violence but which subjects people to treatment that is degrading or dehumanizing and (3) explicit sex without violence that is neither degrading nor dehumanizing. Violence in this context includes both actual physical violence and threats of physical violence. . . .

Some segments of society would consider that all three categories of pornography cause harm to society because they tend to undermine its moral fibre. Others would contend that none of the categories cause harm. Furthermore there is a range of opinion as to what is degrading or dehumanizing. See Pornography and Prostitution in Canada: Report of the Special Committee on Pornography and Prostitution (1985) (the Fraser Report), vol. 1, at p. 51. Because this is not a matter that is susceptible of proof in the traditional way and because we do not wish to leave it to the individual tastes of judges, we must have a norm that will serve as an arbiter in determining what amounts to an undue exploitation of sex. That arbiter is the community as a whole.

The courts must determine as best they can what the community would tolerate others being exposed to on the basis of the degree of harm that may flow from such exposure. . . . In making this determination with respect to the three categories of pornography referred to above, the portrayal of sex coupled with violence will almost always constitute the undue exploitation of sex. Explicit sex which is degrading or dehumanizing may be undue if the risk of harm is substantial. Finally, explicit sex that is not violent and neither degrading nor dehumanizing is generally tolerated in our society and will not qualify as the undue exploitation of sex unless it employs children in its production.

If material is not obscene under this framework, it does not become so by reason of the person to whom it is or may be shown or exposed nor by reason of the place or manner in which it is shown. The availability of sexually explicit materials in theatres and other public places is subject to regulation by competent provincial legislation. Typically such legislation implies restrictions on the material available to children. See Nova Scotia Board of Censors v. McNeil, [1978] 2 S.C.R. 662.

The foregoing deals with the interrelationship of the "community standards test" and "the degrading or dehumanizing" test. How does the "internal necessities" test fit into this scheme? The need to apply this test only arises if a work contains sexually explicit material that by itself would constitute the undue exploitation of sex. The portrayal of sex must then be viewed in context to determine whether that is the dominant theme of the work as a whole. Put another way, is undue exploitation of sex the main object of the work or is this portrayal of sex essential to a wider artistic, literary or other similar purpose? Since the threshold determination must be made on the basis of community standards, that is, whether the sexually explicit aspect is undue, its impact when considered in context must be determined on the same basis. The court must determine whether the sexually explicit material when viewed in the context of the whole work would be tolerated by the community as a whole. Artistic expression rests at the heart of freedom of expression values and any doubt in this regard must be resolved in favor of freedom of expression. . . .

In light of our recent decision in R. v. Keegstra, [1990] 3 S.C.R. 697 [*supra* p. 554], the respondent, and most of the parties intervening in support of the respondent, do not take issue with the proposition that s. 163 of the Criminal Code violates s. 2(b) of the Charter. In *Keegstra,* we were unanimous in advocating a generous approach to the protection afforded by s. 2(b) of the Charter. . . .

In this case, both the purpose and effect of s. 163 are specifically to restrict the communication of certain types of materials based on their content. In my view, there is no doubt that s. 163 seeks to prohibit certain types of expressive activity and thereby infringes s. 2(b) of the Charter.

Does the prevention of the harm associated with the dissemination of certain obscene materials constitute a sufficiently pressing and substantial concern to warrant restriction on the freedom of expression? In this regard, it should be recalled that in *Keegstra,* this Court unanimously accepted that the prevention of the influence of hate propaganda on society at large was a legitimate objective. . . .

This court has thus recognized that the harm caused by the proliferation of materials which seriously offend the values fundamental to our society is a substantial concern which justifies restricting the otherwise full exercise of the freedom of expression. In my view, the harm sought to be avoided in the case of the dissemination of obscene materials is similar. In the words of Nemetz C.J.B.C. in R. v. Red Hot Video Ltd. (1985), 45 C.R. (3d) 36 (B.C.C.A.), there is a growing concern that the exploitation of women and children, depicted in publications and films, can, in certain circumstances, lead to "abject and servile victimization" (at pp. 43-44). As Anderson J.A. also noted in the same case, if true equality between male and female persons is to be achieved, we cannot ignore the threat to equality resulting from exposure to audiences of certain types of violent and degrading material. Material portraying women as a class as objects for sexual exploitation and abuse have a negative impact on "the individual's sense of self-worth and acceptance".

In reaching the conclusion that legislation proscribing obscenity is a valid objective which justifies some encroachment on the right to freedom of expression, I am persuaded in part that such legislation may be found in most free and democratic societies. As Nemetz C.J.B.C. aptly pointed out in *R. v. Red Hot Video, supra,* for centuries democratic societies have set certain limits to freedom of expression. He cited (at p. 40) the following passage of Dickson J.A. (As he then was) in R. v. Great West News Ltd., *supra,* [[1970] 4 C.C.C. 307] at p. 309.

". . . all organized societies have sought in one manner or another to suppress obscenity. The right of the state to legislate to protect its moral fibre and well-being has long been recognized, with roots deep in history. It is within this frame that the Courts and Judges must work." . . .

The enactment of the impugned provision is also consistent with Canada's international obligations (Agreement for the Suppression of the Circulation of Obscene Publications and the Convention for the Suppression of the Circulation of and Traffic in Obscene Publications).

Finally, it should be noted that the burgeoning pornography industry renders the concern even more pressing and substantial than when the impugned provisions were first enacted. I would therefore conclude that the objective of avoiding the harm associated with the dissemination of pornography in this case is sufficiently pressing and substantial to warrant some restriction on full exercise of the right to freedom of expression. The analysis of whether the measure is proportional to the objective must, in my view, be undertaken in light of the conclusion that the objective of the impugned section is valid only in so far as it relates to the harm to society associated with obscene materials. Indeed, the section as interpreted in previous decisions and in these reasons is fully consistent with that objective. The objective of maintaining conventional standards of propriety, independently of any harm to society, is no longer justified in light of the values of individual liberty which underlie the Charter. This, then being the objective of s. 163, which I have found to be pressing and substantial, I must now determine whether the section is rationally connected and proportional to this objective. As outlined above, s. 163(8) criminalizes the exploitation of sex and sex and violence, when, on the basis of the community test, it is undue. The determination of when such exploitation is undue is directly related to the immediacy of a risk of harm to society which is reasonably perceived as arising from its dissemination. . . .

. . .

While a direct link between obscenity and harm to society may be difficult, if not impossible, to establish, it is reasonable to presume that exposure to images bears a causal relationship to changes in attitudes and beliefs. The Meese Commission Report, supra, concluded in respect of sexually violent material (vol. 1, at p. 326):

> . . . the available evidence strongly supports the hypothesis that substantial exposure to sexually violent materials as described here bears a causal relationship to anti-social acts of sexual violence and, for some subgroups, possibly to unlawful acts of sexual violence.

Although we rely for this conclusion on significant scientific empirical evidence, we feel it worthwhile to note the underlying logic of the conclusion. The evidence says simply that the images that people are exposed to bear a causal relationship to their behavior. This is hardly surprising. What would be surprising would be to find otherwise, and we have not so found. We have not, of course, found that the images people are exposed to are a greater cause of sexual violence than all or even many other possible causes the investigation of which has been beyond our mandate. Nevertheless, it would be strange indeed if graphic representations of a form of behavior, especially in a form that almost exclusively portrays such behavior as desirable, did not have at least some effect on patterns of behavior." . . .

Accordingly, I am of the view that there is a sufficiently rational link between the criminal sanction which demonstrates our community's disapproval of the dissemination of materials which potentially victimize women and which restricts the negative influence which such materials have on changes in attitudes and behavior, and the objective. . . .

There are several factors which contribute to the finding that the provision minimally impairs the freedom which is infringed.

First, the impugned provision does not proscribe sexually explicit erotica without violence that is not degrading or dehumanizing. It is designed to catch material that creates a risk of harm to society. It might be suggested that proof of actual harm should be required. It is apparent from what I have said above that it is sufficient in this regard for Parliament to have a reasonable basis for concluding that harm will result and this requirement does not demand actual proof of harm.

Second, materials which have scientific, artistic or literary merit are not captured by the provision. As discussed above, the court must be generous in its application of the "artistic defense". For example, in certain cases, materials such as photographs, prints, books and films which may undoubtedly be produced with some motive for economic profit, may nonetheless claim the protection of the Charter in so far as their defining characteristic is that of aesthetic expression, and thus represent the artist's attempt at individual fulfilment. The existence of an accompanying economic motive does not, of itself, deprive a work of significance as an example of individual artistic or self-fulfilment.

Third, in considering whether the provision minimally impairs the freedom in question, it is legitimate for the court to take into account Parliament's past abortive attempts to replace the definition with one that is more explicit. In *Irwin Toy*, our Court recognized that it is legitimate to take into account the fact that earlier laws and proposed alternatives were thought to be less effective than the legislation that is presently being challenged. The attempt to provide exhaustive instances of obscenity has been shown to be destined to fail (Bill C-54, 2nd Sess., 33rd Parl.). It seems that the only practicable alternative is to strive towards a more abstract definition of obscenity which is contextually sensitive and responsive to progress in the knowledge and understanding to the phenomenon to which the legislation is directed. In my view, the standard of "undue exploitation" is therefore appropriate. The intractable nature of the problem and the impossibility of precisely defining a notion which is inherently elusive makes the possibility of a more explicit provision remote. In this light, it is appropriate to question whether and at what cost, greater legislative precision can be demanded.

Fourth, while the discussion in this appeal has been limited to the definition portion of s. 163, I would note that the impugned section, with the possible exception of subs. 1, which is not in issue here has been held by this Court not to extend its reach to the private use of viewing of obscene materials. . . .

I conclude that while s. 163(8) infringes s. 2(b) of the Charter, freedom of expression, it constitutes a reasonable limit and is saved by virtue of the provisions of s. 1. [Because neither of the lower courts applied the proper definition of obscenity, the Supreme Court of Canada remanded the case back to the trial court and directed a new trial on all charges.]

NOTES AND QUESTIONS

1. *The gender equality rationale.* Does gender equality represent a more persuasive basis for regulating erotica than generalized concerns about public morality? Does the Supreme Court of Canada make a persuasive case that erotica undermines the government's goal of creating and maintaining a truly egalitarian society? Indianapolis, Indiana, made the same arguments in favor of regulating erotica in *Hudnut*, *supra* p. 589, that the Supreme Court of Canada endorses in *Butler.* Is content or viewpoint discrimination in regulating erotica justifiable on equality grounds? Is some pornography more socially harmful than other pornography, because of how it presents women as a class? If you think Judge Easterbrook's argument against this position is persuasive, how can you justify special burdens on erotica in the first place, in that these restrictions rest on viewpoint hostility (whether on generic morals or equality grounds)? *See* Nadine Strossen, *Hate Speech and Pornography: Do We Have to Choose Between Freedom of Speech and Equality?*, 46 Case W. Res. L. Rev. 449, 458-477 (1996) (arguing that

restrictions on sexually explicit speech actually undermine efforts to promote gender equality between the sexes).

2. *Degrading and dehumanizing defined.* What kind of pornography is "dehumanizing" and "degrading"? You might be interested to know that the Canadian Customs Service found that gay and lesbian erotica is the epitome of obscenity under section 163. Little Sisters Book & Art Emporium v. Commissioner, [2000] 2 S.C.R. 1120 (Can.). Is a culturally contingent standard, such as whether material is "degrading," capable of even-handed enforcement? For arguments that it is not, see Ronald J. Krotoszynski, Jr., *The First Amendment in Cross-Cultural Perspective: A Comparative Legal Analysis* 69-79, 82-87 (2006) (discussing problems associated with highly targeted enforcement of both obscenity and hate speech laws in Canada); Steven G. Gey, *Postmodern Censorship Revisited: A Reply to Richard Delgado,* 146 U. Pa. L. Rev. 1077, 1089-1090 (1998) (noting problem of differential enforcement of obscenity laws, and other laws permitting government to restrict speech, to silence unpopular minorities).
3. *Medium-specific regulation and zoning of indecent speech.* Unlike obscene speech, indecent speech is not an unprotected category of speech. As we saw in Chapter 8, however, the Supreme Court has interpreted the First Amendment to permit more restrictions on nonobscene but "indecent" speech in the broadcast medium than in print, on cable television, or the internet. We also saw in Chapter 3 that the Supreme Court upheld a zoning ordinance restricting locations of "adult businesses" by treating it as if it were a content-neutral time, place, and manner restriction rather than a restriction based on the sexual content of the expression offered by these businesses. *See* City of Renton v. Playtime Theatres, 475 U.S. 41 (1986).

AN EXTENDED NOTE ON THE PROBLEM OF "REVENGE PORN"

Should the First Amendment preclude state governments, or the federal government, from adopting criminal laws aimed at preventing the online distribution of embarrassing intimate photographs by vengeful ex-spouses or former boyfriends/girlfriends? Several websites, such as yougotposted.com, godaddy.com, and texxxan.com, exist for the primary purpose of facilitating the distribution of embarrassing, explicit photographs of former intimate partners. Usually, but not always, men post these images of their former wives or girlfriends. *See* Erica Goode, *Once Scorned, But on Revenge Sites, Twice Hurt,* N.Y. Times, Sept. 24, 2013, at A11 (noting that "[r]evenge porn sites feature explicit photos posted by ex-boyfriends, ex-husbands and ex-lovers, often accompanied by disparaging descriptions and identifying details, like where the women live and work, as well as links to their Facebook pages").

Utah, for example, has enacted a statute that criminally punishes the unauthorized distribution of "intimate images" via social media. *See* Utah Code Ann. § 76-5b-203 (2016). In relevant part, the statute, which is typical of enactments in about a dozen other states, proscribes the "distribution of intimate images if the actor, with the intent to cause emotional distress or harm, knowingly or intentionally distributes to any third party any intimate image of an individual who is 18 years of age or older, if: (a) the actor knows that the depicted individual has not given consent to the actor to distribute the intimate image; (b) the intimate image was created by or provided to the actor under circumstances in which the individual has a reasonable expectation of privacy; and (c) actual emotional distress or harm is caused to the person as a result of the distribution under this section." *Id.* at § 76-5b-203(2). Under the statute, "intimate images" encompass "any visual depiction, photograph, film, video, recording, picture, or computer or computer-generated image or picture, whether made or produced by electronic, mechanical, or other means" depicting human genitals, female breasts, or "sexually explicit conduct." *Id.* at § 76-5b-203(1)(b). In turn, "sexually explicit conduct" includes images featuring "partial nudity" or "simulated sexually explicit conduct" that does not depict actual sexual conduct (but seems to do so). *See id.* at § 76-5b-203(1)(b) & (c).

Is this statute constitutional as against a First Amendment challenge? Does simulated sexual activity or partial nudity meet the *Miller* test for obscenity? On the other hand, must a revenge porn statute be limited in scope to materials that are legally obscene? If a statute simply provided specific civil and criminal remedies for legally obscene revenge porn, would it be constitutional? Or would such a narrowly drafted law be subject to an *R.A.V.* objection? (*See R.A.V., supra* p. 562.) On the other hand, would a statute that criminally prohibits posting merely "unflattering" or "upsetting" images be consistent with the First Amendment? For an argument that narrowly drawn anti-revenge porn criminal laws are consistent with the First Amendment, see Danielle Keats Citron & Mary Anne Franks, *Criminalizing Revenge Porn,* 49 Wake Forest L. Rev. 345 (2014). For more skeptical points of view on the need for such laws and their consistency with the First Amendment, see Clay Calvert, *Revenge Porn and Freedom of Expression: Legislative Pushback to an Online Weapon of Emotional and Reputational Destruction,* 24 Fordham Intell. Prop. Media & Ent. L.J. 673, 683-701 (2014), and John A. Humbach, *Privacy and the Right of Free Expression,* 11 First Amend. L. Rev. 16 (2012).

Finally, would the Supreme Court's *New York Times Co. v. Sullivan* (*supra,* p. 471) line of precedent present an obstacle to the application of revenge porn statutes in circumstances involving a public official, a public figure, or someone involved in a matter of public concern? Could government seek to protect a persons's interest in privacy if, in context, the intimate images related to a public official, a public figure, or a matter of public concern? It bears noting that in much of the wider world, a law prohibiting the unauthorized distribution of a nude or even a merely embarrassing personal photograph would be viewed as fully consistent with a strong and meaningful commitment to the freedom of speech. *See* Krotoszynski, *supra* p. 601, at 16-21, 143-44, 156-173. Of course, the First Amendment, as defined and applied by the U.S. federal courts, often compels results that other democratic nations with constitutional free speech guarantees would not embrace.

THEORY-APPLIED PROBLEM

The Contemporary Arts Center (CAC), in Cincinnati, Ohio, hosts a traveling exhibition of photographs by Robert Mapplethorpe, entitled *Robert Mapplethorpe: The Perfect Moment.* Mapplethorpe's oeuvre largely consists of graphic depictions of "homoerotic" art, including photographs of hard-core sex acts associated with images of sadomasochism, bondage, domination, and affiliated sex practices. Mapplethorpe's photographs, mostly in black and white, received very positive critical commentary and, in fact, hang on the walls of some of the nation's most well-respected art museums. For a long period of time, Cincinnati has maintained vigilant efforts to maintain its community standards of decency, and has vigorously enforced state and local laws regulating obscenity. When the local district attorney learns of the planned exhibition, he sues Dennis Barrie, the CAC's director, in a local state court, seeking an injunction against the exhibition of the Mapplethorpe photographs to the public. The district attorney argues that the pictures are patently offensive and offend community standards; he also alleges the photographs present sex and excretory functions in a prurient fashion (again applying contemporary community standards). Finally, the district attorney says that promotional materials for the show "pander" by emphasizing the salacious quality of the photographs and that, regardless of whether the photographs are legally obscene under *Miller*, they may be suppressed on the basis of this pandering. At the hearing on the preliminary injunction, the director offers into evidence five affidavits from recognized art experts stating that the Mapplethorpe photographs possess "significant artistic merit." Applying the *Miller* standard, how should the trial court rule? Should an injunction issue prohibiting the display of photographs in advance of the actual exhibit opening to the public? If the promotional materials for the exhibit emphasized the sexual content, would this be a basis for declaring the materials obscene, regardless of whether the prosecution meets the *Miller* standard?

AN EXTENDED NOTE ON SEXUALLY EXPLICIT EXPRESSIVE CONDUCT: NUDE DANCING AND THE FIRST AMENDMENT

Should non-obscene sexually explicit expressive conduct be subject to content-based government regulations based on the community's moral disapproval of such activity? In two cases involving nude dancing, Barnes v. Glen Theater, 501 U.S. 560 (1991) (*see supra* p. 162) and City of Erie v. Pap's A.M., 529 U.S. 277 (2000) (*see supra* p. 169), the Supreme Court held that nude dancing constitutes protected expression, but nevertheless sustained flat bans against it. These decisions do not directly hold that the government has a compelling interest in banning such expressive conduct (the usual standard required to sustain a content-based speech regulation), but instead uphold bans on nude dancing because the community views it as immoral (*Barnes*) and because such expressive activity often correlates with other illegal activity, such as prostitution, drug dealing, and fighting (*Erie*). Under either rationale, the government may ban nude dancing completely.

In the first decision, *Barnes*, Chief Justice Rehnquist wrote a plurality opinion that sustained the application of Indiana's state law against public nudity on the basis that it constituted merely a content-neutral regulation of expressive conduct:

> Applying the four-part *O'Brien* test . . . we find that Indiana's public indecency statute is justified despite its incidental limitations on some expressive activity. The public indecency statute is clearly within the constitutional power of the State and furthers substantial governmental interests. It is impossible to discern, other than from the text of the statute,

> exactly what governmental interest the Indiana legislators had in mind when they enacted this statute, for Indiana does not record legislative history, and the State's highest court has not shed additional light on the statute's purpose. Nonetheless, the statute's purpose of protecting societal order and morality is clear from its text and history. Public indecency statutes of this sort are of ancient origin and presently exist in at least 47 States. Public indecency, including nudity, was a criminal offense at common law, and this Court recognized the common-law roots of the offense of "gross and open indecency" in Winters v. New York, 333 U.S. 507, 515 (1948). Public nudity was considered an act *malum in se.* Le Roy v. Sidley, 1 Sid. 168, 82 Eng. Rep. 1036 (K.B. 1664). Public indecency statutes such as the one before us reflect moral disapproval of people appearing in the nude among strangers in public places . . . The traditional police power of the States is defined as the authority to provide for the public health, safety, and morals, and we have upheld such a basis for legislation. . . .
>
> Thus, the public indecency statute furthers a substantial government interest in protecting order and morality. But we do not think that when Indiana applies its statute to the nude dancing in these nightclubs it is proscribing nudity because of the erotic message conveyed by the dancers. Presumably numerous other erotic performances are presented at these establishments and similar clubs without any interference from the State, so long as the performers wear a scant amount of clothing. Likewise, the requirement that the dancers don pasties and G-strings does not deprive the dance of whatever erotic message it conveys; it simply makes the message slightly less graphic. The perceived evil that Indiana seeks to address is not erotic dancing, but public nudity. The appearance of people of all shapes, sizes and ages in the nude at a beach, for example, would convey little if any erotic message, yet the State still seeks to prevent it. Public nudity is the evil the State seeks to prevent, whether or not it is combined with expressive activity.

The Chief Justice's opinion, however, only garnered four votes. Justice Souter concurred and voted to sustain the application of Indiana's ban on nudity in public places to nude dancing because of a "simple correlation of such dancing with other evils, rather than a relationship between the other evils and the expressive component of the dancing." Justice White, joined by Justices Marshall, Blackmun, and Stevens, dissented, reasoning that although "the performances in the Kitty Kat Lounge may not be high art, to say the least, and may not appeal to the Court," this fact "is hardly an excuse for distorting settled doctrine" regarding content- and viewpoint-based regulations of speech.

Justice Souter's concurring opinions in *Barnes* uses an analytical device that usually provides little traction to state and local governments in First Amendment cases: the doctrine of secondary effects. Under the doctrine of secondary effects, speech may be regulated, even if the speech itself is not intrinsically harmful, because it produces harmful effects. In most other areas, however, the Supreme Court has held that government must regulate unlawful conduct directly—not speech that correlates with it.

For example, leafleting commonly result in litter on the streets and sidewalks. Governments have, from time to time, attempted to regulate or ban leafleting because of its secondary effect of causing increased litter. *See* Lovell v. City of Griffin, 303 U.S. 444 (1938). In contexts other than "adult entertainment," however, federal courts, including the Supreme Court, reliably have rejected such government arguments out of hand, essentially telling state and local governments to punish those who litter, rather than silence those seeking to distribute leaflets. *See id.* at 451-52; *see also* Schneider v. State, 308 U.S. 147, 161-62 (1939) (invalidating a ban on leafletting because it creates a risk of litter). As the *Schneider* Court explained, "[t]here are obvious methods of preventing littering. Amongst these is the punishment of those who actually throw papers on the streets." 308 U.S. at 162.

Yet, in the area of adult entertainment or erotica (including both fixed media, like books or films, and live performance art), the Supreme Court has permitted local governments to establish special, restrictive zoning regimes for adult businesses because of the alleged "secondary effects" associated with such businesses, presumed to include the sale of illegal drugs, alcohol abuse, prostitution, and breaches of the peace, as well as general concerns about neighborhood "blight." *See, e.g.*, City of Renton v. Playtime Theaters, Inc., 475 U.S. 41, 46, 48-52 (1986). Thus, the Supreme Court has sustained restrictive zoning ordinances that limit adult businesses to within "1,000 feet of another regulated use" or "500 feet of a residential use." Young v. American Mini Theatres, Inc., 427 U.S. 50, 72-73 (1976). The factual predicate for the decision to regulate the purveyors of "adult" entertainments, through restrictive zoning and licensing regulations, need not be empirically rigorous—a study conducted 20 years ago or longer can be sufficient to support regulations aimed at reducing the "blight and crime" associated with adult businesses. *See* City of Los Angeles v. Alameda Books, Inc., 535 U.S. 425, 435-441 (2002).

Despite the doctrinal incoherence and inconsistency, in *City of Erie v. Pap's A.M.*, a plurality of the Supreme Court, in an opinion by Justice O'Connor, invoked the secondary effects doctrine to sustain Erie, Pennsylvania's ban on nude dancing:

> The State's interest in preventing harmful secondary effects is not related to the suppression of expression. In trying to control the secondary effects of nude dancing, the ordinance seeks to deter crime and the other deleterious effects caused by the presence of such an establishment in the neighborhood. . . .
>
> Similarly, even if Erie's public nudity ban has some minimal effect on the erotic message by muting that portion of the expression that occurs when the last stitch is dropped, the dancers at Kandyland and other such establishments are free to perform wearing pasties and G-strings. Any effect on the overall expression is *de minimis*. And as Justice Stevens eloquently stated for the plurality in Young v. American Mimi Theatres, Inc., 427 U.S. 50, 70 (1976), "even though we recognize that the First Amendment will not tolerate the total suppression of erotic materials that have some arguably artistic value, it is manifest that society's interest in protecting this type of expression is of a wholly different, and lesser, magnitude than the interest in untrammeled political debate," and "few of us

would march our sons and daughters off to war to preserve the citizen's right to see" specified anatomical areas exhibited at establishments like Kandyland. If States are to be able to regulate secondary effects, the *de minimis* intrusions on expression such as those at issue here cannot be sufficient to render the ordinance content based. . . .

We conclude that Erie's asserted interest in combating the negative secondary effects associated with adult entertainment establishments like Kandyland is unrelated to the suppression of the erotic message conveyed by nude dancing. The ordinance prohibiting public nudity is therefore valid if it satisfies the four-factor test from *O'Brien* for evaluating restrictions on symbolic speech.

Justice Stevens, joined by Justice Ginsburg, dissented, arguing that "[t]he plurality relies on the so-called 'secondary effects' test to defend the ordinance" but "[t]he present use of that rationale.. finds no support whatsoever in our precedents." Moreover, "Never before have we approved the use of that doctrine to justify a total ban on protected First Amendment expression. On the contrary, we have been quite clear that the doctrine would not support that end." Indeed, this is perhaps the *only* area in which the Supreme Court has permitted the regulation of expressive activity, not because the expression itself causes a social harm that government has the constitutional authority to prevent, but because other social harms tend to follow from it. *Cf.* Brandenburg v. Ohio, 395 U.S. 444, 447 (1969) (holding protected calls for race wars absent a clear and present danger of imminent lawlessness, even though such calls probably correlate with secondary effects, such as race-based assaults, that the government has the power to proscribe).

NOTES AND QUESTIONS

1. *Are secondary effects real?* Even if one were prepared to credit the secondary effects argument, neither Indiana nor Erie presented *any* concrete data showing that the totally nude dancing presented a greater risk of causing serious social harms than the operation of a bowling alley, a McDonald's restaurant, or an Elk's Club. If the empirical basis for regulating "secondary effects" is far from clear, why does the Supreme Court sustain the regulation? Note that in both *Alameda Books* and *Playtime Theatres,* the Supreme Court did not require the local government to document empirically that zoning requirements would actually reduce the "blight and crime" that adult businesses attracted. *See, e.g.*, City of Los Angeles v. Alameda Books, 535 U.S. 425, 435-442 (2002); City of Renton v. Playtime Theatres, Inc., 475 U.S. 41, 50-52 (1986). On the other hand, however, both of these cases—unlike *Pap's A.M.*—did not involve a total ban on the speech activity but rather efforts to limit the locations where such speech activity could take place. For further discussion with actual data on the question, see Alan C. Weinstein & Richard McCleary, *The Association of Adult Businesses with Secondary Effects: Legal Doctrine, Social Theory, and Empirical Evidence*, 20 Cardozo Arts & Ent. L.J. 101 (2011) (documenting the limited empirical evidence supporting the Supreme Court's assumption that the operation of adult businesses invariably causes adverse secondary effects).

2. *Seminude versus fully nude.* Is the message of an almost nude dancer the same as that of a totally nude dancer?
3. *Actual evidence of secondary effects?* Did either Indiana or Erie (or the Supreme Court itself) make a persuasive case that the risk of fights, prostitution, and drug dealing correlates positively with the absence of pasties and G-strings and that the use of pasties and G-strings by erotic dancers directly lowers these undesirable secondary effects?
4. *Content discrimination and nude dancing.* Is this really just a simple case of either content or viewpoint discrimination? Perhaps *both*? Does the government disfavor nude dancing because of its message of unbridled eroticism and sexuality? After all, public nudity exists in a variety of public accommodations in both Indiana and Erie—presumably including country clubs, high school and college locker rooms, gyms, and health spas. If nudity, per se, were the issue, why doesn't the government regulate nudity in other places of public accommodation? Doesn't this selective regulation strongly suggest that the government's concern isn't really related to the hypothetical secondary effects caused by nude dancing? Note, too, on the question of content or viewpoint discrimination, that nudity incident to a major Broadway play or musical, such as *Equus* or *Hair*, does not seem to trigger the same censorial impulse either on the part of local officials or the courts.
5. *Content-neutral regulation of erotica?* If, as Justice Harlan famously once quipped, "one man's vulgarity is another's lyric," why should courts permit state and local governments to regulate erotica more aggressively than other kinds of speech? Should a production of the musical *Hair*, which often features full frontal nudity, enjoy greater protection than dancers at the Kitty Kat Klub because of the aesthetic norms of the ruling caste in South Bend (or, more generally, in Indiana)? If not, how can you square the result in *Barnes* with a meaningful commitment to protect erotica without regard to its content or viewpoint?
6. *Speech/conduct and nude dancing.* Is nude dancing speech? Or is it conduct akin to prostitution? If nude dancing is really conduct, rather than speech, should this imply that the government has a lower burden to meet in regulating it? Note that the Supreme Court has squarely held that recreational dancing *does not* constitute a form of expressive conduct. *See* Dallas v. Stanglin, 490 U.S. 19, 25 (1989) ("We think the activity of these dance-hall patrons—coming together to engage in recreational dancing—is not protected by the First Amendment."). Should this affect the constitutional analysis here? Or is dance as performance art clearly distinguishable from dance as a recreational activity for First Amendment purposes?

B. CHILDREN AND PORNOGRAPHY

The Supreme Court has signaled that protecting children from sexual exploitation constitutes a compelling government interest that justifies substantially broader regulation of child pornography featuring real children than would be permissible under the *Miller* standard. The following cases set forth the special rules that govern materials featuring nude depictions of children (whether pornographic in nature or not).

New York v. Ferber

458 U.S. 747 (1982)

WHITE, J., delivered the opinion of the Court.

At issue in this case is the constitutionality of a New York criminal statute which prohibits persons from knowingly promoting sexual performances by children under the age of 16 by distributing material which depicts such performances.

In recent years, the exploitive use of children in the production of pornography has become a serious national problem. The Federal Government and 47 States have sought to combat the problem with statutes specifically directed at the production of child pornography. At least half of such statutes do not require that the materials produced be legally obscene. Thirty-five States and the United States Congress have also passed legislation prohibiting the distribution of such materials; 20 States prohibit the distribution of material depicting children engaged in sexual conduct without requiring that the material be legally obscene. New York is one of the 20. In 1977, the New York Legislature enacted Article 263 of its Penal Law. N.Y. Penal Law, Art. 263 (McKinney 1980). Section 263.05 criminalizes as a class C felony the use of a child in a sexual performance:

> A person is guilty of the use of a child in a sexual performance if knowing the character and content thereof he employs, authorizes or induces a child less than sixteen years of age to engage in a sexual performance or being a parent, legal guardian or custodian of such child, he consents to the participation by such child in a sexual performance.

A "[s]exual performance" is defined as "any performance or part thereof which includes sexual conduct by a child less than sixteen years of age." § 263.00(1). "Sexual conduct" is in turn defined in § 263.00(3):

> "Sexual conduct" means actual or simulated sexual intercourse, deviate sexual intercourse, sexual bestiality, masturbation, sado-masochistic abuse, or lewd exhibition of the genitals.

A "performance" is defined as "any play, motion picture, photograph or dance" or "any other visual representation exhibited before an audience." § 263.00(4). . . .

This case arose when Paul Ferber, the proprietor of a Manhattan bookstore specializing in sexually oriented products, sold two films to an undercover police officer. The films are devoted almost exclusively to depicting young boys masturbating. Ferber was indicted on two counts of violating § 263.10 and two counts of violating § 263.15, the two New York laws controlling dissemination of child pornography. After a jury trial, Ferber was acquitted of the two counts of promoting an obscene sexual performance, but found guilty of the two counts under § 263.15, which did not require proof that the films were obscene. Ferber's convictions were affirmed without opinion by the Appellate Division of the New York State Supreme Court.

The New York Court of Appeals reversed, holding that § 263.15 violated the First Amendment. . . .

The Court of Appeals proceeded on the assumption that the standard of obscenity incorporated in § 263.10, which follows the guidelines enunciated in Miller v. California, 413 U.S. 15 (1973), constitutes the appropriate line dividing protected from unprotected expression by which to measure a regulation directed at child pornography. It was on the premise that "nonobscene adolescent sex" could not be singled out for special treatment that the court found § 263.15 "strikingly underinclusive." Moreover, the assumption that the constitutionally permissible regulation of pornography could not be more extensive with respect to the distribution of material depicting children may also have led the court to conclude that a narrowing construction of § 263.15 was unavailable.

The Court of Appeals' assumption was not unreasonable in light of our decisions. This case, however, constitutes our first examination of a statute directed at and limited to depictions of sexual activity involving children. We believe our inquiry should begin with the question of whether a State has somewhat more freedom in proscribing works which portray sexual acts or lewd exhibitions of genitalia by children. . . .

The *Miller* standard, like its predecessors, was an accommodation between the State's interests in protecting the "sensibilities of the unwilling recipients" from exposure to pornographic material and the dangers of censorship inherent in unabashedly content-based laws. Like obscenity statutes, laws directed at the dissemination of child pornography run the risk of suppressing protected expression by allowing the hand of the censor to become unduly heavy. For the following reasons, however, we are persuaded that the States are entitled to greater leeway in the regulation of pornographic depictions of children.

First. It is evident beyond the need for elaboration that a State's interest in "safeguarding the physical and psychological well-being of a minor" is "compelling." Globe Newspaper Co. v. Superior Court, 457 U.S. 596, 607 (1982). "A democratic society rests, for its continuance, upon the healthy, well-rounded growth of young people into full maturity as citizens." Prince v. Massachusetts, 321 U.S. 158, 168 (1944). Accordingly, we have sustained legislation aimed at protecting the physical and emotional well-being of youth even when the laws have operated in the sensitive area of constitutionally protected rights. In *Prince v. Massachusetts, supra,* the Court held that a statute prohibiting use of a child to distribute literature on the street was valid notwithstanding the statute's effect on a First Amendment activity. In *Ginsberg v. New York, supra,* we sustained a New York law protecting children from exposure to nonobscene literature. Most recently, we held that the Government's interest in the "well-being of its youth" justified special treatment of indecent broadcasting received by adults as well as children. FCC v. Pacifica Foundation, 438 U.S. 726 (1978).

The prevention of sexual exploitation and abuse of children constitutes a government objective of surpassing importance. [Justice White found that the creation of child pornography causes "physiological, emotional and mental health" harms to children involved in its production.]

Second. The distribution of photographs and films depicting sexual activity by juveniles is intrinsically related to the sexual abuse of children in at least two ways. First, the materials produced are a permanent record of the children's participation and the harm to the child is exacerbated by their circulation. Second, the distribution network for child pornography must be closed if the production of material which requires the sexual exploitation of children is to be effectively controlled. Indeed, there is not serious contention that the legislature was unjustified in believing that it is difficult, if not impossible, to halt the exploitation of children by pursuing only those who produce the photographs and movies. . . .

Third. The advertising and selling of child pornography provide an economic motive for and are thus an integral part of the production of such materials, an activity illegal throughout the Nation. "It rarely has been suggested that the constitutional freedom for speech and press extends its immunity to speech or writing used as an integral part of conduct in violation of a valid criminal statute." Giboney v. Empire Storage & Ice Co., 336 U.S. 490, 498 (1949). . . .

Fourth. The value of permitting live performances and photographic reproductions of children engaged in lewd sexual conduct is exceedingly modest, if not *de minimis.* We consider it unlikely that visual depictions of children performing sexual acts or lewdly exhibiting their genitals would often constitute an important and necessary part of a literary performance or scientific or educational work. As a state judge in this case observed, if it were necessary for literary or artistic value, a person over the statutory age who perhaps looked younger could be utilized. Simulation outside of the prohibition of the statute could provide another alternative. Nor is there any question here of censoring a particular literary theme or portrayal of sexual activity. The First Amendment interest is limited to that of rendering the portrayal somewhat more "realistic" by utilizing or photographing children.

Fifth. Recognizing and classifying child pornography as a category of material outside the protection of the First Amendment is not incompatible with our earlier decisions. . . .

There are, of course, limits on the category of child pornography which, like obscenity, is unprotected by the First Amendment. As with all legislation in this sensitive area, the conduct to be prohibited must be adequately defined by the applicable state law, as written or authoritatively construed. Here the nature of the harm to be combated requires that the state offense be limited to works that *visually* depict sexual conduct by children below a specified age. The category of "sexual conduct" proscribed must also be suitably limited and described.

The test for child pornography is separate from the obscenity standard enunciated in *Miller,* but may be compared to it for the purpose of clarity. The *Miller* formulation is adjusted in the following respects: A trier of fact need not find that the material appeals to the prurient interest of the average person; it is not required that sexual conduct portrayed be done so in a patently offensive manner; and the material at issue need not be considered as whole. We note that the distribution of descriptions or other depictions of sexual conduct, not otherwise obscene, which do not involve live performance or photographic or other visual reproduction of live performances retains First Amendment protection. As with obscenity laws, criminal responsibility may not be imposed without some element of scienter on the part of the defendant. Smith v. California, 361 U.S. 147 (1959); Hamling v. United States, 418 U.S. 87 (1974).

Section 263.15's prohibition incorporates a definition of sexual conduct that comports with the above-stated principles. The forbidden acts to be depicted are listed with sufficient precision and represent the kind of conduct that, if it were the theme of a work, could render it legally obscene: "actual or simulated sexual intercourse, deviate sexual intercourse, sexual bestiality, masturbation, sado-masochistic abuse, or lewd exhibition of the genitals." § 263.00(3). The term "lewd exhibition of the genitals" is not unknown in this area and, indeed, was given in *Miller* as an example of a permissible regulation. 413 U.S., at 25. A performance is defined only to include live or visual depictions: "any play, motion picture, photograph or dance . . . [or] other visual representation exhibited before an audience." § 263.00(4). Section 263.15 expressly includes a scienter requirement.

We hold that § 263.15 sufficiently describes a category of material the production and distribution of which is not entitled to First Amendment protection. It is therefore clear that there is nothing unconstitutionally "underinclusive" about a statute that singles out this category of material for proscription. It also follows that the State is not barred by the First Amendment from prohibiting the distribution of unprotected materials produced outside the State.

It remains to address the claim that the New York statute is unconstitutionally overbroad because it would forbid the distribution of material with serious literary, scientific, or educational value or material which does not threaten the harms sought to be combated by the State. Respondent prevailed on that ground below, and it is to that issue that we now turn. [The majority concluded that § 263.15 was not substantially overbroad.]

Because § 263.15 is not substantially overbroad, it is unnecessary to consider its application to material that does not depict sexual conduct of a type that New York may restrict consistent with the First Amendment. As applied to Paul Ferber and to others who distribute similar material, the statute does not violate the First Amendment as applied to the States through the Fourteenth. The judgment of the New York Court of Appeals is reversed, and the case is remanded to that court for further proceedings not inconsistent with this opinion.

So ordered.

O'CONNOR, J., concurring.

Although I join the court's opinion, I write separately to stress that the Court does not hold that New York must except "material with serious literary, scientific, or educational value," from its statute. The Court merely holds that, even if the First Amendment shelters such material, New York's current statute is not sufficiently overbroad to support respondent's facial attack. The compelling interests identified in today's opinion, suggest that the Constitution might in fact permit New York to ban knowing distribution of works depicting minors engaged in explicit sexual conduct, regardless of the social value of the depictions. For example, a 12-year-old child photographed while masturbating surely suffers the same psychological harm whether the community labels the photograph "edifying" or "tasteless." The audience's appreciation of the depiction is simply irrelevant to New York's asserted interest in protecting children from psychological, emotional, and mental harm. . . .

BRENNAN, J., with whom MARSHALL, J., joins, concurring in the judgment.

I agree with much of what is said in the Court's opinion. As I made clear in the opinion I delivered for the Court in Ginsburg v. New York, 390 U.S. 629 (1968), the State has a special interest in protecting the well-being of its youth. [] This special and compelling interest, and the particular vulnerability of children, afford the State the leeway to regulate pornographic material, the promotion of which is harmful to children, even though the State does not have such leeway when it seeks only to protect consenting adults from exposure to such material. *Ginsburg v. New York.* [] I also agree with the Court that the "tiny fraction," *ante,* at 773, of material of serious artistic, scientific, or educational value that could conceivably fall within the reach of the statute is insufficient to justify striking the statute on the grounds of overbreadth. *See* Broadrick v. Oklahoma, 413 U.S. 601, 630 (1973) (Brennan, J., dissenting).

But in my view application of § 263.15 or any similar statute to depictions of children that in themselves do have serious literary, artistic, scientific, or medical value, would violate the First Amendment. As the Court recognizes, the limited classes of speech, the suppression of which does not raise serious First Amendment concerns, have two attributes. They are of exceedingly "slight social value," and the State has a compelling interest in their regulation. See *Chaplinsky v. New Hampshire,* 315 U.S. 568, 571-572 (1942). The First Amendment value of depictions of children that are in themselves serious contributions to art, literature or science, is, by definition, simply not "*de minimis.* "At the same time, the State's interest in suppression of such materials is likely to be far less compelling. For the Court's assumption of harm to the child resulting from the "permanent record" and "circulation" of the child's "participation," [] lacks much of its force where the depiction is a serious contribution to art or science. The production of materials of serious value is not the "low-profile, clandestine industry" that according to the court produces purely pornographic materials. [] In short, it is inconceivable how a depiction of a child that is itself a serious contribution to the world of art or literature or science can be deemed "material outside the protection of the First Amendment."

I, of course, adhere to my view that, in the absence of exposure, or particular harm, to juveniles or unconsenting adults, the State lacks power to suppress sexually oriented materials. *See, e.g.,* Paris Adult Theatre I v. Slaton, 413 U.S. 49, 73 (1973) (Brennan, J., dissenting). With this understanding, I concur in the Court's judgment in this case.

[Justice STEVENS's concurring opinion is omitted.]

NOTES AND QUESTIONS

1. *Child pornography made without children.* Why does Justice White emphasize, repeatedly, that *Ferber*'s holding is limited to "visual" depictions of real children? Couldn't a book, like Vladimir Nabokov's *Lolita,* although in a purely written form, also help to contribute to a market for child pornography by increasing demand for such wares?
2. *Naked children in artworks.* Should serious works of art be proscribable solely because they depict naked children? For example, photographer Sally Mann created a series of black-and-white posed nudes of her children, Emmett, Jessie, and Virginia, in a series inspired by various classical myths. *See* Sally Mann, *Immediate Family* (1992). Art critics deemed the

works to possess significant merit. Should this factor into the First Amendment analysis at all? For an argument that *Ferber* understates the potential loss of serious artistic work, see Amy Adler, *The Perverse Law of Child Pornography*, 101 Colum. L. Rev. 209, 253-256 (2001) (discussing Mann's work and work of other art photographers that feature nude depictions of children and suggesting that the harm associated with such artistic works is largely a function of cultural factors, rather than intrinsic to the creation and subsequent distribution of such materials); *see also* Connie Samaras, *Feminism, Photography, Censorship, and Sexually Transgressive Imagery: The Work of Robert Mapplethorpe, Joel-Peter Witkin, Jacqueline Livingston, Sally Mann, and Catherine Opie*, 38 N.Y.L. Sch. L. Rev. 75 (1993) (discussing the artistic importance of photographic works featuring images of nude minors).

3. *Devaluing child pornography.* Justice Brennan seems to disagree with Justice O'Connor, and perhaps Justice White, that the First Amendment would tolerate suppression of materials that in any way depict real nude children. Instead, his agreement seems to stem from the fact that the materials in question, taken as a whole, possessed meager social value, even if they were not legally obscene in New York City. What are the potential benefits and costs of adopting Brennan's approach to the problem of nude depictions of real children?
4. *Family photos of naked children.* Does *Ferber* mean that a parent could face a felony conviction for taking pictures of his child in the bath or on a training "potty"? Such pictures are relatively common in contemporary U.S. culture (much to the horror of teenage and adult children who find such photographs enormously embarrassing). On the other hand, should the question be whether materials could be used for a prurient purpose, as opposed to whether the possessor actually made or possessed the materials with a prurient intent?
5. *Is violent speech directed at children an unprotected category of speech, akin to obscenity?* Brown v. Entertainment Merchants Ass'n, 564 U.S. 786 (2011), involved a constitutional challenge to a state prohibiting sale or rental of "violent video games" to minors. The state of California argued that the "interactive" nature of violent video games justified restricting them from minors and provided media effects research purportedly showing that interactive or immersive media experiences can lead to harm. The Court rejected the argument that medium-specific characteristics of video games justified relaxing First Amendment prohibitions on content-based regulation or creating a new category of unprotected speech. Although the Court believed that video games serve First Amendment purposes only fitfully, if at all, it nonetheless gave them full protection, observing that "we have long recognized that it is difficult to distinguish politics from entertainment, and dangerous to try." *Id.* at 790. Video games "communicate ideas—and even social messages—through many familiar literary devices" as well as "through features distinctive to the medium (such as the player's interaction with the virtual world)." *Id.* The Court acknowledged "the challenges of applying the Constitution to ever-advancing

technology," but affirmed the "most basic First Amendment principle, namely that government may not impose content-based limitations except in "well-defined and narrowly limited classes of speech, the prevention and punishment of which has never been thought to raise any Constitutional problem." *Id.* at 790-91. The Court rejected the invitation to expand the categories of unprotected speech simply because the violent video games were "directed at children." *Id.* at 794. Ultimately, the Court declared the video game legislation unconstitutional because California failed to "show a direct causal link between violent video games and harm to minors." *Brown*, 564 U.S. at 799. The media effects research on which California relied was methodologically unsound. The Court also found the legislation particularly unnecessary in light of the evidence on the record that the video game industry already performed a great deal of self-policing by voluntarily refusing to sell to minors video games (voluntarily) labeled as appropriate only for mature audiences. *See id.* at 802-803. The legislation was overinclusive because, in attempting to assist parents in controlling their children's access to violent fare, it prevented access even by those children whose parents did not care whether they purchased such fare. *Id.* at 804-05. For a strong argument that violent material aimed at children should not be protected by the First Amendment, see Kevin W. Saunders, *Violence as Obscenity: Limiting the Media's First Amendment Protection* (1996).

THEORY-APPLIED PROBLEM

In the motion picture *Apt Pupil* (1998), starring Ian McKellen and Brad Renfro, director Bryan Singer (*The Usual Suspects* (1995); *Superman Returns* (2006)) tells the highly disturbing story of a high school student (played by Renfro) obsessed with a former Nazi death camp officer (played by McKellen) and his past; a Stephen King novella inspired the film. In a controversial high school shower scene, director Singer required several young male actors to appear nude; the actors (including Renfro) were, at the time, under 18 years of age. The scene follows a basketball practice and features a fantasy sequence in which Renfro's character imagines himself to be in the showers at a Nazi death camp, surrounded by victims of the Holocaust. The MPAA rated the film "R" for brief nudity, bad language, and violence.

Video Connection is a video rental store in Oklahoma City, Oklahoma, specializing in art, foreign, and "avant-garde" films, including the repertoire of directors such as Fellini and John Waters. Video Connection owns and rents two copies of *Apt Pupil.* On July 1, 2023, a customer presents *Apt Pupil* for rental; when the clerk proceeds to rent the title, she is immediately arrested for "distribution of child pornography," a class B felony under Oklahoma state law. In relevant part, the applicable Oklahoma law prohibits "possession or distribution of any nude photographic or cinematic depiction of a person under 18 years of age, including depiction of the buttocks, genitals, anus, or female breasts." (This statute operates entirely independently of Oklahoma's state law criminalizing obscene materials.) Both the clerk and Video Connection's owners are indicted, tried, and convicted of violating Oklahoma's ban on child pornography. On an appeal of their convictions to the Supreme Court of Oklahoma, the defendants argue that the conviction must be reversed on free speech grounds. The defendants assert that *Free Speech Coalition* (see *infra* p. 619) plainly protects serious films from proscription as child pornography. The local district attorney, in her brief, counters that under *Ferber* and *Osborne*, any nude depiction of a real minor may be criminalized. How should the Supreme Court of Oklahoma rule on the appeal?

AN EXTENDED NOTE ON *STANLEY v. GEORGIA* AND *OSBORNE v. OHIO:* PRIVACY IN THE HOME AND THE FIRST AMENDMENT

In Stanley v. Georgia, 394 U.S. 557 (1969), the Supreme Court held that although government may proscribe obscene materials, adults have a right to possess and review obscene materials in the home as a matter of protected freedom of speech. Writing for the majority, Justice Thurgood Marshall explained that:

> It is now well established that the Constitution protects the right to receive information and ideas. . . .This right to receive information and ideas, regardless of their social worth, see *Winters* v. *New York*, 333 U. S. 507, 510 (1948), is fundamental to our free society. Moreover, in the context of this case — a prosecution for mere possession of printed or filmed matter in the privacy of a person's own home — that right takes on an added dimension. For also fundamental is the right to be free, except in very limited circumstances, from unwanted governmental intrusions into one's privacy.

Id. at 564. Although "the States retain broad power to regulate obscenity," the government's power to proscribe the commercial sale and distribution of obscene materials "simply does not extend to mere possession by the individual in the privacy of his own home." *Id.* at 568. Consistent with this reasoning, the *Stanley* Court unanimously held "that the First and Fourteenth Amendments prohibit making mere private possession of obscene material a crime." *Id.* Thus, although neither a state nor the federal government need tolerate the distribution, display, or public sale of obscene materials, an individual has a First Amendment right, under the Free Speech Clause, to possess and peruse such materials in the privacy of the home.

After *Ferber*, an open question existed regarding the scope of *Stanley*'s application: Did *Stanley* apply to sexually-explicit materials proscrible under the *Ferber* rule? In Osborne v. Ohio, 495 U.S. 103 (1990), the Supreme Court answered this question negatively and declined to extend *Stanley*'s reach to such materials.

Writing for the majority, Justice Byron White explained that:

> The threshold question in this case is whether Ohio may constitutionally proscribe the possession and viewing of child pornography or whether, as Osborne argues, our decision in Stanley v. Georgia, 394 U.S. 557 (1969), compels the contrary result. In *Stanley*, we struck down a Georgia law outlawing the private possession of obscene material. We recognized that the statute impinged upon Stanley's right to receive information in the privacy of his home, and we found Georgia's justifications for its law inadequate.

> *Stanley* should not be read too broadly. We have previously noted that *Stanley* was a narrow holding, see United States v. 12 200-ft. Reels of Film, 413 U.S. 123, 127 (1973), and, since the decision in that case, the value of permitting child pornography has been characterized as "exceedingly modest, if not *de minimis*." New York v. Ferber, 458 U.S. 747, 762 (1982). But assuming, for the sake of argument, that Osborne has a First Amendment interest in viewing and possessing child pornography, we nonetheless find this case distinct from *Stanley* because the interests underlying child pornography prohibitions far exceed the interests justifying the Georgia law at issue in *Stanley*. Every court to address the issue has so concluded.
>
> In *Stanley*, Georgia primarily sought to proscribe the private possession of obscenity because it was concerned that obscenity would poison the minds of its viewers. 394 U.S., at 565. We responded that "[w]hatever the power of the state to control public dissemination of ideas inimical to the public morality, it cannot constitutionally premise legislation on the desirability of controlling a person's private thoughts." The difference here is obvious: The State does not rely on a paternalistic interest in regulating Osborne's mind. Rather, Ohio has enacted § 2907.323(A)(3) in order to protect the victims of child pornography; it hopes to destroy a market for the exploitative use of children.
>
> > It is evident beyond the need for elaboration that a State's interest in 'safeguarding the physical and psychological wellbeing of a minor' is 'compelling.' . . . The legislative judgment, as well as the judgment found in relevant literature, is that the use of children as subjects of pornographic materials is harmful to the physiological, emotional, and mental health of the child. That judgment, we think, easily passes muster under the First Amendment.
>
> *Ferber*, 458 U.S., at 756-758 (citations omitted). It is also surely reasonable for the State to conclude that it will decrease the production of child pornography if it penalizes those who possess and view the product, thereby decreasing demand. . . .
>
> Given the importance of the State's interest in protecting the victims of child pornography, we cannot fault Ohio for attempting to stamp out this vice at all levels in the distribution chain.

Id. at 108-10. Justice White identified other reasons supporting this outcome, including the fact that child pornography "permanently records the victim's abuse" thereby "caus[ing] the child victims continuing harm," as well as "encouraging the destruction of these materials." *Id.* at 111. In sum, "[g]iven the gravity of the State's interests in this context, we find that Ohio may constitutionally proscribe the possession and viewing of child pornography." *Id.*

Justice William J. Brennan, Jr., dissented, joined by Justices Marshall and Stevens, arguing that Ohio's "law, even as construed authoritatively by the Ohio Supreme Court, is still fatally overbroad." *Id.* at 125. Moreover, in his view "our decision in Stanley v. Georgia, 394 U.S. 557 (1969), prevents the State from criminalizing appellant's possession of the photographs at issue in this case." *Id.*

NOTES AND QUESTIONS

1. *Competing principles.* Given that *Ferber* held that suppressing demand for the creation of child pornography was a legitimate government objective, is *Osborne* a logical extension of *Ferber*? Or should the general notion that one's home implicates a zone of privacy justify the application of *Stanley* to these materials? Does Justice White or Justice Brennan have the better view of which principle should be controlling on these facts?
2. *Canada, compared.* Although the Supreme Court of Canada nominally upheld Canada's federal anti–child pornography statute, it engrafted a host of limits and exemptions, including an exemption for any work that possesses even the *slightest* artistic merit. Unlike the United States Supreme Court, Canada's Supreme Court has recognized that even child pornography has some expressive value, which is consistent with its tendency to interpret its Charter as protecting any communicative effort, other than acts of violence. *See* R. v. Sharpe, [2001] 1 S.C.R. 45 (Can.). In *The First Amendment in Cross-Cultural Perspective: A Comparative Legal Analysis of the Freedom of Speech* (2006), Professor Ron Krotoszynski, Jr. details the differences between U.S. and Canadian approaches to regulating child pornography.
3. *Overbreadth.* Osborne attacked the Ohio law as "overbroad," but the majority rejected this claim. The overbreadth doctrine permits a defendant in an obscenity (or other) civil or criminal case to argue that although the government could have written a constitutionally permissible law that regulated his conduct, the law *actually on the books* regulates both unlawful *and* constitutionally protected activity. Such a law will discourage people from exercising First Amendment rights for fear of being subject to civil or criminal sanctions. Because of the "chilling effect" of overbroad laws, the federal courts will permit a defendant to seek invalidation of a law even though the materials at issue could be regulated under a more narrowly tailored law. Thus, if a state legislature enacted a statute that purported to ban "dirty books," a defendant selling legally obscene materials could seek invalidation of the law banning "dirty books" in a criminal prosecution under the "dirty books" statute because the law is overbroad (many books not legally obscene could be deemed "dirty"). A separate, but related, doctrine disallows laws regulating speech if they are vague—this is the so-called void for vagueness doctrine. This doctrine permits a person guilty of behavior that could be criminalized to avoid punishment if the law is written so broadly that it does not give reasonable notice of its coverage. Once again, concerns about a "chilling effect" support this doctrine—if people do not know whether speech might be lawful or unlawful, they might choose not to speak, rather than speak and run a risk of criminal punishment. Thus, the overbreadth and vagueness doctrines work to protect persons not parties to the actual litigation at bar, on the theory that a good many would-be plaintiffs, being risk-averse, will simply not test the limits of the law (even though the speech in question would be fully protected constitutionally).

4. *Protecting children from age-inappropriate sexually explicit material.* To what extent can a state government prohibit adults from obtaining sexually explicit materials not appropriate for children? The Supreme Court has held that the First Amendment permits a state to prohibit the sale of materials "obscene as to minors." *See* Ginsberg v. New York, 390 U.S. 629 (1968). New York state adopted and enforced a "criminal obscenity statute which prohibit[ed] the sale to minors . . . of material defined to be obscene on the basis of its appeal to them whether or not it would be obscene to adults." *Id.* at 631. The Supreme Court sustained New York's law because it served as a permissible means of safeguarding parental control over their children's reading habits and also advanced the state's "independent interest in the well-being of its youth." *Id.* at 639-40. Accordingly, the Supreme Court declined to find that "the statute invades the area of freedom of expression constitutionally secured to minors." *Id.* at 637. On the other hand, however, a state government may not generally prohibit the public display and sale of non-obscene, sexually explicit materials to adults because such materials might fall into the hands of minors. *See* Butler v. Michigan, 352 U.S. 380, 383-84 (1957) ("The incidence of this enactment is to reduce the adult population of Michigan to reading only what is fit for children. It thereby arbitrarily curtails one of those liberties of the individual, now enshrined in the Due Process Clause of the Fourteenth Amendment, that history has attested as the indispensable conditions for the maintenance and progress of a free society.").
5. *Pandering and child pornography.* In U.S. v. Williams, 553 U.S. 285 (2008), the Supreme Court upheld a statute, 18 U.S.C. § 2252A, which "criminalizes, in certain specified circumstances, the pandering or solicitation of child pornography." *Id.* at 288. Writing for a 7–2 majority, Justice Antonin Scalia rejected a First Amendment challenge to this statute because "[o]ffers to engage in illegal transactions are categorically excluded from First Amendment protection." *Id.* at 297. The *Williams* majority construed the statute to prohibit solicitation to commit a crime (i.e., an offer to sell unlawful child pornography) and categorically held "that offers to provide or requests to obtain child pornography are categorically excluded from the First Amendment." *Id.* at 299. Under the statute, however, the materials being offered for sale need not actually have been child pornography; merely offering to sell materials so labelled was sufficient to fall within its scope. The Supreme Court previously had sustained a criminal conviction for "pandering" where a seller offered to sell obscene materials—but where the materials being offered for sale were not, in fact, legally obscene. *See* Ginzburg v. U.S., 383 U.S. 463, 467 (1966). *Williams* constitutes an application and extension of *Ginzburg* in the context of pandering child pornography.

THEORY-APPLIED PROBLEM

The actor Daniel Radcliffe, aka "Harry Potter," starred in a very successful production of the play *Equus* on London's West End during the 2007-2008 theater season. At the time, Radcliffe was only 17 years old. The play, as originally written and blocked by author Peter Shaffer, and as performed by Radcliffe, requires Radcliffe's character, the mentally disturbed stable boy Alan Strang, to appear nude for extended periods on stage, to simulate sex with an actress, and to mutilate six horses with a hoof pick in a state of psychosexual ecstasy. The play, since its debut in London in 1973, has received very favorable critical notices (it won the Tony for "Best New Play" after it opened in New York City), and the new production was no exception.

In July 2008, Radcliffe comes to the United States to perform *Equus.* (At this point, he is 18 years old.) To prepare for its Broadway run, the producers book the Taft Theater, in downtown Cincinnati, Ohio, presumably unaware of the local district attorney's long-standing efforts to keep Cincinnati as smut-free as possible. Ohio, like Indiana, maintains a generic statute that prohibits public nudity. *See* Ohio Rev. Code § 2907.09. In relevant part, the law prohibits public "expos[ure] of one's private parts" or "engag[ing] in conduct that to an ordinary observer would appear to be sexual conduct or masturbation." In the production of *Equus*, Radcliffe does both things, causing the district attorney great anxiety. After the play's opening night, the district attorney seeks an injunction ordering the production closed, and indicts Radcliffe for a second-degree misdemeanor. After learning that persons under 18 had attended the performance, the district attorney initiates a felony prosecution against Radcliffe for public nudity. (The law punishes public nudity in front of minors more severely.) Lawyers for the play's producers and Radcliffe file a motion to dismiss, arguing that the injunction and prosecution violate the Free Speech Clause of the First Amendment. How should the Ohio trial court rule? For bonus points, consider whether Radcliffe could lawfully have performed the role of Alan Strang while under the age of 18. Moreover, if a video recording of the 2007 West End production of *Equus* were available commercially, could one legally sell or possess it in the United States?

C. *NEW MEDIA AND SEXUALLY EXPLICIT SPEECH*

Ashcroft v. Free Speech Coalition

535 U.S. 234 (2002)

KENNEDY, J., delivered the opinion of the Court.

We consider in this case whether the Child Pornography Prevention Act of 1996 (CPPA), 18 U.S.C. § 2251 *et seq.*, abridges the freedom of speech. The CPPA extends the federal prohibition against child pornography to sexually explicit images that appear to depict minors but were produced without using any real children. The statute prohibits, in specific circumstances, possessing or distributing these images which may be created by using adults who look like minors or by using computer imaging. The new technology, according to Congress, makes it possible to create realistic images of children who do not exist.

By prohibiting child pornography that does not depict an actual child, the statute goes beyond New York v. Ferber, 458 U.S. 747 (1982), which distinguished child pornography from other sexually explicit speech because of the State's interest in protecting the child exploited by the production process. As a general rule, pornography can be banned only if obscene, but under *Ferber*, pornography showing minors can be proscribed whether or not the images are obscene under the definition set forth in Miller v. California, 413 U.S. 15 (1973). *Ferber* recognized that "[t]he *Miller* standard, like all general definitions of what may be banned as obscene, does not reflect the State's particular and more compelling interest in prosecuting those who promote the sexual exploitation of children." 458 U.S., at 761.

While we have not had occasion to consider the question, we may assume that the apparent age of persons engaged in sexual conduct is relevant to whether a depiction offends community standards. Pictures of young children engaged in certain acts might be obscene where similar depictions of adults, or perhaps even older adolescents, would not. The CPPA, however, is not directed at speech that is obscene; Congress has proscribed those materials through a separate statute. 18 U.S.C. §§ 1460-1466. Like the law in *Ferber*, the CPPA seeks to reach beyond obscenity, and it makes no attempt to conform to the *Miller* standard. For instance, the statute would reach visual depictions, such as movies, even if they have redeeming social value.

The principal question to be resolved, then, is whether the CPPA is constitutional where it proscribes a significant universe of speech that is neither obscene under *Miller* nor child pornography under *Ferber*.

Before 1996, Congress defined child pornography as the type of depictions at issue in *Ferber*, images made using actual minors. 18 U.S.C. § 2252 (1994 ed.). The CPPA retains that prohibition at 18 U.S.C. § 2256(8)(A) and adds three other prohibited categories of speech, of which the first, § 2256(8)(B), and the third, § 2256(8)(D), are at issue in this case. Section 2256(8)(B) prohibits "any visual depiction, including any photograph, film, video, picture, or computer or computer-generated image or picture," that "is, or appears to be, of a minor engaging in sexually explicit conduct." The prohibition on "any visual depiction" does not depend at all on how the image is produced. The section captures a range of depictions, sometimes called "virtual child pornography," which include computer-generated images, as well as images produced by more traditional means. For instance, the literal terms of the statute embrace a Renaissance painting depicting a scene from classical mythology, a "picture" that "appears to be, of a minor engaging in sexually explicit conduct." The statute also prohibits Hollywood movies, filmed without any child actors, if a jury believes an actor "appears to be" a minor engaging in "actual or simulated . . . sexual intercourse." § 2256(2).

These images do not involve, let alone harm, any children in the production process; but Congress decided the materials threaten children in other, less direct, ways. Pedophiles might use the materials to encourage children to participate in sexual activity. . . .

In addition, Congress identified another problem created by computer-generated images: Their existence can make it harder to prosecute pornographers who do use real minors. As imaging technology improves, Congress found, it becomes more difficult to prove that a particular picture was produced using actual children. To ensure that defendants possessing child pornography using real minors cannot evade prosecution, Congress extended the ban to virtual child pornography.

Section 2256(8)(C) prohibits a more common and lower tech means of creating virtual images, known as computer morphing. Rather than creating original images, pornographers can alter innocent pictures of real children so that the children appear to be engaged in sexual activity. Although morphed images may fall within the definition of virtual child pornography, they implicate the interests of real children and are in that sense closer to the images in *Ferber.* Respondents do not challenge this provision, and we do not consider it.

Respondents do challenge § 2256(8)(D). Like the text of the "appears to be" provision, the sweep of this provision is quite broad. Section 2256(8)(D) defines child pornography to include any sexually explicit image that was "advertised, promoted, presented, described, or distributed in such a manner that conveys the impression" it depicts "a minor engaging in sexually explicit conduct." One Committee Report identified the provision as directed at sexually explicit images pandered as child pornography. *See* S. Rep. No. 104-358, p. 22 (1996) ("This provision prevents child pornographers and pedophiles from exploiting prurient interests in child sexuality and sexual activity through the production or distribution of pornographic material which is intentionally pandered as child pornography"). The statute is not so limited in its reach, however, as it punishes even those possessors who took no part in pandering. Once a work has been described as child pornography, the taint remains on the speech in the hands of subsequent possessors, making possession unlawful even though the content otherwise would not be objectionable.

Fearing that the CPPA threatened the activities of its members, respondent Free Speech Coalition and others challenged the statute in the United States District Court for the Northern District of California. The Coalition, a California trade association for the adult-entertainment industry, alleged that its members did not use minors in their sexually explicit works, but they believed some of these materials might fall within the CPPA's expanded definition of child pornography. . . . The District Court disagreed [with the plaintiffs' First Amendment objections to the CPPA] and granted summary judgment to the Government. . . .

The Court of Appeals for the Ninth Circuit reversed. The court reasoned that the Government could not prohibit speech because of its tendency to persuade viewers to commit illegal acts. The court held the CPPA to be substantially overbroad because it bans materials that are neither obscene nor produced by the exploitation of real children as in *New York v. Ferber*, 458 U.S. 747 (1982).

While the Ninth Circuit found the CPPA invalid on its face, four other Courts of Appeals have sustained it. . . . We granted certiorari.

The First Amendment commands, "Congress shall make no law abridging the freedom of speech." The government may violate this mandate in many ways, *e.g.*, Rosenberger v. Rector and Visitors of Univ. of Va., 515 U.S. 819 (1995); Keller v. State Bar of Cal., 496 U.S. 1 (1990), but a law imposing criminal penalties on protected speech is a stark example of speech suppression. The CPPA's penalties are indeed severe. A first offender may be imprisoned for 15 years. § 2252A(b)(1). A repeat offender faces a prison sentence of not less than 5 years and not more than 30 years in prison. *Ibid.* While even minor punishments can chill protected speech, see Wooley v. Maynard, 430 U.S. 705 (1977), this case provides a textbook example of why we permit facial challenges to statutes that burden expression. With these severe penalties in force, few legitimate movie producers or book publishers, or few other speakers in any capacity, would risk distributing images in or near the uncertain reach of this law. The Constitution gives significant protection from overbroad laws that chill speech within the First Amendment's vast and privileged sphere.

Under this principle, the CPPA is unconstitutional on its face if it prohibits a substantial amount of protected expression. *See* Broadrick v. Oklahoma, 413 U.S. 601, 612 (1973). . . .

Congress may pass valid laws to protect children from abuse, and it has. *E.g.*, 18 U.S.C. §§ 2241, 2251. The prospect of crime, however, by itself does not justify laws suppressing protected speech. *See* Kingsley Int'l Pictures Corp. v. Regents of Univ. of N.Y., 360 U.S. 684, 689 (1959) ("Among free men, the deterrents ordinarily to be applied to prevent crime are education and punishment for violations of the law, not abridgment of the rights of free speech" (internal quotation marks and citation omitted)). It is also well established that speech may not be prohibited because it concerns subjects offending our sensibilities.

As a general principle, the First Amendment bars the government from dictating what we see or read or speak or hear. The freedom of speech has its limits; it does not embrace certain categories of speech, including defamation, incitement, obscenity, and pornography produced with real children. *See* Simon & Schuster, Inc. v. Members of N.Y. State Crime Victims Bd., 502 U.S. 105, 127 (1991) (Kennedy, J., concurring). While these categories may be prohibited without violating the First Amendment, none of them includes the speech prohibited by the CPPA. In his dissent from the opinion of the Court of Appeals, Judge Ferguson recognized this to be the law and proposed that virtual child pornography should be regarded as an additional category of unprotected speech. [] It would be necessary for us to take this step to uphold the statute.

As we have noted, the CPPA is much more than a supplement to the existing federal prohibition on obscenity. Under Miller v. California, 413 U.S. 15 (1973), the Government must prove that the work, taken as a whole, appeals to the prurient interest, is patently offensive in light of community standards, and lacks serious literary, artistic, political, or scientific value. [] The CPPA, however, extends to images that appear to depict a minor engaging in sexually explicit activity without regard to the *Miller* requirements. The materials need not appeal to the prurient interest. Any depiction of sexually explicit activity, no matter how it is presented, is proscribed. The CPPA applies to a picture in a psychology manual, as well as a movie depicting the horrors of sexual abuse. It is not necessary, moreover, that the image be patently offensive. Pictures of what appear to be 17-year-olds engaging in sexually explicit activity do not in every case contravene community standards.

The CPPA prohibits speech despite its serious literary, artistic, political, or scientific value. The statute proscribes the visual depiction of an idea—that of teenagers engaging in sexual activity—that is a fact of modern society and has been a theme in art and literature throughout the ages. Under the CPPA, images are prohibited so long as the persons appear to be under 18 years of age. 18 U.S.C. § 2256(1). This is higher than the legal age for marriage in many States, as well as the age at which persons may consent to sexual relations. It is, of course, undeniable that some youths engage in sexual activity before the legal age, either on their own inclination or because they are victims of sexual abuse.

Both themes—teenage sexual activity and the sexual abuse of children—have inspired countless literary works. William Shakespeare created the most famous pair of teenage lovers, one of whom is just 13 years of age. See Romeo and Juliet, act I, sc. 2, l. 9 ("She hath not seen the change of fourteen years"). In the drama, Shakespeare portrays the relationship as something splendid and innocent, but not juvenile. The work has inspired no less than 40 motion pictures, some of which suggest that the teenagers consummated their relationship. *E.g.*, Romeo and Juliet (B. Luhrmann director, 1996). Shakespeare may not have written sexually explicit scenes for the Elizabethan audience, but were modern directors to adopt a less conventional approach, that fact alone would not compel the conclusion that the work was obscene.

Contemporary movies pursue similar themes. Last year's Academy Awards featured the movie, Traffic, which was nominated for Best Picture. See Predictable and Less So, the Academy Award Contenders, N.Y. Times, Feb. 14, 2001, p. E11. The film portrays a teenager, identified as a 16-year-old, who becomes addicted to drugs. The viewer sees the degradation of her addiction, which in the end leads her to a filthy room to trade sex for drugs. The year before, American Beauty won the Academy Award for Best Picture. *See "American Beauty" Tops the Oscars*, N.Y. Times, Mar. 27, 2000, p. E1. In the course of the movie, a teenage girl engages in sexual relations with her teenage boyfriend, and another yields herself to the gratification of a middle-aged man. The film also contains a scene where, although the movie audience understands the act is not taking place, one character believes he is watching a teenage boy performing a sexual act on an older man.

Our society, like other cultures, has empathy and enduring fascination with the lives and destinies of the young. Art and literature express the vital interest we all have in the formative years we ourselves once knew, when wounds can be so grievous, disappointment so profound, and mistaken choices so tragic, but when moral acts and self-fulfillment are still in reach. Whether or not the films we mention violate the CPPA, they explore themes within the wide sweep of the statute's prohibitions. If these films, or hundreds of others of lesser note that explore those subjects, contain a single graphic depiction of sexual activity within the statutory definition, the possessor of the film would be subject to severe punishment without inquiry into the work's redeeming value. This is inconsistent with an essential First Amendment rule: The artistic merit of a work does not depend on the presence of a single explicit scene. *See* Book Named "John Cleland's Memoirs of a Woman of Pleasure" v. Attorney General of Mass., 383 U.S. 413, 419 (1966) (plurality opinion) ("[T]he social value of the book can neither be weighed against nor canceled by its prurient appeal or patent offensiveness"). Under *Miller*, the First Amendment requires that redeeming value be judged by considering the work as a whole. Where the scene is part of the narrative, the work itself does not for this reason become obscene, even though the scene in isolation might be offensive. *See* Kois v. Wisconsin, 408 U.S. 229, 231 (1972) (*per curiam*). For this reason, and the others we have noted, the CPPA cannot be read to prohibit obscenity, because it lacks the required link between its prohibitions and the affront to community standards prohibited by the definition of obscenity.

In contrast to the speech in *Ferber*, speech that itself is the record of sexual abuse, the CPPA prohibits speech that records no crime and creates no victims by its production. Virtual child pornography is not "intrinsically related" to the sexual abuse of children, as were the materials in *Ferber*. 458 U.S. at 759. While the government asserts that the images can lead to actual instances of child abuse, see *infra*, at 251-254, the causal link is contingent and indirect. The harm does not necessarily follow from the speech, but depends upon some unquantified potential for subsequent criminal acts. . . .

The CPPA, for reasons we have explored, is inconsistent with *Miller* and finds no support in *Ferber.* The Government seeks to justify its prohibitions in other ways. It argues that the CPPA is necessary because pedophiles may use virtual child pornography to seduce children. There are many things innocent in themselves, however, such as cartoons, video games, and candy, that might be used for immoral purposes, yet we would not expect those to be prohibited because they can be misused. The Government, of course, may punish adults who provide unsuitable materials to children, see Ginsberg v. New York, 390 U.S. 629 (1968), and it may enforce criminal penalties for unlawful solicitation. The precedents establish, however, that speech within the rights of adults to hear may not be silenced completely in an attempt to shield children from it. . . .

Here, the Government wants to keep speech from children not to protect them from its content but to protect them from those who would commit other crimes. The principle, however, remains the same: The Government cannot ban speech fit for adults simply because it may fall into the hands of children. The evil in question depends upon the actor's unlawful conduct, conduct defined as criminal quite apart from any link to the speech in question. This establishes that the speech ban is not narrowly drawn. The objective is to prohibit illegal conduct, but this restriction goes well beyond that interest by restricting the speech available to law-abiding adults.

The Government submits further that virtual child pornography whets the appetites of pedophiles and encourages them to engage in illegal conduct. This rationale cannot sustain the provision in question. The mere tendency of speech to encourage unlawful acts is not a sufficient reason for banning it. The government "cannot constitutionally premise legislation on the desirability of controlling a person's private thoughts." Stanley v. Georgia, 394 U.S. 557, 566 (1969). First Amendment freedoms are most in danger when the government seeks to control thought or to justify its laws for that impermissible end. The right to think is the beginning of freedom, and speech must be protected from the government because speech is the beginning of thought.

To preserve these freedoms, and to protect speech for its own sake, the Court's First Amendment cases draw vital distinctions between words and deeds, between ideas and conduct. The government may not prohibit speech because it increases the chance an unlawful act will be committed "at some indefinite future time." Hess v. Indiana, 414 U.S. 105, 108 (1973) (*per curiam*). The government may suppress speech for advocating the use of force or a violation of law only if "such advocacy is directed to inciting or producing imminent lawless action and is likely to incite or produce such action." Brandenburg v. Ohio, 395 U.S. 444, 447 (1969) (*per curiam*). There is here no attempt, incitement, solicitation, or conspiracy. The Government has shown no more than a remote connection between speech that might encourage thoughts or impulses and any resulting child abuse. Without a significantly stronger, more direct connection, the Government may not prohibit speech on the ground that it may encourage pedophiles to engage in illegal conduct.

The Government next argues that its objective of eliminating the market for pornography produced using real children necessitates a prohibition on virtual images as well. Virtual images, the Government contends, are indistinguishable from real ones; they are part of the same market and are often exchanged. In this way, it is said, virtual images promote the trafficking in works produced through the exploitation of real children. The hypothesis is somewhat implausible. If virtual images were identical to illegal child pornography, the illegal images would be driven from the market by the indistinguishable substitutes. Few pornographers would risk prosecution by abusing real children if fictional, computerized images would suffice.

In the case of the material covered by *Ferber*, the creation of the speech is itself the crime of child abuse; the prohibition deters the crime by removing the profit motive. See *Osborne*, 495 U.S., at 109-110. Even where there is an underlying crime, however, the Court has not allowed the suppression of speech in all cases. *E.g.*, *Bartnicki, supra* [Bartnicki v. Vopper, 532 U.S. 514,] 529 [(2001)] (market deterrence would not justify law prohibiting a radio commentator from distributing speech that had been unlawfully intercepted). We need not consider where to strike the balance in this case, because here, there is no underlying crime at all. Even if the Government's market deterrence theory were persuasive in some contexts, it would not justify this statute.

Finally, the Government says that the possibility of producing images by using computer imaging makes it very difficult for it to prosecute those who produce pornography by using real children. Experts, we are told, may have difficulty in saying whether the pictures were made by using real children or by using computer imaging. The necessary solution, the argument runs, is to prohibit both kinds of images. The argument, in essence, is that protected speech may be banned as a means to ban unprotected speech. This analysis turns the First Amendment upside down.

The Government may not suppress lawful speech as the means to suppress unlawful speech. Protected speech does not become unprotected merely because it resembles the latter. The Constitution requires the reverse. "[T]he possible harm to society in permitting some unprotected speech to go unpunished is outweighed by the possibility that protected speech of others may be muted. . . ." Broadrick v. Oklahoma, 413 U.S., at 612. The overbreadth doctrine prohibits the Government from banning unprotected speech if a substantial amount of protected speech is prohibited or chilled in the process. . . .

In sum, § 2256(8)(B) covers materials beyond the categories recognized in *Ferber* and *Miller*, and the reasons the Government offers in support of limiting the freedom of speech have no justification in our precedents or in the law of the First Amendment. The provision abridges the freedom to engage in a substantial amount of lawful speech. For this reason, it is overbroad and unconstitutional.

Respondents challenge § 2256(8)(D) as well. This provision bans depictions of sexually explicit conduct that are "advertised, promoted, presented, described, or distributed in such a manner that conveys the impression that the material is or contains a visual depiction of a minor engaging in sexually explicit conduct." The parties treat the section as nearly identical to the provision prohibiting materials that appear to be child pornography. In the Government's view, the difference between the two is that "the 'conveys the impression' provision requires the jury to assess the material at issue in light of the manner in which it is promoted." Brief for Petitioners 18, n.3. The Government's assumption, however, is that the determination would still depend principally upon the content of the prohibited work.

We disagree with this view. The CPPA prohibits sexually explicit materials that "conve[y] the impression" they depict minors. While that phrase may sound like the "appears to be" prohibition in § 2256(8)(B), it requires little judgment about the content of the image. Under § 2256(8)(D), the work must be sexually explicit, but otherwise the content is irrelevant. Even if a film contains no sexually explicit scenes involving minors, it could be treated as child pornography if the title and trailers convey the impression that the scenes would be found in the movie. The determination turns on how the speech is presented, not on what is depicted. While the legislative findings address at length the problems posed by materials that look like child pornography, they are silent on the evils posed by images simply pandered that way.

The Government does not offer a serious defense of this provision, and the other arguments it makes in support of the CPPA do not bear on § 2256(8)(D). The materials, for instance, are not likely to be confused for child pornography in a criminal trial. The Court has recognized that pandering may be relevant, as an evidentiary matter, to the question whether particular materials are obscene. *See* Ginzburg v. United States, 383 U.S. 463, 474 (1966) ("[I]n close cases evidence of pandering may be probative with respect to the nature of the material in question and thus satisfy the [obscenity] test"). Where a defendant engages in the "commercial exploitation of erotica solely for the sake of their prurient appeal," *id.*, at 466, the context he or she creates may itself be relevant to the evaluation of the materials.

Section 2256(8)(D), however, prohibits a substantial amount of speech that falls outside *Ginzburg*'s rationale. Materials falling within the proscription are tainted and unlawful in the hands of all who receive it, though they bear no responsibility for how it was marketed, sold, or described. The statute, furthermore, does not require that the context be part of an effort at "commercial exploitation." *Ibid.* As a consequence, the CPPA does more than prohibit pandering. It prohibits possession of material described, or pandered, as child pornography by someone earlier in the distribution chain. The provision prohibits a sexually explicit film containing no youthful actors, just because it is placed in a box suggesting a prohibited movie. Possession is a crime even when the possessor knows the movie was mislabeled. The First Amendment requires a more precise restriction. For this reason, § 2256(8)(D) is substantially overbroad and in violation of the First Amendment.

For the reasons we have set forth, the prohibitions of § 2256(8)(B) and 2256(8)(D) are overbroad and unconstitutional. Having reached this conclusion, we need not address respondents' further contention that the provisions are unconstitutional because of vague statutory language.

The judgment of the Court of Appeals is

Affirmed.

THOMAS, J., concurring in the judgment.

In my view, the Government's most persuasive asserted interest in support of the Child Pornography Prevention Act of 1996 (CPPA), 18 U.S.C. § 2251 *et seq.*, is the prosecution rationale—that persons who possess and disseminate pornographic images of real children may escape conviction by claiming that the images are computer generated, thereby raising a reasonable doubt as to their guilt. At this time, however, the Government asserts only that defendants *raise* such defenses, not that they have done so successfully. In fact, the Government points to no case in which a defendant has been acquitted based on a "computer-generated images" defense. While this speculative interest cannot support the broad reach of the CPPA, technology may evolve to the point where it becomes impossible to enforce actual child pornography laws because the Government cannot prove that certain pornographic images are of real children. In the event this occurs, the Government should not be foreclosed from enacting a regulation of virtual child pornography that contains an appropriate affirmative defense or some other narrowly drawn restriction.

O'CONNOR, J., with whom THE CHIEF JUSTICE and SCALIA, J., join as to Part II, concurring in the judgment in part and dissenting in part.

This litigation involves a facial challenge to the CPPA's prohibitions of pornographic images that "appea[r] to be of a minor" and of material that "conveys the impression" that it contains pornographic images of minors. While I agree with the Court's judgment that the First Amendment requires that the latter prohibition be struck down, I disagree with its decision to strike down the former prohibition in its entirety. The "appears to be of a minor" language in § 2256(8)(B) covers two categories of speech: pornographic images of adults that look like children ("youthful adult pornography") and pornographic images of children created wholly on a computer, without using any actual children ("virtual child pornography"). The Court concludes, correctly, that the CPPA's ban on youthful adult pornography is overbroad. In my view, however, respondents fail to present sufficient evidence to demonstrate that the ban on virtual child pornography is overbroad. Because invalidation due to overbreadth is such "strong medicine," Broadrick v. Oklahoma, 413 U.S. 601, 613 (1973), I would strike down the prohibition of pornography that "appears to be" of minors only insofar as it is applied to the class of youthful adult pornography. . . .

REHNQUIST, C.J., with whom SCALIA, J., joins in part, dissenting.

Congress has a compelling interest in ensuring the ability to enforce prohibitions of actual child pornography, and we should defer to its findings that rapidly advancing technology soon will make it all but impossible to do so. Turner Broadcasting System, Inc. v. FCC, 520 U.S. 180, 195 (1997) (we "'accord substantial deference to the predictive judgments of Congress'" in First Amendment cases). . . .

NOTES AND QUESTIONS

1. *Balancing freedom of speech and the government's interest in preventing the exploitation of children.* The free speech interest of adults in access to materials suitable for adults, but not children, evidently prohibits Congress from attempting to protect minors from sexual exploitation by banning "virtual" pornography or material featuring "youthful"-looking actors. Should government be permitted to favor the protection of minors from sexual exploitation over the speech interests of adults? *See* Butler v. Michigan, *supra* p. 618.
2. Romeo and Juliet *as child photography?* On the other hand, Justice Kennedy has a point, doesn't he? Should *Romeo and Juliet*, whether in print or film format, be banned as child pornography if it doesn't feature any real children in its production? In other words, should governmental efforts to protect minors from sexual exploitation be limited to direct regulation of unlawful sex acts, as opposed to regulating speech that might trigger such acts?

3. *Virtual child pornography and enhanced risks to children.* Do computer-generated images not implicate the government's interest in avoiding the creation of a market for child pornography? Recall that in both *Ferber* (*supra* p. 608) and *Osborne* (*supra* p. 615) the Supreme Court credited the government's interest in avoiding the creation of demand for child pornography. Is Justice Kennedy correct to conclude that "virtual" child pornography does not seriously implicate the government's interest in protecting kids from sexual exploitation? Or is Justice O'Connor's position on this question more persuasive?
4. *Self-created sexually explicit images of minors or "sexting."* Should the law distinguish between self-created images of minors engaged in lawful sexual activity and images created by adults for an adult audience? Or does the existence of a sexually explicit photograph of a minor, even if self-created, help to sustain an unlawful, and inherently exploitative, media market in such images? Some state prosecutors have brought child pornography charges against minors who send their peers sexually explicit photographs or "sexts." Erik Eckholm, *Prosecutors Weigh Teenage Sexting: Folly or Felony?*, N.Y. Times, Nov. 14, 2015, at A13 (reporting on a North Carolina case in which local prosecutors "charged the two teenagers with the felony of 'exploiting a minor,' which could have brought them years in prison and decades on the sex offender registry, for privately sharing images of themselves"); *see* Deborah Ahrens, *Schools, Cyberbullies, and the Surveillance State*, 49 Am. Crim. L. Rev. 1669, 1692 (2012) ("While such behavior [sexting] has possible poor outcomes for adults, including public embarrassment and humiliation, minors who transmit sexually-explicit images to one another, including nude pictures of themselves, may face criminal prosecution for offenses such as disseminating child pornography."). Around 20 states have adopted laws regulating sexting by minors among their peers. However, virtually all 50 states maintain and enforce child pornography laws that could be applied to peer-to-peer sexting. For a relevant discussion and comparative law treatment of teen sexting, see Joanne Sweeney, *Sexting and Freedom of Expression: A Comparative Approach*, 102 Ky. L.J. 103 (2013). For an extended argument that sexting between consenting teens should not be subject to criminal sanctions and should instead constitute protected speech activity, see Joanna R. Lampe, Note, *A Victimless Sex Crime: The Case for Decriminalizing Consensual Teen Sexting*, 46 U. Mich. J.L. Reform 703 (2013).
5. *Sexting as protected speech activity.* The Supreme Court of Canada, in R. v. Sharpe, [2001] 1 S.C.R. 45 (Can.), narrowly construed a federal statute proscribing child pornography to exclude self-created images not intended for commercial distribution. Writing for the majority, Chief Justice Beverley McLachlin explained that:

> Private journals, diaries, writings, drawings and other works of the imagination, created by oneself exclusively for oneself, may all trigger the s. 163.1(4) offence. The law, in its prohibition on the possession of such materials, reaches into a realm of exceedingly private expression, where s. 2(b) values may be

> particularly implicated and state intervention may be markedly more intrusive. Further, the risk of harm arising from the private creation and possession of such materials, while not eliminated altogether, is low.

Id. at para. 75. Moreover, "[p]ossession of such materials may implicate the values of self-fulfilment and self-actualization. and therefore . . . reside near the heart of the s. 2(b) guarantee." *Id.* at para. 77. The *Sharpe* Court invalidated section 163.1 insofar as it applied to "self-created expressive material" and "private recordings of lawful sexual activity." *Id.* at para. 115. Thus, Canadian free speech law reflects the view that if minors are old enough lawfully to engage in sexual activity, they are also entitled to create and possess records, including visual records, of such activity.

AN EXTENDED NOTE ON "CHILDPROOFING" THE INTERNET

As a general matter, government efforts to protect children from age-inappropriate materials on the internet cannot encompass regulations that effectively silence speech appropriate for adults. To be sure, obscene communications do not enjoy any special legal privilege simply because many such communications happen to occur over the Web. Similarly, laws against presenting nude pictures of minors apply with full force to the internet. Even so, the Supreme Court has been vigilant in protecting the rights of adults to access noncommercial internet sites, even if those sites contain materials that are inappropriate (perhaps even obscene) as to minors. Thus, legislators may not restrict internet content solely to material fit for children. Reno v. American Civil Liberties Union, 521 U.S. 844 (1997); Ashcroft v. ACLU, 535 U.S. 564 (2002) ("Ashcroft I"); Ashcroft v. ACLU ("Ashcroft II"), 542 U.S. 656 (2004). For further discussion, see *supra* Chapter 8.

Even though the Supreme Court will not accept blanket efforts to childproof the internet (*see Ashcroft*, 542 U.S. at 670-673; *Reno*, 521 U.S. at 867-870, 874-879), there is good cause to believe that a majority of the Justices might accept narrowly tailored, carefully drawn statutes that require good-faith efforts by Webmasters to limit or block access by minors, at least when and if technologies facilitating such blocking can be deployed without significant cost or technical difficulty. Thus, a statute requiring a site visitor to check a box indicating that she is 18 years old or older would likely pass constitutional muster—implementing an age check box would impose little cost and might have some deterrent effect. For a discussion of these issues and the relevant Supreme Court cases addressing them, see Ronald J. Krotoszynski, Jr., *Childproofing the Internet*, 41 Brandeis L.J. 447 (2003).

THEORY-APPLIED PROBLEM: SEXTING AND CYBERSTALKING

"Sexting" describes the practice of sending sexually explicit materials, images, or videos as a text message over a mobile phone. In 2011, two teen girls created a photo, purportedly of a classmate, by pasting a picture of the classmate's head on the picture of a nude body. They posted the "fake" nude photo of their classmate on a Facebook page accessible to most of their high school friends. A prosecutor charged the teens with aggravated stalking, or cyberstalking. *See* Nina Mandell, *Florida Girls in Trouble with Police After Creating Lewd Fake Facebook Profile for Classmate,* N.Y. Daily News, available at http://articles.nydailynews.com/2011-01-14/news/27087490_1_facebook-page-illinois-mother-florida-girls. "Cyberstalking" is defined by state statute as the use of e-mail or other electronic channels to communicate words, images, or language to a specific person, repeatedly, to serve no legitimate purpose, and that causes the person "substantial emotional distress." Fla. Stat. § 784.048 (2010). When one "willfully, maliciously, and repeatedly" cyberstalks another, he or she can be charged with a misdemeanor offense, though the offense becomes a felony when the target is under age 16. If the harassment includes a threat intended to create reasonable fear of bodily injury to the victim or to the victim's family, the crime becomes aggravated stalking. Does this law, as applied to the two teens who created the fake nude photo, violate the First Amendment? See also Miller v. Mitchell, 598 F.3d 139 (3d Cir. 2010), a case in which prosecutors threatened to charge teens with distributing child pornography after they texted explicit images of themselves to "consenting" minors. Does this violate the First Amendment?

CHAPTER 12

THE GOVERNMENT AS SPEAKER, EMPLOYER, AND EDUCATOR

TABLE OF CONTENTS

A. Government-Subsidized Speech and Government Speech
B. Speech by Government Employees
C. Public Schools and Libraries

Previous chapters have dealt with First Amendment principles triggered by government regulations of private speech. This chapter addresses the First Amendment principles that apply when the government subsidizes or finances speech, restricts the speech of its employees or contractors, or imposes regulations on expression in government institutions such as public schools or libraries.

For many years courts took the position that the First Amendment offers no protection to a speaker who violates a condition on the receipt of government funds. When Oliver Wendell Holmes was a Justice on the Massachusetts Supreme Judicial Court in the late nineteenth century, for example, he wrote a famous opinion in which he upheld the firing of a policeman who had violated limitations on political activity in his contract. McAuliffe v. Mayor of New Bedford, 29 N.E. 517 (Mass. 1892). "The petitioner may have a constitutional right to talk politics," Holmes wrote, "but he has no constitutional right to be a policeman." Holmes noted that in the public sphere, as in private employment, the employee "takes the employment on the terms which are offered him." Prior to the twentieth century, the courts' tendency to equate public and private authority to restrict the speech of employees coincided with similarly broad assumptions about the ability of both public and private entities to restrict speech on the property they controlled. *See* Commonwealth v. Davis, 39 N.E. 113, 113 (Mass. 1895), *aff'd*, 167 U.S. 43 (1897) ("For the Legislature absolutely or conditionally to forbid public speaking in a highway or public park is no more an infringement of the rights of a member of the public than for the owner of a private house to forbid it in his house.").As we saw in Chapter 4, the Supreme Court long ago abandoned the notion that the government has the same authority as a private entity to prohibit speech on its property. *See Hague v. CIO, supra* p. 176. As the materials in this chapter will illustrate, the Court has also abandoned the notion that the government has unfettered authority to restrict speech in other contexts involving government financing, including public employment. Unfortunately, the Court has been both less consistent and less clear about the rules constraining the government in these contexts than it has in the public forum area. This chapter attempts to provide some structure to these cases by subdividing the cases into three broad categories: general government subsidies of expression, limitations on the expression of government employees, and restrictions on expression in public schools and libraries. Keep in mind, however, that these categories are somewhat arbitrary, and many cases have elements that fall into several different categories. The Court's jurisprudence in this area is very much a work in progress, and the only definitive statement that can be made is that the First Amendment now limits the extent to which the government can control the content of a speaker's expression, even if the government has paid the speaker.

A. *GOVERNMENT-SUBSIDIZED SPEECH AND GOVERNMENT SPEECH*

Rust v. Sullivan

500 U.S. 173 (1991)

Rehnquist, C.J., delivered the opinion of the Court.

In 1970, Congress enacted Title X of the Public Health Service Act (Act), which provides federal funding for family planning services. The Act authorizes the Secretary to "make grants to and enter into contracts with public or nonprofit private entities to assist in the establishment and operation of voluntary family planning projects which shall offer a broad range of acceptable and effective family planning methods and services." Grants and contracts under Title X must "be made in accordance with such regulations as the Secretary may promulgate."

In 1988, the Secretary promulgated new regulations designed to provide "'clear and operational guidance' to grantees about how to preserve the distinction between Title X programs and abortion as a method of family planning." The regulations attach three principal conditions on the grant of federal funds for Title X projects. First, the regulations specify that a "Title X project may not provide counseling concerning the use of abortion as a method of family planning or provide referral for abortion as a method of family planning." The Title X project is expressly prohibited from referring a pregnant woman to an abortion provider, even upon specific request. One permissible response to such an inquiry is that "the project does not consider abortion an appropriate method of family planning, and therefore does not counsel or refer for abortion." Second, the regulations broadly prohibit a Title X project from engaging in activities that "encourage, promote or advocate abortion as a method of family planning." Forbidden activities include lobbying for legislation that would increase the availability of abortion as a method of family planning, developing or disseminating materials advocating abortion as a method of family planning, providing speakers to promote abortion as a method of family planning, using legal action to make abortion available in any way as a method of family planning, and paying dues to any group that advocates abortion as a method of family planning as a substantial part of its activities. Third, the regulations require that Title X projects be organized so that they are "physically and financially separate" from prohibited abortion activities.

Petitioners are Title X grantees and doctors who supervise Title X funds suing on behalf of themselves and their patients. Petitioners contend that the regulations violate the First Amendment by impermissibly discriminating based on viewpoint because they prohibit "all discussion about abortion as a lawful option—including counseling, referral, and the provision of neutral and accurate information about ending a pregnancy—while compelling the clinic or counselor to provide information that promotes continuing a pregnancy to term."

There is no question but that the statutory prohibition [on speech favoring abortion] is constitutional. The Government can, without violating the Constitution, selectively fund a program to encourage certain activities it believes to be in the public interest, without at the same time funding an alternate program which seeks to deal with the problem in another way. In so doing, the Government has not discriminated on the basis of viewpoint; it has merely chosen to fund one activity to the exclusion of the other. "[A] legislature's decision not to subsidize the exercise of a fundamental right does not infringe the right."

The challenged regulations implement the statutory prohibition by prohibiting counseling, referral, and the provision of information regarding abortion as a method of family planning. They are designed to ensure that the limits of the federal program are observed. The Title X program is designed not for prenatal care, but to encourage family planning. A doctor who wished to offer prenatal care to a project patient who became pregnant could properly be prohibited from doing so because such service is outside the scope of the federally funded program. The regulations prohibiting abortion counseling and referral are of the same ilk; "no funds appropriated for the project may be used in programs where abortion is a method of family planning," and a doctor employed by the project may be prohibited in the course of his project duties from counseling abortion or referring for abortion. This is not a case of the Government "suppressing a dangerous idea," but of a prohibition on a project grantee or its employees from engaging in activities outside of the project's scope.

By requiring that the Title X grantee engage in abortion-related activity separately from activity receiving federal funding, Congress has, consistent with our teachings in *League of Women Voters* and *Regan*, not denied it the right to engage in abortion-related activities. Congress has merely refused to fund such activities out of the public fisc, and the Secretary has simply required a certain degree of separation from the Title X project in order to ensure the integrity of the federally funded program.

The same principles apply to petitioners' claim that the regulations abridge the free speech rights of the grantee's staff. Individuals who are voluntarily employed for a Title X project must perform their duties in accordance with the regulation's restrictions on abortion counseling and referral. The employees remain free, however, to pursue abortion-related activities when they are not acting under the auspices of the Title X project. The regulations, which govern solely the scope of the Title X project's activities, do not in any way restrict the activities of those persons acting as private individuals. The employees' freedom of expression is limited during the time that they actually work for the project; but this limitation is a consequence of their decision to accept employment in a project, the scope of which is permissibly restricted by the funding authority.

This is not to suggest that funding by the Government, even when coupled with the freedom of the fund recipients to speak outside the scope of the Government-funded project, is invariably sufficient to justify government control over the content of expression. For example, this Court has recognized that the existence of a Government "subsidy," in the form of Government-owned property, does not justify the restriction of speech in areas that have "been traditionally open to the public for expressive activity," or have been "expressly dedicated to speech activity." Similarly, we have recognized that the university is a traditional sphere of free expression so fundamental to the functioning of our society that the Government's ability to control speech within that sphere by means of conditions attached to the expenditure of Government funds is restricted by the vagueness and overbreadth doctrines of the First Amendment. It could be argued by analogy that traditional relationships such as that between doctor and patient should enjoy protection under the First Amendment from government regulation, even when subsidized by the Government. We need not resolve that question here, however, because the Title X program regulations do not significantly impinge upon the doctor-patient relationship. Nothing in them requires a doctor to represent as his own any opinion that he does not in fact hold. Nor is the doctor-patient relationship established by the Title X program sufficiently all-encompassing so as to justify an expectation on the part of the patient of comprehensive medical advice. The program does not provide postconception medical care, and therefore a doctor's silence with regard to abortion cannot reasonably be thought to mislead a client into thinking that the doctor does not consider abortion an appropriate option for her. The doctor is always free to make clear that advice regarding abortion is simply beyond the scope of the program. In these circumstances, the general rule that the Government may choose not to subsidize speech applies with full force.

BLACKMUN, J., dissenting, with whom MARSHALL, J., joins, and with whom STEVENS, J., and O'CONNOR, J., join in part.

It cannot seriously be disputed that the counseling and referral provisions at issue in the present cases constitute content-based regulation of speech. Title X grantees may provide counseling and referral regarding any of a wide range of family planning and other topics, save abortion.

The Regulations are also clearly viewpoint-based. While suppressing speech favorable to abortion with one hand, the Secretary compels anti-abortion speech with the other. For example, the Department of Health and Human Services' own description of the Regulations makes plain that "Title X projects are required to facilitate access to prenatal care and social services, including adoption services, that might be needed by the pregnant client to promote her wellbeing and that of her child, while making it abundantly clear that the project is not permitted to promote abortion by facilitating access to abortion through the referral process."

Moreover, the Regulations command that a project refer for prenatal care each woman diagnosed as pregnant, irrespective of the woman's expressed desire to continue or terminate her pregnancy. If a client asks directly about abortion, a Title X physician or counselor is required to say, in essence, that the project does not consider abortion to be an appropriate method of family planning. Both requirements are antithetical to the First Amendment.

The Regulations pertaining to "advocacy" are even more explicitly viewpoint-based. These provide: "A Title X project may not encourage, promote or advocate abortion as a method of family planning." They explain: "This requirement prohibits actions to assist women to obtain abortions or increase the availability or accessibility of abortion for family planning purposes." The Regulations do not, however, proscribe or even regulate antiabortion advocacy. These are clearly restrictions aimed at the suppression of "dangerous ideas."

Remarkably, the majority concludes that "the Government has not discriminated on the basis of viewpoint; it has merely chosen to fund one activity to the exclusion of another." But the majority's claim that the Regulations merely limit a Title X project's speech to preventive or preconceptional services rings hollow in light of the broad range of non-preventive services that the Regulations authorize Title X projects to provide. By refusing to fund those family planning projects that advocate abortion because they advocate abortion, the Government plainly has targeted a particular viewpoint.

NOTES AND QUESTIONS

1. *Can the government treat the professionals it funds merely as means to its ends? Rust* held that the First Amendment does not prohibit the government from heavily restricting the speech of health care workers whose employment is financed by government funds. The Court's theory is that workers in this situation are merely mouthpieces for the government itself; therefore, the government may demand that the workers say only what the government wants them to say. Should the simple fact that the government is hiring someone to speak on its behalf settle the question whether the worker's speech is protected by the First Amendment or should we assess the nature of the government's relationship with the speaker? Professor Robert Post argues that the government should be allowed to regulate the speech of individuals receiving government funds within what he calls "managerial domains," which he defines as domains in which "the state organizes its resources so as to achieve specified ends." Robert C. Post, *Subsidized Speech,* 106 Yale L.J. 151, 164 (1996). Government may regulate the speech of workers within managerial domains because they conceptualize "persons as means to an end rather than as autonomous agents." Nevertheless, Post contends that the government should not be allowed to regulate the speech of health care professionals in cases such as *Rust* because the workers' professional obligations require that they "always qualify their loyalty and commitment to the vertical hierarchy of an organization by their horizontal commitment to general professional norms and standards." *Id.* at 172. *See also* Christina E. Wells, *Abortion Counseling as Vice Activity: The Free Speech Implications of* Rust v. Sullivan *and* Planned Parenthood v. Casey, 95 Colum. L. Rev.1724, 1725-26 (1995) (arguing that federal courts tend to treat regulatory burdens on medical professionals as regulations of activity, rather than speech, even when the regulations directly restrict professional speech); Timothy Zick, *Professional Rights*

Speech, 47 Ariz. State L.J. 1289, 1292 (2015) ("State regulations of professional speech have become more prevalent, more politically tinged, and more likely to structure and dictate the specific content of professional-client interactions."); Claudia E. Haupt, *Professional Speech*, 125 Yale L.J. 1238, 1240 (2016) (arguing that the federal courts have failed to develop and apply an adequate First Amendment framework to safeguard professional speech).

2. *Can government demand that professionals provide false, misleading, or incomplete information?* Should individuals receiving government financing have a First Amendment right to inform members of the public that the government is intentionally misleading them? A controversy arose when South African President Thabo Mbeki expressed the opinion that the HIV virus did not cause AIDS—a point of view widely rejected by the medical and scientific community. Suppose an American government agency adopted this position, and then inserted in the contracts of private scientists receiving government grants from that agency a prohibition on asserting publicly the mainstream scientific position that the HIV virus causes AIDS. Would scientists receiving grants from the agency have a First Amendment right to disobey the contractual directive and espouse publicly the mainstream scientific view?

Legal Services Corp. v. Velazquez

531 U.S. 522 (2001)

KENNEDY, J., delivered the opinion of the Court.

In 1974, Congress enacted the Legal Services Corporation Act. The Act establishes the Legal Services Corporation (LSC) as a District of Columbia nonprofit corporation. LSC's mission is to distribute funds appropriated by Congress to eligible local grantee organizations "for the purpose of providing financial support for legal assistance in noncriminal proceedings or matters to persons financially unable to afford legal assistance."

The grantee organizations hire and supervise lawyers to provide free legal assistance to indigent clients. Each year LSC appropriates funds to grantees or recipients that hire and supervise lawyers for various professional activities, including representation of indigent clients seeking welfare benefits.

This suit requires us to decide whether one of the conditions imposed by Congress on the use of LSC funds violates the First Amendment rights of LSC grantees and their clients. For purposes of our decision, the restriction prohibits legal representation funded by recipients of LSC moneys if the representation involves an effort to amend or otherwise challenge existing welfare law. As interpreted by the LSC and by the Government, the restriction prevents an attorney from arguing to a court that a state statute conflicts with a federal statute or that either a state or federal statute by its terms or in its application is violative of the United States Constitution.

The United States and LSC rely on *Rust* v. *Sullivan* as support for the LSC program restrictions. The Court in *Rust* did not place explicit reliance on the rationale that the counseling activities of the doctors under Title X amounted to governmental speech; when interpreting the holding in later cases, however, we have explained *Rust* on this understanding. As we said in *Rosenberger* [*v. Rector & Visitors of the University of Virginia*, excerpted in this chapter], "[w]hen the government disburses public funds to private entities to convey a governmental message, it may take legitimate and appropriate steps to ensure that its message is neither garbled nor distorted by the grantee."

Neither the latitude for government speech nor its rationale applies to subsidies for private speech in every instance, however. . . . [T]he salient point is that . . . the LSC program was designed to facilitate private speech, not to promote a governmental message. Congress funded LSC grantees to provide attorneys to represent the interests of indigent clients. In the specific context of suits for benefits, an LSC-funded attorney speaks on the behalf of the client in a claim against the government for welfare benefits. The lawyer is not the government's speaker. The attorney defending the decision to deny benefits will deliver the government's message in the litigation. The LSC lawyer, however, speaks on the behalf of his or her private, indigent client.

The Government has designed this program to use the legal profession and the established Judiciary of the States and the Federal Government to accomplish its end of assisting welfare claimants in determination or receipt of their benefits. The advice from the attorney to the client and the advocacy by the attorney to the courts cannot be classified as governmental speech even under a generous understanding of the concept. In this vital respect this suit is distinguishable from *Rust*.

By providing subsidies to LSC, the Government seeks to facilitate suits for benefits by using the State and Federal courts and the independent bar on which those courts depend for the proper performance of their duties and responsibilities. Restricting LSC attorneys in advising their clients and in presenting arguments and analyses to the courts distorts the legal system by altering the traditional role of the attorneys.

Interpretation of the law and the Constitution is the primary mission of the judiciary when it acts within the sphere of its authority to resolve a case or controversy. *Marbury v. Madison*. An informed, independent judiciary presumes an informed, independent bar. The disability [imposed on attorneys by the LSC funding restriction] is inconsistent with the proposition that attorneys should present all the reasonable and well-grounded arguments necessary for proper resolution of the case. By seeking to prohibit the analysis of certain legal issues and to truncate presentation to the courts, the enactment under review prohibits speech and expression upon which courts must depend for the proper exercise of the judicial power. Congress cannot wrest the law from the Constitution which is its source.

The restriction imposed by the statute here threatens severe impairment of the judicial function. [The LSC funding statute] sifts out cases presenting constitutional challenges in order to insulate the Government's laws from judicial inquiry. If the restriction on speech and legal advice were to stand, the result would be two tiers of cases. In cases where LSC counsel were attorneys of record, there would be lingering doubt whether the truncated representation had resulted in complete analysis of the case, full advice to the client, and proper presentation to the court. The courts and the public would come to question the adequacy and fairness of professional representations when the attorney, either consciously to comply with this statute or unconsciously to continue the representation despite the statute, avoided all reference to questions of statutory validity and constitutional authority. A scheme so inconsistent with accepted separation-of-powers principles is an insufficient basis to sustain or uphold the restriction on speech.

SCALIA, J., with whom THE CHIEF JUSTICE, O'CONNOR, J., and THOMAS, J., join, dissenting.

The LSC Act is a federal subsidy program, not a federal regulatory program, and "[t]here is a basic difference between [the two]." *Maher v. Roe.* Regulations directly restrict speech; subsidies do not. Subsidies, it is true, may *indirectly* abridge speech, but only if the funding scheme is "'manipulated' to have a 'coercive effect'" on those who do not hold the subsidized position. *Finley* (Scalia, J., dissenting).

In *Rust v. Sullivan,* the Court applied these principles to a statutory scheme that is in all relevant respects indistinguishable from [the LSC funding restriction challenged here]. . . .

The LSC Act, like the scheme in *Rust,* does not create a public forum. Far from encouraging a diversity of views, it has always, as the Court accurately states, "placed restrictions on its use of funds." Nor does [the LSC funding restriction] discriminate on the basis of viewpoint, since it funds neither challenges to nor defenses of existing welfare law. The provision simply declines to subsidize a certain class of litigation, and under *Rust* that decision "does not infringe the right" to bring such litigation. The Court's repeated claims that [the restriction] "restricts" and "prohibits" speech, and "insulates" laws from judicial review, are simply baseless. No litigant who, in the absence of LSC funding, would bring a suit challenging existing welfare law is deterred from doing so [by the funding restriction]. *Rust* thus controls these cases and compels the conclusion that [the restriction] is constitutional.

The Court contends that *Rust* is different because the program at issue subsidized government speech, while the LSC funds private speech. This is so unpersuasive it hardly needs response. If the private doctors' confidential advice to their patients at issue in *Rust* constituted "government speech," it is hard to imagine what subsidized speech would *not* be government speech. Moreover, the majority's contention that the subsidized speech in these cases is not government speech because the lawyers have a professional obligation to represent the interests of their clients founders on the reality that the doctors in *Rust* had a professional obligation to serve the interests of their patients—which at the time of *Rust* we had held to be highly relevant to the permissible scope of federal regulation. Even respondents agree that "the true speaker in *Rust* was not the government, but a doctor."

Rosenberger v. Rector & Visitors of the University of Virginia

515 U.S. 819 (1995)

KENNEDY, J., delivered the opinion of the Court.

[The University of Virginia maintains a Student Activity Fund (SAF), which is designed] to support a broad range of extracurricular student activities that "are related to the educational purpose of the University." The SAF is based on the

University's "recogni[tion] that the availability of a wide range of opportunities" for its students "tends to enhance the University environment." The Guidelines require that it be administered "in a manner consistent with the educational purpose of the University as well as with state and federal law." The SAF receives its money from a mandatory fee of $14 per semester assessed to each full-time student. The Student Council, elected by the students, has the initial authority to disburse the funds, but its actions are subject to review by a faculty body chaired by a designee of the Vice President for Student Affairs.

Guidelines [for the SAF] recognize 11 categories of student groups that may seek payment to third-party contractors because they "are related to the educational purpose of the University of Virginia." One of these is "student news, information, opinion, entertainment, or academic communications media groups." The Guidelines also specify, however, that the costs of certain activities that are otherwise eligible for funding will not be reimbursed by the SAF. The student activities which are excluded from SAF support are religious activities, philanthropic contributions and activities, political activities, activities that would jeopardize the University's tax-exempt status, those which involve payment of honoraria or similar fees, or social entertainment or related expenses. The prohibition on "political activities" is defined so that it is limited to electioneering and lobbying. The Guidelines provide that "[t]hese restrictions on funding political activities are not intended to preclude funding of any otherwise eligible student organization which . . . espouses particular positions or ideological viewpoints, including those that may be unpopular or are not generally accepted." A "religious activity," by contrast, is defined as any activity that "primarily promotes or manifests a particular belie[f] in or about a deity or an ultimate reality."

Petitioners' organization, Wide Awake Productions (WAP) was established "[t]o publish a magazine of philosophical and religious expression," "[t]o facilitate discussion which fosters an atmosphere of sensitivity to and tolerance of Christian viewpoints," and "[t]o provide a unifying focus for Christians of multicultural backgrounds." WAP publishes Wide Awake: A Christian Perspective at the University of Virginia. The paper's Christian viewpoint was evident from the first issue, in which its editors wrote that the journal "offers a Christian perspective on both personal and community issues, especially those relevant to college students at the University of Virginia." The editors committed the paper to a two-fold mission: "to challenge Christians to live, in word and deed, according to the faith they proclaim and to encourage students to consider what a personal relationship with Jesus Christ means." The first issue had articles about racism, crisis pregnancy, stress, prayer, C. S. Lewis' ideas about evil and free will, and reviews of religious music. In the next two issues, Wide Awake featured stories about homosexuality, Christian missionary work, and eating disorders, as well as music reviews and interviews with University professors. Each page of Wide Awake, and the end of each article or review, is marked by a cross. The advertisements carried in Wide Awake also reveal the Christian perspective of the journal. For the most part, the advertisers are churches, centers for Christian study, or Christian bookstores. By June 1992, WAP had distributed about 5,000 copies of Wide Awake to University students, free of charge. WAP requested the SAF to pay its printer $5,862 for the costs of printing its newspaper. The Appropriations Committee of the Student Council denied WAP's request on the ground that Wide Awake was a "religious activity" within the meaning of the Guidelines, i.e., that the newspaper "promote[d] or manifest[ed] a particular belie[f] in or about a deity or an ultimate reality."

It is axiomatic that the government may not regulate speech based on its substantive content or the message it conveys. Other principles follow from this precept. In the realm of private speech or expression, government regulation may not favor one speaker over another. Discrimination against speech because of its message is presumed to be unconstitutional. These rules informed our determination that the government offends the First Amendment when it imposes financial burdens on certain speakers based on the content of their expression. When the government targets not subject matter but particular views taken by speakers on a subject, the violation of the First Amendment is all the more blatant. Viewpoint discrimination is thus an egregious form of content discrimination. The government must abstain from regulating speech when the specific motivating ideology or the opinion or perspective of the speaker is the rationale for the restriction.

These principles provide the framework forbidding the State from exercising viewpoint discrimination, even when the limited public forum is one of its own creation. In a case involving a school district's provision of school facilities for private uses, we declared that "[t]here is no question that the District, like the private owner of property, may legally preserve the property under its control for the use to which it is dedicated." The necessities of confining a forum to the limited and legitimate purposes for which it was created may justify the State in reserving it for certain groups or for the discussion of certain topics. Once it has opened a limited forum, however, the State must respect the lawful boundaries it has itself set. The State may not exclude speech where its distinction is not "reasonable in light of the purpose served by the forum," nor may it discriminate against speech on the basis of its viewpoint. Thus, in determining whether the State is acting to preserve the limits of the forum it has created so that the exclusion of a class of speech is legitimate, we have observed a distinction between, on the one hand, content discrimination, which may be permissible if it preserves the purposes of that limited forum, and, on the other hand, viewpoint discrimination, which is presumed impermissible when directed against speech otherwise within the forum's limitations.

The SAF is a forum more in a metaphysical than in a spatial or geographic sense, but the same principles are applicable.

The University does acknowledge (as it must in light of our precedents) that "ideologically driven attempts to suppress a particular point of view are presumptively unconstitutional in funding, as in other contexts," but insists that this case does not present that issue because the Guidelines draw lines based on content, not viewpoint. [I]t must be acknowledged, the distinction is not a precise one. It is, in a sense, something of an understatement to speak of religious thought and discussion as just a viewpoint, as distinct from a comprehensive body of thought. The nature of our origins and destiny and their dependence upon the existence of a divine being have been subjects of philosophic inquiry throughout human history. We conclude, nonetheless, that viewpoint discrimination is the proper way to interpret the University's objections to Wide Awake. By the very terms of the SAF prohibition, the University does not exclude religion as a subject matter but selects for disfavored treatment those student journalistic efforts with religious editorial viewpoints. Religion may be a vast area of inquiry, but it also provides, as it did here, a specific premise, a perspective, a standpoint from which a variety of subjects may be discussed and considered. The prohibited perspective, not the general subject matter, resulted in the refusal to make third-party payments, for the subjects discussed were otherwise within the approved category of publications.

The University begins with the unremarkable proposition that the State must have substantial discretion in determining how to allocate scarce resources to accomplish its educational mission. Citing [our decision in *Rust*,] the University argues that content-based funding decisions are both inevitable and lawful. Were the reasoning of [our public forum cases] to apply to funding decisions as well as to those involving access to facilities, it is urged, [the holdings of these cases] "would become a judicial juggernaut, constitutionalizing the ubiquitous content-based decisions that schools, colleges, and other government entities routinely make in the allocation of public funds."

. . . [I]n *Rust v. Sullivan* . . . the government did not create a program to encourage private speech but instead used private speakers to transmit specific information pertaining to its own program. We recognized that when the government appropriates public funds to promote a particular policy of its own it is entitled to say what it wishes. When the government disburses public funds to private entities to convey a governmental message, it may take legitimate and appropriate steps to ensure that its message is neither garbled nor distorted by the grantee.

It does not follow, however, that viewpoint-based restrictions are proper when the University does not itself speak or subsidize transmittal of a message it favors but instead expends funds to encourage a diversity of views from private speakers. A holding that the University may not discriminate based on the viewpoint of private persons whose speech it facilitates does not restrict the University's own speech, which is controlled by different principles.

The distinction between the University's own favored message and the private speech of students is evident in the case before us. The University itself has taken steps to ensure the distinction in the agreement each [student organization] must sign. The University declares that the student groups eligible for SAF support are not the University's agents, are not subject to its control, and are not its responsibility. Having offered to pay the third-party contractors on behalf of private speakers who convey their own messages, the University may not silence the expression of selected viewpoints.

[The Court also rejected the University's argument that financing the religious newspaper would violate the Establishment Clause.]

SOUTER, J., with whom STEVENS, J., GINSBURG, J., and BREYER, J., join, dissenting.

The Court today, for the first time, approves direct funding of core religious activities by an arm of the State. . . . Because there is no warrant for distinguishing among public funding sources for purposes of applying the First Amendment's prohibition of religious establishment, I would hold that the University's refusal to support petitioners' religious activities is compelled by the Establishment Clause.

[Justice O'Connor's and Justice Thomas's concurring opinions are omitted.]

NOTES AND QUESTIONS

1. *Forums, subsidies, and exclusivity.* Like *Rosenberger,* Cornelius v. NAACP Legal Defense & Educ. Fund, 473 U.S. 788 (1985), also involved a metaphysical forum. In contrast to *Rosenberger,* however, the *Cornelius* Court upheld the government restrictions, permitting the government to exclude legal defense and political advocacy organizations from the Combined Federal Campaign, a charity drive aimed at federal employees. The Court held that the Combined Federal Campaign was a nonpublic forum, and emphasized that "[c]ontrol over access to a nonpublic forum can be based on subject matter and speaker identity so long as the distinctions drawn are reasonable in light of the purpose served by the forum and are viewpoint neutral." *Id.* at 806. What distinguishes the program in *Cornelius* from the program in *Rosenberger?* In both cases the government intended to exclude entire categories of participants from the forums, and in both cases the government argued that the exclusion was based on the government's desire to avoid disruption and conflict. Could the paradoxical outcome of the Supreme Court's decision in *Rosenberger* be to encourage public universities and other government funders of private expression to require that speakers receiving government funds express only ideas endorsed by the government? Presumably, if the university officially declared at the program's outset that recipients of student activity funds were speaking on behalf of the university, then the university would be allowed to limit the speech of those recipients, either under the government speech rationale of *Rust* or the nonpublic forum theory of *Cornelius.*
2. *Content versus viewpoint neutrality.* Does the Court's decision in *Rosenberger* "blur the line between viewpoint and content neutrality, suggesting the Court might scrutinize a government's establishment or application of content parameters in a limited public forum more strictly than the 'reasonableness' language [of the constitutional standard] might at first suggest"? *See* Lyrissa Barnett Lidsky, *Public Forum 2.0,* 91 B. U. L. Rev. 1975, 1988 (2011). How do you reconcile *Rosenberger* with *Christian Legal Society v. Martinez, supra* p. 229, where the Court found the university's all-comers policy to be reasonable and viewpoint-neutral, even though it had a greater effect on religious student organizations than on secular ones?

National Endowment for the Arts v. Finley

524 U.S. 569 (1998)

O'Connor, J., delivered the opinion of the Court.

The National Foundation on the Arts and Humanities Act, as amended in 1990, requires the Chairperson of the National Endowment for the Arts (NEA) to ensure that "artistic excellence and artistic merit are the criteria by which [grant] applications are judged, taking into consideration general standards of decency and respect for the diverse beliefs and values of the American public."

[The four individual respondents in this case, Karen Finley, John Fleck, Holly Hughes, and Tim Miller, are performance artists who applied for NEA grants before the "decency and respect" provision was enacted. An advisory panel recommended approval of respondents' projects, both initially and after receiving the NEA Chairman's request to reconsider three of the applications. A majority of the National Council on the Arts subsequently recommended disapproval, and in June 1990, the NEA informed respondents that they had been denied funding. Respondents filed suit, alleging that the NEA had violated their First Amendment rights. A footnote in Justice Souter's dissent describes the art of the three respondents:]

> [The oeuvres d'art for which the four individual plaintiffs in this case sought funding have been described as follows: "Finley's controversial show, 'We Keep Our Victims Ready,' contains three segments. In the second segment, Finley visually recounts a sexual assault by stripping to the waist and smearing chocolate on her breasts and by using profanity to describe the assault. Holly Hughes' monologue 'World Without End' is a somewhat graphic recollection of the artist's realization of her lesbianism and reminiscence of her mother's sexuality. John Fleck, in his stage performance 'Blessed Are All the Little Fishes,' confronts alcoholism and Catholicism. During the course of the performance, Fleck appears dressed as a mermaid, urinates on the stage and creates an altar out of a toilet bowl by putting a photograph of Jesus Christ on the lid. Tim Miller derives his performance 'Some Golden States' from childhood experiences, from his life as a homosexual, and from the constant threat of AIDS. Miller uses vegetables in his performances to represent sexual symbols." Julie Ann Alagna, Note, *1991 Legislation, Reports and Debates Over Federally Funded Art: Arts Community Left with an "Indecent" Compromise*, 48 Wash. & Lee L. Rev. 1545, 1545-46, n. 2 (1991) (citations omitted).]

In this case, we review the Court of Appeals' determination that [the "decency and respect" clause] on its face, impermissibly discriminates on the basis of viewpoint and is void for vagueness under the First and Fifth Amendments. We conclude that [the clause] is facially valid, as it neither inherently interferes with First Amendment rights nor violates constitutional vagueness principles.

Since 1965, the NEA has distributed over $3 billion in grants to individuals and organizations, funding that has served as a catalyst for increased state, corporate, and foundation support for the arts. Throughout the NEA's history, only a handful of the agency's roughly 100,000 awards have generated formal complaints about misapplied funds or abuse of the public's trust. Two provocative works, however, prompted public controversy in 1989 and led to congressional revaluation of the NEA's funding priorities and efforts to increase oversight of its grant-making procedures. The Institute of Contemporary Art at the University of Pennsylvania had used $30,000 of a visual arts grant it received from the NEA to fund a 1989 retrospective of photographer Robert Mapplethorpe's work. The exhibit, entitled The Perfect Moment, included homoerotic photographs that several Members of Congress condemned as pornographic. Members also denounced artist Andres Serrano's work Piss Christ, a photograph of a crucifix immersed in urine. Serrano had been awarded a $15,000 grant from the Southeast Center for Contemporary Art, an organization that received NEA support. [Congress responded to the controversy surrounding the Mapplethorpe and Serrano photographs by eliminating $45,000 from the agency's budget, the precise amount contributed to the two exhibits by NEA grant recipients, and enacting a series of limitations on the discretion of the NEA's grant-making authority. Some of the initial restrictions on the NEA's authority were struck down by lower courts, which led Congress to adopt the "decency and respect" provision at issue here.]

Respondents argue that the provision is a paradigmatic example of viewpoint discrimination because it rejects any artistic speech that either fails to respect mainstream values or offends standards of decency. The premise of respondents' claim is that [the "decency and respect" provision] constrains the agency's ability to fund certain categories of artistic expression. The NEA, however, reads the provision as merely hortatory, and contends that it stops well short of an absolute restriction. The [contested provision] adds "considerations" to the grant-making process; it does not preclude awards to projects that might be deemed "indecent" or "disrespectful," nor place conditions on grants, or even specify that those factors must be given any particular weight in reviewing an application. Indeed, the agency asserts that it has adequately implemented [the provision] merely by ensuring the representation of various backgrounds and points of view on the advisory panels that analyze grant applications. We do not decide whether the NEA's view—that the formulation of diverse advisory panels is sufficient to comply with Congress' command—is in fact a reasonable reading of the statute. It is clear, however, that the text of [the "decency and respect" provision] imposes no categorical requirement. The advisory language stands in sharp contrast to congressional efforts to prohibit the funding of certain classes of speech. When Congress has in fact intended to affirmatively constrain the NEA's grant-making authority, it has done so in no uncertain terms. [*See, for example,* another statutory provision relating to NEA funding stating that "[O]bscenity is without artistic merit, is not protected speech, and shall not be funded".]

Respondent's reliance on our decision in *Rosenberger v. Rector and Visitors of Univ. of Va.* is misplaced. In *Rosenberger*, a public university declined to authorize disbursements from its Student Activities Fund to finance the printing of a Christian student newspaper. We held that by subsidizing the Student Activities Fund, the University had created a limited public forum, from which it impermissibly excluded all publications with religious editorial viewpoints. Although the scarcity of NEA funding does not distinguish this case from *Rosenberger*, the competitive process according to which the grants are allocated does. In the context of arts funding, in contrast to many other subsidies, the Government does not indiscriminately "encourage a diversity of views from private speakers." The NEA's mandate is to make aesthetic judgments, and the inherently content-based "excellence" threshold for NEA support sets it apart from the subsidy at issue in *Rosenberger*—which was available to all student organizations that were "'related to the educational purpose of the University'"—and from comparably objective decisions on allocating public benefits, such as access to a school auditorium or a municipal theater.

Finally, although the First Amendment certainly has application in the subsidy context, we note that the Government may allocate competitive funding according to criteria that would be impermissible were direct regulation of speech or a criminal penalty at stake. So long as legislation does not infringe on other constitutionally protected rights, Congress has wide latitude to set spending priorities. [A]s we held in *Rust*, Congress may "selectively fund a program to encourage certain activities it believes to be in the public interest, without at the same time funding an alternative program which seeks to deal with the problem in another way." *Rust*. In doing so, "the Government has not discriminated on the basis of viewpoint; it has merely chosen to fund one activity to the exclusion of the other." *Ibid.*; *see also Maher v. Roe* ("There is a basic difference between direct state interference with a protected activity and state encouragement of an alternative activity consonant with legislative policy").

[The Court also rejected a vagueness challenge to the "decency and respect" provision, on the grounds that "[i]n the context of selective subsidies, it is not always feasible for Congress to legislate with clarity. Indeed, if this statute is unconstitutionally vague, then so too are all government programs awarding scholarships and grants on the basis of subjective criteria such as 'excellence.'"]

SCALIA, J., with whom THOMAS, J., joins, concurring in the judgment.

"The operation was a success, but the patient died." What such a procedure is to medicine, the Court's opinion in this case is to law. It sustains the constitutionality of [the "decency and respect" provision] by gutting it. The most avid congressional opponents of the provision could not have asked for more. I write separately because, unlike the Court, I think that [the provision] must be evaluated as written, rather than as distorted by the agency it was meant to control. By its terms, it establishes content and viewpoint-based criteria upon which grant applications are to be evaluated. And that is perfectly constitutional.

The Court devotes so much of its opinion to explaining why this statute means something other than what it says that it neglects to cite the constitutional text governing our analysis. The First Amendment reads: "Congress shall make no law . . . *abridging* the freedom of speech." To abridge is "to contract, to diminish; to deprive of." T. Sheridan, A Complete Dictionary of the English Language (6th ed. 1796). With the enactment of [the "decency and respect" provision] Congress did not *abridge* the speech of those who disdain the beliefs and values of the American public, nor did it *abridge* indecent speech. Those who wish to create indecent and disrespectful art are as unconstrained now as they were before the enactment of this statute. *Avant-garde artistes* such as respondents remain entirely free to *epater les bourgeois*; they are merely deprived of the additional satisfaction of having the bourgeoisie taxed to pay for it. It is preposterous to equate the denial of taxpayer subsidy with measures "aimed at the *suppression* of dangerous ideas."

SOUTER, J., dissenting.

The decency and respect proviso mandates viewpoint-based decisions in the disbursement of government subsidies, and the Government has wholly failed to explain why the statute should be afforded an exemption from the fundamental rule of the First Amendment that viewpoint discrimination in the exercise of public authority over expressive activity is unconstitutional. The Court's conclusions that the proviso is not viewpoint based, that it is not a regulation, and that the NEA may permissibly engage in viewpoint-based discrimination, are all patently mistaken. . . .

Scarce money demands choices, of course, but choices "on some acceptable [viewpoint] neutral principle," *Rosenberger*, like artistic excellence and artistic merit;

"nothing in our decision[s] indicate[s] that scarcity would give the State the right to exercise viewpoint discrimination that is otherwise impermissible." If the student activities fund at issue in *Rosenberger* had awarded competitive, merit-based grants to only 50%, or even 5%, of the applicants, on the basis of "journalistic merit taking into consideration the message of the newspaper," it is obvious beyond peradventure that the Court would not have come out differently, leaving the University free to refuse funding after considering a publication's Christian perspective.

NOTES AND QUESTIONS

1. *Protecting the government's editorial and artistic judgments.* While the Court eventually avoided the difficult constitutional issues in *Finley* by holding that the statute in question did not impose viewpoint restrictions on NEA staff decisions, a background theme of the Court's opinion is that the NEA had the right to make content-based funding decisions because it was exercising professional expertise about the artistic excellence of applicants for government grants. For another variation on the theme of editorial judgments and professional expertise by government decision makers, *see* Arkansas Educational Television Commission v. Forbes, 523 U.S. 666 (1998).
2. *Editorial discretion and viewpoint discrimination.* In *Forbes,* the Court rejected a First Amendment claim by a political candidate who was excluded from a televised debate by the producers of a state-owned public television station. The Court held that the producers' editorial discretion insulated them from a First Amendment challenge. "As a general rule, the nature of editorial discretion counsels against subjecting broadcasters to claims of viewpoint discrimination. Programming decisions would be particularly vulnerable to claims of this type because even principled exclusions rooted in sound journalistic judgment can often be characterized as viewpoint-based. To comply with their obligation to air programming that serves the public interest, broadcasters must often choose among speakers expressing different viewpoints."

Pleasant Grove City, Utah v. Summum

555 U.S. 460 (2009)

Alito, J., delivered the opinion of the Court.

This case presents the question whether the Free Speech Clause of the First Amendment entitles a private group to insist that a municipality permit it to place a permanent monument in a city park in which other donated monuments were previously erected. The Court of Appeals held that the municipality was required to accept the monument because a public park is a traditional public forum. We conclude, however, that although a park is a traditional public forum for speeches and other transitory expressive acts, the display of a permanent monument in a public park is not a form of expression to which forum analysis applies. Instead, the placement of a permanent monument in a public park is best viewed as a form of government speech and is therefore not subject to scrutiny under the Free Speech Clause.

I.

. . . Respondent Summum is a religious organization founded in 1975 and headquartered in Salt Lake City, Utah. [Summum asked Pleasant Grove City for] permission to erect a "stone monument" [containing the "aphorisms" of Summum in its 2.5-acre "Pioneer Park." The Park contained 15 monuments at the time, most donated by private groups or individuals. The monuments included "a wishing well," a "September 11 monument," and a "Ten Commandments monument donated by the Fraternal Order of Eagles in 1971."] The City denied the requests and explained that its practice was to limit monuments in the Park to those that "either (1) directly relate to the history of Pleasant Grove, or (2) were donated by groups with longstanding ties to the Pleasant Grove community." The following year, the City passed a resolution putting this policy into writing [and rejected Summum's subsequent request to erect its monument].

In 2005, respondent filed this action against the City and various local officials (petitioners), asserting, among other claims, that petitioners had violated the Free Speech Clause of the First Amendment by accepting the Ten Commandments monument but rejecting the proposed Seven Aphorisms monument. . . .

II.

No prior decision of this Court has addressed the application of the Free Speech Clause to a government entity's acceptance of privately donated, permanent monuments for installation in a public park. . . . Petitioners contend that the pertinent cases are those concerning government speech. Respondent, on the other hand, agrees with the Court of Appeals panel that the applicable cases are those that analyze private speech in a public forum. The parties' fundamental disagreement thus centers on the nature of petitioners' conduct when they permitted privately donated monuments to be erected in Pioneer Park. Were petitioners engaging in their own expressive conduct? Or were they providing a forum for private speech?

If petitioners were engaging in their own expressive conduct, then the Free Speech Clause has no application. The Free Speech Clause restricts government regulation of private speech; it does not regulate government speech. *See Johanns* [*supra* Chapter 6], ("[T]he Government's own speech . . . is exempt from First Amendment scrutiny"). A government entity has the right to "speak for itself." "[I]t is entitled to say what it wishes," *Rosenberger*, and to select the views that it wants to express. *See Rust; Finley.*

Indeed, it is not easy to imagine how government could function if it lacked this freedom. "If every citizen were to have a right to insist that no one paid by public funds express a view with which he disagreed, debate over issues of great concern to the public would be limited to those in the private sector, and the process of government as we know it radically transformed." *Keller v. State Bar of Cal.* [*supra*, Chapter 6].

A government entity may exercise this same freedom to express its views when it receives assistance from private sources for the purpose of delivering a government-controlled message. . . .

This does not mean that there are no restraints on government speech. For example, government speech must comport with the Establishment Clause. The involvement of public officials in advocacy may be limited by law, regulation, or practice. And of course, a government entity is ultimately "accountable to the electorate and the political process for its advocacy."

While government speech is not restricted by the Free Speech Clause, the government does not have a free hand to regulate private speech on government property. [Here the court briefly summarizes the types of public forums and the constitutional standards applicable to them.]

III.

There may be situations in which it is difficult to tell whether a government entity is speaking on its own behalf or is providing a forum for private speech, but this case does not present such a situation. Permanent monuments displayed on public property typically represent government speech.

Governments have long used monuments to speak to the public. Since ancient times, kings, emperors, and other rulers have erected statues of themselves to remind their subjects of their authority and power. . . . A monument, by definition, is a structure that is designed as a means of expression. When a government entity arranges for the construction of a monument, it does so because it wishes to convey some thought or instill some feeling in those who see the structure. Neither the Court of Appeals nor respondent disputes the obvious proposition that a monument that is commissioned and financed by a government body for placement on public land constitutes government speech.

Just as government-commissioned and government-financed monuments speak for the government, so do privately financed and donated monuments that the government accepts and displays to the public on government land. [P]ersons who observe donated monuments routinely—and reasonably—interpret them as conveying some message on the property owner's behalf. In this context, there is little chance that observers will fail to appreciate the identity of the speaker. This is true whether the monument is located on private property or on public property, such as national, state, or city park land.

We think it is fair to say that throughout our Nation's history, the general government practice with respect to donated monuments has been one of selective receptivity. A great many of the monuments that adorn the Nation's public parks were financed with private funds or donated by private parties, including the Statue of Liberty, the Marine Corps War Memorial (the Iwo Jima monument), and the Vietnam Veterans Memorial. . . . By accepting monuments that are privately funded or donated, government entities save tax dollars and are able to acquire monuments that they could not have afforded to fund on their own.

. . . Public parks are often closely identified in the public mind with the government unit that owns the land. City parks . . . commonly play an important role in defining the identity that a city projects to its own residents and to the outside world. . . . Government decision makers select the monuments that portray what they view as appropriate for the place in question, taking into account such content-based factors as esthetics, history, and local culture. The monuments that are accepted, therefore, are meant to convey and have the effect of conveying a government message, and they thus constitute government speech.

IV.

In this case, it is clear that the monuments in Pleasant Grove's Pioneer Park represent government speech. Although many of the monuments were not designed or built by the City and were donated in completed form by private entities, the City decided to accept those donations and to display them in the Park. The City has "effectively controlled" the messages sent by the monuments in the Park by exercising "final approval authority" over their selection. The City has selected those monuments that it wants to display for the purpose of presenting the image of the City that it wishes to project to all who frequent the Park; it has taken ownership of most of the monuments in the Park, including the Ten Commandments monument that is the focus of respondent's concern; and the City has now expressly set forth the criteria it will use in making future selections.

Respondent voices the legitimate concern that the government speech doctrine not be used as a subterfuge for favoring certain private speakers over others based on viewpoint. Respondent's suggested solution is to require a government entity accepting a privately donated monument to go through a formal process of adopting a resolution publicly embracing "the message" that the monument conveys.

We see no reason for imposing a requirement of this sort. The parks of this country contain thousands of donated monuments that government entities have used for their own expressive purposes, usually without producing the sort of formal documentation that respondent now says is required to escape Free Speech Clause restrictions. Requiring all of these jurisdictions to go back and proclaim formally that they adopt all of these monuments as their own expressive vehicles would be a pointless exercise that the Constitution does not mandate.

. . . [The Court rejects the argument that that the City must explicitly "adopt" the monument's "message" for it to be government speech.] Even when a monument features the written word, the monument may be intended to be interpreted, and may in fact be interpreted by different observers, in a variety of ways.

. . . [I]t frequently is not possible to identify a single "message" that is conveyed by an object or structure, and consequently, the thoughts or sentiments expressed by a government entity that accepts and displays such an object may be quite different from those of either its creator or its donor. By accepting a privately donated monument and placing it on city property, a city engages in expressive conduct, but the intended and perceived significance of that conduct may not coincide with the thinking of the monument's donor or creator. . . .

The message that a government entity conveys by allowing a monument to remain on its property may also be altered by the subsequent addition of other monuments in the same vicinity. For example, following controversy over the original design of the Vietnam Veterans Memorial, a compromise was reached that called for the nearby addition of a flagstaff and bronze Three Soldiers statue, which many believed changed the overall effect of the memorial. *See, e.g.*, J. Mayo, War Memorials as Political Landscape: The American Experience and Beyond.

The "message" conveyed by a monument may change over time. A study of war memorials found that "people reinterpret" the meaning of these memorials as "historical interpretations" and "the society around them changes."

A striking example of how the interpretation of a monument can evolve is provided by one of the most famous and beloved public monuments in the United States, the Statue of Liberty. The statue was given to this country by the Third French Republic to express republican solidarity and friendship between the two countries. At the inaugural ceremony, President Cleveland saw the statue as an emblem of international friendship and the widespread influence of American ideals. Only later did the statue come to be viewed as a beacon welcoming immigrants to a land of freedom.

Respondent and the Court of Appeals analogize the installation of permanent monuments in a public park to the delivery of speeches and the holding of marches and demonstrations, and they thus invoke the rule that a public park is a traditional public forum for these activities. But "public forum principles . . . are out of place in the context of this case." *United States v. American Library Assn., Inc.* [*infra* p. 717]. The forum doctrine has been applied in situations in which government-owned property or a government program was capable of accommodating a large number of public speakers without defeating the essential function of the land or the program.

By contrast, public parks can accommodate only a limited number of permanent monuments. . . . [I]t is hard to imagine how a public park could be opened up for the installation of permanent monuments by every person or group wishing to engage in that form of expression. . . .

To be sure, there are limited circumstances in which the forum doctrine might properly be applied to a permanent monument—for example, if a town created a monument on which all of its residents (or all those meeting some other criterion) could place the name of a person to be honored or some other private message. But as a general matter, forum analysis simply does not apply to the installation of permanent monuments on public property.

In sum, we hold that the City's decision to accept certain privately donated monuments while rejecting respondent's is best viewed as a form of government speech. As a result, the City's decision is not subject to the Free Speech Clause, and the Court of Appeals erred in holding otherwise. We therefore reverse.

STEVENS, J., with whom GINSBURG, J., joins, concurring. . . .

Unlike other decisions relying on the government speech doctrine, our decision in this case excuses no retaliation for, or coercion of, private speech. Nor is it likely, given the near certainty that observers will associate permanent displays with the governmental property owner, that the government will be able to avoid political accountability for the views that it endorses or expresses through this means. Finally, recognizing permanent displays on public property as government speech will not give the government free license to communicate offensive or partisan messages. For even if the Free Speech Clause neither restricts nor protects government speech, government speakers are bound by the Constitution's other proscriptions, including those supplied by the Establishment and Equal Protection

Clauses. Together with the checks imposed by our democratic processes, these constitutional safeguards ensure that the effect of today's decision will be limited.

SCALIA, J., with whom THOMAS, J., joins, concurring.

. . . The city ought not fear that today's victory propelled it from the free speech clause frying pan into the establishment clause fire. . . .

NOTES AND QUESTIONS

1. *Distinguishing government speech from private speech.* What qualities or characteristics help us know that the government is speaking? In Salazar v. Buono, 559 U.S. 700 (2010) *infra* p. 1014, the government tried to disclaim ownership of a cross erected in 1934 by the Veterans of Foreign Wars (VFW) on a hill (Sunrise Rock) in the Mojave National Preserve. A Buddhist asked to erect a religious monument in the same spot, and the Park Service said no, stating it was trying to get rid of the cross, which never had government permission to be there. After the Buddhist sued, Congress transferred ownership of the land on which the cross stood to the VFW. There is, of course, no Establishment Clause problem when a private individual erects a religious symbol on his or her own property. However, the government's attempt to convey the monument to private owners turned it into a mirror image of *Summum.* As Professor RonNell Andersen Jones has pointed out, *Summum* involved arguably *private* speech that the government endeavored to characterize as *government* speech in order to avoid a First Amendment Speech Clause problem; in so doing, it potentially created for itself a First Amendment Establishment Clause problem. Conversely, *Buono* involved arguably *government* speech that the government endeavored to characterize as *private* speech in order to avoid a First Amendment Establishment Clause problem; in so doing, it potentially created for itself a First Amendment Speech Clause problem. RonNell Andersen Jones, *Pick Your Poisons: Private Speech, Government Speech, and the Special Problem of Religious Displays,* 2010 BYU L. Rev. 2045 (2010).
2. *Temporary versus permanent displays on government property.* Suppose the Court had held that state actors must maintain viewpoint neutrality in choosing which donated monuments to place on government property. Should temporary displays placed on government property be governed by different constitutional standards than permanent displays? *See* Capitol Square Review and Advisory Bd. v. Pinette, 515 U.S. 753 (1995) (holding that the Ku Klux Klan had a free speech right to erect a cross on a statehouse plaza—a public forum—during Christmas season on the same terms as other groups).
3. *Are trademarks private speech, government speech, or mixed speech?* In Matal v. Tam, 137 S. Ct. 1744 (2017), the Supreme Court squarely rejected the Patent and Trademark Office's (PTO) argument that federal trademarks constitute government speech. Writing for the majority, Justice Samuel Alito reasoned that "[i]f the federal registration of a trademark makes the mark government speech, the

Federal Government is babbling prodigiously and incoherently" and, moreover, "[i]t is saying many unseemly things." *Id.* at 1758. He noted that government does not control the content or message of trademarks, that it does not use trademarks to propagate its own ideas, and that the public does not associate trademarks with the government. *See id.* at 1758-60. Given these circumstances, Justice Alito concluded that the PTO was not speaking when it approved a trademark::

> In sum, the federal registration of trademarks is vastly different from the beef ads in *Johanns*, the monuments in *Summum*, and even the specialty license plates in *Walker*. Holding that the registration of a trademark converts the mark into government speech would constitute a huge and dangerous extension of the government-speech doctrine. For if the registration of trademarks constituted government speech, other systems of government registration could easily be characterized in the same way. . . . Trademarks are private, not government, speech.

Id. at 1760.

4. Are there circumstances where the question of whether a message constitutes private speech or government speech might not be so clear-cut as it was in *Tam*? For example, suppose the government plays a larger role in deciding what messages may be communicated, that the public commonly associates the messages with the government, and, perhaps, that the government has traditionally used a particular kind of speech to propagate messages. The next principal case, involving the affinity license plate program in Texas, raises complex questions about how the federal courts should apply the government speech doctrine in circumstances where a good argument can be made that both a private citizen *and* the government are speaking. In such cases of "mixed speech," which characterization should prevail?

Walker v. Texas Division, Sons of Confederate Veterans, Inc.

576 U.S. 200 (2015)

Justice Breyer delivered the opinion of the Court. . . .

I

[In Texas, all motor vehicles operating on the State's roads must display valid license plates. Drivers may display the State's general-issue license plates, which contain the word "Texas," a license plate number, a silhouette of the State, a graphic of the Lone Star, and the slogan "The Lone Star State." Or drivers may choose a specialty license plate, which contains the word "Texas," a license plate number, and one of a selection of designs prepared by the State. Texas offers a variety of specialty plates for an annual fee. There are three processes for selecting the specialty plates. First, the state legislature may call for the development of a specialty license plate.

Second, the Department of Motor Vehicles Board ("Board") may approve a specialty plate design that a state-designated private vendor has created at the request of an individual or organization. Third, the Board "may create new specialty license plates on its own initiative or on receipt of an application from a" nonprofit entity seeking to sponsor a specialty plate. A nonprofit must include in its application "a draft design of the specialty license plate." Texas law vests authority in the Board to approve or disapprove an application. The relevant statute says that the Board "may refuse to create a new specialty license plate" for many reasons, including "if the design might be offensive to any member of the public . . . or for any other reason established by rule." . . .

In 2010, the Texas division of the Sons of Confederate Veterans (SCV), a nonprofit organization, applied to sponsor a specialty license plate. SCV's draft plate design included the words "SONS OF CONFEDERATE VETERANS" at the bottom, the organization's logo at the side, and a square Confederate battle flag framed by the words "Sons of Confederate Veterans 1896." A faint Confederate battle flag appeared in the background. The license plate number appeared in the middle of the plate with the State's name and silhouette at the top. After public hearing asking for comments on its website and at an open meeting, the Board explained that it found "it necessary to deny th[e] plate design application, specifically the confederate flag portion of the design, because public comments ha[d] shown that many members of the general public find the design offensive, and because such comments are reasonable." The Board added "that a significant portion of the public associate the confederate flag with organizations advocating expressions of hate directed toward people or groups that is demeaning to those people or groups." In 2012, SCV sued the Board, arguing that its decision violated the First Amendment. SCV sought an injunction requiring the Board to approve the proposed plate design. The District Court entered judgment for the Board. A divided panel of the Court of Appeals for the Fifth Circuit reversed.]

II

When government speaks, it is not barred by the Free Speech Clause from determining the content of what it says. *Pleasant Grove City v. Summum*, 555 U.S. 460, 467–468 (2009). That freedom in part reflects the fact that it is the democratic electoral process that first and foremost provides a check on government speech. Thus, government statements (and government actions and programs that take the form of speech) do not normally trigger the First Amendment rules designed to protect the marketplace of ideas. . . .

Were the Free Speech Clause interpreted otherwise, government would not work. . . . "[I]t is not easy to imagine how government could function if it lacked th[e] freedom" to select the messages it wishes to convey. *Summum*. . . .

That is not to say that a government's ability to express itself is without restriction. Constitutional and statutory provisions outside of the Free Speech Clause may limit government speech. And the Free Speech Clause itself may constrain the government's speech if, for example, the government seeks to compel private persons to convey the government's speech. But, as a general matter, when the government speaks it is entitled to promote a program, to espouse a policy, or to take a position. In doing so, it represents its citizens and it carries out its duties on their behalf.

III

In our view, specialty license plates issued pursuant to Texas's statutory scheme convey government speech. Our reasoning rests primarily on our analysis in *Summum*, a recent case that presented a similar problem. . . .

A

In *Summum*, we considered a religious organization's request to erect in a 2.5–acre city park a monument setting forth the organization's religious tenets. In the park were 15 other permanent displays. At least 11 of these . . . had been donated to the city by private entities. . . .

This Court . . . held that the city had not "provid[ed] a forum for private speech" with respect to monuments. Rather, the city, even when "accepting a privately donated monument and placing it on city property," had "engage[d] in expressive conduct." The speech at issue, this Court decided, was "best viewed as a form of government speech" and "therefore [was] not subject to scrutiny under the Free Speech Clause."

We based our conclusion on several factors. First, history shows that "[g]overnments have long used monuments to speak to the public." . . .

Second, we noted that it "is not common for property owners to open up their property for the installation of permanent monuments that convey a message with which they do not wish to be associated." As a result, "persons who observe donated monuments routinely—and reasonably—interpret them as conveying some message on the property owner's behalf." . . . .

Third, . . . we observed that the city government in *Summum* "'effectively controlled' the messages sent by the monuments in the [p]ark by exercising 'final approval authority' over their selection."

In light of these and a few other relevant considerations, the Court concluded that the expression at issue was government speech. And, in reaching that conclusion, the Court rejected the premise that the involvement of private parties in designing the monuments was sufficient to prevent the government from controlling which monuments it placed in its own public park.

B

Our analysis in *Summum* leads us to the conclusion that here, too, government speech is at issue. First, the history of license plates shows that, insofar as license plates have conveyed more than state names and vehicle identification numbers, they long have communicated messages from the States. . . .

Texas . . . has selected various messages to communicate through its license plate designs. By 1919, Texas had begun to display the Lone Star emblem on its plates. . . . In 1977, Texas replaced the Lone Star with a small silhouette of the State. And in 1995, Texas plates celebrated "150 Years of Statehood." Additionally, the Texas Legislature has specifically authorized specialty plate designs stating, among other things, "Read to Succeed," "Houston Livestock Show and Rodeo," "Texans Conquer Cancer," and "Girl Scouts." This kind of state speech has appeared on Texas plates for decades.

Second, Texas license plate designs "are often closely identified in the public mind with the [State]." Each Texas license plate is a government article serving the governmental purposes of vehicle registration and identification. . . .

Texas license plates are, essentially, government IDs. And issuers of ID "typically do not permit" the placement on their IDs of "message[s] with which they do not wish to be associated." Consequently, "persons who observe" designs on IDs "routinely—and reasonably—interpret them as conveying some message on the [issuer's] behalf."

Indeed, a person who displays a message on a Texas license plate likely intends to convey to the public that the State has endorsed that message. If not, the individual could simply display the message in question in larger letters on a bumper sticker right next to the plate. But the individual prefers a license plate design to the purely private speech expressed through bumper stickers. That may well be because Texas's license plate designs convey government agreement with the message displayed.

Third, Texas maintains direct control over the messages conveyed on its specialty plates. Texas law provides that the State "has sole control over the design, typeface, color, and alphanumeric pattern for all license plates." The Board must approve every specialty plate design proposal before the design can appear on a Texas plate. And the Board and its predecessor have actively exercised this authority. Texas asserts, and SCV concedes, that the State has rejected at least a dozen proposed designs. . . .

These considerations, taken together, convince us that the specialty plates here in question are similar enough to the monuments in *Summum* to call for the same result. That is not to say that every element of our discussion in *Summum* is relevant here. For instance, in *Summum* we . . . believed that the speech at issue was government speech rather than private speech in part because we found it "hard to imagine how a public park could be opened up for the installation of permanent monuments by every person or group wishing to engage in that form of expression." Here, a State could theoretically offer a much larger number of license plate designs, and those designs need not be available for time immemorial.

But those characteristics of the speech at issue in *Summum* were particularly important because the government speech at issue occurred in public parks, which are traditional public forums for "the delivery of speeches and the holding of marches and demonstrations" by private citizens. By contrast, license plates are not traditional public forums for private speech. . . .

C

SCV believes . . . the State does not engage in expressive activity through [the] slogans and graphics [on its specialty license plates], but rather provides a forum for private speech by making license plates available to display the private parties' designs. We cannot agree.

. . . [F]orum analysis is misplaced here. Because the State is speaking on its own behalf, the First Amendment strictures that attend the various types of government-established forums do not apply.

The parties agree that Texas's specialty license plates are not a "traditional public forum," such as a street or a park[.] . . .

It is equally clear that Texas's specialty plates are neither a "'designated public forum,'" which exists where "government property that has not traditionally been regarded as a public forum is intentionally opened up for that purpose," nor a "limited public forum," which exists where a government has "reserv[ed a forum] for certain groups or for the discussion of certain topics[.]" . . . [I]n order "to ascertain whether [a government] intended to designate a place not traditionally open to assembly and debate as a public forum," this Court "has looked to the policy and practice of the government" and to "the nature of the property and its compatibility with expressive activity."

Texas's policies and the nature of its license plates indicate that the State did not intend its specialty license plates to serve as either a designated public forum or a limited public forum. First, the State exercises final authority over each specialty license plate design. This authority militates against a determination that Texas has created a public forum. Second, Texas takes ownership of each specialty plate design, making it particularly untenable that the State intended specialty plates to serve as a forum for public discourse. Finally, Texas license plates have traditionally been used for government speech, are primarily used as a form of government ID, and bear the State's name. These features of Texas license plates indicate that Texas explicitly associates itself with the speech on its plates.

For similar reasons, we conclude that Texas's specialty license plates are not a "nonpublic for[um]," which exists "[w]here the government is acting as a proprietor, managing its internal operations." With respect to specialty license plate designs, Texas is not simply managing government property, but instead is engaging in expressive conduct. . . . Texas's specialty license plate designs "are meant to convey and have the effect of conveying a government message." They "constitute government speech."

The fact that private parties take part in the design and propagation of a message does not extinguish the governmental nature of the message or transform the government's role into that of a mere forum-provider. In *Summum*, private entities "financed and donated monuments that the government accept[ed] and display[ed] to the public." Here, similarly, private parties propose designs that Texas may accept and display on its license plates. In this case, as in *Summum*, the "government entity may exercise [its] freedom to express its views" even "when it receives assistance from private sources for the purpose of delivering a government-controlled message." And in this case, as in *Summum*, forum analysis is inapposite.

Of course, Texas allows many more license plate designs than the city in *Summum* allowed monuments. But our holding in *Summum* was not dependent on the precise number of monuments found within the park. . . . Further, there may well be many more messages that Texas wishes to convey through its license plates than there were messages that the city in *Summum* wished to convey through its monuments. Texas's desire to communicate numerous messages does not mean that the messages conveyed are not Texas's own. . . .

For the reasons stated, we hold that Texas's specialty license plate designs constitute government speech and that Texas was consequently entitled to refuse to issue plates featuring SCV's proposed design. Accordingly, the judgment of the United States Court of Appeals for the Fifth Circuit is

Reversed.

Justice ALITO, with whom THE CHIEF JUSTICE, Justice SCALIA, and Justice KENNEDY join, dissenting. . . .

Unfortunately, the Court's decision categorizes private speech as government speech and thus strips it of all First Amendment protection. The Court holds that all the privately created messages on the many specialty plates issued by the State of Texas convey a government message rather than the message of the motorist displaying the plate. Can this possibly be correct?

Here is a test. Suppose you sat by the side of a Texas highway and studied the license plates on the vehicles passing by. You would see, in addition to the standard Texas plates, an impressive array of specialty plates. (There are now more than 350 varieties.) You would likely observe plates that honor numerous colleges and universities. You might see plates bearing the name of a high school, a fraternity or sorority, the Masons, the Knights of Columbus, the Daughters of the American Revolution, a realty company, a favorite soft drink, a favorite burger restaurant, and a favorite NASCAR driver.

As you sat there watching these plates speed by, would you really think that the sentiments reflected in these specialty plates are the views of the State of Texas and not those of the owners of the cars? If a car with a plate that says "Rather Be Golfing" passed by at 8:30 am on a Monday morning, would you think: "This is the official policy of the State—better to golf than to work?" . . .

The Court says that all of these messages are government speech. It is essential that government be able to express its own viewpoint, the Court reminds us, because otherwise, how would it promote its programs, like recycling and vaccinations? So when Texas issues a "Rather Be Golfing" plate, but not a "Rather Be Playing Tennis" or "Rather Be Bowling" plate, it is furthering a state policy to promote golf but not tennis or bowling. And when Texas allows motorists to obtain a Notre Dame license plate but not a University of Southern California plate, it is taking sides in that long-time rivalry.

This capacious understanding of government speech takes a large and painful bite out of the First Amendment. Specialty plates may seem innocuous. They make motorists happy, and they put money in a State's coffers. But the precedent this case sets is dangerous. While all license plates unquestionably contain *some* government speech (*e.g.*, the name of the State and the numbers and/or letters identifying the vehicle), the State of Texas has converted the remaining space on its specialty plates into little mobile billboards on which motorists can display their own messages. And what Texas did here was to reject one of the messages that members of a private group wanted to post on some of these little billboards because the State thought that many of its citizens would find the message offensive. That is blatant viewpoint discrimination.

If the State can do this with its little mobile billboards, could it do the same with big, stationary billboards? Suppose that a State erected electronic billboards along its highways. Suppose that the State posted some government messages on these billboards and then, to raise money, allowed private entities and individuals to purchase the right to post their own messages. And suppose that the State allowed only those messages that it liked or found not too controversial. Would that be constitutional?

What if a state college or university did the same thing with a similar billboard or a campus bulletin board or dorm list serve? What if it allowed private messages that are consistent with prevailing views on campus but banned those that disturbed some students or faculty? Can there be any doubt that these examples of viewpoint discrimination would violate the First Amendment? I hope not, but the future uses of today's precedent remain to be seen. . . .

II

The Court badly misunderstands *Summum*. . . .

The[] characteristics [that] rendered public monuments government speech in *Summum*, are not present in Texas's specialty plate program.

I begin with history. As we said in *Summum*, governments have used monuments since time immemorial to express important government messages, and there is no history of governments giving equal space to those wishing to express dissenting views. . . .

The history of messages on license plates is quite different. After the beginning of motor vehicle registration in 1917, more than 70 years passed before the proliferation of specialty plates in Texas. It was not until the 1990's that motorists were allowed to choose from among 10 messages, such as "Read to Succeed" and "Keep Texas Beautiful."

Up to this point, the words on the Texas plates can be considered government speech. The messages were created by the State, and they plausibly promoted state programs. But when, at some point within the last 20 years or so, the State began to allow private entities to secure plates conveying their own messages, Texas crossed the line. . . .

The Texas specialty plate program also does not exhibit the "selective receptivity" present in *Summum*. To the contrary, Texas's program is *not* selective by design. The Board's chairman, who is charged with approving designs, explained that the program's purpose is "to encourage private plates" in order to "generate additional revenue for the state." And most of the time, the Board "base[s] [its] decisions on rules that primarily deal with reflectivity and readability." . . .

The Court believes that messages on privately created plates are government speech because motorists want a seal of state approval for their messages and therefore prefer plates over bumper stickers. This is dangerous reasoning. There is a big difference between government speech (that is, speech by the government in furtherance of its programs) and governmental blessing (or condemnation) of private speech. Many private speakers in a forum would welcome a sign of government approval. But in the realm of private speech, government regulation may not favor one viewpoint over another.

A final factor that was important in *Summum* was space. A park can accommodate only so many permanent monuments. Often large and made of stone, monuments can last for centuries and are difficult to move. License plates, on the other hand, are small, light, mobile, and designed to last for only a relatively brief time. The only absolute limit on the number of specialty plates that a State could issue is the number of registered vehicles. The variety of available plates is limitless, too. Today Texas offers more than 350 varieties. In 10 years, might it be 3,500?

In sum, the Texas specialty plate program has none of the factors that were critical in *Summum*, and the Texas program exhibits a very important characteristic that was missing in that case: Individuals who want to display a Texas specialty plate, instead of the standard plate, must pay an increased annual registration fee. How many groups or individuals would clamor to pay $8,000 (the cost of the deposit required to create a new plate) in order to broadcast the government's message as opposed to their own? And if Texas really wants to speak out in support of, say, Iowa State University (but not the University of Iowa) or "Young Lawyers" (but not old ones), why must it be paid to say things that it really wants to say? . . .

States have not adopted specialty license plate programs like Texas's because they are now bursting with things they want to say on their license plates. Those programs were adopted because they bring in money. . . .

III

What Texas has done by selling space on its license plates is to create what we have called a limited public forum. It has allowed state property (*i.e.*, motor vehicle license plates) to be used by private speakers according to rules that the State prescribes. Under the First Amendment, however, those rules cannot discriminate on the basis of viewpoint. But that is exactly what Texas did here. The Board rejected Texas SCV's design, "specifically the confederate flag portion of the design, because public comments have shown that many members of the general public find the design offensive, and because such comments are reasonable." These statements indisputably demonstrate that the Board denied Texas SCV's design because of its viewpoint.

The Confederate battle flag is a controversial symbol. To the Texas Sons of Confederate Veterans, it is said to evoke the memory of their ancestors and other soldiers who fought for the South in the Civil War. To others, it symbolizes slavery, segregation, and hatred. Whatever it means to motorists who display that symbol and to those who see it, the flag expresses a viewpoint. The Board rejected the plate design because it concluded that many Texans would find the flag symbol offensive. That was pure viewpoint discrimination. . . .

The Board's decision cannot be saved by its suggestion that the plate, if allowed, "could distract or disturb some drivers to the point of being unreasonably dangerous." This rationale cannot withstand strict scrutiny. Other States allow specialty plates with the Confederate Battle Flag, and Texas has not pointed to evidence that these plates have led to incidents of road rage or accidents. Texas does not ban bumper stickers bearing the image of the Confederate battle flag. Nor does it ban any of the many other bumper stickers that convey political messages and other messages that are capable of exciting the ire of those who loathe the ideas they express.

Messages that are proposed by private parties and placed on Texas specialty plates are private speech, not government speech. Texas cannot forbid private speech based on its viewpoint. That is what it did here. Because the Court approves this violation of the First Amendment, I respectfully dissent.

NOTES AND QUESTIONS

1. SCV*'s lasting effects.* Is Justice Alito correct that the majority opinion in *SCV* "takes a large and painful bite out of the First Amendment?"

2. *Which precedents to use?* Which opinion has the better argument about the appropriate line of applicable precedent (government speech versus public forum doctrine)?
3. *Mixed speech.* Is the problem in SCV that the speech involved is really "mixed"—i.e., both government speech and private speech? How could the Court craft rules if it explicitly recognized that fact? For a thoughtful discussion of the problem of "mixed" speech and its treatment under the First Amendment, see Caroline Mala Corbin, *Mixed Speech: When Speech is Both Private and Governmental,* 83 NYU L. REV. 605 (2008). For a discussion of First Amendment principles applicable to government-sponsored social media sites, *see* Lyrissa Barnett Lidsky, *Public Forum 2.0,* 91 B.U. L. REV. 1975 (2011).
4. *Personalized license plates.* Should the majority's or the dissent's reasoning apply to personalized license plates—i.e., standard state plates that individuals seek to have made with specific personalized messages)? If such plates are "government speech," may a personalized plate, also known as a "vanity plate," bear a sectarian religious message ("JEZSSAVS" or "Jhn3:16")?
5. *Having your [speech] and eating it too?* Can the government have it *both* ways? In other words, may the government refuse to issue personalized plates that contain profanity or scatology ("FuckUT") on the theory that the public will assume the government approves of the offensive message? But, if so, then how can the government issue sectarian personalized plates that would arguably violate the Establishment Clause *(see infra* Chapter 18)? As a matter of constitutional logic, doesn't it have to be one way or the other—not both?

AN EXTENDED NOTE ON GOVERNMENT AS SPEAKER AND SPEECH SUBSIDIZER

Reconciling the cases in this section is not an easy task. Several of these opinions seem to point in different directions, and the factual backgrounds of the cases are often not immediately distinguishable. Consider the following thumbnail sketch of the holdings of these cases. On the one hand, the government is allowed to strictly regulate the content of the speech of individuals that the government hires to speak on its behalf (*Rust*); distinguish among speakers based on the content of speech when the government agent is exercising professional expertise (*Finley*); distinguish among speakers when the government agent is serving an editorial function (*Forbes*); choose which private monuments to "adopt" to convey its own message (*Summum*); and choose which specialty license plates to "adopt" when proposed by private organizations (*SCV*). On the other hand, the government is not allowed to make content-based distinctions among speakers where government funds are used to create a forum that is intended to encourage a diversity of views from private speakers (*Rosenberger*), or where the professional responsibilities of the person or entity hired by the government require that person or entity to express opposition to the government (*Velazquez*). Although this schematic rendering of the Court's holdings may initially seem to draw logical distinctions between the cases, fitting new facts into the various categories will often be difficult. Even in the cases already decided by the Court, it is not immediately evident why one case fits on one side of the line and another case fits on the other side of the line. For example, as Justice Scalia notes in *Velazquez*, it is difficult to distinguish between the lawyer in that case—whom the Court deemed independent of government control—and the doctors and other health professionals in *Rust*—whose speech the Court subjected to virtually complete government control. Nor is it clear why the specialty license plate rules in *SCV* favor a finding of government speech rather than creation of a public forum. The situation becomes even more complicated in the next section, in which the Court creates an entirely different framework for considering constitutional protections for the speech of government employees. Keep in mind that there is substantial overlap between various categories of government speech or government-funded speech, and many factual scenarios could logically be treated under several different categories.

THEORY-APPLIED PROBLEM: THE MEN'S CLUB

The University of Exum is a public university. A group of students at the university wish to become an accredited university group so they can apply for the University's student activities fund and use the University's electronic mailing lists to recruit members and announce group events. This new student group calls itself the "Men's Club" and has as its stated purpose "preventing male decline as women enroll in higher education institutions at greater rates than men and increasingly become the breadwinners for their families." Accreditation of student groups at the University of Exum is granted by a joint faculty-student committee whose assigned task is to grant accreditation to "educationally appropriate student groups that further the educational mission of the University of Exum." Examples of previously accredited groups include the Debate Club, the Art Appreciation Society, and the University Choral Group. The accreditation committee denies accreditation to the Men's Club, stating that it is not an "educationally appropriate student group." The Men's Club is the first student group ever denied accreditation by the University. The Men's Club approaches you for legal advice. What legal strategy do you recommend?

THEORY-APPLIED PROBLEM: PUBLIC SCHOOL BANNERS

Since 2010, the Palm Beach County School District ("District") has used a banner program to recognize business sponsors of its school programs, such as athletics or academic programs. Sponsors have been valuable in giving monetary donations to these programs and the District views these banners, which are hung on fences and gym walls, as a means of recognizing the sponsors' support. The donations are not considered to be payment for advertising. Furthermore, the District's Policy Manual specifically notes that "by permitting the recognition of business sponsors on school campuses, it is not the intent of the District to create or open any school, school property, or facility as a forum for expressive activity or to create a forum for expression that is inconsistent with the educational mission of the District or which could be perceived as bearing the imprimatur or endorsement of the District." David Mech provides a tutoring service in Palm Beach County under the name the "Happy/Fun Math Tutor." He has bachelor's and master's degrees in math. He is also a retired porn star and producer of pornographic films. Beginning in 2013, Mech's business hung a banner with his company's name, location and phone number (after giving a donation of $500) at several local middle and high schools. In 2015, the schools removed the banners after several parents complained upon learning of Mech's past career and current production company. Mech sued the District claiming that the removal of the banners violated his First Amendment rights. The District argued that the banner program amounted to government speech. Can the District credibly argue that the banner program is government speech. This problem is somewhat based on Mech v. School Board of Palm Beach County, 806 F.3d 1070 (11th Cir. 2015).

B. SPEECH BY GOVERNMENT EMPLOYEES

Pickering v. Board of Education

391 U.S. 563 (1968)

MARSHALL, J., delivered the opinion of the Court.

Appellant Marvin L. Pickering, a teacher in Township High School District 205, Will County, Illinois, was dismissed from his position by the appellee Board of Education for sending a letter to a local newspaper in connection with a recently proposed tax increase that was critical of the way in which the Board and the district superintendent of schools had handled past proposals to raise new revenue for the schools. Appellant's dismissal resulted from a determination by the Board, after a full hearing, that the publication of the letter was "detrimental to the efficient operation and administration of the schools of the district" and hence, under the relevant Illinois statute that "interests of the school require[d] [his dismissal]."

The letter constituted, basically, an attack on the School Board's handling of the [proposed tax increase] and its subsequent allocation of financial resources between the schools' educational and athletic programs. It also charged the superintendent of schools with attempting to prevent teachers in the district from opposing or criticizing the proposed bond issue.

. . . [T]he Board charged that numerous statements in the letter were false and that the publication of the statements unjustifiably impugned the "motives, honesty, integrity, truthfulness, responsibility and competence" of both the Board and the school administration. The Board also charged that the false statements damaged the professional reputations of its members and of the school administrators, would be disruptive of faculty discipline, and would tend to foment "controversy, conflict and dissension" among teachers, administrators, the Board of Education, and the residents of the district.

[The Illinois Supreme Court rejected Pickering's claim that the First Amendment prohibited the Board from firing him. The Illinois Court rested its decision] on the ground that [Pickering's] acceptance of a teaching position in the public schools obliged him to refrain from making statements about the operation of the schools "which in the absence of such position he would have an undoubted right to engage in."

To the extent that the Illinois Supreme Court's opinion may be read to suggest that teachers may constitutionally be compelled to relinquish the First Amendment rights they would otherwise enjoy as citizens to comment on matters of public interest in connection with the operation of the public schools in which they work, it proceeds on a premise that has been unequivocally rejected in numerous prior decisions of this Court. At the same time it cannot be gainsaid that the State has interests as an employer in regulating the speech of its employees that differ significantly from those it possesses in connection with regulation of the speech of the citizenry in general. The problem in any case is to arrive at a balance between the interests of the teacher, as a citizen, in commenting upon matters of public concern and the interest of the State, as an employer, in promoting the efficiency of the public services it performs through its employees.

Because of the enormous variety of fact situations in which critical statements by teachers and other public employees may be thought by their superiors, against whom the statements are directed, to furnish grounds for dismissal, we do not deem it either appropriate or feasible to attempt to lay down a general standard against which all such statements may be judged. However, in the course of evaluating the conflicting claims of First Amendment protection and the need for orderly school administration in the context of this case, we shall indicate some of the general lines along which an analysis of the controlling interests should run.

An examination of the statements in appellant's letter objected to by the Board reveals that they, like the letter as a whole, consist essentially of criticism of the Board's allocation of school funds between educational and athletic programs, and of both the Board's and the superintendent's methods of informing, or preventing the informing of, the district's taxpayers of the real reasons why additional tax revenues were being sought for the schools. The statements are in no way directed towards any person with whom appellant would normally be in contact in the course of his daily work as a teacher. Thus no question of maintaining either discipline by immediate superiors or harmony among coworkers is presented here. Appellant's employment relationships with the Board and, to a somewhat lesser extent, with the superintendent are not the kind of close working relationships for which it can persuasively be claimed that personal loyalty and confidence are necessary to their proper functioning. Accordingly, to the extent that the Board's position here can be taken to suggest that even comments on matters of public concern that are substantially correct furnish grounds for dismissal if they are sufficiently critical in tone, we unequivocally reject it.

[The Court then discussed several factually inaccurate statements in Pickering's letter.] What we do have before us is a case in which a teacher has made erroneous public statements upon issues then currently the subject of public attention, which are critical of his ultimate employer but which are neither shown nor can be presumed to have in any way either impeded the teacher's proper performance of his daily duties in the classroom or to have interfered with the regular operation of the schools generally. In these circumstances we conclude that the interest of the school administration in limiting teachers' opportunities to contribute to public debate is not significantly greater than its interest in limiting a similar contribution by any member of the general public.

While criminal sanctions and damage awards have a somewhat different impact on the exercise of the right to freedom of speech from dismissal from employment, it is apparent that the threat of dismissal from public employment is nonetheless a potent means of inhibiting speech. We have already noted our disinclination to make an across-the-board equation of dismissal from public employment for remarks critical of superiors with awarding damages in a libel suit by a public official for similar criticism. However, in a case such as the present one, in which the fact of employment is only tangentially and insubstantially involved in the subject matter of the public communication made by a teacher, we conclude that it is necessary to regard the teacher as the member of the general public he seeks to be.

[Justice White's separate opinion is omitted.]

Connick v. Myers

461 U.S. 138 (1983)

WHITE, J., delivered the opinion of the Court.

In *Pickering v. Board of Education*, we stated that a public employee does not relinquish First Amendment rights to comment on matters of public interest by virtue of government employment. We also recognized that the State's interests as an employer in regulating the speech of its employees "differ significantly from those it possesses in connection with regulation of the speech of the citizenry in general." The problem, we thought, was arriving "at a balance between the interests of the [employee], as a citizen, in commenting upon matters of public concern and the interest of the State, as an employer, in promoting the efficiency of the public services it performs through its employees." We return to this problem today and consider whether the First and Fourteenth Amendments prevent the discharge of a state employee for circulating a questionnaire concerning internal office affairs.

The respondent, Sheila Myers, was employed as an Assistant District Attorney in New Orleans for five and a half years. She served at the pleasure of petitioner Harry Connick, the District Attorney for Orleans Parish. During this period Myers competently performed her responsibilities of trying criminal cases.

In the early part of October 1980, Myers was informed that she would be transferred to prosecute cases in a different section of the criminal court. Myers was strongly opposed to the proposed transfer and expressed her view to several of her supervisors, including Connick. A number of other office matters were discussed and Myers later testified that, in response to [her supervisor's] suggestion that her concerns were not shared by others in the office, she informed him that she would do some research on the matter.

That night Myers prepared a questionnaire soliciting the views of her fellow staff members concerning office transfer policy, office morale, the need for a grievance committee, the level of confidence in supervisors, and whether employees felt pressured to work in political campaigns. [The next day,] Myers distributed the questionnaire to 15 Assistant District Attorneys. Shortly after noon, [one of her supervisors] learned that Myers was distributing the survey. He immediately phoned Connick and informed him that Myers was creating a "mini-insurrection" within the office. Connick returned to the office and told Myers that she was being terminated because of her refusal to accept the transfer. She was also told that her distribution of the questionnaire was considered an act of insubordination. Connick particularly objected to the question which inquired whether employees "had confidence in and would rely on the word" of various superiors in the office, and to a question concerning pressure to work in political campaigns which he felt would be damaging if discovered by the press.

For at least 15 years, it has been settled that a State cannot condition public employment on a basis that infringes the employee's constitutionally protected interest in freedom of expression. Our task, as we defined it in *Pickering*, is to seek "a balance between the interests of the [employee], as a citizen, in commenting upon matters of public concern and the interest of the State, as an employer, in promoting the efficiency of the public services it performs through its employees." The District Court [and Court of Appeals] misapplied our decision in *Pickering* and consequently, in our view, erred in striking the balance for respondent.

The District Court got off on the wrong foot in this case by initially finding that, "[t]aken as a whole, the issues presented in the questionnaire relate to the effective functioning of the District Attorney's Office and are matters of public importance and concern." Connick contends at the outset that no balancing of interests is required in this case because Myers' questionnaire concerned only internal office matters and that such speech is not upon a matter of "public concern," as the term was used in *Pickering*. Although we do not agree that Myers' communication in this case was wholly without First Amendment protection, there is much force to Connick's submission. The repeated emphasis in *Pickering* on the right of a public employee "as a citizen, in commenting upon matters of public concern," was not accidental. This language, reiterated in all of *Pickering*'s progeny, reflects both the historical evolvement of the rights of public employees, and the common-sense realization that government offices could not function if every employment decision became a constitutional matter.

In the precedents in which *Pickering* is rooted, the invalidated statutes and actions sought to suppress the rights of public employees to participate in public affairs. The issue was whether government employees could be prevented or "chilled" by the fear of discharge from joining political parties and other associations that certain public officials might find "subversive."

Pickering v. Board of Education followed from this understanding of the First Amendment. Pickering's subject was "a matter of legitimate public concern" upon which "free and open debate is vital to informed decision-making by the electorate."

Pickering, its antecedents, and its progeny lead us to conclude that if Myers' questionnaire cannot be fairly characterized as constituting speech on a matter of public concern, it is unnecessary for us to scrutinize the reasons for her discharge. When employee expression cannot be fairly considered as relating to any matter of political, social, or other concern to the community, government officials should enjoy wide latitude in managing their offices, without intrusive oversight by the judiciary in the name of the First Amendment. Perhaps the government employer's dismissal of the worker may not be fair, but ordinary dismissals from government service which violate no fixed tenure or applicable statute or regulation are not subject to judicial review even if the reasons for the dismissal are alleged to be mistaken or unreasonable.

We do not suggest, however, that Myers' speech, even if not touching upon a matter of public concern, is totally beyond the protection of the First Amendment. "[T]he First Amendment does not protect speech and assembly only to the extent it can be characterized as political. 'Great secular causes, with smaller ones, are guarded.'" We hold only that when a public employee speaks not as a citizen upon matters of public concern, but instead as an employee upon matters only of personal interest, absent the most unusual circumstances, a federal court is not the appropriate forum in which to review the wisdom of a personnel decision taken by a public agency allegedly in reaction to the employee's behavior.

Whether an employee's speech addresses a matter of public concern must be determined by the content, form, and context of a given statement, as revealed by the whole record. In this case, with but one exception, the questions posed by Myers to her co-workers do not fall under the rubric of matters of "public concern." We view the questions pertaining to the confidence and trust that Myers' co-workers possess in various supervisors, the level of office morale, and the need for a grievance committee as mere extensions of Myers' dispute over her transfer to another section of the criminal court. Unlike the dissent, we do not believe these questions are of public import in evaluating the performance of the District Attorney as an elected official. Myers did not seek to inform the public that the District Attorney's Office was not discharging its governmental responsibilities in the investigation and prosecution of criminal cases. Nor did Myers seek to bring to light actual or potential wrongdoing or breach of public trust on the part of Connick and others. Indeed, the questionnaire, if released to the public, would convey no information at all other than the fact that a single employee is upset with the status quo. While discipline and morale in the workplace are related to an agency's efficient performance of its duties, the focus of Myers' questions is not to evaluate the performance of the office but rather to gather ammunition for another round of controversy with her superiors. These questions reflect one employee's dissatisfaction with a transfer and an attempt to turn that displeasure into a cause celebre.

To presume that all matters which transpire within a government office are of public concern would mean that virtually every remark—and certainly every criticism directed at a public official—would plant the seed of a constitutional case. While as a matter of good judgment, public officials should be receptive to constructive criticism offered by their employees, the First Amendment does not require a public office to be run as a roundtable for employee complaints over internal office affairs.

One question in Myers' questionnaire, however, does touch upon a matter of public concern. Question 11 inquires if assistant district attorneys "ever feel pressured to work in political campaigns on behalf of office supported candidates." We have recently noted that official pressure upon employees to work for political candidates not of the worker's own choice constitutes a coercion of belief in violation of fundamental constitutional rights. Given this history, we believe it apparent that the issue of whether assistant district attorneys are pressured to work in political campaigns is a matter of interest to the community upon which it is essential that public employees be able to speak out freely without fear of retaliatory dismissal.

Because one of the questions in Myers' survey touched upon a matter of public concern and contributed to her discharge, we must determine whether Connick was justified in discharging Myers.

The *Pickering* balance requires full consideration of the government's interest in the effective and efficient fulfillment of its responsibilities to the public. One hundred years ago, the Court noted the government's legitimate purpose in "promot[ing] efficiency and integrity in the discharge of official duties, and [in] maintain[ing] proper discipline in the public service."

We agree with the District Court that there is no demonstration here that the questionnaire impeded Myers' ability to perform her responsibilities. The District Court was also correct to recognize that "it is important to the efficient and successful operation of the District Attorney's office for Assistants to maintain close working relationships with their superiors." Connick's judgment, and apparently also that of his first assistant Dennis Waldron, who characterized Myers' actions as causing a "mini-insurrection," was that Myers' questionnaire was an act of insubordination which interfered with working relationships. When close working relationships are essential to fulfilling public responsibilities, a wide degree of deference to the employer's judgment is appropriate. Furthermore, we do not see the necessity for an employer to allow events to unfold to the extent that the disruption of the office and the destruction of working relationships is [*sic*] manifest before taking action. We caution that a stronger showing may be necessary if the employee's speech more substantially involved matters of public concern.

Also relevant is the manner, time, and place in which the questionnaire was distributed. Here the questionnaire was prepared and distributed at the office; the manner of distribution required not only Myers to leave her work but others to do the same in order that the questionnaire be completed. Although some latitude in when official work is performed is to be allowed when professional employees are involved, and Myers did not violate announced office policy, the fact that Myers, unlike Pickering, exercised her rights to speech at the office supports Connick's fears that the functioning of his office was endangered.

Finally, the context in which the dispute arose is also significant. This is not a case where an employee, out of purely academic interest, circulated a questionnaire so as to obtain useful research. Myers acknowledges that it is no coincidence that the questionnaire followed upon the heels of the transfer notice. When employee speech concerning office policy arises from an employment dispute concerning the very application of that policy to the speaker, additional weight must be given to the supervisor's view that the employee has threatened the authority of the employer to run the office.

BRENNAN, J., with whom MARSHALL, J., BLACKMUN, J., and STEVENS, J., join, dissenting.

The balancing test articulated in *Pickering* comes into play only when a public employee's speech implicates the government's interests as an employer. When public employees engage in expression unrelated to their employment while away from the workplace, their First Amendment rights are, of course, no different from those of the general public. Thus, whether a public employee's speech addresses a matter of public concern is relevant to the constitutional inquiry only when the statements at issue—by virtue of their content or the context in which they were made—may have an adverse impact on the government's ability to perform its duties efficiently.

The Court's decision today is flawed in three respects. First, the Court distorts the balancing analysis required under *Pickering* by suggesting that one factor, the context in which a statement is made, is to be weighed *twice*—first in determining whether an employee's speech addresses a matter of public concern and then in deciding whether the statement adversely affected the government's interest as an employer. Second, in concluding that the effect of respondent's personnel policies on employee morale and the work performance of the District Attorney's Office is not a matter of public concern, the Court impermissibly narrows the class of subjects on which public employees may speak out without fear of retaliatory dismissal. Third, the Court misapplies the *Pickering* balancing test in holding that Myers could constitutionally be dismissed for circulating a questionnaire addressed to at least one subject that *was* "a matter of interest to the community," in the absence of evidence that her conduct disrupted the efficient functioning of the District Attorney's Office.

The Court's decision today inevitably will deter public employees from making critical statements about the manner in which government agencies are operated for fear that doing so will provoke their dismissal. As a result, the public will be deprived of valuable information with which to evaluate the performance of elected officials. Because protecting the dissemination of such information is an essential function of the First Amendment, I dissent.

Garcetti v. Ceballos

547 U.S. 410 (2006)

KENNEDY, J., delivered the opinion of the Court.

Respondent Richard Ceballos has been employed since 1989 as a deputy district attorney for the Los Angeles County District Attorney's Office. During the period relevant to this case, Ceballos was a calendar deputy in the office's Pomona branch, and in this capacity he exercised certain supervisory responsibilities over other lawyers. In February 2000, a defense attorney contacted Ceballos about a pending criminal case. The defense attorney said there were inaccuracies in an affidavit used to obtain a critical search warrant. The attorney informed Ceballos that he had filed a motion to traverse, or challenge, the warrant, but he also wanted Ceballos to review the case.

After examining the affidavit and visiting the location it described, Ceballos determined the affidavit contained serious misrepresentations. The affidavit called a long driveway what Ceballos thought should have been referred to as a separate roadway. Ceballos also questioned the affidavit's statement that tire tracks led from a stripped-down truck to the premises covered by the warrant. His doubts arose from his conclusion that the roadway's composition in some places made it difficult or impossible to leave visible tire tracks.

Ceballos spoke on the telephone to the warrant affiant, a deputy sheriff from the Los Angeles County Sheriff's Department, but he did not receive a satisfactory explanation for the perceived inaccuracies. He relayed his findings to his supervisors, petitioners Carol Najera and Frank Sundstedt, and followed up by preparing a disposition memorandum. The memo explained Ceballos' concerns and recommended dismissal of the case.

Based on Ceballos' statements, a meeting was held to discuss the affidavit. Attendees included Ceballos, Sundstedt, and Najera, as well as the warrant affiant and other employees from the sheriff's department. The meeting allegedly became heated, with one lieutenant sharply criticizing Ceballos for his handling of the case.

Despite Ceballos' concerns, Sundstedt decided to proceed with the prosecution, pending disposition of the defense motion to traverse. The trial court held a hearing on the motion. Ceballos was called by the defense and recounted his observations about the affidavit, but the trial court rejected the challenge to the warrant.

Ceballos claims that in the aftermath of these events he was subjected to a series of retaliatory employment actions. The actions included reassignment from his calendar deputy position to a trial deputy position, transfer to another courthouse, and denial of a promotion. He alleged petitioners violated the First and Fourteenth Amendments by retaliating against him based on his memo.

As the Court's decisions have noted, for many years "the unchallenged dogma was that a public employee had no right to object to conditions placed upon the terms of employment—including those which restricted the exercise of constitutional rights." *Connick*. That dogma has been qualified in important respects. The Court has made clear that public employees do not surrender all their First Amendment rights by reason of their employment. Rather, the First Amendment protects a public employee's right, in certain circumstances, to speak as a citizen addressing matters of public concern. The Court's decisions have sought both to promote the individual and societal interests that are served when employees speak as citizens on matters of public concern and to respect the needs of government employers attempting to perform their important public functions. Underlying our cases has been the premise that while the First Amendment invests public employees with certain rights, it does not empower them to "constitutionalize the employee grievance." *Connick*.

With these principles in mind we turn to the instant case. Respondent Ceballos believed the affidavit used to obtain a search warrant contained serious misrepresentations. He conveyed his opinion and recommendation in a memo to his supervisor. That Ceballos expressed his views inside his office, rather than publicly, is not dispositive. Employees in some cases may receive First Amendment protection for expressions made at work. Many citizens do much of their talking inside their respective workplaces, and it would not serve the goal of treating public employees like "any member of the general public," *Pickering*, to hold that all speech within the office is automatically exposed to restriction.

The memo concerned the subject matter of Ceballos' employment, but this, too, is nondispositive. The First Amendment protects some expressions related to the speaker's job. As the Court noted in *Pickering*: "Teachers are, as a class, the members of a community most likely to have informed and definite opinions as to how funds allotted to the operation of the schools should be spent. Accordingly, it is essential that they be able to speak out freely on such questions without fear of retaliatory dismissal." The same is true of many other categories of public employees.

The controlling factor in Ceballos' case is that his expressions were made pursuant to his duties as a calendar deputy. That consideration—the fact that Ceballos spoke as a prosecutor fulfilling a responsibility to advise his supervisor about how best to proceed with a pending case—distinguishes Ceballos' case from those in which the First Amendment provides protection against discipline. We hold that when public employees make statements pursuant to their official duties, the employees are not speaking as citizens for First Amendment purposes, and the Constitution does not insulate their communications from employer discipline.

Ceballos wrote his disposition memo because that is part of what he, as a calendar deputy, was employed to do. The significant point is that the memo was written pursuant to Ceballos' official duties. Restricting speech that owes its existence to a public employee's professional responsibilities does not infringe any liberties the employee might have enjoyed as a private citizen. It simply reflects the exercise of employer control over what the employer itself has commissioned or created. Contrast, for example, the expressions made by the speaker in *Pickering*, whose letter to the newspaper had no official significance and bore similarities to letters submitted by numerous citizens every day.

Ceballos did not act as a citizen when he went about conducting his daily professional activities, such as supervising attorneys, investigating charges, and preparing filings. In the same way he did not speak as a citizen by writing a memo that addressed the proper disposition of a pending criminal case. When he went to work and performed the tasks he was paid to perform, Ceballos acted as a government employee. The fact that his duties sometimes required him to speak or write does not mean his supervisors were prohibited from evaluating his performance.

Employers have heightened interests in controlling speech made by an employee in his or her professional capacity. Official communications have official consequences, creating a need for substantive consistency and clarity. Supervisors must ensure that their employees' official communications are accurate, demonstrate sound judgment, and promote the employer's mission. Ceballos' memo is illustrative. It demanded the attention of his supervisors and led to a heated meeting with employees from the sheriff's department. If Ceballos' superiors thought his memo was inflammatory or misguided, they had the authority to take proper corrective action.

The Court of Appeals based its holding in part on what it perceived as a doctrinal anomaly. The court suggested it would be inconsistent to compel public employers to tolerate certain employee speech made publicly but not speech made pursuant to an employee's assigned duties. This objection misconceives the theoretical underpinnings of our decisions. Employees who make public statements outside the course of performing their official duties retain some possibility of First Amendment protection because that is the kind of activity engaged in by citizens who do not work for the government. The same goes for writing a letter to a local newspaper, *see Pickering*, or discussing politics with a co-worker, *see* Rankin [v. MacPherson, 483 U.S. 378 (1987)]. When a public employee speaks pursuant to employment responsibilities, however, there is no relevant analogue to speech by citizens who are not government employees.

The Court of Appeals' concern also is unfounded as a practical matter. The perceived anomaly, it should be noted, is limited in scope: It relates only to the expressions an employee makes pursuant to his or her official responsibilities, not to statements or complaints (such as those at issue in cases like *Pickering* and *Connick*) that are made outside the duties of employment. If, moreover, a government employer is troubled by the perceived anomaly, it has the means at hand to avoid it. A public employer that wishes to encourage its employees to voice concerns privately retains the option of instituting internal policies and procedures that are receptive to employee criticism. Giving employees an internal forum for their speech will discourage them from concluding that the safest avenue of expression is to state their views in public.

Two final points warrant mentioning. First, as indicated above, the parties in this case do not dispute that Ceballos wrote his disposition memo pursuant to his employment duties. We thus have no occasion to articulate a comprehensive framework for defining the scope of an employee's duties in cases where there is room for serious debate. We reject, however, the suggestion that employers can restrict employees' rights by creating excessively broad job descriptions. The proper inquiry is a practical one. Formal job descriptions often bear little resemblance to the duties an employee actually is expected to perform, and the listing of a given task in an employee's written job description is neither necessary nor sufficient to demonstrate that conducting the task is within the scope of the employee's professional duties for First Amendment purposes.

Second, Justice Souter suggests today's decision may have important ramifications for academic freedom, at least as a constitutional value. There is some argument that expression related to academic scholarship or classroom instruction implicates additional constitutional interests that are not fully accounted for by this Court's customary employee-speech jurisprudence. We need not, and for that reason do not, decide whether the analysis we conduct today would apply in the same manner to a case involving speech related to scholarship or teaching.

Exposing governmental inefficiency and misconduct is a matter of considerable significance. As the Court noted in *Connick*, public employers should, "as a matter of good judgment," be "receptive to constructive criticism offered by their employees." The dictates of sound judgment are reinforced by the powerful network of legislative enactments—such as whistle-blower protection laws and labor codes—available to those who seek to expose wrongdoing. Cases involving government attorneys implicate additional safeguards in the form of, for example, rules of conduct and constitutional obligations apart from the First Amendment. See, *e.g.*, Cal. Rule Prof. Conduct 5-110 (2005) ("A member in government service shall not institute or cause to be instituted criminal charges when the member knows or should know that the charges are not supported by probable cause"); *Brady v. Maryland*, 373 U.S. 83 (1963). These imperatives, as well as obligations arising from any other applicable constitutional provisions and mandates of the criminal and civil laws, protect employees and provide checks on supervisors who would order unlawful or otherwise inappropriate actions.

We reject, however, the notion that the First Amendment shields from discipline the expressions employees make pursuant to their professional duties. Our precedents do not support the existence of a constitutional cause of action behind every statement a public employee makes in the course of doing his or her job.

SOUTER, J., with whom STEVENS, J., and GINSBURG, J., join, dissenting.

The Court holds that "when public employees make statements pursuant to their official duties, the employees are not speaking as citizens for First Amendment purposes, and the Constitution does not insulate their communications from employer discipline." I respectfully dissent. I agree with the majority that a government employer has substantial interests in effectuating its chosen policy and objectives, and in demanding competence, honesty, and judgment from employees who speak for it in doing their work. But I would hold that private and public interests in addressing official wrongdoing and threats to health and safety can outweigh the government's stake in the efficient implementation of policy, and when they do public employees who speak on these matters in the course of their duties should be eligible to claim First Amendment protection.

Up to a point, then, the majority makes good points: government needs civility in the workplace, consistency in policy, and honesty and competence in public service. But why do the majority's concerns, which we all share, require categorical exclusion of First Amendment protection against any official retaliation for things said on the job? Is it not possible to respect the unchallenged individual and public interests in the speech through a *Pickering* balance? This is, to be sure, a matter of judgment, but the judgment has to account for the undoubted value of speech to those, and by those, whose specific public job responsibilities bring them face to face with wrongdoing and incompetence in government, who refuse to avert their eyes and shut their mouths. And it has to account for the need actually to disrupt government if its officials are corrupt or dangerously incompetent. It is thus no adequate justification for the suppression of potentially valuable information simply to recognize that the government has a huge interest in managing its employees and preventing the occasionally irresponsible one from turning his job into a bully pulpit. Even there, the lesson of *Pickering* (and the object of most constitutional adjudication) is still to the point: when constitutionally significant interests clash, resist the demand for winner-take-all; try to make adjustments that serve all of the values at stake.

Two reasons in particular make me think an adjustment using the basic *Pickering* balancing scheme is perfectly feasible here. First, the extent of the government's legitimate authority over subjects of speech required by a public job can be recognized in advance by setting in effect a minimum heft for comments with any claim to outweigh it. Thus, the risks to the government are great enough for us to hold from the outset that an employee commenting on subjects in the course of duties should not prevail on balance unless he speaks on a matter of unusual importance and satisfies high standards of responsibility in the way he does it. The examples I have already given indicate the eligible subject matter, and it is fair to say that only comment on official dishonesty, deliberately unconstitutional action, other serious wrongdoing, or threats to health and safety can weigh out in an employee's favor.

My second reason for adapting *Pickering* to the circumstances at hand is the experience in Circuits that have recognized claims like Ceballos's here. First Amendment protection less circumscribed than what I would recognize has been available in the Ninth Circuit for over 17 years, and neither there nor in other Circuits that accept claims like this one has there been a debilitating flood of litigation. There has indeed been some: as represented by Ceballos's lawyer at oral argument, each year over the last five years, approximately 70 cases in the different

Courts of Appeals and approximately 100 in the various District Courts. But even these figures reflect a readiness to litigate that might well have been cooled by my view about the importance required before *Pickering* treatment is in order.

The majority accepts the fallacy propounded by the county petitioners and the Federal Government as *amicus* that any statement made within the scope of public employment is (or should be treated as) the government's own speech, and should thus be differentiated as a matter of law from the personal statements the First Amendment protects. The majority invokes the interpretation set out in *Rosenberger* of *Rust,* which held there was no infringement of the speech rights of Title X funds recipients and their staffs when the Government forbade any on-the-job counseling in favor of abortion as a method of family planning. We have read *Rust* to mean that "when the government appropriates public funds to promote a particular policy of its own it is entitled to say what it wishes." *Rosenberger.*

The key to understanding the difference between this case and *Rust* lies in the terms of the respective employees' jobs and, in particular, the extent to which those terms require espousal of a substantive position prescribed by the government in advance. Some public employees are hired to "promote a particular policy" by broadcasting a particular message set by the government, but not everyone working for the government, after all, is hired to speak from a government manifesto. *See Legal Services Corporation v. Velazquez.* There is no claim or indication that Ceballos was hired to perform such a speaking assignment. He was paid to enforce the law by constitutional action: to exercise the county government's prosecutorial power by acting honestly, competently, and constitutionally. The only sense in which his position apparently required him to hew to a substantive message was at the relatively abstract point of favoring respect for law and its evenhanded enforcement, subjects that are not at the level of controversy in this case and were not in *Rust.* Unlike the doctors in *Rust,* Ceballos was not paid to advance one specific policy among those legitimately available, defined by a specific message or limited by a particular message forbidden. The county government's interest in his speech cannot therefore be equated with the terms of a specific, prescribed, or forbidden substantive position comparable to the Federal Government's interest in *Rust,* and *Rust* is no authority for the notion that government may exercise plenary control over every comment made by a public employee in doing his job.

[Citations omitted.]

[Justices Stevens's and Breyer's dissenting opinions are omitted.]

NOTES AND QUESTIONS

1. *Applying the* Connick *standard.* The *Connick* standard is very favorable to public employers seeking to limit the speech of their employees. Under *Connick,* the employee has no First Amendment right whatsoever if the employee's expression does not relate to a matter of public concern, and even if the employee's expression is about a matter of public concern, the employer may still restrict the expression if it would disrupt the workplace in any significant way. In several other decisions involving the free speech rights of government employees, the Court has described the details of the First Amendment analysis in ways that make the standard for assessing free

speech rights in this context even more employer-friendly. For example, the Court places the initial burden on the employee to demonstrate "that his conduct was constitutionally protected, and that this conduct was a 'substantial factor'—or, to put it in other words, that it was a 'motivating factor'" in the decision to fire or sanction the employee. Mt. Healthy City Sch. Dist. Bd. of Educ. v. Doyle, 429 U.S. 274, 287 (1977). Once the employee has met that burden, the government employer must then show "by a preponderance of the evidence that it would have reached the same decision as to [the employee's] re-employment even in the absence of the protected conduct." The employer thus has three chances to avoid liability when an employee has been sanctioned for expression that the employer disfavors. First, the employer may argue that the speech does not pertain to a matter of public concern; second, the employer may argue that the speech disrupts the workplace; and third, the employer may argue that it would have sanctioned the employee regardless of the employee's protected speech.

2. *Defining disruption of the workplace.* In assessing whether an employee's speech has disrupted the workplace, the Court has held that employers must be given substantial deference in quelling potential disruption. This deference is so substantial that courts must even defer to an employer's mistaken impression of what the employee said. In Waters v. Churchill, 511 U.S. 661 (1994), for example, a plurality of the Court held that a public employer may punish an employee in reliance on the employer's reasonable belief that an employee engaged in constitutionally unprotected speech—even if it turns out that the employee's actual remarks were constitutionally protected. The case involved a conversation between two nurses who worked at a public hospital. The first nurse was thinking of transferring to the hospital's obstetrics department, in which the second nurse worked. Three other employees overhead this conversation, and later told their supervisor that the second nurse had made several derogatory comments about the department and one of her supervisors. When the supervisor confronted her, the second nurse denied that she had made some of the negative comments attributed to her. The supervisor nevertheless fired her. Subsequent investigation indicated that the supervisor apparently misunderstood the full context and content of the second nurse's comments. The nurse sued, alleging a violation of her First Amendment rights. Writing for a plurality of the Supreme Court, Justice O'Connor concluded that, unlike First Amendment contexts involving government regulation of private speech, in cases involving government employment "the government's interest in achieving its goals as effectively and efficiently as possible is elevated from a relatively subordinate interest . . . to a significant one." Thus, while the government may not regulate private speech in the interest of efficiency alone, "where the government is employing someone for the very purpose of effectively achieving its goals, such restrictions may well be appropriate." Justice O'Connor specifically recognized that in making the decision to sanction employees based on their speech, government employers may rely "on hearsay, on past similar conduct, on their personal knowledge of people's credibility, and on other factors that the judicial process ignores." The only limit on the employer is that the employer's assessment of the situation must be reasonable.

"We think employer decisionmaking will not be unduly burdened by having courts look to the facts as the employer reasonably found them to be." The employee will prevail under this standard only if the employer acts on the basis of no evidence or very weak evidence of what the employee said. The employer will prevail in a claim governed by the *Connick* standard, however, if the employer merely makes a reasonable mistake about the content of the employee's speech. Is the plurality insufficiently protective of government employees' speech rights? Would it give a government employer free rein to fire an employee based on a false rumor that she had criticized her supervisor's management style? How about a false rumor that she had voted for a Democrat?

3. *Employee or citizen? On-duty or off?* After *Garcetti,* an employee speaking as an employee receives no protection for her speech, but the line between speaking as an employee and speaking as a citizen is by no means always clear. *Garcetti* suggests that when an employer "commission[s] or create[s]" the employee's speech, the speech is subject to the control of the government. In what other circumstances can the government punish or control employee speech in order to further its own message? How critical is the distinction between off-duty speech and on-duty speech? Does it depend on the job? For example, may an assistant attorney general be fired for creating a blog calling a gay student body president a "racist" and a "liar" promoting a "radical homosexual agenda"? *See* Mary-Rose Papandrea, *The Free Speech Rights of "Off-Duty" Government Employees,* 2010 BYU L. Rev. 2117, 2120 (2010) (arguing that "the *Connick/ Pickering* framework should not apply in cases involving off-duty, non-work-related government-employee speech" because it "is not appropriately tailored to address a government employer's legitimate interests").

Lane v. Franks

573 U.S. 228 (2014)

SOTOMAYOR, J., delivered the opinion of the Court.

. . . Today, we consider whether the First Amendment protects a public employee who provided truthful sworn testimony, compelled by subpoena, outside the course of his ordinary job responsibilities. We hold that it does.

In 2006, Central Alabama Community College (CACC) hired petitioner Edward Lane to be the Director of Community Intensive Training for Youth (CITY), a statewide program for underprivileged youth. . . .

At the time of Lane's appointment, CITY faced significant financial difficulties. That prompted Lane to conduct a comprehensive audit of the program's expenses. The audit revealed that Suzanne Schmitz, an Alabama State Representative on CITY's payroll, had not been reporting to her CITY office. . . . contacted Schmitz again and instructed her to show up to the Huntsville office to serve as a counselor. Schmitz refused; she responded that she wished to "'continue to serve the CITY program in the same manner as [she had] in the past.'" Lane fired her shortly thereafter. Schmitz told another CITY employee, Charles Foley, that she intended to "'get [Lane] back'" for firing her.

Schmitz' termination drew the attention of many, including agents of the Federal Bureau of Investigation, which initiated an investigation into Schmitz' employment with CITY. In November 2006, Lane testified before a federal grand jury about his reasons for firing Schmitz. In January 2008, the grand jury indicted Schmitz on four counts of mail fraud and four counts of theft concerning a program receiving federal funds. The indictment alleged that Schmitz had collected $177,251.82 in federal funds even though she performed "'virtually no services,'" "'generated virtually no work product,'" and "'rarely even appeared for work at the CITY Program offices.'". . .

[Schmitz was tried twice. The first jury hung, and the second convicted Schmitz of mail fraud and theft. Lane testified under subpoena at both trials.]

Meanwhile, CITY continued to experience considerable budget shortfalls. [Steve Franks, president of CACC laid off 29 probationary employees, and then hired all back except for Lane and one other.] Franks claims that he "did not rescind Lane's termination . . . because he believed that Lane was in a fundamentally different category than the other employees: he was the director of the entire CITY program, and not simply an employee." In September 2009, CACC eliminated the CITY program and terminated the program's remaining employees. Franks later retired, and respondent Susan Burrow, the current Acting President of CACC, replaced him while this case was pending before the Eleventh Circuit.

In January 2011, Lane sued Franks in his individual and official capacities under Rev. Stat. § 1979, 42 U.S.C. § 1983, alleging that Franks had violated the First Amendment by firing him in retaliation for his testimony against Schmitz. . . .

The District Court granted Franks' motion for summary judgment [on the grounds that Franks was entitled to qualified immunity because a reasonable official in his position had reason to believe, based on *Garcetti*, that Lane's speech was not protected because he learned the information about which he testified while working as the Director and thus his speech was part of his official job duties. The Eleventh Circuit affirmed.]

We granted certiorari to resolve discord among the Courts of Appeals as to whether public employees may be fired—or suffer other adverse employment consequences—for providing truthful subpoenaed testimony outside the course of their ordinary job responsibilities.

II

Speech by citizens on matters of public concern lies at the heart of the First Amendment, which "was fashioned to assure unfettered interchange of ideas for the bringing about of political and social changes desired by the people," Roth v. United States, 354 U.S. 476, 484 (1957). This remains true when speech concerns information related to or learned through public employment. After all, public employees do not renounce their citizenship when they accept employment, and this Court has cautioned time and again that public employers may not condition employment on the relinquishment of constitutional rights. . . . "The interest at stake is as much the public's interest in receiving informed opinion as it is the employee's own right to disseminate it." San Diego v. Roe, 543 U.S. 77, 82 (2004) (*per curiam*).

Our precedents have also acknowledged the government's countervailing interest in controlling the operation of its workplaces. "Government employers, like private employers, need a significant degree of control over their employees' words and actions; without it, there would be little chance for the efficient provision of public services." *Garcetti.*

Pickering provides the framework for analyzing whether the employee's interest or the government's interest should prevail in cases where the government seeks to curtail the speech of its employees. It requires "balanc[ing] . . . the interests of the [public employee], as a citizen, in commenting upon matters of public concern and the interest of the State, as an employer, in promoting the efficiency of the public services it performs through its employees." . . .

In *Garcetti,* we described a two-step inquiry into whether a public employee's speech is entitled to protection:

> "The first requires determining whether the employee spoke as a citizen on a matter of public concern. If the answer is no, the employee has no First Amendment cause of action based on his or her employer's reaction to the speech. If the answer is yes, then the possibility of a First Amendment claim arises. The question becomes whether the relevant government entity had an adequate justification for treating the employee differently from any other member of the general public."

In describing the first step in this inquiry, *Garcetti* distinguished between employee speech and citizen speech. Whereas speech as a citizen may trigger protection, the Court held that "when public employees make statements pursuant to their official duties, the employees are not speaking as citizens for First Amendment purposes, and the Constitution does not insulate their communications from employer discipline." Applying that rule to the facts before it, the Court found that an internal memorandum prepared by a prosecutor in the course of his ordinary job responsibilities constituted unprotected employee speech.

III

Against this backdrop, we turn to the question presented: whether the First Amendment protects a public employee who provides truthful sworn testimony, compelled by subpoena, outside the scope of his ordinary job responsibilities. We hold that it does.

The first inquiry is whether the speech in question—Lane's testimony at Schmitz' [sic] trials—is speech as a citizen on a matter of public concern. It clearly is.

Truthful testimony under oath by a public employee outside the scope of his ordinary job duties is speech as a citizen for First Amendment purposes. That is so even when the testimony relates to his public employment or concerns information learned during that employment.

In rejecting Lane's argument that his testimony was speech as a citizen, the Eleventh Circuit gave short shrift to the nature of sworn judicial statements and ignored the obligation borne by all witnesses testifying under oath. Sworn testimony in judicial proceedings is a quintessential example of speech as a citizen for a simple reason: Anyone who testifies in court bears an obligation, to the court and society at large, to tell the truth. . . .

When the person testifying is a public employee, he may bear separate obligations to his employer—for example, an obligation not to show up to court dressed in an unprofessional manner. But any such obligations as an employee are distinct and independent from the obligation, as a citizen, to speak the truth. That independent obligation renders sworn testimony speech as a citizen and sets it apart from speech made purely in the capacity of an employee.

In holding that Lane did not speak as a citizen when he testified, the Eleventh Circuit read *Garcetti* far too broadly. It reasoned that, because Lane learned of the subject matter of his testimony in the course of his employment with CITY, *Garcetti* requires that his testimony be treated as the speech of an employee rather than that of a citizen. It does not.

The sworn testimony in this case is far removed from the speech at issue in *Garcetti*—an internal memorandum prepared by a deputy district attorney for his supervisors recommending dismissal of a particular prosecution. The *Garcetti* Court held that such speech was made pursuant to the employee's "official responsibilities" because "[w]hen [the employee] went to work and performed the tasks he was paid to perform, [he] acted as a government employee. The fact that his duties sometimes required him to speak or write does not mean that his supervisors were prohibited from evaluating his performance."

But *Garcetti* said nothing about speech that simply relates to public employment or concerns information learned in the course of public employment. The *Garcetti* Court made explicit that its holding did not turn on the fact that the memo at issue "concerned the subject matter of [the prosecutor's] employment," because "[t]he First Amendment protects some expressions related to the speaker's job." In other words, the mere fact that a citizen's speech concerns information acquired by virtue of his public employment does not transform that speech into employee—rather than citizen—speech. The critical question under *Garcetti* is whether the speech at issue is itself ordinarily within the scope of an employee's duties, not whether it merely concerns those duties.

It bears emphasis that our precedents dating back to *Pickering* have recognized that speech by public employees on subject matter related to their employment holds special value precisely because those employees gain knowledge of matters of public concern through their employment. [ ].

The importance of public employee speech is especially evident in the context of this case: a public corruption scandal. The United States, for example, represents that because "[t]he more than 1000 prosecutions for federal corruption offenses that are brought in a typical year . . . often depend on evidence about activities that government officials undertook while in office," those prosecutions often "require testimony from other government employees." It would be antithetical to our jurisprudence to conclude that the very kind of speech necessary to prosecute corruption by public officials—speech by public employees regarding information learned through their employment—may never form the basis for a First Amendment retaliation claim. Such a rule would place public employees who witness corruption in an impossible position, torn between the obligation to testify truthfully and the desire to avoid retaliation and keep their jobs.

Applying these principles, it is clear that Lane's sworn testimony is speech as a citizen.

Lane's testimony is also speech on a matter of public concern. Speech involves matters of public concern "when it can 'be fairly considered as relating to any matter of political, social, or other concern to the community,' or when it 'is a subject of legitimate news interest; that is, a subject of general interest and of value and concern to the public.'" Snyder v. Phelps [*supra* p. 664]. The inquiry turns on the "content, form, and context" of the speech. *Connick.*

The content of Lane's testimony—corruption in a public program and misuse of state funds—obviously involves a matter of significant public concern. [ ].

And the form and context of the speech—sworn testimony in a judicial proceeding—fortify that conclusion. "Unlike speech in other contexts, testimony under oath has the formality and gravity necessary to remind the witness that his or her statements will be the basis for official governmental action, action that often affects the rights and liberties of others." United States v. Alvarez, 567 U.S. 709, 721 (2012) (plurality opinion).

. . . Under *Pickering*, if an employee speaks as a citizen on a matter of public concern, the next question is whether the government had "an adequate justification for treating the employee differently from any other member of the public" based on the government's needs as an employer.

As discussed previously, we have recognized that government employers often have legitimate "interest[s] in the effective and efficient fulfillment of [their] responsibilities to the public," including "'promot[ing] efficiency and integrity in the discharge of official duties,'" and "'maintain[ing] proper discipline in public service.'" We have also cautioned, however, that "a stronger showing [of government interests] may be necessary if the employee's speech more substantially involve[s] matters of public concern." *Connick.*

Here, the employer's side of the *Pickering* scale is entirely empty: Respondents do not assert, and cannot demonstrate, any government interest that tips the balance in their favor. There is no evidence, for example, that Lane's testimony at Schmitz' [sic] trials was false or erroneous or that Lane unnecessarily disclosed any sensitive, confidential, or privileged information while testifying. In these circumstances, we conclude that Lane's speech is entitled to protection under the First Amendment.

[The Court held that even though Lane's speech was protected by the First Amendment, the Eleventh Circuit correctly held that Respondent Franks could reasonably have believed that a government employer could fire an employee under these circumstances. Therefore, Franks was entitled to qualified immunity.]

THOMAS, J., with whom SCALIA, J., and ALITO, J., join, concurring.

. . . The petitioner in this case did not speak "pursuant to" his ordinary job duties because his responsibilities did not include testifying in court proceedings, and no party has suggested that he was subpoenaed as a representative of his employer. Because petitioner did not testify to "fulfil[l] a [work] responsibility," *Garcetti*, he spoke "as a citizen," not as an employee.

We accordingly have no occasion to address the quite different question whether a public employee speaks "as a citizen" when he testifies in the course of his ordinary job responsibilities. For some public employees—such as police officers, crime scene technicians, and laboratory analysts—testifying is a routine and critical part of their employment duties. Others may be called to testify in the context of particular litigation as the designated representatives of their employers. The Court properly leaves the constitutional questions raised by these scenarios for another day.

NOTES AND QUESTIONS

1. *Protecting federal functions?* Would a dismissal of a state employee based on his truthful testimony in federal court be an "unconstitutional state interference with legitimate federal functions"?
2. *The interplay of the government financing and government employee decisions.* Many of the holdings in the Court's government financing and government

employee cases are difficult to reconcile. Consider four cases in particular: First, in *Connick* the Court allowed a District Attorney to sanction a staff attorney for distributing a questionnaire concerning the internal operations of the office. The Court held that questions concerning internal staff morale and staff attorney confidence in supervising attorneys were not matters of public concern, but that questions concerning internal coercion to work in political campaigns were matters of public concern. Second, in *Rust* the Court allowed government-funded agencies to prohibit doctors who receive government funds from informing their patients about particular forms of care that were relevant to the patients' medical conditions. Third, in *Velazquez* the Court prohibited Congress from imposing restrictions on the ability of government-funded attorneys to raise certain kinds of claims on behalf of their clients. The rationale of this decision was that the funding agency cannot override the attorneys' professional obligations to the courts and their clients. Fourth, in *Garcetti* the Court allowed supervising attorneys in a District Attorney's office to sanction a staff attorney for expressing concerns about the prosecution of a case—even though the staff attorney's concerns arguably may have involved fraud on the court. How can these decisions be reconciled? *Rust* seems to treat government-funded speakers as having no First Amendment protection against government constraints that impinge on the funded employee's professional obligations, yet *Velazquez* seems to hold that the First Amendment provides absolute protection of speech undertaken as part of a speaker's professional obligations. Likewise, *Velazquez* seems to hold that the First Amendment protects the government-funded speaker in raising claims that the government specifically forbids the speaker to raise, yet *Garcetti* holds that the government may sanction a government employee for raising claims that the government has specifically forbidden the speaker to raise. Can these seemingly inconsistent results be reconciled by focusing on whether the speech in question occurred within the government office rather than being directed to outsiders? In *Velazquez*, for example, the Court protected the government-funded speakers' ability to speak to an outside body (the courts), and in *Garcetti* the Court noted the "anomaly" that the government would have to tolerate employee speech made to outsiders, but could sanction speech on the same subject made within the workplace as a part of the employee's "professional responsibilities." But if this "insider/outsider" dichotomy is the key to understanding the Court's decisions in this area, then why in *Rust* does the Court uphold restrictions on the doctors' conversations with outsiders (patients), and in *Garcetti* uphold restrictions on speech that is intended to be presented to outsiders (the courts)?

3. *Constitutional protection of internal complaints.* After *Garcetti*, the availability of First Amendment protection under *Pickering* and *Connick* for complaints expressed by an employee to his or her government employer rather than the public at large depends on the employee's precise job description and an assessment of whether the subject matter of the employee's complaint falls within the description of the employee's professional duties. Under the *Garcetti* holding, the employee's speech is not protected if it is within the scope of the employee's job, but it is protected if the speech falls outside the scope of the employee's job description. In *Garcetti*, the Court limited

the scope of Givhan *v.* Western Line Consolidated School District, 439 U.S. 410 (1979). *Givhan* involved a junior high school English teacher, who was fired from her job with a public school system because she had complained about the racially discriminatory hiring practices of the school district as a whole and at the school where she was assigned. The Supreme Court held that her speech was protected by *Pickering*, and noted that "[n]either the [First] Amendment itself nor our decisions indicate that [the employee's] freedom [of speech] is lost to the public employee who arranges to communicate privately with his employer rather than to spread his views before the public." In *Garcetti*, the Court reaffirmed *Givhan*'s holding that the First Amendment protects some speech by employees at the workplace, but held that *Givhan* does not apply in situations in which the employee was speaking "pursuant to his duties." "We hold that when public employees make statements pursuant to their official duties, the employees are not speaking as citizens for First Amendment purposes, and the Constitution does not insulate their communications from employer discipline."

4. *Drawing an arbitrary line?* Dissenting in *Garcetti*, Justice Souter criticized the majority's distinction between expression that falls within a public employee's official duties and expression that falls outside the scope of those duties:

> The difference between a case like *Givhan* and this one is that the subject of Ceballos's speech fell within the scope of his job responsibilities, whereas choosing personnel was not what the teacher was hired to do. The effect of the majority drawing a constitutional line between these two cases, then, is that a schoolteacher is protected when complaining to the principal about hiring policy, but a school personnel officer would not be protected if he protested that the principal disapproved of hiring minority job applicants. This is an odd place to draw a distinction, and while necessary judicial line-drawing sometimes looks arbitrary, any distinction obliges a court to justify its choice. Here, there is no adequate justification for the majority's line categorically denying *Pickering* protection to any speech uttered "pursuant to . . . official duties."

Garcetti, 547 U.S. at 430 (Souter, J., dissenting).

What is the justification for denying protection to a government employee's speech uttered pursuant to official duties?

5. *Should whistleblowing speech enjoy special protection?* Does the value of speech to the public depend on whether the speech relates to a whistleblower's official duties—or on something else? Should the scope of First Amendment protection for government employee speech take into account the value of information to We the People in holding government accountable through the electoral process? For an extended argument that the Supreme Court needs to afford broader, more targeted First Amendment protection to "whistleblowing speech," see Ronald J. Krotoszynski, Jr., *Whistleblowing Speech and the First Amendment*, 93 Ind. L.J. 267 (2018).

6. *The scope of official duties of faculty at public universities.* What implications does *Garcetti* have for faculty at public universities? Assume a law professor at a state university writes on a blog that his law school admits students whose LSAT scores are so low that they are "unqualified to be lawyers"? His employer seeks to discipline him after his speech triggers student protests and a decline in the law school's ability to recruit students. May the law school discipline him? Would the result be different if a high school teacher wrote on her Facebook page that her students "are all too dumb to learn what I'm trying to teach"? Does the concept of academic freedom in the university setting affect the outcome of the first scenario?

U.S. Civil Service Commission v. National Ass'n of Letter Carriers

413 U.S. 548 (1973)

White, J., delivered the opinion of the Court.

[The] single question [in this case is] whether the prohibition in 9(a) of the Hatch Act, against federal employees taking "an active part in political management or in political campaigns," is unconstitutional on its face. [This section provides:]

> An employee in an Executive agency or an individual employed by the government of the District of Columbia may not
>
> **(1)** use his official authority or influence for the purpose of interfering with or affecting the result of an election; or
>
> **(2)** take an active part in political management or in political campaigns.

A divided three-judge court sitting in the District of Columbia had held the section unconstitutional. We reverse the judgment of the District Court.

Each of the plaintiffs alleged that the Civil Service Commission was enforcing, or threatening to enforce, the Hatch Act's prohibition against active participation in political management or political campaigns with respect to certain defined activity in which that plaintiff desired to engage.[3] The Union, for example, stated among other things that its members desired to campaign for candidates for public office. The Democratic and Republican Committees complained of not being able to get federal employees to run for state and local offices.

---

3. The Union alleged that its members were desirous of "a. Running in local elections for such offices as school board member, city council member or mayor. b. Writing letters on political subjects to newspapers. c. Participating as a delegate in a political convention and running for office in a political party. d. Campaigning for candidates for political office." The Democratic and Republican Committees complained that they had been deterred "from seeking desirable candidates who are Federal or state employees covered by the Hatch Act to run on the Democratic or Republican ticket for state and local offices. In addition, numerous individuals who would otherwise desire and be available to become members of Plaintiff Committees have been and continue to be deterred from doing so by said provisions of the Hatch Act." Plaintiff Hummel alleged that he desired to engage in a wide variety of political activities including "(1) participation as a delegate in conventions of a political party; (2) public endorsement of candidates of a political party for local, state and national office; (3) work at polling places on behalf of a political party during elections; (4) holding office in a political club."

We unhesitatingly reaffirm [our earlier holding] that Congress had, and has, the power to prevent [government employees] from holding a party office, working at the polls, and acting as party paymaster for other party workers. An Act of Congress going no farther would in our view unquestionably be valid. So would it be if, in plain and understandable language, the statute forbade activities such as organizing a political party or club; actively participating in fund-raising activities for a partisan candidate or political party; becoming a partisan candidate for, or campaigning for, an elective public office; actively managing the campaign of a partisan candidate for public office; initiating or circulating a partisan nominating petition or soliciting votes for a partisan candidate for public office; or serving as a delegate, alternate or proxy to a political party convention. Our judgment is that neither the First Amendment nor any other provision of the Constitution invalidates a law barring this kind of partisan political conduct by federal employees.

It seems fundamental in the first place that employees in the Executive Branch of the Government, or those working for any of its agencies, should administer the law in accordance with the will of Congress, rather than in accordance with their own or the will of a political party. They are expected to enforce the law and execute the programs of the Government without bias or favoritism for or against any political party or group or the members thereof. A major thesis of the Hatch Act is that to serve this great end of Government—the impartial execution of the laws—it is essential that federal employees, for example, not take formal positions in political parties, not undertake to play substantial roles in partisan political campaigns, and not run for office on partisan political tickets. Forbidding activities like these will reduce the hazards to fair and effective government.

There is another consideration in this judgment: it is not only important that the Government and its employees in fact avoid practicing political justice, but it is also critical that they appear to the public to be avoiding it, if confidence in the system of representative Government is not to be eroded to a disastrous extent.

Another major concern of the restriction against partisan activities by federal employees was perhaps the immediate occasion for enactment of the Hatch Act in 1939. That was the conviction that the rapidly expanding Government work force should not be employed to build a powerful, invincible, and perhaps corrupt political machine. The experience of the 1936 and 1938 campaigns convinced Congress that these dangers were sufficiently real that substantial barriers should be raised against the party in power—or the party out of power, for that matter—using the thousands or hundreds of thousands of federal employees, paid for at public expense, to man its political structure and political campaigns.

A related concern, and this remains as important as any other, was to further serve the goal that employment and advancement in the Government service not depend on political performance, and at the same time to make sure that Government employees would be free from pressure and from express or tacit invitation to vote in a certain way or perform political chores in order to curry favor with their superiors rather than to act out their own beliefs. It may be urged that prohibitions against coercion are sufficient protection; but for many years the joint judgment of the Executive and Congress has been that to protect the rights of federal employees with respect to their jobs and their political acts and beliefs it is not enough merely to forbid one employee to attempt to influence or coerce another. For example, at the hearings in 1972 on proposed legislation for liberalizing the prohibition against political activity, the Chairman of the Civil Service Commission stated that "the prohibitions against active participation in partisan political management and partisan political campaigns constitute the most significant safeguards against coercion. . . ." Perhaps Congress at some time will come to a different view of the realities of political life and Government service; but that is its current view of the matter, and we are not now in any position to dispute it. Nor, in our view, does the Constitution forbid it. . . .

DOUGLAS, J., with whom BRENNAN, J., and MARSHALL, J., concur, dissenting.

There is no definition of what "an active part . . . in political campaigns" means. The Act incorporates over 3,000 rulings of the Civil Service Commission between 1886 and 1940 and many hundreds of rulings since 1940. But even with that gloss on the Act, the critical phrases lack precision. . . .

The present Act cannot be appropriately narrowed to meet the need for narrowly drawn language not embracing First Amendment speech or writing without substantial revision. That rewriting cannot be done by the Commission because Congress refused to delegate to it authority to regulate First Amendment rights.

I would strike this provision of the law down as unconstitutional so that a new start may be made on this old problem that confuses and restricts nearly five million federal, state, and local public employees today that live under the present Act.

NOTES AND QUESTIONS

1. *Off-duty activities and federal government employment.* Is the Supreme Court correct to so readily permit a flat ban on partisan political activity by the many thousands of citizens who happen to work in civil service positions with the federal government? Would a more narrowly tailored restriction not achieve the government's purpose in protecting such workers from coerced partisan activities? If a less complete ban could work, should the government, under the First Amendment, have a duty to use less restrictive means?
2. *State and local employers and restrictions on off-duty speech.* In San Diego v. Roe, 543 U.S. 77 (2004), the Supreme Court upheld the discharge of a San Diego, California, police officer who performed in amateur porn videos and sold his works on Ebay using the handle "'Code3stud@aol.com,' a word play on a high priority police radio call." The U.S. Court of Appeals held that the San Diego police department could not fire Roe for his off-duty expressive activities, reasoning that the activity took place outside the work place, while Roe was off-duty, and was unrelated to his employment. *See* 356 F.3d, at 1110, 1113-1114 (9th Cir. 2004). In a terse *per curiam* opinion, the Supreme Court summarily reversed the Ninth Circuit, holding that "there is no difficulty in concluding that Roe's expression does not qualify as a matter of public concern under any view of the public concern test." This characterization of Roe's speech proved fatal to Roe's First Amendment claim; the majority held that Roe enjoyed *no* First Amendment protection whatsoever for his off-duty speech activity. His employer, the police department, was free to fire Roe because "[t]he speech in question was

detrimental to the mission and functions of the employer." Should a government employer enjoy the same freedom to fire an employee based on the employee's embarrassing or controversial off-duty expressive activity that a private employer possesses? Or should the First Amendment require a government employer to tolerate an employee's off-duty expression even if a private employer would not have to tolerate it?

AN EXTENDED NOTE ON LOYALTY OATHS AND POLITICAL PATRONAGE

From the perspective of the politically engaged government employee, the Supreme Court's First Amendment jurisprudence presents some good news and some bad news. The bad news is that in decisions like *National Ass'n of Letter Carriers*, the Court has been willing to uphold some very restrictive sets of rules, which strictly limit even mundane forms of political participation by government employees. On the other hand, the good news is that the Court has ruled that the First Amendment prohibits the government from imposing on employees ideological litmus tests, and also prohibits the government from enforcing on its employees a mandate of political conformity as a condition of their employment.

Some of the earliest cases in this area dealt with governmental attempts to exclude political leftists from government employment. In Wieman v. Updegraff, 344 U.S. 183 (1952), for example, the Court struck down an Oklahoma statute that required all state employees to sign a "loyalty oath" stating that during the previous five years the employee had not been a member of any organization listed by the Attorney General of the United States as a "communist front" or "subversive." The Court struck down the statute because it did not distinguish between general membership in a political organization and membership driven by the specific intent to aid the organization in the illegal overthrow of the government by force or violence. The Court noted that "[t]here can be no dispute about the consequences visited upon a person excluded from public employment on disloyalty grounds. In the view of the community, the stain is a deep one; indeed, it has become a badge of infamy. Especially is this so in time of cold war and hot emotions when 'each man begins to eye his neighbor as a possible enemy.'"

As the Court moved into the 1960s and beyond, the Court shifted its focus from anti-Communist loyalty oaths to more mainstream forms of political patronage. In Elrod v. Burns, 427 U.S. 347 (1976), the Court took up the issue of political patronage in the context of the old Cook County Democratic Party machine of Mayor Richard Daley. In late 1970 the Republican Sheriff of Cook County was replaced by a Democrat, who upon taking office followed the local political tradition by replacing all non-civil-service employees of the Sheriff's Office with members of his own party. After noting the long history of political patronage in this country, Justice Brennan's plurality opinion turned to the costs the practice imposed on public employees. "In order to maintain their jobs, respondents were required to pledge their political allegiance to the Democratic Party, work for the election of other candidates of the Democratic Party, contribute a portion of their wages to the Party, or obtain the sponsorship of a member of the Party, usually at the price of one of the first three alternatives." The plurality concluded that these costs violated the protections the Court had already provided for public employees in the loyalty oath cases. "[I]f the government could deny a benefit to a person because of his constitutionally protected speech or associations, his exercise of those freedoms would in effect be penalized and inhibited. This would allow the government to 'produce a result which [it] could not command directly.'" Having established that the patronage requirement infringed on First Amendment rights of employees, the plurality then rejected all of the interests that the government offered to justify this infringement. These interests included "the need to insure effective government and the efficiency of public employees," "giving the employees of an incumbent party the incentive to perform well in order to insure their party's incumbency and thereby their jobs," and "the need for political loyalty of employees." The plurality held that limiting patronage dismissals to policymaking positions was sufficient to satisfy the government's legitimate interests. In Justice Stewart's concurring opinion, he agreed with the plurality opinion that a "nonpolicymaking, nonconfidential government employee" could not be "discharged or threatened with discharge from a job that he is satisfactorily performing upon the sole ground of his political beliefs."

Four years after it decided *Elrod*, the Court returned to the issue of political patronage to clarify the scope of the First Amendment defense to politically motivated firings of public employees. In Branti v. Finkel, 445 U.S. 507 (1980), the Court considered a case involving the firing of two assistant public defenders, who had been discharged based solely on their political affiliation. According to the Court, "[b]oth opinions in *Elrod* recognize that party affiliation may be an acceptable requirement for some types of government employment. Thus, if an employee's private political beliefs would interfere with the discharge of his public duties, his First Amendment rights may be required to yield to the State's vital interest in maintaining governmental effectiveness and efficiency." The Court went on to note, however, that it is not always easy to determine when an employee's political beliefs are relevant to that employee's job. The key to that determination, the Court held, was not whether someone is a "nonpolicymaking, nonconfidential government employee," but rather whether political affiliation is "an appropriate requirement for the effective performance of the public office involved." In *Branti* itself, the Court held, "it is manifest that the continued employment of an assistant public defender cannot properly be conditioned upon his allegiance to the political party in control of the county government. The primary, if not the only, responsibility of an assistant public defender is to represent individual citizens in controversy with the State. . . . Thus, whatever policymaking occurs in the public defender's office must relate to the needs of individual clients and not to any partisan political interests."

Both *Elrod* and *Branti* involved politically motivated discharges. In Rutan v. Republican Party of Illinois, 497 U.S. 62 (1990), the Court extended the rationale of those cases to cover politically motivated decisions to hire, promote, and transfer an employee. With regard to promotions and transfers, the Court held that *Elrod* and *Branti* must apply because otherwise employees "will feel a significant obligation to support political positions held by their superiors, and to refrain from acting on the political views they actually hold, in order to progress up the career ladder." With regard to hiring decisions, the Court held that applying the principles of *Elrod* and *Branti* was a logical extension of the long-standing axiom that the government "may not enact a regulation providing that no Republican . . . shall be appointed to federal office." Public Workers v. Mitchell, 330 U.S. 75, 100 (1947).

In O'Hare Truck Service, Inc. v. City of Northlake, 518 U.S. 712 (1996), the Court held that the same First Amendment principles that protect public employees against being discharged for refusing to support a political party or its candidates also extend to independent contractors. The plaintiff in *O'Hare* was a tow truck company that had worked under contract to the city of Northlake, Illinois, for 24 years. When the city's mayor ran for reelection, the plaintiff supported the mayor's opponent. After the mayor won reelection, the plaintiff's company was dropped from the list of tow truck companies used by the city. The Court noted that "[r]ecognizing the distinction [between employees and independent contractors] in these circumstances would invite manipulation by government, which could avoid constitutional liability simply by attaching different labels to particular jobs." The Court recognized that there were a wide range of permissible reasons for the government to exercise its discretion to retain or terminate independent contractors, including the need to "maintain stability, reward good performance, deal with known and reliable persons, or ensure the uninterrupted supply of goods or services." The Court went on to hold, however, that "it does not follow that this discretion can be exercised to impose conditions on expressing, or not expressing, specific political views."

In another application, the Court in Heffernan v. City of Paterson, 578 U.S. 266 (2016), ruled it unconstitutional to demote a government employee based on the *mistaken* belief that the officer had engaged in political activity. The plaintiff in *Heffernan* was a police officer in Paterson, New Jersey, who was demoted after other police officers saw him with a sign for a mayoral candidate, leaving the impression that he supported the candidate. In fact, Heffernan was merely picking up the sign at the request of his bedridden mother. Justice Stephen G. Breyer, writing for the Court, recognized that "[w]hen an employer demotes an employee out of a desire to prevent the employee from engaging in political activity that the First Amendment protects, the employee is entitled to challenge that unlawful action under the First Amendment." That is true "even if, as here, the employer makes a factual mistake about the employee's behavior."

Do decisions such as *Elrod* and *Branti* in effect use the First Amendment to create a national civil service system? In his dissent to *Branti*, Justice Powell argued that "[t]he benefits of political patronage and the freedom of voters to structure their representative government are substantial governmental interests that justify the selection of the assistant public defenders of Rockland County on the basis of political affiliation. The decision to place certain governmental positions within a civil service system is a sensitive political judgment that should be left to the voters and to elected representatives of the people." What are the benefits of political patronage? Is it a sufficient response to this objection that state and local governments can continue to hire and fire employees without proving "cause" so long as they do not do so on the basis of a narrow range of constitutional criteria such as political affiliation, religion, or race? As Justice Brennan summed up the Court's position in *Rutan*: "To the victor belongs only those spoils that may be constitutionally obtained."

THEORY-APPLIED PROBLEM

Luc Beauregard (LB) works as a fireman in the Little Rock, Arkansas municipal fire department. In his spare time, LB is a member of Arkansas Civil War Reenactors (ACWR) and enjoys participating the ACWR's historical reenactment events. ACWR's members recreate famous U.S. Civil War battles—sometimes on their own and sometimes with other, similar organizations. At such events, LB portrays C.S.A. General P.G.T. Beauregard (who is LB's distant relative). LB's participation in ACWR events always takes place when he is off-duty. ACWR maintains a Facebook (Meta) page and LB's photograph, while dressed as C.S.A. General Beauregard, appears on several posts with a caption that identifies him as "Little Rock fireman Luc Beauregard." A local resident in Little Rock notices the social media posts featuring LB and his employment with the city. He brings the Facebook posts, including the photographs, to the attention of the chief of Little Rock's fire department and expresses concern about "the values of our fire department employees if this is how your firefighters are spending their off-time." After reviewing the posts, the chief calls in LB and asks "Is this you?" When LB responds "Yes, it is, I'm a historical reenactor in my spare time," the chief immediately suspends LB. After a hearing, LB is fired for "conduct unbecoming a member of the Little Rock fire department." You work as an associate at the Rose Law Firm, a large (for Little Rock) corporate law firm that handles ACLU of Arkansas matters on a pro bono basis. The firm has agreed to offer pro bono representation to LB at the request of the local ACLU chapter. Your boss asks you to advise her as to whether LB could bring a successful First Amendment challenge to his discharge based on LB's participation in the ACWR events. Does LB have a valid First Amendment claim against the city? What elements must he establish in order to prevail? What, if any, additional facts might you need to assess properly the strength or weakness of his case?

C. *PUBLIC SCHOOLS AND LIBRARIES*

Tinker v. Des Moines Independent Community School District

393 U.S. 503 (1969)

FORTAS, J., delivered the opinion of the Court. Petitioner John F. Tinker, 15 years old, and petitioner Christopher Eckhardt, 16 years old, attended high schools in Des Moines, Iowa. Petitioner Mary Beth Tinker, John's sister, was a 13-year-old student in junior high school.

In December 1965, a group of adults and students in Des Moines held a meeting at the Eckhardt home. The group determined to publicize their objections to the hostilities in Vietnam and their support for a truce by wearing black armbands during the holiday season and by fasting on December 16 and New Year's Eve. Petitioners and their parents had previously engaged in similar activities, and they decided to participate in the program.

The principals of the Des Moines schools became aware of the plan to wear armbands. On December 14, 1965, they met and adopted a policy that any student wearing an armband to school would be asked to remove it, and if he refused he would be suspended until he returned without the armband. Petitioners were aware of the regulation that the school authorities adopted.

On December 16, Mary Beth and Christopher wore black armbands to their schools. John Tinker wore his armband the next day. They were all sent home and suspended from school until they would come back without their armbands. They did not return to school until after the planned period for wearing armbands had expired—that is, until after New Year's Day.

[Petitioners then filed suit in federal court, seeking] an injunction restraining the respondent school officials and the respondent members of the board of directors of the school district from disciplining the petitioners.

[T]he wearing of armbands in the circumstances of this case was entirely divorced from actually or potentially disruptive conduct by those participating in it. It was closely akin to "pure speech" which, we have repeatedly held, is entitled to comprehensive protection under the First Amendment.

First Amendment rights, applied in light of the special characteristics of the school environment, are available to teachers and students. It can hardly be argued that either students or teachers shed their constitutional rights to freedom of speech or expression at the schoolhouse gate.

On the other hand, the Court has repeatedly emphasized the need for affirming the comprehensive authority of the States and of school officials, consistent with fundamental constitutional safeguards, to prescribe and control conduct in the schools. Our problem lies in the area where students in the exercise of First Amendment rights collide with the rules of the school authorities.

The school officials banned and sought to punish petitioners for a silent, passive expression of opinion, unaccompanied by any disorder or disturbance on the part of petitioners. There is here no evidence whatever of petitioners' interference, actual or nascent, with the schools' work or of collision with the rights of other students to be secure and to be let alone. Accordingly, this case does not concern speech or action that intrudes upon the work of the schools or the rights of other students.

Only a few of the 18,000 students in the school system wore the black armbands. Only five students were suspended for wearing them. There is no indication that the work of the schools or any class was disrupted. Outside the classrooms, a few students made hostile remarks to the children wearing armbands, but there were no threats or acts of violence on school premises.

The District Court concluded that the action of the school authorities was reasonable because it was based upon their fear of a disturbance from the wearing of the armbands. But, in our system, undifferentiated fear or apprehension of disturbance is not enough to overcome the right to freedom of expression. Any departure from absolute regimentation may cause trouble. Any variation from the majority's opinion may inspire fear. Any word spoken, in class, in the lunchroom, or on the campus, that deviates from the views of another person may start an argument or cause a disturbance. But our Constitution says we must take this risk, and our history says that it is this sort of hazardous freedom—this kind of openness—that is the basis of our national strength and of the independence and vigor of Americans who grow up and live in this relatively permissive, often disputatious, society.

In order for the State in the person of school officials to justify prohibition of a particular expression of opinion, it must be able to show that its action was caused by something more than a mere desire to avoid the discomfort and unpleasantness that always accompany an unpopular viewpoint. Certainly where there is no finding and no showing that engaging in the forbidden conduct would "materially and substantially interfere with the requirements of appropriate discipline in the operation of the school," the prohibition cannot be sustained.

It is also relevant that the school authorities did not purport to prohibit the wearing of all symbols of political or controversial significance. The record shows that students in some of the schools wore buttons relating to national political campaigns, and some even wore the Iron Cross, traditionally a symbol of Nazism. The order prohibiting the wearing of armbands did not extend to these. Instead, a particular symbol—black armbands worn to exhibit opposition to this Nation's involvement in Vietnam—was singled out for prohibition. Clearly, the prohibition of expression of one particular opinion, at least without evidence that it is necessary to avoid material and substantial interference with schoolwork or discipline, is not constitutionally permissible.

In our system, state-operated schools may not be enclaves of totalitarianism. School officials do not possess absolute authority over their students. Students in school as well as out of school are "persons" under our Constitution. They are possessed of fundamental rights which the State must respect, just as they themselves must respect their obligations to the State. In our system, students may not be regarded as closed-circuit recipients of only that which the State chooses to communicate. They may not be confined to the expression of those sentiments that are officially approved. In the absence of a specific showing of constitutionally valid reasons to regulate their speech, students are entitled to freedom of expression of their views. As Judge Gewin, speaking for the Fifth Circuit, said, school officials cannot suppress "expressions of feelings with which they do not wish to contend."

Under our Constitution, free speech is not a right that is given only to be so circumscribed that it exists in principle but not in fact. Freedom of expression would not truly exist if the right could be exercised only in an area that a benevolent government has provided as a safe haven for crackpots. The Constitution says that Congress (and the States) may not abridge the right to free speech. This provision means what it says. We properly read it to permit reasonable regulation of speech-connected activities in carefully restricted circumstances. But we do not confine the permissible exercise of First Amendment rights to a telephone booth or the four corners of a pamphlet, or to supervised and ordained discussion in a school classroom.

BLACK, J., dissenting.

The Court's holding in this case ushers in what I deem to be an entirely new era in which the power to control pupils by the elected "officials of state supported public schools . . ." in the United States is in ultimate effect transferred to the Supreme Court.

. . . The original idea of schools, which I do not believe is yet abandoned as worthless or out of date, was that children had not yet reached the point of experience and wisdom which enabled them to teach all of their elders. It may be that the Nation has outworn the old-fashioned slogan that "children are to be seen not heard," but one may, I hope, be permitted to harbor the thought that taxpayers send children to school on the premise that at their age they need to learn, not teach.

[The concurring opinions of Justices Stewart and White, and the dissenting opinion of Harlan, J., are omitted.]

NOTES AND QUESTIONS

1. *The general themes of* Tinker. *Tinker* is the foundation of the Court's student-speech cases, and in many ways *Tinker* simply involves the application of long-standing First Amendment principles to the school context. One aspect of *Tinker*, for example, prohibits school authorities from engaging in content or viewpoint regulation of student speech. *See R.A.V. v. St. Paul, supra* p. 562. Another aspect of *Tinker* focuses on the compatibility of student speech with the pedagogical requirements of an educational institution. *See* Grayned v. Rockford, 408 U.S. 104 (1972). Still another aspect of *Tinker* emphasizes the need for time, place, and manner restrictions on disruptive speech. *See* Ward v. Rock Against Racism, 491 U.S. 781 (1989). The overriding theme of the case, however, is that students have many of the same First Amendment rights as adults to express opinions that the government may not like. When reading the next three student-speech cases, reflect on the extent to which the Court has subsequently abandoned this last proposition, in favor of the contrary notion that students generally can be viewed as wards of the state while at school, and in that context should not expect to be afforded anything approaching the same First Amendment rights as adults.
2. *The pragmatics of* Tinker: *The parameters of "disruption."* The linchpin of *Tinker* is its holding that students have First Amendment rights of free speech except when the student speech would "materially and substantially disrupt the work and discipline of the school." The key to enforcing *Tinker*, therefore, is determining when a student's speech becomes so disruptive that it interferes with the educational functions of the school. The subsequent cases applying *Tinker* have given school officials a fair amount of leeway in applying this disruption standard. The lower court cases consistently have held that school officials do not have to wait to silence potentially disruptive speech until the disruption actually occurs, nor do school officials have to produce definitive evidence that disruption will occur. Moreover, the cases routinely apply the disruption analysis to an overall context that includes the hostile responses of listeners to the student speech. Note that this is somewhat inconsistent with the rule the Court applies outside the school context, where the Court generally does not permit governments to regulate potentially disruptive speech based on hostile listeners' response to that speech. *See* Boos v. Barry, 485 U.S. 312, 321 (1988) (striking down a statute regulating signs bringing foreign governments into "public odium" or "public disrepute" within 500 feet of foreign embassies, and holding that the statute was impermissibly content-based because the statute regulated "the content of the speech and the direct impact that speech has on its listeners. The emotive

impact of speech on its audience is not a 'secondary effect.'"). Does the consideration of antagonistic listener responses as part of the assessment of "disruption" in the school context invite the "heckler's veto"? Does this consideration also raise the possibility that speakers who are engaged in the most unpopular speech, or who are in an extreme minority in a particular school, will be protected less vigorously under *Tinker* than more moderate or more popular speakers (because speech by less popular or less numerous speakers will be more likely to engender disruptive responses from hostile listeners)?

Bethel School District No. 403 v. Fraser

478 U.S. 675 (1986)

BURGER, C.J., delivered the opinion of the Court

On April 26, 1983, respondent Matthew N. Fraser, a student at Bethel High School in Pierce County, Washington, delivered a speech nominating a fellow student for student elective office. Approximately 600 high school students, many of whom were 14-year-olds, attended the assembly. Students were required to attend the assembly or to report to the study hall. The assembly was part of a school-sponsored educational program in self-government. Students who elected not to attend the assembly were required to report to study hall. During the entire speech, Fraser referred to his candidate in terms of an elaborate, graphic, and explicit sexual metaphor.

[*Editor's note*: Chief Justice Burger does not quote the speech in his majority opinion. Justice Brennan does quote the speech in his concurring opinion, however. This is the full text of the speech Fraser gave to the assembly:

> I know a man who is firm—he's firm in his pants, he's firm in his shirt, his character is firm—but most . . . of all, his belief in you, the students of Bethel, is firm.
>
> Jeff Kuhlman is a man who takes his point and pounds it in. If necessary, he'll take an issue and nail it to the wall. He doesn't attack things in spurts—he drives hard, pushing and pushing until finally—he succeeds.
>
> Jeff is a man who will go to the very end—even the climax, for each and every one of you.
>
> So vote for Jeff for A.S.B. vice-president—he'll never come between you and the best our high school can be.]

Two of Fraser's teachers, with whom he discussed the contents of his speech in advance, informed him that the speech was "inappropriate and that he probably should not deliver it," and that his delivery of the speech might have "severe consequences."

During Fraser's delivery of the speech, a school counselor observed the reaction of students to the speech. Some students hooted and yelled; some by gestures graphically simulated the sexual activities pointedly alluded to in respondent's speech. Other students appeared to be bewildered and embarrassed by the speech.

One teacher reported that on the day following the speech, she found it necessary to forgo a portion of the scheduled class lesson in order to discuss the speech with the class.

A Bethel High School disciplinary rule prohibiting the use of obscene language in the school provides: "Conduct which materially and substantially interferes with the educational process is prohibited, including the use of obscene, profane language or gestures."

The morning after the assembly, the Assistant Principal called Fraser into her office and notified him that the school considered his speech to have been a violation of this rule. Fraser was presented with copies of five letters submitted by teachers, describing his conduct at the assembly; he was given a chance to explain his conduct, and he admitted to having given the speech described and that he deliberately used sexual innuendo in the speech. Fraser was then informed that he would be suspended for three days, and that his name would be removed from the list of candidates for graduation speaker at the school's commencement exercises.

[The school board's hearing officer affirmed the suspension, and Fraser sued in federal court, claiming a violation of his First Amendment right to free speech. The district court ruled in Fraser's favor, and the United States Court of Appeals for the Ninth Circuit affirmed, holding that Fraser's speech was indistinguishable from the speech at issue in *Tinker.* The Supreme Court reversed.]

The marked distinction between the political "message" of the armbands in Tinker and the sexual content of respondent's speech in this case seems to have been given little weight by the Court of Appeals. In upholding the students' right to engage in a nondisruptive, passive expression of a political viewpoint in *Tinker,* this Court was careful to note that the case did "not concern speech or action that intrudes upon the work of the schools or the rights of other students."

The role and purpose of the American public school system were well described by two historians, who stated: "[P]ublic education must prepare pupils for citizenship in the Republic. . . . It must inculcate the habits and manners of civility as values in themselves conducive to happiness and as indispensable to the practice of self-government in the community and the nation." C. Beard & M. Beard, New Basic History of the United States 228 (1968). In Ambach v. Norwick, 441 U.S. 68, 76-77 (1979), we echoed the essence of this statement of the objectives of public education as the "inculcat[ion of] fundamental values necessary to the maintenance of a democratic political system." . . .

The process of educating our youth for citizenship in public schools is not confined to books, the curriculum, and the civics class; schools must teach by example the shared values of a civilized social order. Consciously or otherwise, teachers—and indeed the older students—demonstrate the appropriate form of civil discourse and political expression by their conduct and deportment in and out of class. Inescapably, like parents, they are role models. The schools, as instruments of the state, may determine that the essential lessons of civil, mature conduct cannot be conveyed in a school that tolerates lewd, indecent, or offensive speech and conduct such as that indulged in by this confused boy.

The pervasive sexual innuendo in Fraser's speech was plainly offensive to both teachers and students—indeed to any mature person. By glorifying male sexuality, and in its verbal content, the speech was acutely insulting to teenage girl students.

The speech could well be seriously damaging to its less mature audience, many of whom were only 14 years old and on the threshold of awareness of human sexuality. Some students were reported as bewildered by the speech and the reaction of mimicry it provoked.

We hold that petitioner School District acted entirely within its permissible authority in imposing sanctions upon Fraser in response to his offensively lewd and indecent speech. Unlike the sanctions imposed on the students wearing armbands in *Tinker*, the penalties imposed in this case were unrelated to any political viewpoint. The First Amendment does not prevent the school officials from determining that to permit a vulgar and lewd speech such as respondent's would undermine the school's basic educational mission.

STEVENS, J., dissenting.

"Frankly, my dear, I don't give a damn."

When I was a high school student, the use of those words in a public forum shocked the Nation. Today Clark Gable's four-letter expletive is less offensive than it was then. Nevertheless, I assume that high school administrators may prohibit the use of that word in classroom discussion and even in extracurricular activities that are sponsored by the school and held on school premises. For I believe a school faculty must regulate the content as well as the style of student speech in carrying out its educational mission. It does seem to me, however, that if a student is to be punished for using offensive speech, he is entitled to fair notice of the scope of the prohibition and the consequences of its violation. The interest in free speech protected by the First Amendment and the interest in fair procedure protected by the Due Process Clause of the Fourteenth Amendment combine to require this conclusion.

It seems fairly obvious that respondent's speech would be inappropriate in certain classroom and formal social settings. On the other hand, in a locker room or perhaps in a school corridor the metaphor in the speech might be regarded as rather routine comment. If this be true, and if respondent's audience consisted almost entirely of young people with whom he conversed on a daily basis, can we—at this distance—confidently assert that he must have known that the school administration would punish him for delivering it?

For three reasons, I think not. First, it seems highly unlikely that he would have decided to deliver the speech if he had known that it would result in his suspension and disqualification from delivering the school commencement address. Second, I believe a strong presumption in favor of free expression should apply whenever an issue of this kind is arguable. Third, because the Court has adopted the policy of applying contemporary community standards in evaluating expression with sexual connotations, this Court should defer to the views of the district and circuit judges who are in a much better position to evaluate this speech than we are.

AN EXTENDED NOTE ON THE "VULGARITY" EXCEPTION TO *TINKER*

Fraser is commonly interpreted as introducing a "vulgarity" exception to the protection of student speech described in *Tinker*, and in fact Chief Justice Burger's majority opinion in *Fraser* focuses on the sexual innuendo in Fraser's speech. Note that in *Fraser* the Court applies this vulgarity exception to a student engaged in the most highly protected form of free speech—a campaign speech on behalf of a political candidate. The significant question in *Fraser* is: When is student speech so "vulgar" that it loses First Amendment protection even when uttered in what would otherwise be one of the most highly protected free speech circumstances? In answering this question, recall Chief Justice Burger's broad rationale for giving the Bethel school officials authority to regulate Fraser's speech: "The undoubted freedom to advocate unpopular and controversial views in schools and classrooms must be balanced against the society's countervailing interest in teaching students the boundaries of socially appropriate behavior. Even the most heated political discourse in a democratic society requires consideration for the personal sensibilities of the other participants and audiences." Many lower courts have taken this rationale to heart, and have interpreted the concept of "vulgarity" to include general concepts of social decorum that have nothing to do with sex or sexuality.

Consider the following scenario. A student running for president of the student council at a public high school gives a speech at an election campaign assembly for all the candidates. His speech includes the following passage:

> The administration plays tricks with your mind and they hope you won't notice. For example, why does Mr. Davidson stutter while he is on the intercom? He doesn't have a speech impediment. If you want to break the iron grip of this school, vote for me for president. I can try to bring back student rights that you have missed and maybe get things that you have always wanted. All you have to do is vote for me, Dean Poling.

At the conclusion of this speech, "many of the students jumped up at the reference to Mr. Davidson (the assistant principal in charge of discipline at the school), clapped their hands, and yelled things like 'way to go, Dean,' and 'we don't like him either.'" The school principal on the other hand, was "quite upset," adding that "I thought that the content of this speech was inappropriate, disruptive of school discipline, and in bad taste." The other candidates on the ballot for student council president were also displeased. They approached a guidance counselor "and complained that Dean Poling had gained an unfair advantage in the election by saying what he had said about Mr. Davidson." School officials responded to these complaints by announcing that Mr. Poling would not be allowed to run for student council president, and that any votes cast for him would not be counted.

Does this scenario seem to fit the model of "vulgarity" set forth in *Fraser*? The Sixth Circuit Court of Appeals thought so. In Poling v. Murphy, 872 F.2d 757 (6th Cir. 1989), *cert. denied*, 493 U.S. 1021 (1990), a divided panel of the Sixth Circuit rejected Mr. Poling's claim that school officials violated his First Amendment rights when they excluded him from the election. The court held that this case was controlled by the rules of *Fraser* and *Kuhlmeier*, rather than *Tinker*. With regard to *Fraser*, the court referred to the school's legitimate concern with teaching its students the "shared values of the civilized social order." According to the court, "these 'shared values' [sometimes] come in conflict with one another; independence of thought and frankness of expression occupy a high place on our scale of values, or ought to, but so too do discipline, courtesy, and respect for authority. Judgments on how best to balance such values may well vary from school to school. Television has not yet so thoroughly homogenized us that conduct deemed unexceptionable in New York City, for example, will necessarily be considered acceptable in rural Tennessee." *Id.* at 762.

Might a geographical dichotomy in attitudes toward profanity or sexual mores explain cases such as B.H. v. Easton Area School District, 725 F.3d 293 (2013)? There, the Third Circuit Court of Appeals, sitting in Philadelphia, ruled in favor of two students who were punished for wearing "I Heart Boobies (Keep A Breast)" bracelets to promote breast cancer awareness at their school. Relying on *Fraser*, the school board argued that the breast cancer bracelets could be misinterpreted as "lewd, vulgar, profane, or plainly offensive student speech." But an *en banc* panel of the Third Circuit clarified that schools, under *Fraser*, "may restrict ambiguously lewd speech only if it cannot plausibly be interpreted as commenting on a social or political matter." The court said the school district could not categorically ban the bracelets because they "are not plainly lewd and express support for . . . [an] unquestionably . . . important social issue." *Id.* at 302.

Note too that the location of a public school student's vulgar or profane speech matters greatly to the First Amendment analysis. In Mahonoy Area School District v. B.L., 141 S. Ct. 2038 (2021), the Supreme Court held that a public high school could not punish social media posts made while off campus by a disappointed would-be varsity cheerleader (B.L.). B.L.'s snapchat posts to her friends, many of whom were also students at the school, included "Fuck school fuck softball fuck cheer fuck everything." *Id.* at 2041. In retaliation for B.L.'s profane and critical posts, the high school removed her from the junior varsity cheerleading squad. The Supreme Court declined to apply *Tinker* and *Fraser* to B.L.'s off-campus speech and instead held that a public school student's off-campus speech was generally protected under the First Amendment. Writing for the 8–1 majority, Justice Breyer explained that although actual disruption to the school's operations constitutes a relevant factor in determining when a public school may punish a student's off-campus speech, it is not the only factor or even the controlling factor:

> Given the many different kinds of off-campus speech, the different potential school-related and circumstance-specific justifications, and the differing extent to which those justifications may call for First Amendment leeway, we can, as a general matter, say little more than this: Taken together, these three features [the lack of *in loco parentis* authority when a public school student is off campus, the free speech implications of permitting a school district to regulate a student 24/7, and the government's interest and duty to safeguard speech] of much off-campus speech mean that the leeway the First Amendment grants to schools in light of their special characteristics is diminished. We leave for future cases to decide where, when, and how these features mean the speaker's off-campus location will make the critical difference. This case can, however, provide one example.

Id. at 2046.

Applying these considerations to B.L.'s profane and critical social media posts, Breyer easily found that the school district had violated B.L.'s First Amendment rights, observing that "it is necessary to protect the superfluous in order to preserve the necessary." *Id.* at 2047. In sum, *Fraser* does not authorize a public school district to punish a student for nondisruptive off-campus speech because the speech is vulgar (or, for that matter, critical of the school and its staff).

Hazelwood School District v. Kuhlmeier

484 U.S. 260 (1988)

WHITE, J., delivered the opinion of the Court.

Respondents are three former Hazelwood East students who were staff members of Spectrum, the school newspaper. They contend that school officials violated their First Amendment rights by deleting two pages of articles from the May 13, 1983, issue of Spectrum.

Spectrum was written and edited by the Journalism II class at Hazelwood East. The newspaper was published every three weeks or so during the 1982-1983 school year. More than 4,500 copies of the newspaper were distributed during that year to students, school personnel, and members of the community.

The costs associated with the newspaper—such as supplies, textbooks, and a portion of the journalism teacher's salary—were borne entirely by the Board.

The practice at Hazelwood East during the spring 1983 semester was for the journalism teacher to submit page proofs of each Spectrum issue to Principal Reynolds for his review prior to publication. On May 10, Emerson delivered the proofs of the May 13 edition to Reynolds, who objected to two of the articles scheduled to appear in that edition. One of the stories described three Hazelwood East students' experiences with pregnancy; the other discussed the impact of divorce on students at the school.

Reynolds was concerned that, although the pregnancy story used false names "to keep the identity of these girls a secret," the pregnant students still might be identifiable from the text. He also believed that the article's references to sexual activity and birth control were inappropriate for some of the younger students at the school. In addition, Reynolds was concerned that a student identified by name in the divorce story had complained that her father "wasn't spending enough time with my mom, my sister and I" prior to the divorce, "was always out of town on business or out late playing cards with the guys," and "always argued about everything" with her mother. Reynolds believed that the student's parents should have been given an opportunity to respond to these remarks or to consent to their publication. He was unaware that Emerson had deleted the student's name from the final version of the article.

Reynolds believed that there was no time to make the necessary changes in the stories before the scheduled press run and that the newspaper would not appear before the end of the school year if printing were delayed to any significant extent. He concluded that his only options under the circumstances were to publish a four-page newspaper instead of the planned six-page newspaper, eliminating the two pages on which the offending stories appeared, or to publish no newspaper at all. Accordingly, he directed Emerson to withhold from publication the two pages containing the stories on pregnancy and divorce.

[The students sued, claiming that the Principal's decision not to publish the two stories violated the students' First Amendment rights.]

We deal first with the question whether Spectrum may appropriately be characterized as a forum for public expression.

The policy of school officials toward Spectrum was reflected in Hazelwood School Board Policy 348.51 and the Hazelwood East Curriculum Guide. Board Policy 348.51 provided that "[s]chool sponsored publications are developed within the adopted curriculum and its educational implications in regular classroom activities." The Hazelwood East Curriculum Guide described the Journalism II course as a "laboratory situation in which the students publish the school newspaper applying skills they have learned in Journalism I." The lessons that were to be learned from the Journalism II course, according to the Curriculum Guide, included development of journalistic skills under deadline pressure, "the legal, moral, and ethical restrictions imposed upon journalists within the school community," and "responsibility and acceptance of criticism for articles of opinion." Journalism II was taught by a faculty member during regular class hours. Students received grades and academic credit for their performance in the course.

One might reasonably infer from the full text of Policy 348.51 that school officials retained ultimate control over what constituted "responsible journalism" in a school-sponsored newspaper. Although the Statement of Policy published in the September 14, 1982, issue of *Spectrum* declared that "*Spectrum*, as a student-press publication, accepts all rights implied by the First Amendment," this statement, understood in the context of the paper's role in the school's curriculum, suggests at most that the administration will not interfere with the students' exercise of those First Amendment rights that attend the publication of a school-sponsored newspaper. It does not reflect an intent to expand those rights by converting a curricular newspaper into a public forum. School officials did not evince either "by policy or by practice," any intent to open the pages of Spectrum to "indiscriminate use," by its student reporters and editors, or by the student body generally. Instead, they "reserve[d] the forum for its intended purpos[e]," as a supervised learning experience for journalism students. Accordingly, school officials were entitled to regulate the contents of Spectrum in any reasonable manner. It is this standard, rather than our decision in *Tinker*, that governs this case.

The question whether the First Amendment requires a school to tolerate particular student speech—the question that we addressed in *Tinker*—is different from the question whether the First Amendment requires a school affirmatively to promote particular student speech. The former question addresses educators' ability to silence a student's personal expression that happens to occur on the school premises. The latter question concerns educators' authority over school-sponsored publications, theatrical productions, and other expressive activities that students, parents, and members of the public might reasonably perceive to bear the imprimatur of the school. These activities may fairly be characterized as part of the school curriculum, whether or not they occur in a traditional classroom setting, so long as they are supervised by faculty members and designed to impart particular knowledge or skills to student participants and audiences.

Educators are entitled to exercise greater control over this second form of student expression to assure that participants learn whatever lessons the activity is designed to teach, that readers or listeners are not exposed to material that may be inappropriate for their level of maturity, and that the views of the individual speaker are not erroneously attributed to the school. Hence, a school may in its capacity as publisher of a school newspaper or producer of a school play "disassociate itself," *Fraser*, not only from speech that would "substantially interfere with [its] work . . . or impinge upon the rights of other students," *Tinker*, but also from speech that is, for example, ungrammatical, poorly written, inadequately researched, biased or prejudiced, vulgar or profane, or unsuitable for immature audiences. A school must be able to set high standards for the student speech that is disseminated under its auspices—standards that may be higher than those demanded by some newspaper publishers or theatrical producers in the "real" world—and may refuse to disseminate student speech that does not meet those standards. In addition, a school must be able to take into account the emotional maturity of the intended audience in determining whether to disseminate student speech on potentially sensitive topics, which might range from the existence of Santa Claus in an elementary school setting to the particulars of teenage sexual activity in a high school setting. A school must also retain the authority to refuse to sponsor student speech that might reasonably be perceived to advocate drug or alcohol use, irresponsible sex, or conduct otherwise inconsistent with "the shared values of a civilized social order," *Fraser*, or to associate the school with any position other than neutrality on matters of political controversy.

Accordingly, we conclude that the standard articulated in *Tinker* for determining when a school may punish student expression need not also be the standard for determining when a school may refuse to lend its name and resources to the dissemination of student expression. Instead, we hold that educators do not offend the First Amendment by exercising editorial control over the style and content of student speech in school-sponsored expressive activities so long as their actions are reasonably related to legitimate pedagogical concerns.

It is only when the decision to censor a school-sponsored publication, theatrical production, or other vehicle of student expression has no valid educational purpose that the First Amendment is so "directly and sharply implicate[d]," [*Epperson v. Arkansas*, *infra* p. 978], as to require judicial intervention to protect students' constitutional rights.

BRENNAN, J., with whom MARSHALL, J., and BLACKMUN, J., join, dissenting.

When the young men and women of Hazelwood East High School registered for Journalism II, they expected a civics lesson. Spectrum, the newspaper they were to publish, "was not just a class exercise in which students learned to prepare papers and hone writing skills, it was a . . . forum established to give students an opportunity to express their views while gaining an appreciation of their rights and responsibilities under the First Amendment to the United States Constitution. . . ." 795 F.2d 1368, 1373 (CA8 1986). "[A]t the beginning of each school year," the student journalists published a Statement of Policy—tacitly approved each year by school authorities—announcing their expectation that "*Spectrum*, as a student-press publication, accepts all rights implied by the First Amendment. . . . Only speech that 'materially and substantially interferes with the requirements of appropriate discipline' can be found unacceptable and therefore prohibited." ([Q]uoting *Tinker*.) The school board itself affirmatively guaranteed the students of Journalism II an atmosphere conducive to fostering such an appreciation and exercising the full panoply of rights associated with a free student press. "School sponsored student publications," it vowed, "will not restrict free expression or diverse viewpoints within the rules of responsible journalism."

This case arose when the Hazelwood East administration breached its own promise, dashing its students' expectations. The school principal, without prior consultation or explanation, excised six articles—comprising two full pages—of the May 13, 1983, issue of Spectrum. He did so not because any of the articles would "materially and substantially interfere with the requirements of appropriate discipline," but simply because he considered two of the six "inappropriate, personal, sensitive, and unsuitable" for student consumption.

In my view the principal broke more than just a promise. He violated the First Amendment's prohibitions against censorship of any student expression that neither disrupts classwork nor invades the rights of others, and against any censorship that is not narrowly tailored to serve its purpose.

Free student expression undoubtedly sometimes interferes with the effectiveness of the school's pedagogical functions. Some brands of student expression do so by directly preventing the school from pursuing its pedagogical mission: The young polemic who stands on a soapbox during calculus class to deliver an eloquent political diatribe interferes with the legitimate teaching of calculus. And the student who delivers a lewd endorsement of a student-government candidate might so extremely distract an impressionable high school audience as to interfere with the orderly operation of the school. See *Bethel.* Other student speech, however, frustrates the school's legitimate pedagogical purposes merely by expressing a message that conflicts with the school's, without directly interfering with the school's expression of its message: A student who responds to a political science teacher's question with the retort, "socialism is good," subverts the school's inculcation of the message that capitalism is better. Even the maverick who sits in class passively sporting a symbol of protest against a government policy, cf. *Tinker,* or the gossip who sits in the student commons swapping stories of sexual escapade could readily muddle a clear official message condoning the government policy or condemning teenage sex. Likewise, the student newspaper that, like Spectrum, conveys a moral position at odds with the school's official stance might subvert the administration's legitimate inculcation of its own perception of community values.

If mere incompatibility with the school's pedagogical message were a constitutionally sufficient justification for the suppression of student speech, school officials could censor each of the students or student organizations in the foregoing hypotheticals, converting our public schools into "enclaves of totalitarianism," *id.*, that "strangle the free mind at its source," *West Virginia Board of Education v. Barnette.* The First Amendment permits no such blanket censorship authority.

NOTES AND QUESTIONS

1. *What is curricular?* Each of the Supreme Court's student-speech cases has one main concept that is central to that case's application. In *Tinker,* that concept is "disruption." In *Fraser,* that concept is "vulgarity." In *Kuhlmeier,* the key concept is "curricular." The crucial language in *Kuhlmeier* grants school officials the authority to regulate or proscribe student speech with regard to "activities [that] may fairly be characterized as part of the school

curriculum, whether or not they occur in a traditional classroom setting, so long as they are supervised by faculty members and designed to impart particular knowledge or skills to student participants and audiences." As with the central concepts of the Court's other student-speech cases, the lower courts have tended to interpret the *Kuhlmeier* concept of "curricular activities" very broadly. Language in one Tenth Circuit Court of Appeals opinion is typical. According to that court, *Kuhlmeier* applies not just to activities that are directly integrated into the school's classroom instruction but also to "activities that might reasonably be perceived to bear the imprimatur of the school and that involve pedagogical concerns." Fleming v. Jefferson County Sch. Dist. R1, 298 F.3d 918, 923 (10th Cir. 2002). Under this broad reading, lower courts have applied the *Kuhlmeier* analysis to several different aspects of the educational experience outside the traditional classroom setting. *See id.* (decorative tiles placed outside a high school); Planned Parenthood of S. Nev., Inc. v. Clark County Sch. Dist., 941 F.2d 817 (9th Cir. 1991) (advertisements in programs distributed at athletic events); Poling v. Murphy, 872 F.2d 757 (6th Cir. 1989) (student government elections); Crosby v. Holsinger, 852 F.2d 801 (4th Cir. 1988) (school mascot); Brody v. Spang, 957 F.2d 1108 (3d Cir. 1992) (commencement exercises); Lundberg v. West Monona Cmty. Sch. Dist., 731 F. Supp. 331 (N.D. Iowa 1989) (same); Golden v. Rossford Exempted Vill. Sch. Dist., 445 F. Supp. 2d 820 (N.D. Ohio 2006) (student assemblies).

2. *College students and professionalism as a basis for discipline*: In Tatro v. Univ. of Minn., 816 N.W.2d 509 (Minn. 2012), the Minnesota Supreme Court upheld a state university's right to discipline a student in a Mortuary Science Program who discussed her human cadaver in an irreverent way using social media, in violation of university policies governing mortuary science students that the court found to be narrowly tailored to achieve professionalism objectives. Can a state university discipline a student in its M.B.A. program for posting on Facebook that "my professor is so boring I want to gouge my eyes out with pencils during her class"? What if the student posts: "The girl who sits next to me in Accounting is a 10"? Does it matter whether the Facebook posts are set to be public or not?
3. Kuhlmeier *and teachers' rights*. The Supreme Court has never addressed the issue of whether teachers below the university level have academic freedom rights protected by the First Amendment. Several lower courts, however, have cited *Kuhlmeier* for the proposition that a school board's control of the curriculum gives it virtually complete authority to dictate how teachers conduct their class and what they teach. *See, e.g.*, Boring v. Buncombe County Bd. of Educ., 136 F.3d 364 (4th Cir.), *cert. denied*, 525 U.S. 813 (1998) (citing *Kuhlmeier* in upholding the transfer of a teacher after the teacher used a controversial play in her theater class); Kirkland v. Northside Indep. Sch. Dist., 890 F.2d 794 (5th Cir. 1989), *cert. denied*, 496 U.S. 926 (1990) (citing *Kuhlmeier* in upholding the nonrenewal of a teacher who used an unapproved supplemental reading list in his class). For extended discussion of the speech rights of public school teachers, *see* Mary-Rose Papandrea, *Social Media, Public School Teachers, and the First Amendment*, 90 N.C. L. Rev. 1597 (2012).

Morse v. Frederick

551 U.S. 393 (2007)

ROBERTS, C.J., delivered the opinion of the Court.

On January 24, 2002, the Olympic Torch Relay passed through Juneau, Alaska, on its way to the winter games in Salt Lake City, Utah. The torchbearers were to proceed along a street in front of Juneau-Douglas High School (JDHS) while school was in session. Petitioner Deborah Morse, the school principal, decided to permit staff and students to participate in the Torch Relay as an approved social event or class trip. Students were allowed to leave class to observe the relay from either side of the street. Teachers and administrative officials monitored the students' actions.

Respondent Joseph Frederick, a JDHS senior, was late to school that day. When he arrived, he joined his friends (all but one of whom were JDHS students) across the street from the school to watch the event. Not all the students waited patiently. Some became rambunctious, throwing plastic cola bottles and snowballs and scuffling with their classmates. As the torchbearers and camera crews passed by, Frederick and his friends unfurled a 14-foot banner bearing the phrase: "BONG HiTS 4 JESUS." The large banner was easily readable by the students on the other side of the street.

Principal Morse immediately crossed the street and demanded that the banner be taken down. Everyone but Frederick complied. Morse confiscated the banner and told Frederick to report to her office, where she suspended him for 10 days. Morse later explained that she told Frederick to take the banner down because she thought it encouraged illegal drug use, in violation of established school policy. Juneau School Board Policy No. 5520 states: "The Board specifically prohibits any assembly or public expression that . . . advocates the use of substances that are illegal to minors. . . ."

Frederick administratively appealed his suspension, but the Juneau School District Superintendent upheld it, limiting it to time served (8 days). In a memorandum setting forth his reasons, the superintendent determined that Frederick had displayed his banner "in the midst of his fellow students, during school hours, at a school-sanctioned activity." He further explained that Frederick "was not disciplined because the principal of the school 'disagreed' with his message, but because his speech appeared to advocate the use of illegal drugs."

The superintendent continued:

> "The common-sense understanding of the phrase 'bong hits' is that it is a reference to a means of smoking marijuana. Given [Frederick's] inability or unwillingness to express any other credible meaning for the phrase, I can only agree with the principal and countless others who saw the banner as advocating the use of illegal drugs. [Frederick's] speech was not political. He was not advocating the legalization of marijuana or promoting a religious belief. He was displaying a fairly silly message promoting illegal drug usage in the midst of a school activity, for the benefit of television cameras covering the Torch Relay. [Frederick's] speech was potentially disruptive to the event and clearly disruptive of and inconsistent with the school's educational mission to educate students about the dangers of illegal drugs and to discourage their use."

II.

At the outset, we reject Frederick's argument that this is not a school speech case—as has every other authority to address the question. The event occurred during normal school hours. It was sanctioned by Principal Morse "as an approved social event or class trip," and the school district's rules expressly provide that pupils in "approved social events and class trips are subject to district rules for student conduct." Teachers and administrators were interspersed among the students and charged with supervising them. The high school band and cheerleaders performed. Frederick, standing among other JDHS students across the street from the school, directed his banner toward the school, making it plainly visible to most students. Under these circumstances, we agree with the superintendent that Frederick cannot "stand in the midst of his fellow students, during school hours, at a school-sanctioned activity and claim he is not at school." There is some uncertainty at the outer boundaries as to when courts should apply school-speech precedents, see *Porter v. Ascension Parish School Bd.*, 393 F.3d 608, 615, n. 22 (CA5 2004), but not on these facts.

III.

The message on Frederick's banner is cryptic. It is no doubt offensive to some, perhaps amusing to others. To still others, it probably means nothing at all. Frederick himself claimed "that the words were just nonsense meant to attract television cameras." But Principal Morse thought the banner would be interpreted by those viewing it as promoting illegal drug use, and that interpretation is plainly a reasonable one.

We agree with Morse. At least two interpretations of the words on the banner demonstrate that the sign advocated the use of illegal drugs. First, the phrase could be interpreted as an imperative: "[Take] bong hits . . ."—a message equivalent, as Morse explained in her declaration, to "smoke marijuana" or "use an illegal drug." Alternatively, the phrase could be viewed as celebrating drug use—"bong hits [are a good thing]," or "[we take] bong hits"—and we discern no meaningful distinction between celebrating illegal drug use in the midst of fellow students and outright advocacy or promotion.

The pro-drug interpretation of the banner gains further plausibility given the paucity of alternative meanings the banner might bear. The best Frederick can come up with is that the banner is "meaningless and funny." Gibberish is surely a possible interpretation of the words on the banner, but it is not the only one, and dismissing the banner as meaningless ignores its undeniable reference to illegal drugs.

. . . [T]he dissent emphasizes the importance of political speech and the need to foster "national debate about a serious issue," as if to suggest that the banner is political speech. But not even Frederick argues that the banner conveys any sort of political or religious message. Contrary to the dissent's suggestion, this is plainly not a case about political debate over the criminalization of drug use or possession.

IV.

The question thus becomes whether a principal may, consistent with the First Amendment, restrict student speech at a school event, when that speech is reasonably viewed as promoting illegal drug use. We hold that she may.

Kuhlmeier does not control this case because no one would reasonably believe that Frederick's banner bore the school's imprimatur. The case is nevertheless instructive because it confirms both principles cited above. *Kuhlmeier* acknowledged that schools may regulate some speech "even though the government could not censor similar speech outside the school." And, like *Fraser*, it confirms that the rule of *Tinker* is not the only basis for restricting student speech.

Drawing on the principles applied in our student speech cases, we have held in the Fourth Amendment context that "while children assuredly do not 'shed their constitutional rights . . . at the schoolhouse gate,' . . . the nature of those rights is what is appropriate for children in school." Vernonia School Dist. 47J v. Acton, 515 U.S. 646, 655-656 (1995) (quoting *Tinker*, *supra*, at 506). Even more to the point, these cases also recognize that deterring drug use by schoolchildren is an "important—indeed, perhaps compelling" interest. Drug abuse can cause severe and permanent damage to the health and well-being of young people[.]

Just five years ago, we wrote: "The drug abuse problem among our Nation's youth has hardly abated since *Vernonia* was decided in 1995. In fact, evidence suggests that it has only grown worse."

Congress has declared that part of a school's job is educating students about the dangers of illegal drug use. It has provided billions of dollars to support state and local drug-prevention programs. . . . Thousands of school boards throughout the country—including JDHS—have adopted policies aimed at effectuating this message. Those school boards know that peer pressure is perhaps "the single most important factor leading schoolchildren to take drugs," and that students are more likely to use drugs when the norms in school appear to tolerate such behavior. Student speech celebrating illegal drug use at a school event, in the presence of school administrators and teachers, thus poses a particular challenge for school officials working to protect those entrusted to their care from the dangers of drug abuse.

Tinker warned that schools may not prohibit student speech because of "undifferentiated fear or apprehension of disturbance" or "a mere desire to avoid the discomfort and unpleasantness that always accompany an unpopular viewpoint." The danger here is far more serious and palpable. The particular concern to prevent student drug abuse at issue here, embodied in established school policy, extends well beyond an abstract desire to avoid controversy.

Petitioners urge us to adopt the broader rule that Frederick's speech is proscribable because it is plainly "offensive" as that term is used in *Fraser*. We think this stretches *Fraser* too far; that case should not be read to encompass any speech that could fit under some definition of "offensive." After all, much political and religious speech might be perceived as offensive to some. The concern here is not that Frederick's speech was offensive, but that it was reasonably viewed as promoting illegal drug use.

THOMAS, J., concurring.

The Court today decides that a public school may prohibit speech advocating illegal drug use. I agree and therefore join its opinion in full. I write separately to state my view that the standard set forth in *Tinker v. Des Moines Independent Community School Dist.*, is without basis in the Constitution.

In my view, the history of public education suggests that the First Amendment, as originally understood, does not protect student speech in public schools.

Although colonial schools were exclusively private, public education proliferated in the early 1800's. By the time the States ratified the Fourteenth Amendment, public schools had become relatively common. If students in public schools were originally understood as having free-speech rights, one would have expected 19th-century public schools to have respected those rights and courts to have enforced them. They did not.

Today, the Court creates another exception. In doing so, we continue to distance ourselves from *Tinker*, but we neither overrule it nor offer an explanation of when it operates and when it does not. I am afraid that our jurisprudence now says that students have a right to speak in schools except when they don't—a standard continuously developed through litigation against local schools and their administrators. In my view, petitioners could prevail for a much simpler reason: As originally understood, the Constitution does not afford students a right to free speech in public schools.

ALITO, J., with whom KENNEDY, J., joins, concurring.

I join the opinion of the Court on the understanding that (a) it goes no further than to hold that a public school may restrict speech that a reasonable observer would interpret as advocating illegal drug use and (b) it provides no support for any restriction of speech that can plausibly be interpreted as commenting on any political or social issue, including speech on issues such as "the wisdom of the war on drugs or of legalizing marijuana for medicinal use."

I do not read the opinion to mean that there are necessarily any grounds for such regulation that are not already recognized in the holdings of this Court. In addition to *Tinker*, the decision in the present case allows the restriction of speech advocating illegal drug use; *Bethel*, permits the regulation of speech that is delivered in a lewd or vulgar manner as part of a middle school program; and *Hazelwood*, allows a school to regulate what is in essence the school's own speech, that is, articles that appear in a publication that is an official school organ. I join the opinion of the Court on the understanding that the opinion does not hold that the special characteristics of the public schools necessarily justify any other speech restrictions.

STEVENS, J., with whom SOUTER, J., and GINSBURG, J., join, dissenting.

I would hold . . . that the school's interest in protecting its students from exposure to speech "reasonably regarded as promoting illegal drug use" cannot justify disciplining Frederick for his attempt to make an ambiguous statement to a television audience simply because it contained an oblique reference to drugs. The First Amendment demands more, indeed, much more.

The Court holds otherwise only after laboring to establish two uncontroversial propositions: first, that the constitutional rights of students in school settings are not coextensive with the rights of adults; and second, that deterring drug use by schoolchildren is a valid and terribly important interest. As to the first, I take the Court's point that the message on Frederick's banner is not *necessarily* protected speech, even though it unquestionably would have been had the banner been unfurled elsewhere. As to the second, I am willing to assume that the Court is correct that the pressing need to deter drug use supports JDHS's rule prohibiting willful conduct that expressly "advocates the use of substances that are illegal to minors." But it is a gross non sequitur to draw from these two unremarkable propositions the remarkable conclusion that the school may suppress student speech that was never meant to persuade anyone to do anything.

In my judgment, the First Amendment protects student speech if the message itself neither violates a permissible rule nor expressly advocates conduct that is illegal and harmful to students. This nonsense banner does neither, and the Court does serious violence to the First Amendment in upholding—indeed, lauding—a school's decision to punish Frederick for expressing a view with which it disagreed.

. . . [T]oday the Court fashions a test that trivializes the two cardinal principles upon which *Tinker* rests. See *ante* ("[S]chools [may] restrict student expression that they reasonably regard as promoting illegal drug use"). The Court's test invites stark viewpoint discrimination. In this case, for example, the principal has unabashedly acknowledged that she disciplined Frederick because she disagreed with the pro-drug viewpoint she ascribed to the message on the banner.

It is also perfectly clear that "promoting illegal drug use" comes nowhere close to proscribable "incitement to imminent lawless action." *Brandenburg.* Encouraging drug use might well increase the likelihood that a listener will try an illegal drug, but that hardly justifies censorship.

No one seriously maintains that drug advocacy (much less Frederick's ridiculous sign) comes within the vanishingly small category of speech that can be prohibited because of its feared consequences. Such advocacy, to borrow from Justice Holmes, "ha[s] no chance of starting a present conflagration." *Gitlow v. New York.*

[I]t takes real imagination to read a "cryptic" message (the Court's characterization, not mine) with a slanting drug reference as an incitement to drug use. . . . The notion that the message on this banner would actually persuade either the average student or even the dumbest one to change his or her behavior is most implausible. That the Court believes such a silly message can be proscribed as advocacy underscores the novelty of its position, and suggests that the principle it articulates has no stopping point. . . .

Even in high school, a rule that permits only one point of view to be expressed is less likely to produce correct answers than the open discussion of countervailing views. In the national debate about a serious issue, it is the expression of the minority's viewpoint that most demands the protection of the First Amendment. Whatever the better policy may be, a full and frank discussion of the costs and benefits of the attempt to prohibit the use of marijuana is far wiser than suppression of speech because it is unpopular.

Justice BREYER, concurring in the judgment in part and dissenting in part.

This Court need not and should not decide this difficult First Amendment issue on the merits. Rather, I believe that it should simply hold that qualified immunity bars the student's claim for monetary damages and say no more.

NOTES AND QUESTIONS

1. *What are the rules for student speech that disagrees with the state's official anti-drug message?* The majority in *Morse* does not hold that all student speech disagreeing with the state's official anti-drug message is unprotected by the First Amendment. But the Court fails to clearly describe when that

speech is protected and when it is not. On the one hand, the Court says that student speech "promoting illegal drug use" may be sanctioned by the school authorities. On the other hand, the Court also suggests that students have a First Amendment right to say favorable things about drugs in the context of "political debate over the criminalization of drug use or possession." How likely is it that this distinction will survive the onslaught of clever students seeking to push the boundaries of what is permissible? Suppose the student in *Morse* changed his posters slightly to say "BONG HITS 4 LEGALIZATION." Would this poster be protected under Chief Justice Roberts's plurality opinion in *Morse*? This modified poster promotes illegal drug use to the same extent as the original poster, but its message is also clearly political. How would Chief Justice Roberts's distinction apply to speech advocating civil disobedience? The entire point of such speech is to advocate illegal behavior, but at the same time such speech carries obvious political messages and ramifications. Would such speech therefore be characterized as unprotected "promotional" speech or as protected "political" speech? Suppose on the day after the Supreme Court issued its *Morse* decision, some of the plaintiff's classmates decided to support his right to free speech by holding up outside the school replica "BONG HiTS 4 JESUS" signs. Would their act of protest be protected under *Morse*? Suppose the principal interpreted their actions as promoting the first student's promotion of illegal drugs. Would the fact that this speech was indirectly pro-drug justify the principal in suspending those students as well?

2. *The applicability of* Tinker *and other student-speech cases to student speech that occurs off-campus.* Although the speech in *Morse* occurred outside the school, on a public sidewalk, and in a crowd that included several members of the general public, the Court treated the case as subject to the same regulatory rules that would have applied if the speech had occurred within the schoolhouse. In Chief Justice Roberts's plurality opinion, he notes that "[t]here is some uncertainty at the outer boundaries as to when courts should apply school-speech precedents." The case Chief Justice Roberts cites for this proposition is Porter v. Ascension Parish School Board, 393 F.3d 608 (5th Cir. 2004), in which the Fifth Circuit declined to apply the Court's student-speech decisions to a case involving sanctions imposed on a 16-year-old student who had composed a violent drawing off-campus. The court held that "[b]ecause Adam's drawing was composed off-campus, displayed only to members of his own household, stored off-campus, and not purposefully taken by him to [his high school] or publicized in a way certain to result in its appearance at [the school], we have found that the drawing is protected by the First Amendment. Furthermore, we have found that it is neither speech directed at the campus nor a purposefully communicated true threat." *Id.* at 620. Note, however, that other lower courts have applied the student-speech decisions to off-campus student speech, including cases involving off-campus newspapers and Web sites. *See* Wynar v. Douglas County Sch. Dist., 728 F.3d 1062 (9th Cir. 2013) (off-campus Web site); Doninger v. Niehoff, 642 F.3d 334,

339-43 (2d Cir. 2011) (off-campus email and blog post); Boucher v. School Bd. of Sch. Dist. of Greenfield, 134 F.3d 821 (7th Cir. 1998) (off-campus newspaper); Bystrom v. Fridley High Sch., 686 F. Supp. 1387 (D. Minn. 1987) (off-campus newspaper); Killion v. Franklin Reg'l Sch. Dist., 136 F. Supp. 2d 446 (W.D. Pa. 2001) (off-campus e-mail); Emmett v. Kent Sch. Dist. No. 415, 92 F. Supp. 2d 1088 (W.D. Wash. 2000) (off-campus Web site); Beussink v. Woodland R-IV Sch. Dist., 30 F. Supp. 2d 1175 (E.D. Mo. 1998) (off-campus Web site). *But see* Doninger v. Niehoff, 642 F.3d 334 (2d Cir. 2011) (holding in favor of student for off-campus parody website).

3. *Fuzzy guidance from the Supreme Court.* The Supreme Court's rather opaque decision in Mahanoy Area School District v. B.L., 141 S. Ct. 2038 (2021) [*supra* p. 696], arguably raises more questions than it answers about the constitutional authority of public school officials to regulate students' off-campus speech activity. Justice Breyer, writing for an 8–1 majority, observes that "we do not believe the special characteristics that give schools additional license to regulate student speech always disappear when a school regulates speech that takes place off campus," but, on the other hand, a "school's regulatory interests remain significant in some off-campus circumstances." *Id.* at 2045. His majority opinion fails to establish clear, categorial rules that delimit when public school officials may regulate or punish a student's off-campus speech. *See id.* at 2046-47 (setting forth a number of considerations that lower courts should consider when analyzing whether public school officials may regulate a public school student's off-campus speech, including, but not limited to, whether the off-campus speech later caused significant and material disruption on campus). Going forward, lower federal and state courts will have to struggle to transform the open-ended balancing exercise set forth in *Mahanoy Area School District* into workable First Amendment rules that generate consistent results.

4. Professor Clay Calvert has shown that some courts of appeals have interpreted the concurrences of Justices Alito and Kennedy in *Morse* to permit schools to censor homophobic and violent expression without applying *Tinker*'s substantial disruption standard. Clay Calvert, *Misuse and Abuse of* Morse v. Frederick *by Lower Courts*, 32 Seattle U. L. Rev. 1 (2008). He points, for example, to the Fifth Circuit's decision in Ponce v. Socorro Independent Sch. Dist., 508 F.3d 765 (5th Cir. 2007), in which the court interpreted *Morse* as standing for the principle that "speech advocating a harm that is demonstrably grave and that derives that gravity from the 'special danger' to the physical safety of students arising from the school environment is unprotected." In other words, the court concluded that "some harms are in fact so great in the school setting that requiring a school administrator to evaluate their disruptive potential is unnecessary."

THEORY-APPLIED PROBLEMS

In order to understand and attempt to reconcile the various strains of the Court's four major student-speech cases, try applying them in the following scenarios:

1. A middle school student draws a Confederate flag on a piece of paper during class and is suspended for three days. *See* West v. Derby Unified Sch. Dist. No. 260, 206 F.3d 1358 (10th Cir.), *cert. denied*, 531 U.S. 825 (2000).
2. A middle school student is suspended for wearing a T-shirt that contains large print reading "George W. Bush," below which is the text, "Chicken-Hawk-in-Chief." Directly below these words is a large picture of the President's face, wearing a helmet, superimposed on the body of a chicken. Surrounding the President are images of oil rigs and dollar symbols. To one side of the President, three lines of cocaine and a razor blade appear. In the "chicken wing" of the President nearest the cocaine, there is a straw. In the other "wing" the President is holding a martini glass with an olive in it. Directly below all these depictions is printed, "1st Chicken Hawk Wing," and below that is text reading "World Domination Tour." *See* Guiles ex rel. Guiles v. Marineau, 461 F.3d 320 (2d Cir. 2006).
3. A school adopts a policy that prohibits all handouts containing "political, religious or organizational symbols." *See* Heinkel ex rel. Heinkel v. School Bd. of Lee County, Fla., 194 Fed. Appx. 604 (11th Cir. 2006).
4. Members of a high school basketball team are suspended from the team after they sign a letter requesting their coach's resignation. *See* Pinard v. Clatskanie Sch. Dist. 6J, 467 F.3d 755 (9th Cir. 2006).
5. School officials punish a student for remaining silent and raising a clenched fist in the air during the class's daily recitation of the Pledge of Allegiance. *See* Holloman ex rel. Holloman v. Harland, 370 F.3d 1252 (11th Cir. 2004).
6. A student is suspended for wearing to school a Marilyn Manson T-shirt depicting a three-headed Jesus accompanied by the words "See No Truth. Hear No Truth. Speak No Truth." *See* Boroff v. Van Wert City Bd. of Educ., 220 F.3d 465 (6th Cir. 2000), *cert. denied*, 532 U.S. 920 (2001).
7. A student is expelled from school after he shows a teacher a poem that includes several examples of violent imagery. *See* LaVine v. Blaine Sch. Dist., 257 F.3d 981 (9th Cir. 2001), *cert. denied*, 536 U.S. 959 (2002).
8. Students who believe that homosexuality is a sin are prohibited by a school anti-harassment policy from expressing their views on the subject. *See* Saxe v. State Coll. Area Sch. Dist., 240 F.3d 200 (3d Cir. 2001).
9. Students are suspended for wearing to school various T-shirts printed with phrases such as "See Dick Drink. See Dick Drive. See Dick Die. Don't Be a Dick," "Coed Naked Band: Do It to the Rhythm," and "Coed Naked Gerbils: Some People Will Censor Anything." *See* Pyle ex rel. Pyle v. South Hadley Sch. Comm., 861 F. Supp. 157 (D. Mass. 1994).
10. A student and his friend created "Satan's web page" which listed "people I wish would die" as well as "people that are cool." It urged viewers, in a hyperbolic fashion, to "Stab someone for no reason . . . " but also included a disclaimer stating "PS: NOW THAT YOU'VE READ MY WEB PAGE PLEASE DON'T GO KILLING PEOPLE AND STUFF THEN BLAMING IT ON ME. OK?" *See* Mahaffey v. Aldrich, 236 F. Supp. 2d 779 (E.D. Mich. 2002).

11. A West Virginia high school student created a MySpace page alleging that a fellow student was infected with a sexually transmitted disease and inviting comments from other students, some of whom posted to MySpace from school computers. The father of the targeted girl complained to the school, and the principal investigated and suspended the student for violating the school's anti-bullying policy. *See* Kowalski v. Berkeley County Schools, 652 F.3d 565 (4th Cir. 2011), *cert. denied*, 565 U.S. 1173 (2012).
12. A school district suspended a student for creating, off campus, a vulgar and "outrageous" parody MySpace profile of her middle school principal making fun of, among other things, his appearance and the size of his penis. The student limited access to the site. The parody was not accessible on campus because the school district blocked access to MySpace. In addition, MySpace removed the profile at the principal's request. The student sued, alleging that the suspension violated the First Amendment. The district court granted summary judgment for the school district on the basis that vulgar and lewd speech that affects campus can be disciplined even without "substantial disruption" as defined by *Tinker.* ex rel. Snyder v. Blue Mountain Sch. Dist., 650 F.3d 915 (3d Cir. 2011) (en banc), *cert. denied*, 565 U.S. 1156 (2012).

Board of Education v. Pico

457 U.S. 853 (1982)

BRENNAN, J., announced the judgment of the Court and delivered an opinion, in which MARSHALL, J., and STEVENS, J., joined, and in which BLACKMUN, J., joined [in part].

In September 1975, petitioners Ahrens, Martin, and Hughes attended a conference sponsored by Parents of New York United (PONYU), a politically conservative organization of parents concerned about education legislation in the State of New York. At the conference these petitioners obtained lists of books described by Ahrens as "objectionable," and by Martin as "improper fare for school students." It was later determined that the [Island Trees] High School library contained nine of the listed books, and that another listed book was in the [Island Trees Memorial] Junior High School library.[3] In February 1976, at a meeting with the Superintendent of Schools and the Principals of the High School and Junior High School, the Board gave an "unofficial direction" that the listed books be removed from the

3. The nine books in the High School library were: Slaughter House Five, by Kurt Vonnegut, Jr.; The Naked Ape, by Desmond Morris; Down These Mean Streets, by Piri Thomas; Best Short Stories of Negro Writers, edited by Langston Hughes; Go Ask Alice, of anonymous authorship; Laughing Boy, by Oliver LaFarge; Black Boy, by Richard Wright; A Hero Ain't Nothin' But A Sandwich, by Alice Childress; and Soul On Ice, by Eldridge Cleaver. The book in the Junior High School library was A Reader for Writers, edited by Jerome Archer. Still another listed book, The Fixer, by Bernard Malamud, was found to be included in the curriculum of a 12th-grade literature course.

library shelves and delivered to the Board's offices, so that Board members could read them. When this directive was carried out, it became publicized, and the Board issued a press release justifying its action. It characterized the removed books as "anti-American, anti-Christian, anti-Sem[i]tic, and just plain filthy," and concluded that "[i]t is our duty, our moral obligation, to protect the children in our schools from this moral danger as surely as from physical and medical dangers."

A short time later, the Board appointed a "Book Review Committee," consisting of four Island Trees parents and four members of the Island Trees schools staff, to read the listed books and to recommend to the Board whether the books should be retained, taking into account the books' "educational suitability," "good taste," "relevance," and "appropriateness to age and grade level." In July, the Committee made its final report to the Board, recommending that five of the listed books be retained and that two others be removed from the school libraries. As for the remaining four books, the Committee could not agree on two, took no position on one, and recommended that the last book be made available to students only with parental approval. The Board substantially rejected the Committee's report later that month, deciding that only one book should be returned to the High School library without restriction, that another should be made available subject to parental approval, but that the remaining nine books should "be removed from elementary and secondary libraries and [from] use in the curriculum." The Board gave no reasons for rejecting the recommendations of the Committee that it had appointed. [Respondents then sued, claiming a violation of their First Amendment rights.]

We emphasize at the outset the limited nature of the substantive question presented by the case before us. For as this case is presented to us, it does not involve textbooks, or indeed any books that Island Trees students would be required to read. Respondents do not seek in this Court to impose limitations upon their school Board's discretion to prescribe the curricula of the Island Trees schools. On the contrary, the only books at issue in this case are *library* books, books that by their nature are optional rather than required reading. Our adjudication of the present case thus does not intrude into the classroom, or into the compulsory courses taught there. Furthermore, even as to library books, the action before us does not involve the *acquisition* of books. Respondents have not sought to compel their school Board to add to the school library shelves any books that students desire to read. Rather, the only action challenged in this case is the *removal* from school libraries of books originally placed there by the school authorities, or without objection from them.

The Court has long recognized that local school boards have broad discretion in the management of school affairs. We are therefore in full agreement with petitioners that local school boards must be permitted "to establish and apply their curriculum in such a way as to transmit community values," and that "there is a legitimate and substantial community interest in promoting respect for authority and traditional values be they social, moral, or political."

At the same time, however, we have necessarily recognized that the discretion of the States and local school boards in matters of education must be exercised in a manner that comports with the transcendent imperatives of the First Amendment.

Of course, courts should not "intervene in the resolution of conflicts which arise in the daily operation of school systems" unless "basic constitutional values" are "directly and sharply implicate[d]" in those conflicts. *Epperson v. Arkansas,* [*infra* p. 978]. But we think that the First Amendment rights of students may be directly and sharply implicated by the removal of books from the shelves of a school library. Our precedents have focused "not only on the role of the First Amendment in fostering individual self-expression but also on its role in affording the public access to discussion, debate, and the dissemination of information and ideas." And we have recognized that "the State may not, consistently with the spirit of the First Amendment, contract the spectrum of available knowledge." *Griswold v. Connecticut.* In keeping with this principle, we have held that in a variety of contexts "the Constitution protects the right to receive information and ideas." *Stanley v. Georgia,* [*supra* Chapter 11].

In sum, just as access to ideas makes it possible for citizens generally to exercise their rights of free speech and press in a meaningful manner, such access prepares students for active and effective participation in the pluralistic, often contentious society in which they will soon be adult members. Of course all First Amendment rights accorded to students must be construed "in light of the special characteristics of the school environment." *Tinker.* But the special characteristics of the school *library* make that environment especially appropriate for the recognition of the First Amendment rights of students.

A school library, no less than any other public library, is "a place dedicated to quiet, to knowledge, and to beauty." *Brown v. Louisiana* (opinion of Fortas, J.). *Keyishian v. Board of Regents* observed that "'students must always remain free to inquire, to study and to evaluate, to gain new maturity and understanding.'" The school library is the principal locus of such freedom.

Petitioners emphasize the inculcative function of secondary education, and argue that they must be allowed *unfettered* discretion to "transmit community values" through the Island Trees schools. But that sweeping claim overlooks the unique role of the school library. It appears from the record that use of the Island Trees school libraries is completely voluntary on the part of students. Their selection of books from these libraries is entirely a matter of free choice; the libraries afford them an opportunity at self-education and individual enrichment that is wholly optional. Petitioners might well defend their claim of absolute discretion in matters of *curriculum* by reliance upon their duty to inculcate community values. But we think that petitioners' reliance upon that duty is misplaced where, as here, they attempt to extend their claim of absolute discretion beyond the compulsory environment of the classroom, into the school library and the regime of voluntary inquiry that there holds sway.

In rejecting petitioners' claim of absolute discretion to remove books from their school libraries, we do not deny that local school boards have a substantial legitimate role to play in the determination of school library content. We thus must turn to the question of the extent to which the First Amendment places limitations upon the discretion of petitioners to remove books from their libraries.

. . . [T]he message of [our] precedents is clear. Petitioners rightly possess significant discretion to determine the content of their school libraries. But that discretion may not be exercised in a narrowly partisan or political manner. If a Democratic school board, motivated by party affiliation, ordered the removal of all books written by or in favor of Republicans, few would doubt that the order violated the constitutional rights of the students denied access to those books. The same conclusion would surely apply if an all-white school board, motivated by racial animus, decided to remove all books authored by blacks or advocating racial equality and integration. Our Constitution does not permit the official suppression of *ideas.* Thus whether petitioners' removal of books from their school libraries denied respondents their First Amendment rights depends upon the motivation behind petitioners' actions. If petitioners *intended* by their removal decision to deny respondents access to ideas with which petitioners disagreed, and if this intent was the decisive factor in petitioners' decision, then petitioners have exercised their discretion in violation of the Constitution. To permit such intentions to control official actions would be to encourage the precise sort of officially prescribed orthodoxy unequivocally condemned in *Barnette.* On the other hand, respondents implicitly concede that an unconstitutional motivation would *not* be demonstrated if it were shown that petitioners had decided to remove the books at issue because those books were pervasively vulgar. And again, respondents concede that if it were demonstrated that the removal decision was based solely upon the "educational suitability" of the books in question, then their removal would be "perfectly permissible." In other words, in respondents' view such motivations, if decisive of petitioners' actions, would not carry the danger of an official suppression of ideas, and thus would not violate respondents' First Amendment rights.

As noted earlier, nothing in our decision today affects in any way the discretion of a local school board to choose books to *add* to the libraries of their schools. Because we are concerned in this case with the suppression of ideas, our holding today affects only the discretion to *remove* books. In brief, we hold that local school boards may not remove books from school library shelves simply because they dislike the ideas contained in those books and seek by their removal to "prescribe what shall be orthodox in politics, nationalism, religion, or other matters of opinion." *West Virginia Board of Education v. Barnette.* Such purposes stand inescapably condemned by our precedents.

[The Court then remanded the case to the District Court for a determination of whether] petitioners' decision to remove the books rested decisively upon disagreement with constitutionally protected ideas in those books, or upon a desire on petitioners' part to impose upon the students of the Island Trees High School and Junior High School a political orthodoxy to which petitioners and their constituents adhered.

BLACKMUN, J., concurring in part and concurring in the judgment.

In my view, then, the principle involved here is both narrower and more basic than the "right to receive information" identified by the plurality. I do not suggest that the State has any affirmative obligation to provide students with information or ideas, something that may well be associated with a "right to receive." And I do not believe, as the plurality suggests, that the right at issue here is somehow associated with the peculiar nature of the school library; if schools may be used to inculcate ideas, surely libraries may play a role in that process. Instead, I suggest that certain forms of state discrimination *between* ideas are improper. In particular, our precedents command the conclusion that the State may not act to deny access to an idea simply because state officials disapprove of that idea for partisan or political reasons.

In my view, we strike a proper balance here by holding that school officials may not remove books for the *purpose* of restricting access to the political ideas or social perspectives discussed in them, when that action is motivated simply by the officials' disapproval of the ideas involved. It does not seem radical to suggest that state action calculated to suppress novel ideas or concepts is fundamentally antithetical to the values of the First Amendment. At a minimum, allowing a school board to engage in such conduct hardly teaches children to respect the diversity of ideas that is fundamental to the American system. In this context, then, the school board must "be able to show that its action was caused by something more than a mere desire to avoid the discomfort and unpleasantness that always accompany an unpopular viewpoint," *Tinker*, and that the board had something in mind in addition to the suppression of partisan or political views it did not share.

WHITE, J., concurring in the judgment.

The District Court found that the books were removed from the school library because the school board believed them "to be, in essence, vulgar." Both Court of Appeals judges in the majority concluded, however, that there was a material issue of fact that precluded summary judgment sought by petitioners. The unresolved factual issue, as I understand it, is the reason or reasons underlying the school board's removal of the books. I am not inclined to disagree with the Court of Appeals on such a fact-bound issue and hence concur in the judgment of affirmance. Presumably this will result in a trial and the making of a full record and findings on the critical issues.

The plurality seems compelled to go further and issue a dissertation on the extent to which the First Amendment limits the discretion of the school board to remove books from the school library. I see no necessity for doing so at this point. When findings of fact and conclusions of law are made by the District Court, that may end the case. If, for example, the District Court concludes after a trial that the books were removed for their vulgarity, there may be no appeal. In any event, if there is an appeal, if there is dissatisfaction with the subsequent Court of Appeals' judgment, and if certiorari is sought and granted, there will be time enough to address the First Amendment issues that may then be presented.

BURGER, C.J., with whom POWELL, J., REHNQUIST, J., and O'CONNOR, J., join, dissenting.

Stripped to its essentials, the issue comes down to two important propositions: *first*, whether local schools are to be administered by elected school boards, or by federal judges and teenage pupils; and *second*, whether the values of morality, good taste, and relevance to education are valid reasons for school board decisions concerning the contents of a school library. In an attempt to place this case within the protection of the First Amendment, the plurality suggests a new "right" that, when shorn of the plurality's rhetoric, allows this Court to impose its own views about what books must be made available to students.

The plurality concludes that under the Constitution school boards cannot choose to retain or dispense with books if their discretion is exercised in a "narrowly partisan or political manner." The plurality concedes that permissible factors are whether the books are "pervasively vulgar," or educationally unsuitable. "Educational suitability," however, is a standardless phrase. This conclusion will undoubtedly be drawn in many—if not most—instances because of the decision-maker's content-based judgment that the ideas contained in the book or the idea expressed from the author's method of communication are inappropriate for teenage pupils.

The plurality also tells us that a book may be removed from a school library if it is "pervasively vulgar." But why must the vulgarity be "pervasive" to be offensive? Vulgarity might be concentrated in a single poem or a single chapter or a single page, yet still be inappropriate. Or a school board might reasonably conclude that even "random" vulgarity is inappropriate for teenage school students. A school board might also reasonably conclude that the school board's retention of such books gives those volumes an implicit endorsement. . . .

We can all agree that as a matter of *educational policy* students should have wide access to information and ideas. But the people elect school boards, who in turn select administrators, who select the teachers, and these are the individuals best able to determine the substance of that policy. The plurality fails to recognize the fact that local control of education involves democracy in a microcosm. In most public schools in the United States the *parents* have a large voice in running the school. Through participation in the election of school board members, the parents influence, if not control, the direction of their children's education. A school board is not a giant bureaucracy far removed from accountability for its actions; it is truly "of the people and by the people." A school board reflects its constituency in a very real sense and thus could not long exercise unchecked discretion in its choice to acquire or remove books. If the parents disagree with the educational decisions of the school board, they can take steps to remove the board members from office. Finally, even if parents and students cannot convince the school board that book removal is inappropriate, they have alternative sources to the same end. Books may be acquired from bookstores, public libraries, or other alternative sources unconnected with the unique environment of the local public schools. . . .

The plurality also limits the new right by finding it applicable only to the *removal* of books once acquired. Yet if the First Amendment commands that certain books cannot be removed, does it not equally require that the same books be *acquired*? Why does the coincidence of timing become the basis of a constitutional holding? According to the plurality, the evil to be avoided is the "official suppression of ideas." It does not follow that the decision to *remove* a book is less "official suppression" than the decision not to acquire a book desired by someone. Similarly, a decision to eliminate certain material from the curriculum, history for example, would carry an equal—probably greater—prospect of "official suppression." Would the decision be subject to our review?

Powell, J., dissenting.

The plurality opinion today rejects a basic concept of public school education in our country: that the States and locally elected school boards should have the responsibility for determining the educational policy of the public schools. After today's decision any junior high school student, by instituting a suit against a school board or teacher, may invite a judge to overrule an educational decision by the official body designated by the people to operate the schools.

A school board's attempt to instill in its students the ideas and values on which a democratic system depends is viewed [by the plurality] as an impermissible suppression of other ideas and values on which other systems of government and other societies thrive. Books may not be removed because they are indecent; extol violence, intolerance, and racism; or degrade the dignity of the individual. Human history, not the least that of the 20th century, records the power and political life of these very ideas. But they are not our ideas or values. Although I would leave this educational decision to the duly constituted board, I certainly would not require a school board to promote ideas and values repugnant to a democratic society or to teach such values to children.

[Judge Rehnquist's dissenting opinion is omitted.]

NOTES AND QUESTIONS

1. *A distinction without a difference?* Is the plurality's proposed distinction between content- and viewpoint-based decisions to remove books from a public school library and declining to add a book in the first place non-sensical? Isn't a decision not to add a book because of hostility to its content and viewpoint indistinguishable from a decision to remove a book from a public school library's shelves?
2. *Do any limits exist on government censorship in the public school curriculum?* How far would the dissenting Justices go in permitting content- and viewpoint-based censorship decisions by local school boards? Could an elected school board remove all books written by authors who support the GOP? Or any and all biographies of presidents affiliated with the Democratic Party?
3. *Banning ideas in the public schools?* May a state government ban ideas that it disagrees with or dislikes from the public schools? For example, a growing number of states have adopted laws that proscribe the teaching of ideas associated with Critical Race Theory (CRT) from the K-12 public schools. Indeed, some of these laws even apply to state-supported colleges and universities. Would the plurality view such a ban as a legitimate curricular decision? What about the dissenters? On the other hand, if a state government or local school board may ban the teaching of CRT, could they also ban teaching economics or biology? On what principled basis can one argue that the First Amendment permits a state or local government to ban the writings of Richard Delgado from the public schools—but not the writings of Adam Smith?
4. *Targeting minority viewpoints?* May a state government ban ideas and perspectives associated with particular minority communities? For a lower court decision holding that the First Amendment and Equal Protection Clause together prohibit efforts to ban educational ideas and approaches because they enjoy support withing particular communities of color, see Gonzalez v. Douglas, 269 F. Supp. 3d. 948 (D. Ariz. 2017).
5. *What about "fixed stars" in our "constitutional constellation"?* Is the plurality's or the dissent's approach more consistent with Justice Robert Jackson's stirring admonition in *Barnette* that "[i]f there is any fixed star in our constitutional constellation, it is that no official, high or petty, can prescribe

what shall be orthodox in politics, nationalism, religion, or other matters of opinion or force citizens to confess by word or act their faith therein." West Virginia Bd. of Educ. v. Barnette, 319 U.S. 624, 642 (1943). Justice Jackson added that "[i]f there are any circumstances which permit an exception, they do not now occur to us." *Id.* Even if a mandatory Pledge of Allegiance exercise lies beyond a state government's prescriptive powers in the public schools, may a local school board make no less ideologically based decisions in shaping the curriculum (such as banning materials that reflect CRT or feminist perspectives)?

United States v. American Library Ass'n

539 U.S. 194 (2003)

REHNQUIST, C.J., announced the judgment of the Court and delivered an opinion, in which O'CONNOR, J., SCALIA, J., and THOMAS, J., joined.

To address the problems associated with the availability of Internet pornography in public libraries, Congress enacted the Children's Internet Protection Act (CIPA). Under CIPA, a public library may not receive federal assistance to provide Internet access unless it installs software to block images that constitute obscenity or child pornography, and to prevent minors from obtaining access to material that is harmful to them. The District Court held these provisions facially invalid on the ground that they induce public libraries to violate patrons' First Amendment rights. We now reverse.

Public libraries pursue the worthy missions of facilitating learning and cultural enrichment. Appellee ALA's Library Bill of Rights states that libraries should provide "[b]ooks and other . . . resources . . . for the interest, information, and enlightenment of all people of the community the library serves." To fulfill their traditional missions, public libraries must have broad discretion to decide what material to provide to their patrons. Although they seek to provide a wide array of information, their goal has never been to provide "universal coverage." Instead, public libraries seek to provide materials "that would be of the greatest direct benefit or interest to the community." To this end, libraries collect only those materials deemed to have "requisite and appropriate quality." See W. Katz, Collection Development: The Selection of Materials for Libraries 6 (1980) ("The librarian's responsibility . . . is to separate out the gold from the garbage, not to preserve everything"); F. Drury, Book Selection xi (1930) ("[I]t is the aim of the selector to give the public, not everything it wants, but the best that it will read or use to advantage"); App. 636 (Rebuttal Expert Report of Donald G. Davis, Jr.) ("A hypothetical collection of everything that has been produced is not only of dubious value, but actually detrimental to users trying to find what they want to find and really need").

We have held in two analogous contexts that the government has broad discretion to make content-based judgments in deciding what private speech to make available to the public. [The Court then discussed Arkansas Educational Television Commission v. Forbes and National Endowment for Arts v. Finley.]

The principles underlying *Forbes* and *Finley* also apply to a public library's exercise of judgment in selecting the material it provides to its patrons. Just as forum analysis and heightened judicial scrutiny are incompatible with the role of public television stations and the role of the NEA, they are also incompatible with the discretion that public libraries must have to fulfill their traditional missions. Public library staffs necessarily consider content in making collection decisions and enjoy broad discretion in making them.

A public library does not acquire Internet terminals in order to create a public forum for Web publishers to express themselves, any more than it collects books in order to provide a public forum for the authors of books to speak. It provides Internet access, not to "encourage a diversity of views from private speakers," *Rosenberger*, but for the same reasons it offers other library resources: to facilitate research, learning, and recreational pursuits by furnishing materials of requisite and appropriate quality.

The District Court disagreed because, whereas a library reviews and affirmatively chooses to acquire every book in its collection, it does not review every Web site that it makes available. Based on this distinction, the court reasoned that a public library enjoys less discretion in deciding which Internet materials to make available than in making book selections. We do not find this distinction constitutionally relevant. A library's failure to make quality-based judgments about all the material it furnishes from the Web does not somehow taint the judgments it does make. A library's need to exercise judgment in making collection decisions depends on its traditional role in identifying suitable and worthwhile material; it is no less entitled to play that role when it collects material from the Internet than when it collects material from any other source. Most libraries already exclude pornography from their print collections because they deem it inappropriate for inclusion. We do not subject these decisions to heightened scrutiny; it would make little sense to treat libraries' judgments to block online pornography any differently, when these judgments are made for just the same reason.

Like the District Court, the dissents fault the tendency of filtering software to "overblock"—that is, to erroneously block access to constitutionally protected speech that falls outside the categories that software users intend to block. Due to the software's limitations, "[m]any erroneously blocked [Web] pages contain content that is completely innocuous for both adults and minors, and that no rational person could conclude matches the filtering companies' category definitions, such as 'pornography' or 'sex.'" Assuming that such erroneous blocking presents constitutional difficulties, any such concerns are dispelled by the ease with which patrons may have the filtering software disabled. When a patron encounters a blocked site, he need only ask a librarian to unblock it or (at least in the case of adults) disable the filter. As the District Court found, libraries have the capacity to permanently unblock any erroneously blocked site, and the Solicitor General stated at oral argument that a "library may . . . eliminate the filtering with respect to specific sites . . . at the request of a patron." With respect to adults, CIPA also expressly authorizes library officials to "disable" a filter altogether "to enable access for bona fide research or other lawful purposes." The Solicitor General confirmed that a "librarian can, in response to a request from a patron, unblock the filtering mechanism altogether," and further explained that a patron would not "have to explain . . . why he was asking a site to be unblocked or the filtering to be disabled." The District Court viewed unblocking and disabling as inadequate because some patrons may be too embarrassed to request them. But the Constitution does not guarantee the right to acquire information at a public library without any risk of embarrassment.

[The Court also rejected the Appellees' claim that CIPA imposes an unconstitutional condition on the receipt of federal assistance.] We need not decide this question because, even assuming that appellees may assert an "unconstitutional conditions" claim, this claim would fail on the merits. Within broad limits, "when the Government appropriates public funds to establish a program it is entitled to define the limits of that program." *Rust v. Sullivan.*

The same is true here. The E-rate and LSTA programs were intended to help public libraries fulfill their traditional role of obtaining material of requisite and appropriate quality for educational and informational purposes. Congress may certainly insist that these "public funds be spent for the purposes for which they were authorized." *Id.* Especially because public libraries have traditionally excluded pornographic material from their other collections, Congress could reasonably impose a parallel limitation on its Internet assistance programs. As the use of filtering software helps to carry out these programs, it is a permissible condition under *Rust.*

Appellees mistakenly contend, in reliance on *Legal Services Corporation v. Velazquez,* that CIPA's filtering conditions "[d]istor[t] the [u]sual [f]unctioning of [p]ublic [l]ibraries." In *Velazquez,* the Court concluded that a Government program of furnishing legal aid to the indigent differed from the program in *Rust*" [i]n th[e] vital respect" that the role of lawyers who represent clients in welfare disputes is to advocate *against* the Government, and there was thus an assumption that counsel would be free of state control. The Court concluded that the restriction on advocacy in such welfare disputes would distort the usual functioning of the legal profession and the federal and state courts before which the lawyers appeared. Public libraries, by contrast, have no comparable role that pits them against the Government, and there is no comparable assumption that they must be free of any conditions that their benefactors might attach to the use of donated funds or other assistance.

KENNEDY, J., concurring in the judgment.

If, on the request of an adult user, a librarian will unblock filtered material or disable the Internet software filter without significant delay, there is little to this case.

If some libraries do not have the capacity to unblock specific Web sites or to disable the filter or if it is shown that an adult user's election to view constitutionally protected Internet material is burdened in some other substantial way, that would be the subject for an as-applied challenge, not the facial challenge made in this case.

There are, of course, substantial Government interests at stake here. The interest in protecting young library users from material inappropriate for minors is legitimate, and even compelling, as all Members of the Court appear to agree. Given this interest, and the failure to show that the ability of adult library users to have access to the material is burdened in any significant degree, the statute is not unconstitutional on its face. For these reasons, I concur in the judgment of the Court.

BREYER, J., concurring in the judgment.

I reach the plurality's ultimate conclusion in a different way.

In ascertaining whether the statutory provisions are constitutional, I would apply a form of heightened scrutiny, examining the statutory requirements in question with special care. The Act directly restricts the public's receipt of information. And it does so through limitations imposed by outside bodies (here Congress) upon two critically important sources of information—the Internet as accessed via public libraries. For that reason, we should not examine the statute's constitutionality as if it raised no special First Amendment concern—as if, like tax or economic regulation, the First Amendment demanded only a "rational basis" for imposing a restriction. Nor should we accept the Government's suggestion that a presumption in favor of the statute's constitutionality applies.

At the same time, in my view, the First Amendment does not here demand application of the most limiting constitutional approach—that of "strict scrutiny." The statutory restriction in question is, in essence, a kind of "selection" restriction (a kind of editing). It affects the kinds and amount of materials that the library can present to its patrons. And libraries often properly engage in the selection of materials, either as a matter of necessity (*i.e.*, due to the scarcity of resources) or by design (*i.e.*, in accordance with collection development policies). To apply "strict scrutiny" to the "selection" of a library's collection (whether carried out by public libraries themselves or by other community bodies with a traditional legal right to engage in that function) would unreasonably interfere with the discretion necessary to create, maintain, or select a library's "collection" (broadly defined to include all the information the library makes available).

Instead, I would examine the constitutionality of the Act's restrictions here as the Court has examined speech-related restrictions in other contexts where circumstances call for heightened, but not "strict," scrutiny—where, for example, complex, competing constitutional interests are potentially at issue or speech-related harm is potentially justified by unusually strong governmental interests. Typically the key question in such instances is one of proper fit.

In such cases the Court has asked whether the harm to speech-related interests is disproportionate in light of both the justifications and the potential alternatives. It has considered the legitimacy of the statute's objective, the extent to which the statute will tend to achieve that objective, whether there are other, less restrictive ways of achieving that objective, and ultimately whether the statute works speech-related harm that, in relation to that objective, is out of proportion.

The Act's restrictions satisfy these constitutional demands. The Act seeks to restrict access to obscenity, child pornography, and, in respect to access by minors, material that is comparably harmful. These objectives are "legitimate," and indeed often "compelling."

At the same time, the Act contains an important exception that limits the speech-related harm that "overblocking" might cause. As the plurality points out, the Act allows libraries to permit any adult patron access to an "overblocked" Web site; the adult patron need only ask a librarian to unblock the specific Web site or, alternatively, ask the librarian, "Please disable the entire filter."

Given the comparatively small burden that the Act imposes upon the library patron seeking legitimate Internet materials, I cannot say that any speech-related harm that the Act may cause is disproportionate when considered in relation to the Act's legitimate objectives.

STEVENS, J., dissenting.

A federal statute penalizing a library for failing to install filtering software on every one of its Internet-accessible computers would unquestionably violate that Amendment. I think it equally clear that the First Amendment protects libraries from being denied funds for refusing to comply with an identical rule. An abridgment of speech by means of a threatened denial of benefits can be just as pernicious as an abridgment by means of a threatened penalty.

The issue in this case does not involve governmental attempts to control the speech or views of its employees. It involves the use of its treasury to impose controls on an important medium of expression. In an analogous situation, we specifically held that when "the Government seeks to use an existing medium of expression and to control it, in a class of cases, in ways which distort its usual functioning," the distorting restriction must be struck down under the First Amendment. *Legal Services Corporation v. Velazquez.* The question, then, is whether requiring the filtering software on all Internet-accessible computers distorts that medium. . . . [T]he over- and underblocking of the software does just that.

The plurality argues that the controversial decision in *Rust v. Sullivan* requires rejection of appellees' unconstitutional conditions claim. But, as subsequent cases have explained, *Rust* only involved and only applies to instances of governmental speech—that is, situations in which the government seeks to communicate a specific message. The discounts under the E-rate program and funding under the Library Services and Technology Act program involved in this case do not subsidize any message favored by the Government. As Congress made clear, these programs were designed "[t]o help public libraries provide their patrons with Internet access," which in turn "provide[s] patrons with a vast amount of valuable information." These programs thus are designed to provide access, particularly for individuals in low-income communities, to a vast amount and wide variety of private speech. They are not designed to foster or transmit any particular governmental message.

The plurality's reliance on *National Endowment for Arts v. Finley* is also misplaced. That case involved a challenge to a statute setting forth the criteria used by a federal panel of experts administering a federal grant program. Unlike this case, the Federal Government was not seeking to impose restrictions on the administration of a nonfederal program.

Also unlike *Finley*, the Government does not merely seek to control a library's discretion with respect to computers purchased with Government funds or those computers with Government-discounted Internet access. CIPA requires libraries to install filtering software on *every* computer with Internet access if the library receives *any* discount from the E-rate program or *any* funds from the LSTA program. If a library has 10 computers paid for by nonfederal funds and has Internet service for those computers also paid for by nonfederal funds, the library may choose not to put filtering software on any of those 10 computers. Or a library may decide to put filtering software on the 5 computers in its children's section. Or a library in an elementary school might choose to put filters on every single one of its 10 computers. But under this statute, if a library attempts to provide Internet service for even *one* computer through an E-rate discount, that library must put filtering software on *all* of its computers with Internet access, not just the one computer with E-rate discount.

This Court should not permit federal funds to be used to enforce this kind of broad restriction of First Amendment rights, particularly when such a restriction is unnecessary to accomplish Congress' stated goal.

SOUTER, J., with whom GINSBURG, J., joins, dissenting.

[We] have to take the statute on the understanding that adults will be denied access to a substantial amount of nonobscene material harmful to children but lawful for adult examination, and a substantial quantity of text and pictures harmful to no one. As the plurality concedes, this is the inevitable consequence of the indiscriminate behavior of current filtering mechanisms, which screen out material to an extent known only by the manufacturers of the blocking software.

The question for me, then, is whether a local library could itself constitutionally impose these restrictions on the content otherwise available to an adult patron through an Internet connection, at a library terminal provided for public use. The answer is no. A library that chose to block an adult's Internet access to material harmful to children (and whatever else the undiscriminating filter might interrupt) would be imposing a content-based restriction on communication of material in the library's control that an adult could otherwise lawfully see. This would simply be censorship. True, the censorship would not necessarily extend to every adult, for an intending Internet user might convince a librarian that he was a true researcher or had a "lawful purpose" to obtain everything the library's terminal could provide. But as to those who did not qualify for discretionary unblocking, the censorship would be complete and, like all censorship by an agency of the Government, presumptively invalid owing to strict scrutiny in implementing the Free Speech Clause of the First Amendment. "The policy of the First Amendment favors dissemination of information and opinion, and the guarantees of freedom of speech and press were not designed to prevent the censorship of the press merely, but any action of the government by means of which it might prevent such free and general discussion of public matters as seems absolutely essential." *Bigelow v. Virginia*, 421 U.S. 809, 829 (1975) (internal quotation marks and brackets omitted).

Public libraries are indeed selective in what they acquire to place in their stacks, as they must be. There is only so much money and so much shelf space, and the necessity to choose some material and reject the rest justifies the effort to be selective with an eye to demand, quality, and the object of maintaining the library as a place of civilized enquiry by widely different sorts of people. Selectivity is thus necessary and complex, and these two characteristics explain why review of a library's selection decisions must be limited: the decisions are made all the time, and only in extreme cases could one expect particular choices to reveal impermissible reasons (reasons even the plurality would consider to be illegitimate), like excluding books because their authors are Democrats or their critiques of organized Christianity are unsympathetic. See *Pico*. Review for rational basis is probably the most that any court could conduct, owing to the myriad particular selections that might be attacked by someone, and the difficulty of untangling the play of factors behind a particular decision.

At every significant point, however, the Internet blocking here defies comparison to the process of acquisition. Whereas traditional scarcity of money and space require a library to make choices about what to acquire, and the choice to be made is whether or not to spend the money to acquire something, blocking is the subject of a choice made after the money for Internet access has been spent or committed. Since it makes no difference to the cost of Internet access whether an adult calls up material harmful for children or the Articles of Confederation, blocking (on facts like these) is not necessitated by scarcity of either money or space. In the instance of the Internet, what the library acquires is electronic access, and the choice to block is a choice to limit access that has already been acquired. Thus, deciding against buying a book means there is no book (unless a loan can be obtained), but blocking the Internet is merely blocking access purchased in its entirety and subject to unblocking if the librarian agrees. The proper analogy therefore is not to passing up a book that might have been bought; it is either to buying a book and then keeping it from adults lacking an acceptable "purpose," or to buying an encyclopedia and then cutting out pages with anything thought to be unsuitable for all adults.

Thus, there is no preacquisition scarcity rationale to save library Internet blocking from treatment as censorship, and no support for it in the historical development of library practice. To these two reasons to treat blocking differently from a decision declining to buy a book, a third must be added. Quite simply, we can smell a rat when a library blocks material already in its control, just as we do when a library removes books from its shelves for reasons having nothing to do with wear and tear, obsolescence, or lack of demand. Content-based blocking and removal tell us something that mere absence from the shelves does not.

NOTES AND QUESTIONS

1. *Undervaluing anonymity?* In *American Library Association*, the Court does little to resolve definitively the question of how the First Amendment applies to the rights of public librarians and public library patrons. To the Justices who provided the key votes for the majority, the fact that library patrons could get unfettered access to the Internet simply by making a request to a librarian essentially eliminated the First Amendment issue from the case. Were these Justices correct in assuming that making such a request is not a significant First Amendment burden? In cases such as McIntyre v. Ohio Elections Commission, 514 U.S. 334 (1995), *supra* p. 282, the Court has held that the right to speak anonymously is protected by the First Amendment. Should the same interest in anonymity apply to library patrons seeking access to certain information or expressive materials? Does the fact that a library patron has to publicly announce a desire to access certain materials on the Internet inhibit expression in the same way that identifying the speaker was found to unconstitutionally inhibit speech in *McIntyre*? Does it matter that the expressive materials

in question in *American Library Ass'n* were sexual in nature? For example, could the government require that all libraries require patrons to identify themselves before checking out radical political or religious materials?

2. *Striking the balance between government control and free speech. American Library Ass'n* is an example of the Court attempting to identify some midpoint between government claims of complete authority to control speech it funds and efforts by speakers to communicate information freely. On one hand, the Court rejected attempts by the plaintiffs to characterize libraries as public forums and refused to grant librarians complete editorial freedom from their government employers in deciding which materials to put in their collections and which materials to leave out. On the other hand, the Court also refused to accept the government's attempt to analogize the case to *Rust.* Several Justices noted that the statute's restriction on the public's receipt of information raised serious First Amendment concerns, which prevented the Court from affording the government the same degree of authority over speech that the Court had granted in *Rust* with regard to government spokespersons. In the end, a majority of the Court rejected both extremes regarding First Amendment rights in public libraries, but its opinion does not strike a clear or precise balance between them.

PART II

The Religion Clauses

CHAPTER 13

INTRODUCTION TO THE RELIGION CLAUSES

TABLE OF CONTENTS

A. The Religion Clauses
B. Saturday Sabbath and Sunday Closing Laws

A. *THE RELIGION CLAUSES*

The First Amendment states that "Congress shall make no law respecting an establishment of religion, or prohibiting the free exercise thereof." This sentence has been read as containing two clauses: The Free Exercise Clause ("Congress shall make no law . . . prohibiting the free exercise [of religion].") and the Establishment Clause ("Congress shall make no law respecting an establishment of religion.").

The Free Exercise Clause facilitates people's practice of religion and is therefore triggered when the government impedes religious practices. Laws that target religion for disfavor might be struck down altogether under the Free Exercise Clause. The Free Exercise Clause might also require exemptions from otherwise applicable laws. Thanks to the Free Exercise Clause, the government cannot ban religious beliefs. It cannot outlaw Judaism, or Islam, or Sikhism. Nor can it generally target religious practices, such as banning Sabbath observances. The question becomes a bit trickier, however, when a law that does not target religion nonetheless makes religious practices like Saturday Sabbath observances more difficult, such as a law that requires subpoenaed witnesses to come to court even if it is Saturday, or a law that mandates all stores close on Sunday. Must Saturday Sabbath observers comply, or does the Free Exercise Clause provide them with a religious exemption?

The Establishment Clause, which is popularly described as mandating "separation of church and state," limits the government from establishing, funding, or practicing religion, or declaring what is religiously true. The Establishment Clause also bars the government from favoring one or some religions over others. Thus, the state cannot allow its Muslim and Christian death row inmates access to religious advisors at their execution but not its Buddhist inmates. Murphy v. Collier, 139 S. Ct. 1475 (2019). The Establishment Clause has also been interpreted as forbidding the government from favoring religion over its secular counterpart, such as by granting a tax break to religious nonprofit publications but not to secular nonprofit publications, or favoring religion at the expense of others. And yet the limits are unclear: "In God We Trust," after all, has been the national motto since 1956.

How the two clauses interact is also an ongoing question. Are they in tension, where the Free Exercise Clause encourages government accommodation of religion while the Establishment Clause puts limits on such encouragement? Or do they both work together to ensure freedom of religion for all, including religious minorities?

The following cases are merely an introduction to these questions. The chapters that follow address each clause in depth.

B. SATURDAY SABBATH AND SUNDAY CLOSING LAWS

Braunfeld v. Brown

366 U.S. 599 (1961)

Mr. Chief Justice WARREN announced the judgment of the Court and an opinion in which Mr. Justice BLACK, Mr. Justice CLARK, and Mr. Justice WHITTAKER concur.

This case concerns the constitutional validity of the application to appellants of the Pennsylvania criminal statute, enacted in 1959, which proscribes the Sunday retail sale of certain enumerated commodities. Among the questions presented are whether the statute is a law respecting an establishment of religion and whether the statute violates equal protection. Since both of these questions, in reference to this very statute, have already been answered in the negative, *Two Guys from Harrison-Allentown, Inc. v. McGinley*, . . . and since appellants present nothing new regarding them, they need not be considered here. Thus, the only question for consideration is whether the statute interferes with the free exercise of appellants' religion.

Appellants are merchants in Philadelphia who engage in the retail sale of clothing and home furnishings within the proscription of the statute in issue. Each of the appellants is a member of the Orthodox Jewish faith, which requires the closing of their places of business and a total abstention from all manner of work from nightfall each Friday until nightfall each Saturday. . . .

Appellants contend that the enforcement against them of the Pennsylvania statute will prohibit the free exercise of their religion because, due to the statute's compulsion to close on Sunday, appellants will suffer substantial economic loss, to the benefit of their non-Sabbatarian competitors, if appellants also continue their Sabbath observance by closing their businesses on Saturday; that this result will either compel appellants to give up their Sabbath observance, a basic tenet of the Orthodox Jewish faith, or will put appellants at a serious economic disadvantage if they continue to adhere to their Sabbath. . . .

Concededly, appellants and all other persons who wish to work on Sunday will be burdened economically by the State's day of rest mandate; and appellants point out that their religion requires them to refrain from work on Saturday as well. Our inquiry then is whether, in these circumstances, the First and Fourteenth Amendments forbid application of the Sunday Closing Law to appellants.

Certain aspects of religious exercise cannot, in any way, be restricted or burdened by either federal or state legislation. Compulsion by law of the acceptance of any creed or the practice of any form of worship is strictly forbidden. The freedom to hold religious beliefs and opinions is absolute. . . . But this is not the case at bar; the statute before us does not make criminal the holding of any religious belief or opinion, nor does it force anyone to embrace any religious belief or to say or believe anything in conflict with his religious tenets.

However, the freedom to act, even when the action is in accord with one's religious convictions, is not totally free from legislative restrictions. . . . Thus, in *Reynolds v. United States*, this Court upheld the polygamy conviction of a member of the Mormon faith despite the fact that an accepted doctrine of his church then imposed upon its male members the *duty* to practice polygamy. And, in *Prince v. Massachusetts*, this Court upheld a statute making it a crime for a girl under eighteen years of age to sell any newspapers, periodicals or merchandise in public places despite the fact that a child of the Jehovah's Witnesses faith believed that it was her religious *duty* to perform this work.

But, again, this is not the case before us because the statute at bar does not make unlawful any religious practices of appellants; the Sunday law simply regulates a secular activity and, as applied to appellants, operates so as to make the practice of their religious beliefs more expensive. Furthermore, the law's effect does not inconvenience all members of the Orthodox Jewish faith but only those who believe it necessary to work on Sunday. And even these are not faced with as serious a choice as forsaking their religious practices or subjecting themselves to criminal prosecution. Fully recognizing that the alternatives open to appellants and others similarly situated—retaining their present occupations and incurring economic disadvantage or engaging in some other commercial activity which does not call for either Saturday or Sunday labor—may well result in some financial sacrifice in order to observe their religious beliefs, still the option is wholly different than when the legislation attempts to make a religious practice itself unlawful.

To strike down, without the most critical scrutiny, legislation which imposes only an indirect burden on the exercise of religion, *i.e.*, legislation which does not make unlawful the religious practice itself, would radically restrict the operating latitude of the legislature. Statutes which tax income and limit the amount which may be deducted for religious contributions impose an indirect economic burden on the observance of the religion of the citizen whose religion requires him to donate a greater amount to his church; statutes which require the courts to be closed on Saturday and Sunday impose a similar indirect burden on the observance of the religion of the trial lawyer whose religion requires him to rest on a weekday. The list of legislation of this nature is nearly limitless. . . .

Of course, to hold unassailable all legislation regulating conduct which imposes solely an indirect burden on the observance of religion would be a gross oversimplification. If the purpose or effect of a law is to impede the observance of one or all religions or is to discriminate invidiously between religions, that law is constitutionally invalid even though the burden may be characterized as being only indirect. But if the State regulates conduct by enacting a general law within its power, the purpose and effect of which is to advance the State's secular goals, the statute is valid despite its indirect burden on religious observance unless the State may accomplish its purpose by means which do not impose such a burden. . . .

However, appellants advance yet another means at the State's disposal which they would find unobjectionable. They contend that the State should cut an exception from the Sunday labor proscription for those people who, because of religious conviction, observe a day of rest other than Sunday. By such regulation, appellants contend, the economic disadvantages imposed by the present system would be removed and the State's interest in having all people rest one day would be satisfied.

A number of States provide such an exemption and this may well be the wiser solution to the problem. But our concern is not with the wisdom of legislation but with its constitutional limitation. Thus, reason and experience teach that to permit the exemption might well undermine the State's goal of providing a day that, as best possible, eliminates the atmosphere of commercial noise and activity. Although not dispositive of the issue, enforcement problems would be more difficult since there would be two or more days to police rather than one and it would be more difficult to observe whether violations were occurring.

Additional problems might also be presented by a regulation of this sort. To allow only people who rest on a day other than Sunday to keep their businesses open on that day might well provide these people with an economic advantage over their competitors who must remain closed on that day; this might cause the Sunday-observers to complain that their religions are being discriminated against. With this competitive advantage existing, there could well be the temptation for some, in order to keep their businesses open on Sunday, to assert that they have religious convictions which compel them to close their businesses on what had formerly been their least profitable day. This might make necessary a state-conducted inquiry into the sincerity of the individual's religious beliefs, a practice which a State might believe would itself run afoul of the spirit of constitutionally protected religious guarantees. Finally, in order to keep the disruption of the day at a minimum, exempted employers would probably have to hire employees who themselves qualified for the exemption because of their own religious beliefs, a practice which a State might feel to be opposed to its general policy prohibiting religious discrimination in hiring. For all of these reasons, we cannot say that the Pennsylvania statute before us is invalid, either on its face or as applied.

Mr. Justice Harlan concurs in the judgment. Mr. Justice Brennan and Mr. Justice Stewart concur in our disposition of appellants' claims under the Establishment Clause and the Equal Protection Clause. Mr. Justice Frankfurter and Mr. Justice Harlan have rejected appellants' claim under the Free Exercise Clause in a separate opinion.

Accordingly, the decision is

Affirmed.

Mr. Justice BRENNAN, concurring and dissenting.

I agree with the Chief Justice that there is no merit in appellants' establishment and equal-protection claims. I dissent, however, as to the claim that Pennsylvania has prohibited the free exercise of appellants' religion. . . .

Mr. Justice STEWART, dissenting.

I agree with substantially all that Mr. Justice Brennan has written. Pennsylvania has passed a law which compels an Orthodox Jew to choose between his religious faith and his economic survival. That is a cruel choice. It is a choice which I think no State can constitutionally demand. For me this is not something that can be swept under the rug and forgotten in the interest of enforced Sunday togetherness. I think the impact of this law upon these appellants grossly violates their constitutional right to the free exercise of their religion.

NOTES AND QUESTIONS

1. *Burden on religion.* How heavy was the religious burden on Braunfeld and his fellow shopkeepers? The Court pointed out that the Sunday closing law did not directly punish Braunfeld from observing his Saturday Sabbath, rather it made it much more expensive for him to do so. Would it matter to Braunfeld if the law directly or indirectly burdened his practice of religion? Should laws that directly burden Sabbath observance be accommodated? For example, what if someone subpoenaed to testify has a Sabbath during the workweek? What if the witness's religion mandated a two-day Sabbath? Three-day Sabbath?
2. *Government's interests.* A law that burdens religious exercise might nonetheless be enforced if the government's interests are sufficiently important. Laws prohibiting murder still apply even if child sacrifice is a religion's central tenet. What are the government's interests in the Sunday closing law? What were the government's interests in *Reynolds* (banning polygamy) and *Prince* (banning child labor)? How do these government interests compare?
3. *Limitless exemptions.* Should the government have to accommodate every religious practice burdened by laws that do not target religion? What about the Court's observation that the "[t]he list of legislation of this nature [*i.e.*, laws that impose an indirect burden on religion] is nearly limitless"?
4. *Accommodation creating burdens for others.* Would allowing Saturday Sabbath observers to close their shops on Saturday rather than Sunday impose any hardships on others? The Court suggests that accommodating Orthodox Jewish shopkeepers would give them a competitive advantage over those who close on Sunday. How does this potential advantage compare to the Orthodox Jewish shopkeepers' economic disadvantage?
5. *Find another job or profession?* What should one make of Chief Justice Warren's suggestion that if closing two days a week makes it economically impossible for people like Braunfeld to operate a viable clothing or furniture store, such persons should "engag[e] in some other commercial activity which does not call for either Saturday or Sunday labor"?
6. *Lurking Establishment Clause issues.* Are Sunday Sabbath observers faced with the same choice: abandon your religious beliefs or possibly lose your business? Why not? Is it fair that some religions are spared this dilemma while others are not? *McGowan v. Maryland,* below, addresses an Establishment Clause challenge to a Sunday closing law—a law which had its roots in enforcing the Fourth Commandment ("Keep Holy the Sabbath").

7. *Secular counterpart.* What if Saturday was the only day someone had to spend with their children or sick parent? Should they be entitled to an exemption? Is it fair that they are not? Does it depend on whether time with family is considered a secular counterpart to Sabbath observance?

McGowan v. Maryland

366 U.S. 420 (1961)

Mr. Chief Justice Warren delivered the opinion of the Court.

The issues in this case concern the constitutional validity of Maryland criminal statutes, commonly known as Sunday Closing Laws or Sunday Blue Laws. These statutes, with exceptions to be noted hereafter, generally proscribe all labor, business and other commercial activities on Sunday. The questions presented are whether the classifications within the statutes bring about a denial of equal protection of the law, . . . and whether the statutes are laws respecting an establishment of religion or prohibiting the free exercise thereof.

Appellants are seven employees of a large discount department store located on a highway in Anne Arundel County, Maryland. They were indicted for the Sunday sale of a three-ring loose-leaf binder, a can of floor wax, a stapler and staples, and a toy submarine in violation of Md. Ann. Code, Art. 27, § 521. Generally, this section prohibited, throughout the State, the Sunday sale of all merchandise except the retail sale of tobacco products, confectioneries, milk, bread, fruits, gasoline, oils, greases, drugs and medicines, and newspapers and periodicals. Recently amended, this section also now excepts from the general prohibition the retail sale in Anne Arundel County of all foodstuffs, automobile and boating accessories, flowers, toilet goods, hospital supplies and souvenirs. It now further provides that any retail establishment in Anne Arundel County which does not employ more than one person other than the owner may operate on Sunday. . . .

Among other things, appellants contended at the trial that the Maryland statutes under which they were charged were contrary to the Fourteenth Amendment for the reasons stated at the outset of this opinion. Appellants were convicted and each was fined five dollars and costs. The Maryland Court of Appeals affirmed, 220 Md. 117, 151 A.2d 156; on appeal brought under 28 U.S.C. § 1257 (2), we noted probable jurisdiction. 362 U.S. 959.

[Chief Justice Warren considered and rejected an equal protection challenge to the Sunday closing laws.]

. . . [A]ppellants contend that the statutes violate the guarantee of separation of church and state in that the statutes are laws respecting an establishment of religion contrary to the First Amendment, made applicable to the States by the Fourteenth Amendment.

The essence of appellants' "establishment" argument is that Sunday is the Sabbath day of the predominant Christian sects; that the purpose of the enforced stoppage of labor on that day is to facilitate and encourage church attendance; that the purpose of setting Sunday as a day of universal rest is to induce people with no religion or people with marginal religious beliefs to join the predominant Christian sects; that the purpose of the atmosphere of tranquility created by Sunday closing is to aid the conduct of church services and religious observance of the sacred day. In substantiating their "establishment" argument, appellants rely on the wording of the present Maryland statutes, on earlier versions of the current Sunday laws and on prior judicial characterizations of these laws by the Maryland Court of Appeals. . . .

In light of the evolution of our Sunday Closing Laws through the centuries, and of their more or less recent emphasis upon secular considerations, it is not difficult to discern that as presently written and administered, most of them, at least, are of a secular rather than of a religious character, and that presently they bear no relationship to establishment of religion as those words are used in the Constitution of the United States.

Throughout this century and longer, both the federal and state governments have oriented their activities very largely toward improvement of the health, safety, recreation and general well-being of our citizens. Numerous laws affecting public health, safety factors in industry, laws affecting hours and conditions of labor of women and children, week-end diversion at parks and beaches, and cultural activities of various kinds, now point the way toward the good life for all. Sunday Closing Laws, like those before us, have become part and parcel of this great governmental concern wholly apart from their original purposes or connotations. The present purpose and effect of most of them is to provide a uniform day of rest for all citizens; the fact that this day is Sunday, a day of particular significance for the dominant Christian sects, does not bar the State from achieving its secular goals. To say that the States cannot prescribe Sunday as a day of rest for these purposes solely because centuries ago such laws had their genesis in religion would give a constitutional interpretation of hostility to the public welfare rather than one of mere separation of church and State.

Finally, we should make clear that this case deals only with the constitutionality of § 521 of the Maryland statute before us. We do not hold that Sunday legislation may not be a violation of the "Establishment" Clause if it can be demonstrated that its purpose—evidenced either on the face of the legislation, in conjunction with its legislative history, or in its operative effect—is to use the State's coercive power to aid religion.

Accordingly, the decision is

Affirmed.

Separate opinion of Mr. Justice FRANKFURTER, whom Mr. Justice HARLAN joins.

Mr. Justice DOUGLAS, dissenting.

The question is not whether one day out of seven can be imposed by a State as a day of rest. The question is not whether Sunday can by force of custom and habit be retained as a day of rest. The question is whether a State can impose criminal sanctions on those who, unlike the Christian majority that makes up our society, worship on a different day or do not share the religious scruples of the majority.

If the "free exercise" of religion were subject to reasonable regulations, as it is under some constitutions, or if all laws "respecting the establishment of religion" were not proscribed, I could understand how rational men, representing a predominantly Christian civilization, might think these Sunday laws did not unreasonably interfere with anyone's free exercise of religion and took no step toward a burdensome establishment of any religion. . . .

With that as my starting point I do not see how a State can make protesting citizens refrain from doing innocent acts on Sunday because the doing of those acts offends sentiments of their Christian neighbors. . . .

The Court picks and chooses language from various decisions to bolster its conclusion that these Sunday laws in the modern setting are "civil regulations." No matter how much is written, no matter what is said, the parentage of these laws is the Fourth Commandment; and they serve and satisfy the religious predispositions of our Christian communities. After all, the labels a State places on its laws are not binding on us when we are confronted with a constitutional decision. We reach our own conclusion as to the character, effect, and practical operation of the regulation in determining its constitutionality.

It seems to me plain that by these laws the States compel one, under sanction of law, to refrain from work or recreation on Sunday because of the majority's religious views about that day. The State by law makes Sunday a symbol of respect or adherence. Refraining from work or recreation in deference to the majority's religious feelings about Sunday is within every person's choice. By what authority can government compel it? . . .

These laws are sustained because, it is said, the First Amendment is concerned with religious convictions or opinion, not with conduct. But it is a strange Bill of Rights that makes it possible for the dominant religious group to bring the minority to heel because the minority, in the doing of acts which intrinsically are wholesome are not antisocial, does not defer to the majority's religious beliefs. . . .

The reverse side of an "establishment" is a burden on the "free exercise" of religion. Receipt of funds from the State benefits the established church directly; laying an extra tax on nonmembers benefits the established church indirectly. Certainly the present Sunday laws place Orthodox Jews and Sabbatarians under extra burdens because of their religious opinions or beliefs. Requiring them to abstain from their trade or business on Sunday reduces their work-week to five days, unless they violate their religious scruples. This places them at a competitive disadvantage and penalizes them for adhering to their religious beliefs. . . .

[T]he special protection which Sunday laws give the dominant religious groups and the penalty they place on minorities whose holy day is Saturday constitute, in my view, state interference with the "free exercise" of religion.

NOTES AND QUESTIONS

1. *Religious establishment.* If Maryland had enacted its Sunday closing laws in order to encourage people to attend Christian church and to respect it as a sacred day, as the plaintiffs alleged, then it would violate the Establishment Clause. The government would be favoring Christianity over other religions. In what way, if any, would this establishment also affect people's practice of their religion?
2. *The "evolving purpose" stratagem.* Is Chief Justice Warren's "evolving purpose" theory persuasive? If mandatory Sunday closing laws have a legislative history associated with enforcing the Fourth Commandment ("Keep Holy the Sabbath"), does a *post hoc* rationalization of the Blue Laws as mere labor regulations serve to sever any religious meaning from such enactments?

3. *A legislative accommodation?* One way of viewing *McGowan* is as a kind of legislative effort to ensure that Sunday worshippers are not faced with a conflict between workplace duties and religious duties. Would this be a more honest rationale for sustaining the Maryland law? Should Maryland's legislature, as a matter of free exercise principles, be permitted to enact a statute that facilitates religious observance by reducing otherwise probable conflicts?
4. *Narrow tailoring?* Even if one might imagine a mandatory accommodation measure, is the Maryland law well crafted to that purpose? If a more limited law would serve this purpose, why doesn't the Supreme Court require Maryland to use more narrowly tailored means?
5. *Accommodations for all?* If a state creates a statutory exemption for one group—most likely the dominant religious group or groups—does it have an obligation to accommodate minority religionists?

Estate of Thornton v. Caldor, Inc.

472 U.S. 703 (1985)

Chief Justice BURGER delivered the opinion of the Court.

We granted certiorari to decide whether a state statute that provides employees with the absolute right not to work on their chosen Sabbath violates the Establishment Clause of the First Amendment.

In early 1975, petitioner's decedent Donald E. Thornton[1] began working for respondent Caldor, Inc., a chain of New England retail stores; he managed the men's and boys' clothing department in respondent's Waterbury, Connecticut, store. At that time, respondent's Connecticut stores were closed on Sundays pursuant to state law. Conn.Gen.Stat. §§ 53-300 to 53-303 (1958).

In 1977, following the state legislature's revision of the Sunday-closing laws, respondent opened its Connecticut stores for Sunday business. In order to handle the expanded store hours, respondent required its managerial employees to work every third or fourth Sunday. Thornton, a Presbyterian who observed Sunday as his Sabbath, initially complied with respondent's demand and worked a total of 31 Sundays in 1977 and 1978. In October 1978, Thornton was transferred to a management position in respondent's Torrington store; he continued to work on Sundays during the first part of 1979. In November 1979, however, Thornton informed respondent that he would no longer work on Sundays because he observed that day as his Sabbath; he invoked the protection of Conn.Gen.Stat. § 53-303e(b) (1985), which provides:

"No person who states that a particular day of the week is observed as his Sabbath may be required by his employer to work on such day. An employee's refusal to work on his Sabbath shall not constitute grounds for his dismissal."

---

1. Thornton died on February 4, 1982, while his appeal was pending before the Supreme Court of Connecticut. The administrator of Thornton's estate has continued the suit on behalf of the decedent's estate.

Thornton rejected respondent's offer either to transfer him to a management job in a Massachusetts store that was closed on Sundays, or to transfer him to a nonsupervisory position in the Torrington store at a lower salary. In March 1980, respondent transferred Thornton to a clerical position in the Torrington store; Thornton resigned two days later and filed a grievance with the State Board of Mediation and Arbitration alleging that he was discharged from his manager's position in violation of Conn.Gen.Stat. § 53-303e(b) (1985).

Respondent defended its action on the ground that Thornton had not been "discharged" within the meaning of the statute; respondent also urged the Board to find that the statute violated Article 7 of the Connecticut Constitution as well as the Establishment Clause of the First Amendment . . .

Under the Religion Clauses, government must guard against activity that impinges on religious freedom, and must take pains not to compel people to act in the name of any religion. In setting the appropriate boundaries in Establishment Clause cases, the Court has frequently relied on our holding in *Lemon* for guidance, and we do so here. To pass constitutional muster under *Lemon* a statute must not only have a secular purpose and not foster excessive entanglement of government with religion, its primary effect must not advance or inhibit religion.

The Connecticut statute challenged here guarantees every employee, who "states that a particular day of the week is observed as his Sabbath," the right not to work on his chosen day. Conn.Gen.Stat. § 53-303e(b) (1985). The State has thus decreed that those who observe a Sabbath any day of the week as a matter of religious conviction must be relieved of the duty to work on that day, no matter what burden or inconvenience this imposes on the employer or fellow workers. The statute arms Sabbath observers with an absolute and unqualified right not to work on whatever day they designate as their Sabbath.

In essence, the Connecticut statute imposes on employers and employees an absolute duty to conform their business practices to the particular religious practices of the employee by enforcing observance of the Sabbath the employee unilaterally designates. The State thus commands that Sabbath religious concerns automatically control over all secular interests at the workplace; the statute takes no account of the convenience or interests of the employer or those of other employees who do not observe a Sabbath. The employer and others must adjust their affairs to the command of the State whenever the statute is invoked by an employee.

There is no exception under the statute for special circumstances, such as the Friday Sabbath observer employed in an occupation with a Monday through Friday schedule—a school teacher, for example; the statute provides for no special consideration if a high percentage of an employer's work force asserts rights to the same Sabbath. Moreover, there is no exception when honoring the dictates of Sabbath observers would cause the employer substantial economic burdens or when the employer's compliance would require the imposition of significant burdens on other employees required to work in place of the Sabbath observers. Finally, the statute allows for no consideration as to whether the employer has made reasonable accommodation proposals.

This unyielding weighting in favor of Sabbath observers over all other interests contravenes a fundamental principle of the Religion Clauses, so well articulated by Judge Learned Hand:

"The First Amendment . . . gives no one the right to insist that in pursuit of their own interests others must conform their conduct to his own religious necessities." Otten v. Baltimore & Ohio R. Co., 205 F.2d 58, 61 (CA2 1953). As such, the statute goes beyond having an incidental or remote effect of advancing religion. The statute has a primary effect that impermissibly advances a particular religious practice.

We hold that the Connecticut statute, which provides Sabbath observers with an absolute and unqualified right not to work on their Sabbath, violates the Establishment Clause of the First Amendment. Accordingly, the judgment of the Supreme Court of Connecticut is

Affirmed.

[Justice REHNQUIST's dissenting opinion is omitted.]

Justice O'CONNOR, with whom Justice MARSHALL joins, concurring.

The Court applies the test enunciated in Lemon v. Kurtzman, 403 U.S. 602, 612-613 (1971), and concludes that Conn.Gen.Stat. § 53-303e(b) (1985) has a primary effect that impermissibly advances religion. I agree, and I join the Court's opinion and judgment. In my view, the Connecticut Sabbath law has an impermissible effect because it conveys a message of endorsement of the Sabbath observance.

All employees, regardless of their religious orientation, would value the benefit which the statute bestows on Sabbath observers—the right to select the day of the week in which to refrain from labor. Yet Connecticut requires private employers to confer this valued and desirable benefit only on those employees who adhere to a particular religious belief. The statute singles out Sabbath observers for special and, as the Court concludes, absolute protection without according similar accommodation to ethical and religious beliefs and practices of other private employees. There can be little doubt that an objective observer or the public at large would perceive this statutory scheme precisely as the Court does today. The message conveyed is one of endorsement of a particular religious belief, to the detriment of those who do not share it. As such, the Connecticut statute has the effect of advancing religion, and cannot withstand Establishment Clause scrutiny.

I do not read the Court's opinion as suggesting that the religious accommodation provisions of Title VII of the Civil Rights Act of 1964 are similarly invalid. These provisions preclude employment discrimination based on a person's religion and require private employers to reasonably accommodate the religious practices of employees unless to do so would cause undue hardship to the employer's business. 42 U.S.C. §§ 2000e(j) and 2000e-2(a)(1). Like the Connecticut Sabbath law, Title VII attempts to lift a burden on religious practice that is imposed by private employers, and hence it is not the sort of accommodation statute specifically contemplated by the Free Exercise Clause. The provisions of Title VII must therefore manifest a valid secular purpose and effect to be valid under the Establishment Clause. In my view, a statute outlawing employment discrimination based on race, color, religion, sex, or national origin has the valid secular purpose of assuring employment opportunity to all groups in our pluralistic society. Since Title VII calls for reasonable rather than absolute accommodation and extends that requirement to all religious beliefs and practices rather than protecting only the Sabbath observance, I believe an objective observer would perceive it as an anti-discrimination law rather than an endorsement of religion or a particular religious practice.

NOTES AND QUESTIONS

1. *Sunday closing law.* This case arose because Connecticut eliminated its Sunday closing law. As a result, Sunday Sabbath observers like Thornton found themselves facing the dilemma that had previously confronted Saturday Sabbath observers: choosing between their employment and their Sabbath observance. Do the burdens on Sabbath observance differ for Thornton compared to Braunfeld?
2. *Favoring religion.* Does the Connecticut law protecting all Sabbath observers favor one religion over others? Does it favor some religions over others? Does it favor religion over its secular counterpart? Is there a secular counterpart to Sabbath observance?
3. *Burden on others.* The Court held that the absolute nature of the law's protection violated the Establishment Clause because it imposed on employers and employees. In what way? How do these burdens compare to burdens that would have been created had Braunfeld been accommodated?
4. *Proposed alternative.* Justice O'Connor maintains that it is possible to accommodate Sabbath observers without violating the Establishment Clause and points to the religious accommodations offered by Title VII of the Civil Rights Act as a model. How does Title VII differ from the Connecticut law in terms of which religious practices are accommodated? How does it differ from the Connecticut law in terms of what burden on others is tolerated?

Chapter 14

Free Exercise of Religion: Exemptions

Table of Contents

A. Pre-*Smith* Caselaw

1. The Belief/Conduct Dichotomy
2. Protection of Religious Conduct

B. The *Smith* Standard

C. Exemptions and Religious Discrimination

1. The Fall of "Neutral and Generally Applicable"
2. The Rise of Religious "Discrimination"

The Supreme Court's initial response to Free Exercise Clause challenges, reflected in cases like *Reynolds*, was to reject categorically the judicial imposition of religious exemptions from generally applicable laws that did not target a particular sect for punishment. In other words, even though religious belief was free from any and all government regulation, conduct of any sort could be the subject of neutral laws of general application. Thus, one of the first doctrinal dichotomies in the Supreme Court's free exercise jurisprudence is the belief/conduct dichotomy: The Free Exercise Clause protects all religious beliefs, but not necessarily all conduct mandated by religious belief.

The Warren Court questioned and ultimately rejected the belief/conduct dichotomy. Writing for the Supreme Court in *Sherbert*, Justice William J. Brennan, Jr., instead suggested that neutral laws of general applicability should be subject to strict judicial scrutiny when such laws impeded religiously motivated conduct. For a period of years from 1963 to 1990, the Supreme Court sometimes applied strict scrutiny, but sometimes did not, to test the constitutionality, as applied, of general laws that substantially burdened religiously motivated conduct. The new dichotomy contrasted "direct" versus "indirect" burdens on religious practice. The Free Exercise Clause generally protected against "direct" burdens but not against "indirect" burdens (for example, the economic losses that would result from closing on

Saturday, as well as Sunday, for observant Jews in a state with mandatory Sunday store-closing laws). Moreover, the "strictness" of the strict scrutiny was very much open to doubt. Preferred religions, such as the Old Order Amish, were able to obtain exemptions from generally applicable state laws. On the other hand, new religious movements, like the Scientologists, did not fare so well. And even the Old Order Amish found that the strictness of strict scrutiny waned in the face of a general government welfare program, like Social Security.

In 1990, in *Smith,* the Supreme Court seemed to return its free exercise jurisprudence to the pre-*Sherbert* regime, finding that neutral laws of general applicability did not violate the Free Exercise Clause.

Twenty years later, the Supreme Court has become increasingly hostile to *Smith.* Despite the expressed desire of several Justices to overrule the case, *Smith* still controls. However, the Supreme Court has (re)defined neutral and generally applicable in such a way as to greatly expand religious liberty protections.

In thinking about the merits of *Smith* versus *Sherbert,* one should consider the overall purpose that the Free Exercise Clause exists to serve. If religious autonomy is the primary rationale for the clause, then the *Sherbert* approach arguably advances free exercise values more effectively than does *Smith.* A focus on equality, however, would not necessarily entail the judicial creation and enforcement of autonomy-enhancing religious exemptions. Instead, judicial scrutiny would focus on overt and covert efforts to impede or punish unpopular religions and religionists. An equalitarian theory of the Free Exercise Clause would also reduce the tension with the Establishment Clause: Just as the Establishment Clause prevents government from preferring or advancing one particular religious sect, the Free Exercise Clause prevents government from *discouraging* any particular religious sect—both clauses exist to prevent government from either proselytizing or proscribing particular religions or religious beliefs.

Although an equality-based theory of the Free Exercise Clause is plausible, most contemporary scholars—and the Supreme Court—embrace the autonomy rationale. As you read these materials, consider whether the rules that the Court provides are capable of neutral and consistent enforcement, regardless of whether the religion at bar is the Roman Catholic Church or the Unification Church (that is, the "Moonies"). Consider also whether the Court has, in fact, neutrally applied its rules.

A. *PRE-*SMITH *CASELAW*

1. *The Belief/Conduct Dichotomy*

The earliest Free Exercise Clause cases involve efforts to suppress the Mormon practice of plural marriage. The federal, state, and territorial governments engaged in a concerted effort to prevent polygamy. Efforts at suppression of the practice led to criminal enforcement actions. Members of the Mormon Church defended against these prosecutions by invoking the Free Exercise Clause (which, even in the 1870s, clearly applied against the federal and territorial governments). As you will see, these efforts did not prove successful. The Supreme Court construed the Free Exercise Clause narrowly to protect religious belief but not necessarily actions mandated by religious belief.

Reynolds v. United States

98 U.S. (8 Otto) 145 (1879)

Mr. Chief Justice WAITE delivered the opinion of the court.

Should the accused have been acquitted if he married the second time, because he believed it to be his religious duty? . . .

As to the defence of religious belief or duty.

On the trial, the plaintiff in error, the accused, proved that at the time of his alleged second marriage he was, and for may years before had been, a member of the Church of Jesus Christ of Latter-Day Saints, commonly called the Mormon Church, and a believer in its doctrines; that it was an accepted doctrine of that church "that it was the duty of male members of said church, circumstances permitting, to practise polygamy; . . . that this duty was enjoined by different books which the members of said church believed to be of divine origin, and among others the Holy Bible, and also that the members of the church believed that the practice of polygamy was directly enjoined upon the male members thereof by the Almighty God, in a revelation to Joseph Smith, the founder and prophet of said church; that the failing or refusing to practise polygamy by such male members of said church, when circumstances would admit, would be punished, and that the penalty for such failure and refusal would be damnation in the life to come." He also proved "that he had received permission from the recognized authorities in said church to enter into polygamous marriage." . . .

Congress cannot pass a law for the government of the Territories which shall prohibit the free exercise of religion. The first amendment to the Constitution expressly forbids such legislation. Religious freedom is guaranteed everywhere throughout the United States, so far as congressional interference is concerned. The question to be determined is, whether the law now under consideration comes within this prohibition.

The word "religion" is not defined in the Constitution. We must go elsewhere, therefore, to ascertain its meaning, and nowhere more appropriately, we think, than to the history of the times in the midst of which the provision was adopted. The precise point of the inquiry is, what is the religious freedom which has been guaranteed.

Before the adoption of the Constitution, attempts were made in some of the colonies and States to legislate not only in respect to the establishment of religion, but in respect to its doctrines and precepts as well. The people were taxed, against their will, for the support of religion, and sometimes for the support of particular sects to whose tenets they could not and did not subscribe. Punishments were prescribed for a failure to attend upon public worship, and sometimes for entertaining heretical opinions. The controversy upon this general subject was animated in many of the States, but seemed at last to culminate in Virginia. In 1784, the House of Delegates of that State having under consideration "a bill establishing provision for teachers of the Christian religion," postponed it until the next session, and directed that the bill should be published and distributed, and that the people be requested "to signify their opinion respecting the adoption of such bill at the next session of assembly."

This brought out a determined opposition. Amongst others, Mr. Madison prepared a "Memorial and Remonstrance," which was widely circulated and signed, and in which he demonstrated "that religion, or the duty we owe the Creator," was not within the cognizance of civil government. . . . At the next session the proposed bill was not only defeated, but another, 'for establishing religious freedom,' drafted by Mr. Jefferson, was passed. . . .

In a little more than a year after the passage of this statute the convention met which prepared the Constitution of the United States. . . . Five of the States, while adopting the Constitution, proposed amendments. Three—New Hampshire, New York, and Virginia—included in one form or another a declaration of religious freedom in the changes they desired to have made, as did also North Carolina, where the convention at first declined to ratify the Constitution until the proposed amendments were acted upon. Accordingly, at the first session of the first Congress the amendment now under consideration was proposed with others by Mr. Madison. It met the view of the advocates of religious freedom, and was adopted. Mr. Jefferson afterwards, in reply to an address to him by a committee of the Danbury Baptist Association, took occasion to say: "Believing with you that religion is a matter which lies solely between man and his God; that he owes account to none other for his faith or his worship; that the legislative powers of the government reach actions only, and not opinions, I contemplate with sovereign reverence that act of the whole American people which declared that their legislature should 'make no law respecting an establishment of religion or prohibiting the free exercise thereof,' thus building a wall of separation between church and State. Adhering to this expression of the supreme will of the nation in behalf of the rights of conscience, I shall see with sincere satisfaction the progress of those sentiments which tend to restore man to all his natural rights, convinced he has no natural right in opposition to his social duties." Coming as this does from an acknowledged leader of the advocates of the measure, it may be accepted almost as an authoritative declaration of the scope and effect of the amendment thus secured. Congress was deprived of all legislative power over mere opinion, but was left free to reach actions which were in violation of social duties or subversive of good order.

Polygamy has always been odious among the northern and western nations of Europe, and, until the establishment of the Mormon Church, was almost exclusively a feature of the life of Asiatic and of African people. At common law, the second marriage was always void (2 Kent, Com. 79), and from the earliest history of England polygamy has been treated as an offence against society. . . . .

By the statute of 1 James I. (c. 11), the offence, if committed in England or Wales, was made punishable in the civil courts, and the penalty was death. As this statute was limited in its operation to England and Wales, it was at a very early period re-enacted, generally with some modifications, in all the colonies. In connection with the case we are now considering, it is a significant fact that on the 8th of December, 1788, after the passage of the act establishing religious freedom, and after the convention of Virginia had recommended as an amendment to the Constitution of the United States the declaration in a bill of rights that 'all men have an equal, natural, and unalienable right to the free exercise of religion, according to the dictates of conscience,' the legislature of that State substantially enacted the statute of James I., death penalty included, because, as recited in the preamble, 'it hath been doubted whether bigamy or poligamy be punishable by the laws of this Commonwealth.' From that day to this we think it may safely be said there never has been a time in any State of the Union when polygamy has not been an offence against society, cognizable by the civil courts and punishable with more or less severity. In the face of all this evidence, it is impossible to believe that the constitutional guaranty of religious freedom was intended to prohibit legislation in respect to this most important feature of social life. Marriage, while from its very nature a sacred obligation, is nevertheless, in most civilized nations, a civil contract, and usually regulated by law. Upon it society may be said to be built, and out of its fruits spring social relations and social obligations and duties, with which government is necessarily required to deal. In fact, according as monogamous or polygamous marriages are allowed, do we find the principles on which the government of the people, to a greater or less extent, rests. . . .

In our opinion, the statute immediately under consideration is within the legislative power of Congress. It is constitutional and valid as prescribing a rule of action for all those residing in the Territories, and in places over which the United States have exclusive control. This being so, the only question which remains is, whether those who make polygamy a part of their religion are excepted from the operation of the statute. If they are, then those who do not make polygamy a part of their religious belief may be found guilty and punished, while those who do, must be acquitted and go free. This would be introducing a new element into criminal law. Laws are made for the government of actions, and while they cannot interfere with mere religious belief and opinions, they may with practices. Suppose one believed that human sacrifices were a necessary part of religious worship, would it be seriously contended that the civil government under which he lived could not interfere to prevent a sacrifice? Or if a wife religiously believed it was her duty to burn herself upon the funeral pile of her dead husband, would it be beyond the power of the civil government to prevent her carrying her belief into practice?

So here, as a law of the organization of society under the exclusive dominion of the United States, it is provided that plural marriages shall not be allowed. Can a man excuse his practices to the contrary because of his religious belief? To permit this would be to make the professed doctrines of religious belief superior to the law of the land, and in effect to permit every citizen to become a law unto himself. Government could exist only in name under such circumstances.

Upon a careful consideration of the whole case, we are satisfied that no error was committed by the court below.

Judgment affirmed.

NOTES AND QUESTIONS

1. *The belief/conduct dichotomy. Reynolds* strongly endorses the belief/conduct dichotomy. Was the rationale persuasive? Should the Free Exercise Clause protect only belief, and not action? What about drinking sacramental wine incident to the Catholic Mass? Or ingesting peyote incident to the rites of the Native American Church? Is "belief" really free if a religion cannot practice its liturgy? Would your answer change if the religion at issue was Rastafarianism? If it does, what does that say about the importance of culture in theorizing free exercise?

2. *Ethnocentrism.* Is polygamy subversive of good order? According to whom? What should one make of the Supreme Court's overt racial language in *Reynolds* (describing polygamy as "almost exclusively a feature of the life of Asiatic and of African people")?
3. *A "Christian nation" and the Establishment Clause.* What should one make of the Supreme Court's rhetoric regarding the United States being a European, Christian nation? How does such a declaration square with the Establishment Clause? Does this suggest that the Supreme Court is bringing a skeptical eye to bear on the beliefs of the defendants? Should the Supreme Court declare particular religious beliefs unacceptable?
4. *The limits of autonomy.* Even if the anti-Mormon rhetoric is problematic, was the Supreme Court correct to assert that it simply is not possible to make every person "a law unto himself"? Or would it be possible to grant at least some religious exemptions from neutral laws of general applicability without making the business of government impossible?

2. *Protection of Religious Conduct*

The Warren Court rejected, at least in part, the belief/conduct dichotomy. In a series of cases starting in the 1960s, the Supreme Court required the government to provide exemptions from neutral laws of general applicability that conflicted with religiously motivated conduct. Even in these cases, however, religionists did not always win judicially crafted exemptions from neutral laws of general applicability. As you read the following cases, consider whether they reflect any general patterns regarding who wins, and who loses, free exercise cases.

Sherbert v. Verner

374 U.S. 398 (1963)

Mr. Justice BRENNAN delivered the opinion of the Court.

Appellant, a member of the Seventh-day Adventist church, was discharged by her South Carolina employer because she would not work on Saturday, the Sabbath Day of her faith.[1] When she was unable to obtain other employment because from conscientious scruples she would not take Saturday work, she filed a claim for unemployment compensation benefits under the South Carolina Unemployment Compensation Act. That law provides that, to be eligible for benefits, a claimant

1. Appellant became a member of the Seventh-day Adventist Church in 1957, at a time when her employer, a textile-mill operator, permitted her to work a five-day week. It was not until 1959 that the work week was changed to six days, including Saturday, for all three shifts in the employer's mill. No question has been raised in this case concerning the sincerity of appellant's religious beliefs. Nor is there any doubt that the prohibition against Saturday labor is a basic tenet of the Seventh-day Adventist creed, based upon that religion's interpretation of the Holy Bible.

must be "able to work . . . available for work"; and further, that a claimant is ineligible for benefits "[i]f . . . he has failed, without good cause . . . to accept available suitable work when offered him by the employment office or the employer. . . ." The appellee Employment Security Commission, in administrative proceedings under the statute, found that appellant's restriction upon her availability for Saturday work brought her within the provision disqualifying for benefits insured workers who fail, without good cause, to accept "suitable work when offered . . . by the employment office or the employer. . . ."

[The South Carolina state courts affirmed the agency's findings and held Sherbert ineligible for benefits.]

We reverse the judgment of the South Carolina Supreme Court and remand for further proceedings not inconsistent with this opinion.

The door of the Free Exercise Clause stands tightly closed against any governmental regulation of religious *beliefs* as such, Cantwell v. Connecticut, 310 U.S. 296, 303. Government may neither compel affirmation of a repugnant belief, Torcaso v. Watkins, 367 U.S. 488; nor penalize or discriminate against individuals or groups because they hold religious views abhorrent to the authorities, Fowler v. Rhode Island, 345 U.S. 67; nor employ the taxing power to inhibit the dissemination of particular religious views, Murdock v. Pennsylvania, 319 U.S. 105; Follett v. McCormick, 321 U.S. 573; *cf.* Grosjean v. American Press Co., 297 U.S. 233. On the other hand, the Court has rejected challenges under the Free Exercise Clause to governmental regulation of certain overt acts prompted by religious beliefs or principles, for "even when the action is in accord with one's religious convictions, [it] is not totally free from legislative restrictions." Braunfeld v. Brown, 366 U.S. 599, 603. The conduct or actions so regulated have invariably posed some substantial threat to public safety, peace or order. *See, e. g.*, Reynolds v. United States, 98 U.S. 145; Jacobson v. Massachusetts, 197 U.S. 11; Prince v. Massachusetts, 321 U.S. 158; Cleveland v. United States, 329 U.S. 14.

Plainly enough, appellant's conscientious objection to Saturday work constitutes no conduct prompted by religious principles of a kind within the reach of state legislation. If, therefore, the decision of the South Carolina Supreme Court is to withstand appellant's constitutional challenge, it must be either because her disqualification as a beneficiary represents no infringement by the State of her constitutional rights of free exercise, or because any incidental burden on the free exercise of appellant's religion may be justified by a "compelling state interest in the regulation of a subject within the State's constitutional power to regulate. . . ." NAACP v. Button, 371 U.S. 415, 438.

We turn first to the question whether the disqualification for benefits imposes any burden on the free exercise of appellant's religion. We think it is clear that it does. . . . Here not only is it apparent that appellant's declared ineligibility for benefits derives solely from the practice of her religion, but the pressure upon her to forego that practice is unmistakable. The ruling forces her to choose between following the precepts of her religion and forfeiting benefits, on the one hand, and abandoning one of the precepts of her religion in order to accept work, on the other hand. Governmental imposition of such a choice puts the same kind of burden upon the free exercise of religion as would a fine imposed against appellant for her Saturday worship. . . .

Significantly South Carolina expressly saves the Sunday worshipper from having to make the kind of choice which we here hold infringes the Sabbatarian's religious liberty. When in times of "national emergency" the textile plants are authorized by the State Commissioner of Labor to operate on Sunday, "no employee shall be required to work on Sunday . . . who is conscientiously opposed to Sunday work; and if any employee should refuse to work on Sunday on account of conscientious . . . objections he or she shall not jeopardize his or her seniority by such refusal or be discriminated against in any other manner." S. C. Code, § 64-4. No question of the disqualification of a Sunday worshipper for benefits is likely to arise, since we cannot suppose that an employer will discharge him in violation of this statute. The unconstitutionality of the disqualification of the Sabbatarian is thus compounded by the religious discrimination which South Carolina's general statutory scheme necessarily effects.

We must next consider whether some compelling state interest enforced in the eligibility provisions of the South Carolina statute justifies the substantial infringement of appellant's First Amendment right. It is basic that no showing merely of a rational relationship to some colorable state interest would suffice; in this highly sensitive constitutional area, "[o]nly the gravest abuses, endangering paramount interests, give occasion for permissible limitation," Thomas v. Collins, 323 U.S. 516, 530. No such abuse or danger has been advanced in the present case. The appellees suggest no more than a possibility that the filing of fraudulent claims by unscrupulous claimants feigning religious objections to Saturday work might not only dilute the unemployment compensation fund but also hinder the scheduling by employers of necessary Saturday work. But that possibility is not apposite here because no such objection appears to have been made before the South Carolina Supreme Court, and we are unwilling to assess the importance of an asserted state interest without the views of the state court. . . .

In these respects, then, the state interest asserted in the present case is wholly dissimilar to the interests which were found to justify the less direct burden upon religious practices in *Braunfeld v. Brown, supra.* The Court recognized that the Sunday closing law which that decision sustained undoubtedly served "to make the practice of [the Orthodox Jewish merchants'] . . . religious beliefs more expensive," 366 U.S., at 605. But the statute was nevertheless saved by a countervailing factor which finds no equivalent in the instant case—a strong state interest in providing one uniform day of rest for all workers. That secular objective could be achieved, the Court found, only by declaring Sunday to be that day of rest. Requiring exemptions for Sabbatarians, while theoretically possible, appeared to present an administrative problem of such magnitude, or to afford the exempted class so great a competitive advantage, that such a requirement would have rendered the entire statutory scheme unworkable. In the present case no such justifications underlie the determination of the state court that appellant's religion makes her ineligible to receive benefits.

In holding as we do, plainly we are not fostering the "establishment" of the Seventh-day Adventist religion in South Carolina, for the extension of unemployment benefits to Sabbatarians in common with Sunday worshippers reflects nothing more than the governmental obligation of neutrality in the face of religious differences, and does not represent that involvement of religious with secular institutions which it is the object of the Establishment Clause to forestall. Nor does the recognition of the appellant's right to unemployment benefits under the state statute serve to abridge any other person's religious liberties. Nor do we, by our decision today, declare the existence of a constitutional right to unemployment benefits on the part of all persons whose religious convictions are the cause of their unemployment. This is not a case in which an employee's religious convictions serve to make him a nonproductive member of society. Finally, nothing we say today constrains the States to adopt any particular form or scheme of unemployment compensation. Our holding today is only that South Carolina may not constitutionally apply the eligibility provisions so as to constrain a worker to abandon his religious convictions respecting the day of rest.

The judgment of the South Carolina Supreme Court is reversed and the case is remanded for further proceedings not inconsistent with this opinion.

It is so ordered.

[Justice STEWART's concurring opinion is omitted.]

Mr. Justice HARLAN, whom Mr. Justice WHITE joins, dissenting.

Today's decision is disturbing both in its rejection of existing precedent and in its implications for the future. . . .

The South Carolina Supreme Court has uniformly applied this law in conformity with its clearly expressed purpose. It has consistently held that one is not 'available for work' if his unemployment has resulted not from the inability of industry to provide a job but rather from personal circumstances, no matter how compelling. . . . Thus in no proper sense can it be said that the State discriminated against the appellant on the basis of her religious beliefs or that she was denied benefits because she was a Seventh-day Adventist. She was denied benefits just as any other claimant would be denied benefits who was not 'available for work' for personal reasons.

With this background, this Court's decision comes into clearer focus. What the Court is holding is that if the State chooses to condition unemployment compensation on the applicant's availability for work, it is constitutionally compelled to *carve out an exception*—and to provide benefits—for those whose unavailability is due to their religious convictions. Such a holding has particular significance in two respects.

First, despite the Court's protestations to the contrary, the decision necessarily overrules Braunfeld v. Brown, 366 U.S. 599, which held that it did not offend the "Free Exercise" Clause of the Constitution for a State to forbid a Sabbatarian to do business on Sunday. . . . [T]he indirect financial burden of the present law is far less than that involved in Braunfeld. Forcing a store owner to close his business on Sunday may well have the effect of depriving him of a satisfactory livelihood if his religious convictions require him to close on Saturday as well. Here we are dealing only with temporary benefits, amounting to a fraction of regular weekly wages and running for not more than 22 weeks. Clearly, any differences between this case and Braunfeld cut against the present appellant.

Second, the implications of the present decision are far more troublesome than its apparently narrow dimensions would indicate at first glance. The meaning of today's holding, as already noted, is that the State must furnish unemployment benefits to one who is unavailable for work if the unavailability stems from the exercise of religious convictions. The State, in other words, must *single out* for financial assistance those whose behavior is religiously motivated, even though it denies such assistance to others whose identical behavior (in this case, inability to work on Saturdays) is not religiously motivated.

It has been suggested that such singling out of religious conduct for special treatment may violate the constitutional limitations on state action. *See* Kurland, *Of Church and State and The Supreme Court*, 29 U. of Chi. L. Rev. 1; *cf.* Cammarano v. United States, 358 U.S. 498, 515 (concurring opinion). My own view, however, is that at least under the circumstances of this case it would be a permissible accommodation of religion for the State, if it *chose* to do so, to create an exception to its eligibility requirements for persons like the appellant. . . . [T]here is, I believe, enough flexibility in the Constitution to permit a legislative judgment accommodating an unemployment compensation law to the exercise of religious beliefs such as appellant's.

For very much the same reasons, however, I cannot subscribe to the conclusion that the State is constitutionally *compelled* to carve out an exception to its general rule of eligibility in the present case. Those situations in which the Constitution may require special treatment on account of religion are, in my view, few and far between, and this view is amply supported by the course of constitutional litigation in this area.

For these reasons I respectfully dissent from the opinion and judgment of the Court.

NOTES AND QUESTIONS

1. *A direct or indirect burden?* Was the burden on *Sherbert* direct, and the equivalent of a fine? Or was it indirect, as in *Braunfeld*, because the state did not require her to work Saturday but made it more expensive to observe a Saturday Sabbath?
2. *The problem of differential treatment.* Is *Sherbert* really about indirect burdens, or is it better conceptualized as a differential treatment case? Justice Brennan notes that South Carolina would not force a Sunday worshipper to choose between "keeping holy the Sabbath" and maintaining eligibility for state unemployment benefits. If South Carolina creates an exemption for Sunday worshippers, can it withhold an exemption from others? Should it matter that a Sunday exemption benefits the dominant religious groups in South Carolina (mainline Protestants and evangelical Christians)?
3. *Penalizing or privileging religiously motivated objections.* Is it unfairly penalizing religion if South Carolina provides unemployment benefits to people who refused jobs that were too far away or outside their field, but not to people who refuse for religious reasons? Is it unfairly privileging religion to recognize deeply held *religious* moral commitments like Sabbath observance as "good cause" to reject Saturday work, but not deeply held *secular* moral commitments such as needing Saturdays off to take care of a sick parent or spend time with one's children?

4. *A broader availability for work requirement.* Suppose South Carolina had a firm rule, without any exceptions or individualized review, that required all persons seeking unemployment benefits to be available any time, any place, for any available work (including work that might give rise to religious objections, such as a distillery or a munitions factory). Would *Sherbert* require South Carolina to recognize religious exemptions for those seeking benefits because religious duty prevents them from meeting the "any job, any time, any place" rule?
5. *The formal neutrality approach.* Professor Phillip C. Kurland famously argued that the best reading of the Establishment and Free Exercise Clauses would be to require "formal neutrality" from the government. Under this approach, religious motivations or purposes could serve neither as the basis for an exemption nor as a basis for imposing a burden. Under this approach, a targeted property tax exemption for property owned by religious organizations, but not other charitable entities, would not be permissible. But neither would a statute that provided property tax exemptions to all charitable entities except religiously affiliated ones. *See* Phillip C. Kurland, *Of Church and State and the Supreme Court,* 29 U. Chi. L. Rev. 1, 6-7 (1961). Although this theory received a great deal of scholarly and judicial attention, it never gained much traction. What is your view?

Wisconsin v. Yoder

406 U.S. 205 (1972)

Mr. Chief Justice Burger delivered the opinion of the Court.

On petition of the State of Wisconsin, we granted the writ of certiorari in this case to review a decision of the Wisconsin Supreme Court holding that respondents' convictions of violating the State's compulsory school-attendance law were invalid under the Free Exercise Clause of the First Amendment to the United States Constitution made applicable to the States by the Fourteenth Amendment. For the reasons hereafter stated we affirm the judgment of the Supreme Court of Wisconsin.

Respondents Jonas Yoder and Wallace Miller are members of the Old Order Amish religion, and respondent Adin Yutzy is a member of the Conservative Amish Mennonite Church. Wisconsin's compulsory school-attendance law required them to cause their children to attend public or private school until reaching age 16 but the respondents declined to send their children, ages 14 and 15, to public school after they completed the eighth grade. . . .

On complaint of the school district administrator for the public schools, respondents were charged, tried, and convicted of violating the compulsory-attendance law in Green County Court and were fined the sum of $5 each. Respondents defended on the ground that the application of the compulsory-attendance law violated their rights under the First and Fourteenth Amendments. The trial testimony showed that respondents believed, in accordance with the tenets of Old Order Amish communities generally, that their children's attendance at high school, public or private, was contrary to the Amish religion and way of life. They believed that by sending their children to high school, they would not only expose themselves to the danger of the censure of the church community, but, as found by the county court, also endanger their own salvation and that of their children. The State stipulated that respondents' religious beliefs were sincere. . . .

. . . [I]n order for Wisconsin to compel school attendance beyond the eighth grade against a claim that such attendance interferes with the practice of a legitimate religious belief, it must appear either that the State does not deny the free exercise of religious belief by its requirement, or that there is a state interest of sufficient magnitude to override the interest claiming protection under the Free Exercise Clause. . . .

We come then to the quality of the claims of the respondents concerning the alleged encroachment of Wisconsin's compulsory school-attendance statute on their rights and the rights of their children to the free exercise of the religious beliefs they and their forebears have adhered to for almost three centuries. In evaluating those claims we must be careful to determine whether the Amish religious faith and their mode of life are, as they claim, inseparable and interdependent. A way of life, however virtuous and admirable, may not be interposed as a barrier to reasonable state regulation of education if it is based on purely secular considerations; to have the protection of the Religion Clauses, the claims must be rooted in religious belief. Although a determination of what is a "religious" belief or practice entitled to constitutional protection may present a most delicate question, the very concept of ordered liberty precludes allowing every person to make his own standards on matters of conduct in which society as a whole has important interests. Thus, if the Amish asserted their claims because of their subjective evaluation and rejection of the contemporary secular values accepted by the majority, much as Thoreau rejected the social values of his time and isolated himself at Walden Pond, their claims would not rest on a religious basis. Thoreau's choice was philosophical and personal rather than religious, and such belief does not rise to the demands of the Religion Clauses.

Giving no weight to such secular considerations, however, we see that the record in this case abundantly supports the claim that the traditional way of life of the Amish is not merely a matter of personal preference, but one of deep religious conviction, shared by an organized group, and intimately related to daily living. . . .

The impact of the compulsory-attendance law on respondents' practice of the Amish religion is not only severe, but inescapable, for the Wisconsin law affirmatively compels them, under threat of criminal sanction, to perform acts undeniably at odds with fundamental tenets of their religious beliefs. *See* Braunfeld v. Brown, 366 U.S. 599, 605 (1961). Nor is the impact of the compulsory-attendance law confined to grave interference with important Amish religious tenets from a subjective point of view. It carries with it precisely the kind of objective danger to the free exercise of religion that the First Amendment was designed to prevent. As the record shows, compulsory school attendance to age 16 for Amish children carries with it a very real threat of undermining the Amish community and religious practice as they exist today; they must either abandon belief and be assimilated into society at large, or be forced to migrate to some other and more tolerant region.

In sum, the unchallenged testimony of acknowledged experts in education and religious history, almost 300 years of consistent practice, and strong evidence of a sustained faith pervading and regulating respondents' entire mode of life support the claim that enforcement of the State's requirement of compulsory formal education after the eighth grade would gravely endanger if not destroy the free exercise of respondents' religious beliefs. . . .

Wisconsin concedes that under the Religion Clauses religious beliefs are absolutely free from the State's control, but it argues that "actions," even though religiously grounded, are outside the protection of the First Amendment. But our decisions have rejected the idea that religiously grounded conduct is always outside the protection of the Free Exercise Clause. It is true that activities of individuals, even when religiously based, are often subject to regulation by the States in the exercise of their undoubted power to promote the health, safety, and general welfare, or the Federal Government in the exercise of its delegated powers. . . . But to agree that religiously grounded conduct must often be subject to the broad police power of the State is not to deny that there are areas of conduct protected by the Free Exercise Clause of the First Amendment and thus beyond the power of the State to control, even under regulations of general applicability. . . . This case, therefore, does not become easier because respondents were convicted for their "actions" in refusing to send their children to the public high school; in this context belief and action cannot be neatly confined in logic-tight compartments.

Nor can this case be disposed of on the grounds that Wisconsin's requirement for school attendance to age 16 applies uniformly to all citizens of the State and does not, on its face, discriminate against religions or a particular religion, or that it is motivated by legitimate secular concerns. . . .

The Court must not ignore the danger that an exception from a general obligation of citizenship on religious grounds may run afoul of the Establishment Clause, but that danger cannot be allowed to prevent any exception no matter how vital it may be to the protection of values promoted by the right of free exercise.

The State advances two primary arguments in support of its system of compulsory education. It notes, as Thomas Jefferson pointed out early in our history, that some degree of education is necessary to prepare citizens to participate effectively and intelligently in our open political system if we are to preserve freedom and independence. Further, education prepares individuals to be self-reliant and self-sufficient participants in society. We accept these propositions.

However, the evidence adduced by the Amish in this case is persuasively to the effect that an additional one or two years of formal high school for Amish children in place of their long-established program of informal vocational education would do little to serve those interests. Respondents' experts testified at trial, without challenge, that the value of all education must be assessed in terms of its capacity to prepare the child for life. It is one thing to say that compulsory education for a year or two beyond the eighth grade may be necessary when its goal is the preparation of the child for life in modern society as the majority live, but it is quite another if the goal of education be viewed as the preparation of the child for life in the separated agrarian community that is the keystone of the Amish faith. *See* Meyer v. Nebraska, 262 U.S., at 400.

The State attacks respondents' position as one fostering "ignorance" from which the child must be protected by the State. No one can question the State's duty to protect children from ignorance but this argument does not square with the facts disclosed in the record. Whatever their idiosyncrasies as seen by the majority, this record strongly shows that the Amish community has been a highly successful social unit within our society, even if apart from the conventional "mainstream." Its members are productive and very law-abiding members of society; they reject public welfare in any of its usual modern forms. The Congress itself recognized their self-sufficiency by authorizing exemption of such groups as the Amish from the obligation to pay social security taxes. . . .

The State, however, supports its interest in providing an additional one or two years of compulsory high school education to Amish children because of the possibility that some such children will choose to leave the Amish community, and that if this occurs they will be ill-equipped for life. . . .

There is nothing in this record to suggest that the Amish qualities of reliability, self-reliance, and dedication to work would fail to find ready markets in today's society. Absent some contrary evidence supporting the State's position, we are unwilling to assume that persons possessing such valuable vocational skills and habits are doomed to become burdens on society should they determine to leave the Amish faith, nor is there any basis in the record to warrant a finding that an additional one or two years of formal school education beyond the eighth grade would serve to eliminate any such problem that might exist.

Insofar as the State's claim rests on the view that a brief additional period of formal education is imperative to enable the Amish to participate effectively and intelligently in our democratic process, it must fall. The Amish alternative to formal secondary school education has enabled them to function effectively in their day-to-day life under self-imposed limitations on relations with the world, and to survive and prosper in contemporary society as a separate, sharply identifiable and highly self-sufficient community for more than 200 years in this country. In itself this is strong evidence that they are capable of fulfilling the social and political responsibilities of citizenship without compelled attendance beyond the eighth grade at the price of jeopardizing their free exercise of religious belief. . . .

The independence and successful social functioning of the Amish community for a period approaching almost three centuries and more than 200 years in this country are strong evidence that there is at best a speculative gain, in terms of meeting the duties of citizenship, from an additional one or two years of compulsory formal education. Against this background it would require a more particularized showing from the State on this point to justify the severe interference with religious freedom. . . .

Our holding in no way determines the proper resolution of possible competing interests of parents, children, and the State in an appropriate state court proceeding in which the power of the State is asserted on the theory that Amish parents are preventing their minor children from attending high school despite their expressed desires to the contrary. Recognition of the claim of the State in such a proceeding would, of course, call into question traditional concepts of parental control over the religious upbringing and education of their minor children recognized in this Court's past decisions. It is clear that such an intrusion by a State into family decisions in the area of religious training would give rise to grave questions of religious freedom comparable to those raised here and those presented in Pierce v. Society of Sisters, 268 U.S. 510 (1925). On this record we neither reach nor decide those issues. . . .

Aided by a history of three centuries as an identifiable religious sect and a long history as a successful and self-sufficient segment of American society, the Amish in this case have convincingly demonstrated the sincerity of their religious beliefs, the interrelationship of belief with their mode of life, the vital role that belief and daily conduct play in the continued survival of Old Order Amish communities and their religious organization, and the hazards presented by the State's enforcement of a statute generally valid as to others. Beyond this, they have carried the even more difficult burden of demonstrating the adequacy of their alternative mode of continuing informal vocational education in terms of precisely those overall interests that the State advances in support of its program of compulsory high school education. In light of this convincing showing, one that probably few other religious groups or sects could make, and weighing the minimal difference between what the State would require and what the Amish already accept, it was incumbent on the State to show with more particularity how its admittedly strong interest in compulsory education would be adversely affected by granting an exemption to the Amish. *Sherbert v. Verner, supra.*

Mr. Justice POWELL and Mr. Justice REHNQUIST took no part in the consideration or decision of this case.

Mr. Justice WHITE, with whom Mr. Justice BRENNAN and Mr. Justice STEWART join, concurring.

Cases such as this one inevitably call for a delicate balancing of important but conflicting interests. I join the opinion and judgment of the Court because I cannot say that the State's interest in requiring two more years of compulsory education in the ninth and tenth grades outweighs the importance of the concededly sincere Amish religious practice to the survival of that sect. . . .

I join the Court because the sincerity of the Amish religious policy here is uncontested, because the potentially adverse impact of the state requirement is great, and because the State's valid interest in education has already been largely satisfied by the eight years the children have already spent in school.

Mr. Justice DOUGLAS, dissenting in part.

I agree with the Court that the religious scruples of the Amish are opposed to the education of their children beyond the grade schools, yet I disagree with the Court's conclusion that the matter is within the dispensation of parents alone. The Court's analysis assumes that the only interests at stake in the case are those of the Amish parents on the one hand, and those of the State on the other. The difficulty with this approach is that, despite the Court's claim, the parents are seeking to vindicate not only their own free exercise claims, but also those of their high-school-age children. . . . I think the emphasis of the Court on the "law and order" record of this Amish group of people is quite irrelevant. A religion is a religion irrespective of what the misdemeanor or felony records of its members might be. I am not at all sure how the Catholics, Episcopalians, the Baptists, Jehovah's Witnesses, the Unitarians, and my own Presbyterians would make out if subjected to such a test. It is, of course, true that if a group or society was organized to perpetuate crime and if that is its motive, we would have rather startling problems akin to those that were raised when some years back a particular sect was challenged here as operating on a fraudulent basis. United States v. Ballard, 322 U.S. 78. But no such factors are present here, and the Amish, whether with a high or low criminal record, certainly qualify by all historic standards as a religion within the meaning of the First Amendment.

The Court rightly rejects the notion that actions, even though religiously grounded, are always outside the protection of the Free Exercise Clause of the First Amendment. In so ruling, the court departs from the teaching of Reynolds v. United States, 98 U.S. 145, 164, where it was said concerning the reach of the Free Exercise Clause of the First Amendment, "Congress was deprived of all legislative power over mere opinion, but was left free to reach actions which were in violation of social duties or subversive of good order." In that case it was conceded that polygamy was a part of the religion of the Mormons. Yet the Court said, "It matters not that his belief [in polygamy] was a part of his professed religion: it was still belief, and belief only." *Id.*, at 167.

Action, which the Court deemed to be antisocial, could be punished even though it was grounded on deeply held and sincere religious convictions. What we do today, at least in this respect, opens the way to give organized religion a broader base than it has ever enjoyed; and it even promises that in time *Reynolds* will be overruled. . . .

NOTES AND QUESTIONS

1. *The continuing relevance of the belief/conduct dichotomy.* After *Yoder*, does anything remain of the *Reynolds* and *Davis* belief/conduct dichotomy? Suppose that a sect requires the ceremonial ingestion of marijuana smoke. Will courts analyze their claim to an exemption from drug laws as seriously as the Old Order Amish claim to an exemption from mandatory school-attendance laws?
2. *The problem of discrimination against unfamiliar religious groups.* In very real ways, such as by repeatedly invoking the 300-year success of the Old Order Amish in the United States, Chief Justice Burger seems to be declaring the Amish to be a "good" religion meriting special considerations. What is the risk that courts will take some claims, and some religions, more seriously than others? Should groups like the Moonies or the Hare Krishnas have the same free exercise rights as the Old Order Amish? Should the federal courts decide which are "good" religions and which are "bad" religions? Which groups need more protection from the courts: older, well-established, well-liked groups or newer, less well-known groups? For a critical commentary, see Mark Tushnet, *"Of Church and State and the Supreme Court Revisited":* Kurland *Revisited*, 1989 Sup. Ct. Rev. 373, 380-382.
3. *A targeted or general exemption?* Chief Justice Burger plainly weighs the state's interest in enforcing a mandatory school-attendance law only against an exemption for the Old Order Amish, rather than against an exemption for any group that might seek an exemption from truancy laws on a religious basis. Is this the correct numerator? Surprising as it might seem, in later cases, the Supreme Court regularly weighs the state's burden against a universal exemption from a general law, rather than a limited exemption.
4. *Viewpoint of Amish children.* Would the Court still have granted the exemption if the Amish children had wanted to continue their public school education? The majority notes that there was no evidence that Amish vocational training would disadvantage them in today's society. Do you agree? Does it matter if boys and girls are taught different skills?

AN EXTENDED NOTE ON "STRICT IN THEORY BUT FEEBLE IN FACT"

The standard enunciated by *Sherbert v. Verner* and *Wisconsin v. Yoder* provided for strict scrutiny for laws that imposed a substantial religious burden. This reflected the view that the Free Exercise Clause ought to mean more than an absence of religious discrimination. Instead, free exercise principles should protect religiously motivated conduct, at least when the government could not proffer a really important reason for applying its general law on the facts presented. In actual practice, however, the Court regularly rejected Free Exercise Clause claims. The one exception was a series of unemployment benefit cases that followed in the footsteps of *Sherbert v. Verner.*

United States v. Lee, 455 U.S. 252 (1982). Lee, an Old Order Amish employer, objected to withholding his employees' social security taxes and to paying his share of his employees' social security taxes on the grounds that "the Amish believe it sinful not to provide for their own elderly and needy and therefore are religiously opposed to the national social security system." Lee unsuccessfully sought a religious exemption from the insurance program. The Supreme Court first held that "[b]ecause the payment of the taxes or receipt of benefits violates Amish religious beliefs, compulsory participation in the social security system interferes with their free exercise rights." Nevertheless, the government's interests were compelling, and the means narrowly tailored: "The design of the system requires support by mandatory contributions from covered employers and employees. This mandatory participation is indispensable to the fiscal vitality of the social security system. . . . [A] comprehensive national social security system providing for voluntary participation would be almost a contradiction in terms and difficult, if not impossible, to administer." Moreover, "Unlike the situation presented in *Wisconsin v. Yoder*, it would be difficult to accommodate the comprehensive social security system with myriad exceptions flowing from a wide variety of religious beliefs." In short, "To maintain an organized society that guarantees religious freedom to a great variety of faiths requires that some religious practices yield to the common good. Religious beliefs can be accommodated, but there is a point at which accommodation would 'radically restrict the operating latitude of the legislature.'"

Bob Jones University v. United States, 461 U.S. 574 (1983). Two private schools lost their tax-exempt status because of their racially discriminatory policies. Based on their interpretation of the Bible, Goldsboro Christian Schools refused to admit African-Americans and Bob Jones University banned interracial dating and marriage among its students. The Supreme Court rejected their request for a free exercise exemption. After observing that "Denial of tax benefits will inevitably have a substantial impact on the operation of private religious schools, but will not prevent those schools from observing their religious tenets," the Court held that the government had a compelling interest in eradicating racial discrimination in education. "The governmental interest at stake here is compelling. As discussed [earlier], the Government has a fundamental, overriding interest in eradicating racial discrimination in education—discrimination that prevailed, with official approval, for the first 165 years of this Nation's history. That governmental interest substantially outweighs whatever burden denial of tax benefits places on petitioners' exercise of their religious beliefs. The interests asserted by petitioners cannot be accommodated with that compelling governmental interest and no 'less restrictive means,' are available to achieve the governmental interest."

Goldman v. Weinberger, 475 U.S. 503 (1986). Goldman was an Orthodox Jew in the United States Air Force. As the dissent noted, "one of the traditional religious obligations of a male Orthodox Jew [is] to cover his head before an omnipresent God." Military dress code prohibited Goldman from wearing his yarmulke while on duty and in uniform. In rejecting Goldman's free exercise claim, the Supreme Court emphasized the deference owed to the military: "[T]o accomplish its mission the military must foster instinctive obedience, unity, commitment, and esprit de corps. The essence of military service 'is the subordination of the desires and interests of the individual to the needs of the service.' . . . In the context of the present case, when evaluating whether military needs justify a particular restriction on religiously motivated conduct, courts must give great deference to the professional judgment of military authorities concerning the relative importance of a particular military interest." The Court then accepted the military's claims: "The considered professional judgment of the Air Force is that the traditional outfitting of personnel in standardized uniforms encourages the subordination of personal preferences and identities in favor of the overall group mission. Uniforms encourage a sense of hierarchical unity by tending to eliminate outward individual distinctions except for those of rank. The Air Force considers them as vital during peacetime as during war. . . . The Air Force has drawn the line essentially between religious apparel that is visible and that which is not, and we hold that those portions of the regulations challenged here reasonably and evenhandedly regulate dress in the interest of the military's perceived need for uniformity."

Bowen v. Roy, 476 U.S. 693 (1986). Parents applied for welfare and food stamp benefits. As a condition of receiving benefits, applicants were required to provide the Social Security number of all household members. The parents refused because using a Social Security number for their 2-year-old daughter, Little Bird of the Snow, would violate their Native American religious beliefs. The Supreme Court rejected their Free Exercise Clause claim, holding that "Never to our knowledge has the Court interpreted the First Amendment to require the Government itself to behave in ways that the individual believes will further his or her spiritual development or that of his or her family. The Free Exercise Clause simply cannot be understood to require the Government to conduct its own internal affairs in ways that comport with the religious beliefs of particular citizens. Just as the Government may not insist that appellees engage in any set form of religious observance, so appellees may not demand that the Government join in their chosen religious practices by refraining from using a number to identify their daughter. . . .

The Free Exercise Clause affords an individual protection from certain forms of governmental compulsion; it does not afford an individual a right to dictate the conduct of the Government's internal procedures."

Lyng v. Northwest Indian Cemetery Protection Ass'n, 485 U.S. 439 (1988). In order to finish a road project linking two California towns, the United States Forest Service planned a six-mile paved road through a section of Six Rivers National Forest. The road, however, "would cause serious and irreparable damage to the sacred areas which are an integral and necessary part of the belief systems and lifeway of Northwest California Indian peoples." The Supreme Court rejected a challenge brought by members of three American Indian tribes. First the Court argued that, as in *Roy*, the government was not forcing anyone to violate their faith but merely conducting its own internal operations. "In both cases, the challenged Government action would interfere significantly with private persons' ability to pursue spiritual fulfillment according to their own religious beliefs. In neither case, however, would the affected individuals be coerced by the Government's action into violating their religious beliefs; nor would either governmental action penalize religious activity by denying any person an equal share of the rights, benefits, and privileges enjoyed by other citizens." Next, the Court argued that the government could not function were it to accommodate every religious belief. "However much we might wish that it were otherwise, government simply could not operate if it were required to satisfy every citizen's religious needs and desires. A broad range of government activities—from social welfare programs to foreign aid to conservation projects—will always be considered essential to the spiritual well-being of some citizens, often on the basis of sincerely held religious beliefs. Others will find the very same activities deeply offensive, and perhaps incompatible with their own search for spiritual fulfillment and with the tenets of their religion. The First Amendment must apply to all citizens alike, and it can give to none of them a veto over public programs that do not prohibit the free exercise of religion." The dissent took issue with the majority's determination that there was no substantial religious burden because "even where the Government uses federal land in a manner that threatens the very existence of a Native American religion, the Government is simply not 'doing' anything to the practitioners of that faith." The dissent concluded, "Because the Court today refuses even to acknowledge the constitutional injury respondents will suffer, and because this refusal essentially leaves Native Americans with absolutely no constitutional protection against perhaps the gravest threat to their religious practices, I dissent. . . ."

Thomas v. Review Bd. of Ind. Emp't Sec. Div., 450 U.S. 707 (1981). In contrast to most cases, the Supreme Court did grant religious exemptions in three unemployment benefits cases, including *Thomas v. Review Board of The Indiana Employment Security Division.* Thomas, a Jehovah's Witness, left his job in a foundry to avoid manufacturing parts for military tanks, claiming that "his religious beliefs prevented him from participating in the production of war materials." He brought a free exercise claim after being denied unemployment benefits. Although the Indiana Supreme Court had questioned the religious basis for his belief, the Supreme Court found that "the guarantee of free exercise is not limited to beliefs which are shared by all the members of a religious sect." It then held that "[u]nless we are prepared to overrule Sherbert, Thomas cannot be denied the benefits due him."

NOTES AND QUESTIONS

1. *Denied benefits and substantial burdens.* Why was denying unemployment compensation a substantial religious burden in *Sherbert* but denying tax exemptions in *Bob Jones University* was not? Perhaps the results could be reconciled if one views *Sherbert* (its broader language notwithstanding) as being a case about religious discrimination. Recall that South Carolina structured its unemployment program so as to protect the rights of Sunday worshippers—they would never face the hard choice of violating their religious duties or forgoing unemployment benefits. If South Carolina's

decision to accommodate, de facto, one group of religionists but not another is the key to the outcome, then *Sherbert* can be reconciled with *Bob Jones University*. If this distinction seems persuasive, however, how then to explain *Braunfeld*?

2. *The applicable standard of review.* Although *Sherbert* and *Yoder* ostensibly established strict scrutiny review for all free exercise claims, *Goldman* suggests that the rule was not quite so categorical. As it turns out, Congress did not think much of the *Goldman* majority's reasoning and was not inclined to defer to the military's judgment regarding the need for uniform appearance. It immediately enacted legislation that permits members of the armed forces to wear religious garb that does not detract from a service member's "neat and conservative" appearance. *See* 10 U.S.C. § 774 (2006); *see also* National Defense Authorization Act for Fiscal Year 1988 and 1989, Pub. L. No. 100-180, 101 Stat. 1019 (1987).
3. *Control over its own internal operations. Lyng* attempts to establish a distinction between the government "coercing" violations of religious beliefs or "penalizing" religious beliefs, on the one hand, and government "merely conducting its own internal operations," on the other. The former trigger the Free Exercise Clause, whereas the latter does not. Did *Sherbert* or the other unemployment benefits cases feature either "coercion" or targeted "penalties"? If not, why isn't the government free to use "*its* [money]" just as freely as the *Lyng* Court holds it may use "*its* land"?

B. THE SMITH *STANDARD*

In 1990, the Supreme Court changed course and appeared to reorient its Free Exercise Clause jurisprudence. This turn did not enjoy unanimous support. Congress responded to *Smith* by enacting the Religious Freedom Restoration Act (RFRA). RFRA represented a legislative effort to overturn *Smith* and restore the *Sherbert/Yoder* standard of review (that is, heightened scrutiny for laws that impose substantial religious burdens). See Chapter 16. Meanwhile, the current Supreme Court has been chipping away at the *Smith* rule, although as of early 2022 it has refrained from overruling it entirely. See Part D.

Employment Division, Department of Human Resources v. Smith

494 U.S. 872 (1990)

Justice SCALIA delivered the opinion of the Court.

This case requires us to decide whether the Free Exercise Clause of the First Amendment permits the State of Oregon to include religiously inspired peyote use within the reach of its general criminal prohibition on use of that drug, and thus permits the State to deny unemployment benefits to persons dismissed from their jobs because of such religiously inspired use.

Oregon law prohibits the knowing or intentional possession of a "controlled substance" unless the substance has been prescribed by a medical practitioner. Schedule I contains the drug peyote, a hallucinogen derived from the plant *Lophophora williamsii Lemaire*. . . .

Respondents Alfred Smith and Galen Black (hereinafter respondents) were fired from their jobs with a private drug rehabilitation organization because they ingested peyote for sacramental purposes at a ceremony of the Native American Church, of which both are members. When respondents applied to petitioner Employment Division (hereinafter petitioner) for unemployment compensation, they were determined to be ineligible for benefits because they had been discharged for work-related "misconduct." The Oregon Court of Appeals reversed that determination, holding that the denial of benefits violated respondents' free exercise rights under the First Amendment.

. . . [T]he Oregon Supreme Court held that respondents' religiously inspired use of peyote fell within the prohibition of the Oregon statute, which "makes no exception for the sacramental use" of the drug. It then considered whether that prohibition was valid under the Free Exercise Clause, and concluded that it was not. [It] ruled that the State could not deny unemployment benefits to respondents for having engaged in that practice. . . .

The Free Exercise Clause of the First Amendment, which has been made applicable to the States by incorporation into the Fourteenth Amendment, see Cantwell v. Connecticut, 310 U.S. 296, 303 (1940), provides that "Congress shall make no law respecting an establishment of religion, or *prohibiting the free exercise thereof*. . . ." U.S. Const., Amdt. 1 (emphasis added). The free exercise of religion means, first and foremost, the right to believe and profess whatever religious doctrine one desires. Thus, the First Amendment obviously excludes all "governmental regulation of religious *beliefs* as such." *Sherbert v. Verner*, *supra*, at 402.

But the "exercise of religion" often involves not only belief and profession but the performance of (or abstention from) physical acts: assembling with others for a worship service, participating in sacramental use of bread and wine, proselytizing, abstaining from certain foods or certain modes of transportation. It would be true, we think (though no case of ours has involved the point), that a State would be "prohibiting the free exercise [of religion]" if it sought to ban such acts or abstentions only when they are engaged in for religious reasons, or only because of the religious belief that they display. It would doubtless be unconstitutional, for example, to ban the casting of "statues that are to be used for worship purposes," or to prohibit bowing down before a golden calf.

Respondents in the present case, however, seek to carry the meaning of "prohibiting the free exercise [of religion]" one large step further. They contend that their religious motivation for using peyote places them beyond the reach of a criminal law that is not specifically directed at their religious practice, and that is concededly constitutional as applied to those who use the drug for other reasons. . . . As a textual matter, we do not think the words must be given that meaning. It is no more necessary to regard the collection of a general tax, for example, as "prohibiting the free exercise [of religion]" by those citizens who believe support of organized government to be sinful, than it is to regard the same tax as "abridging the freedom . . . of the press" of those publishing companies that must pay the tax as a condition of staying in business. It is a permissible reading of the text, in the one case as in the other, to say that if prohibiting the exercise of religion (or burdening the activity of printing) is not the object of the tax but merely the incidental effect of a generally applicable and otherwise valid provision, the First Amendment has not been offended. Compare Citizen Publishing Co. v. United States, 394 U.S. 131, 139 (1969) (upholding application of antitrust laws to press), with Grosjean v. American Press Co., 297 U.S. 233, 250-251 (1936) (striking down license tax applied only to newspapers with weekly circulation above a specified level).

Our decisions reveal that the latter reading is the correct one. We have never held that an individual's religious beliefs excuse him from compliance with an otherwise valid law prohibiting conduct that the State is free to regulate. On the contrary, the record of more than a century of our free exercise jurisprudence contradicts that proposition. . . . We first had occasion to assert that principle in Reynolds v. United States, 98 U.S. 145 (1878), where we rejected the claim that criminal laws against polygamy could not be constitutionally applied to those whose religion commanded the practice. "Laws," we said, "are made for the government of actions, and while they cannot interfere with mere religious belief and opinions, they may with practices. . . . Can a man excuse his practices to the contrary because of his religious belief? To permit this would be to make the professed doctrines of religious belief superior to the law of the land, and in effect to permit every citizen to become a law unto himself." *Id.* at 166-167. Subsequent decisions have consistently held that the right of free exercise does not relieve an individual of the obligation to comply with a "valid and neutral law of general applicability on the ground that the law proscribes (or prescribes) conduct that his religion prescribes (or proscribes)." . . .

The only decisions in which we have held that the First Amendment bars application of a neutral, generally applicable law to religiously motivated action have involved not the Free Exercise Clause alone, but the Free Exercise Clause in conjunction with other constitutional protections, such as freedom of speech and of the press, see Cantwell v. Connecticut, Murdock v. Pennsylvania, or the right of parents, acknowledged in Pierce v. Society of Sisters, 268 U.S. 510 (1925), to direct the education of their children, see Wisconsin v. Yoder, 406 U.S. 205 (1972) (invalidating compulsory school-attendance laws as applied to Amish parents who refused on religious grounds to send their children to school). Some of our cases prohibiting compelled expression, decided exclusively upon free speech grounds, have also involved freedom of religion, *cf.* Wooley v. Maynard, 430 U.S. 705 (1977) (invalidating compelled display of a license plate slogan that offended individual religious beliefs); *West Virginia Bd. of Education v. Barnette.*

The present case does not present such a hybrid situation, but a free exercise claim unconnected with any communicative activity or parental right. Respondents urge us to hold, quite simply, that when otherwise prohibitable conduct is accompanied by religious convictions, not only the convictions but the conduct itself must be free from governmental regulation. We have never held that, and decline to do so now. There being no contention that Oregon's drug law represents an attempt to regulate religious beliefs, the communication of religious beliefs, or the raising of one's children in those beliefs, the rule to which we have adhered ever since *Reynolds* plainly controls. "Our cases do not at their farthest reach support the proposition that a stance of conscientious opposition relieves an objector from any colliding duty fixed by a democratic government." *Gillette v. United States, supra,* at 461. . . .

Respondents argue that even though exemption from generally applicable criminal laws need not automatically be extended to religiously motivated actors, at least the claim for a religious exemption must be evaluated under the balancing test set forth in *Sherbert v. Verner.* Under the Sherbert test, governmental actions that substantially burden a religious practice must be justified by a compelling governmental interest. . . . We have never invalidated any governmental action on the basis of the *Sherbert* test except the denial of unemployment compensation. Although we have sometimes purported to apply the *Sherbert* test in contexts other than that, we have always found the test satisfied. In recent years we have abstained from applying the *Sherbert* test (outside the unemployment compensation field) at all.

Even if we were inclined to breathe into *Sherbert* some life beyond the unemployment compensation field, we would not apply it to require exemptions from a generally applicable criminal law. The *Sherbert* test, it must be recalled, was developed in a context that lent itself to individualized governmental assessment of the reasons for the relevant conduct. As a plurality of the Court noted in *Roy,* a distinctive feature of unemployment compensation programs is that their eligibility criteria invite consideration of the particular circumstances behind an applicant's unemployment: "The statutory conditions [in *Sherbert* and *Thomas*] provided that a person was not eligible for unemployment compensation benefits if, 'without good cause,' he had quit work or refused available work. The 'good cause' standard created a mechanism for individualized exemptions." . . . As the plurality pointed out in *Roy,* our decisions in the unemployment cases stand for the proposition that where the State has in place a system of individual exemptions, it may not refuse to extend that system to cases of "religious hardship" without compelling reason. *Bowen v. Roy, supra,* at 708. . . .

Although, as noted earlier, we have sometimes used the Sherbert test to analyze free exercise challenges to such laws, see *United States v. Lee, Gillette v. United States,* we have never applied the test to invalidate one. We conclude today that the sounder approach, and the approach in accord with the vast majority of our precedents, is to hold the test inapplicable to such challenges. The government's ability to enforce generally applicable prohibitions of socially harmful conduct, like its ability to carry out other aspects of public policy, "cannot depend on measuring the effects of a governmental action on a religious objector's spiritual development." To make an individual's obligation to obey such a law contingent upon the law's coincidence with his religious beliefs, except where the State's interest is "compelling"—permitting him, by virtue of his beliefs, "to become a law unto himself," *Reynolds v. United States,* contradicts both constitutional tradition and common sense.

The "compelling government interest" requirement seems benign, because it is familiar from other fields. But using it as the standard that must be met before the government may accord different treatment on the basis of race, see, *e.g.,* Palmore v. Sidoti, 466 U.S. 429, 432 (1984), or before the government may regulate the content of speech, see, *e.g.,* Sable Communications of California v. FCC, 492 U.S. 115, 126 (1989), is not remotely comparable to using it for the purpose asserted here. What it produces in those other fields—equality of treatment and an unrestricted flow of contending speech—are constitutional norms; what it would produce here—a private right to ignore generally applicable laws—is a constitutional anomaly.

Nor is it possible to limit the impact of respondents' proposal by requiring a "compelling state interest" only when the conduct prohibited is "central" to the individual's religion. *Cf.* Lyng v. Northwest Indian Cemetery Protective Assn., 485 U.S. at 474-476 (Brennan, J., dissenting). It is no more appropriate for judges to determine the "centrality" of religious beliefs before applying a "compelling interest" test in the free exercise field, than it would be for them to determine the "importance" of ideas before applying the "compelling interest" test in the free speech field. What principle of law or logic can be brought to bear to contradict a believer's assertion that a particular act is "central" to his personal faith? Judging the centrality of different religious practices is akin to the unacceptable "business of evaluating the relative merits of differing religious claims." . . . Repeatedly and in many different contexts, we have warned that courts must not presume to determine the place of a particular belief in a religion or the plausibility of a religious claim.

If the "compelling interest" test is to be applied at all, then, it must be applied across the board, to all actions thought to be religiously commanded. Moreover, if "compelling interest" really means what it says (and watering it down here would subvert its rigor in the other fields where it is applied), many laws will not meet the test. Any society adopting such a system would be courting anarchy, but that danger increases in direct proportion to the society's diversity of religious beliefs, and its determination to coerce or suppress none of them. Precisely because "we are a cosmopolitan nation made up of people of almost every conceivable religious preference," Braunfeld v. Brown, 366 U.S. at 606, and precisely because we value and protect that religious divergence, we cannot afford the luxury of deeming presumptively invalid, as applied to the religious objector, every regulation of conduct that does not protect an interest of the highest order. The rule respondents favor would open the prospect of constitutionally required religious exemptions from civic obligations of almost every conceivable kind-ranging from compulsory military service, see, e.g., *Gillette v. United States,* to the payment of taxes, see, e.g., *United States v. Lee;* to health and safety regulation such as manslaughter and child neglect laws, compulsory vaccination laws, drug laws, and traffic laws, see *Cox v. New Hampshire;* to social welfare legislation such as minimum wage laws, see *Tony and Susan Alamo Foundation v. Secretary of Labor,* child labor laws, see, e.g., *Prince v. Massachusetts,* . . . and laws providing for equality of opportunity for the races, see, e.g., *Bob Jones University v. United States.* The First Amendment's protection of religious liberty does not require this.

Values that are protected against government interference through enshrinement in the Bill of Rights are not thereby banished from the political process. Just as a society that believes in the negative protection accorded to the press by the First Amendment is likely to enact laws that affirmatively foster the dissemination of the printed word, so also a society that believes in the negative protection accorded to religious belief can be expected to be solicitous of that value in its legislation as well. It is therefore not surprising that a number of States have made an exception to their drug laws for sacramental peyote use. But to say that a nondiscriminatory religious-practice exemption is permitted, or even that it is desirable, is not to say that it is constitutionally required, and that the appropriate occasions for its creation can be discerned by the courts. It may fairly be said that leaving accommodation to the political process will place at a relative disadvantage those religious practices that are not widely engaged in; but that unavoidable consequence of democratic government must be preferred to a system in which each conscience is a law unto itself or in which judges weigh the social importance of all laws against the centrality of all religious beliefs.

Because respondents' ingestion of peyote was prohibited under Oregon law, and because that prohibition is constitutional, Oregon may, consistent with the Free Exercise Clause, deny respondents unemployment compensation when their dismissal results from use of the drug. The decision of the Oregon Supreme Court is accordingly reversed.

It is so ordered.

Justice O'CONNOR, with whom Justice BRENNAN, Justice MARSHALL, and Justice BLACKMUN join as to Parts I and II, concurring in the judgment.

Although I agree with the result the Court reaches in this case, I cannot join its opinion. In my view, today's holding dramatically departs from well-settled First Amendment jurisprudence, appears unnecessary to resolve the question presented, and is incompatible with our Nation's fundamental commitment to individual religious liberty. . . .

The Court today extracts from our long history of free exercise precedents the single categorical rule that "if prohibiting the exercise of religion . . . is . . . merely the incidental effect of a generally applicable and otherwise valid provision, the First Amendment has not been offended." *Ante,* at 878 (citations omitted). Indeed, the Court holds that where the law is a generally applicable criminal prohibition, our usual free exercise jurisprudence does not even apply. *Ante,* at 884. To reach this sweeping result, however, the Court must not only give a strained reading of the First Amendment but must also disregard our consistent application of free exercise doctrine to cases involving generally applicable regulations that burden religious conduct. . . .

The Court today, however, interprets the Clause to permit the government to prohibit, without justification, conduct mandated by an individual's religious beliefs, so long as that prohibition is generally applicable. *Ante,* at 878. But a law that prohibits certain conduct—conduct that happens to be an act of worship for someone—manifestly does prohibit that person's free exercise of his religion. A person who is barred from engaging in religiously motivated conduct is barred from freely exercising his religion. Moreover, that person is barred from freely exercising his religion regardless of whether the law prohibits the conduct only when engaged in for religious reasons, only by members of that religion, or by all persons. It is difficult to deny that a law that prohibits religiously motivated conduct, even if the law is generally applicable, does not at least implicate First Amendment concerns. . . .

Under our established First Amendment jurisprudence, we have recognized that the freedom to act, unlike the freedom to believe, cannot be absolute. See, *e.g., Cantwell, supra,* at 304; Reynolds v. United States, 98 U.S. 145, 161-167 (1879). Instead, we have respected both the First Amendment's express textual mandate and the governmental interest in regulation of conduct by requiring the government to justify any substantial burden on religiously motivated conduct by a compelling state interest and by means narrowly tailored to achieve that interest. . . . The compelling interest test effectuates the First Amendment's command that religious liberty is an independent liberty, that it occupies a preferred position, and that the Court will not permit encroachments upon this liberty, whether direct or indirect, unless required by clear and compelling governmental interests "of the highest order," *Yoder, supra,* at 215. "Only an especially important governmental interest pursued by narrowly tailored means can justify exacting a sacrifice of First Amendment freedoms as the price for an equal share of the rights, benefits, and privileges enjoyed by other citizens." *Roy, supra,* at 728 (opinion concurring in part and dissenting in part). . . .

In my view, however, the essence of a free exercise claim is relief from a burden imposed by government on religious practices or beliefs, whether the burden is imposed directly through laws that prohibit or compel specific religious practices, or indirectly through laws that, in effect, make abandonment of one's own religion or conformity to the religious beliefs of others the price of an equal place in the civil community. . . .

Finally, the Court today suggests that the disfavoring of minority religions is an "unavoidable consequence" under our system of government and that accommodation of such religions must be left to the political process. *Ante,* at 890. In my view, however, the First Amendment was enacted precisely to protect the rights of those whose religious practices are not shared by the majority and may be viewed with hostility. The history of our free exercise doctrine amply demonstrates the harsh impact majoritarian rule has had on unpopular or emerging religious groups such as the Jehovah's Witnesses and the Amish. . . .

[T]he critical question in this case is whether exempting respondents from the State's general criminal prohibition "will unduly interfere with fulfillment of the governmental interest." . . . Although the question is close, I would conclude that uniform application of Oregon's criminal prohibition is "essential to accomplish," *Lee, supra,* at 257, its overriding interest in preventing the physical harm caused by the use of a Schedule I controlled substance. Oregon's criminal prohibition represents that State's judgment that the possession and use of controlled substances, even by only one person, is inherently harmful and dangerous. Because the health effects caused by the use of controlled substances exist regardless of the motivation of the user, the use of such substances, even for religious purposes, violates the very purpose of the laws that prohibit them. Moreover, in view of the societal interest in preventing trafficking in controlled substances, uniform application of the criminal prohibition at issue is essential to the effectiveness of Oregon's stated interest in preventing any possession of peyote.

For these reasons, I believe that granting a selective exemption in this case would seriously impair Oregon's compelling interest in prohibiting possession of peyote by its citizens. Under such circumstances, the Free Exercise Clause does not require the State to accommodate respondents' religiously motivated conduct. . . . I would therefore adhere to our established free exercise jurisprudence and hold that the State in this case has a compelling interest in regulating peyote use by its citizens and that accommodating respondents' religiously motivated conduct "will unduly interfere with fulfillment of the governmental interest." *Lee, supra,* at 259. Accordingly, I concur in the judgment of the Court.

Justice BLACKMUN, with whom Justice BRENNAN and Justice MARSHALL join, dissenting.

[Justice Blackmun agreed with Justice O'Connor that strict scrutiny should apply but, unlike Justice O'Connor, found that Oregon's interest in suppressing the peyote market did not satisfy strict scrutiny.]

NOTES AND QUESTIONS

1. *The same approach or a new approach?* Was Justice Scalia intellectually honest in suggesting that the Supreme Court had never ordered exemptions from neutral laws of general applicability? What about *Yoder*? Why didn't Justice Scalia simply overrule *Sherbert* and *Yoder*, if that is what he really has in mind?
2. *Exceptions to new* Smith *rule.* Actually, *Smith* did not overrule *Sherbert* and *Yoder*. The new *Smith* rule does not apply to cases like *Sherbert* in which a state is making an individualized determination, nor to "hybrid" rights cases like *Yoder* which implicate free exercise as well as another constitutional right (in *Yoder*'s case, the substantive due process right to control the upbringing of one's children). Many scholars have argued that the exceptions were created expressly to avoid overruling *Sherbert* and *Yoder*. *See, e.g.*, Michael W. McConnell, *Free Exercise Revisionism and the* Smith *Decision*, 57 U. Chi. L. Rev. 1109 (1990) (arguing that the exceptions "have one function only: to enable the Court to reach the conclusion it desired without openly overruling any prior decisions"). Justice Souter's concurrence in *Church of the Lukumi Babalu Aye, Inc. v. City of Hialeah* criticizes the hybrid right claim: "If a hybrid claim is simply one in which another constitutional right is implicated, then the hybrid exception would probably be so vast as to swallow the *Smith* rule, and, indeed, the hybrid exception would cover the situation exemplified by *Smith*, since free speech and associational rights are certainly implicated in the peyote ritual. But if a hybrid claim is one in which a litigant would actually obtain an exemption from a formally neutral, generally applicable law under another constitutional provision, then there would have been no reason for the Court in what *Smith* calls the hybrid cases to have mentioned the Free Exercise Clause at all."
3. *Judicial competence and balancing.* Do you agree with Justice Scalia that federal judges should not engage in ad hoc reviews of general laws and balance those laws against religious objections? Why can't judges evaluate the centrality of religious beliefs? Must they decide on the centrality of religious beliefs in order to determine whether a religious burden is substantial?
4. *Courting anarchy?* Justice Scalia suggests that requiring religious exemptions from neutral laws of general applicability will lead to legal anarchy and that religious individuals will become a law unto themselves. Do you agree? Has his "parade of horribles" come to pass?

5. *The problem of discrimination against unpopular religious groups.* Under *Sherbert,* Christians had better luck than members of minority religions in obtaining exemptions. *See, e.g.*, Ronald J. Krotoszynski, Jr., *If Judges Were Angels: Religious Equality, Free Exercise, and the (Underappreciated) Merits of Smith,* 102 Nw. U.L. Rev. 1189 (2008). Under *Smith,* members of minority religions will now have to appeal to legislatures. Is the problem of religious discrimination likely to be greater in the courts or in politically elected and accountable legislative bodies?
6. *An unpopular decision.* Most, but not all, scholarly commentary has been highly critical of *Smith,* with preeminent scholars of the Religion Clauses describing it as having "eviscerated" the Free Exercise Clause, see Kent Greenawalt, *Religion and the Rehnquist Court,* 99 Nw. U.L. Rev. 145, 149-151 (2004), and another critic describing *Smith* as "produc[ing] widespread disbelief and anger," Douglas Laycock, *The Remnants of Free Exercise,* 1990 S. Ct. Rev. 1, 2-3. *See also* Michael W. McConnell, *Free Exercise Revisionism and the* Smith *Decision,* 57 U. Chi. L. Rev. 1109 (1990). Notwithstanding these strong critiques, *Smith* does have defenders. *See, e.g.*, William P. Marshall, *In Defense of* Smith *and Free Exercise Revisionism,* 58 U. Chi. L. Rev. 308 (1991). Which regime do you prefer: *Sherbert* or *Smith*?

Church of the Lukumi Babalu Aye, Inc. v. City of Hialeah

508 U.S. 520 (1993)

Justice Kennedy delivered the opinion of the Court, except as to Part II-A-2.

The principle that government may not enact laws that suppress religious belief or practice is so well understood that few violations are recorded in our opinions. *Cf.* McDaniel v. Paty, 435 U.S. 618 (1978); Fowler v. Rhode Island, 345 U.S. 67 (1953). Concerned that this fundamental nonpersecution principle of the First Amendment was implicated here, however, we granted certiorari. 503 U.S. 935 (1992).

Our review confirms that the laws in question were enacted by officials who did not understand, failed to perceive, or chose to ignore the fact that their official actions violated the Nation's essential commitment to religious freedom. The challenged laws had an impermissible object; and in all events the principle of general applicability was violated because the secular ends asserted in defense of the laws were pursued only with respect to conduct motivated by religious beliefs. We invalidate the challenged enactments and reverse the judgment of the Court of Appeals.

This case involves practices of the Santeria religion, which originated in the 19th century. When hundreds of thousands of members of the Yoruba people were brought as slaves from western Africa to Cuba, their traditional African religion absorbed significant elements of Roman Catholicism. The resulting syncretion, or fusion, is Santeria, "the way of the saints." The Cuban Yoruba express their devotion to spirits, called *orishas,* through the iconography of Catholic saints, Catholic symbols are often present at Santeria rites, and Santeria devotees attend the Catholic sacraments.

The Santeria faith teaches that every individual has a destiny from God, a destiny fulfilled with the aid and energy of the *orishas*. The basis of the Santeria religion is the nurture of a personal relation with the *orishas*, and one of the principal forms of devotion is an animal sacrifice. . . .

According to Santeria teaching, the *orishas* are powerful but not immortal. They depend for survival on the sacrifice. Sacrifices are performed at birth, marriage, and death rites, for the cure of the sick, for the initiation of new members and priests and during an annual celebration. Animals sacrificed in Santeria rituals include chickens, pigeons, doves, ducks, guinea pigs, goats, sheep, and turtles. The animals are killed by the cutting of the carotid arteries in the neck. The sacrificed animal is cooked and eaten, except after healing and death rituals. . . .

Petitioner Church of the Lukumi Babalu Aye, Inc. (Church), is a not-for-profit corporation organized under Florida law in 1973. The Church and its congregants practice the Santeria religion. . . . In April 1987, the Church leased land in the city of Hialeah, Florida, and announced plans to establish a house of worship as well as a school, cultural center, and museum. [T]he Church's goal was to bring the practice of the Santeria faith, including its ritual of animal sacrifice, into the open. The Church began the process of obtaining utility service and receiving the necessary licensing, inspection, and zoning approvals. . . .

The prospect of a Santeria church in their midst was distressing to many members of the Hialeah community, and the announcement of the plans to open a Santeria church in Hialeah prompted the city council to hold an emergency public session on June 9, 1987. The resolutions and ordinances passed at that and later meetings [effectively and intentionally prevented the Santerians from observing their religious rites, which involved the ritual sacrifice of live animals]. . . .

In September 1987, the city council adopted three substantive ordinances addressing the issue of religious animal sacrifice. Ordinance 87-52 defined "sacrifice" as "to unnecessarily kill, torment, torture, or mutilate an animal in a public or private ritual or ceremony not for the primary purpose of food consumption," and prohibited owning or possessing an animal "intending to use such animal for food purposes." It restricted application of this prohibition, however, to any individual or group that "kills, slaughters or sacrifices animals for any type of ritual, regardless of whether or not the flesh or blood of the animal is to be consumed." The ordinance contained an exemption for slaughtering by "licensed establishment[s]" of animals "specifically raised for food purposes." Declaring, moreover, that the city council "has determined that the sacrificing of animals within the city limits is contrary to the public health, safety, welfare and morals of the community," the city council adopted Ordinance 87-71. That ordinance defined "sacrifice" as had Ordinance 87-52, and then provided that "[i]t shall be unlawful for any person, persons, corporations or associations to sacrifice any animal within the corporate limits of the City of Hialeah, Florida." The final Ordinance, 87-72, defined "slaughter" as "the killing of animals for food" and prohibited slaughter outside of areas zoned for slaughterhouse use. The ordinance provided an exemption, however, for the slaughter or processing for sale of "small numbers of hogs and/or cattle per week in accordance with an exemption provided by state law." All ordinances and resolutions passed the city council by unanimous vote. Violations of each of the four ordinances were punishable by fines not exceeding $500 or imprisonment not exceeding 60 days, or both.

Following enactment of these ordinances, the Church and Pichardo [the church's priest and leader] filed this action pursuant to 42 U.S.C. § 1983 in the United States District Court for the Southern District of Florida. Named as defendants were the city of Hialeah and its mayor and members of its city council in their individual capacities. Alleging violations of petitioners' rights under, *inter alia*, the Free Exercise Clause, the complaint sought a declaratory judgment and injunctive and monetary relief. . . .

. . . . In addressing the constitutional protection for free exercise of religion, our cases establish the general proposition that a law that is neutral and of general applicability need not be justified by a compelling governmental interest even if the law has the incidental effect of burdening a particular religious practice. *Employment Div., Dept. of Human Resources of Ore. v. Smith, supra.* Neutrality and general applicability are interrelated, and, as becomes apparent in this case, failure to satisfy one requirement is a likely indication that the other has not been satisfied. A law falling to satisfy these requirements must be justified by a compelling governmental interest and must be narrowly tailored to advance that interest. These ordinances fail to satisfy the *Smith* requirements. We begin by discussing neutrality. . . . At a minimum, the protections of the Free Exercise Clause pertain if the law at issue discriminates against some or all religious beliefs or regulates or prohibits conduct because it is undertaken for religious reasons. . . .

Although a law targeting religious beliefs as such is never permissible, if the object of a law is to infringe upon or restrict practices because of their religious motivation, the law is not neutral, see *Employment Div., Dept. of Human Resources of Ore. v. Smith*, and it is invalid unless it is justified by a compelling interest and is narrowly tailored to advance that interest. There are, of course, many ways of demonstrating that the object or purpose of a law is the suppression of religion or religious conduct. To determine the object of a law, we must begin with its text, for the minimum requirement of neutrality is that a law not discriminate on its face. A law lacks facial neutrality if it refers to a religious practice without a secular meaning discernible from the language or context. Petitioners contend that three of the ordinances fail this test of facial neutrality because they use the words "sacrifice" and "ritual," words with strong religious connotations. We agree that these words are consistent with the claim of facial discrimination, but the argument is not conclusive. The words "sacrifice" and "ritual" have a religious origin, but current use admits also of secular meanings. The ordinances, furthermore, define "sacrifice" in secular terms, without referring to religious practices.

We reject the contention advanced by the city, see Brief for Respondent 15, that our inquiry must end with the text of the laws at issue. Facial neutrality is not determinative. The Free Exercise Clause, like the Establishment Clause, extends beyond facial discrimination. . . . Official action that targets religious conduct for distinctive treatment cannot be shielded by mere compliance with the requirement of facial neutrality. The Free Exercise Clause protects against governmental hostility which is masked as well as overt. . . .

The record in this case compels the conclusion that suppression of the central element of the Santeria worship service was the object of the ordinances. First, though use of the words "sacrifice" and "ritual" does not compel a finding of improper targeting of the Santeria religion, the choice of these words is support for our conclusion. There are further respects in which the text of the city council's enactments discloses the improper attempt to target Santeria.

It becomes evident that these ordinances target Santeria sacrifice when the ordinances' operation is considered. Apart from the text, the effect of a law in its real operation is strong evidence of its object. To be sure, adverse impact will not always lead to a finding of impermissible targeting. . . . [F]ew if any killings of animals are prohibited other than Santeria sacrifice, which is proscribed because it occurs during a ritual or ceremony and its primary purpose is to make an offering to the *orishas*, not food consumption. Indeed, careful drafting ensured that, although Santeria sacrifice is prohibited, killings that are no more necessary or humane in almost all other circumstances are unpunished. . . .

The ordinance exempts . . . "any licensed [food] establishment" with regard to "any animals which are specifically raised for food purposes," if the activity is permitted by zoning and other laws. This exception, too, seems intended to cover kosher slaughter. Again, the burden of the ordinance, in practical terms, falls on Santeria adherents but almost no others: If the killing is—unlike most Santeria sacrifices—unaccompanied by the intent to use the animal for food, then it is not prohibited by Ordinance 87-52; if the killing is specifically for food but does not occur during the course of "any type of ritual," it again falls outside the prohibition; and if the killing is for food and occurs during the course of a ritual, it is still exempted if it occurs in a properly zoned and licensed establishment and involves animals "specifically raised for food purposes." A pattern of exemptions parallels the pattern of narrow prohibitions. Each contributes to the gerrymander. . . .

We also find significant evidence of the ordinances' improper targeting of Santeria sacrifice in the fact that they proscribe more religious conduct than is necessary to achieve their stated ends. It is not unreasonable to infer, at least when there are no persuasive indications to the contrary, that a law which visits "gratuitous restrictions" on religious conduct, seeks not to effectuate the stated governmental interests, but to suppress the conduct because of its religious motivation. The legitimate governmental interests in protecting the public health and preventing cruelty to animals could be addressed by restrictions stopping far short of a flat prohibition of all Santeria sacrificial practice. If improper disposal, not the sacrifice itself, is the harm to be prevented, the city could have imposed a general regulation on the disposal of organic garbage. It did not do so.

In determining if the object of a law is a neutral one under the Free Exercise Clause, we can also find guidance in our equal protection cases. . . .

Here, as in equal protection cases, we may determine the city council's object from both direct and circumstantial evidence. Arlington Heights v. Metropolitan Housing Development Corp., 429 U.S. 252, 266 (1977). Relevant evidence includes, among other things, the historical background of the decision under challenge, the specific series of events leading to the enactment or official policy in question, and the legislative or administrative history; including contemporaneous statements made by members of the decisionmaking body. *Id.*, at 267-268. These objective factors bear on the question of discriminatory object. Personnel Administrator of Mass. v. Feeney, 442 U.S. 256, 279, n.24 (1979).

That the ordinances were enacted "'because of,' not merely 'in spite of,'" their suppression of Santeria religious practice, *id.*, at 279, is revealed by the events preceding their enactment. Although respondent claimed at oral argument that it had experienced significant problems resulting from the sacrifice of animals within the city before the announced opening of the Church, Tr. of Oral Arg. 27, 46, the city council made no attempt to address the supposed problem before its meeting in June 1987, just weeks after the Church announced plans to open. The minutes and taped excerpts of the June 9 session, both of which are in the record, evidence significant hostility exhibited by residents, members of the city council, and other city officials toward the Santeria religion and its practice of animal sacrifice. The public crowd that attended the June 9 meetings interrupted statements by council members critical of Santeria with cheers and the brief comments of Pichardo with taunts. When Councilman Martinez, a supporter of the ordinances, stated that in pre-revolution Cuba "people were put in jail for practicing this religion," the audience applauded. Taped excerpts of Hialeah City Council Meeting, June 9, 1987.

Other statements by members of the city council were in a similar vein. For example, Councilman Martinez, after noting his belief that Santeria was outlawed in Cuba, questioned: "[I]f we could not practice this [religion] in our homeland [Cuba], why bring it to this country?" Councilman Cardoso said that Santeria devotees at the Church "are in violation of everything this country stands for." Councilman Mejides indicated that he was "totally against the sacrificing of animals" and distinguished kosher slaughter because it had a "real purpose." The "Bible says we are allowed to sacrifice an animal for consumption," he continued, "but for any other purposes, I don't believe that the Bible allows that." The president of the city council, Councilman Echevarria, asked: "What can we do to prevent the Church from opening?"

Various Hialeah city officials made comparable comments. The chaplain of the Hialeah Police Department told the city council that Santeria was a sin, "foolishness," "an abomination to the Lord," and the worship of "demons." He advised the city council: "We need to be helping people and sharing with them the truth that is found in Jesus Christ." He concluded: "I would exhort you . . . not to permit this Church to exist." The city attorney commented that Resolution 87-66 indicated: "This community will not tolerate religious practices which are abhorrent to its citizens. . . ." *Ibid.* Similar comments were made by the deputy city attorney. This history discloses the object of the ordinances to target animal sacrifice by Santeria worshippers because of its religious motivation.

In sum, the neutrality inquiry leads to one conclusion: The ordinances had as their object the suppression of religion. The pattern we have recited discloses animosity to Santeria adherents and their religious practices; the ordinances by their own terms target this religious exercise; the texts of the ordinances were gerrymandered with care to proscribe religious killings of animals but to exclude almost all secular killings; and the ordinances suppress much more religious conduct than is necessary in order to achieve the legitimate ends asserted in their defense. These ordinances are not neutral, and the court below committed clear error in failing to reach this conclusion.

We turn next to a second requirement of the Free Exercise Clause, the rule that laws burdening religious practice must be of general applicability. Employment Div., Dept. of Human Resources of Ore. v. Smith, 494 U.S., at 879-881. All laws are selective to some extent, but categories of selection are of paramount concern when a law has the incidental effect of burdening religious practice. . . .

Respondent claims that Ordinances 87–40, 87–52, and 87–71 advance two interests: protecting the public health and preventing cruelty to animals. The ordinances are underinclusive for those ends. They fail to prohibit nonreligious conduct that endangers these interests in a similar or greater degree than Santeria sacrifice does. The underinclusion is substantial, not inconsequential. Despite the city's proffered interest in preventing cruelty to animals, the ordinances are drafted with care to forbid few killings but those occasioned by religious sacrifice. Many types of animal deaths or kills for nonreligious reasons are either not prohibited or approved by express provision. For example, fishing is legal. Extermination of mice and rats within a home is also permitted. Florida law incorporated by Ordinance 87–40 sanctions euthanasia of "stray, neglected, abandoned, or unwanted animals," Fla.Stat. § 828.058 (1987); destruction of animals judicially removed from their owners "for humanitarian reasons" or when the animal "is of no commercial value," § 828.073(4)(c)(2); the infliction of pain or suffering "in the interest of medical science," § 828.02; the placing of poison in one's yard or enclosure, § 828.08; and the use of a live animal "to pursue or take wildlife or to participate in any hunting," § 828.122(6)(b), and "to hunt wild hogs," § 828.122(6)(e). . . .

The ordinances are also underinclusive with regard to the city's interest in public health, which is threatened by the disposal of animal carcasses in open public places and the consumption of uninspected meat. Neither interest is pursued by respondent with regard to conduct that is not motivated by religious conviction. The health risks posed by the improper disposal of animal carcasses are the same whether Santeria sacrifice or some nonreligious killing preceded it. The city does not, however, prohibit hunters from bringing their kill to their houses, nor does it regulate disposal after their activity.

We conclude, in sum, that each of Hialeah's ordinances pursues the city's governmental interests only against conduct motivated by religious belief. The ordinances "ha[ve] every appearance of a prohibition that society is prepared to impose upon [adherents of Santeria] but not upon itself." This precise evil is what the requirement of general applicability is designed to prevent.

A law burdening religious practice that is not neutral or not of general application must undergo the most rigorous of scrutiny. To satisfy the commands of the First Amendment, a law restrictive of religious practice must advance "interests of the highest order" and must be narrowly tailored in pursuit of those interests. The compelling interest standard that we apply once a law fails to meet the *Smith* requirements is not "water[ed] . . . down" but "really means what it says." Employment Div., Dept. of Human Resources of Ore. v. Smith, 494 U.S., at 888. A law that targets religious conduct for distinctive treatment or advances legitimate governmental interests only against conduct with a religious motivation will survive strict scrutiny only in rare cases. It follows from what we have already said that these ordinances cannot withstand this scrutiny.

As we have discussed, all four ordinances are overbroad or underinclusive in substantial respects. The proffered objectives are not pursued with respect to analogous nonreligious conduct, and those interests could be achieved by narrower ordinances that burdened religion to a far lesser degree. The absence of narrow tailoring suffices to establish the invalidity of the ordinances. . . .

Reversed.

Justice SCALIA, with whom THE CHIEF JUSTICE joins, concurring in part and concurring in the judgment.

The Court analyzes the "neutrality" and the "general applicability" of the Hialeah ordinances in separate sections (Parts II-A and II-B, respectively), and allocates various invalidating factors to one or the other of those sections. If it were necessary to make a clear distinction between the two terms, I would draw a line somewhat different from the Court's. But I think it is not necessary, and would frankly acknowledge that the terms are not only "interrelated," *ante*, at 531, but substantially overlap.

I do not join that section because it departs from the opinion's general focus on the object of the *laws* at issue to consider the subjective motivation of the *lawmakers, i.e.*, whether the Hialeah City Council actually *intended* to disfavor the religion of Santeria. As I have noted elsewhere, it is virtually impossible to determine the singular "motive" of a collective legislative body, see, *e.g.*, Edwards v. Aguillard, 482 U.S. 578, 636-639 (1987) (dissenting opinion), and this Court has a long tradition of refraining from such inquiries. . . .

Justice BLACKMUN, with whom Justice O'CONNOR joins, concurring in the judgment.

The Court holds today that the city of Hialeah violated the First and Fourteenth Amendments when it passed a set of restrictive ordinances explicitly directed at petitioners' religious practice. With this holding I agree. I write separately to emphasize that the First Amendment's protection of religion extends beyond those rare occasions on which the government explicitly targets religion (or a particular religion) for disfavored treatment, as is done in this case. In my view, a statute that burdens the free exercise of religion "may stand only if the law in general, and the State's refusal to allow a religious exemption in particular, are justified by a compelling interest that cannot be served by less restrictive means." Employment Div., Dept. of Human Resources of Ore. v. Smith, 494 U.S. 872, 907 (1990) (dissenting opinion). . . . I continue to believe that *Smith* was wrongly decided, because it ignored the value of religious freedom as an affirmative individual liberty and treated the Free Exercise Clause as no more than an antidiscrimination principle. *See* 494 U.S., at 908-909. Thus, while I agree with the result the Court reaches in this case, I arrive at that result by a different route.

NOTES AND QUESTIONS

1. *Equality and free exercise.* If one adopts an equalitarian approach to interpreting the Free Exercise Clause, do *Smith* and *Lukumi Babalu Aye* sufficiently protect against religious discrimination? Virtually everyone agrees that, whatever else the Free Exercise Clause might mean, it prohibits government from targeting religion for unfavorable treatment. How effectively will the rules announced and applied in *Lukumi Babalu Aye* protect minority religionists from both overt and covert forms of discrimination?
2. *Neutrality.* There was an abundance of proof that the ordinances targeted the Santeria practice of ritual animal sacrifice: the text, the timing of the emergency session, and the hostile comments, for a start. But even without those, when laws are as grossly overinclusive and underinclusive as the Hialeah ordinances, it gives rise to the suspicion that the state's proffered motive

is not the actual motive. In other words, the extreme mismatch between the means and ends suggests something else, such as animus, was at play.

3. *General applicability*. Laws that are riddled with exceptions, as these ordinances were, are obviously not generally applicable. But what about a law that has only one or two exceptions—is it generally applicable? For example, if a police dress code bans beards except for medically necessary beards (required by some skin conditions), is that policy generally applicable? *See* Fraternal Order of Police v. City of Newark, 170 F.3d 359 (3d Cir. 1999). Is it a question of numbers, intent, or something else?
4. *Reliance on equal protection jurisprudence. Smith* made clear that laws neutral on their face are not necessarily neutral under the Free Exercise Clause. The same is true for the Equal Protection Clause, which Justice Kennedy explicitly references. At the same time, in equal protection doctrine, disparate impact alone is not enough to trigger the Equal Protection Clause. Instead, laws neutral on their face that have a discriminatory impact must also have a discriminatory purpose in order to merit heightened scrutiny under the Equal Protection Clause. *See generally* Washington v. Davis, 426 U.S. 229 (1976). Does the Supreme Court mean to import the same requirement of disparate impact plus discriminatory intent into free exercise doctrine when it writes that the ordinances were passed "because of" rather than "in spite of" their disparate impact on the Santeria religious practice?

THEORY-APPLIED PROBLEM

In May 2017, the City of Hialeah adopts an animal cruelty ordinance prohibiting "cruelty towards animals, including the intentional infliction of serious pain and torture, including but not limited to the cutting, mutilation, or maiming of an animal." At the time of adoption, no anti-Santerian statements issue from local government officials. Instead, generic statements about the need to protect "innocent creatures" pepper the legislative record. On May 15, 2017, the day the ordinance takes effect, a local city policeman cites the chief priest of the local Santerian church for violating the anti-animal-cruelty ordinance after observing a Santerian rite involving the intentional killing of a small goat. The police officer's report states, in relevant part, that "the goat appeared to be terrified, was bleating loudly, and attempted to escape, but could not." If the Santerian priest challenged the citation on free exercise grounds, what would be the likely outcome of the claim in the federal courts? If you believe that the citation would probably withstand a Free Exercise Clause challenge, how much protection does *Lukumi Babalu Aye* really provide to minority religionists? Is benign neglect any less harmful to minority religionists than overt forms of discrimination? Or is discrimination qualitatively different from benign neglect?

C. *EXEMPTIONS AND RELIGIOUS DISCRIMINATION*

Although the Supreme Court continues to apply *Smith* to religious liberty challenges, the Court's most recent decisions regularly conclude that the challenged law is not neutral or not generally applicable, and consequently, must be subject to strict scrutiny. Moreover, the post-*Smith* strict scrutiny is much more rigorous than the strict scrutiny the Court has previously applied during the pre-*Smith* era.

1. *The Fall of "Neutral and Generally Applicable"*

A series of cases bringing religious liberty challenges to COVID-19 health regulations illustrates the shift in the Court's application of *Smith.* During the COVID-19 pandemic, many states enacted emergency orders to try and stem infection. These health care measures were regularly challenged by religious objectors, and several cases reached the Court on its "shadow docket." At first, the Supreme Court upheld state COVID-19 restrictions. *See South Bay United Pentecostal Church v. Newsom* (2020) (below); *Calvary Chapel Dayton Valley v. Sisolak* (2020). After Justice Amy Comey Barrett came on the bench, however, both the outcome and the tenor of the decisions changed.

South Bay United Pentecostal Church v. Newsom

140 S. Ct. 1613 (2020)

The application for injunctive relief presented to Justice KAGAN and by her referred to the Court is denied.

Justice THOMAS, Justice ALITO, Justice GORSUCH, and Justice KAVANAUGH would grant the application.

Chief Justice ROBERTS, concurring in denial of application for injunctive relief.

The Governor of California's Executive Order aims to limit the spread of COVID–19, a novel severe acute respiratory illness that has killed thousands of people in California and more than 100,000 nationwide. At this time, there is no known cure, no effective treatment, and no vaccine. Because people may be infected but asymptomatic, they may unwittingly infect others. The Order places temporary numerical restrictions on public gatherings to address this extraordinary health emergency. State guidelines currently limit attendance at places of worship to 25% of building capacity or a maximum of 100 attendees. . . .

Although California's guidelines place restrictions on places of worship, those restrictions appear consistent with the Free Exercise Clause of the First Amendment. Similar or more severe restrictions apply to comparable secular gatherings, including lectures, concerts, movie showings, spectator sports, and theatrical performances, where large groups of people gather in close proximity for extended periods of time. And the Order exempts or treats more leniently only dissimilar activities, such as operating grocery stores, banks, and laundromats, in which people neither congregate in large groups nor remain in close proximity for extended periods.

The precise question of when restrictions on particular social activities should be lifted during the pandemic is a dynamic and fact-intensive matter subject to reasonable disagreement. Our Constitution principally entrusts "[t]he safety and the health of the people" to the politically accountable officials of the States "to guard and protect." Jacobson v. Massachusetts, 197 U.S. 11, 38 (1905). When those officials "undertake[ ] to act in areas fraught with medical and scientific uncertainties," their latitude "must be especially broad." Where those broad limits are not exceeded, they should not be subject to second-guessing by an "unelected federal judiciary," which lacks the background, competence, and expertise to assess public health and is not accountable to the people.

That is especially true where, as here, a party seeks emergency relief in an interlocutory posture, while local officials are actively shaping their response to changing facts on the ground. The notion that it is "indisputably clear" that the Government's limitations are unconstitutional seems quite improbable.

Justice KAVANAUGH, with whom Justice THOMAS and Justice GORSUCH join, dissenting from denial of application for injunctive relief.

I would grant the Church's requested temporary injunction because California's latest safety guidelines discriminate against places of worship and in favor of comparable secular businesses. Such discrimination violates the First Amendment.

In response to the COVID–19 health crisis, California has now limited attendance at religious worship services to 25% of building capacity or 100 attendees, whichever is lower. The basic constitutional problem is that comparable secular businesses are not subject to a 25% occupancy cap, including factories, offices, supermarkets, restaurants, retail stores, pharmacies, shopping malls, pet grooming shops, bookstores, florists, hair salons, and cannabis dispensaries. . . .

In my view, California's discrimination against religious worship services contravenes the Constitution. As a general matter, the "government may not use religion as a basis of classification for the imposition of duties, penalties, privileges or benefits." This Court has stated that discrimination against religion is "odious to our Constitution."

To justify its discriminatory treatment of religious worship services, California must show that its rules are "justified by a compelling governmental interest" and "narrowly tailored to advance that interest." California undoubtedly has a compelling interest in combating the spread of COVID–19 and protecting the health of its citizens. But "restrictions inexplicably applied to one group and exempted from another do little to further these goals and do much to burden religious freedom." Roberts v. Neace, 958 F.3d 409, 414 (CA6 2020) (*per curiam*). What California needs is a compelling justification for distinguishing between (i) religious worship services and (ii) the litany of other secular businesses that are not subject to an occupancy cap.

California has not shown such a justification. The Church has agreed to abide by the State's rules that apply to comparable secular businesses. That raises important questions: "Assuming all of the same precautions are taken, why can someone safely walk down a grocery store aisle but not a pew? And why can someone safely interact with a brave deliverywoman but not with a stoic minister?"

The Church and its congregants simply want to be treated equally to comparable secular businesses. . . . In sum, California's 25% occupancy cap on religious worship services indisputably discriminates against religion, and such discrimination violates the First Amendment. . . .

Roman Catholic Diocese of Brooklyn v. Cuomo

141 S. Ct. 63 (2020)

PER CURIAM.

This emergency application and another, Agudath Israel of America, et al. v. Cuomo, No. 20A90, present the same issue, and this opinion addresses both cases.

Both applications seek relief from an Executive Order issued by the Governor of New York that imposes very severe restrictions on attendance at religious services in areas classified as "red" or "orange" zones. In red zones, no more than 10 persons may attend each religious service, and in orange zones, attendance is capped at 25. The two applications, one filed by the Roman Catholic Diocese of Brooklyn and the other by Agudath Israel of America and affiliated entities, contend that these restrictions violate the Free Exercise Clause of the First Amendment, and they ask us to enjoin enforcement of the restrictions while they pursue appellate review. . . . Both the Diocese and Agudath Israel maintain that the regulations treat houses of worship much more harshly than comparable secular facilities. . . .

Likelihood of success on the merits. . . . [T]he regulations cannot be viewed as neutral because they single out houses of worship for especially harsh treatment.

In a red zone, while a synagogue or church may not admit more than 10 persons, businesses categorized as "essential" may admit as many people as they wish. And the list of "essential" businesses includes things such as acupuncture facilities, camp grounds, garages, as well as many whose services are not limited to those that can be regarded as essential, such as all plants manufacturing chemicals and microelectronics and all transportation facilities. . . . The disparate treatment is even more striking in an orange zone. While attendance at houses of worship is limited to 25 persons, even non-essential businesses may decide for themselves how many persons to admit.

These categorizations lead to troubling results. At the hearing in the District Court, a health department official testified about a large store in Brooklyn that could "literally have hundreds of people shopping there on any given day." Yet a nearby church or synagogue would be prohibited from allowing more than 10 or 25 people inside for a worship service. And the Governor has stated that factories and schools have contributed to the spread of COVID–19, but they are treated less harshly than the Diocese's churches and Agudath Israel's synagogues, which have admirable safety records.

Because the challenged restrictions are not "neutral" and of "general applicability," they must satisfy "strict scrutiny," and this means that they must be "narrowly tailored" to serve a "compelling" state interest. Church of Lukumi, 508 U.S. at 546. Stemming the spread of COVID–19 is unquestionably a compelling interest, but it is hard to see how the challenged regulations can be regarded as "narrowly tailored." They are far more restrictive than any COVID–related regulations that have previously come before the Court, much tighter than those adopted by many other jurisdictions hard-hit by the pandemic, and far more severe than has been shown to be required to prevent the spread of the virus at the applicants' services. The District Court noted that "there ha[d] not been any COVID–19 outbreak in any of the Diocese's churches since they reopened." . . . Similarly, Agudath Israel notes that "[t]he Governor does not dispute that [it] ha[s] rigorously implemented and adhered to all health protocols and that there has been no outbreak of COVID–19 in [its] congregations."

Not only is there no evidence that the applicants have contributed to the spread of COVID–19 but there are many other less restrictive rules that could be adopted to minimize the risk to those attending religious services. Among other things, the maximum attendance at a religious service could be tied to the size of the church or synagogue. Almost all of the 26 Diocese churches immediately affected by the Executive Order can seat at least 500 people, about 14 can accommodate at least 700, and 2 can seat over 1,000. Similarly, Agudath Israel of Kew Garden Hills can seat up to 400. It is hard to believe that admitting more than 10 people to a 1,000–seat church or 400–seat synagogue would create a more serious health risk than the many other activities that the State allows. . . .

Members of this Court are not public health experts, and we should respect the judgment of those with special expertise and responsibility in this area. But even in a pandemic, the Constitution cannot be put away and forgotten. The restrictions at issue here, by effectively barring many from attending religious services, strike at the very heart of the First Amendment's guarantee of religious liberty. Before allowing this to occur, we have a duty to conduct a serious examination of the need for such a drastic measure. . . .

It is so ordered.

Justice GORSUCH, concurring.

Government is not free to disregard the First Amendment in times of crisis. At a minimum, that Amendment prohibits government officials from treating religious exercises worse than comparable secular activities, unless they are pursuing a compelling interest and using the least restrictive means available. Yet recently, during the COVID pandemic, certain States seem to have ignored these long-settled principles.

Today's case supplies just the latest example. New York's Governor has asserted the power to assign different color codes to different parts of the State and govern each by executive decree. In "red zones," houses of worship are all but closed—limited to a maximum of 10 people. In the Orthodox Jewish community that limit might operate to exclude all women, considering 10 men are necessary to establish a minyan, or a quorum. In "orange zones," it's not much different. Churches and synagogues are limited to a maximum of 25 people. These restrictions apply even to the largest cathedrals and synagogues, which ordinarily hold hundreds. And the restrictions apply no matter the precautions taken, including social distancing, wearing masks, leaving doors and windows open, forgoing singing, and disinfecting spaces between services.

At the same time, the Governor has chosen to impose no capacity restrictions on certain businesses he considers "essential." And it turns out the businesses the Governor considers essential include hardware stores, acupuncturists, and liquor stores. Bicycle repair shops, certain signage companies, accountants, lawyers, and insurance agents are all essential too. So, at least according to the Governor, it may be unsafe to go to church, but it is always fine to pick up another bottle of wine, shop for a new bike, or spend the afternoon exploring your distal points and meridians. Who knew public health would so perfectly align with secular convenience? . . .

The only explanation for treating religious places differently seems to be a judgment that what happens there just isn't as "essential" as what happens in secular spaces. Indeed, the Governor is remarkably frank about this: In his judgment laundry and liquor, travel and tools, are all "essential" while traditional religious exercises are not. That is exactly the kind of discrimination the First Amendment forbids. . . .

It is time—past time—to make plain that, while the pandemic poses many grave challenges, there is no world in which the Constitution tolerates color-coded executive edicts that reopen liquor stores and bike shops but shutter churches, synagogues, and mosques.

Justice KAVANAUGH, concurring.

. . . New York's restrictions on houses of worship not only are severe, but also are discriminatory. . . .The State's discrimination against religion raises a serious First Amendment issue and triggers heightened scrutiny, requiring the State to provide a sufficient justification for the discrimination. But New York has not sufficiently justified treating houses of worship more severely than secular businesses.

The State argues that it has not impermissibly discriminated against religion because some secular businesses such as movie theaters must remain closed and are thus treated less favorably than houses of worship. But under this Court's precedents, it does not suffice for a State to point out that, as compared to houses of worship, some secular businesses are subject to similarly severe or even more severe restrictions. Rather, once a State creates a favored class of businesses, as New York has done in this case, the State must justify why houses of worship are excluded from that favored class. Here, therefore, the State must justify imposing a 10-person or 25-person limit on houses of worship but not on favored secular businesses. The State has not done so. . . .

[CHIEF JUSTICE ROBERTS's dissenting opinion is omitted.]

[Justice BREYER's dissenting opinion, with whom Justice SOTOMAYOR and Justice KAGAN join, is omitted.]

Justice SOTOMAYOR, with whom Justice KAGAN joins, dissenting.

Amidst a pandemic that has already claimed over a quarter million American lives, the Court today enjoins one of New York's public health measures aimed at containing the spread of COVID–19 in areas facing the most severe outbreaks. Earlier this year, this Court twice stayed its hand when asked to issue similar extraordinary relief. [*See South Bay United Pentecostal Church v. Newsom* (2020); *Calvary Chapel Dayton Valley v. Sisolak* (2020)] I see no justification for the Court's change of heart, and I fear that granting applications such as the one filed by the Roman Catholic Diocese of Brooklyn (Diocese) will only exacerbate the Nation's suffering.

South Bay and Calvary Chapel provided a clear and workable rule to state officials seeking to control the spread of COVID–19: They may restrict attendance at houses of worship so long as comparable secular institutions face restrictions that are at least equally as strict. New York's safety measures fall comfortably within those bounds. Like the States in South Bay and Calvary Chapel, New York applies "[s]imilar or more severe restrictions . . . to comparable secular gatherings, including lectures, concerts, movie showings, spectator sports, and theatrical performances, where large groups of people gather in close proximity for extended periods of time." Likewise, New York "treats more leniently only dissimilar activities, such as operating grocery stores, banks, and laundromats, in which people neither congregate in large groups nor remain in close proximity for extended periods." That should be enough to decide this case.

The Diocese attempts to get around South Bay and Calvary Chapel by disputing New York's conclusion that attending religious services poses greater risks than, for instance, shopping at big box stores. But the District Court rejected that argument as unsupported by the factual record. Undeterred, Justice Gorsuch offers up his own examples of secular activities he thinks might pose similar risks as religious gatherings, but which are treated more leniently under New York's rules (e.g., going to the liquor store or getting a bike repaired). But Justice Gorsuch does not even try to square his examples with the conditions medical experts tell us facilitate the spread of COVID–19: large groups of people gathering, speaking, and singing in close proximity indoors for extended periods of time. *See* App. to Brief in Opposition in No. 20A87, pp. 46–51 (declaration of Debra S. Blog, Director of the Div. of Epidemiology, NY Dept. of Health); Brief for the American Medical Association et al. as Amicus Curiae 3–6 (Brief for AMA). Unlike religious services, which "have every one of th[ose] risk factors," bike repair shops and liquor stores generally do not feature customers gathering inside to sing and speak together for an hour or more at a time. Id., at 7 ("Epidemiologists and physicians generally agree that religious services are among the riskiest activities"). Justices of this Court play a deadly game in second guessing the expert judgment of health officials about the environments in which a contagious virus, now infecting a million Americans each week, spreads most easily.

In truth, this case is easier than South Bay and Calvary Chapel. While the state regulations in those cases generally applied the same rules to houses of worship and secular institutions where people congregate in large groups, New York treats houses of worship far more favorably than their secular comparators. Compare, e.g., Calvary Chapel, 140 S.Ct., at 2609 (Kavanaugh, J., dissenting) (noting that Nevada subjected movie theaters and houses of worship alike to a 50-person cap) with App. to Brief in Opposition in No. 20A87, p. 53 (requiring movie theaters, concert venues, and sporting arenas subject to New York's regulation to close entirely, but allowing houses of worship to open subject to capacity restrictions). And whereas the restrictions in South Bay and Calvary Chapel applied statewide, New York's fixed-capacity restrictions apply only in specially designated areas experiencing a surge in COVID–19 cases.

The Diocese suggests that, because New York's regulation singles out houses of worship by name, it cannot be neutral with respect to the practice of religion. Thus, the argument goes, the regulation must, ipso facto, be subject to strict scrutiny. It is true that New York's policy refers to religion on its face. But as I have just explained, that is because the policy singles out religious institutions for preferential treatment in comparison to secular gatherings, not because it discriminates against them. Surely the Diocese cannot demand laxer restrictions by pointing out that it is already being treated better than comparable secular institutions.

Finally, the Diocese points to certain statements by Governor Cuomo as evidence that New York's regulation is impermissibly targeted at religious activity—specifically, at combatting heightened rates of positive COVID–19 cases among New York's Orthodox Jewish community. The Diocese suggests that these comments supply "an independent basis for the application of strict scrutiny."

I do not see how. The Governor's comments simply do not warrant an application of strict scrutiny under this Court's precedents. Just a few Terms ago, this Court declined to apply heightened scrutiny to a Presidential Proclamation limiting immigration from Muslim-majority countries, even though President Trump had described the Proclamation as a "Muslim Ban," originally conceived of as a " 'total and complete shutdown of Muslims entering the United States until our country's representatives can figure out what is going on.' " *Trump v. Hawaii* (2018). If the President's statements did not show "that the challenged restrictions violate the 'minimum requirement of neutrality' to religion," it is hard to see how Governor Cuomo's do.

* * *

Free religious exercise is one of our most treasured and jealously guarded constitutional rights. States may not discriminate against religious institutions, even when faced with a crisis as deadly as this one. But those principles are not at stake today. The Constitution does not forbid States from responding to public health crises through regulations that treat religious institutions equally or more favorably than comparable secular institutions, particularly when those regulations save lives. Because New York's COVID–19 restrictions do just that, I respectfully dissent.

Tandom v. Newsom

141 S. Ct. 1294 (2021)

Per Curiam . . .

The Ninth Circuit's failure to grant an injunction pending appeal was erroneous. This Court's decisions have made the following points clear.

First, government regulations are not neutral and generally applicable, and therefore trigger strict scrutiny under the Free Exercise Clause, whenever they treat *any* comparable secular activity more favorably than religious exercise. It is no answer that a State treats some comparable secular businesses or other activities as poorly as or even less favorably than the religious exercise at issue.

Second, whether two activities are comparable for purposes of the Free Exercise Clause must be judged against the asserted government interest that justifies the regulation at issue. . . . Comparability is concerned with the risks various activities pose, not the reasons why people gather.

Third, the government has the burden to establish that the challenged law satisfies strict scrutiny. To do so in this context, it must do more than assert that certain risk factors "are always present in worship, or always absent from the other secular activities" the government may allow. Instead, narrow tailoring requires the government to show that measures less restrictive of the First Amendment activity could not address its interest in reducing the spread of COVID. Where the government permits other activities to proceed with precautions, it must show that the religious exercise at issue is more dangerous than those activities even when the same precautions are applied. Otherwise, precautions that suffice for other activities suffice for religious exercise too. . . .

These principles dictated the outcome in this case. . . . First, California treats some comparable secular activities more favorably than at-home religious exercise, permitting hair salons, retail stores, personal care services, movie theaters, private suites at sporting events and concerts, and indoor restaurants to bring together more than three households at a time. Second, the Ninth Circuit did not conclude that those activities pose a lesser risk of transmission than *applicants'* proposed religious exercise at home. The Ninth Circuit erroneously rejected these comparators simply because this Court's previous decisions involved public buildings as opposed to private buildings. Third, instead of requiring the State to explain why it could not safely permit at-home worshipers to gather in larger numbers while using precautions used in secular activities, the Ninth Circuit erroneously declared that such measures might not "translate readily" to the home. . . .

Applicants are likely to succeed on the merits of their free exercise claim; they are irreparably harmed by the loss of free exercise rights "for even minimal periods of time"; and the State has not shown that "public health would be imperiled" by employing less restrictive measures. Accordingly, applicants are entitled to an injunction pending appeal. . . .

THE CHIEF JUSTICE would deny the application.

Justice KAGAN, with whom Justice BREYER and Justice SOTOMAYOR join, dissenting.

I would deny the application largely for the reasons stated in *South Bay United Pentecostal Church* v. *Newsom* (Kagan, J., dissenting). The First Amendment requires that a State treat religious conduct as well as the State treats comparable secular conduct. Sometimes finding the right secular analogue may raise hard questions. But not today. California limits religious gatherings in homes to three households. If the State also limits all secular gatherings in homes to three households, it has complied with the First Amendment. And the State does exactly that: It has adopted a blanket restriction on at-home gatherings of all kinds, religious and secular alike. California need not, as the *per curiam* insists, treat at-home religious gatherings the same as hardware stores and hair salons—and thus unlike at-home secular gatherings, the obvious comparator here. As the *per curiam*'s reliance on separate opinions and unreasoned orders signals, the law does not require that the State equally treat apples and watermelons.

And even supposing a court should cast so expansive a comparative net, the *per curiam*'s analysis of this case defies the factual record. According to the *per curiam,* "the Ninth Circuit did not conclude that" activities like frequenting stores or salons "pose a lesser risk of transmission" than applicants' at-home religious activities. But Judges Milan Smith and Bade explained for the court that those activities do pose lesser risks for at least three reasons. First, "when people gather in social settings, their interactions are likely to be longer than they would be in a commercial setting," with participants "more likely to be involved in prolonged conversations." Second, "private houses are typically smaller and less ventilated than commercial establishments." And third, "social distancing and mask-wearing are less likely in private settings and enforcement is more difficult." These are not the mere musings of two appellate judges: The district court found each of these facts based on the uncontested testimony of California's public-health experts. No doubt this evidence is inconvenient for the *per curiam*'s preferred result. But the Court has no warrant to ignore the record in a case that turns on risk assessments.

In ordering California to weaken its restrictions on at-home gatherings, the majority yet again "insists on treating unlike cases, not like ones, equivalently." And it once more commands California "to ignore its experts' scientific findings," thus impairing "the State's effort to address a public health emergency." Because the majority continues to disregard law and facts alike, I respectfully dissent from this latest *per curiam* decision.

NOTES AND QUESTIONS

1. *Shadow docket.* All these challenges to COVID-19 public health regulations were shadow docket rulings. Normally, Supreme Court decisions rely on extensive briefing, including amicus briefs, as well as oral argument, and the decisions themselves provide lengthy and detailed reasoning. Shadow docket decisions, often in response to an emergency application, usually lack all these things. Should the Court make major doctrinal changes in shadow docket decisions?
2. *New Justice.* In its first COVID-19 decisions, the Supreme Court found in favor of the state's regulations. After Amy Comey Barrett replaced Ruth Bader Ginsburg on the bench, however, the Court started ruling in favor of the religious objectors. Do you think the change in outcome is due to the change in Justices, or are the later decisions distinguishable from the earlier ones?
3. *Comparator.* Laws that treat religious activities the same as comparable secular activities are likely to be neutral and generally applicable. The question is what counts as a comparable activity. In *South Bay*, the Court held that the comparator for large religious gatherings like worship services were large secular gatherings like movies and concerts; in both "large groups of people gather in close proximity for extended periods of time." Grocery stores, banks, and laundromats, in contrast, were not comparators, as people there "neither congregate in large groups nor remain in close proximity for extended periods." By *Roman Catholic Diocese*, however, a majority of the Court had expanded the comparable activities to include many more secular activities, leading it to conclude that regulations were not neutral since religious activities were being treated more harshly. Is visiting a camp ground, garage, bicycle shop, or liquor store comparable to attending worship services in terms of the risk they pose?
4. *Deference.* How did the majority and dissent reach such different conclusions about the risks posed by various activities? Should the Supreme Court have shown more (or less) deference to the legislature's factual findings? The District Court's? The scientific evidence?
5. *Discrimination.* In *Tandom*, the Court emphasized that even a single secular exemption would defeat the requirement of neutrality and general applicability. Indeed, several Justices argue that this amounts to discrimination against religion. Do *Smith* and *Hialeah* require this view?

2. *The Rise of Religious "Discrimination"*

More and more jurisdictions are passing laws or implementing regulations barring discrimination on the basis of sexual orientation and gender identity. Both for-profit businesses and nonprofit organizations have argued that these antidiscrimination measures violate their religious liberty and that they are entitled to religious exemptions from these antidiscrimination regulations under the Free Exercise Clause. Although many lower courts have rejected these claims, the Supreme Court has proven sympathetic to them.

Masterpiece Cakeshop, Ltd v. Colorado Civil Rights Commission

138 S. Ct. 1719 (2018)

Justice KENNEDY delivered the opinion of the Court.

In 2012 a same-sex couple visited Masterpiece Cakeshop, a bakery in Colorado, to make inquiries about ordering a cake for their wedding reception. The shop's owner told the couple that he would not create a cake for their wedding because of his religious opposition to same-sex marriages—marriages the State of Colorado itself did not recognize at that time. The couple filed a charge with the Colorado Civil Rights Commission alleging discrimination on the basis of sexual orientation in violation of the Colorado Anti–Discrimination Act.

The Commission determined that the shop's actions violated the Act and ruled in the couple's favor. The Colorado state courts affirmed the ruling and its enforcement order, and this Court now must decide whether the Commission's order violated the Constitution.

The case presents difficult questions as to the proper reconciliation of at least two principles. The first is the authority of a State and its governmental entities to protect the rights and dignity of gay persons who are, or wish to be, married but who face discrimination when they seek goods or services. The second is the right of all persons to exercise fundamental freedoms under the First Amendment, as applied to the States through the Fourteenth Amendment.

The freedoms asserted here are both the freedom of speech and the free exercise of religion. . . .

I

A

Masterpiece Cakeshop, Ltd., is a bakery in Lakewood, Colorado, a suburb of Denver. The shop offers a variety of baked goods, ranging from everyday cookies and brownies to elaborate custom-designed cakes for birthday parties, weddings, and other events.

Jack Phillips is an expert baker who has owned and operated the shop for 24 years. Phillips is a devout Christian. He has explained that his "main goal in life is to be obedient to" Jesus Christ and Christ's "teachings in all aspects of his life." And he seeks to "honor God through his work at Masterpiece Cakeshop." One of Phillips' religious beliefs is that "God's intention for marriage from the beginning of history is that it is and should be the union of one man and one woman." To Phillips, creating a wedding cake for a same-sex wedding would be equivalent to participating in a celebration that is contrary to his own most deeply held beliefs.

Phillips met Charlie Craig and Dave Mullins when they entered his shop in the summer of 2012. Craig and Mullins were planning to marry. At that time, Colorado did not recognize same-sex marriages, so the couple planned to wed legally in Massachusetts and afterwards to host a reception for their family and friends in Denver. To prepare for their celebration, Craig and Mullins visited the shop and told Phillips that they were interested in ordering a cake for "our wedding." They did not mention the design of the cake they envisioned.

Phillips informed the couple that he does not "create" wedding cakes for same-sex weddings. He explained, "I'll make your birthday cakes, shower cakes, sell you cookies and brownies, I just don't make cakes for same sex weddings." The couple left the shop without further discussion.

The following day, Craig's mother, who had accompanied the couple to the cakeshop and been present for their interaction with Phillips, telephoned to ask Phillips why he had declined to serve her son. Phillips explained that he does not create wedding cakes for same-sex weddings because of his religious opposition to same-sex marriage. . . . He later explained his belief that "to create a wedding cake for an event that celebrates something that directly goes against the teachings of the Bible, would have been a personal endorsement and participation in the ceremony and relationship that they were entering into."

B

For most of its history, Colorado has prohibited discrimination in places of public accommodation. . . . Today, the Colorado Anti–Discrimination Act (CADA) carries forward the state's tradition of prohibiting discrimination in places of public accommodation. . . .

CADA establishes an administrative system for the resolution of discrimination claims. Complaints of discrimination in violation of CADA are addressed in the first instance by the Colorado Civil Rights Division. The Division investigates each claim; and if it finds probable cause that CADA has been violated, it will refer the matter to the Colorado Civil Rights Commission. The Commission, in turn, decides whether to initiate a formal hearing before a state Administrative Law Judge (ALJ), who will hear evidence and argument before issuing a written decision. The decision of the ALJ may be appealed to the full Commission, a seven-member appointed body. The Commission holds a public hearing and deliberative session before voting on the case. If the Commission determines that the evidence proves a CADA violation, it may impose remedial measures as provided by statute. . . .

C

Craig and Mullins filed a discrimination complaint against Masterpiece Cakeshop and Phillips in September 2012, shortly after the couple's visit to the shop. The complaint alleged that Craig and Mullins had been denied "full and equal service" at the bakery because of their sexual orientation, and that it was Phillips' "standard business practice" not to provide cakes for same-sex weddings.

The Civil Rights Division opened an investigation. The investigator found that "on multiple occasions," Phillips "turned away potential customers on the basis of their sexual orientation. . . . The investigation found that Phillips had declined to sell custom wedding cakes to about six other same-sex couples on this basis . . . . Based on these findings, the Division found probable cause that Phillips violated CADA and referred the case to the Civil Rights Commission.

The Commission found it proper to conduct a formal hearing, and it sent the case to a State ALJ. Finding no dispute as to material facts, the ALJ entertained cross-motions for summary judgment and ruled in the couple's favor. . . .

Phillips raised two constitutional claims before the ALJ. He first asserted that applying CADA in a way that would require him to create a cake for a same-sex wedding would violate his First Amendment right to free speech by compelling him to exercise his artistic talents to express a message with which he disagreed. The ALJ rejected the contention that preparing a wedding cake is a form of protected speech and did not agree that creating Craig and Mullins' cake would force Phillips to adhere to "an ideological point of view." Applying CADA to the facts at hand, in the ALJ's view, did not interfere with Phillips' freedom of speech.

Phillips also contended that requiring him to create cakes for same-sex weddings would violate his right to the free exercise of religion, also protected by the First Amendment. Citing this Court's precedent in *Employment Div., Dept. of Human Resources of Ore. v. Smith*, the ALJ determined that CADA is a "valid and neutral law of general applicability" and therefore that applying it to Phillips in this case did not violate the Free Exercise Clause. The ALJ thus ruled against Phillips and the cakeshop and in favor of Craig and Mullins on both constitutional claims.

The Commission affirmed the ALJ's decision in full. . . .

Phillips appealed to the Colorado Court of Appeals, which affirmed the Commission's legal determinations and remedial order. . . . Relying on this Court's precedent in *Smith*, the court stated that the Free Exercise Clause "does not relieve an individual of the obligation to comply with a valid and neutral law of general applicability" on the ground that following the law would interfere with religious practice or belief. court concluded that requiring Phillips to comply with the statute did not violate his free exercise rights. The Colorado Supreme Court declined to hear the case.

Phillips sought review here, and this Court granted certiorari. He now renews his claims under the Free Speech and Free Exercise Clauses of the First Amendment.

II

A

Our society has come to the recognition that gay persons and gay couples cannot be treated as social outcasts or as inferior in dignity and worth. For that reason the laws and the Constitution can, and in some instances must, protect them in the exercise of their civil rights. The exercise of their freedom on terms equal to others must be given great weight and respect by the courts. At the same time, the religious and philosophical objections to gay marriage are protected views and in some instances protected forms of expression. . . . Nevertheless, while those religious and philosophical objections are protected, it is a general rule that such objections do not allow business owners and other actors in the economy and in society to deny protected persons equal access to goods and services under a neutral and generally applicable public accommodations law. *See* Newman v. Piggie Park Enterprises, Inc., 390 U.S. 400, 402, n. 5 (1968) (*per curiam*). . . .

When it comes to weddings, it can be assumed that a member of the clergy who objects to gay marriage on moral and religious grounds could not be compelled to perform the ceremony without denial of his or her right to the free exercise of religion. This refusal would be well understood in our constitutional order as an exercise of religion, an exercise that gay persons could recognize and accept without serious diminishment to their own dignity and worth. Yet if that exception were not confined, then a long list of persons who provide goods and services for marriages and weddings might refuse to do so for gay persons, thus resulting in a community-wide stigma inconsistent with the history and dynamics of civil rights laws that ensure equal access to goods, services, and public accommodations. . . .

At the time, state law also afforded storekeepers some latitude to decline to create specific messages the storekeeper considered offensive. Indeed, while enforcement proceedings against Phillips were ongoing, the Colorado Civil Rights Division itself endorsed this proposition in cases involving other bakers' creation of cakes, concluding on at least three occasions that a baker acted lawfully in declining to create cakes with decorations that demeaned gay persons or gay marriages. *See* Jack v. Gateaux, Ltd., Charge No. P20140071X (Mar. 24, 2015); Jack v. Le Bakery Sensual, Inc., Charge No. P20140070X (Mar. 24, 2015); Jack v. Azucar Bakery, Charge No. P20140069X (Mar. 24, 2015). . . .

B

The neutral and respectful consideration to which Phillips was entitled was compromised here, however. The Civil Rights Commission's treatment of his case has some elements of a clear and impermissible hostility toward the sincere religious beliefs that motivated his objection.

That hostility surfaced at the Commission's formal, public hearings, as shown by the record. On May 30, 2014, the seven-member Commission convened publicly to consider Phillips' case. At several points during its meeting, commissioners endorsed the view that religious beliefs cannot legitimately be carried into the public sphere or commercial domain, implying that religious beliefs and persons are less than fully welcome in Colorado's business community. One commissioner suggested that Phillips can believe "what he wants to believe," but cannot act on his religious beliefs "if he decides to do business in the state." A few moments later, the commissioner restated the same position: "[I]f a businessman wants to do business in the state and he's got an issue with the—the law's impacting his personal belief system, he needs to look at being able to compromise." Standing alone, these statements are susceptible of different interpretations. On the one hand, they might mean simply that a business cannot refuse to provide services based on sexual orientation, regardless of the proprietor's personal views. On the other hand, they might be seen as inappropriate and dismissive comments showing lack of due consideration for Phillips' free exercise rights and the dilemma he faced. In view of the comments that followed, the latter seems the more likely.

On July 25, 2014, the Commission met again. This meeting, too, was conducted in public and on the record. On this occasion another commissioner made specific reference to the previous meeting's discussion but said far more to disparage Phillips' beliefs. The commissioner stated:

> "I would also like to reiterate what we said in the hearing or the last meeting. Freedom of religion and religion has been used to justify all kinds of discrimination throughout history, whether it be slavery, whether it be the holocaust, whether it be—I mean, we—we can list hundreds of situations where freedom of religion has been used to justify discrimination. And to me it is one of the most despicable pieces of rhetoric that people can use to—to use their religion to hurt others."

To describe a man's faith as "one of the most despicable pieces of rhetoric that people can use" is to disparage his religion in at least two distinct ways: by describing it as despicable, and also by characterizing it as merely rhetorical—something insubstantial and even insincere. The commissioner even went so far as to compare Phillips' invocation of his sincerely held religious beliefs to defenses of slavery and the Holocaust. This sentiment is inappropriate for a Commission charged with the solemn responsibility of fair and neutral enforcement of Colorado's antidiscrimination law—a law that protects against discrimination on the basis of religion as well as sexual orientation.

The record shows no objection to these comments from other commissioners. And the later state-court ruling reviewing the Commission's decision did not mention those comments, much less express concern with their content. Nor were the comments by the commissioners disavowed in the briefs filed in this Court. For these reasons, the Court cannot avoid the conclusion that these statements cast doubt on the fairness and impartiality of the Commission's adjudication of Phillips' case. Members of the Court have disagreed on the question whether statements made by lawmakers may properly be taken into account in determining whether a law intentionally discriminates on the basis of religion. In this case, however, the remarks were made in a very different context—by an adjudicatory body deciding a particular case.

Another indication of hostility is the difference in treatment between Phillips' case and the cases of other bakers who objected to a requested cake on the basis of conscience and prevailed before the Commission.

As noted above, on at least three other occasions the Civil Rights Division considered the refusal of bakers to create cakes with images that conveyed disapproval of same-sex marriage, along with religious text. Each time, the Division found that the baker acted lawfully in refusing service. It made these determinations because, in the words of the Division, the requested cake included "wording and images [the baker] deemed derogatory," Jack v. Gateaux, Ltd., Charge No. P20140071X, at 4; featured "language and images [the baker] deemed hateful," Jack v. Le Bakery Sensual, Inc., Charge No. P20140070X, at 4; or displayed a message the baker "deemed as discriminatory, Jack v. Azucar Bakery, Charge No. P20140069X, at 4.

> The treatment of the conscience-based objections at issue in these three cases contrasts with the Commission's treatment of Phillips' objection. The Commission ruled against Phillips in part on the theory that any message the requested wedding cake would carry would be attributed to the customer,

> not to the baker. Yet the Division did not address this point in any of the other cases with respect to the cakes depicting anti-gay marriage symbolism. Additionally, the Division found no violation of CADA in the other cases in part because each bakery was willing to sell other products, including those depicting Christian themes, to the prospective customers. But the Commission dismissed Phillips' willingness to sell "birthday cakes, shower cakes, [and] cookies and brownies," to gay and lesbian customers as irrelevant. . . .

For the reasons just described, the Commission's treatment of Phillips' case violated the State's duty under the First Amendment not to base laws or regulations on hostility to a religion or religious viewpoint. . . .

III

The Commission's hostility was inconsistent with the First Amendment's guarantee that our laws be applied in a manner that is neutral toward religion. Phillips was entitled to a neutral decisionmaker who would give full and fair consideration to his religious objection as he sought to assert it in all of the circumstances in which this case was presented, considered, and decided. . . .

The outcome of cases like this in other circumstances must await further elaboration in the courts, all in the context of recognizing that these disputes must be resolved with tolerance, without undue disrespect to sincere religious beliefs, and without subjecting gay persons to indignities when they seek goods and services in an open market.

The judgment of the Colorado Court of Appeals is reversed.

It is so ordered.

Justice KAGAN, with whom Justice BREYER joins, concurring.

. . . What makes the state agencies' consideration yet more disquieting is that a proper basis for distinguishing the cases was available—in fact, was obvious. The Colorado Anti–Discrimination Act (CADA) makes it unlawful for a place of public accommodation to deny "the full and equal enjoyment" of goods and services to individuals based on certain characteristics, including sexual orientation and creed. Colo. Rev. Stat. § 24–34–601(2)(a) (2017). The three bakers in the Jack cases did not violate that law. Jack requested them to make a cake (one denigrating gay people and same-sex marriage) that they would not have made for any customer. In refusing that request, the bakers did not single out Jack because of his religion, but instead treated him in the same way they would have treated anyone else—just as CADA requires. By contrast, the same-sex couple in this case requested a wedding cake that Phillips would have made for an opposite-sex couple. In refusing that request, Phillips contravened CADA's demand that customers receive "the full and equal enjoyment" of public accommodations irrespective of their sexual orientation. The different outcomes in the Jack cases and the Phillips case could thus have been justified by a plain reading and neutral application of Colorado law—untainted by any bias against a religious belief. . . .

Justice GORSUCH, with whom Justice ALITO joins, concurring.

In *Employment Div., Dept. of Human Resources of Ore. v. Smith*, this Court held that a neutral and generally applicable law will usually survive a constitutional free exercise challenge. *Smith* remains controversial in many quarters. But we know this with certainty: when the government fails to act neutrally toward the free exercise of religion, it tends to run into trouble. Then the government can prevail only if it satisfies strict scrutiny, showing that its restrictions on religion both serve a compelling interest and are narrowly tailored.

Today's decision respects these principles. As the Court explains, the Colorado Civil Rights Commission failed to act neutrally toward Jack Phillips's religious faith. . . .

[Justice THOMAS's concurring opinion, with whom Justice GORSUCH joins, is omitted.]

Justice GINSBURG, with whom Justice SOTOMAYOR joins, dissenting.

. . . The Court concludes that "Phillips' religious objection was not considered with the neutrality that the Free Exercise Clause requires." This conclusion rests on evidence said to show the Colorado Civil Rights Commission's (Commission) hostility to religion. Hostility is discernible, the Court maintains, from the asserted "disparate consideration of Phillips' case compared to the cases of" three other bakers who refused to make cakes requested by William Jack, an *amicus* here. The Court also finds hostility in statements made at two public hearings on Phillips' appeal to the Commission. The different outcomes the Court features do not evidence hostility to religion of the kind we have previously held to signal a free-exercise violation, nor do the comments by one or two members of one of the four decisionmaking entities considering this case justify reversing the judgment below.

. . . [T]he Colorado Court of Appeals' "difference in treatment of these two instances [was not] based on the government's own assessment of offensiveness." Phillips declined to make a cake he found offensive where the offensiveness of the product was determined solely by the identity of the customer requesting it. The three other bakeries declined to make cakes where their objection to the product was due to the demeaning message the requested product would literally display. As the Court recognizes, a refusal "to design a special cake with words or images . . . might be different from a refusal to sell any cake at all." The Colorado Court of Appeals did not distinguish Phillips and the other three bakeries based simply on its or the Division's finding that messages in the cakes Jack requested were offensive while any message in a cake for Craig and Mullins was not. The Colorado court distinguished the cases on the ground that Craig and Mullins were denied service based on an aspect of their identity that the State chose to grant vigorous protection from discrimination. I do not read the Court to suggest that the Colorado Legislature's decision to include certain protected characteristics in CADA is an impermissible government prescription of what is and is not offensive. . . .

Statements made at the Commission's public hearings on Phillips' case provide no firmer support for the Court's holding today. Whatever one may think of the statements in historical context, I see no reason why the comments of one or two Commissioners should be taken to overcome Phillips' refusal to sell a wedding cake to Craig and Mullins. The proceedings involved several layers of independent decisionmaking, of which the Commission was but one. First, the Division had to find probable cause that Phillips violated CADA. Second, the ALJ entertained the parties' cross-motions for summary judgment. Third, the Commission heard

Phillips' appeal. Fourth, after the Commission's ruling, the Colorado Court of Appeals considered the case *de novo.* What prejudice infected the determinations of the adjudicators in the case before and after the Commission? The Court does not say. . . .

NOTES AND QUESTIONS

1. *Neutrality and hostility.* Even if the public accommodations law itself is neutral and generally applicable, it must also be applied with neutrality. The majority identified two pieces of evidence in support of its conclusion that the adjudication of Masterpiece Cakeshop Ltd's claims were instead marred by hostility. First, it pointed to comments made by two Commissioners. Second, it found that the commission treated Masterpiece Cakeshop Ltd's refusal to bake a cake for a same-sex wedding differently than three other bakeries' refusal to add anti-gay images and Bible verses on cakes for William Jack.
2. *Comments.* Do you agree that the comments made by the two Commissioners are evidence of hostility towards religion? Is it hostility to religion to acknowledge that places of public accommodation should abide by the law, and that religion has in fact been used to justify discrimination in the past? What about labelling the bakery's claim that it has a right to discriminate as a "despicable piece[] of rhetoric"? Does the Commissioner oppose the claim because it is religious, or because it is discriminatory? Does it matter?
3. *Lawmaking body vs. adjudicatory body.* The majority acknowledges that the stray comments of one or two lawmakers are not necessarily evidence that a law is discriminatory, but argues that the Commissioners' comments are evidence that a decision-making process was discriminatory. Why the different treatment?
4. *Wedding cakes vs. anti-gay cakes.* Whose explanation for the different treatment of the bakery refusals (Masterpiece declining to bake a wedding cake for same sex couple compared to three bakeries declining to bake an anti-gay cake for William Jack) is more accurate, the majority or dissent?
5. *Unresolved issues.* Note that the decision never does decide the question of whether bakeries have a right under the Free Exercise Clause or the Free Speech Clause to an exemption from Colorado's anti-discrimination laws. Instead, it a decision that depends on particular facts unlikely to be repeated. Was the Court trying to dodge the issue?

Fulton v. City of Philadelphia

141 S. Ct. 1294 (2021)

Chief Justice ROBERTS delivered the opinion of the Court.

Catholic Social Services is a foster care agency in Philadelphia. The City stopped referring children to CSS upon discovering that the agency would not certify same-sex couples to be foster parents due to its religious beliefs about marriage.

The City will renew its foster care contract with CSS only if the agency agrees to certify same-sex couples. The question presented is whether the actions of Philadelphia violate the First Amendment.

I

The Catholic Church has served the needy children of Philadelphia for over two centuries. . . .

The Philadelphia foster care system depends on cooperation between the City and private foster agencies like CSS. When children cannot remain in their homes, the City's Department of Human Services assumes custody of them. The Department enters standard annual contracts with private foster agencies to place some of those children with foster families.

The placement process begins with review of prospective foster families. Pennsylvania law gives the authority to certify foster families to state-licensed foster agencies like CSS. Before certifying a family, an agency must conduct a home study during which it considers statutory criteria including the family's "ability to provide care, nurturing and supervision to children," "[e]xisting family relationships," and ability "to work in partnership" with a foster agency. The agency must decide whether to "approve, disapprove or provisionally approve the foster family."

When the Department seeks to place a child with a foster family, it sends its contracted agencies a request, known as a referral. The agencies report whether any of their certified families are available, and the Department places the child with what it regards as the most suitable family. The agency continues to support the family throughout the placement.

The religious views of CSS inform its work in this system. CSS believes that "marriage is a sacred bond between a man and a woman." Because the agency understands the certification of prospective foster families to be an endorsement of their relationships, it will not certify unmarried couples—regardless of their sexual orientation—or same-sex married couples. CSS does not object to certifying gay or lesbian individuals as single foster parents or to placing gay and lesbian children. No same-sex couple has ever sought certification from CSS. If one did, CSS would direct the couple to one of the more than 20 other agencies in the City, all of which currently certify same-sex couples. For over 50 years, CSS successfully contracted with the City to provide foster care services while holding to these beliefs.

But things changed in 2018. After receiving a complaint about a different agency, a newspaper ran a story in which a spokesman for the Archdiocese of Philadelphia stated that CSS would not be able to consider prospective foster parents in same-sex marriages. The City Council called for an investigation, saying that the City had "laws in place to protect its people from discrimination that occurs under the guise of religious freedom." The Philadelphia Commission on Human Relations launched an inquiry. And the Commissioner of the Department of Human Services held a meeting with the leadership of CSS. She remarked that "things have changed since 100 years ago," and "it would be great if we followed the teachings of Pope Francis, the voice of the Catholic Church." Immediately after the meeting, the Department informed CSS that it would no longer refer children to the agency. The City later explained that the refusal of CSS to certify same-sex couples violated a non-discrimination provision in its contract with the City as well as the non-discrimination requirements of the citywide Fair Practices Ordinance. The City stated that it would not enter a full foster care contract with CSS in the future unless the agency agreed to certify same-sex couples.

CSS and three foster parents affiliated with the agency filed suit against the City, the Department, and the Commission. . . . The District Court denied preliminary relief. It concluded that the contractual non-discrimination requirement and the Fair Practices Ordinance were neutral and generally applicable under *Employment Division, Department of Human Resources of Oregon v. Smith* . . . . The Court of Appeals for the Third Circuit affirmed. Because the contract between the parties had expired, the court focused on whether the City could insist on the inclusion of new language forbidding discrimination on the basis of sexual orientation as a condition of contract renewal. The court concluded that the proposed contractual terms were a neutral and generally applicable policy under Smith. CSS and the foster parents sought review. They challenged the Third Circuit's determination that the City's actions were permissible under Smith and also asked this Court to reconsider that precedent.

We granted certiorari.

II

A

The Free Exercise Clause of the First Amendment, applicable to the States under the Fourteenth Amendment, provides that "Congress shall make no law . . . prohibiting the free exercise" of religion. As an initial matter, it is plain that the City's actions have burdened CSS's religious exercise by putting it to the choice of curtailing its mission or approving relationships inconsistent with its beliefs. The City disagrees. In its view, certification reflects only that foster parents satisfy the statutory criteria, not that the agency endorses their relationships. But CSS believes that certification is tantamount to endorsement. And "religious beliefs need not be acceptable, logical, consistent, or comprehensible to others in order to merit First Amendment protection." Our task is to decide whether the burden the City has placed on the religious exercise of CSS is constitutionally permissible.

Smith held that laws incidentally burdening religion are ordinarily not subject to strict scrutiny under the Free Exercise Clause so long as they are neutral and generally applicable. CSS urges us to overrule Smith, and the [Alito & Gorsuch] concurrences in the judgment argue in favor of doing so. But we need not revisit that decision here. This case falls outside Smith because the City has burdened the religious exercise of CSS through policies that do not meet the requirement of being neutral and generally applicable.

Government fails to act neutrally when it proceeds in a manner intolerant of religious beliefs or restricts practices because of their religious nature. *See Masterpiece Cakeshop, Ltd. v. Colorado Civil Rights Comm'n.* CSS points to evidence in the record that it believes demonstrates that the City has transgressed this neutrality standard, but we find it more straightforward to resolve this case under the rubric of general applicability.

A law is not generally applicable if it "invite[s]" the government to consider the particular reasons for a person's conduct by providing "'a mechanism for individualized exemptions.'" For example, in *Sherbert v. Verner*, a Seventh-day Adventist was fired because she would not work on Saturdays. Unable to find a job that would allow her to keep the Sabbath as her faith required, she applied for unemployment benefits. The State denied her application under a law prohibiting eligibility to claimants who had "failed, without good cause . . . to accept available suitable work." We held that the denial infringed her free exercise rights and could be justified only by a compelling interest.

Smith later explained that the unemployment benefits law in Sherbert was not generally applicable because the "good cause" standard permitted the government to grant exemptions based on the circumstances underlying each application. Smith went on to hold that "where the State has in place a system of individual exemptions, it may not refuse to extend that system to cases of 'religious hardship' without compelling reason."

A law also lacks general applicability if it prohibits religious conduct while permitting secular conduct that undermines the government's asserted interests in a similar way. In *Church of Lukumi Babalu Aye, Inc. v. Hialeah*, for instance, the City of Hialeah adopted several ordinances prohibiting animal sacrifice, a practice of the Santeria faith. The City claimed that the ordinances were necessary in part to protect public health, which was "threatened by the disposal of animal carcasses in open public places." But the ordinances did not regulate hunters' disposal of their kills or improper garbage disposal by restaurants, both of which posed a similar hazard. The Court concluded that this and other forms of underinclusiveness meant that the ordinances were not generally applicable.

B

The City initially argued that CSS's practice violated section 3.21 of its standard foster care contract. We conclude, however, that this provision is not generally applicable as required by Smith. The current version of section 3.21 specifies in pertinent part:

> "Rejection of Referral. Provider shall not reject a child or family including, but not limited to, . . . prospective foster or adoptive parents, for Services based upon . . . their . . . sexual orientation . . . unless an exception is granted by the Commissioner or the Commissioner's designee, in his/her sole discretion." . . .

Like the good cause provision in Sherbert, section 3.21 incorporates a system of individual exemptions, made available in this case at the "sole discretion" of the Commissioner. The City has made clear that the Commissioner "has no intention of granting an exception" to CSS. But the City "may not refuse to extend that [exemption] system to cases of 'religious hardship' without compelling reason."

The City and intervenor-respondents resist this conclusion on several grounds. They first argue that governments should enjoy greater leeway under the Free Exercise Clause when setting rules for contractors than when regulating the general public. The government, they observe, commands heightened powers when managing its internal operations. And when individuals enter into government employment or contracts, they accept certain restrictions on their freedom as part of the deal. Given this context, the City and intervenor-respondents contend, the government should have a freer hand when dealing with contractors like CSS.

These considerations cannot save the City here. As Philadelphia rightly acknowledges, "principles of neutrality and general applicability still constrain the government in its capacity as manager." We have never suggested that the government may discriminate against religion when acting in its managerial role. . . .

The City and intervenor-respondents add that, notwithstanding the system of exceptions in section 3.21, a separate provision in the contract independently prohibits discrimination in the certification of foster parents. That provision, section 15.1, bars discrimination on the basis of sexual orientation, and it does not on its face allow for exceptions. But state law makes clear that "one part of a contract cannot be so interpreted as to annul another part." Applying that "fundamental" rule here, an exception from section 3.21 also must govern the prohibition in section 15.1, lest the City's reservation of the authority to grant such an exception be a nullity. As a result, the contract as a whole contains no generally applicable non-discrimination requirement.

Finally, the City and intervenor-respondents contend that the availability of exceptions under section 3.21 is irrelevant because the Commissioner has never granted one. That misapprehends the issue. The creation of a formal mechanism for granting exceptions renders a policy not generally applicable, regardless whether any exceptions have been given, because it "invite[s]" the government to decide which reasons for not complying with the policy are worthy of solicitude—here, at the Commissioner's "sole discretion."

. . .

C

In addition to relying on the contract, the City argues that CSS's refusal to certify same-sex couples constitutes an "Unlawful Public Accommodations Practice[ ]" in violation of the Fair Practices Ordinance. . . . The City contends that foster care agencies are public accommodations and therefore forbidden from discriminating on the basis of sexual orientation when certifying foster parents. . . .

We conclude . . . foster care agencies do not act as public accommodations in performing certifications. . . . Certification as a foster parent . . . is not readily accessible to the public. It involves a customized and selective assessment that bears little resemblance to staying in a hotel, eating at a restaurant, or riding a bus. The process takes three to six months. . . . All of this confirms that the one-size-fits-all public accommodations model is a poor match for the foster care system. . . . We therefore have no need to assess whether the ordinance is generally applicable.

III

. . . CSS has demonstrated that the City's actions are subject to "the most rigorous of scrutiny" under those precedents. Because the City's actions are therefore examined under the strictest scrutiny regardless of Smith, we have no occasion to reconsider that decision here.

A government policy can survive strict scrutiny only if it advances "interests of the highest order" and is narrowly tailored to achieve those interests. Put another way, so long as the government can achieve its interests in a manner that does not burden religion, it must do so.

The City asserts that its non-discrimination policies serve three compelling interests: maximizing the number of foster parents, protecting the City from liability, and ensuring equal treatment of prospective foster parents and foster children. The City states these objectives at a high level of generality, but the First Amendment demands a more precise analysis. Rather than rely on "broadly formulated interests," courts must "scrutinize[ ] the asserted harm of granting specific exemptions to particular religious claimants." The question, then, is not whether the City has a compelling interest in enforcing its non-discrimination policies generally, but whether it has such an interest in denying an exception to CSS.

Once properly narrowed, the City's asserted interests are insufficient. Maximizing the number of foster families and minimizing liability are important goals, but the City fails to show that granting CSS an exception will put those goals at risk. If anything, including CSS in the program seems likely to increase, not reduce, the number of available foster parents. . . .

That leaves the interest of the City in the equal treatment of prospective foster parents and foster children. We do not doubt that this interest is a weighty one, for "[o]ur society has come to the recognition that gay persons and gay couples cannot be treated as social outcasts or as inferior in dignity and worth." On the facts of this case, however, this interest cannot justify denying CSS an exception for its religious exercise. The creation of a system of exceptions under the contract undermines the City's contention that its non-discrimination policies can brook no departures. The City offers no compelling reason why it has a particular interest in denying an exception to CSS while making them available to others.

* * *

. . . The refusal of Philadelphia to contract with CSS for the provision of foster care services unless it agrees to certify same-sex couples as foster parents cannot survive strict scrutiny, and violates the First Amendment.

Justice BARRETT, with whom Justice KAVANAUGH joins, and with whom Justice BREYER joins as to all but the first paragraph, concurring.

In *Employment Div., Dept. of Human Resources of Ore. v. Smith*, this Court held that a neutral and generally applicable law typically does not violate the Free Exercise Clause—no matter how severely that law burdens religious exercise. Petitioners, their amici, scholars, and Justices of this Court have made serious arguments that *Smith* ought to be overruled. While history looms large in this debate, I find the historical record more silent than supportive on the question whether the founding generation understood the First Amendment to require religious exemptions from generally applicable laws in at least some circumstances. In my view, the textual and structural arguments against *Smith* are more compelling. As a matter of text and structure, it is difficult to see why the Free Exercise Clause—lone among the First Amendment freedoms—offers nothing more than protection from discrimination.

Yet what should replace *Smith?* The prevailing assumption seems to be that strict scrutiny would apply whenever a neutral and generally applicable law burdens religious exercise. But I am skeptical about swapping *Smith's* categorical antidiscrimination approach for an equally categorical strict scrutiny regime, particularly when this Court's resolution of conflicts between generally applicable laws and other First Amendment rights—like speech and assembly—has been much more nuanced. There would be a number of issues to work through if *Smith* were overruled. To name a few: Should entities like Catholic Social Services—which is an arm of the Catholic Church—be treated differently than individuals? *Cf. Hosanna-Tabor Evangelical Lutheran Church and School v. EEOC.* Should there be a distinction between indirect and direct burdens on religious exercise? *Cf. Braunfeld v. Brown.* What forms of scrutiny should apply? Compare *Sherbert v. Verner* (assessing whether government's interest is " 'compelling' ") with *Gillette v. United States* (assessing whether government's interest is "substantial"). And if the answer is strict scrutiny, would pre-*Smith* cases rejecting free exercise challenges to garden-variety laws come out the same way?

We need not wrestle with these questions in this case, though, because the same standard applies regardless whether *Smith* stays or goes. . . . I therefore see no reason to decide in this case whether *Smith* should be overruled, much less what should replace it. I join the Court's opinion in full.

Justice ALITO, with whom Justice THOMAS and Justice GORSUCH join, concurring in the judgment.

This case presents an important constitutional question that urgently calls out for review: whether this Court's governing interpretation of a bedrock constitutional right, the right to the free exercise of religion, is fundamentally wrong and should be corrected.

In *Employment Div., Dept. of Human Resources of Ore. v. Smith* (1990), the Court abruptly pushed aside nearly 30 years of precedent and held that the First Amendment's Free Exercise Clause tolerates any rule that categorically prohibits or commands specified conduct so long as it does not target religious practice. Even if a rule serves no important purpose and has a devastating effect on religious freedom, the Constitution, according to *Smith,* provides no protection. This severe holding is ripe for reexamination.

I

There is no question that *Smith's* interpretation can have startling consequences. Here are a few examples. Suppose that the Volstead Act, which implemented the Prohibition Amendment, had not contained an exception for sacramental wine. The Act would have been consistent with *Smith* even though it would have prevented the celebration of a Catholic Mass anywhere in the United States. Or suppose that a State, following the example of several European countries, made it unlawful to slaughter an animal that had not first been rendered unconscious. That law would be fine under *Smith* even though it would outlaw kosher and halal slaughter. . . . Or suppose that this Court or some other court enforced a rigid rule prohibiting attorneys from wearing any form of head covering in court. The rule would satisfy *Smith* even though it would prevent Orthodox Jewish men, Sikh men, and many Muslim women from appearing. Many other examples could be added.

We may hope that legislators and others with rulemaking authority will not go as far as *Smith* allows, but the present case shows that the dangers posed by *Smith* are not hypothetical. The city of Philadelphia (City) has issued an ultimatum to an arm of the Catholic Church: Either engage in conduct that the Church views as contrary to the traditional Christian understanding of marriage or abandon a mission that dates back to the earliest days of the Church—providing for the care of orphaned and abandoned children. . . .

This decision might as well be written on the dissolving paper sold in magic shops. The City has been adamant about pressuring CSS to give in, and if the City wants to get around today's decision, it can simply eliminate the never-used exemption power. If it does that, then, voilà, today's decision will vanish—and the parties will be back where they started. The City will claim that it is protected by *Smith*; CSS will argue that *Smith* should be overruled; the lower courts, bound by *Smith*, will reject that argument; and CSS will file a new petition in this Court challenging *Smith*. What is the point of going around in this circle?

We should reconsider *Smith* without further delay. The correct interpretation of the Free Exercise Clause is a question of great importance, and *Smith's* interpretation is hard to defend. It can't be squared with the ordinary meaning of the text of the Free Exercise Clause or with the prevalent understanding of the scope of the free-exercise right at the time of the First Amendment's adoption. It swept aside decades of established precedent, and it has not aged well. Its interpretation has been undermined by subsequent scholarship on the original meaning of the Free Exercise Clause. Contrary to what many initially expected, *Smith* has not provided a clear-cut rule that is easy to apply, and experience has disproved the Smith majority's fear that retention of the Court's prior free-exercise jurisprudence would lead to "anarchy."

It is high time for us to take a fresh look at what the Free Exercise Clause demands. . . .

II

Smith was wrongly decided. As long as it remains on the books, it threatens a fundamental freedom. And while precedent should not lightly be cast aside, the Court's error in *Smith* should now be corrected. . . .

VI

If *Smith* is overruled, what legal standard should be applied in this case? The answer that comes most readily to mind is the standard that *Smith* replaced: A law that imposes a substantial burden on religious exercise can be sustained only if it is narrowly tailored to serve a compelling government interest. . . .

CSS's policy has only one effect: It expresses the idea that same-sex couples should not be foster parents because only a man and a woman should marry. Many people today find this idea not only objectionable but hurtful. Nevertheless, protecting against this form of harm is not an interest that can justify the abridgment of First Amendment rights.

We have covered this ground repeatedly in free speech cases. In an open, pluralistic, self-governing society, the expression of an idea cannot be suppressed simply because some find it offensive, insulting, or even wounding. . . .

The same fundamental principle applies to religious practices that give offense. The preservation of religious freedom depends on that principle. Many core religious beliefs are perceived as hateful by members of other religions or nonbelievers. Proclaiming that there is only one God is offensive to polytheists, and saying that there are many gods is anathema to Jews, Christians, and Muslims. . . .

Suppressing speech—or religious practice—simply because it expresses an idea that some find hurtful is a zero-sum game. While CSS's ideas about marriage are likely to be objectionable to same-sex couples, lumping those who hold traditional beliefs about marriage together with racial bigots is insulting to those who retain such beliefs. In *Obergefell v. Hodges* (2015), the majority made a commitment. It refused to equate traditional beliefs about marriage, which it termed "decent and honorable," with racism, which is neither. And it promised that "religions, and those who adhere to religious doctrines, may continue to advocate with utmost, sincere conviction that, by divine precepts, same-sex marriage should not be condoned." An open society can keep that promise while still respecting the "dignity," "worth," and fundamental equality of all members of the community. . . .

After receiving more than 2,500 pages of briefing and after more than a half-year of post-argument cogitation, the Court has emitted a wisp of a decision that leaves religious liberty in a confused and vulnerable state. Those who count on this Court to stand up for the First Amendment have every right to be disappointed—as am I.

Justice GORSUCH, with whom Justice THOMAS and Justice ALITO join, concurring in the judgment.

The Court granted certiorari to decide whether to overrule *Employment Div., Dept. of Human Resources of Ore. v. Smith* (1990). . . . A majority of our colleagues, however, seek to sidestep the question. . . . On the surface it may seem a nice move, but dig an inch deep and problems emerge. . . .

The majority ignores the FPO's expansive definition of "public accommodations." It ignores the reason the district court offered for why CSS falls within that definition. Instead, it asks us to look to a different public accommodations law—a Commonwealth of Pennsylvania public accommodations statute. And, the majority promises, CSS fails to qualify as a public accommodation under the terms of that law. But why should we ignore the City's law and look to the Commonwealth's? No one knows because the majority doesn't say. . . .

The majority's gloss on state law isn't just novel, it's probably wrong. While the statute lists hotels, restaurants, and swimming pools as examples of public accommodations, it also lists over 40 other kinds of institutions—and the statute emphasizes that these examples are illustrative, not exhaustive. . . .

Still that's not the end of it. Even now, the majority's circumnavigation of Smith remains only half complete. The City argues that, in addition to the FPO, another generally applicable nondiscrimination rule can be found in § 15.1 of its contract with CSS. That provision independently instructs that foster service providers "shall not discriminate or permit discrimination against any individual on the basis of . . . sexual orientation." This provision, the City contends, amounts to a second and separate rule of general applicability exempt from First Amendment scrutiny under Smith. Once more, the majority must find some way around the problem. Its attempt to do so proceeds in three steps.

First, the majority directs our attention to another provision of the contract—§ 3.21. Entitled "Rejection of Referral," this provision prohibits discrimination based on sexual orientation, race, religion, or other grounds "unless an exception is granted" in the government's "sole discretion." Clearly, the majority says, that provision doesn't state a generally applicable rule against discrimination because it expressly contemplates "exceptions."

But how does that help? As § 3.21's title indicates, the provision contemplates exceptions only when it comes to the referral stage of the foster process—where the government seeks to place a particular child with an available foster family. So, for example, the City has taken race into account when placing a child who "used racial slurs" to avoid placing him with parents "of that race." Meanwhile, our case has nothing to do with the referral—or placement—stage of the foster process. This case concerns the recruitment and certification stages—where foster agencies like CSS screen and enroll adults who wish to serve as foster parents. And in those stages of the foster process, § 15.1 seems to prohibit discrimination absolutely.

That difficulty leads the majority to its second step. It asks us to ignore § 3.21's title and its limited application to the referral stage. Instead, the majority suggests, we should reconceive § 3.21 as authorizing exceptions to the City's nondiscrimination rule at every stage of the foster process. . . .

This sets up the majority's final move—where the real magic happens. . . . To avoid nullifying § 3.21's reservation of discretion, the majority insists, it has no choice but to rewrite § 15.1. All so that—voila—§ 15.1 now contains its own parallel reservation of discretion. As rewritten, the contract contains no generally applicable rule against discrimination anywhere in the foster process.

From start to finish, it is a dizzying series of maneuvers. . . . Given all the maneuvering, it's hard not to wonder if the majority is so anxious to say nothing about *Smith's* fate that it is willing to say pretty much anything about municipal law and the parties' briefs. One way or another, the majority seems determined to declare there is no "need" or "reason" to revisit *Smith* today. . . .

It's not as if we don't know the right answer. *Smith* has been criticized since the day it was decided. No fewer than ten Justices—including six sitting Justices—have questioned its fidelity to the Constitution. . . .

We hardly need to "wrestle" today with every conceivable question that might follow from recognizing *Smith* was wrong. (Barrett, J., concurring). To be sure, any time this Court turns from misguided precedent back toward the Constitution's original public meaning, challenging questions may arise across a large field of cases and controversies. But that's no excuse for refusing to apply the original public meaning in the dispute actually before us. Rather than adhere to *Smith* until we settle on some "grand unified theory" of the Free Exercise Clause for all future cases until the end of time, the Court should overrule it now, set us back on the correct course, and address each case as it comes.

. . . *Smith* committed a constitutional error. Only we can fix it. Dodging the question today guarantees it will recur tomorrow. These cases will keep coming until the Court musters the fortitude to supply an answer. Respectfully, it should have done so today.

NOTES AND QUESTIONS

1. *Generally applicable.* The Court held that Philadelphia's regulation was not generally applicable because it allowed for individualized exemptions. In particular, the Commissioner had discretion to grant exemptions, even if the Commissioner had never exercised this power. Do you think this is a fair reading of the statute? Or are you persuaded by Justice Gorsuch's claim that the outcome was the result of multiple maneuvers?
2. *Strict scrutiny: Harm.* Does the Court concede that eliminating discrimination against same-sex couples is a compelling government interest? Justice Alito suggests that the only harm of Catholic Social Services' policy is giving offense. Do you agree?
3. *Strict scrutiny: Tailoring.* If advancing a compelling government interest, why isn't a regulation banning discrimination against same-sex couples narrowly tailored? Is it because no same-sex couple has ever been turned away by Catholic Social Services? If so, would it matter if the reason no one has asked is because they know they will be turned away? Is it because the couple can simply go to another agency? In that case, would a religious foster care agency opposed to mixed race marriages also be entitled to an exemption from a regulation banning discrimination on the basis of race, since such a couple may also simply go to another social service organization?
4. *Government contracts.* The *Fulton* ruling means that as long as Philadelphia partners with private agencies in providing foster care, the city does not have the right to refuse to contract with and fund religious organizations that discriminate. Should the rules be the same when Philadelphia is deciding how to spend its own money? Should the Free Exercise Clause protect a religious organization's right to discriminate with taxpayer monies?
5. *Religious harms.* Justice Alito warns of the harms of the *Smith* regime. Are his predictions likely to occur? Have they? In what ways is banning a Jewish man or Muslim woman from wearing head covering in court similar to or different from banning a government-funded religious social service organization from discriminating?
6. Smith. One of the questions presented in *Fulton* is whether the Supreme Court should overrule *Smith* and its neutral and generally applicable standard. Over the strenuous objections of Justices Alito, Gorsuch, and Thomas, the majority held that it did not need to reach the question. Justice Barrett also seems inclined to eliminate *Smith*, but is not certain what ought to replace it. Should the Court have decided the question? What do you think should be the test for deciding whether religious objectors are entitled to a Free Exercise Clause exemption?

AN EXTENDED NOTE ON SINCERITY

To the extent that the Free Exercise Clause require accommodations for laws that substantially burden religious beliefs, that protection extends to sincere religious beliefs, not fraudulent ones. Courts are often reluctant to judge sincerity, however, because they fear that they will end up judging the validity or plausibility of the belief rather than the believer's sincerity. This risk is particularly high when confronted with the unfamiliar religious beliefs of less familiar religions, such as a Native American belief that the government's use of a social security number might harm a person's spirit. Bowen v. Roy, 476 U.S. 693 (1986).

However, without some inquiry into sincerity, objectors could recast a political belief as a religious one or otherwise claim a religious opposition to any law they dislike. Someone who wishes to indulge in illegal drugs may claim their use a religious necessity. While on the Tenth Circuit, Judge Gorsuch upheld a district court's conclusion that defendants to a marijuana charge did not sincerely believe marijuana was a sacrament and essential to their Church of the Cognizance but were deploying religious belief as a cover for their secular drug dealing. United States v. Quaintance, 608 F.3d 717, 723 (10th Cir. 2010). Someone who opposes mandatory vaccines for ideological reasons may claim that their idiosyncratic religious belief bans them. When Vermont eliminated its philosophical exemptions for mandatory vaccines, for example, requests for religious exemptions increased from .5% to 3.7%. Joshua T. B. Williams et al., *Religious Vaccine Exemptions in Kindergartners: 2011-2018*, 144 Pediatrics (2019).

Unquestioning acceptance that a religious belief is sincere might also facilitate fraud, a charge litigated in United States v. Ballard, 322 U.S. 78 (1944). In the case, Guy, Edna, and Donald Ballard had been convicted of using the mail system to defraud followers. The Ballards had created the I Am movement, where they claimed, among other things, that they were divine messengers for ascended masters such as Saint Germain, and that, according to their criminal indictment, they had "by reason of supernatural attainments, the power to heal persons of ailments and diseases and to make well persons afflicted with any diseases, injuries, or ailments. . . . Each of the representations enumerated in the indictment was followed by the charge that respondents 'well knew' it was false. . . ."

Justice Douglas, writing for the *Ballard* majority, held that the federal fraud statutes may be applied with respect to the Ballards' subjective beliefs; accordingly, a jury may inquire into whether the Ballards subjectively believed the tenets of the "I Am" religion. However, a jury may not inquire into whether those tenets are objectively true. "[W]e do not agree that the truth or verity of respondents' religious doctrines or beliefs should have been submitted to the jury. Whatever this particular indictment might require, the First Amendment precludes such a course, as the United States seems to concede. 'The law knows no heresy, and is committed to the support of no dogma, the establishment of no sect.' Watson v. Jones, 13 Wall. 679, 728. . . . Men may believe what they cannot prove. They may not be put to the proof of their religious doctrines or beliefs. Religious experiences which are as real as life to some may be incomprehensible to others. Yet the fact that they may be beyond the ken of mortals does not mean that they can be made suspect before the law. . . . The religious views espoused by respondents might seem incredible, if not preposterous, to most people. But if those doctrines are subject to trial before a jury charged with finding their truth or falsity, then the same can be done with the religious beliefs of any sect."

In dissent, Justice Jackson protested, noting that "as a matter of either practice or philosophy I do not see how we can separate an issue as to what is believed from considerations as to what is believable. The most convincing proof that one believes his statements is to show that they have been true in his experience. Likewise, that one knowingly falsified is best proved by showing that what he said happened never did happen. How can the Government prove these persons knew something to be false which it cannot prove to be false? If we try religious sincerity severed from religious verity, we isolate the dispute from the very considerations which in common experience provide its most reliable answer. . . ."

NOTES AND QUESTIONS

1. *Evaluating sincerity.* How does a court determine whether someone is sincere or not? For those seeking to avoid work on Saturday, one could look to whether their religion has a Saturday Sabbath or whether they regularly observe it. But not everyone belongs to a familiar religion or necessarily agrees with all its tenets.
2. *Belief versus believability.* Is it possible to distinguish between the plausibility of religious beliefs and whether a person subjectively believes the doctrine to be true? The Church of I Am certainly maintained some highly improbable doctrines. Should the Free Exercise Clause be read to prohibit prosecutions of the sort at issue in *Ballard,* as de facto efforts to regulate religious beliefs?
3. *Just another kind of fraud?* On the other hand, if someone makes a false representation to extract money, why should the criminal law turn a blind eye because the representation happened to relate to the medical healing powers of a sacred amulet, rather than a pill or potion?

Chapter 15

Free Exercise of Religion: Funding

Table of Contents

A. Play in the Joints

B. Discrimination Against Religion

At one point, the main constitutional question about government funding of religious organizations was whether such funding violated the Establishment Clause. *See* Chapter 20. More recently, the main constitutional question is often whether the refusal to fund religious organizations amounts to a Free Exercise Clause violation. At first, the answer to this question was generally no: although the government could not impede religious exercise, it was under no obligation to help fund it. On the contrary, government funding of religious organizations raised serious Establishment Clause concerns. Moreover, there was play in the joints between the two religion clauses: even when the Establishment Clause did not require limits, the government could advance Establishment Clause values without violating the Free Exercise Clause. *Locke v. Davey* (2004).

More recently, free exercise doctrine has increasingly moved toward the rule that religious organizations have an equal right to participate in government funding opportunities and that to deny them that opportunity amounts to discrimination against religion.

A. *PLAY IN THE JOINTS*

Locke v. Davey

540 U.S. 712 (2004)

Chief Justice Rehnquist delivered the opinion of the Court.

The State of Washington established the Promise Scholarship Program to assist academically gifted students with postsecondary education expenses. In accordance with the State Constitution, students may not use the scholarship at an institution where they are pursuing a degree in devotional theology. We hold that such an exclusion from an otherwise inclusive aid program does not violate the Free Exercise Clause of the First Amendment.

The Washington State Legislature found that "[s]tudents who work hard . . . and successfully complete high school with high academic marks may not have the financial ability to attend college because they cannot obtain financial aid or the financial aid is insufficient." Wash. Rev. Code Ann. § 28B.119.005 (West Supp. 2004). In 1999, to assist these high-achieving students, the legislature created the Promise Scholarship Program, which provides a scholarship, renewable for one year, to eligible students for postsecondary education expenses. . . .

To be eligible for the scholarship, a student must meet academic, income, and enrollment requirements. . . . [T]he student must enroll "at least half time in an eligible postsecondary institution in the state of Washington," and may not pursue a degree in theology at that institution while receiving the scholarship. Private institutions, including those religiously affiliated, qualify as " '[e]ligible postsecondary institution[s]' " if they are accredited by a nationally recognized accrediting body. A "degree in theology" is not defined in the statute, but, as both parties concede, the statute simply codifies the State's constitutional prohibition on providing funds to students to pursue degrees that are "devotional in nature or designed to induce religious faith.". . .

Respondent, Joshua Davey, was awarded a Promise Scholarship, and chose to attend Northwest College. Northwest is a private, Christian college affiliated with the Assemblies of God denomination, and is an eligible institution under the Promise Scholarship Program. . . .

At the beginning of the 1999–2000 academic year, Davey met with Northwest's director of financial aid. He learned for the first time at this meeting that he could not use his scholarship to pursue a devotional theology degree. . . .

Davey then brought an action. . . . He argued the denial of his scholarship based on his decision to pursue a theology degree violated, inter alia, the Free Exercise.

The Religion Clauses of the First Amendment provide: "Congress shall make no law respecting an establishment of religion, or prohibiting the free exercise thereof." These two Clauses, the Establishment Clause and the Free Exercise Clause, are frequently in tension. Yet we have long said that "there is room for play in the joints" between them. In other words, there are some state actions permitted by the Establishment Clause but not required by the Free Exercise Clause.

This case involves that "play in the joints" described above. Under our Establishment Clause precedent, the link between government funds and religious training is broken by the independent and private choice of recipients. *See* Zelman v. Simmons–Harris, 536 U.S. 639, 652 (2002). As such, there is no doubt that the State could, consistent with the Federal Constitution, permit Promise Scholars to pursue a degree in devotional theology, and the State does not contend otherwise. The question before us, however, is whether Washington, pursuant to its own constitution, which has been authoritatively interpreted as prohibiting even indirectly funding religious instruction that will prepare students for the ministry, can deny them such funding without violating the Free Exercise Clause.

Davey urges us to answer that question in the negative. He contends that under the rule we enunciated in *Church of Lukumi Babalu Aye, Inc. v. Hialeah*, the program is presumptively unconstitutional because it is not facially neutral with respect to religion. We reject his claim of presumptive unconstitutionality, however; to do otherwise would extend the *Lukumi* line of cases well beyond not only their facts but their reasoning. In *Lukumi*, the city of Hialeah made it a crime to engage in certain kinds of animal slaughter. We found that the law sought to suppress ritualistic animal sacrifices of the Santeria religion. In the present case, the State's disfavor of religion (if it can be called that) is of a far milder kind. It imposes neither criminal nor civil sanctions on any type of religious service or rite. . . . The State has merely chosen not to fund a distinct category of instruction.

Justice Scalia argues, however, that generally available benefits are part of the "baseline against which burdens on religion are measured." Because the Promise Scholarship Program funds training for all secular professions, Justice Scalia contends the State must also fund training for religious professions. But training for religious professions and training for secular professions are not fungible. Training someone to lead a congregation is an essentially religious endeavor. Indeed, majoring in devotional theology is akin to a religious calling as well as an academic pursuit. . . .

Even though the differently worded Washington Constitution draws a more stringent line than that drawn by the United States Constitution, the interest it seeks to further is scarcely novel. In fact, we can think of few areas in which a State's antiestablishment interests come more into play. Since the founding of our country, there have been popular uprisings against procuring taxpayer funds to support church leaders, which was one of the hallmarks of an "established" religion. . . .

Most States that sought to avoid an establishment of religion around the time of the founding placed in their constitutions formal prohibitions against using tax funds to support the ministry. E.g., . . . Pa. Const., Art. II (1776), in 5 id., at 3082 ("[N]o man ought or of right can be compelled to attend any religious worship, or erect or support any place of worship, or maintain any ministry, contrary to, or against, his own free will and consent"); N.J. Const., Art. XVIII (1776), in id., at 2597 (similar); Del. Const., Art. I, § 1 (1792), in 1 id., at 568 (similar); Ky. Const., Art. XII, § 3 (1792), in 3 id., at 1274 (similar); Vt. Const., Ch. I, Art. 3 (1793), in 6 id., at 3762 (similar); Tenn. Const., Art. XI, § 3 (1796), in id., at 3422 (similar); Ohio Const., Art. VIII, § 3 (1802), in 5 id., at 2910 (similar). The plain text of these constitutional provisions prohibited any tax dollars from supporting the clergy. We have found nothing to indicate, as Justice Scalia contends, that these provisions would not have applied so long as the State equally supported other professions or if the amount at stake was de minimis. That early state constitutions saw no problem in explicitly excluding only the ministry from receiving state dollars reinforces our conclusion that religious instruction is of a different ilk.

Far from evincing the hostility toward religion which was manifest in *Lukumi*, we believe that the entirety of the Promise Scholarship Program goes a long way toward including religion in its benefits. The program permits students to attend pervasively religious schools, so long as they are accredited. . . . And under the Promise Scholarship Program's current guidelines, students are still eligible to take devotional theology courses. . . .

In short, we find neither in the history or text of Article I, § 11, of the Washington Constitution, nor in the operation of the Promise Scholarship Program, anything that suggests animus toward religion. Given the historic and substantial state interest at issue, we therefore cannot conclude that the denial of funding for vocational religious instruction alone is inherently constitutionally suspect.

Without a presumption of unconstitutionality, Davey's claim must fail. The State's interest in not funding the pursuit of devotional degrees is substantial and the exclusion of such funding places a relatively minor burden on Promise Scholars. If any room exists between the two Religion Clauses, it must be here. We need not venture further into this difficult area in order to uphold the Promise Scholarship Program as currently operated by the State of Washington.

The judgment of the Court of Appeals is therefore Reversed.

Justice SCALIA, with whom Justice THOMAS joins, dissenting. . . .

When the State makes a public benefit generally available, that benefit becomes part of the baseline against which burdens on religion are measured; and when the State withholds that benefit from some individuals solely on the basis of religion, it violates the Free Exercise Clause no less than if it had imposed a special tax.

That is precisely what the State of Washington has done here. It has created a generally available public benefit, whose receipt is conditioned only on academic performance, income, and attendance at an accredited school. It has then carved out a solitary course of study for exclusion: theology. No field of study but religion is singled out for disfavor in this fashion. Davey is not asking for a special benefit to which others are not entitled. He seeks only equal treatment—the right to direct his scholarship to his chosen course of study, a right every other Promise Scholar enjoys. . . .

[Justice THOMAS's dissenting opinion is omitted].

NOTES AND QUESTIONS

1. *Play in the joints.* The Court explains that there is "play in the joints" between the two religion clauses. The government may accommodate religion even when not required by the Free Exercise Clause—without violating the Establishment Clause. The government may also promote separation of church and state even when not required by the Establishment Clause—without violating the Free Exercise Clause. Providing religious exemptions from neutral and generally applicable laws even if not mandated by the Free Exercise Clause is an example of the former. Washington's Promise Scholarship Program, which denies state money to students training for the ministry, is an example of the latter.
2. *Indirect funding.* The *Locke* Court argues that the Promise Scholarship Program would not violate the Establishment Clause even for students majoring in devotional theological because the choice to spend it on training for

the ministry would be attributable to the student rather than the government. As a result, the government did not fund the religious activity, the private individual did. *Zelman v. Simmons-Harris*, see Chapter 20, established the rule that the genuine and independent choice of private individuals in how to spend their vouchers or scholarships breaks the chain of causation.

3. *Animus towards religion.* According to the majority, Washington refuses to fund religious training not because it bears ill will toward religion, but because of the "historic and substantial state interest" against using tax dollars to support religious leaders, "one of the hallmarks of an 'established' religion." Do you think it would have come to the same conclusion if the scholarship program did not also allow students to take devotional theology classes and attend pervasively sectarian schools?

B. DISCRIMINATION AGAINST RELIGION

Trinity Lutheran Church of Columbia, Inc. v. Comer

137 S. Ct. 2012 (2017)

Chief Justice ROBERTS delivered the opinion of the Court, except as to footnote 3.

The Missouri Department of Natural Resources offers state grants to help public and private schools, nonprofit daycare centers, and other nonprofit entities purchase rubber playground surfaces made from recycled tires. Trinity Lutheran Church applied for such a grant for its preschool and daycare center and would have received one, but for the fact that Trinity Lutheran is a church. The Department had a policy of categorically disqualifying churches and other religious organizations from receiving grants under its playground resurfacing program. The question presented is whether the Department's policy violated the rights of Trinity Lutheran under the Free Exercise Clause of the First Amendment.

I

. . . Due to limited resources, the Department cannot offer grants to all applicants and so awards them on a competitive basis to those scoring highest based on several criteria, such as the poverty level of the population in the surrounding area and the applicant's plan to promote recycling. When the Center applied, the Department had a strict and express policy of denying grants to any applicant owned or controlled by a church, sect, or other religious entity. That policy, in the Department's view, was compelled by Article I, Section 7 of the Missouri Constitution, which provides:

> "That no money shall ever be taken from the public treasury, directly or indirectly, in aid of any church, sect or denomination of religion, or in aid of any priest, preacher, minister or teacher thereof, as such; and that no preference shall be given to nor any discrimination made against any church, sect or creed of religion, or any form of religious faith or worship."

The Center ranked fifth among the 44 applicants in the 2012 Scrap Tire Program. But despite its high score, the Center was deemed categorically ineligible to receive a grant. In a letter rejecting the Center's application, the program director explained that, under Article I, Section 7 of the Missouri Constitution, the Department could not provide financial assistance directly to a church.

The Department ultimately awarded 14 grants as part of the 2012 program. Because the Center was operated by Trinity Lutheran Church, it did not receive a grant.

II

The First Amendment provides, in part, that "Congress shall make no law respecting an establishment of religion, or prohibiting the free exercise thereof." The parties agree that the Establishment Clause of that Amendment does not prevent Missouri from including Trinity Lutheran in the Scrap Tire Program. That does not, however, answer the question under the Free Exercise Clause, because we have recognized that there is "play in the joints" between what the Establishment Clause permits and the Free Exercise Clause compels. *Locke.*

The Free Exercise Clause "protect[s] religious observers against unequal treatment" and subjects to the strictest scrutiny laws that target the religious for "special disabilities" based on their "religious status." *Church of Lukumi Babalu Aye, Inc. v. Hialeah.* Applying that basic principle, this Court has repeatedly confirmed that denying a generally available benefit solely on account of religious identity imposes a penalty on the free exercise of religion that can be justified only by a state interest "of the highest order." . . .

III

A

The Department's policy expressly discriminates against otherwise eligible recipients by disqualifying them from a public benefit solely because of their religious character. . . . [S]uch a policy imposes a penalty on the free exercise of religion that triggers the most exacting scrutiny. *Lukumi.* This conclusion is unremarkable in light of our prior decisions.

. . . [T]he Department's policy puts Trinity Lutheran to a choice: It may participate in an otherwise available benefit program or remain a religious institution. . . .

The Department contends that merely declining to extend funds to Trinity Lutheran does not prohibit the Church from engaging in any religious conduct or otherwise exercising its religious rights. In this sense, says the Department, its policy is unlike the ordinances struck down in *Lukumi,* which outlawed rituals central to Santeria. Here the Department has simply declined to allocate to Trinity Lutheran a subsidy the State had no obligation to provide in the first place. That decision does not meaningfully burden the Church's free exercise rights. And absent any such burden, the argument continues, the Department is free to heed the State's antiestablishment objection to providing funds directly to a church.

It is true the Department has not criminalized the way Trinity Lutheran worships or told the Church that it cannot subscribe to a certain view of the Gospel.

But, as the Department itself acknowledges, the Free Exercise Clause protects against "indirect coercion or penalties on the free exercise of religion, not just outright prohibitions." . . .

Trinity Lutheran is not claiming any entitlement to a subsidy. It instead asserts a right to participate in a government benefit program without having to disavow its religious character. . . . The express discrimination against religious exercise here is not the denial of a grant, but rather the refusal to allow the Church—solely because it is a church—to compete with secular organizations for a grant. . . . Trinity Lutheran is a member of the community too, and the State's decision to exclude it for purposes of this public program must withstand the strictest scrutiny.

B

The Department attempts to get out from under the weight of our precedents by arguing that the free exercise question in this case is instead controlled by our decision in *Locke v. Davey*. It is not. In *Locke*, the State of Washington created a scholarship program to assist high-achieving students with the costs of postsecondary education. The scholarships were paid out of the State's general fund, and eligibility was based on criteria such as an applicant's score on college admission tests and family income. While scholarship recipients were free to use the money at accredited religious and non-religious schools alike, they were not permitted to use the funds to pursue a devotional theology degree—one "devotional in nature or designed to induce religious faith." Davey was selected for a scholarship but was denied the funds when he refused to certify that he would not use them toward a devotional degree. He sued, arguing that the State's refusal to allow its scholarship money to go toward such degrees violated his free exercise rights. . . .

According to the Court, the State had "merely chosen not to fund a distinct category of instruction." Davey was not denied a scholarship because of who he was; he was denied a scholarship because of what he proposed to do—use the funds to prepare for the ministry. Here there is no question that Trinity Lutheran was denied a grant simply because of what it is—a church.

The Court in *Locke* . . . stated that Washington's choice was in keeping with the State's antiestablishment interest in not using taxpayer funds to pay for the training of clergy; in fact, the Court could "think of few areas in which a State's antiestablishment interests come more into play." The claimant in *Locke* sought funding for an "essentially religious endeavor . . . akin to a religious calling as well as an academic pursuit," and opposition to such funding "to support church leaders" lay at the historic core of the Religion Clauses. Here nothing of the sort can be said about a program to use recycled tires to resurface playgrounds.

Relying on *Locke*, the Department nonetheless emphasizes Missouri's similar constitutional tradition of not furnishing taxpayer money directly to churches. But *Locke* took account of Washington's antiestablishment interest only after determining, as noted, that the scholarship program did not "require students to choose between their religious beliefs and receiving a government benefit." As the Court put it, Washington's scholarship program went "a long way toward including religion in its benefits." Students in the program were free to use their scholarships at "pervasively religious schools." Davey could use his scholarship to pursue a secular degree at one institution while studying devotional theology at another. He could also use his scholarship money to attend a religious college and take devotional theology courses there. The only thing he could not do was use the scholarship to pursue a degree in that subject.

In this case, there is no dispute that Trinity Lutheran is put to the choice between being a church and receiving a government benefit. The rule is simple: No churches need apply.[3]

C

The State in this case expressly requires Trinity Lutheran to renounce its religious character in order to participate in an otherwise generally available public benefit program, for which it is fully qualified. Our cases make clear that such a condition imposes a penalty on the free exercise of religion that must be subjected to the "most rigorous" scrutiny.

Under that stringent standard, only a state interest "of the highest order" can justify the Department's discriminatory policy. Yet the Department offers nothing more than Missouri's policy preference for skating as far as possible from religious establishment concerns. In the face of the clear infringement on free exercise before us, that interest cannot qualify as compelling. As we said when considering Missouri's same policy preference on a prior occasion, "the state interest asserted here—in achieving greater separation of church and State than is already ensured under the Establishment Clause of the Federal Constitution—is limited by the Free Exercise Clause."

The State has pursued its preferred policy to the point of expressly denying a qualified religious entity a public benefit solely because of its religious character. Under our precedents, that goes too far. The Department's policy violates the Free Exercise Clause.

Nearly 200 years ago, a legislator urged the Maryland Assembly to adopt a bill that would end the State's disqualification of Jews from public office: . . . [T]he result of the State's policy is nothing so dramatic as the denial of political office. The consequence is, in all likelihood, a few extra scraped knees. But the exclusion of Trinity Lutheran from a public benefit for which it is otherwise qualified, solely because it is a church, is odious to our Constitution all the same, and cannot stand.

The judgment of the United States Court of Appeals for the Eighth Circuit is reversed, and the case is remanded for further proceedings consistent with this opinion.

It is so ordered.

[Justice Thomas's concurring in part opinion, with whom Justice Gorsuch joins, is omitted.]

Justice Gorsuch, with whom Justice Thomas joins, concurring in part.

3. This case involves express discrimination based on religious identity with respect to playground resurfacing. We do not address religious uses of funding or other forms of discrimination.

Missouri's law bars Trinity Lutheran from participating in a public benefits program only because it is a church. I agree this violates the First Amendment and I am pleased to join nearly all of the Court's opinion. I offer only two modest qualifications.

First, the Court leaves open the possibility a useful distinction might be drawn between laws that discriminate on the basis of religious status and religious use. Respectfully, I harbor doubts about the stability of such a line. Does a religious man say grace before dinner? Or does a man begin his meal in a religious manner? Is it a religious group that built the playground? Or did a group build the playground so it might be used to advance a religious mission? The distinction blurs in much the same way the line between acts and omissions can blur when stared at too long. . . .

Second and for similar reasons, I am unable to join the footnoted observation, n. 3, that "[t]his case involves express discrimination based on religious identity with respect to playground resurfacing." Of course the footnote is entirely correct, but I worry that some might mistakenly read it to suggest that only "playground resurfacing" cases, or only those with some association with children's safety or health, or perhaps some other social good we find sufficiently worthy, are governed by the legal rules recounted in and faithfully applied by the Court's opinion. . . .

Justice BREYER, concurring in the judgment.

. . . The Court stated in Everson that "cutting off church schools from" such "general government services as ordinary police and fire protection . . . is obviously not the purpose of the First Amendment." Here, the State would cut Trinity Lutheran off from participation in a general program designed to secure or to improve the health and safety of children. I see no significant difference. . . .

Justice SOTOMAYOR, with whom Justice GINSBURG joins, dissenting.

To hear the Court tell it, this is a simple case about recycling tires to resurface a playground. The stakes are higher. This case is about nothing less than the relationship between religious institutions and the civil government—that is, between church and state. The Court today profoundly changes that relationship by holding, for the first time, that the Constitution requires the government to provide public funds directly to a church. Its decision slights both our precedents and our history, and its reasoning weakens this country's longstanding commitment to a separation of church and state beneficial to both.

I

Founded in 1922, Trinity Lutheran Church (Church) "operates . . . for the express purpose of carrying out the commission of . . . Jesus Christ as directed to His church on earth." . . . The Learning Center serves as "a ministry of the Church and incorporates daily religion and developmentally appropriate activities into . . . [its] program." . . . The Learning Center's facilities include a playground, the unlikely source of this dispute. . . .

II

Properly understood then, this is a case about whether Missouri can decline to fund improvements to the facilities the Church uses to practice and spread its religious views. This Court has repeatedly warned that funding of exactly this kind—payments from the government to a house of worship—would cross the line drawn by the Establishment Clause. So it is surprising that the Court mentions the Establishment Clause only to note the parties' agreement that it "does not prevent Missouri from including Trinity Lutheran in the Scrap Tire Program." Constitutional questions are decided by this Court, not the parties' concessions. The Establishment Clause does not allow Missouri to grant the Church's funding request because the Church uses the Learning Center, including its playground, in conjunction with its religious mission. . . .

The government may not directly fund religious exercise. . . . Put in doctrinal terms, such funding violates the Establishment Clause because it impermissibly "advanc[es] . . . religion." *Agostini v. Felton.*

Nowhere is this rule more clearly implicated than when funds flow directly from the public treasury to a house of worship. . . .

True, this Court has found some direct government funding of religious institutions to be consistent with the Establishment Clause. But the funding in those cases came with assurances that public funds would not be used for religious activity, despite the religious nature of the institution. The Church has not and cannot provide such assurances here. . . . The Church has a religious mission, one that it pursues through the Learning Center. The playground surface cannot be confined to secular use any more than lumber used to frame the Church's walls, glass stained and used to form its windows, or nails used to build its altar.

The Court may simply disagree with this account of the facts and think that the Church does not put its playground to religious use. If so, its mistake is limited to this case. But if it agrees that the State's funding would further religious activity and sees no Establishment Clause problem, then it must be implicitly applying a rule other than the one agreed to in our precedents.

III

Even assuming the absence of an Establishment Clause violation and proceeding on the Court's preferred front—the Free Exercise Clause—the Court errs. It claims that the government may not draw lines based on an entity's religious "status." But we have repeatedly said that it can. When confronted with government action that draws such a line, we have carefully considered whether the interests embodied in the Religion Clauses justify that line. The question here is thus whether those interests support the line drawn in Missouri's Article I, § 7, separating the State's treasury from those of houses of worship. They unquestionably do.

A

The Establishment Clause prohibits laws "respecting an establishment of religion" and the Free Exercise Clause prohibits laws "prohibiting the free exercise thereof." U.S. Const. Amdt. 1. "[I]f expanded to a logical extreme," these prohibitions "would tend to clash with the other." Even in the absence of a violation of one of the Religion Clauses, the interaction of government and religion can raise concerns that sound in both Clauses. For that reason, the government may sometimes act to accommodate those concerns, even when not required to do so by the Free

Exercise Clause, without violating the Establishment Clause. And the government may sometimes act to accommodate those concerns, even when not required to do so by the Establishment Clause, without violating the Free Exercise Clause. . . .

B

Missouri has decided that the unique status of houses of worship requires a special rule when it comes to public funds. Its Constitution reflects that choice and provides:

> "That no money shall ever be taken from the public treasury, directly or indirectly, in aid of any church, sect, or denomination of religion, or in aid of any priest, preacher, minister or teacher thereof, as such; and that no preference shall be given to nor any discrimination made against any church, sect or creed of religion, or any form of religious faith or worship." Art. I, § 7.

Missouri's decision, which has deep roots in our Nation's history, reflects a reasonable and constitutional judgment.

. . . This Nation's early experience with, and eventual rejection of, established religion—shorthand for "sponsorship, financial support, and active involvement of the sovereign in religious activity,"—defies easy summary. . . .

Those who fought to end the public funding of religion based their opposition on a powerful set of arguments, all stemming from the basic premise that the practice harmed both civil government and religion. The civil government, they maintained, could claim no authority over religious belief. For them, support for religion compelled by the State marked an overstep of authority that would only lead to more. Equally troubling, it risked divisiveness by giving religions reason to compete for the State's beneficence. Faith, they believed, was a personal matter, entirely between an individual and his god. Religion was best served when sects reached out on the basis of their tenets alone, unsullied by outside forces, allowing adherents to come to their faith voluntarily. Over and over, these arguments gained acceptance and led to the end of state laws exacting payment for the support of religion.

Take Virginia. After the Revolution, Virginia debated and rejected a general religious assessment. The proposed bill would have allowed taxpayers to direct payments to a Christian church of their choice to support a minister, exempted "Quakers and Menonists," and sent undirected assessments to the public treasury for "seminaries of learning." A Bill Establishing a Provision for Teachers of the Christian Religion, reprinted in Everson.

In opposing this proposal, James Madison authored his famous Memorial and Remonstrance, in which he condemned the bill as hostile to religious freedom. Memorial and Remonstrance Against Religious Assessments (1785). . . . Religion had "flourished, not only without the support of human laws, but in spite of every opposition from them." Compelled support for religion, he argued, would only weaken believers' "confidence in its innate excellence," strengthen others' "suspicion that its friends are too conscious of its fallacies to trust in its own merits," and harm the "purity and efficacy" of the supported religion. He ended by deeming the bill incompatible with Virginia's guarantee of " 'free exercise of . . . Religion according to the dictates of conscience.' "

Madison contributed one influential voice to a larger chorus of petitions opposed to the bill. Others included "the religious bodies of Baptists, Presbyterians, and Quakers." T. Buckley, Church and State in Revolutionary Virginia 1776–1787, p. 148 (1977). . . .

The course of this history shows that those who lived under the laws and practices that formed religious establishments made a considered decision that civil government should not fund ministers and their houses of worship. To us, their debates may seem abstract and this history remote. That is only because we live in a society that has long benefited from decisions made in response to these now centuries-old arguments, a society that those not so fortunate fought hard to build.

In *Locke*, this Court expressed an understanding of, and respect for, this history. *Locke* involved a provision of the State of Washington's Constitution that, like Missouri's nearly identical Article I, § 7, barred the use of public funds for houses of worship or ministers. Consistent with this denial of funds to ministers, the State's college scholarship program did not allow funds to be used for devotional theology degrees. When asked whether this violated the would-be minister's free exercise rights, the Court invoked the play in the joints principle and answered no. The Establishment Clause did not require the prohibition because "the link between government funds and religious training [was] broken by the independent and private choice of [scholarship] recipients." Nonetheless, the denial did not violate the Free Exercise Clause because a "historic and substantial state interest" supported the constitutional provision. The Court could "think of few areas in which a State's antiestablishment interests come more into play" than the "procuring [of] taxpayer funds to support church leaders."

The same is true of this case, about directing taxpayer funds to houses of worship, . . . Recall that a state may not fund religious activities without violating the Establishment Clause. A state can reasonably use status as a "house of worship" as a stand-in for "religious activities." Inside a house of worship, dividing the religious from the secular would require intrusive line-drawing by government, and monitoring those lines would entangle government with the house of worship's activities. And so while not every activity a house of worship undertakes will be inseparably linked to religious activity, "the likelihood that many are makes a categorical rule a suitable means to avoid chilling the exercise of religion." Finally, and of course, such funding implicates the free exercise rights of taxpayers by denying them the chance to decide for themselves whether and how to fund religion. If there is any " 'room for play in the joints' between" the Religion Clauses, it is here. *Locke.*

As was true in *Locke*, a prophylactic rule against the use of public funds for houses of worship is a permissible accommodation of these weighty interests. The rule has a historical pedigree identical to that of the provision in *Locke*. . . . Today, thirty-eight States have a counterpart to Missouri's Article I, § 7. The provisions, as a general matter, date back to or before these States' original Constitutions. That so many States have for so long drawn a line that prohibits public funding for houses of worship, based on principles rooted in this Nation's understanding of how best to foster religious liberty, supports the conclusion that public funding of houses of worship "is of a different ilk." *Locke.*

Missouri has recognized the simple truth that, even absent an Establishment Clause violation, the transfer of public funds to houses of worship raises concerns that sit exactly between the Religion Clauses. To avoid those concerns, and only those concerns, it has prohibited such funding. In doing so, it made the same choice made by the earliest States centuries ago and many other States in the years since. The Constitution permits this choice. . . .

But in this area of law, a decision to treat entities differently based on distinctions that the Religion Clauses make relevant does not amount to discrimination. . . . If the denial of a benefit others may receive is discrimination that violates the Free Exercise Clause, then the accommodations of religious entities we have approved would violate the free exercise rights of nonreligious entities. We have, with good reason, rejected that idea. . . .

A State's decision not to fund houses of worship does not disfavor religion; rather, it represents a valid choice to remain secular in the face of serious establishment and free exercise concerns. That does not make the State "atheistic or antireligious." It means only that the State has "establishe[d] neither atheism nor religion as its official creed."

At bottom, the Court creates the following rule today: The government may draw lines on the basis of religious status to grant a benefit to religious persons or entities but it may not draw lines on that basis when doing so would further the interests the Religion Clauses protect in other ways. Nothing supports this lopsided outcome. . . .

In concluding that Missouri's Article I, § 7, cannot withstand strict scrutiny, the Court describes Missouri's interest as a mere "policy preference for skating as far as possible from religious establishment concerns." The constitutional provisions of thirty-nine States—all but invalidated today—the weighty interests they protect, and the history they draw on deserve more than this judicial brush aside.

Today's decision discounts centuries of history and jeopardizes the government's ability to remain secular.

IV

The Court today dismantles a core protection for religious freedom provided in these Clauses. It holds not just that a government may support houses of worship with taxpayer funds, but that—at least in this case and perhaps in others, see n. 3—it must do so whenever it decides to create a funding program. History shows that the Religion Clauses separate the public treasury from religious coffers as one measure to secure the kind of freedom of conscience that benefits both religion and government. If this separation means anything, it means that the government cannot, or at the very least need not, tax its citizens and turn that money over to houses of worship. The Court today blinds itself to the outcome this history requires and leads us instead to a place where separation of church and state is a constitutional slogan, not a constitutional commitment. I dissent.

Espinoza v. Montana Department of Revenue

140 S. Ct. 2246 (2020)

Chief Justice ROBERTS delivered the opinion of the Court. . . .

The Montana Legislature established a program to provide tuition assistance to parents who send their children to private schools. The program grants a tax credit to anyone who donates to certain organizations that in turn award scholarships to selected students attending such schools. When petitioners sought to use the scholarships at a religious school, the Montana Supreme Court struck down the program. The Court relied on the "no-aid" provision of the State Constitution, which prohibits any aid to a school controlled by a "church, sect, or denomination." The question presented is whether the Free Exercise Clause of the United States Constitution barred that application of the no-aid provision.

I

In 2015, the Montana Legislature sought "to provide parental and student choice in education" by enacting a scholarship program for students attending private schools. The program grants a tax credit of up to $150 to any taxpayer who donates to a participating "student scholarship organization." The scholarship organizations then use the donations to award scholarships to children for tuition at a private school.

So far only one scholarship organization, Big Sky Scholarships, has participated in the program. Big Sky focuses on providing scholarships to families who face financial hardship or have children with disabilities.

The Montana Legislature allotted $3 million annually to fund the tax credits, beginning in 2016. If the annual allotment is exhausted, it increases by 10% the following year. . . .

The Montana Legislature also directed that the program be administered in accordance with Article X, section 6, of the Montana Constitution, which contains a "no-aid" provision barring government aid to sectarian schools. *See* Mont. Code Ann. § 15–30–3101. In full, that provision states:

> "Aid prohibited to sectarian schools. . . . The legislature, counties, cities, towns, school districts, and public corporations shall not make any direct or indirect appropriation or payment from any public fund or monies, or any grant of lands or other property for any sectarian purpose or to aid any church, school, academy, seminary, college, university, or other literary or scientific institution, controlled in whole or in part by any church, sect, or denomination." Mont. Const., Art. X, § 6(1).

Shortly after the scholarship program was created, the Montana Department of Revenue promulgated "Rule 1," over the objection of the Montana Attorney General. That administrative rule prohibited families from using scholarships at religious schools. It did so by changing the definition of "qualified education provider" to exclude any school "owned or controlled in whole or in part by any church, religious sect, or denomination." The Department explained that the Rule was needed to reconcile the scholarship program with the no-aid provision of the Montana Constitution.

. . .

This suit was brought by three mothers whose children attend Stillwater Christian School in northwestern Montana. . . .

The trial court enjoined Rule. . . . In December 2018, the Montana Supreme Court reversed the trial court. The Court first addressed the scholarship program unmodified by Rule 1, holding that the program aided religious schools in violation of the no-aid provision of the Montana Constitution. . . . The Montana Supreme Court went on to hold that the violation of the no-aid provision required invalidating the entire scholarship program. . . .

We granted certiorari.

II

The Religion Clauses of the First Amendment provide that "Congress shall make no law respecting an establishment of religion, or prohibiting the free exercise thereof." We have recognized a " 'play in the joints' between what the Establishment Clause permits and the Free Exercise Clause compels." *Trinity Lutheran Church of Columbia, Inc. v. Comer* (2017) (quoting *Locke v. Davey* (2004)). Here, the parties do not dispute that the scholarship program is permissible under the Establishment Clause. Nor could they. We have repeatedly held that the Establishment Clause is not offended when religious observers and organizations benefit from neutral government programs. . . . Any Establishment Clause objection to the scholarship program here is particularly unavailing because the government support makes its way to religious schools only as a result of Montanans independently choosing to spend their scholarships at such schools. . . .

The question for this Court is whether the Free Exercise Clause precluded the Montana Supreme Court from applying Montana's no-aid provision to bar religious schools from the scholarship program. For purposes of answering that question, we accept the Montana Supreme Court's interpretation of state law—including its determination that the scholarship program provided impermissible "aid" within the meaning of the Montana Constitution—and we assess whether excluding religious schools and affected families from that program was consistent with the Federal Constitution. . . .

Most recently, *Trinity Lutheran* distilled these and other decisions to the same effect into the "unremarkable" conclusion that disqualifying otherwise eligible recipients from a public benefit "solely because of their religious character" imposes "a penalty on the free exercise of religion that triggers the most exacting scrutiny." In *Trinity Lutheran*, Missouri provided grants to help nonprofit organizations pay for playground resurfacing, but a state policy disqualified any organization "owned or controlled by a church, sect, or other religious entity." Because of that policy, an otherwise eligible church-owned preschool was denied a grant to resurface its playground. Missouri's policy discriminated against the Church "simply because of what it is—a church," and so the policy was subject to the "strictest scrutiny," which it failed. We acknowledged that the State had not "criminalized" the way in which the Church worshipped or "told the Church that it cannot subscribe to a certain view of the Gospel." But the State's discriminatory policy was "odious to our Constitution all the same."

Here too Montana's no-aid provision bars religious schools from public benefits solely because of the religious character of the schools. . . . The provision plainly excludes schools from government aid solely because of religious status.

The Department counters that *Trinity Lutheran* does not govern here because the no-aid provision applies not because of the religious character of the recipients, but because of how the funds would be used—for "religious education." . . .

This case also turns expressly on religious status and not religious use. The Montana Supreme Court applied the no-aid provision solely by reference to religious status. The Court repeatedly explained that the no-aid provision bars aid to "schools controlled in whole or in part by churches," "sectarian schools," and "religiously-affiliated schools." . . . The Montana Constitution discriminates based on religious status just like the Missouri policy in *Trinity Lutheran*, which excluded organizations "owned or controlled by a church, sect, or other religious entity."

The Department points to some language in the decision below indicating that the no-aid provision has the goal or effect of ensuring that government aid does not end up being used for "sectarian education" or "religious education." The Department also contrasts what it characterizes as the "completely non-religious" benefit of playground resurfacing in *Trinity Lutheran* with the unrestricted tuition aid at issue here. . . .

Regardless, those considerations were not the Montana Supreme Court's basis for applying the no-aid provision to exclude religious schools; that hinged solely on religious status. Status-based discrimination remains status based even if one of its goals or effects is preventing religious organizations from putting aid to religious uses. . . .

Because the Montana Supreme Court applied the no-aid provision to discriminate against schools and parents based on the religious character of the school, the "strictest scrutiny" is required. . . .

The Montana Supreme Court asserted that the no-aid provision serves Montana's interest in separating church and State "more fiercely" than the Federal Constitution. But "that interest cannot qualify as compelling" in the face of the infringement of free exercise here. A State's interest "in achieving greater separation of church and State than is already ensured under the Establishment Clause . . . is limited by the Free Exercise Clause."

The Department, for its part, asserts that the no-aid provision actually promotes religious freedom. In the Department's view, the no-aid provision protects the religious liberty of taxpayers by ensuring that their taxes are not directed to religious organizations, and it safeguards the freedom of religious organizations by keeping the government out of their operations. An infringement of First Amendment rights, however, cannot be justified by a State's alternative view that the infringement advances religious liberty. . . .

A State need not subsidize private education. But once a State decides to do so, it cannot disqualify some private schools solely because they are religious.

III

The Department argues that, at the end of the day, there is no free exercise violation here because the Montana Supreme Court ultimately eliminated the scholarship program altogether. According to the Department, now that there is no program, religious schools and adherents cannot complain that they are excluded from any generally available benefit.

Two dissenters agree. Justice Ginsburg reports that the State of Montana simply chose to "put all private school parents in the same boat" by invalidating the scholarship program, and Justice Sotomayor describes the decision below as resting on state law grounds having nothing to do with the federal Free Exercise Clause.

The descriptions are not accurate. The Montana Legislature created the scholarship program; the Legislature never chose to end it, for policy or other reasons. The program was eliminated by a court, and not based on some innocuous principle of state law. Rather, the Montana Supreme Court invalidated the program pursuant to a state law provision that expressly discriminates on the basis of religious status.

* * *

The judgment of the Montana Supreme Court is reversed, and the case is remanded for further proceedings not inconsistent with this opinion.

It is so ordered.

[Justice THOMAS's concurring opinion, with whom Justice GORSUCH joins, is omitted.]

[Justice ALITO's concurring opinion is omitted.]

[Justice GORSUCH's concurring opinion is omitted].

Justice GINSBURG, with whom Justice KAGAN joins, dissenting. . . .

Petitioners argue that the Montana Supreme Court's decision fails when measured against *Trinity Lutheran*. I do not see how. Past decisions in this area have entailed differential treatment occasioning a burden on a plaintiff's religious exercise. This case is missing that essential component. Recall that the Montana court remedied the state constitutional violation by striking the scholarship program in its entirety. Under that decree, secular and sectarian schools alike are ineligible for benefits, so the decision cannot be said to entail differential treatment based on petitioners' religion. Put somewhat differently, petitioners argue that the Free Exercise Clause requires a State to treat institutions and people neutrally when doling out a benefit—and neutrally is how Montana treats them in the wake of the state court's decision.

Accordingly, the Montana Supreme Court's decision does not place a burden on petitioners' religious exercise. Petitioners may still send their children to a religious school. And the Montana Supreme Court's decision does not pressure them to do otherwise. Unlike the law in *Trinity Lutheran*, the decision below puts petitioners to no "choice": Neither giving up their faith, nor declining to send their children to sectarian schools, would affect their entitlement to scholarship funding. There simply are no scholarship funds to be had. . . .

Justice BREYER, with whom Justice KAGAN joins as to Part I, dissenting.

The First Amendment's Free Exercise Clause guarantees the right to practice one's religion. At the same time, its Establishment Clause forbids government support for religion. Taken together, the Religion Clauses have helped our Nation avoid religiously based discord while securing liberty for those of all faiths. . . .

The Court [in *Locke v. Davey*] observed that the State's decision not to fund devotional degrees did not penalize religious exercise or require anyone to choose between their faith and a "government benefit." Rather, the State had "merely chosen not to fund a distinct category of instruction" that was "essentially religious." Although Washington's Constitution drew "a more stringent line than that drawn by the United States Constitution," the Court found that the State's position was consistent with the widely shared view, dating to the founding of the Republic, that taxpayer-supported religious indoctrination poses a threat to individual liberty. Given this "historic and substantial state interest," the Court concluded, it would be inappropriate to subject Washington's law to a "presumption of unconstitutionality." And, without such a presumption, the claim that the exclusion of devotional studies violated the Free Exercise Clause "must fail," for "[i]f any room exists between the two Religion Clauses, it must be here.". . .

For our purposes it is enough to say that, among those who gave shape to the young Republic were people, including Madison and Jefferson, who perceived a grave threat to individual liberty and communal harmony in tax support for the teaching of religious truths. These "historic and substantial" concerns have consistently guided the Court's application of the Religion Clauses since. . . . The Court's special attention to these views should come as no surprise, for the risks the Founders saw have only become more apparent over time. In the years since the Civil War, the number of religions practiced in our country has grown to scores. And that has made it more difficult to avoid suspicions of favoritism—or worse—when government becomes entangled with religion. . . .

Justice SOTOMAYOR, dissenting.

The majority holds that a Montana scholarship program unlawfully discriminated against religious schools by excluding them from a tax benefit. The threshold problem, however, is that such tax benefits no longer exist for anyone in the State. . . . Not only is the Court wrong to decide this case at all, it decides it wrongly. . . .

I . . .

Neither differential treatment nor coercion exists here because the Montana Supreme Court invalidated the tax-credit program entirely. Because no secondary school (secular or sectarian) is eligible for benefits, the state court's ruling neither treats petitioners differently based on religion nor burdens their religious exercise. Petitioners remain free to send their children to the religious school of their choosing and to exercise their faith.

To be sure, petitioners may want to apply for scholarships and would prefer that Montana subsidize their children's religious education. But this Court had never before held unconstitutional government action that merely failed to benefit religious exercise. "The crucial word in the constitutional text is 'prohibit': 'For the Free Exercise Clause is written in terms of what the government cannot do to the individual, not in terms of what the individual can exact from the government.' " . . .

II

Even on its own terms, the Court's answer to its hypothetical question is incorrect. The Court relies principally on *Trinity Lutheran,* which found that disqualifying an entity from a public benefit "solely because of [the entity's] religious character" could impose "a penalty on the free exercise of religion." . . .

The Court's analysis of Montana's defunct tax program reprises the error in *Trinity Lutheran.* Contra the Court's current approach, our free exercise precedents had long granted the government "some room to recognize the unique status of religious entities and to single them out on that basis for exclusion from otherwise generally applicable laws."

Until *Trinity Lutheran,* the right to exercise one's religion did not include a right to have the State pay for that religious practice. That is because a contrary rule risks reading the Establishment Clause out of the Constitution. . . .

Here, a State may refuse to extend certain aid programs to religious entities when doing so avoids "historic and substantial" antiestablishment concerns. *Locke.* Properly understood, this case is no different from *Locke* because petitioners seek to procure what the plaintiffs in *Locke* could not: taxpayer funds to support religious schooling. . . . Previously, this Court recognized that a "prophylactic rule against the use of public funds" for "religious activities" appropriately balanced the Religion Clauses' differing but equally weighty interests.

The Court maintains that this case differs from *Locke* because no pertinent " 'historic and substantial' " tradition supports Montana's decision. But the Court's historical analysis is incomplete at best. . . .

[A] State's decision not to fund religious activity does not "disfavor religion; rather, it represents a valid choice to remain secular in the face of serious establishment and free exercise concerns." That is, a "legislature's decision not to subsidize the exercise of a fundamental right does not infringe the right."

Finally, it is no answer to say that this case involves "discrimination." A "decision to treat entities differently based on distinctions that the Religion Clauses make relevant does not amount to discrimination." So too here.

* * *

. . . I respectfully dissent.

NOTES AND QUESTIONS

1. *Footnote 3.* Under the Establishment Clause, it is unconstitutional to directly fund religion or religious exercise. One question in *Trinity Lutheran* then, is whether awarding taxpayer dollars to Trinity Lutheran Church & School for its church playground is better characterized as the constitutional funding of a playground, as the majority maintains, or

the unconstitutional funding of church facilities, as the dissent argues. The *Trinity Lutheran* majority took pains in Footnote 3 to emphasize that its decision is limited to funding the resurfacing of a playground, a secular endeavor. Do you agree? Does this limit survive *Espinoza*?

2. *The Establishment Clause and "play in the joints."* The Court held that excluding churches from a grant program and religious schools from a scholarship program amounts to discrimination against religion. What about the government's antiestablishment interests? Are antiestablishment interests "historic and substantial" or are they no more than a policy preferences? Has the Supreme Court, as Justice Sotomayor complained in *Espinoza,* "read[] the Establishment Clause out of the Constitution"? Is the decision not to fund houses of worship and religious schools discrimination against religion or a valid choice to remain secular? What about the "play in the joints" between the two clauses? Does this play in the joints still exist after *Trinity Lutheran* and *Espinoza*?
3. *Differential treatment of religious and secular counterparts.* In *Espinoza,* the Supreme Court of Montana struck down the entire school funding program, so that the government was funding neither secular nor religious private schools. The majority, however, held that, nonetheless, the decision discriminated against religious schools. How so?
4. *Religious school playgrounds compared to religious schools.* The Supreme Court distinguished *Locke* from *Trinity Lutheran* by arguing that the denial of government funding in *Trinity Lutheran* was based on what they are—their status as a religious school—rather than what they do namely, use government funds for religious exercise. Is it possible to separate the religious status of a church from its religious activities? Is the withholding of taxpayer funds in *Espinoza* a denial based on status or usage? How clear and stable is this distinction?
5. *Analogy with the disqualification of Jews.* What do you think of the analogy made in *Trinity Lutheran* between denying a Christian church government funds for its playground and disqualifying Jews from public office?

Chapter 16

Statutory Protection of Religious Liberty

Table of Contents

A. The Religious Freedom Restoration Act (RFRA) and the Religious Land Use and Institutionalized Persons Act (RLUIPA)

B. Cases

A. *THE RELIGIOUS FREEDOM RESTORATION ACT (RFRA) AND THE RELIGIOUS LAND USE AND INSTITUTIONALIZED PERSONS ACT (RLUIPA)*

Smith was an unpopular opinion, and soon after the decision Congress passed, almost unanimously, the Religious Freedom Restoration Act (RFRA), which attempted to restore the *Sherbert* standard to religious liberty claims. As explained in City of Boerne v. Flores, 521 U.S. 507 (1997):

> Congress enacted RFRA in direct response to the Court's decision in Employment Div., Dept. of Human Resources of Ore. v. Smith, 494 U.S. 872 (1990). . . . The application of the *Sherbert* test, the *Smith* decision explained, would have produced an anomaly in the law, a constitutional right to ignore neutral laws of general applicability. The anomaly would have been accentuated, the Court reasoned, by the difficulty of determining whether a particular practice was central to an individual's religion. We explained, moreover, that it "is not within the judicial ken to question the centrality of particular beliefs or practices to a faith, or the validity of particular litigants' interpretations of those creeds." . . .

These points of constitutional interpretation were debated by Members of Congress in hearings and floor debates. Many criticized the Court's reasoning, and this disagreement resulted in the passage of RFRA. Congress announced:

> **"(1)** [T]he framers of the Constitution, recognizing free exercise of religion as an unalienable right, secured its protection in the First Amendment to the Constitution;
>
> **"(2)** laws 'neutral' toward religion may burden religious exercise as surely as laws intended to interfere with religious exercise;
>
> **"(3)** governments should not substantially burden religious exercise without compelling justification;
>
> **"(4)** in Employment Division v. Smith, 494 U.S. 872 (1990), the Supreme Court virtually eliminated the requirement that the government justify burdens on religious exercise imposed by laws neutral toward religion; and
>
> **"(5)** the compelling interest test as set forth in prior Federal court rulings is a workable test for striking sensible balances between religious liberty and competing prior governmental interests." 42 U.S.C. § 2000bb(a).

The Act's stated purposes are:

> **"(1)** to restore the compelling interest test as set forth in Sherbert v. Verner, 374 U.S. 398 (1963) and Wisconsin v. Yoder, 406 U.S. 205 (1972) and to guarantee its application in all cases where free exercise of religion is substantially burdened; and
>
> **"(2)** to provide a claim or defense to persons whose religious exercise is substantially burdened by government." § 2000bb(b).

RFRA prohibits "[g]overnment" from "substantially burden[ing] a person's exercise of religion even if the burden results from a rule of general applicability unless the government can demonstrate the burden "(1) is in furtherance of a compelling governmental interest; and (2) is the least restrictive means of furthering that compelling governmental interest." § 2000bb-1.

By its terms, RFRA "applies to all Federal and State law, and the implementation of that law, whether statutory or otherwise, and whether adopted before or after [RFRA's enactment]." The Supreme Court held in *Boerne* that Congress had exceeded its authority in passing RFRA. Under its Fourteenth Amendment enforcement power, Congress may enact prophylactic laws to "remedy or prevent unconstitutional actions." However, "There must be a congruence and proportionality between the injury to be prevented or remedied and the means adopted to that end. Lacking such a connection, legislation may become substantive in operation and effect." In other words, Congress rather than the Supreme Court would be dictating the substance of the Free Exercise Clause. "Congress' power under § 5, however, extends only to 'enforc[ing]' the provisions of the Fourteenth Amendment. . . . Legislation which alters the meaning of the Free Exercise Clause cannot be said to be enforcing the Clause. Congress does not enforce a constitutional right by changing what the right is. It has been given the power 'to enforce,' not the power to determine what constitutes a constitutional violation." According to the Court, RFRA was not congruent and proportional: "RFRA is so out of proportion to a supposed remedial or preventive object that it cannot be understood as responsive to, or designed to prevent, unconstitutional behavior. It appears, instead, to attempt a substantive change in constitutional protections." As a consequence,

RFRA is unconstitutional as applied to the states. However, as later cases confirmed, including *Gonzales v. O Centro Espirita Beneficente Uniao Do Vegetal* and *Burwell v. Hobby Lobby Stores, Inc.*, RFRA does apply to federal laws. Moreover, since *Boerne*, roughly half of the states have passed their own version of RFRA, and these state RFRAs apply to their state laws.

Congress also enacted the Religious Land Use and Institutionalized Persons Act (RLUIPA). Like RFRA, it reintroduced the *Sherbert* test for religious liberty claims. Unlike RFRA, RLUIPA applies to only two types of cases: those involving land use (such as zoning regulations) and those involving institutionalized persons (such as prisoners). In addition, rather than rely on the Fourteenth Amendment, Congress enacted RLUIPA pursuant to its power to regulate interstate commerce and to condition federal spending.

B. CASES

Gonzales v. O Centro Espírita Beneficente União do Vegetal

546 U.S. 418 (2006)

Chief Justice ROBERTS delivered the opinion of the Court.

A religious sect with origins in the Amazon Rainforest receives communion by drinking a sacramental tea, brewed from plants unique to the region, that contains a hallucinogen regulated under the Controlled Substances Act by the Federal Government. The Government concedes that this practice is a sincere exercise of religion, but nonetheless sought to prohibit the small American branch of the sect from engaging in the practice, on the ground that the Controlled Substances Act bars all use of the hallucinogen. The sect sued to block enforcement against it of the ban on the sacramental tea, and moved for a preliminary injunction. It relied on the Religious Freedom Restoration Act of 1993 . . .

O Centro Espírita Beneficente União do Vegetal (UDV) is a Christian Spiritist sect based in Brazil, with an American branch of approximately 130 individuals. Central to the UDV's faith is receiving communion through hoasca (pronounced "wass-ca"), a sacramental tea made from two plants unique to the Amazon region. One of the plants, psychotria viridis, contains dimethyltryptamine (DMT), a hallucinogen . . . listed in Schedule I of the Controlled Substances Act. . . .

The Government contends that the Act's description of Schedule I substances as having "a high potential for abuse," "no currently accepted medical use in treatment in the United States," and "a lack of accepted safety for use . . . under medical supervision," 21 U.S.C. § 812(b)(1), by itself precludes any consideration of individualized exceptions such as that sought by the UDV. The Government goes on to argue that the regulatory regime established by the Act—a "closed" system that prohibits all use of controlled substances except as authorized by the Act itself—"cannot function with its necessary rigor and comprehensiveness if subjected to judicial exemptions." Brief for Petitioners 18. According to the Government, there would be no way to cabin religious exceptions once recognized, and "the public will misread" such exceptions as signaling that the substance at issue is not harmful after all. *Id.* at 23. Under the Government's view, there is no need to assess the particulars of the UDV's use or weigh the impact of an exemption for that specific use, because the Controlled Substances Act serves a compelling purpose and simply admits of no exceptions.

RFRA, and the strict scrutiny test it adopted, contemplate an inquiry more focused than the Government's categorical approach. . . . Under the more focused inquiry required by RFRA and the compelling interest test, the Government's mere invocation of the general characteristics of Schedule I substances, as set forth in the Controlled Substances Act, cannot carry the day. It is true, of course, that Schedule I substances such as DMT are exceptionally dangerous. Nevertheless, there is no indication that Congress, in classifying DMT, considered the harms posed by the particular use at issue here—the circumscribed, sacramental use of hoasca by the UDV. . . . Schedule I simply does not provide a categorical answer that relieves the Government of the obligation to shoulder its burden under RFRA.

This conclusion is reinforced by the Controlled Substances Act itself. The Act contains a provision authorizing the Attorney General to "waive the requirement for registration of certain manufacturers, distributors, or dispensers if he finds it consistent with the public health and safety." 21 U.S.C. § 822(d). The fact that the Act itself contemplates that exempting certain people from its requirements would be "consistent with the public health and safety" indicates that congressional findings with respect to Schedule I substances should not carry the determinative weight, for RFRA purposes, that the Government would ascribe to them.

And in fact an exception has been made to the Schedule I ban for religious use. For the past 35 years, there has been a regulatory exemption for use of peyote—a Schedule I substance—by the Native American Church. *See* 21 CFR § 1307.31 (2005). In 1994, Congress extended that exemption to all members of every recognized Indian Tribe. *See* 42 U.S.C. § 1996a(b)(1). Everything the Government says about the DMT in hoasca—that, as a Schedule I substance, Congress has determined that it "has a high potential for abuse," "has no currently accepted medical use," and has "a lack of accepted safety for use . . . under medical supervision," 21 U.S.C. § 812(b)(1)—applies in equal measure to the mescaline in peyote, yet both the Executive and Congress itself have decreed an exception from the Controlled Substances Act for Native American religious use of peyote. If such use is permitted in the face of the congressional findings in § 812(b)(1) for hundreds of thousands of Native Americans practicing their faith, it is difficult to see how those same findings alone can preclude any consideration of a similar exception for the 130 or so American members of the UDV who want to practice theirs. . . .

The well-established peyote exception also fatally undermines the Government's broader contention that the Controlled Substances Act establishes a closed regulatory system that admits of no exceptions under RFRA. The Government argues that the effectiveness of the Controlled Substances Act will be "necessarily . . . undercut" if the Act is not uniformly applied, without regard to burdens on religious exercise. Brief for Petitioners 18. The peyote exception, however, has been in place since the outset of the Controlled Substances Act, and there is no evidence that it has "undercut" the Government's ability to enforce the ban on peyote use by non-Indians.

NOTES AND QUESTIONS

1. *Equal protection for minority religions.* Does *O Centro Espírita* provide an important counterweight to *Smith* and a pointed rejoinder to those who posit that courts are incapable of providing full and equal protection to unfamiliar religions and religious practices under either the Free Exercise Clause itself or civil rights statutes that protect religiously mandated conduct from the impact of generally applicable laws? Or is the outcome better explained by the fact that Congress had already granted an exemption for religious use of peyote?
2. *One exemption vs. all exemptions.* The Court emphasized the very small size of the sect in the United States ("approximately 130 individuals") and the fact that the practical effect of granting the UDV an exemption was quite minimal. Should courts focus on only the requested exemption, or should they consider all possible exemptions? After all, just as the Court pointed to the peyote exemption, won't future challenges point the *hoasca* exemption?
3. *Broad or highly targeted exemptions from general laws?* Is it possible to limit the scope of a religious exemption as narrowly as Chief Justice Roberts posits in *O Centro Espírita*? Suppose a group of college students interested in experimenting with *hoasca* establish the "Church of the Sacred Visions" and attempt to import the drug for their "sacred rites." Could the Customs Service apply the Controlled Substances Act against them? Or would the exemption have to be broadly construed to encompass any other "religious" groups that seek to consume the hallucinogenic *hoasca* tea?
4. *Religion vs. secular counterpart.* Although RFRA could potentially provide a religious exemption for those who wanted to consume sacred *ganja* (that is marijuana), it would not reach a cancer patient who wanted to use marijuana for medical reasons in a state that had not yet legalized medical marijuana. Does RFRA unfairly privilege religious uses over secular uses? Wasn't that the point?

Burwell v. Hobby Lobby Stores, Inc.

573 U.S. 682 (2014)

[Under the Affordable Care Act, employer-sponsored health insurance plans must cover basic preventive care without any cost-sharing from employees. Pursuant to a Department of Health and Human Services regulation that went into effect in 2012, preventive care included all FDA-approved contraception, including morning-after pills and IUDs. Religious employers such as churches, synagogues, mosques, temples and their auxiliaries were automatically exempt from this "contraception mandate," while religiously affiliated non-profit employers became exempt once they notified the Department of Health and Human Services of their religious objections. For-profit corporations, however, were required to comply. Hobby Lobby Stores, Inc. and Conestoga Wood Specialties Corp., both closely held for-profit corporations, brought suit. The owners of these companies were religiously opposed to abortion, and believed that morning-after pills and IUDs caused abortions. They argued that forcing their corporations to include these contraceptives in their health care plan violated the companies' RFRA rights.]

Justice ALITO delivered the opinion of the Court.

We must decide in these cases whether the Religious Freedom Restoration Act of 1993 (RFRA), 107 Stat. 1488, 42 U.S.C. § 2000bb et seq., permits the United States Department of Health and Human Services (HHS) to demand that three closely held corporations provide health-insurance coverage for methods of contraception that violate the sincerely held religious beliefs of the companies' owners. We hold that the regulations that impose this obligation violate RFRA, which prohibits the Federal Government from taking any action that substantially burdens the exercise of religion unless that action constitutes the least restrictive means of serving a compelling government interest.

In holding that the HHS mandate is unlawful, we reject HHS's argument that the owners of the companies forfeited all RFRA protection when they decided to organize their businesses as corporations rather than sole proprietorships or general partnerships. The plain terms of RFRA make it perfectly clear that Congress did not discriminate in this way against men and women who wish to run their businesses as for-profit corporations in the manner required by their religious beliefs.

Since RFRA applies in these cases, we must decide whether the challenged HHS regulations substantially burden the exercise of religion, and we hold that they do. The owners of the businesses have religious objections to abortion, and according to their religious beliefs the four contraceptive methods at issue are abortifacients. If the owners comply with the HHS mandate, they believe they will be facilitating abortions, and if they do not comply, they will pay a very heavy price—as much as $1.3 million per day, or about $475 million per year, in the case of one of the companies. If these consequences do not amount to a substantial burden, it is hard to see what would.

Under RFRA, a Government action that imposes a substantial burden on religious exercise must serve a compelling government interest, and we assume that the HHS regulations satisfy this requirement. But in order for the HHS mandate to be sustained, it must also constitute the least restrictive means of serving that interest, and the mandate plainly fails that test. There are other ways in which Congress or HHS could equally ensure that every woman has cost-free access to the particular contraceptives at issue here and, indeed, to all FDA-approved contraceptives.

In fact, HHS has already devised and implemented a system that seeks to respect the religious liberty of religious nonprofit corporations while ensuring that the employees of these entities have precisely the same access to all FDA-approved contraceptives as employees of companies whose owners have no religious objections to providing such coverage. The employees of these religious nonprofit corporations still have access to insurance coverage without cost sharing for all FDA-approved contraceptives; and according to HHS, this system imposes no net economic burden on the insurance companies that are required to provide or secure the coverage.

Although HHS has made this system available to religious nonprofits that have religious objections to the contraceptive mandate, HHS has provided no reason why the same system cannot be made available when the owners of for-profit corporations have similar religious objections. We therefore conclude that this system constitutes an alternative that achieves all of the Government's aims while providing greater respect for religious liberty. And under RFRA, that conclusion means that enforcement of the HHS contraceptive mandate against the objecting parties in these cases is unlawful.

As this description of our reasoning shows, our holding is very specific. We do not hold, as the principal dissent alleges, that for-profit corporations and other commercial enterprises can "opt out of any law (saving only tax laws) they judge incompatible with their sincerely held religious beliefs." Nor do we hold, as the dissent implies, that such corporations have free rein to take steps that impose "disadvantages . . . on others" or that require "the general public [to] pick up the tab." And we certainly do not hold or suggest that "RFRA demands accommodation of a for-profit corporation's religious beliefs no matter the impact that accommodation may have on . . . thousands of women employed by Hobby Lobby." The effect of the HHS-created accommodation on the women employed by Hobby Lobby and the other companies involved in these cases would be precisely zero. Under that accommodation, these women would still be entitled to all FDA-approved contraceptives without cost sharing. . . .

III

RFRA prohibits the "Government [from] substantially burden[ing] a person's exercise of religion even if the burden results from a rule of general applicability" unless the Government "demonstrates that application of the burden to the person—(1) is in furtherance of a compelling governmental interest; and (2) is the least restrictive means of furthering that compelling governmental interest." 42 U.S.C. §§ 2000bb–1(a), (b) (emphasis added). The first question that we must address is whether this provision applies to regulations that govern the activities of for-profit corporations like Hobby Lobby, Conestoga, and Mardel.

HHS contends that neither these companies nor their owners can even be heard under RFRA. . . . In holding that . . . a "secular, for-profit corporation," lacks RFRA protection, the Third Circuit wrote as follows: "General business corporations do not, separate and apart from the actions or belief systems of their individual owners or employees, exercise religion. They do not pray, worship, observe sacraments or take other religiously-motivated actions separate and apart from the intention and direction of their individual actors." 724 F.3d, at 385 (emphasis added). . . .

As we noted above, RFRA applies to "a person's" exercise of religion, 42 U.S.C. §§ 2000bb–1(a), (b), and RFRA itself does not define the term "person." We therefore look to the Dictionary Act, which we must consult "[i]n determining the meaning of any Act of Congress, unless the context indicates otherwise." 1 U.S.C. § 1. Under the Dictionary Act, "the wor[d] 'person' . . . include[s] corporations, companies, associations, firms, partnerships, societies, and joint stock companies, as well as individuals." . . .

The principal argument advanced by HHS and the principal dissent regarding RFRA protection for Hobby Lobby, Conestoga, and Mardel focuses not on the statutory term "person," but on the phrase "exercise of religion." According to HHS and the dissent, these corporations are not protected by RFRA because they cannot exercise religion. . . .

Is it because of the corporate form? The corporate form alone cannot provide the explanation because, as we have pointed out, HHS concedes that nonprofit corporations can be protected by RFRA . . . If the corporate form is not enough, what about the profit-making objective? . . . If, as Braunfeld recognized, a sole proprietorship that seeks to make a profit may assert a free-exercise claim, why can't Hobby Lobby, Conestoga, and Mardel do the same? Some lower court judges have suggested that RFRA does not protect for-profit corporations because the purpose of such corporations is simply to make money. . . . While it is certainly true that a central objective of for-profit corporations is to make money, modern corporate law does not require for-profit corporations to pursue profit at the expense of everything else, and many do not do so.

For all these reasons, we hold that a federal regulation's restriction on the activities of a for-profit closely held corporation must comply with RFRA.

IV

Because RFRA applies in these cases, we must next ask whether the HHS contraceptive mandate "substantially burden[s]" the exercise of religion. 42 U.S.C. § 2000bb–1(a). We have little trouble concluding that it does.

As we have noted, the Hahns and Greens have a sincere religious belief that life begins at conception. They therefore object on religious grounds to providing health insurance that covers methods of birth control that, as HHS acknowledges, may result in the destruction of an embryo. By requiring the Hahns and Greens and their companies to arrange for such coverage, the HHS mandate demands that they engage in conduct that seriously violates their religious beliefs. . . .

It is true that the plaintiffs could avoid these assessments by dropping insurance coverage altogether and thus forcing their employees to obtain health insurance on one of the exchanges established under ACA. But if at least one of their full-time employees were to qualify for a subsidy on one of the government-run exchanges, this course would also entail substantial economic consequences. The companies could face penalties of $2,000 per employee each year. . . .

[A]mici supporting HHS have suggested that the $2,000 per-employee penalty is actually less than the average cost of providing health insurance, see Brief for Religious Organizations 22, and therefore, they claim, the companies could readily eliminate any substantial burden by forcing their employees to obtain insurance in the government exchanges. We do not generally entertain arguments that were not raised below and are not advanced in this Court by any party . . .

Even if we were to reach this argument, we would find it unpersuasive. As an initial matter, it entirely ignores the fact that the Hahns and Greens and their companies have religious reasons for providing health-insurance coverage for their employees. Before the advent of ACA, they were not legally compelled to provide insurance, but they nevertheless did so—in part, no doubt, for conventional business reasons, but also in part because their religious beliefs govern their relations with their employees. . . .

In taking the position that the HHS mandate does not impose a substantial burden on the exercise of religion, HHS's main argument (echoed by the principal dissent) is basically that the connection between what the objecting parties must do (provide health-insurance coverage for four methods of contraception that may operate after the fertilization of an egg) and the end that they find to be morally wrong (destruction of an embryo) is simply too attenuated. HHS and the dissent note that providing the coverage would not itself result in the destruction of an embryo; that would occur only if an employee chose to take advantage of the coverage and to use one of the four methods at issue.

This argument dodges the question that RFRA presents (whether the HHS mandate imposes a substantial burden on the ability of the objecting parties to conduct business in accordance with their religious beliefs) and instead addresses a very different question that the federal courts have no business addressing (whether the religious belief asserted in a RFRA case is reasonable). The Hahns and Greens believe that providing the coverage demanded by the HHS regulations is connected to the destruction of an embryo in a way that is sufficient to make it immoral for them to provide the coverage. This belief implicates a difficult and important question of religion and moral philosophy, namely, the circumstances under which it is wrong for a person to perform an act that is innocent in itself but that has the effect of enabling or facilitating the commission of an immoral act by another. Arrogating the authority to provide a binding national answer to this religious and philosophical question, HHS and the principal dissent in effect tell the plaintiffs that their beliefs are flawed. For good reason, we have repeatedly refused to take such a step. See, e.g., *Smith*, 494 U.S., at 887 ("Repeatedly and in many different contexts, we have warned that courts must not presume to determine . . . the plausibility of a religious claim"). . . .

Moreover, in Thomas v. Review Bd. of Indiana Employment Security Div., 450 U.S. 707 (1981), we considered and rejected an argument that is nearly identical to the one now urged by HHS and the dissent. In Thomas, a Jehovah's Witness was initially employed making sheet steel for a variety of industrial uses, but he was later transferred to a job making turrets for tanks. Because he objected on religious grounds to participating in the manufacture of weapons, he lost his job and sought unemployment compensation. Ruling against the employee, the state court had difficulty with the line that the employee drew between work that he found to be consistent with his religious beliefs (helping to manufacture steel that was used in making weapons) and work that he found morally objectionable (helping to make the weapons themselves). This Court, however, held that "it is not for us to say that the line he drew was an unreasonable one." Id. at 715. . . .

V

Since the HHS contraceptive mandate imposes a substantial burden on the exercise of religion, we must move on and decide whether HHS has shown that the mandate both "(1) is in furtherance of a compelling governmental interest; and (2) is the least restrictive means of furthering that compelling governmental interest." 42 U.S.C. § 2000bb–1(b).

A

. . . The objecting parties contend that HHS has not shown that the mandate serves a compelling government interest, and it is arguable that there are features of ACA that support that view. As we have noted, many employees—those covered by grandfathered plans and those who work for employers with fewer than 50 employees—may have no contraceptive coverage without cost sharing at all. HHS responds that many legal requirements have exceptions and the existence of exceptions does not in itself indicate that the principal interest served by a law is not compelling. . . .

We find it unnecessary to adjudicate this issue. We will assume that the interest in guaranteeing cost-free access to the four challenged contraceptive methods is compelling within the meaning of RFRA, and we will proceed to consider the final prong of the RFRA test, i.e., whether HHS has shown that the contraceptive mandate is "the least restrictive means of furthering that compelling governmental interest." § 2000bb–1(b)(2).

B

The least-restrictive-means standard is exceptionally demanding, see City of Boerne, 521 U.S., at 532, and it is not satisfied here. HHS has not shown that it lacks other means of achieving its desired goal without imposing a substantial burden on the exercise of religion by the objecting parties in these cases. . . .

The most straightforward way of doing this would be for the Government to assume the cost of providing the four contraceptives at issue to any women who are unable to obtain them under their health-insurance policies due to their employers' religious objections. This would certainly be less restrictive of the plaintiffs' religious liberty, and HHS has not shown, see § 2000bb–1(b)(2), that this is not a viable alternative. . . .

In the end, however, we need not rely on the option of a new, government-funded program in order to conclude that the HHS regulations fail the least-restrictive-means test. HHS itself has demonstrated that it has at its disposal an approach that is less restrictive than requiring employers to fund contraceptive methods that violate their religious beliefs. As we explained above, HHS has already established an accommodation for nonprofit organizations with religious objections. Under that accommodation, the organization can self-certify that it opposes providing coverage for particular contraceptive services. If the organization makes such a certification, the organization's insurance issuer or third-party administrator must "[e]xpressly exclude contraceptive coverage from the group health insurance coverage provided in connection with the group health plan" and "[p]rovide separate payments for any contraceptive services required to be covered" without imposing "any cost-sharing requirements . . . on the eligible organization, the group health plan, or plan participants or beneficiaries." 45 CFR § 147.131(c)(2); 26 CFR § 54.9815–2713A(c)(2).

We do not decide today whether an approach of this type complies with RFRA for purposes of all religious claims. At a minimum, however, it does not impinge on the plaintiffs' religious belief that providing insurance coverage for the contraceptives at issue here violates their religion, and it serves HHS's stated interests equally well.

The principal dissent identifies no reason why this accommodation would fail to protect the asserted needs of women as effectively as the contraceptive mandate, and there is none. . . .

C

HHS and the principal dissent argue that a ruling in favor of the objecting parties in these cases will lead to a flood of religious objections regarding a wide variety of medical procedures and drugs, such as vaccinations and blood transfusions, but HHS has made no effort to substantiate this prediction. . . .

It is HHS's apparent belief that no insurance-coverage mandate would violate RFRA—no matter how significantly it impinges on the religious liberties of employers—that would lead to intolerable consequences. Under HHS's view, RFRA would permit the Government to require all employers to provide coverage for any medical procedure allowed by law in the jurisdiction in question—for instance, third-trimester abortions or assisted suicide.

The owners of many closely held corporations could not in good conscience provide such coverage, and thus HHS would effectively exclude these people from full participation in the economic life of the Nation. RFRA was enacted to prevent such an outcome.

In any event, our decision in these cases is concerned solely with the contraceptive mandate. Our decision should not be understood to hold that an insurance-coverage mandate must necessarily fall if it conflicts with an employer's religious beliefs. Other coverage requirements, such as immunizations, may be supported by different interests (for example, the need to combat the spread of infectious diseases) and may involve different arguments about the least restrictive means of providing them.

The principal dissent raises the possibility that discrimination in hiring, for example on the basis of race, might be cloaked as religious practice to escape legal sanction. Our decision today provides no such shield. The Government has a compelling interest in providing an equal opportunity to participate in the workforce without regard to race, and prohibitions on racial discrimination are precisely tailored to achieve that critical goal. . . .

It is so ordered.

Justice KENNEDY, concurring.

As to RFRA's first requirement, the Department of Health and Human Services (HHS) makes the case that the mandate serves the Government's compelling interest in providing insurance coverage that is necessary to protect the health of female employees, coverage that is significantly more costly than for a male employee. There are many medical conditions for which pregnancy is contraindicated. It is important to confirm that a premise of the Court's opinion is its assumption that the HHS regulation here at issue furthers a legitimate and compelling interest in the health of female employees.

Justice GINSBURG, with whom Justice SOTOMAYOR joins, and with whom Justice BREYER and Justice KAGAN join as to all but Part III–C–1, dissenting.

In a decision of startling breadth, the Court holds that commercial enterprises, including corporations, along with partnerships and sole proprietorships, can opt out of any law (saving only tax laws) they judge incompatible with their sincerely held religious beliefs. Compelling governmental interests in uniform compliance with the law, and disadvantages that religion-based opt-outs impose on others, hold no sway, the Court decides, at least when there is a "less restrictive alternative." And such an alternative, the Court suggests, there always will be whenever, in lieu of tolling an enterprise claiming a religion-based exemption, the government, i.e., the general public, can pick up the tab.

The Court does not pretend that the First Amendment's Free Exercise Clause demands religion-based accommodations so extreme, for our decisions leave no doubt on that score. Instead, the Court holds that Congress, in the Religious Freedom Restoration Act of 1993 (RFRA), 42 U.S.C. § 2000bb et seq., dictated the extraordinary religion-based exemptions today's decision endorses. In the Court's view, RFRA demands accommodation of a for-profit corporation's religious beliefs no matter the impact that accommodation may have on third parties who do not share the corporation owners' religious faith—in these cases, thousands of women employed by Hobby Lobby and Conestoga or dependents of persons those corporations employ. Persuaded that Congress enacted RFRA to serve a far less radical purpose, and mindful of the havoc the Court's judgment can introduce, I dissent.

III

A

RFRA's purpose is specific and written into the statute itself. The Act was crafted to "restore the compelling interest test as set forth in Sherbert v. Verner, 374 U.S. 398, 83 S.Ct. 1790, 10 L.Ed.2d 965 (1963) and Wisconsin v. Yoder, 406 U.S. 205, 92 S.Ct. 1526, 32 L.Ed.2d 15 (1972) and to guarantee its application in all cases where free exercise of religion is substantially burdened." § 2000bb(b)(1). . . .

The legislative history is correspondingly emphatic on RFRA's aim. *See, e.g.*, S. Rep. No. 103–111, p. 12 (1993) (hereinafter Senate Report) (RFRA's purpose was "only to overturn the Supreme Court's decision in *Smith*," not to "unsettle other areas of the law."); 139 Cong. Rec. 26178 (1993) (statement of Sen. Kennedy) (RFRA was "designed to restore the compelling interest test for deciding free exercise claims."). In line with this restorative purpose, Congress expected courts considering RFRA claims to "look to free exercise cases decided prior to *Smith* for guidance." Senate Report 8. *See also* H.R.Rep. No. 103–88, pp. 6–7 (1993) (hereinafter House Report) (same). In short, the Act reinstates the law as it was prior to *Smith*, without "creat[ing] . . . new rights for any religious practice or for any potential litigant." 139 Cong. Rec. 26178 (statement of Sen. Kennedy). Given the Act's moderate purpose, it is hardly surprising that RFRA's enactment in 1993 provoked little controversy. *See* Brief for Senator Murray et al. as Amici Curiae 8 (hereinafter Senators Brief) (RFRA was approved by a 97–to–3 vote in the Senate and a voice vote in the House of Representatives).

B

Despite these authoritative indications, the Court sees RFRA as a bold initiative departing from, rather than restoring, pre-*Smith* jurisprudence. . . .

[T]he Court highlights RFRA's requirement that the government, if its action substantially burdens a person's religious observance, must demonstrate that it chose the least restrictive means for furthering a compelling interest.

"[B]y imposing a least-restrictive-means test," the Court suggests, RFRA "went beyond what was required by our pre-*Smith* decisions." But as RFRA's statements of purpose and legislative history make clear, Congress intended only to restore, not to scrap or alter, the balancing test as this Court had applied it pre-*Smith*. . . .

C

With RFRA's restorative purpose in mind, I turn to the Act's application to the instant lawsuits. That task, in view of the positions taken by the Court, requires consideration of several questions, each potentially dispositive of Hobby Lobby's and Conestoga's claims: Do for-profit corporations rank among "person[s]" who "exercise . . . religion"? Assuming that they do, does the contraceptive coverage requirement "substantially burden" their religious exercise? If so, is the requirement "in furtherance of a compelling government interest"? And last, does the requirement represent the least restrictive means for furthering that interest?

Misguided by its errant premise that RFRA moved beyond the pre-*Smith* case law, the Court falters at each step of its analysis.

1

RFRA's compelling interest test, as noted, applies to government actions that "substantially burden a person's exercise of religion." 42 U.S.C. § 2000bb–1(a) (emphasis added). This reference, the Court submits, incorporates the definition of "person" found in the Dictionary Act, 1 U.S.C. § 1, which extends to "corporations, companies, associations, firms, partnerships, societies, and joint stock companies, as well as individuals." The Dictionary Act's definition, however, controls only where "context" does not "indicat[e] otherwise." § 1. Here, context does so indicate. RFRA speaks of "a person's exercise of religion." 42 U.S.C. § 2000bb–1(a) (emphasis added). *See also* §§ 2000bb–2(4), 2000cc–5(7)(a). Whether a corporation qualifies as a "person" capable of exercising religion is an inquiry one cannot answer without reference to the "full body" of pre-*Smith* "free-exercise caselaw." *Gilardi*, 733 F.3d, at 1212. There is in that case law no support for the notion that free exercise rights pertain to for-profit corporations.

Until this litigation, no decision of this Court recognized a for-profit corporation's qualification for a religious exemption from a generally applicable law, whether under the Free Exercise Clause or RFRA. The absence of such precedent is just what one would expect, for the exercise of religion is characteristic of natural persons, not artificial legal entities. As Chief Justice Marshall observed nearly two centuries ago, a corporation is "an artificial being, invisible, intangible, and existing only in contemplation of law." Trustees of Dartmouth College v. Woodward, 4 Wheat. 518, 636, 4 L.Ed. 629 (1819). Corporations, Justice Stevens more recently reminded, "have no consciences, no beliefs, no feelings, no thoughts, no desires." Citizens United v. Federal Election Comm'n, 558 U.S. 310, 466 (2010) (opinion concurring in part and dissenting in part).

The First Amendment's free exercise protections, the Court has indeed recognized, shelter churches and other nonprofit religion-based organizations. . . . The Court's "special solicitude to the rights of religious organizations," Hosanna-Tabor Evangelical Lutheran Church and School v. EEOC, 132 S.Ct. 694, 706 (2012), however, is just that. No such solicitude is traditional for commercial organizations.

Indeed, until today, religious exemptions had never been extended to any entity operating in "the commercial, profit-making world." Amos, 483 U.S., at 337.

The reason why is hardly obscure. Religious organizations exist to foster the interests of persons subscribing to the same religious faith. Not so of for-profit corporations. Workers who sustain the operations of those corporations commonly are not drawn from one religious community. Indeed, by law, no religion-based criterion can restrict the work force of for-profit corporations. . . . The distinction between a community made up of believers in the same religion and one embracing persons of diverse beliefs, clear as it is, constantly escapes the Court's attention. One can only wonder why the Court shuts this key difference from sight.

Reading RFRA, as the Court does, to require extension of religion-based exemptions to for-profit corporations surely is not grounded in the pre-*Smith* precedent Congress sought to preserve. Had Congress intended RFRA to initiate a change so huge, a clarion statement to that effect likely would have been made in the legislation. . . .

Citing Braunfeld v. Brown, 366 U.S. 599 (1961), the Court questions why, if "a sole proprietorship that seeks to make a profit may assert a free-exercise claim, [Hobby Lobby and Conestoga] can't . . . do the same?" But even accepting, arguendo, the premise that unincorporated business enterprises may gain religious accommodations under the Free Exercise Clause, the Court's conclusion is unsound. In a sole proprietorship, the business and its owner are one and the same. By incorporating a business, however, an individual separates herself from the entity and escapes personal responsibility for the entity's obligations. One might ask why the separation should hold only when it serves the interest of those who control the corporation. . . .

The Court's determination that RFRA extends to for-profit corporations is bound to have untoward effects. Although the Court attempts to cabin its language to closely held corporations, its logic extends to corporations of any size, public or private. . . .

2

Even if Hobby Lobby and Conestoga were deemed RFRA "person[s]," to gain an exemption, they must demonstrate that the contraceptive coverage requirement "substantially burden[s] [their] exercise of religion." 42 U.S.C. § 2000bb–1(a). Congress no doubt meant the modifier "substantially" to carry weight. In the original draft of RFRA, the word "burden" appeared unmodified. The word "substantially" was inserted pursuant to a clarifying amendment offered by Senators Kennedy and Hatch. *See* 139 Cong. Rec. 26180. In proposing the amendment, Senator Kennedy stated that RFRA, in accord with the Court's pre-*Smith* case law, "does not require the Government to justify every action that has some effect on religious exercise." Ibid.

The Court barely pauses to inquire whether any burden imposed by the contraceptive coverage requirement is substantial. . . . I agree with the Court that the Green and Hahn families' religious convictions regarding contraception are sincerely held. . . . But those beliefs, however deeply held, do not suffice to sustain a RFRA claim. RFRA, properly understood, distinguishes between "factual allegations that [plaintiffs'] beliefs are sincere and of a religious nature," which a court must accept as true, and the "legal conclusion . . . that [plaintiffs'] religious exercise is substantially burdened," an inquiry the court must undertake.

That distinction is a facet of the pre-*Smith* jurisprudence RFRA incorporates. Bowen v. Roy, 476 U.S. 693 (1986), is instructive. There, the Court rejected a free exercise challenge to the Government's use of a Native American child's Social Security number for purposes of administering benefit programs. Without questioning the sincerity of the father's religious belief that "use of [his daughter's Social Security] number may harm [her] spirit," the Court concluded that the Government's internal uses of that number "place[d] [no] restriction on what [the father] may believe or what he may do." Id., at 699. Recognizing that the father's "religious views may not accept" the position that the challenged uses concerned only the Government's internal affairs, the Court explained that "for the adjudication of a constitutional claim, the Constitution, rather than an individual's religion, must supply the frame of reference." Id., at 700–701, n. 6. . . . Inattentive to this guidance, today's decision elides entirely the distinction between the sincerity of a challenger's religious belief and the substantiality of the burden placed on the challenger.

Undertaking the inquiry that the Court forgoes, I would conclude that the connection between the families' religious objections and the contraceptive coverage requirement is too attenuated to rank as substantial. The requirement carries no command that Hobby Lobby or Conestoga purchase or provide the contraceptives they find objectionable. Instead, it calls on the companies covered by the requirement to direct money into undifferentiated funds that finance a wide variety of benefits under comprehensive health plans. . . .

Importantly, the decisions whether to claim benefits under the plans are made not by Hobby Lobby or Conestoga, but by the covered employees and dependents, in consultation with their health care providers. . . . It is doubtful that Congress, when it specified that burdens must be "substantia[l]," had in mind a linkage thus interrupted by independent decisionmakers (the woman and her health counselor) standing between the challenged government action and the religious exercise claimed to be infringed. . . .

3

Even if one were to conclude that Hobby Lobby and Conestoga meet the substantial burden requirement, the Government has shown that the contraceptive coverage for which the ACA provides furthers compelling interests in public health and women's well being. Those interests are concrete, specific, and demonstrated by a wealth of empirical evidence. To recapitulate, the mandated contraception coverage enables women to avoid the health problems unintended pregnancies may visit on them and their children. The coverage helps safeguard the health of women for whom pregnancy may be hazardous, even life threatening. And the mandate secures benefits wholly unrelated to pregnancy, preventing certain cancers, menstrual disorders, and pelvic pain. . . .

4

After assuming the existence of compelling government interests, the Court holds that the contraceptive coverage requirement fails to satisfy RFRA's least restrictive means test. . . . A "least restrictive means" cannot require employees to relinquish benefits accorded them by federal law in order to ensure that their commercial employers can adhere unreservedly to their religious tenets.

Then let the government pay (rather than the employees who do not share their employer's faith), the Court suggests. . . . The ACA, however, requires coverage of preventive services through the existing employer-based system of health insurance "so that [employees] face minimal logistical and administrative obstacles." 78 Fed.Reg. 39888. Impeding women's receipt of benefits "by requiring them to take steps to learn about, and to sign up for, a new [government funded and administered] health benefit" was scarcely what Congress contemplated. . . .

And where is the stopping point to the "let the government pay" alternative? Suppose an employer's sincerely held religious belief is offended by health coverage of vaccines, or paying the minimum wage, see Tony and Susan Alamo Foundation v. Secretary of Labor, 471 U.S. 290, 303 (1985), or according women equal pay for substantially similar work, see Dole v. Shenandoah Baptist Church, 899 F.2d 1389, 1392 (C.A.4 1990)? Does it rank as a less restrictive alternative to require the government to provide the money or benefit to which the employer has a religion-based objection?

Because the Court cannot easily answer that question, it proposes something else: Extension to commercial enterprises of the accommodation already afforded to nonprofit religion-based organizations. . . . Ultimately, the Court hedges on its proposal to align for-profit enterprises with nonprofit religion-based organizations. "We do not decide today whether [the] approach [the opinion advances] complies with RFRA for purposes of all religious claims." Counsel for Hobby Lobby was similarly noncommittal. Asked at oral argument whether the Court-proposed alternative was acceptable, counsel responded: "We haven't been offered that accommodation, so we haven't had to decide what kind of objection, if any, we would make to that." Tr. of Oral Arg. 86–87. . . .

In sum, in view of what Congress sought to accomplish, i.e., comprehensive preventive care for women furnished through employer-based health plans, none of the proffered alternatives would satisfactorily serve the compelling interests to which Congress responded.

IV

Among the pathmarking pre-*Smith* decisions RFRA preserved is United States v. Lee, 455 U.S. 252 (1982). Lee, a sole proprietor engaged in farming and carpentry, was a member of the Old Order Amish. He sincerely believed that withholding Social Security taxes from his employees or paying the employer's share of such taxes would violate the Amish faith. This Court held that, although the obligations imposed by the Social Security system conflicted with Lee's religious beliefs, the burden was not unconstitutional. . . . [T]oday's Court dismisses Lee as a tax case. But the *Lee* Court made two key points one cannot confine to tax cases. "When followers of a particular sect enter into commercial activity as a matter of choice," the Court observed, "the limits they accept on their own conduct as a matter of conscience and faith are not to be superimposed on statutory schemes which are binding on others in that activity." . . . Further, the Court recognized in *Lee* that allowing a religion-based exemption to a commercial employer would "operat[e] to impose the employer's religious faith on the employees." . . . Working for Hobby Lobby or Conestoga, in other words, should not deprive employees of the preventive care available to workers at the shop next door, at least in the absence of directions from the Legislature or Administration to do so. . . .

For the reasons stated, I would reverse the judgment of the Court of Appeals for the Tenth Circuit and affirm the judgment of the Court of Appeals for the Third Circuit.

NOTES AND QUESTIONS

1. *RFRA vs. Free Exercise Clause.* The majority and dissent disagree over whether RFRA was meant to restore pre-*Smith* religious liberty protection or exceed it. Who do you think has the better argument?
2. *Corporations as religious rights holders.* This was the first Supreme Court decision that held that for-profit corporations were entitled to religious exemptions. The majority argued that the owners of closely held for-profit corporations should not have to give up their religious rights just because they decide to incorporate. What was the dissent's response? Why do people form corporations? *See generally* Caroline Mala Corbin, *Corporate Religious Liberty*, 30 Const. Commentary 277 (2015).
3. *Substantial burden.* The claim in *Hobby Lobby* was that facilitating someone else's sinful conduct was a substantial religious burden. How does this burden compare to the religious burdens articulated in the free exercise cases you have read so far? Should the courts independently evaluate whether a religious burden is substantial? If they do, would they be passing judgement on religious beliefs? If they prevent ovulation and therefore do not, would they be reading out the requirement that the burden be "substantial"? How deferential should the courts be to claims of substantial burden? What if the plaintiffs make a factual error, such as thinking morning-after pills cause abortions when the scientific consensus is that they do not; should the courts still be deferential?
4. *Compelling state interest.* Although the plurality assumed without deciding that the government had a compelling interest, Justice Kennedy's controlling concurrence contributes the fifth vote for holding that the state's "interest in providing insurance coverage that is necessary to protect the health of female employees" was in fact compelling. Why does the Court maintain that exceptions undermine the government's compelling interests? Would exceptions to the Civil Rights Act undermine the state's compelling interest in ending discrimination? Is grandfathering insurance plans an exception or a means of gradually implementing major changes? Is excluding small employers an exception or a question of scope?
5. *Narrowly tailored means.* The Court held that the contraception mandate was not narrowly tailored because the government could provide the contraception itself instead. Does this reasoning work for religious objections to other laws as well, such as laws mandating social security taxes, minimum wage, or equal pay, or is there something unique about the law mandating contraception coverage? Is a proposed alternative a less restrictive alternative if it is much less effective in accomplishing the government's goals? What if it is just slightly less effective?
6. *Challenge of nonprofits.* The Court also pointed to the accommodation made for religiously affiliated nonprofits as evidence that the mandate was not narrowly tailored. However, even though these nonprofits could

opt-out of contraception coverage by notifying either their insurance carriers or the Department of Health and Human Services of their religious objections, they argued that the accommodation itself violated their rights under RFRA: filing the paperwork in order to receive this accommodation still made them complicit in sin and therefore imposed a substantial religious burden. Although the Supreme Court heard arguments in the lawsuit, its decision in Zubik v. Burwell, 578 U.S. 403 (2016), dodged the issue by sending the case back to the lower courts with instructions to work out a compromise. "[T]he parties on remand should be afforded an opportunity to arrive at an approach going forward that accommodates petitioners' religious exercise while at the same time ensuring that women covered by petitioners' health plans 'receive full and equal health coverage, including contraceptive coverage.' We anticipate that the Courts of Appeals will allow the parties sufficient time to resolve any outstanding issues between them."

Holt v. Hobbs

574 U.S. 352 (2015)

Justice ALITO delivered the opinion of the Court.

Petitioner Gregory Holt, also known as Abdul Maalik Muhammad, is an Arkansas inmate and a devout Muslim who wishes to grow a ½-inch beard in accordance with his religious beliefs. Petitioner's objection to shaving his beard clashes with the Arkansas Department of Correction's grooming policy, which prohibits inmates from growing beards unless they have a particular dermatological condition. We hold that the Department's policy, as applied in this case, violates the Religious Land Use and Institutionalized Persons Act of 2000 (RLUIPA). . . .

Following our decision in *Smith*, Congress enacted RFRA in order to provide greater protection for religious exercise than is available under the First Amendment. . . . In making RFRA applicable to the States and their subdivisions, Congress relied on Section 5 of the Fourteenth Amendment, but in [*City of Boerne*], this Court held that RFRA exceeded Congress' powers under that provision. Congress responded to *City of Boerne* by enacting RLUIPA, which applies to the States and their subdivisions and invokes congressional authority under the Spending and Commerce Clauses. *See* § 2000cc–1(b). RLUIPA concerns two areas of government activity: Section 2 governs land-use regulation, § 2000cc; and Section 3—the provision at issue in this case—governs religious exercise by institutionalized persons, § 2000cc–1. Section 3 mirrors RFRA . . .

Petitioner, as noted, is in the custody of the Arkansas Department of Correction and he objects on religious grounds to the Department's grooming policy, which provides that "[n]o inmates will be permitted to wear facial hair other than a neatly trimmed mustache that does not extend beyond the corner of the mouth or over the lip." App. to Brief for Petitioner 11a. The policy makes no exception for inmates who object on religious grounds, but it does contain an exemption for prisoners with medical needs. . . .

Petitioner sought permission to grow a beard and, although he believes that his faith requires him not to trim his beard at all, he proposed a "compromise" under which he would grow only a ½–inch beard. App. 164. Prison officials denied his request . . .

In addition to showing that the relevant exercise of religion is grounded in a sincerely held religious belief, petitioner also bore the burden of proving that the Department's grooming policy substantially burdened that exercise of religion. Petitioner easily satisfied that obligation. The Department's grooming policy requires petitioner to shave his beard and thus to "engage in conduct that seriously violates [his] religious beliefs." *Hobby Lobby*, 134 S.Ct., at 2775. If petitioner contravenes that policy and grows his beard, he will face serious disciplinary action. Because the grooming policy puts petitioner to this choice, it substantially burdens his religious exercise. Indeed, the Department does not argue otherwise.

Since petitioner met his burden of showing that the Department's grooming policy substantially burdened his exercise of religion, the burden shifted to the Department to show that its refusal to allow petitioner to grow a ½–inch beard "(1) [was] in furtherance of a compelling governmental interest; and (2) [was] the least restrictive means of furthering that compelling governmental interest." § 2000cc–1(a). . . .

The Department contends that enforcing this prohibition is the least restrictive means of furthering prison safety and security in two specific ways. The Department first claims that the no-beard policy prevents prisoners from hiding contraband. The Department worries that prisoners may use their beards to conceal all manner of prohibited items, including razors, needles, drugs, and cellular phone subscriber identity module (SIM) cards. We readily agree that the Department has a compelling interest in staunching the flow of contraband into and within its facilities, but the argument that this interest would be seriously compromised by allowing an inmate to grow a ½–inch beard is hard to take seriously. . . .

[Moreover], the Department cannot show that forbidding very short beards is the least restrictive means of preventing the concealment of contraband. "The least-restrictive-means standard is exceptionally demanding," and it requires the government to "sho[w] that it lacks other means of achieving its desired goal without imposing a substantial burden on the exercise of religion by the objecting part[y]." *Hobby Lobby*, 134 S.Ct., at 2780. The Department failed to establish that it could not satisfy its security concerns by simply searching petitioner's beard. The Department already searches prisoners' hair and clothing, and it presumably examines the ¼–inch beards of inmates with dermatological conditions. It has offered no sound reason why hair, clothing, and ¼–inch beards can be searched but ½–inch beards cannot. . . .

The Department contends that its grooming policy is necessary to further an additional compelling interest, *i.e.*, preventing prisoners from disguising their identities. The Department tells us that the no-beard policy allows security officers to identify prisoners quickly and accurately. It claims that bearded inmates could shave their beards and change their appearance in order to enter restricted areas within the prison, to escape, and to evade apprehension after escaping.

We agree that prisons have a compelling interest in the quick and reliable identification of prisoners, and we acknowledge that any alteration in a prisoner's appearance, such as by shaving a beard, might, in the absence of effective countermeasures, have at least some effect on the ability of guards or others to make a quick identification. But even if we assume for present purposes that the Department's grooming policy sufficiently furthers its interest in the identification of prisoners, that policy still violates RLUIPA as applied in the circumstances present here. The Department contends that a prisoner who has a beard when he is photographed for identification purposes might confuse guards by shaving his beard. But as petitioner has argued, the Department could largely solve this problem by requiring that all inmates be photographed without beards when first admitted to the facility and, if necessary, periodically thereafter. . . .

We emphasize that although RLUIPA provides substantial protection for the religious exercise of institutionalized persons, it also affords prison officials ample ability to maintain security. We highlight three ways in which this is so. First, in applying RLUIPA's statutory standard, courts should not blind themselves to the fact that the analysis is conducted in the prison setting. Second, if an institution suspects that an inmate is using religious activity to cloak illicit conduct, "prison officials may appropriately question whether a prisoner's religiosity, asserted as the basis for a requested accommodation, is authentic." Cutter v. Wilkinson, 544 U.S. 709, 725, n. 13 (2005). *See also* Hobby Lobby, 134 S.Ct., at 2774, n. 28. Third, even if a claimant's religious belief is sincere, an institution might be entitled to withdraw an accommodation if the claimant abuses the exemption in a manner that undermines the prison's compelling interests.

In sum, we hold that the Department's grooming policy violates RLUIPA insofar as it prevents petitioner from growing a ½–inch beard in accordance with his religious beliefs. . . .

It is so ordered.

Justice GINSBURG, with whom Justice SOTOMAYOR joins, concurring.

Unlike the exemption this Court approved in Burwell v. Hobby Lobby Stores, Inc., 134 S.Ct. 2751 (2014), accommodating petitioner's religious belief in this case would not detrimentally affect others who do not share petitioner's belief. *See* 134 S.Ct., at 2787–2788, 2790–2791, and n. 8, 2801 (Ginsburg, J., dissenting). On that understanding, I join the Court's opinion.

NOTES AND QUESTIONS

1. Holt *vs.* Hobby Lobby. In what way do the religious burdens created by the challenged regulations differ in *Holt* and *Hobby Lobby*? In what way do the burdens on others created by granting an exemption differ?
2. *A less restrictive alternative?* Do you agree that regular beard searches and periodic identification photographs were less restrictive alternatives? How much less effective may the alternatives be and still count as a less restrictive alternative?
3. *How much deference?* How deferential was the Supreme Court to prison officials? What does the Court mean when it says that courts should not be blind to the prison setting?

THEORY-APPLIED PROBLEM

Two cashiers work at a small local pharmacy with two cash registers. Both are religiously opposed to contraception and refuse to ring up any purchase of contraception on the grounds that such conduct makes them complicit in sin. Their state has enacted the Equal Access to Medicine Act that requires pharmacies to fill and sell all safe and legal prescriptions. While the law provides an exemption for pharmacists with religious objections, the exemption does not extend to other pharmacy employees. The cashiers file suit, arguing that the law violates their rights under their state's Religious Freedom Restoration Act, which is modeled on the federal law. Not only does the law substantially burden their religious conscience, the cashiers argue, but the state has a less restrictive alternative: let someone else ring up the purchase instead. Will they win? Should they win?

THEORY-APPLIED PROBLEM

Pennsylvania's state legislature, concerned about the quality of the state's public schools, creates a new "choice" program in 2017. The choice program provides vouchers to parents to help with the expenses associated with private and parochial schools. In addition, Pennsylvania creates a new tax deduction for educational expenses incurred for primary, middle, or secondary education. All of these benefits, however, are limited to "accredited institutions that do not practice discrimination on the basis of race, sex, religion, national origin, ethnicity, or sexual orientation in any policies related to admissions, employment, or any other school-sponsored program." The legislature is anxious to avoid subsidizing schools that practice invidious forms of discrimination that, if adopted by the public schools, would violate the Fourteenth Amendment's Equal Protection Clause. The legislative history of the statute does not reflect any targeted animus toward any particular religion or group of religionists.

The Al Said Madrassa (ASM) is located in Philadelphia, Pennsylvania, and is affiliated with a mosque operated by the Brothers of Islam. ASM enjoys state accreditation and offers instruction for grades K through 12. The curriculum is "consistent with the teachings and requirements of Shar'ia" and the school "seeks to foster a comprehensively Islamic environment." The school will admit persons of any race, sex, religion, national origin, ethnicity, or sexual orientation. However, the school features completely sex-segregated dual programs, with entirely separate facilities and faculties and gender-appropriate dress codes and curricula. Girls must wear full dresses and head scarves at all times, and adult women teaching or visiting in the school must wear burkas (full body coverings, with small eye slits). In addition, only men are permitted to teach in the boys program, and only women are permitted to teach in the girls program. Although both programs meet state curricular mandates, significant differences exist in the programs for boys and girls, with the boys' program enjoying broader academic offerings and college preparatory AP courses not available in the girls' school. ASM argues that it prepares women for "gender-appropriate" vocations and that the curriculum reflects religious beliefs about the proper, but quite different, roles of men and women in a well-ordered and godly society. It notes that its practices have deep roots, stretching back for hundreds of years within the Islamic world.

The Pennsylvania State Department of Revenue (Department) holds that ASM is not eligible to receive state-funded school vouchers because it practices pervasive gender discrimination. It alleges that the educational programs, although separate, are far from being equal. The Department also objects to the differential gender-based dress codes that apply to girls and women. In addition, the Department disallows state income tax deductions for educational expenses associated with attending ASM on the grounds that ASM violates the state's nondiscrimination policies. The parents of ASM students respond by bringing a class action suit against the Department, alleging a violation of their Free Exercise Clause rights, as well as their rights under the state Religious Freedom Restoration Act. The parents claim that, as designed and implemented, the Pennsylvania voucher and tax deduction programs discriminate against traditional Islamic schools that observe religiously mandated gender rules, noting that single-sex parochial (Catholic) schools routinely receive vouchers and that the Department allowed parents of parochial school students to claim deductions for educational expenses associated with attending single-sex parochial schools. (The Department says that the parochial schools are different because they provide "fully equivalent" educational opportunities, albeit in a gender-segregated environment, and do not practice comprehensive sex discrimination in staffing single-sex schools.) The plaintiffs allege that, in cultural context, the rules do not constitute gender discrimination. How should the district court rule?

Chapter 17

Free Exercise of Religion: Institutions

Table of Contents

A. Church Property Disputes

B. Employment Disputes

One final matter regarding free exercise requires attention: the problem of disputes within congregations. If a religious organization has a falling out, with the congregation dividing into two (or more) camps, who gets to keep the church building and the fellowship hall? If a dispute arises regarding leadership within the church, what role (if any) may the government play in resolving the dispute? What if a minister brings an employment discrimination claim? In other words, in what ways can government act to resolve disputes within religious organizations without transgressing the Free Exercise Clause?

The problem implicates both religion clauses. It may constitute a free exercise issue if, by interfering in the internal affairs of a religious organization, the court ends up regulating religious beliefs. It may constitute an establishment issue if, by resolving disputes, the court finds itself deciding theological controversies or otherwise favoring one claim to religious truth over another. For example, British law once permitted civil courts to determine whether a church had substantially departed from the tenets of the faith; if it had, the trust creating or funding the church might revert to some other entity or person. Obviously, deciding whether a church has abandoned the essential tenets of its faith requires a court to, at a minimum, define those tenets in the first place. Accordingly, courts in the United States have struggled to establish neutral rules to resolve intra-church disputes that will not require government theology lessons. As you read the following cases, consider whether the categorical approach of *Watson* and *Hosanna-Tabor*, or the "neutral principles" approach of *Jones*, better serves the goal of government neutrality in matters of theology.

A. *CHURCH PROPERTY DISPUTES*

Watson v. Jones

80 (13 Wall) U.S. 679 (1872)

[This litigation grew out of certain disturbances in what is known as the "Third or Walnut Street Presbyterian Church," of Louisville, Kentucky, and which resulted in a division of its members into two distinct bodies, each claiming the exclusive use of the property held and owned by that local church.]

Mr. Justice MILLER now delivered the opinion of the Court.

This case belongs to a class, happily rare in our courts, in which one of the parties to a controversy, essentially ecclesiastical, resorts to the judicial tribunals of the State for the maintenance of rights which the church has refused to acknowledge, or found itself unable to protect. Much as such dissensions among the members of a religious society should be regretted, a regret which is increased when passing from the control of the judicial and legislative bodies of the entire organization to which the society belongs, an appeal is made to the secular authority; the courts when so called on must perform their functions as in other cases.

Religious organizations come before us in the same attitude as other voluntary associations for benevolent or charitable purposes, and their rights of property, or of contract, are equally under the protection of the law, and the actions of their members subject to its restraints. . . .

The questions which have come before the civil courts concerning the rights to property held by ecclesiastical bodies, may, so far as we have been able to examine them, be profitably classified under three general heads, which of course do not include cases governed by considerations applicable to a church established and supported by law as the religion of the state.

1. The first of these is when the property which is the subject of controversy has been, by the deed or will of the donor, or other instrument by which the property is held, by the express terms of the instrument devoted to the teaching, support, or spread of some specific form of religious doctrine or belief.

2. The second is when the property is held by a religious congregation which, by the nature of its organization, is strictly independent of other ecclesiastical associations, and so far as church government is concerned, owes no fealty or obligation to any higher authority.

3. The third is where the religious congregation or ecclesiastical body holding the property is but a subordinate member of some general church organization in which there are superior ecclesiastical tribunals with a general and ultimate power of control more or less complete, in some supreme judicatory over the whole membership of that general organization.

In regard to the first of these classes it seems hardly to admit of a rational doubt that an individual or an association of individuals may dedicate property by way of trust to the purpose of sustaining, supporting, and propagating definite religious doctrines or principles, provided that in doing so they violate no law of morality, and give to the instrument by which their purpose is evidenced, the formalities which the laws require. And it would seem also to be the obvious duty of the court, in a case properly made, to see that the property so dedicated is not diverted from the trust which is thus attached to its use. So long as there are persons qualified within the meaning of the original dedication, and who are also willing to teach the doctrines or principles prescribed in the act of dedication, and so long as there is any one so interested in the execution of the trust as to have a standing in court, it must be that they can prevent the diversion of the property or fund to other and different uses. This is the general doctrine of courts of equity as to charities, and it seems equally applicable to ecclesiastical matters.

In such case, if the trust is confided to a religious congregation of the independent or congregational form of church government, it is not in the power of the majority of that congregation, however preponderant, by reason of a change of views on religious subjects, to carry the property so confided to them to the support of new and conflicting doctrine. A pious man building and dedicating a house of worship to the sole and exclusive use of those who believe in the doctrine of the Holy Trinity, and placing it under the control of a congregation which at the time holds the same belief, has a right to expect that the law will prevent that property from being used as a means of support and dissemination of the Unitarian doctrine, and as a place of Unitarian worship. Nor is the principle varied when the organization to which the trust is confided is of the second or associated form of church government. The protection which the law throws around the trust is the same. And though the task may be a delicate one and a difficult one, it will be the duty of the court in such cases, when the doctrine to be taught or the form of worship to be used is definitely and clearly laid down, to inquire whether the party accused of violating the trust is holding or teaching a different doctrine, or using a form of worship which is so far variant as to defeat the declared objects of the trust.

The second class of cases which we have described has reference to the case of a church of a strictly congregational or independent organization, governed solely within itself, either by a majority of its members or by such other local organism as it may have instituted for the purpose of ecclesiastical government; and to property held by such a church, either by way of purchase or donation, with no other specific trust attached to it in the hands of the church than that it is for the use of that congregation as a religious society.

In such cases where there is a schism which leads to a separation into distinct and conflicting bodies, the rights of such bodies to the use of the property must be determined by the ordinary principles which govern voluntary associations. If the principle of government in such cases is that the majority rules, then the numerical majority of members must control the right to the use of the property. If there be within the congregation officers in whom are vested the powers of such control, then those who adhere to the acknowledged organism by which the body is governed are entitled to the use of the property. The minority in choosing to separate themselves into a distinct body, and refusing to recognize the authority of the governing body, can claim no rights in the property from the fact that they had once been members of the church or congregation. This ruling admits of no inquiry into the existing religious opinions of those who comprise the legal or regular organization; for, if such was permitted, a very small minority, without any officers of the church among them, might be found to be the only faithful supporters of the religious dogmas of the founders of the church. There being no such trust imposed upon the property when purchased or given, the court will not imply one for the purpose of expelling from its use those who by regular succession and order constitute the church, because they may have changed in some respect their views of religious truth. . . .

But the third of these classes of cases is the one which is oftenest found in the courts, and which, with reference to the number and difficulty of the questions involved, and to other considerations, is every way the most important.

It is the case of property acquired in any of the usual modes for the general use of a religious congregation which is itself part of a large and general organization of some religious denomination, with which it is more or less intimately connected by religious views and ecclesiastical government.

The case before us is one of this class, growing out of a schism which has divided the congregation and its officers, and the presbytery and synod, and which appeals to the courts to determine the right to the use of the property so acquired. Here is no case of property devoted forever by the instrument which conveyed it, or by any specific declaration of its owner, to the support of any special religious dogmas, or any peculiar form of worship, but of property purchased for the use of a religious congregation, and so long as any existing religious congregation can be ascertained to be that congregation, or its regular and legitimate successor, it is entitled to the use of the property. In the case of an independent congregation we have pointed out how this identity, or succession, is to be ascertained, but in cases of this character we are bound to look at the fact that the local congregation is itself but a member of a much larger and more important religious organization, and is under its government and control, and is bound by its orders and judgments. There are in the Presbyterian system of ecclesiastical government, in regular succession, the presbytery over the session or local church, the synod over the presbytery, and the General Assembly over all. These are called, in the language of the church organs, "judicatories," and they entertain appeals from the decisions of those below, and prescribe corrective measures in other cases.

In this class of cases we think the rule of action which should govern the civil courts, founded in a broad and sound view of the relations of church and state under our system of laws, and supported by a preponderating weight of judicial authority is, that, whenever the questions of discipline, or of faith, or ecclesiastical rule, custom, or law have been decided by the highest of these church judicatories to which the matter has been carried, the legal tribunals must accept such decisions as final, and as binding on them, in their application to the case before them.

In this country the full and free right to entertain any religious belief, to practice any religious principle, and to teach any religious doctrine which does not violate the laws of morality and property, and which does not infringe personal rights, is conceded to all. The law knows no heresy, and is committed to the support of no dogma, the establishment of no sect. The right to organize voluntary religious associations to assist in the expression and dissemination of any religious doctrine, and to create tribunals for the decision of controverted questions of faith within the association, and for the ecclesiastical government of all the individual members, congregations, and officers within the general association, is unquestioned. All who unite themselves to such a body do so with an implied consent to this government, and are bound to submit to it. But it would be a vain consent and would lead to the total subversion of such religious bodies, if any one aggrieved by one of their decisions could appeal to the secular courts and have them reversed. It is of the essence of these religious unions, and of their right to establish tribunals for the decision of questions arising among themselves, that those decisions should be binding in all cases of ecclesiastical cognizance, subject only to such appeals as the organism itself provides for.

Nor do we see that justice would be likely to be promoted by submitting those decisions to review in the ordinary judicial tribunals. Each of these large and influential bodies (to mention no others, let reference be had to the Protestant Episcopal, the Methodist Episcopal, and the Presbyterian churches), has a body of constitutional and ecclesiastical law of its own, to be found in their written organic laws, their books of discipline, in their collections of precedents, in their usage and customs, which as to each constitute a system of ecclesiastical law and religious faith that tasks the ablest minds to become familiar with. It is not to be supposed that the judges of the civil courts can be as competent in the ecclesiastical law and religious faith of all these bodies as the ablest men in each are in reference to their own. It would therefore be an appeal from the more learned tribunal in the law which should decide the case, to one which is less so. . . .

Under cover of inquiries into the jurisdiction of the synod and presbytery over the congregation, and of the General Assembly over all, [the Kentucky Court of Appeals] went into an elaborate examination of the principles of Presbyterian church government, and ended by overruling the decision of the highest judicatory of that church in the United States, both on the jurisdiction and the merits; and, substituting its own judgment for that of the ecclesiastical court, decides that ruling elders, declared to be such by that tribunal, are not such, and must not be recognized by the congregation, though four-fifths of its members believe in the judgment of the Assembly and desired to conform to its decree.

But we need pursue this subject no further. Whatever may have been the case before the Kentucky court, the appellants in the case presented to us have separated themselves wholly from the church organization to which they belonged when this controversy commenced. They now deny its authority, denounce its action, and refuse to abide by its judgments. They have first erected themselves into a new organization, and have since joined themselves to another totally different, if not hostile, to the one to which they belonged when the difficulty first began. Under any of the decisions which we have examined, the appellants, in their present position, have no right to the property, or to the use of it, which is the subject of this suit.

The novelty of the questions presented to this court for the first time, their intrinsic importance and far-reaching influence, and the knowledge that the schism in which the case originated has divided the Presbyterian churches throughout Kentucky and Missouri, have seemed to us to justify the careful and laborious examination and discussion which we have made of the principles which should govern the case. For the same reasons we have held it under advisement for a year; not uninfluenced by the hope, that since the civil commotion, which evidently lay at the foundation of the trouble, has passed away, that charity, which is so large an element in the faith of both parties, and which, by one of the apostles of that religion, is said to be the greatest of all the Christian virtues, would have brought about a reconciliation. But we have been disappointed. It is not for us to determine or apportion the moral responsibility which attaches to the parties for this result. We can only pronounce the judgment of the law as applicable to the case presented to us, and that requires us to affirm the decree of the Circuit Court as it stands.

Decree affirmed.

NOTES AND QUESTIONS

1. *The rules applicable to resolving disputes regarding church property. Watson* recognizes three distinct classes of church property ownership: (1) church property given in trust for the teaching of a particular faith or doctrine; (2) church property owned by a free-standing and independent congregation; and (3) church property owned by a unit of a hierarchical church. With respect to the second and third categories, the Supreme Court establishes fairly clear rules. A court should ascertain the governing rules for a congregational church and enforce the decision of the entity that has a right to control the property under the charter. For a hierarchical church, the court should enforce the decision of the highest entity with the hierarchy. The first category, however, is potentially problematic because church property held in trust for the teaching of a particular doctrine might require a court to determine whether a church had in fact modified its doctrines.
2. *The difficulty of applying the* Watson *rules.* Even though the rule governing control of property held by a local unit of a hierarchical church is straightforward, in practice its application can be remarkably unpopular. Local courts are unlikely to want to strip local community members of their church in deference to an out-of-state person or entity. In part because of these pressures, state courts have attempted to avoid applying the *Watson* rule with respect to hierarchical churches (with some success—see *Jones, infra*).
3. *Identifying the highest authority within a hierarchical church.* Under *Watson*, if a church is hierarchical in nature, then the decision of the highest official or entity within the hierarchy controls. This approach provides a categorical rule that should, in theory, permit courts to settle property disputes without delving into matters of theology. But is this really the case? Suppose that two persons claim to be Bishop of Rome (or the Supreme Pontiff of the Roman Catholic Church). Historically, during the Great Schism, two popes both claimed to be *the* pope—one in Rome and the other in Avignon, France. How should the courts determine which pope speaks for the hierarchy?

Presbyterian Church in the United States v. Mary Elizabeth Blue Hull Memorial Presbyterian Church

393 U.S. 440 (1969)

Mr. Justice BRENNAN delivered the opinion of the Court.

This is a church property dispute which arose when two local churches withdrew from a hierarchical general church organization. Under Georgia law the right to the property previously used by the local churches was made to turn on a civil court jury decision as to whether the general church abandoned or departed from the tenets of faith and practice it held at the time the local churches affiliated with it. The question presented is whether the restraints of the First Amendment, as applied to the States through the Fourteenth Amendment, permit a civil court to award church property on the basis of the interpretation and significance the civil court assigns to aspects of church doctrine.

Petitioner, Presbyterian Church in the United States, is an association of local Presbyterian churches governed by a hierarchical structure of tribunals which consists of, in ascending order, (1) the Church Session, composed of the elders of the local church; (2) the Presbytery, composed of several churches in a geographical area; (3) the Synod, generally composed of all Presbyteries within a State; and (4) the General Assembly, the highest governing body.

A dispute arose between petitioner, the general church, and two local churches in Savannah, Georgia—the respondents, Hull Memorial Presbyterian Church and Eastern Heights Presbyterian Church—over control of the properties used until they by the local churches. In 1966, the membership of the local churches, in the belief that certain actions and pronouncements of the general church were violations of that organization's constitution and departures from the doctrine and practice in force at the time of affiliation, voted to withdraw from the general church and to reconstitute the local churches as an autonomous Presbyterian organization. The ministers of the two churches renounced the general church's jurisdiction and authority over them, as did all but two of the ruling elders. In response, the general church, through the Presbytery of Savannah, established an Administrative Commission to seek a conciliation. The dissident local churchmen remained steadfast; consequently, the Commission acknowledged the withdrawal of the local leadership and proceeded to take over the local churches' property on behalf of the general church until new local leadership could be appointed.

The local churchmen made no effort to appeal the Commission's action to higher church tribunals—the Synod of Georgia or the General Assembly. Instead, the churches filed separate suits in the Superior Court of Chatham County to enjoin the general church from trespassing on the disputed property, title to which was in the local churches. The cases were consolidated for trial. The general church moved to dismiss the actions and cross-claimed for injunctive relief in its own behalf on the ground that civil courts were without power to determine whether the general church had departed from its tenets of faith and practice. . . .

It is of course true that the State has a legitimate interest in resolving property disputes, and that a civil court is a proper forum for that resolution. Special problems arise, however, when these disputes implicate controversies over church doctrine and practice. The approach of this Court in such cases was originally developed in Watson v. Jones, 13 Wall. 679 (1872), a pre-*Erie R. Co. v. Tompkins* diversity decision decided before the application of the First Amendment to the States but nonetheless informed by First Amendment considerations. There, as here, civil courts were asked to resolve a property dispute between a national Presbyterian organization and local churches of that organization. There, as here, the disputes arose out of a controversy over church doctrine. There, as here, the Court was asked to decree the termination of an implied trust because of departures from doctrine by the national organization. The Watson Court refused pointing out that it was wholly inconsistent with the American concept of the relationship between church and state to permit civil courts to determine ecclesiastical questions. In language which has a clear constitutional ring, the Court said

> 'In this country the full and free right to entertain any religious belief, to practice any religious principle, and to teach any religious doctrine which does not violate the laws of morality and property, and which does not infringe personal rights, is conceded to all. The law knows no heresy, and is committed to the support of no dogma, the establishment of no sect. . . . All who unite themselves to such a body (the general church) do so with an implied consent to (its) government, and are bound to submit to it. But it would be a vain consent and would lead to the total subversion of such religious bodies, if any one aggrieved by one of their decisions could appeal to the secular courts and have them (sic) reversed. It is of the essence of these religious unions, and of their right to establish tribunals for the decision of questions arising among themselves, that those decisions should be binding in all cases of ecclesiastical cognizance, subject only to such appeals as the organism itself provides for.' 13 Wall., at 728-729.

The logic of this language leaves the civil courts no role in determining ecclesiastical questions in the process of resolving property disputes.

Later cases, however, also decided on nonconstitutional grounds, recognized that there might be some circumstances in which marginal civil court review of ecclesiastical determinations would be appropriate. The scope of this review was delineated in Gonzalez v. Roman Catholic Archbishop of Manila, 280 U.S. 1 (1929). There, Gonzalez claimed the right to be appointed to a chaplaincy in the Roman Catholic Church under a will which provided that a member of his family receive that appointment. The Roman Catholic Archbishop of Manila, Philippine Islands, refused to appoint Gonzalez on the ground that he did not satisfy the qualifications established by Canon Law for that office. Gonzalez brought suit in the Court of First Instance of Manila for a judgment directing the Archbishop, among other things, to appoint him chaplain. The trial court entered such an order, but the Supreme Court of the Philippine Islands reversed and 'absolved the Archbishop from the complaint.' This Court affirmed. Mr. Justice Brandeis, speaking for the Court, defined the civil court role in the following words: 'In the absence of fraud, collusion, or arbitrariness, the decisions of the proper church tribunals on matters purely ecclesiastical, although affecting civil rights, are accepted in litigation before the secular courts as conclusive, because the parties in interest made them so by contract or otherwise.' 280 U.S., at 16.

In Kedroff v. St. Nicholas Cathedral of Russian Orthodox Church in North America, 344 U.S. 94 (1952), the Court converted the principle of *Watson* as qualified by *Gonzalez* into a constitutional rule. *Kedroff* grew out of a dispute between the Moscow-based general Russian Orthodox Church and the Russian Orthodox churches located in North America over an appointment to St. Nicholas Cathedral in New York City. The North American churches declared their independence from the general church, and the New York Legislature enacted a statute recognizing their administrative autonomy. The New York courts sustained the constitutionality of the statute and held that the North American churches' elected hierarch had the right to use the cathedral. This Court reversed, finding that the Moscow church had not acknowledged the schism, and holding the statute unconstitutional. The Court said:

> 'The opinion (in *Watson v. Jones*) radiates . . . a spirit of freedom for religious organizations, an independence from secular control or manipulation—in short, power to decide for themselves, free from state interference, matters of church government as well as those of faith and doctrine. Freedom to select the clergy, where no improper methods of choice are proven, we think, must now be said to have federal constitutional protection as a part of the free exercise of religion against state interference.' (Italics supplied.)

. . . This holding invalidating legislative action was extended to judicial action in Kreshik v. St. Nicholas Cathedral, 363 U.S. 190 (1960), where the Court held that the constitutional guarantees of religious liberty required the reversal of a judgment of the New York courts which transferred control of St. Nicholas Cathedral from the central governing authority of the Russian Orthodox Church to the independent Russian Church of America.

Thus, the First Amendment severely circumscribes the role that civil courts may play in resolving church property disputes. It is obvious, however, that not every civil court decision as to property claimed by a religious organization jeopardizes values protected by the First Amendment. Civil courts do not inhibit free exercise of religion merely by opening their doors to disputes involving church property. And there are neutral principles of law, developed for use in all property disputes, which can be applied without 'establishing' churches to which property is awarded. But First Amendment values are plainly jeopardized when church property litigation is made to turn on the resolution by civil courts of controversies over religious doctrine and practice. If civil courts undertake to resolve such controversies in order to adjudicate the property dispute, the hazards are ever present of inhibiting the free development of religious doctrine and of implicating secular interests in matters of purely ecclesiastical concern. . . . [The First] Amendment therefore commands civil courts to decide church property disputes without resolving underlying controversies over religious doctrine. Hence, States, religious organizations, and individuals must structure relationships involving church property so as not to require the civil courts to resolve ecclesiastical questions.

The Georgia courts have violated the command of the First Amendment. The departure-from-doctrine element of the implied trust theory which they applied requires the civil judiciary to determine whether actions of the general church constitute such a 'substantial departure' from the tenets of faith and practice existing at the time of the local churches' affiliation that the trust in favor of the general church must be declared to have terminated. This determination has two parts. The civil court must first decide whether the challenged actions of the general church depart substantially from prior doctrine. In reaching such a decision, the court must of necessity make its own interpretation of the meaning of church doctrines. If the court should decide that a substantial departure has occurred, it must then go on to determine whether the issue on which the general church has departed holds a place of such importance in the traditional theology as to require that the trust be terminated. A civil court can make this determination only after assessing the relative significance to the religion of the tenets from which departure was found. Thus, the departure-from-doctrine element of the Georgia implied trust theory requires the civil court to determine matters at the very core of a religion—the interpretation of particular church doctrines and the importance of those doctrines to the religion. Plainly, the First Amendment forbids civil courts from playing such a role. . . .

The judgment of the Supreme Court of Georgia is reversed, and the case is remanded for further proceedings not inconsistent with this opinion.

It is so ordered.

Mr. Justice HARLAN, concurring.

I am in entire agreement with the Court's rejection of the 'departure-from-doctrine' approach taken by the Georgia courts, as that approach necessarily requires the civilian courts to weigh the significance and the meaning of disputed religious doctrine. I do not, however, read the Court's opinion to go further to hold that the Fourteenth Amendment forbids civilian courts from enforcing a deed or will which expressly and clearly lays down conditions limiting a religious organization's use of the property which is granted. If, for example, the donor expressly gives his church some money on the condition that the church never ordain a woman as a minister or elder, or never amend certain specified articles of the Confession of Faith, he is entitled to his money back if the condition is not fulfilled. In such a case, the church should not be permitted to keep the property simply because church authorities have determined that the doctrinal innovation is justified by the faith's basic principles. *Cf.* Watson v. Jones, 13 Wall. 679, 722-724 (1872).

On this understanding, I join the Court's opinion.

NOTES AND QUESTIONS

1. *Departure-from-doctrine approach.* Is the main problem with the departure-from-doctrine approach a Free Exercise Clause problem or an Establishment Clause problem? In what way do the concerns overlap?
2. *Congregational vs. hierarchical structures. Watson v. Jones* dictated that different approaches were to apply to congregational vs. hierarchical religious bodies. The Presbyterian Church is an example of a hierarchical structure. Do churches, temples, mosques, and other houses of worship always fall neatly into one category or another? If not, how is a court to decide? Does a court risk answering theological questions beyond its competence in making this determination?
3. *Absolute deference.* For disputes in hierarchical structures, must a court always defer to the highest church authority? Note that the Court quotes with approval the following limitation: "In the absence of fraud, collusion, or arbitrariness, the decisions of the proper church tribunals on matters purely ecclesiastical, although affecting civil rights, are accepted in litigation before the secular courts as conclusive, because the parties in interest made them so by contract or otherwise." What counts as fraud, collusion, or arbitrariness?
4. *Alternative approaches?* What if a reviewing court really does not like the decision of the hierarchy? Does it have any options other than enforcing that decision? Consider this question in light of the following case.

Jones v. Wolf

443 U.S. 595 (1979)

Mr. Justice BLACKMUN delivered the opinion of the Court.

This case involves a dispute over the ownership of church property following a schism in a local church affiliated with a hierarchical church organization. The question for decision is whether civil courts, consistent with the First and Fourteenth Amendments to the Constitution, may resolve the dispute on the basis of "neutral principles of law," or whether they must defer to the resolution of an authoritative tribunal of the hierarchical church.

The Vineville Presbyterian Church of Macon, Ga., was organized in 1904, and first incorporated in 1915. Its corporate charter lapsed in 1935, but was revived and renewed in 1939, and continues in effect at the present time. [The property was deeded to the trustees of the Vineville Presbyterian Church, and local congregants provided funds for the construction and maintenance of the church.]

In the same year it was organized, the Vineville church was established as a member church of the Augusta-Macon Presbytery of the Presbyterian Church in the United States (PCUS). The PCUS has a generally hierarchical or connectional form of government, as contrasted with a congregational form.

Under the polity of the PCUS, the government of the local church is committed to its Session in the first instance, but the actions of this assembly or "court" are subject to the review and control of the higher church courts, the Presbytery, Synod, and General Assembly, respectively. The powers and duties of each level of the hierarchy are set forth in the constitution of the PCUS, the Book of Church Order, which is part of the record in the present case.

On May 27, 1973, at a congregational meeting of the Vineville church attended by a quorum of its duly enrolled members, 164 of them, including the pastor, voted to separate from the PCUS. Ninety-four members opposed the resolution. The majority immediately informed the PCUS of the action, and then united with another denomination, the Presbyterian Church in America. Although the minority remained on the church rolls for three years, they ceased to participate in the affairs of the Vineville church and conducted their religious activities elsewhere.

In response to the schism within the Vineville congregation, the Augusta-Macon Presbytery appointed a commission to investigate the dispute and, if possible, to resolve it. The commission eventually issued a written ruling declaring that the minority faction constituted "the true congregation of Vineville Presbyterian Church," and withdrawing from the majority faction "all authority to exercise office derived from the [PCUS]." The majority took no part in the commission's inquiry, and did not appeal its ruling to a higher PCUS tribunal.

Representatives of the minority faction sought relief in federal court, but their complaint was dismissed for want of jurisdiction. Lucas v. Hope, 515 F.2d 234 (CA5 1975), *cert. denied*, 424 U. S. 967 (1976). They then brought this class action in state court, seeking declaratory and injunctive orders establishing their right to exclusive possession and use of the Vineville church property as a member congregation of the PCUS. The trial court, purporting to apply Georgia's "neutral principles of law" approach to church property disputes, granted judgment for the majority. The Supreme Court of Georgia, holding that the trial court had correctly stated and applied Georgia law, and rejecting the minority's challenge based on the First and Fourteenth Amendments, affirmed. We granted certiorari.

Georgia's approach to church property litigation has evolved in response to Presbyterian Church v. Hull Church, 393 U.S. 440 (1969) (*Presbyterian Church I*), *rev'g* Presbyterian Church v. Eastern Heights Church, 224 Ga. 61, 159 S.E.2d 690 (1968). That case was a property dispute between the PCUS and two local Georgia churches that had withdrawn from the PCUS. The Georgia Supreme Court resolved the controversy by applying a theory of implied trust, whereby the property of a local church affiliated with a hierarchical church organization was deemed to be held in trust for the general church, provided the general church had not "substantially abandoned" the tenets of faith and practice as they existed at the time of affiliation. This Court reversed, holding that Georgia would have to find some other way of resolving church property disputes that did not draw the state courts into religious controversies. The court did not specify what that method should be, although it noted in passing that "there are neutral principles of law, developed for use in all property disputes, which can be applied without 'establishing' churches to which property is awarded."

On remand, the Georgia Supreme Court concluded that, without the departure-from-doctrine element, the implied trust theory would have to be abandoned in its entirety. In its place, the court adopted what is now known as the "neutral principles of law" method for resolving church property disputes. The court examined the deeds to the properties, the state statutes dealing with implied trusts, Ga. Code §§ 108-106, 108-107 (1978), and the Book of Church Order to determine whether there was any basis for a trust in favor of the general church. Finding nothing that would give rise to a trust in any of these documents, the court awarded the property on the basis of legal title, which was in the local church, or in the names of trustees for the local church. . . .

The only question presented by this case is which faction of the formerly united Vineville congregation is entitled to possess and enjoy the property located at 2193 Vineville Avenue in Macon, Ga. There can be little doubt about the general authority of civil courts to resolve this question. The State has an obvious and legitimate interest in the peaceful resolution of property disputes, and in providing a civil forum where the ownership of church property can be determined conclusively.

It is also clear, however, that "the First Amendment severely circumscribes the role that civil courts may play in resolving church property disputes." Most importantly, the First Amendment prohibits civil courts from resolving church property disputes on the basis of religious doctrine and practice. As a corollary to this commandment, the Amendment requires that civil courts defer to the resolution of issues of religious doctrine or polity by the highest court of a hierarchical church organization. Subject to these limitations, however, the First Amendment does not dictate that a State must follow a particular method of resolving church property disputes. Indeed, "a State may adopt *any* one of various approaches for settling church property disputes so long as it involves no consideration of doctrinal matters, whether the ritual and liturgy of worship or the tenets of faith."

At least in general outline, we think the "neutral principles of law" approach is consistent with the foregoing constitutional principles. . . .

The primary advantages of the neutral-principles approach are that it is completely secular in operation, and yet flexible enough to accommodate all forms of religious organization and polity. The method relies exclusively on objective, well-established concepts of trust and property law familiar to lawyers and judges. It thereby promises to free civil courts completely from entanglement in questions of religious doctrine, polity, and practice. Furthermore, the neutral-principles analysis shares the peculiar genius of private-law systems in general—flexibility in ordering private rights and obligations to reflect the intentions of the parties. Through appropriate reversionary clauses and trust provisions, religious societies can specify what is to happen to church property in the event of a particular contingency, or what religious body will determine the ownership in the event of a schism or doctrinal controversy. In this manner, a religious organization can ensure that a dispute over the ownership of church property will be resolved in accord with the desires of the members.

This is not to say that the application of the neutral-principles approach is wholly free of difficulty. The neutral-principles method, at least as it has evolved in Georgia, requires a civil court to examine certain religious documents, such as a church constitution, for language of trust in favor of the general church. In undertaking such an examination, a civil court must take special care to scrutinize the document in purely secular terms, and not to rely on religious precepts in determining whether the document indicates that the parties have intended to create a trust. In addition, there may be cases where the deed, the corporate charter, or the constitution of the general church incorporates religious concepts in the provisions relating to the ownership of property. If in such a case the interpretation of the instruments of ownership would require the civil court to resolve a religious controversy, then the court must defer to the resolution of the doctrinal issue by the authoritative ecclesiastical body. *Serbian Orthodox Diocese*, 426 U.S., at 709.

On balance, however, the promise of nonentanglement and neutrality inherent in the neutral-principles approach more than compensates for what will be occasional problems in application. These problems, in addition, should be gradually eliminated as recognition is given to the obligation of "States, religious organizations, and individuals [to] structure relationships involving church property so as not to require the civil courts to resolve ecclesiastical questions." *Presbyterian Church I*, 393 U.S., at 449. We therefore hold that a State is constitutionally entitled to adopt neutral principles of law as a means of adjudicating a church property dispute. . . .

The neutral-principles approach cannot be said to "inhibit" the free exercise of religion, any more than do other neutral provisions of state law governing the manner in which churches own property, hire employees, or purchase goods. Under the neutral-principles approach, the outcome of a church property dispute is not foreordained. At any time before the dispute erupts, the parties can ensure, if they so desire, that the faction loyal to the hierarchical church will retain the church property. They can modify the deeds or the corporate charter to include a right of reversion or trust in favor of the general church. Alternatively, the constitution of the general church can be made to recite an express trust in favor of the denominational church. The burden involved in taking such steps will be minimal. And the civil courts will be bound to give effect to the result indicated by the parties, provided it is embodied in some legally cognizable form.

It remains to be determined whether the Georgia neutral-principles analysis was constitutionally applied on the facts of this case. . . .

If in fact Georgia has adopted a presumptive rule of majority representation, defeasible upon a showing that the identity of the local church is to be determined by some other means, we think this would be consistent with both the neutral-principles analysis and the First Amendment. Majority rule is generally employed in the governance of religious societies. *See* Bouldin v. Alexander, 15 Wall. 131 (1872). Furthermore, the majority faction generally can be identified without resolving any question of religious doctrine or polity. Certainly, there was no dispute in the present case about the identity of the duly enrolled members of the Vineville church when the dispute arose, or about the fact that a quorum was present, or about the final vote. Most importantly, any rule of majority representation can always be overcome, under the neutral-principles approach, either by providing, in the corporate charter or the constitution of the general church, that the identity of the local church is to be established in some other way, or by providing that the church property is held in trust for the general church and those who remain loyal to it. Indeed, the State may adopt any method of overcoming the majoritarian presumption, so long as the use of that method does not impair free-exercise rights or entangle the civil courts in matters of religious controversy.

Neither the trial court nor the Supreme Court of Georgia, however, explicitly stated that it was adopting a presumptive rule of majority representation. Moreover, there are at least some indications that under Georgia law the process of identifying the faction that represents the Vineville church involves considerations of religious doctrine and polity. Georgia law requires that "church property be held according to the terms of the church government," and provides that a local church affiliated with a hierarchical religious association "is part of the whole body of the general church and is subject to the higher authority of the organization and its laws and regulations." All this may suggest that the identity of the "Vineville Presbyterian Church" named in the deeds must be determined according to terms of the Book of Church Order, which sets out the laws and regulations of churches affiliated with the PCUS. Such a determination, however, would appear to require a civil court to pass on questions of religious doctrine, and to usurp the function of the commission appointed by the Presbytery, which already has determined that petitioners represent the "true congregation" of the Vineville church. Therefore, if Georgia law provides that the identity of the Vineville church is to be determined according to the "laws and regulations" of the PCUS, then the First Amendment requires that the Georgia courts give deference to the presbyterial commission's determination of that church's identity.

This Court, of course, does not declare what the law of Georgia is. Since the grounds for the decision that respondents represent the Vineville church remain unarticulated, the judgment of the Supreme Court of Georgia is vacated, and the case is remanded for further proceedings not inconsistent with this opinion.

It is so ordered.

Mr. Justice POWELL, with whom THE CHIEF JUSTICE, Mr. Justice STEWART, and Mr. Justice WHITE join, dissenting.

This case presents again a dispute among church members over the control of a local church's property. Although the Court appears to accept established principles that I have thought would resolve this case, it superimposes on these principles a new structure of rules that will make the decision of these cases by civil courts more difficult. The new analysis also is more likely to invite intrusion into church polity forbidden by the First Amendment.

The Court begins by stating that "[t]his case involves a dispute over the ownership of church property," suggesting that the concern is with legal or equitable ownership in the real property sense. But the ownership of the property of the Vineville church is not at issue. The deeds place title in the Vineville Presbyterian Church, or in trustees of that church, and none of the parties has questioned the validity of those deeds. The question actually presented is which of the factions within the local congregation has the right to control the actions of the titleholder, and thereby to control the use of the property, as the Court later acknowledges.

Since 1872, disputes over control of church property usually have been resolved under principles established by Watson v. Jones, 13 Wall. 679 (1872). Under the new and complex, two-stage analysis approved today, a court instead first must apply newly defined "neutral principles of law" to determine whether property titled to the local church is held in trust for the general church organization with which the local church is affiliated. If it is, then the court will grant control of the property to the councils of the general church. If not, then control by the local congregation will be recognized. In the latter situation, if there is a schism in the local congregation, as in this case, the second stage of the new analysis becomes applicable. Again, the Court fragments the analysis into two substeps for the purpose of determining which of the factions should control the property.

As this new approach inevitably will increase the involvement of civil courts in church controversies, and as it departs from long-established precedents, I dissent. . . .

When civil courts step in to resolve intrachurch disputes over control of church property, they will either support or overturn the authoritative resolution of the dispute within the church itself. The new analysis, under the attractive banner of "neutral principles," actually invites the civil courts to do the latter. The proper rule of decision, that I thought had been settled until today, requires a court to give effect in all cases to the decisions of the church government agreed upon by the members before the dispute arose. . . .

The Court acknowledges that the church law of the Presbyterian Church in the United States (PCUS), of which the Vineville church is a part, provides for the authoritative resolution of this question by the Presbytery. Indeed, the Court indicates that Georgia, consistently with the First Amendment, may adopt the *Watson v. Jones* rule of adherence to the resolution of the dispute according to church law—a rule that would necessitate reversal of the judgment for the respondents. But instead of requiring the state courts to take this approach, the Court approves as well an alternative rule of state law: the Georgia courts are said to be free to "adop[t] a presumptive rule of majority representation, defeasible upon a showing that the identity of the local church is to be determined by some other means."

This showing may be made by proving that the church has "provid[ed], in the corporate charter or the constitution of the general church, that the identity of the local church is to be established in some other way."

On its face, this rebuttable presumption also requires reversal of the state court's judgment in favor of the schismatic faction. The polity of the PCUS commits to the Presbytery the resolution of the dispute within the local church. Having shown this structure of church government for the determination of the identity of the local congregation, the petitioners have rebutted any presumption that this question has been left to a majority vote of the local congregation.

The Court nevertheless declines to order reversal. Rather than decide the case here in accordance with established First Amendment principles, the Court leaves open the possibility that the state courts might adopt some restrictive evidentiary rule that would render the petitioners' evidence inadequate to overcome the presumption of majority control. But, aside from a passing reference to the use of the neutral-principles approach developed earlier in its opinion, the Court affords no guidance as to the constitutional limitations on such an evidentiary rule; the state courts, it says, are free to adopt any rule that is constitutional.

> "Indeed, the state may adopt any method of overcoming the majoritarian presumption, so long as the use of that method does not impair free-exercise rights or entangle the civil courts in matters of religious controversy."

In essence, the Court's instructions on remand therefore allow the state courts the choice of following the long-settled rule of *Watson v. Jones* or of adopting some other rule—unspecified by the Court—that the state courts view as consistent with the First Amendment. Not only questions of state law but also important issues of federal constitutional law thus are left to the state courts for their decision, and, if they depart from *Watson v. Jones*, they will travel a course left totally uncharted by this Court.

Disputes among church members over the control of church property arise almost invariably out of disagreements regarding doctrine and practice. Because of the religious nature of these disputes, civil courts should decide them according to principles that do not interfere with the free exercise of religion in accordance with church polity and doctrine.

The only course that achieves this constitutional requirement is acceptance by civil courts of the decisions reached within the polity chosen by the church members themselves. . . .

Accordingly, in each case involving an intrachurch dispute—including disputes over church property—the civil court must focus directly on ascertaining, and then following, the decision made within the structure of church governance. By doing so, the court avoids two equally unacceptable departures from the genuine neutrality mandated by the First Amendment. First, it refrains from direct review and revision of decisions of the church on matters of religious doctrine and practice that underlie the church's determination of intrachurch controversies, including those that relate to control of church property. Equally important, by recognizing the authoritative resolution reached within the religious association, the civil court avoids interfering indirectly with the religious governance of those who have formed the association and submitted themselves to its authority. . . .

The principles developed in prior decisions thus afford clear guidance in the case before us. The Vineville church is presbyterian, a part of the PCUS. The presbyterian form of church government, adopted by the PCUS, is "a hierarchical structure of tribunals which consists of, in ascending order, (1) the Church Session, composed of the elders of the local church; (2) the Presbytery, composed of several churches in a geographical area; (3) the Synod, generally composed of all Presbyteries within a State; and (4) the General Assembly, the highest governing body." The Book of Church Order subjects the Session to "review and control" by the Presbytery in all matters, even authorizing the Presbytery to replace the leadership of the local congregation, to winnow its membership, and to take control of it. No provision of the Book of Church Order gives the Session the authority to withdraw the local church, removing the dissidents from church office, asserting direct control over the government of the church, and recognizing the petitioners as the legitimate congregation and Session of the church.

NOTES AND QUESTIONS

1. *The neutral principles of law alternative.* What do you make of the *Jones* "neutral principles" approach? Is Justice Powell persuasive when he argues that it cannot be applied without getting into matters of church doctrine? Can *Watson*'s deference approach always be applied without entanglement in religious controversies? Which approach, the *Jones* "neutral principles" approach or the *Watson* deference approach, advances the values of "non-entanglement and neutrality" more effectively? Is one approach generally easier for courts to apply?
2. *Choice of test.* At one point, the Supreme Court holds that courts have a choice of which test to apply: "[A] State may adopt *any* one of various approaches for settling church property disputes so long as it involves no consideration of doctrinal matters, whether the ritual and liturgy of worship or the tenets of faith." What principle should guide courts in choosing which should apply? Is there a risk in giving courts this choice?
3. *Advance planning.* Perhaps the lesson of *Jones* is that, if hierarchal churches wish to retain ownership of local church properties in the event of a schism, they must require all affiliated member churches to record new property deeds with clear statements of trust in favor of the mother church. Should the mother church have the burden of revising land records to protect its interests? Is it more difficult for religious associations compared to other associations to specify what is to happen to its property in the event of a dispute?

B. EMPLOYMENT DISPUTES

AN EXTENDED NOTE ON *SERBIAN EASTERN ORTHODOX DIOCESE V. MILIVOJEVICH*

In Serbian Eastern Orthodox Diocese v. Milivojevich, 426 U.S. 696 (1976), the Supreme Court faced a case in which Bishop Dionisije Milivojevich alleged that his removal as Bishop of the American-Canadian Diocese did not comply with church procedures or rules and was therefore void under the *Gonzalez* "fraud, collusion, or arbitrariness" exception to the rule that civil courts must enforce the decision of the highest body in a hierarchical dispute. *Id.* at 698. The highest bodies of the Serbian Eastern Orthodox Church, the Holy Assembly and Holy Synod, removed Milivojevich in 1964 incident to defrockment proceedings. Milivojevich sued in the Illinois state courts, alleging that the church's proceedings were both substantively and procedurally deficient. The proceedings commenced in state trial court in 1963 and continued over a 13-year period. After a "lengthy trial, the trial court filed [an opinion] which concluded that 'no substantial evidence was produced . . . that fraud, collusion, or arbitrariness existed in any of the actions or decisions preliminary to or during the final proceedings of the decision to defrock Bishop Dionisije made by the highest Hierarchical bodies of the Mother Church.'" *Id.* at 707.

On appeal, however, the Illinois Supreme Court ruled for Milivojevich, holding that the church failed to follow its own rules and official procedures in removing him; accordingly, the court declined to give legal effect to the actions of the Holy Assembly and the Holy Synod because the church's decision was "arbitrary." *Id.* at 708. In order to reach the merits of Bishop Milivojevich's claims, the Illinois Supreme Court reviewed and applied various church documents, including its constitution and bylaws. *Id.* at 698-699, 707-709. The Illinois Supreme Court essentially ordered the church to reinstate Milivojevich to his post as bishop. The Supreme Court of the United States granted a writ of certiorari to review the case.

Writing for an eight-justice majority, Justice Brennan rejected the state supreme court's reasoning in the case. "The fallacy fatal to the judgment of the Illinois Supreme Court is that it rests upon an impermissible rejection of the decisions of the highest ecclesiastical tribunals of this hierarchical church upon the issues in dispute, and impermissibly substitutes its own inquiry into church polity and resolutions based thereon of those disputes." *Id.* at 708. He explained that "where resolution of the disputes cannot be made without extensive inquiry by civil courts into religious law and polity, the First and Fourteenth Amendments mandate that civil courts shall not disturb the decisions of the highest ecclesiastical tribunal within a church of hierarchical polity, but must accept such decisions as binding on them, in the application to the religious issues of doctrine or polity before them." *Id.* at 709.

With respect to the question of "fraud, collusion, or arbitrariness," Justice Brennan found that "[n]o issue of 'fraud' or 'collusion' is involved in this case." *Id.* at 713 n.7. With respect to the "arbitrariness" exception, invoked by the state supreme court, Justice Brennan found that "no 'arbitrariness' exception—in the sense of an inquiry whether the decisions of the highest ecclesiastical tribunal of a hierarchical church complied with church laws and regulations—is consistent with the constitutional mandate that civil courts are bound to accept the decisions of the highest judicatories of a religious organization of hierarchical polity on matters of discipline, faith, internal organization, or ecclesiastical rule, custom, or law." *Id.* Because such inquiries entrain courts into matters of religious doctrine, "a civil court must accept the ecclesiastical decisions of church tribunals as it finds them." *Id.* Applying the rules of the Serbian Eastern Orthodox Church, Justice Brennan held the Holy Assembly of Bishops rested at the top of the church hierarchy and, accordingly, that its decision—however reached—was binding on the civil courts. *See id.* at 716-719. Although the Court did not formally abolish the "fraud, collusion, or arbitrariness" exceptions recognized in the *Gonzalez* dicta, the majority very narrowly construed these exemptions to exclude claims that a church failed to follow its own internal procedures properly. Civil courts do not sit to judge whether a church tribunal has observed its own rules, but with respect to a hierarchical church, instead sit only to identify the person or body that possesses final decisional authority.

Dissenting, then-Justice Rehnquist argued that Illinois state courts faced both the necessity and duty "to ask the real Bishop of the American-Canadian Diocese [to] please stand up." *Id.* at 726 (Rehnquist, J., dissenting). "If civil courts, consistently with the First Amendment, may do that much, the question arises why they may not do what the Illinois courts did here regarding the defrockment of Bishop Dionisije [Milivojevich], and conclude, on the basis of testimony from experts on the canon law at issue, that the decision of the religious tribunal involved was rendered in violation of its own stated rules of procedure." *Id.* at 727. He objected that "[i]f the civil courts are to be bound by any sheet of parchment bearing the ecclesiastical seal and purporting to be a decree of a church court, they can easily be converted into the handmaidens of arbitrary lawlessness." *Id.* A state court may simply enforce a religious organization's own procedural rules, without becoming enmeshed in any questions of religious doctrine, because "an application of neutral principles of law [is] consistent with the decisions of this Court." *Id.* at 734. For Justice Rehnquist, the only relevant First Amendment consideration consists of ascertaining whether the civil courts "remain neutral on matters of religious doctrine." *Id.* at 735.

NOTES AND QUESTIONS

1. *Resolving disputes within hierarchical churches. Milivojevich* represents a strong application of a mandatory rule of near-absolute deference to the decision of the highest authority within a hierarchical church—a position seriously undermined a few years later in *Jones.* The Brennan approach in *Milivojevich* has the virtue of limiting, to the maximum extent possible, the potential for civil courts to become enmeshed in questions of religious dogma—even at the cost of enforcing dubious decisions tainted by arbitrary decision making within the church hierarchy. Is the risk of government imposed religious doctrine so great as to justify a near-complete abdication of judicial review of decisions reached by hierarchical church authorities?
2. *The "fraud, collusion, or arbitrariness" exceptions revisited.* Suppose that a member of the Holy Assembly of Bishops admitted, in a deposition, that he took a bribe to vote to remove Milivojevich. Would that be a sufficient basis for voiding the decision, if one were to apply the substance of Justice Brennan's reasoning in *Milivojevich*?
3. *Enforcing internal church procedural rules.* Is Justice Rehnquist persuasive when he argues that holding a church to its own stated procedures does not (and cannot) seriously implicate the substance of church doctrines? On the other hand, if the dichotomy between substance and procedure is vague, isn't Justice Brennan right to worry that the government may

end up imposing its view of religious doctrine on church entities? For example, if a church rule calls for trial by ordeal, but the body sua sponte declares that the divine will, as ascertained by the assembly, strongly prefers a game of paper, rock, scissors, should the trial courts of Illinois force trial by ordeal?

How do the rules regarding government involvement in internal religious disputes apply in the context of personnel decisions that allegedly violate otherwise applicable civil rights statutes, such as Title VII (which prohibits entities that employ more than 15 persons from engaging in discrimination based on race or sex)? *See* 42 U.S.C. § 2000e-2 (declaring it unlawful to "fail or refuse to hire or to discharge any individual, or otherwise to discriminate against any individual with respect to his compensation, terms, conditions, or privileges of employment, because of such individual's race, color, religion, sex, or national origin"). Or other federal or state antidiscrimination laws, such as the Americans with Disabilities Act, 42 U.S.C. §§ 12101 *et seq.*, or the Age Discrimination Act, 29 U.S.C. §§ 621 *et seq.*? May Congress, a state legislature, or a city council apply such laws to religious organizations and institutions? Or does the Free Exercise Clause and Establishment Clause require that religious organizations enjoy the freedom to choose their employees as they think best?

Hosanna-Tabor Evangelical Lutheran Church and School v. Equal Employment Opportunity Commission

565 U.S. 171 (2012)

Chief Justice ROBERTS delivered the opinion of the Court.

Certain employment discrimination laws authorize employees who have been wrongfully terminated to sue their employers for reinstatement and damages. The question presented is whether the Establishment and Free Exercise Clauses of the First Amendment bar such an action when the employer is a religious group and the employee is one of the group's ministers. . . .

[Cheryl Perich worked at a religiously affiliated school in Redford, Michigan. She was classified as a "called teacher," that is a teacher "called to their vocation by God through a congregation." She held the title "Minister of Religion, Commissioned" within the church and also at her school. Perich's teaching duties included both academic subjects and religion classes. "Perich taught kindergarten during her first four years at Hosanna-Tabor and fourth grade during the 2003-2004 school year. She taught math, language arts, social studies, science, gym, art, and music. She also taught a religion class four days a week [and] led the students in prayer and devotional exercises each day." Perich claimed that the school retaliated against her in violation of the Americans with Disability Act (ADA). After a medical leave and narcolepsy diagnosis, Perich informed the school principal that her doctor had cleared her to return to work. In response, the principal expressed concerns about the safety of Perich's students. The school board requested that Perich resign but she declined. After Perich told the principal that she would sue for disability discrimination, she was fired. Correspondence from the school indicated that she lost her job because she was insubordinate and threatened to take legal action. Under the ADA, it is illegal for an employer to retaliate against an employee for bringing or threatening to bring a disability discrimination suit. Hosanna-Tabor Evangelical Lutheran Church and School (Hosanna-Tabor) responded to this lawsuit by filing a motion to dismiss, invoking a First Amendment-grounded "ministerial exception" to the ADA. "According to the Church, Perich was a minister, and she had been fired for a religious reason—namely, that her threat to sue the Church violated the Synod's belief that Christians should resolve their disputes internally." The district court agreed with the Church's ministerial exception claim, at least as applied on these facts, and accordingly granted summary judgment in Hosanna-Tabor's favor. The U.S. Court of Appeals, however, reversed the grant of summary judgment, 597 F.3d 769, 777 (6th Cir. 2012). It found that although a ministerial exception applied under the ADA, it did not apply in this instance because Perich was not, in fact, a "minister." *Id.* at 778-781. The Supreme Court granted review.]

The First Amendment provides, in part, that "Congress shall make no law respecting an establishment of religion, or prohibiting the free exercise thereof." We have said that these two Clauses "often exert conflicting pressures," Cutter v. Wilkinson, 544 U.S. 709, 719 (2005), and that there can be "internal tension . . . between the Establishment Clause and the Free Exercise Clause," Tilton v. Richardson, 403 U.S. 672, 677 (1971) (plurality opinion). Not so here. Both Religion Clauses bar the government from interfering with the decision of a religious group to fire one of its ministers. . . .

[Chief Justice Roberts provides an extended history of religious establishments in the colonial, revolutionary, and framing eras, including President James Madison's veto of a bill that could have chartered the "Protestant Episcopal Church in the town of Alexandria in what was then the District of Columbia." Chief Justice Roberts places particular emphasis on the fact that the Framers, including Madison, did not believe that the federal government could select or remove ministers consistently with the Religion Clauses.]

Given this understanding of the Religion Clauses—and the absence of government employment regulation generally—it was some time before questions about government interference with a church's ability to select its own ministers came before the courts. This Court touched upon the issue indirectly, however, in the context of disputes over church property. Our decisions in that area confirm that it is impermissible for the government to contradict a church's determination of who can act as its ministers. . . .

Until today, we have not had occasion to consider whether this freedom of a religious organization to select its ministers is implicated by a suit alleging discrimination in employment. The Courts of Appeals, in contrast, have had extensive experience with this issue. Since the passage of Title VII of the Civil Rights Act of 1964, 42 U.S.C. § 2000e *et seq.*, and other employment discrimination laws, the Courts of Appeals have uniformly recognized the existence of a "ministerial exception," grounded in the First Amendment, that precludes application of such legislation to claims concerning the employment relationship between a religious institution and its ministers.

We agree that there is such a ministerial exception. The members of a religious group put their faith in the hands of their ministers. Requiring a church to accept or retain an unwanted minister, or punishing a church for failing to do so, intrudes upon more than a mere employment decision. Such action interferes with the internal governance of the church, depriving the church of control over the selection of those who will personify its beliefs. By imposing an unwanted minister, the state infringes the Free Exercise Clause, which protects a religious group's right to shape its own faith and mission through its appointments. According the state the power to determine which individuals will minister to the faithful also violates the Establishment Clause, which prohibits government involvement in such ecclesiastical decisions. . . .

The EEOC and Perich [] contend that our decision in Employment Div., Dept. of Human Resources of Ore. v. Smith, 494 U.S. 872 (1990), precludes recognition of a ministerial exception. In *Smith*, two members of the Native American Church were denied state unemployment benefits after it was determined that they had been fired from their jobs for ingesting peyote, a crime under Oregon law. We held that this did not violate the Free Exercise Clause, even though the peyote had been ingested for sacramental purposes, because the "right of free exercise does not relieve an individual of the obligation to comply with a valid and neutral law of general applicability on the ground that the law proscribes (or prescribes) conduct that his religion prescribes (or proscribes)." *Id.*, at 879 (internal quotation marks omitted).

It is true that the ADA's prohibition on retaliation, like Oregon's prohibition on peyote use, is a valid and neutral law of general applicability. But a church's selection of its ministers is unlike an individual's ingestion of peyote. *Smith* involved government regulation of only outward physical acts. The present case, in contrast, concerns government interference with an internal church decision that affects the faith and mission of the church itself. *See id.*, at 877 (distinguishing the government's regulation of "physical acts" from its "lend[ing] its power to one or the other side in controversies over religious authority or dogma"). The contention that *Smith* forecloses recognition of a ministerial exception rooted in the Religion Clauses has no merit.

Having concluded that there is a ministerial exception grounded in the Religion Clauses of the First Amendment, we consider whether the exception applies in this case. We hold that it does. . . .

Because Perich was a minister within the meaning of the exception, the First Amendment requires dismissal of this employment discrimination suit against her religious employer. The EEOC and Perich originally sought an order reinstating Perich to her former position as a called teacher. By requiring the Church to accept a minister it did not want, such an order would have plainly violated the Church's freedom under the Religion Clauses to select its own ministers. . . .

The case before us is an employment discrimination suit brought on behalf of a minister, challenging her church's decision to fire her. Today we hold only that the ministerial exception bars such a suit. We express no view on whether the exception bars other types of suits, including actions by employees alleging breach of contract or tortious conduct by their religious employers. There will be time enough to address the applicability of the exception to other circumstances if and when they arise.

. . . The interest of society in the enforcement of employment discrimination statutes is undoubtedly important. But so too is the interest of religious groups in choosing who will preach their beliefs, teach their faith, and carry out their mission.

When a minister who has been fired sues her church alleging that her termination was discriminatory, the First Amendment has struck the balance for us. The church must be free to choose those who will guide it on its way.

The judgment of the Court of Appeals for the Sixth Circuit is reversed.

It is so ordered.

Justice THOMAS, concurring.

I join the Court's opinion. I write separately to note that, in my view, the Religion Clauses require civil courts to apply the ministerial exception and to defer to a religious organization's good-faith understanding of who qualifies as its minister. As the Court explains, the Religion Clauses guarantee religious organizations autonomy in matters of internal governance, including the selection of those who will minister the faith. A religious organization's right to choose its ministers would be hollow, however, if secular courts could second-guess the organization's sincere determination that a given employee is a "minister" under the organization's theological tenets. . . .

[Justice ALITO's concurring opinion, with whom Justice KAGAN joins, is omitted.]

NOTES AND QUESTIONS

1. *Application of* Smith. The Court concedes that the American with Disabilities Act was a neutral law of general applicability. Nonetheless, it distinguished *Smith* on the grounds that "*Smith* involved government regulation of only outward physical acts. The present case, in contrast, concerns government interference with an internal church decision that affects the faith and mission of the church itself." Is this distinction persuasive? How should a court categorize a church decision that ingesting peyote is a sacrament?
2. *Neutral principles of law.* In order to win her retaliation suit, Perich would have had to prove that (1) she engaged in activity protected by the ADA; (2) she suffered a materially adverse action; and (3) there was a causal link between the protected activity and the adverse action. Would it be possible to resolve Perich's ADA claim without delving into questions of religious doctrine? What did the Court have to say about the *Jones v. Wolf* approach?
3. *Absolute nature of exemption.* Under the ministerial exemption, religious institutions do not need to offer a religious justification for their employment decisions. Both churches whose doctrine requires that their clergy be male as well as churches whose doctrine espouses equality between the sexes are exempt from sex discrimination suits brought by ministers.
4. *What suits are barred by the ministerial exemption?* The Court expressed "no view on whether the exception bars other types of suits, including actions by employees alleging breach of contract or tortious conduct by their religious employers." Are those claims different? If they are different, what explains why a sex discrimination or sexual harassment claim is barred but not a breach of contract claim? If they are not different, does this mean that those who qualify as ministers are stripped of all legal protections vis-à-vis their employer?

5. *Who counts as a "minister."* What kinds of jobs might plausibly fall within the "ministerial exception" recognized in *Hosanna-Tabor*? Clearly someone with direct clerical responsibilities falls within the category—but what other kinds of employments qualify for the exemption? Would a choir director, for example, qualify? What about a person working in a church-related day care center? A janitor? Does *Hosanna-Tabor* provide a workable test for deciding precisely who counts as a "minister"?
6. *Entanglement in religious doctrine.* What causes greater entanglement in religious doctrine: deciding whether Hosanna-Tabor retaliated against Perich for threatening to bring an ADA suit or deciding whether Perich qualifies as a minister for purposes of the ministerial exemption?

The *Hosanna-Tabor* decision left open the question of how to determine whether an employee was a "ministerial employee" who could no longer bring a civil rights case against their religious employer. *Our Lady of Guadalupe* starts to answer that question.

Our Lady of Guadalupe v. Morrissey-Berru

140 S. Ct. 2049 (2020)

Justice ALITO delivered the opinion of the Court.

These cases require us to decide whether the First Amendment permits courts to intervene in employment disputes involving teachers at religious schools who are entrusted with the responsibility of instructing their students in the faith. The First Amendment protects the right of religious institutions "to decide for themselves, free from state interference, matters of church government as well as those of faith and doctrine." Applying this principle, we held in *Hosanna-Tabor Evangelical Lutheran Church and School v. EEOC* (2012), that the First Amendment barred a court from entertaining an employment discrimination claim brought by an elementary school teacher, Cheryl Perich, against the religious school where she taught. Our decision built on a line of lower court cases adopting what was dubbed the "ministerial exception" to laws governing the employment relationship between a religious institution and certain key employees. We did not announce "a rigid formula" for determining whether an employee falls within this exception, but we identified circumstances that we found relevant in that case, including Perich's title as a "Minister of Religion, Commissioned," her educational training, and her responsibility to teach religion and participate with students in religious activities.

In the cases now before us, we consider employment discrimination claims brought by two elementary school teachers at Catholic schools whose teaching responsibilities are similar to Perich's. Although these teachers were not given the title of "minister" and have less religious training than Perich, we hold that their cases fall within the same rule that dictated our decision in *Hosanna-Tabor*. The religious education and formation of students is the very reason for the existence of most private religious schools, and therefore the selection and supervision of the teachers upon whom the schools rely to do this work lie at the core of their mission.

Judicial review of the way in which religious schools discharge those responsibilities would undermine the independence of religious institutions in a way that the First Amendment does not tolerate. . . .

The First Amendment provides that "Congress shall make no law respecting an establishment of religion, or prohibiting the free exercise thereof." Among other things, the Religion Clauses protect the right of churches and other religious institutions to decide matters " 'of faith and doctrine' " without government intrusion. . . .

The independence of religious institutions in matters of "faith and doctrine" is closely linked to independence in what we have termed " 'matters of church government.'" This does not mean that religious institutions enjoy a general immunity from secular laws, but it does protect their autonomy with respect to internal management decisions that are essential to the institution's central mission. And a component of this autonomy is the selection of the individuals who play certain key roles.

The "ministerial exception" was based on this insight. Under this rule, courts are bound to stay out of employment disputes involving those holding certain important positions with churches and other religious institutions. The rule appears to have acquired the label "ministerial exception" because the individuals involved in pioneering cases were described as "ministers." . . . Without that power, a wayward minister's preaching, teaching, and counseling could contradict the church's tenets and lead the congregation away from the faith. The ministerial exception was recognized to preserve a church's independent authority in such matters. . . .

In *Hosanna-Tabor,* Cheryl Perich, a kindergarten and fourth grade teacher at an Evangelical Lutheran school, filed suit in federal court, claiming that she had been discharged because of a disability, in violation of the Americans with Disabilities Act of 1990 (ADA). The school responded that the real reason for her dismissal was her violation of the Lutheran doctrine that disputes should be resolved internally and not by going to outside authorities. We held that her suit was barred by the "ministerial exception" and noted that it "concern[ed] government interference with an internal church decision that affects the faith and mission of the church." We declined "to adopt a rigid formula for deciding when an employee qualifies as a minister," and we added that it was "enough for us to conclude, in this our first case involving the ministerial exception, that the exception covers Perich, given all the circumstances of her employment." We identified four relevant circumstances but did not highlight any as essential.

First, we noted that her church had given Perich the title of "minister, with a role distinct from that of most of its members." . . .

Second, Perich's position "reflected a significant degree of religious training followed by a formal process of commissioning."

Third, "Perich held herself out as a minister of the Church by accepting the formal call to religious service, according to its terms," and by claiming certain tax benefits.

Fourth, "Perich's job duties reflected a role in conveying the Church's message and carrying out its mission." . . .

What matters, at bottom, is what an employee does. And implicit in our decision in *Hosanna-Tabor* was a recognition that educating young people in their faith, inculcating its teachings, and training them to live their faith are responsibilities that lie at the very core of the mission of a private religious school. As we put it, Perich had been entrusted with the responsibility of "transmitting the Lutheran faith to the next generation." . . .

Religious education is vital to many faiths practiced in the United States. . . . In the Catholic tradition, religious education is " 'intimately bound up with the whole of the Church's life.' " . . . Similarly, Protestant churches, from the earliest settlements in this country, viewed education as a religious obligation. . . . Religious education is a matter of central importance in Judaism. . . . Religious education is also important in Islam. . . . The Church of Jesus Christ of Latter-day Saints has a long tradition of religious education, with roots in revelations given to Joseph Smith. . . . Seventh-day Adventists "trace the importance of education back to the Garden of Eden." . . .

This brief survey does not do justice to the rich diversity of religious education in this country, but it shows the close connection that religious institutions draw between their central purpose and educating the young in the faith.

When we apply this understanding of the Religion Clauses to the cases now before us, it is apparent that Morrissey-Berru and Biel qualify for the exemption we recognized in *Hosanna-Tabor.* There is abundant record evidence that they both performed vital religious duties. Educating and forming students in the Catholic faith lay at the core of the mission of the schools where they taught, and their employment agreements and faculty handbooks specified in no uncertain terms that they were expected to help the schools carry out this mission and that their work would be evaluated to ensure that they were fulfilling that responsibility. As elementary school teachers responsible for providing instruction in all subjects, including religion, they were the members of the school staff who were entrusted most directly with the responsibility of educating their students in the faith. And not only were they obligated to provide instruction about the Catholic faith, but they were also expected to guide their students, by word and deed, toward the goal of living their lives in accordance with the faith. They prayed with their students, attended Mass with the students, and prepared the children for their participation in other religious activities. Their positions did not have all the attributes of Perich's. Their titles did not include the term "minister," and they had less formal religious training, but their core responsibilities as teachers of religion were essentially the same. And both their schools expressly saw them as playing a vital part in carrying out the mission of the church, and the schools' definition and explanation of their roles is important. In a country with the religious diversity of the United States, judges cannot be expected to have a complete understanding and appreciation of the role played by every person who performs a particular role in every religious tradition. A religious institution's explanation of the role of such employees in the life of the religion in question is important.

In holding that Morrissey-Berru and Biel did not fall within the *Hosanna-Tabor* exception, the Ninth Circuit misunderstood our decision. . . .

The Ninth Circuit's rigid test produced a distorted analysis. First, it invested undue significance in the fact that Morrissey-Berru and Biel did not have clerical titles. . . . It is true that Perich's title included the term "minister," but we never said that her title (or her reference to herself as a "minister") was necessary to trigger the *Hosanna-Tabor* exception. . . .

Second, the Ninth Circuit assigned too much weight to the fact that Morrissey-Berru and Biel had less formal religious schooling than Perich. . . . The schools in question here thought that Morrissey-Berru and Biel had a sufficient understanding of Catholicism to teach their students, and judges have no warrant to second-guess that judgment or to impose their own credentialing requirements.

Third, the *St. James* panel inappropriately diminished the significance of Biel's duties because they did not evince "close guidance and involvement" in "students' spiritual lives." . . .

Respondents go further astray in suggesting that an employee can never come within the *Hosanna-Tabor* exception unless the employee is a "practicing" member of the religion with which the employer is associated. . . . When a school with a religious mission entrusts a teacher with the responsibility of educating and forming students in the faith, judicial intervention into disputes between the school and the teacher threatens the school's independence in a way that the First Amendment does not allow.

* * *

For these reasons, the judgment of the Court of Appeals in each case is reversed, and the cases are remanded for proceedings consistent with this opinion.

It is so ordered.

Justice THOMAS, with whom Justice GORSUCH joins, concurring.

I agree with the Court that Morrissey-Berru's and Biel's positions fall within the "ministerial exception," because, as Catholic school teachers, they are charged with "carry[ing] out [the religious] mission" of the parish schools . . . . I write separately, however, to reiterate my view that the Religion Clauses require civil courts to defer to religious organizations' good-faith claims that a certain employee's position is "ministerial." . . .

This deference is necessary because, as the Court rightly observes, judges lack the requisite "understanding and appreciation of the role played by every person who performs a particular role in every religious tradition." What qualifies as "ministerial" is an inherently theological question, and thus one that cannot be resolved by civil courts through legal analysis. . . .

Justice SOTOMAYOR, with whom Justice GINSBURG joins, dissenting.

Two employers fired their employees allegedly because one had breast cancer and the other was elderly. Purporting to rely on this Court's decision in *Hosanna-Tabor Evangelical Lutheran Church and School v. EEOC* (2012), the majority shields those employers from disability and age-discrimination claims. In the Court's view, because the employees taught short religion modules at Catholic elementary schools, they were "ministers" of the Catholic faith and thus could be fired for any reason, whether religious or nonreligious, benign or bigoted, without legal recourse. The Court reaches this result even though the teachers taught primarily secular subjects, lacked substantial religious titles and training, and were not even required to be Catholic. In foreclosing the teachers' claims, the Court skews the facts, ignores the applicable standard of review, and collapses *Hosanna-Tabor*'s careful analysis into a single consideration: whether a church thinks its employees play an important religious role. Because that simplistic approach has no basis in law and strips thousands of schoolteachers of their legal protections, I respectfully dissent. . . .

The "ministerial exception" . . . is a judge-made doctrine. This Court first recognized it eight years ago in *Hosanna-Tabor*, concluding that the First Amendment categorically bars certain antidiscrimination suits by religious leaders against their religious employers. When it applies, the exception is extraordinarily potent: It gives an employer free rein to discriminate because of race, sex, pregnancy, age, disability, or other traits protected by law when selecting or firing their "ministers," even when the discrimination is wholly unrelated to the employer's religious beliefs or practices. That is, an employer need not cite or possess a religious reason at all; the ministerial exception even condones animus. . . .

Hosanna-Tabor focused on four "circumstances" to determine whether a fourth-grade teacher, Cheryl Perich, was employed at a Lutheran school as a "minister": (1) "the formal title given [her] by the Church," (2) "the substance reflected in that title," (3) "her own use of that title," and (4) "the important religious functions she performed for the Church." Confirming that the ministerial exception applies to a circumscribed sub-category of faith leaders, the Court analyzed those four "factors," to situate Perich as a minister within the Lutheran Church's structure. . . .

Hosanna-Tabor's well-rounded approach ensured that a church could not categorically disregard generally applicable antidiscrimination laws for nonreligious reasons. By analyzing objective and easily discernable markers like titles, training, and public-facing conduct, *Hosanna-Tabor* charted a way to separate leaders who "personify" a church's "beliefs" or who "minister to the faithful" from individuals who may simply relay religious tenets. This balanced First Amendment concerns of state-church entanglement while avoiding an overbroad carve-out from employment protections.

. . . But then the Court recasts *Hosanna-Tabor* itself: Apparently, the touchstone all along was a two-Justice concurrence. To that concurrence, "[w]hat matter[ed]" was "the religious function that [Perich] performed" and her "functional status." *Hosanna-Tabor* (opinion of Alito, J.). Today's Court yields to the concurrence's view with identical rhetoric. "What matters," the Court echoes, "is what an employee does."

But this vague statement is no easier to comprehend today than it was when the Court declined to adopt it eight years ago. It certainly does not sound like a legal framework. Rather, the Court insists that a "religious institution's explanation of the role of [its] employees in the life of the religion in question is important." . . . But because the Court's new standard prizes a functional importance that it appears to deem churches in the best position to explain, one cannot help but conclude that the Court has just traded legal analysis for a rubber stamp.

Indeed, the Court reasons that "judges cannot be expected to have a complete understanding and appreciation" of the law and facts in ministerial-exception cases, and all but abandons judicial review. . . . That is, the Court's apparent deference here threatens to make nearly anyone whom the schools might hire "ministers" unprotected from discrimination in the hiring process. That cannot be right. Although certain religious functions may be important to a church, a person's performance of some of those functions does not mechanically trigger a categorical exemption from generally applicable antidiscrimination laws.

Faithfully applying *Hosanna-Tabor*'s approach and common sense confirms that the teachers here are not Catholic "ministers" as a matter of law. . . .

First, and as the Ninth Circuit explained, neither school publicly represented that either teacher was a Catholic spiritual leader or "minister." Neither conferred a title reflecting such a position. Rather, the schools referred to both Biel and Morrissey-Berru as "lay" teachers. . . .

Second (and further undermining the schools' claims), neither teacher had a "significant degree of religious training" or underwent a "formal process of commissioning." . . . Nor did either school require such training or commissioning as a prerequisite to gaining (or keeping) employment. In Biel's case, the record reflects that she attended a single conference that lasted "four or five hours," briefly discussed "how to incorporate God into . . . lesson plans," and otherwise "showed [teachers] how to do art and make little pictures or things like that." . . . In turn, Our Lady of Guadalupe did not ask Morrissey-Berru to undergo any religious training for her first 13 years of teaching, until it asked her to attend the uncompleted program described above. This consideration instructs that the teachers here did not fall within the ministerial exception.

Third, neither Biel nor Morrissey-Berru held herself out as having a leadership role in the faith community. . . .

That leaves only the fourth consideration in *Hosanna-Tabor*: the teachers' function. . . . Although the Court does not resolve this functional question with "a stopwatch," it still considers the "amount of time an employee spends on particular activities" in "assessing that employee's status." Here, the time Biel and Morrissey-Berru spent on secular instruction far surpassed their time teaching religion. For the vast majority of class, they taught subjects like reading, writing, spelling, grammar, vocabulary, math, science, social studies, and geography. In so doing, both were like any public school teacher in California, subject to the same statewide curriculum guidelines. In other words, both Biel and Morrissey-Berru had almost exclusively secular duties, making it especially improper to deprive them of all legal protection when their employers have not offered any religious reason for the alleged discrimination.

Nevertheless, the Court insists that the teachers are ministers because "implicit in our decision in *Hosanna-Tabor* was a recognition that educating young people in their faith, inculcating its teachings, and training them to live their faith are responsibilities that lie at the very core of the mission of a private religious school." But teaching religion in school alone cannot dictate ministerial status. If it did, then *Hosanna-Tabor* wasted precious pages discussing titles, training, and other objective indicia to examine whether Cheryl Perich was a minister. . . .

Were there any doubt left about the proper result here, recall that neither school has shown that it required its religion teachers to be Catholic. The Court does not explain how the schools here can show, or have shown, that a non-Catholic "personif[ies]" Catholicism or leads the faith. . . .

Pause, for a moment, on the Court's conclusion: Even if the teachers were not Catholic, and even if they were forbidden to participate in the church's sacramental worship, they would nonetheless be "ministers" of the Catholic faith simply because of their supervisory role over students in a religious school. That stretches the law and logic past their breaking points. (Indeed, it is ironic that Our Lady of Guadalupe School seeks complete immunity for age discrimination when its teacher handbook promised not to discriminate on that basis.) As the Government once put it, even when a school has a "pervasively religious atmosphere," its faculty are unlikely ministers when "there is no requirement that its teachers even be members of [its] religious denomination." It is hard to imagine a more concrete example than these cases.

* * *

The Court's conclusion portends grave consequences. . . . So long as the employer determines that an employee's "duties" are "vital" to "carrying out the mission of the church," then today's laissez-faire analysis appears to allow that employer to make employment decisions because of a person's skin color, age, disability, sex, or any other protected trait for reasons having nothing to do with religion.

I respectfully dissent.

NOTES AND QUESTIONS

1. Hosanna-Tabor *factors.* Do you think that *Our Lady of Guadalupe* followed or departed from the guidelines laid out by *Hosanna-Tabor*?
2. *Effect.* Does *Our Lady of Guadalupe* mean that any elementary school teacher responsible for religion classes is a "ministerial employee"? Why or why not?
3. *Risks of each approach.* In *Our Lady of Guadalupe,* the majority expressed concern about the courts making theological determinations beyond their competence about who is religiously important, while the dissent expressed concern about eliminating civil rights protections for thousands upon thousands of teachers. Which do you think is the greater risk?

THEORY-APPLIED PROBLEM

After the Episcopal Church (USA) approves the ordination of women as well as gay and lesbian priests and bishops, the congregation of St. John's Episcopal Church, in Pascagoula, Mississippi, becomes embroiled in a bitter dispute. The Board of Vestry votes to remain part of the Episcopal Church. The congregation, enraged at this outcome, votes by a margin of 174-33 to break with the Episcopal Church (USA) and align instead with the Congregation of Anglicans in North America (CANA), which has denounced the ordination of gays and lesbians.

The deed in question, properly recorded in 1909, simply states that the property "shall be used in perpetuity for an Episcopal church and shall always observe the true doctrines of the Anglican Communion of Churches." The church's charter provides for the regular election of vestrymen by popular vote at regular intervals, corresponding to annual terms of office; the rules do not provide any means of recalling a vestry member once elected. The Episcopal Diocese of Mississippi finds that the minority group of 33 represents the bona fide congregation, endorses the authority of the local Board of Vestry, and claims ownership on the Board's behalf of the St. John's church, buildings, and assets. The dissenting majority faction also claims ownership on the grounds that they are the ones that truly represent an "Episcopal" church.

The Jackson County Chancery Court, applying neutral principles of state law, rules in favor of the dissident majority, holding that the deed established a trust in favor of the Anglican theological doctrines as they existed in 1909. Because the Episcopal Church did not ordain women, gays, or lesbians as either priests or bishops in 1909, the state court judge rules that because of departure from true Anglican doctrine, the trust failed.

The Episcopal Diocese of Mississippi appeals the chancery court decision to the Mississippi Court of Appeals. How should the appellate state court rule? May it affirm the lower court ruling without violating the Free Exercise Clause? Is the trial court ruling consistent with *Jones*? With *Watson*?

Chapter 18

Defining and Enforcing the Establishment Clause

Table of Contents

A. Early Efforts to Define the Separation of Church and State
B. Modern Tests for Impermissible Religious Establishments
   1. The "*Lemon* Test"
   2. The Endorsement Analysis
   3. The Coercion Analysis
   4. The History and Tradition Analysis

The Establishment Clause is one of the most controversial and frequently litigated components of the First Amendment. Although disputes about the proper relationship between church and state have been a feature of this country's history since the earliest settlements by Western Europeans, it may surprise many students to learn that the Supreme Court has only been actively interpreting and applying the Establishment Clause since 1947. As if to make up for lost time, the Court has generated a huge body of case law in that 75-year period, covering virtually every aspect of life in which government action intersects with religious belief and practice.

As in every other area of the First Amendment, there are endless debates about both the history and the theory of the constitutional law that governs the relationship between church and state. These debates inform the actual holdings of the cases and the doctrine on which those holdings are based. This chapter begins with a brief discussion of the history of religious establishment in the United States, before turning to a discussion of various different standards being used by different members of the Supreme Court to enforce the Establishment Clause. Many observers of the Court's church/state jurisprudence have been frustrated in recent years because the Justices on the Supreme Court have failed to coalesce around one Establishment Clause standard.

One explanation for the Court's failure to articulate a single standard is that the Court continues to be sharply divided about the underlying theory of the Establishment Clause. In brief, there are two broad schools of thought about the meaning of the Establishment Clause. The basic differences between these schools of thought can be illustrated by their contrasting attitudes toward the concept of separation of church and state. The concept of church/state separation was advanced early in the country's history by Thomas Jefferson. While serving as President, Jefferson wrote a letter to the Danbury Baptist Association, in which he argued that when the citizens of the United States adopted the First Amendment they intended to build "a wall of separation between Church & State." Thomas Jefferson, "A Bill for Establishing Religious Freedom," in *The Portable Thomas Jefferson* 303 (Merrill D. Peterson ed., 1975). Jefferson borrowed the "wall of separation" metaphor from Roger Williams, who founded the first Baptist Church in the United States and was also one of the founders of the state of Rhode Island, which from its origins was unusual in welcoming into the state members of every religious denomination. Williams once wrote that "when they have opened a gap in the hedge or wall of Separation between the Garden of the Church and the Wilderness of the world, God hath ever broke down the wall itself, removed the Candlestick, and made his Garden a Wilderness." Roger Williams, *Mr. Cotton's Letter Examined and Answered* (1644), reprinted in 1 *The Complete Writings of Roger Williams* 313, 392 (Russel & Russel, Inc., 1963).

Modern supporters of the "wall of separation" between church and state tend to argue that in order to preserve the purity and independence of both church and state the government should be a secular entity that is neutral with regard to any one sect and to religion in general. In other words, the government should neither support nor oppose any religious doctrine or institution.

From this perspective, religion is an intensely private matter that should not be subject to either pressure or manipulation by the government. As indicated by the excerpts in Section A below, this was the position of Jefferson's good friend James Madison (who wrote the First Amendment), and also the stance adopted by the Supreme Court in its first modern Establishment Clause decision, *Everson v. Board of Education.*

Until very recently, most members of the Court have continued to express support for the separation of church and state, although the Court's enforcement of this theory has often been deeply inconsistent. These inconsistencies have been accentuated in recent years because several members of the Court have begun expressing strong disagreement with the very goal of separating church and state. They argue that the United States is (and always has been) a deeply religious country, and that the government should reflect this fact. Thus, in his dissent in *Wallace v. Jaffree* (excerpted in this chapter and in Chapter 21), then-Justice Rehnquist argued that the Establishment Clause should be interpreted to permit the government to endorse and finance religion in general, as long as it refrains from endorsing or financing only particular religious sects favored by the government. Another variation on this theme is Justice Scalia's argument in *McCreary County v. ACLU* (excerpted in Chapter 22) that the Establishment Clause should be interpreted to permit the government to favor those who belong to monotheistic faiths and should also be allowed to "disregard" atheists, agnostics, and those who belong to polytheistic faiths. The limitations of space do not permit a full survey of the theoretical materials in this casebook, but the basic theoretical dispute between those who support and those who oppose the separation of church and state lies just below the surface of virtually every decision included in the next four chapters.

After discussing the history and doctrine of the Establishment Clause in this chapter, Chapter 19 focuses on an area of tension between free exercise and establishment: government attempts to facilitate religious practice that may or may not go too far and violate the Establishment Clause. Chapter 20 addresses decisions involving government efforts to finance religious activities or institutions. Chapter 21 discusses religion in the public school context, and Chapter 22 addresses government-sponsored prayers and religious symbols outside the public school context.

A. *EARLY EFFORTS TO DEFINE THE SEPARATION OF CHURCH AND STATE*

The history of religious freedom in the United States is not always enlightening or encouraging. In pre-revolutionary times, when religious groups who came to this country seeking religious freedom for themselves became the dominant religious group in their new home, they often fell into the habit of oppressing members of other faiths. The history of the American colonies is riddled with examples of religious oppression, and that oppression did not end with the American Revolution. When John Jay, the first Chief Justice of the Supreme Court, was governor of New York, for example, he proposed to ban Catholics from that state. *See* Thomas J. Curry, *The First Freedoms: Church and State in America to the Passage of the First Amendment* 162 (1986). Similarly, Massachusetts proposed to banish Anabaptists and to execute Catholic priests who strayed back into Massachusetts after having been excluded from that state. *See* Alexis de Tocqueville, *Democracy in America* 42-43 & nn. 26-27 (George Lawrence trans., Perennial Classics 1969) (1848).

Religious oppression in the young Republic took many different forms. Five states refused to grant full rights to Catholics. *See* 1 Anson Stokes, *Church and State in the United States* 402 (1950) (North Carolina); *id.* at 406 (New York); *id.* at 430 (New Hampshire); *id.* at 435 (New Jersey); *id.* at 441 (Vermont). Other states, such as Virginia, mandated that all persons be married in the Anglican Church. *See* Sanford H. Cobb, *The Rise of Religious Liberty in America: A History* 494 (Burt Franklin 1970) (1902). More commonly, religious oppression took the form of Protestant financial establishments in states such as Massachusetts, whose constitution required towns in the state "to make suitable provision, at their own expense, for the institutions of the public worship of God, and for the support and maintenance of public Protestant teachers of piety, religion and morality. . . ." *See* Declaration of Rights in the 1780 Massachusetts Constitution, in 3 Francis Newton Thorpe, ed., *The Federal and State Constitutions, Colonial Charters, and Other Organic Laws* 1890 (1909).

On the other hand, the political landscape of the early Republic also included more hopeful examples such as Rhode Island, which never had an established church and from the outset granted full liberty of conscience to members of all faiths. And many of the most influential leaders of the new country were freethinkers, including rationalists like Ethan Allen and Thomas Paine and Deists like James

Madison, Thomas Jefferson, and (most likely) George Washington. The religious and political context in which the First Amendment was written was complicated and fluid, and although several broad trends and themes can be discerned in the historical data, many of these trends and themes have led observers to contradictory conclusions about the meaning of the Establishment Clause.

At the time the First Amendment was written, some states still maintained official religious establishments, mostly in the form of mandatory tax collections for the financial support of churches. All of the states that continued to maintain religious establishments, however, had moved from the establishment of a single church to so-called multiple establishments, which permitted the taxpayer to designate the church that the taxpayer's taxes would support.

It is common practice to cluster the states into three groups: The New England states, with political regimes derived from traditional Puritan establishments, maintained official establishments that lasted well into the first decades of the nineteenth century. The Southern states, which started out with Anglican establishments, soon pursued disestablishment to accommodate both the surge of Protestant dissenters and the hostility toward an Anglican church that was closely associated with the former colonial ruler. The Middle Atlantic states tended to have weak establishments or no establishments at all. Indeed, four states, all in the middle of the country, never maintained official establishments: Rhode Island, Pennsylvania, Delaware, and New Jersey. By 1791, eight of the original thirteen states had eliminated their official religious establishments. The other five states would eliminate their official establishments soon thereafter, culminating with Massachusetts, which would be the last state to eliminate its official establishment in 1833.

What is one to make of this history? It does not represent a consistent story of religious liberty and disestablishment. The one clear message of this history, however, is that at the time the Bill of Rights was drafted the trend throughout the country was towards eliminating all religious establishments.

Perhaps the best illustration of the disestablishment trend in the United States during this period is the dispute in Virginia over Governor Patrick Henry's proposal to revive Virginia's religious establishment, in the form of a "Bill establishing a provision for Teachers of the Christian Religion." This proposed Bill was a fairly benign form of religious establishment compared to previous versions, in the sense that it did not favor any Christian sect (although it did favor Christianity generally), establish any articles of faith, or speak in terms of an explicit establishment of an official religion for the state of Virginia. Nevertheless, James Madison vigorously opposed the Bill, and in the course of his opposition produced the Memorial and Remonstrance Against Religious Assessments, one of the primary documents expounding on the peculiarly American form of religious liberty. Madison's rhetorical and political skills were instrumental in mustering substantial opposition to Henry's bill, not only among the usual opponents such as Baptists, Quakers, and secularists, but also among many Presbyterians, Episcopalians, and Methodists, who had originally supported the bill. Upon defeat of the assessment bill, Madison then proposed and the Virginia legislature passed Thomas Jefferson's Statute for Religious Freedom, which in many ways provides a model for the theory of the Establishment Clause that has dominated the Supreme Court's jurisprudence for the last 70 years.

Everson v. Board of Education

330 U.S. 1 (1947)

Mr. Justice Black delivered the opinion of the Court.

[*Everson* involved a challenge to a state statute that authorized the reimbursement of bus fares paid for transporting children to private schools, most of which were Catholic. After holding that the Establishment Clause was incorporated into the Fourteenth Amendment and therefore applicable to the states, the Court considered the history of the adoption of the Clause.]

A large proportion of the early settlers of this country came here from Europe to escape the bondage of laws which compelled them to support and attend government-favored churches. The centuries immediately before and contemporaneous with the colonization of America had been filled with turmoil, civil strife, and persecutions, generated in large part by established sects determined to maintain their absolute political and religious supremacy. With the power of government supporting them, at various times and places, Catholics had persecuted Protestants, Protestants had persecuted Catholics, Protestant sects had persecuted other Protestant sects, Catholics of one shade of belief had persecuted Catholics of another shade of belief, and all of these had from time to time persecuted Jews. In efforts to force loyalty to whatever religious group happened to be on top and in league with the government of a particular time and place, men and women had been fined, cast in jail, cruelly tortured, and killed. Among the offenses for which these punishments had been inflicted were such things as speaking disrespectfully of the views of ministers of government-established churches, non-attendance at those churches, expressions of non-belief in their doctrines, and failure to pay taxes and tithes to support them.

These practices of the Old World were transplanted to and began to thrive in the soil of the new America. The very charters granted by the English Crown to the individuals and companies designated to make the laws which would control the destinies of the colonials authorized these individuals and companies to erect religious establishments which all, whether believers or non-believers, would be required to support and attend. An exercise of this authority was accompanied by a repetition of many of the Old-World practices and persecutions. Catholics found themselves hounded and proscribed because of their faith; Quakers who followed their conscience went to jail; Baptists were peculiarly obnoxious to certain dominant Protestant sects; men and women of varied faiths who happened to be in a minority in a particular locality were persecuted because they steadfastly persisted in worshipping God only as their own consciences dictated. And all of these dissenters were compelled to pay tithes and taxes to support government-sponsored churches whose ministers preached inflammatory sermons designed to strengthen and consolidate the established faith by generating a burning hatred against dissenters.

These practices became so commonplace as to shock the freedom-loving colonials into a feeling of abhorrence. . . . But Virginia, where the established church had achieved a dominant influence in political affairs and where many excesses attracted wide public attention, provided a great stimulus and able leadership for the movement. The people there, as elsewhere, reached the conviction that individual religious liberty could be achieved best under a government which was stripped of all power to tax, to support, or otherwise to assist any or all religions, or to interfere with the beliefs of any religious individual or group.

The movement toward this end reached its dramatic climax in Virginia in 1785-86 when the Virginia legislative body was about to renew Virginia's tax levy for the support of the established church. Thomas Jefferson and James Madison led the fight against this tax. Madison wrote his great Memorial and Remonstrance against the law. In it, he eloquently argued that a true religion did not need the support of law; that no person, either believer or non-believer, should be taxed to support a religious institution of any kind; that the best interest of a society required that the minds of men always be wholly free; and that cruel persecutions were the inevitable result of government-established religions. Madison's Remonstrance received strong support throughout Virginia, and the Assembly postponed consideration of the proposed tax measure until its next session. When the proposal came up for consideration at that session, it not only died in committee, but the Assembly enacted the famous "Virginia Bill for Religious Liberty" originally written by Thomas Jefferson. The preamble to that Bill stated among other things that

> "Almighty God hath created the mind free; that all attempts to influence it by temporal punishments or burthens, or by civil incapacitations, tend only to beget habits of hypocrisy and meanness, and are a departure from the plan of the Holy author of our religion, who being Lord both of body and mind, yet chose not to propagate it by coercions on either . . . ; that to compel a man to furnish contributions of money for the propagation of opinions which he disbelieves, is sinful and tyrannical; that even the forcing him to support this or that teacher of his own religious persuasion, is depriving him of the comfortable liberty of giving his contributions to the particular pastor, whose morals he would make his pattern. . . ."

And the statute itself enacted

> "That no man shall be compelled to frequent or support any religious worship, place, or ministry whatsoever, nor shall be enforced, restrained, molested, or burthened in his body or goods, nor shall otherwise suffer on account of his religious opinions or belief. . . ."

This Court has previously recognized that the provisions of the First Amendment, in the drafting and adoption of which Madison and Jefferson played such leading roles, had the same objective and were intended to provide the same protection against governmental intrusion on religious liberty as the Virginia statute. Prior to the adoption of the Fourteenth Amendment, the First Amendment did not apply as a restraint against the states. Most of them did soon provide similar constitutional protections for religious liberty. But some states persisted for about half a century in imposing restraints upon the free exercise of religion and in discriminating against particular religious groups. . . .

The "establishment of religion" clause of the First Amendment means at least this: Neither a state nor the Federal Government can set up a church. Neither can pass laws which aid one religion, aid all religions, or prefer one religion over another. Neither can force nor influence a person to go to or to remain away from church against his will or force him to profess a belief or disbelief in any religion.

No person can be punished for entertaining or professing religious beliefs or disbeliefs, for church attendance or non-attendance. No tax in any amount, large or small, can be levied to support any religious activities or institutions, whatever they may be called, or whatever form they may adopt to teach or practice religion. Neither a state nor the Federal Government can, openly or secretly, participate in the affairs of any religious organizations or groups and vice versa. In the words of Jefferson, the clause against establishment of religion by law was intended to erect "a wall of separation between church and State." *Reynolds v. United States*, 98 U.S. at 164.

[Although all nine members of the *Everson* Court agreed with Justice Black's separationist account of the Establishment Clause, they disagreed about the application of the Clause to the facts of *Everson* itself. Five Justices voted to uphold the New Jersey program using government funds to transport children to private religious schools, and four Justices dissented.]

James Madison

Memorial and Remonstrance Against Religious Assessments

(1785)

We, the subscribers, citizens of the said Commonwealth, . . . remonstrate against the ["Bill establishing a provision for Teachers of the Christian Religion,"]

1. Because we hold it for a fundamental and undeniable truth, "that Religion or the duty which we owe to our Creator and the Manner of discharging it, can be directed only by reason and conviction, not by force or violence." The Religion then of every man must be left to the conviction and conscience of every man; and it is the right of every man to exercise it as these may dictate. This right is in its nature an unalienable right. It is unalienable; because the opinions of men, depending only on the evidence contemplated by their own minds, cannot follow the dictates of other men: It is unalienable also; because what is here a right towards men, is a duty towards the Creator. It is the duty of every man to render to the Creator such homage, and such only, as he believes to be acceptable to him. This duty is precedent both in order of time and degree of obligation, to the claims of Civil Society. Before any man can be considered as a member of Civil Society, he must be considered as a subject of the Governor of the Universe: And if a member of Civil Society, who enters into any subordinate Association, must always do it with a reservation of his duty to the general authority; much more must every man who becomes a member of any particular Civil Society, do it with a saving of his allegiance to the Universal Sovereign. We maintain therefore that in matters of Religion, no man's right is abridged by the institution of Civil Society, and that Religion is wholly exempt from its cognizance. True it is, that no other rule exists, by which any question which may divide a Society, can be ultimately determined, but the will of the majority; but it is also true, that the majority may trespass on the rights of the minority. . . .

3. Because, it is proper to take alarm at the first experiment on our liberties. We hold this prudent jealousy to be the first duty of citizens, and one of [the] noblest characteristics of the late Revolution. The freemen of America did not wait till usurped power had strengthened itself by exercise, and entangled the question

in precedents. They saw all the consequences in the principle, and they avoided the consequences by denying the principle. We revere this lesson too much, soon to forget it. Who does not see that the same authority which can establish Christianity, in exclusion of all other Religions, may establish with the same ease any particular sect of Christians, in exclusion of all other Sects? That the same authority which can force a citizen to contribute three pence only of his property for the support of any one establishment, may force him to conform to any other establishment in all cases whatsoever? . . .

5. Because the bill implies either that the Civil Magistrate is a competent Judge of Religious truth; or that he may employ Religion as an engine of Civil policy. The first is an arrogant pretension falsified by the contradictory opinions of Rulers in all ages, and throughout the world: The second an unhallowed perversion of the means of salvation.

6. Because the establishment proposed by the Bill is not requisite for the support of the Christian Religion. To say that it is, is a contradiction to the Christian Religion itself; for every page of it disavows a dependence on the powers of this world: it is a contradiction to fact; for it is known that this Religion both existed and flourished, not only without the support of human laws, but in spite of every opposition from them; and not only during the period of miraculous aid, but long after it had been left to its own evidence, and the ordinary care of Providence: Nay, it is a contradiction in terms; for a Religion not invented by human policy, must have pre-existed and been supported, before it was established by human policy. It is moreover to weaken in those who profess this Religion a pious confidence in its innate excellence, and the patronage of its Author; and to foster in those who still reject it, a suspicion that its friends are too conscious of its fallacies, to trust it to its own merits.

7. Because experience witnesseth that ecclesiastical establishments, instead of maintaining the purity and efficacy of Religion, have had a contrary operation. During almost fifteen centuries, has the legal establishment of Christianity been on trial. What have been its fruits? More or less in all places, pride and indolence in the Clergy; ignorance and servility in the laity; in both, superstition, bigotry and persecution. Enquire of the Teachers of Christianity for the ages in which it appeared in its greatest lustre; those of every sect, point to the ages prior to its incorporation with Civil policy. Propose a restoration of this primitive state in which its Teachers depended on the voluntary rewards of their flocks; many of them predict its downfall. On which side ought their testimony to have greatest weight, when for or when against their interest?

8. Because the establishment in question is not necessary for the support of Civil Government. If it be urged as necessary for the support of Civil Government only as it is a means of supporting Religion, and it be not necessary for the latter purpose, it cannot be necessary for the former. If Religion be not within [the] cognizance of Civil Government, how can its legal establishment be said to be necessary to civil Government? What influence in fact have ecclesiastical establishments had on Civil Society? In some instances they have been seen to erect a spiritual tyranny on the ruins of Civil authority; in many instances they have been seen upholding the thrones of political tyranny; in no instance have they been seen the guardians of the liberties of the people. Rulers who wished to subvert the public liberty, may

have found an established clergy convenient auxiliaries. A just government, instituted to secure & perpetuate it, needs them not. Such a government will be best supported by protecting every citizen in the enjoyment of his Religion with the same equal hand which protects his person and his property; by neither invading the equal rights of any Sect, nor suffering any Sect to invade those of another.

9. Because the proposed establishment is a departure from that generous policy, which, offering an asylum to the persecuted and oppressed of every Nation and Religion, promised a lustre to our country, and an accession to the number of its citizens. What a melancholy mark is the Bill of sudden degeneracy? Instead of holding forth an asylum to the persecuted, it is itself a signal of persecution. It degrades from the equal rank of Citizens all those whose opinions in Religion do not bend to those of the Legislative authority. Distant as it may be, in its present form, from the Inquisition it differs from it only in degree. The one is the first step, the other the last in the career of intolerance. The magnanimous sufferer under this cruel scourge in foreign Regions, must view the Bill as a Beacon on our Coast, warning him to seek some other haven, where liberty and philanthrophy in their due extent may offer a more certain repose from his troubles. . . .

11. Because, it will destroy that moderation and harmony which the forbearance of our laws to intermeddle with Religion, has produced amongst its several sects. Torrents of blood have been spilt in the old world, by vain attempts of the secular arm to extinguish Religious discord, by proscribing all difference in Religious opinions. Time has at length revealed the true remedy. Every relaxation of narrow and rigorous policy, wherever it has been tried, has been found to assuage the disease. The American Theatre has exhibited proofs, that equal and complete liberty, if it does not wholly eradicate it, sufficiently destroys its malignant influence on the health and prosperity of the State. If with the salutary effects of this system under our own eyes, we begin to contract the bonds of Religious freedom, we know no name that will too severely reproach our folly. At least let warning be taken at the first fruits of the threatened innovation. The very appearance of the Bill has transformed that "Christian forbearance, love and charity," which of late mutually prevailed, into animosities and jealousies, which may not soon be appeased. What mischiefs may not be dreaded should this enemy to the public quiet be armed with the force of a law?

NOTES AND QUESTIONS

1. *Madison's views.* James Madison is known as the Chief Architect of the First Amendment. His Memorial & Remonstrance presents several arguments as to why it is beneficial for church and state to remain separate.
2. *Establishment harms civil peace.* According to paragraph 11, separation of church and state leads to "moderation and harmony." In contrast, attempts to establish religion led to "torrents of blood" in the Old World. Indeed, how has the "public quiet" been affected by Virginia's proposed "Bill establishing a provision for Teachers of the Christian Religion"?
3. *Establishment harms religious minorities.* According to paragraph 9, establishment is the first step to what? Even if state-established religion does not lead to persecution of religious minorities, it creates second-class citizens:

"It degrades from the equal rank of Citizens all those whose opinions do not bend to those of the Legislative authority."

4. *Establishment harms favored religion.* A close relationship with the government or support from the government is not always beneficial to the favored religion either. According to paragraph 6, what does establishment do to a church's reputation? According to paragraph 7, what does history reveal about established churches and their clergy?

B. MODERN TESTS FOR IMPERMISSIBLE RELIGIOUS ESTABLISHMENTS

1. The "Lemon Test"

One of the oldest Establishment Clause doctrinal tests is the three-part *Lemon* test: "Three such tests may be gleaned from our cases. First, the statute must have a secular legislative purpose; second, its principal or primary effect must be one that neither advances nor inhibits religion; finally, the statute must not foster 'an excessive government entanglement with religion.'" Lemon v. Kurtzman, 403 U.S. 602, 612-13 (1971). Although some components of the three-part *Lemon* test have been part of the Court's Establishment Clause jurisprudence since the early 1960s, the *Lemon* test became the subject of controversy almost from the moment it was articulated. Some of the attacks on *Lemon* are quite vivid. Justice Scalia, for example, once likened *Lemon* to "some ghoul in a late-night horror movie that repeatedly sits up in its grave and shuffles abroad, after being repeatedly killed and buried." *Lamb's Chapel v. Center Moriches Union Free Sch. Dist.* (Scalia, J., concurring in the judgment). The *Lemon* test's continued vitality is in question. Although a clear majority has never squarely rejected the *Lemon* framework, the Supreme Court does not routinely and reliably apply it in major Establishment Clause cases. Thus, even if *Lemon* has not been officially repudiated, its continuing precedential force is in serious doubt.

2. The Endorsement Analysis

The endorsement test was developed by Justice O'Connor, but later adopted by the Court in cases involving government-sponsored religious displays. She introduced her views in a concurrence, writing, "The Establishment Clause prohibits government from making adherence to a religion relevant in any way to a person's standing in the political community. . . . Endorsement sends a message to nonadherents that they are outsiders, not full members of the political community, and an accompanying message to adherents that they are insiders, favored members of the political community. Disapproval sends the opposite message." For Justice O'Connor, the question was whether a "reasonable person" would conclude that the government had the purpose or effect of endorsing religion. Moreover, "the reasonable observer in the endorsement inquiry must be deemed aware of the history and context of the community and forum in which the religious display appears. Nor can the knowledge attributed to the reasonable observer be limited to the information gleaned simply from viewing the challenged display." County of Allegheny v. ACLU, 492 U.S. 573 (1989) (O'Connor, J., concurring). Some lower courts have treated the endorsement test as distinct from the *Lemon* test. Others view it as a refinement of the *Lemon* test: instead of asking whether the government's challenged action had the purpose or effect of advancing religion, the question is whether a reasonable person would find that the challenged government action had the purpose or effect of endorsing religion.

3. *The Coercion Analysis*

A few Justices have argued that the Establishment Clause has not been violated by government-sponsored religious displays or practices unless the state has coerced someone into participating in a religious exercise. Others had steadfastly maintained that while coercion is sufficient it is not necessary to violate the Establishment Clause. For example, Justice Blackmun in concurrence wrote: "The Court repeatedly has recognized that a violation of the Establishment Clause is not predicated on coercion." Lee v. Weisman, 505 U.S. 577, 604 (1992). Adding to the confusion is that not all Justices define coercion in the same way. Justice Scalia, for example, had a very narrow definition. A supporter of the coercion requirement, he argued that only those actions that entail the coercion of religious belief or practice "by force of law and threat of penalty" were unconstitutional. In contrast, Justice Kennedy, writing for the majority in a case challenging short prayers at a public middle school graduation, took a broader view of coercion. "[T]here are heightened concerns with protecting freedom of conscience from subtle coercive pressure in the elementary and secondary public schools. . . . The undeniable fact is that the school district's supervision and control of a high school graduation ceremony places public pressure, as well as peer pressure, on attending students to stand as a group or, at least, maintain respectful silence during the invocation and benediction. This pressure, though subtle and indirect, can be as real as any overt compulsion." Lee v. Weisman, 505 U.S. 577 (1992). Notably, Justice Kennedy did not opine on whether coercion is a prerequisite, and the Supreme Court has not yet explicitly held that coercion is necessary for an Establishment Clause violation, although it has moved closer to that position in Town of Greece v. Galloway, 572 U.S. 565 (2014).

4. *The History and Tradition Analysis*

In Marsh v. Chambers, 463 U.S. 783 (1983), the Supreme Court debuted yet another approach to Establishment Clause cases. Marsh was challenging Nebraska's practice of opening its legislative sessions with a prayer delivered by a state-funded chaplain. The Court upheld the prayer practice, emphasizing the long history of legislative prayers. "The opening of sessions of legislative and other deliberative public bodies with prayer is deeply embedded in the history and tradition of this country." The Court also pointed out that the same Congress that approved the First Amendment also approved Congressional chaplains. "On September 25, 1789, three days after Congress authorized the appointment of paid chaplains, final agreement was reached on the language of the Bill of Rights. Clearly the men who wrote the First Amendment Religion Clause did not view paid legislative chaplains and opening prayers as a violation of that Amendment, for the practice of opening sessions with prayer has continued without interruption ever since that early session of Congress." This historical approach has not been confined to longstanding practices dating to the founding era. Instead, the "history and tradition" analysis has become the favored approach to Establishment Clause cases for a majority of the current Supreme Justices.

THEORY-APPLIED PROBLEMS

Even a cursory perusal of the Establishment Clause standards summarized in this chapter will indicate the conflicting outcomes that are possible under the various standards. To further clarify what these standards mean, and how they may lead to different results in specific cases, consider how each of these standards would apply to the following five church/state disputes based on cases that have been litigated under the Establishment Clause. Do not worry for the moment about how the Court has actually resolved these disputes; the next four chapters will discuss the outcomes of the specific cases. For the moment, focus on what each standard means, how the cases would be resolved if each standard were applied consistently to different types of church/state disputes, and what each standard implies about a comprehensive theory of the proper relationship between church and state.

1. The government passes a statute that obligates private employers to accommodate the religious activities of their employees in situations in which a religious obligation of an employee conflicts with a requirement of the job. The statute is challenged by a nonreligious employee who has been forced by her employer to work on Sundays because a religious employee with less seniority is given that day off because of the employee's religious obligations.
2. The government operates a program that provides supplemental educational resources to private schools within the school district, almost all of which are religious. Under this program, the government supplies to the private schools publicly funded teachers for classes in art, music, calculus, and other elective subjects. The publicly funded teachers teach these subjects on the premises of the religious schools to classes comprised entirely of the religious school students. This program is challenged by a local taxpayer who objects to spending tax money to finance a portion of the religious schools' curriculums.
3. The administration at a public high school invites a local minister to give a brief, nondenominational prayer at the school's graduation ceremony. This invitation is challenged by a graduating senior who does not want to sit through the prayer.

4. A state statute requires schoolchildren to recite the Pledge of Allegiance every morning in public school classrooms, including the words "one nation under God." This statute is challenged by a parent who does not want his child exposed to the religious portion of the Pledge.
5. A city erects a holiday display every year in a public park. The display includes secular holiday symbols such as a Santa Claus, candy canes, and sleighs, but also includes a manger scene that depicts the baby Jesus, Mary and Joseph, and the wise men. The display is challenged by a local citizen who objects to the religious component of the display.

CHAPTER 19

THE ESTABLISHMENT CLAUSE AND VOLUNTARY RELIGIOUS ACCOMMODATIONS

The Supreme Court's Establishment Clause decisions can be grouped into three broad categories. The first category, which is the subject of this chapter, involves cases where the government's voluntary religious accommodation risks violating the Establishment Clause. The second category includes cases involving government financing of religious activities and institutions. They are covered in Chapter 20. The third category, covered in Chapters 21 and 22, includes cases in which the government practices or endorses religion.

PLAY IN THE JOINTS

It does not necessarily violate the Establishment Clause for the legislature to provide religious accommodations that are not required by the Free Exercise Clause. Thus, there is "play in the joints" of the two religion clauses. At the same time, some religious accommodations, like the absolute protection for Sabbath observance struck down in *Estate of Thornton v. Caldor* do violate the Establishment Clause. Some of the factors the Supreme Court has considered in deciding which side of the line an accommodation falls include: the burden on religious exercise the accommodation relieves; the burden the accommodation imposes on nonbeneficiaries; and whether the accommodation favors one religion over others or religion over secular counterparts that might also benefit from a similar accommodation.

Texas Monthly, Inc. v. Bullock

489 U.S. 1 (1989)

Justice BRENNAN announced the judgment of the Court and delivered an opinion, in which Justice MARSHALL and Justice STEVENS join.

Texas exempts from its sales tax "[p]eriodicals that are published or distributed by a religious faith and that consist wholly of writings promulgating the teaching of the faith and books that consist wholly of writings sacred to a religious faith." Tex.Tax Code Ann. § 151.312 (1982). The question presented is whether this exemption violates the Establishment Clause or the Free Press Clause of the First Amendment when the State denies a like exemption for other publications. We hold that, when confined exclusively to publications advancing the tenets of a religious faith, the exemption runs afoul of the Establishment Clause; accordingly, we need not reach the question whether it contravenes the Free Press Clause as well. . . .

In proscribing all laws "respecting an establishment of religion," the Constitution prohibits, at the very least, legislation that constitutes an endorsement of one or another set of religious beliefs or of religion generally. It is part of our settled jurisprudence that "the Establishment Clause prohibits government from abandoning secular purposes in order to put an imprimatur on one religion, or on religion as such, or to favor the adherents of any sect or religious organization." Gillette v. United States, 401 U.S. 437, 450 (1971). The core notion animating the requirement that a statute possess "a secular legislative purpose" and that "its principal or primary effect . . . be one that neither advances nor inhibits religion," Lemon v. Kurtzman, 403 U.S., at 612, is not only that government may not be overtly hostile to religion but also that it may not place its prestige, coercive authority, or resources behind a single religious faith or behind religious belief in general, compelling nonadherents to support the practices or proselytizing of favored religious organizations and conveying the message that those who do not contribute gladly are less than full members of the community.

It does not follow, of course, that government policies with secular objectives may not incidentally benefit religion. The nonsectarian aims of government and the interests of religious groups often overlap, and this Court has never required that public authorities refrain from implementing reasonable measures to advance legitimate secular goals merely because they would thereby relieve religious groups of costs they would otherwise incur. . . . [I]n the case most nearly on point, Walz v. Tax Comm'n of New York City, 397 U.S. 664 (1970), we sustained a property tax exemption that applied to religious properties no less than to real estate owned by a wide array of nonprofit organizations, despite the sizable tax savings it accorded religious groups.

In all of these cases, however, we emphasized that the benefits derived by religious organizations flowed to a large number of nonreligious groups as well. Indeed, were those benefits confined to religious organizations, they could not have appeared other than as state sponsorship of religion; if that were so, we would not have hesitated to strike them down for lacking a secular purpose and effect. *See, e.g.,* Estate of Thornton v. Caldor, Inc., 472 U.S. 703 (1985) (finding violative of the Establishment Clause a statute providing Sabbath observers with an unconditional right not to work on their chosen Sabbath). . . .

Finally, we emphasized in Walz that in granting a property tax deduction, the State "has not singled out one particular church or religious group or even churches as such; rather, it has granted exemption to all houses of religious worship within a broad class of property owned by nonprofit, quasi-public corporations which include hospitals, libraries, playgrounds, scientific, professional, historical, and patriotic groups." 397 U.S., at 673. The breadth of New York's property tax exemption was essential to our holding that it was "not aimed at establishing, sponsoring, or supporting religion," *id.*, at 674, but rather possessed the legitimate secular purpose and effect of contributing to the community's moral and intellectual diversity and encouraging private groups to undertake projects that advanced the community's well-being and that would otherwise have to be funded by tax revenues or left undone. . . .

Texas' sales tax exemption for periodicals published or distributed by a religious faith and consisting wholly of writings promulgating the teaching of the faith lacks sufficient breadth to pass scrutiny under the Establishment Clause. . . . [W]hen government directs a subsidy exclusively to religious organizations that is not required by the Free Exercise Clause and that either burdens nonbeneficiaries markedly or cannot reasonably be seen as removing a significant state-imposed deterrent to the free exercise of religion, as Texas has done, see *infra*, at 901-902, it "provide[s] unjustifiable awards of assistance to religious organizations" and cannot but "conve[y] a message of endorsement" to slighted members of the community. Corporation of Presiding Bishop of Church of Jesus Christ of Latter-day Saints v. Amos, 483 U.S. 327, 348 (1987) (O'Connor, J., concurring in judgment). This is particularly true where, as here, the subsidy is targeted at writings that promulgate the teachings of religious faiths. It is difficult to view Texas' narrow exemption as anything but state sponsorship of religious belief, regardless of whether one adopts the perspective of beneficiaries or of uncompensated contributors.

How expansive the class of exempt organizations or activities must be to withstand constitutional assault depends upon the State's secular aim in granting a tax exemption. If the State chose to subsidize, by means of a tax exemption, all groups that contributed to the community's cultural, intellectual, and moral betterment, then the exemption for religious publications could be retained, provided that the exemption swept as widely as the property tax exemption we upheld in Walz. By contrast, if Texas sought to promote reflection and discussion about questions of ultimate value and the contours of a good or meaningful life, then a tax exemption would have to be available to an extended range of associations whose publications were substantially devoted to such matters; the exemption could not be reserved for publications dealing solely with religious issues, let alone restricted to publications advocating rather than criticizing religious belief or activity, without signaling an endorsement of religion that is offensive to the principles informing the Establishment Clause. *See* Estate of Thornton v. Caldor, Inc., 472 U.S., at 711 (O'Connor, J., concurring) (because the statute bestows an advantage on Sabbath observers "without according similar accommodation to ethical and religious beliefs and practices of other private employees," "[t]he message conveyed is one of endorsement of a particular religious belief, to the detriment of those who do not share it"; the statute therefore "has the effect of advancing religion, and cannot withstand Establishment Clause scrutiny"); Welsh v. United States, 398 U.S., at 356-361 (Harlan, J., concurring in result) (conscientious objector status cannot be limited to those whose opposition to war has religious roots, but must extend to those whose convictions have purely moral or philosophical sources). . . .

Because Texas' sales tax exemption for periodicals promulgating the teaching of any religious sect lacks a secular objective that would justify this preference along with similar benefits for nonreligious publications or groups, and because it effectively endorses religious belief, the exemption manifestly fails this test. . . . We conclude that Texas' sales tax exemption for religious publications violates the First Amendment, as made applicable to the States by the Fourteenth Amendment. Accordingly, the judgment of the Texas Court of Appeals is reversed, and the case is remanded for further proceedings.

It is so ordered.

[Justice WHITE's opinion, concurring in the judgment, is omitted.]

Justice BLACKMUN, with whom Justice O'CONNOR joins, concurring in the judgment. . . .

Perhaps it is a vain desire, but I would like to decide the present case without necessarily sacrificing either the Free Exercise Clause value or the Establishment Clause value. It is possible for a State to write a tax-exemption statute consistent with both values: for example, a state statute might exempt the sale not only of religious literature distributed by a religious organization but also of philosophical literature distributed by nonreligious organizations devoted to such matters of conscience as life and death, good and evil, being and nonbeing, right and wrong. Such a statute, moreover, should survive Press Clause scrutiny because its exemption would be narrowly tailored to meet the compelling interests that underlie both the Free Exercise and Establishment Clauses. . . .

In this case, by confining the tax exemption exclusively to the sale of religious publications, Texas engaged in preferential support for the communication of religious messages. Although some forms of accommodating religion are constitutionally permissible, see Corporation of Presiding Bishop of Church of Jesus Christ of Latter-day Saints v. Amos, 483 U.S. 327 (1987), this one surely is not. A statutory preference for the dissemination of religious ideas offends our most basic understanding of what the Establishment Clause is all about and hence is constitutionally intolerable.

Justice SCALIA, with whom THE CHIEF JUSTICE and Justice KENNEDY join, dissenting.

Where accommodation of religion is the justification, by definition religion is being singled out. . . . It is not always easy to determine when accommodation slides over into promotion, and neutrality into favoritism, but the withholding of a tax upon the dissemination of religious materials is not even a close case. The subjects of the exemption before us consist exclusively of "writings promulgating the teaching of the faith" and "writings sacred to a religious faith." If there is any close question, it is not whether the exemption is permitted, but whether it is constitutionally compelled in order to avoid "interference with the dissemination of religious ideas." *Gillette*, 401 U.S., at 462.

NOTES AND QUESTIONS

1. *Which Establishment test(s) did the Court rely on?* The opinion alludes to both the *Lemon* test and the endorsement test. What prong of the *Lemon* test did the Court focus on? Did the decision clarify the relationship between the two tests?

2. *Lack of burden on religious exercise.* The Court writes that the government violates the Establishment Clause "when government directs a subsidy exclusively to religious organizations that is not required by the Free Exercise Clause and . . . cannot reasonably be seen as removing a significant state-imposed deterrent to the free exercise of religion." Did the tax exemption for religious periodicals remove a significant religious burden?
3. *Significant burden on nonbeneficiaries.* The Court also writes that a government accommodation not required by free exercise runs afoul of the Establishment Clause if the accommodation "burdens nonbeneficiaries markedly." Was that the case here?
4. *Favoring religion over secular counterparts.* The majority and concurrence both emphasize that the state may not provide a benefit to religious periodicals and withhold it from secular periodicals. What if there were no secular counterpart? Would it still violate the Establishment Clause to single out religion?
5. *What exemption would pass muster?* The majority and concurrence both suggest that a broader tax exemption, that also included secular periodicals, would have passed constitutional muster. In what way would that change a reasonable observer's view of the tax benefit?

Corporation of the Presiding Bishop of the Church of Jesus Christ of Latter-Day Saints v. Amos

483 U.S. 327 (1987)

Justice WHITE delivered the opinion of the Court.

Section 702 of the Civil Rights Act of 1964, 78 Stat. 255, as amended, 42 U.S.C. § 2000e-1, exempts religious organizations from Title VII's prohibition against discrimination in employment on the basis of religion. The question presented is whether applying the § 702 exemption to the secular nonprofit activities of religious organizations violates the Establishment Clause of the First Amendment. The District Court held that it does, and these cases are here on direct appeal pursuant to 28 U.S.C. § 1252.2. We reverse.

The Deseret Gymnasium (Gymnasium) in Salt Lake City, Utah, is a nonprofit facility, open to the public, run by the Corporation of the Presiding Bishop of The Church of Jesus Christ of Latter-day Saints (CPB), and the Corporation of the President of The Church of Jesus Christ of Latter-day Saints (COP). The CPB and the COP are religious entities associated with The Church of Jesus Christ of Latter-day Saints (Church), an unincorporated religious association sometimes called the Mormon or LDS Church.

Appellee Mayson worked at the Gymnasium for some 16 years as an assistant building engineer and then as building engineer. He was discharged in 1981 because he failed to qualify for a temple recommend, that is, a certificate that he is a member of the Church and eligible to attend its temples.

Mayson and others purporting to represent a class of plaintiffs brought an action against the CPB and the COP alleging, among other things, discrimination on the basis of religion in violation of § 703 of the Civil Rights Act of 1964,

42 U.S.C. § 2000e-2.5. The defendants moved to dismiss this claim on the ground that § 702 shields them from liability. The plaintiffs contended that if construed to allow religious employers to discriminate on religious grounds in hiring for nonreligious jobs, § 702 violates the Establishment Clause. . . .

"This Court has long recognized that the government may (and sometimes must) accommodate religious practices and that it may do so without violating the Establishment Clause." Hobbie v. Unemployment Appeals Comm'n of Fla., 480 U.S. 136, 144-145 (1987) (footnote omitted). It is well established, too, that "[t]he limits of permissible state accommodation to religion are by no means co-extensive with the noninterference mandated by the Free Exercise Clause." Walz v. Tax Comm'n, 397 U.S. 664, 673 (1970). . . . At some point, accommodation may devolve into "an unlawful fostering of religion," but these are not such cases, in our view.

The private appellants contend that we should not apply the three-part *Lemon* approach, which is assertedly unsuited to judging the constitutionality of exemption statutes such as § 702. Brief for Appellants in No. 86-179, pp. 24-26. The argument is that an exemption statute will always have the effect of advancing religion and hence be invalid under the second (effects) part of the *Lemon* test. [W]e need not reexamine *Lemon* as applied in this context, for the exemption involved here is in no way questionable under the *Lemon* analysis.

Lemon requires first that the law at issue serve a "secular legislative purpose." *Id.*, at 612. This does not mean that the law's purpose must be unrelated to religion—that would amount to a requirement "that the government show a callous indifference to religious groups," Zorach v. Clauson, 343 U.S. 306, 314 (1952), and the Establishment Clause has never been so interpreted. Rather, *Lemon*'s "purpose" requirement aims at preventing the relevant governmental decisionmaker—in this case, Congress—from abandoning neutrality and acting with the intent of promoting a particular point of view in religious matters.

Under the *Lemon* analysis, it is a permissible legislative purpose to alleviate significant governmental interference with the ability of religious organizations to define and carry out their religious missions. Appellees argue that there is no such purpose here because § 702 provided adequate protection for religious employers prior to the 1972 amendment, when it exempted only the religious activities of such employers from the statutory ban on religious discrimination. We may assume for the sake of argument that the pre-1972 exemption was adequate in the sense that the Free Exercise Clause required no more. Nonetheless, it is a significant burden on a religious organization to require it, on pain of substantial liability, to predict which of its activities a secular court will consider religious. The line is hardly a bright one, and an organization might understandably be concerned that a judge would not understand its religious tenets and sense of mission. Fear of potential liability might affect the way an organization carried out what it understood to be its religious mission.

After a detailed examination of the legislative history of the 1972 amendment, the District Court concluded that Congress' purpose was to minimize governmental "interfer[ence] with the decision-making process in religions." 594 F. Supp., at 812. We agree with the District Court that this purpose does not violate the Establishment Clause.

The second requirement under *Lemon* is that the law in question have "a principal or primary effect . . . that neither advances nor inhibits religion." 403 U.S.

at 612. Undoubtedly, religious organizations are better able now to advance their purposes than they were prior to the 1972 amendment to § 702. But religious groups have been better able to advance their purposes on account of many laws that have passed constitutional muster. . . . A law is not unconstitutional simply because it allows churches to advance religion, which is their very purpose. For a law to have forbidden "effects" under *Lemon*, it must be fair to say that the government itself has advanced religion through its own activities and influence. . . .

We find unpersuasive the District Court's reliance on the fact that § 702 singles out religious entities for a benefit. Although the Court has given weight to this consideration in its past decisions, it has never indicated that statutes that give special consideration to religious groups are per se invalid. That would run contrary to the teaching of our cases that there is ample room for accommodation of religion under the Establishment Clause. Where, as here, government acts with the proper purpose of lifting a regulation that burdens the exercise of religion, we see no reason to require that the exemption comes packaged with benefits to secular entities. . . .

It cannot be seriously contended that § 702 impermissibly entangles church and state; the statute effectuates a more complete separation of the two and avoids the kind of intrusive inquiry into religious belief that the District Court engaged in in this case. The statute easily passes muster under the third part of the *Lemon* test.

The judgment of the District Court is reversed, and the cases are remanded for further proceedings consistent with this opinion.

It is so ordered.

Justice BRENNAN, with whom Justice MARSHALL joins, concurring in the judgment.

I write separately to emphasize that my concurrence in the judgment rests on the fact that these cases involve a challenge to the application of § 702's categorical exemption to the activities of a nonprofit organization. I believe that the particular character of nonprofit activity makes inappropriate a case-by-case determination whether its nature is religious or secular.

These cases present a confrontation between the rights of religious organizations and those of individuals. Any exemption from Title VII's proscription on religious discrimination necessarily has the effect of burdening the religious liberty of prospective and current employees. An exemption says that a person may be put to the choice of either conforming to certain religious tenets or losing a job opportunity, a promotion, or, as in these cases, employment itself. The potential for coercion created by such a provision is in serious tension with our commitment to individual freedom of conscience in matters of religious belief.

At the same time, religious organizations have an interest in autonomy in ordering their internal affairs, so that they may be free to: "select their own leaders, define their own doctrines, resolve their own disputes, and run their own institutions. Religion includes important communal elements for most believers. They exercise their religion through religious organizations, and these organizations must be protected by the [Free Exercise] [C]lause." Laycock, *Towards a General Theory of the Religion Clauses: The Case of Church Labor Relations and the Right to Church Autonomy*, 81 Colum. L. Rev. 1373, 1389 (1981).

. . . For many individuals, religious activity derives meaning in large measure from participation in a larger religious community. Such a community represents an ongoing tradition of shared beliefs, an organic entity not reducible to a mere aggregation of individuals. Determining that certain activities are in furtherance of an organization's religious mission, and that only those committed to that mission should conduct them, is thus a means by which a religious community defines itself. Solicitude for a church's ability to do so reflects the idea that furtherance of the autonomy of religious organizations often furthers individual religious freedom as well.

The authority to engage in this process of self-definition inevitably involves what we normally regard as infringement on free exercise rights, since a religious organization is able to condition employment in certain activities on subscription to particular religious tenets. We are willing to countenance the imposition of such a condition because we deem it vital that, if certain activities constitute part of a religious community's practice, then a religious organization should be able to require that only members of its community perform those activities.

This rationale suggests that, ideally, religious organizations should be able to discriminate on the basis of religion only with respect to religious activities, so that a determination should be made in each case whether an activity is religious or secular. This is because the infringement on religious liberty that results from conditioning performance of secular activity upon religious belief cannot be defended as necessary for the community's self-definition. . . .

What makes the application of a religious-secular distinction difficult is that the character of an activity is not self-evident. As a result, determining whether an activity is religious or secular requires a searching case-by-case analysis. This results in considerable ongoing government entanglement in religious affairs. Furthermore, this prospect of government intrusion raises concern that a religious organization may be chilled in its free exercise activity. While a church may regard the conduct of certain functions as integral to its mission, a court may disagree. A religious organization therefore would have an incentive to characterize as religious only those activities about which there likely would be no dispute, even if it genuinely believed that religious commitment was important in performing other tasks as well. As a result, the community's process of self-definition would be shaped in part by the prospects of litigation. A case-by-case analysis for all activities therefore would both produce excessive government entanglement with religion and create the danger of chilling religious activity.

The risk of chilling religious organizations is most likely to arise with respect to nonprofit activities. The fact that an operation is not organized as a profit-making commercial enterprise makes colorable a claim that it is not purely secular in orientation. . . . Nonprofit activities therefore are most likely to present cases in which characterization of the activity as religious or secular will be a close question. If there is a danger that a religious organization will be deterred from classifying as religious those activities it actually regards as religious, it is likely to be in this domain. . . .

Sensitivity to individual religious freedom dictates that religious discrimination be permitted only with respect to employment in religious activities. Concern for the autonomy of religious organizations demands that we avoid the entanglement and the chill on religious expression that a case-by-case determination would produce. We cannot escape the fact that these aims are in tension. Because of the nature of nonprofit activities, I believe that a categorical exemption for such enterprises appropriately balances these competing concerns. As a result, I concur in the Court's judgment that the nonprofit Deseret Gymnasium may avail itself of an automatic exemption from Title VII's proscription on religious discrimination.

[Justice BLACKMUN concurred in the judgment.]

Justice O'CONNOR, concurring in the judgment.

Although I agree with the judgment of the Court, I write separately to note that this action once again illustrates certain difficulties inherent in the Court's use of the test articulated in Lemon v. Kurtzman, 403 U.S. 602, 612-613 (1971). . . . [T]he Court seems to suggest that the "effects" prong of the *Lemon* test is not at all implicated as long as the government action can be characterized as "allowing" religious organizations to advance religion, in contrast to government action directly advancing religion. This distinction seems to me to obscure far more than to enlighten. Almost any government benefit to religion could be recharacterized as simply "allowing" a religion to better advance itself, unless perhaps it involved actual proselytization by government agents. . . . It is for this same reason that there is little significance to the Court's observation that it was the Church rather than the Government that penalized Mayson's refusal to adhere to Church doctrine. The Church had the power to put Mayson to a choice of qualifying for a temple recommend or losing his job because the Government had lifted from religious organizations the general regulatory burden imposed by § 702.

The necessary first step in evaluating an Establishment Clause challenge to a government action lifting from religious organizations a generally applicable regulatory burden is to recognize that such government action does have the effect of advancing religion. The necessary second step is to separate those benefits to religion that constitutionally accommodate the free exercise of religion from those that provide unjustifiable awards of assistance to religious organizations. As I have suggested in earlier opinions, the inquiry framed by the *Lemon* test should be "whether government's purpose is to endorse religion and whether the statute actually conveys a message of endorsement." *Wallace*, 472 U.S., at 69. To ascertain whether the statute conveys a message of endorsement, the relevant issue is how it would be perceived by an objective observer, acquainted with the text, legislative history, and implementation of the statute. *Id.*, at 76. Of course, in order to perceive the government action as a permissible accommodation of religion, there must in fact be an identifiable burden on the exercise of religion that can be said to be lifted by the government action . . .

The above framework, I believe, helps clarify why the amended § 702 raises different questions as it is applied to nonprofit and for-profit organizations. As Justice BRENNAN observes in his concurrence: "The fact that an operation is not organized as a profit-making commercial enterprise makes colorable a claim that it is not purely secular in orientation." These cases involve a Government decision to lift from a nonprofit activity of a religious organization the burden of demonstrating that the particular nonprofit activity is religious as well as the burden of refraining from discriminating on the basis of religion. Because there is a probability that a nonprofit activity of a religious organization will itself be involved in the organization's religious mission, in my view the objective observer should perceive the Government action as an accommodation of the exercise of religion rather than as a Government endorsement of religion.

It is not clear, however, that activities conducted by religious organizations solely as profit-making enterprises will be as likely to be directly involved in the religious mission of the organization. While I express no opinion on the issue, I emphasize that under the holding of the Court, and under my view of the appropriate Establishment Clause analysis, the question of the constitutionality of the § 702 exemption as applied to for-profit activities of religious organizations remains open.

NOTES AND QUESTIONS

1. *Title VII exemption.* Title VII of the Civil Rights Act bans discrimination in employment on the basis of religion; however, § 702 exempts religious organizations from this prohibition. The exemption was originally limited to religious positions, thereby allowing a Jewish day school to discriminate on the basis of religion when hiring a Judaic studies teacher, for example. The exemption was expanded in 1972 to cover to all positions, including janitors.
2. Lemon *and secular purpose and effect.* According to the majority, how can granting a religious accommodation advance a secular purpose or have a secular effect? How does Justice O'Connor's endorsement analysis change the question?
3. *Burden on religious exercise.* Both the majority and Justice O'Connor's concurrence emphasize that in order to comply with the Establishment Clause, an accommodation must relieve an identifiable burden on religious practice. What burden does Title VII impose on religious organizations vis-à-vis nonreligious jobs? The argument is not that the organization needs people who adhere to their beliefs to fill those positions, as might be the case with religious positions.
4. *Burden on nonbeneficiaries.* Exempting religious organizations from Title VII allows them to discriminate on the basis of religion. This discrimination imposes significant costs on people like Mayson who are not hired or who are fired because of their religion. In *Estate of Thornton v. Caldor*, an accommodation that significantly burdened nonbeneficiaries was found unconstitutional (see *supra* p. 735). Why wasn't the § 702 accommodation also unconstitutional?
5. *Favoring religion.* On the one hand, § 702 grants a benefit to religious groups—the right to discriminate on the basis of religion—without granting the same benefit to secular groups. On the other hand, if an environmental group is allowed to hire only those people who identify as environmentalists, why shouldn't a religious group be able to hire only those people who share its beliefs?
6. *Nonprofits vs. for-profits.* The holding applies to the nonprofit activities of religious organizations. Justice Brennan argues it is limited to nonprofits while Justice O'Connor leaves the question open. Do you think the reasoning applies to the for-profit activities of religious organizations? What about for-profit corporations?

Cutter v. Wilkinson

544 U.S. 709 (2005)

Justice GINSBURG delivered the opinion of the Court.

Section 3 of the Religious Land Use and Institutionalized Persons Act of 2000 (RLUIPA), 114 Stat. 804, 42 U.S.C. § 2000cc-1(a)(1) [to] (2), provides in part: "No government shall impose a substantial burden on the religious exercise of a person residing in or confined to an institution," unless the burden furthers "a compelling governmental interest," and does so by "the least restrictive means." Plaintiffs below, petitioners here, are current and former inmates of institutions operated by the Ohio Department of Rehabilitation and Correction and assert that they are adherents of "nonmainstream" religions: The Satanist, Wicca, and Asatru religions, and the Church of Jesus Christ Christian. They complain that Ohio prison officials (respondents here), in violation of RLUIPA, have failed to accommodate their religious exercise. . . .

In response to petitioners' complaints, respondent prison officials have mounted a facial challenge to the institutionalized-persons provision of RLUIPA; respondents contend, inter alia, that the Act improperly advances religion in violation of the First Amendment's Establishment Clause. The District Court denied respondents' motion to dismiss petitioners' complaints, but the Court of Appeals reversed that determination. The appeals court held, as the prison officials urged, that the portion of RLUIPA applicable to institutionalized persons, 42 U.S.C. § 2000cc-1, violates the Establishment Clause. We reverse the Court of Appeals' judgment.

"This Court has long recognized that the government may . . . accommodate religious practices . . . without violating the Establishment Clause." Hobbie v. Unemployment Appeals Comm'n of Fla., 480 U.S. 136, 144-145 (1987). Just last term, in Locke v. Davey, 540 U.S. 712 (2004) the Court reaffirmed that "there is room for play in the joints between" the Free Exercise and Establishment Clauses, allowing the government to accommodate religion beyond free exercise requirements, without offense to the Establishment Clause. *Id.*, at 718 (quoting Walz v. Tax Comm'n of City of New York, 397 U.S. 664, 669 (1970)). "At some point, accommodation may devolve into 'an unlawful fostering of religion.'" But § 3 of RLUIPA, we hold, does not, on its face, exceed the limits of permissible government accommodation of religious practices. . . .

RLUIPA is the latest of long-running congressional efforts to accord religious exercise heightened protection from government-imposed burdens, consistent with this Court's precedents. Ten years before RLUIPA's enactment, the Court held, in Employment Div., Dept. of Human Resources of Ore. v. Smith, 494 U.S. 872, 878-882 (1990), that the First Amendment's Free Exercise Clause does not inhibit enforcement of otherwise valid laws of general application that incidentally burden religious conduct. In particular, we ruled that the Free Exercise Clause did not bar Oregon from enforcing its blanket ban on peyote possession with no allowance for sacramental use of the drug. Accordingly, the State could deny unemployment benefits to persons dismissed from their jobs because of their religiously inspired peyote use.

Responding to *Smith,* Congress enacted the Religious Freedom Restoration Act of 1993 (RFRA), 107 Stat. 1488, 42 U.S.C. § 2000bb *et seq.* RFRA "prohibits '[g]overnment' from 'substantially burden[ing]' a person's exercise of religion even if the burden results from a rule of general applicability unless the government can demonstrate the burden '(1) is in furtherance of a compelling governmental interest; and (2) is the least restrictive means of furthering that compelling governmental interest.'" City of Boerne v. Flores, 521 U.S. 507, 515-516 (1997) (brackets in original) (quoting § 2000bb-1). "[U]niversal" in its coverage, RFRA "applie[d] to all Federal and State law," *id.*, at 516 (quoting former § 2000bb-3 (a)), but notably lacked a Commerce Clause underpinning or a Spending Clause limitation to recipients of federal funds. In *City of Boerne,* this Court invalidated RFRA as applied to States and their subdivisions, holding that the Act exceeded Congress' remedial powers under the Fourteenth Amendment. *Id.*, at 532-536.

Congress again responded, this time by enacting RLUIPA. Less sweeping than RFRA, and invoking federal authority under the Spending and Commerce Clauses, RLUIPA targets two areas: Section 2 of the Act concerns land-use regulation, 42 U.S.C. § 2000cc; § 3 relates to religious exercise by institutionalized persons, § 2000cc-1. Section 3, at issue here, provides that "[n]o [state or local] government shall impose a substantial burden on the religious exercise of a person residing in or confined to an institution," unless the government shows that the burden furthers "a compelling governmental interest" and does so by "the least restrictive means." § 2000cc-1(a)(1)-(2). The Act defines "religious exercise" to include "any exercise of religion, whether or not compelled by, or central to, a system of religious belief." § 2000cc-5(7)(A). Section 3 applies when "the substantial burden [on religious exercise] is imposed in a program or activity that receives Federal financial assistance," or "the substantial burden affects, or removal of that substantial burden would affect, commerce with foreign nations, among the several States, or with Indian tribes." § 2000cc-1(b)(1)-(2). "A person may assert a violation of [RLUIPA] as a claim or defense in a judicial proceeding and obtain appropriate relief against a government." § 2000cc-2(a). . . .

The Religion Clauses of the First Amendment provide: "Congress shall make no law respecting an establishment of religion, or prohibiting the free exercise thereof." The first of the two Clauses, commonly called the Establishment Clause, commands a separation of church and state. The second, the Free Exercise Clause, requires government respect for, and noninterference with, the religious beliefs and practices of our Nation's people. While the two Clauses express complementary values, they often exert conflicting pressures. *See Locke,* 540 U.S. at 718 ("These two Clauses . . . are frequently in tension."); *Walz,* 397 U.S., at 668-669 ("The court has struggled to find a neutral course between the two Religion Clauses, both of which are cast in absolute terms, and either of which, if expanded to a logical extreme, would tend to clash with the other.")

Our decisions recognize that "there is room for play in the joints" between the Clauses, *id.*, at 669, some space for legislative action neither compelled by the Free Exercise Clause nor prohibited by the Establishment Clause. . . . In accord with the majority of Courts of Appeals that have ruled on the question, we hold that § 3 of RLUIPA fits within the corridor between the Religion Clauses: On its face, the Act qualifies as a permissible legislative accommodation of religion that is not barred by the Establishment Clause.

Foremost, we find RLUIPA's institutionalized-persons provision compatible with the Establishment Clause because it alleviates exceptional government-created burdens on private religious exercise. . . . Furthermore, the Act on its face does not founder on shoals our prior decisions have identified: Properly applying RLUIPA, courts must take adequate account of the burdens a requested accommodation may impose on nonbeneficiaries, see Estate of Thornton v. Caldor, Inc., 472 U.S. 703 (1985); and they must be satisfied that the Act's prescriptions are and will be administered neutrally among different faiths, see *Kiryas Joel*, 512 U.S. 687. . . .

We do not read RLUIPA to elevate accommodation of religious observances over an institution's need to maintain order and safety. Our decisions indicate that an accommodation must be measured so that it does not override other significant interests. In *Caldor*, the Court struck down a Connecticut law that "arm[ed] Sabbath observers with an absolute and unqualified right not to work on whatever day they designate[d] as their Sabbath." 472 U.S., at 709. We held the law invalid under the Establishment Clause because it "unyielding[ly] weigh[ted]" the interests of Sabbatarians "over all other interests." *Id.*, at 710.

We have no cause to believe that RLUIPA would not be applied in an appropriately balanced way, with particular sensitivity to security concerns. While the Act adopts a "compelling governmental interest" standard, see *supra*, at 2118, "[c]ontext matters" in the application of that standard. *See* Grutter v. Bollinger, 539 U.S. 306, 327 (2003). Lawmakers supporting RLUIPA were mindful of the urgency of discipline, order, safety, and security in penal institutions. *See, e.g.*, 139 Cong. Rec. 26190 (1993) (remarks of Senator Hatch). They anticipated that courts would apply the Act's standard with "due deference to the experience and expertise of prison and jail administrators in establishing necessary regulations and procedures to maintain good order, security and discipline, consistent with consideration of costs and limited resources." Joint Statement S7775 (quoting S. Rep. No. 103-111, p. 10 (1993), U.S. Code Cong. & Admin. News 1993, pp. 1892, 1899, 1900).

Finally RLUIPA does not differentiate among bona fide faiths. In *Kiryas Joel*, we invalidated a state law that carved out a separate school district to serve exclusively a community of highly religious Jews, the Satmar Hasidim. We held that the law violated the Establishment Clause, 512 U.S., at 690, in part because it "single[d] out a particular religious sect for special treatment," *id.*, at 706 (footnote omitted). RLUIPA presents no such defect. In confers no privileged status on any particular religious sect, and singles out no bona fide faith for disadvantageous treatment.

The Sixth Circuit misread our precedents to require invalidation of RLUIPA as "impermissibly advancing religion by giving greater protection to religious rights than to other constitutionally protected rights." 349 F.3d, at 264. Our decision in *Amos* counsels otherwise. There, we upheld against an Establishment Clause challenge a provision exempting "religious organizations from Title VII's prohibition against discrimination in employment on the basis of religion." 483 U.S., at 329. The District Court in *Amos*, reasoning in part that the exemption improperly "single[d] out religious entities for a benefit," *id.*, at 338, had "declared the statute unconstitutional as applied to secular activity," *id.*, at 333. Religious accommodations, we held, need not "come packaged with benefits to secular entities." *Id.*, at 338; *see* Madison, 355 F.3d, at 318 ("There is no requirement that legislative protections for fundamental rights march in lockstep.").

Were the Court of Appeals' view the correct reading of our decisions, all manner of religious accommodations would fall. Congressional permission for members of the military to wear religious apparel while in uniform would fail, see 10 U.S.C. § 774, as would accommodations Ohio itself makes. Ohio could not, as it now does, accommodate "traditionally recognized" religions, 221 F. Supp. 2d, at 832: The State provides inmates with chaplains "but not with publicists or political consultants," and allows "prisoners to assemble for worship, but not for political rallies." Reply Brief for United States 5.

In upholding RLUIPA's institutionalized-persons provision, we emphasize that respondents "have raised a facial challenge to [the Act's] constitutionality, and have not contended that under the facts of any of [petitioners'] specific cases . . . [that] applying RLUIPA would produce unconstitutional results." 221 F. Supp. 2d, at 831. The District Court, noting the underdeveloped state of the record, concluded: A finding "that it is factually impossible to provide the kind of accommodations that RLUIPA will require without significantly compromising prison security or the levels of service provided to other inmates" cannot be made at this juncture. *Id.*, at 848 (emphasis added). We agree. . . .

We see no reason to anticipate that abusive prisoner litigation will overburden the operations of state and local institutions. The procedures mandated by the Prison Litigation Reform Act of 1995, we note, are designed to inhibit frivolous filings.

Should inmate requests for religious accommodations become excessive, impose unjustified burdens on other institutionalized persons, or jeopardize the effective functioning of an institution, the facility would be free to resist the imposition. In that event, adjudication in as-applied challenges would be in order.

For the reasons stated, the judgment of the United States Court of Appeals for the Sixth Circuit is reversed, and the case is remanded for further proceedings consistent with this opinion.

It is so ordered.

NOTES AND QUESTIONS

1. *Facial challenge to RLUIPA.* Congress passed RLUIPA after the Supreme Court struck down the Religious Freedom Restoration Act's application to the states in *Boerne* (see *supra* pp. 823-825). While RFRA was passed pursuant to Congress's Fourteenth Amendment enforcement power, RLUIPA was passed pursuant to its spending and commerce clause powers. Note that the challenge in *Cutter* was a facial rather than an as-applied challenge. *Cutter* demonstrates that if Congress acts pursuant to a valid constitutional power, it can enact civil rights legislation that mandates accommodation of religious practices.
2. *Burdens on religion.* The Court does not describe the "exceptional government-created burdens on private religious exercise," but it ought not be difficult to imagine how incarceration might severely impair prisoners' ability to practice their religion.
3. *Burdens on nonbenficiaries.* The Court emphasized that accommodating prisoners' religious practices would not impose on others by

compromising order or safety in prison. In fact, the Court essentially advises that RLUIPA be applied with "due deference to the experience and expertise of prison and jail administrators in establishing necessary regulations and procedures to maintain good order, security and discipline, consistent with consideration of costs and limited resources." But if courts defer to prison officials, would they really be applying strict scrutiny as RLUIPA requires? Is the decision's suggestion that strict scrutiny is not always as strict in some cases as in others limited to the prison context? Should strict scrutiny vary with the perceived importance of the government's interests? Of the popularity of the plaintiff religious group? Both? Neither?

4. *Favoring religion.* RLUIPA does not favor some religions over others, as it "does not differentiate among bona fide faiths." At the same time, the Court acknowledged that the "play in the joints" is sufficient to permit legislatively enacted accommodations for only religiously motivated conduct. In other words, the law requires that a refusal to provide a prisoner a Bible be scrutinized in a way that a refusal to provide a family photograph will not. Is this result consistent with *Texas Monthly*? How else are the two cases distinguishable?
5. *Play in the joints.* In theory, the "play in the joints" that exists between the two religion clauses not only allows the government to provide accommodations that are not required by the Free Exercise Clause, but also allows the government to curtail aid to religion that is not required by the Establishment Clause. Locke v. Davey, 540 U.S. 712 (2004), see *supra* pp. 803, provides an example. In *Locke*, the State of Washington would not award a postsecondary scholarship to students pursuing a degree in devotional theology, i.e., training for the ministry. The Supreme Court rejected the Free Exercise Clause claim of Davey Locke, one of those students. After finding that it would not violate the Establishment Clause for the state to fund Davey's studies, it held that ban was allowed by the "play in the joints." "Even though the differently worded Washington Constitution draws a more stringent line than that drawn by the United States Constitution, the interest it seeks to further is scarcely novel. In fact, we can think of few areas in which a State's antiestablishment interests come more into play. Since the founding of our country, there have been popular uprisings against procuring taxpayer funds to support church leaders, which was one of the hallmarks of an 'established' religion. . . . Most States that sought to avoid an establishment of religion around the time of the founding placed in their constitutions formal prohibitions against using tax funds to support the ministry." The Court held that "Given the historic and substantial state interest at issue, we therefore cannot conclude that the denial of funding for vocational religious instruction alone is inherently constitutionally suspect" and that "If any room exists between the two Religion Clauses, it must be here." However, that "play in the joints," at least in terms of pursuing establishment goals beyond what is required by the Establishment Clause, has been called into question by more recent cases, where religious schools excluded from government funding

programs have successfully brought Free Exercise Clause challenges. *See* Trinity Lutheran Church v. Comer, 137 S. Ct. 2012 (2017) and Espinoza v. Montana Dep't of Revenue, 140 S. Ct. 2246 (2020).

AN EXTENDED NOTE ON THE VIETNAM-ERA CONSCIENTIOUS OBJECTOR CASES *SEEGER* AND *WELSH*

The conscientious objector cases provide additional insight into the question of whether the government may provide an exemption for some religionists but not others. The federal government had, from time to time, maintained a national system of compulsory military service from the Civil War until the conclusion of the Vietnam War. Congress, by statute, ended involuntary military conscription in June 1973 and put the nation's armed forces on an all-volunteer basis. However, when the policy of a mandatory draft was in effect, Congress consistently provided an exemption for those persons who held a conscientious religiously based objection to military service predicated on opposition to all forms of war. Among the faith communities categorically opposed to war, and whose adherents were accordingly eligible to claim conscientious objector status, were Quakers, Mennonites, Moravian Brethren, and some Seventh Day Adventists and Jehovah's Witnesses.

During the Vietnam War period, the relevant statutory language granted conscientious objector status to any person "who, by reason of religious training and belief, is conscientiously opposed to participation in war in any form. Religious training and belief in this connection means an individual's belief in a relation to a Supreme Being involving duties superior to those arising from any human relation, but does not include essentially political, sociological, or philosophical views or a merely personal moral code." Universal Military Training and Service Act of 1948, § 6(j), 62 Stat. 612, 50 U.S.C. App. § 456(j). Thus, Congress expressly tried to exclude philosophical or abstract moral objections to war as a basis for securing conscientious objector status.

The federal government applied the exemption narrowly and routinely rejected applications for conscientious objector status when an applicant disclaimed a traditional belief in God. In United States v. Seeger, 380 U.S. 163 (1965) and Welsh v. United States, 398 U.S. 333 (1970), defendants had unsuccessfully sought to claim conscientious objector status while emphatically and overtly disclaiming any theistic or formal religious basis for their opposition to war. Notwithstanding the clear language of the statute, however, the Supreme Court held that both Seeger and Welsh qualified for conscientious objector status under Section 456(j). In both cases, the Supreme Court read the statute broadly in order to avoid Establishment Clause problems.

In *Seeger*, Daniel Seeger had "declared that he was conscientiously opposed to participation in war in any form by reason of his 'religious' belief; that he preferred to leave the question as to his belief in a Supreme Being open, 'rather than answer 'yes' or 'no'; that his 'skepticism or disbelief in the existence of God' did 'not necessarily mean lack of faith in anything whatsoever'; that his was a 'belief in and devotion to goodness and virtue for their own sakes, and a religious faith in a purely ethical creed.' R. 69-70, 73. He cited such personages as Plato, Aristotle and Spinoza for support of his ethical belief in intellectual and moral integrity 'without belief in God, except in the remotest sense.'" *Id.* at 166. Plainly, Seeger lacked a belief premised on a "Supreme Being," as required by the statute. The statute, by exempting only members of religions that believed in a Supreme Being (as opposed to religions such as Buddhism, Taoism and Ethical Culture that do not necessary center around a Supreme Being), appeared to violate the Establishment Clause prohibition on favoring some religions over others.

The Court held that Seeger was covered by the statute. Writing for the *Seeger* majority, Justice Tom C. Clark explained:

> We have concluded that Congress, in using the expression "Supreme Being" rather than the designation "God," was merely clarifying the meaning of religious training and belief so as to embrace all religions and to exclude essentially political, sociological, or philosophical views. We believe that under this construction, the test of belief "in a relation to a Supreme Being" is whether a given belief that is sincere and meaningful occupies a place in the life of its possessor parallel to that filled by the orthodox belief in God of one who clearly qualifies for the exemption. Where such beliefs have parallel positions in the lives of their respective holders we cannot say that one is "in a relation to a Supreme Being" and the other is not. We have concluded that the beliefs of the objectors in these cases [including Seeger] meet these criteria. . . .

Id. at 165-166.

Thus, to avoid striking down the entire statute as unconstitutional, the Supreme Court found Seeger to be eligible for conscientious objector status, holding that the governing test was "essentially an objective one, namely, does the claimed belief occupy the same place in the life of the objector as an orthodox belief in God holds in the life of one clearly qualified for exemption?" *Id.* at 184; *see also id.* at 187 ("We think it clear that the beliefs which prompted [Seeger's] objection occupy the same place in his life as the belief in a traditional deity holds in the lives of his friends, the Quakers."). Justice Clark cautioned that "it must be remembered that in resolving these exemption problems one deals with the beliefs of different individuals who will articulate them in a multitude of ways" and that "[i]n such an intensely personal area, of course, the claim of the registrant that his belief is an essential part of a religious faith must be given great weight." *Id.* at 184.

Elliott Welsh presented an even harder case than did Daniel Seeger. Although the statute had been amended to eliminate language about a Supreme Being, it still limited conscientious objectors status to those "who, by reason of religious training and belief, is conscientiously opposed to participation in war in any form." The Selective Service denied Welsh conscientious objector status because "Welsh could sign [the required affirmation] only after striking the words 'my religious training and.'" *Welsh,* 398 U.S. at 336. Thus, Welsh expressly disclaimed an overtly religious basis for his objection to war and participation in the military services. If the Court held that the statute did not cover Welsh, it would likely face the question of whether it violated the Establishment Clause to grant exemptions to those with deeply held religious objections to war but refuse exemptions to those with deeply held nonreligious objections to war. In other words, may the government favor religion over its secular counterpart?

To avoid answering this difficult Establishment Clause question, the Supreme Court held that Welsh was entitled to claim conscientious objector status even though Welsh's objection to military service was, at least in part, based on political, sociological, and philosophical beliefs. *See id.* at 342-344. The Court reasoned that as long as the moral beliefs in question hold the same place and importance as traditional religious beliefs as a form of compelled and binding moral commitment, a person may claim the benefit of the conscientious objector policy. Accordingly, Justice Hugo L. Black, writing for the *Welsh* majority, concluded that Section 456(j) "exempts from military service all those whose consciences, spurred by deeply held moral, ethical, or religious beliefs, would give them no rest or peace if they allowed themselves to become a part of an instrument of war." *Id.* at 344.

In sum, in order to avoid Establishment Clause problems that arguably would have required the complete invalidation of the conscientious objector exemption from conscription, the Supreme Court instead interpreted the exemption broadly to provide an exemption to anyone who held a "moral, ethical, or religious" objection to war under any and all circumstances. *But cf.* Gillette v. United States, 401 U.S. 437, 454-462 (1971) (holding that Congress could constitutionally limit eligibility for conscientious objector status to persons who "oppose participation in war in any form" and that this restriction on eligibility does not violate either the Establishment Clause or Free Exercise Clause). The logic of *Welsh* and *Seeger* suggests that when Congress provides statutory exemptions for religious organizations and their adherents, it cannot do so on a highly selective basis. So long as Congress crafts an exemption broadly, making it available to all persons who hold a religious belief or the material equivalent of such a belief, such exemptions may constitutionally help to advance Free Exercise Clause values without running afoul of the Establishment Clause.

THEORY-APPLIED PROBLEM

Maryland's legislature is considering revisions to the official state holiday calendar, which provides all state workers (including local public school teachers) with certain automatic vacation days, in addition to individualized vacation benefits. The Senate Government Affairs Committee commissions a survey of possible new holidays; the survey asks state and local government employees to list the top five holidays that they would like to have off as a matter of course. Of the respondents, 93 percent list "Good Friday" as one of the "top five" most desired holidays. In addition, the State Personnel Manager reports that state agencies have a larger number of requests for vacation time on Good Friday, as well as very high rates of absenteeism from those workers unable to obtain approved vacation. In light of this information, Maryland adds "Good Friday" to the official list of state holidays. The chief sponsor of the bill in the state Senate, when introducing the measure, says that "[w]e need to recognize the needs of our workforce, and Maryland's employees want to observe Good Friday." The Maryland ACLU promptly files a federal lawsuit seeking to invalidate the creation of the Good Friday state holiday. Maryland defends the law by arguing that it is a permissible accommodation of the dominant religious groups in the state. The ACLU argues that the state cannot enshrine an overtly Christian holy day as a secular holiday and that a more generic accommodation of religious practices should be required (that is, a "floating holiday" approach). How should the district court rule?

CHAPTER 20

THE ESTABLISHMENT CLAUSE AND GOVERNMENT FINANCING OF RELIGION

TABLE OF CONTENTS

A. Separation Versus Neutrality: *Everson v. Board of Education*

B. Tax Deductions for Religious Organizations

C. Direct Aid

D. Voucher Programs

This chapter deals with the area of church/state relations that first instigated the movement against religious establishments in this country. Most of the early battles over religious establishments involved disputes over the collection of state taxes to finance religious institutions. By the time the Bill of Rights was ratified, most states had eliminated their financial establishments, and by 1833 all states had done so. In the modern era, disputes over government financial support for religion usually arise over tax exemption programs, government financial support to church-related social services providers, and government grants to private religious education.

The Court's rhetoric in the earlier financing cases tended to describe a system of strict separation between church and state. Recall the phrase from *Everson* to the effect that "[n]o tax in any amount, large or small, can be levied to support any religious activities or institutions, whatever they may be called, or whatever form they may adopt to teach or practice religion." The Court's implementation of this principle has been far less strict. In *Everson* itself, for example, the Court voted 5–4 to uphold a New Jersey statute that provided free transportation of students to parochial schools.

As for aid to religious schools, subsequent decisions during the next 50 years following the Court's *Everson* decision did little to clarify the situation. During the last decade, a new majority on the Supreme Court has fundamentally revamped

Establishment Clause jurisprudence to make it far easier for the government to finance private religious institutions—especially religious schools.

Mitchell v. Helms overruled decades of precedent barring direct governmental subsidies to religious schools in the form of educational materials. Justice O'Connor provided the fifth vote in *Mitchell* to uphold the direct subsidy program but continued to insist that the Constitution prohibits religious schools from diverting government financial support to explicitly religious activities. Four Justices in *Mitchell* would permit such diversions, and it is not clear whether a current Supreme Court majority would subscribe to the non-diversion requirement.

In *Mueller v. Allen,* the Court developed the theory that government funds can be filtered to religious schools through the parents of students at those schools. In the tax deduction scheme of *Mueller,* parents serve as a kind of constitutional circuit-breaker, insulating the government from Establishment Clause challenges despite the fact that the program in question provided a large portion of its financial benefits to private religious education. In *Zelman v. Simmons-Harris,* the *Mueller* majority once again used the private-choice logic to justify a multi-million-dollar voucher program of subsidies to parents sending children to private schools, virtually all of which were religious. The only limits on the parental-subsidy model that remains after *Zelman* is that the subsidies formally be available on a neutral basis, such that secular schools could also apply for a subsidy, and that the parents' decision to direct the subsidy to a religious school be the result of a genuine and independent choice.

A. *SEPARATION VERSUS NEUTRALITY:* EVERSON V. BOARD OF EDUCATION

Everson v. Board of Education marked both the beginning of the Supreme Court's modern Establishment Clause era generally and its modern jurisprudence regarding government financial aid to religion. As noted above, the Court unanimously agreed on a broad statement of principles regarding the Establishment Clause, including the proposition that "[n]o tax in any amount, large or small, can be levied to support any religious activities or institutions, whatever they may be called, or whatever form they may adopt to teach or practice religion." But having agreed on this absolutist principle, the Court then split 5–4 on the application of that principle to a New Jersey statute providing publicly funded K through12 school transportation for students attending private religious schools. Writing on behalf of the majority, Justice Black found no constitutional problem with the program.

Everson v. Board of Education of Ewing TP. et al.

330 U.S. 1 (1947)

Mr. Justice Black delivered the opinion of the Court.

A New Jersey statute authorizes its local school districts to make rules and contracts for the transportation of children to and from schools. The appellee, a township board of education, acting pursuant to this statute authorized reimbursement to parents of money expended by them for the bus transportation of their children on regular busses operated by the public transportation system. Part of this money was for the payment of transportation of some children in the community to Catholic parochial schools. These church schools give their students, in addition to secular education, regular religious instruction conforming to the religious tenets and modes of worship of the Catholic Faith. The superintendent of these schools is a Catholic priest.

The appellant, in his capacity as a district taxpayer, filed suit in a State court challenging the right of the Board to reimburse parents of parochial school students. . . . The New Jersey statute is challenged as a 'law respecting an establishment of religion.' The First Amendment, as made applicable to the states by the Fourteenth, Murdock v. Commonwealth of Pennsylvania, 319 U.S. 105 (1943), commands that a state 'shall make no law respecting an establishment of religion, or prohibiting the free exercise thereof.' These words of the First Amendment reflected in the minds of early Americans a vivid mental picture of conditions and practices which they fervently wished to stamp out in order to preserve liberty for themselves and for their posterity. Doubtless their goal has not been entirely reached; but so far has the Nation moved toward it that the expression 'law respecting an establishment of religion,' probably does not so vividly remind present-day Americans of the evils, fears, and political problems that caused that expression to be written into our Bill of Rights. Whether this New Jersey law is one respecting the 'establishment of religion' requires an understanding of the meaning of that language, particularly with respect to the imposition of taxes. Once again, therefore, it is not inappropriate briefly to review the background and environment of the period in which that constitutional language was fashioned and adopted. . . .

The 'establishment of religion' clause of the First Amendment means at least this: Neither a state nor the Federal Government can set up a church. Neither can pass laws which aid one religion, aid all religions, or prefer one religion over another. Neither can force nor influence a person to go to or to remain away from church against his will or force him to profess a belief or disbelief in any religion. No person can be punished for entertaining or professing religious beliefs or disbeliefs, for church attendance or non-attendance. No tax in any amount, large or small, can be levied to support any religious activities or institutions, whatever they may be called, or whatever form they may adopt to teach or practice religion. Neither a state nor the Federal Government can, openly or secretly, participate in the affairs of any religious organizations or groups and vice versa. In the words of Jefferson, the clause against establishment of religion by law was intended to erect 'a wall of separation between Church and State.' Reynolds v. United States, supra, 98 U.S. at 164.

We must consider the New Jersey statute in accordance with the foregoing limitations imposed by the First Amendment. But we must not strike that state statute down if it is within the state's constitutional power even though it approaches the verge of that power. New Jersey cannot consistently with the 'establishment of religion' clause of the First Amendment contribute tax-raised funds to the support of an institution which teaches the tenets and faith of any church. On the other hand, other language of the amendment commands that New Jersey cannot hamper its citizens in the free exercise of their own religion. Consequently, it cannot exclude individual Catholics, Lutherans, Mohammedans, Baptists, Jews, Methodists, Non-believers, Presbyterians, or the members of any other faith, because of their faith, or lack of it, from receiving the benefits of public welfare legislation. While we do not mean to intimate that a state could not provide transportation only to children attending public schools, we must be careful, in protecting the citizens of New Jersey against state-established churches, to be sure that we do not inadvertently prohibit New Jersey from extending its general State law benefits to all its citizens without regard to their religious belief.

Measured by these standards, we cannot say that the First Amendment prohibits New Jersey from spending tax raised funds to pay the bus fares of parochial school pupils as a part of a general program under which it pays the fares of pupils attending public and other schools. It is undoubtedly true that children are helped to get to church schools. There is even a possibility that some of the children might not be sent to the church schools if the parents were compelled to pay their children's bus fares out of their own pockets when transportation to a public school would have been paid for by the State. The same possibility exists where the state requires a local transit company to provide reduced fares to school children including those attending parochial schools, or where a municipally owned transportation system undertakes to carry all school children free of charge. Moreover, state-paid policemen, detailed to protect children going to and from church schools from the very real hazards of traffic, would serve much the same purpose and accomplish much the same result as state provisions intended to guarantee free transportation of a kind which the state deems to be best for the school children's welfare. And parents might refuse to risk their children to the serious danger of traffic accidents going to and from parochial schools, the approaches to which were not protected by policemen. Similarly, parents might be reluctant to permit their children to attend schools which the state had cut off from such general government services as ordinary police and fire protection, connections for sewage disposal, public highways and sidewalks. Of course, cutting off church schools from these services, so separate and so indisputably marked off from the religious function, would make it far more difficult for the schools to operate. But such is obviously not the purpose of the First Amendment. That Amendment requires the state to be a neutral in its relations with groups of religious believers and non-believers; it does not require the state to be their adversary. State power is no more to be used so as to handicap religions, than it is to favor them.

This Court has said that parents may, in the discharge of their duty under state compulsory education laws, send their children to a religious rather than a public school if the school meets the secular educational requirements which the state has power to impose. *See* Pierce v. Society of Sisters, 268 U.S. 510 (1925). It appears that these parochial schools meet New Jersey's requirements. The State contributes no money to the schools. It does not support them. Its legislation, as applied, does no more than provide a general program to help parents get their children, regardless of their religion, safely and expeditiously to and from accredited schools.

The First Amendment has erected a wall between church and state. That wall must be kept high and impregnable. We could not approve the slightest breach. New Jersey has not breached it here.

Affirmed.

Mr. Justice JACKSON, dissenting.

. . . The Township of Ewing is not furnishing transportation to the children in any form; it is not operating school busses itself or contracting for their operation; and it is not performing any public service of any kind with this taxpayer's money. All school children are left to ride as ordinary paying passengers on the regular busses operated by the public transportation system. What the Township does, and what the taxpayer complains of, is at stated intervals to reimburse parents for the fares paid, provided the children attend either public schools or Catholic Church schools. This expenditure of tax funds has no possible effect on the child's safety or expedition in transit. As passengers on the public busses they travel as fast and no faster, and are as safe and no safer, since their parents are reimbursed as before. . . .

It is of no importance in this situation whether the beneficiary of this expenditure of tax-raised funds is primarily the parochial school and incidentally the pupil, or whether the aid is directly bestowed on the pupil with indirect benefits to the school. The state cannot maintain a Church and it can no more tax its citizens to furnish free carriage to those who attend a Church. The prohibition against establishment of religion cannot be circumvented by a subsidy, bonus or reimbursement of expense to individuals for receiving religious instruction and indoctrination. . . .

[The state] may socialize utilities and economic enterprises and make taxpayers' business out of what conventionally had been private business. It may make public business of individual welfare, health, education, entertainment or security. But it cannot make public business of religious worship or instruction, or of attendance at religious institutions of any character. There is no answer to the proposition more fully expounded by Mr. Justice RUTLEDGE that the effect of the religious freedom Amendment to our Constitution was to take every form of propagation of religion out of the realm of things which could directly or indirectly be made public business and thereby be supported in whole or in part at taxpayers' expense. That is a difference which the Constitution sets up between religion and almost every other subject matter of legislation, a difference which goes to the very root of religious freedom and which the Court is overlooking today. This freedom was first in the Bill of Rights because it was first in the forefathers' minds; it was set forth in absolute terms, and its strength is its rigidity. It was intended not only to keep the states' hands out of religion, but to keep religion's hands off the state, and above all, to keep bitter religious controversy out of public life by denying to every denomination any advantage from getting control of public policy or the public purse. Those great ends I cannot but think are immeasurably compromised by today's decision.

This policy of our Federal Constitution has never been wholly pleasing to most religious groups. They all are quick to invoke its protections; they all are irked when they feel its restraints. . . . But we cannot have it both ways. Religious teaching cannot be a private affair when the state seeks to impose regulations which infringe on it indirectly, and a public affair when it comes to taxing citizens of one faith to aid another, or those of no faith to aid all. If these principles seem harsh in prohibiting aid to Catholic education, it must not be forgotten that it is the same Constitution that alone assures Catholics the right to maintain these schools at all when predominant local sentiment would forbid them. Pierce v. Society of Sisters, 268 U.S. 510. Nor should I think that those who have done so well without this aid would want to see this separation between Church and State broken down. If the state may aid these religious schools, it may therefore regulate them. Many groups have sought aid from tax funds only to find that it carried political controls with it. Indeed this Court has declared that 'It is hardly lack of due process for the Government to regulate that which it subsidizes.' Wickard v. Filburn, 317 U.S. 111. . . .

Mr. Justice RUTLEDGE, with whom Mr. Justice FRANKFURTER, Mr. Justice JACKSON and Mr. Justice BURTON agree, dissenting.

'Congress shall make no law respecting an establishment of religion, or prohibiting the free exercise thereof. . . .' U.S.Const.Am. Art. I.

'Well aware that Almighty God hath created the mind free; . . . that to compel a man to furnish contributions of money for the propagation of opinions which he disbelieves, is sinful and tyrannical; . . .

'We, the General Assembly, do enact, That no man shall be compelled to frequent or support any religious worship, place, or ministry whatsoever, nor shall be enforced, restrained, molested, or burthened in his body or goods, nor shall otherwise suffer on account of his religious opinions or belief. . . .'

I cannot believe that the great author of those words, or the men who made them law, could have joined in this decision. Neither so high nor so impregnable today as yesterday is the wall raised between church and state by Virginia's great statute of religious freedom and the First Amendment, now made applicable to all the states by the Fourteenth. New Jersey's statute sustained is the first, if indeed it is not the second breach to be made by this Court's action. That a third, and a fourth, and still others will be attempted, we may be sure. . . .

Not simply an established church, but any law respecting an establishment of religion is forbidden. The Amendment was broadly but not loosely phrase . . . The Amendment's purpose was not to strike merely at the official establishment of a single sect, creed or religion, outlawing only a formal relation such as had prevailed in England and some of the colonies. Necessarily it was to uproot all such relationships. But the object was broader than separating church and state in this narrow sense. It was to create a complete and permanent separation of the spheres of religious activity and civil authority by comprehensively forbidding every form of public aid or support for religion. . . . The prohibition broadly forbids state support, financial or other, of religion in any guise, form or degree. It outlaws all use of public funds for religious purposes. . . .

As the Remonstrance discloses throughout, Madison opposed every form and degree of official relation between religion and civil authority. For him religion was a wholly private matter beyond the scope of civil power either to restrain or to support. Denial or abridgment of religious freedom was a violation of rights both of conscience and of natural equality. State aid was no less obnoxious or destructive to freedom and to religion itself than other forms of state interference. 'Establishment' and 'free exercise' were correlative and coextensive ideas, representing only different facets of the single great and fundamental freedom. The Remonstrance, following the Virginia statute's example, referred to the history of religious conflicts and the effects of all sorts of establishments, current and historical, to suppress religion's free exercise. With Jefferson, Madison believed that to tolerate any fragment of establishment would be by so much to perpetuate restraint upon that freedom. Hence he sought to tear out the institution not partially but root and branch, and to bar its return forever.

In no phase was he more unrelentingly absolute than in opposing state support or aid by taxation. Not even 'three pence' contribution was thus to be exacted from any citizen for such a purpose. Remonstrance, Par. 3. . . .

Here parents pay money to send their children to parochial schools and funds raised by taxation are used to reimburse them. This not only helps the children to get to school and the parents to send them. It aids them in a substantial way to get the very thing which they are sent to the particular school to secure, namely, religious training and teaching. . . . New Jersey's action therefore exactly fits the type of exaction and the kind of evil at which Madison and Jefferson struck. . . .

This is not therefore just a little case over bus fares. In paraphrase of Madison, distant as it may be in its present form from a complete establishment of religion, it differs from it only in degree; and is the first step in that direction. Id., Par. 9.[53]

No one conscious of religious values can by unsympathetic toward the burden which our constitutional separation puts on parents who desire religious instruction mixed with secular for their children. They pay taxes for others' children's education, at the same time the added cost of instruction for their own. Nor can one happily see benefits denied to children which others receive, because in conscience they or their parents for them desire a different kind of training others do not demand.

But if those feelings should prevail, there would be an end to our historic constitutional policy and command. No more unjust or discriminatory in fact is it to deny attendants at religious schools the cost of their transportation than it is to deny them tuitions, sustenance for their teachers, or any other educational expense which others receive at public cost. Hardship in fact there is which none can blink. But, for assuring to those who undergo it the greater, the most comprehensive freedom, it is one written by design and firm intent into our basic law.

Of course discrimination in the legal sense does not exist. The child attending the religious school has the same right as any other to attend the public school. But he foregoes exercising it because the same guaranty which assures this freedom forbids the public school or any agency of the state to give or aid him in securing the religious instruction he seeks.

Were he to accept the common school, he would be the first to protest the teaching there of any creed or faith not his own. And it is precisely for the reason that their atmosphere is wholly secular that children are not sent to public schools under the Pierce doctrine. But that is a constitutional necessity, because we have staked the very existence of our country on the faith that complete separation between the state and religion is best for the state and best for religion. Remonstrance, Par. 8, 12.

That policy necessarily entails hardship upon persons who forego the right to educational advantages the state can supply in order to secure others it is precluded from giving. Indeed this may hamper the parent and the child forced by conscience to that choice. But it does not make the state unneutral to withhold what the Constitution forbids it to give. . . .

Two great drives are constantly in motion to abridge, in the name of education, the complete division of religion and civil authority which our forefathers made. One is to introduce religious education and observances into the public schools. The other, to obtain public funds for the aid and support of various private religious schools. In my opinion both avenues were closed by the Constitution. Neither should be opened by this Court. . . .

The judgment should be reversed.

NOTES AND QUESTIONS

1. *Separation or neutrality.* The decision presents two approaches to government funding of religion. The first is strict separation, holding that no taxpayer money whatsoever be directed towards religion. Certainly much of the majority opinion's language supports this approach. Yet the holding itself suggests an alternate: If the government's goal is secular, and the money is made available on a neutral basis, why shouldn't religious organizations also participate? Which approach do you favor?
2. *Funding for police and fire protection.* If you believe in a strict separation between church and state, should this preclude funding for fire and police protection of religious schools? How do you distinguish this aid to religion from the aid in *Everson*?
3. *Funding for math and ethics education.* If you support a more neutral approach to government funding, would you also support government subsidies to math teachers in religious schools in order to improve state math achievement? What about government subsidies to religious schools as part of a state-wide effort to improve ethics?
4. *Direct vs. indirect funding.* In *Everson*, the government reimbursed the parents of schoolchildren in parochial schools rather than the parochial schools themselves. Do you think this makes any difference?
5. For 50 years after *Everson* the Court's religious financing cases were characterized by similarly sharp disputes within the Court about particular programs under which government money was given to religious enterprises. Subsequent decisions during the next 50 years following the Court's *Everson* decision did little to clarify the situation. *Compare* Zobrest v. Catalina Foothills Sch. Dist., 509 U.S. 1 (1993) (upholding the provision of a government-funded interpreter to a deaf student attending a Catholic high school); Mueller v. Allen, 463 U.S. 388 (1983) (upholding a state program providing tax deductions for private and public school students, most of which went to religious school students); Hunt v. McNair, 413 U.S. 734 (1973) (upholding the issuance of state revenue bonds to benefit Baptist colleges); Tilton v. Richardson, 403 U.S. 672 (1971) (upholding federal construction grants for religious colleges and universities); Roemer v. Board of Pub. Works, 426 U.S. 736 (1976) (upholding a general state subsidy to religious colleges and universities); *and* Board of Educ. v. Allen, 392 U.S. 236 (1968) (upholding a state program loaning secular textbooks to students at private religious schools), *with* School Dist. of the City of Grand Rapids v. Ball, 473 U.S. 373 (prohibiting a city from sending

public school teachers into private religious schools to teach remedial education classes); Wolman v. Walter, 433 U.S. 229 (1977) (striking down a state program providing instructional materials other than books to private religious schools); Meek v. Pittenger, 421 U.S. 349 (1975) (same); Committee for Pub. Educ. v. Nyquist, 413 U.S. 756 (1973) (striking down state maintenance, repair, and tuition reimbursement grants to private religious schools); *and* Lemon v. Kurtzman, 403 U.S. 602 (1971) (striking down state programs providing reimbursement to religious schools for teacher salaries, textbooks, and instructional aids).

B. TAX DEDUCTIONS FOR RELIGIOUS ORGANIZATIONS

Walz v. Tax Commission of the City of New York

397 U.S. 664 (1970)

Mr. Chief Justice BURGER delivered the opinion of the Court.

Appellant, owner of real estate in Richmond County, New York, sought an injunction in the New York courts to prevent the New York City Tax Commission from granting property tax exemptions to religious organizations for religious properties used solely for religious worship. The exemption from state taxes provides in relevant part:

> "Exemptions from taxation may be granted only by general laws. Exemptions may be altered or repealed except those exempting real or personal property used exclusively for religious, educational or charitable purposes as defined by law and owned by any corporation or association organized or conducted exclusively for one or more of such purposes and not operating for profit."

The essence of appellant's contention was that the New York City Tax Commission's grant of an exemption to church property indirectly requires the appellant to make a contribution to religious bodies and thereby violates provisions prohibiting establishment of religion under the First Amendment which under the Fourteenth Amendment is binding on the States.

The course of constitutional neutrality in this area cannot be an absolutely straight line; rigidity could well defeat the basic purpose of these provisions, which is to insure that no religion be sponsored or favored, none commanded, and none inhibited. The general principle deducible from the First Amendment and all that has been said by the Court is this: that we will not tolerate either governmentally established religion or governmental interference with religion. Short of those expressly proscribed governmental acts there is room for play in the joints productive of a benevolent neutrality which will permit religious exercise to exist without sponsorship and without interference.

The legislative purpose of a property tax exemption is neither the advancement nor the inhibition of religion; it is neither sponsorship nor hostility. New York, in common with the other States, has determined that certain entities that exist in a harmonious relationship to the community at large, and that foster its "moral or mental improvement," should not be inhibited in their activities by property taxation or the hazard of loss of those properties for nonpayment of taxes. It has not singled out one particular church or religious group or even churches as such; rather, it has granted exemption to all houses of religious worship within a broad class of property owned by nonprofit, quasi-public corporations which include hospitals, libraries, playgrounds, scientific, professional, historical, and patriotic groups. The State has an affirmative policy that considers these groups as beneficial and stabilizing influences in community life and finds this classification useful, desirable, and in the public interest. Qualification for tax exemption is not perpetual or immutable; some tax-exempt groups lose that status when their activities take them outside the classification and new entities can come into being and qualify for exemption.

We find it unnecessary to justify the tax exemption on the social welfare services or "good works" that some churches perform for parishioners and others—family counseling, aid to the elderly and the infirm, and to children. Churches vary substantially in the scope of such services; programs expand or contract according to resources and need. As public-sponsored programs enlarge, private aid from the church sector may diminish. The extent of social services may vary, depending on whether the church serves an urban or rural, a rich or poor constituency. To give emphasis to so variable an aspect of the work of religious bodies would introduce an element of governmental evaluation and standards as to the worth of particular social welfare programs, thus producing a kind of continuing day-to-day relationship which the policy of neutrality seeks to minimize. Hence, the use of a social welfare yardstick as a significant element to qualify for tax exemption could conceivably give rise to confrontations that could escalate to constitutional dimensions.

Granting tax exemptions to churches necessarily operates to afford an indirect economic benefit and also gives rise to some, but yet a lesser, involvement than taxing them. In analyzing either alternative the questions are whether the involvement is excessive, and whether it is a continuing one calling for official and continuing surveillance leading to an impermissible degree of entanglement. Obviously a direct money subsidy would be a relationship pregnant with involvement and, as with most governmental grant programs, could encompass sustained and detailed administrative relationships for enforcement of statutory or administrative standards, but that is not this case. The hazards of churches supporting government are hardly less in their potential than the hazards of government supporting churches; each relationship carries some involvement rather than the desired insulation and separation. We cannot ignore the instances in history when church support of government led to the kind of involvement we seek to avoid.

Mr. Justice BRENNAN, concurring.

Government has two basic secular purposes for granting real property tax exemptions to religious organizations. First, these organizations are exempted because they, among a range of other private, nonprofit organizations contribute to the well-being of the community in a variety of nonreligious ways, and thereby bear burdens that would otherwise either have to be met by general taxation, or be left undone, to the detriment of the community. Thus, New York exempts "[r]eal property owned by a corporation or association organized exclusively for the moral or mental improvement of men and women, or for religious, bible, tract, charitable, benevolent, missionary, hospital, infirmary, educational, public playground, scientific, literary, bar association, medical society, library, patriotic, historical or cemetery purposes, for the enforcement of laws relating to children or animals, or for two or more such purposes. . . ."

Appellant seeks to avoid the force of this secular purpose of the exemptions by limiting his challenge to "exemptions from real property taxation to religious organizations on real property used exclusively for religious purposes." Appellant assumes, apparently, that church-owned property is used for exclusively religious purposes if it does not house a hospital, orphanage, weekday school, or the like. Any assumption that a church building itself is used for exclusively religious activities, however, rests on a simplistic view of ordinary church operations. As the appellee's brief cogently observes, "the public welfare activities and the sectarian activities of religious institutions are . . . intertwined. . . . Often a particular church will use the same personnel, facilities and source of funds to carry out both its secular and religious activities." Thus, the same people who gather in church facilities for religious worship and study may return to these facilities to participate in Boy Scout activities, to promote antipoverty causes, to discuss public issues, or to listen to chamber music. Accordingly, the funds used to maintain the facilities as a place for religious worship and study also maintain them as a place for secular activities beneficial to the community as a whole. Even during formal worship services, churches frequently collect the funds used to finance their secular operations and make decisions regarding their nature.

Second, government grants exemptions to religious organizations because they uniquely contribute to the pluralism of American society by their religious activities. Government may properly include religious institutions among the variety of private, nonprofit groups that receive tax exemptions, for each group contributes to the diversity of association, viewpoint, and enterprise essential to a vigorous, pluralistic society. To this end, New York extends its exemptions not only to religious and social service organizations but also to scientific, literary, bar, library, patriotic, and historical groups, and generally to institutions "organized exclusively for the moral or mental improvement of men and women." The very breadth of this scheme of exemptions negates any suggestion that the State intends to single out religious organizations for special preference. The scheme is not designed to inject any religious activity into a nonreligious context, as was the case with school prayers. No particular activity of a religious organization — for example, the propagation of its beliefs — is specially promoted by the exemptions. They merely facilitate the existence of a broad range of private, non-profit organizations, among them religious groups, by leaving each free to come into existence, then to flourish or wither, without being burdened by real property taxes.

Although governmental purposes for granting religious exemptions may be wholly secular, exemptions can nonetheless violate the Establishment Clause if they result in extensive state involvement with religion. Accordingly, those who urge the exemptions' unconstitutionality argue that exemptions are the equivalent of governmental subsidy of churches. General subsidies of religious activities would, of course, constitute impermissible state involvement with religion. Tax exemptions and general subsidies, however, are qualitatively different. Though both provide economic assistance, they do so in fundamentally different ways. A subsidy involves the direct transfer of public monies to the subsidized enterprise and uses resources exacted from taxpayers as a whole. An exemption, on the other hand, involves no such transfer. It assists the exempted enterprise only passively, by relieving a privately funded venture of the burden of paying taxes. In other words, "(i)n the case of direct subsidy, the state forcibly diverts the income of both believers and nonbelievers to churches," while "(i)n the case of an exemption, the state merely refrains from diverting to its own uses income independently generated by the churches through voluntary contributions." Giannella, *Religious Liberty, Nonestablishment, and Doctrinal Development, pt. II,* 81 Harv. L. Rev. 513, 553 (1968). Thus, "the symbolism of tax exemption is significant as a manifestation that organized religion is not expected to support the state; by the same token the state is not expected to support the church." Freund, *Public Aid to Parochial Schools,* 82 Harv. L. Rev. 1680, 1687 n. 16 (1969). Tax exemptions, accordingly, constitute mere passive state involvement with religion and not the affirmative involvement characteristic of outright governmental subsidy.

Mr. Justice DOUGLAS, dissenting.

There is a line between what a State may do in encouraging "religious" activities, and what a State may not do by using its resources to promote "religious" activities, or bestowing benefits because of them. Yet that line may not always be clear. Closing public schools on Sunday is in the former category; subsidizing churches, in my view, is in the latter. Indeed I would suppose that in common understanding one of the best ways to "establish" one or more religions is to subsidize them, which a tax exemption does.

State aid to places of worship, whether in the form of direct grants or tax exemption, takes us back to the Assessment Bill and the Remonstrance. The church *qua* church would not be entitled to that support from believers and from nonbelievers alike. Yet the church *qua* nonprofit, charitable institution is one of many that receive a form of subsidy through tax exemption.

Churches perform some functions that a State would constitutionally be empowered to perform. I refer to nonsectarian social welfare operations such as the care of orphaned children and the destitute and people who are sick. A tax exemption to agencies performing those functions would therefore be as constitutionally proper as the grant of direct subsidies to them. Under the First Amendment a State may not, however, provide worship if private groups fail to do so.

That is a major difference between churches on the one hand and the rest of the nonprofit organizations on the other. Government could provide or finance operas, hospitals, historical societies, and all the rest because they represent social welfare programs within the reach of the police power. In contrast, government may not provide or finance worship because of the Establishment Clause any more than it may single out "atheistic" or "agnostic" centers or groups and create or finance them. . . .

Texas Monthly, Inc. v. Bullock

489 U.S. 1 (1989)

[*See supra* p. 891.]

NOTES AND QUESTIONS

1. *General or targeted tax benefits?* There is a key difference between *Walz*'s and *Texas Monthly*'s approaches to tax deductions for religious organizations. In *Walz*, tax deductions to religious organizations were incorporated into programs granting deductions to a broad range of secular and religious organizations. *Texas Monthly*, in contrast, involved a tax deduction program that explicitly provided benefits to religious organizations alone.
2. *State support for associations.* Justice Brennan's concurrence in *Walz* noted two secular reasons to support nonprofit organizations like churches. First, they "contribute to the well-being of the community in a variety of nonreligious ways, and thereby bear burdens that would otherwise either have to be met by general taxation, or be left undone, to the detriment of the community." Second, they "contribute to the pluralism of American society." What if, however, the former were not true. Is the latter sufficient justification for government financial aid?
3. *Tax deductions.* Are tax deductions better characterized as direct financial aid or indirect financial aid? Justice Brennan's *Walz* concurrence suggests the latter: "A subsidy involves the direct transfer of public monies to the subsidized enterprise and uses resources exacted from taxpayers as a whole. An exemption, on the other hand, involves no such transfer." Do you agree? Does it make a difference? The Court has not always been consistent in how it characterizes tax deductions.

C. DIRECT AID

In his Memorial and Remonstrance, James Madison declared that not even three pence of taxpayer money should go directly to houses of worship. In recent years, it has become more commonplace to allocate public funds to religious groups that provide various social services to members of the public, provided the money is used for purely secular purposes. The George W. Bush Administration implemented through a series of executive orders an aggressive plan to encourage religious organizations to participate in federally funded social service programs. This is how the Supreme Court described the Administration's "Faith-Based Initiatives":

> In 2001, the President issued an executive order creating the White House Office of Faith-Based and Community Initiatives within the Executive

> Office of the President. Exec. Order No. 13199, 3 CFR 752 (2001 Comp.). The purpose of this new office was to ensure that "private and charitable community groups, including religious ones . . . have the fullest opportunity permitted by law to compete on a level playing field, so long as they achieve valid public purposes" and adhere to "the bedrock principles of pluralism, nondiscrimination, evenhandedness, and neutrality." Ibid. The office was specifically charged with the task of eliminating unnecessary bureaucratic, legislative, and regulatory barriers that could impede such organizations' effectiveness and ability to compete equally for federal assistance. Id., at 752-753.

By separate executive orders, President Bush also created Executive Department Centers for Faith-Based and Community Initiatives within several federal agencies and departments. These centers were given the job of ensuring that faith-based community groups would be eligible to compete for federal financial support without impairing their independence or autonomy, as long as they did "not use direct Federal financial assistance to support any inherently religious activities, such as worship, religious instruction, or proselytization." Exec. Order No. 13279, 3 CFR §2(f), p. 260 (2002 Comp.). Although renamed the Office of Faith-Based and Neighborhood Partnerships, President Obama did not significantly alter the program. Faith-based organizations could still compete on equal footing for federal social service grants without having to change their religious identity or cease offering (privately funded) religious activities to social service beneficiaries. President Obama even left intact the ability of faith-based organizations that receive federal grants to discriminate on the basis of religion in hiring. His regulations did require that social service beneficiaries get a written notice of their rights, which include the right not to be discriminated against on account of their religious beliefs, the right not to participate in any religious activities, and the right to request an alternate nonreligious provider.

The Trump Administration's White House Faith and Opportunity Initiative jettisoned many of these safeguards on grants to faith-based organizations. For example, it eliminated the obligation of faith-based providers who receive federal funds to inform potential clients of secular alternatives. It is still too early to know in what direction the Biden Administration will take faith-based funding, although it has re-established a White House Office of Faith-Based and Neighborhood Partnerships.

Meanwhile, the Supreme Court has become increasingly receptive to funding religious organizations. That was not always the case. At one time, the Court barred direct cash grants to pervasively sectarian organizations—like houses or worship and religious schools—based on the belief that because the religious and the secular were so intertwined at pervasively secular institutions, the government's money would inevitably be used for religious purposes in violation of the Establishment Clause. In contrast, today the Supreme Court has held that not only is there no Establishment Clause problem with awarding government grants to religious entities on an equal basis with secular ones, but that it violates the Free Exercise Clause if religious entities are excluded solely due to their religious status. *See* Chapter 15.

Bowen, Secretary of Health & Human Services v. Kendrick

487 U.S. 589 (1988)

Chief Justice REHNQUIST delivered the opinion of the Court.

I.

The Adolescent Family Life Act (AFLA or Act) was passed by Congress in 1981 in response to the "severe adverse health, social, and economic consequences" that often follow pregnancy and childbirth among unmarried adolescents.

In pertinent part, grant recipients are to provide two types of services: "care services," for the provision of care to pregnant adolescents and adolescent parents, § 300z-1(a)(7), and "prevention services," for the prevention of adolescent sexual relations, § 300z-1(a)(8).

In drawing up the AFLA and determining what services to provide under the Act, Congress was well aware that "the problems of adolescent premarital sexual relations, pregnancy, and parenthood are multiple and complex." Indeed, Congress expressly recognized that legislative or governmental action alone would be insufficient:

> "[S]uch problems are best approached through a variety of integrated and essential services provided to adolescents and their families by other family members, religious and charitable organizations, voluntary associations, and other groups in the private sector as well as services provided by publicly sponsored initiatives." § 300z(a)(8)(B).

Accordingly, the AFLA expressly states that federally provided services in this area should promote the involvement of parents, and should "emphasize the provision of support by other family members, religious and charitable organizations, voluntary associations, and other groups."

In addition, AFLA requires grant applicants, among other things, to describe how they will, "as appropriate in the provision of services[,] involve families of adolescents[, and] involve religious and charitable organizations, voluntary associations, and other groups in the private sector as well as services provided by publicly sponsored initiatives." This broad-based involvement of groups outside of the government was intended by Congress to "establish better coordination, integration, and linkages" among existing programs in the community to aid in the development of "strong family values and close family ties," and to "help adolescents and their families deal with complex issues of adolescent premarital sexual relations and the consequences of such relations."

Since 1981, when the AFLA was adopted, the Secretary has received 1,088 grant applications and awarded 141 grants. It is undisputed that a number of grantees or subgrantees were organizations with institutional ties to religious denominations.

II.

The District Court in this lawsuit held the AFLA unconstitutional both on its face and as applied. Few of our cases in the Establishment Clause area have explicitly distinguished between facial challenges to a statute and attacks on the statute as applied. Several cases have clearly involved challenges to a statute "on its face." For example, in *Edwards v. Aguillard* we considered the validity of the Louisiana "Creationism Act," finding the Act "facially invalid." Indeed, in that case it was clear that only a facial challenge could have been considered, as the Act had not been implemented. Other cases, as well, have considered the validity of statutes without the benefit of a record as to how the statute had actually been applied.

There is, then, precedent in this area of constitutional law for distinguishing between the validity of the statute on its face and its validity in particular applications. This said, we turn to consider whether the District Court was correct in concluding that the AFLA was unconstitutional on its face.

As we see it, it is clear from the face of the statute that the AFLA was motivated primarily, if not entirely, by a legitimate secular purpose—the elimination or reduction of social and economic problems caused by teenage sexuality, pregnancy, and parenthood. Appellees cannot, and do not, dispute that, on the whole, religious concerns were not the sole motivation behind the Act, nor can it be said that the AFLA lacks a legitimate secular purpose.

As usual in Establishment Clause cases, the more difficult question is whether the primary effect of the challenged statute is impermissible.

Given [the] statutory framework, there are two ways in which the statute, considered "on its face," might be said to have the impermissible primary effect of advancing religion. First, it can be argued that the AFLA advances religion by expressly recognizing that "religious organizations have a role to play" in addressing the problems associated with teenage sexuality. In this view, even if no religious institution receives aid or funding pursuant to the AFLA, the statute is invalid under the Establishment Clause because, among other things, it expressly enlists the involvement of religiously affiliated organizations in the federally subsidized programs, it endorses religious solutions to the problems addressed by the Act, or it creates symbolic ties between church and state. Secondly, it can be argued that the AFLA is invalid on its face because it allows religiously affiliated organizations to participate as grantees or subgrantees in AFLA programs. From this standpoint, the Act is invalid because it authorizes direct federal funding of religious organizations which, given the AFLA's educational function and the fact that the AFLA's "viewpoint" may coincide with the grantee's "viewpoint" on sexual matters, will result unavoidably in the impermissible "inculcation" of religious beliefs in the context of a federally funded program.

We consider the former objection first. Putting aside for the moment the possible role of religious organizations as grantees, these provisions of the statute reflect at most Congress' considered judgment that religious organizations can help solve the problems to which the AFLA is addressed. Nothing in our previous cases prevents Congress from making such a judgment or from recognizing the important part that religion or religious organizations may play in resolving certain secular problems. Particularly when, as Congress found, "prevention of adolescent sexual activity and adolescent pregnancy depends primarily upon developing strong family values and close family ties," it seems quite sensible for Congress to recognize that religious organizations can influence values and can have some influence on family life, including parents' relations with their adolescent children. To the extent that this congressional recognition has any effect of advancing religion, the effect is at most "incidental and remote." In addition, although the AFLA does require potential grantees to describe how they will involve religious organizations in the provision of services under the Act, it also requires grantees to describe the involvement of "charitable organizations, voluntary associations, and other groups in the private sector." In our view, this reflects the statute's successful maintenance of "a course of neutrality among religions, and between religion and non-religion."

This brings us to the second ground for objecting to the AFLA: the fact that it allows religious institutions to participate as recipients of federal funds. The AFLA defines an "eligible grant recipient" as a "public or nonprofit private organization or agency" which demonstrates the capability of providing the requisite services. As this provision would indicate, a fairly wide spectrum of organizations is eligible to apply for and receive funding under the Act, and nothing on the face of the Act suggests it is anything but neutral with respect to the grantee's status as a sectarian or purely secular institution. In this regard, then, the AFLA is similar to other statutes that this Court has upheld against Establishment Clause challenges in the past.

Of course, even when the challenged statute appears to be neutral on its face, we have always been careful to ensure that direct government aid to religiously affiliated institutions does not have the primary effect of advancing religion. One way in which direct government aid might have that effect is if the aid flows to institutions that are "pervasively sectarian." We stated in *Hunt* that

> "[a]id normally may be thought to have a primary effect of advancing religion when it flows to an institution in which religion is so pervasive that a substantial portion of its functions are subsumed in the religious mission. . . ."

The reason for this is that there is a risk that direct government funding, even if it is designated for specific secular purposes, may nonetheless advance the pervasively sectarian institution's "religious mission." Accordingly, a relevant factor in deciding whether a particular statute on its face can be said to have the improper effect of advancing religion is the determination of whether, and to what extent, the statute directs government aid to pervasively sectarian institutions.

In this lawsuit, nothing on the face of the AFLA indicates that a significant proportion of the federal funds will be disbursed to "pervasively sectarian" institutions. Indeed, the contention that there is a substantial risk of such institutions receiving direct aid is undercut by the AFLA's facially neutral grant requirements, the wide spectrum of public and private organizations which are capable of meeting the AFLA's requirements, and the fact that, of the eligible religious institutions, many will not deserve the label of "pervasively sectarian."

[We] disagree with the District Court's conclusion that the AFLA is invalid because it authorizes "teaching" by religious grant recipients on "matters [that] are fundamental elements of religious doctrine," such as the harm of premarital sex and the reasons for choosing adoption over abortion. On an issue as sensitive and important as teenage sexuality, it is not surprising that the Government's secular concerns would either coincide or conflict with those of religious institutions. But the possibility or even the likelihood that some of the religious institutions who receive AFLA funding will agree with the message that Congress intended to deliver to adolescents through the AFLA is insufficient to warrant a finding that the statute on its face has the primary effect of advancing religion. Nor does the alignment of the statute and the religious views of the grantees run afoul of our proscription against "fund[ing] a specifically religious activity in an otherwise substantially secular setting." *Hunt*, 413 U.S., at 743.

As yet another reason for invalidating parts of the AFLA, the District Court found that the involvement of religious organizations in the Act has the impermissible effect of creating a "crucial symbolic link" between government and religion. If we were to adopt the District Court's reasoning, it could be argued that any time a government aid program provides funding to religious organizations in an area in which the organization also has an interest, an impermissible "symbolic link" could be created, no matter whether the aid was to be used solely for secular purposes. This would jeopardize government aid to religiously affiliated hospitals, for example, on the ground that patients would perceive a "symbolic link" between the hospital—part of whose "religious mission" might be to save lives—and whatever government entity is subsidizing the purely secular medical services provided to the patient. We decline to adopt the District Court's reasoning and conclude that, in this litigation, whatever "symbolic link" might in fact be created by the AFLA's disbursement of funds to religious institutions is not sufficient to justify striking down the statute on its face.

This, of course, brings us to the third prong of the *Lemon* Establishment Clause "test"—the question whether the AFLA leads to "'an excessive government entanglement with religion.'" There is no doubt that the monitoring of AFLA grants is necessary if the Secretary is to ensure that public money is to be spent in the way that Congress intended and in a way that comports with the Establishment Clause. Accordingly, this litigation presents us with yet another "Catch-22" argument: the very supervision of the aid to assure that it does not further religion renders the statute invalid.

[Here there is] no reason to fear that . . . monitoring involved here will cause the Government to intrude unduly in the day-to-day operation of the religiously affiliated AFLA grantees. Unquestionably, the Secretary will review the programs set up and run by the AFLA grantees, and undoubtedly this will involve a review of, for example, the educational materials that a grantee proposes to use. The Secretary may also wish to have Government employees visit the clinics or offices where AFLA programs are being carried out to see whether they are in fact being administered in accordance with statutory and constitutional requirements. But in our view, this type of grant monitoring does not amount to "excessive entanglement," at least in the context of a statute authorizing grants to religiously affiliated organizations that are not necessarily "pervasively sectarian."

For the foregoing reasons we conclude that the AFLA does not violate the Establishment Clause "on its face."

III.

We turn now to consider whether the District Court correctly ruled that the AFLA was unconstitutional as applied. [A]lthough there is no dispute that the record contains evidence of specific incidents of impermissible behavior by AFLA grantees, we feel that this lawsuit should be remanded to the District Court for consideration of the evidence presented by appellees insofar as it sheds light on the manner in which the statute is presently being administered.

Justice BLACKMUN, with whom Justice BRENNAN, Justice MARSHALL, and Justice STEVENS join, dissenting.

In 1981, Congress enacted the Adolescent Family Life Act (AFLA), thereby "involv[ing] families[,] . . . religious and charitable organizations, voluntary associations, and other groups," in a broad-scale effort to alleviate some of the problems associated with teenage pregnancy. It is unclear whether Congress ever envisioned that public funds would pay for a program during a session of which parents and teenagers would be instructed:

> "You want to know the church teachings on sexuality. . . . You are the church. You people sitting here are the body of Christ. The teachings of you and the things you value are, in fact, the values of the Catholic Church."

Or of curricula that taught:

> "The Church has always taught that the marriage act, or intercourse, seals the union of husband and wife, (and is a representation of their union on all levels.) [sic] Christ commits Himself to us when we come to ask for the sacrament of marriage. We ask Him to be active in our life. God is love. We ask Him to share His love in ours, and God procreates with us, He enters into our physical union with Him, and we begin new life."

Or the teaching of a method of family planning described on the grant application as "not only a method of birth regulation but also a philosophy of procreation," and promoted as helping "spouses who are striving . . . to transform their married life into testimony[,] . . . to cultivate their matrimonial spirituality[, and] to make themselves better instruments in God's plan," and as "facilitat[ing] the evangelization of homes."

Whatever Congress had in mind, however, it enacted a statute that facilitated and, indeed, encouraged the use of public funds for such instruction, by giving religious groups a central pedagogical and counseling role without imposing any restraints on the sectarian quality of the participation. As the record developed thus far in this litigation makes all too clear, federal tax dollars appropriated for AFLA purposes have been used, with Government approval, to support religious teaching. Today the majority upholds the facial validity of this statute and remands the action to the District Court for further proceedings concerning appellees' challenge to the manner in which the statute has been applied. Because I am firmly convinced that our cases require invalidating this statutory scheme, I dissent. . . .

Notwithstanding the fact that Government funds are paying for religious organizations to teach and counsel impressionable adolescents on a highly sensitive subject of considerable religious significance, often on the premises of a church or parochial school and without any effort to remove religious symbols from the sites, 657 F. Supp., at 1565-1566, the majority concludes that the AFLA is not facially invalid. The majority acknowledges the constitutional proscription on government-sponsored religious indoctrination but, on the basis of little more than an indefensible assumption that AFLA recipients are not pervasively sectarian and consequently are presumed likely to comply with statutory and constitutional mandates, dismisses as insubstantial the risk that indoctrination will enter counseling. Similarly, the majority rejects the District Court's conclusion that the subject matter renders the risk of indoctrination unacceptable, and does so, it says, because "the likelihood that some of the religious institutions who receive AFLA funding will agree with the message that Congress intended to deliver to adolescents through the AFLA" does not amount to the advancement of religion. I do not think the statute can be so easily and conveniently saved.

The District Court concluded that asking religious organizations to teach and counsel youngsters on matters of deep religious significance, yet expect them to refrain from making reference to religion is both foolhardy and unconstitutional. The majority's rejection of this view is illustrative of its doctrinal misstep in relying so heavily on the college-funding cases. The District Court reasoned:

> "To presume that AFLA counselors from religious organizations can put their beliefs aside when counseling an adolescent on matters that are part of religious doctrine is simply unrealistic . . . Moreover, the statutory scheme is fraught with the possibility that religious beliefs might infuse instruction and never be detected by the impressionable and unlearned adolescent to whom the instruction is directed" (emphasis in original). 657 F. Supp., at 1563.

The majority rejects the District Court's assumptions as unwarranted outside the context of a pervasively sectarian institution. In doing so, the majority places inordinate weight on the nature of the institution receiving the funds, and ignores altogether the targets of the funded message and the nature of its content. . . .

The AFLA, unlike any statute this Court has upheld, pays for teachers and counselors, employed by and subject to the direction of religious authorities, to educate impressionable young minds on issues of religious moment. Time and again we have recognized the difficulties inherent in asking even the best-intentioned individuals in such positions to make "a total separation between secular teaching and religious doctrine." Lemon v. Kurtzman, 403 U.S., at 619. . . . Where the targeted audience is composed of children, of course, the Court's insistence on adequate safeguards has always been greatest. . . .

Whereas there may be secular values promoted by the AFLA, including the encouragement of adoption and premarital chastity and the discouragement of abortion, it can hardly be doubted that when promoted in theological terms by religious figures, those values take on a religious nature. Not surprisingly, the record is replete with observations to that effect. It should be undeniable by now that religious dogma may not be employed by government even to accomplish laudable secular purposes such as "the promotion of moral values, the contradiction to the materialistic trends of our times, the perpetuation of our institutions and the teaching of literature." Abington School District v. Schempp, 374 U.S. 203, 223 (1963) (holding unconstitutional daily reading of Bible verses and recitation of the Lord's Prayer in public schools); Stone v. Graham, 449 U.S. 39 (1980) (holding unconstitutional posting of Ten Commandments despite notation explaining secular application thereof).[10] It is true, of course, that the Court has recognized that

---

10. Religion plays an important role to many in our society. By enlisting its aid in combating certain social ills, while imposing the restrictions required by the First Amendment on the use of public funds to promote religion, we risk secularizing and demeaning the sacred enterprise. Whereas there is undoubtedly a role for churches of all denominations in helping prevent the problems often associated with early sexual activity and unplanned pregnancies, any attempt to confine that role within the strictures of a government-sponsored secular program can only taint the religious mission with a "corrosive secularism." Grand Rapids School District v. Ball, 473 U.S. 373, 385 (1985). The First Amendment protects not only the State from being captured by the Church, but also protects the Church from being corrupted by the State and adopted for its purposes.

the Constitution does not prohibit the government from supporting secular social-welfare services solely because they are provided by a religiously affiliated organization. But such recognition has been closely tied to the nature of the subsidized social service: "the State may send a cleric, indeed even a clerical order, to perform a *wholly secular task.*" There is a very real and important difference between running a soup kitchen or a hospital, and counseling pregnant teenagers on how to make the difficult decisions facing them. The risk of advancing religion at public expense, and of creating an appearance that the government is endorsing the medium and the message, is much greater when the religious organization is directly engaged in pedagogy, with the express intent of shaping belief and changing behavior, than where it is neutrally dispensing medication, food, or shelter. . . .

For some religious organizations, the answer to a teenager's question "Why shouldn't I have an abortion?" or "Why shouldn't I use barrier contraceptives?" will undoubtedly be different from an answer based solely on secular considerations. Public funds may not be used to endorse the religious message.

NOTES AND QUESTIONS

1. *Symbolic link.* The majority argues that government financial aid in the form of direct social service grants to religiously affiliated organizations does not automatically create an unconstitutional symbolic link between church and state. Is this always the case? What features makes this true for AFLA?
2. *Pervasively sectarian.* The majority also held that direct financial aid to a pervasively sectarian organization would violate the Establishment Clause. What characterizes a pervasively sectarian organization? According to *Bowen,* why would directly funding a pervasively sectarian organization inevitably advance religion? Does the rule still hold after *Mitchell v. Helms?*
3. *Alignment of government and religious values.* According to the majority, the fact that the government's message on premarital sex coincides with religious beliefs does not necessarily mean it advances religion. After all, there may be secular reasons for the message as well. For example, avoiding teen pregnancies is a secular reason to advocate for teen abstinence. What is the secular value underlying the government's opposition to abortion?
4. *Teaching abstinence vs. providing food.* The dissent argues that "There is a very real and important difference between running a soup kitchen or a hospital" and counseling teenagers on sexual abstinence. In particular, the majority and dissent disagree about the ability of people of faith to teach "highly sensitive subject[s] of considerable religious significance" without interjecting their religious beliefs into the lessons. Who do you think is more likely to be correct about the risk of religious indoctrination?
5. *Faith-based initiatives and the problem of religiously motivated discrimination.* If government funds faith-based providers that supply social services to the public, may such entities discriminate with respect to hiring and employment? What if the discrimination is not just favoring co-religionists? For example, could a religiously affiliated foster home for abused and neglected children that receives placements from the state's Department of Social Services refuse to employ openly gay or lesbian persons? Or

could it refuse to place children with gay or lesbian foster parents? If the state itself could not directly adopt and enforce such policies for a state-run foster home, can it achieve the same results through the expedient of contracting out these services to faith-based service providers?

6. *The risk of undue dependence on government funds.* How might government money affect how a religiously affiliated entity undertakes its mission more generally? Independent of the constitutional permissibility of using faith-based providers of social services, is such a close relationship between church and state good for religious organizations? If a religious organization relies heavily on government funds to maintain and support its social outreach programs, how likely will it be to stick to its theological and doctrinal guns when the state conditions its largesse on a practice or policy offensive to the tenets of the faith?

Mitchell v. Helms

530 U.S. 793 (2000)

Justice THOMAS announced the judgment of the Court and delivered an opinion, in which THE CHIEF JUSTICE, Justice SCALIA, and Justice KENNEDY join.

As part of a longstanding school-aid program known as Chapter 2, the Federal Government distributes funds to state and local governmental agencies, which in turn lend educational materials and equipment to public and private schools, with the enrollment of each participating school determining the amount of aid that it receives. The question is whether Chapter 2, as applied in Jefferson Parish, Louisiana, is a law respecting an establishment of religion, because many of the private schools receiving Chapter 2 aid in that parish are religiously affiliated. We hold that Chapter 2 is not such a law.

I

Several restrictions apply to aid to private schools. Most significantly, the "services, materials, and equipment" provided to private schools must be "secular, neutral, and nonideological." In addition, private schools may not acquire control of Chapter 2 funds or title to Chapter 2 materials, equipment, or property. A private school receives the materials and equipment listed in [the federal statute] by submitting to the LEA [Local Educational Authorities] an application detailing which items the school seeks and how it will use them; the LEA, if it approves the application, purchases those items from the school's allocation of funds, and then lends them to that school.

In Jefferson Parish (the Louisiana governmental unit at issue in this case), as in Louisiana as a whole, private schools have primarily used their allocations for nonrecurring expenses, usually materials and equipment. In the 1986-1987 fiscal year, for example, 44% of the money budgeted for private schools in Jefferson Parish was spent by LEA's for acquiring library and media materials, and 48% for instructional equipment. Among the materials and equipment provided have been library books, computers, and computer software, and also slide and movie projectors, overhead projectors, television sets, tape recorders, VCR's, projection screens, laboratory equipment, maps, globes, filmstrips, slides, and cassette recordings.

It appears that, in an average year, about 30% of Chapter 2 funds spent in Jefferson Parish are allocated for private schools. For the 1985-1986 fiscal year, 41 private schools participated in Chapter 2. For the following year, 46 participated, and the participation level has remained relatively constant since then. Of these 46, 34 were Roman Catholic; 7 were otherwise religiously affiliated; and 5 were not religiously affiliated.

II

A

[T]he question whether governmental aid to religious schools results in governmental indoctrination is ultimately a question whether any religious indoctrination that occurs in those schools could reasonably be attributed to governmental action. We have also indicated that the answer to the question of indoctrination will resolve the question whether a program of educational aid "subsidizes" religion, as our religion cases use that term.

In distinguishing between indoctrination that is attributable to the State and indoctrination that is not, we have consistently turned to the principle of neutrality, upholding aid that is offered to a broad range of groups or persons without regard to their religion. If the religious, irreligious, and areligious are all alike eligible for governmental aid, no one would conclude that any indoctrination that any particular recipient conducts has been done at the behest of the government. For attribution of indoctrination is a relative question. If the government is offering assistance to recipients who provide, so to speak, a broad range of indoctrination, the government itself is not thought responsible for any particular indoctrination. To put the point differently, if the government, seeking to further some legitimate secular purpose, offers aid on the same terms, without regard to religion, to all who adequately further that purpose, then it is fair to say that any aid going to a religious recipient only has the effect of furthering that secular purpose. The government, in crafting such an aid program, has had to conclude that a given level of aid is necessary to further that purpose among secular recipients and has provided no more than that same level to religious recipients. . . .

B

Respondents . . . offer two rules that they contend should govern our determination of whether Chapter 2 has the effect of advancing religion. They argue first, and chiefly, that "direct, nonincidental" aid to the primary educational mission of religious schools is always impermissible. Second, they argue that provision to religious schools of aid that is divertible to religious use is similarly impermissible. Respondents' arguments are inconsistent with our more recent case law . . . and we therefore reject them.

Although some of our earlier cases, particularly [*Grand Rapids v.*] *Ball*, did emphasize the distinction between direct and indirect aid, the purpose of this distinction was merely to prevent "subsidization" of religion. Of course, we have seen "special Establishment Clause dangers" when *money* is given to religious schools or entities directly rather than . . . indirectly. But direct payments of money are not at issue in this case, and we refuse to allow a "special" case to create a rule for all cases.

Respondents also contend that the Establishment Clause requires that aid to religious schools not be impermissibly religious in nature or be divertible to religious use. We agree with the first part of this argument but not the second. Respondents' "no divertibility" rule is inconsistent with our more recent case law and is unworkable. So long as the governmental aid is not itself "unsuitable for use in the public schools because of religious content," and eligibility for aid is determined in a constitutionally permissible manner, any use of that aid to indoctrinate cannot be attributed to the government and is thus not of constitutional concern.

The issue is not divertibility of aid but rather whether the aid itself has an impermissible content. Where the aid would be suitable for use in a public school, it is also suitable for use in any private school. Similarly, the prohibition against the government providing impermissible content resolves the Establishment Clause concerns that exist if aid is actually diverted to religious uses. . . . [J]ust as a government [sign-language] interpreter [as in *Zobrest*] does not herself inculcate a religious message—even when she is conveying one—so also a government computer or overhead projector does not itself inculcate a religious message, even when it is conveying one.

A concern for divertibility, as opposed to improper content, is misplaced not only because it fails to explain why the sort of aid that we have allowed is permissible, but also because it is boundless—enveloping all aid, no matter how trivial—and thus has only the most attenuated (if any) link to any realistic concern for preventing an "establishment of religion." Presumably, for example, government-provided lecterns, chalk, crayons, pens, paper, and paintbrushes would have to be excluded from religious schools under respondents' proposed rule. But we fail to see how indoctrination by means of (*i.e.*, diversion of) such aid could be attributed to the government. In fact, the risk of improper attribution is *less* when the aid lacks content, for there is no risk (as there is with books), of the government inadvertently providing improper content.

C

The dissent serves up a smorgasbord of 11 factors that, depending on the facts of each case "in all its particularity," could be relevant to the constitutionality of a school-aid program. One of the dissent's factors deserves special mention: whether a school that receives aid (or whose students receive aid) is pervasively sectarian. The dissent is correct that there was a period when this factor mattered, particularly if the pervasively sectarian school was a primary or secondary school. But that period is one that the Court should regret, and it is thankfully long past.

There are numerous reasons to formally dispense with this factor. First, its relevance in our precedents is in sharp decline. Although our case law has consistently mentioned it even in recent years, we have not struck down an aid program in reliance on this factor since 1985. . . .

Finally, hostility to aid to pervasively sectarian schools has a shameful pedigree that we do not hesitate to disavow. . . . Opposition to aid to "sectarian" schools acquired prominence in the 1870's with Congress' consideration (and near passage) of the Blaine Amendment, which would have amended the Constitution to bar any aid to sectarian institutions. Consideration of the amendment arose at a time of pervasive hostility to the Catholic Church and to Catholics in general, and it was an open secret that "sectarian" was code for "Catholic." . . .

In short, nothing in the Establishment Clause requires the exclusion of pervasively sectarian schools from otherwise permissible aid programs, and other doctrines of this Court bar it. This doctrine, born of bigotry, should be buried now.

Justice O'CONNOR, with whom Justice BREYER joins, concurring in the judgment.

I write separately because, in my view, the plurality announces a rule of unprecedented breadth for the evaluation of Establishment Clause challenges to government school-aid programs. Reduced to its essentials, the plurality's rule states that government aid to religious schools does not have the effect of advancing religion so long as the aid is offered on a neutral basis and the aid is secular in content. The plurality also rejects the distinction between direct and indirect aid, and holds that the actual diversion of secular aid by a religious school to the advancement of its religious mission is permissible. Although the expansive scope of the plurality's rule is troubling, two specific aspects of the opinion compel me to write separately. First, the plurality's treatment of neutrality comes close to assigning that factor singular importance in the future adjudication of Establishment Clause challenges to government school-aid programs. Second, the plurality's approval of actual diversion of government aid to religious indoctrination is in tension with our precedents and, in any event, unnecessary to decide the instant case.

I do not quarrel with the plurality's recognition that neutrality is an important reason for upholding government-aid programs against Establishment Clause challenges. Our cases have described neutrality in precisely this manner, and we have emphasized a program's neutrality repeatedly in our decisions approving various forms of school aid. Nevertheless, we have never held that a government-aid program passes constitutional muster *solely* because of the neutral criteria it employs as a basis for distributing aid.

I also disagree with the plurality's conclusion that actual diversion of government aid to religious indoctrination is consistent with the Establishment Clause. Although "[o]ur cases have permitted some government funding of secular functions performed by sectarian organizations," our decisions "provide no precedent for the use of public funds to finance religious activities." [W]e have long been concerned that secular government aid not be diverted to the advancement of religion.

Like Justice Souter, I do not believe that we should treat a per-capita-aid program the same as . . . true private-choice programs. . . . I believe the distinction between a per-capita school-aid program and a true private-choice program is significant for purposes of endorsement. In terms of public perception, a government program of direct aid to religious schools based on the number of students attending each school differs meaningfully from the government distributing aid directly to individual students who, in turn, decide to use the aid at the same religious schools. In the former example, if the religious school uses the aid to inculcate religion in its students, it is reasonable to say that the government has communicated a message of endorsement. Because the religious indoctrination is supported by government assistance, the reasonable observer would naturally perceive the aid program as *government* support for the advancement of religion.

Finally, the distinction between a per-capita-aid program and a true private-choice program is important when considering aid that consists of direct monetary subsidies. This Court has "recognized special Establishment Clause dangers where the government makes direct money payments to sectarian institutions." If, as the plurality contends, a per-capita-aid program is identical in relevant constitutional respects to a true private-choice program, then there is no reason that, under the plurality's reasoning, the government should be precluded from providing direct money payments to religious organizations (including churches) based on the number of persons belonging to each organization. And, because actual diversion is permissible under the plurality's holding, the participating religious organizations (including churches) could use that aid to support religious indoctrination. To be sure, the plurality does not actually hold that its theory extends to direct money payments. That omission, however, is of little comfort. In its logic—as well as its specific advisory language—the plurality opinion foreshadows the approval of direct monetary subsidies to religious organizations, even when they use the money to advance their religious objectives.

[Having rejected the plurality's approach, Justice O'Connor upholds the program: "The Chapter 2 aid is allocated on the basis of neutral, secular criteria; the aid must be supplementary and cannot supplant non-Federal funds; no Chapter 2 funds ever reach the coffers of religious schools; the aid must be secular; any evidence of actual diversion is *de minimis*; and the program includes adequate safeguards. Regardless of whether these factors are constitutional requirements, they are surely sufficient to find that the program at issue here does not have the impermissible effect of advancing religion. For the same reasons, 'this carefully constrained program also cannot reasonably be viewed as an endorsement of religion.' Accordingly, I concur in the judgment."]

Justice SOUTER, with whom Justice STEVENS and Justice GINSBURG join, dissenting.

The establishment prohibition of government religious funding serves more than one end. It is meant to guarantee the right of individual conscience against compulsion, to protect the integrity of religion against the corrosion of secular support, and to preserve the unity of political society against the implied exclusion of the less favored and the antagonism of controversy over public support for religious causes.

These objectives are always in some jeopardy since the substantive principle of no aid to religion is not the only limitation on government action toward religion. Because the First Amendment also bars any prohibition of individual free exercise of religion, and because religious organizations cannot be isolated from the basic government functions that create the civil environment, it is as much necessary as it is difficult to draw lines between forbidden aid and lawful benefit. For more than 50 years, this Court has been attempting to draw these lines. Owing to the variety of factual circumstances in which the lines must be drawn, not all of the points creating the boundary have enjoyed self-evidence.

The insufficiency of evenhandedness neutrality as a stand-alone criterion of constitutional intent or effect has been clear from the beginning of our interpretative efforts, for an obvious reason. . . .

[I]f we looked no further than evenhandedness, and failed to ask what activities the aid might support, or in fact did support, religious schools could be blessed with government funding as massive as expenditures made for the benefit of their public school counterparts, and religious missions would thrive on public money. This is why the consideration of less than universal neutrality has never been recognized as dispositive and has always been teamed with attention to other facts bearing on the substantive prohibition of support for a school's religious objective.

At least three main lines of enquiry addressed particularly to school aid have emerged to complement evenhandedness neutrality. First, we have noted that two types of aid recipients heighten Establishment Clause concern: pervasively religious schools and primary and secondary religious schools. Second, we have identified two important characteristics of the method of distributing aid: directness or indirectness of distribution and distribution by genuinely independent choice. Third, we have found relevance in at least five characteristics of the aid itself: its religious content; its cash form; its divertibility or actually diversion to religious support; its supplantation of traditional items of religious school expense; and its substantiality.

1

Two types of school aid recipients have raised special concern. First, we have recognized the fact that the overriding religious mission of certain schools, those sometimes called "pervasively sectarian," is not confined to a discrete element of the curriculum. Based on record evidence and long experience, we have concluded that religious teaching in such schools is at the core of the instructors' individual and personal obligations, *cf.* Canon 803, §2, Text & Commentary 568 ("It is necessary that the formation and education given in a Catholic school be based upon the principles of Catholic doctrine; teachers are to be outstanding for their correct doctrine and integrity of life"), and that individual religious teachers will teach religiously. As religious teaching cannot be separated from secular education in such schools or by such teachers, we have concluded that direct government subsidies to such schools are prohibited because they will inevitably and impermissibly support religious indoctrination.

Second, we have expressed special concern about aid to primary and secondary religious schools. On the one hand, we have understood how the youth of the students in such schools makes them highly susceptible to religious indoctrination. On the other, we have recognized that the religious element in the education offered in most sectarian primary and secondary schools is far more intertwined with the secular than in university teaching, where the natural and academic skepticism of most older students may separate the two. Thus, government benefits accruing to these pervasively religious primary and secondary schools raise special dangers of diversion into support for the religious indoctrination of children and the involvement of government in religious training and practice.

2

We have also evaluated the portent of support to an organization's religious mission that may be inherent in the method by which aid is granted, finding pertinence in at least two characteristics of distribution. First, we have asked whether aid is direct or indirect, observing distinctions between government schemes with individual beneficiaries and those whose beneficiaries in the first instance might be religious schools. Direct aid obviously raises greater risks, although recent cases have discounted this risk factor, looking to other features of the distribution mechanism.

Second, we have distinguished between indirect aid that reaches religious schools only incidentally as a result of numerous individual choices and aid that is in reality directed to religious schools by the government or in practical terms selected by religious schools themselves. In these cases, we have declared the constitutionality of programs providing aid directly to parents or students as tax deductions or scholarship money, where such aid may pay for education at some sectarian institutions, but only as the result of "genuinely independent and private choices of aid recipients."

3

In addition to the character of the school to which the benefit accrues, and its path from government to school, a number of features of the aid itself have figured in the classifications we have made. First, we have barred aid with actual religious content, which would obviously run afoul of the ban on the government's participation in religion. In cases where we have permitted aid, we have regularly characterized it as "neutral" in the sense of being without religious content.

Second, we have long held government aid invalid when circumstances would allow its diversion to religious education. The risk of diversion is obviously high when aid in the form of government funds makes its way into the coffers of religious organizations, and so from the start we have understood the Constitution to bar outright money grants of aid to religion.

Divertibility is not, of course, a characteristic of cash alone, and when examining provisions for ostensibly secular supplies we have considered their susceptibility to the service of religious ends. In upholding a scheme to provide students with secular textbooks, we emphasized that "each book loaned must be approved by the public school authorities; only secular books may receive approval."

With the same point in mind, we held that buildings constructed with government grants to universities with religious affiliation must be barred from religious use indefinitely to prevent the diversion of government funds to religious objectives. We were accordingly constrained to strike down aid for repairing buildings of nonpublic schools because they could be used for religious education.

Third, our cases have recognized the distinction, adopted by statute in the Chapter 2 legislation, between aid that merely supplements and aid that supplants expenditures for offerings at religious schools, the latter being barred. Although we have never adopted the position that any benefit that flows to a religious school is impermissible because it frees up resources for the school to engage in religious indoctrination, from our first decision holding it permissible to provide textbooks for religious schools we have repeatedly explained the unconstitutionality of aid that supplants an item of the school's traditional expense.

Finally, we have recognized what is obvious (however imprecise), in holding "substantial" amounts of aid to be unconstitutional whether or not a plaintiff can show that it supplants a specific item of expense a religious school would have borne. . . .

The plurality's mistaken assumptions explain and underscore its sharp break with the Framers' understanding of establishment and this Court's consistent interpretative course. Under the plurality's regime, little would be left of the right of conscience against compelled support for religion; the more massive the aid the more potent would be the influence of the government on the teaching mission; the more generous the support, the more divisive would be the resentments of those resisting religious support, and those religions without school systems ready to claim their fair share.

[T]here is no mistaking the abandonment of doctrine that would occur if the plurality were to become a majority. It is beyond question that the plurality's notion of evenhandedness neutrality as a practical guarantee of the validity of aid to sectarian schools would be the end of the principle of no aid to the schools' religious mission. And if that were not so obvious it would become so after reflecting on the plurality's thoughts about diversion and about giving attention to the pervasiveness of a school's sectarian teaching.

The plurality is candid in pointing out the extent of actual diversion of Chapter 2 aid to religious use in the case before us, and equally candid in saying it does not matter. To the plurality there is nothing wrong with aiding a school's religious mission; the only question is whether religious teaching obtains its tax support under a formally evenhanded criterion of distribution. The principle of no aid to religious teaching has no independent significance.

And if this were not enough to prove that no aid in religious school aid is dead under the plurality's First Amendment, the point is nailed down in the plurality's attack on the legitimacy of considering a school's pervasively sectarian character when judging whether aid to the school is likely to aid its religious mission. The relevance of this consideration is simply a matter of common sense: where religious indoctrination pervades school activities of children and adolescents, it takes great care to be able to aid the school without supporting the doctrinal effort. This is obvious. The plurality nonetheless condemns any enquiry into the pervasiveness of doctrinal content as a remnant of anti-Catholic bigotry (as if evangelical Protestant schools and Orthodox Jewish yeshivas were never pervasively sectarian), and it equates a refusal to aid religious schools with hostility to religion (as if aid to religious teaching were not opposed in this very case by at least one religious respondent and numerous religious *amici curiae* in a tradition claiming descent from Roger Williams). My concern with these arguments goes not so much to their details as it does to the fact that the plurality's choice to employ imputations of bigotry and irreligion as terms in the Court's debate makes one point clear: that in rejecting the principle of no aid to a school's religious mission the plurality is attacking the most fundamental assumption underlying the Establishment Clause, that government can in fact operate with neutrality in its relation to religion. I believe that it can, and so respectfully dissent.

NOTES AND QUESTIONS

1. *Earlier cases on direct aid.* Earlier cases, decided during the primacy of *Lemon*, generally disallowed the provision of any instructional materials, equipment, or funding that provided generalized support to pervasively

sectarian schools or that could be "diverted" to support a pervasively sectarian school's religious mission. *See* Wolman v. Walter, 433 U.S. 229 (1977) (permitting Ohio to provide textbooks, testing services, and diagnostic services to students enrolled in pervasively sectarian K-12 schools, but invalidating on Establishment Clause grounds Ohio's provision of "instructional materials and equipment" and financial support for field trips, because such government assistance "necessarily results in aid to the sectarian school enterprise as a whole"); Meek v. Pittenger, 421 U.S. 349 (1975) (allowing state-supplied "auxiliary services" and textbooks in secular subjects to students in pervasively sectarian K-12 schools, but disallowing the provision of "instructional material and equipment," including audiovisual equipment, maps, and laboratory equipment, to such schools because "[s]ubstantial aid to the educational function of such schools . . . necessarily results in aid to the sectarian school enterprise as a whole").

2. *Defining government neutrality.* The theme of government neutrality has been repeatedly used by the Court over the years to describe the central mandate of the Establishment Clause, but the term *neutrality* seems to have meant very different things to different Justices and commentators. The most prominent early proponent of the neutrality theory of the Establishment Clause was Philip Kurland. His version of neutrality—sometimes referred to as "strict neutrality"—also can be found in Justice Black's famous early description of the Establishment Clause standard in *Everson,* which is quoted earlier in this chapter. Under the more recent version of "formal neutrality," on the other hand, government programs that provide benefits to religious individuals or organizations would not violate the Establishment Clause as long as they offer the same aid under the same conditions to both religious and nonreligious recipients. Thus, according to the *Mitchell* plurality, the government can provide (noncash) aid directly to private religious schools, as long as the aid is not "impermissibly religious in nature" and the program that authorizes the aid is formally open to secular as well as sectarian schools. It does not matter that all or most of the funds go to religious schools. Nor does it matter, according to the plurality, if the schools are pervasively sectarian in the sense that religion permeates every aspect of the school's curriculum or if the pervasively sectarian schools divert government aid to explicitly religious uses. However, Justice O'Connor's concurrence rather than the plurality controls. Why is that?
3. *"Diversion" as a limit on direct government support.* Justice O'Connor "disagree[s] with the plurality's conclusion that actual diversion of government aid to religious indoctrination is consistent with the Establishment Clause." What other limits on direct government aid does Justice O'Connor list? One thing Justice O'Connor does not disallow is direct aid to pervasively sectarian schools. But won't aid to pervasively sectarian schools always be diverted to explicitly religious uses?
4. *Blaine Amendment.* In 1875, Congress considered but ultimately did not pass an amendment known as the "Blaine Amendment" that would have explicitly barred directing any public funds to religious organizations.

However, 37 states have some form of constitutional prohibition on aid to religious education. Supporters of government funding for religious institutions have recently attacked the legacy of the Blaine Amendment as evidence of (to use Justice Thomas's characterization from *Mitchell*) "pervasive hostility to the Catholic Church and to Catholics in general." The history of the state constitutional provisions barring state aid to religious institutions is actually a much more complicated affair. It is true that many state provisions (and their federal analogue) were motivated partly by anti-Catholic bias. But it is not true that state no-aid provisions were exclusively motivated by anti-Catholic animus. As is evident from the Virginia experience in 1785-1786, there is a long history of anti-establishment sentiment in this country.

5. *Neutrality as the only limit on government support of religious education.* Does the simple (and easily satisfied) requirement that all government aid programs be formally neutral adequately protect against whatever concerns about establishment remain in the modern era?

Trinity Lutheran Church of Columbia, Inc. v. Comer

137 S. Ct. 2012 (2017)

[As described on pp. 807, the State of Missouri provided funding to resurface playgrounds but declined to award a cash grant to a church because the Missouri Constitution prohibited the state from funding churches.]

NOTES AND QUESTIONS

1. Mitchell *and direct money grants to religious schools.* Even the *Mitchell* plurality, which had argued that direct aid to religious schools in the form of educational materials did not violate the Establishment Clause if awarded on a neutral basis, looked askance at direct cash awards to religious schools, acknowledging that "Of course, we have seen 'special Establishment Clause dangers' when *money* is given to religious schools or entities directly rather than . . . indirectly," and Justice O'Connor, in her controlling concurrence, emphasizes that precedent bars giving funding to religious schools for religious activities. Has that concern evaporated?
2. *Church playgrounds.* The Supreme Court majority assumes that the government's monies given directly to the church school will be used for a secular purpose: improving a playground. Is a church playground a secular endeavor?
3. *Substantial and historic interest or policy preference.* The majority rejects the claim that avoiding direct money grants to churches is a compelling government interest, instead characterizing it solely as a "policy preference." Is that characterization of the state's decision to avoid cash grants to churches consistent with precedent? With history?
4. *Play in the joints.* If voluntarily promoting Establishment Clause values is merely a "policy preference," is voluntarily promoting Free Exercise

Clause values (e.g., by granting a religious exemption that the Free Exercise Clause does not require) also merely a "policy preference"? If so, should these voluntary exemptions violate the Establishment Clause?

D. *VOUCHER PROGRAMS*

In Mueller v. Allen, 463 U.S. 388 (1983),the Court upheld a tax exemption program that extended benefits to parents of students attending private religious schools. In this case the Court relied heavily on the fact that the deductions went to parents who independently decided where to send their children to school. Thus, the Court reasoned, this system of private choice could not be attributable to the government and therefore could not possibly violate the Establishment Clause. In *Zelman v. Simmons-Harris*, the Court combined this notion of private choice with a theory of formal neutrality and produced the model for the new era of government financing decisions under the Establishment Clause. In this new era, the government is allowed to fund religious institutions (including schools) so long as it allows secular institutions to apply for funds from the same programs and so long as it configures the financing program in a way that funnels the money to religious institutions through parents or other private individuals. In reading these decisions, consider whether these two formal limitations are effective in enforcing the spirit of the First Amendment's prohibition on religious establishments.

Zelman v. Simmons-Harris

536 U.S. 639 (2002)

Chief Justice Rehnquist delivered the opinion of the Court.

The State of Ohio has established a pilot program designed to provide educational choices to families with children who reside in the Cleveland City School District. The question presented is whether this program offends the Establishment Clause of the United States Constitution. We hold that it does not.

There are more than 75,000 children enrolled in the Cleveland City School District. The majority of these children are from low-income and minority families. Few of these families enjoy the means to send their children to any school other than an inner-city public school. For more than a generation, however, Cleveland's public schools have been among the worst performing public schools in the Nation. In 1995, a Federal District Court declared a crisis of magnitude and placed the entire Cleveland school district under state control. Shortly thereafter, the state auditor found that Cleveland's public schools were in the midst of a crisis that is perhaps unprecedented in the history of American education. Cleveland City School District Performance Audit 21 (Mar. 1996). The district had failed to meet any of the 18 state standards for minimal acceptable performance. Only 1 in 10 ninth graders could pass a basic proficiency examination, and students at all levels performed at a dismal rate compared with students in other Ohio public schools. More than two-thirds of high school students either dropped or failed out before graduation. Of those students who managed to reach their senior year, one of every four still failed to graduate. Of those students who did graduate, few could read, write, or compute at levels comparable to their counterparts in other cities.

It is against this backdrop that Ohio enacted, among other initiatives, its Pilot Project Scholarship Program. The program provides financial assistance to families in any Ohio school district that is or has been under federal court order requiring supervision and operational management of the district by the state superintendent. Cleveland is the only Ohio school district to fall within that category.

The program provides two basic kinds of assistance to parents of children in a covered district. First, the program provides tuition aid for students in kindergarten through third grade, expanding each year through eighth grade, to attend a participating public or private school of their parent's choosing. Second, the program provides tutorial aid for students who choose to remain enrolled in public school.

The tuition aid portion of the program is designed to provide educational choices to parents who reside in a covered district. Any private school, whether religious or nonreligious, may participate in the program and accept program students so long as the school is located within the boundaries of a covered district and meets statewide educational standards. Participating private schools must agree not to discriminate on the basis of race, religion, or ethnic background, or to "advocate or foster unlawful behavior or teach hatred of any person or group on the basis of race, ethnicity, national origin, or religion." Any public school located in a school district adjacent to the covered district may also participate in the program. Adjacent public schools are eligible to receive a $2,250 tuition grant for each program student accepted in addition to the full amount of per-pupil state funding attributable to each additional student. All participating schools, whether public or private, are required to accept students in accordance with rules and procedures established by the state superintendent.

Tuition aid is distributed to parents according to financial need. Families with incomes below 200% of the poverty line are given priority and are eligible to receive 90% of private school tuition up to $2,250. For these lowest-income families, participating private schools may not charge a parental co-payment greater than $250. For all other families, the program pays 75% of tuition costs, up to $1,875, with no co-payment cap. These families receive tuition aid only if the number of available scholarships exceeds the number of low-income children who choose to participate. Where tuition aid is spent depends solely upon where parents who receive tuition aid choose to enroll their child. If parents choose a private school, checks are made payable to the parents who then endorse the checks over to the chosen school.

The program has been in operation within the Cleveland City School District since the 1996-1997 school year. In the 1999-2000 school year, 56 private schools participated in the program, 46 (or 82%) of which had a religious affiliation. None of the public schools in districts adjacent to Cleveland have elected to participate. More than 3,700 students participated in the scholarship program, most of whom (96%) enrolled in religiously affiliated schools. Sixty percent of these students were from families at or below the poverty line. In the 1998-1999 school year, approximately 1,400 Cleveland public school students received tutorial aid. This number was expected to double during the 1999-2000 school year.

There is no dispute that the program challenged here was enacted for the valid secular purpose of providing educational assistance to poor children in a demonstrably failing public school system. Thus, the question presented is whether the Ohio program nonetheless has the forbidden effect of advancing or inhibiting religion.

To answer that question, our decisions have drawn a consistent distinction between government programs that provide aid directly to religious schools, and programs of true private choice, in which government aid reaches religious schools only as a result of the genuine and independent choices of private individuals.

[Our previous cases] make clear that where a government aid program is neutral with respect to religion, and provides assistance directly to a broad class of citizens who, in turn, direct government aid to religious schools wholly as a result of their own genuine and independent private choice, the program is not readily subject to challenge under the Establishment Clause. A program that shares these features permits government aid to reach religious institutions only by way of the deliberate choices of numerous individual recipients. The incidental advancement of a religious mission, or the perceived endorsement of a religious message, is reasonably attributable to the individual recipient, not to the government, whose role ends with the disbursement of benefits.

Respondents suggest that even without a financial incentive for parents to choose a religious school, the program creates a public perception that the State is endorsing religious practices and beliefs. But we have repeatedly recognized that no reasonable observer would think a neutral program of private choice, where state aid reaches religious schools solely as a result of the numerous independent decisions of private individuals, carries with it the *imprimatur* of government endorsement. The argument is particularly misplaced here since the reasonable observer in the endorsement inquiry must be deemed aware of the history and context underlying a challenged program. Any objective observer familiar with the full history and context of the Ohio program would reasonably view it as one aspect of a broader undertaking to assist poor children in failed schools, not as an endorsement of religious schooling in general.

Justice Souter speculates that because more private religious schools currently participate in the program, the program itself must somehow discourage the participation of private nonreligious schools. But Cleveland's preponderance of religiously affiliated private schools certainly did not arise as a result of the program; it is a phenomenon common to many American cities. Indeed, by all accounts the program has captured a remarkable cross-section of private schools, religious and nonreligious. It is true that 82% of Cleveland's participating private schools are religious schools, but it is also true that 81% of private schools in Ohio are religious schools. To attribute constitutional significance to this figure, moreover, would lead to the absurd result that a neutral school-choice program might be permissible in some parts of Ohio, such as Columbus, where a lower percentage of private schools are religious schools, but not in inner-city Cleveland, where Ohio has deemed such programs most sorely needed, but where the preponderance of religious schools happens to be greater. Cf. Brief for State of Florida et al. as *Amici Curiae* 17 ("[T]he percentages of sectarian to nonsectarian private schools within Florida's 67 school districts vary from zero to 100 percent[.]"). Likewise, an identical private choice program might be constitutional in some States, such as Maine or Utah, where less than 45% of private schools are religious schools, but not in other States, such as Nebraska or Kansas, where over 90% of private schools are religious schools.

Respondents and Justice Souter claim that even if we do not focus on the number of participating schools that are religious schools, we should attach constitutional significance to the fact that 96% of scholarship recipients have enrolled in religious schools. They claim that this alone proves parents lack genuine choice, even if no parent has ever said so. We need not consider this argument in detail, since it was flatly rejected in *Mueller*, where we found it irrelevant that 96% of parents taking deductions for tuition expenses paid tuition at religious schools. Indeed, we have recently found it irrelevant even to the constitutionality of a direct aid program that a vast majority of program benefits went to religious schools. The constitutionality of a neutral educational aid program simply does not turn on whether and why, in a particular area, at a particular time, most private schools are run by religious organizations, or most recipients choose to use the aid at a religious school. As we said in *Mueller*, "[s]uch an approach would scarcely provide the certainty that this field stands in need of, nor can we perceive principled standards by which such statistical evidence might be evaluated."

Justice O'Connor, concurring.

These cases are different from prior indirect aid cases in part because a significant portion of the funds appropriated for the voucher program reach religious schools without restrictions on the use of these funds. The share of public resources that reach religious schools is not, however, as significant as respondents suggest. Data from the 1999-2000 school year indicate that 82 percent of schools participating in the voucher program were religious and that 96 percent of participating students enrolled in religious schools, but these data are incomplete. These statistics do not take into account all of the reasonable educational choices that may be available to students in Cleveland public schools. When one considers the option to attend community schools, the percentage of students enrolled in religious schools falls to 62.1 percent. If magnet schools are included in the mix, this percentage falls to 16.5 percent.

Even these numbers do not paint a complete picture. The Cleveland program provides voucher applicants from low-income families with up to $2,250 in tuition assistance and provides the remaining applicants with up to $1,875 in tuition assistance. In contrast, the State provides community schools $4,518 per pupil and magnet schools, on average, $7,097 per pupil. Even if one assumes that all voucher students came from low-income families and that each voucher student used up the entire $2,250 voucher, at most $8.2 million of public funds flowed to religious schools under the voucher program in 1999-2000. Although just over one-half as many students attended community schools as religious private schools on the state fisc, the State spent over $1 million more on students in community schools than on students in religious private schools because per-pupil aid to community schools is more than double the per-pupil aid to private schools under the voucher program. Moreover, the amount spent on religious private schools is minor compared to the $114.8 million the State spent on students in the Cleveland magnet schools.

Although $8.2 million is no small sum, it pales in comparison to the amount of funds that federal, state, and local governments already provide religious institutions. Religious organizations may qualify for exemptions from the federal corporate income tax; the corporate income tax in many States; and property taxes in all 50 States; and clergy qualify for a federal tax break on income used for housing expenses. In addition, the Federal Government provides individuals, corporations, trusts, and estates a tax deduction for charitable contributions to qualified religious groups. Finally, the Federal Government and certain state governments provide tax credits for educational expenses, many of which are spent on education at religious schools.

These tax exemptions, which have "much the same effect as [cash grants] . . . of the amount of tax [avoided]," are just part of the picture. Federal dollars also reach religiously affiliated organizations through public health programs such as Medicare and Medicaid, through educational programs such as the Pell Grant program, and the G.I. Bill of Rights, and through child care programs such as the Child Care and Development Block Grant Program (CCDBG). These programs are well-established parts of our social welfare system, and can be quite substantial.

Against this background, the support that the Cleveland voucher program provides religious institutions is neither substantial nor atypical of existing government programs. While this observation is not intended to justify the Cleveland voucher program under the Establishment Clause, it places in broader perspective alarmist claims about implications of the Cleveland program and the Court's decision in these cases.

Justice STEVENS, dissenting.

Is a law that authorizes the use of public funds to pay for the indoctrination of thousands of grammar school children in particular religious faiths a "law respecting an establishment of religion" within the meaning of the First Amendment? In answering that question, I think we should ignore three factual matters that are discussed at length by my colleagues.

First, the severe educational crisis that confronted the Cleveland City School District when Ohio enacted its voucher program is not a matter that should affect our appraisal of its constitutionality. In the 1999-2000 school year, that program provided relief to less than five percent of the students enrolled in the district's schools. The solution to the disastrous conditions that prevented over 90 percent of the student body from meeting basic proficiency standards obviously required massive improvements unrelated to the voucher program. Of course, the emergency may have given some families a powerful motivation to leave the public school system and accept religious indoctrination that they would otherwise have avoided, but that is not a valid reason for upholding the program.

Second, the wide range of choices that have been made available to students *within the public school system* has no bearing on the question whether the State may pay the tuition for students who wish to reject public education entirely and attend private schools that will provide them with a sectarian education. The fact that the vast majority of the voucher recipients who have entirely rejected public education receive religious indoctrination at state expense does, however, support the claim that the law is one "respecting an establishment of religion." The State may choose to divide up its public schools into a dozen different options and label them magnet schools, community schools, or whatever else it decides to call them, but the State is still required to provide a public education and it is the State's decision to fund private school education over and above its traditional obligation that is at issue in these cases.

Third, the voluntary character of the private choice to prefer a parochial education over an education in the public school system seems to me quite irrelevant to the question whether the government's choice to pay for religious indoctrination is constitutionally permissible. Today, however, the Court seems to have decided that the mere fact that a family that cannot afford a private education wants its children educated in a parochial school is a sufficient justification for this use of public funds.

For the reasons stated by Justice Souter and Justice Breyer, I am convinced that the Court's decision is profoundly misguided. Admittedly, in reaching that conclusion I have been influenced by my understanding of the impact of religious strife on the decisions of our forbears to migrate to this continent, and on the decisions of neighbors in the Balkans, Northern Ireland, and the Middle East to mistrust one another. Whenever we remove a brick from the wall that was designed to separate religion and government, we increase the risk of religious strife and weaken the foundation of our democracy.

Justice SOUTER, with whom Justice STEVENS, Justice GINSBURG, and Justice BREYER join, dissenting.

The Court's majority holds that the Establishment Clause is no bar to Ohio's payment of tuition at private religious elementary and middle schools under a scheme that systematically provides tax money to support the schools' religious missions. The occasion for the legislation thus upheld is the condition of public education in the city of Cleveland. The record indicates that the schools are failing to serve their objective, and the vouchers in issue here are said to be needed to provide adequate alternatives to them. If there were an excuse for giving short shrift to the Establishment Clause, it would probably apply here. But there is no excuse. Constitutional limitations are placed on government to preserve constitutional values in hard cases, like these.

Today, however, the majority holds that the Establishment Clause is not offended by Ohio's Pilot Project Scholarship Program, under which students may be eligible to receive as much as $2,250 in the form of tuition vouchers transferable to religious schools. In the city of Cleveland the overwhelming proportion of large appropriations for voucher money must be spent on religious schools if it is to be spent at all, and will be spent in amounts that cover almost all of tuition. The money will thus pay for eligible students' instruction not only in secular subjects but in religion as well, in schools that can fairly be characterized as founded to teach religious doctrine and to imbue teaching in all subjects with a religious dimension. Public tax money will pay at a systemic level for teaching the covenant with Israel and Mosaic law in Jewish schools, the primacy of the Apostle Peter and the Papacy in Catholic schools, the truth of reformed Christianity in Protestant schools, and the revelation to the Prophet in Muslim schools, to speak only of major religious groupings in the Republic.

How can a Court consistently leave *Everson* on the books and approve the Ohio vouchers? The answer is that it cannot. It is only by ignoring *Everson* that the majority can claim to rest on traditional law in its invocation of neutral aid provisions and private choice to sanction the Ohio law. It is, moreover, only by ignoring the meaning of neutrality and private choice themselves that the majority can even pretend to rest today's decision on those criteria.

II.

A.

Consider first the criterion of neutrality. As recently as two Terms ago, a majority of the Court recognized that neutrality conceived of as evenhandedness toward aid recipients had never been treated as alone sufficient to satisfy the Establishment Clause, *Mitchell.* But at least in its limited significance, formal neutrality seemed to serve some purpose. Today, however, the majority employs the neutrality criterion in a way that renders it impossible to understand.

In order to apply the neutrality test, it makes sense to focus on a category of aid that may be directed to religious as well as secular schools, and ask whether the scheme favors a religious direction. Here, one would ask whether the voucher provisions, allowing for as much as $2,250 toward private school tuition (or a grant to a public school in an adjacent district), were written in a way that skewed the scheme toward benefiting religious schools.

This, however, is not what the majority asks. The majority looks not to the provisions for tuition vouchers, but to every provision for educational opportunity: "The program permits the participation of *all* schools within the district, [as well as public schools in adjacent districts], religious or nonreligious." The majority then finds confirmation that "participation of *all* schools" satisfies neutrality by noting that the better part of total state educational expenditure goes to public schools, thus showing there is no favor of religion.

The illogic is patent. If regular, public schools (which can get no voucher payments) "participate" in a voucher scheme with schools that can, and public expenditure is still predominantly on public schools, then the majority's reasoning would find neutrality in a scheme of vouchers available for private tuition in districts with no secular private schools at all. Neutrality as the majority employs the term is, literally, verbal and nothing more. This, indeed, is the only way the majority can gloss over the very nonneutral feature of the total scheme covering "*all* schools": public tutors may receive from the State no more than $324 per child to support extra tutoring (that is, the State's 90% of a total amount of $360), whereas the tuition voucher schools (which turn out to be mostly religious) can receive up to $2,250.

Why the majority does not simply accept the fact that the challenge here is to the more generous voucher scheme and judge its neutrality in relation to religious use of voucher money seems very odd. It seems odd, that is, until one recognizes that comparable schools for applying the criterion of neutrality are also the comparable schools for applying the other majority criterion, whether the immediate recipients of voucher aid have a genuinely free choice of religious and secular schools to receive the voucher money. And in applying this second criterion, the consideration of "*all* schools" is ostensibly helpful to the majority position.

B.

The majority addresses the issue of choice the same way it addresses neutrality, by asking whether recipients or potential recipients of voucher aid have a choice of public schools among secular alternatives to religious schools. Again, however, the majority asks the wrong question and misapplies the criterion. The majority has confused choice in spending scholarships with choice from the entire menu of possible educational placements, most of them open to anyone willing to attend a public school. I say "confused" because the majority's new use of the choice criterion, which it frames negatively as "whether Ohio is coercing parents into sending their children to religious schools," ignores the reason for having a private choice enquiry in the first place. Cases since *Mueller* have found private choice relevant under a rule that aid to religious schools can be permissible so long as it first passes through the hands of students or parents. The majority's view that all educational choices are comparable for purposes of choice thus ignores the whole point of the choice test: it is a criterion for deciding whether indirect aid to a religious school is legitimate because it passes through private hands that can spend or use the aid in a secular school. The question is whether the private hand is genuinely free to send the money in either a secular direction or a religious one. The majority now has transformed this question about private choice in channeling aid into a question about selecting from examples of state spending (on education) including direct spending on magnet and community public schools that goes through no private hands and could never reach a religious school under any circumstance. When the choice test is transformed from where to spend the money to where to go to school, it is cut loose from its very purpose.

Defining choice as choice in spending the money or channeling the aid is, moreover, necessary if the choice criterion is to function as a limiting principle at all. If "choice" is present whenever there is any educational alternative to the religious school to which vouchers can be endorsed, then there will always be a choice and the voucher can always be constitutional, even in a system in which there is not a single private secular school as an alternative to the religious school. And because it is unlikely that any participating private religious school will enroll more pupils than the generally available public system, it will be easy to generate numbers suggesting that aid to religion is not the significant intent or effect of the voucher scheme.

That is, in fact, just the kind of rhetorical argument that the majority accepts in these cases. In addition to secular private schools (129 students), the majority considers public schools with tuition assistance (roughly 1,400 students), magnet schools (13,000 students), and community schools (1,900 students), and concludes that fewer than 20% of pupils receive state vouchers to attend religious schools. (In fact, the numbers would seem even more favorable to the majority's argument if enrollment in traditional public schools without tutoring were considered, an alternative the majority thinks relevant to the private choice enquiry.) Justice O'Connor focuses on how much money is spent on each educational option and notes that at most $8.2 million is spent on vouchers for students attending religious schools, which is only 6% of the State's expenditure if one includes separate funding for Cleveland's community ($9.4 million) and magnet ($114.8 million) public schools.

The variations show how results may shift when a judge can pick and choose the alternatives to use in the comparisons, and they also show what dependably comfortable results the choice criterion will yield if the identification of relevant choices is wide open. If the choice of relevant alternatives is an open one, proponents of voucher aid will always win, because they will always be able to find a "choice" somewhere that will show the bulk of public spending to be secular. The choice enquiry will be diluted to the point that it can screen out nothing, and the result will always be determined by selecting the alternatives to be treated as choices.

If, contrary to the majority, we ask the right question about genuine choice to use the vouchers, the answer shows that something is influencing choices in a way that aims the money in a religious direction: of 56 private schools in the district participating in the voucher program (only 53 of which accepted voucher students in 1999-2000), 46 of them are religious; 96.6% of all voucher recipients go to religious schools, only 3.4% to nonreligious ones. Unfortunately for the majority position, there is no explanation for this that suggests the religious direction results simply from free choices by parents. One answer to these statistics, for example, which would be consistent with the genuine choice claimed to be operating, might be that 96.6% of families choosing to avail themselves of vouchers choose to educate their children in schools of their own religion. This would not, in my view, render the scheme constitutional, but it would speak to the majority's choice criterion. Evidence shows, however, that almost two out of three families using vouchers to send their children to religious schools did not embrace the religion of those schools. The families made it clear they had not chosen the schools because they wished their children to be proselytized in a religion not their own, or in any religion, but because of educational opportunity. . . . There is, in any case, no way to interpret the 96.6% of current voucher money going to religious schools as reflecting a free and genuine choice by the families that apply for vouchers. The 96.6% reflects, instead, the fact that too few nonreligious school desks are available and few but religious schools can afford to accept more than a handful of voucher students. And contrary to the majority's assertion, public schools in adjacent districts hardly have a financial incentive to participate in the Ohio voucher program, and none has. For the overwhelming number of children in the voucher scheme, the only alternative to the public schools is religious. And it is entirely irrelevant that the State did not deliberately design the network of private schools for the sake of channeling money into religious institutions. The criterion is one of genuinely free choice on the part of the private individuals who choose, and a Hobson's choice is not a choice, whatever the reason for being Hobsonian. . . .

Justice BREYER, with whom Justice STEVENS and Justice SOUTER join, dissenting.

The First Amendment begins with a prohibition, that "Congress shall make no law respecting an establishment of religion," and a guarantee, that the government shall not prohibit "the free exercise thereof." These Clauses embody an understanding, reached in the 17th century after decades of religious war, that liberty and social stability demand a religious tolerance that respects the religious views of all citizens, permits those citizens to "worship God in their own way," and allows all families to "teach their children and to form their characters" as they wish. The Clauses reflect the Framers vision of an American Nation free of the religious strife that had long plagued the nations of Europe. Whatever the Framers might have thought about particular 18th century school funding practices, they undeniably intended an interpretation of the Religion Clauses that would implement this basic First Amendment objective.

In part for this reason, the Court's 20th-century Establishment Clause cases—both those limiting the practice of religion in public schools and those limiting the public funding of private religious education—focused directly upon social conflict, potentially created when government becomes involved in religious education.

When it decided these 20th-century Establishment Clause cases, the Court did not deny that an earlier American society might have found a less clear-cut church/state separation compatible with social tranquility. Indeed, historians point out that during the early years of the Republic, American schools—including the first public schools—were Protestant in character. Their students recited Protestant prayers, read the King James version of the Bible, and learned Protestant religious ideals. Those practices may have wrongly discriminated against members of minority religions, but given the small number of such individuals, the teaching of Protestant religions in schools did not threaten serious social conflict.

The 20th-century Court was fully aware, however, that immigration and growth had changed American society dramatically since its early years. By 1850, 1.6 million Catholics lived in America, and by 1900 that number rose to 12 million. There were similar percentage increases in the Jewish population. Not surprisingly, with this increase in numbers, members of non-Protestant religions, particularly Catholics, began to resist the Protestant domination of the public schools. Scholars report that by the mid-19th century religious conflict over matters such as Bible reading grew intense, as Catholics resisted and Protestants fought back to preserve their domination. Dreading Catholic domination, native Protestants terrorized Catholics. In some States "Catholic students suffered beatings or expulsions for refusing to read from the Protestant Bible, and crowds . . . rioted over whether Catholic children could be released from the classroom during Bible reading."

The principle underlying these cases—avoiding religiously based social conflict—remains of great concern. As religiously diverse as America had become when the Court decided its major 20th-century Establishment Clause cases, we are exponentially more diverse today. America boasts more than 55 different religious groups and subgroups with a significant number of members. Major religions include, among others, Protestants, Catholics, Jews, Muslims, Buddhists, Hindus, and Sikhs. And several of these major religions contain different subsidiary sects with different religious beliefs. Newer Christian immigrant groups are "expressing their Christianity in languages, customs, and independent churches that are barely recognizable, and often controversial, for European-ancestry Catholics and Protestants." . . .

In a society as religiously diverse as ours, the Court has recognized that we must rely on the Religion Clauses of the First Amendment to protect against religious strife, particularly when what is at issue is an area as central to religious belief as the shaping, through primary education, of the next generation's minds and spirits.

I concede that the Establishment Clause currently permits States to channel various forms of assistance to religious schools, for example, transportation costs for students, computers, and secular texts.

School voucher programs differ, however, in both *kind* and *degree* from aid programs upheld in the past. They differ in kind because they direct financing to a core function of the church: the teaching of religious truths to young children. For that reason the constitutional demand for "separation" is of particular constitutional concern.

Vouchers also differ in *degree*. The aid programs recently upheld by the Court involved limited amounts of aid to religion. But the majority's analysis here appears to permit a considerable shift of taxpayer dollars from public secular schools to private religious schools. That fact, combined with the use to which these dollars will be put, exacerbates the conflict problem. State aid that takes the form of peripheral secular items, with prohibitions against diversion of funds to religious teaching, holds significantly less potential for social division. In this respect as well, the secular aid upheld in *Mitchell* differs dramatically from the present case.

The Court, in effect, turns the clock back. It adopts, under the name of "neutrality," an interpretation of the Establishment Clause that this Court rejected more than half a century ago. In its view, the parental choice that offers each religious group a kind of equal opportunity to secure government funding overcomes the Establishment Clause concern for social concord. An earlier Court found that "equal opportunity" principle insufficient; it read the Clause as insisting upon greater separation of church and state, at least in respect to primary education. In a society composed of many different religious creeds, I fear that this present departure from the Court's earlier understanding risks creating a form of religiously based conflict potentially harmful to the Nation's social fabric. Because I believe the Establishment Clause was written in part to avoid this kind of conflict, and for reasons set forth by Justice Souter and Justice Stevens, I respectfully dissent.

NOTES AND QUESTIONS

1. *Constitutional requirements for vouchers.* In order to comply with the Establishment Clause, school vouchers must be available on a neutral basis (which is also the case for direct aid), and they must end up at religious institutions as the result of the "genuine and independent choice" of private individuals. Unlike direct aid, voucher aid may be used for religious purposes. What do each of these, "neutrality" and "genuine and independent choice," actually require?
2. *Neutrality.* Does *Zelman* require more than formal neutrality? In other words, as long as the funding program is formally open to any educational institution, does it matter that as a practical matter only religious schools apply for the government funds? When analyzing what percentage of the financial aid is directed to religious as opposed to secular schools, whose analysis is more persuasive, that of Justice O'Connor, who considers all educational options, or that of Justice Souter, who considers only the voucher program?
3. *Neutrality among religions.* Is Ohio's program neutral in terms of various religions? In other words, does the voucher program favor some religions over others?

4. *Genuine and independent choice.* Justice Souter points out that for most parents, the only alternative to the failing public schools is a religious school. In addition, "almost two out of three families using vouchers to send their children to religious schools did not embrace the religion of those schools." In other words, most parents chose a private religious school not because of the religious education but in spite of it. Does this affect the genuineness and independence of their choice?
5. *Endorsement.* The majority argues that no reasonable person would conclude that Ohio was endorsing religion in part because "where the tuition aid is spent depends solely upon where parents who receive tuition aid choose to enroll their child." That is, "no reasonable observer would think a neutral program of private choice, where state aid reaches religious schools solely as the result of the numerous independent decisions of private individuals, carries with it the imprimatur of government endorsement." Do you agree?
6. *Conditions on aid.* Private schools that accept voucher money may not discriminate on the basis of race, religion, or ethnic background, nor may they "advocate or foster unlawful behavior or teach hatred of any person or group" on those bases. Participating schools are not barred from discriminating on the basis of sex or sexual orientation or teaching hatred on the basis of sex or sexual orientation. Should schools have to compromise their religious beliefs in order to participate in the voucher program? Should taxpayers have to help fund schools that compromise the nation's commitment to equality?
7. *Memorial and Remonstrance.* If we view these recent disputes over government funding of religion as a replay of the political battle between Patrick Henry and James Madison over religious assessments in Virginia in 1785-1786, then have the latter-day Patrick Henry forces won this round? What are the significant differences (if any) between a modern voucher program that allocates virtually all of its funding to finance religious education and a Virginia-style statute explicitly providing for the funding of religious education? Does the fact that the modern Supreme Court has never come close to enforcing Madison's strict injunction against granting even "three pence" of government money to religious organizations mean that this was always an unrealistic objective? Are the arguments Madison raised in Virginia in 1785 still compelling today, or does the modern political and social context diminish the importance of many of his concerns?
8. *Do voucher programs advance neutrality?* Could supporters of the voucher program argue that a school system with vouchers would actually be more substantively neutral than a school system without vouchers because the vouchers would provide alternatives for religious parents who objected to the secular orientation of the public schools? On the other hand, could opponents of the voucher system argue that vouchers are inherently nonneutral in the sense that they subsidize religious education, thereby encouraging religious belief and practice?

AN EXTENDED NOTE ON STANDING TO CHALLENGE GOVERNMENT FINANCING OF RELIGION

In general, taxpayer standing has not been recognized as sufficient to establish a case or controversy under Article III's grant of jurisdiction to federal courts. *See* Frothingham v. Mellon, 262 U.S. 447 (1923). In Flast v. Cohen, 392 U.S. 83 (1968); however, the Supreme Court created an exception to this general rule in cases in which plaintiffs were challenging the use of tax funds for religious activities in violation of the Establishment Clause. In *Flast,* the Court held that plaintiffs would be granted standing to pursue a lawsuit in federal court if they could establish a nexus between their taxpayer status and the nature of the claims in the lawsuit:

> The nexus demanded of federal taxpayers has two aspects to it. First, the taxpayer must establish a logical link between that status and the type of legislative enactment attacked. Thus, a taxpayer will be a proper party to allege the unconstitutionality only of exercises of congressional power under the taxing and spending clause of Art. I, 8, of the Constitution. It will not be sufficient to allege an incidental expenditure of tax funds in the administration of an essentially regulatory statute. Secondly, the taxpayer must establish a nexus between that status and the precise nature of the constitutional infringement alleged. Under this requirement, the taxpayer must show that the challenged enactment exceeds specific constitutional limitations imposed upon the exercise of the congressional taxing and spending power and not simply that the enactment is generally beyond the powers delegated to Congress by Art. I, 8. When both nexuses are established, the litigant will have shown a taxpayer's stake in the outcome of the controversy and will be a proper and appropriate party to invoke a federal court's jurisdiction.

The Court noted that claims under the Establishment Clause would satisfy the second taxpayer standing nexus because opposition to the use of tax funds for religious purposes was at the heart of Establishment Clause history.

> Our history vividly illustrates that one of the specific evils feared by those who drafted the Establishment Clause and fought for its adoption was that the taxing and spending power would be used to favor one religion over another or to support religion in general. James Madison, who is generally recognized as the leading architect of the religion clauses of the First Amendment, observed in his famous Memorial and Remonstrance Against Religious Assessments that "the same authority which can force a citizen to contribute three pence only of his property for the support of any one establishment, may force him to conform to any other establishment in all cases whatsoever." Writings of James Madison 183, 186 (Hunt ed. 1901). The concern of Madison and his supporters was quite clearly that religious liberty ultimately would be the victim if government could employ its taxing and spending powers to aid one religion over another or to aid religion in general. The Establishment Clause was designed as a specific bulwark against such potential abuses of governmental power, and that clause of the First Amendment operates as a specific constitutional

> limitation upon the exercise by Congress of the taxing and spending power conferred by Art. I, 8.

In recent years, the Court has limited the scope of the *Flast v. Cohen* taxpayer standing rule. The first major limitation of *Flast* occurred in Valley Forge Christian College v. Americans United for Separation of Church & State, Inc., 454 U.S. 464 (1982), where the Court held that *Flast* did not give taxpayers standing to challenge transfers of public property to religious organizations under the Constitution's Property Clause, art. IV, §3, cl. 2. Thus, the Court held that taxpayers had no standing to challenge a decision of the Secretary of Health, Education, and Welfare to convey to a Christian college a 77-acre tract of government-owned land, which was worth approximately $577,500.

The second major limitation of *Flast* was imposed by Hein v. Freedom from Religion Foundation, 551 U.S. 587 (2007), where the Court denied taxpayer standing to a challenge to the actions of executive branch officials in carrying out the Bush Administration's Faith-Based and Community Initiatives program. The plaintiffs in *Hein* challenged specific grants under the Initiative, and also challenged the constitutionality of several conferences held by government officials to encourage religious organizations to participate in the Initiative. The challenges to specific grants were settled at the summary judgment stage of the proceedings in the District Court, and not appealed. With regard to the remaining issue in the lawsuit, the Supreme Court held that the plaintiffs did not have taxpayer standing status to challenge the conferences.

There is no majority opinion for the Supreme Court in *Hein*. The court split three ways. Three Justices (Chief Justice Roberts, and Justices Alito and Kennedy) ruled that *Flast v. Cohen* does not apply to lawsuits challenging expenditures of government funds that were not specifically earmarked by Congress. The plurality held that the plaintiffs in *Hein* could not rely on *Flast* because "the expenditures at issue here were not made pursuant to any Act of Congress. Rather, Congress provided general appropriations to the Executive Branch to fund its day-to-day activities. These appropriations did not expressly authorize, direct, or even mention the expenditures of which respondents complain. Those expenditures resulted from executive discretion, not congressional action." The other six Justices rejected the plurality's distinction between executive allocations of generally appropriated funds and specific congressional authorizations of expenditures, but these six justices split on the viability of *Flast* itself. Justices Scalia and Thomas argued that *Flast* should be overruled. The other four Justices (Souter, Stevens, Breyer, and Ginsburg) dissented. They argued that *Flast* should apply to all expenditures of funds that violate the Establishment Clause, regardless of whether the ultimate determination to allocate funds illegally was made by executive officials or under the specific terms of a statute. The dissenters noted that this had been the Court's practice in cases such as *Bowen*, and concluded that "if the Executive could accomplish through the exercise of discretion exactly what Congress cannot do through legislation, Establishment Clause protection would melt away."

The Supreme Court once again considered the continuing precedential value of *Flast* in Arizona Christian School Tuition Organization v. Winn, 563 U.S. 125 (2011). Writing for a 5–4 majority, Justice Kennedy held that taxpayer standing under *Flast* does not exist to challenge tax credits that benefit religiously affiliated schools. Arizona "provides tax credits for contributions to school tuition organizations, or STOs" and the STOs, in turn, "use these contributions to provide scholarships to students attending private schools, many of which are religious." *Id.* at 129. "Respondents are a group of Arizona taxpayers who challenge the STO tax credit as a violation of the First and Fourteenth Amendments." *Id.* The plaintiffs who challenged Arizona's STO program invoked *Flast* to establish standing as taxpayers seeking to litigate an Establishment Clause claim.

Justice Kennedy rejected the application of *Flast* to tax credit programs, such as Arizona's STO program, even though he acknowledged that "[i]t is easy to see that tax credits and governmental expenditures can have similar economic consequences, at least for beneficiaries whose tax liability is sufficiently large to take full advantage of the credit. Yet tax credits and governmental expenditures do not both implicate individual taxpayers in sectarian activities." *Id.* at 141-42. The majority found that tax expenditures are less direct and particularized than direct affirmative subsidies to religious organizations using government funds. This "distinction between governmental expenditures and tax credits refutes respondents' assertion of standing" because "[w]hen Arizona taxpayers choose to contribute to STO's, they spend their own money, not money the state has collected from respondents or other taxpayers." *Id.* at 142. Thus, "[t]he STO tax credit is not tantamount to a religious tax or to a tithe and does not visit the injury identified in *Flast.*" *Id.* at 142-43. "It follows that respondents have neither alleged an injury for standing purposes under general rules nor met the *Flast* exception." *Id.*

Justice Scalia, joined by Justice Thomas, wrote a concurring opinion, arguing that *Flast* should be squarely overruled: "*Flast* is an anomaly in our jurisprudence, irreconcilable with the Article III restrictions on federal judicial power that our opinions have established. I would repudiate that misguided decision and enforce the Constitution." *Id.* at 146-47 (Scalia, J., dissenting). Justice Scalia nevertheless joined the "Court's opinion because it finds respondents lack standing by applying *Flast* rather than distinguishing it away on unprincipled grounds." *Id.* at 147.

In dissent, Justice Kagan, joined by Justices Ginsburg, Breyer, and Sotomayor, squarely rejected Justice Kennedy's attempt to distinguish between direct appropriations and tax credits for purposes of applying *Flast*:

> This novel distinction in standing law between appropriations and tax expenditures has as little basis in principle as it has in our precedent. Cash grants and targeted tax breaks are means of accomplishing the same government objective—to provide financial support to select individuals or organizations. Taxpayers who oppose state aid of religion have equal reason to protest whether that aid flows from the one form of subsidy or the other. Either way, the government has financed the religious activity. And so either way, taxpayers should be able to challenge the subsidy.
>
> Still worse, the Court's arbitrary distinction threatens to eliminate *all* occasions for a taxpayer to contest the government's monetary support of religion. Precisely because appropriations and tax breaks can achieve identical objectives, the government can easily substitute one for the other. Today's opinion thus enables the government to end-run *Flast*'s guarantee of access to the Judiciary. From now on, the government need

> follow just one simple rule—subsidize through the tax system—to preclude taxpayer challenges to state funding of religion.

Id. at 148 (Kagan, J., dissenting).

In sum, *Flast* seems limited essentially to its specific facts: taxpayer standing will be available only for challenges to specific congressional or state legislative appropriations that violate the Establishment Clause.

THEORY-APPLIED PROBLEM

You work on a pro bono basis as a lawyer for the Mississippi Chapter of the American Civil Liberties Union (ACLU), based in Jackson, Mississippi. The ACLU's staff director forwards you an e-mail from Ms. Janet Givens, an inmate at the Central Mississippi Correctional Facility (CMCF), in Pearl, Missisisippi, seeking the ACLU's assistance. Ms. Givens was convicted of possession of heroin and sentenced to serve five to seven years in the CMCF. Under the applicable statute and regulations, however, she should be eligible for parole after serving three years of her sentence. The state parole board's regulations provide that "for persons convicted of drug offenses, clear and convincing evidence of successful substance abuse treatment shall be required as a condition of favorable action on an inmate's application for parole." The explanatory notes add: "Normally, evidence of successful substance abuse treatment would include successful completion of a state-approved drug rehabilitation program, such as Narcotics Anonymous or a similarly successful program."

Ms. Givens has served just over two years of her sentence, but she has not yet participated in a state-approved drug rehabilitation program. The only such free program at CMCF is sponsored by a local evangelical church and is called "InnerTruth" (IT). IT offers "freedom from addiction through the healing power of Christ." Unfortunately, Givens is an avowed and somewhat evangelical atheist. However, in order to be eligible for parole, she enrolled in IT. Alas, things did not go very well. At her first IT meeting, she strongly objected to "dragging God's name into this messy business of addictions" and expressed vehement disagreement with the "vengeance obsessed, hypercontrolling, and just plain mean" depiction of Jesus propounded at the session. Givens regards IT's fundamentalist view of Jesus, and God for that matter, as entirely irreconcilable with her own beliefs about free will; more generally, she has found the program's religious content to be profoundly offensive to her personal religious beliefs. Givens subsequently asks CMCF officials to permit her to enroll in a nonsectarian drug abuse treatment program. Responding to this request, the CMCF's chief staff counselor tells Givens that "the budget is real tight at the moment" and that "no funding exists for an alternative program to InnerTruth." The counselor urges Givens to reconsider participating in IT—at least if she wants to be eligible for early release through parole.

Givens has asked the ACLU to sue the Mississippi Department of Corrections on her behalf, arguing that the state's parole program for convicted drug offenders, at least as currently implemented, violates the Establishment Clause. How do you advise her regarding the merits of her claim? Is Givens likely to prevail? Why or why not? For bonus points: What test will a federal court likely apply to resolve the merits of the Establishment Clause claim?

CHAPTER 21

THE ESTABLISHMENT CLAUSE AND PUBLIC SCHOOLS

TABLE OF CONTENTS

A. Government Endorsement of Religion in the Public Schools: School Prayer
B. Government Endorsement of Religion in the Public Schools: Religion in the Public School Curriculum
C. Religious Speech in Public Schools

Government endorsement of religion can take various forms, ranging from officially sanctioned government prayer to the use of religious symbols such as crosses on government property to the granting of special privileges to religious entities. The category of government endorsement cases can be further subdivided into two subcategories: cases involving government endorsement of religion in the public schools, and cases involving government endorsement of religion in the adult world. The school cases should be considered separately from other cases because the Court has consistently recognized that "there are heightened concerns with protecting freedom of conscience from subtle coercive pressure in the elementary and secondary public schools." Lee v. Weisman, 505 U.S. 577, 592 (1992).

Thus, although the Court may say that it applies the same constitutional standard to alleged Establishment Clause violations in every context, that standard may take on additional rigor when the alleged violations take place in public schools. This phenomenon is evident from the basic holdings of the cases excerpted below.

The materials in this chapter start with the Court's school prayer decisions. Note how uncharacteristically uniform the Court's conclusions are in this segment of Establishment Clause jurisprudence. The Supreme Court has issued five full opinions on the subject of school prayer or school Bible reading over a 40-year period, and in every case a large majority of the Court has held the religious exercise unconstitutional. The same consistency is evident in the Court's decisions regarding government attempts to limit on religious grounds the teaching of mainstream science. Once we turn in the next chapter to the Court's decisions regarding religious endorsement outside the public school context, however, this consistency breaks down, and it is more difficult to discern any coherent pattern to the Court's decisions.

A. *GOVERNMENT ENDORSEMENT OF RELIGION IN THE PUBLIC SCHOOLS: SCHOOL PRAYER*

Engel v. Vitale

370 U.S. 421 (1962)

[Public schools in New York directed teachers to lead students in the following prayer, which was composed by the New York Board of Regents:

> Almighty God, we acknowledge our dependence upon Thee, and we beg Thy blessings upon us, our parents, our teachers and our Country.

The New York courts upheld the prayer but also required school systems to accommodate students who objected to the prayer, either by allowing the students to remain silent or excusing them altogether from the religious exercise. Objecting students and parents appealed to the United States Supreme Court, which held the prayer exercise unconstitutional.]

Mr. Justice Black delivered the opinion of the Court.

We think that by using its public school system to encourage recitation of the Regents' prayer, the State of New York has adopted a practice wholly inconsistent with the Establishment Clause. There can, of course, be no doubt that New York's program of daily classroom invocation of God's blessings as prescribed in the Regents' prayer is a religious activity. It is a solemn avowal of divine faith and supplication for the blessings of the Almighty. The nature of such a prayer has always been religious, none of the respondents has denied this and the trial court expressly so found.

The petitioners contend among other things that the state laws requiring or permitting use of the Regents' prayer must be struck down as a violation of the Establishment Clause because that prayer was composed by governmental officials as a part of a governmental program to further religious beliefs. For this reason, petitioners argue, the State's use of the Regents' prayer in its public school system breaches the constitutional wall of separation between Church and State. We agree with that contention since we think that the constitutional prohibition against laws respecting an establishment of religion must at least mean that in this country it is no part of the business of government to compose official prayers for any group of the American people to recite as a part of a religious program carried on by government. . . .

By the time of the adoption of the Constitution, our history shows that there was a widespread awareness among many Americans of the dangers of a union of Church and State. These people knew, some of them from bitter personal experience, that one of the greatest dangers to the freedom of the individual to worship in his own way lay in the Government's placing its official stamp of approval upon one particular kind of prayer or one particular form of religious services. They knew the anguish, hardship and bitter strife that could come when zealous religious groups struggled with one another to obtain the Government's stamp of approval from each King, Queen, or Protector that came to temporary power. The Constitution was intended to avert a part of this danger by leaving the government of this country in the hands of the people rather than in the hands of any monarch. But this safeguard was not enough. Our Founders were no more willing to let the content of their prayers and their privilege of praying whenever they pleased be influenced by the ballot box than they were to let these vital matters of personal conscience depend upon the succession of monarchs. The First Amendment was added to the Constitution to stand as a guarantee that neither the power nor the prestige of the Federal Government would be used to control, support or influence the kinds of prayer the American people can say—that the people's religions must not be subjected to the pressures of government for change each time a new political administration is elected to office. Under that Amendment's prohibition against governmental establishment of religion, as reinforced by the provisions of the Fourteenth Amendment, government in this country, be it state or federal, is without power to prescribe by law any particular form of prayer which is to be used as an official prayer in carrying on any program of governmentally sponsored religious activity.

There can be no doubt that New York's state prayer program officially establishes the religious beliefs embodied in the Regents' prayer. The respondents' argument to the contrary, which is largely based upon the contention that the Regents' prayer is "nondenominational" and the fact that the program, as modified and approved by state courts, does not require all pupils to recite the prayer but permits those who wish to do so to remain silent or be excused from the room, ignores the essential nature of the program's constitutional defects. Neither the fact that the prayer may be denominationally neutral nor the fact that its observance on the part of the students is voluntary can serve to free it from the limitations of the Establishment Clause, as it might from the Free Exercise Clause, of the First Amendment, both of which are operative against the States by virtue of the Fourteenth Amendment. Although these two clauses may in certain instances overlap, they forbid two quite different kinds of governmental encroachment upon religious freedom. The Establishment Clause, unlike the Free Exercise Clause, does not depend upon any showing of direct governmental compulsion and is violated by the enactment of laws which establish an official religion whether those laws operate directly to coerce nonobserving individuals or not. This is not to say, of course, that laws officially prescribing a particular form of religious worship do not involve coercion of such individuals. When the power, prestige and financial support of government is placed behind a particular religious belief, the indirect coercive pressure upon religious minorities to conform to the prevailing officially approved religion is plain. But the purposes underlying the Establishment Clause go much further than that. Its first and most immediate purpose rested on the belief that a union of government and religion tends to destroy government and to degrade religion. The history of governmentally established religion, both in England and in this country, showed that whenever government had allied itself with one particular form of religion, the inevitable result had been that it had incurred the hatred, disrespect and even contempt of those who held contrary beliefs. That same history showed that many people had lost their respect for any religion that had relied upon the support for government to spread its faith. The Establishment Clause thus stands as an expression of principle on the part of the Founders of our Constitution that religion is too personal, too sacred, too holy, to permit its "unhallowed perversion" by a civil magistrate. Another purpose of the Establishment Clause rested upon an awareness of the historical fact that governmentally established religions and religious persecutions go hand in hand. The Founders knew that only a few years after the Book of Common Prayer became the only accepted form of religious services in the established Church of England, an Act of Uniformity was passed to compel all Englishmen to attend those services and to make it a criminal offense to conduct or attend religious gatherings of any other kind—a law which was consistently flouted by dissenting religious groups in England and which contributed to widespread persecutions of people like John Bunyan who persisted in holding "unlawful (religious) meetings . . . to the great disturbance and distraction of the good subjects of this kingdom. . . ." And they knew that similar persecutions had received the sanction of law in several of the colonies in this country soon after the establishment of official religions in those colonies. It was in large part to get completely away from this sort of systematic religious persecution that the Founders brought into being our Nation, our Constitution, and our Bill of Rights with its prohibition against any governmental establishment of religion. The New York laws officially prescribing the Regents' prayer are inconsistent both with the purposes of the Establishment Clause and with the Establishment Clause itself.

It has been argued that to apply the Constitution in such a way as to prohibit state laws respecting an establishment of religious services in public schools is to indicate a hostility toward religion or toward prayer. Nothing, of course, could be more wrong. The history of man is inseparable from the history of religion. And perhaps it is not too much to say that since the beginning of that history many people have devoutly believed that "More things are wrought by prayer than this world dreams of." It was doubtless largely due to men who believed this that there grew up a sentiment that caused men to leave the cross-currents of officially established state religions and religious persecution in Europe and come to this country filled with the hope that they could find a place in which they could pray when they pleased to the God of their faith in the language they chose. And there were men of this same faith in the power of prayer who led the fight for adoption of our Constitution and also for our Bill of Rights with the very guarantees of religious freedom that forbid the sort of governmental activity which New York has attempted here. These men knew that the First Amendment, which tried to put an end to governmental control of religion and of prayer, was not written to destroy either. They knew rather that it was written to quiet well-justified fears which nearly all of them felt arising out of an awareness that governments of the past had shackled men's tongues to make them speak only the religious thoughts that government wanted them to speak and to pray only to the God that government wanted them to pray to. It is neither sacrilegious nor antireligious to say that each separate government in this country should stay out of the business of writing or sanctioning official prayers and leave that purely religious function to the people themselves and to those the people choose to look to for religious guidance.[21]

Mr. Justice STEWART, dissenting.

A local school board in New York has provided that those pupils who wish to do so may join in a brief prayer at the beginning of each school day, acknowledging

---

21. There is of course nothing in the decision reached here that is inconsistent with the fact that school children and others are officially encouraged to express love for our country by reciting historical documents such as the Declaration of Independence which contain references to the Deity or by singing officially espoused anthems which include the composer's professions of faith in a Supreme Being, or with the fact that there are many manifestations in our public life of belief in God. Such patriotic or ceremonial occasions bear no true resemblance to the unquestioned religious exercise that the State of New York has sponsored in this instance.

their dependence upon God and asking His blessing upon them and upon their parents, their teachers, and their country. The Court today decides that in permitting this brief non-denominational prayer the school board has violated the Constitution of the United States. I think this decision is wrong.

The Court does not hold, nor could it, that New York has interfered with the free exercise of anybody's religion. For the state courts have made clear that those who object to reciting the prayer must be entirely free of any compulsion to do so, including any "embarrassments and pressures." *Cf.* West Virginia State Board of Education v. Barnette, 319 U.S. 624. But the Court says that in permitting school children to say this simple prayer, the New York authorities have established "an official religion."

With all respect, I think the Court has misapplied a great constitutional principle. I cannot see how an "official religion" is established by letting those who want to say a prayer say it. On the contrary, I think that to deny the wish of these school children to join in reciting this prayer is to deny them the opportunity of sharing in the spiritual heritage of our Nation.

The Court's historical review of the quarrels over the Book of Common Prayer in England throws no light for me on the issue before us in this case. England had then and has now an established church. Equally unenlightening, I think, is the history of the early establishment and later rejection of an official church in our own States. For we deal here not with the establishment of a state church, which would, of course, be constitutionally impermissible, but with whether school children who want to begin their day by joining in prayer must be prohibited from doing so. Moreover, I think that the Court's task, in this as in all areas of constitutional adjudication, is not responsibly aided by the uncritical invocation of metaphors like the "wall of separation," a phrase nowhere to be found in the Constitution. What is relevant to the issue here is not the history of an established church in sixteenth century England or in eighteenth century America, but the history of the religious traditions of our people, reflected in countless practices of the institutions and officials of our government.

At the opening of each day's Session of this Court we stand, while one of our officials invokes the protection of God. Since the days of John Marshall our Crier has said, "God save the United States and this Honorable Court." Both the Senate and the House of Representatives open their daily Sessions with prayer. Each of our Presidents, from George Washington to John F. Kennedy, has upon assuming his Office asked the protection and help of God.

Countless similar examples could be listed, but there is no need to belabor the obvious. It was all summed up by this Court just ten years ago in a single sentence: "We are a religious people whose institutions presuppose a Supreme Being." Zorach v. Clauson, 343 U.S. 306, 313.

School District of Abington Township v. Schempp

374 U.S. 203 (1963)

Mr. Justice CLARK delivered the opinion of the Court.

[A Pennsylvania statute] requires that "At least ten verses from the Holy Bible shall be read, without comment, at the opening of each public school on each school day. Any child shall be excused from such Bible reading, or attending such

Bible reading, upon the written request of his parent or guardian." The Schempp family, husband and wife and two of their three children, brought suit to enjoin enforcement of the statute. [The Schempps] are members of the Unitarian Church in Germantown, Philadelphia, Pennsylvania, where they, as well as another son, Ellory, regularly attend religious services.

On each school day at the Abington Senior High School between 8:15 and 8:30 a.m., while the pupils are attending their home rooms or advisory sections, opening exercises are conducted pursuant to the statute. The exercises are broadcast into each room in the school building through an intercommunications system and are conducted under the supervision of a teacher by students attending the school's radio and television workshop. Selected students from this course gather each morning in the school's workshop studio for the exercises, which include readings by one of the students of 10 verses of the Holy Bible, broadcast to each room in the building. This is followed by the recitation of the Lord's Prayer, likewise over the intercommunications system, but also by the students in the various classrooms, who are asked to stand and join in repeating the prayer in unison. The exercises are closed with the flag salute and such pertinent announcements as are of interest to the students. Participation in the opening exercises, as directed by the statute, is voluntary. The student reading the verses from the Bible may select the passages and read from any version he chooses, although the only copies furnished by the school are the King James version, copies of which were circulated to each teacher by the school district. During the period in which the exercises have been conducted the King James, the Douay and the Revised Standard versions of the Bible have been used, as well as the Jewish Holy Scriptures. There are no prefatory statements, no questions asked or solicited, no comments or explanations made and no interpretations given at or during the exercises. The students and parents are advised that the student may absent himself from the classroom or, should he elect to remain, not participate in the exercises.

At the first trial Edward Schempp and the children testified as to specific religious doctrines purveyed by a literal reading of the Bible "which were contrary to the religious beliefs which they held and to their familial teaching." Edward Schempp testified at the second trial that he had considered having Roger and Donna excused from attendance at the exercises but decided against it for several reasons, including his belief that the children's relationships with their teachers and classmates would be adversely affected.

Applying the Establishment Clause principles to the cases at bar we find that the States are requiring the selection and reading at the opening of the school day of verses from the Holy Bible and the recitation of the Lord's Prayer by the students in unison. These exercises are prescribed as part of the curricular activities of students who are required by law to attend school. They are held in the school buildings under the supervision and with the participation of teachers employed in those schools. The trial court has found that such an opening exercise is a religious ceremony and was intended by the State to be so. We agree with the trial court's finding as to the religious character of the exercises. Given that finding, the exercises and the law requiring them are in violation of the Establishment Clause.

[T]he State contends that the program is an effort to extend its benefits to all public school children without regard to their religious belief. Included within its secular purposes, it says, are the promotion of moral values, the contradiction to the materialistic trends of our times, the perpetuation of our institutions and the teaching of literature. The case came up on demurrer, of course, to a petition which alleged that the uniform practice under the rule had been to read from the King James version of the Bible and that the exercise was sectarian. The short answer, therefore, is that the religious character of the exercise was admitted by the State. But even if its purpose is not strictly religious, it is sought to be accomplished through readings, without comment, from the Bible. Surely the place of the Bible as an instrument of religion cannot be gainsaid, and the State's recognition of the pervading religious character of the ceremony is evident from the rule's specific permission of the alternative use of the Catholic Douay version as well as the recent amendment permitting nonattendance at the exercises. None of these factors is consistent with the contention that the Bible is here used either as an instrument for nonreligious moral inspiration or as a reference for the teaching of secular subjects.

It is insisted that unless these religious exercises are permitted a "religion of secularism" is established in the schools. We agree of course that the State may not establish a "religion of secularism" in the sense of affirmatively opposing or showing hostility to religion, thus "preferring those who believe in no religion over those who do believe." We do not agree, however, that this decision in any sense has that effect. In addition, it might well be said that one's education is not complete without a study of comparative religion or the history of religion and its relationship to the advancement of civilization. It certainly may be said that the Bible is worthy of study for its literary and historic qualities. Nothing we have said here indicates that such study of the Bible or of religion, when presented objectively as part of a secular program of education, may not be effected consistently with the First Amendment. But the exercises here do not fall into those categories. They are religious exercises, required by the States in violation of the command of the First Amendment that the Government maintain strict neutrality, neither aiding nor opposing religion.

Mr. Justice BRENNAN, concurring.

The secular purposes which devotional exercises are said to serve fall into two categories—those which depend upon an immediately religious experience shared by the participating children; and those which appear sufficiently divorced from the religious content of the devotional material that they can be served equally by nonreligious materials. With respect to the first objective, much has been written about the moral and spiritual values of infusing some religious influence or instruction into the public school classroom. To the extent that only *religious* materials will serve this purpose, it seems to me that the purpose as well as the means is so plainly religious that the exercise is necessarily forbidden by the Establishment Clause. The fact that purely secular benefits may eventually result does not seem to me to justify the exercises, for similar indirect nonreligious benefits could no doubt have been claimed for the released time program invalidated in [Illinois ex rel. McCollum v. Board of Education, 333 U.S. 203 (1948)].

The second justification assumes that religious exercises at the start of the school day may directly serve solely secular ends—for example, by fostering harmony and tolerance among the pupils, enhancing the authority of the teacher, and inspiring better discipline. To the extent that such benefits result not from the content of the readings and recitation, but simply from the holding of such a solemn exercise at the opening assembly or the first class of the day, it would seem that less sensitive materials might equally well serve the same purpose. I have previously suggested that [our earlier precedents] forbid the use of religious means to achieve secular ends where nonreligious means will suffice. That principle is readily applied to these cases. It has not been shown that readings from the speeches and messages of great Americans, for example, or from the documents of our heritage of liberty, daily recitation of the Pledge of Allegiance, or even the observance of a moment of reverent silence at the opening of class, may not adequately serve the solely secular purposes of the devotional activities without jeopardizing either the religious liberties of any members of the community or the proper degree of separation between the spheres of religion and government. Such substitutes would, I think, be unsatisfactory or inadequate only to the extent that the present activities do in fact serve religious goals. While I do not question the judgment of experienced educators that the challenged practices may well achieve valuable secular ends, it seems to me that the State acts unconstitutionally if it either sets about to attain even indirectly religious ends by religious means, or if it uses religious means to serve secular ends where secular means would suffice.

It has been suggested that a tentative solution to these problems may lie in the fashioning of a "common core" of theology tolerable to all creeds but preferential to none. But as one commentator has recently observed, "[h]istory is not encouraging to" those who hope to fashion a "common denominator of religion detached from its manifestation in any organized church." Sutherland, *Establishment According to Engel*, 76 HARV. L. REV. 25, 51 (1962). Thus, the notion of a "common core" litany or supplication offends many deeply devout worshippers who do not find clearly sectarian practices objectionable. Father Gustave Weigel has recently expressed a widely shared view: "The moral code held by each separate religious community can reductively be unified, but the consistent particular believer wants no such reduction." And, as the American Council on Education warned several years ago, "The notion of a common core suggests a watering down of the several faiths to the point where common essentials appear. This might easily lead to a new sect—a public school sect—which would take its place alongside the existing faiths and compete with them." *Engel* is surely authority that nonsectarian religious practices, equally with sectarian exercises, violate the Establishment Clause. Moreover, even if the Establishment Clause were oblivious to nonsectarian religious practices, I think it quite likely that the "common core" approach would be sufficiently objectionable to many groups to be foreclosed by the prohibitions of the Free Exercise Clause.

Stone v. Graham

449 U.S. 39 (1992)

PER CURIAM.

A Kentucky statute requires the posting of a copy of the Ten Commandments, purchased with private contributions, on the wall of each public classroom in the State. Petitioners, claiming that this statute violates the Establishment and Free Exercise Clauses of the First Amendment, sought an injunction against its enforcement. The state trial court upheld the statute, finding that its "avowed purpose" was "secular and not religious," and that the statute would "neither advance nor inhibit any religion or religious group" nor involve the State excessively in religious matters. The Supreme Court of the Commonwealth of Kentucky affirmed by an equally divided court. We reverse.

The Commonwealth insists that the statute in question serves a secular legislative purpose, observing that the legislature required the following notation in small print at the bottom of each display of the Ten Commandments: "The secular application of the Ten Commandments is clearly seen in its adoption as the fundamental legal code of Western Civilization and the Common Law of the United States."

The pre-eminent purpose for posting the Ten Commandments on schoolroom walls is plainly religious in nature. The Ten Commandments are undeniably a sacred text in the Jewish and Christian faiths, and no legislative recitation of a supposed secular purpose can blind us to that fact. The Commandments do not confine themselves to arguably secular matters, such as honoring one's parents, killing or murder, adultery, stealing, false witness, and covetousness. *See* Exodus 20: 12-17; Deuteronomy 5: 16-21. Rather, the first part of the Commandments concerns the religious duties of believers: worshipping the Lord God alone, avoiding idolatry, not using the Lord's name in vain, and observing the Sabbath Day. *See* Exodus 20: 1-11; Deuteronomy 5: 6-15.

This is not a case in which the Ten Commandments are integrated into the school curriculum, where the Bible may constitutionally be used in an appropriate study of history, civilization, ethics, comparative religion, or the like. Posting of religious texts on the wall serves no such educational function. If the posted copies of the Ten Commandments are to have any effect at all, it will be to induce the schoolchildren to read, meditate upon, perhaps to venerate and obey, the Commandments. However desirable this might be as a matter of private devotion, it is not a permissible state objective under the Establishment Clause.

It does not matter that the posted copies of the Ten Commandments are financed by voluntary private contributions, for the mere posting of the copies under the auspices of the legislature provides the "official support of the State . . . Government" that the Establishment Clause prohibits. Nor is it significant that the Bible verses involved in this case are merely posted on the wall, rather than read aloud as in *Schempp* and *Engel*, for "it is no defense to urge that the religious practices here may be relatively minor encroachments on the First Amendment."

NOTES AND QUESTIONS

1. *Religious purpose.* Does the state always have a religious purpose when it sponsors prayers or posts the Ten Commandments, both of which are inherently religious texts? What about Justice Brennan's argument that the government's true goals are religious when "it uses religious means to serve secular ends when secular means would suffice." Do you agree? If so, may the government ever use religious symbols?
2. *Religion not completely barred.* Americans often misunderstand the Establishment Clause limits on religion in school. One poll showed that 23% thought that public school teachers cannot read from the Bible as an

example of literature. Pew Research Center, U.S. Religious Knowledge Survey (2010). *Abington,* however, notes that "Nothing we have said here indicates that such study of the Bible or of religion, when presented objectively as part of a secular program of education" is unconstitutional. *Stone v. Graham* reiterates this sentiment, noting that "the Bible may be constitutionally used in an appropriate study of history, civilization, ethics, comparative religion, or the like."

3. *Coercion. Engel* is the first of many cases to hold that coercion is sufficient but not necessary for an Establishment Clause violation. Assuming every child were a willing and eager participant, in what way(s) would school-sponsored prayers still violate the Establishment Clause?
4. *Prayers as indirectly coercive. Engel* also concludes that, even though participation was optional, the recitation of the Regent's Prayer exerted "indirect coercive pressure" on students. What form does that pressure take? Is it fair to attribute that pressure to the government? Why did Schempp in *Abington* have his children participate in the religious exercises despite the fact that those exercises clashed with the family's religious beliefs?
5. *Hostility to religion?* Does barring school-sponsored recitation of the Regent's prayer or the Lord's Prayer indicate hostility to religion? Does it not favor nonreligion over religion, and endorse "a religion of secularism"? What might a devout Buddhist say? What type of prayer would avoid the problem of favoring some religions over others? Is it possible to construct a prayer that would satisfy all religions?

AN EXTENDED NOTE ON THE CONSTITUTIONAL STATUS OF "MOMENT OF SILENCE" REQUIREMENTS IN THE PUBLIC SCHOOLS

Both *Engel* and *Schempp* involved spoken and explicitly religious exercises in the public school classroom. In *Engel,* the state actually wrote the prayer; in *Schempp,* students chose the prayers, but the state assembled the captive audience of students to listen to the prayers. What would be the result, however, if the state did nothing more than assemble the students in a classroom and require them to remain silent for a brief period, during which many of the students individually decided to pray? In Wallace v. Jaffree, 472 U.S. 38 (1985), the Supreme Court struck down an Alabama statute that authorized teachers in public school classrooms to announce "that a period of silence not to exceed one minute in duration shall be observed for meditation or voluntary prayer." The ground for the Court's decision, however, was fairly narrow. The Court ruled that the Alabama Legislature passed the statute in question with impermissible religious motives, thereby violating the first part of the three-part *Lemon* test, which requires that all statutes must have a secular purpose. When Alabama passed the statute, it already had on its books another statute requiring that in every public school classroom "a period of silence, not to exceed one minute in duration, shall be observed for meditation." (This earlier statute was not challenged by the plaintiffs in *Wallace,* and the Court did not rule on its constitutionality.) The Court held that the only plausible reason the legislature passed a second statute requiring a moment of silent meditation and mentioning "voluntary prayer" was "for the sole purpose of expressing the State's endorsement of prayer activities for one minute at the beginning of each school day."

The open question after *Wallace* is whether a "clean" silent meditation statute—that is, one that did not implicitly or explicitly endorse prayer—would pass constitutional muster. In her concurring opinion to *Wallace,* Justice O'Connor asserted that it would:

> A state-sponsored moment of silence in the public schools is different from state-sponsored vocal prayer or Bible reading. First, a moment of silence is not inherently religious. Silence, unlike prayer or Bible reading, need not be associated with a religious exercise. Second, a pupil who participates in a moment of silence need not compromise his or her beliefs. During a moment of silence, a student who objects to prayer is left to his or her own thoughts, and is not compelled to listen to the prayers or thoughts of others. For these simple reasons, a moment of silence statute does not stand or fall under the Establishment Clause according to how the Court regards vocal prayer or Bible reading. . . . It is difficult to discern a serious threat to religious liberty from a room of silent, thoughtful schoolchildren.

The lower courts that have considered the matter have tended to agree with Justice O'Connor's assessment. *See* Brown v. Gilmore, 258 F.3d 265 (4th Cir.), *cert. denied,* 534 U.S. 996 (2001) (upholding a Virginia statute mandating a "minute of silence" in the state's public schools); Bown v. Gwinnett County Sch. Dist., 112 F.3d 1464 (11th Cir. 1997) (upholding a Georgia state statute requiring one minute of silent reflection in the state's public school classrooms). *But see* May v. Cooperman, 780 F.2d 240 (3d Cir. 1985) (holding that a New Jersey statute requiring students in public schools to observe a one-minute period of silence at the beginning of each school day lacked a secular purpose and was therefore unconstitutional). *See also* Holloman v. Harland, 370 F.3d 1252 (11th Cir. 2004) (holding unconstitutional an individual public school teacher's practice of enforcing a moment of silence at the beginning of the school day and soliciting prayer requests from students as a means of indicating that the moment of silence was regarded as a religious activity).

In the absence of "smoking gun" evidence that a state legislature or local school board has adopted a moment of silence policy to encourage or facilitate school prayer, should this practice be deemed invalid on Establishment Clause grounds? Or is the Establishment Clause objection primarily related to the practice of organized, official religious observances in the public schools? For one perspective, see Eric J. Segall, *Mired in the* Marsh: *Legislative Prayers, Moments of Silence, and the Establishment Clause,* 63 U. Miami L. Rev. 713, 738 (2009) (arguing that "starting each day with a moment of silent reflection allows each person to use that time in a way that most benefits his or her conscience without infringing on the rights of others" and that "unlike the case with school prayer, even if the intent behind the moment is to encourage prayer, as long as there was no direct coercion, there probably would not be a constitutional violation").

On the other hand, could a public school district purport to ban all voluntary prayer or religious observances on school property? Would such a policy be consistent with general free speech principles? Moreover, what bearing might the Free Exercise Clause, addressed *supra* in Chapter 14, have on this question? Do these considerations suggest that a moment of silence—without the presence of organized prayer by school officials or teachers—should be no more objectionable than recess periods, lunch breaks, and study halls (that is, times during the school day when students presumably can and sometimes do pray)? Or is a moment of silence clearly distinguishable, on its face, from a recess period, a lunch break, or a study hall?

Lee v. Weisman

505 U.S. 577 (1992)

Justice Kennedy delivered the opinion of the Court.

School principals in the public school system of the city of Providence, Rhode Island, are permitted to invite members of the clergy to offer invocation and benediction prayers as part of the formal graduation ceremonies for middle schools and for high schools. The question before us is whether including clerical members who offer prayers as part of the official school graduation ceremony is consistent with the Religion Clauses of the First Amendment, provisions the Fourteenth Amendment makes applicable with full force to the States and their school districts.

Deborah Weisman graduated from Nathan Bishop Middle School, a public school in Providence, at a formal ceremony in June 1989. She was about 14 years old. For many years it has been the policy of the Providence School Committee and the Superintendent of Schools to permit principals to invite members of the clergy to give invocations and benedictions at middle school and high school graduations.

It has been the custom of Providence school officials to provide invited clergy with a pamphlet entitled "Guidelines for Civic Occasions," prepared by the National Conference of Christians and Jews. The Guidelines recommend that public prayers at nonsectarian civic ceremonies be composed with "inclusiveness and sensitivity." . . . The principal gave Rabbi Gutterman the pamphlet before the graduation and advised him the invocation and benediction should be nonsectarian. Agreed Statement of Facts ¶17, *id.*, at 13. . . .

. . . It is beyond dispute that, at a minimum, the Constitution guarantees that government may not coerce anyone to support or participate in religion or its exercise, or otherwise act in a way which "establishes a [state] religion or religious faith, or tends to do so." *Lynch, supra*, at 678. The State's involvement in the school prayers challenged today violates these central principles.

That involvement is as troubling as it is undenied. A school official, the principal, decided that an invocation and a benediction should be given; this is a choice attributable to the State, and from a constitutional perspective it is as if a state statute decreed that the prayers must occur. The principal chose the religious participant, here a rabbi, and that choice is also attributable to the State.

The State's role did not end with the decision to include a prayer and with the choice of a clergyman. Principal Lee provided Rabbi Gutterman with a copy of the "Guidelines for Civic Occasions," and advised him that his prayers should be nonsectarian. Through these means the principal directed and controlled the content of the prayers. Even if the only sanction for ignoring the instructions were that the rabbi would not be invited back, we think no religious representative who valued his or her continued reputation and effectiveness in the community would incur the State's displeasure in this regard. It is a cornerstone principle of our

Establishment Clause jurisprudence that "it is no part of the business of government to compose official prayers for any group of the American people to recite as a part of a religious program carried on by government," *Engel v. Vitale*, 370 U.S. 421, 425 (1962), and that is what the school officials attempted to do.

Petitioners argue, and we find nothing in the case to refute it, that the directions for the content of the prayers were a good-faith attempt by the school to ensure that the sectarianism which is so often the flashpoint for religious animosity be removed from the graduation ceremony.

It must not be forgotten then, that while concern must be given to define the protection granted to an objector or a dissenting nonbeliever, these same Clauses exist to protect religion from government interference. James Madison, the principal author of the Bill of Rights, did not rest his opposition to a religious establishment on the sole ground of its effect on the minority. A principal ground for his view was: "[E]xperience witnesseth that ecclesiastical establishments, instead of maintaining the purity and efficacy of Religion, have had a contrary operation." Memorial and Remonstrance Against Religious Assessments (1785).

. . . The degree of school involvement here made it clear that the graduation prayers bore the imprint of the State and thus put school-age children who objected in an untenable position. We turn our attention now to consider the position of the students, both those who desired the prayer and she who did not. . . .

The lessons of the First Amendment are as urgent in the modern world as in the 18th century when it was written. One timeless lesson is that if citizens are subjected to state-sponsored religious exercises, the State disavows its own duty to guard and respect that sphere of inviolable conscience and belief which is the mark of a free people. To compromise that principle today would be to deny our own tradition and forfeit our standing to urge others to secure the protections of that tradition for themselves.

As we have observed before, there are heightened concerns with protecting freedom of conscience from subtle coercive pressure in the elementary and secondary public schools. Our decisions in Engel v. Vitale, 370 U.S. 421 (1962), and *School Dist. of Abington, supra*, recognize, among other things, that prayer exercises in public schools carry a particular risk of indirect coercion. The concern may not be limited to the context of schools, but it is most pronounced there. What to most believers may seem nothing more than a reasonable request that the nonbeliever respect their religious practices, in a school context may appear to the nonbeliever or dissenter to be an attempt to employ the machinery of the State to enforce a religious orthodoxy.

We need not look beyond the circumstances of this case to see the phenomenon at work. The undeniable fact is that the school district's supervision and control of a high school graduation ceremony places public pressure, as well as peer pressure, on attending students to stand as a group or, at least, maintain respectful silence during the invocation and benediction. This pressure, though subtle and indirect, can be as real as any overt compulsion. Of course, in our culture standing or remaining silent can signify adherence to a view or simple respect for the views of others. And no doubt some persons who have no desire to join a prayer have little objection to standing as a sign of respect for those who do. But for the dissenter of high school age, who has a reasonable perception that she is being forced by the

State to pray in a manner her conscience will not allow, the injury is no less real. There can be no doubt that for many, if not most, of the students at the graduation, the act of standing or remaining silent was an expression of participation in the rabbi's prayer. That was the very point of the religious exercise. It is of little comfort to a dissenter, then, to be told that for her the act of standing or remaining in silence signifies mere respect, rather than participation. What matters is that, given our social conventions, a reasonable dissenter in this milieu could believe that the group exercise signified her own participation or approval of it.

Finding no violation under these circumstances would place objectors in the dilemma of participating, with all that implies, or protesting. We do not address whether that choice is acceptable if the affected citizens are mature adults, but we think the State may not, consistent with the Establishment Clause, place primary and secondary school children in this position. Research in psychology supports the common assumption that adolescents are often susceptible to pressure from their peers towards conformity, and that the influence is strongest in matters of social convention. To recognize that the choice imposed by the State constitutes an unacceptable constraint only acknowledges that the government may no more use social pressure to enforce orthodoxy than it may use more direct means.

The injury caused by the government's action, and the reason why Daniel and Deborah Weisman object to it, is that the State, in a school setting, in effect required participation in a religious exercise. It is, we concede, a brief exercise during which the individual can concentrate on joining its message, meditate on her own religion, or let her mind wander. But the embarrassment and the intrusion of the religious exercise cannot be refuted by arguing that these prayers, and similar ones to be said in the future, are of a *de minimis* character. To do so would be an affront to the rabbi who offered them and to all those for whom the prayers were an essential and profound recognition of divine authority. And for the same reason, we think that the intrusion is greater than the two minutes or so of time consumed for prayers like these. Assuming, as we must, that the prayers were offensive to the student and the parent who now object, the intrusion was both real and, in the context of a secondary school, a violation of the objectors' rights. That the intrusion was in the course of promulgating religion that sought to be civic or nonsectarian rather than pertaining to one sect does not lessen the offense or isolation to the objectors. At best it narrows their number, at worst increases their sense of isolation and affront. *See supra*, at 2658.

There was a stipulation in the District Court that attendance at graduation and promotional ceremonies is voluntary. Petitioners and the United States, as *amicus*, made this a center point of the case, arguing that the option of not attending the graduation excuses any inducement or coercion in the ceremony itself. The argument lacks all persuasion. Law reaches past formalism. And to say a teenage student has a real choice not to attend her high school graduation is formalistic in the extreme. True, Deborah could elect not to attend commencement without renouncing her diploma; but we shall not allow the case to turn on this point. Everyone knows that in our society and in our culture high school graduation is one of life's most significant occasions. . . .

The importance of the event is the point the school district and the United States rely upon to argue that a formal prayer ought to be permitted, but it becomes one of the principal reasons why their argument must fail. Their contention, one of considerable force were it not for the constitutional constraints applied to state action, is that the prayers are an essential part of these ceremonies because for many persons an occasion of this significance lacks meaning if there is no recognition, however brief, that human achievements cannot be understood apart from their spiritual essence. We think the Government's position that this interest suffices to force students to choose between compliance or forfeiture demonstrates fundamental inconsistency in its argumentation. It fails to acknowledge that what for many of Deborah's classmates and their parents was a spiritual imperative was for Daniel and Deborah Weisman religious conformance compelled by the State. While in some societies the wishes of the majority might prevail, the Establishment Clause of the First Amendment is addressed to this contingency and rejects the balance urged upon us. The Constitution forbids the State to exact religious conformity from a student as the price of attending her own high school graduation. This is the calculus the Constitution commands. . . . It is a tenet of the First Amendment that the State cannot require one of its citizens to forfeit his or her rights and benefits as the price of resisting conformance to state-sponsored religious practice. . . .

We do not hold that every state action implicating religion is invalid if one or a few citizens find it offensive. People may take offense at all manner of religious as well as nonreligious messages, but offense alone does not in every case show a violation. We know too that sometimes to endure social isolation or even anger may be the price of conscience or nonconformity. But, by any reading of our cases, the conformity required of the student in this case was too high an exaction to withstand the test of the Establishment Clause. The prayer exercises in this case are especially improper because the State has in every practical sense compelled attendance and participation in an explicit religious exercise at an event of singular importance to every student, one the objecting student had no real alternative to avoid.

For the reasons we have stated, the judgment of the Court of Appeals is

Affirmed.

Justice Blackmun, with whom Justices Stevens and O'Connor join, concurring.

[I]t is not enough that the government restrain from compelling religious practices: It must not engage in them either. The Court repeatedly has recognized that a violation of the Establishment Clause is not predicated on coercion. The Establishment Clause proscribes public schools from "conveying or attempting to convey a message that religion or a particular religious belief is favored or preferred," even if the schools do not actually "impos[e] pressure upon a student to participate in a religious activity."

When the government puts its imprimatur on a particular religion, it conveys a message of exclusion to all those who do not adhere to the favored beliefs. A government cannot be premised on the belief that all persons are created equal when it asserts that God prefers some.

Justice Souter, with whom Justice Stevens and O'Connor join, concurring.

Over the years, this Court has declared the invalidity of many noncoercive state laws and practices conveying a message of religious endorsement. For example, in *County of Allegheny, supra,* we forbade the prominent display of a nativity scene on public property; without contesting the dissent's observation that the créche coerced no one into accepting or supporting whatever message it proclaimed, five

Members of the Court found its display unconstitutional as a state endorsement of Christianity. Likewise, in Wallace v. Jaffree, 472 U.S. 38 (1985), we struck down a state law requiring a moment of silence in public classrooms not because the statute coerced students to participate in prayer (for it did not), but because the manner of its enactment "convey[ed] a message of state approval of prayer activities in the public schools." *Id.*, at 61. In Epperson v. Arkansas, 393 U.S. 97 (1968), we invalidated a state law that barred the teaching of Darwin's theory of evolution because, even though the statute obviously did not coerce anyone to support religion or participate in any religious practice, it was enacted for a singularly religious purpose. *See also* Edwards v. Aguillard, 482 U.S. 578, 593 (1987). Our precedents may not always have drawn perfectly straight lines. They simply cannot, however, support the position that a showing of coercion is necessary to a successful Establishment Clause claim.

. . . While petitioners insist that the prohibition extends only to the "coercive" features and incidents of establishment, they cannot easily square that claim with the constitutional text. The First Amendment forbids not just laws "respecting an establishment of religion," but also those "prohibiting the free exercise thereof." Yet laws that coerce nonadherents to "support or participate in any religion or its exercise," would virtually by definition violate their right to religious free exercise. Thus, a literal application of the coercion test would render the Establishment Clause a virtual nullity.

Justice SCALIA, with whom THE CHIEF JUSTICE, Justice WHITE, and Justice THOMAS, join, dissenting.

In holding that the Establishment Clause prohibits invocations and benedictions at public-school graduation ceremonies, the Court—with nary a mention that it is doing so—lays waste a tradition that is as old as public-school graduation ceremonies themselves, and that is a component of an even more longstanding American tradition of nonsectarian prayer to God at public celebrations generally. As its instrument of destruction, the bulldozer of its social engineering, the Court invents a boundless, and boundlessly manipulable, test of psychological coercion. Today's opinion shows more forcefully than volumes of argumentation why our Nation's protection, that fortress which is our Constitution, cannot possibly rest upon the changeable philosophical predilections of the Justices of this Court, but must have deep foundations in the historic practices of our people.

The Court presumably would separate graduation invocations and benedictions from other instances of public "preservation and transmission of religious beliefs" on the ground that they involve "psychological coercion." I find it a sufficient embarrassment that our Establishment Clause jurisprudence regarding holiday displays, see *County of Allegheny*, has come to "requir[e] scrutiny more commonly associated with interior decorators than with the judiciary." American Jewish Congress v. Chicago, 827 F.2d 120, 129 (CA7 1987) (Easterbrook, J., dissenting). But interior decorating is a rock-hard science compared to psychology practiced by amateurs. A few citations of "[r]esearch in psychology" that have no particular bearing upon the precise issue here cannot disguise the fact that the Court has gone beyond the realm where judges know what they are doing. The Court's argument that state officials have "coerced" students to take part in the invocation and benediction at graduation ceremonies is, not to put too fine a point on it, incoherent.

The Court declares that students' "attendance and participation in the [invocation and benediction] are in a fair and real sense obligatory." But what exactly is this "fair and real sense"? According to the Court, students at graduation who want "to avoid the fact or appearance of participation" in the invocation and benediction are *psychologically* obligated by "public pressure, as well as peer pressure. . . . to stand as a group or, at least, maintain respectful silence" during those prayers. This assertion—*the very linchpin of the Court's opinion*— is almost as intriguing for what it does not say as for what it says. It does not say, for example, that students are psychologically coerced to bow their heads, place their hands in a Dürer-like prayer position, pay attention to the prayers, utter "Amen," or in fact pray. (Perhaps further intensive psychological research remains to be done on these matters.) It claims only that students are psychologically coerced "to stand . . . *or*, at least, maintain respectful silence." . . .

The deeper flaw in the Court's opinion does not lie in its wrong answer to the question whether there was state-induced "peer-pressure" coercion; it lies, rather, in the Court's making violation of the Establishment Clause hinge on such a precious question. The coercion that was a hallmark of historical establishments of religion was coercion of religious orthodoxy and of financial support *by force of law and threat of penalty*. Typically, attendance at the state church was required; only clergy of the official church could lawfully perform sacraments; and dissenters, if tolerated, faced an array of civil disabilities. Thus, for example, in the Colony of Virginia, where the Church of England had been established, ministers were required by law to conform to the doctrine and rites of the Church of England; and all persons were required to attend church and observe the Sabbath, were tithed for the public support of Anglican ministers, and were taxed for the costs of building and repairing churches.

The Establishment Clause was adopted to prohibit such an establishment of religion at the federal level (and to protect state establishments of religion from federal interference). I will further acknowledge for the sake of argument that, as some scholars have argued, by 1790 the term "establishment" had acquired an additional meaning—"financial support of religion generally, by public taxation"—that reflected the development of "general or multiple" establishments, not limited to a single church. But that would still be an establishment coerced *by force of law*. And I will further concede that our constitutional tradition, from the Declaration of Independence and the first inaugural address of Washington, quoted earlier, down to the present day, has, with a few aberrations, ruled out of order government-sponsored endorsement of religion—even when no legal coercion is present, and indeed even when no ersatz, "peer-pressure" psycho-coercion is present—where the endorsement is sectarian, in the sense of specifying details upon which men and women who believe in a benevolent, omnipotent Creator and Ruler of the world are known to differ (for example, the divinity of Christ). But there is simply no support for the proposition that the officially sponsored nondenominational invocation and benediction read by Rabbi Gutterman—with no one legally coerced to recite them—violated the Constitution of the United States. To the contrary, they are so characteristically American they could have come from the pen of George Washington or Abraham Lincoln himself.

The reader has been told much in this case about the personal interest of Mr. Weisman and his daughter, and very little about the personal interests on the other side. They are not inconsequential. Church and state would not be such a difficult subject if religion were, as the Court apparently thinks it to be, some purely personal avocation that can be indulged entirely in secret, like pornography, in the privacy of one's room. For most believers it is *not* that, and has never been. Religious men and women of almost all denominations have felt it necessary to acknowledge and beseech the blessing of God as a people, and not just as individuals, because they believe in the "protection of divine Providence," as the Declaration of Independence put it, not just for individuals but for societies; because they believe God to be, as Washington's first Thanksgiving Proclamation put it, the "Great Lord and Ruler of Nations." One can believe in the effectiveness of such public worship, or one can deprecate and deride it. But the longstanding American tradition of prayer at official ceremonies displays with unmistakable clarity that the Establishment Clause does not forbid the government to accommodate it.

The narrow context of the present case involves a community's celebration of one of the milestones in its young citizens' lives, and it is a bold step for this Court to seek to banish from that occasion, and from thousands of similar celebrations throughout this land, the expression of gratitude to God that a majority of the community wishes to make. The issue before us today is not the abstract philosophical question whether the alternative of frustrating this desire of a religious majority is to be preferred over the alternative of imposing "psychological coercion," or a feeling of exclusion, upon nonbelievers. Rather, the question is *whether a mandatory choice in favor of the former has been imposed by the United States Constitution.* As the age-old practices of our people show, the answer to that question is not at all in doubt.

I must add one final observation: The Founders of our Republic knew the fearsome potential of sectarian religious belief to generate civil dissension and civil strife. And they also knew that nothing, absolutely nothing, is so inclined to foster among religious believers of various faiths a toleration—no, an affection—for one another than voluntarily joining in prayer together, to the God whom they all worship and seek. Needless to say, no one should be compelled to do that, but it is a shame to deprive our public culture of the opportunity, and indeed the encouragement, for people to do it voluntarily. The Baptist or Catholic who heard and joined in the simple and inspiring prayers of Rabbi Gutterman on this official and patriotic occasion was inoculated from religious bigotry and prejudice in a manner that cannot be replicated. To deprive our society of that important unifying mechanism, in order to spare the nonbeliever what seems to me the minimal inconvenience of standing or even sitting in respectful nonparticipation, is as senseless in policy as it is unsupported in law.

For the foregoing reasons, I dissent.

Santa Fe Independent School District v. Doe

530 U.S. 290 (2000)

Justice STEVENS delivered the opinion of the Court.

[Prior to 1995, the Santa Fe High School student who occupied the school's elective office of student council chaplain delivered a prayer over the public address system before each varsity football game for the entire season. This practice, along with others, was challenged in District Court as a violation of the Establishment Clause of the First Amendment. Because of their fear of retaliation, the plaintiffs sued under a "John Doe" pseudonym. (This practice is not uncommon in Establishment Clause cases, and is discussed in more detail in the notes after this case.) While proceedings against the original prayer policy were pending in the District Court, the school district adopted a different policy that permitted, but did not require, prayer initiated and led by a student at all home games. The District Court entered an order modifying that policy to permit only nonsectarian, nonproselytizing prayer. The Court of Appeals held that, even as modified by the District Court, the football prayer policy was invalid.]

We granted the District's petition for certiorari, limited to the following question: "Whether petitioner's policy permitting student-led, student-initiated prayer at football games violates the Establishment Clause." We conclude, as did the Court of Appeals, that it does. . . .

The actual or perceived endorsement of the message . . . is established by factors beyond just the text of the policy. Once the student speaker is selected and the message composed, the invocation is then delivered to a large audience assembled as part of a regularly scheduled, school-sponsored function conducted on school property. The message is broadcast over the school's public address system, which remains subject to the control of school officials. It is fair to assume that the pregame ceremony is clothed in the traditional indicia of school sporting events, which generally include not just the team, but also cheerleaders and band members dressed in uniforms sporting the school name and mascot. The school's name is likely written in large print across the field and on banners and flags. The crowd will certainly include many who display the school colors and insignia on their school T-shirts, jackets, or hats and who may also be waving signs displaying the school name. It is in a setting such as this that "[t]he board has chosen to permit" the elected student to rise and give the "statement or invocation."

Regardless of the listener's support for, or objection to, the message, an objective Santa Fe High School student will unquestionably perceive the inevitable pregame prayer as stamped with her school's seal of approval.

The text and history of this policy, moreover, reinforce our objective student's perception that the prayer is, in actuality, encouraged by the school. When a governmental entity professes a secular purpose for an arguably religious policy, the government's characterization is, of course, entitled to some deference. But it is nonetheless the duty of the courts to "distinguis[h] a sham secular purpose from a sincere one."

According to the District, the secular purposes of the policy are to "foste[r] free expression of private persons . . . as well [as to] solemniz[e] sporting events, promot[e] good sportsmanship and student safety, and establis[h] an appropriate environment for competition." We note, however, that the District's approval of only one specific kind of message, an "invocation," is not necessary to further any of these purposes. Additionally, the fact that only one student is permitted to give a content-limited message suggests that this policy does little to "foste[r] free expression." Furthermore, regardless of whether one considers a sporting event an appropriate occasion for solemnity, the use of an invocation to foster such solemnity is impermissible when, in actuality, it constitutes prayer sponsored by the school. And it is unclear what type of message would be both appropriately "solemnizing" under the District's policy and yet nonreligious.

Most striking to us is the evolution of the current policy from the long-sanctioned office of "Student Chaplain" to the candidly titled "Prayer at Football Games" regulation. This history indicates that the District intended to preserve the practice of prayer before football games.

The District further argues that attendance at the commencement ceremonies at issue in *Lee* "differs dramatically" from attendance at high school football games, which it contends "are of no more than passing interest to many students" and are "decidedly extracurricular," thus dissipating any coercion. Attendance at a high school football game, unlike showing up for class, is certainly not required in order to receive a diploma. Moreover, we may assume that the District is correct in arguing that the informal pressure to attend an athletic event is not as strong as a senior's desire to attend her own graduation ceremony.

There are some students, however, such as cheerleaders, members of the band, and, of course, the team members themselves, for whom seasonal commitments mandate their attendance, sometimes for class credit. The District also minimizes the importance to many students of attending and participating in extracurricular activities as part of a complete educational experience. As we noted in *Lee*, "[l]aw reaches past formalism." To assert that high school students do not feel immense social pressure, or have a truly genuine desire, to be involved in the extracurricular event that is American high school football is "formalistic in the extreme." We stressed in *Lee* the obvious observation that "adolescents are often susceptible to pressure from their peers towards conformity, and that the influence is strongest in matters of social convention." High school home football games are traditional gatherings of a school community; they bring together students and faculty as well as friends and family from years present and past to root for a common cause. Undoubtedly, the games are not important to some students, and they voluntarily choose not to attend. For many others, however, the choice between whether to attend these games or to risk facing a personally offensive religious ritual is in no practical sense an easy one. The Constitution, moreover, demands that the school may not force this difficult choice upon these students for "[i]t is a tenet of the First Amendment that the State cannot require one of its citizens to forfeit his or her rights and benefits as the price of resisting conformance to state-sponsored religious practice."

Chief Justice REHNQUIST, with whom Justice SCALIA and Justice THOMAS join, dissenting.

The Court distorts existing precedent to conclude that the school district's student-message program is invalid on its face under the Establishment Clause. But even more disturbing than its holding is the tone of the Court's opinion; it bristles with hostility to all things religious in public life. Neither the holding nor the tone of the opinion is faithful to the meaning of the Establishment Clause, when it is recalled that George Washington himself, at the request of the very Congress which passed the Bill of Rights, proclaimed a day of "public thanksgiving and prayer, to be observed by acknowledging with grateful hearts the many and signal favors of Almighty God." [The Chief Justice then devoted much of his dissent to the argument that the majority should not have permitted a facial challenge to the policy, but rather should have waited until the policy was put into practice.] Had the policy been put into practice, the students may have chosen a speaker according to wholly secular criteria—like good public speaking skills or social popularity—and the student speaker may have chosen, on her own accord, to deliver a religious message. Such an application of the policy would likely pass constitutional muster.

NOTES AND QUESTIONS

1. *Attributable to the state.* Unlike the earlier school prayers cases, the prayers in *Lee* and *Santa Fe* were given by private individuals. Nonetheless, in both cases the Court held that the prayers were still attributable to the government. What features allowed the Court to reach this conclusion?
2. *Religious purpose.* Do you agree with the Court in *Santa Fe* that the purpose of the school's policy allowing a student speaker at football games was to encourage prayers? Why or why not?
3. *Coercion: mandatory attendance.* According to the *Lee* decision, one factor contributing to the coerciveness of graduation prayers was that students' presence at graduation was not voluntary. While strictly speaking students were not required to attend, "law reaches beyond formalism." Is it more accurate to describe attendance as valued rather than mandatory, so that the issue is not so much that students must attend but that student should not have to forgo attendance? Would the prayers be constitutional if attendance were purely voluntary? Also, how would you characterize attendance at school football games?
4. *Coercion: social pressure.* Justice Kennedy held that the social and peer pressure at school graduation, "though subtle and indirect, can be as real as any overt compulsion." Are these types of subtle and indirect pressures as coercive as those backed by the force of law? Whether as real or not, they are surely harder to measure. Is the test "incoherent," as Justice Scalia accuses?
5. *Necessary and legal coercion.* Justice Scalia suggests that legal coercion is necessary to violate the Establishment Clause, at least in this case. Would this interpretation render the Establishment Clause a "virtual nullity" as Justice Souter contends? If this narrow version of the Establishment Clause controlled, what would it actually prevent the government from doing? Could the government require public school teachers to lead their classes in officially sanctioned daily prayers, so long as dissenting students are not sanctioned for refusing to participate? *See Engel v. Vitale.* Could a state declare that Christianity, or the Abrahamic tradition, was the official state religion? How would such a proclamation differ from the state declaring that the cello was the official state musical instrument or that Caucasian was the official state race?
6. *Anonymous litigation in Establishment Clause cases.* Cases involving school prayer raise passions like few other Establishment Clause disputes. The risks of retaliation against Establishment Clause plaintiffs in these cases are often quite serious—especially in religiously homogeneous communities in which the plaintiffs are in a distinct minority. Two families litigated *Santa Fe.* One family was Mormon and the other was Catholic. Note that they litigated the case under a "John Doe" alias. In Justice Stevens's majority opinion in *Santa Fe,* he notes that the District Court entered the anonymity order to protect the Does from intimidation and harassment.

The fear of harassment was well founded. Stevens quotes the Fifth Circuit's conclusion that the decision to permit the plaintiffs to litigate anonymously was one that the school officials "apparently neither agreed with nor particularly respected." Stevens also quotes the order that the District Court was forced to enter a month after the complaint was filed:

> [A]ny further attempt on the part of District or school administration, officials, counsellors, teachers, employees or servants of the School District, parents, students or anyone else, overtly or covertly to ferret out the identities of the Plaintiffs in this cause, by means of bogus petitions, questionnaires, individual interrogation, or downright "snooping," will cease immediately. ANYONE TAKING ANY ACTION ON SCHOOL PROPERTY, DURING SCHOOL HOURS, OR WITH SCHOOL RESOURCES OR APPROVAL FOR PURPOSES OF ATTEMPTING TO ELICIT THE NAMES OR IDENTITIES OF THE PLAINTIFFS IN THIS CAUSE OF ACTION, BY OR ON BEHALF OF ANY OF THESE INDIVIDUALS, WILL FACE THE HARSHEST POSSIBLE CONTEMPT SANCTIONS FROM THIS COURT, AND MAY ADDITIONALLY FACE CRIMINAL LIABILITY. The Court wants these proceedings addressed on their merits, and not on the basis of intimidation or harassment of the participants on either side.

Santa Fe, 530 U.S. at 294 n.1 (emphasis in original). For other cases discussing the need to sue pseudonymously in religious rights cases, see Doe v. Stegall, 653 F.2d 180 (5th Cir. 1981); Doe v. Harlan County Sch. Dist., 96 F. Supp. 2d 667 (E.D. Ky. 2000).

7. *School prayer in the university context.* All of the school prayer cases considered by the Supreme Court have involved public schools below the university level. At the lower court level, courts have been equally vigilant in restricting the direct infusion of religion into public university classrooms, although a few courts have been somewhat more lenient with regard to religious exercises at university graduation ceremonies. Should there be a distinction between college and university students, on the one hand, and K through 12 students, on the other?

B. *GOVERNMENT ENDORSEMENT OF RELIGION IN THE PUBLIC SCHOOLS: RELIGION IN THE PUBLIC SCHOOL CURRICULUM*

Epperson v. Arkansas

393 U.S. 97 (1968)

Mr. Justice FORTAS delivered the opinion of the Court.

This appeal challenges the constitutionality of the "anti-evolution" statute which the State of Arkansas adopted in 1928 to prohibit the teaching in its public schools and universities of the theory that man evolved from other species of life. The statute was a product of the upsurge of "fundamentalist" religious fervor of the twenties. The Arkansas statute was an adaptation of the famous Tennessee "monkey law" which that State adopted in 1925. The constitutionality of the Tennessee law was upheld by the Tennessee Supreme Court in the celebrated *Scopes* case in 1927.[2]

The Arkansas law makes it unlawful for a teacher in any state-supported school or university "to teach the theory or doctrine that mankind ascended or descended from a lower order of animals," or "to adopt or use in any such institution a textbook that teaches" this theory. Violation is a misdemeanor and subjects the violator to dismissal from his position.

The present case concerns the teaching of biology in a high school in Little Rock. According to the testimony, until the events here in litigation, the official textbook furnished for the high school biology course did not have a section on the Darwinian Theory. Then, for the academic year 1965-1966, the school administration, on recommendation of the teachers of biology in the school system, adopted and prescribed a textbook which contained a chapter setting forth "the theory about the origin . . . of man from a lower form of animal."

Susan Epperson, a young woman who graduated from Arkansas' school system and then obtained her master's degree in zoology at the University of Illinois, was employed by the Little Rock school system in the fall of 1964 to teach 10th grade biology at Central High School. At the start of the next academic year, 1965, she was confronted by the new textbook (which one surmises from the record was not unwelcome to her). She faced at least a literal dilemma because she was supposed to use the new textbook for classroom instruction and presumably to teach the statutorily condemned chapter; but to do so would be a criminal offense and subject her to dismissal.

She instituted the present action in the Chancery Court of the State, seeking a declaration that the Arkansas statute is void and enjoining the State and the defendant officials of the Little Rock school system from dismissing her for violation of the statute's provisions. H. H. Blanchard, a parent of children attending the public schools, intervened in support of the action.

[The Chancery Court held that the statute violated the Fourteenth Amendment to the United States Constitution. On appeal, the Supreme Court of Arkansas reversed. In a two-sentence opinion, it sustained the statute as an exercise of the State's power to specify the curriculum in public schools. It did not address itself to the competing constitutional considerations.]

We do not rest our decision upon the asserted vagueness of the statute. On either interpretation of its language, Arkansas' statute cannot stand. It is of no moment whether the law is deemed to prohibit mention of Darwin's theory, or to forbid any or all of the infinite varieties of communication embraced within the

---

2. Scopes v. State, 154 Tenn. 105, 289 S.W. 363 (1927). The Tennessee court, however, reversed Scopes' conviction on the ground that the jury and not the judge should have assessed the fine of $100. Since Scopes was no longer in the State's employ, it saw "nothing to be gained by prolonging the life of this bizarre case." It directed that a *nolle prosequi* be entered, in the interests of "the peace and dignity of the state." 154 Tenn., at 121, 289 S.W., at 367.

term "teaching." Under either interpretation, the law must be stricken because of its conflict with the constitutional prohibition of state laws respecting an establishment of religion or prohibiting the free exercise thereof. The overriding fact is that Arkansas' law selects from the body of knowledge a particular segment which it proscribes for the sole reason that it is deemed to conflict with a particular religious doctrine; that is, with a particular interpretation of the Book of Genesis by a particular religious group.

Government in our democracy, state and national, must be neutral in matters of religious theory, doctrine, and practice.

As early as 1872, this Court said: "The law knows no heresy, and is committed to the support of no dogma, the establishment of no sect." Watson v. Jones, 13 Wall. 679, 728. There is and can be no doubt that the First Amendment does not permit the State to require that teaching and learning must be tailored to the principles or prohibitions of any religious sect or dogma.

In the present case, there can be no doubt that Arkansas has sought to prevent its teachers from discussing the theory of evolution because it is contrary to the belief of some that the Book of Genesis must be the exclusive source of doctrine as to the origin of man. No suggestion has been made that Arkansas' law may be justified by considerations of state policy other than the religious views of some of its citizens. It is clear that fundamentalist sectarian conviction was and is the law's reason for existence.[16]

Its antecedent, Tennessee's "monkey law," candidly stated its purpose: to make it unlawful "to teach any theory that denies the story of the Divine Creation of man as taught in the Bible, and to teach instead that man has descended from a lower order of animals."[17] Perhaps the sensational publicity attendant upon the *Scopes* trial induced Arkansas to adopt less explicit language.[18] It eliminated Tennessee's

---

16. The following advertisement is typical of the public appeal which was used in the campaign to secure adoption of the statute:

> **"THE BIBLE OR ATHEISM, WHICH?**
>
> "All atheists favor evolution. If you agree with atheism vote against Act No. 1. If you agree with the Bible vote for Act No. 1. . . . Shall conscientious church members be forced to pay taxes to support teachers to teach evolution which will undermine the faith of their children? The Gazette said Russian Bolshevists laughed at Tennessee. True, and that sort will laugh at Arkansas. Who cares? Vote FOR ACT NO. 1." The Arkansas Gazette, Little Rock, Nov. 4, 1928, p. 12, cols. 4-5.

Letters from the public expressed the fear that teaching of evolution would be "subversive of Christianity," *id.*, Oct. 24, 1928, p. 7, col. 2; *see also id.*, Nov. 4, 1928, p. 19, col. 4; and that it would cause school children "to disrespect the Bible," *id.*, Oct. 27, 1928, p. 15, col. 5. One letter read: "The cosmogony taught by (evolution) runs contrary to that of Moses and Jesus, and as such is nothing, if anything at all, but atheism. . . . Now let the mothers and fathers of our state that are trying to raise their children in the Christian faith arise in their might and vote for this anti-evolution bill that will take it out of our tax supported schools. When they have saved the children, they have saved the state." *Id.*, at cols. 4-5.

17. Arkansas' law was adopted by popular initiative in 1928, three years after Tennessee's law was enacted and one year after the Tennessee Supreme Court's decision in the *Scopes* case, *supra.*

18. In its brief, the State says that the Arkansas statute was passed with the holding of the *Scopes* case in mind. Brief for Appellee 1.

reference to "the story of the Divine Creation of man" as taught in the Bible, but there is no doubt that the motivation for the law was the same: to suppress the teaching of a theory which, it was thought, "denied" the divine creation of man.

Arkansas' law cannot be defended as an act of religious neutrality. Arkansas did not seek to excise from the curricula of its schools and universities all discussion of the origin of man. The law's effort was confined to an attempt to blot out a particular theory because of its supposed conflict with the Biblical account, literally read. Plainly, the law is contrary to the mandate of the First, and in violation of the Fourteenth, Amendment to the Constitution.

AN EXTENDED NOTE ON THE *SCOPES* TRIAL

For much of the last century, certain religious groups have resisted the exclusion of biblical theories of creation from public school science curricula. This resistance generated one of the more colorful and well-known constitutional battles: the Tennessee "monkey trial" of John Scopes, which is noted in a footnote to the *Epperson* decision. Scopes was a public school teacher in a small Tennessee town who was convicted of violating the Tennessee anti-evolution statute by teaching the theory of evolution in his high school science class. The Tennessee statute made it "unlawful for any teacher in any of the Universitis [*sic*], Normals and all other public schools of the State which are supported in whole or in part by the public school funds of the State, to teach any theory that denies the story of the Divine Creation of man as taught in the Bible, and to teach instead that man has descended from a lower order of animals." Act of Mar. 13, 1925, ch. 27, 1925 Tenn. Pub. Acts 50.

The Scopes trial brought the dispute between science and religion to center stage, complete with appearances by larger-than-life characters such as Clarence Darrow and William Jennings Bryan, and a running commentary by a third outsized figure in the form of H.L. Mencken. The popular memory of this battle is that science and sophisticated rationalism defeated ignorance and parochial sophistry. Much of this popular understanding is probably attributable to the Jerome Lawrence and Robert E. Lee play about the trial. *See* Jerome Lawrence & Robert E. Lee, *Inherit the Wind* (1955). This play was later made into a famous movie, with Spencer Tracy playing the role of the fictionalized Darrow character. For the background to the actual trial and the story of how the trial gradually achieved near-mythical status, see Edward J. Larson, *Summer for the Gods: The Scopes Trial and America's Continuing Debate Over Science and Religion* (1997). To the chagrin of modern opponents of evolution, Mencken's harsh judgment about Darrow's public humiliation of Bryan probably sums up much of the country's common understanding of the battle between evolution and creationism: "On the one side was bigotry, ignorance, hatred, superstition, every sort of blackness that the human mind is capable of. On the other side was sense. And sense achieved a great victory." H.L. Mencken, "Aftermath," in *The Impossible H.L. Mencken: A Selection of His Best Newspaper Stories* 611 (Marion Elizabeth Rodgers ed., 1991).

Contrary to popular perception, no federal court ever ruled on the constitutionality of the Scopes conviction. Scopes was convicted and fined $100 in state court for violating the Tennessee anti-evolution statute, and the Tennessee Supreme Court overturned this verdict on the ground that the jury, rather than the judge, had imposed the fine. Although the Tennessee Supreme Court reversed the verdict, it also expressed the view that the Tennessee statute did not constitute an establishment of religion in violation of either the federal or the state constitution. *See* Scopes v. State, 289 S.W. 363, 367 (Tenn. 1927) ("We are not able to see how the prohibition of teaching the theory that man has descended from a lower order of animals gives preference to any religious establishment or mode of worship. So far as we know, there is no religious establishment or organized body that has in its creed or confession of faith any article denying or affirming such a theory."). But having asserted the constitutionality of the Tennessee statute, the court avoided further embarrassment to the state by noting that "[w]e see nothing to be gained by prolonging the life of this bizarre case" and "suggested" that the Attorney General enter a nolle prosequi in the case. *Id.* Thus, in *Scopes* the constitutional issues were addressed only in dicta in the state court, and never even reached the United States Supreme Court. It would be another 40 years before the Supreme Court would finally review a Scopes-style creationism statute in *Epperson* and announce its determination that, contrary to the Tennessee court's dicta, the Establishment Clause of the United States Constitution does not permit states to prohibit the teaching of evolution in public schools.

Edwards v. Aguillard

482 U.S. 578 (1987)

Justice BRENNAN delivered the opinion of the Court.

The question for decision is whether Louisiana's "Balanced Treatment for Creation-Science and Evolution-Science in Public School Instruction" Act (Creationism Act) is facially invalid as violative of the Establishment Clause of the First Amendment.

The Creationism Act forbids the teaching of the theory of evolution in public schools unless accompanied by instruction in "creation science." No school is required to teach evolution or creation science. If either is taught, however, the other must also be taught. The theories of evolution and creation science are statutorily defined as "the scientific evidences for [creation or evolution] and inferences from those scientific evidences."

[T]he Act's stated purpose is to protect academic freedom. This phrase might, in common parlance, be understood as referring to enhancing the freedom of teachers to teach what they will. The Court of Appeals, however, correctly concluded that the Act was not designed to further that goal.[6] We find no merit in the State's argument that the "legislature may not [have] use[d] the terms 'academic freedom' in the correct legal sense. They might have [had] in mind, instead, a basic concept of fairness; teaching all of the evidence." Even if "academic freedom" is read to mean "teaching all of the evidence" with respect to the origin of human beings, the Act does not further this purpose. The goal of providing a more comprehensive science curriculum is not furthered either by outlawing the teaching of evolution or by requiring the teaching of creation science.

---

6. The Act actually serves to diminish academic freedom by removing the flexibility to teach evolution without also teaching creation science, even if teachers determine that such curriculum results in less effective and comprehensive science instruction.

While the Court is normally deferential to a State's articulation of a secular purpose, it is required that the statement of such purpose be sincere and not a sham.

It is clear from the legislative history that the purpose of the legislative sponsor, Senator Bill Keith, was to narrow the science curriculum. During the legislative hearings, Senator Keith stated: "My preference would be that neither [creationism nor evolution] be taught." Such a ban on teaching does not promote—indeed, it undermines—the provision of a comprehensive scientific education.

It is equally clear that requiring schools to teach creation science with evolution does not advance academic freedom. The Act does not grant teachers a flexibility that they did not already possess to supplant the present science curriculum with the presentation of theories, besides evolution, about the origin of life. Indeed, the Court of Appeals found that no law prohibited Louisiana public school teachers from teaching any scientific theory. As the president of the Louisiana Science Teachers Association testified, "[a]ny scientific concept that's based on established fact can be included in our curriculum already, and no legislation allowing this is necessary." The Act provides Louisiana school teachers with no new authority. Thus the stated purpose is not furthered by it.

Thus we agree with the Court of Appeals' conclusion that the Act does not serve to protect academic freedom, but has the distinctly different purpose of discrediting "evolution by counterbalancing its teaching at every turn with the teaching of creationism. . . ."

As in *Stone* [*v. Graham*] and *Abington* [*v. Schempp*], we need not be blind in this case to the legislature's preeminent religious purpose in enacting this statute. There is a historic and contemporaneous link between the teachings of certain religious denominations and the teaching of evolution. It was this link that concerned the Court in *Epperson v. Arkansas*, which also involved a facial challenge to a statute regulating the teaching of evolution. These same historic and contemporaneous antagonisms between the teachings of certain religious denominations and the teaching of evolution are present in this case. The preeminent purpose of the Louisiana Legislature was clearly to advance the religious viewpoint that a supernatural being created humankind.

In this case, the purpose of the Creationism Act was to restructure the science curriculum to conform with a particular religious viewpoint. Out of many possible science subjects taught in the public schools, the legislature chose to affect the teaching of the one scientific theory that historically has been opposed by certain religious sects. As in *Epperson*, the legislature passed the Act to give preference to those religious groups which have as one of their tenets the creation of humankind by a divine creator. The "overriding fact" that confronted the Court in *Epperson* was "that Arkansas' law selects from the body of knowledge a particular segment which it proscribes for the sole reason that it is deemed to conflict with . . . a particular interpretation of the Book of Genesis by a particular religious group." The Establishment Clause, however, "forbids *alike* the preference of a religious doctrine *or* the prohibition of theory which is deemed antagonistic to a particular dogma." *Epperson*. Because the primary purpose of the Creationism Act is to advance a particular religious belief, the Act endorses religion in violation of the First Amendment.

Justice SCALIA, with whom THE CHIEF JUSTICE joins, dissenting.

We have relatively little information upon which to judge the motives of those who supported the Act. About the only direct evidence is the statute itself and transcripts of the seven committee hearings at which it was considered. Unfortunately, several of those hearings were sparsely attended, and the legislators who were present revealed little about their motives. We have no committee reports, no floor debates, no remarks inserted into the legislative history, no statement from the Governor, and no postenactment statements or testimony from the bill's sponsor or any other legislators. Nevertheless, there is ample evidence that the majority is wrong in holding that the Balanced Treatment Act is without secular purpose.

The Act had its genesis (so to speak) in legislation introduced by Senator Bill Keith in June 1980.

Before summarizing the testimony of Senator Keith and his supporters, I wish to make clear that I by no means intend to endorse its accuracy. But my views (and the views of this Court) about creation science and evolution are (or should be) beside the point. Our task is not to judge the debate about teaching the origins of life, but to ascertain what the members of the Louisiana Legislature believed. The vast majority of them voted to approve a bill which explicitly stated a secular purpose; what is crucial is not their *wisdom* in believing that purpose would be achieved by the bill, but their *sincerity* in believing it would be. . . .

It is undoubtedly true that what prompted the legislature to direct its attention to the misrepresentation of evolution in the schools (rather than the inaccurate presentation of other topics) was its awareness of the tension between evolution and the religious beliefs of many children. But even appellees concede that a valid secular purpose is not rendered impermissible simply because its pursuit is prompted by concern for religious sensitivities. If a history teacher falsely told her students that the bones of Jesus Christ had been discovered, or a physics teacher that the Shroud of Turin had been conclusively established to be inexplicable on the basis of natural causes, I cannot believe (despite the majority's implication to the contrary) that legislators or school board members would be constitutionally prohibited from taking corrective action, simply because that action was prompted by concern for the religious beliefs of the misinstructed students.

In sum, even if one concedes, for the sake of argument, that a majority of the Louisiana Legislature voted for the Balanced Treatment Act partly in order to foster (rather than merely eliminate discrimination against) Christian fundamentalist beliefs, our cases establish that that alone would not suffice to invalidate the Act, so long as there was a genuine secular purpose as well. We have, moreover, no adequate basis for disbelieving the secular purpose set forth in the Act itself, or for concluding that it is a sham enacted to conceal the legislators' violation of their oaths of office. I am astonished by the Court's unprecedented readiness to reach such a conclusion, which I can only attribute to an intellectual predisposition created by the facts and the legend of *Scopes v. State*—an instinctive reaction that any governmentally imposed requirements bearing upon the teaching of evolution must be a manifestation of Christian fundamentalist repression. In this case, however, it seems to me the Court's position is the repressive one. The people of Louisiana, including those who are Christian fundamentalists, are quite entitled, as a secular matter, to have whatever scientific evidence there may be against evolution presented in their schools, just as Mr. Scopes was entitled to present whatever scientific evidence there was for it. Perhaps what the Louisiana Legislature has done is unconstitutional because there is no such evidence, and the scheme they have established will amount to no more than a presentation of the Book of Genesis. But we cannot say that on the evidence before us in this summary judgment context, which includes ample uncontradicted testimony that "creation science" is a body of scientific knowledge rather than revealed belief. *Infinitely less* can we say (or should we say) that the scientific evidence for evolution is so conclusive that no one could be gullible enough to believe that there is any real scientific evidence to the contrary, so that the legislation's stated purpose must be a lie. Yet that illiberal judgment, that *Scopes*-in-reverse, is ultimately the basis on which the Court's facile rejection of the Louisiana Legislature's purpose must rest.

NOTES AND QUESTIONS

1. *Secular purpose.* In order to satisfy the *Lemon* test, is it enough that a statute have a secular purpose, or must the primary purpose be secular? Must it be the latter because it is always possible to come up with a secular justification? Is the answer different for the endorsement test? What if the Arkansas law or the Creationism Act was motivated in part by a desire to avoid controversy in the public schools?
2. *Some definitions.* The National Academy of Sciences and Institute of Medicine define "science" as "the use of evidence to construct testable explanation and prediction of natural phenomena, as well as the knowledge generated through this process." National Academy of Sciences and Institute of Medicine, *Science, Evolution, and Creationism* (2008). Does creationism meet that criteria? Note too that "theory" has a special meaning in science. According to the National Academy of Sciences and the Institute of Medicine: "The formal scientific definition of theory is quite different from the everyday meaning of the word. It refers to a comprehensive explanation of some aspect of nature that is supported by a vast body of evidence." *Id.* In addition to the theory of evolution, other scientific theories include the heliocentric theory (the earth revolves around the sun), cell theory (living things are made up of cells), and the theory of plate tectonics. *Id.*
3. *The scientific community's response to Justice Scalia.* Justice Scalia's *Edwards* dissent did not fare very well with the scientific community. "[T]hough it may form only part of his rationale, Scalia's argument relies crucially upon a false concept of science. . . . I regret to say that Justice Scalia does not understand the subject matter of evolutionary biology. He has simply adopted the creationists' definition and thereby repeated their willful mistake. . . . He equates creation and evolution because creationists can't explain life's beginning while evolutionists can't resolve the ultimate origin of the inorganic components that later aggregate to life. But this inability is the very heart of creationist logic and the central reason why their doctrine is not science, while science's inability to specify the ultimate origin of matter is irrelevant because we are not trying to do any such thing. We know that we can't, and we do not even consider such a question as part of science." Stephen Jay Gould, *Justice Scalia's Misunderstanding*, 5 Const. Commentary 1, 8, 10 (1988).

4. *Favoring one religion over others.* Doesn't a school favor one religion over others if it teaches Biblical creationism? After all, other Christian denominations and other religions have different origin stories. Indeed, evolution does not necessarily clash with religious belief. While it describes how species change and develop, it does not address the ultimate origins of life. Moreover, someone could, for example, believe that God chose natural selection as the means to create new species.
5. *Neutrality.* When evolution and religious belief do clash, is the state acting neutrally when it offers the secular view without acknowledging the religious view? Consider Stephen Carter's critique of the *Edwards* holding as an example of the conflict between two completely different ways of viewing the world: the empirical, rationalist outlook that forms the heart of the French Enlightenment worldview, and the religious worldview that is defined by faith and a belief in the primacy of an essentially unknowable supernatural power. *See* Stephen L. Carter, *Evolution, Creationism, and Treating Religion as a Hobby*, 1987 Duke L.J. 977. Carter criticizes the Supreme Court for its *Edwards* decision, and suggests that the larger problem with the decision is the inability of the secular legal and political structure to come to terms with the basic attributes of religion. According to Carter, "The liberal critic may be right to say that creationism is bad science. But why should that issue be the crucial one? Creationists are not irrational merely because they are unscientific. Creationism was not created from thin air; creation theory developed as a consequence of the preferred hermeneutical method of many Christian fundamentalists for understanding the world." *Id.* at 980. The hermeneutical assumptions to which Carter refers are derived from the assumption of biblical inerrancy. If one assumes that the Bible is the literally true, received word of God, Carter argues, "what chance is there that the theory of evolution is correct? Virtually none." *Id.* Carter argues that the root of the conflict is the "reliance of liberalism on dialogue and rationality as indispensable components of its political theory, and the often unstated premise of many liberal theorists that reasoning and religious belief are mutually exclusive means for understanding the world." *Id.* at 986. Is Carter right? Is the reliance on "dialogue and rationality" itself an Establishment Clause violation? Do the scientific method and its essential requisites of empiricism and rationality form a sufficiently comprehensive worldview to fall within the ambit of the term "religion"?
6. *The third generation of creationism: Intelligent Design.* Creationism has, perhaps ironically, evolved since the Scopes "Monkey Trial" in the 1920s. The theory has gone through two major transformations in response to the legal decisions summarized above. The first generation of creationism statutes barred the teaching of evolution altogether. These statutes were the basis of the *Scopes* trial in 1927 and were finally held unconstitutional by the 1968 Supreme Court decision, *Epperson v. Arkansas.* The second generation of creationism statutes no longer challenged the teaching of evolution, but required public school teachers who taught evolution to give creationist theory equal time. These so-called balanced treatment statutes were held unconstitutional in 1987 in *Edwards v. Aguillard.* Both of the first two generations of creationism statutes relied heavily on

so-called young-earth creationist doctrine, which suggests that the earth is only approximately 6,000 years old, all geological phenomena can be explained by catastrophism (a flood), and diverse new species do not evolve from common ancestors.

In response to *Edwards*, a third generation of creationism has developed in the form of so-called Intelligent Design doctrine. There are two main distinctions between Intelligent Design creationism and its predecessors. First, unlike earlier versions of creationism, Intelligent Design doctrine does not attempt to make an affirmative case for supernatural creation but instead relies mostly on the claim that evolutionary theory is flawed. (Intelligent Design proponents do continue to advance the most important claim made by previous generations of creationists, however, which is the contention that higher species have not evolved from common ancestors.) Second, unlike earlier versions of creationism, which explicitly asserted that God created the world in essentially its present form, Intelligent Design does not identify the "intelligent designer" by the name "God." Intelligent Design hopes to escape the Establishment Clause restrictions imposed by *Epperson* and *Edwards* by avoiding mentioning the religious concept of God by name. Intelligent Design proposals come in various forms, including efforts to have school boards directly advance the theory in science classes in addition to the traditional scientific renditions of evolution theory, the incorporation of Intelligent Design precepts in state science standards, and the placement of disclaimers in science textbooks. Thus far, these proposals have failed to survive judicial scrutiny in the lower courts.

The most important decision involving a school board's attempt to incorporate Intelligent Design precepts into a public school curriculum is Kitzmiller v. Dover Area School District, 400 F. Supp. 2d 707 (M.D. Pa. 2005). In *Kitzmiller*, a Dover, Pennsylvania, school board attempted to interject Intelligent Design into the curriculum by reading to students official disclaimers implying that evolutionary theory might be flawed. The school board also placed Intelligent Design textbooks in the school library. The judge ruled that the Dover policy was unconstitutional both on secular purpose and secular effect grounds as an impermissible endorsement of religion. The judge concluded "that the religious nature of ID [the common abbreviation for Intelligent Design] would be readily apparent to an objective observer, adult or child." *Id.* at 718. The decision is important not only for its basic holding but also because the court ruled on the merits of the scientific claims made by Intelligent Design proponents. After hearing extensive expert testimony on the subject, the judge ruled that

> ID is not science. We find that ID fails on three different levels, any one of which is sufficient to preclude a determination that ID is science. They are: (1) ID violates the centuries-old ground rules of science by invoking and permitting supernatural causation; (2) the argument of irreducible complexity, central to ID, employs the same flawed and illogical contrived dualism [between religion and science] that doomed creation science in the 1980's; and (3) ID's negative attacks on evolution have been refuted by the scientific community. . . . [I]t is additionally

> important to note that ID has failed to gain acceptance in the scientific community, it has not generated peer-reviewed publications, nor has it been the subject of testing or research.

Id. at 735; *see also id.* at 738 ("ID fails to meet the essential ground rules that limit science to testable, natural explanations."). In November 2005, the citizens of Dover voted to turn out of office all eight members of the Dover school board who had supported the anti-evolution policy. The new school board decided not to appeal the *Kitzmiller* decision.

7. *Disavowal of evolution on public school science textbooks.* The Cobb County, Georgia, public schools, facing objections from parents over the inclusion of Darwin's theory of evolution in new science textbooks being used in local public schools, adopted a policy of placing stickers on the books. The stickers stated: "This textbook contains material on evolution. Evolution is a theory, not a fact, regarding the origin of living things. This material should be approached with an open mind, studied carefully, and critically considered." Selman v. Cobb Cnty. Sch. Dist., 390 F. Supp. 1286, 1292 (N.D. Ga. 2005), *rev'd,* 449 F.3d 1320 (11th Cir. 2006). In subsequent litigation, a federal district court ordered removal of the stickers because they constituted an endorsement of religion. *See id.* at 1306-1312. On appeal, however, the Eleventh Circuit found the record inadequate and vacated and remanded the district court's decision. On remand, the school district elected to settle the case. May a school district distance itself from Darwin's theory of evolution in this way? Or is the effort to disavow evolution itself objectionable on Establishment Clause grounds?

C. RELIGIOUS SPEECH IN PUBLIC SCHOOLS

Widmar v. Vincent

454 U.S. 263 (1981)

Justice POWELL delivered the opinion of the Court.

This case presents the question whether a state university [the University of Missouri at Kansas City], which makes its facilities generally available for the activities of registered student groups, may close its facilities to a registered student group desiring to use the facilities for religious worship and religious discussion.

From 1973 until 1977 a registered religious group named Cornerstone regularly sought and received permission to conduct its meetings in University facilities.[2] In 1977, however, the University informed the group that it could no longer meet in University buildings. The exclusion was based on a regulation, adopted by the Board of Curators in 1972, that prohibits the use of University buildings or grounds "for purposes of religious worship or religious teaching."

---

2. Cornerstone is an organization of evangelical Christian students from various denominational backgrounds. . . . A typical Cornerstone meeting included prayer, hymns, Bible commentary, and discussion of religious views and experiences.

The University first argues that it cannot offer its facilities to religious groups and speakers on the terms available to other groups without violating the Establishment Clause of the Constitution of the United States. We agree that the interest of the University in complying with its constitutional obligations may be characterized as compelling. It does not follow, however, that an "equal access" policy would be incompatible with this Court's Establishment Clause cases.

In this case two prongs of the [*Lemon*] test are clearly met. Both the District Court and the Court of Appeals held that an open-forum policy, including nondiscrimination against religious speech, would have a secular purpose and would avoid entanglement with religion. But the District Court concluded, and the University argues here, that allowing religious groups to share the limited public forum would have the "primary effect" of advancing religion.

The University's argument misconceives the nature of this case. The question is not whether the creation of a religious forum would violate the Establishment Clause. The University has opened its facilities for use by student groups, and the question is whether it can now exclude groups because of the content of their speech. In this context we are unpersuaded that the primary effect of the public forum, open to all forms of discourse, would be to advance religion.

We are not oblivious to the range of an open forum's likely effects. It is possible—perhaps even foreseeable—that religious groups will benefit from access to University facilities. But this Court has explained that a religious organization's enjoyment of merely "incidental" benefits does not violate the prohibition against the "primary advancement" of religion.

We are satisfied that any religious benefits of an open forum at UMKC would be "incidental" within the meaning of our cases. Two factors are especially relevant.

First, an open forum in a public university does not confer any imprimatur of state approval on religious sects or practices. As the Court of Appeals quite aptly stated, such a policy "would no more commit the University . . . to religious goals" than it is "now committed to the goals of the Students for a Democratic Society, the Young Socialist Alliance," or any other group eligible to use its facilities.

Second, the forum is available to a broad class of nonreligious as well as religious speakers; there are over 100 recognized student groups at UMKC. The provision of benefits to so broad a spectrum of groups is an important index of secular effect. If the Establishment Clause barred the extension of general benefits to religious groups, "a church could not be protected by the police and fire departments, or have its public sidewalk kept in repair." At least in the absence of empirical evidence that religious groups will dominate UMKC's open forum, we agree with the Court of Appeals that the advancement of religion would not be the forum's "primary effect."

Lamb's Chapel v. Center Moriches Union Free School District

508 U.S. 384 (1993)

Justice WHITE delivered the opinion of the Court.

New York [Education Law] authorizes local school boards to adopt reasonable regulations for the use of school property for 10 specified purposes when the property is not in use for school purposes. Among the permitted uses is the holding of "social, civic and recreational meetings and entertainments, and other uses pertaining to the welfare of the community; but such meetings, entertainment and uses shall be non-exclusive and shall be open to the general public." The list of permitted uses does not include meetings for religious purposes, and a New York appellate court ruled that local boards could not allow student bible clubs to meet on school property because "[r]eligious purposes are not included in the enumerated purposes for which a school may be used under section 414."

Pursuant to [the state law], the Board of Center Moriches Union Free School District (District) has issued rules and regulations with respect to the use of school property when not in use for school purposes. The rules allow only 2 of the 10 purposes authorized by [state law]: social, civic, or recreational uses (Rule 10) and use by political organizations if [properly authorized] (Rule 8). Rule 7, however, consistent with the judicial interpretation of state law, provides that "[t]he school premises shall not be used by any group for religious purposes."

The issue in this case is whether, against this background of state law, it violates the Free Speech Clause of the First Amendment, made applicable to the States by the Fourteenth Amendment, to deny a church access to school premises to exhibit for public viewing and for assertedly religious purposes, a film series dealing with family and child-rearing issues faced by parents today.[2]

The District, as a respondent, would save its judgment below on the ground that to permit its property to be used for religious purposes would be an establishment of religion forbidden by the First Amendment. This Court suggested in *Widmar v. Vincent,* that the interest of the State in avoiding an Establishment Clause violation "may be [a] compelling" one justifying an abridgment of free speech otherwise protected by the First Amendment; but the Court went on to hold that permitting use of university property for religious purposes under the open access policy involved there would not be incompatible with the Court's Establishment Clause cases.

We have no more trouble than did the *Widmar* Court in disposing of the claimed defense on the ground that the posited fears of an Establishment Clause violation are unfounded. The showing of this film series would not have been during school hours, would not have been sponsored by the school, and would have been open to the public, not just to church members. The District property had repeatedly been used by a wide variety of private organizations. Under these circumstances, as in *Widmar,* there would have been no realistic danger that the community would think that the District was endorsing religion or any particular creed, and any benefit to religion or to the Church would have been no more than incidental.

---

2. [*Editor's Note: Relocated Footnote.*] Shortly before the first of these requests, the Church had applied for permission to use school rooms for its Sunday morning services and for Sunday School. The hours specified were 9 a.m. to 1 p.m. and the time period one year beginning in the next month. 959 F.2d 381, 383 (CA2 1992). Within a few days the District wrote petitioner that the application "requesting use of the high school for your Sunday services" was denied, citing both N.Y. Educ. Law §414 and the District's Rule 7 barring uses for religious purposes. The Church did not challenge this denial in the courts and the validity of this denial is not before us.

NOTES AND QUESTIONS

1. *If religion dominated.* What if the empirical evidence in *Widmar* reveals that religious groups dominate the open forum? Would that change the Establishment Clause analysis? Is it possible for a religious group to "so dominate a public forum that a formal policy of equal access is transformed into a demonstration of approval"? *Pinette* (O'Connor, J., concurring).
2. *Religion as a subject or viewpoint.* Free Speech Clause forum doctrine does not always treat subject matter regulations and viewpoint regulations in the same way. In nonpublic forums, the government may restrict the forum to certain subjects as long as the limit is reasonable. However, any attempt to exclude viewpoints triggers strict scrutiny. *See supra* Chapter 5. *Lamb's Chapel* holds that the regulation barring access for "religious purposes" was a viewpoint restriction that could not survive strict scrutiny. Is religion better characterized as a subject matter or a viewpoint? What if the exclusion were limited to religious worship? In other words, is a regulation allowing Lamb's Chapel to screen a religious film about childrearing but not hold religious worship services a subject matter or viewpoint regulation?
3. *May (must) government distance itself from sectarian proselytizing?* Suppose a religious group seeks to use a government public forum at a school to proselytize. Suppose that the speech takes the form of an attack against unbelievers; for example, the cover of a student-edited, university-supported publication proclaims in large, bold letters: "Why Papists Will Surely Burn in Hell." Does a public university have an obligation to distance itself from such overtly sectarian speech? *Cf. Pinette* (Justice O'Connor, concurring) ("The [Establishment] Clause is more than a negative prohibition against certain narrowly defined forms of government favoritism; it also imposes affirmative obligations that may require a State, in some situations, to take steps to avoid being perceived as supporting or endorsing a private religious message.").
4. *Extension in* Rosenberger. The reasoning of *Widmar* and *Lamb's Chapel*, which involved access to physical spaces, was extended to access to funding in *Rosenberger v. Rector & Visitors of the University of Virginia*, where the school allowed its student activity fund to subsidize student extracurricular activities yet declined to subsidize an evangelical student newspaper. The Court held that when the university created the student activity fund, it had essentially designated a public forum, albeit a public forum "more in a metaphysical than in a spatial or geographic sense," but in which the same rules applied. *Id.* at 830. The Court held that denying funds to religious speakers would constitute unconstitutional viewpoint discrimination under the Free Speech Clause of the First Amendment. The Court rejected the university's theory that the Establishment Clause prohibited the university from providing government funds to the religious magazine on the ground that the program was neutral with regard to the perspective of speakers receiving funds. "The neutrality of the program distinguishes the student fees from a tax levied for the direct support

of a church or group of churches." *Id.* at 840. Should the same reasoning apply to funding as to facilities? To after-school access as opposed to school extracurriculars?

5. *The difficulty in fashioning a truly neutral policy.* If the government attempts to advance Establishment Clause values by excluding religious speakers from a limited-purpose public forum, it engages in a form of content/viewpoint discrimination. On the other hand, if it permits religious activities and even services to take place on public property, it is directly subsidizing overtly sectarian activities. This Scylla and Charybdis does not admit of an obvious or easy solution; the framing device completely prefigures the constitutional outcome.
6. *Free speech and religion.* Note that these cases brought by religious plaintiffs rely on the Free Speech Clause rather than the Free Exercise Clause. What are the advantages and disadvantages of viewing religious liberty rights through the lens of free speech rather than free exercise?

AN EXTENDED NOTE ON OPEN ACCESS REQUIREMENTS

In Board of Education v. Mergens, 496 U.S. 226 (1990), the Supreme Court upheld the federal Equal Access Act, 20 U.S.C. §§4071-4074 (1994), which makes it "unlawful for any public secondary school which receives Federal financial assistance and which has a limited open forum to deny equal access or a fair opportunity to, or discriminate against, any students who wish to conduct a meeting within that limited open forum on the basis of the religious, political, philosophical, or other content of the speech at such meetings." A "limited open forum" exists "whenever such school grants an offering to or opportunity for one or more noncurriculum related student groups to meet on school premises during noninstructional time." The Court emphasized several factors that were important considerations in upholding the statute: (1) the meetings were held in noninstructional time; (2) the meetings did not interfere with the educational program of the school; (3) the meetings were not endorsed by the school; (4) school officials did not participate in the meetings; (5) the religious club was merely one of many different student-initiated voluntary clubs, including many secular clubs; and (6) unwilling students were not coerced into attending the religious meetings.

Should a "neutral" access policy of this sort be seen as consistent with the purposes and objectives of the Establishment Clause? Alternatively, if a government entity, such as a local public library, makes meeting space generally available to the public, can it *exclude* those with religious viewpoints from the meeting space? Wouldn't such an exclusion constitute content, if not viewpoint, discrimination? To exclude such viewpoints appears to reflect hostility toward religion and religiously motivated points of view. On the other hand, does a policy of mandatory neutrality toward religious groups seeking to meet on public property have the effect of promoting religion? Or should equal treatment be viewed as a genuinely neutral policy that facially neither advances nor inhibits religion? Does the Free Exercise Clause have any bearing on the constitutional validity of such policies? (For the answer to this question, see *infra* Chapter 16.)

THEORY-APPLIED PROBLEMS

Litigants have raised Establishment Clause claims against a diverse array of religious exercises in public schools, and the Court has used a variety of theoretical approaches to resolve these challenges. One recurrent consideration in the cases is whether private religious exercise or expression should be attributed to the government and therefore limited by the Establishment Clause. In many cases the Court has found it easy to attribute the religious exercise to the government because government officials wrote the prayer (*Engel*), mandated the Bible reading by students (*Schempp*), legally required the posting of religious materials (*Stone*), officially invited the clergyman who recited the offending prayer (*Lee*), or formally organized the vote at which students were allowed to choose to include prayer at an official school function (*Santa Fe*). In other cases the Court has decided that the religious expression in question was not attributable to the government because the expression took place in a context in which many other varieties of expression also occurred (*Widmar, Lamb's Chapel*), or the government put in place certain institutional impediments to prevent official participation or encouragement of the private religious exercise (*Mergens*). Another recurring consideration is whether young impressionable students would feel pressure to participate in a religious exercise. For example, in *Schempp, Lee,* and *Santa Fe,* the Court expressed great concern that permitting private religious speech at a public school or at an official public school function would exert pressure on religious minorities, especially in communities where one or a few religious faiths predominated. The Court also expressed concern that dissenting students in the audience essentially would be captive to the private religious expression. Therefore, the students' Bible readings in *Schempp,* the rabbi's prayer in *Lee,* and the student prayers in *Santa Fe* were all deemed constitutionally impermissible, even though the religious speech in question was that of private individuals. Consider the following variations on the theme of religious expression in public school, and ask yourself on which side of the constitutional line they should fall.

1. A student reads aloud a paper on "Why I Love Jesus" in a public high school English class. (*See* C.H. ex rel. Z.H. v. Oliva, 195 F.3d 167 (3d Cir.), *vacated and reh'g en banc granted by* 197 F.3d 63 (3d Cir. 1999), *on reh'g en banc,* 226 F.3d 198 (3d Cir. 2000); Denooyer v. Merinelli, No. 92-2080, 1993 WL 477030 (6th Cir. Nov. 18, 1993) (per curiam).)
2. At a public high school graduation ceremony, a student elected as valedictorian of the graduating class bows her head during the valedictory address and recites a short prayer. (*See* Lassonde v. Pleasanton Unified Sch. Dist., 320 F.3d 979 (9th Cir. 2003); Cole v. Oroville Union High Sch. Dist., 228 F.3d 1092 (9th Cir. 2000).)
3. A state-mandated moment of silence is observed in a public high school classroom in which 95 percent of students bow and quietly pray.
4. A moment of silence is observed at a public high school graduation ceremony, at which numerous members of the audience spontaneously recite the Lord's Prayer, then applaud after "amen." (*See* Chaudhuri v. Tennessee, 130 F.3d 232 (6th Cir. 1997), *cert. denied,* 523 U.S. 1024 (1998).)

5. The incident described in example 4 occurs repeatedly over a period of several years, and school officials do nothing in response.
6. Every morning before the school day starts, a large group of students at a public high school gather to pray around the flagpole in front of the school (which all students have to pass by before entering the school).
7. Several teachers participate (before the school day starts) in the flagpole prayer described in example 6. (*See* Daugherty v. Vanguard Charter Sch. Acad., 116 F. Supp. 2d 897 (W.D. Mich. 2000).)
8. Most of the students on a public high school basketball team pray together on center court immediately before each game. (*See* Doe v. Duncanville Indep. Sch. Dist., 70 F.3d 402 (5th Cir. 1995).)
9. Most of the students on a public high school basketball team pray together in the locker room immediately before each game.
10. The coach of the public high school basketball team prays in the center of the basketball court immediately before school games and asks the students to join him.
11. Several public school teachers wear "We Are One in Christ" T-shirts to class during a school spirit day. (*See* Harper v. Poway Unified Sch. Dist., 445 F.3d 1166 (9th Cir. 2006), *dismissed as moot,* 485 F.3d 1052 (9th Cir. 2007).)
12. An overwhelming majority of the students at a public school wear "We Are One in Christ" T-shirts to class during a school spirit day.
13. Several female Muslim students wear the hijab to class in a public high school. (*See* Isaacs ex rel. Isaacs v. Board of Educ. of Howard County, Md., 40 F. Supp. 2d 335 (D. Md. 1999).)
14. A Muslim teacher wears the hijab to teach her class in a public high school. (*See* United States v. Board of Educ., 911 F.2d 882 (3d Cir. 1990).)
15. A teacher places a large Bible on the corner of his desk, where the class is likely to notice it. (*See* Roberts v. Madigan, 921 F.2d 1047 (10th Cir. 1990), *cert. denied,* 505 U.S. 1218 (1992).)
16. A teacher invites her class at a public elementary school to decorate the classroom for Christmas and permits the inclusion of religious elements among the decorations.
16. A choir at a public school performs a repertoire that includes mostly religious music. (*See* Bauchman v. West High Sch., 132 F.3d 542 (10th Cir. 1997), *cert. denied,* 524 U.S. 953 (1998).)

Chapter 22

The Establishment Clause and Government Endorsement of Religion

Table of Contents

A. Government-Sponsored Religious Displays
B. Government-Sponsored Prayers Outside School
C. Government/Religion Power Sharing

A. *GOVERNMENT-SPONSORED RELIGIOUS DISPLAYS*

Lynch v. Donnelly

465 U.S. 668 (1984)

Chief Justice Burger delivered the opinion of the Court.

We granted certiorari to decide whether the Establishment Clause of the First Amendment prohibits a municipality from including a crèche, or Nativity scene, in its annual Christmas display.

Each year, in cooperation with the downtown retail merchants' association, the city of Pawtucket, R. I., erects a Christmas display as part of its observance of the Christmas holiday season. The display is situated in a park owned by a nonprofit organization and located in the heart of the shopping district. The display is essentially like those to be found in hundreds of towns or cities across the Nation—often on public grounds—during the Christmas season. The Pawtucket display comprises many of the figures and decorations traditionally associated with Christmas, including, among other things, a Santa Claus house, reindeer pulling Santa's sleigh, candy-striped poles, a Christmas tree, carolers, cutout figures representing such characters as a clown, an elephant, and a teddy bear, hundreds of colored lights, a large banner that reads "SEASONS GREETINGS," and the crèche at issue here. All components of this display are owned by the City.

The crèche, which has been included in the display for 40 or more years, consists of the traditional figures, including the Infant Jesus, Mary and Joseph, angels, shepherds, kings, and animals, all ranging in height from 5″ to 5′. In 1973, when the present crèche was acquired, it cost the City $1,365; it now is valued at $200. The erection and dismantling of the crèche costs the City about $20 per year; nominal expenses are incurred in lighting the crèche. No money has been expended on its maintenance for the past 10 years.

There is an unbroken history of official acknowledgment by all three branches of government of the role of religion in American life from at least 1789. . . . Our history is replete with official references to the value and invocation of Divine guidance in deliberations and pronouncements of the Founding Fathers and contemporary leaders. Beginning in the early colonial period long before Independence, a day of Thanksgiving was celebrated as a religious holiday to give thanks for the bounties of Nature as gifts from God. President Washington and his successors proclaimed Thanksgiving, with all its religious overtones, a day of national celebration and Congress made it a National Holiday more than a century ago. Ch. 167, 16 Stat. 168 (1870). That holiday has not lost its theme of expressing thanks for Divine aid any more than has Christmas lost its religious significance.

Executive Orders and other official announcements of Presidents and of the Congress have proclaimed both Christmas and Thanksgiving National Holidays in religious terms. And, by Acts of Congress, it has long been the practice that federal employees are released from duties on these National Holidays, while being paid from the same public revenues that provide the compensation of the Chaplains of the Senate and the House and the military services. *See* J. Res. 5, 23 Stat. 516 (1885). Thus, it is clear that Government has long recognized—indeed it has subsidized—holidays with religious significance.

Other examples of reference to our religious heritage are found in the statutorily prescribed national motto "In God We Trust," 36 U.S.C. § 186, which Congress and the President mandated for our currency, see 31 U.S.C. § 324, and in the language "One nation under God," as part of the Pledge of Allegiance to the American flag. That pledge is recited by thousands of public school children—and adults—every year.

Art galleries supported by public revenues display religious paintings of the 15th and 16th centuries, predominantly inspired by one religious faith. The National Gallery in Washington, maintained with Government support, for example, has long exhibited masterpieces with religious messages, notably the Last Supper, and paintings depicting the Birth of Christ, the Crucifixion, and the Resurrection, among many others with explicit Christian themes and messages. The very chamber in which oral arguments on this case were heard is decorated with a notable and permanent—not seasonal—symbol of religion: Moses with Ten Commandments. Congress has long provided chapels in the Capitol for religious worship and meditation. There are countless other illustrations of the Government's acknowledgment of our religious heritage and governmental sponsorship of graphic manifestations of that heritage. . . .

This history may help explain why the Court consistently has declined to take a rigid, absolutist view of the Establishment Clause. . . .

In the line-drawing process we have often found it useful to inquire whether the challenged law or conduct has a secular purpose, whether its principal or primary effect is to advance or inhibit religion, and whether it creates an excessive entanglement of government with religion. *Lemon, supra.* But, we have repeatedly emphasized our unwillingness to be confined to any single test or criterion in this sensitive area.

The District Court inferred from the religious nature of the crèche that the City has no secular purpose for the display. In so doing, it rejected the City's claim that its reasons for including the crèche are essentially the same as its reasons for sponsoring the display as a whole. The District Court plainly erred by focusing almost exclusively on the crèche. When viewed in the proper context of the Christmas Holiday season, it is apparent that, on this record, there is insufficient evidence to establish that the inclusion of the crèche is a purposeful or surreptitious effort to express some kind of subtle governmental advocacy of a particular religious message. In a pluralistic society a variety of motives and purposes are implicated. The City, like the Congresses and Presidents, however, has principally taken note of a significant historical religious event long celebrated in the Western World. The crèche in the display depicts the historical origins of this traditional event long recognized as a National Holiday.

The narrow question is whether there is a secular purpose for Pawtucket's display of the crèche. The display is sponsored by the City to celebrate the Holiday and to depict the origins of that Holiday. These are legitimate secular purposes. The District Court's inference, drawn from the religious nature of the crèche, that the City has no secular purpose was, on this record, clearly erroneous.

The District Court found that the primary effect of including the crèche is to confer a substantial and impermissible benefit on religion in general and on the Christian faith in particular. Comparisons of the relative benefits to religion of different forms of governmental support are elusive and difficult to make. But to conclude that the primary effect of including the crèche is to advance religion in violation of the Establishment Clause would require that we view it as more beneficial to and more an endorsement of religion than, for example, expenditure of public funds for transportation of students to church-sponsored schools, *Everson v. Board of Education, supra*; and the tax exemptions for church properties sanctioned in *Walz, supra.* It would also require that we view it as more of an endorsement of religion than the Sunday Closing Laws upheld in McGowan v. Maryland, 366 U.S. 420 (1961). We are unable to discern a greater aid to religion deriving from inclusion of the crèche than from these benefits and endorsements previously held not violative of the Establishment Clause. . . .

The dissent asserts some observers may perceive that the City has aligned itself with the Christian faith by including a Christian symbol in its display and that this serves to advance religion. We can assume, *arguendo,* that the display advances religion in a sense; but our precedents plainly contemplate that on occasion some advancement of religion will result from governmental action. The Court has made it abundantly clear, however, that "not every law that confers an 'indirect,' 'remote,' or 'incidental' benefit upon [religion] is, for that reason alone, constitutionally invalid." *Nyquist, supra,* 413 U.S., at 771. Here, whatever benefit to one faith or religion or to all religions, is indirect, remote and incidental; display of the crèche is no more an advancement or endorsement of religion than the Congressional and Executive recognition of the origins of the Holiday itself as "Christ's Mass," or the exhibition of literally hundreds of religious paintings in governmentally supported museums.

. . . We hold that, notwithstanding the religious significance of the crèche, the City of Pawtucket has not violated the Establishment Clause of the First Amendment. Accordingly, the judgment of the Court of Appeals is reversed.

It is so ordered.

Justice O'CONNOR, concurring

The Establishment Clause prohibits government from making adherence to a religion relevant in any way to a person's standing in the political community. . . . Endorsement sends a message to nonadherents that they are outsiders, not full members of the political community, and an accompanying message to adherents that they are insiders, favored members of the political community. Disapproval sends the opposite message. *See generally* Abington School District v. Schempp, 374 U.S. 203 (1963). . . .

The central issue in this case is whether Pawtucket has endorsed Christianity by its display of the crèche. To answer that question, we must examine both what Pawtucket intended to communicate in displaying the crèche and what message the City's display actually conveyed. The purpose and effect prongs of the Lemon test represent these two aspects of the meaning of the City's action. . . .

The purpose prong of the Lemon test requires that a government activity have a secular purpose. That requirement is not satisfied, however, by the mere existence of some secular purpose, however dominated by religious purposes. In Stone v. Graham, 449 U.S. 39 (1980), for example, the Court held that posting copies of the Ten Commandments in schools violated the purpose prong of the Lemon test, yet the State plainly had some secular objectives, such as instilling most of the values of the Ten Commandments and illustrating their connection to our legal system . . .

The evident purpose of including the crèche in the larger display was not promotion of the religious content of the crèche but celebration of the public holiday through its traditional symbols. Celebration of public holidays, which have cultural significance even if they also have religious aspects, is a legitimate secular purpose.

The District Court's finding that the display of the crèche had no secular purpose was based on erroneous reasoning. The District Court believed that it should ascertain the City's purpose in displaying the creche separate and apart from the general purpose in setting up the display. . . .

Pawtucket's display of its crèche, I believe, does not communicate a message that the government intends to endorse the Christian beliefs represented by the crèche. Although the religious and indeed sectarian significance of the crèche, as the district court found, is not neutralized by the setting, the overall holiday setting changes what viewers may fairly understand to be the purpose of the display—as a typical museum setting, though not neutralizing the religious content of a religious painting, negates any message of endorsement of that content. The display celebrates a public holiday, and no one contends that declaration of that holiday is understood to be an endorsement of religion. The holiday itself has very strong secular components and traditions. Government celebration of the holiday, which is extremely common, generally is not understood to endorse the religious content of the holiday, just as government celebration of Thanksgiving is not so understood. The crèche is a traditional symbol of the holiday that is very commonly displayed along with purely secular symbols, as it was in Pawtucket.

These features combine to make the government's display of the crèche in this particular physical setting no more an endorsement of religion than such governmental "acknowledgments" of religion as legislative prayers of the type approved in Marsh v. Chambers, 463 U.S. 783 (1983), government declaration of Thanksgiving as a public holiday, printing of "In God We Trust" on coins, and opening court sessions with "God save the United States and this honorable court." Those government acknowledgments of religion serve, in the only ways reasonably possible in our culture, the legitimate secular purposes of solemnizing public occasions, expressing confidence in the future, and encouraging the recognition of what is worthy of appreciation in society. For that reason, and because of their history and ubiquity, those practices are not understood as conveying government approval of particular religious beliefs. The display of the crèche likewise serves a secular purpose—celebration of a public holiday with traditional symbols. It cannot fairly be understood to convey a message of government endorsement of religion. . . .

Giving the challenged practice the careful scrutiny it deserves, I cannot say that the particular crèche display at issue in this case was intended to endorse or had the effect of endorsing Christianity. I agree with the Court that the judgment below must be reversed.

Justice BRENNAN, with whom Justice MARSHALL, Justice BLACKMUN, and Justice STEVENS join, dissenting.

The Court advances two principal arguments to support its conclusion that the Pawtucket crèche satisfies the *Lemon* test. Neither is persuasive.

First. The Court, by focusing on the holiday "context" in which the nativity scene appeared, seeks to explain away the clear religious import of the crèche and the findings of the District Court that most observers understood the crèche as both a symbol of Christian beliefs and a symbol of the city's support for those beliefs. Thus, although the Court concedes that the city's inclusion of the nativity scene plainly serves "to depict the origins" of Christmas as a "significant historical religious event," and that the crèche "is identified with one religious faith," we are nevertheless expected to believe that Pawtucket's use of the crèche does not signal the city's support for the sectarian symbolism that the nativity scene evokes. The effect of the crèche, of course, must be gauged not only by its inherent religious significance but also by the overall setting in which it appears. But it blinks reality to claim, as the Court does, that by including such a distinctively religious object as the crèche in its Christmas display, Pawtucket has done no more than make use of a "traditional" symbol of the holiday, and has thereby purged the crèche of its religious content and conferred only an "incidental and indirect" benefit on religion.

[E]ven in the context of Pawtucket's seasonal celebration, the crèche retains a specifically Christian religious meaning. I refuse to accept the notion implicit in today's decision that non-Christians would find that the religious content of the crèche is eliminated by the fact that it appears as part of the City's otherwise secular celebration of the Christmas holiday. The nativity scene is clearly distinct in its purpose and effect from the rest of the Hodgson Park display for the simple reason that it is the only one rooted in a biblical account of Christ's birth. It is the chief symbol of the characteristically Christian belief that a divine Savior was brought into the world and that the purpose of this miraculous birth was to illuminate a path toward salvation and redemption. For Christians, that path is exclusive, precious and holy. But for those who do not share these beliefs, the symbolic re-enactment of the birth of a divine being who has been miraculously incarnated as a man stands as a dramatic reminder of their differences with Christian faith.[14]

When government appears to sponsor such religiously inspired views, we cannot say that the practice is "'so separate and so indisputably marked off from the religious function,' . . . that [it] may fairly be viewed as reflect[ing] a neutral posture toward religious institutions." To be so excluded on religious grounds by one's elected government is an insult and an injury that, until today, could not be countenanced by the Establishment Clause.

Second. The Court also attempts to justify the crèche by entertaining a beguilingly simple, yet faulty syllogism. The Court begins by noting that government may recognize Christmas day as a public holiday; the Court then asserts that the crèche is nothing more than a traditional element of Christmas celebrations; and it concludes that the inclusion of a crèche as part of a government's annual Christmas celebration is constitutionally permissible. The Court apparently believes that once it finds that the designation of Christmas as a public holiday is constitutionally acceptable, it is then free to conclude that virtually every form of governmental association with the celebration of the holiday is also constitutional. The vice of this dangerously superficial argument is that it overlooks the fact that the Christmas holiday in our national culture contains both secular and sectarian elements. To say that government may recognize the holiday's traditional, secular elements of gift-giving, public festivities and community spirit, does not mean that government may indiscriminately embrace the distinctively sectarian aspects of the holiday. Indeed, in its eagerness to approve the crèche, the Court has advanced a rationale so simplistic that it would appear to allow the Mayor of Pawtucket to participate in the celebration of a Christmas Mass, since this would be just another unobjectionable way for the City to "celebrate the holiday." As is demonstrated below, the

---

14. For Christians, of course, the essential message of the nativity is that God became incarnate in the person of Christ. But just as fundamental to Jewish thought is the belief in the "non-incarnation of God, . . . [t]he God in whom [Jews] believe, to whom [Jews] are pledged, does not unite with human substance on earth." M. Buber, Israel and the World (1948) (reprinted in F. Talmage, Disputation and Dialogue: Readings in the Jewish-Christian Encounter 281-282 (1975)) (emphasis deleted). This distinction, according to Buber, "constitute[s] the ultimate division between Judaism and Christianity." *Id.*, at 281. *See also* R. Reuther, Faith and Fratricide 246 (1974).

Similarly, those who follow the tenets of Unitarianism might well find Pawtucket's support for the symbolism of the crèche, which highlights the trinitarian tradition in Christian faith, to be an affront to their belief in a single divine being. *See* J. Williams, What Americans Believe and How They Worship 316-317 (3d ed. 1969). *See also* C. Olmstead, History of Religion in the United States 296-299 (1960).

Court's logic is fundamentally flawed both because it obscures the reason why public designation of Christmas Day as a holiday is constitutionally acceptable, and blurs the distinction between the secular aspects of Christmas and its distinctively religious character, as exemplified by the crèche.

When government decides to recognize Christmas Day as a public holiday, it does no more than accommodate the calendar of public activities to the plain fact that many Americans will expect on that day to spend time visiting with their families, attending religious services, and perhaps enjoying some respite from pre-holiday activities. The Free Exercise Clause, of course, does not necessarily compel the government to provide this accommodation, but neither is the Establishment Clause offended by such a step. Because it is clear that the celebration of Christmas has both secular and sectarian elements, it may well be that by taking note of the holiday, the government is simply seeking to serve the same kinds of wholly secular goals—for instance, promoting goodwill and a common day of rest—that were found to justify Sunday Closing Laws in *McGowan* [*v. Maryland*]. If public officials go further and participate in the *secular* celebration of Christmas—by, for example, decorating public places with such secular images as wreaths, garlands or Santa Claus figures—they move closer to the limits of their constitutional power but nevertheless remain within the boundaries set by the Establishment Clause. But when those officials participate in or appear to endorse the distinctively religious elements of this otherwise secular event, they encroach upon First Amendment freedoms. For it is at that point that the government brings to the forefront the theological content of the holiday, and places the prestige, power, and financial support of a civil authority in the service of a particular faith.

The inclusion of a crèche in Pawtucket's otherwise secular celebration of Christmas clearly violates these principles. Unlike such secular figures as Santa Claus, reindeer and carolers, a nativity scene represents far more than a mere "traditional" symbol of Christmas. The essence of the crèche's symbolic purpose and effect is to prompt the observer to experience a sense of simple awe and wonder appropriate to the contemplation of one of the central elements of Christian dogma—that God sent His son into the world to be a Messiah. Contrary to the Court's suggestion, the crèche is far from a mere representation of a "particular historic religious event." It is, instead, best understood as a mystical re-creation of an event that lies at the heart of Christian faith. To suggest, as the Court does, that such a symbol is merely "traditional" and therefore no different from Santa's house or reindeer is not only offensive to those for whom the crèche has profound significance, but insulting to those who insist for religious or personal reasons that the story of Christ is in no sense a part of "history" nor an unavoidable element of our national "heritage."

For these reasons, the crèche in this context simply cannot be viewed as playing the same role that an ordinary museum display does. The Court seems to assume that prohibiting Pawtucket from displaying a crèche would be tantamount to forbidding a state college from including the Bible or Milton's Paradise Lost in a course on English literature. But in those cases the religiously-inspired materials are being considered solely as literature. The purpose is plainly not to single out the particular religious beliefs that may have inspired the authors, but to see in these writings the outlines of a larger imaginative universe shared with other forms of literary expression. The same may be said of a course devoted to the study of art; when the course turns to Gothic architecture, the emphasis is not on the religious beliefs which the cathedrals exalt, but rather upon the "aesthetic consequences of [such religious] thought."

AN EXTENDED NOTE ON GOVERNMENT-SPONSORED SEASONAL HOLIDAY DISPLAYS

Litigation over the constitutionality of holiday displays is now almost as much of a traditional feature of the holiday season as the displays themselves. One of the major reasons that litigation is so frequent is that the standard used by the Supreme Court to adjudicate holiday displays is so contextual and indefinite. A good illustration of how problematic these cases have been for the Court can be found in the Court's other main holiday display case, County of Allegheny v. ACLU, 492 U.S. 573 (1989). The case involved Establishment Clause challenges to two holiday displays on Allegheny County property. One display included a crèche, which contained a traditional representation of the manger scene in Bethlehem surrounded by poinsettias and topped with an angel bearing a banner that proclaimed "Gloria in Excelsis Deo!" The crèche was placed on the Grand Staircase inside the county courthouse. The second display was under an arch outside the city-county building, another government property located a block away from the county courthouse. The second display contained an 18-foot menorah, placed alongside a 45-foot Christmas tree and a sign entitled "Salute to Liberty."

The Court split into three groups on the issue of whether these displays were constitutional. Justice Kennedy, joined by the Chief Justice and Justices Scalia and White, asserted that both displays were constitutional. Justices Brennan, Marshall, and Stevens argued that both displays were unconstitutional. Justices Blackmun and O'Connor, who both relied on Justice O'Connor's endorsement test, distinguished the crèche from the menorah. They held that the crèche display was an unconstitutional endorsement of religion, but the menorah display was "simply a recognition of cultural diversity." *Id.* at 619. Justices Blackmun and O'Connor were therefore the only two Justices to agree on the result in the case, but even they could not get their respective objective observers to see the same religious significance in the menorah display. Although Justice Blackmun recognized that the menorah is a religious symbol, he also asserted that a menorah has secular symbolic value. Blackmun argued that by placing the menorah beside a disclaimer sign and a Christmas tree, which he viewed as a wholly secular symbol, the city had brought the menorah's secular symbolism to the fore and had conveyed only the "city's secular recognition of different traditions for celebrating the winter-holiday season." *Id.* at 620. Justice O'Connor disagreed, noting that she did not "strain to argue that the menorah has a 'secular dimension.'" *Id.* at 634 (O'Connor, J., concurring). Instead, O'Connor recognized that the menorah is a religious symbol and Chanukah is a religious holiday. But this acknowledgment of the religious nature of the symbol did not keep O'Connor from finding that this particular use of an admittedly religious symbol celebrating an admittedly religious holiday conveyed a purely secular message to an objective observer. O'Connor concluded that the city's placement of the religious symbol beside the tree and the sign was merely an "effort to acknowledge the cultural diversity of our country and to convey tolerance of different choices in matters of religious belief or nonbelief by recognizing that the winter holiday season is celebrated in diverse ways by our citizens." *Id.* at 636 (O'Connor, J., concurring).

As this brief description indicates, there is no precise standard for distinguishing the permissible use of overtly religious symbols to acknowledge the society's religious diversity from the impermissible use of the same symbols to endorse religion. The lack of a precise standard, coupled with the different factual contexts raised in every display case, means that the likelihood of litigation over new displays ranges from high to inevitable. The likelihood that lower courts will produce inconsistent rulings in these cases is equally high.

NOTES AND QUESTIONS

1. *Secular purpose.* Is it possible to depict the origins of Christmas without displaying a crèche? Is it necessary to depict the origins of Christmas in order to celebrate it? Do we generally celebrate holidays by depicting their origins?
2. *Effect and context.* The effect of a government-sponsored religious display may turn on the context in which it appears. Most reasonable people would not conclude that art museums were endorsing or promoting religion by displaying images of the birth of Jesus. Does the same hold true for including the birth of Jesus in a state-sponsored holiday display? Why was the holiday crèche in *Lynch* constitutional but the one in *Allegheny* was not? Does displaying a crèche surrounded by secular items always serve to neutralize any message of endorsement? What if the crèche were displayed with only one other secular item?
3. *Christmas as national holiday.* Both the majority and the dissent in *Lynch* agree that the government does not violate the Establishment Clause by designating Christmas as a national holiday. Why not? Would declaring Good Friday a national holiday also be constitutional? Is the difference that everyone celebrates Christmas? Does everyone celebrate Christmas? How does Christmas compare to Thanksgiving?
4. *Crèche vs. menorah.* When comparing the display of a crèche to the display of a menorah, does it matter that 70.6 percent of Americans identify as Christian compared to 1.9 percent who identify as Jewish? Pew Research Center, Public & Religious Life, Religious Landscape Study, http://www.pewforum.org/religious-landscape-study/. In what way?
5. *Ceremonial deism.* The majority suggests that displaying a crèche is merely an acknowledgment of our religious heritage on par with mentioning God in our national motto ("In God We Trust"). Are the two comparable? In any event, is including God in our national motto problematic? The official national motto used to be "E Pluribus Unum" (Out of Many, One). It was changed in 1956, during the Cold War, in order to differentiate the United States from the atheistic USSR. Does this history change your answer? The Cold War era also saw the addition of "under God" to the Pledge of Allegiance. Although the Pledge's constitutionality was

challenged in Elk Grove Unified School District v. Newdow, 542 U.S. 1 (2004), the Court found that Newdow lacked standing and therefore did not reach the Establishment Clause question.

6. *Reasonable person.* The endorsement test asks whether a reasonable person would conclude that the government's display had the purpose or effect of endorsing religion. Does the reasonable person have a religion? Would a reasonable Christian view the crèche or "In God We Trust" differently from a reasonable Muslim, Buddhist, or atheist? How would you feel if instead of the crèche surrounded by secular objects, the town of Pawtucket displayed a five foot menorah or a five foot Buddha surrounded by toys?
7. *Protecting religion.* Among its other goals, the Establishment Clause was designed to protect the sponsored religion from degradation. Has Christianity been tarnished or demeaned by a government sponsored holiday display that pairs a crèche with Santa's house, festive reindeer, and a clown?

McCreary County, Kentucky v. American Civil Liberties Union of Kentucky

545 U.S. 844 (2005)

[In the initial action that eventually led to this lawsuit, two Kentucky Counties posted large copies of the Ten Commandments in their courthouses. The ACLU sued to enjoin the displays on the ground that they violated the First Amendment's Establishment Clause. In response, the Counties adopted nearly identical resolutions calling for a more extensive exhibit meant to show that the Commandments are Kentucky's "precedent legal code." The resolutions noted several grounds for taking that position, including the state legislature's acknowledgment of Christ as the "Prince of Ethics." The displays around the Commandments were modified to include eight smaller, historical documents containing religious references as their sole common element, for example, the Declaration of Independence's "endowed by their Creator" passage. The District Court held that the new display lacked a secular purpose under *Lemon.* After changing counsel, the Counties revised the exhibits again. The new exhibit, entitled "The Foundations of American Law and Government Display," consisted of nine framed documents of equal size. One set out the Commandments explicitly identified as the "King James Version," quoted them at greater length, and explained that they have profoundly influenced the formation of Western legal thought and this Nation. Along with the Commandments, the counties posted framed copies of, among other things, the Star Spangled Banner's lyrics and the Declaration of Independence, accompanied by statements about their historical and legal significance. Both the District Court and the Court of Appeals held the third display unconstitutional under the *Lemon* secular purpose analysis, and the Supreme Court affirmed.]

Justice SOUTER delivered the opinion of the Court.

Ever since *Lemon v. Kurtzman* summarized the three familiar considerations for evaluating Establishment Clause claims, looking to whether government action has "a secular legislative purpose" has been a common, albeit seldom dispositive, element of our cases. Though we have found government action motivated by an illegitimate purpose only four times since *Lemon*, and "the secular purpose requirement alone may rarely be determinative . . ., it nevertheless serves an important function."

We take *Stone* [*v. Graham*] as the initial legal benchmark, our only case dealing with the constitutionality of displaying the Commandments. *Stone* recognized that the Commandments are an "instrument of religion" and that, at least on the facts before it, the display of their text could presumptively be understood as meant to advance religion: although state law specifically required their posting in public school classrooms, their isolated exhibition did not leave room even for an argument that secular education explained their being there. But *Stone* did not purport to decide the constitutionality of every possible way the Commandments might be set out by the government, and under the Establishment Clause detail is key. Hence, we look to the record of evidence showing the progression leading up to the third display of the Commandments.

The display rejected in *Stone* had two obvious similarities to the first one in the sequence here: both set out a text of the Commandments as distinct from any traditionally symbolic representation, and each stood alone, not part of an arguably secular display. *Stone* stressed the significance of integrating the Commandments into a secular scheme to forestall the broadcast of an otherwise clearly religious message, and for good reason, the Commandments being a central point of reference in the religious and moral history of Jews and Christians. They proclaim the existence of a monotheistic god (no other gods). They regulate details of religious obligation (no graven images, no sabbath breaking, no vain oath swearing). And they unmistakably rest even the universally accepted prohibitions (as against murder, theft, and the like) on the sanction of the divinity proclaimed at the beginning of the text. Displaying that text is thus different from a symbolic depiction, like tablets with 10 roman numerals, which could be seen as alluding to a general notion of law, not a sectarian conception of faith. Where the text is set out, the insistence of the religious message is hard to avoid in the absence of a context plausibly suggesting a message going beyond an excuse to promote the religious point of view. The display in *Stone* had no context that might have indicated an object beyond the religious character of the text, and the Counties' solo exhibit here did nothing more to counter the sectarian implication than the postings at issue in *Stone*. Actually, the posting by the Counties lacked even the *Stone* display's implausible disclaimer that the Commandments were set out to show their effect on the civil law. What is more, at the ceremony for posting the framed Commandments in Pulaski County, the county executive was accompanied by his pastor, who testified to the certainty of the existence of God. The reasonable observer could only think that the Counties meant to emphasize and celebrate the Commandments' religious message.

This is not to deny that the Commandments have had influence on civil or secular law; a major text of a majority religion is bound to be felt. The point is simply that the original text viewed in its entirety is an unmistakably religious statement dealing with religious obligations and with morality subject to religious sanction. When the government initiates an effort to place this statement alone in public view, a religious object is unmistakable.

[The Court then discussed the history of the three displays.] These new statements of purpose [issued in conjunction with the third display] were presented only as a litigating position, there being no further authorizing action by the Counties' governing boards. And although repeal of the earlier county authorizations would not have erased them from the record of evidence bearing on current purpose, the extraordinary resolutions for the second display passed just months earlier were not repealed or otherwise repudiated. Indeed, the sectarian spirit of the common resolution found enhanced expression in the third display, which quoted more of the purely religious language of the Commandments than the first two displays had done; ("I the LORD thy God am a jealous God") (text of Second Commandment in third display); ("the LORD will not hold him guiltless that taketh his name in vain") (from text of Third Commandment); and ("that thy days may be long upon the land which the LORD thy God giveth thee") (text of Fifth Commandment). No reasonable observer could swallow the claim that the Counties had cast off the objective so unmistakable in the earlier displays.

Nor did the selection of posted material suggest a clear theme that might prevail over evidence of the continuing religious object. In a collection of documents said to be "foundational" to American government, it is at least odd to include a patriotic anthem, but to omit the Fourteenth Amendment, the most significant structural provision adopted since the original Framing. And it is no less baffling to leave out the original Constitution of 1787 while quoting the 1215 Magna Carta even to the point of its declaration that "fish-weirs shall be removed from the Thames." If an observer found these choices and omissions perplexing in isolation, he would be puzzled for a different reason when he read the Declaration of Independence seeking confirmation for the Counties' posted explanation that the "Ten Commandments . . . influence is clearly seen in the Declaration"; in fact the observer would find that the Commandments are sanctioned as divine imperatives, while the Declaration of Independence holds that the authority of government to enforce the law derives "from the consent of the governed." If the observer had not thrown up his hands, he would probably suspect that the Counties were simply reaching for any way to keep a religious document on the walls of courthouses constitutionally required to embody religious neutrality.

In holding the preliminary injunction adequately supported by evidence that the Counties' purpose had not changed at the third stage, we do not decide that the Counties' past actions forever taint any effort on their part to deal with the subject matter. We hold only that purpose needs to be taken seriously under the Establishment Clause and needs to be understood in light of context; an implausible claim that governmental purpose has changed should not carry the day in a court of law any more than in a head with common sense. It is enough to say here that district courts are fully capable of adjusting preliminary relief to take account of genuine changes in constitutionally significant conditions.

[Justice O'CONNOR's concurring opinion is omitted.]

Justice SCALIA, with whom THE CHIEF JUSTICE and Justice THOMAS join and with whom Justice KENNEDY joins, dissenting.

Besides appealing to the demonstrably false principle that the government cannot favor religion over irreligion, today's opinion suggests that the posting of the Ten Commandments violates the principle that the government cannot favor one religion over another. That is indeed a valid principle where public aid or assistance to religion is concerned or where the free exercise of religion is at issue, but it necessarily applies in a more limited sense to public acknowledgment of the Creator. If religion in the public forum had to be entirely nondenominational, there could be no religion in the public forum at all. One cannot say the word "God," or "the Almighty," one cannot offer public supplication or thanksgiving, without contradicting the beliefs of some people that there are many gods, or that God or the gods pay no attention to human affairs. With respect to public acknowledgment of religious belief, it is entirely clear from our Nation's historical practices that the Establishment Clause permits this disregard of polytheists and believers in unconcerned deities, just as it permits the disregard of devout atheists. The Thanksgiving Proclamation issued by George Washington at the instance of the First Congress was scrupulously nondenominational—but it was monotheistic.

Perhaps in recognition of the centrality of the Ten Commandments as a widely recognized symbol of religion in public life, the Court is at pains to dispel the impression that its decision will require governments across the country to sandblast the Ten Commandments from the public square. The constitutional problem, the Court says, is with the Counties' *purpose* in erecting the Foundations Displays, not the displays themselves. The Court adds in a footnote: "One consequence of taking account of the purpose underlying past actions is that the same government action may be constitutional if taken in the first instance and unconstitutional if it has a sectarian heritage."

This inconsistency may be explicable in theory, but I suspect that the "objective observer" with whom the Court is so concerned will recognize its absurdity in practice. By virtue of details familiar only to the parties to litigation and their lawyers, McCreary and Pulaski Counties, Kentucky, and Rutherford County, Tennessee, have been ordered to remove the same display that appears in courthouses from Mercer County, Kentucky to Elkhart County, Indiana. Displays erected in silence (and under the direction of good legal advice) are permissible, while those hung after discussion and debate are deemed unconstitutional. Reduction of the Establishment Clause to such minutiae trivializes the Clause's protection against religious establishment; indeed, it may inflame religious passions by making the passing comments of every government official the subject of endless litigation.

Van Orden v. Perry

545 U.S. 677 (2005)

[Among the 21 historical markers and 17 monuments surrounding the Texas State Capitol is a 6-foot-high monolith inscribed with the Ten Commandments. The monolith stands 6 feet high and 31/2 feet wide. It is located to the north of the Capitol building, between the Capitol and the Supreme Court building. Its primary content is the text of the Ten Commandments. An eagle grasping the American flag, an eye inside of a pyramid, and two small tablets with what appears to be an ancient script are carved above the text of the Ten Commandments. Below the text are two Stars of David and the superimposed Greek letters Chi and Rho, which represent Christ. The bottom of the monument bears the inscription "PRESENTED TO THE PEOPLE AND YOUTH OF TEXAS BY THE FRATERNAL ORDER OF

EAGLES OF TEXAS 1961." The legislative record surrounding the State's acceptance of the monument is limited to legislative journal entries. After the monument was accepted, the State selected a site for the monument based on the recommendation of the state organization responsible for maintaining the Capitol grounds. The Eagles paid the cost of erecting the monument, the dedication of which was presided over by two state legislators.]

Chief Justice REHNQUIST announced the judgment of the Court and delivered an opinion, in which Justice SCALIA, Justice KENNEDY, and Justice THOMAS join.

Our cases, Januslike, point in two directions in applying the Establishment Clause. One face looks toward the strong role played by religion and religious traditions throughout our Nation's history. The other face looks toward the principle that governmental intervention in religious matters can itself endanger religious freedom.

This case, like all Establishment Clause challenges, presents us with the difficulty of respecting both faces. Our institutions presuppose a Supreme Being, yet these institutions must not press religious observances upon their citizens. One face looks to the past in acknowledgment of our Nation's heritage, while the other looks to the present in demanding a separation between church and state. Reconciling these two faces requires that we neither abdicate our responsibility to maintain a division between church and state nor evince a hostility to religion by disabling the government from in some ways recognizing our religious heritage.

Whatever may be the fate of the *Lemon* test in the larger scheme of Establishment Clause jurisprudence, we think it not useful in dealing with the sort of passive monument that Texas has erected on its Capitol grounds. Instead, our analysis is driven both by the nature of the monument and by our Nation's history.

In this case we are faced with a display of the Ten Commandments on government property outside the Texas State Capitol. Such acknowledgments of the role played by the Ten Commandments in our Nation's heritage are common throughout America. We need only look within our own Courtroom. Since 1935, Moses has stood, holding two tablets that reveal portions of the Ten Commandments written in Hebrew, among other lawgivers in the south frieze. Representations of the Ten Commandments adorn the metal gates lining the north and south sides of the Courtroom as well as the doors leading into the Courtroom. Moses also sits on the exterior east facade of the building holding the Ten Commandments tablets.

Of course, the Ten Commandments are religious—they were so viewed at their inception and so remain. The monument, therefore, has religious significance. According to Judeo-Christian belief, the Ten Commandments were given to Moses by God on Mt. Sinai. But Moses was a lawgiver as well as a religious leader. And the Ten Commandments have an undeniable historical meaning, as the foregoing examples demonstrate. Simply having religious content or promoting a message consistent with a religious doctrine does not run afoul of the Establishment Clause.

There are, of course, limits to the display of religious messages or symbols. For example, we held unconstitutional a Kentucky statute requiring the posting of the Ten Commandments in every public schoolroom. Stone v. Graham, 449 U.S. 39 (1980) (*per curiam*). In the classroom context, we found that the Kentucky statute had an improper and plainly religious purpose. As evidenced by *Stone*'s almost exclusive reliance upon two of our school prayer cases, it stands as an example of the fact that we have "been particularly vigilant in monitoring compliance with the Establishment Clause in elementary and secondary schools." Neither *Stone* itself nor subsequent opinions have indicated that *Stone*'s holding would extend to a legislative chamber, or to capitol grounds.[11]

[Justices SCALIA's and THOMAS's concurring opinions are omitted.]

Justice BREYER, concurring in the judgment.

In *School Dist. of Abington Township v. Schempp*, Justice Goldberg, joined by Justice Harlan, wrote, in respect to the First Amendment's Religion Clauses, that there is "no simple and clear measure which by precise application can readily and invariably demark the permissible from the impermissible." One must refer instead to the basic purposes of those Clauses. They seek to "assure the fullest possible scope of religious liberty and tolerance for all." They seek to avoid that divisiveness based upon religion that promotes social conflict, sapping the strength of government and religion alike. They seek to maintain that "separation of church and state" that has long been critical to the "peaceful dominion that religion exercises in [this] country," where the "spirit of religion" and the "spirit of freedom" are productively "united," "reign[ing] together" but in separate spheres "on the same soil." A. de Tocqueville, Democracy in America 282-283 (1835) (H. Mansfield & D. Winthrop transls. and eds. 2000).

The Court has made clear, as Justices Goldberg and Harlan noted, that the realization of these goals means that government must "neither engage in nor compel religious practices," that it must "effect no favoritism among sects or between religion and nonreligion," and that it must "work deterrence of no religious belief." The government must avoid excessive interference with, or promotion of, religion. But the Establishment Clause does not compel the government to purge from the public sphere all that in any way partakes of the religious. Such absolutism is not only inconsistent with our national traditions, but would also tend to promote the kind of social conflict the Establishment Clause seeks to avoid. . . .

If the relation between government and religion is one of separation, but not of mutual hostility and suspicion, one will inevitably find difficult borderline cases. And in such cases, I see no test-related substitute for the exercise of legal judgment. That judgment is not a personal judgment. Rather, as in all constitutional cases, it must reflect and remain faithful to the underlying purposes of the Clauses, and it must take account of context and consequences measured in light of those

---

11. Nor does anything suggest that *Stone* would extend to displays of the Ten Commandments that lack a "plainly religious," "pre-eminent purpose," [*Stone v. Graham*,] at 41. *See Edwards v. Aguillard*, . . . ("[*Stone*] did not mean that no use could ever be made of the Ten Commandments, or that the Ten Commandments played an exclusively religious role in the history of Western Civilization"). Indeed, we need not decide in this case the extent to which a primarily religious purpose would affect our analysis because it is clear from the record that there is no evidence of such a purpose in this case.

purposes. While the Court's prior tests provide useful guideposts—and might well lead to the same result the Court reaches today, no exact formula can dictate a resolution to such fact-intensive cases.

The case before us is a borderline case. It concerns a large granite monument bearing the text of the Ten Commandments located on the grounds of the Texas State Capitol. On the one hand, the Commandments' text undeniably has a religious message, invoking, indeed emphasizing, the Deity. On the other hand, focusing on the text of the Commandments alone cannot conclusively resolve this case. Rather, to determine the message that the text here conveys, we must examine how the text is *used*. And that inquiry requires us to consider the context of the display.

In certain contexts, a display of the tablets of the Ten Commandments can convey not simply a religious message but also a secular moral message (about proper standards of social conduct). And in certain contexts, a display of the tablets can also convey a historical message (about a historic relation between those standards and the law)—a fact that helps to explain the display of those tablets in dozens of courthouses throughout the Nation, including the Supreme Court of the United States.

Here the tablets have been used as part of a display that communicates not simply a religious message, but a secular message as well. The circumstances surrounding the display's placement on the capitol grounds and its physical setting suggest that the State itself intended the latter, nonreligious aspects of the tablets' message to predominate. And the monument's 40-year history on the Texas state grounds indicates that that has been its effect. . . .

The physical setting of the monument, moreover, suggests little or nothing of the sacred. The monument sits in a large park containing 17 monuments and 21 historical markers, all designed to illustrate the "ideals" of those who settled in Texas and of those who have lived there since that time. The setting does not readily lend itself to meditation or any other religious activity. But it does provide a context of history and moral ideals. It (together with the display's inscription about its origin) communicates to visitors that the State sought to reflect moral principles, illustrating a relation between ethics and law that the State's citizens, historically speaking, have endorsed. That is to say, the context suggests that the State intended the display's moral message—an illustrative message reflecting the historical "ideals" of Texans—to predominate.

If these factors provide a strong, but not conclusive, indication that the Commandments' text on this monument conveys a predominantly secular message, a further factor is determinative here. As far as I can tell, 40 years passed in which the presence of this monument, legally speaking, went unchallenged (until the single legal objection raised by petitioner). And I am not aware of any evidence suggesting that this was due to a climate of intimidation. Hence, those 40 years suggest more strongly than can any set of formulaic tests that few individuals, whatever their system of beliefs, are likely to have understood the monument as amounting, in any significantly detrimental way, to a government effort to favor a particular religious sect, primarily to promote religion over nonreligion, to "engage in" any "religious practice," to "compel" any "religious practice," or to "work deterrence" of any "religious belief." Those 40 years suggest that the public visiting the capitol grounds has considered the religious aspect of the tablets' message as part of what is a broader moral and historical message reflective of a cultural heritage. . . .

Justice STEVENS, with whom Justice GINSBURG joins, dissenting.

The sole function of the monument on the grounds of Texas' State Capitol is to display the full text of one version of the Ten Commandments. The monument is not a work of art and does not refer to any event in the history of the State. It is significant because, and only because, it communicates the following message:

> "I AM the LORD thy God.
> "Thou shalt have no other gods before me.
> "Thou shalt not make to thyself any graven images.
> "Thou shalt not take the Name of the Lord thy God in vain.
> "Remember the Sabbath day, to keep it holy.
> "Honor thy father and thy mother, that thy days may be long upon the land which the Lord thy God giveth thee.
> "Thou shalt not kill.
> "Thou shalt not commit adultery.
> "Thou shalt not steal.
> "Thou shalt not bear false witness against thy neighbor.
> "Thou shalt not covet thy neighbor's house.
> "Thou shalt not covet thy neighbor's wife, nor his manservant, nor his maidservant, nor his cattle, nor anything that is thy neighbor's."

Viewed on its face, Texas' display has no purported connection to God's role in the formation of Texas or the founding of our Nation; nor does it provide the reasonable observer with any basis to guess that it was erected to honor any individual or organization. The message transmitted by Texas' chosen display is quite plain: This State endorses the divine code of the "Judeo-Christian" God.

For those of us who learned to recite the King James version of the text long before we understood the meaning of some of its words, God's Commandments may seem like wise counsel. The question before this Court, however, is whether it is counsel that the State of Texas may proclaim without violating the Establishment Clause of the Constitution. If any fragment of Jefferson's metaphorical "wall of separation between church and State" is to be preserved—if there remains any meaning to the "wholesome 'neutrality' of which this Court's [Establishment Clause] cases speak,"—a negative answer to that question is mandatory.

The reason this message stands apart is that the Decalogue is a venerable religious text. As we held 25 years ago, it is beyond dispute that "[t]he Ten Commandments are undeniably a sacred text in the Jewish and Christian faiths." *Stone v. Graham*. For many followers, the Commandments represent the literal word of God as spoken to Moses and repeated to his followers after descending from Mount Sinai. The message conveyed by the Ten Commandments thus cannot be analogized to an appendage to a common article of commerce ("In God we Trust") or an incidental part of a familiar recital ("God save the United States and this honorable Court"). Thankfully, the plurality does not attempt to minimize the religious significance of the Ten Commandments. Attempts to secularize what is unquestionably a sacred text defy credibility and disserve people of faith.

[D]espite the Eagles' best efforts to choose a benign nondenominational text,[15] the Ten Commandments display projects not just a religious, but an inherently sectarian message. There are many distinctive versions of the Decalogue, ascribed to by different religions and even different denominations within a particular faith; to a pious and learned observer, these differences may be of enormous religious significance.[16] *See* Lubet, *The Ten Commandments in Alabama*, 15 Constitutional Commentary 471, 474-476 (Fall 1998). In choosing to display this version of the Commandments, Texas tells the observer that the State supports this side of the doctrinal religious debate. The reasonable observer, after all, has no way of knowing that this text was the product of a compromise, or that there is a rationale of any kind for the text's selection.

The Establishment Clause, if nothing else, forbids government from "specifying details upon which men and women who believe in a benevolent, omnipotent Creator and Ruler of the world are known to differ." Given that the chosen text inscribed on the Ten Commandments monument invariably places the State at the center of a serious sectarian dispute, the display is unquestionably unconstitutional under our case law.

Even if, however, the message of the monument, despite the inscribed text, fairly could be said to represent the belief system of all Judeo-Christians, it would still run afoul of the Establishment Clause by prescribing a compelled code of conduct from one God, namely a Judeo-Christian God, that is rejected by prominent polytheistic sects, such as Hinduism, as well as nontheistic religions, such as Buddhism. And, at the very least, the text of the Ten Commandments impermissibly

---

15. Despite the Eagles' efforts, not all of the monuments they donated in fact conform to a "universally-accepted" text. Compare, *e.g.*, Appendix, *infra* (including the command that "Thou shalt not make to thyself any graven images"), with *Freedom from Religion Foundation*, 898 P.2d at 1016 (omitting that command altogether). The distinction represents a critical divide between the Protestant and Catholic faiths. During the Reformation, Protestants destroyed images of the Virgin Mary and of Jesus Christ that were venerated in Catholic churches. Even today there is a notable difference between the imagery in different churches, a difference that may in part be attributable to differing understandings of the meaning of what is the Second Commandment in the King James Bible translation and a portion of the First Commandment in the Catholic translation. *See* Finkelman, *The Ten Commandments on the Courthouse Lawn and Elsewhere*, 73 Ford. L. Rev. 1477, 1493-1494 (2005).

16. For example, in the Jewish version of the Sixth Commandment God commands: "You shall not murder"; whereas, the King James interpretation of the same command is: "Thou shalt not kill." Compare W. Plaut, The Torah: A Modern Commentary 534 (1981), with Appendix, *infra*. The difference between the two versions is not merely semantic; rather, it is but one example of a deep theological dispute. *See* Finkelman, *supra*, at 1481-1500; P. Maier, *Enumerating the Decalogue; Do We Number the Ten Commandments Correctly?* 16 Concordia J. 18, 18-26 (1990). Varying interpretations of this Commandment explain the actions of vegetarians who refuse to eat meat, pacifists who refuse to work for munitions makers, prison officials who refuse to administer lethal injections to death row inmates, and pharmacists who refuse to sell morning-after pills to women. *See* Finkelman, *supra*, at 1494-1496; Brief for American Jewish Congress et al. as *Amici Curiae* 22-23. Although the command is ambiguous, its power to motivate likeminded interpreters of its message cannot be denied.

commands a preference for religion over irreligion. Any of those bases, in my judgment, would be sufficient to conclude that the message should not be proclaimed by the State of Texas on a permanent monument at the seat of its government.

[Justice SOUTER's and Justice O'CONNOR's dissenting opinions are omitted.]

NOTES AND QUESTIONS

1. *A principled distinction or ad hoc decision making?* In light of the different outcomes of *McCreary County* and *Van Orden*, how should an attorney advise a city or county regarding a plaque or monument depicting the Ten Commandments? Is the key factor the existence of an explicit and plausible disavowal by the government officials of any intent to endorse the religious message of the Commandments? Or is what surrounds the plaque or monument the key? Might the age of the monument be the deciding factor? Is the divisiveness caused by the placement of a particular display crucial?
2. *Religion in the public square.* Dissenting from *McCreary County*, Justice Scalia writes that "if religion in the public forum has to be entirely nondenominational there could be no religion in the public forum at all." Of course, his point is limited to government-sponsored religion. We know from the equal access cases, see *supra* pp. 990-992, that the Free Speech Clause protects private religious speech in any forum open to the public. Justice Scalia concludes that because nondenominational religion is impossible, the Establishment Clause does not bar the government from favoring some religions over others, and favoring those that center around God in particular. If Justice Scalia is correct about the impossibility of nondenominational religion, what other conclusion might you draw about government-sponsored religion?
3. *Context.* Justice Rehnquist wrote for the four Justices in *Van Orden v. Perry*, with Justice Breyer providing the fifth vote. Justice Breyer emphasizes the importance of context. Context might include the background to enactment, which informed the decision in *McCreary*. Context might refer to the setting, such as a museum, school, or grounds of the State Capitol. Context might also encompass what is physically around the display. What else might context include?
4. *Divisiveness.* Justice Breyer's *Van Orden* concurrence also highlights the issue of divisiveness. According to Justice Breyer, the lack of complaints about the Ten Commandments monument for forty years showed that it conveyed a secular message and not a divisive religious one. What, if anything, does the apparent need to permit Establishment Clause plaintiffs to sue anonymously say about the viability of Justice Breyer's proposed "divisiveness" test for Establishment Clause violations? Should religious minorities be required to seek out public confrontations in order to establish a viable Establishment Clause claim?
5. *May government favor one sect's version of a religious text?* As Justice Stevens explains in dissent, different faith traditions have different Ten

Commandments, with the variations reflecting theological differences. Is the existence of multiple versions of the Ten Commandments relevant? In his *McCreary County* dissent, Justice Scalia thought not: "I doubt that most religious adherents are even aware that there are competing versions with doctrinal consequences (I certainly was not)." Suppose a municipality is considering posting a Ten Commandments plaque or monument, and both Protestant and Catholic residents seek to have their version of the Commandments engraved on the display; would the simple fact that the municipality chooses one and rejects the other be evidence of an impermissible Establishment Clause violation?

6. *Source of law.* Are the Ten Commandments an important source for American law? Are all the commandments incorporated into our laws? Is murder, theft, and perjury also forbidden in countries that do not rely on the Ten Commandments for their laws? Does the United States Constitution refer to the Ten Commandments? What about the fact that the Declaration of Independence refers to a "Creator"?
7. *Other examples of government appropriation of religious symbols.* In addition to the Ten Commandments, several other examples of official government references to religion or religious symbols have been the subject of lower court rulings. *See* O'Hair v. Murray, 588 F.2d 1144 (5th Cir. 1979) (upholding a federal statute requiring the motto "In God We Trust" to be inscribed on coins and currency); Murray v. Austin, 947 F.2d 147 (5th Cir. 1991) (holding that Establishment Clause is not violated by the use of Christian cross in city insignia); Harris v. Zion, 927 F.2d 1401 (7th Cir. 1991), *cert. denied,* 505 U.S. 1229 (1992) (holding unconstitutional the use of a Latin cross in city insignias); ACLU v. Capitol Square Review & Advisory Bd., 243 F.3d 289 (6th Cir. 2001) (upholding the constitutionality of Ohio's state motto "With God All Things Are Possible" on the grounds that (1) no reasonable observer would perceive motto to be an endorsement of Christianity, (2) the motto serves a secular legislative purpose by boosting morale and serving as a symbol of a common identity, and (3) the motto has a secular effect because it "merely pays lip service to the puissance of God").
8. *Does government appropriation potentially degrade religious symbols?* Finally, consider one of the points made in Judge Boyce's dissenting opinion in *Capitol Square*: "When Jesus' key to eternal salvation is lumped in the Ohio statutes with the Buckeye tree and tomato juice, the signal sent is that religion is no more important than those two nice but ultimately inconsequential things. To many, religion is much more important, perhaps the most important force in their lives. I fear that Ohio has given Christianity a crutch it is better left without." *Id.* at 312. Does Judge Boyce have a valid point here? Does government appropriation of religious symbols have the effect of repurposing them for secular ends? And, if so, does this process of reinterpretation do more to debase than to edify religious iconography?

American Legion v. American Humanist Association was not the first time the Supreme Court addressed the constitutionality of a Latin cross on government land. Salazar v. Buono, 559 U.S. 700 (2010), involved a seven-foot-tall Latin cross on Sunrise Rock, a rocky outcrop located in the Mojave National Preserve that the Veterans of

Foreign Wars (VFW) had erected in 1934 to honor American soldiers who died in World War I. Frank Buono, a retired National Park Service employee, initiated litigation challenging the continued placement of the cross on federal lands. After Buono prevailed in the lower federal courts, Congress enacted a statute that transferred the park land on which the cross was located to the VFW, in hopes of preventing its removal from Sunrise Rock. While the federal district court enjoined the land transfer on Establishment Clause grounds, the Supreme Court allowed it. The Court, splintering badly, had no majority and could not agree on a rationale for deciding the case.

In its most recent decision addressing government-sponsored religious displays, the Court upheld a Latin cross on public land in *American Legion v. American Humanist Association.*

American Legion v. American Humanist Association

139 S. Ct. 2069 (2019)

Justice ALITO announced the judgment of the Court and delivered the opinion of the Court with respect to Parts I, II–B, II–C, III, and IV, and an opinion with respect to Parts II–A and II–D, in which THE CHIEF JUSTICE, Justice BREYER, and Justice KAVANAUGH join.

Since 1925, the Bladensburg Peace Cross (Cross) has stood as a tribute to 49 area soldiers who gave their lives in the First World War. Eighty-nine years after the dedication of the Cross, respondents filed this lawsuit, claiming that they are offended by the sight of the memorial on public land and that its presence there and the expenditure of public funds to maintain it violate the Establishment Clause of the First Amendment. To remedy this violation, they asked a federal court to order the relocation or demolition of the Cross or at least the removal of its arms. The Court of Appeals for the Fourth Circuit agreed that the memorial is unconstitutional and remanded for a determination of the proper remedy. We now reverse.

Although the cross has long been a preeminent Christian symbol, its use in the Bladensburg memorial has a special significance. After the First World War, the picture of row after row of plain white crosses marking the overseas graves of soldiers who had lost their lives in that horrible conflict was emblazoned on the minds of Americans at home, and the adoption of the cross as the Bladensburg memorial must be viewed in that historical context. For nearly a century, the Bladensburg Cross has expressed the community's grief at the loss of the young men who perished, its thanks for their sacrifice, and its dedication to the ideals for which they fought. It has become a prominent community landmark, and its removal or radical alteration at this date would be seen by many not as a neutral act but as the manifestation of "a hostility toward religion that has no place in our Establishment Clause traditions." . . .

I

The cross came into widespread use as a symbol of Christianity by the fourth century, and it retains that meaning today. But there are many contexts in which the symbol has also taken on a secular meaning . . .

The image used in the Bladensburg memorial—a plain Latin cross—also took on new meaning after World War I. "During and immediately after the war, the army marked soldiers' graves with temporary wooden crosses or Stars of David"—a departure from the prior practice of marking graves in American military cemeteries with uniform rectangular slabs. G. Piehler, Remembering War the American Way 101 (1995); App. 1146. The vast majority of these grave markers consisted of crosses, and thus when Americans saw photographs of these cemeteries, what struck them were rows and rows of plain white crosses. As a result, the image of a simple white cross "developed into a 'central symbol' " of the conflict. *Ibid.* . . .

After the 1918 armistice, the War Department announced plans to replace the wooden crosses and Stars of David with uniform marble slabs like those previously used in American military cemeteries. But the public outcry against that proposal was swift and fierce. . . . A Member of Congress likewise introduced a resolution noting that "these wooden symbols have, during and since the World War, been regarded as emblematic of the great sacrifices which that war entailed, have been so treated by poets and artists and have become peculiarly and inseparably associated in the thought of surviving relatives and comrades and of the Nation with these World War graves." H. Res. 15, 68th Cong., 1 (1924), App. 1163–1164. This national debate and its outcome confirmed the cross's widespread resonance as a symbol of sacrifice in the war.

Recognition of the cross's symbolism extended to local communities across the country. In late 1918, residents of Prince George's County, Maryland, formed a committee for the purpose of erecting a memorial for the county's fallen soldiers. . . . Although we do not know precisely why the committee chose the cross, it is unsurprising that the committee—and many others commemorating World War I—adopted a symbol so widely associated with that wrenching event. . . .

The completed monument is a 32-foot tall Latin cross that sits on a large pedestal. The American Legion's emblem is displayed at its center, and the words "Valor," "Endurance," "Courage," and "Devotion" are inscribed at its base, one on each of the four faces. The pedestal also features a 9- by 2.5-foot bronze plaque explaining that the monument is "Dedicated to the heroes of Prince George's County, Maryland who lost their lives in the Great War for the liberty of the world." . . .

At the dedication ceremony, a local Catholic priest offered an invocation. United States Representative Stephen W. Gambrill delivered the keynote address, honoring the " 'men of Prince George's County' " who " 'fought for the sacred right of all to live in peace and security.' . . .

As the area around the Cross developed, the monument came to be at the center of a busy intersection. In 1961, the Maryland-National Capital Park and Planning Commission (Commission) acquired the Cross and the land on which it sits in order to preserve the monument and address traffic-safety concerns . . . . Over the next five decades, the Commission spent approximately $ 117,000 to maintain and preserve the monument. In 2008, it budgeted an additional $ 100,000 for renovations and repairs to the Cross. . . .

II

A

Lemon ambitiously attempted to distill from the Court's existing case law a test that would bring order and predictability to Establishment Clause decisionmaking. That test, as noted, called on courts to examine the purposes and effects of a challenged government action, as well as any entanglement with religion that it might entail. *Lemon.* The Court later elaborated that the "effect[s]" of a challenged action should be assessed by asking whether a "reasonable observer" would conclude that the action constituted an "endorsement" of religion. . . .

If the *Lemon* Court thought that its test would provide a framework for all future Establishment Clause decisions, its expectation has not been met. In many cases, this Court has either expressly declined to apply the test or has simply ignored it. . . .

This pattern is a testament to the *Lemon* test's shortcomings. . . . The test has been harshly criticized by Members of this Court, lamented by lower court judges, and questioned by a diverse roster of scholars.

For at least four reasons, the *Lemon* test presents particularly daunting problems in cases, including the one now before us, that involve the use, for ceremonial, celebratory, or commemorative purposes, of words or symbols with religious associations. Together, these considerations counsel against efforts to evaluate such cases under *Lemon* and toward application of a presumption of constitutionality for longstanding monuments, symbols, and practices.

B

First, these cases often concern monuments, symbols, or practices that were first established long ago, and in such cases, identifying their original purpose or purposes may be especially difficult. . . .

Second, as time goes by, the purposes associated with an established monument, symbol, or practice often multiply. . . . The existence of multiple purposes is not exclusive to longstanding monuments, symbols, or practices, but this phenomenon is more likely to occur in such cases. Even if the original purpose of a monument was infused with religion, the passage of time may obscure that sentiment. As our society becomes more and more religiously diverse, a community may preserve such monuments, symbols, and practices for the sake of their historical significance or their place in a common cultural heritage. . . .

Third, just as the purpose for maintaining a monument, symbol, or practice may evolve, "[t]he 'message' conveyed . . . may change over time." . . . With sufficient time, religiously expressive monuments, symbols, and practices can become embedded features of a community's landscape and identity. The community may come to value them without necessarily embracing their religious roots. . . . consider the many cities and towns across the United States that bear religious names. Religion undoubtedly motivated those who named Bethlehem, Pennsylvania; Las Cruces, New Mexico; Providence, Rhode Island; Corpus Christi, Texas; Nephi, Utah, and the countless other places in our country with names that are rooted in religion. Yet few would argue that this history requires that these names be erased from the map. . . .

Fourth, when time's passage imbues a religiously expressive monument, symbol, or practice with this kind of familiarity and historical significance, removing it may no longer appear neutral, especially to the local community for which it has taken on particular meaning. A government that roams the land, tearing down monuments with religious symbolism and scrubbing away any reference to the divine will strike many as aggressively hostile to religion. . . .

These four considerations show that retaining established, religiously expressive monuments, symbols, and practices is quite different from erecting or adopting new ones. The passage of time gives rise to a strong presumption of constitutionality.

C

. . . Immediately following the war, "[c]ommunities across America built memorials to commemorate those who had served the nation in the struggle to make the world safe for democracy." G. Piehler, The American Memory of War, App. 1124. Although not all of these communities included a cross in their memorials, the cross had become a symbol closely linked to the war. . . . And as already noted, the fallen soldiers' final resting places abroad were marked by white crosses or Stars of David. The solemn image of endless rows of white crosses became inextricably linked with and symbolic of the ultimate price paid by 116,000 soldiers. And this relationship between the cross and the war undoubtedly influenced the design of the many war memorials that sprang up across the Nation.

This is not to say that the cross's association with the war was the sole or dominant motivation for the inclusion of the symbol in every World War I memorial that features it. But today, it is all but impossible to tell whether that was so. . . . And no matter what the original purposes for the erection of a monument, a community may wish to preserve it for very different reasons, such as the historic preservation and traffic-safety concerns the Commission has pressed here. . . .

Finally, as World War I monuments have endured through the years and become a familiar part of the physical and cultural landscape, requiring their removal would not be viewed by many as a neutral act. And an alteration like the one entertained by the Fourth Circuit—amputating the arms of the Cross, see 874 F.3d at 202, n. 7—would be seen by many as profoundly disrespectful. One member of the majority below viewed this objection as inconsistent with the claim that the Bladensburg Cross serves secular purposes, see 891 F.3d at 121 (Wynn, J., concurring in denial of en banc), but this argument misunderstands the complexity of monuments. A monument may express many purposes and convey many different messages, both secular and religious. *Cf. Van Orden*, 545 U.S. at 690, 125 S.Ct. 2854 (plurality opinion) (describing simultaneous religious and secular meaning of the Ten Commandments display). Thus, a campaign to obliterate items with religious associations may evidence hostility to religion even if those religious associations are no longer in the forefront. . . .

D

While the *Lemon* Court ambitiously attempted to find a grand unified theory of the Establishment Clause, in later cases, we have taken a more modest approach that focuses on the particular issue at hand and looks to history for guidance. Our cases involving prayer before a legislative session are an example. . . .

IV

The cross is undoubtedly a Christian symbol, but that fact should not blind us to everything else that the Bladensburg Cross has come to represent. For some, that monument is a symbolic resting place for ancestors who never returned home. For others, it is a place for the community to gather and honor all veterans and their sacrifices for our Nation. For others still, it is a historical landmark. For many of these people, destroying or defacing the Cross that has stood undisturbed for nearly a century would not be neutral and would not further the ideals of respect and tolerance embodied in the First Amendment. For all these reasons, the Cross does not offend the Constitution.

* * *

We reverse the judgment of the Court of Appeals for the Fourth Circuit and remand the cases for further proceedings.

It is so ordered.

Justice BREYER, with whom Justice KAGAN joins, concurring.

I have long maintained that there is no single formula for resolving Establishment Clause challenges. . . .

I agree with the Court that allowing the State of Maryland to display and maintain the Peace Cross poses no threat to those ends. The Court's opinion eloquently explains why that is so: The Latin cross is uniquely associated with the fallen soldiers of World War I; the organizers of the Peace Cross acted with the undeniably secular motive of commemorating local soldiers; no evidence suggests that they sought to disparage or exclude any religious group; the secular values inscribed on the Cross and its place among other memorials strengthen its message of patriotism and commemoration; and, finally, the Cross has stood on the same land for 94 years, generating no controversy in the community until this lawsuit was filed. Nothing in the record suggests that the lack of public outcry "was due to a climate of intimidation." . . . And, as the Court explains, ordering its removal or alteration at this late date would signal "a hostility toward religion that has no place in our Establishment Clause traditions."

The case would be different, in my view, if there were evidence that the organizers had "deliberately disrespected" members of minority faiths or if the Cross had been erected only recently, rather than in the aftermath of World War I. . . .

Nor do I understand the Court's opinion today to adopt a "history and tradition test" that would permit any newly constructed religious memorial on public land. . . .

Justice KAVANAUGH, concurring.

. . . Consistent with the Court's case law, the Court today applies a history and tradition test in examining and upholding the constitutionality of the Bladensburg Cross. . . . As this case again demonstrates, this Court no longer applies the old test articulated in *Lemon*. . . .

Justice KAGAN, concurring in part.

. . . Although I agree that rigid application of the *Lemon* test does not solve every Establishment Clause problem, I think that test's focus on purposes and effects is crucial in evaluating government action in this sphere—as this very suit shows. I therefore do not join Part II–A. I do not join Part II–D out of perhaps an excess of caution. . . .

Justice THOMAS, concurring in the judgment.

. . . "[t]he mere presence of the monument along [respondents'] path involves no coercion and thus does not violate the Establishment Clause." *Van Orden*, 545 U.S. at 694, 125 S.Ct. 2854 (opinion of THOMAS, J.). The *sine qua non* of an establishment of religion is " 'actual legal coercion.' . . .

As to the long-discredited test set forth in *Lemon*, the plurality rightly rejects its relevance to claims, like this one, involving "religious references or imagery in public monuments, symbols, mottos, displays, and ceremonies." I agree with that aspect of its opinion. I would take the logical next step and overrule the *Lemon* test in all contexts. . . .

* * *

[Justice GORSUCH, with whom Justice THOMAS joins, concurring in the judgment; opinion omitted.]

Justice GINSBURG, with whom Justice SOTOMAYOR joins, dissenting.

An immense Latin cross stands on a traffic island at the center of a busy three-way intersection in Bladensburg, Maryland. "[M]onumental, clear, and bold" by day, the cross looms even larger illuminated against the night-time sky. Known as the Peace Cross, the monument was erected by private citizens in 1925 to honor local soldiers who lost their lives in World War I. "[T]he town's most prominent symbol" was rededicated in 1985 and is now said to honor "the sacrifices made [in] all wars," by "all veterans." Both the Peace Cross and the traffic island are owned and maintained by the Maryland-National Capital Park and Planning Commission (Commission), an agency of the State of Maryland.

Decades ago, this Court recognized that the Establishment Clause of the First Amendment to the Constitution demands governmental neutrality among religious faiths, and between religion and nonreligion. *See Everson v. Bd. of Ewing* (1947). Numerous times since, the Court has reaffirmed the Constitution's commitment to neutrality. Today the Court erodes that neutrality commitment, diminishing precedent designed to preserve individual liberty and civic harmony in favor of a "presumption of constitutionality for longstanding monuments, symbols, and practices."

The Latin cross is the foremost symbol of the Christian faith, embodying the "central theological claim of Christianity: that the son of God died on the cross, that he rose from the dead, and that his death and resurrection offer the possibility of eternal life." Brief for Baptist Joint Committee for Religious Liberty et al. as *Amici Curiae* 7 (Brief for *Amici* Christian and Jewish Organizations). Precisely because the cross symbolizes these sectarian beliefs, it is a common marker for the graves of Christian soldiers. For the same reason, using the cross as a war memorial does not transform it into a secular symbol, as the Courts of Appeals have uniformly recognized. Just as a Star of David is not suitable to honor Christians who died serving their country, so a cross is not suitable to honor those of other faiths who died defending their nation. Soldiers of all faiths "are united by their love of country, but they are not united by the cross." Brief for Jewish War Veterans of the United States of America, Inc., as *Amicus Curiae* 3 (Brief for *Amicus* Jewish War Veterans).

By maintaining the Peace Cross on a public highway, the Commission elevates Christianity over other faiths, and religion over nonreligion. Memorializing the service of American soldiers is an "admirable and unquestionably secular" objective. But the Commission does not serve that objective by displaying a symbol that bears "a starkly sectarian message."

I

The Establishment Clause essentially instructs: "[T]he government may not favor one religion over another, or religion over irreligion." . . . And by demanding neutrality between religious faith and the absence thereof, the Establishment Clause shores up an individual's "right to select any religious faith or none at all." *Wallace v. Jaffree* (1985).

In cases challenging the government's display of a religious symbol, the Court has tested fidelity to the principle of neutrality by asking whether the display has the "effect of 'endorsing' religion." The display fails this requirement if it objectively "convey[s] a message that religion or a particular religious belief is favored or preferred." . . .

As I see it, when a cross is displayed on public property, the government may be presumed to endorse its religious content. The venue is surely associated with the State; the symbol and its meaning are just as surely associated exclusively with Christianity. . . . To non-Christians, nearly 30% of the population of the United States, Pew Research Center, America's Changing Religious Landscape 4 (2015), the State's choice to display the cross on public buildings or spaces conveys a message of exclusion: It tells them they "are outsiders, not full members of the political community," . . .

A presumption of endorsement, of course, may be overcome. . . . The "typical museum setting," for example, "though not neutralizing the religious content of a religious painting, negates any message of endorsement of that content." *Lynch v. Donnelly* (1984) (O'Connor, J., concurring). Similarly, when a public school history teacher discusses the Protestant Reformation, the setting makes clear that the teacher's purpose is to educate, not to proselytize. The Peace Cross, however, is not of that genre.

II

"For nearly two millennia," the Latin cross has been the "defining symbol" of Christianity, . . .

An exclusively Christian symbol, the Latin cross is not emblematic of any other faith. . . . The principal symbol of Christianity around the world should not loom over public thoroughfares, suggesting official recognition of that religion's paramountcy.

The Commission urges in defense of its monument that the Latin cross "is not merely a reaffirmation of Christian beliefs"; rather, "when used in the context of a war memorial," the cross becomes "a universal symbol of the sacrifices of those who fought and died." . . .

The Commission's "[a]ttempts to secularize what is unquestionably a sacred [symbol] defy credibility and disserve people of faith." . . .

Because of its sacred meaning, the Latin cross has been used to mark Christian deaths since at least the fourth century. . . . As a commemorative symbol, the Latin cross simply "makes no sense apart from the crucifixion, the resurrection, and Christianity's promise of eternal life."

The cross affirms that, thanks to the soldier's embrace of Christianity, he will be rewarded with eternal life. "To say that the cross honors the Christian war dead does not identify a secular meaning of the cross; it merely identifies a common application of the religious meaning." Scarcely "a universal symbol of sacrifice," the cross is "the symbol of one particular sacrifice."

Every Court of Appeals to confront the question has held that "[m]aking a . . . Latin cross a war memorial does not make the cross secular," it "makes the war memorial sectarian." . . .

The Peace Cross is no exception. That was evident from the start. At the dedication ceremony, the keynote speaker analogized the sacrifice of the honored soldiers to that of Jesus Christ, calling the Peace Cross "symbolic of Calvary," where Jesus was crucified. . . .

C

The Commission nonetheless urges that the Latin cross is a "well-established" secular symbol commemorating, in particular, "military valor and sacrifice [in] World War I." Calling up images of United States cemeteries overseas showing row upon row of cross-shaped gravemarkers, the Commission overlooks this reality: The cross was never perceived as an appropriate headstone or memorial for Jewish soldiers and others who did not adhere to Christianity. . . .

When the War Department began preparing designs for permanent headstones in 1919, "no topic managed to stir more controversy than the use of religious symbolism." . . . Throughout the headstone debate, no one doubted that the Latin cross and the Star of David were sectarian gravemarkers, and therefore appropriate only for soldiers who adhered to those faiths. . . .

The overwhelming majority of World War I memorials contain no Latin cross.

In fact, the "most popular and enduring memorial of the [post-World War I] decade" was "[t]he mass-produced *Spirit of the American Doughboy* statue." Budreau, Bodies of War, at 139. . . . The Peace Cross, as Plaintiffs' expert historian observed, was an "aberration . . . even in the era [in which] it was built and dedicated."

Like cities and towns across the country, the United States military comprehended the importance of "pay[ing] equal respect to all members of the Armed Forces who perished in the service of our country," *Buono*, 559 U.S. at 759, 130 S.Ct. 1803 (Stevens, J., dissenting), and therefore avoided incorporating the Latin cross into memorials. . . .

APPENDIX

The Bladensburg Peace Cross. App. 887.

Headstones in the Henri-Chappelle American Cemetery and Memorial in Belgium. American Battle Monuments Commission, Henri-Chappelle American Cemetery and Memorial 16 (1986).

NOTES AND QUESTIONS

1. *Controlling test.* Which Establishment Clause test do the various justices rely on? Is there a clear majority for any particular test? Which test do you think should control?
2. *Context.* In previous decisions involving government-sponsored religious displays, the Court emphasized the physical context in which a religious symbol appeared. A nativity scene (representing the birth and adoration of the baby Jesus) alone, with nothing to detract from its religious message, was constitutionally different from a nativity scene surrounded by secular objects. *Compare* County of Allegheny v. ACLU, 492 U.S. 573 (1989) *with* Lynch v. Donnelly, 465 U.S. 668 (1984). How does the majority justify upholding a large Latin cross with no surrounding secular objects?
3. *Meaning of Latin cross.* Whose characterization of the Latin cross do you find more accurate, the majority's or the dissent's?
4. *Risk that uniting church and state degrades religion.* Does it degrade Christianity to argue that a Latin cross memorial is not first and foremost a sacred Christian symbol? Or is the concern that the union of church and state will undermine the integrity of religion overblown?
5. *Original purpose.* Why might people in 1920 choose a Latin cross as a WWI memorial as opposed to, for example, something like the Spirit of the American Doughboy statue? Can any inference be drawn from the fact that secular alternatives existed?
6. *Removal of Latin cross.* The majority repeatedly argues that removing the cross from government property would evince hostility to religion. Do you think Jews, Muslims, Buddhists, atheists, or other religious minorities would agree with that assessment?

B. GOVERNMENT-SPONSORED PRAYERS OUTSIDE SCHOOL

Marsh v. Chambers

463 U.S. 783 (1983)

Chief Justice Burger delivered the opinion of the Court.

The question presented is whether the Nebraska Legislature's practice of opening each legislative day with a prayer by a chaplain paid by the State violates the Establishment Clause of the First Amendment. . . . Robert E. Palmer, a Presbyterian minister, has served as chaplain since 1965 at a salary of $319.75 per month for each month the legislature is in session.

II.

The opening of sessions of legislative and other deliberative public bodies with prayer is deeply embedded in the history and tradition of this country. From colonial times through the founding of the Republic and ever since, the practice of legislative prayer has coexisted with the principles of disestablishment and religious freedom. In the very courtrooms in which the United States District Judge and later three Circuit Judges heard and decided this case, the proceedings opened with an announcement that concluded, "God save the United States and this Honorable Court." The same invocation occurs at all sessions of this Court. . . .

Although prayers were not offered during the Constitutional Convention, the First Congress, as one of its early items of business, adopted the policy of selecting a chaplain to open each session with prayer. . . . On Sept. 25, 1789, three days after Congress authorized the appointment of paid chaplains, final agreement was reached on the language of the Bill of Rights. Clearly the men who wrote the First Amendment Religion Clause did not view paid legislative chaplains and opening prayers as a violation of that Amendment, for the practice of opening sessions with prayer has continued without interruption ever since that early session of Congress. It has also been followed consistently in most of the states, including Nebraska, where the institution of opening legislative sessions with prayer was adopted even before the State attained statehood.

Standing alone, historical patterns cannot justify contemporary violations of constitutional guarantees, but there is far more here than simply historical patterns. In this context, historical evidence sheds light not only on what the draftsmen intended the Establishment Clause to mean, but also on how they thought that Clause applied to the practice authorized by the First Congress-their actions reveal their intent. . . .

In Walz v. Tax Comm'n, 397 U.S. 664, 678 (1970), we considered the weight to be accorded to history: "It is obviously correct that no one acquires a vested or protected right in violation of the Constitution by long use, even when that span of time covers our entire national existence and indeed predates it. Yet an unbroken practice . . . is not something to be lightly cast aside."

No more is Nebraska's practice of over a century, consistent with two centuries of national practice, to be cast aside. It can hardly be thought that in the same week Members of the First Congress voted to appoint and to pay a Chaplain for each House and also voted to approve the draft of the First Amendment for submission to the States, they intended the Establishment Clause of the Amendment to forbid what they had just declared acceptable. . . .

Respondent cites Justice Brennan's concurring opinion in Abington School Dist. v. Schempp, 374 U.S. 203, 237 (1963), and argues that we should not rely too heavily on "the advice of the Founding Fathers" because the messages of history often tend to be ambiguous and not relevant to a society far more heterogeneous than that of the Framers, Respondent also points out that John Jay and John Rutledge opposed the motion to begin the first session of the Continental Congress with prayer. Brief for Respondent 60.

We do not agree that evidence of opposition to a measure weakens the force of the historical argument; indeed it infuses it with power by demonstrating that the subject was considered carefully and the action not taken thoughtlessly, by force of long tradition and without regard to the problems posed by a pluralistic society. . . .

In light of the unambiguous and unbroken history of more than 200 years, there can be no doubt that the practice of opening legislative sessions with prayer has become part of the fabric of our society. To invoke Divine guidance on a public body entrusted with making the laws is not, in these circumstances, an "establishment" of religion or a step toward establishment; it is simply a tolerable acknowledgment of beliefs widely held among the people of this country. As Justice Douglas observed, "[w]e are a religious people whose institutions presuppose a Supreme Being." Zorach v. Clauson, 343 U.S. 306, 313 (1952).

III.

We turn then to the question of whether any features of the Nebraska practice violate the Establishment Clause. Beyond the bare fact that a prayer is offered, three points have been made: first, that a clergyman of only one denomination-Presbyterian-has been selected for 16 years; second, that the chaplain is paid at public expense; and third, that the prayers are in the Judeo-Christian tradition.[14] Weighed against the historical background, these factors do not serve to invalidate Nebraska's practice.

The Court of Appeals was concerned that Palmer's long tenure has the effect of giving preference to his religious views. . . . To the contrary, the evidence indicates that Palmer was reappointed because his performance and personal qualities were acceptable to the body appointing him. . . . Absent proof that the chaplain's reappointment stemmed from an impermissible motive, we conclude that his long tenure does not in itself conflict with the Establishment Clause.

Nor is the compensation of the chaplain from public funds a reason to invalidate the Nebraska Legislature's chaplaincy; remuneration is grounded in historic practice initiated, as we noted earlier, by the same Congress that adopted the Establishment Clause of the First Amendment. . . .

The content of the prayer is not of concern to judges where, as here, there is no indication that the prayer opportunity has been exploited to proselytize or advance any one, or to disparage any other, faith or belief. That being so, it is not for us to embark on a sensitive evaluation or to parse the content of a particular prayer. . . .

The unbroken practice for two centuries in the National Congress, for more than a century in Nebraska and in many other states, gives abundant assurance that there is no real threat "while this Court sits."

The judgment of the Court of Appeals is

Reversed.

Justice BRENNAN, with whom Justice MARSHALL joins, dissenting.

I

The Court makes no pretense of subjecting Nebraska's practice of legislative prayer to any of the formal "tests" that have traditionally structured our inquiry under the Establishment Clause. That it fails to do so is, in a sense, a good thing, for it simply confirms that the Court is carving out an exception to the Establishment Clause rather than reshaping Establishment Clause doctrine to accommodate legislative prayer. For my purposes, however, I must begin by demonstrating

---

14. Palmer characterizes his prayers as "nonsectarian," "Judeo Christian," and with "elements of the American civil religion." App. 75 and 87. (Deposition of Robert E. Palmer). Although some of his earlier prayers were often explicitly Christian, Palmer removed all references to Christ after a 1980 complaint from a Jewish legislator. Id., at 49.

what should be obvious: that, if the Court were to judge legislative prayer through the unsentimental eye of our settled doctrine, it would have to strike it down as a clear violation of the Establishment Clause.

The most commonly cited formulation of prevailing Establishment Clause doctrine is found in Lemon v. Kurtzman, 403 U.S. 602 (1971). . . . That the "purpose" of legislative prayer is preeminently religious rather than secular seems to me to be self-evident. "To invoke Divine guidance on a public body entrusted with making the laws," is nothing but a religious act. Moreover, whatever secular functions legislative prayer might play-formally opening the legislative session, getting the members of the body to quiet down, and imbuing them with a sense of seriousness and high purpose-could so plainly be performed in a purely nonreligious fashion that to claim a secular purpose for the prayer is an insult to the perfectly honorable individuals who instituted and continue the practice.

The "primary effect" of legislative prayer is also clearly religious. As we said in the context of officially sponsored prayers in the public schools, "prescribing a particular form of religious worship," even if the individuals involved have the choice not to participate, places "indirect coercive pressure upon religious minorities to conform to the prevailing officially approved religion. . . ." Engel v. Vitale, 370 U.S. 421, 431 (1962). More importantly, invocations in Nebraska's legislative halls explicitly link religious belief and observance to the power and prestige of the State. . . .

Finally, there can be no doubt that the practice of legislative prayer leads to excessive "entanglement" between the State and religion. . . . In the case of legislative prayer, the process of choosing a "suitable" chaplain, whether on a permanent or rotating basis, and insuring that the chaplain limits himself or herself to "suitable" prayers, involves precisely the sort of supervision that agencies of government should if at all possible avoid.

In sum, I have no doubt that, if any group of law students were asked to apply the principles of *Lemon* to the question of legislative prayer, they would nearly unanimously find the practice to be unconstitutional.

II

The path of formal doctrine, however, can only imperfectly capture the nature and importance of the issues at stake in this case. A more adequate analysis must therefore take into account the underlying function of the Establishment Clause, and the forces that have shaped its doctrine. . . .

Legislative prayer clearly violates the principles of neutrality and separation that are embedded within the Establishment Clause. It is contrary to the fundamental message of *Engel* and *Schempp*. It intrudes on the right to conscience by forcing some legislators either to participate in a "prayer opportunity," with which they are in basic disagreement, or to make their disagreement a matter of public comment by declining to participate. It forces all residents of the State to support a religious exercise that may be contrary to their own beliefs. It requires the State to commit itself on fundamental theological issues. It has the potential for degrading religion by allowing a religious call to worship to be intermeshed with a secular call to order. And it injects religion into the political sphere by creating the potential that each and every selection of a chaplain, or consideration of a particular prayer, or even reconsideration of the practice itself, will provoke a political battle along religious lines and ultimately alienate some religiously identified group of citizens.

We have also recognized that Government cannot, without adopting a decidedly *anti*-religious point of view, be forbidden to recognize the religious beliefs and practices of the American people as an aspect of our history and culture. Certainly, bona fide classes in comparative religion can be offered in the public schools. And certainly, the text of Abraham Lincoln's Second Inaugural Address which is inscribed on a wall of the Lincoln Memorial need not be purged of its profound theological content. The practice of offering invocations at legislative sessions cannot, however, simply be dismissed as "a tolerable *acknowledgment of beliefs* widely held among the people of this country." "Prayer is religion *in act*." "Praying means to take hold of a word, the end, so to speak, of a line that leads to God." Reverend Palmer and other members of the clergy who offer invocations at legislative sessions are not museum pieces, put on display once a day for the edification of the legislature. Rather, they are engaged by the legislature to lead it-as a body-in an act of religious worship. If upholding the practice requires denial of this fact, I suspect that many supporters of legislative prayer would feel that they had been handed a pyrrhic victory. . . .

Finally, our cases recognize that, in one important respect, the Constitution is *not* neutral on the subject of religion: Under the Free Exercise Clause, religiously motivated claims of conscience may give rise to constitutional rights that other strongly-held beliefs do not . . . This is not, however, a case in which a State is accommodating individual religious interests. We are not faced here with the right of the legislature to allow its members to offer prayers during the course of general legislative debate. We are certainly not faced with the right of legislators to form voluntary groups for prayer or worship. We are not even faced with the right of the state to employ members of the clergy to minister to the private religious needs of individual legislators. Rather, we are faced here with the regularized practice of conducting official prayers, on behalf of the entire legislature, as part of the order of business constituting the formal opening of every single session of the legislative term. If this is Free Exercise, the Establishment Clause has no meaning whatsoever.

III

The Court's main argument for carving out an exception sustaining legislative prayer is historical. The Court cannot-and does not-purport to find a pattern of "undeviating acceptance," *Walz*, 397 U.S. at 681 (BRENNAN, J., concurring), of legislative prayer. It also disclaims exclusive reliance on the mere longevity of legislative prayer. The Court does, however, point out that, only three days before the First Congress reached agreement on the final wording of the Bill of Rights, it authorized the appointment of paid chaplains for its own proceedings, and the Court argues that in light of this "unique history," the actions of Congress reveal its intent as to the meaning of the Establishment Clause. I agree that historical practice is "of considerable import in the interpretation of abstract constitutional language," *Walz*, 397 U.S. at 681, (Brennan, J., concurring). This is a case, however, in which-absent the Court's invocation of history-there would be no question that the practice at issue was unconstitutional.[30] . . .

---

30. [FN30, slightly moved.] Indeed, the sort of historical argument made by the Court should be advanced with some hesitation in light of certain other skeletons in the congressional closet. *See, e.g.*, . . . Act of July 23, 1866, 14 Stat. 216 (reaffirming the racial segregation of the public schools in the District of Columbia; enacted exactly one week after Congress proposed Fourteenth Amendment to the States).

[T]he Court assumes that the Framers of the Establishment Clause would not have themselves authorized a practice that they thought violated the guarantees contained in the clause. This assumption, however, is questionable. Legislators, influenced by the passions and exigencies of the moment, the pressure of constituents and colleagues, and the press of business, do not always pass sober constitutional judgment on every piece of legislation they enact, and this must be assumed to be as true of the members of the First Congress as any other. Indeed, the fact that James Madison, who voted for the bill authorizing the payment of the first congressional chaplains, later expressed the view that the practice was unconstitutional, is instructive on precisely this point. Madison's later views may not have represented so much a change of *mind* as a change of *role*, from a member of Congress engaged in the hurley-burley of legislative activity to a detached observer engaged in unpressured reflection. Since the latter role is precisely the one with which this Court is charged, I am not at all sure that Madison's later writings should be any less influential in our deliberations than his earlier vote. . . .

[A] ny practice of legislative prayer, even if it might look "non-sectarian" to nine Justices of the Supreme Court, will inevitably and continuously involve the state in one or another religious debate. Prayer is serious business-serious theological business-and it is not a mere "acknowledgment of beliefs widely held among the people of this country" for the State to immerse itself in that business. Some religious individuals or groups find it theologically problematic to engage in joint religious exercises predominantly influenced by faiths not their own. Some might object even to the attempt to fashion a "non-sectarian" prayer. Some would find it impossible to participate in any "prayer opportunity," marked by Trinitarian references. Some would find a prayer *not* invoking the name of Christ to represent a flawed view of the relationship between human beings and God. . . . And some might object on theological grounds to the Court's requirement that prayer, even though religious, not be proselytizing. But, in this case, we are faced with potential religious objections to an activity at the very center of religious life, and it is simply beyond the competence of government, and inconsistent with our conceptions of liberty, for the state to take upon itself the role of ecclesiastical arbiter.

Justice STEVENS, dissenting.

In a democratically elected legislature, the religious beliefs of the chaplain tend to reflect the faith of the majority of the lawmakers' constituents. Prayers may be said by a Catholic priest in the Massachusetts Legislature and by a Presbyterian minister in the Nebraska Legislature, but I would not expect to find a Jehovah's Witness or a disciple of Mary Baker Eddy or the Reverend Moon serving as the official chaplain in any state legislature. Regardless of the motivation of the majority that exercises the power to appoint the chaplain, it seems plain to me that the designation of a member of one religious faith to serve as the sole official chaplain of a state legislature for a period of 16 years constitutes the preference of one faith over another in violation of the Establishment Clause of the First Amendment.

NOTES AND QUESTIONS

1. *History and tradition.* If the same Congress that approved the Establishment Clause believed that legislative prayers were consistent with the Establishment Clause, why shouldn't we? Moreover, if the practice has existed since the founding of the country, isn't the message communicated more about a deeply embedded tradition than about religion?
2. *Change in nation's religious composition.* The dissent notes that "our religious composition makes us a vastly more diverse people than were our forefathers." In *"Nonpreferential" Aid to Religion: A False Claim about Original Intent,* 27 WM. & MARY L. REV. 875 (1986), Douglas Laycock concludes, "In 1791, almost no one thought that government support of Protestantism was inconsistent with religious liberty, because almost no one could imagine a more broadly pluralist state." What might the Framers think if confronted with today's diversity?
3. *The (primary) Framer's intent.* If, as Chief Justice Burger's *Marsh* opinion suggests, we should look to the Framers' own words and actions to determine the meaning of the phrase "respecting an establishment of religion," then should we pay special attention to the precise views of the author of the First Amendment? As Justice Brennan points out in his *Marsh* dissent, James Madison had a very specific opinion on the constitutionality of legislative prayers, which can be found in the following passage from Madison's "Detached Memoranda" (abbreviations and punctuation are as in the original):

> Is the appointment of Chaplains to the two Houses of Congress consistent with the Constitution, and with the pure principle of religious freedom?
>
> In strictness the answer on both points must be in the negative. The Constitution of the U.S. forbids everything like an establishment of a national religion. The law appointing Chaplains establishes a religious worship for the national representatives, to be performed by Ministers of religion, elected by a majority of them; and these are to be paid out of the national taxes. Does not this involve the principle of a national establishment, applicable to a provision for a religious worship for the Constituent as well as of the representative Body, approved by the majority, and conducted by Ministers of religion paid by the entire nation.
>
> The establishment of the chaplainship to Congs is a palpable violation of equal rights, as well as of Constitutional principles: The tenets of the chaplains elected [by the majority] shut the door of worship agst the members whose creeds & consciences forbid a participation in that of the majority. To say nothing of other sects, this is the case with that of Roman Catholics & Quakers who have always had members in one or both of the Legislative branches. Could a Catholic clergyman ever hope to be appointed a Chaplain? To say that his religious principles are

> obnoxious or that his sect is small, is to lift the evil at once and exhibit in its naked deformity the doctrine that religious truth is to be tested by numbers. [O]r that the major sects have a right to govern the minor.

4. *Bound by original understanding?* Should we interpret the Constitution just as the Framers or founding generation did? What about the fact that the same Congress that proposed the Fourteenth Amendment's Equal Protection Clause also approved funding for segregated schools in Washington, D.C.?
5. *Applying the Establishment Clause tests.* How would these state-funded prayers fare under the various Establishment Clause tests? Is it true, as Justice Brennan argues, that if "any groups of law students" were asked to apply *Lemon*, "they would nearly unanimously find the practice to be unconstitutional"? What about the endorsement test? Or the coercion test? If you were a Nebraska representative up for reelection, would you feel pressure to participate?
6. *Exception or new approach?* Is the emphasis on history and tradition approach limited to legislative prayers? To practices that date to the founding? Or does this represent an alternative approach to the Establishment Clause? Looking back over the cases you have read, what role did history and tradition play?

Town of Greece v. Galloway

572U.S. 565 (2014)

Justice Kennedy delivered the opinion of the Court, except as to Part II–B.

The Court must decide whether the town of Greece, New York, imposes an impermissible establishment of religion by opening its monthly board meetings with a prayer. It must be concluded, consistent with the Court's opinion in Marsh v. Chambers, 463 U.S. 783 (1983), that no violation of the Constitution has been shown.

I

Greece, a town with a population of 94,000, is in upstate New York. For some years, it began its monthly town board meetings with a moment of silence. In 1999, the newly elected town supervisor, John Auberger, decided to replicate the prayer practice he had found meaningful while serving in the county legislature. Following the roll call and recitation of the Pledge of Allegiance, Auberger would invite a local clergyman to the front of the room to deliver an invocation. After the prayer, Auberger would thank the minister for serving as the board's "chaplain for the month" and present him with a commemorative plaque. The prayer was intended to place town board members in a solemn and deliberative frame of mind, invoke divine guidance in town affairs, and follow a tradition practiced by Congress and dozens of state legislatures. App. 22a–25a.

The town followed an informal method for selecting prayer givers, all of whom were unpaid volunteers. A town employee would call the congregations listed in a local directory until she found a minister available for that month's meeting. The town eventually compiled a list of willing "board chaplains" who had accepted invitations and agreed to return in the future. The town at no point excluded or denied an opportunity to a would-be prayer giver. Its leaders maintained that a minister or layperson of any persuasion, including an atheist, could give the invocation. But nearly all of the congregations in town were Christian; and from 1999 to 2007, all of the participating ministers were too.

Greece neither reviewed the prayers in advance of the meetings nor provided guidance as to their tone or content, in the belief that exercising any degree of control over the prayers would infringe both the free exercise and speech rights of the ministers. The town instead left the guest clergy free to compose their own devotions. Some of the ministers spoke in a distinctly Christian idiom; and a minority invoked religious holidays, scripture, or doctrine. . . .

Respondents Susan Galloway and Linda Stephens attended town board meetings to speak about issues of local concern, and they objected that the prayers violated their religious or philosophical views. . . .

II

In Marsh v. Chambers, 463 U.S. 783 (1983), the Court found no First Amendment violation in the Nebraska Legislature's practice of opening its sessions with a prayer delivered by a chaplain paid from state funds. The decision concluded that legislative prayer, while religious in nature, has long been understood as compatible with the Establishment Clause. As practiced by Congress since the framing of the Constitution, legislative prayer lends gravity to public business, reminds lawmakers to transcend petty differences in pursuit of a higher purpose, and expresses a common aspiration to a just and peaceful society. . . .

Marsh is sometimes described as "carving out an exception" to the Court's Establishment Clause jurisprudence, because it sustained legislative prayer without subjecting the practice to "any of the formal 'tests' that have traditionally structured" this inquiry. Id., at 796, 813 (Brennan, J., dissenting). The Court in *Marsh* found those tests unnecessary because history supported the conclusion that legislative invocations are compatible with the Establishment Clause. . . .

Marsh stands for the proposition that it is not necessary to define the precise boundary of the Establishment Clause where history shows that the specific practice is permitted. Any test the Court adopts must acknowledge a practice that was accepted by the Framers and has withstood the critical scrutiny of time and political change. . . .

The Court's inquiry, then, must be to determine whether the prayer practice in the town of Greece fits within the tradition long followed in Congress and the state legislatures. Respondents assert that the town's prayer exercise falls outside that tradition and transgresses the Establishment Clause for two independent but mutually reinforcing reasons. First, they argue that *Marsh* did not approve prayers containing sectarian language or themes, such as the prayers offered in Greece that referred to the "death, resurrection, and ascension of the Savior Jesus Christ," App. 129a, and the "saving sacrifice of Jesus Christ on the cross," id., at 88a. Second, they argue that the setting and conduct of the town board meetings create social pressures that force nonadherents to remain in the room or even feign participation in order to avoid offending the representatives who sponsor the prayer and will vote on matters citizens bring before the board. . . .

A

The Congress that drafted the First Amendment would have been accustomed to invocations containing explicitly religious themes of the sort respondents find objectionable. . . . The decidedly Christian nature of these prayers must not be dismissed as the relic of a time when our Nation was less pluralistic than it is today. Congress continues to permit its appointed and visiting chaplains to express themselves in a religious idiom. It acknowledges our growing diversity not by proscribing sectarian content but by welcoming ministers of many creeds. . . .

Marsh nowhere suggested that the constitutionality of legislative prayer turns on the neutrality of its content. . . . To hold that invocations must be nonsectarian would force the legislatures that sponsor prayers and the courts that are asked to decide these cases to act as supervisors and censors of religious speech. . . . Government may not mandate a civic religion that stifles any but the most generic reference to the sacred any more than it may prescribe a religious orthodoxy. . . . Once it invites prayer into the public sphere, government must permit a prayer giver to address his or her own God or gods as conscience dictates, unfettered by what an administrator or judge considers to be nonsectarian.

In rejecting the suggestion that legislative prayer must be nonsectarian, the Court does not imply that no constraints remain on its content. The relevant constraint derives from its place at the opening of legislative sessions, where it is meant to lend gravity to the occasion and reflect values long part of the Nation's heritage. Prayer that is solemn and respectful in tone, that invites lawmakers to reflect upon shared ideals and common ends before they embark on the fractious business of governing, serves that legitimate function. If the course and practice over time shows that the invocations denigrate nonbelievers or religious minorities, threaten damnation, or preach conversion, many present may consider the prayer to fall short of the desire to elevate the purpose of the occasion and to unite lawmakers in their common effort. That circumstance would present a different case than the one presently before the Court. . . .

Absent a pattern of prayers that over time denigrate, proselytize, or betray an impermissible government purpose, a challenge based solely on the content of a prayer will not likely establish a constitutional violation. *Marsh*, indeed, requires an inquiry into the prayer opportunity as a whole, rather than into the contents of a single prayer. 463 U.S., at 794–795.

Finally, the Court disagrees with the view taken by the Court of Appeals that the town of Greece contravened the Establishment Clause by inviting a predominantly Christian set of ministers to lead the prayer. The town made reasonable efforts to identify all of the congregations located within its borders and represented that it would welcome a prayer by any minister or layman who wished to give one. That nearly all of the congregations in town turned out to be Christian does not reflect an aversion or bias on the part of town leaders against minority faiths. So long as the town maintains a policy of nondiscrimination, the Constitution does not require it to search beyond its borders for non-Christian prayer givers in an effort to achieve religious balancing. . . .

B

Respondents further seek to distinguish the town's prayer practice from the tradition upheld in *Marsh* on the ground that it coerces participation by nonadherents. They and some amici contend that prayer conducted in the intimate setting of a town board meeting differs in fundamental ways from the invocations delivered in Congress and state legislatures, where the public remains segregated from legislative activity and may not address the body except by occasional invitation. Citizens attend town meetings, on the other hand, to accept awards; speak on matters of local importance; and petition the board for action that may affect their economic interests, such as the granting of permits, business licenses, and zoning variances. Respondents argue that the public may feel subtle pressure to participate in prayers that violate their beliefs in order to please the board members from whom they are about to seek a favorable ruling. In their view the fact that board members in small towns know many of their constituents by name only increases the pressure to conform.

On the record in this case the Court is not persuaded that the town of Greece, through the act of offering a brief, solemn, and respectful prayer to open its monthly meetings, compelled its citizens to engage in a religious observance.

It is presumed that the reasonable observer is acquainted with this tradition and understands that its purposes are to lend gravity to public proceedings and to acknowledge the place religion holds in the lives of many private citizens, not to afford government an opportunity to proselytize or force truant constituents into the pews. . . . Respondents suggest that constituents might feel pressure to join the prayers to avoid irritating the officials who would be ruling on their petitions, but this argument has no evidentiary support. . . . Adults often encounter speech they find disagreeable; and an Establishment Clause violation is not made out any time a person experiences a sense of affront from the expression of contrary religious views in a legislative forum, especially where, as here, any member of the public is welcome in turn to offer an invocation reflecting his or her own convictions.

It is so ordered.

[Justice ALITO, with whom Justice SCALIA joins, concurred.]

[Justice THOMAS, with whom Justice SCALIA joined as to Part II, concurring in part and concurring in the judgment.]

Justice BREYER, dissenting.

As we all recognize, this is a "fact-sensitive" case. . . . I also here emphasize several factors that I believe underlie the conclusion that, on the particular facts of this case, the town's prayer practice violated the Establishment Clause.

First, Greece is a predominantly Christian town, but it is not exclusively so. A map of the town's houses of worship introduced in the District Court shows many Christian churches within the town's limits. It also shows a Buddhist temple within the town and several Jewish synagogues just outside its borders, in the adjacent city of Rochester, New York. Id., at 24.Yet during the more than 120 monthly meetings at which prayers were delivered during the record period (from 1999 to 2010), only four prayers were delivered by non-Christians. And all of these occurred in 2008, shortly after the plaintiffs began complaining about the town's Christian prayer practice and nearly a decade after that practice had commenced.

Second, the town made no significant effort to inform the area's non-Christian houses of worship about the possibility of delivering an opening prayer. . . .

Third, in this context, the fact that nearly all of the prayers given reflected a single denomination takes on significance. That significance would have been the same had all the prayers been Jewish, or Hindu, or Buddhist, or of any other denomination. The significance is that, in a context where religious minorities exist and where more could easily have been done to include their participation, the town chose to do nothing. . . .

Justice KAGAN, with whom Justice GINSBURG, Justice BREYER, and Justice SOTOMAYOR join, dissenting.

For centuries now, people have come to this country from every corner of the world to share in the blessing of religious freedom. Our Constitution promises that they may worship in their own way, without fear of penalty or danger, and that in itself is a momentous offering. Yet our Constitution makes a commitment still more remarkable—that however those individuals worship, they will count as full and equal American citizens. A Christian, a Jew, a Muslim (and so forth)—each stands in the same relationship with her country, with her state and local communities, and with every level and body of government. So that when each person performs the duties or seeks the benefits of citizenship, she does so not as an adherent to one or another religion, but simply as an American.

I respectfully dissent from the Court's opinion because I think the Town of Greece's prayer practices violate that norm of religious equality—the breathtakingly generous constitutional idea that our public institutions belong no less to the Buddhist or Hindu than to the Methodist or Episcopalian. . . . The practice at issue here differs from the one sustained in *Marsh* because Greece's town meetings involve participation by ordinary citizens, and the invocations given—directly to those citizens—were predominantly sectarian in content. Still more, Greece's Board did nothing to recognize religious diversity: In arranging for clergy members to open each meeting, the Town never sought (except briefly when this suit was filed) to involve, accommodate, or in any way reach out to adherents of non-Christian religions. So month in and month out for over a decade, prayers steeped in only one faith, addressed toward members of the public, commenced meetings to discuss local affairs and distribute government benefits. In my view, that practice does not square with the First Amendment's promise that every citizen, irrespective of her religion, owns an equal share in her government.

. . . I agree with the majority that the issue here is "whether the prayer practice in the Town of Greece fits within the tradition long followed in Congress and the state legislatures."

Where I depart from the majority is in my reply to that question. . . . [T]he Board's meetings are also occasions for ordinary citizens to engage with and petition their government, often on highly individualized matters. That feature calls for Board members to exercise special care to ensure that the prayers offered are inclusive—that they respect each and every member of the community as an equal citizen. But the Board, and the clergy members it selected, made no such effort. Instead, the prayers given in Greece, addressed directly to the Town's citizenry, were more sectarian, and less inclusive, than anything this Court sustained in *Marsh*. . . .

Let's count the ways in which these pictures diverge. First, the governmental proceedings at which the prayers occur differ significantly in nature and purpose. The Nebraska Legislature's floor sessions—like those of the U.S. Congress and other state assemblies—are of, by, and for elected lawmakers. Members of the public take no part in those proceedings; any few who attend are spectators only, watching from a high-up visitors' gallery. (In that respect, note that neither the Nebraska Legislature nor the Congress calls for prayer when citizens themselves participate in a hearing—say, by giving testimony relevant to a bill or nomination.) Greece's town meetings, by contrast, revolve around ordinary members of the community. Each and every aspect of those sessions provides opportunities for Town residents to interact with public officials. And the most important parts enable those citizens to petition their government. In the Public Forum, they urge (or oppose) changes in the Board's policies and priorities; and then, in what are essentially adjudicatory hearings, they request the Board to grant (or deny) applications for various permits, licenses, and zoning variances. So the meetings, both by design and in operation, allow citizens to actively participate in the Town's governance—sharing concerns, airing grievances, and both shaping the community's policies and seeking their benefits.

Second (and following from what I just said), the prayers in these two settings have different audiences. In the Nebraska Legislature, the chaplain spoke to, and only to, the elected representatives . . . The very opposite is true in Greece: Contrary to the majority's characterization, the prayers there are directed squarely at the citizens. . . . In essence, the chaplain leads, as the first part of a town meeting, a highly intimate (albeit relatively brief) prayer service, with the public serving as his congregation.

And third, the prayers themselves differ in their content and character. . . . [N]o one can fairly read the prayers from Greece's Town meetings as anything other than explicitly Christian—constantly and exclusively so. . . . About two-thirds of the prayers given over this decade or so invoked "Jesus," "Christ," "Your Son," or "the Holy Spirit"; in the 18 months before the record closed, 85% included those references. *See generally id.*, at 27a–143a. Many prayers contained elaborations of Christian doctrine or recitations of scripture.

Those three differences, taken together, remove this case from the protective ambit of *Marsh* and the history on which it relied. . . .

Let's say that a Muslim citizen of Greece goes before the Board to share her views on policy or request some permit. Maybe she wants the Board to put up a traffic light at a dangerous intersection; or maybe she needs a zoning variance to build an addition on her home. But just before she gets to say her piece, a minister deputized by the Town asks her to pray "in the name of God's only son Jesus Christ." App. 99a. She must think—it is hardly paranoia, but only the truth—that Christian worship has become entwined with local governance. And now she faces a choice—to pray alongside the majority as one of that group or somehow to register her deeply felt difference. She is a strong person, but that is no easy call—especially given that the room is small and her every action (or inaction) will be noticed. She does not wish to be rude to her neighbors, nor does she wish to aggravate the Board members whom she will soon be trying to persuade. And yet she does not want to acknowledge Christ's divinity, any more than many of her neighbors would want to deny that tenet. So assume she declines to participate with the others in the first act of the meeting—or even, as the majority proposes, that she stands up and leaves the room altogether. At the least, she becomes a different kind of citizen, one who will not join in the religious practice that the Town Board has chosen as reflecting its own and the community's most cherished beliefs. And she thus stands at a remove, based solely on religion, from her fellow citizens and her elected representatives.

Everything about that situation, I think, infringes the First Amendment. . . . That the clergy thus put some residents to the unenviable choice of either pretending to pray like the majority or declining to join its communal activity, at the very moment of petitioning their elected leaders. That the practice thus divides the citizenry, creating one class that shares the Board's own evident religious beliefs and another (far smaller) class that does not. And that the practice also alters a dissenting citizen's relationship with her government, making her religious difference salient when she seeks only to engage her elected representatives as would any other citizen. . . .

In this country, when citizens go before the government, they go not as Christians or Muslims or Jews (or what have you), but just as Americans (or here, as Grecians). That is what it means to be an equal citizen, irrespective of religion. And that is what the Town of Greece precluded by so identifying itself with a single faith. . . .

When the citizens of this country approach their government, they do so only as Americans, not as members of one faith or another. And that means that even in a partly legislative body, they should not confront government-sponsored worship that divides them along religious lines. I believe, for all the reasons I have given, that the Town of Greece betrayed that promise. I therefore respectfully dissent from the Court's decision.

NOTES AND QUESTIONS

1. Marsh *as starting point.* Both the majority and the dissents accepted the constitutionality of legislative prayers, and focused on whether the *Greece* prayers could be considered part of the same tradition as the prayers upheld in *Marsh.* What would have been the outcome had they applied the *Lemon* test or endorsement test instead? Have those tests been supplanted?
2. *Sectarian prayers.* Were the prayers in *Marsh* sectarian? Did *Marsh* require that the prayers be nonsectarian? The majority argues that prayers during the Founding era were sectarian, and that "[t]he decidedly Christian nature of these prayers must not be dismissed as the relic of a time when our Nation was less pluralistic than it is today." Why not? Wasn't the Nation much less pluralistic than it is today?
3. *The constitutionality of requiring nonsectarian prayers.* The majority suggests that for Greece to require its prayers be nonsectarian would violate the Free Exercise or Free Speech Clause. A Free Exercise Clause violation requires a substantial religious burden. What is the burden on religious exercise at stake here? Regulating religious viewpoints would indeed violate the Free Speech Clause if Greece has opened up a forum for private

speech. Has it? Does Greece, for example, encourage all viewpoints on "the fractious business of governing"?

4. *Any constraints?* The majority notes that not anything goes: "[A] pattern of prayers that over time denigrate, proselytize, or betray an impermissible government purpose" would violate the Establishment Clause. Why is requiring nonproselytizing prayers less problematic than requiring nonsectarian ones?
5. *Discriminatory intent.* For the majority, as long as every religious tradition in theory may be reflected in the prayer, the prayer practice does not violate the Establishment Clause if in fact most of them are Christian. According to the majority, only if the predominance of Christianity was the result of intentional exclusion of non-Christian religions is the Establishment Clause violated. The dissents argue that the Establishment Clause is also violated if the predominance of Christianity was the result of the indifference: Once Greece realized that Christianity dominated, it ought to have done more. Which approach better advances Establishment Clause values? *See generally* Caroline Mala Corbin, *Intentional Discrimination in Establishment Clause Jurisprudence*, 67 ALA. L. REV. 299 (2015).
6. *Coercion.* The majority holds that there is no "evidentiary support" that anyone feels coerced into participating in Greece's prayers. Has the Court required evidence of actual coercion before? Must someone, such as Justice Kagan's hypothetical Muslim petitioner, have actually suffered retaliation for refusing to participate in order to feel pressure to join in?
7. *Harm.* What is the harm, if any, of sectarian prayer? Is it that they are simply offensive to those whose beliefs are different? Or is it something more?

C. *GOVERNMENT/RELIGION POWER SHARING*

Larkin v. Grendel's Den

459 U.S. 116 (1982)

Chief Justice BURGER delivered the opinion of the Court.

Appellee operates a restaurant located in the Harvard Square area of Cambridge, Mass. The Holy Cross Armenian Catholic Parish is located adjacent to the restaurant; the back walls of the two buildings are 10 feet apart. In 1977, appellee applied to the Cambridge License Commission for approval of an alcoholic beverages license for the restaurant.

[Massachusetts law] provides: "Premises . . . located within a radius of five hundred feet of a church or school shall not be licensed for the sale of alcoholic beverages if the governing body of such church or school files written objection thereto." Holy Cross Church objected to appellee's application, expressing concern over "having so many licenses so near." The License Commission voted to deny the application, citing only the objection of Holy Cross Church and noting that the church "is within 10 feet of the proposed location."

The purpose of [the Massachusetts law giving churches the right to object to the sale of alcoholic beverages] is to "protec[t] spiritual, cultural, and educational centers from the 'hurly-burly' associated with liquor outlets." There can be little doubt that this embraces valid secular legislative purposes. However, these valid secular objectives can be readily accomplished by other means—either through an absolute legislative ban on liquor outlets within reasonable prescribed distances from churches, schools, hospitals, and like institutions, or by ensuring a hearing for the views of affected institutions at licensing proceedings where, without question, such views would be entitled to substantial weight.

[This law] gives churches the right to determine whether a particular applicant will be granted a liquor license, or even which one of several competing applicants will receive a license. The churches' power under the statute is standardless, calling for no reasons, findings, or reasoned conclusions. That power may therefore be used by churches to promote goals beyond insulating the church from undesirable neighbors; it could be employed for explicitly religious goals, for example, favoring liquor licenses for members of that congregation or adherents of that faith. We can assume that churches would act in good faith in their exercise of the statutory power, yet [Massachusetts law] does not by its terms require that churches' power be used in a religiously neutral way. "[T]he potential for conflict inheres in the situation," and appellants have not suggested any "effective means of guaranteeing" that the delegated power "will be used exclusively for secular, neutral, and nonideological purposes." In addition, the mere appearance of a joint exercise of legislative authority by Church and State provides a significant symbolic benefit to religion in the minds of some by reason of the power conferred. It does not strain our prior holdings to say that the statute can be seen as having a "primary" and "principal" effect of advancing religion.

Turning to the third phase of the inquiry called for by *Lemon v. Kurtzman*, we see that we have not previously had occasion to consider the entanglement implications of a statute vesting significant governmental authority in churches. This statute enmeshes churches in the exercise of substantial governmental powers contrary to our consistent interpretation of the Establishment Clause. Ordinary human experience and a long line of cases teach that few entanglements could be more offensive to the spirit of the Constitution.

[Justice REHNQUIST's dissenting opinion is omitted.]

AN EXTENDED NOTE ON *BOARD OF EDUCATION OF KIRYAS JOEL v. GRUMET*

The other major decision raising the issue of government/religion power sharing is Board of Education of Kiryas Joel v. Grumet, 512 U.S. 687 (1994). In *Kiryas Joel*, the Court held unconstitutional a New York statute that created a special school district for the Satmar Hasidim, practitioners of a strict form of Judaism. Members of the sect "interpret the Torah strictly; segregate the sexes outside the home; speak Yiddish as their primary language; eschew television, radio, and English language publications; and dress in distinctive ways that include head coverings and special garments for boys and modest dresses for girls. Children are educated in private religious schools, most boys at the United Talmudic Academy, where they receive a thorough grounding in the Torah and limited exposure to secular subjects, and most girls at Bais Rochel, an affiliated school with a curriculum designed to prepare girls for their roles as wives and mothers." *Id.* at 691. The New York statute created a special school district exclusively to allow members of this sect to obtain services for their handicapped children within their own religious community. Before the statute was enacted, members of the sect who had handicapped children were forced to send their children to schools run by the public school district in which the Satmars lived. The Court held that the New York statute "resembles the issue raised in *Larkin* to the extent that the earlier case teaches that a State may not delegate its civic authority to a group chosen according to a religious criterion." *Id.* at 698.

> The fundamental source of constitutional concern here is that the legislature itself may fail to exercise governmental authority in a religiously neutral way. The anomalously case-specific nature of the legislature's exercise of state authority in creating this district for a religious community leaves the Court without any direct way to review such state action for the purpose of safeguarding a principle at the heart of the Establishment Clause, that government should not prefer one religion to another, or religion to irreligion. . . . Because the religious community of Kiryas Joel did not receive its new governmental authority simply as one of many communities eligible for equal treatment under a general law, we have no assurance that the next similarly situated group seeking a school district of its own will receive one. . . . Nor can the historical context in this case furnish us with any reason to suppose that the Satmars are merely one in a series of communities receiving the benefit of special school district laws. Early on in the development of public education in New York, the State rejected highly localized school districts for New York City when they were promoted as a way to allow separate schooling for Roman Catholic children. And in more recent history, the special Act in this case stands alone.

Id. at 703-704. The Court went on to point out that there were several alternatives to the creation of a special school district to serve the Satmars, including having the broader school district provide special educational services at a neutral site near one of the village's parochial schools.

NOTES AND QUESTIONS

1. Rajneeshpuram *and the problem of a municipality controlled by a religious sect.* Does the fact that a political entity, such as the town of Kiryas Joel, has a distinctive religious character, mean that it cannot constitutionally exercise government power? Is this the best reading of *Larkin* and *Grumet*? Or is there a difference between empowering a religious group to exercise state power and a simple coincidence that most people within a particular political subdivision happen to share a common faith? *Cf.* Oregon v. City of Rajneeshpuram, 598 F. Supp. 1208, 1216-1217 (D. Ore. 1984) (holding the incorporation of a religiously identified commune invalid on Establishment Clause grounds because "control over the City of Rajneeshpuram by these

religious organizations is different enough from the control exercised by the religious leaders in a city of private landowners of one religion as to allow a constitutional distinction to be made between the two situations"). Rajneeshpuram was a religious commune in rural Oregon; only adherents of the faith, followers in good standing of the Bhagwan Shree Rajneesh, were permitted to reside in the community, and all land within the city was owned by the religious organization. *See id.* at 1210-1211. Should the fact that a religious organization owns all of the land within a municipality and uses this ownership to categorically exclude nonbelievers affect the constitutional analysis? For an argument that it should, see *id.* at 1216 (holding that "[t]he provision of services by a municipal government in a city whose residents are private landowners of one religious faith has the direct and primary effect of aiding the individual landowners" whereas when "all of the real property in the City of Rajneeshpuram is owned or controlled by religious organizations, the provision of municipal services by the City of Rajneeshpuram necessarily has the effect of aiding not only the individual residents of the City of Rajneeshpuram, but also of directly, obviously, and immediately benefitting the religious organizations themselves").

2. *Expressly rejecting certain religious beliefs.* May government take the opposite step—that is, go out of its way to *reject* the exercise of government power by members of a particular faith? On November 2, 2010, Oklahoma voters passed the "Save Our State Amendment," a statewide referendum proposition that prohibited the Oklahoma state courts from recognizing or giving any effect to "international law or Sharia law." *See* Awad v. Ziriax, 670 F.3d 1111, 1116-1118 (10th Cir. 2012). The measure passed with the support of over 70 percent of the voters. *Id.* at 1118. The U.S. Court of Appeals for the Tenth Circuit applied the strict scrutiny test set forth in Larson v. Valente, 456 U.S. 228, 255 (1982), and concluded that the state of Oklahoma "failed to assert a compelling interest" and, accordingly, the amendment "failed to satisfy strict scrutiny," as required under *Larson. Id.* at 1130. The Tenth Circuit also found that the Save Our State Amendment was not narrowly tailored: "Even if the state could identify and support a reason to single out and restrict Sharia law in its courts, the amendment's complete ban of Sharia law is hardly an exercise of narrow tailoring." *Id.* at 1131. One could see *Larkin* and *Grumet* as the other side of the same coin at issue in *Awad*: Government can neither attempt to delegate power to a particular religion or group or religionists nor try to prohibit members of a religion from using the law on equal terms to protect their interests (even if religiously motivated or inspired).

3. *May government prohibit religious leaders from holding public office?* Just as government may not prohibit members of a particular religious group from seeking the protection of the state's law and courts, so too a state may not ban persons who hold religious offices from serving in a government office. *See* McDaniel v. Paty, 435 U.S. 618, 626-628 (1978). Strictly speaking, however, the *McDaniel* decision rests on Free Exercise, rather than Establishment Clause, grounds. The fact that the Free Exercise Clause prohibits government from banning religious ministers or priests from serving in public office clearly limits the potential scope of *Larkin* and *Grumet.*

4. *A formal neutrality approach.* In this line of cases, the Supreme Court appears to be saying that, consistent with the imperatives of the Establishment Clause, government may not discriminate in favor of a particular religion or group of religionists in allocating state power and, under the Free Exercise Clause, it may not ban adherents of particular religions from holding government office simply because of their religious beliefs. Is this a sensible approach?

Table of Cases

Principle cases are indicated by bold.

A

Abrams v. United States, 250 U.S. 616 (1919), 37

ACLU v. Alvarez, 679 F.3d 583 (7th Cir. 2012), 372

ACLU v. Capitol Square Review & Advisory Bd., 243 F.3d 289 (6th Cir. 2001), 1014

Action for Children's Television v. FCC, 58 F.3d 654 (D.C. Cir. 1995), 433

Adderley v. Florida, 385 U.S. 39 (1966), 4, 222

AETC v. Forbes, 523 U.S. 666 (1998), 230

Alexander v. United States, 509 U.S. 544 (1993), 27, 408

Amalgamated Food Employees v. Logan Valley Plaza, Inc., 391 U.S. 308 (1968), 240

American Booksellers Ass'n, Inc. v. Hudnut, 771 F.2d 323 (7th Cir. 1985), *aff'd mem.*, 475 U.S. 1001 (1986), 589

American Knights of the Ku Klux Klan v. City of Goshen, 50 F. Supp. 2d 835 (N.D. Ind. 1999), 288

American Legion v. American Humanist Association, 139 S. Ct. 2069 (2019), 1015

Anderson v. Liberty Lobby, Inc., 477 U.S. 242 (1986), 479

Arizona Christian School Tuition Organization v. Winn, 563 U.S. 125 (2011), 953

Arkansas Educational Television Commission v. Forbes, 523 U.S. 666 (1998), 646, 660

Ashcroft v. ACLU ("Ashcroft I"), 535 U.S. 564 (2002), 587, 629

Ashcroft v. ACLU ("Ashcroft II"), 542 U.S. 656 (2004), 629

Ashcroft v. Free Speech Coalition, 535 U.S. 234 (2002), 619

Associated Press v. Walker, 388 U.S. 130 (1967), 481

AvePoint, Inc. v. Power Tools, Inc., 981 F. Supp. 2d 496 (W.D. Va. 2013), 498

Awad v. Ziriax, 670 F.3d 1111 (10th Cir. 2012), 1041

B

B.H. v. Easton Area School District, 725 F.3d 293 (2013), 696

Barnes v. Glen Theatre, Inc., 501 U.S. 560 (1991), 5, 139, **162**, 603

Barr v. American Ass'n of Political Consultants, 140 S. Ct. 2335 (2020), 346

Bartnicki v. Vopper, 532 U.S. 514 (2001), 515

Bates v. State Bar of Ariz., 433 U.S. 350, 383-84 (1977), 325

Bauchman v. West High Sch., 132 F.3d 542 (10th Cir. 1997), *cert. denied*, 524 U.S. 953 (1998), 994

Bauer v. Brinkman, 958 N.W.2d 194 (Iowa 2021), 494

Beauharnais v. Illinois, 343 U.S. 250 (1952), 479, **523**

Berisha v. Lawson, 141 S.Ct. 2424 (2021), 499

Berger v. City of Seattle, 569 F.3d 1029 (9th Cir. 2009), 238

Bethel School District No. 403 v. Fraser, 478 U.S. 675 (1986), 552, **692**, 700

Beussink v. Woodland R-IV Sch. Dist., 30 F. Supp. 2d 1175 (E.D. Mo. 1998), 708

Biden v. Knight First Amendment Inst. At Columbia Univ., 593 U.S. ___ (2021), 462

Bigelow v. Virginia, 421 U.S. 809 (1975), 313, 318

Board of Educ. v. Allen, 392 U.S. 236 (1968), 916

Board of Education v. Mergens, 496 U.S. 226 (1990), 992, 993
Board of Education v. Pico, 457 U.S. 853 (1982), 710
Board of Education of Kiryas Joel v. Grumet, 512 U.S. 687 (1994), 1039
Board of Regents of the University of Wisconsin v. Southworth, 529 U.S. 217 (2000), 281
Boardley v. U.S. Dep't of Interior, 615 F.3d 508 (D.C. Cir. 2010), 239
Bob Jones University v. United States, 461 U.S. 574 (1983), 755
Boehner v. McDermott, 484 F.3d 573 (D.C. Cir. 2007), 516
Bolger v. Youngs Drug Products Corp., 463 U.S. 60 (1983), 352
Boos v. Barry, 485 U.S. 312 (1988), 105, 139, 691
Boring v. Buncombe County Bd. of Educ., 136 F.3d 364 (4th Cir.), *cert. denied*, 525 U.S. 813 (1998), 701
Boroff v. Van Wert City Bd. of Educ., 220 F.3d 465 (6th Cir. 2000), *cert. denied*, 532 U.S. 920 (2001), 709
Bose Corp. v. Consumers Union, 466 U.S. 485 (1984), 479
Bostock v. Clayton County, 140 S. Ct. 1731 (2020), 540
Boucher v. School Bd. of Sch. Dist. of Greenfield, 134 F.3d 821 (7th Cir. 1998), 708
Bowen v. Roy, 476 U.S. 693 (1986), 756, 801
Bowen, Secretary of Health & Human Services v. Kendrick, 487 U.S. 589 (1988), 923
Bown v. Gwinnett County Sch. Dist., 112 F.3d 1464 (11th Cir. 1997), 967
Boy Scouts of America v. Dale, 530 U.S. 640 (2000), 300, 537
Brandenburg v. Ohio, 395 U.S. 444 (1969), 4, **55**, 533, 576, 606
Branti v. Finkel, 445 U.S. 507 (1980), 686
Branzburg v. Hayes, 408 U.S. 665 (1972), 373
Braunfeld v. Brown, 366 U.S. 599 (1961), 728
Bridges v. California, 314 U.S. 252 (1941), 20, 52
Broadrick v. Oklahoma, 413 U.S. 601 (1973), 25, 26
Brockett v. Spokane Arcades, Inc., 472 U.S. 491 (1985), 26
Brody v. Spang, 957 F.2d 1108 (3d Cir. 1992), 701
Brown v. Entertainment Merchants Ass'n, 564 U.S. 786 (2011), 24, 81, 84, **106**, 460, 588, 613
Brown v. Gilmore, 258 F.3d 265 (4th Cir.), *cert. denied*, 534 U.S. 996 (2001), 967
Brown v. Louisiana, 383 U.S. 131 (1966), 222
Buckley v. Valeo, 424 U.S. 1 (1976), 118, 287
Burns v. Town of Palm Beach, 999 F.3d 1317 (11th Cir. 2021), 151
Burson v. Freeman, 504 U.S. 191 (1992), 105
Burwell v. Hobby Lobby Stores, Inc., 573 U.S. 682 (2014), 827
Butler v. Michigan, 352 U.S. 380 (1957), 587, 618, 627
Bystrom v. Fridley High Sch., 686 F. Supp. 1387 (D. Minn. 1987), 708

C

C.H. ex rel. Z.H. v. Oliva, 195 F.3d 167 (3d Cir.), *vacated and reh'g en banc granted by* 197 F.3d 63 (3d Cir. 999), *on reh'g en banc*, 226 F.3d 198 (3d Cir. 2000), 993
Cannon v. University of Chicago, 441 U.S. 677 (1979), 540
Cantwell v. Connecticut, 310 U.S. 296 (1940), 52, 67, **181**, 202
Capitol Square Review and Advisory Bd. v. Pinette, 515 U.S. 753 (1995), 651, 991
Calvary Chapel Dayton Valley v. Sisolak (2020), 774
Case C-131/12, Google Spain SL, Google Inc. v. Agencia Española de Protectión de Datos (AEPD), Mario Costeja Gonzáles, Court of Justice (Grand Chamber), 13 May 2014, 514
CBS, Inc. v. Young, 522 F.2d 234 (6th Cir. 1975), 422
Central Hudson Gas & Electric Corp. v. Public Service Commission of New York, 447 U.S. 557 (1980), 320
Chapadeau v. Utica Observer-Dispatch, Inc., 341 N.E.2d 569 (N.Y. 1975), 487
Chaplinsky v. New Hampshire, 315 U.S. 568 (1942), 31, **65**, 81, 580
Chaudhuri v. Tennessee, 130 F.3d 232 (6th Cir. 1997), *cert. denied*, 523 U.S. 1024 (1998), 993

Chicago Lawyers' Committee for Civil Rights Under the Law, Inc. v. Craigslist, Inc., 519 F.3d 666 (7th Cir. 2008), 497
Christian Legal Society v. Martinez, 561 U.S. 661 (2010), 222, 229, 642
Church of the Am. Knights of the Ku Klux Klan v. Kerid, 356 F.3d 197, 206-207 (2d Cir. 2004), 288
Church of the Lukumi Babalu Aye, Inc. v. City of Hialeah, 508 U.S. 520 (1993), 765, **766**
Citizens United v. Federal Election Commission, 558 U.S. 310 (2010), 16, 27, **118**, 287, 362, 364, 368, 372, 460, 537
City of Boerne v. Flores, 521 U.S. 507 (1997), 823, 904
City of Chicago v. Morales, 527 U.S. 41 (1999), 27
City of Cincinnati v. Discovery Network, Inc., 507 U.S. 410 (1993), 139, **341**
City of Erie v. Pap's A.M., 429 U.S. 277 (2000), 169, 603, 605
City of Houston v. Hill, 482 U.S. 451 (1987), 67
City of Lakewood v. Plain Dealer Publg. Co., 486 U.S. 750, 757 (1988), 179
City of Littlejohn v. Z.J. Gifts D-4, L.L.C., 541 U.S. 774 (2004), 588
City of Los Angeles v. Alameda Books, Inc., 535 U.S. 425 (2002), 138, 605, 606
City of Nyssa v. Dufloth, 121 P.3d 639 (Or. 2005), 593
City of Renton v. Playtime Theatres, 475 U.S. 41 (1986), 601, 605, 606
Clark v. Community for Creative Non-Violence, 468 U.S. 288 (1984), 139, 145, **184**
Cohen v. California, 403 U.S. 15 (1971), 4, 68, 192, **542**
Cohen v. Cowles Media Co., 501 U.S. 663 (1991), 516
Cole v. Oroville Union High Sch. Dist., 228 F.3d 1092 (9th Cir. 2000), 993
Columbia Broad. Sys., Inc. v. Democratic Natl. Comm'n, 412 U.S. 94 (1973), 428
Committee for Pub. Educ. v. Nyquist, 413 U.S. 756 (1973), 917
Commonwealth v. Davis, 162 Mass. 510 (1895), 175
Commonwealth v. Davis, 39 N.E. 113, 113 (Mass. 1895), *aff'd*, 167 U.S. 43 (1897), 631
Connick v. Myers, 461 U.S. 138 (1983), 664, 680
Consolidated Edison Co. v. Pub. Serv. Comm'n, 447 U.S. 530 (1980), 355
Cornelius v. NAACP Legal Defense and Education Fund, 473 U.S. 488 (1985), 223, 642
Corporation of the Presiding Bishop of the Church of Jesus Christ of Latter-Day Saints v. Amos, 483 U.S. 327 (1987), 895
County of Allegheny v. ACLU, 492 U.S. 573 (1989), 887, 1002, 1024
Court in Heffernan v. City of Paterson, 578 U.S. 266 (2016), 687
Courthouse News Serv. v. Schaefer, 2 F.4th 318 (2021), 394
Cox v. Louisiana, 379 U.S. 536 (1965), 179, 211
Cox v. New Hampshire, 312 U.S. 569 (1941), 4, 28, **179**, 212
Crosby v. Holsinger, 852 F.2d 801 (4th Cir. 1988), 701
Crowe v. Oregon State Bar, 989 F.3d 784 (9th Cir. 2021), 279
Curtis Publg. Co. v. Butts, 388 U.S. 130 (1967), 480, 481
Cutter v. Wilkinson, 544 U.S. 709 (2005), 901

D

Dahlstrom v. Sun-Times Media, LLC., 777 F.3d 937 (7th Cir. 2015), 516
Dallas v. Stanglin, 490 U.S. 19 (1989), 607
Daugherty v. Vanguard Charter Sch. Acad., 116 F. Supp. 2d 897 (W.D. Mich. 2000), 994
Davis v. Massachusetts, 167 U.S. 43 (1897), 175
Debs v. United States, 249 U.S. 211 (1919), 36
Deeb v. Saati, 778 Fed. App'x 683 (11th Cir. 2019), 494
Dennis v. United States, 341 U.S. 494 (1951), 52
Denooyer v. Merinelli, No. 92-2080, 1993 WL 477030 (6th Cir. Nov. 18, 1993), 993
Denver Area Educational Telecommunications Consortium, Inc. v. FCC, 518 U.S. 727 (1996), 450
Discount Tobacco City & Lottery Inc. v. U.S., 674 F.3d 509 (6th Cir. 2012), 330

Doe v. Backpage.com, 817 F.3d 12 (1st Cir. 2016), cert. denied, 137 S.Ct. 622 (2017), 497

Doe v. Duncanville Indep. Sch. Dist., 70 F.3d 402 (5th Cir. 1995), 994

Doe v. GTE Corp., 347 F.3d 655 (7th Cir. 2003), 497

Doe v. Harlan County Sch. Dist., 96 F. Supp. 2d 667 (E.D. Ky. 2000), 978

Doe v. Reed, 561 U.S. 186 (2010), 287

Doe v. Stegall, 653 F.2d 180 (5th Cir. 1981), 978

Doninger v. Niehoff, 642 F.3d 334 (2d Cir. 2011), 707, 708

Doran v. Salem Inn, Inc., 422 U.S. 922 (1975), 580

Dow Jones & Co. v. Gutnick (2002) 210 C.L.R. 575, 422

Dun & Bradstreet v. Greenmoss Builders, 472 U.S. 749 (1985), 488

E

Edenfield v. Fane, 507 U.S. 761 (1993), 326

Edwards v. Aguillard, 482 U.S. 578 (1987), 982

Edwards v. South Carolina, 372 U.S. 229 (1963), 207, 221, 238

Elk Grove Unified School District v. Newdow, 542 U.S. 1 (2004), 1004

Elonis v. United States, 135 S. Ct. 2001 (2015), 74

Elrod v. Burns, 427 U.S. 347 (1976), 685

Emmett v. Kent Sch. Dist. No. 415, 92 F. Supp. 2d 1088 (W.D. Wash. 2000), 708

Employment Division, Department of Human Resources v. Smith, 494 U.S. 872 (1990), 740, **758**, 867

Engel v. Vitale, 370 U.S. 421 (1962), 958, 977, 993

Epperson v. Arkansas, 393 U.S. 97 (1968), 978

Espinoza v. Montana Department of Revenue, 140 S. Ct. 2246 (2020), 815, 906

Estate of Thornton v. Caldor, Inc. 472 U.S. 703 (1985), 735, 891, 900

Everson v. Board of Education, 330 U.S. 1 (1947), 878, **881**, 909, **910**

Expressions Hair Design v. Schneiderman, 137 S. Ct. 1144 (2017), 339, 340

F

Fair Housing Council of San Fernando Valley v. Roommates. com LLC, 521 F.3d 1157, 36 Med. L. Rptr. 1545 (9th Cir. 2008), 496

FCC v. CBS Corp., 567 U.S. 953 (2012), 440

FCC v. League of Women Voters, 468 U.S. 364 (1984), 429

FCC v. Pacifica Foundation, 438 U.S. 726 (1978), 429

Federal Communications Commission v. Fox Television Stations, Inc., 567 U.S. 239 (2012), 434

Feiner v. New York, 340 U.S. 315 (1951), 203

Ferber v. New York, 458 U.S. 747 (1982), 81, 628

Fields v. City of Philadelphia, 862 F.3d 353 (3d Cir. 2017), 372

First National Bank of Boston v. Bellotti, 435 U.S. 765 (1978), 21, 45, 355, **356**, 537

Flast v. Cohen, 392 U.S. 83 (1968), 952

Fleming v. Jefferson County Sch. Dist. R1, 298 F.3d 918 (10th Cir. 2002), 701

Flynt v. Rumsfeld, 355 F.3d 697 (D.C. Cir. 2004), 403

Forsyth County, Ga. v. Nationalist Movement, 505 U.S. 123 (1992), 4, **212**

Fox Television Stations, Inc. v. FCC, 489 F. 3d 444 (2d Cir. 2007), *rev'd*, 556 U.S. 502 (2009), 434

Fraternal Order of Police v. City of Newark, 170 F.3d 359 (3d Cir. 1999), 773

Frisby v. Schultz, 487 U.S. 474 (1988), 189, 222

Frohwerk v. United States, 249 U.S. 204 (1919), 36

Frothingham v. Mellon, 262 U.S. 447 (1923), 952

Fulton v. City of Philadelphia, 141 S. Ct. 1294 (2021), 790

G

Gaeta v. New York News, Inc., 465 N.E.2d 802 (N.Y. 1984), 487

Garcetti v. Ceballos, 547 U.S. 410 (2006), 668, 680

Garrison v. Louisiana, 379 U.S. 64 (1964), 478

Gentile v. State Bar of Nevada, 501 U.S. 1030 (1991), 422
Gertz v. Robert Welch, Inc., 418 U.S. 323 (1974), 482
Gertz v. Robert Welch, Inc., 680 F.2d 527 (7th Cir. 1982), 488, 490
Gibson v. Florida Legislative Investigation Comm., 372 U.S. 539 (1963), 292
Ginsberg v. New York, 390 U.S. 629 (1968), 587, 618
Gitlow v. New York, 268 U.S. 652 (1925), 43
Givhan *v.* Western Line Consolidated School District, 439 U.S. 410 (1979), 681
Glickman v. Wileman Bros., 521 U.S. 457 (1997), 279
Globe Newspaper Co. v. Superior Court, 457 U.S. 596 (1982), 395
Golden v. Rossford Exempted Vill. Sch. Dist., 445 F. Supp. 2d 820 (N.D. Ohio 2006), 701
Goldman v. Weinberger, 475 U.S. 503 (1986), 756
Gonzales v. O Centro Espírita Beneficente União do Vegetal, 546 U.S. 418 (2006), 825
Gonzalez v. Douglas, 269 F. Supp. 3d. 948 (D. Ariz. 2017), 716
Gonzalez v. Google, 2 F.4th 871 (9th Cir. 2021), 497
Gooding v. Wilson, 405 U.S. 518 (1972), 25, 69, **548**
Grant v. Torstar Corp. (Can.), [2009] 3 S.C.R. 640, 497
Grayned v. City of Rockford, 408 U.S. 104 (1972), 26, 691
Greater New Orleans Broadcasting Association v. U.S., 527 U.S. 173 (1999) (GNOB), 329, 330
Greer v. Spock, 424 U.S. 828 (1976), 222
Guiles v. Marineau, 461 F.3d 320 (2d Cir. 2006), 709

H

Hague v. CIO, 307 U.S. 496 (1939), 25, **176**, 218, 631
Halter v. Nebraska, 205 U.S. 34 (1907), 146,
Harper v. Poway Unified Sch. Dist., 445 F.3d 1166 (9th Cir. 2006), *dismissed as moot*, 485 F.3d 1052 (9th Cir. 2007), 994
Harris v. Zion, 927 F.2d 1401 (7th Cir. 1991), *cert. denied*, 505 U.S. 1229 (1992), 1014
Harte-Hanks Communs, Inc. v. Connaughton, 491 U.S. 657 (1989), 480
Hazelwood School District v. Kuhlmeier, 484 U.S. 260 (1988), 697
Healy v. James, 408 U.S. 169 (1972), 293
Hein v. Freedom from Religion Foundation, 551 U.S. 587 (2007), 953
Heinkel ex rel. Heinkel v. School Bd. of Lee County, Fla., 194 Fed. Appx. 604 (11th Cir. 2006), 709
Herceg v. Hustler Magazine, 814 F.2d 1017 (5th Cir. 1987), 63
Hess v. Indiana, 314 U.S. 105 (1973), 58, 552
Hill v. Colorado, 530 U.S. 703 (2000), 105, 201
Hishon v. King & Spaulding, 467 U.S. 69 (1984), 535, 540
Hodge v. Talkin, 799 F.3d 1145 (D.C. Cir. 2015), 230
Holder v. Humanitarian Law Project, 561 U.S. 1 (2010), 26, 62, 105, **112**
Holloman v. Harland, 370 F.3d 1252 (11th Cir. 2004), 709, 967
Holt v. Hobbs, 574 U.S. 352 (2015), 840
Hosanna-Tabor Evangelical Lutheran Church and School v. Equal Employment Opportunity Commission, 565 U.S. 171 (2012), 864
Houchins v. KQED, Inc., 438 U.S. 1 (1978), 398
Hudgens v. NLRB, 424 U.S. 507 (1976), 242
Hunt v. McNair, 413 U.S. 734 (1973), 916
Hurley v. Irish-American Gay, Lesbian and Bisexual Group of Boston, 515 U.S. 557 (1995), 151, **269**
Hustler Magazine, Inc. v. Falwell, 485 U.S. 46 (1989), 500

I

In re Boulevard Entm't, Inc., 334 F.3d 1336 (Fed. Cir. 2003), 347
In re Complaint of Syracuse Peace Council, 2 FCC Rec. 5043 (1987), 429
In re Fox, 702 F. 3d 633 (Fed. Cir. 2012), 347
In re Grand Jury Proceedings, 5 F.3d 397 (9th Cir. 1993), 382

In re Grand Jury Proceedings, 810 F.2d 580 (6th Cir. 1987), 382
In re Grand Jury Subpoena, No. 16-03-217, 384
In re Providence Journal Co., 820 F.2d 1354 (1st Cir. 1987), 409
In re Tam, 808 F.3d 1321, 1330 (Fed. Cir. 2015) (en banc), *aff'd*, 137 S. Ct. 1744 (2017), 347
In re WTHR-TV, 693 N.E.2d 1 (Ind. 1998), 382
Isaacs ex rel. Isaacs v. Board of Educ. of Howard County, Md., 40 F. Supp. 2d 335 (D. Md. 1999), 994

J

J.S. v. Bethlehem Area Sch. Dist., 807 A.2d 803 (Pa. 2002), 507
J.S. v. Village Voice Media Holdings, 359 P.3d 714 (Wash. 2015), 497
Jackson v. Mayweather, 10 Cal. App. 5th 1240 (Cal. Ct. App. 2017), 515
Janus v. American Federation of State, County, and Municipal Employees, Council 31, 138 S. Ct. 2448 (2018), 272
Johanns v. Livestock Mktg Ass'n, 544 U.S. 550 (2005), 281
Jones v. Dirty World Entertainment, 755 F.3d 398 (6th Cir. 2014), 497
Jones v. Wolf, 443 U.S. 595 (1979), 855, 867
Jordan v. Jewel Food Stores, Inc., 743 F. 3d 509 (2014), 360
Judge v. Saltz Plastic Surgery, 367 P.3d 1006 (Utah 2016), 515

K

Keller v. State Bar of California, 496 U.S. 1 (1990), 279
Killion v. Franklin Reg'l Sch. Dist., 136 F. Supp. 2d 446 (W.D. Pa. 2001), 708
Kingsley International Pictures Corp. v. Regents, 360 U.S. 684 (1959), 104, 580
Kinney v. Barnes, 443 S.W. 3d 87 (2014), 412, 413, 495
Kirkland v. Northside Indep. Sch. Dist., 890 F.2d 794 (5th Cir. 1989), *cert. denied*, 496 U.S. 926 (1990), 701
Kitzmiller v. Dover Area School District, 400 F. Supp. 2d 707 (M.D. Pa. 2005), 987
Klayman v. Zuckerberg, 753 F.3d 1354 (D.C. Cir. 2014), 497
Kovacs v. Cooper, 336 U.S. 77 (1949), 180
Kowalski v. Berkeley County Schools, 652 F.3d 565 (4th Cir. 2011), *cert. denied*, 565 U.S. 1173 (2012), 710
Kunz v. New York, 340 U.S. 290 (1951), 179, **529**

L

Lamb's Chapel v. Center Moriches Union Free School District, 508 U.S. 384 (1993), 886, **989**, 993
Lane v. Franks, 573 U.S. 228 (2014), 675
Larkin v. Grendel's Den, 459 U.S. 116 (1982), 1038
Larson v. Valente, 456 U.S. 228 (1982), 1041
Lassonde v. Pleasanton Unified Sch. Dist., 320 F.3d 979 (9th Cir. 2003), 993
LaVine v. Blaine Sch. Dist., 257 F.3d 981 (9th Cir. 2001), *cert. denied*, 536 U.S. 959 (2002), 709
Leathers v. Medlock, 499 U.S. 439 (1990), 371
Lee v. Weisman, 505 U.S. 577 (1992), 887, 957, **968**, 993
Legal Services Corp. v. Velazquez, 531 U.S. 522 (2001), 636, 660, 680
Lehman v. Shaker Heights, 418 U.S. 298 (1974), 222
Lemon v. Kurtzman, 403 U.S. 602 (1971), 886, **917**
Little Sisters Book & Art Emporium v. Commissioner, [2000] 2 S.C.R. 1120 (Can.), 601
Lloyd Corp. v. Tanner, 407 U.S. 551 (1972), 241
Lochner v. New York, 198 U.S. 45 (1908), 317
Locke v. Davey, 540 U.S. 712 (2004), 803, 905
Lovell v. City of Griffin, 303 U.S. 444 (1938), 178, 605
Lundberg v. West Monona Cmty. Sch. Dist., 731 F. Supp. 331 (N.D. Iowa 1989), 701
Lynch v. Donnelly, 465 U.S. 668 (1984), 995, 1015, 1024
Lyng v. Northwest Indian Cemetery Protection Ass'n, 485 U.S. 439 (1988), 756

M

Madsen v. Women's Health Ctr., Inc., 512 U.S. 753 (1994), 28

Mahaffey v. Aldrich, 236 F. Supp. 2d 779 (E.D. Mich. 2002), 709
Mahanoy Area School Dist. v. B.L., 141 S. Ct. 2038 (2021), 552, 696, 708
Marsh v. Alabama, 326 U.S. 501 (1946), 240
Marsh v. Chambers, 463 U.S. 783 (1983), 887, **1024**
Martin v. Hearst Corp., 777 F.3d 546 (2d Cir. 2015), 514
Martin v. Struthers, 319 U.S. 141, 146 (1943), 178
Masses Publishing Co. v. Patten, 244 F. 535 (S.D.N.Y. 1917), 41
Masses Publg. Co. v. Patten, 246 F. 24 (2d Cir. 1917), 41
Masson v. New Yorker Magazine, 501 U.S. 496 (1991), 480
Masterpiece Cakeshop. Ltd. v. Colorado Civil Rights Commission, 138 S. Ct. 1719 (2018), 259, **783**
Matal v. Tam, 137 S. Ct. 1744 (2017), 347, 651
May v. Cooperman, 780 F.2d 240 (3d Cir. 1985), 967
McAuliffe v. Mayor of New Bedford, 29 N.E. 517 (Mass. 1892), 631
McConnell v. Federal Election Comm'n, 540 U.S. 93 (2003), 287, 429
McCreary County, Kentucky v. American Civil Liberties Union of Kentucky, 545 U.S. 844 (2005), 878, **1004**
McCullen v. Coakley, 134 S. Ct. 2518 (2014), 193, 222
McDaniel v. Paty, 435 U.S. 618 (1978), 1041
McGowan v. Maryland, 366 U.S. 420 (1961), 732
McIntyre v. Ohio Elections Commission, 514 U.S. 334 (1995), 282, 723
McKee v. Cosby, Jr. 139 S.Ct. 675 (2019), 499
Meek v. Pittenger, 421 U.S. 349 (1975), 917, 938
Members of City Council of City of Los Angeles v. Taxpayers for Vincent, 466 U.S. 789 (1984), 25, 27
Memoirs v. Massachusetts, 383 U.S. 413 (1966), 581
Meritor Savings Bank v. Vinson, 477 U.S. 57 (1986), 537, 540
Metromedia, Inc. v. San Diego, 453 U.S. 490 (1981), 188
Miami Herald v. Tornillo, 418 U.S. 241 (1974), 260, 428, 449
Milkovich v. Lorain Journal Co., 497 U.S. 1 (1990), 490
Mills v. Alabama, 384 U.S. 214 (1966), 369
Miller v. California, 413 U.S. 15 (1973), 4, 581, **582**
Miller v. Mitchell, 598 F.3d 139 (3d Cir. 2010), 630
Minersville School District v. Gobitis, 310 U.S. 586 (1940), 244
Mitchell v. Helms, 530 U.S. 793 (2000), 910, **930**, 939
Morse v. Frederick, 551 U.S. 393 (2007), 552, **702**
Mt. Healthy City Sch. Dist. Bd. of Educ. v. Doyle, 429 U.S. 274, 287 (1977), 674
Mueller v. Allen, 463 U.S. 388 (1983), 910, 916
Murphy v. Collier, 139 S. Ct. 1475 (2019), 727
Murray v. Austin, 947 F.2d 147 (5th Cir. 1991), 1014
Mutual Film Corp. v. Industrial Comm'n, 236 U.S. 230 (1915), 317

N

NAACP v. Alabama ex rel. Patterson, 357 U.S. 449 (1958), 45, 51, **288**
NAACP v. Button, 371 U.S. 415 (1963), 293
NAACP v. Claiborne Hardware Co., 458 U.S. 886 (1982), 54, 61, 73
National Endowment for the Arts v. Finley, 524 U.S. 569 (1998), 642, 660
National Institute of Family and Life Advocates v. Becerra, 138 S. Ct. 2361 (2018), 250
Near v. Minnesota, 283 U.S. 697 (1931), 404
Nebraska Press Ass'n v. Stuart, 427 U.S. 539 (1976), 27, 395, **414**
NetChoice, LLC v. Moody, No. 4:21CV220-RH-MAF, 2021 WL 2690876 (N.D. Fla. June 30, 2021), 462
NetChoice, LLC v. Paxton, No. 1:21-CV-840-RP, 2021 WL 5755120 (W.D. Tex. Dec. 1, 2021), 462
New York v. Ferber, 458 U.S. 747 (1982), 32, **608**
New York State Club Ass'n, Inc. v. City of New York, 487 U.S. 1 (1988), 299

New York Times Co. v. Gonzales, 382 F. Supp. 2d 457 (S.D.N.Y. 2005), *vacated & remanded* New York Times Co. v. Gonzales, 459 F.3d 160, 163 (2d Cir. 2006), 387
New York Times Co. v. Sullivan, 376 U.S. 254 (1964), 16, 42, 68, **471**, 533
New York Times Co. v. United States, 403 U.S. 713 (1971), 410
Norton v. City of Springfield, 803 F.3d 411 (7th Cir. 2015), 105
Noto v. United States, 367 U.S. 290 (1961), 54
Nwanguma v. Trump, 903 F.3d 604 (6th Cir. 2018), 58

O

O'Hair v. Murray, 588 F.2d 1144 (5th Cir. 1979), 1014
O'Hare Truck Service, Inc. v. City of Northlake, 518 U.S. 712 (1996), 687
Oberwetter v. Hilliard, 639 F.3d 545 (D.C. Cir. 2011), 239
Obsidian Financial Group LLC v. Cox, 740 F.3d 1284 (9th Cir. 2014), 488
Ohralik v. Ohio State Bar Ass'n, 436 U.S. 447 (1978), 325
Oregon v. City of Rajneeshpuram, 598 F. Supp. 1208 (D. Ore. 1984), 1040
Oregon v. Henry, 732 P.2d 9 (Or. 1987), 593
Our Lady of Guadelupe v. Morrissey-Berru, 140 S. Ct. 2049 (2020), 868
Packingham v. North Carolina, 137 S. Ct. 1730 (2017), 5
Patterson v. Colorado, 205 U.S. 454, 462 (1907), 13
Pell v. Procunier, 417 U.S. 817 (1974), 398
People v. New Times Pblg. Co, 35 Colo. 253 (1906), 13
Perry Education Ass'n v. Perry Local Educators' Ass'n, 460 U.S. 37 (1983), 218
Philadelphia Newspapers, Inc. v. Hepps, 475 U.S. 767 (1986), 478, 488
Pickering v. Board of Education, 391 U.S. 563 (1968), 662
Pierre-Paul v. ESPN, 44 Media L. Rep. 2452 (S.D. Fla. 2016), 515
Pinard v. Clatskanie Sch. Dist. 6J, 467 F.3d 755 (9th Cir. 2006), 709
Planned Parenthood v. American Coalition of Life Activists, 290 F.3d 1059 (9th Cir. 2002), 81
Planned Parenthood of S. Nev., Inc. v. Clark County Sch. Dist., 941 F.2d 817 (9th Cir. 1991), 701
Pleasant Grove City, Utah v. Summum, 555 U.S. 460 (2009), 230, **646**, 660
Police Dept. of the City of Chicago v. Mosley, 408 U.S. 92 (1972), 24, **90**,
Poling v. Murphy, 872 F.2d 757 (6th Cir. 1989), *cert. denied*, 493 U.S. 1021 (1990), 695, 701
Ponce v. Socorro Independent Sch. Dist., 508 F.3d 765 (5th Cir. 2007), 708
Porter v. Ascension Parish School Board, 393 F.3d 608 (5th Cir. 2004), 707
Posadas de Puerto Rico Associates v. Tourism Co., 478 U.S. 328 (1986), 326
Prager University v. Google LLC, 951 F.3d 991 (9th Cir. 2020), 242
Presbyterian Church in the United States v. Mary Elizabeth Blue Hull Memorial Presbyterian Church, 393 U.S. 440 (1969), 850
Presley v. Georgia, 558 U.S. 209 (2010), 396
Press-Enterprise Co. v. Superior Court, 464 U.S. 501 (1984) ("Press-Enterprise I"), 395
Press-Enterprise Co. v. Superior Court, 478 U.S. 1 (1986) ("Press-Enterprise II"), 396
Procter & Gamble Co. v. Bankers Trust Co., 78 F.3d 219 (6th Cir. 1996)
PruneYard Shopping Center et al. v. Robins, 447 U.S. 74 (1980), 264
Publicker Indus., Inc. v. Cohen, 733 F.2d 1059 (3d Cir. 1984), 394
Pyle ex rel. Pyle v. South Hadley Sch. Comm., 861 F. Supp. 157 (D. Mass. 1994), 709

Q

Queen v. Dr. Brown, 88 Eng. Rep. 911 (Q.B. 1706), 8
Queen v. Tutchin, 90 Eng. Rep. 1133 (Q.B. 1704), 8

R

R. v. Butler, (1992) 1 S.C.R. 452 (Can.), 594
R. v. Keegstra, [1990] 3 S.C.R. 697 (Can.), 152, **554**
R. v. Oakes, [1986] S.C.R. 103, 88
R. v. Sharpe, [2001] 1 S.C.R. 45 (Can.), 86, 617, 628

R.A.V. v. City of St. Paul 505 U.S. 377 (1992), 68, 73, 104, 139, 479, 533, 553, **562**, 691
R.J. Reynolds Tobacco Co. v. FDA, 696 F.3d 1205 (D.C. Cir. 2012), 258, 330
Radio & Television News Ass'n v. U.S. Dist. Court, 781 F.2d 1443 (9th Cir. 1986), 422
Radio-Television News Directors Ass'n v. FCC, 229 F.3d 269 (D.C. Cir. 2000), 428
Railway Express Agency, Inc. v. New York City, 336 U.S. 106 (1949), 313, **316**
Red Lion Broad. Co. v. FCC, 395 U.S. 367 (1969), 264, 424
Redrup v. New York, 386 U.S. 767 (1967), 581
Reed v. Town of Gilbert, 576 U.S. 155 (2019), 94, 137
Regina v. Hicklin, [1868] L.R. 3 Q.B. 360, 580
Reno v. American Civil Liberties Union, 521 U.S. 844 (1997), 5, **456**, 629
Renton v. Playtime Theatres, Inc., 475 U.S. 41 (1986), 135
Reynolds v. United States, 98 U.S. (8Otto) 145 (1879), 739, **741**
Rice v. Paladin Enterprises, 128 F.3d 233 (4th Cir. 1997), 63
Richmond Newspapers, Inc. v. Virginia, 448 U.S. 555 (1980), 387
Roberts v. Madigan, 921 F.2d 1047 (10th Cir. 1990), *cert. denied*, 505 U.S. 1218 (1992), 994
Roberts v. United States Jaycees, 468 U.S. 609 (1984), 293
Roemer v. Board of Pub. Works, 426 U.S. 736 (1976), 916
Roman Catholic Diocese of Brooklyn v. Cuomo, 141 S. Ct. 63 (2020), 776
Rosenberger v. Rector & Visitors of University of Virginia, 515 U.S. 819 (1995), 229, **638**, 660, 991
Rosenblatt v. Baer, 383 U.S. 75 (1966), 481
Rosenfeld v. New Jersey, 408 U.S. 901 (1972), 549
Roth v. United States, 354 U.S. 476, 514 (1957), 24, 580
Rumsfeld v. Forum for Acad. & Institutional Rights, 547 U.S. 47 (2006), 151, 268
Rust v. Sullivan, 500 U.S. 173 (1991), 632, 660, 680
Rutan v. Republican Party of Illinois, 497 U.S. 62 (1990), 686

S

Salazar v. Buono, 559 U.S. 700 (2010), 651, 1014
Salem Inn, Inc. v. Frank, 501 F.2d 18 (2d Cir. 1974), 580
San Diego v. Roe, 543 U.S. 77 (2004), 684
Santa Fe Independent School District v. Doe, 530 U.S. 290 (2000), 974, 993
Saxbe v. Washington Post Co., 417 U.S. 843 (1974), 398
Saxe v. State Coll. Area Sch. Dist., 240 F.3d 200 (3d Cir. 2001), 709
Scales v. United States, 367 U.S. 203 (1961), 53
Schenck v. United States, 249 U.S. 47 (1919), 14, 27, **33**
Schneider v. New Jersey, 308 U.S. 147 (1939), 138, 178, 192, 605
Schneiderman v. United States, 320 U.S. 118 (1943), 52
School Dist. of the City of Grand Rapids v. Ball, 473 U.S. 373, 916
School District of Abington Township v. Schempp, 374 U.S. 203 (1963), 961, 993
Scopes v. State, 289 S.W. 363 (Tenn. 1927), 982
Seaton v. TripAdvisor, 728 F.3d 592 (6th Cir. 2013), 495
Seattle Times Co. v. Rhinehart, 467 U.S. 20 (1984), 396
Selman v. Cobb Cnty. Sch. Dist., 390 F. Supp. 1286, 1292 (N.D. Ga. 2005), *rev'd*, 449 F.3d 1320 (11th Cir. 2006), 988
Serbian Eastern Orthodox Diocese v. Milivojevich, 426 U.S. 696 (1976), 861
Shaffer v. United States, 255 F. 886 (9th Cir. 1919), 33
Shelton v. Tucker, 364 U.S. 479 (1960), 292
Sheppard v. Maxwell, 384 U.S. 333 (1966), 394, 414
Sherbert v. Verner, 374 U.S. 398 (1963), 739, 740, **744**
Shuttlesworth v. City of Birmingham, 394 U.S. 147 (1969), 179
Simon & Schuster, Inc. v. Members of New York State Crime Victims Board, 502 U.S. 105 (1991), 105
Smith v. Goguen, 415 U.S. 566 (1974), 26

Snyder v. Blue Mountain Sch. Dist., 650 F.3d 915 (3d Cir. 2011) (en banc), *cert. denied*, 565 U.S. 1156 (2012), 710

Snyder v. Phelps, 562 U.S. 443 (2011), 504, 546

Sorrell v. IMS Health Inc., 564 U.S. 552 (2011), 331

South Bay United Pentecostal Church v. Newsom, 140 S. Ct. 1613 (2020), 774

Southeastern Promotions, Ltd. v. Conrad, 420 U.S. 546 (1975), 223

Spence v. Washington, 418 U.S. 405 (1974), 139, 145, **146**

Spencer v. Glover, 397 P.3d 780 (Utah App. 2017), 495

St. Amant v. Thompson, 390 U.S. 727 (1968), 480

Stand Up America Now v. City of Dearborn, 969 F. Supp. 2d 843 (E.D. Mich. 2013), 535

Stanley v. Georgia, 394 U.S. 557 (1969), 615

State ex rel. Sports Mgmt. News, Inc. v. Nachtigal, 921 P.2d 1304 (Or. 1996), 412

State v. Ciancanelli, 121 P.3d 613 (Or. 2005), 593

State v. Arlene's Flowers, 441 P.3d 1203 (Wash. 2019), 259

Stone v. Graham, 449 U.S. 39 (1992), 964, 993

Street v. New York, 394 U.S. 576 (1969), 146

Stromberg v. California, 283 U.S. 359 (1931), 16, 45

Stuart v. Camnitz, 774 F.3d 238 (4th Cir. 2014), 259

T

Talley v. California, 362 U.S. 60 (1960), 286

Tandom v. Newsom, 141 S. Ct. 1294 (2021), 780

Tatro v. Univ. of Minn., 816 N.W.2d 509 (Minn. 2012), 701

Taylor v. Mississippi, 319 U.S. 583 (1943), 52

Telecommunications Research & Action Ctr. v. FCC, 801 F.2d 501 (D.C. Cir. 1986), 428

Terminiello v. Chicago, 337 U.S. 1 (1949), 210

Texas v. Johnson, 491 U.S. 397 (1989), 5, 69, 139, **153**

Texas Monthly, Inc. v. Bullock, 489 U.S. 1 (1989), 891, 905, **921**

The Florida Star v. B. J. F., 491 U.S. 524 (1989), 508

Thomas v. Chicago Park Dist., 534 U.S. 316 (2002), 28, 179, 181

Thomas v. Review Bd. of Ind. Emp't Sec. Div., 450 U.S. 707 (1981), 756

Thornhill v. Alabama, 310 U.S. 88 (1940), 52

Tilton v. Richardson, 403 U.S. 672 (1971), 916

Time, Inc. v. Firestone, 424 U.S. 448 (1976), 487

Time, Inc. v. Pape, 401 U.S. 279 (1971), 480

Tinker v. Des Moines Independent Community School District, 393 U.S. 503 (1969), 552, **688**, 700

Town of Greece v. Galloway, 572 U.S. 565 (2014), 887, **1031**

Trinity Lutheran Church of Columbia, Inc. v. Comer, 137 S. Ct. 2012 (2017), 807, 906, **939**

Turner Broad. Sys., Inc. v. FCC, 520 U.S. 180 (1997) ("Turner II"), 450

Turner Broadcasting System, Inc. v. FCC, 512 U.S. 622 (1994) ("Turner I"), 24, **441**

U

U.S. v. Sterling, 818 F. Supp. 2d 945 (E.D. Va. 2011), 385

U.S. v. Sterling, 724 F.3d 482 (4th Cir. 2013), 385

U.S. v. Williams, 553 U.S. 285 (2008), 618

U.S. Civil Service Commission v. National Ass'n of Letter Carriers, 413 U.S. 548 (1973), 682, 685

U.S. Postal Service v. Council of Greenburgh Civic Ass'ns, 453 U.S. 114 (1981), 222

United States v. Alvarez, 567 U.S. 709 (2012), 85, **109**, 134, 364, 494, 522

United States v. American Library Ass'n, 539 U.S. 194 (2003), 230, **717**

United States v. Ballard, 322 U.S. 78 (1944), 801

United States v. Board of Educ., 911 F.2d 882 (3d Cir. 1990), 994

United States v. Caronia, 703 F.3d 149 (2012), 349
United States v. Dickinson, 465 F.2d 496 (5th Cir. 1972), 410
United States v. Eichman, 496 U.S. 310 (1990), 159
United States v. Glassdoor, 875 F. 3d 1179 (9th Cir. 2017), 384
United States v. Grace, 461 U.S. 171 (1983), 178, 222
United States v. Jeffries, 692 F.3d 473 (6th Cir. 2012), 75
United States v. Kokinda, 497 U.S. 720 (1990), 222
United States v. Lee, 455 U.S. 252 (1982), 755
United States v. O'Brien, 391 U.S. 367 (1968), 5, **140**, 145, 187
United States v. Playboy Entertainment Group, Inc., 529 U.S. 803 (2000), 451
United States v. Quaintance, 608 F.3d 717 (10th Cir. 2010), 801
United States v. Rosen, 445 F. Supp. 2d 602 (E.D. Va. 2006), 412
United States v. Rosen, 557 F.3d 192 (4th Cir. 2009), 413
United States v. Seeger, 380 U.S. 163 (1965), 906
United States v. Smith, 135 F.3d 963 (5th Cir. 1998), 382
United States v. Stevens, 559 U.S. 460 (2010), 24, 68, **81**
United States v. Stevens, 881 F.3d 1249 (10th Cir. 2018), 75
United States v. United Foods, 533 U.S. 405 (2001), 280
United States v. Williams, 535 U.S. 285 (2010), 26

V

Valentine v. Chrestensen, 316 U.S. 52 (1942), 314
Valley Forge Christian College v. Americans United for Separation of Church & State, Inc., 454 U.S. 464 (1982), 953
Van Orden v. Perry, 545 U.S. 677 (2005), 1007
Virginia v. Black, 538 U.S. 343 (2003), 73, 74, 534, 554, **571**
Virginia v. Hicks, 539 U.S. 113, 119 (2003), 25
Virginia State Board of Pharmacy v. Virginia Citizens Consumer Council, Inc., 425 U.S. 728 (1976), 319

W

Walker v. City of Birmingham, 388 U.S. 307 (1967), 409
Walker v. Texas Division, Sons of Confederate Veterans, Inc., 576 U.S. 200 (2015), 652
Wallace v. Jaffree, 472 U.S. 38 (1985), 878, 966
Walz v. Tax Commission of the City of New York, 397 U.S. 664 (1970), 917
Ward v. Rock Against Racism, 491 U.S. 781 (1989), 129, 145, 188, 360, 691
Washington v. Davis, 426 U.S. 229 (1976), 773
Watchtower Bible & Tract Society of New York, Inc. v. Stratton, 536 U.S. 150 (2002), 286
Waters v. Churchill, 511 U.S. 661 (1994), 674
Watson v. Jones, 80 (13 Wall) U.S. 679 (1872), 846
Watts v. United States, 394 U.S. 705 (1969), 71, 576
Welsh v. United States, 398 U.S. 333 (1970), 906, 907
West v. Derby Unified Sch. Dist. No. 260, 206 F.3d 1358 (10th Cir.), *cert. denied*, 531 U.S. 825 (2000), 709
West Virginia State Board of Education v. Barnette, 319 U.S. 624 (1943), 244, 528, 717
Whitney v. California, 274 U.S. 357 (1927), 19, **46**
Widmar v. Vincent, 454 U.S. 263 (1981), 988, 993
Wieman v. Updegraff, 344 U.S. 183 (1952), 685
Williams-Yulee v. Florida Bar, 575 U.S. 433 (2013), 105, 117
Wisconsin v. Mitchell, 508 U.S. 476 (1993), 568
Wisconsin v. Yoder, 406 U.S. 205 (1972), 749
Wolman v. Walter, 433 U.S. 229 (1977), 917, 938
Wooley v. Maynard, 430 U.S. 705 (1977), 248

Wynar v. Douglas County Sch. Dist., 728 F.3d 1062 (9th Cir. 2013), 707

Y

Yates v. United States, 354 U.S. 298 (1957), 52
Yick Wo v. Hopkins, 118 U.S. 356 (1886), 145
Young v. American Mini Theatres, Inc., 427 U.S. 50 (1976), 138, 605

Z

Zauderer v. Office of Disciplinary Counsel, 471 U.S. 626 (1985), 325
Zelman v. Simmons-Harris, 536 U.S. 639 (2002), 807, **940**
Zeran v. America Online, Inc., 129 F.3d 327 (4th Cir. 1997), 496
Zobrest v. Catalina Foothills Sch. Dist., 509 U.S. 1 (1993), 916
Zubik v. Burwell, 578 U.S. 403 (2016), 840

Table of Authorities

Adler, Amy, The Perverse Law of Child Pornography, 101 Colum. L. Rev. 209, 253-256 (2001), 613
Ahrens, Deborah, Schools, Cyberbullies, and the Surveillance State, 49 Am. Crim. L. Rev. 1669, 1692 (2012), 628
Anderson, David A., Incitement and Tort Law, 37 Wake Forest L. Rev. 957 (2002), 62
______, The Origins of the Press Clause, 30 UCLA L. Rev. 455 (1983), 10, 11, 368
______, Freedom of the Press, 80 Tex. L. Rev. 510 (2002), 384
Baker, C. Edwin, Unreasoned Reasonableness: Mandatory Parade Permits and Time, Place and Manner Regulations, 78 Nw. U. L. Rev. 937 (1983), 180
Bambauer, Jane, Is Data Speech?, 66 Stan. L. Rev. 57 (2014), 339
BeVier, Lillian, Rehabilitating Public Forum Doctrine: In Defense of Categories, 1993 Sup. Ct. Rev. 79, 223
Bhagwat, Ashutosh, *Sorrell v. IMS Health*: Details, Detailing, and the Death of Privacy, 36 Vt. L. Rev. 855, 856 (2012), 339
Bi, Kathryn, Comment, What Is "False or Misleading" Off-Label Promotion?, 82 U. Chi. L. Rev. 975 (2015), 351
Bickel, Alexander, The Morality of Consent 72 (1975), 67
Black, Hugo L., The Bill of Rights, 35 N.Y.U. L. Rev. 865 (1960), 4
Blackstone, William, Commentaries on the Laws of England, 6, 9, 404
Blasi, Vincent, The Checking Value in First Amendment Theory, 1977 Am. B. Found. Research J. 521, 17
______, Toward a Theory of Prior Restraint: The Central Linkage, 66 Minn. L. Rev. 11, (1981), 28
______, The First Amendment and the Idea of Civic Courage, 29 Wm. & Mary L. Rev. 653 (1988), 51
______, The Pathological Perspective and the First Amendment, 85 Colum. L. Rev. 449 (1985), 37, 46
______, Reading Holmes Through the Lens of Schauer: The *Abrams* Dissent, 72 Notre Dame L. Rev. 1343 (1997), 57
______, Free Speech and Good Character, 46 UCLA L. Rev. 1567 (1999), 51
Bonomi, Patricia U., "Religious Dissent and The Case for American Exceptionalism," in Religion in a Revolutionary Age (Hoffman & Albert eds. 1994), 21
Bork, Robert, Neutral Principles and Some First Amendment Problems, 47 Ind. L.J. 1 (1971), 17, 46, 593
Browne, Kingsley R., Title VII as Censorship: Hostile-Environment Harassment and the First Amendment, 52 Ohio St. L.J. 481 (1991), 522
Buel, Richard, "Freedom of the Press in Revolutionary America: The Evolution of Libertarianism, 1760-1820," in The Press and the American Revolution (Bernard Bailyn & John Hench eds. 1980), 10
______, Securing the Revolution (1972), 12
Caine, Burton, The Trouble with Fighting Words: *Chaplinsky v. New Hampshire* Is a Threat to First Amendment Values and Should Be Overruled, 88 Marq. L. Rev. 441 (2004), 70
Calvert, Clay, Misuse and Abuse of *Morse v. Frederick* by Lower Courts, 32 Seattle U. L. Rev.1 (2008), 708

______, Revenge Porn and Freedom of Expression: Legislative Pushback to an Online Weapon of Emotional and Reputational Destruction, 24 Fordham Intell. Prop. Media & Ent. L.J. 673, 683-701 (2014), 602
Carpenter, Dale, Expressive Association and Anti-Discrimination Law After *Dale*: A Tripartite Approach, 85 Minn. L. Rev. 1515 (2001), 309
Carter, Stephen L., Evolution, Creationism, and Treating Religion as a Hobby, 1987 Duke L.J. 977, 986
Chafee, Zechariah, Book Review, 62 Harv. L. Rev. 891 (1949), 17
______, Free Speech in the United States (1941), 41, 42
______, Freedom of Speech in War Time, 32 Harv. L. Rev. 932 (1919), 10
Chen, Alan K., Statutory Speech Bubbles, First Amendment Overbreadth, and Improper Legislative Purpose, 38 Harv. C.R.-C.L. L. Rev. 31 (2003), 25
Citron, Danielle Keats, Hate Crimes in Cyberspace (2014), 79, 288
Citron, Danielle Keats & Mary Anne Franks, Criminalizing Revenge Porn, 49 Wake Forest L. Rev. 345 (2014), 602
Cobb, Sanford H., The Rise of Religious Liberty in America: A History (Burt Franklin 1970) (1902), 879
Collins, Ronald K.L. & David M. Skover, Curious Concurrence: Justice Brandeis's Vote in *Whitney v. California*, 2005 Sup. Ct. Rev. 333 (2006), 51
Comment, Supreme Court No-Clear-Majority Decisions: A Study in Stare Decisis, 24 U. Chi. L. Rev. 99 (1956), 440
Corbin, Caroline Mala, Mixed Speech: When Speech is Both Private and Governmental, 83 NYU L. Rev. 605 (2008), 660
______, Compelled Disclosures, 65 Ala. L. Rev. 1277 (2014), 259
______, Corporate Religious Liberty, 30 Const. Commentary 277 (2015), 839
______, Intentional Discrimination in Establishment Clause Jurisprudence, 67 Ala. L. Rev. 299 (2015), 1038
Crump, David, Camouflaged Incitement: Freedom of Speech, Communicative Torts, and the Borderland of the *Brandenburg* Test, 29 Ga. L. Rev. 1 (1994), 58
Curry, Thomas J., The First Freedoms: Church and State in America to the Passage of the First Amendment (1986), 879
Curtis, Michael Kent, Lincoln, Vallandingham, and Anti-War Speech in the Civil War, 7 Wm. & Mary B.R. J. 105 (1988), 13
De Tocqueville, Alexis, Democracy in America (1969), 879
Delgado, Richard, Campus Anti-Racism Rules: Constitutional Narratives in Collision, 85 Nw. U. L. Rev. 343 (1991), 522
Ely, John Hart, Flag Desecration: A Case Study in the Roles of Categorization and Balancing in First Amendment Analysis, 88 Harv. L. Rev. 1482 (1975), 138, 144, 160
______, Democracy and Distrust (1980), 67
Emerson, Thomas I., The Doctrine of Prior Restraint, 20 Law & Contemp. Probs. 648 (1955), 179
______, The System of Freedom of Expression 80 (1970), 144
______, Toward a General Theory of the First Amendment 60 (1966), 23
Epstein, Richard, The Constitutional Perils of Moderation: The Case of the Boy Scouts, 74 S. Cal. L. Rev. 119 (2000), 309
Farber, Daniel A., Content Regulation and the First Amendment: A Revisionist View, 68 Geo. L.J. 727 (1980), 104
Farber, Daniel A. & John E. Nowak, The Misleading Nature of Public Forum Analysis: Content and Context in First Amendment Adjudication, 70 Va. L. Rev. 1219 (1984), 223
Fine, Nathan, Labor and Farmer Parties in the United States, 1828-1928 (1928), 32
Fish, Stanley, "The Dance of Theory," in Eternally Vigilant: Free Speech in the Modern Era (Lee C. Bollinger & Geoffrey R. Stone eds. 2002), 22
______, There's No Such Thing as Free Speech, and It's a Good Thing, Too (1994), 528

Gard, Stephen W., Fighting Words as Free Speech, 58 Wash. U. L.Q. 531 (1980), 70, 188
Gey, Steven G., The Apologetics of Suppression: The Regulation of Pornography as Act and Idea, 86 Mich. L. Rev. 1564 (1988), 593
______, The Case Against Post-Modern Censorship Theory, 145 U. Pa. L. Rev. 193 (1996), 522
______, Postmodern Censorship Revisited: A Reply to Richard Delgado, 146 U. Pa. L. Rev. 1077 (1998), 601
______, The Nuremburg Files and the First Amendment Value of Threats, 78 Tex. L. Rev. 541 (2000), 74
Goldberger, David, Judicial Scrutiny in Public Forum Cases: Misplaced Trust in the Judgment of Public Officials, 32 Buff. L. Rev. 175 (1983), 188
______, A Reconsideration of *Cox v. New Hampshire*: Can Demonstrators Be Required to Pay the Costs of Using America's Public Forums?, 62 Tex. L. Rev. 403 (1983), 217
Goldstein, Robert Justin, Political Repression in Modern America: From 1870 to 1976 (2001), 32, 42
Goodman, Ellen P., Visual Gut Punch: Persuasion, Emotion, and the Constitutional Meaning of Graphic Disclosure, 99 Cornell L. Rev. 513 (2014), 330
Gould, Stephen Jay, Justice Scalia's Misunderstanding, 5 Const. Commentary 1 (1988), 985
Greene, Stephanie M. & Noah, Lars, Debate: Off Label Drug Promotion and the First Amendment, 162 U. Pa. L. Rev. Online 239 (2014), 351
Greenawalt, Kent, Free Speech Justifications, 89 Colum. L. Rev. 119 (1989), 18
______, Speech, Crime, and the Uses of Language (1989), 62
______, Insults and Epithets: Are They Protected Speech?, 42 Rutgers L. Rev. 287 (1990), 70
______, Religion and the Rehnquist Court, 99 Nw. U. L. Rev. 145, 149-151 (2004), 766
Gunther, Gerald, Learned Hand and the Origins of Modern First Amendment Doctrine: Some Fragments of History, 27 Stan. L. Rev. 719 (1975), 41, 54
Hamburger, Philip, The Development of the Law of Seditious Libel and the Control of the Press, 37 Stan. L. Rev. 661 (1985), 7, 8
Haupt, Claudia, Professional Speech, 125 Yale L. J. 1238 (2016), 326, 636
Healy, The Great Dissent: How Oliver Wendell Holmes Changed His Mind—And Changed the History of Free Speech in America (2013), 41
Heyman, Steven J., Righting the Balance: An Inquiry into the Foundations and Limits of Freedom of Expression, 78 B.U. L. Rev. 1275 (1998), 74
______, To Drink from the Cup of Fury: Funeral Picketing, Public Discourse and the First Amendment, 47 Ct. L. Rev. 101 (2012), 507
Hudson, David, The Secondary Effects Doctrine: "The Evisceration of First Amendment Freedoms," 37 Washburn L.J. 55 (1997), 138
Humbach, John A., Privacy and the Right of Free Expression, 11 First Amend. L. Rev. 16 (2012), 602
Inazu, John, Liberty's Refuge: The Forgotten Freedom of Assembly (2012), 292
Jefferson, Thomas, A Bill for Establishing Religious Freedoms, in 2 The Papers of Thomas Jefferson (Julian P. Boyd ed, 1950), 275, 878
Jeffries, John, Rethinking Prior Restraints, 92 Yale L.J. 409 (1983), 409
Jones RonNell Anderson, Pick Your Poisons: Private Speech, Government Speech, and the Special Problem of Religious Displays, 2010 BYU L. Rev. 2045, 651
Kagan, Elena, Private Speech, Public Purpose: The Role of Governmental Motive in First Amendment Doctrine, 63 U. Chi. L. Rev. 413 (1996), 179, 566
______, The Changing Faces of First Amendment Neutrality: *R.A.V. v. St. Paul, Rust v. Sullivan*, and the Problem of Content-Based Underinclusion, 1992 Sup. Ct. Rev. 29, 567
Kalven, Harry, The Concept of the Public Forum: *Cox v. Louisiana*, 1965 Sup. Ct. Rev. 1, 178

Karst, Kenneth, Threats and Meanings: How the Facts Govern First Amendment Doctrine, 58 Stan. L. Rev. 1337 (2006), 74
Keighley, Jennifer M., Can You Handle the Truth? Compelled Commercial Speech and the First Amendment, 15 U. Pa. J. Const. L. 539 (2012), 331
Kendrick, Leslie, First Amendment Expansionism, 56 Wm. & Mary L. Rev. 1199 (2015), 340
Kosseff, Jeff, The United States of Anonymous: How the First Amendment Shaped Online Speech (2022), 288
Kozinski, Alex & Stuart Banner, Who's Afraid of Commercial Speech, 76 Va. L. Rev. 627 (1990), 324
Krotoszynski, Ronald J., Into the Woods: Broadcasters, Bureaucrats, and Children's Television Programming, 45 Duke L.J. 1193 (1996), 355
______, Childproofing the Internet, 41 Brandeis L.J. 447 (2003), 629
______, The First Amendment in Cross-Cultural Perspective: A Comparative Legal Analysis (2006), 153, 528, 529, 533, 601, 602, 617
______, If Judges Were Angels: Religious Equality, Free Exercise, and the (Underappreciated) Merits of Smith, 102 Nw. U.L. Rev. 1189 (2008), 766
______, Reclaiming the Petition Clause: Seditious Libel, "Offensive" Protest, and the Right to Petition the Government for Redress of Grievances (2012), 212
______, Privacy Revisited: A Global Perspective on the Right to Be Left Alone (2016), 577, 617
______, The First Amendment as a Procrustean Bed?: On How and Why Bright Line First Amendment Tests Can Stifle the Scope and Vibrancy of Democratic Deliberation, 2020 U. Chi. Legal F. 145, 340
______, Whistleblowing Speech and the First Amendment, 93 Ind. L. J. 267 (2018), 681
Kurland, Philip B., Of Church and State and the Supreme Court, 29 U. Chi. L. Rev. 1 (1961), 749
Lakier, Genevieve, The Invention of Low-Value Speech, 128 Harv. L. Rev. 2166 (2015), 68
Lampe, Joanna R., Note, A Victimless Sex Crime: The Case for Decriminalizing Consensual Teen Sexting, 46 U. Mich. J.L. Reform 703 (2013), 628
Larson, Edward J., Summer for the Gods: The Scopes Trial and America's Continuing Debate over Science and Religion (1997), 981
Lawrence, Jerome & Robert E. Lee, Inherit the Wind (1955), 981
Laycock, Douglas, "Nonpreferential" Aid to Religion: A False Claim About Original Intent, 27 Wm. & Mary L. Rev. 875 (1986), 1030
______, Towards a General Theory of the Religion Clauses: The Case of Church Labor Relations and the Right to Church Autonomy, 81 Colum. L. Rev. 1373, 1389 (1981), 897
______, The Remnants of Free Exercise, 1990 S. Ct. Rev. 1, 766
Lee, William E., Probing Secrets: The Press and Inchoate Liability for Newsgathering Crimes, 36 Am. J. of Crim L. 129 (2009), 413
Lemley, Mark A. & Eugene Volokh, Freedom of Speech and Injunctions in Intellectual Property Cases, 48 Duke L.J. 147 (1998), 411
Levitas, Daniel, Scaling Waller: How Courts Have Eroded the Sixth Amendment Public Trial Right, 59 Emory L. J. 493 (2009), 397
Levy, Leonard W., Emergence of a Free Press 4-8 (1985), 6, 10, 13
______, Freedom of the Press from Zenger to Jefferson (Leonard Levy ed. 1966), 404
Lewis, Anthony, A Preferred Position for Journalism?, 7 Hofstra L. Rev. 595 (1979), 383
Lidsky, Lyrissa Barnett, Where's the Harm? Free Speech and the Regulation of Lies, 65 Wash. & Lee. L. Rev. 1091 (2008), 85, 533
______, Public Forum 2.0, 91 B.U. L. Rev. 1975 (2011), 642, 660
______, Not a Free Press Court?, 2012 B.Y.U. L. Rev. 1819 (2012), 460

Lidsky, Lyrissa Barnett & Thomas F. Cotter, Authorship, Audiences, and Anonymous Speech, 82 Notre Dame L. Rev.1537 (2007), 288
Lidsky, Lyrissa Barnett & RonNell Andersen Jones, Of Reasonable Readers and Unreasonable Speakers: Libel Law in a Networked World, 23 Va. J. Soc. Pol'y & L. 155 (2016), 488
Linder, Douglas O., Freedom of Association After *Roberts v. United States Jaycees*, 82 Mich. L. Rev. 1878 (1984), 299
Logan, David, Rescuing Our Democracy by Rethinking New York Times Co. v. Sullivan, 81 Ohio St. L.J. 759 (2020), 499
MacKinnon, Catharine A., The Sexual Harassment of Working Women (1979), 537
Madigan, James P., Questioning the Coercive Effect of Self-Identifying Speech, 87 Iowa L. Rev. 75 (2001), 309
Madison, James, Memorial and Remonstrance Against Religious Assessments (1785), 883915, 951, 969
______, Report Accompanying the Virginia Resolution, reprinted in 4 The Debates in the Several State Conventions on the Adoption of the Federal Constitution (J. Elliott ed. 1836), 15
Magarian, Gregory P., The First Amendment, The Public-Private Distinction and Nongovernmental Suppression of Wartime Political Debate, 73 Geo. Wash. L. Rev. 101 (2004), 242
______, Managed Speech: The Roberts Court's First Amendment (2017), 331
______, The Marrow of Tradition: The Roberts Court and Categorical Speech Exclusions, 56 Wm. & Mary L. Rev. 1339 (2015), 86
Malloy, S. Elizabeth Wilborn & Ronald J. Krotoszynski, Jr., Recalibrating the Cost of Harm Advocacy: Getting Beyond *Brandenburg*, 41 Wm. & Mary L. Rev. 1159 (2000), 62
Mann, Sally, Immediate Family (1992), 612
Marshall, William P., In Defense of *Smith* and Free Exercise Revisionism, 58 U. Chi. L. Rev. 308 (1991), 766
Matsuda, Mari, Public Response to Racist Speech: Considering the Victim's Story, 87 Mich. L. Rev. 2320 (1989), 522
Mayton, William T., Toward a Theory of First Amendment Process, Injunctions of Speech, Subsequent Punishment, and the Costs of the Prior Restraint Doctrine, 67 Cornell L. Rev. 245 (1982), 28
______, Seditious Libel and the Lost Guarantee of Freedom of Expression, 84 Colum. L. Rev. 91 (1984), 11, 13
McConnell, Michael W., Free Exercise Revisionism and the Smith Decision, 57 U. Chi. L. Rev. 1109 (1990), 765, 766
McDonald Barry P., Regulating Student Cyberspeech, 77 Mo. L Rev.727 (2012), 553
Meiklejohn, Alexander, Free Speech and Its Relation to Self-Government (1948), 16, 117
______, The First Amendment Is an Absolute, 1961 Sup. Ct. Rev. 245, 17
Mencken, H.L., "Aftermath," in The Impossible H.L. Mencken: A Selection of His Best Newspaper Stories 611 (Marion Elizabeth Rodgers ed., 1991), 981
Mill, John Stuart, On Liberty (Bromwich & Kale eds. 2003), 18, 478
Milton, John, Areopagitica (George Sabine ed. 1951), 6
Murray, Robert, Red Scare: A Study in National Hysteria (1964), 42
Orentlicher, David, Off-Label Drug Marketing, the First Amendment, and Federalism, 50 Wash. U. J.L. & Pol'y, 89 (2016)), 350
Papandrea, Mary Rose, Student Speech Rights in the Digital Age, 60 Fla. L. Rev. 1027 (2008), 553
______, The Free Speech Rights of "Of-Duty" Government Employees, 2010 BYU L. Rev. 2117 (2010), 675

______, Social Media, Public School Teachers, and the First Amendment, 90 N.C. L. Rev. 1597 (2012), 701
Peters, Shawn Francis, Judging Jehovah's Witnesses: Religious Persecution and the Dawn of the Rights Revolution (2000), 178
Peterson, Merrill D. ed., The Portable Thomas Jefferson (1975), 878
Piety Tamara, Brandishing the First Amendment: Commercial Expression in America (2012), 338
Posner, Richard A., Not a Suicide Pact: The Constitution in a Time of National Emergency (2006), 62
Post, Robert,
Racist Speech, Democracy, and the First Amendment, 32 Wm. & Mary L. Rev. 267 (1991), 4
______, Recuperating First Amendment Doctrine, 47 Stan. L. Rev. 1249 (1995), 145, 152
______, Subsidized Speech, 106 Yale L.J. 151 (1996), 635
Rabban, David, The Emergence of Modern First Amendment Doctrine, 50 U. Chi. L. Rev. 1205 (1983), 41
______, The Ahistorical Historian: Leonard Levy on Freedom of Expression in Early American History, 37 Stan. L. Rev. 795 (1995), 10, 11, 13
Redish, Martin H., The Content Distinction in First Amendment Analysis, 34 Stan. L. Rev. 113 (1981), 93, 134
______, The Proper Role of the Prior Restraint Doctrine in First Amendment Theory, 70 Va. L. Rev. 53 (1984), 408
______, The Value of Free Speech 130 U. Pa. L. Rev. 591 (1982), 20, 67
Rehnquist, William H., All the Laws But One: Civil Liberties in Wartime (1998), 46
Reilly, Wendy B., Note, Fighting the Fighting Words Standard: A Call for Its Destruction, 52 Rutgers L. Rev. 947 (2000), 70
Richards, David A.J., Free Speech and Obscenity Law: Toward a Moral Theory of the First Amendment, 123 U. Pa. L. Rev. 45 (1974), 19
Rutzick, Mark C., Offensive Language and the Evolution of First Amendment Protection, 9 Harv. C.R.-C.L. L. Rev. 1 (1974), 67, 70
Samaras, Connie, Feminism, Photography, Censorship, and Sexually Transgressive Imagery: The Work of Robert Mapplethorpe, Joel-Peter Withkin, Jacqueline Livingston, Sally Mann, and Catherine Opie, 38 N.Y.L. Sch. L. Rev. 75 (1993), 613
Saunders, Kevin, Violence as Obscenity: Limiting the Media's First Amendment Protection (1996), 614
Schauer, Frederick, Fear, Risk and the First Amendment: Unraveling the Chilling Effect, 58 B.U. L. Rev. 685 (1978), 28
______, Free Speech: A Philosophical Enquiry (1982), 22
______, The Boundaries of the First Amendment: A Preliminary Exploration of Constitutional Salience, 117 Harv. L. Rev. 1765 (2004), 4, 28-29, 86, 152, 338
______, Intentions, Conventions, and the First Amendment: The Case of Cross-Burning, 2003 Sup. Ct. Rev. 197, 74
______, Costs and Challenge of the Hostile Audience, 94 Notre Dame L. Rev. 1671 (2019), 203
Scheiber, Harry N., The Wilson Administration and Civil Liberties (1960), 32, 33
Scheineson, Marc J. & Cuevas, Guillermo, *United States v. Caronia,* The Increasing Strength of Commercial Free Speech and Potential New Emphasis on Classifying Off-Label Promotion as "False and Misleading", 68 Food & Drug L.J. 201 (2013), 351
Segall, Eric, Mired in the Marsh: Legislative Prayers, Moments of Silence, and the Establishment Clause, 63 U. Miami L. Rev. 713 (2009), 967
Shanor, Amanda, First Amendment Coverage, 93 N.Y.U. L. Rev. 318 (2018), 152

Shiffrin, Seanna Valentine, What Is Really Wrong with Compelled Association?, 99 Nw. U. L. Rev. 839 (2005), 299
Shiffrin, Steven H., The First Amendment, Democracy and Romance (1999), 21
______, Dissent, Injustice, and the Meanings of America (1999), 21
Siebert, Fredrick Seaton, Freedom of the Press in England 1476-1776 (1952), 6, 7
Smith, Jeffrey A., Prior Restraint: Original Intentions and Modern Interpretations, 28 Wm. & Mary L. Rev. 439 (1987), 408
Smith, Steven D., Radically Subversive Speech and the Authority of Law, 94 Mich. L. Rev. 348 (1995), 46
Smolla, Rodney A., Free Speech in an Open Society (1992), 411
______, Should the *Brandenburg v. Ohio* Incitement Test Apply in Media Violence Tort Cases?, 27 N. Ky. L. Rev. 1 (2000), 62
______, Off Label Drug Advertising and the First Amendment, 50 Wake Forest L. Rev. 81, 91 (2015), 350
Song, Doori, Qualified Immunity and the Clear, but Unclear First Amendment Right to Film Police, 33 Notre Dame J. of Law, Ethics & Pub'l Pol' 337 (2019), 372
Stewart, Potter, Or of the Press, 26 Hastings L.J. 631 (1975), 368
Stokes, Anson, 1 Church and State in the United States 402 (1950), 879
Stone, Geoffrey R., Fora Americana, 1974 Sup. Ct. Rev. 233, 223
______, Restrictions of Speech Because of Its Content: The Peculiar Case of Subject-Matter Restrictions, 46 U. Chi. L. Rev. 81 (1978), 104
______, Content Regulation and the First Amendment, 25 Wm. & Mary L. Rev. 207 (1983), 93
______, Flagburning and the First Amendment, 75 Iowa L. Rev. 111 (1990), 160
______, Perilous Times, Free Speech in Wartime (2004), 13, 32, 42, 47
Strasser, Mark P., Those Are Fighting Words, Aren't They? On Adding Injury to Insult, 71 Case W. L. Rev. 249 (2020), 70
Strossen, Nadine, Hate Speech and Pornography: Do We Have to Choose Between Freedom of Speech and Equality?, 46 Case W. Res. L. Rev. 449, 458-477 (1996), 600-01
______, The Regulation of Extremist Speech in the Era of Mass Digital Communications, 36 Pepp. L. Rev. 361 (2009), 61-62
Strum, Phillipa ed., Brandeis on Democracy (1995), 51
Sullivan, Kathleen, Comment, Two Concepts of Freedom of Speech, 124 Harv. L. Rev. 143 (2010), 331
Sunstein, Cass, Democracy and the Problem of Free Speech (1993), 264, 567
Sweeney, Joanne, Sexting and Freedom of Expression: A Comparative Approach, 102 Ky. L.J. 103 (2013), 628
Thorpe, Francis Newton, ed., The Federal and State Constitutions, Colonial Charters, and Other Organic Laws (1909), 879
Tribe, Laurence, American Constitutional Law (2d ed. 1988), 580
Tsesis, Alexander, Inflammatory Speech: Offense Versus Incitement, 97 Minn. L. Rev. 1145 (2013), 61
Tushnet, Mark, "Of Church and State and the Supreme Court Revisited": Kurland Revisited, 1989 Sup. Ct. Rev. 373, 754
Van Alstyne, William W., The Hazards to the Press of Claiming a "Preferred Position," 28 Hastings L.J. 761 (1977), 383
______, Remembering Melville Nimmer: Some Cautionary Notes on Commercial Speech, 43 UCLA L. Rev. 1635 (1996), 345
Villasenor, John, Anonymous Expression and "Unmasking" in Civil and Criminal Proceedings, 23 Minn. J.L. Sci. & Tech 77 (2022), 384
Volokh, Eugene, Freedom of Speech and Workplace Harassment, 39 UCLA L. Rev. 1791 (1992), 522
______, How Harassment Law Restricts Free Speech, 47 Rutgers L. Rev. 563 (1995), 540

______, Crime-Facilitating Speech, 57 Stan. L. Rev. 1095 (2005), 62
______, Freedom for the Press as an Industry or the Press as a Technology? From the Framing to Today, 160 U. Pa. L. Rev. 1 (2011), 368
______, Gruesome Speech, 100 Cornell L. Rev. 901 (2015), 588
______, Anti-Libel Injunctions, 168 Penn. L. Rev. 73 (2019), 412
______, Treating Social Media Platforms Like Common Carriers?, 1 Journal of Free Speech Law 377 (2021), 269
Waldron, Jeremy, The Harm in Hate Speech (2012), 522
Ward, Stephen W., Fighting Words as Free Speech, 58 Wash. U. L. Q. 531 (1980), 67
Weinstein, Alan C. & Richard McCleary, The Association of Adult Businesses with Secondary Effects: Legal Doctrine, Social Theory, and Empirical Evidence, 20 Cardozo Arts & Ent. L.J. 101 (2011), 606
Wells, Christina E., Reinvigorating Autonomy: Freedom and Responsibility in the Supreme Court's First Amendment Jurisprudence, 32 Harv. Civ. Rt.-Civ. Lib. L. Rev. 159 (1997), 20
______, Abortion Counseling as Vice Activity: The Free Speech Implications of *Rust v. Sullivan* and *Planned Parenthood v. Casey*, 95 Colum. L. Rev.1724, 1725-26 (1995), 635
______, Fear and Loathing in Constitutional Decision-Making, 2005 Wis. L. Rev. 115, 50, 57
______, Privacy and Funeral Protests, 87 N.C. L. Rev. 151 (2008), 507
______, Contextualizing Disclosure's Effects: Wikileaks, Balancing and the First Amendment, 97 Iowa L. Rev. Bull. 51 (2012), 413
Werbach, Kevin D., Supercommons: Toward A Unified Theory of Wireless Communication, 82 Tx. L. Rev. (2004), 429
West, Sonja, Awakening the Press Clause, 58 UCLA L. Rev. 1025 (2011), 384
White, G. Edward, Justice Holmes and the Modernization of Free Speech Jurisprudence: The Human Dimension, 80 Cal. L. Rev. 391 (1992), 18, 41
Willard, Nancy, School Response to Cyberbullying and Sexting: The Legal Challenges, 2011 BYU Ed. & L.J. 75, 553
Williams, Roger, Complete Writings of Roger Williams (Russell & Russell, Inc. 1963), 878
Woodward, Bob & Armstonr, Scott, The Brethren: Inside the Supreme Court (1979), 581
Yoo, Christopher S., The Rise and Demise of the Technology-Specific Approach to the First Amendment, 91 Geo. L.J. 245 (2003), 429
Zick, Timothy, Cross Burning, Cockfighting, and Symbolic Meaning: Toward a First Amendment Ethnography, 45 Wm. & Mary L. Rev. 2261 (2004), 169, 309
______, Space, Place and Speech: The Expressive Topography, 74 Geo. Wash. L. Rev. 439 (2006), 223
______, Speech and Spatial Tactics, 84 Tex. L. Rev. 581 (2006), 212
______, Speech Out of Doors: Preserving First Amendment Liberties in Public Places (2008), 24, 223, 238, 242
______, Falsely Shouting Fire in a Global Theater: Emerging Complexities of Transborder Expression, 65 Vand. L. Rev. 125 (2012), 61
______, Rights Speech, 48 U.C. Davis L. Rev. 1 (2014), 258
______, Professional Rights Speech, 47 Ariz. State L.J. 1289, 1292 (2015), 258, 326, 635-36
______, Justice Scalia and Abortion Speech, 15 First Am. L. Rev. 288 (2017), 201
______, Managing Dissent, 95 Wash. U. L. Rev. 1423 (2018), 183
______, The Dynamic Free Speech Clause: Free Speech and Its Relation to Other Constitutional Rights (2018), 93
______, The First Amendment in the Trump Era (2019), 13
______, The Costs of Dissent, 89 Geo Was. L. Rev. 233 (2021), 21, 217

A

ABRAMS CASE, 18, 37, 41-42, 51, 57, 110
ACTUAL MALICE, 472, 475, 491
ADULT BUSINESSES, 135-139, 161-173, 588-589, 603-607
ADVOCACY OF ACTION, 4, 16, 24, 28, 31-51, 56, 61-65, 360, 560, 706
ADVOCACY OF BELIEF, 51-54, 57-58, 113-116, 223-224, 284-286, 292, 580, 635, 997
ANTIDISCRIMINATION LAWS, 243, 259, 299, 303, 307-309, 535-541, 569, 772, 785-800
ASSEMBLY, 25, 47, 51-53, 91, 176-179, 209-210, 212, 218-219, 290, 292, 374, 506, 666
ASSOCIATION,
- Generally, 47, 51-54, 57, 243, 288-311
- Anonymous political speech, 282-287, 389
- Boy Scouts, 300-309, 537
- Compelled disclosure, 250-259, 287, 290-291, 373-384
- Compelled monetary subsidies, 278-279, 281
- Criticism of employer, 662-668, 673-675
- Disclosure of political associations, 288-293, 296
- Exclusion from membership, 293-300, 309, 535-537
- Flag salute, 245, 247-249, 962
- Gender discrimination, 535-540, 594-601
- License plate message, 248-250, 258, 265-268, 621, 760
- Patronage and, 685-687
- Right not to be associated with ideas, 244-247, 249, 264-266, 272-282, 528
- Unlawful advocacy, 32-41, 43-44, 51, 54-58, 61-62

AUDIENCE,
- Captive, 148, 191, 531, 542, 547, 587
- Hostile, 183, 202-207, 210, 215-217, 692

B

BAD TENDENCY, 33, 35, 203
BARNETTE CASE, 148, 151, 157, 244-248, 250, 258, 264, 266, 268, 528, 590, 700, 716-717, 760
BEAUHARNAIS CASE, 479, 522-529, 532-534, 555-556, 571
BIAS-MOTIVATED CRIME ORDINANCE, 79, 288, 553, 561-565, 568-571
BLACK ARMBANDS, 148, 688-692
BRANDENBURG TEST, 4, 54-58, 60-63, 116, 155, 555, 624
BROADCASTING, 263-264, 330, 423, 425, 429, 432
- Airwaves regulation, 264, 423, 425-440
- Cable television, 61, 118, 441-456
- Fairness doctrine, 426-429

C

CABLE TELEVISION, 441-456
- Compared with broadcast, 449-450
- Editorial autonomy, 13, 230, 260-265, 269, 428, 449-450
- Must carry provision, 441-450
- Public access channels, 441-442

CAMPAIGN FUNDING, 118-119, 121-128, 286, 665
CAMPAIGN-POLITICAL, 118-128, 285, 287, 296, 346, 352, 429, 664-665, 682-685, 690, 695
- Ban on taking active part in (Hatch Act), 682-685
- Equalizing freedom of (political) speech, 122. *See also* Election

CAMPUS, 58, 293, 309-310, 540-541, 552-553, 689, 696, 707-708
CANADA, 86-88, 554-560, 594-607
CANTWELL CASE, 52, 66-67, 181-183, 202-210, 745, 759-760
CENTRAL HUDSON CASE, 320-326, 329-330, 337, 340, 344-345, 360, 364
CEREMONIAL DEISM, 1003-1004
CHALLENGES,
- Facial and as-applied, 26-27

CHAPLINSKY CASE, 24, 31, 65-68, 70, 81-86, 92, 150, 206, 208, 431, 483, 531, 546, 548-549, 562-563
CHILD PORNOGRAPHY PREVENTION ACT OF 1996, 619-629
CHILDREN, 24, 84-87, 106-110, 244, 247-248, 278, 326, 355, 397, 429-434, 451, 456, 460, 550, 580, 588, 607
- Pornography depicting, 24, 32, 65, 81, 86-87, 607-614, 619-620, 627-628, 630, 717
- Sexual performances by, 607-614
- Transportation to parochial school, 910-917

CHRISTMAS DISPLAYS, 995-1004
CITY OF BOERNE CASE, 823-825, 832, 840, 902, 904
CIVIL RIGHTS PROTESTS, 61, 73, 207-212, 471-478
CLEAR AND PRESENT DANGER, 31, 33-42, 44-45, 49-57, 183, 202, 204, 209-210, 245, 415, 419, 422, 431, 474, 524, 526, 556, 576, 606
  Brandenburg formulation and beyond, 54-58, 60-63, 155, 533, 555, 578, 606, 624
  Dennis formulation, 50, 52-57, 419
COMMERCIAL SPEECH AND ECONOMIC REGULATION,
  Generally, 28, 65, 86, 280, 298, 313, 320-326, 331, 340, 356
  Artificiality of rigid commercial/non-commercial distinction, 351-356, 360-362
  Big Tech, 461-467
  Central Hudson Test, 320-324, 329-330, 337, 340, 342, 348, 350, 360
  Commercial advertising, 29, 254, 263, 281-282, 313-326
  Contraceptive advertising, 352-355
  Core commercial speech, 351-360
  Data as speech, 331-340
  Defining commercial speech, 353, 355
  Drug advertising, 319-320, 333-334, 338-379, 346-351
  False, deceptive, or misleading, 316, 324, 325, 349-351, 353, 355, 365, 369
  Gambling advertising, 326-330
  Nondisclosure laws, 508-519
  Paternalism, 337-338
  Public utility communications, 355-356
  Tobacco advertising, 320, 326, 330-331
  Trademarks, 313, 346-349, 651-652
COMMUNICATIONS DECENCY ACT OF 1996, 450-461, 496
COMMUNISM, 52, 57, 483, 492, 576, 591
  Advocacy of, 4, 16, 24, 28, 31-33, 42-43, 52-54
  Communist party, 52-53, 116
  Communist propaganda, 32, 38, 42-43, 47
COMPELLED SPEECH,243, 244-259, 262-263, 268-269, 278-279, 281, 760
  Anti-abortion speech, 80, 201, 250-252, 634
  License plate, 248-250, 652-660, 760
CONDUCT, 135, 139, 146-170, 184-188, 231, 272
  Coerced, 245-247, 274, 280-281, 684, 887-888
  Expressive, 5, 23-24, 69, 87, 90-92, 131, 135, 139-140, 146, 153, 161, 169-170, 184, 188, 231, 272, 561, 568, 569, 576, 603, 607, 647-649, 654, 656
  Relating to flags, 146-151, 153-160
  Symbolic, 5, 139-146, 155-158, 160, 162, 168, 170-171, 185, 187, 233, 279, 304, 308, 606
CONTENT-BASED RESTRICTIONS, 24-29, 85, 89, 93-104, 108-117, 129, 134, 136-138, 145, 159, 161, 168, 171, 195, 199-202, 215, 219-220, 252, 258, 333, 338, 346, 371, 440-441, 445, 449-450, 452-460, 552, 562, 564-567, 574, 588, 592, 603, 613, 614, 641, 660
CONTENT-NEUTRAL RESTRICTIONS, 89, 103-105, 112-117, 135, 180, 188, 222, 242, 445, 642
  False speech, 109-117
  General principles, 89-105
  Money as "speech", 118, 121-124, 128
  Public property, 4, 23-25, 99-101, 147, 150, 160, 163, 176, 188, 190, 213-223, 225, 253, 320, 341-344, 442, 506, 526, 535, 648, 650, 953, 971, 992, 1021
  Secondary effects, 135-139, 166-167, 169, 171-173, 338, 604-607
  Speaker identity, irrelevance of, 118-129
  Symbolic conduct, 69, 87, 90-92, 131, 135, 156, 162, 185
  Ward Test, 129-134
CONTRACEPTIVE ADVERTISING, 352-355
CORPORATE ELECTORAL SPEECH, 21, 45, 118-127, 356-360, 362-365, 372, 537
CORPORATE SPEAKERS, 16-17, 117-128, 355-356, 362-365
COUNTERSPEECH THEORY, 110-112, 494-495, 501
CREATIONISM CONTROVERSY, 923-924, 981-988
CROSS BURNING, 73-74, 169, 309, 571-577
CYBERSPACE. *See* Internet

D

DANGEROUS IDEAS/INFORMATION, 6, 9, 11, 15, 32-33, 35, 40, 48-49, 419, 524, 590-591, 633, 635, 645
DEFAMATION, 7, 24, 32, 65, 82, 85-86, 92, 368, 383, 411-412, 423
  Generally, 469-490
  Candidates, 58, 125, 285, 471, 473-475, 481-482, 485, 501, 516, 519, 592, 682, 683, 810, 822, 1041

Damages, 61, 470-478, 485-486, 488-490, 500-501, 503, 506, 509
Group libel, 479, 523, 534
Intentional infliction of emotional distress, 469-471, 499-507, 547
Involuntary public figures, 484-488
Media-non-media distinction, 488, 494-495
Negligence, 480, 486-487, 509, 512
Private persons and libel, 482-490, 513
Public figures and libel, 471-482
Public issues and libel, 384, 488, 490, 493, 504-505, 511, 514-515, 547, 602
Public officials and libel, 16, 72, 187-188, 204, 471-482
DISCLOSURE, 86, 250-259, 267, 282-293, 296, 330, 373-384
Contributions to political campaigns, 118, 121, 125, 128, 224, 227, 272, 275, 287, 356, 369
Identity, 287
Membership list, 288-293
DRAFT CARD BURNING, 5, 139-145, 151, 169, 304
Fuck the draft, 68, 432, 542
DRUGS, 319-320, 332-337, 349-351, 397, 552, 605, 623, 702-707, 833
Peyote, 743, 758-766, 826-827, 866-867, 901

E

EDUCATION, 49, 62, 148, 219, 544, 552, 688-708, 712, 714, 972, 978-992
Amish high school children, 347, 740, 749-754, 760, 764
Dismissal of faculty for political views, 662-664
ELECTIONS, 11-12, 47, 48, 120-126, 134, 224, 282-287, 326, 357-358, 370
Anonymous contributions, 287
Ballot measures, 285, 287
Candidate contribution restrictions, 286-287
Candidate expenditure restrictions, 118-128, 273, 286
Corporate speech and, 362-364
Disclosure requirements, 285-287
Federal Election Campaign Act of 1971, 121, 286-287
Political parties, 53, 245, 274, 526, 665, 683
ELECTRONIC MEDIA, 389, 429, 441
Access to the mass media, 260-264
Editorial advertising, 428-429
Fairness doctrine, 426
Indecent speech, 453, 601, 645, 694
EMPLOYEES, 662
Federal, 682-685
Government, 662-682
Hatch Act, 682-683
Non-policy making, 685-686
Policymaking, 686. *See also* Public Employees
ESPIONAGE ACT OF 1917, 32-33, 36, 41-42, 387, 412-413
ESTABLISHMENT OF RELIGION,
Blaine Amendment, 933, 938-939
Coercion Test, 959, 966-970, 972-977, 1020, 1031, 1038
Conflict with free exercise, 803-807, 814, 817, 822, 891-895, 900-901
De facto establishments, 996-997, 1014, 999, 1003-1004
Disbursements inclusive of parochial schools and church related activities, 807, 940-951
Endorsement of religion, 737, 784, 791-792, 877, 886-887, 892-894, 899-900, 933-934, 942, 951, 957-988, 996-1000, 1002-1006, 1008, 1014, 1017, 1021, 1031, 1037
Entanglement, 736, 857, 861, 868, 872, 886, 898, 918, 926, 989, 997, 1017, 1027, 1039
Establishment of a state church, 734, 879, 881-882, 886, 912, 914, 959, 961
Establishment of a nationally-preferred religion, 878-879, 1030
Federal aid to church-related colleges, 916-917, 953
Interpreter, 916, 932
Lemon test, 736-737, 877, 886-887, 894, 869-897, 899-900, 917, 926, 928, 937, 985, 989, 997-999, 1004-1005, 1008, 1016-1020, 1027, 1031, 1037, 1079
Legislature, 887, 967, 999, 1024, 1026-1033, 1037
Menorah, 1002-1004
Nativity scene, 971, 995-1004
Neutrality test, 746, 749, 769, 770, 772, 780, 789, 790, 792, 794, 848, 857, 861, 894, 909-917, 922, 931, 933, 935, 937-940, 946-947, 950-951, 963, 981, 986, 1021-1021, 1033, 1042
Nondiscrimination, 794, 798, 1033
Nonendorsement principle, 951, 957, 971-972
Public property, 971, 995-1024

Released-time program, 949, 963
Religious gerrymandering, 903, 1039-1042
School prayer cases, 919, 957-978
School voucher programs, 807, 940-951
Subsidies/financial aid, 803-807, 813-815, 821-822, 891-895, 901-903, 910, 916, 940, 943, 947
Sunday closings, 727-735, 738, 746, 997, 1001
Tax deduction for education expenses, 910, 916, 921, 944
Wall of separation, 742, 878, 883, 911, 958, 961, 1011
EXPRESSIVE CONDUCT, 5, 23-24, 69, 87, 90-92, 131, 135, 139, 151-158, 161-170, 186, 231, 272, 561, 565, 576, 603-607, 647, 649, 654. *See also* unconventional forms of communication

F

FAIRNESS DOCTRINE, 263-264, 426, 428
FALWELL, JERRY, 500
FEDERAL COMMUNICATIONS COMMISSION (FCC), 24, 423-428, 441-461
FIGHTING WORDS, 24, 28, 31, 65-70, 81, 86, 92, 104, 139, 155, 159, 183, 200, 525, 531-533, 549, 551, 561-567, 569-570, 580
Compared with libel and obscenity, 24, 28, 65-70, 470, 525, 531
Likely to provoke a reaction, 65-70, 551, 562
Profanity, 66-67, 306, 542-553, 659-660
Racist, 4, 522, 528, 532, 540, 553-568
FIRE,
Falsely shouted in a theater, 34-35, 45, 57, 61, 431, 527, 531-532
FLAG BURNING (DESECRATION/ MISUSE), 4-5, 16, 146-149, 153-160
Breach of peace to desecrate, 69, 139, 144, 146, 148, 153-155, 157
Communicative conduct relating to, 5, 69, 139, 146
Desecration, 146-160
Peace symbol on, 146-153
State interest in preserving as symbol, 154-157
FLYNT, LARRY, 500
FORUM, 4, 91, 99-102, 127-130, 163
Forum analysis, 175-183
Four forum approach, 184-201, 218-239
Limited forum, 102, 220, 222, 226, 228-229, 348, 640, 642, 644, 656, 659, 989, 992
Nonpublic forum, 221, 226-227, 232-239, 642, 991
FREE EXERCISE CLAUSE, 727-728, 730, 737, 739-773
Amish, 740, 749-754, 883
Animal sacrifices, 766-773
Burdens, 775, 780, 792, 795-800, 805-808, 819
Military, 756-758, 762, 904, 906-908, 996, 1016, 1022
Mormons, 309, 729, 740-744, 754, 895, 977
Native American use of national forest, 756-758, 762
Polygamy, 729-730, 740-744, 754, 760
Prisons, 825, 840-842, 901-906
Religious discrimination, 773-800, 807-822
Religious Freedom Restoration Act, 758, 823-842, 902, 904
Santeria, 766-772
Sherbert test, 739-740, 744-745, 748-749, 753, 755-758, 761, 765-766, 792-793, 796, 823-825
limited in its application, 759, 761-763
limited to unemployment compensation, 744-749, 757-758, 761-763, 793, 831, 866
Sincerity, 800-802
Social Security tax, 740, 752, 755-756, 801, 837-839
Sunday closing, 728-735, 738, 746, 997, 1001
Taxation, 357-359, 371, 639, 645, 662-663, 720, 728, 745, 755, 759-762, 799, 800, 805-809, 813, 821-838, 844, 869, 881-883, 892-895, 905, 909-922, 973
Unemployment compensation cases, 744-749, 755, 757-766, 831
Yarmulke, 756
FREEDOM OF EXPRESSION,
Compelled disclosure of beliefs/ associations, 244-245, 274, 281, 287-288, 290-292, 296, 757
Compelled expression (right not to speak), 243-250, 258-259, 263-279, 286-287
FREEDOM OF PRESS, 4, 6-7, 9-10, 14-15, 43, 125, 262-264, 315, 317, 359, 367-379, 383-384, 388, 390, 394-395, 403-410
Access to government information,
Access to judicial proceedings, 387-395, 397-403, 414-422

FUNDS,
Government, 631-632, 634-635, 660, 680, 721, 804
Private recipients of public funds, 632-638, 642-646, 660-661
Public funds used for religious purposes, 804, 814, 822, 883, 910, 927, 929-930, 936, 950, 953-954
Receipt of Title X, 632-635, 637, 673

G
GOVERNMENT NEUTRALITY IN RELIGIOUS DISPUTES, 845-861
Civil court accepts decision of highest judicatories, 850, 855-857, 862-863
Compulsory deference, 854, 861-864
Controversy over church doctrine and practice, 850-851, 853-854, 856, 859, 861
Fraud, collusion, arbitrariness, 854, 861-863
Neutral principles of law, 853, 855-857, 859, 861, 863, 867
GOVERNMENT SUBSIDIES, 621, 632, 637, 642, 644-645, 910, 916, 920
Religious schools, 910, 916-920, 934-935, 954
Subsidized speech, 637-638, 642

H
HARASSMENT IN THE WORKPLACE, 64, 198, 288, 522, 537-541, 630, 709, 867, 977-978
HATE-CRIME STATUTES, 79, 288, 561, 568-577
HATE SPEECH, 479, 521-523, 527-529, 533-534, 553-561, 566-570, 577, 600-601
Campus speech regulation, 293, 522, 696-697, 707-708, 710
Hostile environment harassment litigation under Title VII, 522, 535, 537-538, 540-541
Mitchell case, 554, 568-571
Off-campus student speech, 696-697, 707-708
R.A.V. case, 68, 73, 101, 104, 139, 445, 479, 533, 553-554, 561-566, 572-576, 602, 691
HECKLER'S VETO, 203, 206, 211, 216-217, 692
HUDNUT CASE, 589-593, 600

I
INCITEMENT, 4, 10, 24, 28-29, 31, 33, 41, 43, 45, 47, 49, 51-52, 54, 56-58, 61-63, 65, 73, 81, 86, 159, 204-206, 208, 528-529
Generally, 29, 33, 45-51, 54-58
INDECENT EXPRESSION, 5, 429-434, 436-441, 451-461, 577, 580, 601, 609, 644-645, 694, 716
INJUNCTIONS, 28, 405, 412, 414, 495-497, 700
INTERNET, 5, 61, 79, 111, 230, 242, 263, 288, 368-369, 384, 423, 433, 436, 456-461, 465, 494, 496, 587-588, 601, 629-630, 717-724

K
KU KLUX KLAN, 54-55, 73, 213, 267, 288, 537, 571-572, 651

LEARNED HAND, 41, 49, 419, 736
LIBEL, 6, 16, 28-29, 40, 42, 68, 150, 212, 282-285, 396, 404, 406, 412, 431, 469-498, 500-503, 523-534, 563, 580, 664
Actual malice, 472, 475-476, 478-483, 487-489, 491, 496, 499, 503
Burden of proof in civil cases, 479-480, 482, 484
Chilling effect of civil libel actions, 28, 123, 501, 561
Criminal, 8, 14, 406, 474, 525-526
Gertz case, 482, 490, 492-493, 592
Group, 479, 521-529
Issue of public concern, 384, 469, 478, 482-488, 490, 492-493, 504-506, 514-515, 547, 602, 663-667, 673-674, 676-679, 680, 684
Of public figure, 36, 362, 481-488, 493, 498-503, 516, 602
Of public official, 16, 72, 187, 206, 211-212, 220, 263, 368, 377, 471-481, 484-486, 501, 503, 648, 664-666, 678
Opinion, 490-498, 501, 503, 507
Tourism, 497-498
LIBRARY, 218, 222, 230, 239, 457, 710-724, 919, 987, 992
Book selection, 710-717
Internet, 5, 61, 79, 111, 124, 230, 242, 263, 288, 368-369, 433, 436, 456-461, 465, 494, 496, 587-588, 601, 629, 717-724

Public, 218, 222, 239, 712, 717-724
School, 710-717
LICENSE PLATES, 249-250, 652-660

M
MARKETPLACE THEORY, 12, 19-22, 25, 42, 46, 93, 100-103, 117-118, 122, 127-128, 156-157, 256, 260-261, 266, 283, 318, 329-330, 335, 337, 345, 426, 428, 431, 441, 450, 462, 491, 501, 553, 560, 581, 591, 653
MEDIA, 242, 263, 320, 367-372
Access to jail, 218, 222, 226, 398-403
Broadcast, 423-440
Coverage of trial, 387-397, 414-423
Discrimination between, 428-429, 441, 459
Electronic, 423-440, 449-450, 456-467
Exposure of jurors, 367, 375, 388, 394, 414-423
Social media, 461-467
MEMBERSHIP IN ORGANIZATIONS. *See* Association
MENORAH, 1002-1004
MUST-CARRY RULES, 441-450

N
NAZI SPEECH, 80, 240, 267, 299, 527, 533, 562, 590, 614, 690
NEW YORK TIMES CASE, 16, 42, 72, 90, 92, 119, 127, 262, 270, 381, 471-481, 491, 493, 499, 501, 533, 602
NEWSPAPERS, 10-13, 36, 55, 98, 128, 242, 260-267, 269, 270, 285, 300, 318, 343-345, 355, 359, 369-423, 428, 450, 464, 472, 474, 478, 496, 501-519, 609, 662, 682, 697-701
Abortion advertisement, 313, 318-319
Prior restraints and, 9, 179, 374, 395, 403-412
Right of reply statute, 260-264, 428
Tax subsidy, 125, 891-895
NEWSRACKS, 100, 333, 341-346
NO-AID THEORY, 891-895, 909-917
NONENDORSEMENT PRINCIPLE, 933-934, 942, 951, 957-1042
NUDE DANCING,
Generally, 5, 139, 161-173, 338, 603-607
Content-neutral regulation of nudity, 138-139, 173, 607
NUDITY, 5, 162-173, 436-439, 584, 602-607, 614, 619
NUREMBERG FILES, 74

O
O'BRIEN TEST, 5, 92, 140-145, 148, 151, 154-155, 159, 161, 163-173, 186-188, 249, 304, 308, 448, 450, 543, 584, 603, 606
OBSCENITY AND PORNOGRAPHY, 4, 24, 32, 68, 86, 431, 470, 579-593
Adult speech, 587, 612, 615-618, 624-629
As "low" value speech, 24, 68, 173, 580-581
Children, 587-588, 593, 618-630
Community standards, 457, 459-460, 581, 584-588, 590, 596-597, 603, 620, 622-623
Definitions, 582-589, 607-618
Distribution or exhibition, 562-581
Feminism and pornography, 589-601, 613
Intent, 607, 618, 621, 626
Miller test, 584-586
Pandering, 603, 618, 626
Possession of, 615-618
Prior restraints and, 588-589
Revenge porn, 601-603
Scienter, 610-611
Victimization of women, 579, 589-591, 596, 598-600
Virtual child pornography, 620-628
OFFENSIVE LANGUAGE, 4, 68, 542-553
OUTRAGEOUS OPINION, 499, 501-503, 506, 547, 710
OVERBREADTH, 25-27, 192, 412, 440, 562, 565, 612, 617, 625, 627, 634

P
PANDERING, 603, 618, 621, 626
PARADE PERMIT FEES, 4, 180, 212-217
PARKS, 4, 24-25, 130, 177-178, 183-188, 192, 219, 222-223, 234, 238-240, 530, 648-650, 655
Camping in, 139, 184-187, 192
Public, 178, 218, 222-223, 648, 650, 655
PARODY, 499-503, 518, 708, 710
PENTAGON PAPERS, 410-412
PERFORMANCE DANCE, 5, 139, 161-173, 603-607
PERMIT AND LICENSE REQUIREMENTS, 6, 9, 104, 163, 179-184, 212, 216, 264, 403-410, 424-431, 437, 439-444, 529-530, 532, 588, 650, 652
Generally, 4, 179-183, 530, 532
Forsyth case, 212-217
Kunz case, 529-534

Leafletting and pamphleting restrictions, 138, 178-179, 192-193, 197, 201, 231-232, 241, 282-287, 315-316, 370, 378, 526-572, 605
Littering abatement motives, 99-100, 133, 138, 342, 345, 605
Public forum access rights and, 99-100, 130, 178, 189, 194, 218-223, 225-228
Standardless licensing decisions, 178-181, 212
Time, place and manner restrictions, 4, 25, 28, 91, 128-134, 136-137, 145, 176, 180-181, 184-201, 212, 214, 219-220, 320, 342, 360, 372, 390, 393, 507, 601, 691
PLEDGE OF ALLEGIANCE, 244-248, 528, 709, 717, 889, 964, 996, 1003, 1031
POLITICAL HYPERBOLE, 70-75, 77, 492, 494, 503, 553, 573, 576
PRIOR RESTRAINTS, 9-10, 14, 23, 27, 35, 178-179, 191, 403-412, 418-419, 421-422, 532
Alternatives to, 419-420
Classic, 396, 403
Injunctions, 404-407, 409-412
Licensing, 6-10, 27-28, 176, 178-179, 283, 403, 425, 429, 530
National security and, 6, 15, 410-412
Obscenity and, 588-590
Permit system, 27-28, 91, 94, 119, 121, 180-181, 532
Presumption against validity of, 411-412, 422-423, 530, 532
Time, place and manner restrictions, 4, 91, 128-130, 132, 180-181, 217
PRIVACY, 130, 181, 184, 189-192, 201, 283, 287, 290, 331-339, 377, 384, 397-399, 414, 432-433, 453, 461, 469, 500, 507, 509-516, 544, 547, 587, 602, 615-617
PRIVATE PROPERTY AND FIRST AMENDMENT RIGHTS, 24, 94, 148, 178, 225, 240-242, 249, 263-267, 317, 423, 530-531, 648
Generally, 240-242, 264-268
Handbill distribution, 12, 105, 133, 201, 241-242, 265, 282-286, 314-315, 341-345
Owners' First Amendment rights, protection of, 102, 240-242, 264-268
PROFANITY, 58, 66-68, 306, 432, 542, 548, 552, 577, 643, 660, 696
PUBLIC EMPLOYEES, 272-279, 662-687
Compelled disclosure of beliefs/associations, 654-655, 672-673
Confidential information, 667, 673
Criticism of management/government policy, 650-653, 656-657
Independent contractors, 673-674
Partisan political activity, 672-674
Patronage, 672-674
Political expression, 621-622, 625, 653-654, 664, 667, 669-672
School teachers, 650-652, 657, 668-669, 687
Subversive advocacy/associations, 653, 672
PUBLIC FIGURES, 249, 466-467, 472
False statements about, 481-482, 484-485, 487, 493, 498-499, 501, 503
Parodies of, 500-503
PUBLIC FORUM DOCTRINE, 4, 91, 99-100, 102, 127, 129-130, 163, 175-179, 218-223, 225-228, 230, 238
Generally, 218-239
Abortion, 189-201, 243-259, 313
Auditoriums, 220, 223, 239, 458
Charities, unequal access of, 224-229
Created for a limited purpose, 226, 228-230, 640
Funerals, 202, 504-507
Military bases, 218, 222, 226, 390, 393
National Parks, 238-239
Picketing near a home, 189-192, 201, 222
School libraries, 710-717
School mail facilities, 218-221
Shopping centers, 240-242, 264-269
Supreme Court, 230-238
PUBLIC FUNDING, 242, 400, 637, 641, 647, 673, 719, 811-814, 821, 914, 916, 921, 927-929, 933, 938, 943-945, 949, 1015, 1026

R

RACIST SPEECH, 4, 54-57, 73-74, 169, 213, 267, 288, 309, 522, 528, 537, 572-577
RED FLAG LAWS, 16, 42, 154, 270
RED SCARE, 42, 52, 576, 591
RELIGIOUS FREEDOM RESTORATION ACT, 758, 825-844, 902, 904
RELIGIOUS TEST, 745
SCHENCK CASE, 14, 27, 33-45, 47, 116, 406, 431, 531
SCHOOLS, PAROCHIAL AND PRIVATE, 218, 220, 755, 807-822, 843-844, 881, 888, 909, 911-916, 920, 930-951, 954, 1040

Bus transportation, 910-917
Computers, 910, 930-939
Diagnostic services, 938
Direct v. indirect subsidies, 811, 881-886, 937-940, 945, 997, 1020
Textbooks, 916-917, 936, 938, 987-988
Vouchers, 807, 843-844, 940-951
SCHOOLS, PRIMARY AND SECONDARY PUBLIC,
Administration, 688-691, 692-695, 697-700, 702-706
Amish high school children, 740, 749-754, 760
Authority to refuse to sponsor student speech, 692-701, 706-708, 974-975, 978-979
Board library decisions, 717-724
Student protest, 207-212, 222, 688-692, 696-697, 702-708, 712
SECONDARY EFFECTS, 135-139, 162-173, 338, 604-607
SEDITION ACT OF 1798, 11-13, 18, 33, 40, 42, 404, 474
SEDITION ACT OF 1918, 37, 39
SEDITIOUS LIBEL,
Generally, 6-8, 10-13, 40, 42, 283, 404
Common law, First Amendment's effect on, 6-8, 10-13
SELF-GOVERNMENT, 15-16, 19, 93, 127, 128, 149, 391, 553, 579, 692-693
Free speech and, 15-17, 21, 47, 120, 426, 489, 593
SEXUAL HARASSMENT, 537-541, 867
Litigation under Title VII, 309, 522-523, 535-540
SHOPPING CENTERS AND MALLS, 241-242, 264-269, 272
SIDEWALKS, 24-25, 101, 138-139, 178, 183, 189, 192-207, 219, 222-223, 231-239, 264, 341-342, 344, 506, 605, 912
SPEECH EXACTIONS, 279-293
SPENCE CASE, 139, 145-152, 154, 156, 270, 272
STREETS AND PARKS, 4, 24-25, 65, 101, 130, 138, 157, 177-183, 189, 192-194, 197, 199-200, 202-204, 211, 218-219, 222, 314-316, 327, 341, 344-345, 390, 393, 442, 450, 506, 529-532, 591, 605
SYMBOLIC SPEECH, 141, 157-158, 170-171, 187, 279, 308, 336, 606
Generally, 139-145, 184-189
SYNDICALISM, 31, 42-51, 54-58
Brandenburg case, 54-58
Whitney case, 19, 46-51, 54-57, 110, 545

T

TAXPAYER SUITS, 800, 884, 915, 921, 951-955
TERRORISM, 46-47, 54, 61-63, 113-117
UNCONSTITUTIONAL CONDITIONS CASES, 719, 721
UNCONVENTIONAL FORMS OF COMMUNICATION, 141, 145-149, 157-158, 166, 170-173, 187, 270, 279
UNIVERSITIES, 268, 309, 540-541, 642, 657, 682, 916, 936, 979, 981
Academic freedom, 671, 682, 701, 982-983
Church, 755, 757-758, 762, 953
Newspapers, 673, 718, 941
Prayer, 978

V

VAGUENESS, 25-27, 146, 261, 412, 427, 437-440, 617, 634, 643, 645, 979
VIEWPOINT DISCRIMINATION, 100, 173, 196, 221, 229, 254, 257-258, 347-348, 561-562, 564, 566, 570-571, 574, 576, 592-594, 607, 640, 644-646, 657-659, 706, 991-992
VIDEO GAME VIOLENCE, 106-108
As speech, 81-86

W

WHITNEY CASE, 19, 46-51, 54-57, 110, 545
WOMEN,
Abortion, 80, 192-201, 243, 250-259, 267, 313, 318
Discrimination, 521-523, 535, 537-540, 542
Pornography, 579-602
Sexual harassment, 499, 537-541
Street harassment, 203-212, 540-541, 546-553

Y

YODER CASE, 749-755, 758, 760, 764-766, 824, 834

Z

ZENGER TRIAL, 9-10, 404
ZONING ORDINANCES, 102, 135-139, 167, 172, 588, 601, 605-606, 825, 1034-1042